Evidence

A Canadian Casebook

FOURTH EDITION

HAMISH STEWART
General Editor
Faculty of Law
University of Toronto

BENJAMIN BERGER
Osgoode Hall Law School
York University

EMMA CUNLIFFE
Faculty of Law
University of British Columbia

RONALDA MURPHY
Schulich School of Law
Dalhousie University

STEVEN PENNEY
Faculty of Law
University of Alberta

Toronto, Canada
2016

Emond Montgomery Publications Limited
60 Shaftesbury Avenue
Toronto ON M4T 1A3
http://www.emond.ca/lawschool

Printed in Canada.

We acknowledge the financial support of the Government of Canada. Canadä

Emond Montgomery Publications has no responsibility for the persistence or accuracy of URLs for external or third-party Internet websites referred to in this publication, and does not guarantee that any content on such websites is, or will remain, accurate or appropriate.

Vice president, publishing: Anthony Rezek
Publisher: Danann Hawes
Managing editor, development: Kelly Dickson
Senior editor, production: Jim Lyons
Production editor: Laura Bast
Copy editor: Rose Knecht
Proofreader: Boris Roginsky
Permissions editor: Lisa Brant
Typesetter: Nancy Ennis

Library and Archives Canada Cataloguing in Publication

Evidence (2016)
   Evidence : a Canadian casebook / general editor, Hamish Stewart (Faculty of Law, University of Toronto); contributing editors, Benjamin Berger (Osgoode Hall Law School, York University), Emma Cunliffe (Faculty of Law, University of British Columbia), Ronalda Murphy (Schulich School of Law, Dalhousie University), Steven Penney (Faculty of Law, University of Alberta). — Fourth edition.

Includes bibliographical references.
ISBN 978-1-55239-680-3 (hardback)

   1. Evidence (Law)—Canada—Cases.   I. Stewart, Hamish, editor   II. Title.

KE8440 E82 2016   345.71'06   C2016-900667-0
KF8935 ZA2 E95 2016

Acknowledgments

A book of this nature borrows heavily from other published material. We have attempted to request permission from, and to acknowledge in the text, all sources of such material. We wish to make specific references here to the authors, publishers, journals, and institutions that have generously given permission to reproduce in this text works already in print. If we have inadvertently overlooked an acknowledgment or failed to secure a permission, we offer our sincere apologies and undertake to rectify the omission in the next edition.

Canada Law Book   Hamish Stewart, "Public Interest Immunity After Bill C-36" (2003) 47 Crim LQ 249. Reproduced by permission of Canada Law Book, a division of Thomson Reuters Canada Limited.

Preface to the Fourth Edition

This casebook presents the law of evidence in Canada primarily through extracts from decisions of the Supreme Court of Canada and other appellate courts. In the absence of any significant statutory reform, the law of evidence in Canada continues to be developed by judges through the interplay of common law rules originally derived from English law, the values enshrined in the *Canadian Charter of Rights and Freedoms*, and the principles developed by the Supreme Court of Canada over the last 30 years and described in the prefaces to the previous editions.

It has been a pleasure to work with Professors Steven Penney and Ronalda Murphy on the last three editions of the book. We will miss Professor Marilyn Pilkington and Professor James Stribopoulos (as he then was), who made such significant contributions to the second and third editions and who have moved on to other endeavours. But we are very pleased to welcome Professor Benjamin Berger of Osgoode Hall Law School, York University, and Professor Emma Cunliffe of the Allard School of Law, University of British Columbia, to the editorial team. I particularly appreciate their taking a fresh look not only at the chapters for which they were primarily responsible but also at other parts of the book.

Professor Murphy would like to thank Dylan Baker for research assistance. Professors Berger and Cunliffe would like to thank Amy Brubacher for her research and editing assistance. And finally, all of us thank the staff at Emond Publishing, particularly Kelly Dickson and Laura Bast, for their careful and professional editing of our work.

H.S.
May 2016

Preface to the Third Edition

Five years have passed since the second edition of this casebook appeared. During that time, the Supreme Court of Canada has, for the most part, continued to develop the common law of evidence by moving away from strict rules toward the balancing of factors relevant to admissibility. In this vein, the decision in *Khelawon*, excerpted in chapter 4, revisits the principled approach to hearsay and provides somewhat more structure for the trial judge's decision about admissibility while preserving the central idea that, where traditional exceptions are not available, the trial judge should consider the necessity and reliability of hearsay statements on a case-by-case basis. The court's implicit weakening of the confessions rule in criminal cases, discussed in chapter 8, and its recognition of the possibility of a journalist–source privilege, discussed in chapter 9, are to similar effect. The reformulation of the test for exclusion of unconstitutionally obtained evidence (see *Grant*, excerpted in chapter 8) is a further effort to replace a highly structured rule of evidence with an approach that encourages judicial balancing of the factors relevant to the purpose of the law in question. But the movement toward flexibility is not uniform. Over the past few years, the court has strongly reinforced the traditional solicitor–client privilege and has refused to entertain any balancing of interests where a claim of police–informer privilege is at stake (see chapter 9). Whether the flexible discretionary approach is preferable to the traditional rules-based approach is the subject of much debate among Canadian evidence scholars, judges, and practitioners. We hope this book will provide its readers with some of the tools for participation in that debate.

I am very grateful to all the members of the editorial team for their work on the third edition of the book. I would particularly like to thank Professor James Stribopoulos, who is chiefly responsible for the hypothetical case of *R v. Galloway* that is described in chapter 1 and revisited at the end of each subsequent chapter. This detailed and quite realistic case study should provide instructors and students with many opportunities to discuss and to apply the rules of evidence. I would also like to thank the instructors who have commented on the previous edition, particularly Professor Martha Shaffer of the University of Toronto and Professor Benjamin Berger of Osgoode Hall Law School. Finally, we would all like to thank Bernard Sandler, Nancy Ennis, and David Handelsman at Emond Montgomery.

H.S.
July 2011

Preface to the Second Edition

The law of evidence continues to develop in the direction of a principled approach in which the trial judge's central task in determining admissibility is to balance the probative value of the evidence against its detrimental effects on the trial process (see, for example, *R v. Handy*, excerpted in chapter 7). But this development is by no means uniform, and at times it seems that the principled approach has developed structural rigidities of its own (see, for example, the elaboration of the principled approach to hearsay discussed in chapter 4). This revised edition of *Evidence: A Canadian Casebook* attempts to capture the major changes in the law of evidence, for better or for worse, since the first edition appeared three-and-a-half years ago.

For the second edition, I am pleased to welcome Ronalda Murphy, Steven Penney, Marilyn Pilkington, and James Stribopoulos to the editorial team. Each of the new contributors has brought his or her own strengths and interests to the casebook and has not only updated but substantially improved the material.

I thank all the teachers, students, and other readers who offered corrections to and comments on the first edition. I am particularly grateful to Ronda Bessner and Michael Code for their detailed feedback. I would also like to thank the capable and patient editorial and production team at Emond Montgomery, in particular Peggy Buchan and Jim Lyons. Last, but not least, for research assistance, Professor Murphy would like to thank Audrey Parsons, and Professor Penney would like to thank Natasha MacKay.

H.S.
January 2006

Preface to the First Edition

In most law school courses, the "facts" of the cases studied are taken as given: they are presented as found by a trial court or tribunal or as understood by an appellate court. The law of evidence is concerned with how facts are established in legal proceedings. In most contested cases, the parties will offer the tribunal different versions of the facts. The law of evidence establishes rules and principles governing the means that the parties can use to try to establish their versions of the facts, and the reasoning that the trier of fact is permitted to engage in while determining the facts.

These materials are intended for use in a second- or third-year course in evidence taught in a common law Canadian law school. Familiarity with subjects frequently taught in first year, particularly constitutional law, criminal law, and contracts, is assumed. Some familiarity with the trial process is also assumed; instructors who wish to spend more time on the trial process, particularly in law schools where civil procedure is not taught in first year, might supplement the brief overview presented in chapter 1 with other material.

There is no separate law of evidence in civil cases; all of the principles and doctrines explored in these materials are applicable, *mutatis mutandis*, in civil proceedings. But the admissibility of evidence is usually much more critical in criminal cases than in civil cases; consequently, many of the leading cases in the Canadian law of evidence are criminal cases.

Most of the recent leading cases in the law of criminal evidence involve homicides, sexual assaults, and other sexual offences. Homicide cases have always been central to the law of evidence, but the proportion of leading cases in evidence that involve sexual assault and related offences has increased over time. There are at least three reasons for this increase. First, over the past 15 to 20 years, there has been a recognition that sexual assault and sexual abuse are persistent, pervasive phenomena in our society; there has been a corresponding increase in the number of sexual offences prosecuted. Second, persons charged with sexual offences tend to plead guilty less frequently than persons charged with other offences. Third, Parliament's efforts to amend evidentiary doctrines governing sexual offences have often met with resistance from the criminal bar and from the courts. (Many of these issues are canvassed in L'Heureux-Dubé J's important dissenting judgment in *R v. Seaboyer*, [1991] 2 SCR 577, which is excerpted in chapter 3.) Thus, there are many cases involving sexual offences in the criminal justice system; many of these cases are fiercely contested by the Crown and by the accused; and since the admissibility of evidence is often crucial to the outcome, many of these cases have become leading cases on various points of evidence law. These cases can be disturbing to read, but if one wishes to understand the law of evidence and to reflect on its possible future development, there is no substitute for reading them.

Professor Alan W. Mewett, the original compiler of these materials, taught for several years at Saskatchewan, Osgoode, and Queen's before joining the law faculty at the University of Toronto, where he spent the last 33 years of his life. He was a mentor and friend to many members of the criminal bar, and to younger criminal law scholars such as Professor Martha Shaffer and Professor Kent Roach of the University of Toronto, Professor Janet Mosher of Osgoode Hall Law School, Professor Peter Sankoff of the University of Auckland, and myself. These teaching materials are dedicated to Alan Mewett's memory.

H.S.

June 2002

Summary Table of Contents

PART III   EXCLUSIONARY RULES BASED ON POLICY

PART IV   FURTHER ASPECTS OF PROOF

Detailed Table of Contents

PART I   INTRODUCTION: BASIC CONCEPTS

PART II   EXCLUSIONARY RULES BASED ON UNRELIABILITY AND PREJUDICE

PART III   EXCLUSIONARY RULES BASED ON POLICY

PART IV   FURTHER ASPECTS OF PROOF

Table of Cases

A page number in boldface type indicates that the text of the case or a portion thereof is reproduced. A page number in lightface type indicates that the case is quoted briefly or discussed. Cases mentioned within excerpts are not listed.

PART I

Introduction: Basic Concepts

CHAPTER ONE

Sources and Goals of the Law of Evidence

I. THE SCOPE OF THE LAW OF EVIDENCE

The word "evidence" has a variety of meanings. In this casebook, "evidence" refers most often to information that is offered by a party at trial as a means of establishing its claims: see further Hock Lai Ho, "The Legal Concept of Evidence" in Edward N Zalta, ed, *The Stanford Encyclopedia of Philosophy*, Winter 2015 ed, online: Stanford Encyclopedia of Philosophy <http://plato .stanford.edu/archives/win2015/entries/evidence-legal>. The law of evidence refers to those statutory, common law, and constitutional rules that regulate which information may be offered in a court proceeding, what inferences may be drawn from that information, and how facts are proven. The law of evidence is therefore also necessarily concerned with burdens and standards of proof, and presumptions.

The eminent English scholar William Twining has made two observations about the traditional common law approach to teaching and writing about evidence. First, that approach has focused on the law and legal doctrine virtually to the exclusion of studying questions about factual reasoning. Second, scholarship and teaching of the law of evidence has tended to focus on questions of admissibility (that is, what information is admitted, and what is excluded) in contested trials. (William Twining, *Rethinking Evidence: Exploratory Essays*, 2nd ed (Cambridge: Cambridge University Press, 2006) at 241-42.) Factual reasoning is a core legal skill, and worthy of a course in its own right. While this casebook does not offer a sustained analysis of factual reasoning—for such a treatment, see Terence Anderson, David Schum & William Twining, *Analysis of Evidence*, 2nd ed (Cambridge: Cambridge University Press, 2005)—it engages carefully with legal rules beyond those regulating admissibility and beyond the contested trial, including the regulation of inferences, admissions by a party, and judicial notice.

The law of evidence operates primarily within the framework provided by the substantive law. How does one determine what facts must be proven? The party asserting a cause of action, offence, or defence must lead evidence to establish *facts* that support each of the elements required in accordance with the *substantive law*. The law of evidence is thus concerned primarily with the means of proof that can be put before the trier of fact at trial, the permissible uses that the trier of fact can make of the proof, and how evidence and inferences may be presented and tested.

However, the law of evidence operates not only at the trial of substantive issues, but whenever facts must be established. Thus evidence law applies to the proof of facts that provide a basis for applying *jurisdictional law* (to determine which court or tribunal has jurisdiction over the matter), *procedural law* (to determine issues that arise regarding the process of that court or tribunal), and *remedial law* (to determine the appropriate remedy, insofar as the remedy is within the jurisdiction of the court or tribunal). Evidence law operates within, and is conditioned by, the context of the facts that are in issue and the purpose for which they are being proved. As will become clear throughout this book (consider, for example, Chapter 3, Section II, which considers the concept of relevance in sexual assault trials), evidence law also operates within a broader social context, and it cannot be wholly separated from that context. This social context gives rise to risks such as the possible operation of unfair or discriminatory stereotypes. It also leads to concerns about ensuring that litigants have fair access to the information necessary to pursue their claims. Some aspects of the law of evidence seek to ameliorate such risks and concerns on the premise that this amelioration advances the truth-seeking functions of the trial while also securing other important rights and values.

An excellent illustration of both the importance and the inherent limits of building a factual case that adequately addresses the central legal and evidentiary issues at stake in a case is provided by Sonia Lawrence in her analysis of *Canada (Attorney General) v Bedford*, 2013 SCC 72 ("Expert-Tease: Advocacy, Ideology and Experience in Bedford and Bill C-36" (2015) 30 CJLS 5). Lawrence documents the work done by those who challenged the constitutionality of *Criminal Code* provisions to build an evidentiary foundation—based especially on expert evidence—to support their claim that the *Criminal Code* infringed the security of the person of those who engage in sex work. The evidentiary record was at the heart of efforts to persuade the Supreme Court of Canada to strike down those provisions. However, in subsequent parliamentary consultations on law reform, that evidentiary record played little role in informing how Parliament would respond to the court's decision.

The *Bedford* example illustrates the complexity of the evidentiary record in much contemporary Canadian litigation, and the extent to which evidence lies at the heart of advocacy. The Supreme Court of Canada has reformed the law of evidence considerably in recent years. These reforms reflect the imperatives of Charter guarantees of rights and freedoms, the growing judicial recognition that inflexible rules of admission and exclusion operated unjustly at times, and the increasing complexity of evidentiary records, particularly expert evidence.

This casebook focuses on the core of the law of evidence, and aims to equip the reader not only to understand the law of evidence as it stands today, but also to adapt and respond to the change and reform that is a constant feature of the law of evidence.

II. THE FUNDAMENTAL RULE OF THE LAW OF EVIDENCE

There is one overarching rule of evidence law: Everything that is relevant to a fact in issue is admissible unless there is a legal reason for excluding it. Courts and commentators have expressed this overarching rule in several ways:

> (1) that nothing is to be received which is not logically probative of some matter requiring to be proved; and (2) that everything which is thus probative should come in, unless a clear ground of policy or law excludes it.

(James Bradley Thayer, *A Preliminary Treatise on Evidence at the Common Law* (Boston: Little, Brown, 1898) at 530 (cited as reflecting "the law in Canada" in *Morris v R*, [1983] 2 SCR 190 at 201, per Lamer J, dissenting).)

> Once evidence is found to be relevant, it is generally admissible and the jury is left to decide how much weight to give a particular item of evidence. Similarly, once evidence is determined to be relevant with respect to a particular live issue, the jury should normally be free to weigh the evidence in drawing conclusions about that live issue. This is subject to specific exclusionary rules and the judge's discretion to exclude evidence that is more prejudicial than probative.

(*R v White*, 2011 SCC 13 at para 54, per Rothstein J.)

These very general statements raise at least three questions. First, what does it mean for something to be relevant? Second, what kinds of reasons justify the exclusion of relevant evidence? Third, what is the significance of a piece of evidence being admitted?

III. RELEVANCE

Two considerations determine whether a piece of evidence is relevant. The first, usually referred to as "factual relevance," might be described as a matter of logic or of cognition, or perhaps as a matter of empirical knowledge. The test for factual relevance is whether the evidence makes a fact in issue more or less likely to be true. McCormick described the test as follows: "does the evidence offered render the desired inference *more probable than it would be without the evidence*?" (Charles T McCormick, *Handbook of the Law of Evidence* (St Paul, Minn: West, 1954) at 318; see also US Federal Rule of Evidence 401.)

The second consideration that determines relevance is the issues to which the facts are relevant. The purpose of a trial is to determine the facts and apply the law to those facts, but not just any facts: only those facts that are legally significant. Whether a fact is legally significant depends on the nature of the action. In a criminal prosecution, the facts to be determined depend on the elements of the offence charged and on the elements of any defences that are in play. Some offences, such as murder, require proof of subjective fault; others, such as manslaughter, do not. So evidence tending to prove or disprove the accused's subjective knowledge that his or her actions would cause death is always relevant in a murder trial. In a manslaughter trial, on the other hand, the accused's subjective foresight of death does not have to be proved or disproved, so evidence that related to that factual issue would be legally irrelevant (unless it also related to some other factual issue that was in dispute). Similarly, in a civil case the facts in issue will be defined by the nature of the cause of action and any defences, as set forth in the pleadings. Evidence tending *only* to prove or disprove facts lying outside of the facts that have to be proved to sustain the cause of action, or defend against it, will be legally irrelevant.

The two considerations are generally distinguished by the following terms: the first is called "relevance" and the second is called "materiality" or "legal relevance." "*Relevance* is established at law if, as a matter of logic and experience, the evidence tends to prove the proposition for which it is advanced. The evidence is *material* if it is directed at a matter in issue in the case." (*R v Collins* (2001), 150 OAC 220, 160 CCC (3d) 85 at para 18, per Charron JA.) Cases concerning the meaning of relevance in the first sense are presented in Chapter 3, Relevancy, Probative Value, and Prejudicial Effect.

IV. REASONS FOR EXCLUDING RELEVANT EVIDENCE

One might think that everything that is relevant to a material proposition should be admissible: whenever relevant evidence is excluded, the trier of fact is deprived of some information that could have a bearing on its determination of the facts. Nonetheless, the law recognizes many grounds for exclusion, which may be tentatively grouped as follows.

First, relevant evidence may be inadmissible because to admit it would distort the fact-finding function of the court. Many of the major exclusionary rules are based on the concern that certain types of evidence, though relevant, tend to cause the trier of fact to reason irrationally or inappropriately. For example, the rule against hearsay is largely based on the concern that out-of-court statements offered for their truth, though relevant, are insufficiently reliable to enter into the trier of fact's reasoning. The rule preventing the Crown from leading evidence in chief of the accused's bad character is based in part on the concern that the trier of fact, on learning that the accused is a bad person, will tend to rely on that information to resolve any reasonable doubt that might otherwise arise on the evidence relating to the current charge. The concern about distorting the fact-finding process is a concern about the fairness of the trial. In addition to specific exclusionary rules based on this concern, a judge has a discretion to exclude evidence where its "probative value" is outweighed by its "prejudicial impact." This general discretion is discussed separately below.

Second, relevant evidence may be inadmissible because its admission would unnecessarily prolong a trial or confuse the issues. Perhaps the most notable rule founded on this concern is the so-called collateral facts bar (see Chapter 6, Credibility), which in essence prevents a party from proving independently that an opposing party's witness is lying about matters that are unrelated to the matter in issue. Evidence that a witness tends to tell lies is always relevant, because it goes to his or her credibility, which in turn goes to the tendency of his or her testimony to establish a fact in issue. Nonetheless, the exclusion of the evidence is justified on the basis that to permit an open-ended inquiry into the general credibility of every witness would create trials within trials, confusing the issues and unduly prolonging trials without significantly enhancing their truth-finding function.

Third, relevant evidence may be inadmissible because its admission would undermine some important value other than fact-finding. Thus, for example, evidence that unfairly surprises the opposite party may be excluded. Where a party to a civil action has failed to disclose relevant evidence in the discovery process, the evidence will not be admissible at trial except on terms that prevent prejudice to the opposing party (see Ontario *Rules of Civil Procedure*, RRO 1990, Reg 194, r 53.08). Section 24(2) of the *Canadian Charter of Rights and Freedoms*, Part I of the *Constitution Act, 1982*, being Schedule B to the *Canada Act 1982* (UK), 1982, c 11, provides for the exclusion of evidence obtained in violation of the Charter where "the admission of it in the proceedings would bring the administration of justice into disrepute." Evidence obtained in a manner that infringes the Charter is often relevant and highly probative—indeed it is frequently determinative—of the facts at issue, but it may nonetheless be excluded as a means of enforcing constitutional values (see Chapter 8, Statements of an Accused and Illegally Obtained Evidence). The law of evidence also recognizes various forms of privilege that foster certain relationships by protecting confidential communications from disclosure, even where the disclosure would advance the fact-finding function of the trial. A classic example is the accused person who confesses to his lawyer. This confession may place certain constraints on the lawyer's conduct of the accused's defence (see, for example, Law Society of Upper Canada, *Rules of Professional Conduct*, Commentary to r 5.1-1), but the lawyer cannot be compelled to divulge the confession because obtaining legal advice and representation would be undermined if the solicitor (or the client) could be compelled to disclose his confidential communications. The privilege is important to long-term fairness in the administration of justice, which outweighs the interest of the administration of justice in getting at the truth in any individual case. Privilege is considered in Chapter 9, Privilege.

Fourth, relevant evidence may be excluded because the manner in which it is acquired, or presented, is inconsistent with the nature of the trial process. In the common law adversarial trial, it is for the parties to investigate and to present the case; the trial judge is to be neutral, disinterested, and concerned with ensuring that the trial is fair to both parties; and the trier of fact is to be neutral, disinterested, and charged with the task of determining the facts based on the evidence. Thus, the trier of fact is not supposed to perform its own investigations into the facts of the case. No matter how relevant or probative the evidence discovered in this way might be, it would be inadmissible because it was acquired in a manner that is inconsistent with the adversarial process. It may deprive the parties of the opportunity to test the evidence, and undermine the neutrality of the trier of fact. Rules concerning the form and manner of the examination and cross-examination of witnesses, the order of presentation of evidence, and the proper manner of addressing and charging a jury might also be seen as related to the need to have a fair trial conducted by impartial adjudicators.

Finally, as you will study more closely in Chapter 3, it is now well established in criminal cases that evidence should be excluded where its "probative value" is outweighed by its "prejudicial effect." In this context, "prejudicial effect" refers to the possibility that the evidence may distort the fact-finding process, resulting in unfairness to the accused. The issue may arise where evidence is admissible for one purpose but inadmissible for another purpose. Thus, for example, a witness's record of convictions is admissible as a means of testing credibility. If an accused decides to testify, his or her criminal record could thus be used to assess credibility, but it must not be used as evidence that the accused is a bad person and that he therefore likely committed the crime on which he now stands charged. A trial judge determining the admissibility of such evidence must choose between (1) admitting the evidence and providing the trier of fact with a limiting instruction as to how it can be used and (2) excluding all or part of the evidence. The second option should be chosen where the prejudicial effect of the evidence on one issue exceeds in some measure its probative value on the other. The rule that excessively prejudicial evidence should be excluded is sometimes treated as an aspect of the test for relevancy, but the preferable view is that the balance between probative value and prejudicial effect is the last test to be applied before evidence is admitted. See also Chapter 3, Section II.

McCormick referred to the reasons for excluding relevant evidence as "counterbalancing factors" and he summarized them as follows (Charles T McCormick, *Handbook of the Law of Evidence* (St Paul, Minn: West, 1954) at 319-20):

> There are several counterbalancing factors which may move the court to exclude relevant … evidence if they outweigh its probative value. First, the danger that the facts offered may unduly arouse the jury's emotions of prejudice, hostility or sympathy. Second, the probability that the proof and the answering evidence that it provokes may create a side-issue that will unduly distract the jury from the main issues. Third, the likelihood that the evidence will consume an undue amount of time. Fourth, the danger of unfair surprise to the opponent when, having no reasonable ground to anticipate this development of proof, he would be unprepared to meet it.

Where evidence is relevant to a defence raised by the accused in a criminal trial, the evidence will be excluded if its "prejudicial effect" substantially outweighs its "probative value." In this context, "prejudicial effect" refers to a distortion in reasoning or unfair prejudice to social and individual interests such as a sexual assault complainant's rights to equality, privacy, and dignity. In summary, to be admissible, a piece of evidence must pass the following tests:

1. a. Is the evidence factually relevant, that is, does it tend to prove or disprove the fact for which it is tendered?
   b. Is the evidence legally relevant (material), that is, is the fact that the evidence tends to prove or disprove legally significant in establishing an element of the cause of action, offence, or defence at issue?
2. Is the evidence inadmissible on any ground of law or policy?
3. Does the prejudicial effect of the evidence outweigh its probative value? (If the evidence is tendered by the accused in a criminal trial, does the prejudicial effect of the evidence substantially outweigh its probative value?)

For evidence to be admissible, the answers to questions 1a and 1b must be "yes," and the answers to questions 2 and 3 must be "no." If *either* question 1a *or* question 1b is answered "no," then the evidence is inadmissible; and if *either* question 2 *or* question 3 is answered "yes," then the evidence is also inadmissible.

V. ADMISSIBILITY AND WEIGHT

Suppose a party has proffered a piece of evidence that has been determined to be relevant and that is not subject to exclusion on any ground of law, policy, or prejudice. What is the significance of admissibility? If evidence is admissible, the trier of fact should consider it in reaching a factual determination, but the trier of fact is not required to accept or to believe any particular piece of evidence or to draw from it the inferences that the party invites it to draw. In other words, there is a difference between the admissibility of evidence and the weight that is attached to it. It is for the trial judge to determine whether evidence is admissible; once it is admissible, it is for the trier of fact, subject to any cautions that the trial judge might give, to determine what importance to attach to the evidence in determining the facts in issue. (An exception to this usual rule arises where, as a matter of law, the proof of one fact is presumed to constitute the proof of another fact. See, for example, s 258(1)(a) or s 139(3) of the *Criminal Code*, RSC 1985, c C-46. To the extent that such a presumption shifts an element of the burden of proof to the accused, it may infringe the presumption of innocence guaranteed in the Charter. The court must then determine whether the infringement is justified in accordance with s 1 of the Charter.) (See Chapter 11, Burden and Quantum of Proof, Sections IV and V.)

VI. THE SOURCES OF THE LAW OF EVIDENCE

The law of evidence in common law jurisdictions in Canada has four sources: the common law, statutes, Indigenous law, and the Constitution.

A. The Common Law

The law of evidence in Canadian common law jurisdictions is still governed largely by the common law, that is, by judicial efforts to explain, rationalize, and develop principles governing the admissibility, exclusion, and application of evidence. Some of the most important evidentiary rules, such as the rule against hearsay (Chapter 4, Hearsay), the rules relating to burden and quantum of proof (Chapter 11, Burden and Quantum of Proof), and the rules relating to expert evidence (Chapter 5, Opinion Evidence), derive almost entirely from the common law. In recent years the Supreme Court of Canada has been actively modifying and developing the common law of evidence. It has replaced some categorical exclusionary rules with a more functional and principle-driven approach (for example, in the law of similar fact evidence (see Chapter 7, Character, Section II.C), hearsay (see Chapter 4), and corroboration (see Chapter 6, Credibility, Section V)). In addition, the court has addressed stereotypical thinking embedded in the law of evidence and replaced outmoded assumptions with new starting points for determining the relevance of evidence. For example, the court has adopted a new approach to assessing children's evidence (see Chapter 2, Witnesses, Section I.C), and new approaches to the relevance of evidence relating to sexual assault (*R v Seaboyer; R v Gayme*, [1991] 2 SCR 577, 66 CCC (3d) 321; see Chapter 3, Section II) and spousal assault (*R v Lavallee*, [1990] 1 SCR 852, 55 CCC (3d) 97; see Chapter 5, Section III).

It is important to remember that the rules of evidence are a means for securing the dual ends of truth and fairness; they are not an end in themselves. Thus Lord Devlin acknowledged, in a child wardship case, that special measures may be warranted in order to serve the cause of justice in the context of the case:

> [A] principle of judicial enquiry, whether fundamental or not, is only a means to an end. If it can be shown in any particular class of case that the observance of a principle of this sort does not serve the ends of justice, it must be dismissed, otherwise it would become the master instead of the servant of justice. Obviously the ordinary principles of judicial enquiry are requirements for all ordinary cases and it can only be in an extraordinary class of case that any one of them can be discarded.

(*Official Solicitor v K*, [1965] AC 201 at 238 (HL).)

B. Statutes

The common law rules of evidence can, of course, be modified by statute and often have been, but no Canadian common law jurisdiction has enacted a comprehensive code of evidence that is comparable to the Federal Rules of Evidence in the United States. The Law Reform Commission of Canada addressed the issue in its Report on Evidence (1975), and a Federal/Provincial Task Force on Uniform Rules of Evidence (1982) proposed more comprehensive legislation, but neither proposal was implemented. Accordingly, while every jurisdiction in Canada has an evidence act, those acts are not self-contained and cannot be understood without reference to the common law background. For example, s 3 of the *Canada Evidence Act*, RSC 1985, c C-5 states:

> A person is not incompetent to give evidence by reason of interest or crime.

This provision makes no sense at all, except against the common law background in which the parties to an action were incompetent by reason of their interest, and certain convicted criminals were incompetent because their criminality was deemed to be fatal to their credibility. The evidence acts thus modify or add to the common law of evidence, but do not create a comprehensive code to displace it.

In addition to the evidence acts, individual statutes may contain provisions concerning the evidentiary rules applicable to the matters they govern. The *Criminal Code*, for example, contains many evidentiary rules that apply only in criminal proceedings; the *Controlled Drugs and Substances Act*, SC 1996, c 19 contains certain evidentiary rules applicable only to proceedings under that Act; the *Child and Family Services Act*, RSO 1990, c C.11 provides, in s 50(1), that evidence of the past conduct of a person toward a child, which generally would not be admissible if the person were an accused, is admissible in proceedings under the Act. Similarly, statutes governing administrative tribunals or the legislation that creates provincial inferior courts or specific administrative tribunals may contain provisions concerning the admissibility of evidence. See, for example, the *Statutory Powers Procedure Act*, RSO 1990, c S.22, s 15, which generally authorizes tribunals, many of which operate less formally than courts, to admit testimony and documents even though they would not be admissible in court. This broad authority is subject only to the law of privilege and to any specific statutory provisions to the contrary.

Accordingly, the common law rules of evidence are often tailored, by statute, to address the special circumstances of particular types of subject matter and processes. The rules of evidence may even be tailored to different phases of the same proceeding. Thus the requirements for the admissibility of evidence establishing guilt in a criminal case are more rigorous than those governing the admissibility of evidence on sentencing: see *Criminal Code*, ss 723 and 724.

By virtue of the principle of parliamentary supremacy, statutory provisions may modify, reform, and displace the common law. Nonetheless, the Supreme Court of Canada, without finding an infringement of the Charter, has been prepared to read statutory evidence requirements as being subject to the court's general common law discretion to exclude evidence whose prejudicial impact on the fairness of the trial outweighs its probative value on an issue in the case. (See *R v Corbett*, [1988] 1 SCR 670 re *Canada Evidence Act*, s 12; *R v Potvin*, [1989] 1 SCR 525 re *Criminal Code*, s 715.)

C. Indigenous Law

There are plural legal traditions in Canada: the common law adopted from England, the civil law in Quebec, and Indigenous legal traditions, which pre-date the other two traditions and continue to exist, except where they have been explicitly extinguished (see *Calder v British Columbia (AG)*, [1973] SCR 313 at 318, 328, and 375; *Mitchell v MNR*, 2001 SCC 33, [2001] 1 SCR 911 at 927). The Supreme Court of Canada has held that, in litigation to determine the scope of unextinguished Aboriginal rights, the Aboriginal sources of evidence must be respected and balanced with other sources admissible at common law. In *Delgamuukw v BC*, [1997] 3 SCR 1010 at 1069, the Supreme Court of Canada held that oral histories passed down by elders are a valid source of evidence for the determination of Aboriginal rights:

> Notwithstanding the challenges created by the use of oral histories as proof of historical facts, the laws of evidence must be adapted in order that this type of evidence can be accommodated and placed on an equal footing with the types of historical evidence that courts are familiar with, which largely consists of historical documents.

The court has recognized the unique evidentiary barriers faced by Indigenous claimants, and the validity of their sources of evidence, which must be fairly assessed and balanced with other forms of evidence to determine whether the validity of the Aboriginal claim has been established on a balance of probabilities. (See *R v Marshall*, [1999] 3 SCR 456; *R v Van der Peet*, [1996] 2 SCR 507 at para 68, per Lamer CJ.)

And yet there are notes within the court's jurisprudence that suggest that the court continues to regard common law principles of evidence as representing a norm against which the evidence brought by Indigenous claimants will be measured. Consider the following statement from *Mitchell v MNR*, 2001 SCC 33 at para 38, [2001] 1 SCR 911:

> Again, however, it must be emphasized that a consciousness of the special nature of aboriginal claims does not negate the operation of general evidentiary principles. While evidence adduced in support of aboriginal claims must not be undervalued, neither should it be interpreted or weighed in a manner that fundamentally contravenes the principles of evidence law, which, as they relate to the valuing of evidence, are often synonymous with the "general principles of common sense" ... .

For as long as this kind of affirmation of the "common sense" character of the prevailing common law principles of evidence persists, it is difficult to be entirely sanguine about the status of Indigenous law as a valued source of our laws of evidence.

D. The Constitution

Section 52(1) of the *Constitution Act, 1982* provides:

> The Constitution is the supreme law of Canada, and any law that is inconsistent with the provisions of the Constitution is, to the extent of the inconsistency, of no force or effect.

Thus the law of evidence, like any other law, is constrained by constitutional requirements. A statutory evidence provision that is inconsistent with the Constitution is of no force or effect. Further, in a criminal prosecution, which involves state action, a common law rule of evidence that is inconsistent with the Charter is of no force or effect, and the court can formulate a new rule to replace it (see *R v Seaboyer; R v Gayme*, [1991] 2 SCR 577; *R v Swain*, [1991] 1 SCR 933; *R v Daviault*, [1994] 3 SCR 63; *R v Stone*, [1999] 2 SCR 290). In an action between private parties, involving no government action, a common law rule will be developed in accordance with Charter values (see *Hill v Church of Scientology of Toronto*, [1995] 2 SCR 1130).

1. Division of Legislative Authority

Sections 91 and 92 of the *Constitution Act, 1867* (UK), 30 & 31 Vict, c 3, reprinted in RSC 1985, Appendix II, No 5, define the subjects on which the federal and provincial governments can legislate. The limitations on legislative powers created by ss 91 and 92 apply to the rules of evidence as well as to substantive law: only Parliament can create or modify rules of evidence for matters falling under federal jurisdiction, and only the provincial legislatures can create or modify rules of evidence for matters falling under provincial jurisdiction. Thus, for example, because of Parliament's jurisdiction over criminal law and procedure, the provincial legislatures cannot create evidentiary rules for criminal proceedings; because of provincial jurisdiction over "Property and Civil Rights in the Province," the federal government cannot create evidentiary rules concerning contractual disputes or tort actions (except those involving the federal Crown).

It follows that the division of legislative authority also governs the applicability of evidence statutes. In criminal and federal regulatory matters, and in disputes involving the federal Crown, the *Canada Evidence Act* will apply. In matters within provincial jurisdiction, the appropriate provincial evidence act will apply.

In some instances, however, the applicable evidence law in a matter within federal jurisdiction will be determined in accordance with provincial evidence provisions that are incorporated by reference into the *Canada Evidence Act* by virtue of s 40. Section 40 provides that

> [i]n all proceedings over which Parliament has legislative authority, the laws of evidence in force in the province in which those proceedings are taken, including the laws of proof of service of any warrant, summons, subpoena or other document, subject to this Act and other Acts of Parliament, apply to those proceedings.

In what situations would s 40 apply? How does it interact with s 8(2) of the *Criminal Code*, which states that "[t]he criminal law of England that was in force in a province immediately before April 1, 1955 continues in force in the province except as altered, varied, modified or affected by this Act or any other Act of the Parliament of Canada"?

2. The Canadian Charter of Rights and Freedoms

The *Canadian Charter of Rights and Freedoms* came into force on April 17, 1982. It has had a fundamental impact on the law of evidence in Canadian criminal proceedings in at least four ways.

First, the Charter provides express constitutional protection for some evidentiary principles in criminal proceedings: the presumption that an accused is innocent until proven guilty according to law in a fair and public hearing by an independent and impartial tribunal (s 11(d)), the right not to be compelled as a witness against oneself (s 11(c)), and the right against self-incrimination in subsequent proceedings (s 13).

Second, s 7 of the Charter has proved to be an important vehicle for the constitutionalization of evidentiary principles. Section 7 provides:

> Everyone has the right to life, liberty and security of the person and the right not to be deprived thereof except in accordance with the principles of fundamental justice.

In criminal proceedings, liberty is always at stake, so s 7 is always applicable. All criminal proceedings must therefore be conducted in accordance with the principles of fundamental justice. The question then becomes: are any of the common law rules of evidence so important or so basic to the justice system that they have become principles of fundamental justice? The Supreme Court has considered arguments of this type on several occasions, and while it has usually rejected the claim, there is no doubt that some very basic principles of evidence have been embedded in s 7 (see, for example, *R v Seaboyer; R v Gayme*, [1991] 2 SCR 577 in Chapter 3, *R v Hebert*, [1990] 2 SCR 151 in Chapter 8, and *R v S (RJ)*, [1995] 1 SCR 451 in Chapter 8). Common law or statutory evidence rules that are inconsistent with the principles of fundamental justice must either be justified under s 1 or be declared of no force or effect.

Third, the Charter protects important rights in the investigation of offences: "the right to be secure against unreasonable search or seizure" (s 8), "the right not to be arbitrarily detained or imprisoned" (s 9), and "the right on arrest or detention … to retain and instruct counsel without delay and to be informed of that right" (s 10(b)). Common law or statutory evidence rules that are inconsistent with these rights must again either be justified under s 1 or be declared of no force or effect; state action that is not authorized by statute or common law and is inconsistent with these rights cannot be justified, since it is not "prescribed by law" as required in s 1. The scope of rights relating to investigation of offences is reviewed in a course on criminal procedure.

Fourth, where evidence is obtained in a manner that infringes a Charter right, the Charter provides for a remedy in the following terms:

> 24(1) Anyone whose rights or freedoms, as guaranteed by this Charter, have been infringed or denied may apply to a court of competent jurisdiction to obtain such remedy as the court considers appropriate and just in the circumstances.
>
> (2) Where, in proceedings under subsection (1), a court concludes that evidence was obtained in a manner that infringed or denied any rights or freedoms guaranteed by this Charter, the evidence shall be excluded if it is established that, having regard to all the circumstances, the admission of it in the proceedings would bring the administration of justice into disrepute.

This exclusionary rule will be considered in Chapter 8, Section II.

VII. THE TRIAL PROCESS

It is impossible to understand the rules of evidence in common law jurisdictions without a basic understanding of the common law trial. This book is intended for use in the second or third year of a Canadian law school program, and students should already have some familiarity with the trial process from a course in civil procedure or the legal process. What follows is, therefore, a very brief overview of the main features of a common law trial.

A. Witnesses

The witness (see Chapter 2) is at the centre of the common law trial, whether the subject matter of the trial is criminal or civil. With very few exceptions, all facts have to be proved or disproved through the testimony of witnesses. Testimony is elicited through questions put by counsel (or by the parties themselves if they are unrepresented) and, occasionally, by the trial judge. The questions asked by the party calling a witness constitute the examination in chief; the questions asked by other parties constitute cross-examination. The principal difference between examination in chief and cross-examination is in the permissible form of questioning: leading questions are generally not permitted in examination in chief, but are the usual method of cross-examination (see Chapter 2, Section IV). At the conclusion of cross-examination, the party who called the witness may re-examine the witness to address any matters arising from the cross-examination that were not addressed in the examination in chief.

B. Criminal Proceedings

In Canadian law, every criminal trial begins with a charging document called the indictment, or the information. The charging document specifies the offence charged and contains some statement, usually quite brief, of the facts that are to be alleged by the Crown. (The law of criminal pleadings in Canada is quite complex and is considered in a course devoted to criminal procedure.) Before the trial begins, the Crown has a constitutional duty to disclose all relevant and non-privileged information to the defence (see *R v Stinchcombe*, [1991] 3 SCR 326, 68 CCC (3d) 1), but there is no corresponding disclosure obligation on the defence. At the outset of the trial, the accused will be called upon to plead "guilty" or "not guilty." (Other pleas are possible, but again these are best considered in a criminal procedure course.) A plea of guilty is a formal admission of the facts necessary to establish the Crown's allegations (see Chapter 10, Proof Without Evidence). A plea of not guilty indicates that the accused will dispute the Crown's case, thus requiring the Crown to adduce sufficient evidence to establish each element of the offence.

The criminal court may be constituted by a judge and a jury or by a judge sitting alone. In a trial with a jury, the trial judge decides all the legal questions that arise, including the admissibility of evidence and the propriety of any questions asked or answers given. At the end of the trial, the judge instructs the jury as to the applicable substantive law and as to the burden and quantum of proof on whatever factual issues are to be decided. Counsel for the parties may make objections to the judge's charge to the jury and, if warranted, the judge will reinstruct the jury. The jury is the trier of fact: it determines what the facts are and applies the law to those facts, but the jury does not report its factual findings. Instead, the jury simply reports whether it has found the accused guilty or not guilty on each charge. In a trial by judge alone, the judge performs the functions of judge and jury, deciding legal questions and finding facts. The judge is required to provide reasons for decision, which, having regard to the particular circumstances of the case, provide an explanation of the basis of the decision in a manner that is reasonably intelligible to the parties and enables meaningful appellate review of the correctness of the decision (see *R v Sheppard*, 2002 SCC 26, [2002] 1 SCR 869). Despite the centrality of the jury to common law rules of evidence, less than 1 percent of criminal cases in Canada are resolved by a jury verdict. (See, further, Lisa Dufraimont, "Evidence Law and the Jury: A Reassessment" (2008) 53 McGill LJ 199.)

In a criminal case, subject to very few exceptions, the Crown is required to prove the facts it alleges beyond a reasonable doubt (see Chapter 11). If the accused pleads not guilty, the Crown calls its witnesses first. This part of the trial is called the Crown's case in chief. The Crown's witnesses will be examined in chief by Crown counsel, cross-examined by defence counsel, and, if appropriate, re-examined by Crown counsel on matters arising during the cross-examination. At the close of the Crown's case, the accused may bring a motion for a directed verdict of acquittal. The ground for such a motion is that the Crown's evidence, even if believed, is insufficient to establish the elements of the offence, so that the accused must be acquitted (see *United States of America v Shephard*, [1977] 2 SCR 1067, (1976), 30 CCC (2d) 424). If the trial judge grants the motion, traditionally he or she would direct the jury to acquit the accused, but the Supreme Court has held that the judge should withdraw the case from the jury and enter the acquittal himself or herself (see *R v Rowbotham; R v Roblin*, [1994] 2 SCR 463, 90 CCC (3d) 449).

Once the Crown's case is complete, the accused may (but need not) call witnesses. The accused himself or herself may (but need not) testify. The defence witnesses will be examined in chief by defence counsel, cross-examined by Crown counsel, and re-examined by defence counsel. At the end of the accused's case, the Crown may, in rare circumstances, be permitted to call evidence in reply, with the accused in even rarer circumstances having a right to further reply.

After all the evidence has been heard, the trier of fact will be addressed by counsel for the accused and by counsel for the Crown. (On the order of these addresses, see *Criminal Code*, s 651 and *R v Rose*, [1998] 3 SCR 262, 129 CCC (3d) 449.) If the defence calls evidence, counsel for the accused addresses the trier of fact first. The trial judge then instructs the jury, and the jury retires to consider its verdict. In Canada, it is a criminal offence for jurors to disclose their deliberations, except under limited circumstances (see *Criminal Code*, s 649). If the trier of fact acquits the accused, he or she is of course free to go (unless the accused is in custody in relation to another matter). If the trier of fact finds the accused guilty, he or she is remanded for sentencing by the trial judge.

1. Voir Dire to Determine Conditions Precedent to the Admission of Evidence

In a trial by jury, it may be necessary to hold a "*voir dire*" (a trial within the trial) to determine the facts that are a condition precedent to the admissibility of evidence. Thus, for example, before a witness refers to a confession made by the accused, it must be established that the confession was voluntarily made. (See the discussion in Chapter 8, Section I.) The *voir dire* is held in the absence of the jury, since knowing that the accused had confessed would be highly prejudicial if the confession is held to be inadmissible. On some other evidentiary issues, a *voir dire* will be heard in the presence of the jury. Thus, for example, a *voir dire* as to whether a child is competent to testify will be heard in the presence of the jury. If the judge finds that the child is competent to testify, the jury can make use of the evidence on the *voir dire* in assessing the weight to give to the child's testimony. If the judge finds that the child is not competent, there is no likelihood of prejudice resulting from the jury having heard the evidence on competence. (See Chapter 2.)

For an excellent overview of the Canadian criminal trial, see Alan W Mewett & Shaun Nakatsuru, *An Introduction to the Criminal Process in Canada*, 4th ed (Toronto: Carswell, 2000). Overviews of procedural developments in Canadian criminal law are provided by Don Stuart, *Charter Justice in Canadian Criminal Law*, 5th ed (Toronto: Carswell, 2010) and by Kent Roach, *Due Process and Victims' Rights* (Toronto: University of Toronto Press, 1999).

2. Appealing on the Basis of Evidence Rulings in Criminal Cases

The rights of the accused and the Crown to appeal from verdicts in proceedings by indictment are laid out in part XXI of the *Criminal Code*. Generally speaking, the accused may appeal from conviction on a question of law, as well as on other grounds, while the Crown may appeal from acquittal only on a question of law. A trial judge's decision to admit or to exclude evidence is a question of law. Decisions about admissibility are therefore frequent grounds of appeal for both the Crown and the accused. Most of the cases included in these materials are reports of appellate decisions. Where an appellate court holds that evidence was admitted or excluded in error, it will nonetheless dismiss the appeal unless the error resulted in a substantial wrong or a miscarriage of justice (*Criminal Code*, s 686(1)(b)(iii)). Where an appeal is allowed, the court may quash the conviction, substitute a verdict, or order a new trial so that the matter can be determined on a proper evidentiary foundation (*Criminal Code*, ss 686(2), (3), and (4)).

3. Fresh Evidence on Appeal

An appeal is argued on the basis of the record of evidence at the trial, but in an appropriate case, the appellate court has the power to hear additional evidence (*Criminal Code*, s 683; *Palmer v R*, [1980] 1 SCR 759).

C. Civil Proceedings

Civil proceedings begin with a statement of claim from the plaintiff, a statement of defence from the defendant, and further pleadings from any other parties to the action. Following the exchange of pleadings, rules of civil procedure in each jurisdiction provide for pre-trial discovery. While pleadings and discovery in civil cases are properly considered in a course on civil procedure, they merit a brief discussion here as they also have implications for the proof of facts at trial. The pleadings frame the issues in the action and provide the basis for determining whether evidence is relevant to a material issue. An admission of fact in a pleading dispenses with the need to prove that fact at trial, and thereby makes that issue immaterial. The party's affidavit on production disclosing documents relevant to the action is often an important source of evidence. A party may give notice to another party to admit certain facts, including the authenticity of documents, and a party who unreasonably fails to do so, requiring that the facts be proven at trial, may suffer costs consequences. An admission made in the oral examination for discovery, or in response to a notice to admit, can be read into the record at trial and will dispense with the need for further proof. In addition, the examination for discovery enables the examining party to assess the strengths and weaknesses of the case. Moreover, if the party changes his or her story at trial, the transcript of the examination for discovery can be used to impeach his or her credibility. (See, for example, Ontario *Rules of Civil Procedure*, rr 31.11 and 51, and Ontario *Evidence Act*, ss 20 and 21.)

Most civil cases are heard by a judge sitting alone, but jury trials are by no means unusual. The functional division between the judge and the jury in a civil trial is the same as in a criminal trial: the judge decides all questions of law, including decisions about the admissibility of evidence, and the jury determines the facts and applies the law to them. As in a criminal case, the parties to a civil case call witnesses who are examined in chief by the party calling them, are cross-examined by the other parties, and may be re-examined. The jury's factual findings in a civil case may be more detailed than in a criminal case; the jury may, for instance, be asked to answer a series of questions bearing on the defendant's liability, rather than simply finding the defendant liable or not liable.

Appeals in civil cases, as in criminal cases, may be founded on alleged errors in admitting or excluding evidence.

1. Evidence in Interlocutory Proceedings in Civil Matters

Prior to trial of a civil action, it may be necessary to determine procedural issues, such as a motion to add a party, a motion for an interlocutory injunction, or a motion to compel further discovery. Where facts must be established in support of an interlocutory motion, the evidence is generally presented in sworn statements or affidavits. Where necessary, the witness (deponent) in the affidavit may be required to attend and be cross-examined before a special examiner (see, for example, Ontario *Rules of Civil Procedure*, r 39).

D. The Competing Goals of the Trial Process

Ideally, the trial would determine the facts correctly, inexpensively, expeditiously, fairly, and without damaging other social values. In practice, these goals are likely to come into conflict with each other: for example, correctly determining the facts may take a very long time or might be quite costly; or it might involve compromising other social values such as the privacy of witnesses or the security of the state. The rules of evidence, like other procedural rules, are therefore concerned not just with truth-seeking but also with a range of other values. The law of evidence acts as a filter preventing the trier of fact from hearing some information and limiting what it can do with the information it does hear. As you read through the judicial reasoning that forms the bulk of this book, you should ask yourself whether the Canadian law of evidence does a good job of balancing the various goals of the trial process.

1. The Adversary System and the Roles of Counsel and the Court

Our trial process is based on the adversary system, the essential attributes of which are defined by the respective roles of the parties and the court. In contrast to the inquisitorial system, the adversary process is not shaped by an official. Rather, the parties and their counsel determine the issues to be litigated, the evidence to be offered, and the strategy to be pursued. The judge is a neutral adjudicator of legal questions, and more passive than a judge in an inquisitorial jurisdiction. The judge does not investigate or conduct research into the facts at issue (*Phillips v Ford Motor Co of Canada Ltd*, [1971] 2 OR 637 (CA)), does not call witnesses (unless, in a criminal trial, it is necessary to do so to ensure that justice is done (*R v Cleghorn*, [1967] 2 QB 584)), and generally should exercise restraint in questioning witnesses, so as not to interfere with the fair conduct of the trial. The judge's role is to supervise the proceedings: to determine the admissibility and sufficiency of evidence, to decide any procedural issues, and to intervene as necessary to ensure the fairness and efficiency of the proceeding. Finally, the role of the judge is to listen to the evidence and submissions and to decide: to review the evidence for the jury and instruct the jury on the law, or, when the judge sits without a jury, to determine the applicable legal principles, find the facts, and apply the law to the facts, giving sufficient reasons to indicate the basis of the decision.

In support of the adversary system, it is argued that the opportunity for parties to participate in shaping the case enhances the legitimacy of the proceeding. A party who has had a full opportunity to raise issues, tender proof, and submit arguments is more likely to have confidence in the process. Moreover, it is assumed that the self-interest of the parties will motivate them to leave no stone unturned in presenting a strong case and testing the evidence of the other side. The tendering and challenging of evidence throughout the trial also tends to keep the trier of fact in a state of suspended judgment until all admissible evidence is before the court, thus counteracting the human tendency to form an early hypothesis about the case and screen out the facts that do not fit that hypothesis.

Notwithstanding the conceptual strengths of the adversary system, its effectiveness is handicapped to some extent by practical constraints. The parties may not have access to equal resources to investigate the facts and present the case (see Mark Cooney, "Evidence as Partisanship" (1994) 28 Law & Soc'y Rev 833). In some instances, parties may not be equally motivated on either side of the case. The trier of fact must rely on evidence filtered through witnesses rather than first-hand investigation. Techniques of questioning witnesses may distort the truth-finding process in some cases, and methods of assessing credibility may reflect culturally limited assumptions. Whatever the state of the evidence, the trier of fact must make an immediate and definitive decision at the completion of the trial. The "winner takes all" approach raises the stakes of the litigation, and the adversary nature of the pro-ceedings may disrupt continuing relationships.

It is important to acknowledge modifications to the adversary system that seek to address some of its handicaps and enhance its effectiveness as a fair means of getting at the truth. The discovery process in civil cases (see, for example, r 31 of the Ontario *Rules of Civil Proced-ure*) and the obligation of the Crown to make full disclosure to the defence in criminal pros-ecutions (*R v Stinchcombe*, [1991] 3 SCR 326; *R v McNeil*, 2009 SCC 3, [2009] 1 SCR 66) avoid the potential unfairness of trial by ambush. The professional standards expected of lawyers and judges restrain abuses of the process. Adverse cultural or stereotypical assumptions that could distort the process can be challenged, usually through expert evidence, or excluded through common law and statutory rules. Plea bargaining in criminal cases and the introduc-tion of mediation and pre-trial conferences in civil cases encourage the resolution of dis-putes, and, in civil cases, rules of costs provide incentives to be realistic in assessing the value of a civil case for settlement purposes. The requirement, in criminal cases, that the Crown prove guilt beyond a reasonable doubt strives to ensure, but does not always secure, that the innocent are not convicted. It must be noted, however, that fairness often depends upon the validity of the assumption that triers of fact are able to compartmentalize their analysis when evidence is admissible for one purpose but cannot be used for another. It is indeed troubling that some empirical studies challenge the validity of that fundamental assumption (see *R v Corbett*, [1988] 1 SCR 670).

The most intractable problem with the adversary system is the frequent disparity in the resources of the parties, including at times the inability of one or both parties to retain coun-sel. The problem is addressed to a limited extent through the availability of legal aid and the tradition of members of the bar providing professional services on a *pro bono* or voluntary basis, and access to relevant information is facilitated by the rules regarding discovery and disclosure. However, the number of unrepresented parties in our courts is an increasing con-cern. Problems with access to justice strike at the core of the adversary system.

VIII. R v GALLOWAY: A CASE STUDY

Throughout the casebook we will be returning to the fictional case of Martin Galloway, who is charged with first-degree murder in the death of his wife, Angela. Developments in the Gallo-way trial will be introduced at the end of each chapter, and questions that introduce particular evidentiary challenges in litigation relating to topics dealt with in the chapter will be posed.

With each new problem, those facts necessary to address the issue raised will be provided. For now, by way of introduction, below are some background facts to help orient you with respect to this case and the key issues that lie at the heart of this litigation.

Martin Galloway, the accused, is charged with first-degree murder in the death of his wife, Angela. She was killed on Easter Sunday, March 27, 2016. There is no dispute that Angela Galloway was brutally murdered; the issue at trial will be whether the accused is the person who killed her.

At the time of the murder, the Galloways had been married for approximately seven years and had two children, then aged five and three. The deceased had been involved in competitive dog training and used thxe drive shed of their rural home (located 30 feet northwest of their residence) to train her dogs. Although the Galloway home is in the country, neighbours live on each side of them, in homes situated within earshot.

At approximately 11:00 p.m. on Sunday, March 27, 2016, the accused telephoned 911 and reported that he had found his wife in the drive shed. She was unconscious and appeared to have suffered a serious head injury. He was directed to return to her and perform CPR. Emergency personnel arrived 15 minutes later. One of the firefighters was an off-duty police officer; upon seeing Angela Galloway, he concluded she was dead and secured the scene.

The accused cooperated with the police and was interviewed by them on three separate occasions, initially on March 28 and then again on April 18 and June 2, 2016. In each of his statements, the accused told police that he and his wife had spent March 27 (Easter Sunday) with their children before visiting his in-laws for dinner, returning home around 7:00 p.m. That evening a friend, Tom Jenkins, dropped by their home to see the accused (who is a chiropractor) for a back adjustment. Mr. Jenkins left around 9:00 p.m. The accused told police that after Mr. Jenkins left, he and his wife watched *Nova* on PBS. (The accused was able to describe the program in detail to police.) At 10:00 p.m. his wife went out to the drive shed to train her dog for an upcoming competition. The accused used the hot tub in the basement of the home, tidied up the house, and got ready for bed. When his wife had not returned by 11:00 p.m., the accused went out to speak to her, as he was anxious to go to bed. He told police he opened the side door to the drive shed and found his wife. After calling 911 from the house, he returned to the drive shed and performed CPR. He told police that his wife was initially face down on her left side, that he rolled her onto her back, unzipped her jacket and performed several cycles of CPR.

The Crown's case against Mr. Galloway boils down to the following arguments that it intends to substantiate with supporting evidence:

1. First, the Crown contends that the crime scene was staged to make it appear as though the drive shed was broken into. In that respect, the Crown will point to the following:
   a. the purported point of entry was a broken window to the drive shed that is visible from the home and the street, whereas a far more discreet window at the back of the drive shed was untouched;
   b. those who perpetrate break-ins avoid residences where the occupants are home—the Galloway home was well lit on the night in question and two cars were in the driveway;
   c. late on an Easter Sunday evening is an especially strange time for a break-in, as residents are very likely to be home;
   d. no property of any apparent value, including rings on Mrs. Galloway's hands, was taken (notably, a snow blower was pushed outside of the drive shed, just beyond a roll-up door, but it was not removed from the property); and

    e. the amount of trauma visited upon Mrs. Galloway was more consistent with a crime of passion, not the sort of force one would expect from a burglar simply trying to make good his escape.

2. Second, the Crown contends that Mr. Galloway was the only person with the opportunity to commit the crime. In that regard, the Crown will emphasize that none of the neighbours heard or saw anything unusual on the evening in question prior to the arrival of emergency personnel.

3. Third, the Crown contends that Mr. Galloway lied about performing CPR. It asserts that he simply did not have enough blood on his person to have performed CPR on the blood-soaked victim. (When police arrived, there were only a few spots of blood on the accused's T-shirt.)

4. Finally, and most importantly from the perspective of the Crown, during the six-month period leading up to the murder, Mr. Galloway was involved in a passionate affair with another woman: Margaret Jenkins. The Crown will point to the affair as supplying Mr. Galloway with the motive to kill his wife.

In contrast, it will be the position of the defence at trial that the accused is innocent. The defence will point to the broken window in the drive shed and the snow blower pushed outside of the drive shed's open roll-up door as evidence of the break-in. In addition, the defence hopes to rely on a body of evidence that seems to point away from Mr. Galloway as the killer, including: unidentified fingerprints on the deceased's vinyl jacket; an unidentified partial palm print on the snow blower; unidentified footwear impressions on the windowsill and inside the drive shed; and fibres found on a stud, inside the drive shed, just below the broken window.

FURTHER READING

Anderson, Terence, David Schum & William Twining. *Analysis of Evidence*, 2nd ed (Cambridge: Cambridge University Press, 2005).

Brooks, Neil W. "The Judge and the Adversary System" in A Linden, ed, *The Canadian Judiciary* (Toronto: Osgoode Hall Law School, York University, 1976) at 90, reproduced in J Walker et al, *The Civil Litigation Process*, 8th ed (Toronto: Emond, 2016) 19.

Dufraimont, Lisa. "Evidence Law and the Jury: A Reassessment" (2008) 53 McGill LJ 199.

Ho, Hock Lai. "The Legal Concept of Evidence" in Edward N Zalta, ed, *The Stanford Encyclopedia of Philosophy*, Winter 2015 ed, online: Stanford Encyclopedia of Philosophy <http://plato.stanford.edu/archives/win2015/entries/evidence-legal>.

Mewett, Alan W & Shaun Nakatsuru. *An Introduction to the Criminal Process in Canada*, 4th ed (Toronto: Carswell, 2000).

Witnesses

In common law trials, the general rule is that the parties must prove or disprove all facts in issue through the oral (*viva voce*) evidence of witnesses. This general rule applies not only to facts directly observed by witnesses but also to physical and documentary evidence—in general, any object or document that is offered in evidence must be identified by a witness before it can be admissible. (There are some statutory exceptions to this general rule—e.g. s 51 of the *Controlled Drugs and Substances Act*, SC 1996, c 19.)

In order to testify, a witness must be competent and must either swear an oath to tell the truth or satisfy one of the statutory substitutes for the oath. This chapter introduces some of the issues surrounding these requirements: see Section I.

At common law, the parties, their spouses, and convicted felons were incompetent to testify because their testimony was deemed to be inherently unreliable. These testimonial disabilities have been removed, wholly or partially, by statute: *Alberta Evidence Act*, RSA 2000, c A-18, ss 3 and 4; *Evidence Act*, RSBC 1996, c 124, ss 3, 6, and 7; *Manitoba Evidence Act*, CCSM c E150, ss 3 and 4; *Evidence Act*, RSNB 1973, c E-11, ss 2, 3, 4, and 5; *Evidence Act*, RSNL 1990, c E-16, ss 2, 4, and 9; *Evidence Act*, RSNS 1989, c 154, ss 44, 45, and 48; *Evidence Act*, RSO 1990, c E.23, ss 6, 7, and 8; *Evidence Act*, RSPEI 1988, c E-11, ss 2, 3, and 4; *Evidence Act*, SS 2006, c E-11.2, ss 5 and 6. Convicts and the parties to civil cases are now in general competent witnesses. The testimonial disability of an accused person remains in force to the extent that the accused is an incompetent witness for the prosecution in criminal proceedings. Indeed, this disability now takes the form of the accused's constitutional right not to be compelled to be a witness. Some aspects of the accused's testimonial status are discussed in Section II.

The chapter concludes with a brief description of some aspects of testimony: see Sections III and IV.

I. THE OATH AND ITS SUBSTITUTES

In order to testify, a witness must be "competent"—that is, legally capable of testifying. With very few exceptions, every adult is a competent witness and may be compelled by subpoena to attend court for the purpose of testifying for any party to a proceeding. Once called to the witness stand, the witness must give some formal indication that he or she will be truthful. At common law, that formal indication was to take an oath to tell the truth. From the mid-18th century (see *Omychund v Barker* (1744), 1 Atk 21, 26 ER 15 (CA)), the oath did not have to be a Christian one, but the witness had to believe in some supreme being who would ensure retribution for breaking the oath. As John Stuart Mill observed in *On Liberty* (1859) ch 2, this rule was unfair to those non-believers who were honest enough to admit their lack of belief. Evidence acts now provide that evidence may be received on the basis of a solemn affirmation as a substitute for the oath: see e.g. *Canada Evidence Act*, RSC 1985, c C-5, s 14(1); *Alberta Evidence Act*, RSA 2000, c A-18, ss 15-18; *Evidence Act*, RSBC 1996, c 124, ss 20, 21; *Manitoba Evidence Act*, CCSM c E150, ss 13-18; *Evidence Act*, RSNB 1973, c E-11, ss 12-15; *Evidence Act*, RSNS 1989, c E-18, s 62(1); *Evidence Act*, RSO 1990, c E.23, s 17(1); *Evidence Act*, RSPEI 1988, c E-11, s 13; *Evidence Act*, SS 2006, c E-1.2, s 25(1). Note that some of the provincial acts still require a "conscientious objection" to the oath as a precondition for taking a solemn affirmation, although the federal act does not. In Sections I.A and I.B, we consider some aspects of the oath and solemn affirmation. In Section I.C, we consider the substitutes for the oath or affirmation where the witness is a child or a person whose mental capacity is challenged.

A. The Oath

If the witness's understanding of the oath is challenged, what must the party proposing the witness show in order to satisfy the trial judge that the witness is competent to testify?

R v Bannerman
(1966), 48 CR 110 (Man CA)
Miller CJM, Shultz JA, and Dickson J ad hoc (17 February 1966)

DICKSON J: The accused was tried before Keith Co. Ct. J on two charges, one of unlawfully having sexual intercourse with a girl under 14 years of age, and one of gross indecency with her brother on the same occasion. He was convicted on both charges and was sentenced to 20 years' imprisonment on the first charge and to two years' imprisonment, concurrent with the first sentence, on the second charge. At the time of trial the girl, Karen Vera Spence, was 12 years of age, and the boy, Frankie Keith Spence, 13 according to his evidence, but 12 according to the evidence of his mother. The children are of Indian extraction; the accused is not.

The accused appeals both conviction and sentence.

The first ground of appeal is that the judge erred in permitting Frankie Spence to be sworn when there was no sufficient inquiry made concerning his capacity to know the nature and consequences of an oath.

After questions which elicited that the boy was 13 and in Grade IV at Norquay School, the examination by Mr. Mitchell, Crown counsel, continued:

Q Do you know what it is to swear to tell the truth on the Bible? A No.

Mr. Walsh: The answer to that is "No."

Q That is correct, Mr. Walsh. The answer to that is "no."

If I asked you a question and asked you to tell the truth about what happened what would you tell me, the right thing that happened or the wrong thing? A The right thing.

Q If you put your right hand on the Bible and His Honour asked you if you would swear to tell the truth do you know what is meant? A Yes.

All right, put your hand on the Bible. What would this mean? A To tell the whole truth.

Mr. Mitchell: Does Your Honour wish to examine further of this witness as to whether he is capable of understanding an oath?

By the Court:

Q Did you ever go to church or Sunday school? A I go to catechism.

Q Do they tell you there you must tell the truth? A Yes.

Q And what do they say if you don't tell the truth? A I don't know.

Q That it is bad? A Yes.

Q Do you believe that it is? A Yes.

The Court: I think he can be sworn.

Mr. Walsh: I think not, Your Honour. I submit that is not sufficient to indicate the knowledge of the nature and consequences of an oath as set out in the *Sankey* case.

Mr. Mitchell: The *Sankey* case only goes to the discretionary opinion of the Court.

The Court: I look at this boy, he is a very bright looking boy, an intelligent boy. He goes to catechism and knows what the truth is and knows on all occasions he should tell the truth and particularly when he swears he shall tell the truth, is that correct?

The Witness: Yes.

Q And you know it is wrong not to tell the truth, don't you? A Yes.

Mr. Walsh: May I ask some questions?

The Court: Yes.

Q You are fourteen years of age? A Thirteen.

Q And you are in grade 4? A Yes.

Q When did you pass into grade 4? A Last year.

Q Last September? A Yes.

Q Now what would happen to you if you didn't tell the truth, do you know? A No.

Mr. Walsh: That is all I have to ask.

Mr. Mitchell: May the witness be sworn, Your Honour?

The Court: I see the magistrate had him sworn. I didn't realize that. I think I would rule he should be sworn. I think he knows what it means.

Counsel for the accused contends that the boy, although understanding the "nature" of an oath, did not understand the "consequences" of an oath and therefore the inquiry fell short of what is required by law.

[Dickson J reviewed a number of cases on point, quoted the version of s 16 of the *Canada Evidence Act* in force at the time, and continued:]

It is plain that the boy understood the nature and consequences of an oath. He understood that the consequence of taking an oath to be such that it placed him under a moral obligation to tell the truth, a breach of which moral obligation would be "bad" and "wrong." He knew that "on all occasions he should tell the truth and particularly when he swears he shall tell the truth." That could, in this case, have been a sufficient base for the judge to exercise his judicial discretion and to conclude that it was proper for the boy to be sworn. This judge had the very great advantage of observing and talking to the child. That this was of special importance is apparent from the judge's comments. Where a trial judge with these advantages examines a child as to its understanding of the nature of an oath and determines that the child is competent to testify, his discretion, unless manifestly abused, should not be interfered with. We must avoid appearing to be laying down what and how many questions must be asked. Each case will depend on its own facts, and the impression that the child makes upon the judge will be of great importance.

It was not necessary for the child to answer the question: "Q Now what would happen to you if you didn't tell the truth, do you know?," by replying, as suggested by counsel for the accused, that he would "go to hell." Counsel for the accused also suggested that an answer evidencing a belief in superhuman punishment *would* follow the telling of a lie was a condition precedent to the swearing of the boy.

The belief as to the spiritual consequences of an oath, supposing this to mean the spiritual consequences of telling a lie on oath, will necessarily differ according to the theological belief of the witness. An oriental child who, breaking a saucer against the witness box, responds to the oath: "You shall tell the truth and the whole truth; the saucer is cracked and if you don't tell the truth your soul will be cracked like the saucer"; or one who takes the "chicken oath," in which there is cut off the head of the fowl; or one who takes the "paper oath" in which the witness, having written his name on a piece of paper, burns it, may give different answers to the question: "What happens if you tell a lie?," and may all answer differently to the child raised in the Christian tradition.

What are the spiritual consequences of telling a lie under oath? No human being can say. When Frankie was asked what would happen to him if he didn't tell the truth and said that he did not know, he was simply giving the answer which any person asked this question must give, however learned and devout he may be. The more learned and devout the more probable that the answer would be the same as that given by this child.

As I have mentioned, counsel for the accused contended that Frankie Spence should have replied, "I will go to hell," or given some other answer acknowledging the sureness of Divine punishment. It seems to me that such thinking is wrong theologically and in other respects.

It is not Christian theology that a lie told on oath *will* be punished by hell fire. Nor is it Christian theology that superhuman retribution in this world or the next will *inevitably* follow false swearing.

An article of Christian theology is "the forgiveness of sins." It is Christian teaching that God will reward and punish according to one's deserts. Only God can judge what those may be. Only God could know "what would happen" to young Spence "if he didn't tell the truth."

. . .

In my opinion all that is required when one speaks of an understanding of the "consequences" of an oath is that the child appreciates it is assuming a moral obligation: See Best, Odgers, Archbold, and Halsbury, *supra*. The object of the law in requiring an oath is to get at the truth relative to the matters in dispute by getting a hold on the conscience of the witness.

I would hold that the trial judge's inquiry was sufficient to show that Frankie Spence understood the nature and consequences of an oath.

[Shultz JA agreed with Dickson J in separate reasons. Miller CJM dissented, holding that "[t]he evidence shows that the witness did not know the nature of an oath, and certainly did not know the consequences of failing to tell the truth under oath. The sanction involved in the word 'consequences' is a religious one." The appeal was dismissed.]

NOTES

Bannerman's further appeal to the Supreme Court was dismissed: [1966] SCR v, 50 CR 76.

In *R v Fletcher* (1982), 1 CCC (3d) 370 (Ont CA), a five-judge panel of the Ontario Court of Appeal said that for a child to take an oath, all that had to be determined was "whether the child has a sufficient appreciation of the solemnity of the occasion, and the added responsibility to tell the truth, which is involved in taking the oath." In *R v Leonard* (1990), 54 CCC (3d) 225 (Ont CA), the court held that a child had not been properly sworn for the following reasons:

[The trial judge's] inquiry did not show that the child appreciated the solemnity of the occasion. It did not show that she understood the added responsibility to tell the truth over and above the duty to tell the truth as part of the ordinary duty of normal social conduct. It did not show that she had an understanding of what it means to tell the truth in court. Nor did it show that she had an appreciation of what happens in both a practical and moral sense when a lie is told in court. Thus we are of the opinion that the inquiry did not establish her understanding of the nature of an oath.

These cases all involved child witnesses. The cases are nonetheless relevant to adult witnesses because they are ultimately concerned with whether the witness, child or adult, understands the nature of an oath.

B. The Solemn Affirmation

R v Walsh
(1978), 45 CCC (2d) 199 (Ont CA)
Brooke, Martin, and Lacourcière JJA (11 December 1978)

[The Crown appealed from the accused's acquittal on a charge of possession of stolen property.]

MARTIN JA: The trial Judge ruled that a proposed Crown witness who did not suffer from any mental disorder or defect, but who professed to be a "satanist" was incompetent to testify because he did not recognize any social duty to tell the truth in Court, although the proposed witness knew that he could be prosecuted and punished if he gave false evidence. The question presented by this appeal is whether the trial Judge was correct in so ruling.

When Crown counsel at the trial stated that he was going to call Stephen Harford (hereafter Harford) as a witness, defence counsel requested a *voir dire* to determine the competency of the proposed witness. Doctor Conn, a psychiatrist, testified on the *voir dire* that, at the request of Crown counsel, he had examined Harford. He testified that Harford suffers from a sociopathic type of personality, but did not suffer from psychosis or insanity. Doctor Conn did not suggest that the personality disorder from which Harford suffered was so severe as to constitute a mental disorder or mental illness of any kind. He said that Harford's intelligence was, at least, within the normal range, if not in excess of normal. He had what is called "average or better intelligence." He also testified that Harford was intellectually capable of distinguishing truth from falsehood, and would be able to understand questions and recall events. Harford would not, however, have the normal emotional response to wrongdoing in committing a falsehood. He expressed the opinion that the Bible would have little meaning for Harford in binding his conscience.

The learned trial Judge, initially, on the basis of Dr. Conn's evidence, ruled that Harford was competent to testify, and he was called to the witness-box. On being instructed by the Clerk of the Court to place his hand on the Bible to be sworn, Harford said he did not wish to do so, that he did not believe in the Bible, and believed in Satanism.

The trial Judge with the concurrence of both Crown counsel and defence counsel, then embarked on a second *voir dire*, during which Harford was examined and cross-examined with respect to his beliefs. Harford gave the following answers in examination-in-chief, and in cross-examination:

Q. All right. Now when you say you are a Satanist, what exactly are your beliefs?
A. I don't really feel I should say that.
His Honour: Answer the question, sir.
Witness: I am a god for a thing, a Satanist, I do what I feel I should. If I feel I shouldn't I won't.
Q. Well perhaps I should, and this may be a bit unusual, but I should go into more detail and what do you mean by truth?
A. What I feel is true. If I see something happening with my own eyes that is truth.

. . .

Q. Now you mentioned something about truth, that if you feel you should tell the truth you will tell the truth?

A. Yes.

Q. Now in this proceeding that we are now dealing with, what is your feeling as to truth?

A. I don't follow.

Q. If you were allowed to testify, I will ask you questions and defence counsel will ask questions. How will you answer those questions?

A. I'll answer them truthfully the way I saw them.

Q. Well perhaps I should go further. Why do you feel that you should answer or will answer the questions we put to you in this proceeding truthfully?

A. Because they are what happened.

Q. Are you aware of what is called the law of perjury.

A. Yes.

Q. Do you know what that is?

A. Yes.

Q. What is it?

A. Where you state something to the police and then you go to court and you don't say what you stated you can be charged with perjury. Is that what you mean?

Q. Are you aware that you can be punished if you don't tell the truth in court proceedings?

A. Yes.

Q. What, if any, obligation do you feel towards the community, that is, if my friends will allow me, the people, the government or the public, brought a charge against the accused for possession of stolen goods, and what, if any, obligation or duty do you feel towards the public in giving your answers in the proceedings?

A. I don't. It's for myself.

Q. What duty do you feel towards yourself?

A. I don't know, none really, just for myself I will tell the truth of what happened.

Q. Do you have any internal pressures or thing laying upon you that causes you to say you will tell the truth?

A. No.

Q. Can you give me any reason as to why you will tell the truth?

A. (No answer)

Q. What are your reasons for telling the truth in these proceedings?

A. You benefit from the truth. You don't benefit if you lie.

Q. How will you benefit from telling the truth in these proceedings?

A. I will be able to go through life saying I told the truth instead of saying I told a lie.

Q. And if you told a lie, how do you think that would affect you as you go through life?

A. I would not be able to live with myself.

Q. Why not?

A. Just to know that I lied.

Q. Do you have in your mind any benefit that you may obtain from not telling the truth?

A. No.

• • •

Q. You have indicated in examination that you would tell the truth if you felt a benefit, because there was a benefit from telling the truth, is that right?

A. Yes.

Q. Then would it be correct to assume that if there was no benefit to you, you conceptualise yourself a god those are the words you gave?

A. Sort of, yes.

Q. Would it be fair to say then if you felt there was no benefit in telling the truth, that there would be no benefit to you, as a god, that you would not tell the truth, is that fair to say?

A. It would depend on how I felt. If I don't feel like telling the truth, I won't but if I feel like telling the truth, I will.

Q. And that feeling, the feeling that you have about telling the truth or not telling the truth—

A. Right.

Q. —is really a question of whether it benefits you or not?

A. Somewhat, yes.

Q. Is that correct?

A. Yes.

Q. So that it therefore follows if it does not benefit you to tell the truth you won't tell the truth, isn't that correct?

A. Right.

Mr. Girard: Q. For example, if this Court ordered you to tell the truth and you as a god felt that you are not going to tell the truth because it does not benefit you, you still assert the right of superseding this Court's order to you?

A. (No answer)

Q. Is that what you are telling us?

A. I don't know. I guess that would have to occur. It has not occurred yet so I don't know how I would take it.

Q. Well if you were ordered to tell the truth—

A. Um-huh.

Q. —to testify, and if you choose not to tell the truth, are you not placing yourself above the order of this Court?

A. I guess I am.

Q. And because you are a god, in your words, you assert that right?

A. Um-huh.

Q. So you know from one point of [view] there may be a duty on you from within to tell the truth but you don't really, you don't really appreciate that from the point of view of necessarily having to do it, depending upon how you feel?

A. Um-huh.

Q. And irregardless (sic) of what this Court does or says, to force you to tell the truth, if you feel there is something you won't tell the truth about for your own personal reasons, you won't?

A. That's right. But I'm saying I will tell the truth.

• • •

His Honour: I gather, Mr. Harford, that you conceive to tell the truth is dependent upon whether you regard the answer that you might give as providing a benefit to yourself?

A. (No answer)

His Honour: As long as you perceive the answer is providing a benefit to yourself you are prepared to answer truthfully?

Witness: A. (No answer)

His Honour: Is that correct?

Witness: A. Yes, sir.

His Honour: And if in your wisdom you perceive it not to provide a benefit to yourself you would be prepared to lie?

Witness: A. I don't follow that.

His Honour: In other words, in giving an answer if you can perceive of no benefit accruing to yourself then you in those circumstances would be prepared to lie?

Witness: A. Yes.

It will be observed that although the witness acknowledged that in a hypothetical situation he would be prepared to lie if he perceived no benefit to himself in telling the truth, he, none the less, asserted that he would tell the truth in the case before the Court, because he could not live with himself otherwise. He never refused to affirm under s. 14 of the *Canada Evidence Act* and, indeed was not given the opportunity to affirm. Harford was competent mentally to testify, the requirements of s. 14 of the *Canada Evidence Act* were satisfied and he should have been affirmed. We do not wish in any way, however, to be thought to assent to the proposition that even if Harford had said that he would tell the truth or not as he pleased with respect to the very matter upon which he was called to give evidence, he would thereby become incompetent to testify, or that the Court would be powerless to deal with him by the coercive measures of contempt proceedings. We are also of the view that to affirm while at the same time asserting that he would not tell the truth would be equivalent to a refusal to affirm. Any other view would mean that a witness could deprive the prosecution or the defence of relevant evidence at his whim. I merely point out that this is not the situation here.

At the conclusion of the second *voir dire*, the trial Judge ruled that Harford was incompetent to testify. In our view, he erred in holding that Harford was not competent to testify because he disclaimed any social duty to tell the truth in Court.

. . .

At common law all testimony was required to be given on oath. Belief in a Supreme Being who in this life or hereafter will punish false swearing was a condition of competency, since in the absence of such a belief an oath would not bind the conscience of the witness. Legislation was first enacted to permit certain Christian sects whose religious tenets forbid the taking of a judicial oath, to affirm. Those persons who had no religious beliefs remained incompetent to testify in England until the *Evidence Amendment Act, 1869* (UK), c. 68, s. 4, was enacted: see Nokes, *An Introduction to Evidence*, 4th ed. (1967), p. 399.

Section 14 of the *Canada Evidence Act*, RSC 1970, c. E-10, is modelled on the English Act of 1869 with the omission of certain words. Section 14 reads:

14(1) Where a person called or desiring to give evidence objects, on grounds of conscientious scruples, to take an oath, or is objected to as incompetent to take an oath, such person may make the following affirmation:

I solemnly affirm that the evidence to be given by me shall be the truth, the whole truth, and nothing but the truth.

(2) Upon the person making such solemn affirmation, his evidence shall be taken and have the same effect as if taken under oath.

The words "is objected to as incompetent" in s. 14 do not refer to mental incompetency but to incompetency to take an oath on the ground that the oath would not bind the conscience of the witness because of an absence of religious belief. Harford was incompetent to take an oath since it would not bind his conscience, but he was not incompetent to testify on affirmation.

In his reasons for holding that Harford was incompetent to testify the learned trial Judge said:

I think it is abundantly apparent from the evidence of not only Dr. Conn, but of the proposed witness himself, that if there is in fact any duty to tell the truth, that duty is not to society, Mr. Bonn [defence counsel], nor to this Court, but to the witness himself.

In my view, that does not come within the test prescribed by *Hawke*. I well realize the difficulties engendered, however at this point I am going to rule the witness Harford as being incompetent to testify in these proceedings.

In *R v. Hawke* (1975), 22 CCC (2d) 19, Dubin JA speaking for the Court said at p. 30:

Prior to the introduction of what is now s. 14 of the *Canada Evidence Act* a person who could not be sworn could not testify. Pursuant to that section the Court may now have the benefit of the testimony of a witness under affirmation where it is held that the witness under affirmation where it is held that the witness ought not to be sworn on the grounds of conscientious scruples, or because the witness would not be bound by the sanction of an oath. However, the determination that a witness may be affirmed does not flow automatically upon determination that the witness ought not to be sworn. A further inquiry is necessary to determine whether the witness appreciates the duty of speaking the truth before the witness may be affirmed; the extent and nature of the inquiry depending upon the circumstances.

We are, with deference to the trial Judge, of the view that the above passage does not provide authority for his ruling that Harford was incompetent to testify. That passage must be considered in the context of the question before the Court in that case. The Crown on a charge of murder proposed to call as a witness a young woman with a long history of mental illness, who had been confined in a psychiatric facility until shortly before the killing which gave rise to the charge, and who at that time was being treated on an outpatient basis. Defence counsel stated that he intended to challenge the competency of the proposed witness. He then requested, but was refused, a brief adjournment in order to call two psychiatrists, under whose care the witness had been, to testify on the issue of competency. The trial Judge held, erroneously, that the issue of competency was resolved by s. 14 of the *Canada Evidence Act*.

Dubin JA, in the passage quoted above was dealing with the propriety of affirming a witness whose mental competency was in issue. He was not, in our view, enunciating a rule that in the case of an adult witness not suffering from any mental disorder or defect, it is necessary in every case, notwithstanding the requirements of s. 14 are satisfied, to conduct an inquiry to ensure that the witness appreciates the duty of speaking the truth before that witness may be affirmed. In any event, the *voir dire* in this case established that the witness appreciated the duty of speaking the truth in the relevant sense, since he was aware that he was liable to penal sanctions if he gave false evidence.

As previously indicated, we are all of the view that Harford was competent to testify on affirmation, that the trial Judge erred in holding that he was incompetent to testify, and should have directed that he be affirmed. Accordingly, the Crown is entitled to a new trial if it desires it. The appeal is allowed, the acquittal is set aside and a new trial is ordered.

QUESTIONS

1. Do you think that Harford's willingness to tell the truth was sufficient for him to affirm?

2. If *Bannerman* and *Walsh* are both correct, is there any practical difference between the oath and the solemn affirmation?

C. Unsworn Evidence

At common law, children and others who were unable to understand the meaning of an oath were incompetent to testify. Evidence acts now provide for substitutes for the oath in such cases. Section 16.1 of the *Canada Evidence Act*, reproduced below, governs the testimony of children. Section 16 of the Act, also reproduced below, governs the testimony of "a person whose mental capacity is challenged."

In *Khan*, the Supreme Court of Canada considered the meaning of an earlier version of s 16, which applied to "a child of tender years."

R v Khan
[1990] 2 SCR 531, 59 CCC (3d) 92
Lamer CJC and Wilson, Sopinka, Gonthier, and McLachlin JJ
(13 September 1990)

McLACHLIN J: This case raises the question of the admissibility of a child's unsworn evidence and statements made by a child to an adult concerning sexual assault.

The Facts

On March 26, 1985, Mrs. O. and her daughter T., who was three and a half years old, attended at the office of their family doctor, Dr. Khan, for a general examination of the mother and a routine immunization of T.

Dr. Khan examined T. first, in the presence of her mother. He then told her to wait in his private office while he conducted the examination of her mother. Dr. Khan and T. were alone in his private office for a period of five to seven minutes while the mother undressed and put on a hospital gown. T. was alone in the office for the following fifteen minutes while her mother's examination was being conducted. T. did not come into contact with any other male person during this period.

When the mother rejoined T., she noticed the child picking at a wet spot on her sleeve. They left and went to a nearby drug store. Upon leaving the store, approximately 15 minutes after leaving Dr. Khan's office, mother and child had essentially the following conversation:

> Mrs. O So you were talking to Dr. Khan, were you? What did he say?
>
> T. He asked me if I wanted a candy. I said yes. And do you know what?
>
> Mrs. O What?
>
> T. He said "open your mouth." And do you know what? He put his birdie in my mouth, shook it and peed in my mouth.
>
> Mrs. O Are you sure?
>
> T. Yes.
>
> Mrs. O You're not lying to me, are you?
>
> T. No. He put his birdie in my mouth. And he never did give me my candy.

The mother testified that the word "birdie" meant penis to T. As a result of the police investigation T.'s jogging suit was examined and the spot on the sleeve was determined to have been produced by a deposit of semen and, in some areas, a mixture of semen and saliva that had soaked through the fabric before it dried. The concentration of the mixture suggested to the forensic biologist that the substances were probably mixed before they were applied to the material.

The appellant was charged with sexual assault. At trial he elected to call no evidence. With respect to the Crown's case, the trial judge made two significant rulings. The trial judge held that T. was not competent to give unsworn evidence and also refused to admit the evidence of the mother as to the above-noted conversation on the basis that the statement was not contemporaneous with the event. The trial judge acquitted the appellant of the charges. The Crown appealed the acquittal to the Court of Appeal for Ontario, which allowed the appeal, set aside the acquittal and ordered a new trial: 42 CCC (3) 197.

Relevant Statutory Provision

Canada Evidence Act, RSC 1970, c. E-10, s. 16 (since repealed and replaced by 1987, c. 24, s. 18):

> 16(1) In any legal proceeding where a child of tender years is offered as a witness, and such child does not, in the opinion of the judge, justice or other presiding officer, understand the nature of an oath, the evidence of such child may be received, though not given upon oath, if, in the opinion of the judge, justice or other presiding officer, as the case may be, the child is possessed of sufficient intelligence to justify the reception of the evidence, and understands the duty of speaking the truth.
>
> (2) No case shall be decided upon such evidence alone, and it must be corroborated by some other material evidence.

Judgments

District Court of Ontario

Locke Dist. Ct. J did not admit the testimonial evidence of the child, T. He also rejected the argument that the statements T. made to her mother were admissible as an exception to the hearsay rule because they were "spontaneous statements." Therefore, Locke Dist. Ct. J did not admit the evidence of the mother with regard to the conversation that took place shortly after leaving the doctor's office. He concluded: "In all of the circumstances, and however suspicious I remain to this moment, the Crown has fallen just short of proof of the accused's guilt beyond a reasonable doubt."

Court of Appeal

Robins JA, writing for the court, found that the trial judge erred when considering the admission of the child's testimony. He found that the trial judge applied the more strenuous test for admission of sworn testimony when he should have applied the less strenuous test applicable to unsworn testimony. Robins JA also held that the trial judge erred when considering the admissibility of the spontaneous statements. In his opinion because the child was of tender years and because a sexual event was alleged greater latitude should have been given in respect of the lapse of time between the event and the declaration.

Issues

1. Did the Court of Appeal err in concluding that the trial judge misdirected himself in ruling that the child witness was incompetent to give unsworn testimony?

2. Did the Court of Appeal err in holding, contrary to the ruling of the trial judge, that a "spontaneous declaration" allegedly made by the child to her mother after the alleged sexual assault was admissible?

Analysis

1. Did the trial judge err in law in holding that the child was incompetent to give unsworn evidence?

T. was called as a witness at the trial. She was four years and eight months old. Questioning revealed that she did not understand what the Bible was and did not understand the nature of telling the truth "in court." The Crown did not contend that she was competent to give evidence under oath. It submitted, however, that her unsworn evidence should be received under s. 16 of the *Canada Evidence Act*:

· · ·

The trial judge refused to receive T.'s unsworn evidence on the ground that while she possessed sufficient intelligence to justify the reception of the evidence, he was not satisfied that she understood the duty of speaking the truth.

The Court of Appeal, *per* Robins JA, concluded that the trial judge had erred in rejecting T.'s testimony. It found he made two errors.

The first error, in the view of the Court of Appeal, was to apply the test in *Bannerman v. The Queen* (1966), 48 CR 110 (Man. CA); affirmed [1966] SCR v, 50 CR 76n, a case where the issue was the reception of evidence *under oath*, and in particular the statement of Dickson J that "[t]he object of the law in requiring an oath is to get at the truth relative to the matters in dispute by getting a hold on the conscience of the witness." (at p. 138).

Robins JA stated, at p. 206:

To satisfy the less stringent standards applicable to unsworn evidence, the child need only understand the duty to speak the truth in terms of ordinary everyday social conduct. This can be demonstrated through a simple line of questioning directed to whether the child understands the difference between the truth and a lie, knows that it is wrong to lie, understands the necessity to tell the truth, and promises to do so. It is to be borne in mind that under s. 16(2) the child's unsworn evidence must be corroborated by some other material evidence. Any frailties that may be inherent in the child's testimony go to the weight to be given the testimony rather than its admissibility.

The second error, the Court of Appeal concluded, was to place too much weight on the fact that the child was very young, in effect drawing a distinction between children of very tender years and older children. It is clear that the trial judge was concerned by the very young age of the witness. He pointed out that most of the cases concerned children of 10 to 13 years and that he could find no case of the evidence of a child under five being received. While acknowledging that theoretically a child of any age could be proffered in court, he noted in his concluding comments: "T. ... , however intelligent she may be to this day, is still very much an infant who is just beginning to embark upon childhood. She is still mentally and physically normal but very immature."

I agree with the Court of Appeal that the trial judge made the two errors to which it referred. He erred first in applying the *Bannerman* test to s. 16 of the *Evidence Act* and emphasizing that T. did not understand what it meant to lie "to the court." While the distinction between the ability to testify under oath and the ability to give unsworn evidence under s. 16 has been narrowed by rejection in cases such as *Bannerman* of the need for a religious understanding of the oath, it has not been eliminated. Before a person can give evidence under oath, it must be established that the oath in some way gets a hold on his conscience, that there is an appreciation of the significance of testifying in court under oath. It was wrong to apply this test, which T. clearly did not meet, to s. 16, where the only two requirements for reception of the evidence are sufficient intelligence and an understanding of the duty to tell the truth.

The trial judge also erred in placing critical weight on the child's young age. The Act makes no distinction between children of different ages. The trial judge in effect found that T. met the two requirements for permitting a child to testify under s. 16, but, emphasizing her immaturity, rejected her evidence. He found that T. had sufficient intelligence, and conceded that she "seemed to be aware at least of the consequences of telling a lie." This is clear from T.'s evidence, as revealed by the following portions of the transcript:

Q. Yes, and do you know what it is to tell the truth? You're sort of shrugging your shoulders there and smiling. Do you know what it is to tell a lie?
A. U-hmm.
Q. What's a lie?
A. If you say you cleaned up the room and you didn't, and your mother and your father went to see it and it's messy, that's a lie.
Q. I see. What happens when you tell a lie?
A. The parent spank their bum.

. . .

Q. I see. You're doing just fine. Tell me, what else happens to you if you tell a lie?

A. I get spanked and I get sent in my room and I get cleaned up and I cry and I come back out and I not cry, and that's okay.

Q. And then everything is fine, is it?

A. (Nod)

Having found that the two requirements for reception of the evidence under s. 16 had been fulfilled, the trial judge erred in letting himself be swayed by the young age of the child. Were that a determinative consideration, there would be danger that offences against very young children could never be prosecuted.

[The remainder of this case is reproduced in Chapter 4, Section III.B.]

After the trial in *Khan*, s 16 of the *Canada Evidence Act* was amended to read as follows:

16(1) Where a proposed witness is a person of fourteen years of age or older whose mental capacity is challenged, the court shall, before permitting the person to give evidence, conduct an inquiry to determine

(a) whether the person understands the nature of an oath or a solemn affirmation; and

(b) whether the person is able to communicate the evidence.

(2) A person referred to in subsection (1) who understands the nature of an oath or a solemn affirmation and is able to communicate the evidence shall testify under oath or solemn affirmation.

(3) A person referred to in subsection (1) who does not understand the nature of an oath or a solemn affirmation but is able to communicate the evidence may testify on promising to tell the truth.

(4) A person referred to in subsection (1) who neither understands the nature of an oath or a solemn affirmation nor is able to communicate the evidence shall not testify.

(5) A party who challenges the mental capacity of a proposed witness of fourteen years of age or more has the burden of satisfying the court that there is an issue as to the capacity of the proposed witness to testify under an oath or a solemn affirmation.

In *Marquard*, the Supreme Court considered the meaning of the phrase "communicate the evidence" in the revised version of s 16.

R v Marquard
[1993] 4 SCR 223, 108 DLR (4th) 47
Lamer CJC and La Forest, L'Heureux-Dubé, Sopinka, Gonthier, Cory, McLachlin, Iacobucci, and Major JJ (21 October 1993)

McLACHLIN J (Lamer CJC, Sopinka, Cory, Iacobucci, and Major JJ concurring): In the early morning hours of June 4, 1988, Debbie-Ann LeBlanc, aged three and one-half years, suffered a severe facial burn. From her birth until the time of her injury, Debbie-Ann had lived with her grandmother, the appellant, Mrs. Marquard. The appellant had legal custody of Debbie-Ann with the consent of Debbie-Ann's mother.

The appellant was charged with aggravated assault of her granddaughter, contrary to s. 245.2(1) of the *Criminal Code*, RSC 1970, c. C-34, as amended by 1980-81-82-83, c. 125, s. 19 (now RSC 1985, c. C-46, s. 268(1)). At trial, 17 months after the incident, the Crown alleged that Mrs. Marquard had put the child's face against a hot stove door in order to discipline her. The oven door was hot, it was suggested, because Mrs. Marquard had forgotten to turn the oven off before going to bed the night before because she had been drinking. The child, unsworn, testified: "My nanna put me on the stove."

Mrs. Marquard and her husband both testified about how they discovered that Debbie-Ann had been burned. There were only slight differences between the accounts they gave at trial. They testified that they had been awakened at 6:30 a.m. by the child screaming for her "nanna." They ran to the living-room where they found the child kneeling in front of a couch with her face down. Mrs. Marquard detected the smell of burned hair and skin. There was also smoke about the ceiling. A butane cigarette lighter lay beside the child on the couch. Mr. Marquard stated that he noticed that the cigarette was charred and that there appeared to be moisture on the filter end, as if the cigarette had been in someone's mouth. The testimony of Mr. and Mrs. Marquard diverged with respect to who had reached the child first and how they noticed the child's burn. Mrs. Marquard said she had reached Debbie-Ann first and when she patted the child's head, a clump of hair fell away. Mr. Marquard said he had been the first to reach the child, and when he picked her up, he saw a clump of her hair on the couch. He realized the child was burned after Mrs. Marquard brushed off the side of Debbie-Ann's face. Mrs. Marquard testified that, after they had discovered the child's burn, she said: "My God, baby girl, what did you do?" The child responded: "Nanna, I tried to light a cigarette." At this point, they wrapped her and took her to Wellesley Hospital. Mr. and Mrs. Marquard testified that Mrs. Marquard had a loving and caring relationship with Debbie-Ann and that the child had never been physically disciplined.

The trial was by judge and jury. In addition to the evidence recounted above, the Crown called a number of expert witnesses to corroborate its version of the events as did the defence. The expert evidence related to the functioning of butane lighters, the nature of the burn, whether the child was telling the truth at the trial, and the psychological effects of abuse. At the end of the evidence, the addresses of counsel and the judge's charge, the jury returned a verdict of guilty after deliberating for two days. The judge sentenced Mrs. Marquard to five years' imprisonment. The Ontario Court of Appeal upheld the conviction but reduced the sentence of imprisonment to two years less a day and added a three-year probationary period to her sentence. The court stated:

> The appellant has raised a number of issues both as to the admission of evidence and the charge to the jury. As to the evidentiary issues, having regard to the manner in which the trial was conducted by the defence we cannot give affect [sic] to these objections now. As to the charge to the jury, we think the trial judge left the issues fairly to the jury, there may be some imperfections in the charge but we are not persuaded that there was any error that would cause us to doubt that this verdict of the jury should stand.

Before this court, Mrs. Marquard argued that the trial was unfair on a number of grounds. She asked that her conviction be quashed and an acquittal entered, or alternatively, that a new trial be directed.

I have concluded that while a number of the matters complained of by the appellant do not constitute errors, the cumulative effect of the errors which were committed in the course of the trial mandates that a new trial be directed. I will deal with each allegation of error in turn.

1. The Inquiry Under s. 16(1)(b) of the Canada Evidence Act

The appellant, Mrs. Marquard, submits that the trial judge erred in failing to conduct an adequate inquiry into whether the complainant could rationally communicate evidence about the injury. The trial judge questioned Debbie-Ann on her schooling and on her appreciation of the duty to tell the truth. Several times the child reiterated that "You have to tell the truth." Asked whether it was important or unimportant to tell the truth, she responded that it was important. At the end of the questioning, the judge asked defence counsel whether she had omitted any questions. He replied: "I can't say that there's anything I think Your Honour has omitted." In further questioning by Crown counsel, Debbie-Ann demonstrated that she knew the difference between the truth and a lie. The judge indicated that while she did not believe the child capable of understanding an oath, her unsworn evidence should be accepted. Some further questioning on remembering took place, and Debbie-Ann told the judge that yesterday "I went down to the donut shop, and I got a drink and bubble gum." After promising to tell the truth, the child's evidence was taken.

The trial judge was proceeding under s. 16(1)(b) of the *Canada Evidence Act*, RSC 1985, c. C-5; repealed and substituted RSC 1985, c. 19 (3rd Supp.), s. 18, which provides:

> 16(1) Where a proposed witness is a person under fourteen years of age or a person whose mental capacity is challenged, the court shall, before permitting the person to give evidence, conduct an inquiry to determine
>
> . . .
>
> (b) whether the person is able to communicate the evidence.

The appellant's argument turns on the meaning of the phrase "conduct an inquiry to determine … whether the person is able to communicate the evidence." She contends that it is not enough to explore the child's ability to understand the truth and communicate. The judge must, in her submission, satisfy herself that the child is competent to testify about the events at issue in the trial. To this end, the trial judge must test the child's ability to perceive and interpret the events in question at the time they took place, as well as her ability to recollect accurately and communicate them at trial. All the latter, she submits, are embraced by the phrase "able to communicate the evidence" in s. 16 of the Act.

The Crown, on the other hand, takes the position that Parliament, in choosing the infinitive "to communicate," evinced the intention to exclude all other aspects of testimonial competence. The ability of the witness to perceive and interpret the events at the time they occurred and the ability of the witness to recollect them at the time of trial are not part of the test. The only requirement is that the child be able to "communicate" her evidence.

It seems to me that the proper interpretation of s. 16 lies between these two extremes. In the case of a child testifying under s. 16 of the *Canada Evidence Act*, testimonial competence is not presumed. The child is placed in the same position as an adult whose competence has been challenged. At common law, such a challenge required the judge to inquire into the competence of the witness to testify.

Testimonial competence comprehends: (1) the capacity to observe (including interpretation); (2) the capacity to recollect, and (3) the capacity to communicate: *McCormick on Evidence*, 4th ed. (St. Paul, Minn.: West Publishing Co., 1992), vol. 1, pp. 242-8; *Wigmore on Evidence* (Chadbourn rev. 1979), vol. 2, pp. 636-8. The judge must satisfy himself or herself that the witness possesses these capacities. Is the witness capable of observing what was happening? Is he or she capable of remembering what he or she observes? Can he or she communicate what he or she remembers? The goal is not to ensure that the evidence is credible, but only to assure that it meets the minimum threshold of being receivable. The inquiry is into *capacity* to perceive, recollect and communicate, not whether the witness *actually* perceived, recollects and can communicate about the events in question. Generally speaking, the best gauge of capacity is the witness's performance at the time of trial. The procedure at common law has generally been to allow a witness who demonstrates capacity to testify at trial to testify. Defects in ability to perceive or recollect the particular events at issue are left to be explored in the course of giving the evidence, notably by cross-examination.

I see no indication in the wording of s. 16 that Parliament intended to revise this time-honoured process. The phrase "communicate the evidence" indicates more than mere verbal ability. The reference to "the evidence" indicates the ability to testify about the matters before the court. It is necessary to explore in a general way whether the witness is capable of perceiving events, remembering events and communicating events to the court. If satisfied that this is the case, the judge may then receive the child's evidence, upon the child's promising to tell the truth under s. 16(3). It is not necessary to determine in advance that the child perceived and recollects the very events at issue in the trial as a condition of ruling that her evidence be received. That is not required of adult witnesses, and should not be required for children.

My colleague, Justice L'Heureux-Dubé, contends that the standard I have outlined is one which is inconsistent with "the trend to do away with presumptions of unreliability and to expand the admissibility of children's evidence and may, in fact, subvert the purpose of legislative reform in this area." I disagree. The test I have expounded is not based on presumptions about the incompetency of children to be witnesses nor is it intended as a test which would make it difficult for children to testify. Rather, the test outlines the basic abilities that individuals need to possess if they are to testify. The threshold is not a high one. What is required is the basic ability to perceive, remember and communicate. This established, deficiencies of perception, recollection of the events at issue may be dealt with as matters going to the weight of the evidence.

The examination conducted in this case was sufficient to permit the trial judge to conclude that Debbie-Ann was capable of perceiving events, remembering events and recounting events to the court. This in turn permitted the trial judge to receive her evidence, upon Debbie-Ann's promise to tell the truth. What Debbie-Ann actually perceived and recollected of the events in question was a matter for the jury to determine after listening to her evidence in chief and in cross-examination.

I would add this. It has repeatedly been held that a large measure of deference is to be accorded to the trial judge's assessment of a child's capacity to testify. Meticulous second-guessing on appeal is to be eschewed. As Dickson J (as he then was) put it in the oft-cited case of *R v. Bannerman* (1966), 48 CR 110 at p. 135 (Man. CA); affirmed [1966] SCR v, 50 CR 76n, a trial judge's discretion in determining that a child is competent to testify "unless manifestly abused, should not be interfered with."

I conclude that the trial judge did not err in the inquiry she conducted under s. 16(1)(b) of the *Canada Evidence Act* or in receiving the evidence of the child.

· · ·

[L'Heureux-Dubé J dissented. She held that "[u]nder s. 16, once the child's ability to communicate (understood as the ability to respond to questions) has been established, any limitations due to deficiencies in recollection or perception go to weight rather than admissibility." Gonthier J, La Forest J concurring, agreed with McLachlin J in the result but with L'Heureux-Dubé J on the meaning of s 16.]

NOTES AND QUESTIONS

At the new trial, Marquard was acquitted: see *R v Marquard*, [1995] OJ No 3050 (QL) (Gen Div). Moldaver J, as he then was, received the child's evidence but was not satisfied beyond a reasonable doubt of its accuracy and reliability. He was particularly concerned about the differences between the child's description of the event and the medical evidence concerning the nature of the burn to the child's face.

As a result of changes to the *Canada Evidence Act* that came into force in 2006, s 16 now applies only to persons "of fourteen years of age or older whose mental capacity is challenged." The evidence of children is now governed by s 16.1, which provides as follows:

16.1(1) A person under fourteen years of age is presumed to have the capacity to testify.

(2) A proposed witness under fourteen years of age shall not take an oath or make a solemn affirmation despite a provision of any Act that requires an oath or a solemn affirmation.

(3) The evidence of a proposed witness under fourteen years of age shall be received if they are able to understand and respond to questions.

(4) A party who challenges the capacity of a proposed witness under fourteen years of age has the burden of satisfying the court that there is an issue as to the capacity of the proposed witness to understand and respond to questions.

(5) If the court is satisfied that there is an issue as to the capacity of a proposed witness under fourteen years of age to understand and respond to questions, it shall, before permitting them to give evidence, conduct an inquiry to determine whether they are able to understand and respond to questions.

(6) The court shall, before permitting a proposed witness under fourteen years of age to give evidence, require them to promise to tell the truth.

(7) No proposed witness under fourteen years of age shall be asked any questions regarding their understanding of the nature of the promise to tell the truth for the purpose of determining whether their evidence shall be received by the court.

(8) For greater certainty, if the evidence of a witness under fourteen years of age is received by the court, it shall have the same effect as if it were taken under oath.

In *DAI*, the Supreme Court of Canada considered some aspects of the new ss 16 and 16.1.

R v DAI
2012 SCC 5, [2012] 1 SCR 149
McLachlin CJC and Binnie, LeBel, Deschamps, Fish, Abella, Charron, Rothstein,
and Cromwell JJ (10 February 2012)

McLACHLIN CJC (Deschamps, Abella, Charron, Rothstein, and Cromwell JJ concurring):
[1] Sexual assault is an evil. Too frequently, its victims are the vulnerable in our society—children and the mentally handicapped. Yet rules of evidence and criminal procedure, based on the norm of the average witness, may make it difficult for these victims to
testify in courts of law. The challenge for the law is to permit the truth to be told, while
protecting the right of the accused to a fair trial and guarding against wrongful conviction.

[2] Parliament has addressed this challenge by a series of amendments to the *Canada
Evidence Act*, R.S.C. 1985, c. C-5, that modify the normal rules of testimonial capacity
for children and adults with mental disabilities. This Court has considered the provisions
relating to children on a number of occasions. This appeal involves the provisions relating
to adults with mental disabilities.

[3] At the heart of this case is a young woman, K.B., aged 26, with the mental age of
a three- to six-year-old. The Crown alleges that she was repeatedly sexually assaulted by
her mother's partner at the time, D.A.I. The prosecution sought to call the young woman
to testify about the alleged assaults. It also sought to adduce evidence through her school
teacher and a police officer of what she told them.

[4] The trial judge excluded this evidence, on the ground that K.B. was not competent
to testify in a court of law (A.R., vol. I, at p. 2). As a result, the case collapsed and D.A.I.
was acquitted (2008 CanLII 21725 (Ont. S.C.J.)). The Ontario Court of Appeal affirmed
the acquittal (2010 ONCA 133, 260 O.A.C. 96).

[5] I respectfully disagree. In my view, the trial judge made a fundamental error of
law in interpreting and applying the provisions of the *Canada Evidence Act* governing the
testimonial competence of adult witnesses with mental disabilities. This error of law viti-
ates the trial judge's ruling that K.B. could not be allowed to testify. Subsequent evidence
on other matters cannot overcome this fatal defect. I would therefore set aside the acquittal
of D.A.I. and order a new trial.

. . .

II. *Legal Analysis*

A. *Testimonial Competence: A Threshold Requirement*

[15] Before turning to s. 16(3) of the *Canada Evidence Act*, it is important to distinguish between three different concepts that are sometimes confused: (1) the witness's
competence to testify; (2) the admissibility of his or her evidence; and (3) the weight of
the witness's testimony. The evidentiary rules governing all three concepts share a common purpose: ensuring that convictions are based on solid evidence and that the accused
has a fair trial. However, each concept plays a distinct role in achieving this goal.

[16] The first concept, and the one most relevant to this appeal, is the principle of
competence to testify. Competence addresses the question of whether a proposed witness
has the capacity to provide evidence in a court of law. The purpose of this principle is to

exclude at the outset worthless testimony, on the ground that the witness lacks the basic capacity to communicate evidence to the court. Competence is a threshold requirement. As a matter of course, witnesses are presumed to possess the basic "capacity" to testify. However, in the case of children or adults with mental disabilities, the party challenging the competence of a witness may be called on to show that there is an issue as to the capacity of the proposed witness.

[17] The second concept is admissibility. The rules of admissibility determine what evidence given by a competent witness may be received into the record of the court. Evidence may be inadmissible for various reasons. Only evidence that is relevant to the case may be considered by the judge or jury. Evidence may also be inadmissible if it falls under an exclusionary rule, for example the confessions rule or the rule against hearsay evidence. Among the purposes of the rules of admissibility are improving the accuracy of fact finding, respecting policy considerations, and ensuring the fairness of the trial.

[18] The third concept—the responsibility of the trier of fact to decide what evidence, if any, to accept—is based on the assumption that the witness is competent and the rules of admissibility have been properly applied. Fulfillment of these requirements does not establish that the evidence should be accepted. It is the task of the judge or jury to weigh the probative value of each witness's evidence on the basis of factors such as demeanour, internal consistency, and consistency with other evidence, and to thus determine whether the witness's evidence should be accepted in whole, in part, or not at all. Unless the trier of fact is satisfied that the prosecution has established all elements of the offence beyond a reasonable doubt, there can be no conviction.

[19] Together, the rules governing competence, admissibility and weight of the evidence work to ensure that a verdict of guilty is based on accurate and credible evidence and that the accused person has a fair trial. The point for our purposes is a simple one: the requirement of competence is only the first step in the evidentiary process. It is the initial threshold for receiving evidence. It seeks a minimal requirement—a basic ability to provide truthful evidence. A finding of competence is not a guarantee that the witness's evidence will be admissible or accepted by the trier of fact.

B. The Requirements for Competence of Adult Witnesses with Mental Disabilities: Section 16 of the Canada Evidence Act

[20] Against this background, I come to the provision at issue in this case, s. 16(3) of the *Canada Evidence Act*, which governs the capacity to testify of adults with mental disabilities. ...

[21] Section 16(1) sets out what a judge must do when a challenge is raised. First, the judge must determine "whether the person understands the nature of an oath or a solemn declaration" and "whether the person is able to communicate the evidence" (s. 16(1)). If these requirements are met, the witness testifies under oath or affirmation, as other witnesses do (s. 16(2)). If these requirements are not met, the judge moves on to s. 16(3). Section 16(3) provides that "[a] person ... who does not understand the nature of an oath or a solemn affirmation but is able to communicate the evidence may ... testify on promising to tell the truth."

[22] In brief, s. 16(1) provides that an adult witness whose competence to testify is challenged should testify under oath or affirmation, if the witness "understands the nature

of an oath or a solemn affirmation" and can "communicate the evidence." Here K.B. did not meet the first requirement. The inquiry therefore moved to s. 16(3), which states that if an adult witness cannot take the oath or affirm under s. 16(1), then she must be permitted to testify *if she is "able to communicate the evidence" and promises to tell the truth.*

[23] On its face, s. 16 says that in a case such as this where the witness cannot take the oath or affirm, the judge has only one further issue to consider—whether the witness can communicate the evidence. If the answer to that question is yes, the judge must then ask the witness whether she promises to tell the truth. If she does, she is competent to testify. It is not necessary to inquire into whether the witness understands the duty to tell the truth.

[24] The respondent argues, however, that the plain words of s. 16(3) do not suffice. They must be supplemented, he says, by the requirement that an adult witness with mental disabilities who cannot take an oath or affirm must not only be able to communicate the evidence and promise to tell the truth, but must also *understand the nature of a promise to tell the truth.*

[25] I cannot accept this submission. The words of an Act are to be interpreted in their entire context: *Rizzo & Rizzo Shoes Ltd. (Re)*, [1998] 1 S.C.R. 27, at para. 21. The wording of s. 16(3), its history, its internal logic and its statutory context all point to the conclusion that s. 16(3) should be read as it stands, without reading in a further requirement that the witness demonstrate an understanding of the nature of the obligation to tell the truth. All that is required is that the witness be able to communicate the evidence and in fact promise to tell the truth.

[26] First, as already mentioned, this interpretation goes beyond the words used by Parliament. To insist that the witness demonstrate understanding of the nature of the obligation to tell the truth is to import a requirement into the section that Parliament did not place there. The first and cardinal principle of statutory interpretation is that one must look to the plain words of the provision. Where ambiguity arises, it may be necessary to resort to external factors to resolve the ambiguity: R. Sullivan, *Sullivan on the Construction of Statutes* (5th ed. 2008), at p. 44. However, Parliament has clearly stated the requirements for finding adult witnesses with mental disabilities to be competent. Section 16 shows no ambiguity.

[27] Second, the history of s. 16 supports the view that Parliament intended to remove barriers that had prevented adults with mental disabilities from testifying prior to the 1987 amendments (S.C. 1987, c. 24). The amendments altered the common law rule, by virtue of which only witnesses under oath could testify. To take the oath or affirm, a witness must have an understanding of the duty to tell the truth: *R. v. Brasier* (1779), 1 Leach 199, 168 E.R. 202. Adults with mental disabilities might not be able to do this. To remove this barrier, Parliament provided an alternative basis for competence for this class of individuals. Section 16(1) of the 1987 provision continued to maintain the oath or affirmation as the first option for adults with mental disabilities, but s. 16(3) provided for competence based simply on the ability to communicate the evidence and a promise to tell the truth.

[28] This history suggests that Parliament intended to eliminate an understanding of the abstract nature of the oath or solemn affirmation as a prerequisite for testimonial capacity. Failure to show that the witness *could demonstrate an understanding of the obligation to tell the truth* was no longer the end of the matter. Provided the witness (1) was

able to *communicate the evidence*, and (2) promised to tell the truth, she should be allowed to testify.

[29] The drafters of s. 16(3) did not intend this provision to require an abstract understanding of the duty to tell the truth (see Appendix A). The original text of Bill C-15, which adopted the 1987 amendments, was changed by the Legislative Committee on Bill C-15 precisely to avoid that interpretation. The version of s. 16(3) first put before Parliament allowed testimony on promising to tell the truth if the witness was "sufficiently intelligent that the reception of the evidence is justified." A discussion was held on the meaning of "sufficient intelligence," after which the Committee concluded that all that was needed for a witness to be sufficiently intelligent was to understand the moral difference between telling the truth and lying. The Committee, fearing that this would open the door to abstract inquiries, ultimately replaced "sufficient intelligence" by "able to communicate the evidence." The deliberations that followed emphasized the practical ability to communicate the evidence. There was no suggestion that ability to communicate the evidence accompanied by a promise to tell the truth implicitly imposed a requirement that the witness demonstrate a more abstract understanding of the duty to tell the truth.

[30] The historic background against which s. 16(3) was enacted explains why Parliament might have wished in 1987 to lower the requirements of testimonial competence for adults with mental disabilities, who are nonetheless capable of communicating the evidence. While adults with mental disabilities received little consideration in the pre-1987 case law, the inappropriateness of questioning children on abstract understandings of the truth had been noted and criticized. In *R. v. Bannerman* (1966), 48 C.R. 110 (Man. C.A.), Dickson J. *ad hoc* (as he then was) rejected the practice of examining child witnesses on their religious beliefs and the philosophical meaning of truth. Meanwhile, awareness of the sexual abuse of children and adults with mental disabilities was growing. To rule out the evidence of children and adults with mental disabilities at the stage of competence— the effect of the requirement of an abstract understanding of the nature of the obligation to tell the truth—meant their stories would never be told and their cases never prosecuted. These concerns explain why Parliament moved to simplify the competence test for adult witnesses with mental disabilities.

[31] Third, and flowing from this history, the internal logic of s. 16 negates the suggestion that "promising to tell the truth" in s. 16(3) must be read as implying an understanding of the obligation to tell the truth. Two procedures are provided by s. 16. The preferred option is testimony under oath or affirmation (s. 16(1)), and the alternative procedure is testimony on a promise to tell the truth (s. 16(3)). If the witness is required under s. 16(3) to demonstrate that she understands the obligation to tell the truth, s. 16(3) adds little, if anything, to s. 16(1). In both cases, the witness is required to articulate abstract concepts of the nature of truth and the nature of the obligation to tell the truth in court. The result is essentially to render s. 16(3) a dead letter and to negate the dual structure of the provision. This runs against the principle of statutory interpretation that Parliament does not speak in vain: *Attorney General of Quebec v. Carrières Ste-Thérèse Ltée*, [1985] 1 S.C.R. 831, at p. 838.

[32] Fourth, s. 16(4) indicates that ability to communicate the evidence is the only quality that an adult with mental disabilities must possess in order to testify under s. 16(3). Section 16(4) provides that the proposed witness is unable to testify if she neither understands the nature of an oath or solemn affirmation nor is able to communicate the evidence.

It follows that the witness is competent to testify if she is able to communicate the evidence; she may testify on promising to tell the truth under s. 16(3). The qualities envisaged in s. 16 as basis for testimonial competence are mentioned in s. 16(4). Imposing an additional qualitative requirement to understand the nature of a promise to tell the truth would flout the utility of s. 16(4).

[33] Fifth, the legislative context speaks against reading s. 16(3) as requiring that an adult witness with mental disabilities understand the nature of the obligation to tell the truth. If this requirement is added to s. 16(3), the result is a different standard for the competence of adults with mental disabilities under s. 16(3) and children under s. 16.1 (enacted in 2005 (S.C. 2005, c. 32) pursuant to the "Brief on Bill C-2: Recognizing the Capacities & Needs of Children as Witnesses in Canada's Criminal Justice System" (Child Witness Project, March 2005) (the "Bala Report")). As will be discussed more fully below, s. 16(3) governing the competence of adults with mental disabilities, and ss. 16.1(3), (5) and (6) governing the competence of children, set forth essentially the same requirements. Broadly speaking, both condition testimonial capacity on: (1) the ability to communicate or answer questions; and (2) a promise to tell the truth. While it was open to Parliament to enact different requirements for children and adults with the minds of children, consistency of Parliamentary intent should be assumed, absent contrary indications. No explanation has been offered as to why Parliament would consider a promise to tell the truth a meaningful procedure for children, but an empty gesture for adults with mental disabilities.

[34] The foregoing reasons make a strong case that s. 16(3) should be read as requiring only two requirements for competence of an adult with mental disabilities: (1) ability to communicate the evidence; and (2) a promise to tell the truth. However, two arguments have been raised in opposition to this interpretation: first, without a further requirement of an understanding of the obligation to tell the truth, a promise to tell the truth is an "empty gesture"; second, Parliament's failure in 2005 to extend to adults with mental disabilities the s. 16.1(7) prohibition on the questioning of children means that it intended this questioning to continue for adults. I will examine each argument in turn.

[35] The first argument is that unless an adult witness with mental disabilities is required to demonstrate that she understands the nature of the obligation to tell the truth, the promise is an "empty gesture." However, this submission's shortcoming is that it departs from the plain words of s. 16(3), on the basis of an assumption that is unsupported by any evidence and contrary to Parliament's intent. Imposing an additional qualitative condition for competence that is not provided in the text of s. 16(3) would demand compelling demonstration that a promise to tell the truth cannot amount to a meaningful procedure for adults with mental disabilities. No such demonstration has been made. On the contrary, common sense suggests that the act of promising to tell the truth may be useful, even in the absence of the witness's ability to explain what telling the truth means in abstract terms.

[36] Promising is an act aimed at bringing home to the witness the seriousness of the situation and the importance of being careful and correct. The promise thus serves a practical, prophylactic purpose. A witness who is able to communicate the evidence, as required by s. 16(3), is necessarily able to relate events. This in turn implies an understanding of what really happened—i.e. the truth—as opposed to fantasy. When such a witness promises to tell the truth, this reinforces the seriousness of the occasion and the

need to do so. In dealing with the evidence of children in s. 16.1, Parliament held that a promise to tell the truth was all that is required of a child capable of responding to questions. Parliament did not think a child's promise, without more, is an empty gesture. Why should it be otherwise for an adult with the mental ability of a child?

[37] The second argument raised in support of the proposition that "promising to tell the truth" in s. 16(3) implies a requirement that the witness must show that she understands the nature of the obligation to tell the truth is that Parliament has not enacted a ban on questioning adult witnesses with mental disabilities on the nature of the obligation to tell the truth, as it did for child witnesses in 2005 in s. 16.1(7). To understand this argument, we must briefly trace the history of s. 16.1.

[38] In 2005, following the Bala Report, Parliament once more modified the *Canada Evidence Act's* provisions on testimonial competence, but this time only with respect to children. The central focus of the 2005 legislation relating to the *Canada Evidence Act* was the competence of *child* witnesses, with the aim of altering the restrictive gloss the case law had placed on the previous provisions relating to the capacity of children to testify. Chief among this case law was *R. v. Khan* (1988), 42 C.C.C. (3d) 197 (Ont. C.A.), which insisted that a child understand the nature of the obligation to tell the truth before the child could testify. Section 16.1, in unequivocal language, rejected this requirement.

[McLachlin CJC quoted s 16.1 and continued:]

[39] Section 16.1, like s. 16(3) governing adult witnesses with mental disabilities, imposed two preconditions for the testimony of children: (1) that the child be able to understand and respond to questions (s. 16.1(5)); and (2) that the child promise to tell the truth (s. 16.1(6)). But, taking direct aim at *Khan's* insistence that children be questioned on their understanding of the nature of the obligation to tell the truth, s. 16.1(7) went on to state explicitly that children not *"be asked any questions regarding their understanding of the nature of the promise to tell the truth for the purpose of determining whether their evidence shall be received by the court."*

[40] The argument is that if Parliament had intended adult witnesses with mental disabilities to be competent to testify simply on the basis of the ability to communicate and the making of a promise, it would have enacted a ban on questioning them on their understanding of the nature of the obligation to tell the truth, as it did for child witnesses under s. 16.1(7). The absence of such a provision, it is said, requires us to draw the inference that Parliament intended that *adult* witnesses with mental disabilities *must* be questioned on the obligation to tell the truth.

[41] First, this argument overlooks the fact that Parliament's concern in enacting the 2005 amendment to the *Canada Evidence Act* was exclusively with children. The changes arose out of the Bala Report on the problems associated with prosecuting crimes against children. The Parliamentary debates on s. 16.1 attest to the fact that the focus of the 2005 amendment was on children, and only children.

[42] Moreover, it is apparent from the Parliamentary works on Bill C-2 that s. 16.1(7) was intended to confirm the existing formal requirement of a promise alone, and not to modify the law: see Appendix B.

· · ·

[44] Second, as already mentioned, the wording of s. 16(3) governing the competence of adult witnesses had since 1987 required only a promise to tell the truth. There was no need for Parliament to add a provision on questioning an adult witness's understanding of the nature of the obligation to tell the truth in s. 16(3). The fact that Parliament did so 18 years later for children's evidence under s. 16.1(7) reflects concern with the fact that courts in children's cases, such as *Khan*, were continuing to engage in this type of questioning, instead of accepting a simple promise to tell the truth. It does not evince an intention that Parliament intended the words "promising to tell the truth" to have different meanings in ss. 16(3) and 16.1(6).

[45] Third, the argument that the enactment of s. 16.1(7) for children but not for adults endorsed as applicable to adult witnesses the earlier judicial interpretation of the provisions relating to children does not take into account s. 45 of the federal *Interpretation Act*, R.S.C. 1985, c. I-21 … .

[46] Section 45(3) of the *Interpretation Act* provides that the amendment of an enactment (in this case the adoption of s. 16.1(7)) shall not be deemed to involve any declaration as to the meaning of the previous law (in this case s. 16(3)). Therefore, no inference as to the meaning of s. 16(3) flows from the mere adoption of s. 16.1(7) with respect to children.

[47] Additionally, s. 45(4) of the *Interpretation Act* states that the re-enactment of a provision (in this case, s. 16 with respect to adults with mental disabilities) is not sufficient to infer that Parliament adopted the provision's judicial interpretation which prevailed at the time of the re-enactment. It follows that the fact that s. 16 was re-enacted for adults with mental disabilities in 2005 does not, alone, imply that Parliament intended to countenance the judicial interpretation of this section which required understanding the obligation to tell the truth.

[48] Fourth, the argument that the absence of the equivalent of s. 16.1(7) in s. 16(3) means that adult witnesses with mental disabilities must demonstrate an understanding of the nature of the duty to speak the truth is logically flawed. The argument rests on the premise that s. 16(3), unless amended, requires an inquiry into the witness's understanding of the obligation to tell the truth. On this basis, it asserts that, unless the ban on questioning in s. 16.1(7) dealing with children is read into s. 16(3), such questioning must be conducted. Thus, my colleague Binnie J. states that "[t]he Crown invites us, in effect, to apply the 'don't ask' rule governing children to adults whose mental capacity is challenged" (para. 127).

[49] The fallacy in this argument is the starting assumption that s. 16(3) requires importing a "don't ask" rule. As explained earlier, it does not. Section 16(3) sets two requirements for the competence of adults with mental disabilities: the ability to communicate the evidence and a promise to tell the truth. It is self-sufficient. Nothing further need be imported.

[50] Fifth, and following from the previous point, the argument relies on the assumption that unless it can be shown that adult witnesses with mental disabilities are the same as, or like, child witnesses, adult witnesses with mental disabilities must be treated differently, and subjected to an inquiry into their understanding of the nature of the obligation to tell the truth before they can be held competent to testify. Thus Binnie J. states that before s. 16(3) can be read as importing the "don't ask" rule, it is for the Crown to establish that there is no difference between children and adults with mental disabilities on the test

of what reasonable people would accept. He opines that an assertion of equivalency is "pure assertion on a key issue" (para. 130).

[51] There are several answers to this "equivalency" argument. First, like the previous argument, it rests on the mistaken assumption that the Crown asks us to import a "don't ask" rule into s. 16(3). The plain words of s. 16(3) do not require an understanding of the obligation to tell the truth, and it is for the party seeking to depart from the text of s. 16(3) to demonstrate that adults with mental disabilities should be treated differently from children. Second, the argument suffers from inconsistency. It claims that the equivalency of the vulnerabilities of these two groups of witnesses is "pure assertion on a key issue," but at the same time claims that the previous judge-made law for children (*Khan*) should apply to adult witnesses with mental disabilities. Third, one may question how equivalency, were it needed, should be established: Is the proper approach to competence what reasonable people would conclude, or judicial opinion informed by assessment of the situation and expert opinion?

[52] The final and most compelling answer to the equivalency argument is simply this: When it comes to testimonial competence, precisely what, one may ask, is the difference between an adult with the mental capacity of a six-year-old, and a six-year-old with the mental capacity of a six-year-old? Parliament, by applying essentially the same test to both under s. 16(3) and s. 16.1(3) and (6) of the *Canada Evidence Act*, implicitly finds no difference. In my view, judges should not import one.

[53] I conclude that s. 16(3) of the *Canada Evidence Act*, properly interpreted, establishes two requirements for an adult with mental disabilities to take the stand: the ability to communicate the evidence and a promise to tell the truth. A further requirement that the witness demonstrate that she understands the nature of the obligation to tell the truth should not be read into the provision.

C. The Jurisprudence

[McLachlin CJC considered a number of earlier cases and held that "insofar as the authorities suggest that 'promising to tell the truth' in s. 16(3) should be read as requiring an abstract inquiry into an understanding of the obligation to tell the truth, they should be rejected. All that is required is that the witness be able to communicate the evidence and promise to tell the truth." She continued:]

D. Policy Considerations

[64] I have concluded that s. 16(3) imposes two requirements for the testimonial competence of an adult with mental disabilities: (1) the ability to communicate the evidence; and (2) a promise to tell the truth. It is unnecessary and indeed undesirable to conduct an abstract inquiry into whether the witness generally understands the difference between truth and falsity and the obligation to give true evidence in court. Mentally limited people may well understand the difference between the truth and a lie and know they should tell the truth, without being able to articulate in general terms the nature of truth or why and how it fastens on the conscience in a court of law. Section 16(3), in assessing the witness's capacity, focuses on the concrete acts of communicating and promising. The witness is not required to explain the difference between the truth and a lie, or what makes a promise binding. I have argued that this result follows from the plain words of s. 16 of

the *Canada Evidence Act*, and that judges should not by implication add other elements to the dual requirements of an ability to communicate evidence and a promise to tell the truth imposed by s. 16(3).

[65] The discussion of the proper interpretation of s. 16(3) of the *Canada Evidence Act* would not be complete, however, without addressing the policy concerns underlying the issue. Two potentially conflicting policies are in play. The first is the social need to bring to justice those who sexually abuse people of limited mental capacity—a vulnerable group all too easily exploited. The second is to ensure a fair trial for the accused and to prevent wrongful convictions.

[66] The first policy consideration is self-evident and requires little amplification. Those with mental disabilities are easy prey for sexual abusers. In the past, mentally challenged victims of sexual offences have been frequently precluded from testifying, not on the ground that they could not relate what happened, but on the ground that they lacked the capacity to articulate in abstract terms the difference between the truth and a lie and the nature of the obligation imposed by promising to tell the truth. As discussed earlier, such witnesses may well be capable of telling the truth and in fact understanding that when they do promise, they should tell the truth. To reject this evidence on the ground that they cannot explain the nature of the obligation to tell the truth in philosophical terms that even those possessed of normal intelligence may find challenging is to exclude reliable and relevant evidence and make it impossible to bring to justice those charged with crimes against the mentally disabled.

[67] The inability to prosecute such crimes and see justice done, whatever the outcome, may be devastating to the family of the alleged victim, and to the victim herself. But the harm does not stop there. To set the bar too high for the testimonial competence of adults with mental disabilities is to permit violators to sexually abuse them with near impunity. It is to jeopardize one of the fundamental desiderata of the rule of law: that the law be enforceable. It is also to effectively immunize an entire category of offenders from criminal responsibility for their acts and to further marginalize the already vulnerable victims of sexual predators. Without a realistic prospect of prosecution, they become fair game for those inclined to abuse.

[68] What then of the policy considerations on the other side of the equation? Here again, the starting point is clear. The *Canadian Charter of Rights and Freedoms* guarantees a fair trial to everyone charged with a crime. This right cannot be abridged; an unfair trial can never be condoned.

[69] It is neither necessary nor wise to enter on the vast subject of what constitutes a fair trial. One searches in vain for exhaustive definitions in the jurisprudence. Rather, the approach taken in the jurisprudence is to ask whether particular rules or occurrences render a trial unfair. It is from that perspective that we must approach this issue in this case.

[70] The question is this: Does allowing an adult witness with mental disabilities to testify when the witness can communicate the evidence and promises to tell the truth render a trial unfair? In my view, the answer to this question is no.

[71] The common law, upon which our current rules of evidence are founded, recognized a variety of rules governing the capacity to testify in different circumstances. The golden thread uniting these varying and different rules is the principle that the evidence must meet a minimal threshold or reliability as a condition of being heard by a judge or jury. Generally speaking, this threshold of reliability is met by establishing that the witness

has the capacity to understand and answer the questions put to her, and by bringing home to the witness the need to tell the truth by securing an oath, affirmation or promise. There is no guarantee that any witness—even those of normal intelligence who can take the oath or affirm—will in fact tell the truth, all the truth, or nothing but the truth. What the trial process seeks is merely a basic indication of reliability.

[72] Many cases, including *Khan*, have warned against setting the threshold for the testimonial competence too high for adults with mental disabilities: *R. v. Caron* (1994), 72 O.A.C. 287; *Farley* [*R v Farley* (1995), 23 OR (3d) 445]; *Parrott* [*R v Parrott* (1999), 175 Nfld & PEIR 89]. This reflects the fact that such witnesses may be capable of giving useful, relevant and reliable evidence. It also reflects the fact that allowing the witness to testify is only the first step in the process. The witness's evidence will be tested by cross-examination. The trier of fact will observe the witness's demeanour and the way she answers the questions. The result may be that the trier of fact does not accept the witness's evidence, accepts only part of her evidence, or reduces the weight accorded to her evidence. This is a task that judges and juries perform routinely in a myriad of cases involving witnesses of unchallenged as well as challenged mental ability.

[73] The requirement that the witness be able to communicate the evidence and promise to tell the truth satisfies the low threshold for competence in cases such as this. Once the witness is allowed to testify, the ultimate protection of the accused's right to a fair trial lies in the rules governing admissibility of evidence and in the judge's or jury's duty to carefully assess and weigh the evidence presented. Together, these additional safeguards offer ample protection against the risk of wrongful conviction.

E. Summary of the Section 16(3) Test

[74] To recap, s. 16(3) of the *Canada Evidence Act* imposes two conditions for the testimonial competence of adults with mental disabilities:

(1) the witness must be able to communicate the evidence; and

(2) the witness must promise to tell the truth.

Inquiries into the witness's understanding of the nature of the obligation this promise imposes are neither necessary nor appropriate. It is appropriate to question the witness on her ability to tell the truth in concrete factual circumstances, in order to determine if she can communicate the evidence. It is also appropriate to ask the witness whether she in fact promises to tell the truth. However, s. 16(3) does not require that an adult with mental disabilities demonstrate an understanding of the nature of the truth *in abstracto*, or an appreciation of the moral and religious concepts associated with truth telling.

[75] The following observations may be useful when applying s. 16(3) in the context of s. 16 of the *Canada Evidence Act*.

[76] First, the *voir dire* on the competence of a proposed witness is an independent inquiry: it may not be combined with a *voir dire* on other issues, such as the admissibility of the proposed witness's out-of-court statements.

[77] Second, although the *voir dire* should be brief, it is preferable to hear all available relevant evidence that can be reasonably considered before preventing a witness to testify. A witness should not be found incompetent too hastily.

[78] Third, the primary source of evidence for a witness's competence is the witness herself. Her examination should be permitted. Questioning an adult with mental disabilities requires consideration and accommodation for her particular needs; questions should be phrased patiently in a clear, simple manner.

[79] Fourth, the members of the proposed witness's surrounding who are personally familiar with her are those who best understand her everyday situation. They may be called as fact witnesses to provide evidence on her development.

[80] Fifth, expert evidence may be adduced if it meets the criteria for admissibility, but preference should always be given to expert witnesses who have had personal and regular contact with the proposed witness.

[81] Sixth, the trial judge must make two inquiries during the *voir dire* on competence: (a) does the proposed witness understand the nature of an oath or affirmation, and (b) can she communicate the evidence?

[82] Seventh, the second inquiry into the witness's ability to communicate the evidence requires the trial judge to explore in a general way whether she can relate concrete events by understanding and responding to questions. It may be useful to ask if she can differentiate between true and false everyday factual statements.

[83] Finally, the witness testifies under oath or affirmation if she passes both parts of the test, and on promising to tell the truth if she passes the second part only.

III. Application

[84] During the *voir dire* on K.B.'s testimonial capacity, the Crown posed a line of questions going to whether she could tell the difference between true and false factual statements in concrete circumstances. These were relevant to K.B.'s basic ability to communicate the evidence:

MR. SEMENOFF:

Q. How old are you now, [K.B.]?

A. I'm 22, you know that.

Q. 22? When's your birthday?

A. [Birth date].

Q. [Birth date]. Are you going to school now or are you done with school?

A. I'm not done in school yet.

Q. What school do you go to, [K.B.]?

A. [Name of school].

Q. How long—do you know how long you've been going to [name of school]?

A. I don't know.

Q. Did you go to any school before you went to [name of school]?

A. From [name of previous school].

Q. From [name of previous school]. Okay. Did you have a teacher from that school, a Ms. [W.]?

A. Ms. [R.].

Q. Oh, [R.]. Okay. And I call her Ms. [W.], do you know what her name is, is it [R.] or is it Ms. [W.]?

A. [R.].

Q. Okay.

. . .

    Q. [K.B.], if I were to tell you that the room that we're in that the walls in the room are black[,] would that be a truth or a lie, [K.B.]?

    A. A lie.

    Q. Why would it be a lie?

    A. It's different colours in here.

    Q. There are different colours in here. What colour are the walls?

    A. Purple.

    Q. Purple. Okay. If I were to tell you that the gown that I'm wearing that that is black, would that be a truth or a lie?

    A. The truth.

    Q. And why is that?

    A. I don't know.

    Q. You don't know. Is it a good thing or a bad thing to tell the truth?

    A. Good thing.

    Q. Is it a good thing or a bad thing to tell a lie?

    A. Bad thing.

(A.R., vol. I, at pp. 111-13)

However, the trial judge went on to question K.B. on her understanding of the meaning of truth, religious concepts, and the consequences of lying.

[THE COURT:]

    [Q.] Do you go to church, [K.B.]?

    A. No.

    Q. No. Have you ever been taught about God or anything like that?

    A. No.

    Q. No? All right. What happens if you steal something?

    A. I don't know.

    Q. You don't know. If you steal something and no one sees it, will anything happen to you? Nothing will happen. Why won't anything happen?

    A. I don't know.

    Q. You don't know. Tell me what you think about the truth.

    A. I don't know.

    Q. You don't know. All right. Is it important to tell the truth?

    A. I don't know.

    Q. You don't know. Tell me what a promise is when you make a—

    A. I don't know.

    Q. —promise. What's a promise?

    A. I don't know.

    Q. You don't know what a promise is. Okay. Have you ever been in court before?

    A. Once.

    Q. Once? And do you think it's an important thing to be in court?

    A. I don't know.

    Q. You don't know. All right. Do you know what an oath is, to take an oath?

    A. I don't know.

Q. No. Do you have any idea what it means to tell the truth?

A. I don't know.

Q. You don't know. If you tell a lie does anything happen to you? Nothing happens.

A. No.

. . .

[THE COURT:]

[Q.] Do you know why you're here today?

A. I don't know. To talk about [D.A.I.].

Q. Yes, and do you think that's really important?

A. Maybe yeah.

Q. Maybe yeah? Remember earlier I was asking you about a promise?

A. No.

Q. Have you ever made a promise to anybody?

A. I don't know.

Q. That you promised you'll be good, did you ever say that? Have you ever heard that expression "I promise to be good, mommy"?

A. Okay.

Q. All right. So do you know what a promise is, that you're going to do something the right way? Do you understand that?

A. Okay.

Q. Can you tell me whether you understand that, [K.B.]?

A. I don't know.

Q. Does anything happen if you break a promise?

A. I don't know.

Q. You told me you don't go to church, right?

A. Right.

Q. And no one has ever told you about God; is that correct? No one has ever told you about God?

A. No.

Q. Has anyone ever told you that if you tell big lies you'll go to jail?

A. Right.

Q. If you tell big lies will you go to jail?

A. No.

(*Ibid.*, at pp. 117-19 and 155-56)

[85] As these passages demonstrate, the trial judge was not satisfied with the Crown's questions on K.B.'s ability to recount events and distinguish between telling the truth and lying in concrete, real-life situations. He went on to question her on the nature of truth, religious obligations and the consequences of failing to tell the truth. Because K.B. was unable to satisfactorily answer these more abstract questions, he ruled that she could not be allowed to promise to tell the truth and refused to allow her to testify.

[86] This ruling was based on an erroneous interpretation of s. 16(3), which the trial judge read as requiring an understanding of the duty to speak the truth. Hence, K.B. was precluded from testifying on promising to tell the truth. The trial judge summed up his conclusions as follows:

Having questioned [K.B.] at length I am fully satisfied that [K.B.] *has not satisfied the prerequisite that she understands the duty to speak to the truth.* She cannot communicate what truth involves or what a lie involves, or what consequences result from truth or lies, and in such circumstances, quite independent of the evidence of [Dr. K.], I am not satisfied that she can be permitted to testify *under a promise to tell the truth.* [Emphasis added; *ibid.*, at p. 3.]

[87] The fatal error of the trial judge is that he did not consider the second part of the test under s. 16. He failed to inquire into whether K.B. had the ability to communicate the evidence under s. 16(3), insisting instead on an understanding of the duty to speak the truth that is not prescribed by s. 16(3). This error, an error of law, led him to rule K.B. incompetent and hence to the total exclusion of her evidence from the trial. This fundamental error vitiated the trial.

. . .

[90] I would allow the appeal, set aside the acquittal, and direct a new trial.

BINNIE J (LeBel and Fish JJ concurring) (dissenting):

[91] I agree with the Chief Justice that, in this case, "[t]wo potentially conflicting policies are in play," the first being to "bring to justice" those accused of sexual abuse and the second being "to ensure a fair trial for the accused and to prevent wrongful convictions" (para. 65). In my view, by turning Parliament's direction permitting a person "whose mental capacity is challenged" to testify only "on promising to tell the truth" into an empty formality—a mere mouthing of the words "I promise" without any inquiry as to whether the promise has any significance to the potential witness—the majority judgment unacceptably dilutes the protection Parliament intended to provide to accused persons.

[92] I prefer the contrary interpretation of s. 16(3) of the *Canada Evidence Act*, R.S.C. 1985, c. C-5, expressed by our Chief Justice herself in her concurring judgment in *R. v. Rockey*, [1996] 3 S.C.R. 829, where, as McLachlin J., drawing a distinction between "the ability to communicate the evidence and the ability to promise to tell the truth" (para. 25), wrote:

The only inference that can be drawn from this evidence is that while [the potential witness] Ryan understood the difference between what is "so" and "not so," he had no conception of any moral obligation to say what is "right" or "so" in giving evidence or otherwise. In these circumstances, *no judge could reasonably have concluded that Ryan was able to promise to tell the truth.* [Emphasis added; para. 27.]

McLachlin J.'s views on the requirements of s. 16(3) were not disagreed with by the majority, and indeed on this point she simply reflected the Court's earlier unanimous opinion in *R. v. Khan*, [1990] 2 S.C.R. 531, at pp. 537-38.

[93] The majority judgment in the present case repudiates the earlier jurisprudence and the balanced approach it achieved. It entirely eliminates any inquiry into whether the potential witness has any "conception of any moral obligation to say what is 'right.' "

[94] I agree with the Chief Justice that "allowing the witness to testify is only the first step in the process" (para. 72). More particularly, my colleague continues:

The witness's evidence will be tested by cross-examination. The trier of fact will observe the witness's demeanour and the way she answers the questions. [*Ibid.*]

In this case, the exchanges between the challenged witness, K.B., and the trial judge, demonstrated the futility of any such cross-examination. The trial judge noted that K.B. "did not 'compute' questions before giving answers, that she was not processing the information being communicated to her, and that she had serious problems relating to her ability to communicate and to recollect," 2008 CanLII 21726 (Ont. S.C.J.) (the "hearsay decision"), at para. 7). As a practical matter, it is not possible to cross-examine such a witness meaningfully. The trial judge concluded correctly on this point that "there is no secure method of testing K.B.'s credibility" (para. 56). The result of the majority judgment in this case is to create unfair prejudice to the accused.

[95]   What is fundamental, as was emphasized here by the Ontario Court of Appeal, is that the trial judge had the opportunity to observe the witness's demeanour and the way she answers the questions (McLachlin C.J., at para. 72). We do not have that advantage. The trial judge concluded, based on his direct observation, that, in light of the severity of her mental disability, K.B.'s evidence could not be relied upon for the truth-seeking purposes of a criminal trial and it ought to be altogether excluded. In a judge-alone trial, it goes without saying, where the trial judge found that K.B.'s testimony did not meet even a threshold of admissibility, he would not—had the evidence been admitted—have accepted it as the basis for a proper conviction. An acquittal was inevitable.

NOTE

The *Victims Bill of Rights Act*, SC 2015, c 13, which came in to force in 2015, added the following subsection to s 16 of the *Canada Evidence Act*:

> 16(3.1) A person referred to in subsection (3) shall not be asked any questions regarding their understanding of the nature of the promise to tell the truth for the purpose of determining whether their evidence shall be received by the court.

In light of *DAI*, what is the effect, if any, of this amendment?

II. THE TESTIMONIAL COMPETENCY OF THE ACCUSED AND HIS OR HER SPOUSE

At common law, the accused person and his or her spouse were incompetent witnesses for either party in both civil and criminal proceedings. As noted above, in civil proceedings, these disabilities have been removed by statute in every common law province and territory. The situation in criminal proceedings is more complex. In Section II.A, we consider the testimonial competency of the accused's spouse historically and as recently affected by legislative changes. In Section II.B, we consider the testimonial position of the accused person.

A. Spousal Competency in Criminal Proceedings

As noted above, at common law, the accused and his or her spouse were incompetent witnesses for either the prosecution or the defence. Statutory changes in the late 19th century made both the accused and his spouse competent witnesses for the defence. For example, the *Canada Evidence Act*, RSC 1985, c C-5, now provides:

4(1) Every person charged with an offence, and, except as otherwise provided in this section, the wife or husband, as the case may be, of the person so charged, is a competent witness for the defence, whether the person so charged is charged solely or jointly with any other person.

However, the accused and his spouse remained incompetent witnesses for the prosecution. In *Salituro*, extracted below, Iacobucci J described the rationales for the incompetency of the accused's spouse and suggested that these rationales were weak in the Charter era.

R v Salituro
[1991] 3 SCR 654, 68 CCC (3d) 289
Lamer CJ and Gonthier, Cory, McLachlin and Iacobucci JJ (28 November 1991)

IACOBUCCI J (for the court):

(1) The Origins of the Rule in General

The first clear authority for the rule that a spouse is not a competent witness is Lord Coke's *Institutes of the Laws of England*, originally published in 1628. The rule was initially concerned only with the testimonial incompetence of wives: a wife was an incompetent witness for or against her husband. Lord Coke described the rule as follows (1 Inst. 6b.):

> *Note*, it hath been resolved by the justices, that a wife cannot be produced either against or for her husband, *quia sunt duae animae in carne unâ*; and it might be a cause of implacable discord and dissention between the husband and the wife, and a meane of great inconvenience …

The rule that a wife was an incompetent witness for or against her husband followed naturally from the legal position of a wife at the time. On marriage, a woman lost her independent legal identity. Blackstone, *supra* [*Commentaries on the Laws of England*, 4th ed (1770)], described the legal status of a married woman as follows, at p. 442 of Book One:

> By marriage, the husband and wife are one person in law; that is, the very being or legal existence of the woman is suspended during the marriage, or at least is incorporated and consolidated into that of the husband; under whose wing, protection, and cover, she performs every thing; and is therefore called in our law-french a *femme-covert, foemina viro co-operta*; is said to be *covert-baron*, or under the protection and influence of her husband, her *baron*, or lord; and her condition during her marriage is called her *coverture*. [Emphasis in original.]

The general testimonial incompetence of a wife for or against her husband was accepted in *Lord Audley's Case* (1631), Hutt. 115 at p. 116, 123 ER 1140 at p. 1141.

(2) Justifications for the Rule

Since that time, at least four distinct justifications have been advanced for the rule but only two of these survive today. The most important justification is that the rule protects marital harmony. The danger to marital harmony of making a spouse a competent witness was first mentioned by Lord Coke, and was most recently emphasized in the decision of the Court of Appeal in the case at bar, in *R v. Bailey, supra* [(1983), 4 CCC (3d) 21 (Ont. CA)], and in *R v. Sillars, supra* [(1978), 45 CCC (2d) 283 (BCCA)]. A second reason sometimes mentioned is what Wigmore called the "*natural repugnance* to every fair-minded person to compelling a wife or husband to be the means of the other's condemnation" (*Wigmore on Evidence* (McNaughton rev. 1961), vol. 8, p. 217, s. 2228 (emphasis in original)).

The two justifications which have not survived are that a spouse is an incompetent witness because husband and wife are in law a single person (although this justification survived into the 18th century), and that husband and wife are disqualified from being a witness for or against each other because their interests are identical.

The policy grounds supporting the rule have come in for sustained attack. Wigmore scathingly criticizes the variety of inconsistent arguments used to support the rule (at p. 213):

> The record of judicial ratiocination defining the grounds and policy of this privilege forms one of the most curious and entertaining chapters of the law of evidence. It is curious because the variety of ingenuity displayed, in the invention of reasons "ex post facto" for a rule so simple and so long accepted, could hardly have been believed but for the recorded utterances … We behold the fantastic spectacle of a fundamental rule of evidence, which had only questionable reasons for existence, surviving nonetheless through two centuries upon the strength of certain artificial dogmas—pronouncements wholly irreconcilable with each other, with the facts of life and with the rule itself, and yet repeatedly invoked, with smug judicial positiveness, like magic formulas to still the specter of forensic doubt.

In the study paper "Competence and Compellability" by the Evidence Project of the Law Commission of Canada, the rule was characterized as more a product of history than the reflection of any clear policy decision (*Evidence* (1972), Study Paper No. 1, at p. 5):

> … the rule, rather than the reflection of a clear-cut fundamental policy decision, appears to be simply a product of history. This is confirmed when we note that a fundamental policy decision surely would be based on concern not only for the married couple but for the family unit as a whole, and yet no one has suggested legislation making fathers and sons or mothers and daughters incompetent witnesses for the prosecution against their parents or children.

There is, in my opinion, a more fundamental difficulty with the reasons for the rule. The grounds which have been used in support of the rule are inconsistent with respect for the freedom of all individuals, which has become a central tenet of the legal and moral fabric of this country particularly since the adoption of the Charter. In *R v. Big M Drug Mart Ltd.*, [1985] 1 SCR 295, Dickson J (as he then was) defined freedom in this way (at p. 336): "Freedom must surely be founded in respect for the inherent dignity and the inviolable rights of the human person." The common law rule making a spouse an incompetent witness involves a conflict between the freedom of the individual to choose whether or not to testify and the interests of society in preserving the marriage bond. It is unnecessary for me to consider the difficult question of how this conflict ought to be resolved, because in this appeal we are concerned only with spouses who are irreconcilably separated. Where spouses are irreconcilably separated, there is no marriage bond to protect and we are faced only with a rule which limits the capacity of the individual to testify.

To give paramountcy to the marriage bond over the value of individual choice in cases of irreconcilable separation may have been appropriate in Lord Coke's time, when a woman's legal personality was incorporated in that of her husband on marriage, but it is inappropriate in the age of the Charter. As Wilson J put it in *R v. Morgentaler*, [1988] 1 SCR 30 at p. 166, the Charter requires that individual choices not be restricted unnecessarily:

The idea of human dignity finds expression in almost every right and freedom guaranteed in the Charter. Individuals are afforded the right to choose their own religion and their own philosophy of life, the right to choose with whom they will associate and how they will express themselves, the right to choose where they will live and what occupation they will pursue. These are all examples of the basic theory underlying the Charter, namely, that the state will respect choices made by individuals and, to the greatest extent possible, will avoid subordinating those choices to any one conception of the good life.

Through its family and divorce laws, our society has recognized that spouses have the right to seek dissolution of the marriage where relations between them have irrevocably broken down. The recognition that a marriage may be dissolved is reflected in the long history of divorce legislation. Divorce without a special Act of Parliament has been possible in England since the 1857 *Matrimonial Causes Act*, 1857 (UK), c. 85. In Canada, there was a Divorce Act as early as 1758 in Nova Scotia and later in other provinces; the first federal Divorce Act was the *Divorce Act*, SC 1967-68, c. 24; later RSC 1970, c. D-8: see "Competence and Compellability," *ibid.*, at p. 6, and more generally Alastair Bissett-Johnson and David C. Day, *The New Divorce Law* (1986).

Despite the suggestion in *Salituro* that the rule of spousal incompetency was inconsistent with Charter values, the Supreme Court of Canada declined to abrogate or to modify the rule, preferring to leave such a major change to Parliament: see e.g. *R v Hawkins*, [1996] 3 SCR 1043, 30 OR (3d) 641, 111 CCC (3d) 129.

There were several exceptions to the rule of spousal incompetency. The spouse was a competent witness for the prosecution in cases involving the spouse's "person, liberty, or health": see *The Lord Audley's Case* (1631), 3 State Tr 4015, 123 ER 1140. Under the *Canada Evidence Act*, the accused's spouse was a competent and compellable witness for the prosecution where the accused was charged with certain other offences where the victim or complainant was under 14 years of age or with a sexual offence. In *Salituro*, the Supreme Court of Canada created a common law exception under which an "irreconcilably separated" spouse was a competent witness for the prosecution. Finally, in *Hawkins*, the court suggested that if the marriage was a "sham," entered into for the purpose of avoiding the obligation to testify, the spouse might be competent for the prosecution, although on the facts of the case the marriage between the accused and the proposed Crown witness was found to be genuine.

There were two main controversies about the scope of the rule of spousal incompetency. First, who was a "spouse" for the purposes of the rule? In general, the rule applied only to legally married couples. This restriction was challenged several times as a violation of the equality guarantee in s 15 of the *Canadian Charter of Rights and Freedoms*, but most of these challenges failed: see e.g. *R v Martin*, 2009 SKCA 37; *R v Nguyen*, 2015 ONCA 278.

Second, was a comptent spouse also compellable? This question did not arise under the statutory exceptions, which expressly made the spouse "competent and compellable," but it was unclear whether a spouse who was competent under a common law exception was also compellable. If the spouse was competent but not compellable, then he or she would be permitted to choose whether to testify against his or her husband or wife; but if the spouse was competent and compellable, then he or she could be compelled to testify like any other witness. In the leading case on point, McLachlin JA (as she then was) held on policy grounds that a spouse who was a competent witness under the common law exception for offences involving his or her "person, liberty, or health" was also compellable: see *R v McGinty*, [1986] 4 WWR 97, 27 CCC (3d) 36 (YKCA).

These controversies are likely moot as a result of a recent amendment to the *Canada Evidence Act*. Section 4(2), in force since August 2015, now provides:

> 4(1) No person is incompetent, or uncompellable, to testify for the prosecution by reason only that they are married to the accused.

What exactly is the effect of this amendment? Is there any possible constitutional objection to it?

Section 4(3) of the Act provides:

> 4(3) No husband is compellable to disclose any communication made to him by his wife during their marriage, and no wife is compellable to disclose any communication made to her by her husband during their marriage.

This "spousal communication privilege" is considered in more detail in Chapter 9, Privilege and Related Issues.

B. The Testimonial Competency of the Accused

At common law, the accused was incompetent to testify in his own defence. When that incompetency was removed, what is now section 4(6) of the *Canada Evidence Act* was enacted. The provision currently reads as follows:

> 4(6) The failure of the person charged, or of the wife or husband of that person, to testify shall not be made the subject of comment by the judge or by counsel for the prosecution.

What is the purpose of this provision? When does a "comment" by a trial judge offend it?

McConnell and Beer v R
[1968] SCR 802, 69 DLR (2d) 149
Fauteux, Judson, Ritchie, Hall, and Spence JJ (24 June 1968)

RITCHIE J (Fauteux and Judson JJ concurring): This is an appeal from a judgment of the Court of Appeal for Ontario affirming the conviction of the appellants on a charge that they did, without lawful excuse, have in their possession instruments for house-breaking contrary to s. 295(1) of the *Criminal Code*.

· · ·

The facts which gave rise to this prosecution were that at 12:35 a.m. on September 3, 1966, the appellant Beer was sitting behind the steering wheel of a motor vehicle owned by his wife which was parked at the rear of some dry cleaning premises in Sault Ste. Marie. The head lights were turned off, the motor was running and the appellant McConnell was some 60 feet away under an open window of the premises in question. A search of the motor vehicle revealed an iron bar, a screw driver and a table knife either on or under the front seat of the vehicle. Beer admitted ownership of these instruments and told the police that the screw driver was being used because they were having trouble with the ignition and that the bar was used for taking off hub caps. Mrs. Beer gave evidence to the effect that her husband had been using the screw driver to work on the car and that the bar had been moved from the trunk to underneath the front seat at the time of a camping trip during the previous summer when the table knife had also used. The arrangements that Beer may have made during the previous summer do not appear to me to be an explanation for having the tools where they were found at the time and place in question, and the fact that at the time of the arrest, a complete jack, including a wheel nut wrench with a chisel affair on the other end of it was found in the back trunk of the car, appears to me to weaken considerably the explanation for the presence of the bar under the front seat. In addition to this, Beer's evidence in explanation of the presence of the bar was elicited on cross-examination of a Crown witness and is self-serving so that in my view its admissibility was highly questionable.

McConnell admitted his association with Beer but explained his presence under the open window of the dry cleaning establishment by saying that he was relieving himself. While this may afford a reason for his being where he was, it does not seem to me to afford any explanation for being associated with Beer in the possession of the instruments in question.

. . .

In the present case neither of the accused gave evidence at the trial, and in the course of his charge the learned trial judge pointed out to the jury that they did not have to accept the unsworn explanation which McConnell had given to the police for his presence under the open window.

Upon counsel for the accused taking objection to this portion of the charge, the learned trial judge recalled the jury and said:

> Gentlemen of the Jury, it was pointed out that in the course of my charge to you I stated that you did not have to accept the explanations of the accused because those explanations were not made under oath. You are not to take it from that that there is any onus upon the accused to prove their innocence by going into the witness box and testifying in their defence. There is no such onus on these or any accused persons in any criminal trial of proving their innocence by going into the witness box and testifying in their own defence. You are not to be influenced in your decision by either of the accused not going into the witness box and testifying, but the Court does point out that these explanations were given and when made were not made under oath and it is not only for that reason alone but for any other number of reasons that may occur to you, to decide if you will accept these explanations.

It was argued before the Court of Appeal, as it was before this Court, that these observations offended against the provision of s. 4(5) [now s 4(6)] of the *Canada Evidence Act* and that a new trial should accordingly be had.

. . .

Mr. Justice Evans, in the course of his reasons for judgment in the Court of Appeal, with which MacKay JA agreed, expressed himself in the following terms:

> The principle underlying the prohibition in Section 4(5) is the protection of the accused. Originally it was part of the same enactment by which the disability of an accused person to testify was removed. *R v. Romano* 24 CCC 30. In a jury case when an accused does not testify on his own behalf, this fact is immediately known to the jury and one would be most naive

to believe that it is not considered by them in their deliberations. To hold that an accidental slip or an innocuous statement indicating the failure of the accused to testify must ipso facto result in a reversible error does violence to the intent and meaning of the Statute.

I am of the opinion that the impugned statement must be considered solely in the light of possible prejudice to the accused. If there is no possibility of prejudice then it does not amount to misdirection because it is a statement of law and amounts to an explanation of the legal rights of an accused who has already adopted a position of which the jury is aware. The absence of such a legal explanation might well react unfavourably to the accused particularly when defence counsel fails to explain to the jury his client's legal right to remain silent.

. . .

In the present case I have carefully considered the "comment" objected to and I am unable to find that it could be considered in any way prejudicial to the appellants. It is favourable to the accused persons to adopt the position which they did adopt coupled with a clear warning by the Trial Judge that no prejudicial inference is to be drawn from their election to remain out of the witness box. There is no suggestion in the remarks of the Trial Judge that there was evidence peculiarly within the knowledge of the appellants which they could give and which they failed to give.

Mr. Justice Evans did, however, express the view that "once it was determined that the comment violated the statutory provisions it was a fatal defect and a new trial was mandatory." Although Mr. Justice MacKay agreed with Evans JA that the remarks of the trial judge did not constitute a "comment" so as to offend against s. 4(5), he did not agree that the effect of such a comment, if made, was to make "a new trial mandatory." Mr. Justice MacKay said:

I desire, however, to express the view that even if the comments of the learned trial judge in reference to the appellants not giving evidence could be construed as offending against section 4(5) of the *Canada Evidence Act*, that this would be a proper case to apply the provisions of section 592(1)(b)(iii) of the *Criminal Code*.

In his dissenting opinion, Mr. Justice Wells took the view that in recharging the jury as he did the learned trial judge had made a direct comment on the failure of the accused to testify and that in so doing he had violated the provisions of s. 4(5) of the *Canada Evidence Act*, and that a new trial was accordingly necessary. Mr. Justice Wells, who found the matter to be concluded by the decision of this Court in *Bigaouette v. The King*, [1927] SCR 112, expressed himself as follows:

Looking at what the learned trial judge said in the case at bar, it would appear to me that in this case there is a much more direct comment on the failure of the accused to testify in their own defence. It is not a mere pointing out that certain matters are not contradicted, it deals directly with their failure to testify at their trial. In my opinion, this direct comment comes squarely within the prohibition of the Statute and renders a new trial necessary. The matter is decisively concluded in my opinion by the judgment of the late Chief Justice which I have quoted from in *Bigaouette v. The King*.

. . .

In the *Bigaouette* case the accused was charged with the murder of his mother and he admitted that he was in the house at the time when the death was said to have occurred and in the *Gallagher* case [(1922), 37 CCC 83 (Alta. SCAD)] the accused was the last person known to have been seen with the deceased whose murder he was accused of having committed; in each case the learned trial judge was found to have commented on the accused's failure to testify in explanation of these circumstances. There is nothing of this kind in the present case. Here the language used by the trial judge to which objection is taken was not so much a "comment" on the failure of the persons charged to testify as a statement of their right to refrain from doing so, and it does not appear to me that it should be taken to have been the intention of Parliament in enacting s. 4(5) of the *Canada Evidence Act* to preclude judges from explaining to juries the law with respect to the rights of accused persons in this regard. I am accordingly in agreement with Mr. Justice Evans "that the remarks of the trial judge viewed in context and on a reasonable interpretation do not amount to a comment in breach of the section."

I think it is to be assumed that the section in question was enacted for the protection of accused persons against the danger of having their right not to testify presented to the jury in such fashion as to suggest that their silence is being used as a cloak for their guilt.

As has been indicated by Mr. Justice Evans, it would be "most naive" to ignore the fact that when an accused fails to testify after some evidence of guilt has been tendered against him by the Crown, there must be at least some jurors who say to themselves "If he didn't do it, why didn't he say so." It is for this reason that it seems to me to be of the greatest importance that a trial judge should remain unhampered in his right to point out to the jury, when the occasion arises to do so in order to protect the rights of the accused, that there is no onus on the accused to prove his innocence by going into the witness box. To construe s. 4(5) of the *Canada Evidence Act* as interfering with that right would, in my opinion, run contrary to the purpose of the section itself.

[Ritchie J concluded in the alternative that if the comment was contrary to s 4(5), the trial judge's error could be cured by s 592(1)(b)(iii), now s 686(1)(b)(iii), of the *Criminal Code*, RSC 1985, c C-46.]

HALL J (Spence J concurring) (dissenting): … In his reasons, speaking for the majority in the Court of Appeal, Evans JA said:

> In a jury case when an accused does not testify on his own behalf, this fact is immediately known to the jury and one would be most naive to believe that it is not considered by them in their deliberations.

My brother Ritchie, in referring to this, states that it was in part to protect the accused from such speculations that s. 4(5) of the *Canada Evidence Act* was enacted. With deference, I cannot agree. The accused is accorded the protection he is entitled to by the mandatory directions which the trial judge must give that an accused is presumed to be innocent and that the burden of proving the guilt of an accused beyond a reasonable doubt rests upon the Crown. The learned trial judge adequately discharged his duty to the accused in the instant case when he said:

> For these reasons, therefore, both Mr. McConnell and Mr. Beer are presumed to be innocent until the Crown, his accuser, proves him guilty, and this presumption of innocence remains with the accused from the time they were charged and throughout this trial until the end and this presumption of innocence only ceases to apply at the end of the trial if, after hearing all evidence, you are satisfied that Mr. McConnell or Mr. Beer is guilty beyond a reasonable doubt.

The onus or burden of proving the guilt of these two accused persons beyond a reasonable doubt rests upon the Crown and never shifts. There is no burden upon either of these two persons to prove his innocence. The Crown must prove beyond a reasonable doubt that they are guilty of the offence before they can be convicted.

The protection which an accused is entitled to under s. 4(5) is compliance with the positive injunction not to *comment* imposed upon the judge and counsel for the prosecution, in other words, no *comment* on the subject from either of them.

In the present case, Wells JA (now CJHC) took the view that in recharging the jury as he did, the learned judge had made a comment on the failure of the accused to testify, and in so doing, had violated the provisions of s. 4(5) of the *Canada Evidence Act* and that a new trial was, accordingly, necessary.

I am in full agreement with Wells JA. Section 4(5) of the *Canada Evidence Act* is clear and unambiguous. In it Parliament has defined an area that is forbidden ground to the judge and to counsel for the prosecution. It is not a difficult matter for either or both to keep from entering the prohibited zone. If they refrain from doing what Parliament says they must not do, Courts of appeal and this Court will not be required to rationalize and refine these transgressions as they try to measure the depth of the imprint left on the minds of jurors as being consequential or inconsequential. No measurement of the effect of departing from the standards set by Parliament becomes necessary where the judge and counsel for the prosecution obey the law.

What the learned judge said in the instant case was clearly a comment. In my view, in dealing with a case of this kind, it is a case of comment or no comment. If there was no comment within the meaning of the statute as in the Wright and Kelly cases, that ends the matter. If there was a comment as in *Bigaouette*, an error fatal to the validity of the proceedings has occurred and the remedy is not in trying to speculate whether it had a material or no effect on the jury, but in a new trial. The accused in no way contributed to the result. It flows solely from the failure of the judge or of counsel for the prosecution to obey the law which Parliament has clearly laid down.

. . .

There are no compelling reasons in the instant case to depart from the law as laid down in *Bigaouette* in 1927.

If Parliament intended to qualify the word "comment" in the said section to have it mean "comment adversely or prejudicially," it could have amended the statute accordingly or may still do so. It is not for the Court to do it.

I would allow the appeal, quash the conviction and direct a new trial.

In 1982, some years after the decision in *McConnell and Beer*, the *Canadian Charter of Rights and Freedoms* came into effect. Sections 11(c) and (d) of the Charter read as follows:

11. Any person charged with an offence has the right

. . .

(c) not to be compelled to be a witness in proceedings against that person in respect of the offence;

(d) to be presumed innocent until proven guilty according to law in a fair and public hearing by an independent and impartial tribunal ... .

Furthermore, as we will see in Chapter 8, Statements of an Accused and Illegally Obtained Evidence, the Supreme Court has recognized a pre-trial right to silence as a principle of fundamental justice under s 7 of the Charter. Do these constitutional provisions have any implications for the propriety of drawing inferences from the accused's silence at trial? In *Noble*, below, the Supreme Court considered that question in the context of a judge-alone trial.

R v Noble

[1997] 1 SCR 874, 146 DLR (4th) 385, 114 CCC (3d) 385

Lamer CJ and La Forest, L'Heureux-Dubé, Sopinka, Gonthier, Cory, McLachlin, Iacobucci and Major JJ (24 April 1997)

SOPINKA J (L'Heureux-Dubé, Cory, Iacobucci and Major JJ concurring):

Analysis

While it is clear that the accused is neither a competent nor a compellable witness for the Crown, it is a separate question whether the silence of the accused at trial may be used against him in reaching a verdict. Specifically, if the trier of fact is otherwise not convinced of guilt beyond a reasonable doubt, may the silence of the accused at trial be treated as a distinct piece of evidence which the trier of fact may use to become convinced of guilt beyond a reasonable doubt? Put in other ways, may silence be placed on the evidentiary scales or may it be used as a "make-weight"? In my view, the answer to this question is found in two common law rights which were subsequently enshrined in the *Charter*: the right to silence and the presumption of innocence.

The Right to Silence

[Sopinka J reviewed *R v Hebert*, [1990] 2 SCR 151, and *R v Chambers*, [1990] 2 SCR 1293.]

The right to silence is based on society's distaste for compelling a person to incriminate him- or herself with his or her own words. Following this reasoning, in my view the use of silence to help establish guilt beyond a reasonable doubt is contrary to the rationale behind the right to silence. Just as a person's words should not be conscripted and used against him or her by the state, it is equally inimical to the dignity of the accused to use his or her silence to assist in grounding a belief in guilt beyond a reasonable doubt. To use silence in this manner is to treat it as communicative evidence of guilt. To illustrate this point, suppose an accused did commit the offence for which he was charged. If he testifies and is truthful, he will be found guilty as the result of what he said. If he does not testify and is found guilty in part because of his silence, he is found guilty because of what he did not say. No matter what the non-perjuring accused decides, communicative evidence emanating from the accused is used against him. The failure to testify tends to place the accused in the same position as if he had testified and admitted his guilt. In my view, this is tantamount to conscription of self-incriminating communicative evidence and is contrary to the underlying purpose of the right to silence. In order to respect the dignity of the accused, the silence of the accused should not be used as a piece of evidence against him or her.

The Presumption of Innocence

The presumption of innocence, enshrined at trial in s. 11(d) of the *Charter*, provides further support for the conclusion that silence of the accused at trial cannot be placed on the evidentiary scales against the accused. Lamer J (as he then was) stated in *Dubois v. The Queen*, [1985] 2 SCR 350, at p. 357, that:

> Section 11(d) imposes upon the Crown the burden of proving the accused's guilt beyond a reasonable doubt as well as that of making out the case against the accused before he or she need respond, either by testifying or calling other evidence.

If silence may be used against the accused in establishing guilt, part of the burden of proof has shifted to the accused. In a situation where the accused exercises his or her right to silence at trial, the Crown need only prove the case to some point short of beyond a reasonable doubt, and the failure to testify takes it over the threshold. The presumption of innocence, however, indicates that it is not incumbent on the accused to present any evidence at all, rather it is for the Crown to prove him or her guilty. Thus, in order for the burden of proof to remain with the Crown, as required by the *Charter*, the silence of the accused should not be used against him or her in building the case for guilt. Belief in guilt beyond a reasonable doubt must be grounded on the testimony and any other tangible or demonstrative evidence admitted during the trial.

Some reference to the silence of the accused by the trier of fact may not offend the *Charter* principles discussed above: where in a trial by judge alone the trial judge is convinced of the guilt of the accused beyond a reasonable doubt, the silence of the accused may be referred to as evidence of the absence of an explanation which could raise a reasonable doubt. If the Crown has proved the case beyond a reasonable doubt, the accused need not testify, but if he doesn't, the Crown's case prevails and the accused will be convicted. It is only in this sense that the accused "need respond" once the Crown has proved its case beyond a reasonable doubt. Another permissible reference to the silence of the accused was alluded to by the Court of Appeal in this case. In its view, such a reference is permitted by a judge trying a case alone to indicate that he need not speculate about possible defences that might have been offered by the accused had he or she testified. As McEachern CJBC stated (at p. 171):

> In other words, the court will not speculate that the accused may have some unstated defence, such as, in this case, that someone may have stolen his driver's licence.

Such treatment of the silence of the accused does not offend either the right to silence or the presumption of innocence. If silence is simply taken as assuring the trier of fact that it need not speculate about unspoken explanations, then belief in guilt beyond a reasonable doubt is not in part grounded on the silence of the accused, but rather is grounded on the evidence against him or her. The right to silence and its underlying rationale are respected, in that the communication or absence of communication is not used to build the case against the accused. The silence of the accused is not used as inculpatory evidence, which would be contrary to the right to silence, but simply is not used as exculpatory evidence. Moreover, the presumption of innocence is respected, in that it is not incumbent on the accused to defend him- or herself or face the possibility of conviction on the basis of his or her silence. Thus, a trier of fact may refer to the silence of the accused simply as evidence of the absence of an explanation which it must consider in reaching a verdict. On the other hand, if there exists in evidence a rational explanation or inference that is capable of raising a reasonable doubt about guilt, silence cannot be used to reject this explanation.

The reasons of the Chief Justice and McLachlin J, when read with my reasons, indicate that there are three ways in which the silence of the accused might be considered by the trier of fact:

(1) Once the Crown has proffered a case to meet, the silence of the accused can be used in determining whether an accused is guilty beyond a reasonable doubt.

(2) Inferences of guilt may be drawn from the accused's silence "only where a case to meet has been put forth and the accused is enveloped in a 'cogent network of inculpatory facts.'"

(3) The silence of the accused means that the evidence of the Crown is uncontradicted and therefore must be evaluated on this basis without regard for any explanation of those facts that does not arise from the facts themselves.

The Chief Justice appears to adopt both positions (1) and (2) in different parts of his reasons. Clearly, the first position uses the silence of the accused and violates both the right to silence and the presumption of innocence. If the Crown's evidence, although sufficient to pass the case to meet test, would, on evaluation, fall short of proof beyond a reasonable doubt but for the evidence of the accused, then the silence of the accused becomes evidence for the Crown which enables the Crown to discharge its burden of proof beyond a reasonable doubt.

The second position appears to invite the use of silence when the level of the Crown's proof passes the case to meet test but falls slightly short of proof beyond a reasonable doubt. In other words, the Crown has a strong case but it needs a little extra push. The extra push will be supplied by the silence of the accused. Of course, if the Crown's case does not need the extra push, there would be no justification for this position. Whether the evidence of the accused bridges the entire gap or only part of the gap between the standard of a case to meet and proof beyond a reasonable doubt, the silence of the accused becomes evidence for the Crown in discharge of its burden of proof. In both instances, the right to silence and the presumption of innocence are violated.

The third position which I have attempted to explain in my reasons simply recognizes that fact that the evidence of the Crown stands alone. It must be evaluated on this basis. Contradictions that have not been offered cannot be supplied. No inference of guilt is drawn from the silence of the accused. Rather, the silence of the accused fails to provide any basis for concluding otherwise, once the uncontradicted evidence points to guilt beyond a reasonable doubt.

It is not entirely clear which position McLachlin J adopts. Her reasons appear to conclude that the judge or jury may take into account that the Crown's evidence is unchallenged and decide the case on this basis. This appears to accord with position (3) and not with positions (1) or (2). This would not support either the reasons or the result by the Chief Justice.

Sopinka J went on to hold that although the Charter prohibited adverse inferences from silence, s 4(6) of the *Canada Evidence Act* would prevent a trial judge from instructing a jury not
to draw an adverse inference from the accused's failure to testify at trial. Because *Noble* was
a judge-alone trial, this holding was, strictly speaking, *obiter dicta*. In *R v Prokofiew*, 2012 SCC
49, [2012] 2 SCR 639, the Supreme Court of Canada revisited that question.

R v Prokofiew
2012 SCC 49, [2012] 2 SCR 639

McLachlin CJ and LeBel, Deschamps, Fish, Abella, Rothstein, Cromwell,
Moldaver, and Karakatsanis JJ (12 October 2012)

MOLDAVER J (Deschamps, Abella, Rothstein, and Karakatsanis JJ concurring):

[1] The issue in this case is whether a trial judge is prohibited by s. 4(6) of the *Canada
Evidence Act*, R.S.C. 1985, c. C-5 ("*CEA*"), from affirming an accused's right to silence.
At trial, the Crown alleged that Mr. Prokofiew and his co-accused, Mr. Solty, participated
in a fraudulent scheme involving the fictitious sale of heavy equipment to generate harmonized sales tax that was then not remitted to the federal government as required. The
fraudulent nature of the scheme was never challenged. The involvement of Messrs. Prokofiew and Solty in the scheme was also conceded. The question for the jury was whether
either or both accused were aware of the fraudulent nature of the scheme. Mr. Prokofiew
did not testify, but was incriminated by Mr. Solty's testimony. In his closing address,
Mr. Solty's counsel invited the jury to infer Mr. Prokofiew's guilt from the latter's failure
to testify. The trial judge refrained from giving a remedial instruction to the jury about
Mr. Prokofiew's right to silence. Mr. Prokofiew was convicted and sentenced and his appeal was dismissed by Doherty J.A. on behalf of a unanimous five-person panel of the
Ontario Court of Appeal (2010 ONCA 423, 100 O.R. (3d) 401). Largely for the reasons
given by Doherty J.A., I would dismiss Mr. Prokofiew's further appeal to this Court.

[2] I have had the benefit of reading the reasons of my colleague Justice Fish and I
agree with much of his analysis. Where I disagree with him is in the result. I will explain
our disagreement and why the appeal should be dismissed, but before doing so, I will
address the matters on which my colleague and I agree—albeit with some additional
observations.

I. *Matters of Agreement*

[3] My colleague and I agree that s. 4(6) of the *Canada Evidence Act*, R.S.C. 1985,
c. C-5 ("*CEA*"), does not prohibit a trial judge from affirming an accused's right to silence.
In so concluding, I should not be taken—nor do I understand my colleague to suggest—
that such an instruction must be given in every case where an accused exercises his or
her right to remain silent at trial. Rather, it will be for the trial judge, in the exercise of
his or her discretion, to provide such an instruction where there is a realistic concern that
the jury may place evidential value on an accused's decision not to testify.

[4] In cases where the jury is given an instruction on the accused's right to remain silent
at trial, the trial judge should, in explaining the right, make it clear to the jury that an

accused's silence is not evidence and that it cannot be used as a makeweight for the Crown in deciding whether the Crown has proved its case. In other words, if, after considering the whole of the evidence, the jury is not satisfied that the charge against the accused has been proven beyond a reasonable doubt, the jury cannot look to the accused's silence to remove that doubt and give the Crown's case the boost it needs to push it over the line.

[5] The case at hand provides an example of a situation where such an instruction would be warranted—cut-throat defences where one accused testifies and points the finger at the other, while the other exercises his right not to testify. My colleague and I agree that, in summing up to the jury, Mr. Solty's counsel could have relied on the fact that his client had testified to argue that Mr. Solty was innocent and had "nothing to hide." Moreover, he could have emphasized that Mr. Solty's testimony stood uncontradicted and that the jury could consider this in assessing whether they believed his evidence or whether it left them in a state of reasonable doubt.

[6] What Mr. Solty's counsel could not do is mislead the jury on a matter of law. He could not invite the jury to use Mr. Prokofiew's silence at trial as evidence, much less evidence of guilt.

[7] In cases where there is a risk of counsel misleading the jury on a co-accused's right to remain silent at trial, trial judges would do well to spell out the governing principles and ensure that counsel's remarks conform to those principles. That way, the potential harm can be prevented from occurring, thereby sparing the need for a remedial instruction.

[8] In the context of the charge as a whole, I think it might be helpful to explain how a jury may use a lack of contradictory evidence in deciding whether the Crown has proved its case beyond a reasonable doubt.

[9] Apart from a few notable exceptions—such as when an accused raises the defence of not criminally responsible on account of a mental disorder under s. 16 of the *Criminal Code*, R.S.C. 1985, c. C-46—in every criminal trial, juries are instructed that an accused has no obligation to prove anything. The onus of proof rests upon the Crown from beginning to end and it never shifts.

[10] Juries are also told that in deciding whether the Crown has proved its case to the criminal standard, they are to look to the whole of the evidence—and, having done so, they may only convict if they are satisfied, on the basis of evidence they find to be both credible and reliable, that the Crown has established the accused's guilt beyond a reasonable doubt. In coming to that conclusion, a jury may not use an accused's silence at trial as evidence, much less evidence of guilt, and, where appropriate, the jury should be so instructed.

[11] That said, in assessing the credibility and reliability of evidence upon which the Crown can and does rely, a jury is entitled to take into account, among other things, the fact that the evidence stands uncontradicted, if that is the case—and the jury may be so instructed. Of course, the fact that evidence is uncontradicted does not mean that the jury must accept it, and an instruction to that effect should be given.

II. Is a New Trial Required?

. . .

[22] My colleague points out that the trial judge did not give an explicit instruction to the jury about the impropriety of using Mr. Prokofiew's silence at trial as evidence of guilt. I agree. However, I do not agree that the jury received no assistance from the trial judge

on the matter. On the contrary, I am satisfied that the trial judge implicitly endorsed the remarks Mr. Prokofiew's counsel made in direct response to the improper remarks made by Mr. Solty's counsel. At the very least, the trial judge went a long way in that direction.

[23] In response to the impugned remarks, counsel for Mr. Prokofiew juxtaposed other jurisdictions in the world where accused persons were required to disprove their guilt with the situation in Canada:

> That is not, thankfully, the way things are done here in Canada. We have the luxury and we have the thankfulness that we have a system that requires the State to prove our guilt before a conviction or a finding of guilt can be entered.
>
> In this situation, this is the situation why Mr. Prokofiew does not have to call evidence, and this is why Mr. Prokofiew did not call evidence. [A.R., vol. V, at p. 27]

[24] In his instructions to the jury, the trial judge picked up on this theme and endorsed it as follows:

> Mr. Solty and Mr. Prokofiew do not have to present evidence or prove anything in this case. In particular, they do not have to prove that they are innocent of the crimes charged [sic]. From start to finish, it is the Crown that must prove guilt beyond a reasonable doubt. It is Crown counsel who must prove Mr. Solty's guilt and/or Mr. Prokofiew's guilt beyond a reasonable doubt, not Mr. Prokofiew or Mr. Solty who must prove their innocence. [A.R., vol. V, at p. 133]

Doherty J.A. observed that this jury instruction "tied the presumption of innocence into the burden of proof in a manner that spoke almost directly to the irrelevance of the appellant's failure to testify" (para. 49). I agree.

[25] In the face of an instruction that effectively endorsed the remarks of Mr. Prokofiew's counsel on the very issue of concern, I fail to see how it can be said that the trial judge left the jury to cast about on its own, with free rein to treat Mr. Prokofiew's failure to testify as evidence of his guilt and to convict him, at least in part, for that reason.

[26] In sum, while I agree that an explicit remedial instruction from the trial judge would have been preferable—and would have been warranted in these circumstances—I am satisfied that the instructions that were given in the instant case, when considered as a whole, were adequate. Like Doherty J.A., I am confident that the jury would have understood, in the context of the entirety of the instructions, that the Crown could prove Mr. Prokofiew's guilt only on the evidence and, as Mr. Prokofiew's silence at trial did not constitute evidence, it could not be used to prove his guilt. However, I do not fault the trial judge for concluding—wrongly but understandably—that he was prohibited by s. 4(6) of the CEA from making any reference at all to Mr. Prokofiew's failure to testify. My colleague has addressed that matter and it should not pose a problem in future cases.

[Moldaver J held that the trial judge had also erred in improperly admitting various items of documentary evidence but that this error "was minor and the verdict would inevitably have been the same had he not made it." The accused's appeal was therefore dismissed.]

FISH J (McLachlin CJC and LeBel and Cromwell JJ concurring) (dissenting):

I

[37] At the conclusion of their joint trial before judge and jury, Ewaryst Prokofiew and Peter Solty were both convicted of fraud and conspiracy to defraud the Government of Canada of $3.25 million.

[38] Mr. Prokofiew did not testify. Mr. Solty did, proclaiming his innocence and incriminating Mr. Prokofiew.

[39] In his closing address to the jury, Mr. Solty's counsel implied that Mr. Prokofiew's silence indicated that he had something to hide. There is no dispute as to the significance of counsel's words: The Crown concedes in its factum that "counsel for Mr. Solty suggested [to the jury] that [Mr. Prokofiew] *had not testified because he was guilty of the alleged offences*" (R.F., at para. 2 (emphasis added)).

[40] The trial judge recognized that no such inference was permitted and he wanted to make this clear to the jury. He concluded there was a "significant risk" that the jury might otherwise, as suggested by Mr. Solty's counsel, infer from Mr. Prokofiew's silence that he was guilty as charged (A.R., vol. I, at p. 7).

[41] In response to defence counsel's request for a "strong [remedial] direction," the trial judge replied: "You can count on it" (A.R., vol. V, at p. 92).

[42] "[T]here are few rights more fundamental than the right to remain silent," the judge added, "and it must be made clear to the jury … that they may not consider Mr. Prokofiew's silence … as indicative of guilt when they come to considering his guilt or innocence" (A.R., vol. 5, at p. 92).

[43] After considering two decisions of this Court, however, the trial judge held—wrongly but understandably, as we shall see—that he was prohibited by s. 4(6) of the *Canada Evidence Act*, R.S.C. 1985, c. C-5, from making any reference at all to Mr. Prokofiew's failure to testify. He therefore refrained from giving the remedial instruction that he had earlier thought necessary to prevent the jury from drawing the impermissible inference they had been invited to draw by Mr. Solty's counsel.

[44] The Court of Appeal for Ontario, correctly in my view, held that s. 4(6) prohibits comments *prejudicial to the accused*—but not the remedial instruction requested by defence counsel and contemplated by the judge (2010 ONCA 423, 100 O.R. (3d) 401). The Court of Appeal held as well, again correctly, that the trial judge had erred in admitting hearsay evidence. It is undisputed in this Court that the hearsay evidence was inadmissible and ought to have been excluded.

[45] The Court of Appeal nonetheless dismissed Mr. Prokofiew's appeal on the ground that both errors were harmless. With respect, I am of a different view. For the reasons that follow, I would quash Mr. Prokofiew's conviction, allow the appeal and order a new trial.

II

[46] Having concluded that a new trial should be had, I shall refer to the facts only to the extent necessary to explain my conclusion.

[47] Mr. Prokofiew and Mr. Solty were alleged by the Crown to have participated knowingly in a fraudulent scheme involving the sale of non-existent "heavy equipment" between the Maritimes and Ontario. Harmonized Sales Tax (HST) was collected on these fictitious sales but never remitted to the government. In all, the perpetrators of the scheme defrauded the Government of Canada of more than three million dollars.

[48] It was uncontested at trial that the scheme was fraudulent and that Mr. Prokofiew and Mr. Solty had both participated in it. The only live issue was whether they were aware of its fraudulent nature.

[49] Mr. Solty testified that he was an innocent participant. He was induced, he said, to participate in the fraud by Mr. Prokofiew, who orchestrated the scheme.

[50] Mr. Prokofiew did not testify.

[51] In his address to the jury, counsel for Mr. Solty contrasted in the following terms Mr. Prokofiew's silence with Mr. Solty's decision to testify:

> It's clear that Mr. Solty never ran and [n]ever tried to hide from his involvement in this case. … And when it came to his turn to tell his side of the story, he did not, like Ewaryst Prokofiew, shirk from that challenge. And why did he do all this? Especially when there was absent no obligation for him to do anything? Because, I suggest, he had nothing to hide. Because he's innocent. Innocent people don't make themselves scarce when the troubles begin. They stand up with their friends and colleagues and try and deal with the problem. I suggest to you that at every turn, Peter Solty acted in a manner that is consistent with an innocent person.
>
> • • •
>
> Lastly, Peter Solty took the stand and told his story, warts and all. Ewaryst Prokofiew did not. Mr. Solty accused him of massive monetary fraud, and backed up that accusation with the hand-written invoices and other documentation that he provided to the police. What was Mr. Prokofiew's response? Ask yourself why Ewaryst Prokofiew did not testify. Did he have something to hide or did he simply have no response that could help him since there is no point in trying to contradict the truth? [A.R., vol. V, at pp. 10-11 and 16-17]

[52] The trial judge was concerned that these comments could undermine Mr. Prokofiew's right to a fair trial. As earlier mentioned, he felt there was a "significant risk" that the jury would infer that Mr. Prokofiew's silence could be taken as evidence of guilt, in contravention of *R. v. Noble*, [1997] 1 S.C.R. 874 (A.R., vol. I, at p. 7). It was therefore necessary, said the judge, to make clear to the jury that no such inference was permitted—"that they may not consider Mr. Prokofiew's silence … as indicative of [his] guilt" (A.R., vol. V, at p. 92).

[53] However, after hearing submissions and reviewing *Noble* and *R. v. Crawford*, [1995] 1 S.C.R. 858, the trial judge concluded that s. 4(6) of the *Canada Evidence Act* precluded him from commenting *in any way* on an accused's silence at trial. He therefore made no reference in his jury instructions to Mr. Prokofiew's failure to testify.

[Fish J summarized the Court of Appeal's reasons for dismissing Prokofiew's appeal from conviction and continued.]

III

[64] *Noble* establishes that a trier of fact may not draw an adverse inference from the accused's failure to testify and that the accused's silence at trial may not be treated as evidence of guilt. To do so would violate the presumption of innocence and the right to silence. It would to that extent and for that reason shift the burden of proof to the accused, turning the accused's constitutional right to silence into a "snare and a delusion" (*Noble*, at para. 72).

[65] We are now urged by the Crown to overrule *Noble*. Upon careful consideration of Crown counsel's full and able argument, and the helpful submissions of all counsel on this issue, I would decline to do so.

[66] I see no persuasive reason to overturn *Noble*. *Noble* is a recent and important precedent regarding a fundamental constitutional principle. The Court's decision in that case is constitutionally mandated and has not proven unworkable in practice. Nothing of significance has occurred since 1997 to cause the Court to reconsider its decision. And it is well established that the Court must exercise particular caution in contemplating the reversal of a precedent where the effect, as here, would be to diminish the protection of the *Canadian Charter of Rights and Freedoms*: *R. v. Henry*, 2005 SCC 76, [2005] 3 S.C.R. 609, at para. 44.

[67] These questions remain: Does s. 4(6) of the *Canada Evidence Act* prohibit *any comment at all* by the trial judge on the failure of the accused to testify—as the trial judge found in this case? If not, what can trial judges tell juries about the failure of an accused to testify? Was a remedial instruction required in this case? If so, is the absence of a remedial instruction fatal to the verdict?

[68] Section 4(6) of the *Canada Evidence Act* provides:

> The failure of the person charged, or of the wife or husband of that person, to testify shall not be made the subject of comment by the judge or by the counsel for the prosecution.

[69] In *Crawford*, Justice Sopinka stated that s. 4(6) "encompasses both comment prejudicial to the accused, as well as a direction that the jury must not draw an unfavourable conclusion from the accused's failure to testify" (para. 22).

[70] And he reiterated this observation in *Noble*:

> Section 4(6), whose validity is not at issue in the present case, prevents a trial judge from commenting on the silence of the accused. The trial judge is therefore prevented from instructing the jury on the impermissibility of using silence to take the case against the accused to one that proves guilt beyond a reasonable doubt. [para. 95]

[71] I agree with Justice Doherty that both comments were *obiter dicta*. Section 4(6) was not at issue in either *Crawford* or *Noble*. *Crawford* dealt with what an accused or defence counsel may say in relation to a co-accused's pre-trial silence, while *Noble* held that an accused's silence at trial cannot be used as evidence of guilt.

[72] In both cases, Justice Sopinka's references to s. 4(6) merely formed part of his description of the legislative background in describing ancillary issues relating to an accused's silence. His comments were brief and unnecessary to the result. *Dicta* of this sort may be set aside where, as in this instance, there are good reasons to do so: *Henry*, at para. 57.

[73] First, the impugned observations in *Noble* and *Crawford* ignored—indeed, contradicted—judgments of the Court that explicitly defined and applied s. 4(6) (*McConnell*, at p. 809; *Avon*, at p. 655; *R. v. Potvin*, [1989] 1 S.C.R. 525, at pp. 557-58). These well-established precedents cannot be taken to have been overruled without mention—*en passant*, as it were—by *obiter* comments in *Crawford* and *Noble*.

[74] Second, as *McConnell*, *Avon* and *Potvin* demonstrate, a purposive interpretation of s. 4(6) compels the conclusion that trial judges may inform the jury of the accused's right to silence and the protection it affords. More specifically, applying *Noble*, trial judges

may instruct the jury that, as a matter of law, no adverse inference may be drawn from the failure of the accused to testify.

. . .

[78] Quite properly, the Crown has conceded before us that s. 4(6) should be interpreted in accordance with *McConnell, Avon* and *Potvin*.

[79] In short, s. 4(6) of the *Canada Evidence Act* does not prohibit an affirmation by the trial judge of the accused's right to silence. And, in appropriate circumstances, an instruction that no adverse inference may be drawn from the silence of the accused at trial is not a prohibited "comment" on the accused's failure to testify within the meaning of that provision.

IV

[80] I turn now to consider whether the trial judge in this case erred in failing to instruct the jury that no adverse inference could be drawn from the appellant's failure to testify. Unlike the Court of Appeal, and with the greatest of respect, I believe that he did. And I believe as well that this error, though understandable in light of *Crawford* and *Noble*, is fatal to the jury's verdict.

[81] The Court of Appeal recognized that "no one knows for sure what the jury used or did not use," but found that the absence of a remedial instruction would only be fatal where the "appellant shows a real risk that his silence was misused" (para. 42).

[82] In concluding that Mr. Prokofiew had not discharged that burden, the Court of Appeal pointed to various passages of the judge's charge. Essentially, in the passages considered by the Court of Appeal (paras. 46-48), the trial judge instructed the jury that their verdict must be based on "the evidence put before you, and only on that evidence" (A.R., vol. V, at p. 125); that both Mr. Prokofiew and Mr. Solty were presumed innocent throughout the trial; that they did not have to prove their innocence; and that the presumption of their innocence "is only defeated if and when Crown counsel has satisfied all of you, beyond a reasonable doubt, that either or both Mr. Prokofiew and Mr. Solty are guilty of either or both of the crimes with which they are each charged" (p. 132).

[83] Relying on the entirety of the judge's instructions, and notably on the instructions mentioned, the court was satisfied "that the jury would understand that the Crown could prove the appellant's guilt based only on the evidence, and that the appellant's silence at trial—or indeed, any other non-evidentiary matter—could not be used to infer the appellant's guilt" (para. 51).

[84] The Court of Appeal also characterized as a "direct response" (para. 44) to the prejudicial comments by counsel for Mr. Solty, the following passages from the closing address of counsel for Mr. Prokofiew:

> Mr. Prokofiew, as [counsel for Mr. Solty] pointed out, chose not to testify in this case. There are many jurisdictions in the world that are, frankly, not as kind as ours; that when a person has an allegation against them, that they have to stand up; you're alleged to do this; or you prove to us, you tell us why you are not guilty. That is not, thankfully, the way things are done here in Canada. We have the luxury and we have the thankfulness that we have a system that requires the State to prove our guilt before a conviction or a finding of guilt can be entered.
>
> In this situation, this is the situation why Mr. Prokofiew does not have to call evidence, and this is why Mr. Prokofiew did not call evidence. In the context of counsel for Mr. Solty's

statement, well, yes, Mr. Solty testified, but with respect, Mr. Solty had no choice but to testify. He was implicated at every turn of these transactions. He was in transactions up to his neck. And as a result, with respect to him, he had no choice but to take the stand. In response to Mr. Prokofiew, as I will mention in my submission, the evidence comes down to the evidence of Mr. Tulloch, and juxtaposed by the evidence of Peter Solty. With the greatest respect to them, their evidence does not come close to establishing guilt beyond a reasonable doubt in this case. And in the context of what Mr. Solty testified to will simply adjust the position of the evidence of Mr. Tulloch. Nothing more, nothing less. [A.R., vol. V, at pp. 27-28]

[85] With respect, unlike the Court of Appeal, I believe these comments by counsel for Mr. Prokofiew lend little curative weight to the absence of a remedial instruction by the trial judge.

[86] It is true that "[a]ppellate review of the trial judge's charge will encompass the addresses of counsel as they may fill gaps left in the charge" (*R. v. Daley*, 2007 SCC 53, [2007] 3 S.C.R. 523, at para. 58). However, we are not dealing in this case with a failure by the trial judge to mention evidence that is brought to the jury's attention by counsel in their closing submissions. Nor are we concerned with uncontested or uncontroversial matters inadvertently omitted from the judge's charge. Or with any other gap of the kind contemplated by *Daley*.

[87] That is not our case. Here, the jurors were faced with *conflicting* comments by counsel that complicated—rather than complemented—the "gap" in the judge's charge. They were left to determine for themselves, with no assistance from the judge, the evidentiary and legal effect of Mr. Prokofiew's failure to testify at trial.

[88] It is true that the addresses of counsel may in some circumstances adequately complement the judge's charge. But that cannot be so where counsel for two antagonistic accused make diametrically opposite submissions on a fundamental principle of law, as in this case.

[89] We have no basis for supposing that the jury understood, in the absence of an explicit instruction by the judge, which counsel had stated the law correctly. The jury had no informed reason to believe one lawyer rather than the other. The guiding hand of the trial judge was essential—and absent.

[90] Most importantly, *neither* the judge's instructions cited by the Court of Appeal *nor* the comments by counsel for Mr. Prokofiew address the impermissibility of drawing an adverse inference from Mr. Prokofiew's silence.

[91] The essence of the matter is that Mr. Solty's counsel had invited the jurors to draw the impermissible inference that Mr. Prokofiew was using his silence to "cloak his guilt" (*Avon*, at p. 655). In the Crown's words, "he suggested [to the jury] that [Mr. Prokofiew] had not testified because he was guilty of the alleged offences" (R.F., at para. 2).

[92] The impugned comments by Mr. Solty's counsel, as the trial judge recognized, cried out for an explicit, remedial instruction. They received no remedial instruction at all. I agree with the Court of Appeal that "no one knows for sure what the jury used or did not use" (para. 42). What we do know for sure is that they were left free to treat Mr. Prokofiew's failure to testify as evidence of his guilt and to convict him, at least in part, for that reason.

[93] In my respectful view, this alone is fatal to their verdict.

[94] Trial judges must take care to ensure that the right to silence becomes neither a snare nor a delusion (*Noble*, at para. 72). To this end, whenever there is a "significant risk"—as the trial judge found in this case—that the jury will otherwise treat the silence of the accused as evidence of guilt, an appropriate remedial direction ought to be given to the jury. That was not done here.

[95] Standard instructions on the definition of evidence, the presumption of innocence, the Crown's burden of proof, and the reasonable doubt standard will not suffice. That is particularly true where, as here, counsel for one accused has suggested unmistakably to the jury that the guilt of a co-accused may be inferred from that person's failure to testify.

[Fish J held that the trial judge's error "was exacerbated by the erroneous admission of hearsay evidence." He held that the Crown's case was not overwhelming and that the verdict would not necessarily have been the same absent the errors; accordingly, s. 686(1)(b)(iii) was inapplicable and a new trial was required.]

III. THE EXAMINATION OF WITNESSES

A. Examination and Cross-Examination

As noted at the outset of this chapter, the general rule for common law trials is that all evidence must be given or identified by the oral testimony of a witness. That oral evidence is brought out through questions asked by counsel for the parties. The party offering a witness will ask the witness a series of questions intended to elicit evidence helpful to the party's case. This series of questions is called the "examination in chief." The opposing party's counsel is then permitted to ask a series of questions, known as "cross-examination," usually intended either to bring out aspects of the case helpful to the opposing party or to discredit the witness's evidence in whole or in part.

The principal difference between examination in chief and cross-examination is in the form of questioning. During examination in chief, leading questions are generally not permitted: the witness is supposed to tell his or her own story without too much prompting from counsel. During cross-examination, leading questions are not only permitted but are almost always used. A leading question is one which is structured to drive the witness to a narrow range of answers, sometimes to one answer only; or, as it is sometimes put, a leading question is one that suggests its own answer. Consider the following four questions:

1. "What did you see next?"
2. "You saw a car, didn't you?"
3. "What was the weather like?"
4. "It was raining, wasn't it?"

The first and third questions are open-ended—the form of the question does not suggest any particular answer. These questions would be perfectly acceptable in examination in chief. The second and fourth questions are leading—they strongly suggest a particular answer (although, of course, they also permit the opposite answer). These questions would not be permitted in examination in chief, but would be permitted in cross-examination.

Cross-examination of non-accused witnesses can be quite wide-ranging—they may be cross-examined not only as to facts relevant to the case but as to matters that might cast doubt on their credibility, such as discreditable conduct and associations unrelated to the case at hand. Independent proof of false statements by witnesses is, however, limited by the collateral facts bar (see Chapter 6, Credibility). The accused as witness is in a somewhat different position. To protect the accused from irrelevant and prejudicial allegations, cross-examination of the accused on discreditable conduct is typically not permitted (but see Chapter 7, Character). Similarly, to protect the accused's constitutional right to silence, as a rule, he may not be cross-examined about his failure to respond to questions from the police or his failure to advance a defence before trial; to protect the presumption of innocence, he may not be cross-examined about his motive for giving exculpatory testimony.

B. Testimonial Factors

Examination and cross-examination are usually directed at the facts relevant to the disposition of the case. But examination and cross-examination may also be directed at facts relevant to the assessment of a witness's testimony. In order to accept or reject a witness's evidence, the trier of fact must make inferences regarding the following questions:

1. *The witness's use of language.* What does the witness mean by the words he or she uses? What criteria is the witness applying when the witness reports, for example, that a colour was "dark," that a person was "tall," or that another person was "angry"?

2. *The witness's sincerity.* Does the witness believe what he or she is saying?

3. *The witness's memory.* What factors might influence the witness's recall of the events in question? Did they happen recently or long ago? Was there anything about the events that might make them easier or more difficult to recall? Has the witness's recall been affected by intervening events—for example, discussions with other witnesses or suggestions by the police or other investigators?

4. *The witness's perception.* Was there anything interfering with—or enhancing—the witness's ability to see or hear the events in question? Was the witness intoxicated or distracted? How good were the conditions for observation?

In short, the trier of fact must make inferences about the witness's (1) use of language, (2) sincerity, (3) memory, and (4) perception. Professor Schiff usefully labelled these the "testimonial factors" that the trier of fact must consider in evaluating a witness's testimony, while Dean Wigmore called them the "elements of a testimonial assertion": see Stanley Schiff, *Evidence in the Litigation Process*, 4th student ed (Toronto: Carswell, 1993) at 143-46, 209-13; and JH Wigmore, *Evidence*, vol 2 (JH Chadbourn rev) (Boston: Little, Brown, 1979) at §478. For a helpful discussion of these factors, see Andrew L-T Choo, *Hearsay and Confrontation in Criminal Trials* (Oxford: Clarendon Press, 1996) at 16-32.

Some commentators and judges use the term "credibility" to refer to the ensemble of factors that might affect the extent to which the fact-finder believes a witness's evidence, including not only the fact-finder's assessment of the witness's testimonial factors but also qualities of the witness that the law recognizes as affecting his or her character for credibility in general—for example, his or her criminal record: see Chapter 6. But one witness may testify honestly and yet be in error or mistaken in some way, while another witness may not be a credible person but be truthful on the particular occasion of his or her testimony. For this reason, many judges distinguish between a witness's "credibility" and his or her "reliability." According to this distinction, assessing a witness's "credibility" involves determining whether he or she is testifying honestly, and therefore involves his or her character and sincerity; assessing "reliability," on the other hand, involves determining whether the witness's testimony, even if it is the product of a sincere effort to tell the truth, is accurate. In *R v Morrissey* (1995), 22 OR (3d) 514, 97 CCC (3d) 193 (CA), Doherty JA expressed this distinction as follows:

> Testimonial evidence can raise veracity and accuracy concerns. The former relate to the witness's sincerity, that is, his or her willingness to speak the truth as the witness believes it to be. The latter concerns relate to the actual accuracy of the witness's testimony. The accuracy of a witness's testimony involves considerations of the witness's ability to accurately observe, recall and recount the events in issue. When one is concerned with a witness's veracity, one speaks of the witness's credibility. When one is concerned with the accuracy of a witness's testimony, one speaks of the reliability of that testimony. Obviously a witness whose evidence on a point is not credible cannot give reliable evidence on that point. The evidence of a credible, that is, honest witness, may, however, still be unreliable.

The common law has traditionally regarded cross-examination as the most important device for casting doubt on a witness's credibility and reliability by bringing out weaknesses in the witness's testimonial factors. The trier of fact may consider the witness's demeanour as he or she testifies, and may consider the fact that the witness has given some indication of his or her commitment to tell the truth, but these two devices are probably less important than the witness's response to questions asked in examination in chief and in cross-examination. Subject to the rules of evidence, particularly those discussed in Chapter 5, Opinion Evidence, and Chapter 6, the parties may also lead evidence relating to a witness's testimonial factors.

C. Refreshing and Recording Memory

A witness is entitled to refresh his or her memory before testifying or while testifying. There is no special rule relating to the device that refreshes the witness's memory—while the device will usually be a document of some sort, in principle it can be anything. In *R v Fliss*, 2002 SCC 16 at para 45, [2002] 1 SCR 535, Binnie J said:

> There is ... no doubt that the [witness] was entitled to refresh his memory by any means that would rekindle his recollection, whether or not the stimulus itself constituted admissible evidence. This is because it is his recollection, not the stimulus, that becomes evidence. The stimulus may be hearsay, it may itself be largely inaccurate, it may be nothing more than the sight of someone who had been present or hearing some music that had played in the background.

In a similar vein, in *United States v Rappy*, 157 F (2d) 964 at 967 (2nd Cir 1947), Learned Hand J said that the device used to refresh a witness's memory could be "a song, a scent, a photograph, an allusion, even a past statement known to be false."

If the device that stimulates a witness's recollection is inadmissible at the instance of the party calling the witness, should it become admissible where the opposing party wants to explore the way in which the witness refreshed his or her memory?

Present memory refreshed should be distinguished from past recollection recorded (though Canadian courts have not always done so). Where a witness cannot remember the events in question, he or she may testify from a record of his or her past recollection. (The record is usually, but need not be, made by the witness himself or herself: see *R v Davey* (1969), 2 CRNS 288 (BCSC).) In *R v Meddoui* [1990] 2 WWR 289, 111 AR 295, 61 CCC (3d) 345 (CA) at 352, Kerans JA summarized the conditions for the admissibility of past recollection recorded:

1. The past recollection must have been recorded in some reliable way.

2. At the time, it must have been sufficiently fresh and vivid to be probably accurate.

3. The witness must be able now to assert that the record accurately represented his knowledge and recollection at the time. The usual phrase requires the witness to affirm that he "knew it to be true at the time."

4. The original record itself must be used, if it is procurable.

Kerans JA based these conditions on the discussion in Wigmore, *Evidence*, vol 3 (Chadbourn rev) (Boston: Little, Brown, 1970) at §§ 734-755. The Supreme Court of Canada adopted Kerans JA's statement of the law in *Fliss*, above at para 62.

Is past recollection recorded hearsay? (See Chapter 4, Hearsay.) How can a witness who offers his or her evidence in the form of a past recollection recorded be properly cross-examined?

IV. SOME ASPECTS OF CROSS-EXAMINATION

Cross-examination can extend to any matter at issue in the action, including the credibility of the witness, and is not limited to matters that have been covered in the examination in chief. Cross-examination may provide a means of obtaining relevant evidence as well as testing the evidence given by the witness in chief. Counsel is entitled to conduct the cross-examination through leading questions—that is, questions that suggest the desired answer or that assume the existence of a fact not yet proved in evidence.

The common law has traditionally had a high regard for the cross-examination of witnesses as a method of getting at the truth, and more specifically as a method of casting doubt on the truth of a witness's testimony-in-chief. Cross-examination may be directed at any of the testimonial factors discussed in Section III.B, above. Cross-examination of a non-accused witness may include questions about the witness's discreditable conduct unrelated to the case. Cross-examination of an accused person is more limited because of the general rule excluding evidence of the accused's bad character, unless the accused has put his good character at issue (see Chapter 7).

In this section, we consider two topics related to cross-examination. First, if a party intends to lead evidence to contradict a witness's testimony, must the party first cross-examine the witness on that testimony? What are the consequences if the party does not address the issue in cross-examination? Second, what foundation, if any, must the party have for questions put to an opposing witness in cross-examination? Must the party be prepared to prove the facts supporting questions put in cross-examination? The related question of the extent to which a party may lead evidence to contradict an answer given by a witness on cross-examination is considered in Chapter 6.

A. The Obligation to Cross-Examine a Witness Whom One Intends to Contradict

In a well-known passage from *Browne v Dunn* (1893), 6 R 67 (HL), Lord Herschell LC said:

> Now, my Lords, I cannot help saying that it seems to me to be absolutely essential to the proper conduct of a cause, where it is intended to suggest that a witness is not speaking the truth on a particular point, to direct his attention to the fact by some questions put in cross-examination showing that that imputation is intended to be made, and not to take his evidence and pass it by as a matter altogether unchallenged, and then, when it is impossible for him to explain, as perhaps he might have been able to do if such questions had been put to him, the circumstances which it is suggested indicate that the story he tells ought not to be believed, to argue that he is a witness unworthy of credit. My Lords, I have always understood that if you intend to impeach a witness you are bound, whilst he is in the box, to give him an opportunity of making any explanation which is open to him; and, as it seems to me, that is not only a rule of professional practice in the conduct of a case, but is essential to fair play and fair dealing with witnesses.

Assuming that *Browne v Dunn* established a "duty to cross-examine" in English law, there was some doubt about whether there was also such a duty in Canada: see *R v Dyck*, [1970] 2 CCC 283 (BCCA); *Palmer v R*, [1980] 1 SCR 759; *R v Speid* (1988), 42 CCC (3d) 12 (Ont CA). But Canadian courts are now generally of the view that the "rule in *Browne v Dunn*" is part of the law of evidence: see e.g. *Gardiner v R*, 2010 NBCA 46. In *R v McNeill* (2000), 48 OR (3d) 212, 144 CCC (3d) 551 (CA), Moldaver JA, as he then was, assumed the existence of the duty and addressed the consequences of non-compliance as follows:

[47] In cases such as this one, where the concern lies in a witness's inability to present his or her side of the story, it seems to me that the first option worth exploring is whether the witness is available for recall. If so, then assuming the trial judge is otherwise satisfied, after weighing the pros and cons, that recall is appropriate, the aggrieved party can either take up the opportunity or decline it. If the opportunity is declined, then, in my view, no special instruction to the jury is required beyond the normal instruction that the jury is entitled to believe all, part or none of a witness's evidence, regardless of whether the evidence is uncontradicted.

[48] The mechanics of when the witness should be recalled and by whom should be left to the discretion of the trial judge.

[49] In those cases where it is impossible or highly impracticable to have the witness recalled or where the trial judge otherwise determines that recall is inappropriate, it should be left to the trial judge to decide whether a special instruction should be given to the jury. If one is warranted, the jury should be told that in assessing the weight to be given to the uncontradicted evidence, they may properly take into account the fact that the opposing witness was not questioned about it. The jury should also be told that they may take this into account in assessing the credibility of the opposing witness.

[50] Depending on the circumstances, there may be other permissible ways of rectifying the problem. The two options that I have mentioned are not meant to be exhaustive. As a rule, however, I am of the view that they will generally prove to be the fairest and most effective solutions.

What are the advantages and disadvantages of the rule in *Browne v Dunn*? Should testimony that has not been tested on cross-examination attract a presumption of credibility, or are the devices considered by Moldaver JA sufficient to forward the purposes of the rule?

B. Foundation for Cross-Examination

Are there any limits on allegations a party can put to a witness on cross-examination? Can the trial judge require that a party undertake to lead evidence to establish the factual foundation of its questions on cross-examination?

R v Lyttle
2004 SCC 5, [2004] 1 SCR 193
McLachlin CJ and Major, Binnie, Arbour, LeBel, Deschamps, and Fish JJ
(12 February 2004)

MAJOR and FISH JJ:

[12] On February 19, 1999, Stephen Barnaby was viciously beaten by five men with baseball bats, four of them said to have been masked. He was found outside an apartment building, collapsed, shivering, with broken bones and with other severe injuries to his head and legs. He had no wallet, no house keys and no identification.

[13] Barnaby told a uniformed officer, with whom he spoke briefly soon after the attack, that he had been beaten over a gold chain.

[14] Detective Sean Lawson, initially assigned to the case, stated in his "Occurrence Report" that the attack was believed to be over a drug debt and the victim was being less than truthful. His suspicion in this regard was based on a conversation with Barnaby at the hospital, on the ferocity of the beating, on the fact that Barnaby had a drug-related conviction, and on other elements of Detective Lawson's own preliminary investigation.

[15] On the following morning, referring to the Barnaby attack in his "Daily Major" report summarizing all serious crimes that had occurred during his shift, Detective-Sergeant Ian Ganson wrote: "believed to be [over] a drug debt ... further inquiries." Ganson, it should be noted, never spoke directly with Barnaby. He merely relied, in the usual way, on information he had received from subordinate investigators and uniformed officers.

[16] Lawson's "Occurrence Report" and Ganson's "Daily Major" report were disclosed to the defence in a timely manner, as required by law. See *R. v. Stinchcombe*, [1991] 3 S.C.R. 326.

[17] Detective Michael Korb and his partner, Detective Martin Ottaway, took over the investigation the day after the attack and obtained a statement from Barnaby at the hospital. Korb and Ottaway were aware of the "drug deal gone bad" theory mentioned by Lawson and Ganson, but both testified that it did not influence their investigation. Unlike Lawson and Ganson, Korb and Ottaway believed Barnaby's version of the assault and the reasons for it.

[18] Barnaby, at a photographic line-up, identified the appellant as the unmasked attacker.

[The trial judge ruled that defence counsel could not cross-examine the Crown witnesses on the drug-debt theory unless she committed to leading some evidence during the defence case to support that theory. He said: "I am not saying you can or cannot ask any questions. It is your case, it is your defence, you conduct it as you see fit. *I am just saying that there will be strict adherence to the rules of evidence, which require that if you ask a question of the nature we have discussed, that, at some point, you are required to produce some foundation or substantive basis for asking that question.* You cannot simply pick out of the air an allegation of that nature and hope that it will persuade the jury. There has to be factual underpinning for it. And that if it comes later in the trial, fine, no problem" (emphasis in original). In response to this ruling, defence counsel carried out the proposed cross-examination and then called Lawson and Ganson as defence witnesses. As a result, the defence was deprived of the opportunity to address the jury last (see *Criminal Code,* s 651(3)). The jury convicted the accused of several offences. His appeal to the Ontario Court of Appeal was dismissed.]

[46]   This appeal concerns the constraint on cross-examination arising from the ethical and legal duties of counsel when they allude in their questions to disputed and unproven facts. Is a good faith basis sufficient or is counsel bound, as the trial judge held in this case, to provide an evidentiary foundation for the assertion?

[47]   Unlike the trial judge, and with respect, we believe that a question can be put to a witness in cross-examination regarding matters that need not be proved independently, provided that counsel has a good faith basis for putting the question. It is not uncommon for counsel to believe what is in fact true, without being able to prove it *otherwise than by cross-examination*; nor is it uncommon for reticent witnesses to concede suggested facts—in the mistaken belief that they are already known to the cross-examiner and will therefore, in any event, emerge.

[48]   In this context, a "good faith basis" is a function of the information available to the cross-examiner, his or her belief in its likely accuracy, and the purpose for which it is used. Information falling short of admissible evidence may be put to the witness. In fact, the information may be incomplete or uncertain, provided the cross-examiner does not put suggestions to the witness recklessly or that he or she knows to be false. The cross-examiner may pursue any hypothesis that is honestly advanced on the strength of reasonable inference, experience or intuition. The purpose of the question must be consistent with the lawyer's role as an officer of the court: to suggest what counsel genuinely thinks possible on known facts or reasonable assumptions is in our view permissible; to assert or to imply in a manner that is calculated to mislead is in our view improper and prohibited.

[49]   In *Bencardino* [*R v Bencardino* (1973), 15 CCC (2d) 342], at p. 347, Jessup JA applied the English rule to this effect:

> ... whatever may be said about the forensic impropriety of the three incidents in cross-examination, I am unable to say any illegality was involved in them. As Lord Radcliffe said in *Fox v. General Medical Council*, [1960] 1 WLR 1017 at p. 1023:
>
> > An advocate is entitled to use his discretion as to whether to put questions in the course of cross-examination which are based on material which he is not in a position to prove directly. The penalty is that, if he gets a denial or some answer that does not suit him, the answer stands against him for what it is worth.

[50]   More recently, in *R v. Shearing,* [2002] 3 SCR 33, 2002 SCC 58, while recognizing the need for exceptional restraint in sexual assault cases, Binnie J reaffirmed, at paras. 121-22,

the general rule that "in most instances the adversarial process allows wide latitude to cross-examiners to resort to unproven assumptions and innuendo in an effort to crack the untruthful witness … ." As suggested at the outset, however, wide latitude does not mean unbridled licence, and cross-examination remains subject to the requirements of good faith, professional integrity and the other limitations set out above (paras. 44-45). See also *Seaboyer* [[1991] 2 SCR 577], at p. 598; *Osolin* [[1993] 4 SCR 595], at p. 665.

[51] A trial judge must balance the rights of an accused to receive a fair trial with the need to prevent unethical cross-examination. There will thus be instances where a trial judge will want to ensure that "counsel [is] not merely taking a random shot at a reputation imprudently exposed or asking a groundless question to waft an unwarranted innuendo into the jury box." See *Michelson v. United States*, 335 US 469 (1948), at p. 481, *per* Jackson J.

[52] Where a question implies the existence of a disputed factual predicate that is manifestly tenuous or suspect, a trial judge may properly take appropriate steps, by conducting a *voir dire* or otherwise, to seek and obtain counsel's assurance that a good faith basis exists for putting the question. If the judge is satisfied in this regard and the question is not otherwise prohibited, counsel should be permitted to put the question to the witness.

. . .

[66] As long as counsel has a good faith basis for asking an otherwise permissible question in cross-examination, the question should be allowed. In our view, no distinction need be made between expert and lay witnesses within the broad scope of this general principle. Counsel, however, bear important professional duties and ethical responsibilities, not just at trial, but on appeal as well. This point was emphasized by Lord Reid in *Rondel v. Worsley*, [1969] 1 AC 191 (HL), at pp. 227-28, when he said:

> Every counsel has a duty to his client fearlessly to raise every issue, advance every argument, and ask every question, however distasteful, which he thinks will help his client's case. But, as an officer of the court concerned in the administration of justice, he has an overriding duty to the court, to the standards of his profession, and to the public, which may and often does lead to a conflict with his client's wishes or with what the client thinks are his personal interests. *Counsel must not mislead the court, he must not lend himself to casting aspersions on the other party or witnesses for which there is no sufficient basis in the information in his possession,* he must not withhold authorities or documents which may tell against his clients but which the law or the standards of his profession require him to produce … . [Emphasis added.]

[67] By requiring an evidentiary foundation on the basis of *Howard*, the trial judge erred in law. Over the course of the two *voir dires* the existence of a good faith basis for the defence's "drug debt" theory had, in any event, become apparent. This basis included, but was not limited to, the police reports, the complainant Barnaby's drug conviction, his admission at the preliminary hearing that he had dealt in drugs, and the drug conviction of the complainant's acquaintance who drove him to the alleged scene of the attack.

V. Conclusion

[68] In order to determine whether there has been no substantial wrong or miscarriage of justice as a result of a trial judge's error, an appellate court must determine "whether there is any reasonable possibility that the verdict would have been different had the error at issue not been made." See *R v. Bevan*, [1993] 2 SCR 599, at p. 617.

[69] In *R v. Anandmalik* (1984), 6 OAC 143, at p. 144, the Ontario Court of Appeal recognized that the importance of cross-examination becomes even more critical when credibility is the central issue in the trial:

> In a case where the guilt or innocence of the [accused] largely turned on credibility, it was a serious error to limit the [accused] of his substantial right to fully cross-examine the principal Crown witness. It would not be appropriate in the circumstances to invoke or apply the curative provisions of s. 613(1)(b)(iii) [now s 686(1)(b)(iii)].

[70] The Manitoba Court of Appeal echoed these sentiments in *R v. Wallick* (1990), 69 Man. R (2d) 310, at p. 311:

> Cross-examination is a most powerful weapon of the defence, particularly when the entire case turns on credibility of the witnesses. An accused in a criminal case has the right of cross-examination in the fullest and widest sense of the word as long as he does not abuse that right. Any improper interference with the right is an error which will result in the conviction being quashed.

[71] It follows that where, as here, a trial judge improperly interfered with an accused's right to cross-examine, infused a mistrial chill into the proceedings, and placed conditions on a legitimate line of questioning that forfeited the accused's statutory right to address the jury last, a substantial wrong occurred and an unfair trial resulted.

[72] This alone is sufficient to dispose of the appeal in the appellant's favour.

PROBLEM (R v GALLOWAY)

At Martin Galloway's trial, the Crown wishes to call evidence from a number of witnesses, including Mia Galloway, Nate Smith, and Margaret Jenkins.

Mia Galloway

Mia is the Galloways' oldest child. She was five years old at the time of the events in question and, by the time of the trial, had just turned six. Mia has been living with her maternal grandparents since the murder of her mother, Angela, and the arrest of her father, Martin. Although Mia's maternal grandparents were supportive of Martin in the immediate aftermath of their daughter's death, once they learned that he had been having an affair, their attitude toward him understandably changed. After Martin's arrest, they became antagonistic toward him, convinced not only that he was unfaithful to their daughter but also that he is guilty of her murder.

Several months after the murder, Mia was interviewed by police in the company of her grandmother. The police were interested in asking Mia whether her parents were getting along in the period prior to her mother's death. However, at the mere mention of her mother, Mia broke down crying. Her grandmother intervened, saying, "Tell them, honey, tell them, Mommy and Daddy were arguing all the time before Mommy died, it's okay, tell them!" When the detective asked Mia whether what her grandmother was saying is true, she responded by saying, "Yes, whatever Nanna says."

When Mia is called to the stand, the trial judge asks her a series of questions, including her name, age, the grade she is in, and the school she attends. Mia appears to understand each of the questions asked and responds appropriately.

In light of the role played by Mia's grandmother in the making of her statement to police, is the trial judge obligated, before permitting Mia to testify, to conduct an inquiry to ensure that her evidence is the result of her own independent recollection and not the product of any improper influence by her grandmother? Is Mia competent to testify? If Mia does testify, should she take an oath or affirm?

Nate Smith

Nate Smith resides with his parents, who live immediately next door to the Galloways. He is 19 years old. From time to time, Nate would do odd jobs for the Galloways, for which they would pay him. At approximately 10:30 a.m. on the morning of Sunday, March 27, 2016, while the Galloway children were involved in an Easter egg hunt in the family's garden, Nate was conducting a spring cleanup of the Galloway property. He was interviewed by police and informed them that while in the garden he heard Angela and Martin arguing about something, although he can't say what. He reported that Angela was "really, really mad at Mr. Galloway."

The Crown wishes to call Nate to testify about what he observed between the couple on the morning of Angela's murder. Despite his chronological age, Nate is intellectually challenged because of a brain injury he suffered in a snowmobile accident that took place when he was 13. The accident left him with severe brain damage, detrimentally impacting his cognitive functioning; intellectually, he functions at a level comparable to the average five-year-old.

Before Nate is sworn, the judge proceeds to question him as follows:

THE COURT: Good morning, Nate. Have a seat right there. Nate, before we start I have to ask you a few questions. Do you understand?

N. Smith: [Reporter's note–witness nods]

THE COURT: How old are you? Take your time.

N. Smith: Nineteen.

THE COURT: Do you understand that you are in a courtroom?

N. Smith: Kind of.

THE COURT: You don't understand what this place is?

N. Smith: I would like to go now, please.

THE COURT: You can go home soon, but first I need to ask you some more questions. Is that okay?

N. Smith: I guess.

THE COURT: You will go home soon, I promise, but first a couple more questions. Do you know the difference between the truth and a lie?

N. Smith: … Stuart lies.

THE COURT: Who is Stuart?

N. Smith: My brother.

THE COURT: What did he lie about?

N. Smith: He took my yogurt.

THE COURT: Do you know what the truth is?

N. Smith: I know.

THE COURT: So you know what it is to tell the truth?

N. Smith: Stuart is a liar … always, always, he steals my food.

THE COURT: Is it okay to tell a lie?

N. Smith: No.

THE COURT: Is it wrong to lie?

N. Smith: No.

THE COURT: Is it okay to tell a lie?

N. Smith: No.

THE COURT: What is the difference between a lie and the truth?

N. Smith: Stuart lies.

THE COURT: Is it wrong for Stuart to lie?

N. Smith: Stuart is bad.

THE COURT: So you understand that it is wrong to lie?

N. Smith: Yes.

THE COURT: If I ask you to promise to tell me only the truth, will you?

N. Smith: Yes.

THE COURT: Do you promise to tell me only the truth in answering the questions you are asked?

N. Smith: Yes.

THE COURT: Do you promise?

N. Smith: Yes.

Based on the above inquiry, should the trial judge rule Nate competent to testify?

Margaret Jenkins

Police surveillance officers observed Martin Galloway and Margaret Jenkins embracing and kissing within a week of Angela Galloway's murder. Initially, along with Martin, police considered Margaret a suspect. Within a month of the homicide, Margaret approached police with her lawyer. She told them about the affair but denied any involvement in the murder. Margaret told police that she is unsure whether Martin killed his wife. After being given a promise of immunity from prosecution, Margaret agreed to wear a wire during her meetings with Martin. (The police obtained a warrant to authorize this.)

Over the next few months, hundreds of hours of conversation between Margaret and Martin were recorded. In these recordings Martin's affection for Margaret is made clear, but at no time does Martin explicitly admit any involvement in his wife's murder.

Margaret reported that during the period that she was working with the police she sometimes had conversations with Martin that she did not manage to record (because she did not have time to secrete the recording device on her person and turn it on). During one such conversation, Margaret claimed that Martin had said, "I can't believe the cops think I killed Angela, I would have to be a genius to do that and eliminate all evidence connecting me to the crime; then again, you know how smart I am." According to Margaret, as he concluded this sentence, Martin shot her a villainous grin. Margaret mentioned this strange comment to police only after Martin's arrest.

During cross-examination, defence counsel suggests that Margaret has made this aspect of her evidence up. Margaret flatly denies this suggestion. Defence counsel suggests to Margaret that she is lying about this, and suggests that she told her co-worker Amanda that "Martin is a no good SOB. After he was arrested I found out that he was also sleeping with his kids' nanny!" Although Margaret confirms that Amanda is a co-worker, she denies ever making such a statement to her.

What, if any, ethical restrictions are there on the sorts of suggestions that a lawyer is entitled to make to a witness during cross-examination? For example:

1. Imagine that Martin tells defence counsel that he never made the statement that Margaret attributes to him, but speculates that Margaret might have made this up because she discovered that he was also cheating on her. Would this be enough for defence counsel to make this sort of suggestion to Margaret during cross-examination?
2. Without specific information that Margaret had told her co-worker Amanda about Martin's affair with the nanny and being angry about it, would it be permissible for defence counsel to make such a suggestion to Margaret during cross-examination?

CHAPTER THREE

Relevancy, Probative Value, and Prejudicial Effect

I. RELEVANCY

Nothing is admissible in evidence unless it is relevant. How should relevance be determined?

R v Watson
(1996), 108 CCC (3d) 310 (Ont CA)
Morden ACJO and Arbour and Doherty JJA (2 August 1996)

[The accused was charged with second-degree murder and was convicted of manslaughter. On April 12, 1991, the victim, referred to as "Sada" in the excerpts below, was at his business premises with his friends Reid, Thorpe, and Whinstanley. The accused, together with two other men, Headley and Cain, arrived at about 6:00 p.m. Not long afterward, the victim was shot and killed, and Cain was shot and wounded. There was a conflict in the expert evidence as to how many bullets struck the victim. Dr. Fletis, the pathologist who performed the autopsy, testified that the victim was shot seven times, but Mr. Barbetta, a firearms expert, testified that the victim was shot five times.]

DOHERTY JA: ...

II. The Trial Proceedings

...

(b) The positions of the parties

It was the position of the Crown that Headley, Cain and the appellant arrived at the deceased's premise at about 6:00 p.m. on April 12th. They were all armed and were there to kill the deceased. Headley and Cain made their way to the back of the warehouse area with the deceased and opened fire, catching the deceased in a crossfire. On the Crown theory, the deceased was shot by Headley and Cain, and Cain was shot in the chest with a bullet fired by Headley. The Crown's position was that the appellant, knowing that the deceased was to be killed, remained on guard in the front area of the business premise while Cain and Headley shot the deceased. The three then made good their escape in the appellant's car. The Crown contended that the appellant was liable for murder as an aider and abetter to the murder actually committed by Headley and Cain. The Crown also took the position that on the evidence, the jury should be instructed on the included offence of manslaughter.

It was the defence position that the appellant had nothing to do with the shooting and should be acquitted. According to the defence, Headley, Cain and the appellant went to the rental unit together. Unknown to the appellant, Headley was armed with a loaded six-shot 357 magnum. Cain was not armed. At the deceased's invitation, Headley went to the back of the warehouse area with the deceased for some purpose unknown to the appellant. The appellant remained in the front office. The deceased, again unknown to the appellant, was armed with a handgun. Shortly after Headley and the deceased went to the back part of the warehouse, a dispute of unknown origin erupted between them. Both drew their guns and fired. Headley hit the deceased five times. The deceased fired at Headley but hit Cain who was standing some distance away. A second shot fired by the deceased hit the ceiling. Headley and Cain fled toward the front of the rental unit. Headley stopped to pick up the deceased's gun. The appellant, who had remained in the front office throughout, saw his friends coming towards him, panicked, knocked over a plant and fled the scene with Headley and Cain.

In cross-examination, Mr. Barbetta agreed that all five of the shots which hit the deceased could have been fired from one gun by one person standing in a stationary position and that the deceased could have fired the shot which hit Cain after being struck by one or more shots. In re-examination, Mr. Barbetta made it clear that the defence hypothesis was no more than a possibility.

As this review of the competing positions demonstrates, there were two central issues at trial:

- was there a plan afoot to kill or, at least, do harm to the deceased when Headley, Cain and the appellant entered the rental unit?
- if there was such a plan, was the appellant privy to it?

The number of times the deceased was shot became a prominent issue at the trial. One of the guns used to shoot the deceased was a six-shot 357 magnum. If, as Dr. Fletis testified, the deceased was shot seven times, he had to have been shot with two different guns as there was no time to reload a weapon. If the deceased was shot with two different guns, the strong inference was that both Headley and Cain had weapons and shot the deceased. This inference supported the Crown's theory that Headley and Cain went to the back of the warehouse area with the deceased, intent upon killing him. A finding that Headley and Cain, acting in concert, ambushed and shot the deceased seconds after going to the back of the warehouse and then made good their escape with the appellant could support the contention that Headley, Cain and the appellant intended to kill the deceased when they arrived at his rental unit.

If the deceased was shot five times, as Mr. Barbetta believed, it was possible, even allowing for the shot fired by Headley in the direction of Reid, that Headley fired all five shots into the deceased. This conclusion could lead credence to the defence theory that Headley was acting alone when he shot the deceased, and could undermine the Crown's theory that Headley, Cain and the appellant arrived at the premises with the intention of killing the deceased. The defence did not suggest that a finding that the deceased was shot five times, and not seven, compelled the conclusion that only Headley shot the deceased and had acted alone. The defence argued only that this finding was capable of supporting the defence theory and putting the Crown theory in doubt.

As indicated above, it was also part of the defence theory that the deceased was armed and had fired one or perhaps two shots during the exchange of gunfire which resulted in his death. One shot, according to the defence theory, hit Cain. The defence argued that if the jury concluded that the deceased had a gun and used it, these findings would support the defence in two ways. First, they would account for the two weapons fired without putting one in the hands of Cain. Second, the findings would make the defence contention that the deceased was killed during a spontaneous gun battle between Headley and the deceased more credible. Findings that the deceased was armed and fired his gun could, according to the defence position, leave a reasonable doubt as to whether the deceased's death was planned by Headley, Cain and the appellant before Headley went to the back of the warehouse with the deceased.

. . .

III. The Grounds of Appeal

(a) The admissibility of the evidence of Clive Mair

At the conclusion of the Crown's case, the defence sought a number of evidentiary rulings before deciding whether to call any defence. One involved the proposed evidence of Clive Mair. Mr. Mair was a good friend of the deceased and saw him on a regular basis up to the day before his death. Mr. Mair was interviewed by the police six days after the homicide and gave them a lengthy signed statement. In the course of that statement he said:

> ... I've never seen any guns but Sada [the deceased] had one with him all the time. *The gun Sada had was a 9 millimetre or something and he always carried it on him. It was always on his left side. It was his dog—you know like a credit card. He never left home without it.* He never took it out—never let anyone touch it, it wasn't in a holster just inside his pants. [Emphasis added.]

In other parts of the statement, Mair said that the deceased was not a violent man.

[The trial judge accepted the Crown's argument that Mair's evidence was irrelevant and therefore inadmissible, commenting that there was "no viable issue of self-defence" on the evidence in the case.]

For the purposes of his ruling, the trial judge assumed that Mair would give evidence which was consistent with his statement. As I will discuss later in these reasons, there was cause to doubt whether he would do so. However, like the trial judge, I regard it as appropriate to begin my assessment of the admissibility of the evidence proffered by the defence on the premise that Mair's testimony would be consistent with his statement. I also follow the trial judge's lead by beginning that assessment with an examination of the relevance of the proposed evidence. In doing so, I do not, as the trial judge did, limit my inquiry to the relevance of the evidence to claim that Headley acted in self-defence. The evidence was not tendered for that purpose. Relevance must be assessed in the context of the entire case and the respective positions taken by the Crown and the defence: *R v. Sims* (1994), 87 CCC (3d) 402 (BCCA) at 420-427. There is no rule limiting prior misconduct by the deceased to cases in which self-defence is raised.

In *R v. Corbett* (1988), 41 CCC (3d) 385 (SCC), La Forest J (in dissent) at p. 416 described the significance of relevance to our law of evidence:

> All relevant evidence is admissible, subject to a discretion to exclude matters that may unduly prejudice, mislead or confuse the trier of fact, take up too much time, or that should otherwise be excluded on clear grounds of law or policy.

In explaining what he meant by relevance, La Forest J referred to *R v. Morris* (1983), 7 CCC (3d) 97 (SCC), and then said at pp. 417-418:

> It should be noted that this passage [from *R v. Morris*] followed a general discussion of the concept of relevance in which *the court affirmed that no minimum probative value is required for evidence to be deemed relevant. The court made it clear that relevance does not involve considerations of sufficiency of probative value*. ... A cardinal principle of our law of evidence, then, is that any matter that has any tendency, as a matter of logic and human experience, to prove a fact in issue, is admissible in evidence, subject, of course, to the overriding judicial discretion to exclude such matters for the practical and policy reasons already identified. [Emphasis added.]

While La Forest J dissented in the result in *Corbett*, his discussion of the significance and meaning of relevance is consistent with previous and subsequent majority decisions of the Supreme Court of Canada: *R v. Morris, supra*, per McIntyre J, at pp. 98-99, per Lamer J (dissenting in the result) at pp. 105-106; *R v. Seaboyer* (1991), 66 CCC (3d) 321 (SCC) at 389-392. Relevance as explained in these authorities requires a determination of whether as a matter of human experience and logic the existence of "Fact A" makes the existence or non-existence of "Fact B" more probable than it would be without the existence of "Fact A." If it does then "Fact A" is relevant to "Fact B." As long as "Fact B" is itself a material fact in issue or is relevant to a material fact in issue in the litigation then "Fact A" is relevant and *prima facie* admissible.

In this case the relevance inquiry must proceed through two steps:

- Does the fact that the deceased always carried a gun make it more likely that he was in possession of a gun when he was shot?
- Does the fact that the deceased was in possession of a gun when he was shot make it less likely that the appellant was party to a plan to kill or do harm to the deceased, formed some time prior to his arrival with Headley and Cain at the rental unit?

The first inquiry is straightforward. Does the fact that the deceased always carried a gun, as a matter of logic and human experience, make it more likely that he was carrying a gun when he was shot? The second inquiry assumes an affirmative answer to the first and looks for a connection between the fact that the deceased had a gun when he was shot and one of the material issues at trial—the appellant's alleged participation in a plan to kill or do harm to the deceased. Clearly the deceased's possession of a gun when he was shot had no direct connection to the question of whether the appellant participated in a plan to kill or do harm to the deceased. The absence of a direct connection does not, however, determine relevance. If it did, most circumstantial evidence would be inadmissible. If the deceased's possession of a gun when he was shot triggers a chain of inferences, based on logic or experience, which ultimately makes the appellant's participation in a plan to kill or do harm to the deceased less likely, then the second stage of the relevance inquiry is satisfied.

Where a person's conduct in given circumstances is in issue, evidence that the person repeatedly acted in a certain way when those circumstances arose in the past has been received as circumstantial evidence that the person acted in conformity with past practice on the occasion in question: *Cross and Tapper on Evidence*, 8th ed. (Markham, Ont.: Butterworths, 1995) at pp. 25-26; *Wigmore on Evidence* (Tillers rev. 1983), vol. 1A, pp. 1607-1610; R. Delisle, *Evidence: Principles and Problems*, 4th ed. (Scarborough, Ont.: Carswell, 1996) at p. 38; *McCormick on Evidence*, 4th ed. (1992), vol. 1, pp. 825-830. For example, in McCormick at p. 826 it is said:

> ... Surely any sensible person in investigating whether a given individual did a particular act would be greatly helped in his inquiry by evidence as to whether that individual was in the habit of doing it.

The position taken in these authorities is, in my opinion, consistent with human experience and logic. The fact that a person is in the habit of doing a certain thing in a given situation suggests that on a specific occasion in which those circumstances arose the person acted in accordance with established practice. It makes the conclusion that the person acted in a particular way more likely than it would be without the evidence of habit. Evidence of habit is therefore properly viewed as circumstantial evidence that a person acted in a certain way on the occasion in issue.

Evidence of habit is closely akin to, but not identical to, evidence of disposition. Evidence of habit involves an inference of conduct on a given occasion based on an established pattern of past conduct. It is an inference of conduct from conduct. Evidence of disposition involves an inference of the existence of a state of mind (disposition) from a person's conduct on one or more previous occasions and a further inference of conduct on the specific occasion based on the existence of that state of mind. Evidence of habit proceeds on the basis that repeated conduct in a given situation is a reliable predictor of conduct in that situation. Evidence of disposition is premised on the belief that a person's disposition is a reliable predictor of conduct in a given situation.

The distinction between evidence of habit and evidence of disposition is demonstrated by a comparison of this case and the facts in *Scopelliti* [*R v Scopelliti* (1981), 63 CCC (2d) 81, excerpted in Chapter 7 below]. Here the defence wanted to show that the deceased habitually carried a gun in the past and to invite the jury to infer from that prior conduct that he had a gun when he was shot. In *Scopelliti*, the defence wanted to show that the deceased had on occasions in the past been the aggressor in physical confrontations with others and to invite the jury to infer, first that the deceased was a physically aggressive person (his disposition), and second that the deceased's actions at the relevant time were in keeping with his physically aggressive nature. Like evidence of habit, evidence of disposition can constitute circumstantial evidence of conduct on a specific occasion. The inferences necessary to render disposition evidence relevant to prove conduct on a specific occasion may be more difficult to draw than those required where evidence of habit is tendered.

The recognition that evidence of habit is relevant to prove conduct on a specific occa-sion begs the more fundamental question—what is a habit? McCormick at p. 826 describes habit as:

> the person's *regular* practice of responding to a *particular* kind of situation with a *specific* type of conduct. [Emphasis added.]

Habit therefore involves a repeated and specific response to a particular situation.

Mair's graphic assertion that the deceased carried a gun "like a credit card. He never left home without it" strongly suggests repeated and specific conduct. Mair's statement does not suggest that the deceased's possession of a weapon was limited to any particular situation. To the contrary, Mair indicated that the deceased always carried a gun. The general nature of the habit described by Mair does not affect the relevance of the evidence, but would, along with other aspects of the evidence (e.g. the duration and regularity of the habit), go to the weight to be given to the evidence by the jury.

Having concluded that evidence that the deceased always carried a gun was relevant to the question of whether he had a gun when he was shot, I turn to the second level of the relevance inquiry. Mair's evidence may put the deceased in possession of a gun at the material time, but standing alone it cannot support the inference that he fired the gun at that time. In fact, Mair's evidence did not suggest that the deceased had ever used his gun. The further inference from possession to use of the weapon is essential to make Mair's evidence relevant to any issue in the trial. The availability of that inference requires a consideration of the rest of the evidence.

There were at most three people at the back of the warehouse. The deceased and Cain were shot and the evidence does not suggest that Cain shot himself. He must have been shot by either Headley or the deceased. Headley definitely shot the deceased and at least two of the bullets which hit the deceased came from a different gun than the one used to shoot Cain. There were, therefore, two possibilities. Either Cain was shot by the deceased or Headley fired two different guns hitting the deceased with one and Cain with the other. In my opinion, a jury, having concluded that the deceased was armed, could have inferred that Cain was shot not by his friend Headley, but by the deceased who was the target of Headley's assault.

I am further satisfied, had the jury inferred that the deceased was armed and fired a weapon, that those inferences could logically have influenced the jury's conclusion as to the origins of the shooting. If the deceased was unarmed, the circumstances strongly suggest a preconceived plan to shoot the deceased. If the deceased was armed and used his weapon, then the possibility that the shooting was a result of a spontaneous confronta-tion between Headley and the deceased, both of whom were armed, becomes a viable one. If the shooting was the product of an armed confrontation between the two men it could reasonably be inferred that the confrontation arose during the discussion involving Headley and the deceased. If the confrontation arose in this manner, it offered strong support for the appellant's contention that he was not party to any plan to kill or do harm to the de-ceased. Therefore, evidence supporting the inferences that the deceased was armed and used a weapon during the confrontation made the defence position as to the appellant's non-involvement in any plan to kill or do harm to the deceased more viable than it would have been if those inferences were not available. Mair's proposed evidence, which pro-vided the basis for those inferences, was, therefore, relevant to a material fact in issue. In so concluding, I do not pass on the cogency of the inferences relied on by the defence or attempt to measure the effect of the proposed evidence on the jury's assessment of the appellant's liability. I limit myself to the inquiry demanded by our concept of relevancy.

In coming to the conclusion that the evidence that the deceased always carried a weapon was relevant to the ultimate question of whether the appellant was privy to any plan to kill or do harm to the deceased, I have not relied on the evidence of the hand washings performed on the deceased or Mr. Barbetta's evidence concerning the various scenarios which were consistent with the physical evidence. In so far as that evidence is not inconsistent with the deceased having fired a gun, it does fortify my conclusion with respect to the relevance of Mair's potential evidence.

A finding that evidence is relevant does not determine its admissibility. Relevant evidence will be excluded if it runs afoul of a specific exclusionary rule, or if a balancing of its probative value against its prejudicial effect warrants its exclusion: *R v. Corbett, supra; R v. Bevan* (1993), 82 CCC (3d) 310 (SCC) at 326; *R v. Terry* (1996), 106 CCC (3d) 508 (SCC) at pp. 518-9. Where the evidence found to be relevant is offered by the defence in a criminal case, it will be excluded under the second of these exclusionary rules only where the prejudice substantially outweighs the probative value: *R v. Seaboyer, supra*, at p. 391; *R v. Arcangioli* (1994), 87 CCC (3d) 289 (SCC) at 297.

The evidence that the deceased always carried a gun suggested that he was a potentially dangerous person and reflected adversely on his character. Evidence suggesting that an accused is a person of bad character is subject to a specific exclusionary rule to which there are exceptions. There is, however, no such exclusionary rule in criminal cases where otherwise relevant evidence suggests that the deceased (or some other third party) is a person of bad character: *R v. Arcangioli, supra*. Where such evidence is relevant, it will be received unless the trial judge concludes that its potential to prejudice the jury substantially outweighs its probative value. In this context, prejudice refers to the possibility that the jury will misuse the evidence by concluding that the deceased's bad character somehow justified or excused the otherwise criminal conduct of the accused. Put bluntly, there is a concern that the jury will base their verdict in part at least on an assessment that the deceased's bad character rendered the deceased unworthy of the protection of the law.

Evidence that the deceased habitually carried a gun certainly had some prejudicial potential. As the trial judge found the evidence to be irrelevant, he did not balance that potential prejudice against the probative value of the evidence. In my view, that balancing process favoured admission.

The proposed evidence of Mair had significant probative value for the defence on the question of whether the deceased was armed at the relevant time. That factual issue was in turn a crucial first step in the laying of an evidentiary foundation for the defence position that the deceased was killed in a spontaneous gun battle involving only Headley and the deceased. The defence position was not viable unless it could put the deceased in possession of a weapon when he was at the back of the warehouse with Headley. Mair's evidence could, therefore, be significantly probative on one aspect of the defence position and was crucial to the viability of the ultimate position taken by the defence.

This was also not a case where, absent the impugned evidence, the record would not have suggested that the deceased was a person of bad character. Apart from Mair's proposed evidence, there was considerable evidence, none of which was or could have been objected to, which suggested that the deceased had a criminal lifestyle. Even without

Mair's proposed evidence, the trial judge would have had to caution the jury against the misuse of that evidence. In fact, he did so. The admission of Mair's evidence would not, therefore, have introduced an element of potential prejudice into the trial which was not already present. In my view, the limiting instruction given by the trial judge with respect to the other evidence which reflected badly on the deceased's character would also have served to eliminate the potential prejudice flowing from the admission of Mair's proposed evidence.

Finally, I observe that this case was unlike the typical case where the court is concerned about the potential prejudicial effect of evidence of a deceased's bad character. In the typical case (like *Scopelliti*), the accused seeks to justify or at least partially excuse the killing of the deceased usually on the basis of self-defence or provocation. In those cases, the risk that the jury may conclude, because of the deceased's bad character, that the deceased got what was deserved is potentially very high. In the present case, the defence did not suggest that the deceased's killing was justified or should be excused. The evidence of his habitual possession of a weapon was offered not to justify Headley's shooting of the deceased, but to extricate the appellant from any involvement in that shooting.

Mair's proposed evidence was relevant and it cannot be said that its potential prejudicial effect substantially outweighed its potential probative value. The trial judge erred in holding that the evidence was inadmissible.

[Doherty JA held that the trial judge's error was not curable under s. 686(1)(b)(iii) of the *Criminal Code*. The accused's appeal was allowed and a new trial was ordered.]

PROBLEMS ON RELEVANCY

It has been suggested that regardless of the legal test for relevance, "given imperfect and incomplete information it is often necessary to draw on 'common-sense' assumptions or pre-existing beliefs in order to decide whether to draw an inference and, if so, what weight to attach to it" (Christine Boyle, "A Principled Approach to Relevance: The Cheshire Cat in Canada" in Paul Roberts and Mike Redmayne, eds, *Innovations in Evidence and Proof: Integrating Theory, Research and Teaching* (Oxford: Hart, 2007) 87 at 111). As you consider the following problems, ask yourself what the assumptions about human behaviour that lie behind the arguments for and against relevance are and how you might, if necessary, challenge those assumptions.

1. In *Morris v R*, [1983] 2 SCR 190, 7 CCC (3d) 97, the accused was charged with conspiring to import heroin from Hong Kong. He denied involvement in the conspiracy. While searching his residence, the police discovered an undated newspaper clipping describing events in the heroin trade in Pakistan. Was the clipping relevant?

2. The accused was charged with sexual assault. He, the complainant, and their friend D had been drinking through the evening and into the early morning. They went to the accused's house, where the complainant and D passed out on a bed. The complainant testified that she awoke to find the accused attempting to have sexual intercourse with her. She told him to get off, and he did so. She then woke D up, and they left the house, intending to call the police. The accused testified and denied any sexual contact with the complainant. He testified that after the complainant and D had passed out, he walked to his mother's house,

which was closer to his work than his own house. In cross-examination, Crown counsel asked the following questions:

Q: Would you agree with me that the complainant is a fairly attractive woman?
A: I wouldn't know.
Q: You wouldn't know?
A: No.
Q: You don't think she's somewhat nice-looking?
A: I don't—I don't judge people by their appearance.
Q: You don't judge women by their appearance?
A: Anybody.
Q: Anybody.
A: Yes, I just see people as equal.

Was this line of questioning relevant? See *R v Moose* (2004), 190 CCC (3d) 521 (Man CA); and compare *R v MF*, 2009 ONCA 617.

3. The accused is charged with the first-degree murder of James, another resident of the rooming house in which he lived. The case against him is strong but circumstantial. In the days following the killing, the accused described to several friends a dream that he had had in which he had killed someone. Six days after the killing, he left Canada and went to stay with his girlfriend in California. The police searched his room (in the rooming house) and found the following handwritten, undated, unsigned poem:

Crazy thoughts pass through my head.
Now I have killed a life, it's dead.
I drained his blood with my
knife, how stupid am I to
take his life. He had done
nothing wrong but I took his life and now he's gone. Why?
Why did I do it? How? How
could I? Shit.

Is the evidence of the dream and of the poem relevant? Is there any more information you would like to have before making a ruling on this point? See *R v Terry*, [1996] 2 SCR 207, 106 CCC (3d) 508, aff'g (1994), 91 CCC (3d) 209 (BCCA).

II. PROBATIVE VALUE AND PREJUDICIAL EFFECT

At common law, a trial judge has the power to exclude otherwise admissible evidence on the ground that its prejudicial effect exceeds its probative value. This power is applicable to evidence tendered by either party in civil cases (see e.g. *Gray v Insurance Corp of British Columbia*, 2010 BCCA 459, 326 DLR (4th) 564) and to evidence tendered by the Crown in criminal cases.

The most characteristic type of prejudicial effect is the possibility that evidence, though relevant and in principle admissible to support one kind of inference, might be used to support an impermissible inference. For example, evidence of the accused's bad conduct unrelated to the offence charged is sometimes relevant to disputed issues at trial. But it is impermissible for the fact-finder to use this evidence to support the inference that the accused is more likely to be guilty because he is a bad person. The possibility that the evidence might be misused in this way is one kind of prejudicial effect. (This admissibility of the accused's bad acts is discussed in much more detail in Chapter 7, below.)

It was once held that otherwise admissible evidence tendered by the defence could never be excluded on the ground that its probative value was outweighed by its prejudicial effect (see e.g. *R v Valley* (1986), 26 CCC (3d) 207 (Ont CA)). In *Seaboyer*, the Supreme Court of Canada reviewed the power to exclude on the ground of excessive prejudice, and considered the application of this power to evidence offered by the defence, in the context of a constitutional challenge to an evidentiary statute intended to promote an important societal value.

R v Seaboyer; R v Gayme
[1991] 2 SCR 577, 83 DLR (4th) 193, 66 CCC (3d) 321
Lamer CJ and La Forest, L'Heureux-Dubé, Sopinka, Gonthier, Cory, McLachlin,
Stevenson, and Iacobucci JJ (22 August 1991)

McLACHLIN J (Lamer CJ, La Forest, Sopinka, Cory, Stevenson, and Iacobucci JJ concurring): These cases raise the issue of the constitutionality of ss. 276 and 277 of the *Criminal Code*, RSC 185, c. C-46 (formerly ss. 246.6 and 246.7), commonly known as the "rape-shield" provisions. The provisions restrict the right of the defence on a trial for a sexual offence to cross-examine and lead evidence of a complainant's sexual conduct on other occasions. The question is whether these restrictions offend the guarantees accorded to an accused person by the *Canadian Charter of Rights and Freedoms*.

My conclusion is that one of the sections in issue, s. 276, offends the *Charter*. While its purpose—the abolition of outmoded, sexist based use of sexual conduct evidence—is laudable, its effect goes beyond what is required or justified by that purpose. At the same time, striking down s. 276 does not imply reversion to the old common law rules, which permitted evidence of the complainant's sexual conduct even though it might have no probative value to the issues on the case and, on the contrary, might mislead the jury. Instead, relying on the basic principles that actuate our law of evidence, the courts must seek a middle way that offers the maximum protection to the complainant compatible with the maintenance of the accused's fundamental right to a fair trial.

· · ·

The Background

I deal first with *Seaboyer*. The accused was charged with sexual assault of a woman with whom he had been drinking in a bar. On the preliminary inquiry the judge refused to allow the accused to cross-examine the complainant on her sexual conduct on other occasions. The appellant contends that he should have been permitted to cross-examine as to other acts of sexual intercourse which may have caused bruises and other aspects of the complainant's condition which the Crown had put in evidence. While the theory of the defence has not been detailed at this early stage, such evidence might arguably be relevant to consent, since it might provide other explanations for the physical evidence tendered by the Crown in support of the use of force against the complainant.

The *Gayme* case arose in different circumstances. The complainant was 15, the appellant 18. They were friends. The Crown alleges that the appellant sexually assaulted her at his school. The defence, relying on the defences of consent and honest belief in consent, contends that there was no assault and that the complainant was the sexual aggressor. In pursuance of this defence, the appellant at the preliminary inquiry sought to cross-examine and present evidence on prior and subsequent sexual conduct of the complainant. Accordingly, he brought a motion for an order declaring that ss. 276 and 277 of the *Code* were unconstitutional. The judge rejected the motion, on the ground that he lacked jurisdiction to hear it, and committed the appellant for trial.

[The two accused applied to Galligan J for orders quashing the committals for trial. Galligan J granted the orders. The Crown's appeal to the Ontario Court of Appeal was allowed, and the committals for trial were restored, on the ground that the preliminary inquiry judge lacked jurisdiction to determine the constitutional validity of ss 276 and 277. However, the Court of Appeal was unanimously of the view that s 276 could in some circumstances violate an accused's *Charter* rights. The accused appealed to the Supreme Court of Canada. The court agreed with the Court of Appeal on the jurisdictional issue and so dismissed the appeal. The court nevertheless went on to consider the constitutional issues that had been raised.]

The Issues

. . .

1. Do ss. 276 and 277 infringe ss. 7 and 11(d) of the *Charter*?

2. If so, are they saved by s. 1?

3. Does the constitutional exemptions doctrine apply?

4. If the legislation is invalid, what is the law?

. . .

Relevant Legislation

Criminal Code, s. 276:

276(1) In proceedings in respect of an offence under section 271, 272 or 273, no evidence shall be adduced by or on behalf of the accused concerning the sexual activity of the complainant with any person other than the accused unless

(a) it is evidence that rebuts evidence of the complainant's sexual activity or absence thereof that was previously adduced by the prosecution;

(b) it is evidence of specific instances of the complainant's sexual activity tending to establish the identity of the person who had sexual contact with the complainant on the occasion set out in the charge; or

(c) it is evidence of sexual activity that took place on the same occasion as the sexual activity that forms the subject-matter of the charge, where that evidence relates to the consent that the accused alleges he believed was given by the complainant.

· · ·

Criminal Code, s. 276:

> 277 In proceedings in respect of an offence under section 271, 272 or 273, evidence of
> sexual reputation, whether general or specific, is not admissible for the purpose of challeng-
> ing or supporting the credibility of the complainant.

· · ·

Discussion

1. *Do sections 276 and 277 of the Criminal Code infringe sections 7 and 11(d) of the Charter?*

(a) *The approach to sections 7 and 11(d) of the Charter*

Everyone, under s. 7 of the *Charter*, has the right to life, liberty and security of person
and the right not to be deprived thereof except in accordance with the principles of fundamental justice.

The first branch of s. 7 need not detain us. It is not disputed that ss. 276 and 277 of the
Criminal Code have the capacity to deprive a person of his or her liberty. A person convicted of sexual assault may be sentenced to life imprisonment. In so far as ss. 276 and
277 may affect conviction, they may deprive a person of his or her liberty.

The real issue under s. 7 is whether the potential for deprivation of liberty flowing from
ss. 276 and 277 takes place in a manner that conforms to the principles of fundamental
justice. The principles of fundamental justice are the fundamental tenets upon which our
legal system is based. We find them in the legal principles which have historically been
reflected in the law of this and other similar states: *R v. Beare*, [1988] 2 SCR 387. The
sections which follow s. 7, like the right to a fair trial enshrined in s. 11(d), reflect particular principles of fundamental justice: *Re BC Motor Vehicle Act*, [1985] 2 SCR 486.
Thus, the discussion of ss. 7 and 11(d) is inextricably intertwined.

The principles of fundamental justice reflect a spectrum of interests, from the rights
of the accused to broader societal concerns. Section 7 must be construed having regard
to those interests and "against the applicable principles and policies that have animated
legislative and judicial practice in the field" (*Beare, supra*, at p. 70, *per* La Forest J). The
ultimate question is whether the legislation, viewed in a purposive way, conforms to the
fundamental precepts which underlie our system of justice.

One way of putting this question is to ask whether the challenged legislation infringes
the *Charter* guarantee in purpose or effect: *R v. Big M Drug Mart Ltd.*, [1985] 1 SCR 295.
"Purpose," on this test, must be defined generously in terms of the ultimate aim of the
legislation. "Effect" refers to the actual consequences of the legislation. Where the *Charter*
guarantee relates to individual rights, as does s. 7, the inquiry as to effect will necessarily
concern not only the over-all effect of the measure as it operates in the justice system, but
will extend to consideration of its impact on the individuals whose rights the *Charter*
protects, typically the person charged with an offence.

A final point must be made on the ambit of s. 7 of the *Charter*. It has been suggested
that s. 7 should be viewed as concerned with the interest of complainants as a class to
security of person and to equal benefit of the law as guaranteed by ss. 15 and 28 of the
Charter: Yola Althea Grant, "The Penetration of the Rape Shield: *R v. Seaboyer* and *R v.*

Gayme in the Ontario Court of Appeal" (1989-90), 3 *CJWL* 592, at p. 600. Such an approach is consistent with the view that s. 7 reflects a variety of societal and individual interests. However, all proponents in this case concede that a measure which denies the accused the right to present a full and fair defence would violate s. 7 in any event.

(b) The positions of the parties

(i) The arguments in favour of the legislation

The supporters of the legislation submit that it conforms to, and indeed furthers, the principles of fundamental justice, both in purpose and effect.

The main purpose of the legislation is to abolish the old common law rules which permitted evidence of the complainant's sexual conduct which was of little probative value and calculated to mislead the jury. The common law permitted questioning on the prior sexual conduct of a complainant without proof of relevance to a specific issue in the trial. Evidence that the complainant had relations with the accused and others was routinely presented (and accepted by judges and juries) as tending to make it more likely that the complainant had consented to the alleged assault and as undermining her credibility generally. These inferences were based not on facts, but on the myths that unchaste women were more likely to consent to intercourse and in any event, were less worthy of belief. These twin myths are now discredited. The fact that a woman has had intercourse on other occasions does not in itself increase the logical probability that she consented to intercourse with the accused. Nor does it make her a liar. In an effort to rid the criminal law of these outmoded and illegitimate notions, legislatures throughout the United States and in England, Australia and Canada passed "rape-shield" laws. (I note that the term "rape-shield" is less than fortunate; the legislation offers protection not against rape, but against the questioning of complainants in trials for sexual offences.)

Three subsidiary purposes of such legislation may be discerned. The first, and the one most pressed before us, was the preservation of the integrity of the trial by eliminating evidence which has little or no probative force but which unduly prejudices the judge or jury against the complainant. If we accept, as we must, that the purpose of the criminal trial is to get at the truth in order to convict the guilty and acquit the innocent, then it follows that irrelevant evidence which may mislead the jury should be eliminated in so far as possible. There is no doubt that evidence of the complainant's sexual activities has often had this effect. Empirical studies in the United States suggest that juries often misused evidence of unchastity and improperly considered "victim-precipitating" conduct, such as going to a bar or getting into a car with the defendant, to "penalize" those complainants who did not fit the stereotype of the "good woman" either by convicting the defendant of a lesser charge or by acquitting the defendant: Harriett R. Galvin, "Shielding Rape Victims in the State and Federal Courts: A Proposal for the Second Decade" (1986), 70 *Minn. L Rev.* 763, at p. 796. It follows that society has a legitimate interest in attempting to eliminate such evidence.

The second rationale cited in support of rape-shield legislation is that it encourages the reporting of crime. Despite the fact that the statistics do not demonstrate with any certainty that reporting of sexual offences has increased in Canada as a consequence of rape-shield provisions, I accept that it is a legitimate legislative goal to attempt to encourage such reporting by eliminating to the greatest extent possible those elements of the trial which cause embarrassment or discomfort to the complainant. As time passes and the existence of such provisions becomes better known, they may well have some effect in promoting reporting. Certainly, failure to consider the position of the complainant in the trial process may have the opposite effect.

A third and related reason sometimes offered for rape-shield legislation is protection of the witness's privacy. This is really the private aspect upon which the social interest in encouraging the reporting of sexual offences is based. In addition to furthering reporting, our system of justice has an interest in preventing unnecessary invasion of witnesses' privacy.

The goals of the legislation—the avoidance of unprobative and misleading evidence, the encouraging of reporting and the protection of the security and privacy of the witnesses—conform to our fundamental conceptions of justice. The concern with the legislation is not as to its purpose, which is laudable, but with its effect. The reasons for these concerns emerge from a consideration of the appellants' position, to which I now turn.

(ii) The arguments against the legislation

The appellants contend that the legislation, however laudable its goals, in fact infringes their right to present evidence relevant to their defence and hence violates their right to a fair trial, one of the most important of the principles of fundamental justice.

The precept that the innocent must not be convicted is basic to our concept of justice. One has only to think of the public revulsion felt at the improper conviction of Donald Marshall in this country or the Birmingham Six in the United Kingdom to appreciate how deeply held is this tenet of justice. Lamer J (as he then was) put it this way in *Reference re: Section 94(2) of Motor Vehicle Act* ... [*Re BC Motor Vehicle Act*, [1985] 2 SCR 486 at 513, 23 CCC (3d) 289 at 310 (SCC)]:

> It has from time immemorial been part of our system of laws that the innocent not be punished. This principle has long been recognized as an essential element of a system for the administration of justice which is founded upon a belief in the dignity and worth of the human person and on the rule of law.

Dickson J (as he then was) expressed the same view in *R v. Sault Ste. Marie (City)*, [1978] 2 SCR 1299, when he stated at p. 1310: "there is a generally held revulsion against punishment of the morally innocent."

It is this fundamental principle—that the innocent not be punished—that is urged in support of the contention that ss. 276 and 277 violate the *Charter*. The interest is both individual, in that it affects the accused, and societal, for no just society can tolerate the conviction and punishment of the innocent.

The right of the innocent not to be convicted is reflected in our society's fundamental commitment to a fair trial, a commitment expressly embodied in s. 11(d) of the *Charter*. It has long been recognized that an essential facet of a fair hearing is the "opportunity adequately to state [one's] case": *Duke v. The Queen*, [1972] SCR 917, at p. 923, dealing with s. 2(e) of the *Canadian Bill of Rights*, RSC 1970, App. III. This applies with particular force to the accused, who may not have the resources of the state at his or her disposal. Thus, our courts have traditionally been reluctant to exclude even tenuous defence evidence: David H. Doherty, "'Sparing' the Complainant 'Spoils' the Trial" (1984), 40 CR

(3d) 55, at p. 58, citing *R v. Wray*, [1971] SCR 272, and *R v. Scopelliti* (1981), 34 OR (2d) 524 (CA). For the same reason, our courts have held that even informer privilege and solicitor-client privilege may yield to the accused's right to defend himself on a criminal charge: *Canada (Solicitor-General) v. Ontario (Royal Commission of Inquiry into Confidentiality of Health Records*, [1981] 2 SCR 494; *R v. Dunbar and Logan* (1982), 68 CCC (2d) 13 (Ont. CA).

In other jurisdictions too the right to defend oneself of a criminal charge is regarded as a principle of fundamental importance. The constitution of the United States enshrines the right in the due process guarantees of the Fifth and Fourteenth Amendments and the express right to confront one's accuser embodied in the Sixth Amendment. The jurisprudence of the United States Supreme Court affirms the right's fundamental importance: see *Davis v. Alaska*, 415 US 308 (1974); *Alford v. United States*, 882 US 687 (1931).

The right of the innocent not to be convicted is dependent on the right to present full answer and defence. This, in turn, depends on being able to call the evidence necessary to establish a defence and to challenge the evidence called by the prosecution. As one writer has put it:

> If the evidentiary bricks needed to build a defence are denied the accused, then for that accused the defence has been abrogated as surely as it would be if the defence itself was held to be unavailable to him. (Doherty, *supra*, at p. 67)

In short, the denial of the right to call and challenge evidence is tantamount to the denial of the right to rely on a defence to which the law says one is entitled. The defence which the law gives with one hand, may be taken away with the other. Procedural limitations make possible the conviction of persons who the criminal law says are innocent.

(iii) The issue between the parties

All the parties agree that the right to a fair trial—one which permits the trier of fact to get at the truth and properly and fairly dispose of the case—is a principle of fundamental justice. Nor is there any dispute that encouraging reporting of sexual offences and protection of the complainant's privacy are legitimate goals provided they do not interfere with the primary objective of a fair trial. Where the parties part company is on the issue of whether ss. 276 and 277 of the *Criminal Code* in fact infringe the right to a fair trial. The supporters of the legislation urge that it furthers the right to a fair trial by eliminating evidence of little or no worth and considerable prejudice. The appellants, on the other hand, say that the legislation goes too far and in fact eliminates relevant evidence which should be admitted notwithstanding the possibility of prejudice.

This raises two questions. First, what are the fundamental principles governing the right to introduce relevant defence evidence which may also be prejudicial? Second, does the legislation infringe these principles?

(c) The principles governing the right to call defence evidence

It is fundamental to our system of justice that the rules of evidence should permit the judge and jury to get at the truth and properly determine the issues. This goal is reflected in the basic tenet of relevance which underlies all our rules of evidence: see *Morris v. The Queen*, [1983] 2 SCR 190, and *R v. Corbett*, [1988] 1 SCR 670. In general, nothing is to be received which is not logically probative of some matter requiring to be proved and every-thing which is probative should be received, unless its exclusion can be justified on some other ground. A law which prevents the trier of fact from getting at the truth by excluding relevant evidence in the absence of a clear ground of policy or law justifying the exclusion runs afoul of our fundamental conceptions of justice and what constitutes a fair trial.

The problem which arises is that a trial is a complex affair, raising many different issues. Relevance must be determined not in a vacuum, but in relation to some issue in the trial. Evidence which may be relevant to one issue may be irrelevant to another issue. What is worse, it may actually mislead the trier of fact on the second issue. Thus, the same piece of evidence may have value to the trial process but bring with it the danger that it may prejudice the fact-finding process on another issue.

The law of evidence deals with this problem by giving the trial judge the task of balanc-ing the value of the evidence against its potential prejudice. Virtually all common law jurisdictions recognize a power in the trial judge to exclude evidence on the basis that its probative value is outweighed by the prejudice which may flow from it.

Professor McCormick, in *McCormick's Handbook of the Law of Evidence* (2nd ed. 1972), puts this principle, sometimes referred to as the concept of "legal relevancy," as follows, at pp. 438-40:

> Relevant evidence, then, is evidence that in some degree advances the inquiry, and thus has probative value, and is *prima facie* admissible. But relevance is not always enough. There may remain the question, is its value worth what it costs? There are several counterbalancing factors which may move the court to exclude relevant evidence if they outweigh its probative value. In order of their importance, they are these. First, the danger that the facts offered may unduly arouse the jury's emotions of prejudice, hostility or sympathy. Second, the prob-ability that the proof and the answering evidence that it provokes may create a side issue that will unduly distract the jury from the main issues. Third, the likelihood that the evidence offered and the counter proof will consume an undue amount of time. Fourth, the danger of unfair surprise to the opponent when, having no reasonable ground to anticipate this development of the proof, he would be unprepared to meet it. Often, of course, several of these dangers such as distraction and time consumption, or prejudice and surprise, emerge from a particular offer of evidence. This balancing of intangibles—probative values against probative dangers—is so much a matter where wise judges in particular situations may differ that a leeway of discretion is generally recognized.

This court has affirmed the trial judge's power to exclude Crown evidence the preju-dicial effect of which outweighs its probative value in a criminal case, but a narrower formula than that articulated by McCormick has emerged. In *Wray, supra*, at p. 293, the court stated that the judge may exclude only "evidence gravely prejudicial to the accused, the admissibility of which is tenuous, and whose probative force in relation to the main issue before the Court is trifling." More recently, in *Sweitzer v. The Queen*, [1982] 1 SCR 949, at p. 953, an appeal involving a particularly difficult brand of circumstantial evidence offered by the Crown, the court said that "admissibility will depend upon the probative effect of the evidence balanced against the prejudice caused to the accused by its admis-sion ... ." In *Morris, supra*, at p. 193, the court without mentioning *Sweitzer* cited the narrower *Wray* formula. But in *R v. Potvin*, [1989] 1 SCR 525, La Forest J (Dickson CJ concurring) affirmed in general terms "the rule that the trial judge may exclude admissible evidence if its prejudicial effect substantially outweighs its probative value" (p. 531).

I am of the view that the more appropriate description of the general power of a judge to exclude relevant evidence on the ground of prejudice is that articulated in *Sweitzer* and generally accepted throughout the common law world. It may be noted that the English case from which the *Wray* formula was adopted has been superseded by more expansive formulae substantially in the language of *Sweitzer*.

The Canadian cases cited above all pertain to evidence tendered by the Crown against the accused. The question arises whether the same power to exclude exists with respect to defence evidence. Canadian courts, like courts in most common law jurisdictions, have been extremely cautious in restricting the power of the accused to call evidence in his or her defence, a reluctance founded in the fundamental tenet of our judicial system that an innocent person must not be convicted. It follows from this that the prejudice must substantially outweigh the value of the evidence before a judge can exclude evidence relevant to a defence allowed by law.

These principles and procedures are familiar to all who practise in our criminal courts. They are common sense rules based on basic notions of fairness, and as such properly lie at the heart of our trial process. In short, they form part of the principles of fundamental justice enshrined in s. 7 of the *Charter*. They may be circumscribed in some cases by other rules of evidence, but as will be discussed in more detail below, the circumstances where truly relevant and reliable evidence is excluded are few, particularly where the evidence goes to the defence. In most cases, the exclusion of relevant evidence can be justified on the ground that the potential prejudice to the trial process of admitting the evidence clearly outweighs its value.

This then is the yardstick by which ss. 276 and 277 of the *Code* are to be measured. Do they exclude evidence the probative value of which is not substantially outweighed by its potential prejudice? If so, they violate the fundamental principles upon which our justice system is predicated and infringe s. 7 of the *Charter*.

The parties, as I understand their positions, agree on this view of the principles of fundamental justice. The Attorney-General for Ontario, for the respondent, does not assert that the *Charter* permits exclusion of evidence of real value to an accused's defence. Rather, he contends that any evidence which might be excluded by ss. 276 and 277 of the *Code* would be of such trifling value in relation to the prejudice that might flow from its reception that its exclusion would enhance rather than detract from the fairness of the trial. Others who defend the legislation, do so on the ground that it does not exclude evidence relevant to the defence, that the exceptions contained in the provisions "encompass *all* potential situations where evidence of a complainant's sexual history with men other than the accused would be *relevant* to support a legitimate defence" (emphasis in original): see Grant, *supra*, at p. 601. It is to this issue, which I see as the crux of the case, which I now turn.

(d) The effect of the legislation—what evidence is excluded?

Section 277 excludes evidence of sexual reputation for the purpose of challenging or supporting the credibility of the plaintiff. The idea that a complainant's credibility might be affected by whether she has had other sexual experience is today universally discredited. There is no logical or practical link between a woman's sexual reputation and whether she is a truthful witness. It follows that the evidence excluded by s. 277 can serve no legitimate purpose in the trial. Section 277, by limiting the exclusion to a purpose which is clearly illegitimate, does not touch evidence which may be tendered for valid purposes, and hence does not infringe the right to a fair trial.

I turn then to s. 276. Section 276, unlike s. 277, does not condition exclusion on use of the evidence for an illegitimate purpose. Rather, it constitutes a blanket exclusion, subject to three exceptions—rebuttal evidence, evidence going to identity, and evidence relating to consent to sexual activity on the same occasion as the trial incident. The question is whether this may exclude evidence which is relevant to the defence and the probative value of which is not substantially outweighed by the potential prejudice to the trial process. To put the matter another way, can it be said *a priori*, as the Attorney-General for Ontario contends, that any and all evidence excluded by s. 276 will necessarily be of such trifling a weight in relation to the prejudicial effect of the evidence that it may fairly be excluded?

In my view, the answer to this question must be negative. The Canadian and American jurisprudence affords numerous examples of evidence of sexual conduct which would be excluded by s. 276 but which clearly should be received in the interests of a fair trial, notwithstanding the possibility that it may divert a jury by tempting it to improperly infer consent or lack of credibility in the complainant.

Consider the defence of honest belief. It rests on the concept that the accused may honestly but mistakenly (and not necessarily reasonably) have believed that the complainant was consenting to the sexual act. If the accused can raise a reasonable doubt as to his intention on the basis that he honestly held such a belief, he is not guilty under our law and is entitled to an acquittal. The basis of the accused's honest belief in the complainant's consent may be sexual acts performed by the complainant at some other time or place. Yet s. 276 would preclude the accused leading such evidence.

Another category of evidence eliminated by s. 276 relates to the right of the defence to attack the credibility of the complainant on the ground that the complainant was biased or had motive to fabricate the evidence. In *State v. Jalo*, 557 P.2d 1359 (Or. Ct. App. 1976), a father accused of sexual acts with his young daughter sought to present evidence that the source of the accusation was his earlier discovery of the fact that the girl and her brother were engaged in intimate relations. The defence contended that when the father stopped the relationship, the daughter, out of animus toward him, accused him of the act. The father sought to lead this evidence in support of his defence that the charges were a concoction motivated by animus. Notwithstanding its clear relevance, this evidence would be excluded by s. 276. The respondent submits that the damage caused by its exclusion would not be great, because all that would be forbidden would be evidence of the sexual activities of the children, and the father could still testify that his daughter was angry with him. But surely the father's chance of convincing the jury of the validity of his defence would be greatly diminished if he were reduced to saying, in effect: "My daughter was angry with me, but I can't say why or produce any corroborating evidence." As noted above, to deny a defendant the building blocks of his defence is often to deny him the defence itself.

Other examples abound. Evidence of sexual activity excluded by s. 276 may be relevant to explain the physical conditions on which the Crown relies to establish intercourse or the use of force, such as semen, pregnancy, injury or disease—evidence which may go to consent: see Galvin, *supra*, at pp. 818-23; J.A. Tanford and A.J. Bocchino, "Rape Victim Shield Laws and the Sixth Amendment" (1980), 128 *U Pa. L Rev.* 544, pp. 584-5; D.W. Elliott, "Rape Complainants' Sexual Experience with Third Parties," [1984] *Crim. L Rev.* 4, at p. 7; *State v. Carpenter*, 447 NW 2d 436 (Minn. Ct. App. 1989), at pp. 440-2; *Commonwealth v. Majorana*, 470 A.2d 80 (Pa. 1983), at pp. 84-5; *People v. Mikula*, 269 NW 2d 195 (Mich. Ct. App. 1978), at pp. 198-9; *State ex rel. Pope v. Superior Court*, 545 P.2d 946 (Ariz. 1976), at p. 953. In the case of young complainants where there may be a tendency to believe their story on the ground that the detail of their account must have come from the alleged encounter, it may be relevant to show other activity which provides an explanation for the knowledge: see *R v. LeGallant* (1985), 47 CR (3d) 170 (B.C.S.C.), at pp. 175-6; *R v. Greene* (1990), 76 CR (3d) 119 (Ont. Dist. Ct.), at p. 122; *State v. Pulizzano*, 456 NW 2d 325 (Wis. 1990), at pp. 333-5; *Commonwealth v. Black*, 487 A.2d 396 (Pa. Super. Ct. 1985), at p. 400, fn. 10; *State v. Oliveira*, 576 A.2d 111 (RI 1990), at pp. 113-4; *State v. Carver*, 678 P.2d 842 (Wash. Ct. App. 1984); *State v. Howard*, 426 A.2d 457 (NH 1981); *State v. Reinart*, 440 NW 2d 503 (ND 1989); *Summitt v. State*, 697 P.2d 1374 (Nev. 1985).

Even evidence as to pattern of conduct may on occasion be relevant. Since this use of evidence of prior sexual conduct draws upon the inference that prior conduct infers similar subsequent conduct, it closely resembles the prohibited use of the evidence and must be carefully scrutinized: *R v. Wald* (1989), 47 CCC (3d) 315 (Alta. CA), at pp. 339-40; *Re Seaboyer and The Queen* (1987), 61 OR 290 (CA), at p. 300; Tanford and Bocchino, *supra*, at pp. 586-9; Galvin, *supra*, at pp. 831-48; Elliott, *supra*, at pp. 7-8; A. Ordover, "Admissibility of Patterns of Similar Sexual Conduct: The Unlamented Death of Character for Chastity" (1977), 63 *Cornell L Rev.* 90, at pp. 112-9; *Winfield v. Commonwealth*, 301 SE 2d 15 (Va. 1983), at pp. 19-21; *State v. Shoffner*, 302 SE 2d 830 (NC Ct. App. 1983), at pp. 832-3; *State v. Gonzalez*, 757 P.2d 925 (Wash. 1988), at pp. 929-31; *State v. Hudlow*, 659 P.2d 514 (Wash. 1983), at p. 520. Yet such evidence might be admissible in nonsexual cases under the similar fact rule. Is it fair then to deny it to an accused, merely because the trial relates to a sexual offence?

Consider the example offered by Tanford and Bocchino, *supra*, at p. 588, commenting on the situation in the United States:

A woman alleges that she was raped. The man she has accused of the act claims that she is a prostitute who agreed to sexual relations for a fee of twenty dollars, and afterwards, threatening to accuse him of rape, she demanded an additional one hundred dollars. The man refused to pay the extra amount. She had him arrested for rape, and he had her arrested for extortion. In the extortion trial, the state would be permitted to introduce evidence of the woman's previous sexual conduct—the testimony of other men that, using the same method, she had extorted money from them. When the woman is the complaining witness in the rape prosecution, however, evidence of this *modus operandi* would be excluded in most states. The facts are the same in both cases, as is the essential issue whether the woman is a rape victim or a would-be extortionist. Surely the relevance of the testimony should also be identical. If the woman's sexual history is relevant enough to be admitted against her when she is a defendant, entitled to the protections of the Constitution, then certainly it is relevant enough to be admitted in a trial at which she is merely a witness, entitled to no constitutional protection. Relevance depends on the issues that must be resolved at trial, not on the particular crime charged.

These examples leave little doubt that s. 276 has the potential to exclude evidence of critical relevance to the defence. Can it honestly be said, as the Attorney-General for Ontario contends, that the value of such evidence will always be trifling when compared with its potential to mislead the jury? I think not. The examples show that the evidence may well be of great importance to getting at the truth and determining whether the accused is guilty or innocent under the law—the ultimate aim of the trial process. They demonstrate that s. 276, enacted for the purpose of helping judges and juries arrive at the proper and just verdict in the particular case, overshoots the mark, with the result that it may have the opposite effect of impeding them in discovering the truth.

The conclusion that s. 276 overreaches is supported by consideration of how it impacts on the justifications for s. 276 set out above. The first and most important justification for s. 276 is that it prevents the judge or jury from being diverted by irrelevant evidence of other sexual conduct of the complainant which will unfairly prejudice them against the complainant and thus lead to an improper verdict. Accepting that evidence that diverts the trier of fact from the real issue and prejudices the chance of a true verdict can properly be excluded even if it possesses some relevance, the fact remains that a provision which categorically excludes evidence without permitting the trial judge to engage in the exercise of whether the possible prejudicial effect of the evidence outweighs its value to the truth-finding process runs the risk of overbreadth: see Doherty, *supra*, at p. 65.

The argument based on the reporting of sexual offences similarly fails to justify the wide reach of s. 276. As Doherty points out at p. 65, it is counterproductive to encourage reporting by a rule which impairs the ability of the trier of fact to arrive at a just result and determine the truth of the report. Reporting is but the first step in the judicial process, not an end in itself. But even if it is assumed that increased reporting will result in increased convictions, the argument is unpersuasive. Elliott, at p. 14, discounts this justification for prohibitions of relevant evidence on the ground that it "cross[es] a hitherto uncrossed line" to rule out legitimate tactics which may help an innocent man escape conviction. To accept that persuasive evidence for the defence can be categorically excluded on the ground that it may encourage reporting and convictions is, Elliott points out, to say either (a) that we assume the defendant's guilt, or (b) that the defendant must be hampered in his defence so that genuine rapists can be put down. Neither alternative conforms to our notions of fundamental justice. Finally, the justification of maintaining the privacy of the witness fails to support the rigid exclusionary rule embodied in s. 276 of the *Code*. First, it can be argued that important as it is to take all measures possible to ease the plight of the witness, the constitutional right to a fair trial must take precedence in case of conflict. As Doherty puts it (at p. 66):

> Every possible procedural step should be taken to minimize the encroachment on the witness's privacy, but in the end if evidence has sufficient cogency the witness must endure a degree of embarrassment and perhaps psychological trauma. This harsh reality must be accepted as part of the price to be paid to ensure that only the guilty are convicted.

Secondly, s. 276 goes further than required to protect privacy because it fails to permit an assessment of the effect on the witness of the evidence—an effect which may be great in some cases and small in others—in relation to the cogency of the evidence.

The failings of s. 276 are inherent in its concept. Commentators have identified two fundamental flaws in rape-shield provisions similar to s. 276. The first is that such provisions fail to distinguish between the different purposes for which evidence may be tendered. The legislation may misdefine the evil to be addressed as evidence of sexual activity, when in fact the evil to be addressed is the narrower evil of the misuse of evidence of sexual activity for irrelevant and misleading purposes, namely, the inference that the complainant consented to the act or that she is an unreliable witness. The result of this misdefinition of the problem is a blanket prohibition of evidence of sexual activity, regardless of whether the evidence is tendered for an illegitimate purpose or for a valid one. This defect is noted by Professor Galvin in her analysis of the various statutes in force in the United States (at p. 812):

> The basic problem with existing rape-shield legislation is its failure to distinguish between benign and invidious uses of sexual conduct evidence. This failure stems from a misperception by the drafters of the precise wrong to be redressed by reform legislation. The result is not merely bad evidence law; in many instances, the result is constitutional problems that stem from unnecessarily broad enactments. These various problems could have been avoided … if the legislators had clearly understood the underlying evidentiary concepts and had properly incorporated those concepts in the rape-shield statutes.

Section 276 takes the form of a basic prohibition of evidence of other sexual activity, regardless of the purpose for which it is tendered. It then stipulates three exceptions—evidence to rebut prosecution evidence of sexual activity; evidence tending to establish the identity of the person who committed the act; and evidence of sexual activity on the same occasion relating to consent. While there is some concession to the need to permit evidence of sexual activity for legitimate purposes, the exceptions exclude other purposes where the evidence would not be merely misleading, but truly relevant and helpful. In so far as they do so, the legislation falls into the trap identified by Professor Galvin.

A second and related criticism of provisions such as s. 276 is that they adopt a "pigeonhole" approach which is incapable of dealing adequately with the fundamental evidentiary problem at stake, that of determining whether or not the evidence is truly relevant, and not merely irrelevant and misleading. This amounts, in effect, to predicting relevancy on the basis of a series of categories. Courts and scholars frequently have alluded to the impossibility of predicting relevance in advance by a series of rules or categories. In *R v. Morin*, [1988] 2 SCR 345, at pp. 370-71, Sopinka J, speaking for the majority of this court, stated:

> It is difficult and arguably undesirable to lay down stringent rules for the determination of the relevance of a particular category of evidence. Relevance is very much a function of the other evidence and issues in a case. Attempts in the past to define the criteria for the admission of similar facts have not met with much success … . The test must be sufficiently flexible to accommodate the varying circumstances in which it must be applied.

Scholars have criticized rape-shield legislation adopting the format of a blanket exclusion supplemented by exceptions on the ground that this approach is inherently incapable of permitting the court sufficient latitude to properly determine relevance in the individual case. Professor Galvin says of this type of provision (the "Michigan" model), at p. 814:

> [M]any of the statutes fail to afford the accused the opportunity to present sexual conduct evidence which is indisputably relevant and necessary to the presentation of a legitimate defence theory. On one level, the problem is simply a failure to codify a sufficient number of exceptions; the case law amply demonstrates the need to amend many of these statutes by providing more bases for admitting sexual conduct evidence. More significant, however, is the fact that the common element linking each of these relevant uses of sexual conduct evidence seems to have escaped the notice of the drafters—none requires reliance on the invidious common-law notions that a woman's consent to sexual relations with one man implies either consent to relations with others or a lack of credibility.

In short, the problem with legislation like s. 276, as Professor Galvin sees it, is its failure to rely on the governing concept of whether the evidence is being tendered for an irrelevant, illegitimate purpose, and its reliance instead on categories of admissible evidence which can never anticipate the multitude of circumstances which may arise in trials for sexual offences. The failing is summed up succinctly by Doherty, *supra*, at p. 57, where he characterizes s. 276 as calling for "a mechanical 'pigeon-holing' approach to the question of admissibility based on criteria which may in a given case have little to do with the potential value of the evidence."

To summarize, s. 276 has the potential to exclude otherwise admissible evidence which may in certain cases be relevant to the defence. Such evidence is excluded absolutely, without any means of evaluating whether in the circumstances of the case the integrity of the trial process would be better served by receiving it than by excluding it. Accepting that the rejection of relevant evidence may sometimes be justified for policy reasons, the fact remains that s. 276 may operate to exclude evidence where the very policy which imbues the section—finding the truth and arriving at the correct verdict—suggests the evidence should be received. Given the primacy in our system of justice of the principle that the innocent should not be convicted, the right to present one's case should not be curtailed in the absence of an assurance that the curtailment is clearly justified by even stronger contrary considerations. What is required is a law which protects the fundamental right to a fair trial while avoiding the illegitimate inferences from other sexual conduct that the complainant is more likely to have consented to the act or less likely to be telling the truth.

· · ·

(g) Summary

I conclude that the operation of s. 276 of the *Criminal Code* permits the infringement of the rights enshrined in ss. 7 and 11(d) of the *Charter*. In achieving its purpose—the abolition of the outmoded, sexist based use of sexual conduct evidence—it overshoots the mark and renders inadmissible evidence which may be essential to the presentation of legitimate defences and hence to a fair trial. In exchange for the elimination of the possibility that the judge and jury may draw illegitimate inferences from the evidence, it exacts as a price the real risk that an innocent person may be convicted. The price is too great in relation to the benefit secured, and cannot be tolerated in a society that does not countenance in any form the conviction of the innocent. Support for this conclusion is found in other rules of evidence which have adapted to meet the dangers of arbitrarily excluding valuable evidence, as well as the law in other jurisdictions, which by one means or another rejects the idea that rape-shield legislation, however legitimate its aims, should be cast so widely as to deprive the accused of the tools with which to build a legitimate defence.

Section 277 does not, by contrast, offend the *Charter*.

2. Is section 276 saved by section 1 of the Charter?

Is s. 276 of the *Criminal Code* justified in a free and democratic society, notwithstanding the fact that it may lead to infringements of the *Charter*?

The first step under s. 1 is to consider whether the legislation addresses a pressing and substantial objective: *R v. Oakes*, [1986] 1 SCR 103. As already discussed, it does.

The second requirement under s. 1 is that the infringement of rights be proportionate to the pressing objective. This inquiry involves three considerations. The first—whether there exists a rational connection between the legislative measure and the objective—is arguably met; s. 276 does help to exclude unhelpful and potentially misleading evidence of the complainant's prior sexual conduct. The second consideration under proportionality is whether the legislation impairs the right as little as possible. It has been suggested that legislatures must be given some room to manoeuvre, particularly where the legislation is attempting to fix a balance between competing groups in society: *Irwin Toy Ltd. v. Quebec (Attorney-General)*, [1989] 1 SCR 927. Assuming that this case, although criminal and as such a contest between the state and the accused, might fall into this class, it still cannot be said that the degree of impairment effected by s. 276 is appropriately restrained. In creating exceptions to the exclusion of evidence of the sexual activity of the complainant on other occasions, Parliament correctly recognized that justice requires a measured approach, one which admits evidence which is truly relevant to the defence notwithstanding potential prejudicial effect. Yet Parliament at the same time excluded other evidence of sexual conduct which might be equally relevant to a legitimate defence and which appears to pose no greater danger of prejudice than the exceptions it recognizes. To the extent the section excludes relevant defence evidence whose value is not clearly outweighed by the danger it presents, the section is overbroad.

I turn finally to the third aspect of the proportionality requirement—the balance between the importance of the objective and the injurious effect of the legislation. The objective of the legislation, as discussed above, is to eradicate the erroneous inferences from evidence of other sexual encounters that the complainant is more likely to have consented to the sexual act in issue or less likely to be telling the truth. The subsidiary aims are to promote fairer trials and increased reporting of sexual offences and to minimize the invasion of the complainant's privacy. In this way the personal security of women and their right to equal benefit and protection of the law are enhanced. The effect of the legislation, on the other hand, is to exclude relevant defence evidence, the value of which outweighs its potential prejudice. As indicated in the discussion of s. 7, all parties agree that a provision which rules out probative defence evidence which is not clearly outweighed by the prejudice it may cause to the trial strikes the wrong balance between the rights of complainants and the rights of the accused.

The line must be drawn short of the point where it results in an unfair trial and the possible conviction of an innocent person. Section 276 fails this test.

I conclude that s. 276 is not saved by s. 1 of the *Charter*.

· · ·

4. *What follows from striking down section 276?*

The first question is whether the striking down of s. 276 revives the old common law rule of evidence permitting liberal and often inappropriate reception of evidence of the complainant's sexual conduct. Some inappropriate uses of such evidence are precluded by s. 277, which I have found to be valid. But other common law rules fall outside s. 277. Does striking s. 276 revive them?

The answer to this question is no. The rules in question are common law rules. Like other common law rules of evidence, they must be adapted to conform to current reality. As all counsel on these appeals accepted, the reality in 1991 is that evidence of sexual conduct and reputation in itself cannot be regarded as logically probative of either the complainant's credibility or consent. Although they still may inform the thinking of many, the twin myths which s. 276 sought to eradicate are just that—myths—and have no place in a rational and just system of law. It follows that the old rules which permitted evidence of sexual conduct and condoned invalid inferences from it solely for these purposes have no place in our law.

The inquiry as to what the law is in the absence of s. 276 of the *Code* is thus remitted to consideration of the fundamental principles governing the trial process and the reception of evidence. Harking back to Thayer's maxim, relevant evidence should be admitted, and irrelevant evidence excluded, subject to the qualification that the value of the evidence must outweigh its potential prejudice to the conduct of a fair trial. Moreover, the focus must be not on the evidence itself, but on the use to which it is put. As Professor Galvin puts it, our aim is "to abolish the outmoded, sexist-based use of sexual conduct evidence while permitting other uses of such evidence to remain": *supra*, p. 809.

[McLachlin J considered Galvin's proposal at some length and continued:]

While accepting the premise and the general thrust of Galvin's proposal, I suggest certain modifications. There seems little purpose in having separate rules for the use of sexual conduct evidence for illegitimate inferences of consent and credibility in the Canadian context. Again, I question whether evidence of other sexual conduct with the accused should automatically be admissible in all cases; sometimes the value of such evidence might be little or none. The word "complainant" is more compatible with the presumption of innocence of the accused than the word "victim." Professor Galvin's reference to the defence of reasonable belief in consent must be adapted to meet Canadian law, which does not require reasonableness. And the need to warn the jury clearly against improper uses of the evidence should be emphasized, in my view.

In the absence of legislation, it is open to this court to suggest guidelines for the reception and use of sexual conduct evidence. Such guidelines should be seen for what they are—an attempt to describe the consequences of the application of the general rules of evidence governing relevance and the reception of evidence—and not as judicial legislation cast in stone.

In my view the trial judge under this new regime shoulders a dual responsibility. First, the judge must assess with a high degree of sensitivity whether the evidence proffered by the defence meets the test of demonstrating a degree of relevance which outweighs the damages and disadvantages presented by the admission of such evidence. The examples presented earlier suggest that while cases where such evidence will carry sufficient probative value will exist, they will be exceptional. The trial judge must ensure that evidence is tendered for a legitimate purpose, and that it logically supports a defence. The fishing expeditions which unfortunately did occur in the past should not be permitted. The trial judge's discretion must be exercised to ensure that neither the *in camera* procedure nor the trial become forums for demeaning and abusive conduct by defence counsel.

The trial judge's second responsibility will be to take special care to ensure that, in the exceptional case where circumstances demand that such evidence be permitted, the jury is fully and properly instructed as to its appropriate use. The jurors must be cautioned that they should not draw impermissible inferences from evidence of previous sexual activity. While such evidence may be tendered for a purpose logically probative of the defence to be presented, it may be important to remind jurors that they not allow the allegations of past sexual activity to lead them to the view that the complainant is less worthy of belief, or was more likely to have consented for that reason. It is hoped that a sensitive and responsive exercise of discretion by the judiciary will reduce and even eliminate the concerns which provoked legislation such as s. 276, while at the same time preserving the right of an accused to a fair trial.

I would summarize the applicable principles as follows:

1. On a trial for a sexual offence, evidence that the complainant has engaged in consensual sexual conduct on other occasions (including past sexual conduct with the accused) is not admissible solely to support the inference that the complainant is by reason of such conduct:

   (a) more likely to have consented to the sexual conduct at issue in the trial;

   (b) less worthy of belief as a witness.

2. Evidence of consensual sexual conduct on the part of the complainant may be admissible for purposes other than an inference relating to the consent or credibility of the complainant where it possesses probative value on an issue in the trial and where that probative value is not substantially outweighed by the danger of unfair prejudice flowing from the evidence.

   By way of illustration only, and not by way of limitation, the following are examples of admissible evidence:

   (A) Evidence of specific instances of sexual conduct tending to prove that a person other than the accused caused the physical consequences of the rape alleged by the prosecution;

   (B) Evidence of sexual conduct tending to prove bias or motive to fabricate on the part of the complainant;

(C) Evidence of prior sexual conduct, known to the accused at the time of the act charged, tending to prove that the accused believed that the complainant was consenting to the act charged (without laying down absolute rules, normally one would expect some proximity in time between the conduct that is alleged to have given rise to an honest belief and the conduct charged);

(D) Evidence of prior sexual conduct which meets the requirements for the reception of similar act evidence, bearing in mind that such evidence cannot be used illegitimately merely to show that the complainant consented or is an unreliable witness;

(E) Evidence tending to rebut proof introduced by the prosecution regarding the complainant's sexual conduct.

3. Before evidence of consensual sexual conduct on the part of a victim is received, it must be established on a *voir dire* (which may be held *in camera*) by affidavit or the testimony of the accused or third parties, that the proposed use of the evidence of other sexual conduct is legitimate.

4. Where evidence that the complainant has engaged in sexual conduct on other occasions is admitted on a jury trial, the judge should warn the jury against inferring from the evidence of the conduct itself, either that the complainant might have consented to the act alleged, or that the complainant is less worthy of credit.

· · ·

I would dismiss these appeals and affirm the order of the Court of Appeal that these cases proceed to trial. I would answer the constitutional questions as follows:

1. Whether s. 246.6 (now s. 276) or s. 246.7 (now s. 277) of the *Criminal Code* is inconsistent with ss. 7 or 11(d) of the *Canadian Charter of Rights and Freedoms*?

Yes, s. 276 is inconsistent with ss. 7 and 11(d). Section 277 is not.

2. If ss. 246.6 or 246.7 of the *Criminal Code* is inconsistent with ss. 7 or 11(d) of the *Canadian Charter of Rights and Freedoms*, whether that inconsistency is justified on the basis of s. 1 thereof.

No.

L'HEUREUX-DUBÉ J (Gonthier J concurring) dissenting in part:

· · ·

Sexual Assault

Sexual assault is not like any other crime. In the vast majority of cases the target is a woman and the perpetrator is a man. (98.7% of those charged with sexual assault are men: *Crime Statistics 1986*, quoted in T. Dawson, "Sexual Assault Law and Past Sexual Conduct of the Primary Witness: The Construction of Relevance," 2 *CJWL* 310 (1988), at p. 326, note 72.) Unlike other crimes of a violent nature, it is for the most part unreported. Yet, by all accounts, women are victimized at an alarming rate and there is some evidence that an already frighteningly high rate of sexual assault is on the increase. The prosecution and conviction rates for sexual assault are among the lowest for all violent crimes. Perhaps more than any other crime, the fear and constant reality of sexual assault affects how women conduct their lives and how they define their relationship with the larger society. Sexual assault is not like any other crime.

Conservative estimates inform us that, in Canada, at least one woman in five will be sexually assaulted during her lifetime: see J. Brickman and J. Briere, "Incidence of Rape and Sexual Assault in an Urban Canadian Population," 7 *Int'l J of Women's Stud.* 195 (1985). The report of the Committee on Sexual Offences Against Children and Youths warns that one in two females will be the victim of unwanted sexual acts (Sexual Offences Against Children (1984)). While social scientists agree that the incidence of sexual assault is great, they also agree that it is impossible, for a variety of reasons, to measure accurately the actual rate of victimization. However, Brickman and Briere, *supra*, report that police figures "may be multiplied anywhere from five to 20 times to correct for victim under-reporting": see also LeGrand, "Rape and Rape Laws: Sexism in Society and Law," 61 *Cal. L Rev.* 919 (1973), at p. 939, and L. Clark and D. Lewis, *Rape: The Price of Coercive Sexuality* (1977), at p. 57. While there is a large gap between reported incidents and actual victimization, there is a further gap between what researchers tell us are the actual numbers and what the actual numbers are.

There are a number of reasons why women may not report their victimization: fear of reprisal, fear of a continuation of their trauma at the hands of the police and the criminal justice system, fear of a perceived loss of status and lack of desire to report due to the typical effects of sexual assault such as depression, self-blame or loss of self-esteem. Although all of the reasons for failing to report are significant and important, more relevant to the present inquiry are the numbers of victims who choose not to bring their victimization to the attention of the authorities due to their perception that the institutions, with which they would have to become involved, will view their victimization in a stereotypical and biased fashion. In the report of the Solicitor General of Canada, *Canadian Urban Victimization Survey: Reported and Unreported Crimes* (1984), the statistics in this regard are noted at p. 10:

> Analysis of reasons for failure to report incidents confirms many of the concerns which have already been noted by rape crisis workers—that women fear revenge from the offender (a factor in 33% of the unreported incidents) and, even more disturbingly, that they often fail to report because of their concern about the attitude of police or courts to this type of offence (43% of unreported incidents).

See also L. Holmstrom and A. Burgess, *The Victim of Rape: Institutional Reactions* (1983), at p. 58, and P. Marshall, "Sexual Assault, The Charter and Sentencing Reform" (1988), 63 CR (3d) 216 at p. 217.

The woman who comes to the attention of the authorities has her victimization measured against the current rape mythologies, i.e., who she should be in order to be recognized as having been, in the eyes of the law, raped; who her attacker must be in order to be recognized, in the eyes of the law, as a potential rapist; and how injured she must be in order to be believed. If her victimization does not fit the myths, it is unlikely that an arrest will be made or a conviction obtained. As prosecutors and police often suggest, in an attempt to excuse their application of stereotype, there is no point in directing cases toward the justice system if juries and judges will acquit on the basis of their stereotypical perceptions of the "supposed victim" and her "supposed" victimization. K. Williams, *The Prosecution of Sexual Assaults* (1978), discusses, at p. 42, the attrition rate for sexual assault cases as they progress through the system:

> [T]he DC Task Force on Rape reported their concern that sexual assault cases did not fare well in the courts. They were not sure, however, whether this reflected normal attrition, experienced with all cases, or whether rape cases were particularly prone to dismissal. The latter seems to be true. In our analysis, rape cases were less likely to result in conviction than cases of robbery, burglary, and murder. The only crime with an attrition rate at all comparable was aggravated assault. There is an explanation for a large part of the attrition rate of assault cases, but it does not apply to rape. Over 60 percent of the rejections at screening and over one-half of the later dismissals in aggravated assault cases can be attributed to the complaining witness's decision to stop cooperating with the prosecutor. The attrition that results from such a decision on the part of the victim does *not* account for the attrition in rape cases. Attrition in rape cases is more likely to be the result of the prosecutor's judgment that the victim's credibility is questionable .... Few cases ... go to trial .... Most fall out of the system before they reach that stage.

[Emphasis added.] [Italics in original.]

More specifically, police rely in large measure upon popular conceptions of sexual assault in order to classify incoming cases as "founded" or "unfounded." It would appear as though most forces have developed a convenient shorthand regarding their decisions to proceed in any given case. This shorthand is composed of popular myth regarding rapists (distinguishing them from men as a whole), and stereotype about women's character and sexuality. Holmstrom and Burgess, *supra*, at pp. 174-99, conveniently set out and explain the most common of these myths and stereotypes:

1. *Struggle and Force: Woman As Defender of Her Honor.* There is a myth that a woman cannot be raped against her will, that if she really wants to prevent a rape she can.

The prosecution attempts to show that she did struggle, or had no opportunity to do so, while the defence attempts to show that she did not.

Women know that there is no response on their part that will assure their safety. The experience and knowledge of women is borne out by the *Canadian Urban Victimization Survey: Female Victims of Crime* (1985). At p. 7 of the report the authors note:

> Sixty percent of those who tried reasoning with their attackers, and 60% of those who resisted actively by fighting or using weapon [*sic*] were injured. Every sexual assault incident is unique and so many factors are unknown (physical size of victims and offenders, verbal or physical threats, etc.) that no single course of action can be recommended unqualifiedly.

2. *Knowing the Defendant: The Rapist As a Stranger.* There is a myth that rapists are strangers who leap out of bushes to attack their victims ... the view that interaction between friends or between relatives does not result in a rape is prevalent.

The defence uses the existence of a relationship between the parties to blame the victim. (Feild and Bienen [H.S. Feild and L.B. Bienen, *Jurors and Rape* (Lexington, MA: Lexington Books, 1980)] report at p. 76 that "a significant proportion of reported rapes involve an assailant known by the victim": see also J. Check and N. Malamuth, "Sex Role Stereotyping and Reactions to Depictions of Stranger Versus Acquaintance Rape," 45 *J of Personality and Soc. Psychology* 344 (1983), at pp. 344-5.)

3. *Sexual Reputation: The Madonna-Whore Complex.* ... [W]omen ... are categorized into one-dimensional types. They are maternal or they are sexy. They are good or they are bad. They are madonnas or they are whores.

The legal rules use these distinctions.

4. *General Character: Anything Not 100 Percent Proper and Respectable.* ... Being on welfare or drinking or drug use could be used to discredit anyone, but where women are involved, these issues are used to imply that the woman consented to sex with the defendant or that she contracted to have sex for money.

5. *Emotionality of Females.* Females are assumed to be "more emotional" than males. The expectation is that if a woman is raped, she will get hysterical during the event and she will be visibly upset afterward. If she is able to "retain her cool," then people assume that "nothing happened" ... .

6. *Reporting Rape.* Two conflicting expectations exist concerning the reporting of rape. One is that if a woman is raped she will be too upset and ashamed to report it, and hence most of the time this crime goes unreported. The other is that if a woman is raped she will be so upset that she will report it. Both expectations exist simultaneously.

7. *Woman as Fickle and Full of Spite.* Another stereotype is that the feminine character is especially filled with malice. Woman is seen as fickle and as seeking revenge on past lovers.

8. *The Female Under Surveillance: Is the Victim Trying to Escape Punishment?* ... It is assumed that the female's sexual behavior, depending on her age, is under the surveillance of her parents or her husband, and also more generally of the community. Thus, the defense argues, if a woman says she was raped it must be because she consented to sex that she was not supposed to have. She got caught, and now she wants to get back in the good graces of whomever's [*sic*] surveillance she is under.

9. *Disputing That Sex Occurred.* That females fantasize rape is another common stereotype. Females are assumed to make up stories that sex occurred when in fact nothing happened ... . Similarly, women are thought to fabricate the sexual activity not as part of a fantasy life, but out of spite.

10. *Stereotype of the Rapist.* One stereotype of the rapist is that of a stranger who leaps out of the bushes to attack his victim and later abruptly leaves her ... . [S]tereotypes of the rapist can be used to blame the victim. She tells what he did.

And because it often does not match what jurors think rapists do, his behavior is held against her.

A corollary of this myth is the belief that rapists are not "normal" and are "mentally ill."

This court has previously examined the application of myth and stereotype to women in the realm of the criminal law. In *R v. Lavallee*, [1990] 1 SCR 852, this court considered the negative impact of stereotypes about battered women and held at p. 125 that "[e]xpert evidence can assist the jury in dispelling these myths." L. Vandervort, "Mistake of Law and Sexual Assault: Consent and Mens Rea," 2 *CJWL* 233 (1987), at p. 258, note 43, suggests that, "[t]he criminal justice system can play a major role in the process of replacing 'mythical' views of sexual assault, and the social definitions of sexual assault based on these myths, with views based on fact and the results of empirical studies."

This list of stereotypical conceptions about women and sexual assault is by no means exhaustive. Like most stereotypes, they operate as a way, however flawed, of understanding the world and, like most such constructs, operate at a level of consciousness that makes it difficult to root them out and confront them directly. This mythology finds its way into the decisions of the police regarding their "founded"/"unfounded" categorization, operates in the mind of the Crown when deciding whether or not to prosecute, influences a judge's or juror's perception of guilt or innocence of the accused and the "goodness" or "badness" of the victim, and finally, has carved out a niche in both the evidentiary and substantive law governing the trial of the matter.

[After reviewing the impact of these myths on police behaviour, L'Heureux-Dubé J turned to their impact on the trial process. She considered a body of social-science research, based mainly on US data, indicating, among other effects, that jurors are less likely to convict when they are aware of the complainant's sexual history or when they learn that the complainant and the accused were previously acquainted. L'Heureux-Dubé J then reviewed the common law rules of evidence applicable to sexual offences, considered some earlier statutory changes, and continued:]

Relevance and Admissibility at Common Law and Under the Legislative Provisions

. . .

Once the mythical bases of relevancy determinations in this area of the law are revealed (discussed at greater length later in these reasons), the irrelevance of most evidence of prior sexual history is clear. Nevertheless, Parliament has provided broad avenues for its admissibility in the setting out of the exceptions to the general rule in s. 246.6 (now s. 276). Moreover, *all* evidence of the complainant's previous sexual history with the accused is *prima facie* admissible under those provisions. Evidence that is excluded by these provisions is simply, in a myth and stereotype-free decision-making context, irrelevant.

The first exception, in subs. (1)(a), has the potential for allowing the admission of a wide variety of sexual history evidence. It encompasses situations where the Crown directly or indirectly introduces in evidence the issue of the complainant's sexual history. If the Crown chooses to do so, the door is open for rebuttal evidence. It would allow the defence to adduce sexual history evidence to explain semen, pregnancy, injury or disease that the Crown contends was a consequence of the offence. Such evidence is, however, limited to rebutting this explicit or implicit contention of the Crown. Subsection (1)(b) allows the receipt of evidence which goes to show the identity of the person who had sexual relations with the complainant on the pertinent occasion. This subsection and subs. (1)(a) overlap to some degree in that rebuttal evidence regarding the physical consequences of the assault would, depending upon the circumstances of the case, be admissible under one or either subsection. Noteworthy, however, is the caveat in subs. (1)(b) that such evidence must go to establishing the identity of the person who had sexual contact with the complainant on the occasion set out in the charge. While these provisions are inherently broad, their interpretation must nevertheless remain true to the wording of the exception otherwise they will have little effect. As for the last exception, subs. (1)(c), it allows the receipt of relevant and proximate sexual history evidence that goes to the issue of the consent the accused honestly thought he had been given. In summary, as Grange JA pointed out (at p. 307), for the majority of the Court of Appeal, "[t]here is nothing startling or unique about our legislation."

As to s. 246.7 (now s. 277), it merely excludes evidence of sexual reputation used to impeach or support the credibility of the complainant. The notion that reputation for "unchasteness" is relevant to credibility is insupportable and its legislative exclusion uncontentious. Furthermore, evidence of sexual reputation is inherently unreliable. Due to the nature of the activity that forms the subject-matter of the reputation, the alleged reputation is often nothing more than "speculation and exaggeration": see Galvin, *supra*, at p. 801, and Ordover, "Admissibility of Patterns of Similar Sexual Conduct: The Unlamented Death of Character for Chastity," 63 *Cornell L Rev.* 90 (1977), at p. 105. In fact, both the appellant Seaboyer and the intervener, the Canadian Civil Liberties Association, concede that the exclusion mandated by s. 277 is uncontentious. Indeed, my colleague reaches the same conclusion at p. 21 of her reasons.

The literature and case-law in this area abound with examples of the supposed relevant evidence that is excluded by s. 276. For the most part, however, the "relevant" evidence provided in these examples is, on a principled inquiry, irrelevant; any semblance of relevance depends in large measure upon acceptance of stereotype about women and rape. Much of the remainder is admissible under the provision. One hesitates, however, to construct an argument around the speculative scenarios offered. Many of the scenarios are pure fantasy and have absolutely no grounding in life or experience. Speculating in this manner depends, to some degree, upon the acceptance of stereotypes about women and sexual assault and the will to propagate them. The point is well made by Sheehy, ... ["Canadian Judges and the Law of Rape: Should the Charter Insulate Bias?" (1989), 21 *Ottawa L. Rev.* 741], at pp. 755-7:

> The indeterminate exceptions [that evidence of sexual history is generally irrelevant] posed by the *Wald* case constitute an open invitation to the "pornographic imagination" with which we have all been culturally endowed. The beliefs which spring from this collective imagination are not only without empirical foundation: they also systematically deny control and credibility to those who do not belong to the dominant culture. *Even more problematic is the fact that these beliefs are insidious because they are taken for granted and are therefore almost irresistible to the trier of fact who has absorbed our culture ... .*

> *In fact, the examples used by defence counsel, academics, and judges to illustrate situations where sexual history evidence is said to be highly "relevant" resemble … "pornographic vignettes" … . These hypotheticals play upon internalized assumptions about what women really want and male desires for specific sexual scenarios … . They evoke highly emotive reactions which bear no relationship to "truth" and they bring out the worst in us.*

(Emphasis added; footnotes omitted.)

I also heartily concur in the submissions at p. 17 of the factum of the intervener Women's Legal Education and Action Fund on this point:

> *… in all of the hypothetical situations outlined in the Appellants' factums, evidence of sexual history and/or sexual reputation is either totally irrelevant, admissible pursuant to the exceptions provided for in s. 276, or, in the alternative, of very low probative value and highly prejudicial to the interests of the administration of justice …*

(Emphasis added.)

I will, therefore, resist as much as possible joining the discourse at this level and will restrict myself to perhaps a more general discussion of the effect of the provisions.

As I stated above, many of the examples set up by opponents to the legislation are based upon a misapprehension of the scope of the exceptions and, indeed, some of the earlier case-law striking down these provisions is, unfortunately, guilty of the same error. In *R v. Coombs* (1985), 23 CCC (3d) 356 (Nfld. SCTD), and *R v. Oquataq* [(1985), 18 CCC (3d) 440 (NWTSC)], the defence wished to adduce evidence of prior sexual history in response to Crown evidence of physical injury of the complainant. In both cases such evidence would have been admissible under s. 276. In *Coombs, supra,* the trial judge held that the evidence was not admissible under the legislation and, as such evidence was relevant and necessary for the accused to make full answer and defence, the provisions excluding it were unconstitutional. In *Oquataq, supra,* the same type of evidence was also held to be inadmissible under subs. (1)(a) with the same constitutional result. Many of the examples offered by the appellants of "relevant" evidence that is excluded by s. 276 suffer from a similar misapprehension.

I will now turn my attention specifically to the categories of relevant evidence that the appellants suggest are excluded by the provision. I will discuss only those categories that are commonly referred to in the literature. I will consider the possible ramifications of the *Canadian Charter of Rights and Freedoms* subsequent to this discussion.

Many argue that the most convincing support for the argument that the provision is drawn too narrowly is provided by so-called "similar fact evidence," or "pattern of conduct evidence," i.e., that the complainant has had consensual sexual relations in circumstances that look an awful lot like those supporting the assault allegation and, hence, such evidence is probative of consent. I am of the firm opinion that such evidence is almost invariably irrelevant and, in any event, is nothing more than a prohibited propensity argument, besides being highly prejudicial to the integrity and fairness of the trial process.

Such arguments depend for their vitality on the notion that women consent to sex based upon such extraneous considerations as the location of the act, the race, age or profession of the alleged assaulter and/or considerations of the nature of the sexual act engaged in. Though it feels somewhat odd to have to state this next proposition explicitly, consent is to a person and not to a circumstance. The use of the words "pattern" and "similar fact" deny this reality. Such arguments are implicitly based upon the notion that women will, in the right circumstances, consent to anyone and, more fundamentally, that "unchaste" women have a propensity to consent. While my colleague suggests that this proposition is "now discredited" and "[has] no place in a rational and just system of law," she nevertheless concludes that the exclusion of "pattern" evidence is unconstitutional. In my view, the mythical bases of these arguments deny their relevance.

Although Galvin, *supra*, comes to what is, in my opinion, an erroneous conclusion, namely that "pattern" evidence may be relevant if it is narrowly confined, she nevertheless accurately discusses the problems inherent in this type of evidence. She states at p. 834:

> In the context of a trial for rape, evidence that the complainant previously slept with rock stars or with men she met in singles' bars could only be used to show her propensity to consent in such circumstances; her identity is not a disputed issue. The ... "common plan or scheme" exception to the propensity rule is similarly inapplicable in this context, because a complainant's pattern of similar sexual encounters can hardly be said to occur as the result of a pre-existing plan or scheme on her part. Moreover, as with all propensity evidence, the danger of jury prejudice is high; the complainant may be viewed as a "loose" woman who "got what she deserved," irrespective of her behavior on this particular occasion.

Furthermore, if there is any evidence of this nature that has any legitimate claim to relevance and this is already a highly dubious proposition, it is amply covered by the fact that previous sexual contact between the accused and the complainant is admissible under the provision. Another argument often used in an attempt to get "pattern" or "propensity" evidence admitted is to call the behaviour "habitual." Borrowing from *McCormick on Evidence*, 3rd ed. (1984), s. 195 at pp. 574-5 (quoted in Galvin, *supra*, at p. 778):

> Habit ... is more specific [than character]. It denotes one's regular response to a repeated situation ... . Thus, a person may be in the habit of bounding down a certain stairway two or three steps at a time, of patronizing a particular pub after each day's work, or of driving his automobile without using a seatbelt.

(Footnotes omitted.)

It is impossible, in my view, to draw an analogy between this behaviour and volitional sexual conduct. The rationale underlying the admissibility of habit evidence has no application in this context.

A similar argument, often made in support of the contention that prior sexual history is relevant and admissible but excluded by the provision, is based upon an extension of the Ontario Court of Appeal's reasoning in *R v. Scopelliti* (1981), 63 CCC (2d) 481, 34 OR (2d) 524. In that case the Court of Appeal held at p. 492 that:

> Obviously, evidence of previous acts of violence by the deceased, not known to the accused, is not relevant to show the reasonableness of the accused's apprehension of an impending attack. *However, there is impressive support for the proposition that, where self-defence is raised, evidence of the deceased's character (i.e., disposition) for violence is admissible to show the probability of the deceased having been the aggressor and to support the accused's evidence that he was attacked by the deceased.*

(Emphasis added.)

Assuming that the Ontario Court of Appeal is correct in its analysis and assuming that such an analysis applies generally, adopting such an argument in the context of this case would lend support to the stereotypical proposition that "unchaste" women have a propensity to consent. I must also confess an inability to grasp how violent behaviour and consensual sexual behaviour are at all analogous. Furthermore, a history of violent conduct is less likely to trigger the invocation of stereotype about the person who engages in such behaviour. Even so, it is interesting to note that the admissibility of evidence of the deceased's propensity for violence in trials for murder is a matter of some controversy as there is great danger that such evidence may be misused by jurors to improperly blame the deceased: see McCormick, *supra*, at pp. 571-3, quoted in Galvin, *supra*, at p. 782.) For all of these reasons, the rule in *Scopelliti*, *supra*, is of no avail in the present context.

A second category of so-called relevant evidence is also widely set up as conclusively demonstrating the infirmity of the provision, namely, evidence of mistaken belief in consent. Again, I am of the firm opinion that no relevant evidence regarding the defence of honest but mistaken belief in consent is excluded by the provision under attack here.

Although, in Canada, the defence is one of honest belief and not one of reasonable belief, the exception in subs. (1)(c) amply provides for this defence. In *R v. Bulmer*, [1987] 1 SCR 782, this court discussed the effect of s. 244(4) (now s. 265(4)), which codifies this defence, on the defence of honest but mistaken belief in consent articulated by this court in *Pappajohn v. The Queen*, [1980] 2 SCR 120. For clarity I will reproduce this section.

> 265(4) Where an accused alleges that he believed that the complainant consented to the conduct that is the subject-matter of the charge, a judge, if satisfied that there is sufficient evidence and that, if believed by the jury, the evidence would constitute a defence, shall instruct the jury, when reviewing all the evidence relating to the determination of the honesty of the accused's belief, to consider the presence or absence of reasonable grounds for that belief.

This court concluded that the "Pappajohn" defence had not been legislatively altered. While one may then wonder why Parliament included the codification of this defence in its package of reforms, the decision of this court in *Bulmer*, *supra*, does not force the conclusion that subs. (1)(c) of s. 276 excludes relevant evidence. McIntyre J, for the majority in *Bulmer*, *supra*, held at pp. 790-91 that before the defence of honest but mistaken belief can be put to the jury, the trial judge must conclude that there is an "air of reality" to the defence:

> There will not be an air of reality about a mere statement that "I thought she was consenting" not supported to some degree by other evidence or circumstances arising in the case ... .
> The question he [the trial judge] must answer is this. In all the circumstances of this case, is there any reality in the defence? ...
>
> When the defence of mistake of fact—or for that matter any other defence—is raised, two distinct steps are involved. The first step for the trial judge is to decide if the defence should be put to the jury. It is on this question, as I have said, that the "air of reality" test is applied.

Further, when the trier of fact turns his or her mind to the issue of whether the belief was honestly held, McIntyre J stated at p. 792:

This section [s. 244(4), now s. 265(4)], in my view, does not change the law as applied in *Pappajohn*. It does not require that the mistaken belief be reasonable or reasonably held. It simply makes it clear that in determining the issue of the honesty of the asserted belief, the presence or absence of reasonable grounds for the belief are relevant factors for the jury's consideration.

It is my view that, assuming that both the trier of fact and the trier of law are operating in an intellectual environment that is free of rape myth and stereotype about women, any evidence excluded by this subsection would not satisfy the "air of reality" that must accompany this defence nor would it provide reasonable grounds for the jury to consider in assessing whether the belief was honestly held. The structure of the exception provided for in s. 276(1)(c) is, thus, not offensive to such a defence. Evidence of prior acts of prostitution or allegations of prostitution are properly excluded by the provision. In my opinion, this evidence is never relevant and, besides its irrelevance, is hugely prejudicial. I vehemently disagree with the assertion of the appellant Seaboyer that "a prostitute is generally more willing to consent to sexual intercourse and is less credible as a witness because of that mode of life" (at p. 21 of his factum, quoting the Federal/Provincial Task Force, ... [Federal/Provincial Task Force on Uniform Rules of Evidence, *Report of the Federal Provincial Task Force on the Uniform Rules of Evidence* (Toronto: Carswell, 1982)]). Nor do I particularly understand the phenomenon whereby many complainants in sexual assault cases are asked if they are prostitutes. (See, for example, Z. Adler, "The Relevance of Sexual History Evidence in Rape: Problems of Subjective Interpretation," [1985] *Crim. LR* 769 at p. 778.)

Many also argue that the provision does not allow evidence going to show motive to fabricate or bias. Clearly, most such alleged motives or bias will not be grounded in the complainant's past sexual history. Moreover, much of this evidence depends for its relevance on certain stereotypical visions of women; that they lie about sexual assault and that women who allege sexual assault often do so in order to get back in the good graces of those who may have her [*sic*] sexual conduct under scrutiny. Thus, again, refutation of stereotype strikes at the heart of the argument. As to evidence that a complainant has made prior false allegations of sexual assault, such evidence is admissible under the existing provision since this evidence does not involve the admission of her previous sexual history.

As I stated at the outset, the evidence which is excluded by the provision is simply irrelevant. It is based upon discriminatory beliefs about women and sexual assault. In addition, the impugned provision provides wide avenues for the introduction of sexual history evidence that is relevant. Paradoxically, some of the exceptions may be cast overly broadly with the unfortunate result that a large body of evidence may still be improperly admitted on the basis of specious relevancy claims.

If I am wrong in concluding that no relevant sexual history evidence is excluded by the contested provision, I am of the view that such exclusion is proper due to its extremely prejudicial effect on the trial of the legal issues.

[L'Heureux-Dubé J referred to McCormick's categories of prejudice and to other authorities on prejudicial effects, and continued:]

Rather than negatively affecting decisions of guilt and innocence, the exclusion of evidence of sexual history rationalizes such determinations. The discussion at the outset of these reasons conclusively demonstrated that sexual history evidence pre-empts considered decision making. The words of Catton [K. Catton, "Evidence Regarding the Prior Sexual History of an Alleged Rape Victim—Its Effect on the Perceived Guilt of the Accused," 33 *U of T Fac. L Rev.* 165 (1975)], at p. 173 … , bear repeating: "Any information at all implying that the victim had a prior sex history had the effect of reducing the perceived guilt of the accused regardless of whether this information was verified."

The guilt or innocence determination is transformed into an assessment of whether or not the complainant should be protected by the law of sexual assault. In my view, it is indisputable that this evidence has such a prejudicial effect. Many a defence lawyer knows the effect of such evidence and, thus, strives to get it admitted. Indeed, during debate in the House of Commons regarding the first effort of Parliament to rationalize this area of law, one member, Mr. Jarvis, commented:

> The myth is that a "bad woman" is incapable of being raped … . We have to deal with the myth that the credibility of a "bad woman" is immediately in question. I was never sure what that phrase meant. *As a lawyer, all I knew was that it was of benefit to hurl as much dirt as possible in the direction of such a woman, hoping that some of it would stick and that the jury would disbelieve what she said.*

(Emphasis added). (*House of Commons Debates*, November 19, 1975, at p. 9252.)

If, indeed, we are searching for the truth, such a result is repugnant and that which produces it properly inadmissible.

[L'Heureux-Dubé J therefore held that s 276 did not violate s 7 of the Charter, on the ground that the provision "excludes only irrelevant or prejudicial evidence." She held in the alternative that s 276 was "easily justified under s. 1" of the Charter.]

NOTES AND QUESTIONS

How exactly do McLachlin J and L'Heureux-Dubé J differ in their answers to the following questions?

1. Under what circumstances did former s 276 have the effect of excluding relevant evidence?
2. How, and to what extent, is the evidence excluded by the former s 276 prejudicial?
3. What should be done if the evidence is relevant but prejudicial?

For discussions of *Seaboyer*, see Martha Shaffer, "Seaboyer v. R: A Case Comment" (1992), 5 CJWL 29; Christine Boyle & Marilyn MacCrimmon, "R v. Seaboyer: A Lost Cause?" (1991), 7 CR (4th) 225; Kent Roach, *Due Process and Victims' Rights* (Toronto: University of Toronto Press, 1999) 167-75.

In response to the decision in *Seaboyer*, Parliament replaced s 276 with a new section setting out criteria for admissibility of a complainant's prior sexual activity, and enacted ss 276.1 through 276.5, which create a procedure for applications under s 276. Sections 276(1) and (2) of the *Criminal Code* now read:

276(1) In proceedings in respect of [a sexual offence], evidence that the complainant has engaged in sexual activity, whether with the accused or with any other person, is not admissible to support an inference that, by reason of the sexual nature of that activity, the complainant

(a) is more likely to have consented to the sexual activity that forms the subject-matter of the charge; or

(b) is less worthy of belief.

(2) In proceedings in respect of an offence referred to in subsection (1), no evidence shall be adduced by or on behalf of the accused that the complainant has engaged in sexual activity other than the sexual activity that forms the subject-matter of the charge, whether with the accused or with any other person, unless the judge ... determines, in accordance with the procedures set out in sections 276.1 and 276.2, that the evidence

(a) is of specific instances of sexual activity;

(b) is relevant to an issue at trial; and

(c) has significant probative value that is not substantially outweighed by the danger of prejudice to the proper administration of justice.

Section 276(3) lists a number of factors that a judge must consider in making this determination, including "the interests of justice, including the right of the accused to make a full answer and defence," "society's interest in encouraging the reporting of sexual assault offences," and "the right of the complainant and of every individual to personal security and to the full protection and benefit of the law."

How does this provision differ from the old common law, from the previous version of s 276, and (if at all) from the new common law rule articulated in *Seaboyer*? Are these provisions constitutional? See *R v Darrach*, 2000 SCC 46, [2000] 2 SCR 443, 148 CCC (3d) 97, aff'g (1998), 38 OR (3d) 1, 122 CCC (3d) 225 (CA). For discussions of the application of the current version of s 276, see Hamish Stewart, *Sexual Offences in Canadian Law* (Toronto: Canada Law Book, 2004) (loose-leaf) at §8:200; Janine Benedet, "Probity, Prejudice and the Continuing Misuse of Sexual History Evidence" (2009) 64 CR (6th) 72; Senem Ozkin, "Balancing of Interests: Admissibility of Prior Sexual History Under Section 276" (2011) 57 Crim LQ 327.

At the same time that the new version of s 276 was enacted, Parliament also enacted s 273.1, which defines "consent" for the purposes of sexual assault, and s 273.2, which limits the defence of mistaken belief in consent to situations where the accused has taken "reasonable steps, in the circumstances known to the accused at the time, to ascertain that the complainant was consenting." In *R v Ewanchuk*, [1999] 1 SCR 330, the Supreme Court of Canada interpreted these provisions and made three comments that are highly relevant to the application of the new s 276. The court held, first, that ss 273.1 and 273.2 excluded any notion of "implied consent" from the law of sexual assault. Second, for the purpose of determining the *actus reus* of the offence, "consent" meant the complainant's subjective willingness to engage in the sexual activity in question. And, third, for the purpose of determining the *mens rea* of the offence, the defence of mistaken belief in consent was available only if the accused believed that the complainant had, by words or conduct, *communicated* her consent to the accused. If these substantive provisions, as interpreted in *Ewanchuk*, had been in force when *Seaboyer* was decided, how would the constitutional arguments have been affected? How do they affect the admissibility of evidence under the current version of s 276?

As the majority in *Seaboyer* indicates, trial judges have a common law power to exclude evidence offered by the Crown where the prejudicial effect of that evidence outweighs its probative value. *Seaboyer* makes it clear that a similar power exists where the evidence is offered by the defence, but the balance is different: in McLachlin J's words, "the prejudice must substantially outweigh the value of the evidence before a judge can exclude evidence relevant to a defence allowed by law." In what sense is this power "discretionary"? Can a trial judge find that the prejudicial effect of a piece of evidence offered by the Crown exceeds its probative value and nonetheless decide to admit it? What is the rationale for the asymmetry between evidence offered by the Crown and evidence offered by the defence? See also *R v Grant*, 2015 SCC 9, [2015] 1 SCR 475.

Seaboyer goes further and states that the principles of fundamental justice require trial judges to have this discretionary power. This assertion raises several important questions. First, *Seaboyer* suggests that any statutory or common law rule that does not permit the trial judge to exercise this discretion is inconsistent with the principles of fundamental justice. Second, *Seaboyer* opens up the possibility that other common law rules of evidence might be principles of fundamental justice. Under what conditions should a common law rule of evidence be elevated to a constitutionally protected principle of fundamental justice? In *Seaboyer* itself, the relevant principle is connected with the right to a fair trial: are any other arguments possible? Could an infringement of s 7 of the Charter resulting from statutory modification of a common law evidentiary rule that has become a principle of fundamental justice ever be justified under s 1? For further discussion, see Hamish Stewart, "Section 7 of the Charter and the Common Law Rules of Evidence" (2008) 40 SCLR (2d) 415. As you read through Parts II and III of this casebook, you should ask whether there are any other common law rules or principles of evidence that deserve to be recognized as principles of fundamental justice.

What exactly are the "probative value" and the "prejudicial effect" of a piece of evidence? The trier of fact will ultimately decide how much weight to attach to all the *admissible* evidence, and will be instructed to avoid improper uses of that evidence; however, since the balancing of probative value and prejudicial effect is an aspect of admissibility, the trial judge must make some preliminary assessment of these factors before the trier of fact hears the evidence. Probative value, then, is probably best understood as the trial judge's estimate of how important the evidence, used for a legitimate purpose, is likely to be in the jury's reasoning. Similarly, prejudicial effect is probably best understood as the trial judge's estimate of how likely it is that the jury, even if properly instructed, will use the evidence for an improper purpose, or as the trial judge's estimate of the detrimental effect of the evidence on other aspects of the trial process. For further discussion, see Hamish Stewart, "The Law of Evidence and the Protection of Rights" in François Tanguay-Renaud and James Stribopoulos, eds, *Rethinking Criminal Law Theory* (Oxford: Hart, 2012) 177 at 183-92.

A prejudicial effect is *not* created merely by evidence that is unfavourable to a party's case. To take a simple example, testimony identifying the accused given by a disinterested witness who is personally acquainted with the accused and who had a good opportunity to observe him is very unfortunate for the accused, but it is not prejudicial and may be very probative. Rather, a prejudicial effect is an *improper* use or effect of the evidence. In *R v Clarke* (1998), 129 CCC (3d) 1 (Ont CA), Rosenberg JA drew on *Seaboyer*, on the work of McCormick, and on his own sense of the trial process to identify the following five forms of prejudice:

1. The danger that the evidence will arouse the jury's emotions of prejudice, hostility or sympathy.

2. The danger that the proposed evidence and any evidence in response will create a side issue that will unduly distract the jury from the main issue in the case.

3. The likelihood that the evidence will consume an undue amount of time.

4. The danger of unfair surprise to the opponent who had no reasonable ground to anticipate the issue and was unprepared to meet it.

· · ·

5. The danger that the evidence will be presented in such a form as to usurp the function of the jury.

McCormick called these "counterbalancing factors" rather than forms of prejudice: see Charles T MacCormick, *Evidence* (St Paul, Minn: West, 1954) at 319-20. Is there any advantage to using McCormick's terminology (reserving the word "prejudice" for the first and perhaps the second)? Can you think of anything else that should count as a counterbalancing factor or as a form of prejudice?

PROBLEM: RELEVANCY AND PREJUDICIAL EFFECT IN R v GALLOWAY

During the course of their investigation, the police (with Martin Galloway's informed consent) conducted a thorough search of the entire Galloway residence and property.

In the course of searching the residence, the police took note of approximately 200 books that were located in various places throughout the house. In the basement, in a box with other personal belongings that clearly belonged to Martin, the police found the following books:

- *The Anarchist Arsenal: Improvised Incendiary and Explosives Techniques* (a how-to manual for creating various explosives)
- *How to Make Your Own Professional Lock Tools* (a how-to manual for picking locks)
- *Ten Perfect Murders* (a how-to manual describing how to kill and get away with it).

The last book included ten examples of how to kill and escape responsibility. Various examples were outlined, from tampering with a victim's vehicle to poisoning a victim with difficult-to-detect chemicals. Staging a break-in was *not* among the examples.

The Crown wants to introduce all three books into evidence at Martin's trial.

Are they relevant? If they are relevant, is their probative value outweighed by their prejudicial effect?

PART II

Exclusionary Rules Based on Unreliability and Prejudice

Hearsay

I. INTRODUCTION: WHAT IS HEARSAY?

The rule against hearsay is one of the best known but least understood features of the common law trial. In the first part of this chapter, we consider some judicial and academic efforts to define hearsay, and we consider the rationale for the rule against hearsay. We then consider some of the common law and statutory exceptions to the rule against hearsay. Finally, we consider the Supreme Court of Canada's principled approach to the admission of hearsay.

A. Defining Hearsay

Hearsay is often defined along the following lines: "Hearsay evidence is an out-of-court state-ment offered for the truth of its contents." That is, where the witness testifies that another person, the declarant, said something, the witness's evidence is hearsay if, but only if, the trier of fact is asked to accept the declarant's statement as true. The following three cases provide examples of hearsay evidence.

R v Gibson (1887), 18 QBD 537. The accused was charged with wounding by throwing a stone at the complainant. Identity was in issue. The complainant could not say who had thrown the stone, but testified that a bystander said, "The person who threw the stone went in there," indicating the accused's house. The accused and his father were discovered in the house. The bystander was not called as a witness. His statement could assist the trier of fact in identifying the accused as the offender only if it was true. The prosecution conceded on appeal that the complainant's evidence of the bystander's statement was hearsay.

Bond v Martinos, [1970] 2 OR 319, 10 DLR (3d) 536 (CA). The defendant's vehicle struck the plaintiff's vehicle in a rear-end collision. The plaintiff alleged that he had suffered a lower back injury as a result of the accident. The defendant's position was that the plaintiff suffered from a pre-existing condition and that his injury had not been caused by the accident. There was uncontradicted medical evidence to the effect that the plaintiff did indeed have a pre-existing condition, but that "it was a condition which could be dormant and symptom-free and which could be activated so as to produce symptoms such as the plaintiff complained of if the plaintiff were exposed to a traumatic experience of the nature which occurred." The plaintiff's neighbour Miller testified to the effect that "the plaintiff, Bond, never did any gar-dening, never cut the grass on his lawn and that someone in the family—he could not say whether it was the plaintiff himself, his wife or one of the children—had stated that the rea-son why the plaintiff did no gardening was because of back trouble." Relying heavily on Miller's evidence, the trial judge found that the plaintiff had not established that the collision had caused the injury. The plaintiff was therefore awarded quite modest damages and was awarded nothing for loss of earnings. He appealed. The Court of Appeal held that Miller's evidence was "purely hearsay and quite inadmissible" and ordered a new trial.

R v Williams (1985), 50 OR (2d) 321, 18 CCC (3d) 356 (CA). The accused was charged with arson. She testified and denied having set the fire. The theory of the defence was that the fire had been set by Miller, one of the accused's neighbours. Miller was called as a defence witness and denied having set the fire. At this point, a *voir dire* was held to determine the admissibility of certain statements attributed to Miller. The accused and two other witnesses testified that Miller had admitted to them that he had set the fire. The trial judge ruled that this evidence was inadmissible hearsay. The accused was convicted, and her appeal to the Court of Appeal was dismissed. Martin JA agreed with the trial judge's ruling, calling the accused's testimony concerning Miller's admission "a classic example of hearsay" and holding that it was not ad-missible under the declaration against interest exception (this exception is discussed in Sec-tion II.B, below).

B. Non-Hearsay Words

While an out-of-court statement offered for the truth of its contents is hearsay, an out-of-court statement that is offered for some other purpose is *not* hearsay and is not subject to the general exclusionary rule. That is, where the witness testifies that the declarant said something, but the declarant's statement is relevant for some reason apart from its truth, then the witness's evidence is not hearsay. *Subramaniam*, *Wildman*, and *Creaghe* distinguish between hearsay and non-hearsay on this basis: in each case the disputed statement is *not* hearsay because it is offered for a purpose other than its truth. In *Subramaniam*, the statement is relevant even if false; in *Wildman*, the truth of the statement is not disputed, but it is relevant for another reason; and in *Creaghe*, the legal significance of the statement does not depend on its truth.

Subramaniam v Public Prosecutor
[1956] 1 WLR 965 (PC)
Lord Radcliffe, Lord Tucker, and Mr. L.M.D. De Silva (9 July 1956)

[The accused was convicted of being in possession of 20 rounds of ammunition, contrary to reg. 4(1)(b) of the Emergency Regulations, 1951, of the Federation of Malaya, and was sentenced to death.]

MR. L.M.D. DE SILVA: … It was common ground that on April 29, 1955, at a place in the Rengam District in the State of Johore, the appellant was found in a wounded condition by certain members of the security forces; that when he was searched there was found around his waist a leather belt with three pouches containing 20 live rounds of ammunition; no weapon of any description was found upon him or in the immediate vicinity.

The defence put forward on behalf of the appellant was that he had been captured by terrorists, that at all material times he was acting under duress, and that at the time of his capture by the security forces he had formed the intention to surrender, with which intention he had come to the place where he was found.

• • •

The appellant gave evidence in defence. He called witnesses to give evidence as to his character and to support his story as to how he had been occupied for some months before his capture by the terrorists. The appellant described his capture thus:—"when I was just walking down a small hill, where there was lallang at the sides, a Chinese came out and asked me to halt; I did not know then that he was a communist; he came from behind me. I asked him why are you stopping me? I want to return home. He spoke in Malay and I replied in Malay. He then asked me: 'Do you know who I am?' and so saying he drew out a revolver from behind him; to all appearance he was a civilian; he pointed that pistol at me and said 'I am a communist' and it was then I knew that he was one. He asked me to produce my I. Card; when he looked at my I.C. he spoke something in his own language and two others came out; the three then surrounded me; of the other two one had a pistol and the other had a rifle about a yard long; they told me I could not return home; two of them had knives like sickles."

He then described how he was forced to accompany the terrorists, one of whom walked in front and two behind, who told him he was being taken to their leader. At this stage an intervention by the trial judge is recorded thus:—

"*Court*: I tell Murugason hearsay evidence is not admissible and all the conversation with bandits is not admissible unless they are called."

Murugason was counsel assigned to defend the appellant.

In ruling out peremptorily the evidence of conversation between the terrorists and the appellant the trial judge was in error. Evidence of a statement made to a witness by a person who is not himself called as a witness may or may not be hearsay. It is hearsay and inadmissible when the object of the evidence is to establish the truth of what is contained in the statement. It is not hearsay and is admissible when it is proposed to establish by the evidence, not the truth of the statement, but the fact that it was made. The fact that the statement was made, quite apart from its truth, is frequently relevant in considering the mental state and conduct thereafter of the witness or of some other person in whose presence the statement was made. In the case before their Lordships statements could have been made to the appellant by the terrorists, which, whether true or not, if they had been believed by the appellant, might reasonably have induced in him an apprehension of instant death if he failed to conform to their wishes.

In the rest of the evidence given by the appellant statements made to him by the terrorists appear now and again to have been permitted, probably inadvertently, to go in. But, a complete, or substantially complete, version according to the appellant of what was said to him by the terrorists and by him to them has been shut out. This version, if believed, could and might have afforded cogent evidence of duress brought to bear upon the appellant. Its admission would also have meant that the complete story of the appellant would have been before the trial judge and assessors and enabled them more effectively to have come to a correct conclusion as to the truth or otherwise of the appellant's story.

In the course of his evidence the appellant stated that he was given the ammunition belt to wear but no weapon, the object, according to him, being that others could use the ammunition. The evidence of the appellant, such as it was, suggested generally that he was in fear, that he planned unsuccessfully to escape, and that he had no alternative but to do as the terrorists asked him to do. He said, amongst other things, "I could not refuse wearing the belt; if I had refused they would have done anything to me." Those words, in the context in which they occur, may well have been used by the appellant to indicate, as best he could, that owing to what the terrorists said and did he was in reasonable fear of instant death if he refused to do what the terrorists demanded of him.

[The Board held that the exclusion of this evidence had prevented the accused from advancing his defence of duress, and that the result of the trial might have been different if the evidence had been admitted. The appeal was allowed.]

R v Wildman
(1981), 60 CCC (2d) 289 (Ont CA)
Houlden, Weatherston, and Thorson JJA (21 June 1981)

HOULDEN JA: After trial before a Supreme Court Judge and jury, the appellant was convicted of first degree murder. The charge arose out of the death of Tricia Paquette on or about February 15, 1978.

In October, 1973, the appellant was married to Joyce Paquette. The appellant testified that his wife had been an alcoholic since she was 17 years of age. The appellant had known his wife for about six months and had lived with her for about five months prior to the marriage. Mrs. Wildman had a child Tricia Paquette by a prior marriage. Two children were born of the marriage of the appellant and Joyce Wildman. There was testimony at the trial that the appellant favoured his own children over Tricia.

The appellant's marriage was a stormy one. He and his wife separated on several occasions. From time to time, the Children's Aid Society had to intervene to protect the children, and on occasion, the marital squabbles were so violent that the police were called.

In August, 1977, the appellant and his wife separated. Mrs. Wildman took Tricia with her, and the appellant kept the other two children. The appellant testified that in October, 1977, his wife returned to the apartment that he occupied at 25 Duke St., Brantford, and, except for the odd night, Mrs. Wildman and Tricia lived with him until January 6, 1978.

On January 6th, the appellant entered a Toronto hospital for an operation. On his return to Brantford on January 20th, he discovered that his wife and the three children had moved out of the apartment and all the furnishings had been removed.

About the end of January, 1978, the appellant's wife commenced proceedings for divorce and custody. The appellant was not agreeable to his wife having custody of the two children of the marriage. He applied for Legal Aid and retained Karl Beyer as his lawyer to defend the proceedings.

Tricia Paquette was eight years of age when she was killed. On Wednesday, February 15, 1978, Tricia, according to certain pupils of the school that she attended, was present in the schoolyard prior to 9:00 a.m.; however, she did not attend classes that day or return home that night. Her body was found on Sunday, February 19, 1978, on the north bank of the Grand River. She had been killed by some 19 blows to the head. A hatchet was recovered from the Grand River near the scene of the killing. The medical evidence indicated that the blows to the head were consistent with the injuries having been inflicted by a hatchet. There was no sign of any sexual molestation.

· · ·

8. The final ground of appeal is that the trial judge erred in excluding evidence that defence counsel sought to adduce through the witnesses Beverley Thelma McIsaac and Ronald Gerald McIsaac. This is the only ground of appeal raised by the appellant to which we asked Mr. Hunt to respond. He conceded that the trial judge had erred in excluding this evidence but submitted that no substantial wrong or miscarriage of justice had been occasioned thereby.

This ground of appeal arises out of the following events that occurred at the trial: The Crown called as a witness Margaret Ruth MacDonald who in February, 1978, lived next door to Joyce Wildman, the appellant's wife.

[MacDonald testified that on February 20, 1978, Wildman had visited the bookstore where she worked and had told her "someone had put an axe in Tricia's head."]

The next witness called by the Crown was Beverley Thelma McIsaac. In December, 1977, Mrs. McIsaac had moved to the premises at 25 Duke St., Brantford. She, her husband, Ronald McIsaac and their two children lived in the lower part of 25 Duke St., and the appellant lived in the upper part. According to Mrs. McIsaac, from December 7th to January 6th, the appellant's two children were living with the appellant at 25 Duke St. Tricia was living elsewhere with Mrs. Wildman. Mrs. McIsaac said that Joyce Wildman and Tricia were in the premises "off and on."

On January 6th, the appellant went to Toronto for his operation. From January 6th to January 18th, according to Mrs. McIsaac, Mrs. Wildman and the three children lived in the upper apartment at 25 Duke St. On January 18th, Mrs. Wildman left the premises at 25 Duke St., removing the furniture and taking the children with her. On January 20th, the appellant returned to 25 Duke St., and from that time until he was arrested, he lived by himself in the upper apartment.

In the course of cross-examining Mrs. McIsaac, Mr. Staats, counsel for the appellant, in the absence of a jury, sought the trial judge's ruling and direction on a matter that he wished to put to the witness. Mr. Staats informed the trial judge that it dealt with a telephone call that Mrs. McIsaac had received at her home on February 16th when the appellant was present. According to Mr. Staats, he expected the witness to testify that the telephone call was from Joyce Wildman and that Mrs. Wildman made an accusation that Beverley Thelma McIsaac, Ronald McIsaac and the appellant had killed Tricia with a hatchet. Mr. Staats also expected Mrs. McIsaac to testify that she had related this conversation to the appellant.

Mr. Staats advised the trial judge that the evidence was being tendered not to prove the truth of the statement, but to prove that the statement was made and its effect on the state of mind of the appellant. He referred the trial judge to the decision of the Privy Council in *Subramaniam v. Public Prosecutor*, [1956] 1 WLR 965, and quoted the following passage from that decision (at p. 970):

> The fact that the statement [a statement made to a witness by a person who is not himself called as a witness] was made, quite apart from its truth, is frequently relevant in considering the mental state and conduct thereafter of the witness or of some other person in whose presence the statement was made.

Mr. Staats summed up his submission on the admissibility of the evidence in these words:

> In my submission, in this case, it is as a result of the telephone call to Mrs. McIsaac, the contents of which were related to Mr. Wildman, it does go to the state of mind, or the subsequent conduct of Mr. Wildman, as we know from Mrs. MacDonald.

The statement by Mrs. McIsaac of what she had been told on the telephone, if tendered to establish the truth of what was said, would be hearsay; but counsel was not tendering the evidence for that purpose. Furthermore, what Mrs. McIsaac told the appellant based on that conversation was not hearsay, since Mrs. McIsaac was called as a witness and could testify as to what she had said to the appellant.

The trial judge ruled that the evidence was hearsay and refused to permit Mrs. McIsaac to be cross-examined about the telephone call. In making his ruling, he said: "If it was in fact Joyce Wildman, she can be called ... ." However, as we have pointed out, Crown counsel was of the opinion that Mrs. Wildman was not a competent and compellable witness, and there was probably good reason why defence counsel did not wish, even if Mrs. Wildman was agreeable to giving evidence, to call her as a defence witness.

With respect, we think that the trial judge erred in refusing to permit Mr. Staats to question Mrs. McIsaac about the telephone call from Joyce Wildman. In *Subramaniam v. Public Prosecutor, supra,* Mr. L.M.D. De Silva, delivering the advice of the Board, said (at p. 970):

> Evidence of a statement made to a witness by a person who is not himself called as a witness may or may not be hearsay. It is hearsay and inadmissible when the object of the evidence is to establish the truth of what is contained in the statement. It is not hearsay and is admissible when it is proposed to establish by the evidence, not the truth of the statement, but the fact that it was made.

Here the evidence was being adduced not to establish the truth of what Mrs. Wildman had said, but for some other relevant purpose, namely, to show how the appellant had acquired knowledge on February 16th of the circumstances of Tricia's death and to explain the appellant's subsequent conduct, particularly his statement to the witness Margaret Ruth MacDonald on February 20, 1978: see also *R v. Willis,* [1960] 1 All ER 331 at p. 334.

The next witness for the prosecution was Ronald Gerald McIsaac, the husband of Beverley Thelma McIsaac. Towards the end of his cross-examination defence counsel, in the jury's absence, informed the court that this witness, too, had spoken to Joyce Wildman in the course of the earlier described telephone conversation between her and Mrs. McIsaac. Mr. Staats made the following submission to the trial judge:

> As I indicated, I do not propose to ask him the contents of that phone call, only if it was received and then did he and Wildman discuss a hatchet thereafter.
>
> The Crown obviously has introduced a great deal of the conversations between Mr. Wildman and Mr. McIsaac concerning the quoting of this and other items, about conversations about hatchets and what he told them after he got back from identifying the body on the Sunday. And I submit that this is in no different position really than discussion about a hatchet, after that phone call.

In accordance with his earlier ruling, the trial judge did not permit these questions to be asked since he believed that they were designed to elicit hearsay responses. For the reasons we have given in connection with the evidence of Mrs. McIsaac, we think that the trial judge erred in holding that this evidence was hearsay.

About 1:00 p.m. on February 19th, Ronald McIsaac was taken by the police to the river bank to identify the body. When he returned home, he refused to tell the appellant anything about what he had seen. The appellant called the police station and was told that the body was Tricia's.

Later in the day on February 19th, the police took a statement from the appellant. In his statement, the appellant made no mention of any telephone call from his wife to Mrs. McIsaac on February 16th. In the course of taking the statement, the police asked the appellant about a hatchet, but they did not tell him that Tricia had been killed with a hatchet. The taking of the statement was completed about 8:40 p.m. and the appellant was then taken home.

[Houlden JA quoted from the accused's testimony concerning his conversations with MacDonald and the McIsaacs. The accused referred to his conversation with the McIsaacs about a hatchet, but because of the trial judge's ruling, he was unable to refer to the telephone call that the McIsaacs said they had received.]

The trial lasted for almost three weeks. In the course of his long and detailed charge to the jury, the trial judge made the following reference to Crown counsel's submission regarding the evidence of Mrs. MacDonald:

… Wildman, according to her, said,

"She's crazy. She's blaming me for murdering Tricia."

and then he said,

"Someone put an axe in Tricia's head."

and the Crown says, how could he know this unless he was there? The police had not made an announcement other than that a body had been found and that it was battered, and a blunt instrument had been used. According to Staff Superintendent Burtis, the first mention of an axe by the police was on the 28th.

If Mr. and Mrs. McIsaac had been permitted to give their evidence about the telephone calls from Joyce Wildman, the jury would have heard the evidence that the defence submitted provided an answer to the Crown's question.

Mr. Carter argued that the McIsaacs' testimony about the telephone call from Joyce Wildman would also have lessened the damaging impact of the testimony given on cross-examination by a defence witness, Karl Beyer, the appellant's lawyer in the divorce proceedings. Mr. Beyer testified that on February 16, 1978, the day following Tricia's disappearance and three days before her body was found, the appellant told him "that his wife had accused him of killing Tricia with an axe." Mr. Beyer's testimony was potentially much more damning to the defence than Mrs. MacDonald's. (The defence might have been able to explain the appellant's knowledge about the means of Tricia's death when he spoke to Mrs. Mac-Donald on February 20, 1978, by the fact that on the previous day her battered body had been found and the police had questioned the appellant about an axe which he once owned.) However, there were only two possible explanations for the fact that he knew on the 16th that Tricia had been killed with an axe—either he had killed her, or he was told, through the McIsaacs, that Tricia had been killed with an axe by the actual murderer, his wife. There was conclusive evidence that Mrs. Wildman was not the person who killed Tricia.

Mr. Beyer gave the following testimony:

Q. Do you recall any information that Mr. Wildman did in fact pass on to you about the death of Tricia?

A. Yes. He—he told me on—I'm fairly sure that it was the first telephone call that I received from him after Tricia disappeared, and his would have been on the 16th of February, he told me that—and this was in connection with access to Jocelyn and Sheri, he told me that his wife had accused him of killing Tricia with an axe.

Q. That's something Mr. Wildman told you?

A. Yes.

In his charge to the jury the trial judge said:

Mr. Beyer was called by the defence, and he was acting for Wildman. In cross-examination by Mr. Swanson he said that the accused spoke to him—and I do not recall whether it was on the telephone or in person—on February the 16th—no, he said he had a call from Wildman and that Wildman said that his wife was accusing him of killing Tricia with an axe. That is Thursday the 16th. The child's body had not yet been found.

You alone are the judges of the facts. You will have to judge whether that was said and how Joyce could know. Did she tell this to John or accuse him of this? You have to judge, did Mr. Beyer hear that, or is it correctly reported by him, and you may think that Mr. Beyer has no interest in this matter.

. . .

If you do not accept the evidence that Joyce told him on Thursday, February the 16th, that Tricia was killed with an axe, how could he know? The Crown says that the only person or persons who could know were the person or persons who in fact used that axe to kill Tricia. You will recall that the gentleman who owned the hairdressing establishment was called, and he said that Joyce was working there from fairly early in the morning on Wednesday the 15th until 4.00 o'clock in the afternoon.

If you accept his evidence, then Joyce was not at the river that morning with Tricia.

If Mr. and Mrs. McIsaac had been permitted to give their testimony about the telephone calls from Joyce Wildman, the question, "If you do not accept the evidence that Joyce told him on Thursday, February the 16th, that Tricia was killed with an axe, how could he know?" would not have had the same cogency.

After about four hours of deliberation, the jury returned and asked for certain evidence to be read to them, including the complete testimony of Karl Beyer. The Reporter who had transcribed the evidence was not available, but a tape of Mr. Beyer's testimony was available. The trial judge informed the jury that he would read them his notes of Mr. Beyer's evidence, but if they found that the notes were not full enough, he would play the tape for them.

The trial judge read his notes to the jury. He then said to the jury: "Now, if you are not satisfied with that, would you like to hear the tape?" The foreman of the jury responded in these words:

Sir, I would like to hear, I would like to hear the last portion of the tape pertaining to the discussion re the remarks attributed to Mrs. Wildman, made to Mr. Beyer by Mr. Wildman regarding the hatchet.

The trial judge had the tape played for the jury. The jury then retired for a further two hours and arrived at their verdict of guilty.

[The Court of Appeal held that the evidence of the accused's guilt was so overwhelming that, despite the trial judge's erroneous ruling, the proviso in s 613(1)(b)(iii), now s 686(1)(b)(iii), of the *Criminal Code* should be applied to dismiss the accused's appeal. Wildman appealed to the Supreme Court of Canada. Lamer J, for the court, agreed with the Court of Appeal's analysis of the hearsay issue, but held that the proviso should not have been applied, and ordered a new trial. See *R v Wildman*, [1984] 2 SCR 311, 14 CCC (3d) 321.]

Creaghe v Iowa Home Mutual Casualty Company
323 F (2d) 981 (10th Cir 1963)
Phillips, Hill, and Seth Cir JJ (4 November 1963)

SETH CIR J: The plaintiff-appellant has an unsatisfied judgment against Muril J. Osborn obtained in a damage action which arose from a collision between the plaintiff's car and Osborn's truck. In the case at bar, appellant alleges that the appellee insurance company was the insurer of Osborn's truck at the time of the accident, and seeks to collect this judgment from it. The appellee admits that at one time it issued a liability policy to Osborn, but asserts that he cancelled it shortly before the accident. Osborn was not a party to this suit and did not appear as a witness. Motions for directed verdict were made by both parties. The judge reserved his ruling and submitted interrogatories to the jury. These were answered favorably for appellant, but the court found that there was no material fact for the jury and gave appellee a directed verdict. The plaintiff-appellant has taken this appeal.

The appellant asserts that the evidence was not sufficient to show compliance with the policy provisions as to cancellation nor with the rules of the Colorado Public Utilities Commission on the subject. Appellant also urges that appellee cannot rely upon cancellation because it did not promptly refund the unearned premiums. Appellant also argues that the trial court committed error in admitting certain testimony relating to statements made by the insured on the occasion when the cancellation purportedly took place.

The record shows that the policy in question was one which Osborn was required to have as an operator of a commercial vehicle. A copy of such policy had to be filed with the Colorado Public Utilities Commission and the policy could not be cancelled without first giving the Commission a ten-day notice. The policy states that the insured may cancel it by a surrender of the policy or by mailing notice of cancellation. The policy also provides that the premium adjustment be made as soon as practicable after cancellation becomes effective.

When one of appellee's agents wrote the policy in appellee's company, only one-half of the premium was paid to the agent. The unpaid balances were on account between the agent and the insured, and did not involve appellee. The policy was thereafter changed from time to time as the coverage expanded, and the agent retained the policy in order to make the changes. As the coverage increased, so did the premium due. Osborn sent the agent a check for a part of the balance due after the initial payment, but it was returned by the bank marked insufficient funds. The agent testified that he called Osborn about the check, and was told by Osborn that he was going to cancel the insurance and would come by to pick up the returned check. Osborn did come to the agent's office on October 19 and, in the presence of the agent and a secretary, stated he wanted the insurance cancelled immediately. The check was returned to Osborn and the agent told him he did not know whether there would be a refund or not. The policy was then in the possession of the agent because of changes in coverage mentioned above, and thus there was no change in the possession of the policy as Osborn did not have it to physically surrender it. The agent then sent the policy to the appellee insurance company and advised it of the cancellation. Appellee notified the Colorado Public Utilities Commission of the cancellation. The date of receipt of this notice was not determined, but on October 29 the Commission responded to the notice. The collision between Osborn's truck and appellant's car occurred on November 25.

Disregarding for the moment questions of admissibility, the record shows undisputed facts which establish cancellation of the policy by the insured, and a period of time greater than ten days between notice to the Colorado Commission of cancellation and the accident. The policy provisions as to cancellation were complied with because the agent already had the policy, and the testimony of the agent as to Osborn's desire is a sufficient showing of compliance under the circumstances. As mentioned above, Osborn, the one-time insured, did not testify. *Angelo v. Traviglia*, Ohio Com. Pl., 155 NE.2d 717.

The record also shows that notice of cancellation was sent by the company to the Utilities Commission, and that more than ten days had elapsed thereafter before the accident took place.

The trial judge found that there was no question of fact for the jury, and with this we agree.

• • •

Appellant challenges the action of the trial court in admitting the testimony of the agent of appellee and his employee as to what took place, and what was said by the insured, on the occasion when he came to the agent's office to receive back the check. The agent's testimony and that of his employee was, as mentioned, that the insured stated he wanted the policy cancelled, also that his check for some of the premiums in addition to those initially made was then returned. Appellant asserts that this testimony was hearsay.

The hearsay rule does not exclude *relevant* testimony as to what the contracting parties said with respect to the making or the terms of an oral agreement. The presence or absence of such words and statements of themselves are part of the issues in the case. This use of such testimony does not require a reliance by the jury or the judge upon the competency of the person who originally made the statements for the truth of their content. Neither the truth of the statements nor their accuracy are then involved. In the case at bar we are not concerned with whether the insured was truthful or not when he told the agent he wanted the policy cancelled and that he did not need it any more. It is enough for the issues here presented to determine only whether or not he made such statements to the agent. The fact that these statements were made was testified to by the agent, and his competency and truthfulness as to this testimony was subject to testing through cross-examination by counsel for appellant, and this was done at considerable length. The fact that the statements with which we are here concerned related to an oral termination of a written contract does not lead to a rule different from that prevailing for the formation of an oral agreement. The reasons for the rule permitting such testimony are the same in both instances.

[Seth Cir J reviewed a number of cases and concluded:]

The general authorities cited demonstrate that the testimony with which we are here concerned is admissible since it is part of, or is the oral agreement to cancel the insurance policy. Oral agreements can only be established by testimony as to the conversation which was had between the parties. This testimony may be given by a witness to such conversation, as was the agent of the appellee in this instance.

The testimony plus the other proof on the point provided evidence of a cancellation which was equivalent to the actual surrender of the policy then already in the agent's possession. The testimony of the agent and his employee is not contradicted; it is not inconsistent with other facts in the record. With this record before us, we cannot say that the trial court was in error in admitting the testimony in question. The trial court was also correct in directing the verdict as was done. We have considered the other points raised by appellant and find no error.

Affirmed.

C. Implied Assertions and Hearsay by Conduct

The basic distinction between hearsay words and non-hearsay words does not cover all the situations in which an out-of-court statement might be considered hearsay. An out-of-court statement, though irrelevant or expressly asserting no facts at all, might implicitly assert facts, or might imply a belief in facts, that are relevant to the matters in dispute. Is such evidence hearsay?

R v Baldree

2013 SCC 35, [2013] 2 SCR 520

McLachlin CJ and LeBel, Fish, Abella, Rothstein, Cromwell, Moldaver, Karakatsanis, and Wagner JJ (19 June 2013)

FISH J [McLachlin CJ and LeBel, Fish, Abella, Rothstein, Cromwell, Karakatsanis, and Wagner JJ concurring]:

I

[1] An out-of-court statement by a person not called as a witness in the proceedings is properly characterized as hearsay where it is tendered in evidence to make proof of the truth of its contents.

[2] It is undisputed on this appeal that hearsay evidence is presumptively inadmissible as a matter of law.

[3] The sole issue is whether this exclusionary rule applies to "express hearsay" only, or to "implied hearsay" as well. As a matter of logic and of principle, I am satisfied that it does.

[4] In both instances, the relevance of the out-of-court statement is not *that the statement was made*, but rather *what the content of the statement purports to prove*. And, in both instances, what the statement purports to prove is the truth of what the person not called as a witness is alleged to have asserted—expressly or by implication.

[5] With respect to their logical relevance, there is thus no substantive distinction between express and implied hearsay. The principled reasons for their presumptive inadmissibility apply equally to both.

[6] For these reasons and the reasons that follow, I agree with the majority in the Court of Appeal that the impugned out-of-court statement in issue here ought to have been excluded by the trial judge. It falls within no traditional exception to the hearsay rule and lacks the indicia of necessity and reliability that might otherwise render it admissible.

[7] Accordingly, I would dismiss the Crown's appeal to this Court against the judgment of the Court of Appeal.

II

[8] The respondent was convicted at his trial before judge alone of possessing marijuana and cocaine for the purposes of trafficking, contrary to s. 5(2) of the *Controlled Drugs and Substances Act*, S.C. 1996, c. 19.

[9] His appeal was allowed by a majority of the Ontario Court of Appeal and a new trial ordered. The Crown appeals to this Court as of right, pursuant to s. 693(1)(a) of the *Criminal Code*, R.S.C. 1985, c. C-46, on the questions of law on which the dissent of Watt J.A. was based.

[10] Since I agree with the Court of Appeal that a new trial is warranted, I shall refer to the facts only to the extent necessary to dispose of this appeal.

[11] On May 11, 2006, Cornwall police officers Sergeant Shawn Martelle and Constable Robert Ouellette responded to a suspected break-in at the apartment of a certain Eric Lepage. They knocked on the door and a man, who identified himself as Chris Baldree, allowed them in. The officers entered and immediately detected an odour of marijuana, and discovered marijuana "joints" and small marijuana buds in an ashtray.

[12] In the closet of the spare bedroom, Sgt. Martelle found an open safe containing a sandwich bag filled with 90 grams of cocaine—and, beside the safe, a large cardboard box with one ziplock bag containing 511 grams of marijuana.

[13] Mr. Baldree was arrested along with three other people found in the apartment. The police seized from him a cellular telephone and some cash found in his possession.

[14] At the police station, Mr. Baldree's phone was ringing. Sgt. Martelle answered. At trial, he described the call as follows:

A. A male voice on the other end of the, of the phone advised that he was at 327 Guy Street and that he was a friend of Megan and asked for Chris. Knowing that there were two Chris that I had just arrested, I asked, "Chris who?" the male advised, "Baldree" and requested one ounce of weed. I then stated that I was now running the, the show here and that Mr. Baldree was not here and I was gonna take his … .

THE COURT: All right, sorry, asked for Chris.

A. Yes, I'm sorry Your Honour.

THE COURT: Yes.

A. And I questioned him, I asked him, "Chris who?" and he answered, "Baldree."

THE COURT: Yes.

A. He asked for one ounce of weed. I then asked him how much Chris charges him, he says he pays $150. I then advised him I would deliver same, 327 Guy, and that was the end of the conversation. [A.R., vol. II, at p. 76].

The police made no effort at all to contact the caller at the address he provided.

[15] Counsel for the accused promptly objected to this testimony on the ground that it was inadmissible hearsay. The trial judge disagreed. He found the evidence to be "non-

hearsay," a convenient term I shall adopt throughout, on the basis of *R. v. Ly*, [1997] 3 S.C.R. 698, and *R. v. Edwards* (1994), 91 C.C.C. (3d) 123 (Ont. C.A.), aff'd on other grounds, [1996] 1 S.C.R. 128.

[16] In the judge's view:

> Whether these calls can be referred to as admissible hearsay or simply statements of state of mind, the law holds that they are admissible as circumstantial evidence to indicate a person engaged in drug trafficking. They are not tendered in evidence for the truth of the fact that the individual phoning is in fact the individual whom the individual states to be or that the individual in fact will carry out the trafficking of the drugs. As stated, it is circumstantial evidence of an individual engaged in the trafficking of drugs. [A.R., vol. I, at pp. 22-23]

[17] Having concluded that Sgt. Martelle's testimony was not hearsay, the trial judge found it unnecessary to weigh its probative value against its prejudicial effect.

. . .

IV

[30] The defining features of hearsay are (1) the fact that the statement is adduced to prove the truth of its contents and (2) the absence of a contemporaneous opportunity to cross-examine the declarant: *R. v. Khelawon*, 2006 SCC 57, [2006] 2 S.C.R. 787, at para. 56. As Justice Charron explained in *Khelawon*, at para. 35, the hearsay rule reflects the value our criminal justice system places on live, in-court testimony:

> Our adversary system puts a premium on the calling of witnesses, who testify under oath or solemn affirmation, whose demeanour can be observed by the trier of fact, and whose testimony can be tested by cross-examination. We regard this process as the optimal way of testing testimonial evidence. Because hearsay evidence comes in a different form, it raises particular concerns. The general exclusionary rule is a recognition of the difficulty for a trier of fact to assess what weight, if any, is to be given to a statement made by a person who has not been seen or heard, and who has not been subject to the test of cross-examination. The fear is that untested hearsay evidence may be afforded more weight than it deserves.

[31] In short, hearsay evidence is presumptively inadmissible because of the difficulties inherent in testing the reliability of the declarant's assertion. Apart from the inability of the trier of fact to assess the declarant's demeanour in making the assertion, courts and commentators have identified four specific concerns. They relate to the declarant's perception, memory, narration, and sincerity: *Khelawon*, at para. 2; *R. v. Starr*, 2000 SCC 40, [2000] 2 S.C.R. 144, at para. 159.

[32] First, the declarant may have *misperceived* the facts to which the hearsay statement relates; second, even if correctly perceived, the relevant facts may have been *wrongly remembered*; third, the declarant may have narrated the relevant facts in an *unintentionally misleading manner*; and finally, the declarant may have *knowingly made a false assertion*. The opportunity to fully probe these potential sources of error arises only if the declarant is present in court and subject to cross-examination.

[33] Over the years, a number of common law exceptions were recognized, based on the belief that an overly rigid application of the exclusionary rule would impede the truth-finding process. As J.H. Wigmore explains:

> The theory of the Hearsay rule … is that the many possible sources of inaccuracy and untrustworthiness which may lie underneath the bare untested assertion of a witness can best be brought to light and exposed, if they exist, by the test of cross-examination. But this test or security may in a given instance be superfluous; it may be sufficiently clear, in that instance, that the statement offered is free from the risk of inaccuracy and untrustworthiness, so that the test of cross-examination would be a work of supererogation. Moreover, the test may be impossible of employment—for example, by reason of the death of the declarant—, so that, if his testimony is to be used at all, there is a necessity for taking it in the untested shape.

(*Wigmore on Evidence* (2nd ed. 1923), vol. III, at §1420, quoted with approval in *R. v. Smith*, [1992] 2 S.C.R. 915, at p. 929.)

[Fish J summarized the Supreme Court of Canada's "principled approach" to the admissibility of hearsay (which is considered in detail in Section III, below). He continued:]

[35] The hearsay rule, like many others, is easier to state than to apply.

[36] No evidence is hearsay on its face. As mentioned at the outset, its admissibility depends on the *purpose* for which it is sought to be admitted. Evidence is hearsay—and presumptively inadmissible—if it is tendered to make proof of the truth of its contents.

V

[37] Plainly, in this case, the Crown adduced Sgt. Martelle's evidence as proof of the truth of its contents. Since the declarant was not called to testify, Sgt. Martelle's testimony constituted hearsay and was therefore presumptively inadmissible. Accordingly, in my view, the trial judge erred in failing to subject the evidence to a principled analysis.

[38] Sergeant Martelle testified, it will be recalled, that someone claiming to be a resident of 327 Guy Street called the cell phone which Sgt. Martelle had seized from Chris Baldree, asked for Mr. Baldree, and requested an ounce of marijuana for the price of $150.

[39] I agree with Feldman J.A. that the Crown did not offer this testimony as circumstantial evidence that the respondent was engaged in drug trafficking. Rather, the Crown asked the trier of fact to conclude, based on Sgt. Martelle's testimony, that the unknown caller intended to purchase marijuana from the respondent *because he believed the respondent to be a drug dealer*. The relevance of the statement thus hinges on the truth of the declarant's underlying belief. Any inference that can be drawn from the statement necessarily assumes its veracity.

[40] Had the caller stated that he wanted to buy drugs from Mr. Baldree because *Mr. Baldree sells drugs*, this would have amounted to an express assertion that Mr. Baldree is a drug dealer. Thus framed, the caller's assertion would doubtless have constituted hearsay.

[41] But the caller stated instead that he was calling because he wished to *purchase drugs from Mr. Baldree*. His assertion that Mr. Baldree is a drug dealer was no less manifest in substance, though implicit rather than explicit in form. In the Crown's submission, implied assertions are not caught by the hearsay rule and the telephone conversation was presumptively admissible for that reason.

[42] In my view, the hearsay nature of this evidence cannot be made to depend on how the declarant framed his request. Such a formalistic analysis disregards the purposive approach to the hearsay rule adopted by this Court. Indeed, "it seems absurd that anything

should turn on the grammatical form of the declarant's assertions": L. Dufraimont, Annotation to *R. v. Baldree* (2012), 92 C.R. (6th) 331, at p. 334.

[43] There is no principled or meaningful distinction between (a) "I am calling Mr. Baldree because I want to purchase drugs from him" and (b) "I am calling Mr. Baldree because he sells drugs." In either form, this out-of-court statement is being offered for an identical purpose: to prove the truth of the declarant's assertion that Mr. Baldree sells drugs. No trier of fact would need to be a grammarian in order to understand the import of this evidence.

[44] The need for a functional approach to implied assertions is readily apparent, bearing in mind the core hearsay dangers of perception, memory, narration, and sincerity.

[45] It has been argued that the danger of lack of sincerity is sometimes diminished for implied assertions. This is because "[i]f a declarant possesses no intention of asserting anything, it would seem to follow that he also possesses no intention of misrepresenting anything": P.R. Rice, "Should Unintended Implications of Speech be Considered Nonhearsay? The Assertive/Nonassertive Distinction Under Rule 801(a) of the Federal Rules of Evidence" (1992), 65 *Temp. L. Rev.* 529, at p. 531.

[46] But the other hearsay dangers clearly remain operative, and may in fact increase when an individual "states" something by implication:

> Looked at from the point of view of the four hearsay dangers, there is a much reduced risk of lies if the declarant did not intend to convey that which his statement is relied upon to prove, particularly if he it [*sic*] was not his purpose to make a representation of fact at all. But the other hearsay dangers remain, that is, the risk of misperception, false memory (unless the implied assertion concerns the declarant's own state of mind) and ambiguity. Indeed the last danger may be magnified. When X says: "Is Z in there?" does this imply that Z is not with X and nothing more, or that Z is not with X and X wants Z, or Z is in danger, or X wants to know where Z is? *The upshot is that in many situations implied assertions depend for their value on the reliability of the declarant just as much as express assertions.* [Emphasis added.]

(H.M. Malek et al., eds., *Phipson on Evidence* (17th ed. 2010), at p. 889)

Moreover, even insincerity remains a concern with implied assertions:

> If the justification for the assertive/nonassertive distinction is the absence of the insincerity problem, and through that guarantee of sincerity a reduced level of perception, memory, and ambiguity problems, this justification cannot be applied to implied statements from speech. Speech is a mechanism of communication; it is virtually always used for the purpose of communicating something to someone. It is illogical to conclude that the question of sincerity is eliminated and that the problem of unreliability is reduced for unintended implications of speech if that speech might have been insincere in the first instance, relative to the direct message intentionally communicated. If potential insincerity is injected into the utterance of words that form the basis for the implied communication, the implication from the speech is as untrustworthy as the utterance upon which it is based. [Rice, at p. 534]

[47] In short, "if the standard for comparing express and implied assertions is the quantity of dangers each entails, they are indistinguishable": T. Finman, "Implied Assertions as Hearsay: Some Criticisms of the Uniform Rules of Evidence" (1962), 14 *Stan. L. Rev.* 682, at p. 689.

[48] Accordingly, there is no principled reason, in determining their admissibility, to distinguish between express and implied assertions adduced for the truth of their contents. Both function in precisely the same way. And the benefits of cross-examining the declarant are not appreciably different when dealing with one form of testimony than the other. If an out-of-court statement implicates the traditional hearsay dangers, it constitutes hearsay and must be dealt with accordingly.

[49] In the present matter, the trial judge and the dissenting judge in the Court of Appeal both found that this Court had decided otherwise in *Ly*. With respect, I disagree.

[50] *Ly* concerned the admissibility of a telephone conversation between a police officer who had called a suspected "dial-a-dope" operation and the person who answered his call. The officer had called to arrange for the purchase and delivery of drugs. And the appellant, drugs in hand, later showed up at the agreed-upon time and place—where he was promptly arrested and charged with possession of drugs for the purpose of trafficking.

[51] The trial judge characterized as hearsay, and excluded for that reason, evidence of the police officer's conversation with the person who had answered his call. On an appeal by the Crown, the Alberta Court of Appeal disagreed. It found that the impugned conversation was admissible as "part of the narrative," since "[i]t was impossible to understand the development of the later events without the evidence of the telephone conversation which preceded them" ([*R v Ly* (1996), 193 AR 149 (CA)], at para. 3).

[52] In brief oral reasons, this Court agreed with the Court of Appeal that evidence of the conversation was improperly excluded at trial. The Court noted that the conversation was tendered to explain why the appellant appeared at the designated time and place in possession of the drugs—and not, as in the case that concerns us here, for the truth of its contents: *Ly*, at para. 3.

[53] I see nothing in *Ly* to suggest—let alone decide—that an implied assertion tendered for the truth of its contents stands on a different footing, with respect to the hearsay rule, than an explicit assertion to the same effect. Unlike *Ly*, that is the issue here.

[54] And the issue now comes before us for the first time, though it has for at least half a century divided lower courts in several provinces: see, for example, *R. v. Fialkow*, [1963] 2 C.C.C. 42 (Ont. C.A.); *Edwards*; *Wilson* [*R v Wilson* (1996), 29 OR (3d) 97 (CA)]; *R. v. Lucia*, 2010 ONCA 533 (CanLII); *R. v. Cook* (1978), 10 B.C.L.R. 84 (C.A.); *R. v. Nguyen*, 2003 BCCA 556, 188 B.C.A.C. 218; *R. v. Parchment*, 2004 BCSC 1806 (CanLII); *R. v. Williams*, 2009 BCCA 284, 273 B.C.A.C. 86; *R. v. Graham*, 2013 BCCA 75 (CanLII); *R. v. Ramsum*, 2003 ABQB 45, 329 A.R. 370.

VI

[55] The highest courts of England and Wales, and Australia, have likewise concluded that the hearsay rule governs implied assertions, only to have these decisions reversed by statute: see *Kearley* [*R v Kearley*, [1992] 2 All ER 345]; *R. v. Bannon* (1995), 132 A.L.R. 87 (H.C.); *Criminal Justice Act 2003* (U.K.), 2003, c. 44, s. 115; *Evidence Act 1995* (Aust.), No. 2, s. 59(1).

[56] In Canada, Parliament has not found it necessary or appropriate to adopt legislation classifying implied assertions as non-hearsay. This is, of course, entirely understandable in view of our principled and more flexible approach to exclusion.

[57]   As noted by Feldman J.A., the facts in *Kearley*, the leading British decision, were similar to the facts in this case. In *Kearley*, the police raided the home of the accused on suspicion that he was selling drugs. Drugs were found, but in insufficient quantities to support an inference of drug trafficking. While the police were present at the accused's residence, they intercepted ten telephone calls from callers asking to purchase drugs from him. Seven people also came to the apartment seeking to buy narcotics.

[58]   The majority of the House of Lords concluded that the drug purchase calls and the in-person statements were inadmissible hearsay. Because they were phrased as requests for drugs, the statements did not directly assert but instead implied that the accused was a drug dealer. However, whether stated expressly or impliedly, their Lordships found the information communicated to be the same. In Lord Ackner's words:

> [I]f the inquirer had said in the course of making his request, "I would like my usual supply of amphetamine at the price which I paid you last week" … , the hearsay rule prevents the prosecution from calling police officers to recount the conversation which I have described. …
>
> If [however] the simple request or requests for drugs to be supplied by the appellant, as recounted by the police, contains in substance, but only by implication, the same assertion, then I can find neither authority nor principle to suggest that the hearsay rule should not be equally applicable and exclude such evidence. What is sought to be done is to use the oral assertion, even though it may be an implied assertion, as evidence of the truth of the proposition asserted. That the proposition is asserted by way of necessary implication rather than expressly cannot, to my mind, make any difference. [pp. 363-64]

[59]   Two main reasons have been urged against applying the hearsay rule to implied assertions.

[60]   First, as Watt J.A. states (at para. 83) and as the Crown argues, excluding implied assertions as hearsay has the potential of broadening the exclusionary rule, given that "[v]irtually every human action is based on some set of assumptions implicitly accepted and, on this approach, 'asserted' by the actor" (A.F., at para. 62, quoting *McWilliams' Canadian Criminal Evidence* (4th ed. (loose-leaf)), at p. 7-21).

[61]   Second, as critics of *Kearley* have pointed out, applying the hearsay rule to implied assertions such as drug purchase calls has the potential to deprive the trier of fact of reliable evidence and thereby impede the truth-finding process: see, for example, D. Birch, "Criminal Justice Act 2003 (4) Hearsay: Same Old Story, Same Old Song?," [2004] *Crim. L.R.* 556, at pp. 564-65.

[62]   The short answer to the first argument is that we are not concerned on this appeal with the application of the hearsay rule to assertions implied through non-verbal conduct. Our concern, rather, is with a quintessentially *verbal* statement.

[63]   The issue of the applicability of the hearsay rule to inferences that can be drawn from non-verbal conduct is best left for another day. For present purposes, I find it sufficient to say that "one can engage in conduct without ever intending to communicate *anything* to *anyone* [but] the same is not true of speech or a combination of speech and conduct (for example, placing a bet) because the sole purpose of speech is communication": Rice, at p. 536 (emphasis in original).

[64]   The second concern mentioned above is greatly attenuated, I again emphasize, by Canada's principled approach to hearsay.

[65] In *Kearley*, having found the evidence in that case to be hearsay, it was automatically excluded because it did not fall within a traditional exception to the hearsay rule.

[66] The Canadian approach suffers from no such inflexibility. Under our law, hearsay evidence that is not admissible under a traditional exception may nonetheless be admitted pursuant to a principled analysis of its necessity and reliability. This "sensible scheme" recognizes that "some implied assertions, like some express assertions, will be highly reliable even in the absence of cross-examination": Finman, at p. 693. Pursuant to its terms, implied assertions that are necessary and reliable may be admitted while those that are unreliable or unnecessary will be excluded.

[Fish J held that the phone call was not admissible under any exception to the rule against hearsay and that the curative proviso in s 686(1)(b)(iii) of the *Criminal Code* was not applicable. The appeal was therefore dismissed.]

[Moldaver J's reasons for judgment, concurring in the result, are omitted.]

D. The Rationale for the Rule Against Hearsay

At common law, hearsay is inadmissible (subject to several established exceptions). In *R v Blastland*, [1986] 1 AC 41, Lord Bridge of Harwich summarized the common law's traditional aversion to hearsay evidence as follows:

> Hearsay is not excluded because it has no logically probative value. Given that the subject matter of the hearsay is relevant to some issue in the trial, it may clearly be potentially probative. The rationale of excluding it as inadmissible, rooted as it is in the system of trial by jury, is a recognition of the great difficulty, even more acute for a juror than for a trained judicial mind, of assessing what, if any, weight can properly be given to a statement by a person whom the jury have not seen or heard and which has not been subject to any test of reliability by cross-examination. As Lord Normand put it, delivering the judgment of the Privy Council in *Teper v. The Queen* [1952] AC 480, 486:
>
> > "The rule against the admission of hearsay evidence is fundamental. It is not the best evidence and it is not delivered on oath. The truthfulness and accuracy of the person whose words are spoken to by another witness cannot be tested by cross-examination, and the light which his demeanour would throw on his testimony is lost."
>
> The danger against which this fundamental rule provides a safeguard is that untested hearsay evidence will be treated as having a probative force which it does not deserve.

Thus, the rationale for the rule against hearsay is linked to the problem of assessing a witness's credibility and reliability.

In assessing a witness's credibility, the trier of fact should consider the following "testimonial factors" (see Chapter 2, Section III):

- the witness's sincerity: is the witness telling the truth (as he or she saw it)?
- the witness's use of language: what does the witness mean by the words used?
- the witness's memory: can the witness accurately and completely remember what he or she is testifying to?

- the witness's perceptual ability: could the witness accurately and completely perceive what he or she is testifying to?

Evidence in court is given under oath or an equivalent; the opposite party may cross-examine the witness; and the trier of fact may observe the witness. These three features of testimonial evidence assist the trier of fact in assessing the witness's credibility. In contrast, hearsay is not given under oath; the declarant cannot be observed while giving the evidence; and the opposite party cannot cross-examine him or her. The trier of fact must assess first the credibility of the witness who reports the hearsay, and then the credibility of the declarant—who is not sworn to tell the truth, cannot be observed while giving the evidence, and cannot be cross-examined. The trier of fact therefore has fewer tools in assessing the declarant's sincerity, use of language, memory, and perceptual ability. Hence the common law's mistrust of hearsay.

In a classic article, Morgan referred to the trier of fact's inability to assess directly the declarant's sincerity, use of language, memory, and perceptual ability as the "hearsay dangers." See EM Morgan, "Hearsay Dangers and the Application of the Hearsay Concept" (1948), 62 Harv L Rev 177. In *B (KG)*, below, Lamer CJ refers to the absence of the oath, the opportunity to observe the declarant, and the lack of cross-examination as "hearsay dangers." In either formulation, it is the secondhand nature of hearsay that is the basis of the exclusionary rule. See also Andrew L-T Choo, *Hearsay and Confrontation in Criminal Trials* (Oxford: Clarendon Press, 1996) ch 2.

Do the "hearsay dangers" apply, and to what extent, when the declarant is also a witness or a potential witness? Do they apply where the declarant is a party to the action?

Why do the "hearsay dangers" not apply to non-hearsay words?

E. Hearsay Definitions

In light of the preceding cases, and of the rationale for the presumptive inadmissibility of hearsay, are any of the following definitions of hearsay entirely satisfactory?

1. "Written or oral statements, or communicative conduct made by persons otherwise than in testimony at the proceeding in which it is offered ... if such statements or conduct are tendered either as proof of their truth or as proof of the assertions implicit therein." (Sopinka, Lederman & Bryant, *The Law of Evidence in Canada* (Toronto: Butterworths, 1992) at 156.)

2. "[A]ssertions, offered testimonially, which have not been in some way subjected to the test of cross-examination." (JH Wigmore, *Evidence*, vol 5 (Chadbourn rev) at §1362.)

3. "Evidence offered by a party-litigant—whether a witness' oral testimony or a writing—setting out an assertion or an implied assertion of some relevant matter previously made by a person, which evidence the party-litigant offers to prove the matter. 'Implied assertion' means (a) a person's verbal statement about something not the relevant matter, and also his non-verbal conduct which he intends as a substitute for the verbal statement, when the party-litigant offers evidence of the words or conduct to prove the person's state of mind caused by the relevant matter, and (b) a person's non-verbal conduct which he does not intend as a substitute for any verbal

statement when the party-litigant offers evidence of the conduct to prove the person's state of mind caused by the relevant matter." (Stanley Schiff, *Evidence in the Litigation Process*, 4th student ed, vol 1 (Toronto: Carswell, 1993) at 301.)

4. "[T]he hearsay rule is that, subject to certain specified exceptions, evidence relating to what some other person wrote or said to the witness in the witness box is not admissible as proof of the facts spoken or written." (JJ Robinette, "The Hearsay Rule" in *Special Lectures of the Law Society of Upper Canada 1955: Evidence* (Toronto: Richard De Boo, 1955) at 279.)

5. "The essential defining features of hearsay are … (1) the fact that the statement is adduced to prove the truth of its contents and (2) the absence of a contemporaneous opportunity to cross-examine the declarant." (*R v Khelawon*, 2006 SCC 57, [2006] 2 SCR 787 at para 35.)

F. Problems: Hearsay or Non-Hearsay?

PROBLEM 1

Will is being prosecuted for bigamy. It is common ground that Will went through a form of marriage with Tanya; but the Crown alleges that at the time, Will was already validly married to Diane.

(a) Admissible documentary evidence of the alleged marriage to Diane is lacking. To prove the marriage between Will and Diane, the Crown proposes to call Martin, who presided over the ceremony. Martin will testify that when he asked Will, "Do you, Will, take Diane to be your wife?," etc., Will replied, "I do." Is Martin's evidence hearsay?

(b) Will's defence is that he believed Diane was dead. Jones is prepared to testify that at the reception following the ceremony between Will and Tanya, Will said, "Diane has just moved to Ottawa." Diane is, in fact, still alive and living in Toronto. Is Jones's evidence hearsay?

PROBLEM 2

Picasso purchased a painting by Dali from Sam's Gallery. Klee claims ownership of the painting, alleging that he had merely lent the painting to Sam, as a favour, to enhance the gallery's current showing of Dali's works. Sam claims that Klee gave him the painting as a gift. Picasso says he had no knowledge of any dealings between Klee and Sam. When the painting was purchased, it had a card attached, which read, "Property of Sam's Gallery. Price: $1,000.00." Is the card hearsay if it offered to support an inference that

(a) Sam was the true owner?
(b) Picasso was a good faith purchaser for value without notice of Klee's claim?

PROBLEM 3

Joe orally agreed to sell Bill a car. It is common ground that Joe offered to sell his car to Bill and that Bill accepted Joe's offer, but there is a dispute over the purchase price. Joe claims that the agreed price was $7,000; Bill says that it was $6,000. Which, if any, of the following statements are hearsay if offered to prove the terms of the oral agreement?

  (a)   Bill testifies that Joe said, "I offer to sell you my car for $6,000."
  (b)   Joe testifies that he said, "I offer to sell you my car for $7,000."
  (c)   Fred, who was present when the transaction occurred, testifies that Joe said, "I offer to sell you my car for $7,000."
  (d)   Pete, Joe's friend, testifies that a few hours later, Joe told him, "I just found a sucker to take my old car for $7,000!"

PROBLEM 4

The accused is charged with trafficking in cocaine. A police officer testifies that he received a tip from a very reliable informant providing a description of the accused and stating that the accused would be selling cocaine at the corner of Bloor and Spadina at 10:30 p.m. on January 3. The officer testifies further that he observed the accused at the stated time and place transferring small white packets to various people in exchange for rolled-up bills. The officer arrested the accused, searched him, and found him in possession of a substantial quantity of cocaine and cash. Is the officer's testimony regarding the informant's tip hearsay if he offered to support an inference that

  (a)   the accused was a cocaine trafficker?
  (b)   the officer had reasonable grounds to make the arrest?

PROBLEM 5

The accused is charged with maliciously setting fire to his wife's store and with intent to defraud. There is no doubt that the fire was deliberately set; the factual issue is whether the accused had set the fire. A police officer testifies that about half an hour after the fire had started, he heard an unidentified woman speak the following words to a man who resembled the accused: "Your place burning and you going away from the fire." Is the officer's evidence hearsay? See *Teper v R*, [1952] 2 All ER 447 (PC).

PROBLEM 6

The steamship *Douglas* sank in the river Thames. On the night of October 27, 1881, the steamship *Mary Nixon* collided with the wreck of the *Douglas* and was damaged. The owner of the *Mary Nixon* sued the owner of the *Douglas*, claiming that the defendants were negligent in that they did not place any warning lights near the wreck. At the trial, the defendants wanted to call the captain of the tugboat *Endeavour*. This witness would testify that the mate of the *Douglas* asked him to go to the harbourmaster at Gravesend and request him to take care of the wreck, and that he came back to the mate of the *Douglas* and told him that the harbourmaster had undertaken to light the wreck. (Under the *Removal of Wrecks Act*, 1877, the harbourmaster had the power, but not the obligation, to undertake this duty.) The plaintiff objected to the proposed testimony on the ground that it was hearsay. Was the plaintiff's objection well founded? See *The Douglas* (1882), 7 PD 151.

PROBLEM 7

Able witnessed the robbery of a convenience store. Based on her description of the offender, the police charged Baker with the robbery. The police then conducted a proper line-up, during which Able identified Baker as the offender. At Baker's trial, the Crown wishes to call the police officers who conducted the line-up to testify that Able previously identified Baker as the offender. Is this evidence hearsay if, in her testimony at Baker's trial,

    (a)   Able positively identifies Baker?
    (b)   Able says that she is "50 percent certain" that Baker was the robber?
    (c)   Able can no longer identify Baker as the robber but states that she is sure she identified the right person at the line-up?
    (d)   Able positively states that Baker was not the robber?
    (e)   Able gives no evidence about the line-up?

See *R v Osbourne*, [1973] 1 QB 678; *R v Swanston* (1982), 65 CCC (2d) 453 (BCCA); *Alexander v R* (1981), 145 Commonwealth LR 395; *R v Langille* (1990), 75 OR (2d) 65, 59 CCC (3d) 544 (CA); *R v Tat* (1997), 35 OR (3d) 641, 117 CCC (3d) 481, 14 CR (5th) 116 (CA); Hamish Stewart, "Prior Identifications and Hearsay: A Note on R v. Tat" (1998), 3 Can Crim L Rev 61; Ronald Delisle, "Annotation [to *R v. Tat*]" (1998), 14 CR (5th) 118; *R v Starr*, [2000] 2 SCR 144, 147 CCC (3d) 449.

PROBLEM 8

The accused is charged with sexual assault. The complainant states in her evidence that when the accused initiated sexual contact, she said, "No." The accused states in his evidence that when he initiated sexual contact, the complainant said, "Yes." Is the complainant's evidence hearsay or non-hearsay? Is the accused's evidence hearsay or non-hearsay? On what concept of consent does your answer depend? What effect, if any, do the provisions of ss 273.1 and 273.2 of the *Criminal Code* and the reasoning in *R v Ewanchuk*, [1999] 1 SCR 330, 131 CCC (3d) 481 have on your answer?

PROBLEM 9

The accused was charged with the buggery and murder of a young boy. His defence was that the acts had been committed by another man named Mark. Mark was not called by the Crown, and the defence's application to call Mark and treat him as a hostile witness was refused. Instead of calling Mark as a witness, the accused sought to call witnesses who would have reported statements made by Mark indicating that Mark had knowledge of the murder before the victim's body was found. One witness would testify that on the day of the murder, Mark came home "shaking like a leaf, covered in mud, and wet from his knees downwards, and that he had told her that a young boy had been murdered." Was the proposed evidence hearsay? See *R v Blastland*, [1986] 1 AC 41.

PROBLEM 10

The accused is charged with trafficking in marijuana. A police officer testifies that he saw the accused give a woman a small package in exchange for money. The officer stopped the woman, told her that he had just seen her buy marijuana, and asked her to give him what she had bought. She opened her purse and gave him a gram of marijuana. She was not called as a witness. Is the officer's evidence concerning the woman's actions hearsay? See *R v MacKinnon*, 2002 BCCA 249, 165 CCC (3d) 73.

PROBLEM 11

The accused and another were charged with robbery and attempted murder. Identity was in issue. The getaway car had been purchased for $400 cash two days before the robbery. The couple who sold the car were called as Crown witnesses. They were unable to identify the purchaser. However, they testified that the purchaser "told them that he worked in chain link fencing," that he had "big dogs," and that "his dog was going to have pups." It was subsequently established in evidence that "the accused, Evans, had a large dog and that it was going to have pups and that Evans had been employed as a chain link fencer." Was the sellers' evidence of the purchaser's statements hearsay? See *R v Evans*, [1993] 3 SCR 653, 85 CCC (3d) 97.

II. SOME EXCEPTIONS TO THE RULE AGAINST HEARSAY

There are numerous common law and statutory exceptions to the rule against hearsay. The precise number of exceptions is uncertain. Rules 803 and 804 of the United States *Federal Rules of Evidence* provide some 29 exceptions, based on the common law exceptions, while the first edition of Sopinka, Lederman, and Bryant's text discusses 11, more or less. This section provides an introduction to some of the more frequently encountered exceptions, but it is by no means a complete survey of the recognized exceptions. As you read the cases, you should ask: To what extent does each exception respond to the rationale for the exclusion of hearsay?

A. Res Gestae, or Spontaneous Utterances

R v Bedingfield
(1879), 14 Cox CC 341 (footnotes omitted)
Crown Court, Norwich Winter Assizes, Cockburn CJ (1879)

. . .

It appeared that the prisoner had relations with the deceased woman, and had conceived a violent resentment against her on account of her refusing him something he very much desired, and also as appearing to wish to put an end to these relations; he had uttered violent threats against her, and had distinctly threatened to kill her by cutting her throat. She carried on the business of a laundress, with two women as assistants, the prisoner living a little distance from her. On the night before the day on which the act in question occurred, the deceased, from something that had been said, entertained apprehensions about him, and desired a policeman to keep his eye on her house, and he being near at ten at night heard the voice of a man in great anger. Early next morning, earlier than he had ever been there before, he came to her house, and they were together in a room some time. He went out, and she was found by one of the assistants lying senseless on the floor, her head resting on a footstool. He went to a spirit shop and bought some spirits, which he took to the house, and went again into the room where she was, both the assistants being at that time in the yard. In a minute or two the deceased came suddenly out of the house towards the women with her throat cut, and on meeting one of them she said something, pointing backwards to the house. In a few minutes she was dead. In the course of the opening speech on the part of the prosecution it was proposed to state what she said. It was objected on the part of the prisoner that it was not admissible, and Cockburn CJ said he had carefully considered the question and was clear that it could not be admitted, and therefore ought not to be stated, as it might have a fatal effect. I regret, he said, that according to the law of England, any statement made by the deceased should not be admissible. Then could it be admissible having been made in the absence of the prisoner, as part of the *res gestae*, but it is not so admissible, for it was not part of anything done, or something said while something was being done, but something said after something done. It was not as if, while being in the room, and while the act was being done, she had said something which was heard.

Counsel for the prosecution consequently did not state what the deceased said, but said they should tender it in evidence, and accordingly, when the witness was called—one of the assistants who heard the statement—she was first asked as to the circumstances, and stated that "the deceased came out of the house bleeding, very much at the throat, and seeming very much frightened," and then said something, and died in ten minutes.

It was then proposed to prove what she said, but Cockburn CJ said it was not admissible. Anything, he said, uttered by the deceased at the time the act was being done would be admissible, as, for instance, if she had been heard to say something, as "Don't, Harry!" But here it was something stated by her after it was all over, whatever it was, and after the act was completed.

$\cdots$

The defence set up by the prisoner being that the woman had first cut his throat and then her own with a razor she had borrowed from him professedly for another purpose, a curious question of circumstantial evidence arose as to whether this was the truth of the case, or the converse view set up by the prosecution that the prisoner had first cut the woman's throat and then his own. The statement made by him would, therefore have been very material, and its rejection, as it turned out, nearly caused a miscarriage of justice. The doubt of the prisoner's guilt was indeed removed by the fact that the deceased ran out to make complaint or outcry, and the fact that the razor was found under his body, and under his hand,—almost in his hand—for the marks of his fingers were upon it, and it was evidence that he had held it in his hand, and that his hand had only just relaxed its grasp with the weakness caused by loss of blood.

Cockburn CJ in summing up the case to the jury, pressed both these facts upon their attention, especially the first, pointing out that it was the deceased woman, not the prisoner, who ran out, as though to make outcry or complaint.

Verdict, Guilty; Sentence, Death

Ratten v R

[1972] AC 378 (PC)

Lord Reid, Lord Hodson, Lord Wilberforce, Lord Diplock, and
Lord Cross of Chelsea (11 October 1972)

LORD WILBERFORCE: The appellant was convicted, on August 20, 1970, after a trial before Winneke CJ and a jury, of the murder of his wife. His application to the Full Court of the Supreme Court of Victoria for leave to appeal was dismissed on September 16, 1970. By special leave he now appeals to the Board.

The appellant lived with his wife, the deceased, and three young children, in Echuca, a small country town in the State of Victoria. The deceased was eight months pregnant. The appellant, for over a year, had been carrying on a liaison with another woman and it was suggested by the prosecution, though not admitted by the appellant, that his relations with her had reached a critical state.

The death of the deceased took place in the kitchen of her house on May 7, 1970, as the result of a gunshot wound. The evidence established the times of certain events as follows:

(i) At 1:09 p.m., the appellant's father S.R. Ratten telephoned to the appellant from Melbourne; the call was a trunk call and so was timed and the time recorded. It lasted 2.9 minutes. The conversation was perfectly normal: Mr. S.R. Ratten heard the voice of the deceased woman in the background apparently making comments of a normal character.

(ii) At about 1:15 p.m. a telephone call was made from the house and answered at the local exchange. The facts regarding this call are critical and will be examined later.

(iii) At about 1:20 p.m. a police officer, calling from the local police station, telephoned the appellant's house and spoke to the appellant. By this time the appellant's wife had been shot. Thus the shooting of the deceased, from which she died almost immediately, must have taken place between 1:12 p.m. and about 1:20 p.m.

The death of the deceased was caused by a wound from a shotgun held by the appellant. The appellant's account was that the discharge was accidental and occurred while he was cleaning his gun. There were in the kitchen, when the police arrived soon after the shooting, two double barrelled shotguns and a rifle, with cleaning materials. The gun from which the shot was fired was an old one, not normally used by the appellant, which had been sent in February/March 1970 to a gunsmith for examination. It was returned unloaded and placed in the appellant's garage where it remained until brought into the kitchen on May 7, 1970. The appellant was unable to explain how it came to be loaded. It was in fact found by the police to have been loaded in each of its two barrels and both barrels had been fired. The right barrel had misfired, but there was an imprint of the firing pin on the cartridge. The left barrel was discharged. The appellant was thoroughly experienced in the use of firearms.

It is clear that on the facts summarised above there was a *prima facie* case against the appellant, and the case against him would depend on whether the prosecution could satisfy the jury, on this circumstantial evidence, that the killing was deliberate or whether the jury would accept his account of an accident.

It was relevant and important to inquire what was the action of the appellant immediately after the shooting. His evidence, which he first gave in a signed statement to the police on May 8, 1970, was that he immediately telephoned for an ambulance and that shortly afterwards the police telephoned him upon which he asked them to come immediately. He denied that any telephone call had been made by his wife, and also denied that he had telephoned for the police. It should be added that he gave evidence from the witness box at the trial, maintaining his account of events.

In these circumstances, and in order to rebut the appellant's account, the prosecution sought to introduce evidence from a telephonist at the local exchange as to the call made from the house at about 1:15 p.m.

The evidence as given by the telephonist (Miss Janet L. Flowers) was as follows:

> … I plugged into a number at Echuca, 1494 and I said—I opened the speak key and I said to the person "Number please" and the reply I got was "Get me the police please." I kept the speak key open as the person was hysterical.
>
> *His Honour*—You what?
>
> *Witness*—I kept the speak key open as the person was in an hysterical state [later, the witness added that the person sobbed] and I connected the call to Echuca 41 which is the police station. As I was connecting the call the person gave her address as 59 Mitchell Street.

The witness then said that the caller hung up but that she (the witness) after consulting her superior spoke to the police and told them that they were wanted at 59 Mitchell Street. It was in consequence of this that, as narrated above, the police telephoned to the house at about 1:20 p.m. and spoke to the accused. Echuca 1494 was the number of the appellant's house.

[Lord Wilberforce held that the appeal had to be decided on the assumption that the phone call was made by the victim. He continued:]

The next question related to the further facts sought to be proved concerning the telephone call. The objection taken against this evidence was that it was hearsay and that it did not come within any of the recognised exceptions to the rule against hearsay evidence.

In their Lordship's opinion the evidence was not hearsay evidence and was admissible as evidence of a fact relevant to the issue.

The mere fact that evidence of a witness includes evidence as to words spoken by another person who is called, is no objection to its admissibility. Words spoken are facts just as much as any other action by a human being. If the speaking of the words is a relevant act, a witness may give evidence that they were spoken. A question of hearsay only arises when the words spoken are relied on "testimonially," *i.e.*, as establishing some fact narrated by those words. …

The evidence relating to the act of telephoning by the deceased was, in their Lordship's view, factual and relevant. It can be analysed into the following elements.

(1) At about 1:15 p.m. the number Echuca 1494 rang. I plugged into that number.

(2) I opened the speak key and said "Number please."

(3) A female voice answered.

(4) The voice was hysterical and sobbed.

(5) The voice said "Get me the police please."

The factual items numbered (1)–(3) were relevant in order to show that, contrary to the evidence of the appellant, a call was made, only some 3-5 minutes before the fatal shooting, by a woman. It not being suggested that there was anybody in the house other than the appellant, his wife and small children, this woman, the caller, could only have been the deceased. Items (4) and (5) were relevant as possibly showing (if the jury thought fit to draw the inference) that the deceased woman was at this time in a state of emotion or fear (cf. *Averson v. Lord Kinnaird* (1805), 6 East 188, 193, *per* Lord Ellenborough CJ). They were relevant and necessary, evidence in order to explain and complete the fact of the call being made. A telephone call is a composite act, made up of manual operations together with the utterance of words (cf. *McGregor v. Stokes*, [1952] VLR 347 and remarks of Salmond J therein quoted). To confine the evidence to the first would be to deprive the act of most of its significance. The act had content when it was known that the call was made in a state of emotion. The knowledge that the caller desired the police to be called helped to indicate the nature of the emotion—anxiety or fear at an existing or impending emergency. It was a matter for the jury to decide what light (if any) this evidence, in the absence of any explanation from the appellant, who was in the house, threw upon what situation was occurring, or developing at the time.

If then, this evidence had been presented in this way, as evidence purely of relevant facts, its admissibility could hardly have been plausibly challenged. But the appellant submits that in fact this was not so. It is said that the evidence was tendered and admitted as evidence of an assertion by the deceased that she was being attacked by the accused, and that it was, so far, hearsay evidence, being put forward as evidence of the truth of facts asserted by his statement. It is claimed that the Chief Justice so presented the evidence to the jury and that, therefore, its admissibility, as hearsay, may be challenged.

Their Lordships, as already stated, do not consider that there is any hearsay element in the evidence, nor in their opinion was it so presented by the trial judge, but they think it right to deal with the appellant's submission on the assumption that there is: i.e., that the words said to have been used involve an assertion of the truth of some facts stated in them and that they may have been so understood by the jury. The Crown defended the admissibility of the words as part of the "res gestae" a contention which led to the citation of numerous authorities.

The expression "res gestae," like many Latin phrases, is often used to cover situations insufficiently analysed in clear English terms. In the context of the law of evidence it may be used in at least three different ways:

1. When a situation of fact (e.g. a killing) is being considered, the question may arise when does the situation begin and when does it end. It may be arbitrary and artificial to confine the evidence to the firing of the gun or the insertion of the knife, without knowing in a broader sense, what was happening. Thus in

O'Leary v. The King (1946), 73 CLR 566 evidence was admitted of assaults, prior to a killing, committed by the accused during what was said to be a continuous orgy. As Dixon J said at p. 577:

> Without evidence of what, during that time, was done by those men who took any significant part in the matter and especially evidence of the behaviour of the prisoner, the transaction of which the alleged murder formed an integral part could not be truly understood and, isolated from it, could only be presented as an unreal and not very intelligible event.

2. The evidence may be concerned with spoken words as such (apart from the truth of what they convey). The words are then themselves the *res gestae* or part of the *res gestae*, i.e., are the relevant facts or part of them.

3. A hearsay statement is made either by the victim of an attack or by a bystander—indicating directly or indirectly the identity of the attacker. The admissibility of the statement is then said to depend on whether it was made as part of the *res gestae*. A classical instance of this is the much debated case of *Reg. v. Bedingfield* (1879), 14 Cox CC 341, and there are other instances of its application in reported cases. These tend to apply different standards, and some of them carry less than conviction. The reason, why this is so, is that concentration tends to be focused upon the opaque or at least imprecise Latin phrase rather than upon the basic reason for excluding the type of evidence which this group of cases is concerned with. There is no doubt what this reason is: it is twofold. The first is that there may be uncertainty as to the exact words used because of their transmission through the evidence of another person than the speaker. The second is because of the risk of concoction of false evidence by persons who have been victims of assault or accident. The first matter goes to weight. The person testifying to the words used is liable to cross-examination: the accused person (as he could not at the time when earlier reported cases were decided) can give his own account if different. There is no such difference in kind or substance between evidence of what was said and evidence of what was done (for example between evidence of what the victim said as to an attack and evidence that he (or she) was seen in a terrified state or was heard to shriek) as to require a total rejection of one and admission of the other.

The possibility of concoction, or fabrication, where it exists, is on the other hand an entirely valid reason for exclusion, and is probably the real test which judges in fact apply. In their Lordships' opinion this should be recognised and applied directly as the relevant test: the test should be not the uncertain one whether the making of the statement was in some sense part of the event or transaction. This may often be difficult to establish: such external matters as the time which elapses between the events and the speaking of the words (or vice versa), and differences in location being relevant factors but not, taken by themselves, decisive criteria. As regards statements made after the event it must be for the judge, by preliminary ruling, to satisfy himself that the statement was so clearly made in circumstances of spontaneity or involvement in the event that the possibility of concoction can be disregarded. Conversely, if he considers that the statement was made by way of narrative of a detached prior event so that the speaker was so disengaged from it as to be able to construct or adapt his account, he should exclude it. And the same must in principle be true of statements made before the event. The test should be not the uncertain one, whether the making of the statement should be regarded as part of the event or transaction. This may often be difficult to show. But if the drama, leading up to the climax, has commenced and assumed such intensity and pressure that the utterance can safely be regarded as a true reflection of what was unrolling or actually happening, it ought to be received. The expression "res gestae" may conveniently sum up these criteria, but the reality of them must always be kept in mind: it is this that lies behind the best reasoned of the judges' rulings. ...

In the present case, in their Lordships' judgment, there was ample evidence of the close and intimate connection between the statement ascribed to the deceased and the shooting which occurred very shortly afterwards. They were closely associated in place and in time. The way in which the statement came to be made (in a call for the police) and the tone of voice used, showed intrinsically that the statement was being forced from the deceased by an overwhelming pressure of contemporary event. It carried its own stamp of sponta- neity and this was endorsed by the proved time sequence and the proved proximity of the deceased to the accused with his gun. Even on the assumption that there was an ele- ment of hearsay in the words used, they were safely admitted. The jury was, additionally, directed with great care as to the use to which they might be put. On all counts, therefore, their Lordships can find no error in law in the admission of the evidence. They should add that they see no reason why the judge should have excluded it as prejudicial in the exercise of discretion.

QUESTIONS

1. Do you agree with the Board's view that the victim's statements, as reported by the telephone operator, were not hearsay? If they were not hearsay, what sense can be made of the Board's alternative ground for holding them admissible?

2. What was the basis for the finding that the "pressure of contemporary event" made the statements admissible as part of the res gestae?

R v Clark
(1983), 42 OR (2d) 609, 7 CCC (3d) 46, 35 CR (3d) 357 (CA)
MacKinnon ACJO and Dubin and Cory JJA (25 August 1983)

[On 7 July 1980, the accused went to her ex-husband's residence and killed her ex- husband's new wife. She was convicted of second-degree murder, and appealed.]

DUBIN JA: ... The defence was self-defence and/or provocation. The appellant testified that she knocked on the door of the deceased's premises and told the deceased that she wanted the two lawn chairs. They attended at the garage but could not find the chairs. According to the appellant, the deceased said, "Howard's been over you a long time, just don't make any more excuses." The appellant replied, "Don't be too sure." The appellant testified that as they came out of the garage the deceased gave the appellant a push and said not to "come around any more." She stated that she then stood with her back to the garage door and with her eyes closed. When she heard footsteps, she opened her eyes and saw the deceased quite close, holding a knife. The appellant was startled and afraid. She testified that she grabbed the knife with her left hand and pushed the deceased with the other. The deceased fell. As the appellant tried to run way, she tripped over the deceased and fell down. She was not sure whether she had hit the deceased but saw that her own hand was bleeding. She said that the deceased then grabbed her, and she felt that she was hanging on to the deceased near a chair which was near the garage entrance. She testified that she did not know that she had injured the deceased, who was at that time sitting on the chair.

. . .

Spontaneous Exclamations

It was submitted that the learned trial judge erred in admitting certain of the evidence to be found in the testimony of Fawn Pitcher, referred to briefly earlier.

On 7th July 1980 Miss Pitcher was staying with her aunt, who resided across the street from the Ade residence. While in the kitchen of those premises she heard someone calling for help. She first thought that it was children fooling around in a pool, but when the noise continued she went to the back gate of her premises and realized that the cries were coming from the deceased's residence across the street.

In order to appreciate the evidentiary issues raised, as well as to indicate the overall importance of her testimony in this case, I set out hereunder in some detail the relevant portions of Miss Pitcher's testimony:

> "Q. Okay, just take it slowly, and tell the jury, please, what it was that you heard, please. A. Okay, I was in the back kitchen making my breakfast. It was around 10:00 and I heard somebody calling for help. First I thought it was kids fooling around a pool. I was sort of annoyed at it, and it kept up, and I thought no, so I went outside and I realized it wasn't a child in a pool. I went out to the back gate and I realized where the cries were coming from, across the road. ...
>
> "Q. Fawn, could you tell me, then, what you saw and heard as you went across the street to find out what was going on? A. Okay, as I came out the back gate to my aunt's place and up her side lawn I saw a woman standing at the top of the driveway in the picture shown, and she was yelling: '*Help, help! I've been murdered! I've been stabbed!*' And I didn't see anyone else around. I walked across the road, down through their ditch and up into the lawn and I saw the accused sort of agitated, going back and forth towards the deceased."

. . .

It was the submission by counsel for the appellant that the words spoken by the deceased, "Help! I've been murdered! I've been stabbed!" were inadmissible hearsay. No objection was taken by counsel at trial to the admissibility of that evidence, but if the evidence was in fact inadmissible and highly prejudicial the failure to object is not fatal.

[Dubin JA reviewed a number of cases, including *Ratten*, and continued:]

It is clear in this case that the challenged evidence was tendered as evidence of the truth of that which was stated, and, thus, if admissible, as a true exception to the hearsay rule. The basis of its admissibility as such is discussed in *Wigmore on Evidence*, vol. 6, para. 1747, p. 195, as follows:

"§1747.(1) *General principle of the exception.* This general principle is based on the experience that, under certain external circumstances of physical shock, a stress of nervous excitement may be produced which stills the reflective faculties and removes their control, so that the utterance which then occurs is a spontaneous and sincere response to the actual sensations and perceptions already produced by the external shock. Since this utterance is made under the immediate and uncontrolled domination of the senses, and during the brief period when considerations of self-interest could not have been brought fully to bear by reasoned reflection, the utterance may be taken as particularly trustworthy (or, at least, as lacking the usual grounds of untrustworthiness), and thus as expressing the real tenor of the speaker's belief as to the facts just observed by him; and may therefore be received as testimony to those facts."

The exception is now recognized in *Phipson on Evidence*, 13th ed. (1982), p. 460, as follows:

"A spontaneous hearsay statement relevant to an issue made by the victim of an attack or a bystander is admissible in evidence provided that the risk of concoction or distortion can be excluded."

And at p. 464:

"Although Lord Wilberforce [in *Ratten*, supra] referred to the hearsay statement relating to the 'identity of the attacker' being admissible it is submitted that the subject matter is not limited solely to identity. This may usually be the subject matter of the statement as the authorities show, but it is not always so. Indeed in *Ratten* itself it was not the identity of the attacker which was proved by the telephone call, but the attack itself. It is submitted therefore that the statement may relate to any relevant matter. *The significance of Ratten was to clarify this exception to the hearsay rule and to move the test from asking whether the statement was part of the res gestae or the transaction to asking whether its spontaneity was such that concoction or distortion could safely be excluded.*" (The italics are mine.)

Thus, although what was stated by Robertson CJO in *R v. Leland* [[1951] OR 12, 98 CCC 337 (CA)], ... appears to have been consistent with the then state of the authorities, it cannot, in my respectful opinion, now be viewed as an authoritative statement of the law. This case can of course be readily distinguishable from *Leland*, in that it is apparent from the evidence of Miss Pitcher that the words attributed by her as having been spoken by the deceased were spoken while the event was still transpiring and thus were contemporaneous with the unfolding events. But I would prefer to rest my judgment on a broader base, as it is now apparent from the foregoing that the narrow test of exact contemporaneity should no longer be followed.

The circumstances, as outlined by Miss Pitcher, under which the words were said to have been spoken by the deceased were such as to exclude the possibility of concoction or distortion and, if Miss Pitcher's evidence were accepted by the jury, the words spoken, "Help! I've been murdered! I've been stabbed!" were evidence of the belief of the deceased as to what had occurred and evidence as to the truth of the facts stated by her as a true exception to the hearsay rule. Such was also the view of this court in *Mahoney v. R* (1979),

50 CCC (2d) 380, affirmed [1982] 1 SCR 834, 67 CCC (2d) 197. The words, "Go call the police, go call an ambulance," to which no exception was taken on appeal, were of course admissible as a verbal act and not as an exception to the hearsay rule.

For these reasons, I would reject the submission made by counsel for the appellant on this issue.

[The appeal was dismissed.]

NOTES AND QUESTIONS

1. In *Clark*, what inference did the Crown want the jury to draw from the deceased's exclamation? How probative of the inference was the exclamation?

2. In *R v Folland* (1999), 43 OR (3d) 290, 132 CCC (3d) 14 (CA), the complainant, the accused, and a man named Harris painted the complainant's apartment and consumed a great deal of alcohol. The complainant went to sleep in her bedroom while the accused and Harris apparently slept in the living room. The complainant awoke in the early morning to find someone having sexual intercourse with her. The assailant did not ejaculate. She identified the assailant as the accused. But when the complainant went to the living room, Harris insisted that he had been the assailant, threatened the complainant, and tried to prevent the complainant from calling the police. She was ultimately able to contact the police, and when they arrived, Harris again stated that the accused had nothing to do with it and that he had raped the complainant. Underwear with traces of semen was found in the complainant's bed. (Fresh evidence tendered on appeal established that the semen was that of Harris.) There was evidence that Harris and the complainant had previously been intimate and that DNA traces could remain on the underwear even after it had been washed. Harris later retracted his claim that he was the assailant, and he was not called at trial by the Crown or by the defence. The accused testified and denied having raped the complainant. Were any of Harris's statements on the night in question admissible under the *res gestae* exception?

3. Under what circumstances (if any) should an accused person be permitted to lead evidence of his own exculpatory statements as part of the *res gestae*? Would it matter what the Crown's theory of the case was, or whether the accused was going to testify? In considering these questions, bear these two points in mind: the statements would be admissible for their truth if led by the Crown (see Section II.E, below); but prior consistent statements are generally inadmissible, the main exception being to rebut an allegation of recent fabrication (see Chapter 6, Section I.C). For attempts by the accused to put his own statements into evidence as part of the *res gestae*, see *R v Risby* (1976), 32 CCC (2d) 242 (BCCA); *R v Keeler*, 1977 ALTASCAD 126, 36 CCC (2d) 8 (CA).

B. Statements Against Interest

Statements against interest should not be confused with party admissions. See Section II.F, below.

1. The English and American Background

The law governing the admissibility of statements against interest is often traced to the *Sussex Peerage Case* (1844), 11 Cl & Fin 85, 8 ER 1034. The *Royal Marriage Act*, 12 Geo 3, c 11, stated that no descendant of George II could marry without the consent of the Privy Council, that any such marriage was void, and that anyone who presided at such a marriage was subject to criminal penalties. The succession to the Duchy of Sussex turned on the validity of the marriage of Prince Augustus Frederick, a descendant of George II, to Lady Augusta Murray, celebrated in Rome on April 4, 1793 by the Rev. Mr. Gunn, a minister of the Church of England, without the consent of the Privy Council. The party seeking to uphold the validity of this marriage had to establish that it had actually occurred, and then had to persuade the court that the *Royal Marriage Act* did not apply to it because it was performed outside England. At the time of the trial, both parties to the marriage and Gunn were dead. The party seeking to uphold the validity of the marriage offered into evidence a statement made by Gunn to his son, and argued that the statement was admissible because Gunn had exposed himself to penal liability in making it. The House of Lords held that statements against pecuniary interest were admissible under an exception to the rule against hearsay but statements against penal interest were not. The evidence of Gunn's son was therefore inadmissible. Based on other evidence, the House found that the marriage had occurred but that it was invalid because the *Royal Marriage Act* applied regardless of the location of the wedding.

This approach to statements against interest was confirmed in *R v Blastland*, [1986] 1 AC 41, [1985] 2 All ER 1095. See Problem 9 in Section I.F, above. The accused was charged with murdering a young boy. Another suspect named Mark had made, and then retracted, statements to the police admitting his involvement in the victim's death. Mark was not called as a witness. The trial judge ruled that Mark's statements were inadmissible hearsay, and the Court of Appeal agreed. In commenting on the refusal of leave to appeal on this ground, Lord Bridge of Harwich said, "To admit in criminal trials statements confessing to the crime for which the defendant is being tried made by third parties not called as witnesses would be to create a very significant and, many might think, a dangerous new exception."

In *Donnelly v United States*, 228 US 243 (1913), the accused was charged with murder and sought to introduce the confession of an individual named Dick, who had died before the accused's trial. The statement was ruled inadmissible and Donnelly was convicted. The majority followed the *Sussex Peerage Case* and early American authority, and held that Dick's confession had been properly excluded because it was not a statement against pecuniary interest. In a well-known dissent, Holmes J said:

> The confession of Joe Dick, since deceased, that he committed the murder for which the plaintiff in error was tried, coupled with circumstances pointing to its truth, would have a very strong tendency to make any one outside of a court of justice believe that Donnelly did not commit the crime. I say this, of course, on the supposition that it should be proved that the confession really was made, and that there was no ground for connecting Donnelly with Dick. The rules of evidence in the main are based on experience, logic and common sense, less hampered by history than some parts of the substantive law. There is no decision by this court against the admissibility of such a confession; the English cases since the separation of the two countries do not bind us; the exception to the hearsay rule in the case of declarations against interest is well known; no other statement is so much against interest as a confession of murder, it is far more calculated to convince than dying declarations, which would be let in to hang a man, *Mattox v. United States*,

146 US 140; and when we surround the accused with so many safeguards, some of which seem to me excessive, I think we ought to give him the benefit of a fact that, if proved, commonly would have such weight. The history of the law and the arguments against the English doctrine are so well and fully stated by Mr. Wigmore that there is no need to set them forth at greater length. 2 Wigmore, *Evidence*, §§1476, 1477.

The law in the United States was altered by what is now r 804(3) of the *Federal Rules of Evidence*.

In *O'Brien*, the Supreme Court of Canada considered several aspects of the exception for declarations against interest.

R v O'Brien

[1978] 1 SCR 591, 35 CCC (2d) 209

Laskin CJ and Martland, Judson, Ritchie, Spence, Pigeon, Dickson, Beetz, and
de Grandpré JJ (24 June 1977)

DICKSON J: Martin Edward O'Brien and Paul Jensen were jointly charged with possession of a narcotic for the purpose of trafficking. O'Brien was arrested and convicted; Jensen fled the country. Following O'Brien's conviction, Jensen returned to Canada. He told O'Brien's counsel, Mr. Simons, that he, Jensen, alone had committed the act. He agreed to testify to that effect. Before the hearing, Jensen died. Leave to adduce fresh evidence was obtained from the British Columbia Court of Appeal. Mr. Simons repeated Jensen's statement before that court. On the strength of Mr. Simons' testimony the court allowed the appeal and directed an acquittal. The substantial question upon which this Crown appeal turns is whether Mr. Simons' evidence was inadmissible as hearsay.

Leave to appeal against the judgment of the Court of Appeal was granted on the following question of law:

> That the Court of Appeal for British Columbia erred at law in holding that hearsay evidence given before that court by Sidney B. Simons pursuant to leave granted in accordance with section 610 of the Criminal Code would have been capable of raising a reasonable doubt in the mind of the trial judge as to the guilt of the accused.

Mr. Justice McFarlane, of the British Columbia Court, was of opinion that the evidence of Mr. Simons was not hearsay.

It is settled law that evidence of a statement made to a witness by a person who is not himself called as a witness is hearsay and inadmissible when the object of the evidence is to establish the truth of what is contained in the statement; it is not hearsay and is admissible when it is proposed to establish by the evidence, not the truth of the statement but the fact that it was made. This succinct formulation of the hearsay rule which one finds in *Subramaniam v. Public Prosecutor*, [1956] 1 WLR 965 at p. 970 (PC), was repeated with approval in *Ratten v. The Queen*, [1971] 3 All ER 801 at p. 805 (PC). The reasons supporting the exclusion of hearsay evidence were stated by Lord Normand in *Teper v. The Queen*, [1952] AC 480 at p. 486 (PC):

> The rule against the admission of hearsay evidence is fundamental. It is not the best evidence and it is not delivered on oath. The truthfulness and accuracy of the person whose words

> are spoken to by another witness cannot be tested by cross-examination, and the light which
> his demeanour would throw on his testimony is lost.

The evidence of Mr. Simons was offered for the purpose of proving the truth of the matter asserted. It was sought, through that evidence, to prove that Jensen, and not O'Brien, had committed the act with which O'Brien stood charged, or at least to raise a reasonable doubt as to O'Brien's guilt. That is the classic touchstone of inadmissible hearsay.

Before this court counsel for O'Brien sought to support the admissibility of Mr. Simons' testimony as falling within an exception to the hearsay rule. It was contended that a hearsay statement by a deceased person against his interest constitutes such an exception. The exception rests upon necessity and presumed trustworthiness. The witness is dead; there is no other evidence available on the point. It is considered that declarations made by persons against their own interests are "extremely unlikely to be false" *per* Fletcher Moulton LJ, in *Tucker v. Oldbury Urban Council*, [1912] 2 KB 317 at p. 321.

· · ·

Dean Wigmore has made a devastating onslaught on a rule which would admit declarations against pecuniary interest but deny admission to declarations against penal interest: *Wigmore on Evidence*, 3rd ed., vol. V, paras. 1476, 1477. His attack is founded upon logic and upon the historical argument that *The Sussex Peerage* case was a departure from the earlier rule that admissions against interest generally were accepted in a proper case; *The Sussex Peerage* case was a "backward step," in the words of Traynor J, in *People v. Spriggs* [60 Cal.2d 868]. Dean Wigmore is not alone in his approach: see Baker, *The Hearsay Rule*, 64; Morgan, "Declarations Against Interest," 5 Vand. L Rev. 451; Jefferson, "Declarations Against Interest: An Exception to the Hearsay Rule," 58 Harv. L Rev. 1.

The effect of the rule in *The Sussex Peerage* case, as it has been generally understood, is to render admissible a statement by a deceased that he had received payment of a debt from another or that he held a parcel of land as tenant and not as owner, but to render inadmissible a confession by a deceased that he and not someone else was the real perpetrator of the crime. The distinction is arbitrary and tenuous. There is little or no reason why declarations against penal interest and those against pecuniary or proprietary interest should not stand on the same footing. A person is as likely to speak the truth in a matter affecting his liberty as in a matter affecting his pocketbook. For these reasons and the ever-present possibility that a rule of absolute prohibition could lead to grave injustice I would hold that, in a proper case, a declaration against penal interest is admissible according to the law of Canada; the rule as to absolute exclusion of declarations against penal interest, established in *The Sussex Peerage* case, should not be followed.

There is a further question. Can it be said that Jensen's declaration to Mr. Simons qualifies as a declaration against penal interest? The requirements to be met before admission of an extra judicial statement were stated by Hamilton LJ, in *Ward v. H.S. Pitt & Co.; Lloyd v. Powell Duffryn Steam Coal Company* [[1913] 2 KB 130]. In *Demeter v. The Queen* (1977), 34 CCC (2d) 137, this Court held that the principles enunciated by the Court of Appeal for Ontario in that case furnished a valuable guide for consideration in the event this court should determine that a declaration against penal interest was not to be held inadmissible under the rule against the reception of hearsay evidence.

The second and third requirements in *Ward*'s case were [at 137-38]:

2. It is essential that such fact should have been "to the deceased's immediate prejudice," that is against his interest at the time when he stated it. If it may be construed for his interest or against it (*Massey v. Allen*, 13 Ch.D 558) or may only be against his interest in certain future events (*Ex parte Edwards*, 14 QBD 415) it is inadmissible.

3. It is essential that the deceased should have known the fact to be against his interest when he made it, because it is on the guarantee of truth based on a man's conscious statement of a fact, "even though it be to his own hindrance," that the whole theory of admissibility depends. It is "a necessary element, that the subject-matter of the declaration ... must have been within the direct personal knowledge of the person making the declaration" (*per* Lord Selborne LC in *Sturla v. Freccia* (1880), 5 App. Cas. 623, 633); "to support the admissibility it must be shewn that the statement was, to the knowledge of the deceased, contrary to his interest" (*per* Fletcher Moulton in *Tucker v. Oldbury Urban Council*, [1912] 2 KB 317, 321).

· · ·

In the case at bar, Jensen did not make his declaration of guilt until ten months after the respondent had been convicted and sentenced and not until almost six months after the charges which he himself faced had been stayed.

It might be useful to recall the chronology and the time intervals:

December 13, 1972	Date of alleged offence. Jensen left the country upon hearing that O'Brien had been arrested.
April 2, 1974	O'Brien convicted.
April 11, 1974	Jensen returned to Canada and was arrested.
April 26, 1974	O'Brien sentenced.
September 24, 1974	Charges against Jensen stayed.
October, 1974	Mr. Simons' office in communication with Jensen at which time Jensen agreed to attend to discuss. He did not appear.
March 12, 1975	Jensen attended at the office of Mr. Simons.
April 16, 1975	Jensen died from drug overdose.

Jensen had consulted counsel. According to Mr. Simons' notes of the interview, Jensen told him "no affidavits—OK to talk to Martin's [O'Brien's] lawyer—lawyer says to take *Canada Evidence Act*." There was presumably always the possibility that the stay of proceedings against Jensen might be lifted—the record is silent as to the reason for the stay—but the entire circumstances in which the statement was made negative the conclusion Jensen apprehended exposing himself to prosecution. The statement was made in the privacy of Mr. Simons' office. The public confession was to be in circumstances in which his words could not be used nor be receivable in evidence against him in any criminal trial. The following passage is taken from the transcript of the proceedings before the Court of Appeal:

Bull JA: ... and I am willing to accept it, that this man would not swear an affidavit as to these things because he thereby would not have the protection of the *Canada Evidence Act*.

Maclean JA: Yes, because he would take the risk.

Bull JA: Because he would be taking a risk, and I do not blame him.

Maclean JA: Yes, friendship would not have gone that far.

As Professor Morgan has stressed in his article, in *The Sussex Peerage* case one of Lord Lyndhurst's reasons for holding the testimony inadmissible was that the offered declarations were made to declarant's own son, "and in so making them, it cannot be presumed that he would have exposed himself to prosecution, or that he made them under any belief that he should do so."

The guarantee of trustworthiness of a statement made out of court flows from the fact that the statement is to the "deceased's immediate prejudice." To be admissible there must be a realization by the declarant that the statement may well be used against him. That is the very thing Jensen wished to avoid. He had no intention of furnishing evidence against himself. His obvious desire was not to create damaging evidence, detrimental to his penal interest. Yet, that is the very basis upon which admissibility of extra judicial declarations of penal interest rests. In my opinion, the statements of Jensen to Mr. Simons failed to meet the requirements for admissibility. Viewed from Jensen's subjectivity, the statements were not against interest. Failure to fall within the exception is, therefore, fatal to the admissibility of Mr. Simons' hearsay.

[The Crown's appeal was allowed and O'Brien's conviction was restored.]

QUESTIONS

1. To what extent must the declarant be "unavailable" for the exception to apply?
2. Does it matter whether the declarant's statement is on its face exculpatory or inculpatory? In *Pelletier*, the Ontario Court of Appeal considered this question.

R v Pelletier
(1978), 38 CCC (2d) 515 (Ont CA)
Jessup, Brooke, and MacKinnon JJA (11 January 1978)

JESSUP JA: The main question raised by this appeal is whether a declaration against penal interest was admissible as being more incriminatory than exculpatory and because, in the circumstances, the declarant was not available.

[Cormier, David, and Pelletier were roommates. Cormier was killed on the night of April 4-5, 1975. The police initially arrested David and charged him with manslaughter. David gave the police the following statement:]

> On Friday, the 4th of April, I drank beer and wine during the day. I room with Michel Pelletier and Elie Cormier. During the evening, I went out with Michel Pelletier. We went to the Frontenac. Elie did not come out at night. He said he was sick and I think he was feeling good from drinking alcohol. From the Frontenac, Michel and I, we went to the Prospect Hotel around 9:00 p.m. That is the hour that the dance starts. Me, I did not dance. I left the Prospect Hotel at approximately 10:00 p.m. I returned home walking. When I arrived at the room, Elie started mouthing off and I did too. I do not know what we were talking about. Elie took me by the neck and I pushed him and that is when he must have fallen. My throat is sore since that time. I went to the bathroom and when I returned, Elie was on the floor in

the doorway of the bedroom. I passed over him and I told myself "he is already sleeping." I layed [*sic*] down in my bed.

I got up the next morning around 6 or 7 o'clock and I took a glass of wine with Michel. Michel told me to awaken Elie, he was still on the floor. I called to him, but he did not answer. I went to him and touched him and I saw that his hands were white. I said to myself "he has no more blood." I called Michel. I told him "come and see Elie."

Michel came to see Elie and said "it seems that he is dead." I also said "I believe he is dead." Michel left to phone the police.

He came back, I do not know where he went, I knew that he went to phone.

The police came and removed Elie.

On the same day Antoine David was arrested and charged with manslaughter arising out of the death of Elie Cormier. Prior to his preliminary hearing the charge was withdrawn and on September 22, 1975, an information was sworn charging the appellant with manslaughter. In consequence, the appellant returned voluntarily from the Province of Quebec and surrendered himself to the Regional Police in Sudbury.

[Both the Crown and the defence made efforts to procure David's attendance at Pelletier's trial. David's family and police forces in other jurisdictions were contacted, and the Crown took out a material witness warrant, but David could not be found.]

The learned trial judge refused to admit the statement of Antoine David which was sought to be admitted by trial counsel for the appellant.

In *R v. O'Brien* (1977), 35 CCC (2d) 209, the Supreme Court of Canada held that in a proper case a declaration against penal interest is admissible at the trial of an accused who seeks to prove the declaration. And in *Demeter v. The Queen* (1977), 34 CCC (2d) 137 at p. 141, the same court said of the five tests or conditions of admissibility suggested by this court in *R v. Demeter* (1975), 25 CCC (2d) 417 at pp. 439-40:

> These furnish a valuable guide for consideration in the event that this court should determine that a declaration against penal interest is not to be held inadmissible under the rule against the reception of hearsay evidence.

Of those five tests I think only No. 3 and No. 5 require consideration in this case.

With respect to No. 3, notwithstanding that David's declaration puts forward self-defence, it is an admission of an assault made to the police when they were investigating manslaughter by assault and it places the deceased's body where it was found by the police. Moreover, I think the declaration is to be regarded in the light of all the evidence. There is no direct evidence that the appellant assaulted the deceased and in the light of David's admission a jury might well infer that it was he rather than the appellant who followed up his initial assault by inflicting the fatal blows: *R v. Agawa and Mallet* (1976), 28 CCC (2d) 379, is to be distinguished. In that case there was an abundance of direct evidence that Mallet had stabbed the deceased a number of times so that on the whole evidence the contention in his declaration that he had acted in self-defence made the declaration primarily in his favour. In the present case in my opinion, having regard to the whole evidence, the declaration of David, considered in its totality, is against his interest.

Test or condition 5 suggested by this court in *Demeter* was, in my opinion, not intended to be stated in exhaustive terms. The logical approach of Wigmore and McCormick commends itself. In *Wigmore on Evidence*, 3rd ed. vol. 5, para. 1456, the author states: "Whenever the witness is practically unavailable, his statements should be received." *McCormick on Evidence*, 2nd ed., p. 678, states: "Any reason why the declarant cannot be brought in at the trial should suffice, such as physical incapacity, absence of the witness from the jurisdiction or inability of the party to find him ..." In my opinion, in this case, having regard to the evidence quoted and particularly that of the police officer, the declarant Antoine David was unavailable within the meaning of the rule that would permit his declaration to be admitted.

[Pelletier's appeal was allowed and a new trial was ordered.]

Lucier v R
[1982] 1 SCR 28, 65 CCC (2d) 150
Laskin CJ and Martland, Ritchie, Dickson, Beetz, Estey, McIntyre, Chouinard, and Lamer JJ (26 January 1982)

[The accused had been convicted of arson, and his appeal to the Manitoba Court of Appeal had been dismissed (50 CCC (2d) 535).]

RITCHIE J: ... The facts of this case are essentially undisputed and reveal that the appellant's house was destroyed by fire at a time when he was absent from the locality and shortly after he had increased his fire insurance policy by the sum of $20,000. The circumstances immediately preceding this fire are recounted by the appellant's friend, one Dumont, who had himself been in the house at the time of the fire with the result that he was seriously burned and upon escaping to his sister's house nearby he was ultimately removed to a hospital in Winnipeg. There he was visited by a constable of the RCMP to whom he made a statement admitting that he had personally set the house afire and that he had been hired to do so for the purpose by the appellant who had undertaken to pay him $500 for the task. Dumont later made a further statement to another RCMP officer which was to the same effect in that he admitted responsibility for setting the fire and implicated the accused in the undertaking. Both these statements were made to persons in authority after Dumont had been duly cautioned and they were in my view contrary to his penal interest. A few days later Dumont died and it is the question of whether or not his statements should be admitted against the appellant which lies at the root of this appeal. After a careful review of the leading cases on the somewhat vexed question as to the admissibility of statements made against penal interest, the Court of Appeal concluded that the Dumont statements were admissible.

. . .

Having regard to the judgment of this court in the *Demeter* and *O'Brien* cases, it must now be recognized that in a proper case statements tendered on behalf of the accused and made by an unavailable person may be admitted at trial if they can be shown to have been made against the penal interest of the person making them; but neither the two cases to which I have just referred nor any of the wealth of authorities cited in the courts below apply such a rule to statements which have an inculpatory effect on the accused. On the contrary, wherever such statements have been admitted it will be found that they have an exculpatory effect. The difference is a very real one because a statement implicating the accused in the crime with which he is charged emanating from the lips of one who is no longer available to give evidence robs the accused of the invaluable weapon of cross-examination which has always been one of the mainstays of fairness in our courts.

In the present case the statements made by Dumont which were tendered by the prosecutor are obviously inculpatory of the appellant and in my opinion this is not a "proper case" for admitting them so that the learned trial judge did err in permitting their introduction into evidence and I would accordingly allow this appeal on the first ground specified in the notice of appeal, quash the conviction and direct a new trial in accordance with the alternative relief sought by the appellant.

QUESTIONS

Ritchie J's reasons appear to suggest that the Crown cannot rely on the hearsay exception for statements against interest, at least for the purpose of inculpating the accused. What would be the rationale for this limitation? Is there another way to rationalize the court's holding that Dumont's out-of-court statement should not have been admitted under this exception?

2. Note on Statements Against Interest

The first principle from *Ward*, not mentioned by Dickson J in his judgment in *O'Brien*, is that the fact stated must be one within the peculiar knowledge of the declarant.

The "five tests" referred to in *Pelletier* are from *R v Demeter* (1976), 10 OR (2d) 321 at 343-44 (CA):

In any event of the law, we think that, in addition to the principles applied in determining if a declaration is against pecuniary or proprietary interest, the following principles would have to be applied in determining whether a declaration is against penal interest:

1. The declaration would have to be made to such a person and in such circumstances that the declarant should have apprehended a vulnerability to penal consequences as a result. In *Sussex Peerage* the Lord Chancellor would not have admitted the declaration in any event of the rule because it was made to the declarant's son. In ordinary circumstances where a declaration is made for instance to an unestranged son, wife or mother, the psychological assurance of reliability is lacking because of risk of penal consequences is not real and the declarant may have motives such as a desire for self-aggrandizement or to shock which makes the declaration unreliable.

2. The vulnerability to penal consequences would have to be not remote.

3. "… the declaration sought to be given in evidence must be considered in its totality. If upon the whole tenor the weight is in favour of the declarant, it is not against his interest": *Re Van Beelen*, p. 208; *R v. Agawa* … [(1976), 11 OR (2d) 176, 28 CCC (2d) 379 (CA)].

4. In a doubtful case a Court might properly consider whether or not there are other circumstances connecting the declarant with the crime and whether or not there is any connection between the declarant and the accused.

5. The declarant would have to be unavailable by reason of death, insanity, grave illness which prevents the giving of testimony even from a bed, or absence in a jurisdiction to which none of the processes of the Court extends. A declarant would not be unavailable in the circumstances that existed in *R v. Agawa*.

Are these tests consistent with the three principles from *Ward*? If not, which should be used? Do these principles and tests adequately overcome the hearsay dangers associated with a statement against interest by a declarant who cannot be cross-examined by Crown counsel or observed by the trier of fact?

In *R v Folland* (see Section II.A, above) were Harris's statements admissible as statements against penal interest?

C. Prior Judicial Proceedings

1. Testimony from Prior Criminal Proceedings

Section 715 of the *Criminal Code* makes testimony taken at a prior proceeding admissible under certain circumstances. It reads as follows:

715(1) Where, at the trial of an accused, a person whose evidence was given at a previous trial on the same charge, or whose evidence was taken in the investigation of the charge against the accused or on the preliminary inquiry into the charge, refuses to be sworn or to give evidence, or if facts are proved on oath from which it can be inferred reasonably that the person

(a) is dead,

(b) has since become and is insane,

(c) is so ill that he is unable to travel or testify, or

(d) is absent from Canada,

and where it is proved that the evidence was taken in the presence of the accused, it may be admitted as evidence in the proceedings without further proof, unless the accused proves that the accused did not have full opportunity to cross-examine the witness.

(2) Evidence that has been taken on the preliminary inquiry or other investigation of a charge against an accused may be admitted as evidence in the prosecution of the accused for any other offence on the same proof and in the same manner in all respects, as it might, according to law, be admitted as evidence in the prosecution of the offence with which the accused was charged when the evidence was taken.

(3) For the purposes of this section, where evidence was taken at a previous trial or preliminary hearing or other proceeding in respect of an accused in the absence of the accused, who was absent by reason of having absconded, the accused is deemed to have been present during the taking of the evidence and to have had full opportunity to cross-examine the witness.

In *R v Potvin*, [1989] 1 SCR 525, 47 CCC (3d) 289, the accused challenged the constitutionality of s 715. Wilson J, speaking for the majority of the court, rejected this challenge.

R v Potvin
[1989] 1 SCR 525, 47 CCC (3d) 289
Dickson CJ and Lamer, Wilson, La Forest, and Sopinka JJ (23 March 1989)

WILSON J (Lamer and Sopinka JJ concurring): ... The appellant argues that an accused's ability to cross-examine all adverse witnesses at trial before the trier of fact is a principle of fundamental justice and a requirement of a fair trial. Basic to this argument is acceptance of the proposition that the trier of fact will be unable to assess the credibility of a witness in the absence of his or her physical presence at the time the evidence is presented to the trier of fact. That credibility is the issue under the section seems clear from the fact that it specifically requires that the previous evidence of the witness that is to be admitted at the trial has been taken in the presence of the accused who had a full opportunity to cross-examine on the evidence at the time.

I think the appellant's submission that s. 643(1) [now s 715(1) of the *Criminal Code*] violates s. 7 [of the *Canadian Charter of Rights and Freedoms*] must fail. This Court held in the *Re B.C. Motor Vehicle Act*, [1985] 2 SCR 486, at p. 503, that the principles of fundamental justice are to be found in the basic tenets of our justice system. Our justice system has, however, traditionally held evidence given under oath at a previous proceeding to be admissible at a criminal trial if the witness was unavailable at the trial for a reason such as death, provided the accused had an opportunity to cross-examine the witness when the evidence was originally given. The common law origins of the predecessor section to the present s. 643(1) were noted by Bain J in *R v. Hamilton* (1898), 2 CCC 390 (Man. QB), at p. 406, where he said:

> It is a rule founded on common law principles that, if a witness be proved to be dead, secondary evidence of a statement he made under oath on a former trial between the same parties will be received, provided that the facts in issue are substantially the same, and that the person against whom the evidence is to be given had the right and opportunity of cross-examining the witness: *Reg. v. Smith*, 2 Stark. 208 and note; Taylor on Evidence, §§464.

Likewise, Wigmore in his treatise on *Evidence* (Chadbourn rev. 1974), vol. 5, has explained at §1370 why the practice of admitting testimony which has already been subjected to cross-examination is consistent with the requirements of the hearsay rule:

> §1370. **Cross-examined statements not an exception to the hearsay rule.** The hearsay rule excludes testimonial statements not subjected to cross-examination (§1362 *supra*). When, therefore, a statement has *already been subjected to cross-examination* and is hence admitted—as in the case of a deposition or testimony at a former trial—it comes in because the rule is satisfied, not because an exception to the rule is allowed. The statement may have been made before the present trial, but if it has been already subjected to proper cross-examination, it has satisfied the rule and needs no exception in its favour. This is worth clear appreciation, because it involves the whole theory of the rule: ...

The practice of admitting previously taken evidence if the accused had an opportunity on the previous occasion to cross-examine the witness has been sanctioned by courts in the United Kingdom (see *R v. Hall*, [1973] 1 All ER 1 (CA), at p. 7) and in the United States (see *Ohio v. Roberts*, 448 US 56 (1980)). The American authorities on this question, collected in F. Dougherty, "Admissibility or Use in Criminal Trials of Testimony Given at

Preliminary Proceeding by Witness not Available at Trial" (1985), 38 ALR 4th 378, are of interest in that the Sixth Amendment of the American Bill of Rights specifically guarantees the accused the right "to be confronted with the witnesses against him." This right of confrontation has been held to be satisfied by the accused's having had an opportunity to cross-examine the witness at the time the previous evidence was given. It is clear to me from this survey that the right asserted by the appellant to confront an unavailable witness before the trier of fact at trial cannot be said to be a traditional or basic tenet of our justice system.

To the extent that s. 7 guarantees the accused a fair trial, can the admission of the previously obtained testimony under s. 643(1) be said to be unfair to the accused? In the absence of circumstances which negated or minimized the accused's opportunity to cross-examine the witness when the previous testimony was given, I think not. In this regard I would respectfully adopt the following statement of Vancise JA of the Saskatchewan Court of Appeal in *R v. Rodgers* (1987), 35 CCC (3d) 50, at pp. 60-61:

> Does this procedure offend the basic tenets and principles on which the principles of fundamental justice are based? Put another way, are these procedural safeguards sufficient to make the taking of the evidence accord with the principles of fundamental justice which are founded upon a belief "in the dignity and worth of a human person and on the rule of law"? In my opinion, they are. The conditions under which the evidence is given, including the solemnity of the occasion, are such as to guarantee its trustworthiness and to protect the rights of an accused. The evidence is given in open court in the presence of the accused, taken on oath or solemn affirmation, and the person against whose interest it is sought to be introduced has reasonable opportunity to cross-examine. The evidence is certified as to correctness by the judge before whom it was given. This is not a mechanism for the introduction of evidence which is not admissible, but rather a system for the use of evidence which would otherwise be lost. Its use, or admissibility, is provided for in a way which accords full safety to the rights of an accused. Those safeguards, together with the limited circumstances in which the procedure can be resorted to, justify its acceptance into evidence. The procedure is one which accords with the principles of fundamental justice, and in my opinion, s. 7 of the Charter has not been offended.

> ● ● ●

> What rights then does an accused have under s. 7 of the *Charter* with respect to the admission of previous testimony? It is, in my view, basic to our system of justice that the accused have had a full opportunity to cross-examine the witness when the previous testimony was taken if a transcript of such testimony is to be introduced as evidence in a criminal trial for the purpose of convicting the accused. This is in accord with the traditional view that it is the opportunity to cross-examine and not the fact of cross-examination which is crucial if the accused is to be treated fairly. As Professor Delisle has noted: Annotation (1986), 50 CR (3d) 195, at p. 196:

> > If the opposing party has had an opportunity to fully cross-examine he ought not to be justified in any later complaint if he did not fully exercise that right.

> I would respectfully adopt the following observations of Martin JA of the Ontario Court of Appeal in *Davidson* [R v Davidson (1988), 42 CCC (3d) 289 (Ont CA)], at pp. 298-99:

An accused is not necessarily deprived of his or her constitutional right to a fair trial, where the evidence taken at a preliminary hearing from a crucial witness who has since died is read as evidence at the trial. However, if in a particular case, an accused proves that he or she did not have "full opportunity" to cross-examine the witness at the preliminary hearing because, for example, he or she was deprived of the right to counsel or because of improper restrictions by the court on the cross-examination by counsel, then the conditions of s. 643 have not been met, and the evidence taken at the preliminary hearing is not admissible under the section. Furthermore, the accused's constitutional right to a fair trial guaranteed by s. 11(d) of the Charter would also require the exclusion of evidence where the accused did not have full opportunity to cross-examine the witness at the preliminary hearing.

I would respectfully agree with Martin JA that the accused would have a constitutional right to have the evidence of prior testimony obtained in the absence of a full opportunity to cross-examine the witness excluded. When the evidence is sought to be introduced in order to obtain a criminal conviction which could result in imprisonment, the accused is threatened with a deprivation of his or her liberty and security of the person and this can only be done in accordance with the principles of fundamental justice. It is, as I have said, a principle of fundamental justice that the accused have had a full opportunity to cross-examine the adverse witness.

I would add that the new constitutional dimension of this matter under the *Charter* casts doubt on the continued validity of pre-*Charter* decisions which did not construe the right to full opportunity to cross-examine in the broad and generous manner befitting its constitutional status. For examples of a restrictive approach to the content of this right see *Rose v. The King* (1946), 88 CCC 114 (Que. KB), at pp. 124-25, 153-54, and 178-79; *Lambert v. The Queen* (1974), 28 CRNS 238 (Que. CA), at pp. 244-45; *R v. Devlin* (1976), 32 CCC (2d) 334 (NBSC App. Div.), at p. 338.

The appellant submits that the provision of a full opportunity to cross-examine at the preliminary inquiry does not necessarily ensure fairness. More specifically, he argues that 1) the trier of fact is deprived of the ability to assess the credibility of the witness through observing his or her demeanour; 2) when the evidence is taken at a preliminary inquiry the credibility of that evidence is not in issue; and 3) the accused at the preliminary inquiry may have strategic reasons for not testing the credibility, or even conducting any cross-examination, of a witness. Despite the fact that these observations may be sound and could operate to the detriment of the accused, I do not think they are of such magnitude and effect as to deprive the accused of the basics of a fair trial. I say this for the following reasons.

I note that although it is possible that an accused might suffer a detriment because of the trier of fact's inability to assess the credibility of a witness on a face to face basis, it is also true that this feature of s. 643(1) could work to an accused's benefit. In any event, because s. 643(1) can only be invoked when its stringent pre-requisites are met by the party seeking to introduce the previous testimony, it is not a provision that the Crown can use at will to its advantage or as a device to protect Crown witnesses who may not prove to be credible before the trier of fact.

Although it is true that credibility is not specifically an issue to be determined at a preliminary inquiry (see *United States of America v. Shephard*, [1977] 2 SCR 1067, *per* Ritchie J, at pp. 1080 and 1084; *Mezzo v. The Queen*, [1986] 1 SCR 802, *per* McIntyre J, at pp. 836-37), this does not mean that an accused is taken unawares or unfairly surprised by the admission of testimony taken at a preliminary inquiry if a witness subsequently becomes unavailable. If a judge presiding at a preliminary inquiry seeks to curtail cross-examination designed to test a witness's credibility and that witness's testimony is subsequently admitted at trial under s. 643(1), this may very well constitute an infringement of the accused's right under s. 7 of the *Charter* to have had a full opportunity to cross-examine the witness.

As for the detriment an accused might suffer from the tactical decision of his or her counsel not to press certain issues at the preliminary inquiry with a witness who may subsequently become unavailable at the trial, I am in complete agreement with the observation of Martin JA in *Davidson, supra*, at p. 298:

> In my view, an accused is not deprived of "full opportunity" to cross-examine a witness at the preliminary hearing merely because his counsel, for tactical reasons, has conducted the cross-examination of a witness differently than he would have conducted the cross-examination at the trial, provided that there has been no improper restriction of the cross-examination by the provincial judge holding the preliminary hearing.

In short, I find that s. 643(1) of the *Criminal Code*, in so far as it allows evidence given at a preliminary inquiry to be admitted at a criminal trial when a witness is unavailable or unwilling to testify, does not infringe s. 7 of the *Charter* because it provides that the evidence will only be admitted if the accused has had a full opportunity to cross-examine the witness at the time the evidence was given.

[Wilson J also held that s 715 gave the trial judge "a statutory discretion to prevent any unfairness that could otherwise result from a purely mechanical application of the section." She held that the discretion could be exercised where "there has been unfairness in the manner in which the evidence was obtained" or where admission of the evidence would affect "the fairness of the trial itself."]

NOTE

Wigmore was of the view that the kind of evidence made admissible by s 715 of the Code was not hearsay at all because it had been subjected to cross-examination. Do you agree?

In *R v Hawkins*, [1996] 3 SCR 1043, which is excerpted in Chapter 2, Section I.A and in Section III.B in this chapter, the Crown's principal witness at the preliminary inquiry was Graham, Hawkins's girlfriend. After the preliminary inquiry but before the trial, Hawkins and Graham married. The trial judge held, and the Supreme Court agreed, that Graham was therefore incompetent for the Crown (see Chapter 2, Section I). The Crown sought to adduce Graham's testimony from the preliminary hearing under s 715 of the *Criminal Code*. On a pre-trial motion, Le Sage Dist Ct J refused to admit this evidence. Arbour JA in the Court of Appeal held that in the circumstances the marriage was equivalent to Graham's refusing to be sworn under s 715(1), and that her preliminary hearing testimony should therefore have been admitted. But the Supreme Court of Canada held, unanimously on this point, that Graham's earlier testimony was not admissible under s 715. Lamer CJ and Iacobucci J said:

Graham's marriage clearly cannot be read into the section as grounds for admitting the transcripts of her preliminary inquiry evidence. The marriage of Graham and Hawkins does not represent a refusal to give evidence: the common law rule of spousal incompetency disqualifies a spouse from giving evidence, regardless of the spouse's choice. Indeed, there is no way of knowing whether Graham actually would have refused to testify; she may have chosen to testify for the defence.

In light of these comments, how strictly will the conditions established by s 715(1) be applied? Would it be fair to characterize Arbour JA's approach as "purposive" and the Supreme Court's approach as "literal"?

2. Testimony from Prior Civil Proceedings

The admissibility of testimony from prior civil proceedings is governed by rules of court. In British Columbia, the relevant rule, r 12-5(54), reads:

> (54) If a witness is dead, or is unable to attend and testify because of age, infirmity, sickness or imprisonment or is out of the jurisdiction or his or her attendance cannot be secured by subpoena, the court may permit a transcript of any evidence of that witness taken in any proceeding, hearing or inquiry at which the evidence was taken under oath, whether or not involving the same parties, to be put in as evidence, but reasonable notice must be given of the intention to give that evidence.

(*Supreme Court Civil Rules*, BC Reg 168/2009.)

The relevant rules in Alberta read:

> 8.17(3) Evidence taken in any other action may be presented at trial but only if the party proposing to submit the evidence gives each of the other parties written notice of that party's intention 5 days or more before the trial is scheduled to start and obtains the Court's permission to submit the evidence.
>
> 8.19 Evidence at trial may be used in a subsequent application or subsequent proceedings in that action.

(*Alberta Rules of Court*, Alta Reg 124/2010.)

What is the difference between the British Columbia rule and the Alberta rules? What factors should structure a trial judge's exercise of discretion under each rule?

The admissibility at trial of evidence taken on examination for discovery is also governed by the rules of court. In Ontario, the relevant rule of civil procedure reads:

> 31.11(6) Where a person examined for discovery,
>
> (a) has died;
>
> (b) is unable to testify because of infirmity or illness;
>
> (c) for any other sufficient reason cannot be compelled to attend at the trial; or
>
> (d) refuses to take an oath or make an affirmation or to answer any proper question,
>
> any party may, with leave of the trial judge, read into evidence all or part of the evidence given on the examination for discovery as the evidence of the person examined, to the extent that it would be admissible if the person were testifying in court.

(7) In deciding whether to grant leave under subrule (6), the trial judge shall consider,
    (a) the extent to which the person was cross-examined on the examination for discovery;
    (b) the importance of the evidence in the proceeding;
    (c) the general principle that evidence should be presented orally in court; and
    (d) any other relevant factor.

(*Rules of Civil Procedure*, RRO 1990, Reg 194.)

For a similar result at common law, see *Walkerton (Town) v Erdman* (1894), 23 SCR 352. Under the *Alberta Rules of Court*, only the adverse party may use evidence from examination for discovery: see r 5.31(1). What would be the rationale for this limit? Is it a wise one?

3. *Verdicts from Prior Criminal Proceedings*

In a much-criticized decision, the Court of Appeal in England held that a criminal conviction was *not* admissible as evidence that the accused had committed the offence in a civil action involving the same facts. See *Hollington v F Hewthorn and Co Ltd*, [1943] 2 All ER 35 (CA). The decision was not followed in Canada: see *Demeter v British Pacific Life Ins Co* (1983), 43 OR (2d) 33, 150 DLR (3d) 249 (HCJ), aff'd (1984), 48 OR (2d) 266, 13 DLR (4th) 318 (CA).

The Ontario *Evidence Act* now provides as follows:

22.1(1) Proof that a person has been convicted or discharged anywhere in Canada of a crime is proof, in the absence of evidence to the contrary, that the crime was committed by the person, if,
    (a) no appeal of the conviction or discharge was taken and the time for an appeal has expired; or
    (b) an appeal of the conviction or discharge was taken but was dismissed or abandoned and no further appeal is available.
(2) Subsection (1) applies whether or not the convicted or discharged person is a party to the proceeding.

Compare *Alberta Evidence Act*, RSA 2000, c A-18, s 26. What is the effect of these provisions on the rule in *Hollington v Hewthorn*?

Consider the following questions in light of the policy reasons for and against allowing a party to relitigate a factual issue that has already been decided against him or her.

The plaintiff sued the defendant for damages arising out of a sexual assault for which the defendant had been convicted. At the criminal trial, the defendant had pleaded not guilty and had testified in his own defence. On the plaintiff's motion for summary judgment, both parties relied solely on a transcript of the criminal trial; no other evidence was offered. The issue on a motion for summary judgment is whether there is a genuine issue for trial. Would you grant the motion? See *F (K) (Litigation Guardian of) v White* (2001), 53 OR (3d) 391, 198 DLR (4th) 541 (CA).

An employee of a city's department of parks and recreation was convicted of a sexual assault on a young boy. The offence occurred in the course of his employment, and he was dismissed by the city. His union grieved the dismissal. The arbitrator who heard the grievance accepted the conviction as *prima facie* evidence that the offence had occurred, but rejected the city's submission that the conviction was conclusive proof. Both parties therefore led evidence on this issue. The employee testified at the arbitration and denied having assaulted the complainant. The complainant did not testify. The arbitrator found that the offence had not occurred, and ordered the city to reinstate the employee. Did the arbitrator make any error that would justify judicial review of his decision? See *Toronto (City) v CUPE, Local 79*, 2003 SCC 63, [2003] 3 SCR 77, 232 DLR (4th) 385, and compare *Caci v Dorkin*, 2008 ONCA 750, 93 OR (3d) 701.

Should the fact that a person has been acquitted of an offence be *prima facie* evidence in civil proceedings that he or she did not commit the offence? Should the reasons for the acquittal matter? See *Polgrain Estate v Toronto East General Hospital*, 2008 ONCA 427, 90 OR (3d) 630, 293 DLR (4th) 266.

If a person is acquitted of a criminal offence, the Crown is precluded by the principles of double jeopardy from re-trying that person for that offence or for any included offence of which the accused could have been convicted: see *Criminal Code*, ss 608, 609; Charter, s 11(h). In a trial on a different offence, to what extent is the Crown precluded from proving the facts of the offence of which the accused was acquitted? See *R v Gushue*, [1980] 1 SCR 798; *R v Grdic*, [1985] 1 SCR 810; *R v Mahalingan*, 2008 SCC 63, [2008] 3 SCR 316.

For a discussion of *res judicata* in civil matters and its relationship to the rules of evidence, see Sopinka, Lederman & Bryant, *The Law of Evidence in Canada* (Toronto: Butterworths, 1992) at 988-1013.

What, if anything, do *res judicata* and issue estoppel have to do with the rule against hearsay?

D. Statements Concerning Bodily and Mental Condition

Youlden v London Guarantee and Accident Co
(1910), 26 OLR 75 (Ont HCJ)
Middleton J (12 March 1910)

MIDDLETON J: The deceased had been insured with the defendants for some years, the policy having been issued on the 7th January, 1902, and the renewal premium paid on the 2nd January, 1909.

On the 23rd June, 1909, shortly after his dinner, the deceased—a member of a firm carrying on a foundry business in Kingston—was at the railway station, superintending and assisting in the loading of a retort upon a railway car. The retort weighed about three and a half tons, and had to be transferred from a dray to the railway car by means of jacks and other appliances. For the purpose of making a way for removing the retort, a heavy stick of timber, lying upon the railway premises, was desired to be used. This weighed from five to six hundred pounds. Youlden attempted to carry one end of this, while the other end was carried by two men. His partner Selby went to his assistance; and shortly afterwards Youlden remarked to him that he was afraid he had injured himself. He then sat in the shade at the station for a time, and, feeling faint, he went with Selby to an hotel and took a glass of whisky and soda, and thereafter did no more work, but returned to the shop upon a rig, and sat around doing little or nothing until six o'clock, when he went home. The same evening, without taking any supper, he went to a garden party, where a presentation was to be made in which he was much interested. During the evening he partook sparingly of ice-cream, and went home at a little after ten o'clock. His, wife, hearing that he was unwell, followed him home; and shortly thereafter he lay down upon a sofa to rest for the night, in a dressing-gown. During the night he was uncomfortable and restless, could not sleep, and, his wife said, "looked miserable and grey." Nevertheless, he went to the office in the morning, but stayed there only a short time, returning in about half an hour: A doctor was called, and found him weak and in pain. He had then had a violent motion of the bowels, and appeared to be generally collapsed. By the evening his temperature was high and there was further bowel trouble. The case developed into a case of acute enteritis, which would not yield to treatment, and finally caused his death.

The plaintiff alleges that a strain was caused by the exertion of lifting the timber, and that, this strain brought about a physical condition which enabled bacteria in the digestive tract to develop to such an extent that death resulted from his inability to resist their attack, by reason of the reduced vitality following the strain in lifting the timber.

At the trial I admitted in evidence, against the protest of the defendants' counsel, the statement made by the deceased to his partner Selby, shortly after he had lifted the timber, that he thought he had hurt himself. It is argued that, apart from this, there is no evidence of the existence of a strain. The medical men stated that there was no physical condition indicating a strain; that the injury, if it existed, was internal only; and that the only knowledge they had of its existence would be from statements made to them by the patient of his symptoms, and the history of the case. The symptoms made it quite plain that the malady was caused by the invasion of the system by pernicious bacteria. This invasion, in the opinion of the doctors, might well be occasioned by any injury to the system which rendered it unable to manifest the normal resistance of a healthy and uninjured individual; but the result might follow equally from anything which would bring about a marked reduction of vitality, or it might follow from the introduction of pernicious bacteria in the food taken—the latter being the general origin of such a malady. The ice-cream taken the evening before, if impure or tainted, would adequately account for the condition found.

It, therefore, becomes a matter of great importance to examine the propriety of my ruling ...

The Irish Court of Appeal, *Wright v. Kerrigan*, [1911] 2 IR 301, had before it a claim under the *Workmen's Compensation Act*, where part of the evidence tendered was a statement of the deceased to a doctor as to how the injury was received. Cherry LJ, mentions this evidence, saying: "Hearsay evidence is in some cases admissible, and the learned Recorder appears to me to have acted strictly in accordance with the settled rules of evidence. ... He ruled out statements as to the circumstances of the accident. He admitted the statements made by the deceased man to his medical attendant ... as to his symptoms and their cause. Such statements are usually held to be admissible upon the ground that there is no other means possible of proving bodily or mental feelings than by the statements of the person who experiences them."

In *Amys v. Barton*, [1911] WN 205, the accuracy of this statement of the law was canvassed by the Court of Appeal, and Cozens-Hardy MR pointed out that the words "and their cause" in the statement by Cherry LJ could not be supported, but appeared to approve of the rule as stated, with this exception.

In the 9th edition (1910) of *Powell on Evidence*, p. 358, the admissibility of statements for the limited purpose of proving the physical condition of the person making the statement is asserted; and I think for this purpose the evidence was properly admitted, and it is sufficient to establish that, shortly after the deceased had been engaged in lifting the timber, he had, as he said, indications that he had been hurt.

The statement, perhaps, did not go so far as to indicate that the lifting of the timber was the cause of the injury; but I think that this is an inference which may be drawn from the fact of the injury, and falls within the principle indicated in *Richard Evans & Co. Limited v. Astley*, [1911] AC 674, 678, where it is said: "The applicant must prove his case. This does not mean that he must demonstrate his case. If the more probable cause is that for which he contends, and there is anything pointing to it, then there is evidence for a Court to act upon. Any conclusion short of certainty may be miscalled conjecture or surmise, but Courts, like individuals, habitually act upon a balance of probabilities." See also the decisions of the Supreme Court of Canada in *McKeand v. Canadian Pacific R.W. Co.*, not yet reported, and in *Grand Trunk R.W. Co. v. Griffith* (1911), 45 SCR 380.

Acting upon this principle, I find that the symptoms indicate that the deceased, at this time, did suffer an injury in lifting the timber in question; and I further find that this injury was the cause of his death. I believe this to be the cause, because, as I understand the medical evidence, it is a possible cause, and it is the only one of the several possible causes which is shewn to have actually existed. There is no evidence that the ice-cream eaten was tainted; and the evidence satisfies me that up to the happening of the accident the deceased appeared to be in perfect health. This brings the case within the decision of the Court of Appeal in *In re Etherington and Lancashire and Yorkshire Accident Insurance Co.*, [1909] 1 KB 591.

[The plaintiff's action was dismissed on other grounds.]

———————————

On the authority of cases such as *Youlden*, statements about a declarant's bodily and mental condition, contemporaneous with the condition described, have been admitted because there is no other way to determine the facts asserted in the statements, and because their spontaneity indicates reliability. Is that a sufficient rationale?

What further inferences can properly be drawn from a statement admitted to show the declarant's bodily and mental condition?

R v Wysochan
(1930), 54 CCC 172 (Sask CA)
Haultain CJS (10 June 1930)

HAULTAIN CJS: Appeal against conviction.

The appellant was convicted on March 20, 1930, before Bigelow J, of the wilful murder of one Antenia Kropa on December 25, 1929, at Humboldt in this Province, and was sentenced to death.

The main ground of appeal raises the question of the admissibility of evidence of words spoken by A. Kropa some time after she was shot. It appears that A. Kropa, her husband S. Kropa, and the appellant were the only persons present at or about the time the shooting took place.

As to what took place at the time, it will be sufficient to say that according to S. Kropa's evidence the shooting must have been done by the appellant, while on the other hand according to the evidence of the appellant the shooting must have been done by S. Kropa.

The evidence shows that S. Kropa ran out of the house at or about the time the shooting took place, and that after reporting the matter to some friends and the police he returned to the house half an hour later.

The evidence objected to relates to words spoken by A. Kropa at the time. The evidence is, that she said to one Tony Sokolowski, "Tony where is my husband" and that when S. Kropa, the husband, was near her she stretched out her hand to him and said:—"Stanley, help me out because there is a bullet in my body." Further, when she was put into a sleigh to be taken to the hospital and was being covered up, she said, "Stanley, help me, I am too hot."

In his charge to the jury the trial judge, in commenting on this evidence, said as follows:—

> "Now, if that was so gentlemen, Mr. Wilson has very properly argued that that would be a most unusual and unreasonable, and I think, improbable thing for her to do, if it was her husband who had shot her. There is no doubt that this woman was killed that night, and there are one of two alternatives before you. Either it was Kropa or the accused, and if it was not Kropa, it does not require any argument or logic for you to come to the conclusion it was the accused, and that is why this evidence is put before you to show that when her husband appeared on the scene she stretched out her arms to him and asked for help. Would it not have been a most improbable thing had he been the author of her death that night?"

It may be observed at the outset that the statements in question were not part of a dying declaration, nor were they part of the *res gestae*. They rather come within the class of utterances described in 3 *Wigmore on Evidence*, Can. ed., p. 2315, para. 1790, as follows:—"Utterances as indicating Circumstantially the Speaker's Own State of Mind. The condition of a speaker's mind, as to knowledge, belief, rationality, emotion, or the like, may be evidenced by his utterances, either used testimonially as assertions to be believed, or used circumstantially as affording indirect inferences. Utterances of the former sort may be received under the Exception for Statements of a Mental Condition (*ante* para. 1714). … The usual resort is to utterances which circumstantially indicate a specific state of mind causing them."

In *Gilbert v. The King* (1907), 12 Can. CC 127, at pp. 131-2, Harvey J is reported as saying in the court below, as follows:—"The charge is one of deliberately shooting the deceased while the defence is that the shooting was purely accidental. If it were shewn that after the shooting the state of mind of the man shot were one of friendliness to the accused, it surely would be deemed to have an important bearing on the question in issue, and in the same way evidence indicating aversion and fear have as important a bearing in the opposite direction. Wigmore, in his work on Evidence, points out very fully the difference between the admission of utterances as proof of the truth of the facts stated and their admission to prove a state of mind which he terms their circumstantial use as opposed to the other or testimonial use, and states, in par. 1790, that to the use circumstantially the hearsay rule makes no opposition 'because the utterance is not used for the sake of inducing belief in any assertion it may contain.'"

The evidence in question seems to come well within the principle above stated. The utterances in question contained no statement of facts necessary to be proved. They are only evidence more or less strong of a certain feeling or attitude of mind, and it was for the jury to decide what inferences might be drawn from them.

A number of objections were taken to the judge's charge to the jury on the grounds of misdirection and non-direction. The evidence, in the opinion of the court, was fully stated in the summing-up, and while on certain points the charge was not favourable to the accused, the jury were adequately instructed as to the defences open to him, and were invariably told that they were after all the sole judges of fact, and that they should not convict if they had any reasonable doubt of the prisoner's guilt.

The appeal must therefore be dismissed.

NOTES AND QUESTIONS

Assume the court is correct in stating that Antenia Kropa's statement was potentially admissible under the state of mind exception to the rule against hearsay. How was that state of mind relevant? What inference did the Crown want the jury to draw from it? Was that further inference captured by the state of mind exception?

Ten days after his appeal was dismissed, Wysochan was executed. He was represented throughout the proceedings, *pro bono*, by John Diefenbaker, who would later become prime minister of Canada. For a more detailed description of the evidence and the proceedings in the *Wysochan* case, see Denis Smith, *Rogue Tory: The Life and Legend of John Diefenbaker* (Toronto: Macfarlane Walter & Ross, 1995) at 66-69.

In *R v Griffin*, 2009 SCC 28, [2009] 2 SCR 42, Griffin and Harris were charged with first-degree murder in the shooting death of Denis Poirier. The Crown's theory of the case was that the killing was "retribution for Poirier's failure to repay a large drug-related debt, and that Griffin was the shooter while Harris acted as the lookout." The Crown witness Jennifer Williams identified Griffin as the shooter. She also gave the following testimony concerning a meeting with Poirier about ten days before the shooting:

> … Poirier met with his girlfriend Williams at the bar of the Clarion Hotel. Poirier left the bar at regular intervals throughout the evening to make phone calls and check his messages, and he grew increasingly stressed as the evening went on. Around 11 p.m., Poirier suggested that Williams depart, and as she was leaving he said to her: "If anything happens to me it's your cousin's family." A first cousin of Williams had a child with a first cousin of Griffin, and Williams immediately understood that Poirier was referring to Griffin. Poirier did not explain to Williams why he feared for his safety but she understood he was afraid of Griffin.

Assuming that this evidence was potentially admissible under a hearsay exception to show Poirier's state of mind, what further inferences (if any) could properly be drawn from it? Do those further inferences have a hearsay quality?

E. Statements of Intention

The "statement of intention" exception is sometimes regarded as an aspect of the exception for statements concerning bodily and mental condition, in that an intention might be thought of as a mental state. But it is often the case that the intention is relevant not in itself, but only if it was acted upon. When, if ever, should the trier of fact be permitted to infer that the declarant acted on a statement of intention?

Mutual Life Insurance Company v Hillmon
145 US 285 (1892)
Fuller CJ and Field, Harlan, Gray, Blatchford, Lamar, Brewer, and Brown JJ
(1892)

MR. JUSTICE GRAY: … This question is of the admissibility of the letters written by Walters on the first day of March, 1879, which were offered in evidence by the defendants, and excluded by the court. In order to determine the competency of these letters, it is important to consider the state of the case when they were offered to be read.

The matter chiefly contested at the trial was the death of John W. Hillmon, the insured; and that depended upon the question whether the body found at Crooked Creek on the night of March 18, 1879, was his body, or the body of one Walters.

Much conflicting evidence had been introduced as to the identity of the body. The plaintiff had also introduced evidence that Hillmon and one Brown left Wichita in Kansas on or about March 5, 1879, and travelled together through Southern Kansas in search of a site for a cattle ranch, and that on the night of March 18, while they were in camp at Crooked Creek, Hillmon was accidentally killed, and that his body was taken thence and buried. The defendants had introduced evidence, without objection, that Walters left his home and his betrothed in Iowa in March, 1878, and was afterwards in Kansas until March, 1879; that during that time he corresponded regularly with his family and his betrothed; that the last letters received from him were one received by his betrothed on March 3 and postmarked at Wichita March 2, and one received by his sister about March 4 or 5, and dated at Wichita a day or two before; and that he had not been heard from since.

· · ·

"Dearest Alvina: Your kind and ever welcome letter was received yesterday afternoon about an hour before I left Emporia. I will stay here until the fore part of next week, and then will leave here to see a part of the country that I never expected to see when I left home, as I am going with a man by the name of Hillmon, who intends to start a sheep ranch, and as he promised me more wages than I could make at anything else I concluded to take it, for a while at least, until I strike something better. There is so many folks in this country that have got the Leadville fever, and if I could not of got the situation that I have now I would have went there myself; but as it is at present I get to see the best portion of Kansas, Indian Territory, Colorado, and Mexico. The route that we intend to take would cost a man to travel from $150 to $200, but it will not cost me a cent; besides, I get good wages. I will drop you a letter occasionally until I get settled down; then I want you to answer it."

· · ·

The evidence that Walters was at Wichita on or before March 5, and had not been heard from since, together with the evidence to identify as his the body found at Crooked Creek on March 18, tended to show that he went from Wichita to Crooked Creek between those dates. Evidence that just before March 5 he had the intention of leaving Wichita with Hillmon would tend to corroborate the evidence already admitted, and to show that he went from Wichita to Crooked Creek with Hillmon. Letters from him to his family and his betrothed were the natural, if not the only attainable, evidence of his intention.

· · ·

But upon another ground suggested they should have been admitted. A man's state of mind or feeling can only be manifested to others by countenance, attitude or gesture, or by sounds or words, spoken or written. The nature of the fact to be proved is the same, and evidence of its proper tokens is equally competent to prove it, whether expressed by aspect or conduct, by voice or pen. When the intention to be proved is important only as qualifying an act, its connection with that act must be shown, in order to warrant the admission of declarations of the intention. But whenever the intention is of itself a distinct and material fact in a chain of circumstances, it may be proved by contemporaneous oral or written declarations of the party.

The existence of a particular intention in a certain person at a certain time being a material fact to be proved, evidence that he expressed that intention at that time is as direct evidence of the fact, as his own testimony that he then had that intention would be. After his death there can hardly be any other way of proving it; and while he is still alive, his own memory of his state of mind at a former time is no more likely to be clear and true than a bystander's recollection of what he then said, and is less trustworthy than letters written by him at the very time and under circumstances precluding a suspicion of misrepresentation.

The letters in question were competent, not as narratives of facts communicated to the writer by others, nor yet as proof that he actually went away from Wichita, but as evidence that, shortly before the time when other evidence tended to show that he went away, he had the intention of going, and of going with Hillmon, which made it more probable both that he did go and that he went with Hillmon, than if there had been no proof of such intention. In view of the mass of conflicting testimony introduced upon the question whether it was the body of Walters that was found in Hillmon's camp, this evidence might properly influence the jury in determining that question.

The rule applicable to this case has been thus stated by this court: "Wherever the bodily or mental feelings of an individual are material to be proved, the usual expressions of such feelings are original and competent evidence. Those expressions are the natural reflexes of what it might be impossible to show by other testimony. If there be such other testimony, this may be necessary to set the facts thus developed in their true light, and to give them their proper effect. As independent explanatory or corroborative evidence, it is often indispensable to the due administration of justice. Such declarations are regarded as verbal acts, and are as competent as any other testimony, when relevant to the issue. Their truth or falsity is an inquiry for the jury." *Insurance Co. v. Mosley*, 5 Wall. 397, 404, 405.

. . .

Upon principle and authority, therefore, we are of opinion that the two letters were competent evidence of the intention of Walters at the time of writing them, which was a material fact bearing upon the question in controversy; and that for the exclusion of these letters, as well as for the undue restriction of the defendants' challenges, the verdicts must be set aside, and a new trial had.

NOTE

For further information about *Hillmon*, see the Hillmon Case website: <http://www.thehillmoncase.com>.

R v Wainwright
(1875), 13 Cox CC 171 (Central Crim Ct)
Cockburn CJ (November 1875)

[Henry Wainwright was charged with the murder of Harriet Louisa Lane; Thomas George Wainwright was charged as an aider and abettor of the murder.]

During the examination of a witness for the prosecution, named Ellen Willmore, the admissibility of certain evidence was discussed. The witness was the person who had last seen Harriet Louisa Lane on the afternoon of the 11th of September, 1874, when the latter left her lodgings at 3, Sydney-square, Mile End. After that date Harriet Louisa Lane was not seen again alive, and that was the date fixed upon by the prosecution as the time when the murder was perpetrated. The witness having described what occurred at the parting between her and Harriet Louisa Lane on that afternoon, was asked whether Harriet Louisa Lane, at the time of her departure from the house, made a statement to her.

Besley, interposing. This is a convenient time to take an objection, not to this question, but to one which it is intended shall follow upon it. It will be an interrogation as to what Harriet Louisa Lane then said as to where she was going. It is contended that although the preliminary question may be put, the further question "what statement did she make" is objectionable, on the ground that this evidence comes into the class of hearsay evidence, and that it is inadmissible, because made in the absence of the prisoner who is sought to be affected by it. The circumstances do not warrant the court in accepting it, as a statement, which is part of the *res gestae*, and, therefore, as an exception to the rule precluding the admissibility of that kind of evidence. In determining the objection which is now made, regard should be had to the character of the act charged. It is a charge of wilful murder and the expressed intention of Harriet Louisa Lane to do an act, which she may or may not have done, cannot be evidence on this trial.

THE LORD CHIEF JUSTICE.   All that is proposed to ask now is the question, "When going away did she make a statement?" That question can be put, but not the question, "What statement did she make?" The question at present only goes to the extent of ascertaining whether a statement was made and there it stops; what was the statement, it would be inadmissible. You are constantly meeting with such a question, "Did so and so make a statement to you and in consequence of that communication did you do anything." The fact that some statement was made is undoubtedly admissible.

The *Attorney-General*.   The woman is leaving her house when she makes a statement, which is a declaration of intention, and it is submitted that that is a statement accompanying an act. It is part of the act of leaving, and on that ground it is proposed to ask the question to which objection has been made.

THE LORD CHIEF JUSTICE.   It was no part of the act of leaving, but only an incidental remark. It was only a statement of intention which might or might not have been carried out. She would have gone away under any circumstances. You may get the fact that on leaving she made a statement, but you must not go beyond it.

The question was then put to the witness as to whether Harriet Louisa Lane had made a statement to her, and the answer was that she did. The response to the question which had been disallowed, would have been, "she said she was going to 115, Whitechapel-road." These were the premises in the occupation of Henry Wainwright where the deceased had been interred ... .

[Notwithstanding this ruling, Henry Wainwright was convicted of the murder and was executed.]

R v Thomson
[1912] 3 KB 19 (Cr App)
Lord Alverstone CJ, Darling and Avory JJ (10 June 1912)

The appellant was tried before Phillimore J upon a charge of using an instrument upon a woman on March 21, 1912, for the purpose of procuring miscarriage. The woman died on March 31, but not as a result of the operation. The defence set up was that the appellant had done nothing to the woman, but that she had performed the operation upon herself.

At the trial counsel for the accused proposed to ask one of the witnesses for the prosecution in cross-examination whether the deceased woman had made in the month of February, 1912, a statement that she intended to perform an operation upon herself in order to procure miscarriage, and on March 29, a statement that she had performed such an operation upon herself. The learned judge ruled that this evidence was inadmissible and that these questions could not be asked. The accused was found guilty and sentenced to three years' penal servitude.

. . .

LORD ALVERSTONE CJ: The point is one of importance and at first appeared to be difficult. Counsel for the appellant was not allowed in cross-examination to put questions to a witness for the prosecution as to what the deceased woman had told her some time before the miscarriage as to her intentions and also a few days before her death as to what she had done. If put in a popular way, the argument for the appellant, that what the woman had said she had done to herself ought to be admissible evidence for the defence, might be attractive; but upon consideration it is seen to be a dangerous argument, and, in the opinion of the Court, the rejection of evidence of that kind is much more in favour of the accused than of the prosecution. If such evidence is admissible for one side it must also be admissible for the other.

In our opinion there is no principle upon which this evidence is admissible any more than any other hearsay evidence. If it were admissible, then all those decisions in which it was considered whether statements were admissible in evidence as dying declarations, or as part of the res gestae, or as admissions against pecuniary or proprietary interest, would have been unnecessary. ... In this case it cannot be argued that the statements were admissible as part of the *res gestae*; the statements sought to be proved were not made at the time when anything was being done to the woman.

In our opinion the ruling of the learned judge in rejecting this evidence was correct and this appeal must be dismissed.

QUESTION

What is the difference between the English and the American approach to statements of intention, as articulated in the three preceding cases?

R v P (R)
(1990), 58 CCC (3d) 334 (H Ct J)
Doherty J (28 May 1990)

DOHERTY J: I will begin with the reasons for my ruling with respect to the admissibility of utterances made by the deceased to various witnesses.

I. The Problem

The Crown seeks to introduce several statements said to have been made by the deceased to various Crown witnesses. I have been provided with a summary of what the Crown anticipates these various witnesses will say was said to them by the deceased (ex. I). The deceased and the accused lived together for about three years prior to her disappearance in late February, 1988. These utterances by the deceased are said to be capable of demonstrating her state of mind. Some of the utterances also relate things which the deceased said Mr. P did to her. Much of this reported conduct is reprehensible, and some of it could well be viewed as bizarre. The contents of some of these utterances suggest that Mr. P's treatment of the deceased was that of a domineering tyrant. There is no suggestion of violence against the deceased by Mr. P in these statements.

The Crown contends that the various utterances of the deceased go to her state of mind beginning at some point in 1987, and through to the days and weeks immediately preceding her disappearance in late February, 1988. The Crown argues that the statements are evidence of various mental states:

(1) the deceased's fear of Mr. P;

(2) her unhappiness and dissatisfaction with the relationship she had with Mr. P;

(3) her determination to end that relationship;

(4) her intention that the termination of the relationship would be permanent and that she would have no further involvement of any kind with Mr. P.

After reviewing the statements, I am satisfied that the utterances do afford evidence of all but the first of these states of mind.

The Crown contends that these mental states are, in turn, circumstantially relevant to a material fact in issue. The Crown advances the following reasoning process:

(1) the identification of the killer is the ultimate material fact in issue in this trial;

(2) proof of motive is relevant to proof of identification: *Lewis v. The Queen* (1979), 47 CCC (2d) 24 at p. 35, 98 DLR (3d) 111, [1979] 2 SCR 821;

(3) it will be alleged that Mr. P was motivated to kill the deceased because he was enraged by and felt humiliated by her decision to leave him and to terminate

their relationship completely. Accordingly to the Crown, Mr. P killed the deceased as retribution for her decision to permanently sever their relationship;

(4) according to the Crown, the deceased's decision to permanently end their relationship is the event which triggered the motive which in turn led Mr. P to kill her;

(5) evidence of the deceased's fear of Mr. P, her dissatisfaction and unhappiness with the relationship, her decision to end that relationship, and her resolve to have nothing more to do with Mr. P, provide circumstantial evidence which is probative of the state of their relationship, her termination of that relationship, and the permanent nature of that termination from her point of view. These facts are, in turn, probative of the existence of the alleged motive although standing alone they do not establish the motive.

. . .

III. Are the Utterances Relevant?

Relevant evidence can be defined as evidence having any tendency to make the existence of any fact that is of consequence to the determination of the action more probable or less probable than it would be without the evidence: *Morris v. The Queen* [[1983] 2 SCR 190], *per* Lamer J, at pp. 103-5 (dissenting on another ground); Rule 401, *Federal Rules of Evidence* (1974), cited in *McCormick on Evidence*, 3rd ed. (1984), p. 1055; R. Delisle, *Evidence Principles and Problems*, 2nd ed. (1989), pp. 9-11.

In the case at bar, relevance has two aspects. Are the statements relevant to the deceased's state of mind in that they permit one to draw a reasonable conclusion as to her state of mind? If so, is her state of mind relevant directly or indirectly to the fact in issue?: *United States v. Brown*, 490 F.2d 758 at pp. 774-5 (1974) (1st Cir.). I have already indicated that the statements clear the first relevance hurdle.

Relevance is a matter of inductive logic requiring that the trial judge examine the proffered evidence in light of his own knowledge and understanding of human conduct: *McCormick, ibid.*, p. 544; *Delisle, ibid.*, p. 10. Relevance is situational and depends not only on the ultimate issue in the case (e.g., identification), but also on the other factual issues which either of the litigants raises as relevant to the ultimate issue. Consequently, the deceased's mental state may bear no direct relevance to the ultimate issue of identification but it will none the less be relevant to that issue if it is relevant to another fact (e.g., motive) which is directly relevant to the ultimate issue of identification.

In this case, the deceased's various mental states as described above make it more probable that her relationship with Mr. P was unsatisfactory to her, that she determined to end it, and that she, in fact, did end it on what, in her mind, was a permanent basis, than would be the case if there was no evidence of her state of mind. These facts, in turn, make it more probable that Mr. P had the motive ascribed to him by the Crown than would be the case without this evidence. By that, I mean the fact that his partner in the relationship was dissatisfied with the relationship, determined to end it, and had done so on what she believed to be a permanent basis, makes it more probable that the event which the Crown says precipitated Mr. P's motive (her departure and decision to permanently end the relationship) occurred. The occurrence of these events in turn makes it more probable that the motive existed than would be the case if the triggering event did not occur. This route to relevance does not depend on the accused knowing of the deceased's state of mind. If he is aware of her intentions, then the evidence has an added relevance and affords more direct proof of motive. The evidence of the utterances put before me does not prove Mr. P was aware of the deceased's state of mind, had formed the alleged motive, or that he acted as a result of that motive. Evidence may, however, be relevant even though it does not go directly to the proof of a material fact, or even alone provide the basis for an inference that the material fact exists. Evidence may become relevant by its combination with other evidence adduced in the case. Such is the essence of circumstantial evidence. The utterances of the deceased, in so far as they describe or permit a reasonable inference as to her state of mind in the period immediately preceding her disappearance, with respect to her view of her relationship with Mr. P, her determination to end that relationship, and her decision to sever all connection with Mr. P are legally relevant as a step along the road to proof of the motive alleged. Alone, however, they are not capable of proving motive and if at the end of the day the Crown's case has moved no further down the road to proof of motive, the evidence of the deceased's state of mind will have no probative value. My ruling presumes, as indicated by the Crown in argument, that there will be evidence which permits the further inferences necessary to prove motive.

· · ·

IV. Are the Utterances Excluded by Any Rule of Evidence?

Assuming relevance, evidence of utterances made by a deceased (although the rule is not limited to deceased persons) which evidence her state of mind are admissible. If the statements are explicit statements of a state of mind, they are admitted as exceptions to the hearsay rule. If those statements permit an inference as to the speaker's state of mind, they are regarded as original testimonial evidence and admitted as circumstantial evidence from which a state of mind can be inferred. The result is the same whichever route is taken, although circumstantial evidence of a state of mind poses added problems rising out of the inference drawing process: ...

I acknowledge that there is authority to the contrary, none of which is, however, binding on me, e.g., R v. Thomson, [1912] 3 KB 19.

· · ·

Evidence of the deceased's state of mind may, in turn, be relevant as circumstantial evidence that the deceased subsequently acted in accordance with that avowed state of mind. Where a deceased says, "I will go to Ottawa tomorrow," the statement affords direct evidence of the state of mind—an intention to go to Ottawa tomorrow—and circumstantial evidence that the deceased in fact went to Ottawa on that day. If either the state of mind, or the fact to be inferred from the existence of the state of mind is relevant, the evidence is receivable subject to objections based on undue prejudice. R v. Moore (1984), 15 CCC (3d) 541 at pp. 569-70 (Ont. CA); leave to appeal to the Supreme Court of Canada refused CCC loc. cit.; Home v. Corbeil [[1955] 4 DLR 750 (Ont HC)]; R v. McKenzie (1986), 32 CCC (3d) 527 at pp. 532-5 (BC CA); R v. Belowitz, an unreported judgment of Bowlby J released October 22, 1987, at pp. 8-11; R v. Maskery and Ditta [unreported, Ont HCJ, November 28, 1985]; McCormick, ibid., pp. 846-51; Mutual Life Ins. Co. v. Hillmon, 145 US 285 at p. 296 (1892); A. Sheppard, Evidence (1988), pp. 467-9.

An utterance indicating that a deceased had a certain intention or design will afford evidence that the deceased acted in accordance with that stated intention or plan where it is reasonable to infer that the deceased did so. The reasonableness of the inference will depend on a number of variables including the nature of the plan described in the utterance, and the proximity in time between the statement as to the plan and the proposed implementation of the plan.

The rules of evidence as developed to this point do not exclude evidence of utterances by a deceased which reveal her state of mind, but rather appear to provide specifically for their admission where relevant. The evidence is not, however, admissible to show the state of mind of persons other than the deceased (unless they were aware of the statements), or to show that persons other than the deceased acted in accordance with the deceased's stated intentions, save perhaps cases where the act was a joint one involving the deceased and another person. The evidence is also not admissible to establish that past acts or events referred to in the utterances occurred. *McCormick, ibid.*, pp. 845, 851-4; *Giles v. United States*, 432 A.2d 739 at pp. 745-6 (1981) (DC App.); *People v. Madson*, [638 P (2d) 18 (1981)]; *United States v. Brown, supra*, at pp. 762-3.

Before I turn to the final question, which is whether the accused has established that all or part of this evidence, though otherwise admissible, should be excluded because of its prejudicial potential, I will review the substance of the evidence proffered.

S.S., the sister of the deceased, had conversations with the deceased some time in 1987, during which the deceased expressed her dissatisfaction with her relationship with Mr. P, and her fear that Mr. P would report her to the immigration authorities. In these conversations, the deceased also said that Mr. P had taped her telephone calls, opened her mail, and required her to write letters of apology to Mr. P with promises of future good behaviour. These statements were made in the context of the deceased explaining her dissatisfaction with her relationship with Mr. P.

In January and February, 1988, S.S. spoke to her sister on a number of occasions. In January, her sister indicated that she intended to move out of the residence she shared with Mr. P. Later in February, after she had apparently moved out, she instructed her sister not to reveal her telephone number or her address to P and still later in the month of February, she indicated she was happy to be free of Mr. P and had no desire to ever see him again. The deceased indicated that she wished to start a new life without Mr. P. There was a final conversation on February 17, 1988, during which the deceased indicated she would meet her sister on February 21st to celebrate the beginning of her new life. She also indicated to her sister that she had told Mr. P that it was her intention to pick up her remaining belongings at Mr. P's residence.

The deceased also befriended one Robert Fisher in January, 1988. In late January, she told Mr. Fisher she intended to move out of Mr. P's residence. She also said that Mr. P treated her "like a slave." She went on to indicate that Mr. P was a jealous man who did not allow her to have friends, and who listened to her telephone conversations. The deceased said that Mr. P would tell people that she was not home, when in fact she was, and that he regularly threatened to turn her over to the Department of Immigration. The deceased advised Mr. Fisher that she was planning to leave Mr. P and to visit the Department of Immigration, presumably to pre-empt any efforts by Mr. P to put her immigration status in jeopardy.

Between February 15 and February 19, 1988, the deceased spoke to a friend, Ms. Kil. She indicated that she was not going to return to her boy-friend and that her new telephone number and address were not to be given to her boy-friend. Ms. Kil did not know the identity of the boy-friend.

In February, 1988, the deceased spoke to Sabrina Dao, also a friend, and told her not to give her telephone number or address to Mr. P.

In late January, 1988, the deceased spoke to a person named Peter Carpenter and told him that she planned to move to a new residence in Scarborough.

Beginning with the last utterance first, the statement to Mr. Carpenter clearly comes within the rule which permits statements going to evidence, a plan or design on the part of the speaker. The statement also affords evidence that the deceased did move. The statements to Ms. Dao and Ms. Kil constitute circumstantial evidence from which a trier of fact could infer that as of the dates of those conversations, the deceased had formed a fixed intention to remain permanently away from Mr. P and to keep Mr. P out of her life.

The deceased's statements to Mr. Fisher in January, 1988, also constitute evidence of the deceased's intention, design or plan to leave Mr. P. They go much further in that they provide detail as to why she had reached that decision. In providing that detail, her utterances refer to prior conduct on the part of Mr. P. Clearly, the statements are not admissible to prove that Mr. P engaged in that prior conduct. Their inadmissibility for that purpose does not, however, render them any less relevant as evidence of the deceased's state of mind: *United States v. Brown, supra,* at p. 763.

The statement to S.S. on February 17, 1988, evidences that the deceased was happy to have left Mr. P and determined to remain separate from him. The earlier statements to S.S. in February, 1988, also provide evidence of the deceased's determination to permanently terminate her relationship with Mr. P.

The statement to S.S. in January, 1988, regarding the deceased's intention to move out of Mr. P's residence is a classic familiar example of a statement showing intention or design which is admissible both to show the intention and design and as evidence that the speaker followed through with that intention or design.

The statements made some time in 1987 to S.S. go to show the deceased's dissatisfaction with her relationship with Mr. P. They also contain considerable detail concerning conduct which Mr. P allegedly engaged in which led to the deceased's dissatisfaction. While these statements may come within the rules which permit statements going to a speaker's state of mind, they are significantly less probative in that they relate to a state of mind at some point in 1987, rather than a state of mind in January and February, 1988. Some of the comments made in 1987 also describe discreditable conduct on the part of Mr. P. The evidence is, of course, not admissible to prove that those events occurred.

V. Should Any of the Utterances Be Excluded Because of Their Prejudicial Potential?

A trial judge may, in his discretion, exclude evidence which is otherwise admissible where the potential prejudicial effect of that evidence outweighs its potential probative force: *R v. B. (C.R.)* (1990), 55 CCC (3d) 1, [1990] 1 SCR 717; *R v. D. (L.E.)* (1989), 50 CCC (3d) 142 at pp. 156-7, [1989] 2 SCR 111; *R v. Potvin* (1989), 47 CCC (3d) 289 at pp. 313-5, [1989] 1 SCR 525, *per* La Forest J.

Prejudice can refer to several things. In the context of this case, it means the danger, despite instructions to the contrary, that the jury will use the evidence of the deceased's utterances for purposes other than drawing inferences and conclusions as to her state of mind and as to her subsequent conduct. In particular, the jury may infer from some of the utterances that Mr. P was a tyrannical person, obsessed with controlling the deceased even to the extent of engaging in illegal and bizarre conduct. From that, they may infer that he is the sort of person who would kill someone who dared challenge his authority over that person. This line of reasoning, while not illogical, is not permitted: *R v. D. (L.E.)*, *supra*, at p. 157.

The balancing process envisioned by the claim that prejudicial potential outweighs probative potential is no longer designed only to root out the most extreme cases where prejudicial potential is "grave" and probative value is "trifling": *R v. Wray*, [1970] 4 CCC 1 at p. 17, 11 DLR (3d) 673, [1971] SCR 272. The onus, however, is on the accused to demonstrate that the balance favours exclusion of otherwise admissible evidence. Where the prejudice asserted rests in the potential misuse of the evidence by the jury, one's assessment of the jury's ability to properly follow directions will play a key role in determining whether the accused has shown that the balance favours exclusion. Views as to the jury's ability to follow the law rather than their instincts or prejudices differ: *R v. Corbett* (1988), 41 CCC (3d) 385 at pp. 403 and 426, [1988] 1 SCR 670; *Shepard v. United States*, 290 US 96 at p. 104 (1933); *People v. Hamilton*, 362 P.2d 473 at pp. 481 and 478 (1961); *R v. Belowitz*, *supra*, at pp. 20-1. I incline to the view that lawyers and judges tend to underestimate the intellectual power and discipline of juries.

In determining where the balances lies in this case, I adopt the approach detailed by Mr. Marc Rosenberg in his most enlightening paper, "Rationalizing the Rules of Evidence: The Supreme Court Revolution," delivered in November, 1989, to the Ontario Criminal Lawyers Association annual convention. Mr. Rosenberg writes at p. 49:

> [T]he steps which the trial judge must go through are as follows:
>
> 1. The judge must determine the probative value of the evidence by assessing its tendency to prove a fact in issue in the case including the credibility of witnesses.
>
> 2. The judge must determine the prejudicial effect of the evidence because of its tendency to prove matters which are not in issue [or I add because of the risk that the jury may use the evidence improperly to prove a fact in issue].
>
> 3. The judge must balance the probative value against the prejudicial effect having regard to the importance of the issues for which the evidence is legitimately offered against the risk that the jury will use it for other improper purposes, taking into account the effectiveness of any limiting instructions.

The American case-law reveals an extensive experience in balancing probative force against prejudicial effect in cases where utterances of the deceased victim are tendered by the Crown through other witnesses, e.g., see *United States v. Brown*, *supra*, at pp. 764-6 and 773-81, and cases referred to therein. These authorities pronounce an approach which is consistent with Mr. Rosenberg's. They also recognize the editing of potentially prejudicial and otherwise irrelevant parts of the utterances as a means short of exclusion which may reduce the potential prejudice to a tolerable level: *United States v. Brown*, *supra*, at p. 779; *People v. Madson*, *supra*, at p. 31, note 16.

Following that approach, I conclude:

(1) The utterances made in 1987 are not of great probative value. They refer not to any plan or design, but to a state of mind existing in 1987. While a state of mind in 1987 may have some value in determining the deceased's state of mind in January and February, 1988, that value is limited. The statements in this case are also rendered redundant for that purpose in that there are several statements alleged to have been made in January and February, 1988, which speak to the deceased's state of mind at that time. Some of the 1987 statements also refer to the prior conduct of Mr. P. As I have indicated, that conduct is such that the jury could draw the conclusion that Mr. P was a possessive tyrant, determined to control the deceased at all costs. There is a high risk that the jury would use this evidence for the improper purpose of concluding that Mr. P had acted improperly and bizarrely towards the deceased in the past and that he was therefore disposed to act in the same manner towards her when she left him. The balance favours exclusion of these utterances.

(2) The statements made in January and February, 1988, have considerable probative potential both as they relate to the deceased's state of mind and as circumstantial evidence that she had terminated her relationship with Mr. P on a permanent basis. The statements made to SS in January and February, 1988, carry little, if any, potential for prejudice to the accused. The same is true of the statements made to Ms. Kil, Ms. Dao and Mr. Carpenter. The balance favours admission of these utterances.

(3) The utterances made to Mr. Fisher in January, 1988, have considerable probative potential in the same way as the statements made to other witnesses in January and February, 1988. The utterances to Fisher were, however, combined with statements as to what Mr. P had done to the deceased in the past. These parts of the utterances have considerable potential to prejudice the case against Mr. P for the same reasons as set out in respect to the 1987 utterances. I propose to dissect the deceased's utterances to Mr. Fisher so as to differentiate for admissibility purposes between her utterances which reveal her state of mind and her statements as to the conduct of the accused which, according to her, precipitated that state of mind. I will admit her statements to the effect that she planned to leave Mr. P's residence, and her statements that her plans to leave his residence and her plans to go to the Department of Immigration were to remain a secret. I will not permit evidence through Mr. Fisher of the deceased's statements concerning Mr. P's treatment of her and his conduct towards her. In particular, her reference to P treating her "like a slave" will not be admitted nor will the evidence concerning P's interference with her privacy.

NOTES AND QUESTIONS

The accused was, after three trials, convicted as charged. See *R v Pan; R v Sawyer*, 2001 SCC 42, [2001] 2 SCR 344, 200 DLR (4th) 577.

How does Doherty J's view of this exception differ from the American and English views?

The statement of intention exception was modified in *R v Starr*, which is reproduced in Section III.B, below.

F. Statements by Parties

A statement by a party offered by an opposing party is admissible for its truth. This exception should not be confused with the exception for statements against interest, discussed in

Section II.B, above; nor should it be confused with formal admissions made in pleadings, in the course of a guilty plea, or pursuant to s 655 of the *Criminal Code* (see Chapter 10, Section I.A). In his helpful and entertaining *Irreverent Introduction to Hearsay* (American Bar Association, 1977) at 23-24, Irving Younger offered the following formal definition of a party admission: "An admission is a statement made or an act done by a party to a lawsuit which is or which amounts to a prior acknowledgement that some fact is not as he now claims it to be." He then suggested the following "trial lawyer's rule of thumb … *Anything the other side ever said or did will be admissible so long as it has something to do with the case.*"

The statements of the accused person in criminal proceedings are the subject of special rules of admissibility, discussed in Chapter 8, below. However, the statements of parties to civil proceedings are not subject to those rules. In *Yorkton Agricultural & Industrial Exhibition Association Ltd v Morley* (1967), 66 DLR (2d) 37 (Sask CA), the eight-year-old defendant and his friends burned down the plaintiff's barn. The only evidence as to the cause of the fire came from statements that they made to a police officer and an insurance adjuster. The trial judge held that the defendant had to show that the defendant's statements were voluntary, as if he was an accused person in a criminal proceeding. The Court of Appeal disagreed with this approach. Brownridge JA, Maguire JA concurring, held in *obiter dicta* that the limits on the admissibility of confessions in criminal proceedings were not applicable in civil proceedings. Hall JA, concurring in the result, held that the young age of the defendant might go to the weight to be attached to his statement, but did not affect its admissibility. The plaintiff's action was dismissed on other grounds.

The exception for statements by a party may be motivated by the theory that a statement against a party's interest is more likely to be reliable than a self-serving statement by a party, but, perhaps more importantly, the exception is motivated by the adversarial nature of the common law trial. In *R v Evans*, [1993] 3 SCR 653, 85 CCC (3d) 97, Sopinka J explained this idea as follows:

> [I]n lieu of seeking independent circumstantial guarantees of trustworthiness, it is sufficient that the evidence is tendered against a party. Its admissibility rests on the theory of the adversary system that what a party has previously stated can be admitted against the party in whose mouth it does not lie to complain of the unreliability of his or her own statements. As stated by Morgan, "[a] party can hardly object that he had no opportunity to cross-examine himself or that he is unworthy of credence save when speaking under sanction of oath" (Morgan, "Basic Problems of Evidence" ([American Law Institute,] 1963), pp. 265-6, quoted in *McCormick on Evidence* [(4th ed. 1992, vol. 2], p. 140). The rule is the same for both criminal and civil cases subject to the special rules governing confessions which apply in criminal cases.

For a discussion of the admissibility of statements by agents for a corporation against the corporation, see *R v Strand Electric Ltd*, [1969] 1 OR 190, [1969] 2 CCC 264 (CA).

G. Business Records

At common law, the following exception was available to make business records admissible:

> Statements made by a deceased person in the course of his duty and in the ordinary routine of his business are admissible in certain circumstances. To be admissible on this ground the statement must (1) relate to some act or transaction performed by the person making it in the ordinary

course of his business and duty; (2) be made in the ordinary course of his business under a duty to make it; and (3) be made at or near the time at which the act or transaction to which it relates was performed.

(15 *Halsbury's Laws of England* (3rd ed) at para. 555.)

In most Canadian jurisdictions, the common law business records exception has been overtaken by statutory exceptions. See e.g. *Canada Evidence Act*, RSC 1985, c C-5, ss 29, 30, 31; *Evidence Act*, RSBC 1996, c 124, s 42; *Manitoba Evidence Act*, CCSM c E150, s 49; *Evidence Act*, RSNS 1989, c 154, s 23; *Evidence Act*, RSO 1990, c E.23, ss 31, 33, 34, 35; *Evidence Act*, RSPEI 1988, c E-11, s 32; and *Evidence Act*, SS 2006, c E-11.2, s 50.

In Alberta, which still lacks a statutory business records exception, the Court of Appeal has defined the common law business records exception as follows (*R v Monkhouse*, 1987 ABCA 227, [1988] 1 WWR 725 at 732):

In his useful book, *Documentary Evidence in Canada* (Carswell Co., 1984), Mr. J.D. Ewart summarizes the common law rule after the decision in *Ares v. Venner* [excerpted in Section III.A, below] as follows at p. 54:

[T]he modern rule can be said to make admissible a record containing (i) an original entry (ii) made contemporaneously (iii) in the routine (iv) of business (v) by a recorder with personal knowledge of the thing recorded as a result of having done or observed or formulated it (vi) who had a duty to make the record and (vii) who had no motive to misrepresent. Read in this way, the rule after *Ares* does reflect a more modern, realistic approach for the common law to take towards business duty records.

To this summary, I would respectfully make one modification. The "original entry" need not have been made personally by a recorder with knowledge of the thing recorded. ... it is sufficient if the recorder is functioning in the usual and ordinary course of a system in effect for the preparation of business records.

For a thorough discussion of the relationship between statutory and common law hearsay exceptions for business records, see *R v Wilcox*, 2001 NSCA 45, 152 CCC (3d) 157.

SOME QUESTIONS ABOUT THE EXCEPTIONS

1. Is there any pattern or logic to the exceptions to the rule against hearsay that we have considered so far?

2. Does the rationale for each of the common law exceptions deal adequately with the hearsay dangers?

3. If you were drafting a statutory restatement of the law of hearsay, would you adopt any or all of the common law exceptions we have considered?

4. If you were a judge, what arguments would persuade you to create a new common law exception?

III. THE PRINCIPLED APPROACH TO HEARSAY

Given the seemingly arbitrary and ad hoc development of the hearsay exceptions at common law, it has often been suggested that some sort of rationalization of the exceptions should be undertaken. In this section of the materials, we consider the extent to which the Supreme Court of Canada has undertaken such a rationalization.

A. Intimations of Reform

Myers v Director of Public Prosecutions
[1965] AC 1001, [1964] 2 All ER 881 (HL) (footnotes omitted)
Lord Reid, Lord Morris of Borth-y-Gest, Lord Hodson, Lord Pearce, and
Lord Donovan (17 June 1964)

LORD REID: My Lords, the appellant was convicted, together with another man, on several counts relating to the theft of motor cars. His scheme was to buy for small sums, but, curiously, not very small sums, wrecked cars together with their log books issued by the local authorities on registration. Having bought a wrecked car he then stole a car as nearly as possible identical with the wrecked car and proceeded to disguise the stolen car so that it corresponded in every respect with the particulars of the wrecked car noted in its log book. He could then, as he thought, safely sell the disguised stolen car together with the genuine log book of the wrecked car.

The log book contains a chassis number and an engine number, and these had therefore to be transferred, together with the wrecked car's number plates, from it to the stolen car. As the chassis number and engine number appear on small plates which can be detached from the chassis or engine it was not difficult to substitute the genuine chassis and number plates taken from the wrecked car for those on the stolen car.

But a great deal of evidence of various kinds was adduced against the appellant in a trial which lasted, I think, 29 days, and the appellant was shown to be involved in the thefts of nearly 20 cars. Owners of the stolen cars identified the disguised cars as their cars by dents, scratches or other features. The appellant's defence was that he had rebuilt the wrecked cars which he bought and had had nothing to do with the stolen cars. This was contradicted by the evidence of expert insurance assessors, who had examined some of the wrecked cars before they were written off and sold to the appellant and who testified that for various reasons the disguised cars could not possibly be the wrecked cars rebuilt. In some cases the stolen cars had been repainted to correspond with the colour of the wrecked car and in these cases there was evidence that below the paint of the disguised car there was paint of the original colour of the stolen car. And in premises occupied by the appellant there had been found number plates and other parts of the stolen cars which had been discarded in the process of disguising them.

But there was also very cogent evidence in the case of a few cars derived from records kept by Austins, the manufacturers, at their Longbridge Works, and the question of law in this case is whether that evidence was rightly admitted. It appeared that when each car is being assembled it is accompanied by a card on which it is the duty of the workman concerned to copy particulars of the car. So there is copied on to the card the chassis number and the engine number which the workman sees on the car. But there is also another number, known as the block number, which is indelibly stamped on the engine: and this, too, is entered on the card. These cards were photographed on to microfilms and then destroyed and the microfilms were produced by a witness responsible for these records who also transcribed the particulars from the microfilms. If these records were admissible evidence they proved that when a particular car left the works it bore three particular numbers—the chassis and engine numbers on detachable plates and the block number. But when the disguised car was examined it bore two numbers which the records showed belonged to the wrecked car and one, the block number, which the records showed belonged to the stolen car. As the latter number was incapable of alteration this evidence proved conclusively that the disguised car was the stolen car and not the wrecked car rebuilt.

The reason why this evidence is maintained to have been inadmissible is that its cogency depends on hearsay. The witness could only say that a record made by someone else showed that, if the record was correctly made, a car had left the works bearing three particular numbers. He could not prove that the record was correct or that the numbers which it contained were in fact the numbers on the car when it was made. This is a highly technical point, but the law regarding hearsay evidence is technical, and I would say absurdly technical. So I must consider whether in the existing state of the law that objection to the admissibility of this evidence must prevail.

. . .

I have never taken a narrow view of the functions of this House as an appellate tribunal. The common law must be developed to meet changing economic conditions and habits of thought, and I would not be deterred by expressions of opinion in this House in old cases. But there are limits to what we can or should do. If we are to extend the law it must be by the development and application of fundamental principles. We cannot introduce arbitrary conditions or limitations: that must be left to legislation. And if we do in effect change the law, we ought in my opinion only to do that in cases where our decision will produce some finality or certainty. If we disregard technicalities in this case and seek to apply principle and common sense, there are a number of other parts of the existing law of hearsay susceptible of similar treatment, and we shall probably have a series of appeals in cases where the existing technical limitations produce an unjust result. If we are to give a wide interpretation to our judicial functions questions of policy cannot be wholly excluded, and it seems to me to be against public policy to produce uncertainty. The only satisfactory solution is by legislation following on a wide survey of the whole field, and I think that such a survey is overdue. A policy of make do and mend is no longer adequate. The most powerful argument of those who support the strict doctrine of precedent is that if it is relaxed judges will be tempted to encroach on the proper field of the legislature, and this case to my mind offers a strong temptation to do that which ought to be resisted. I must now explain why I think that to hold this evidence competent would be to change the law.

[Lord Reid therefore held that the records should not have been received into evidence. He nonetheless upheld the conviction on the basis of the proviso in s 4(1) of the *Criminal Appeal Act* of 1907, which is similar to s 686(1)(b)(iii) of the Canadian *Criminal Code*.]

LORD PEARCE: My Lords, the evidence whose admission is the ground of complaint was fair, clear, reliable and sensible. The question is whether the court was bound by a technical rule to exclude it. No one doubts that the general exclusion of hearsay evidence, subject to exceptions permitted where common sense and the pursuit of truth demand it, is an important and valuable principle. But it is a disservice to that general principle if the courts limit the necessary exceptions so rigidly that the general rule creates a frequent and unnecessary injustice. This case is of importance since a similar situation may arise, not only in the many cases of car-stealing but also in cases of long firm frauds, hire-purchase frauds and the like.

. . .

In the present case, if the anonymous workman who copied down the number could be proved to be dead, the records would be admissible as declarations in the course of duty. Since we do not know whether he is dead or not, the court, it is argued, cannot inform itself from the records; but in this case the fact that he is not on oath and is not subject to cross-examination has no practical importance whatever. It would be no advantage, if he could have been identified, to put him on oath and cross-examine him about one out of many hundreds of repetitious and routine entries made three years before. He could say that to the best of his belief the number was correct; but everybody already knows that. If he pretends to any memory in the matter, he is untruthful; but, even if he is, that in no way reflects on whether he copied down a number correctly in the day's work three years before. Nor is it of any importance how he answers the routine question in cross-examination: "You may have made a mistake?" Everybody knows that he may have made a mistake. The jury knew it without being told, the judge told them so at least once and both counsel told them so, probably more than once. The only questions that could helpfully be asked on the matter were whether the particular system of recording was good and whether in practice it had been found prone to error. These questions could not be answered by the individual workman but they could be dealt with by Mr. Legg if the defence wished to probe into the matter. He and not the workmen would know how efficient the system had been found in practice and how often, if at all, it had been shown subsequently that mis-recordings must have occurred. The evidence produced is therefore as good as evidence on this point can be; it is the best evidence, though it is of course subject, like every other man-made record, to the admitted universal human frailty of occasional clerical error. The fact that the engine and chassis numbers which emanated from precisely the same source are admissible because they have been embodied in a public document, namely the log-book, shows up the absurdity of excluding these records. Has the machinery of justice really got itself into such a position that it must blind its eyes to the truth in such a situation? It is indeed a sad thing if it must condemn an accused by excluding evidence that to eyes of any reasonable man would prove his innocence. For the same situation would arise and the same technicality would be a bar, if the accused could have proved by Austin's records (if they had been admissible) that the car was not stolen, in spite of deceptive human evidence to the contrary. It is no answer to say that in such a case a prosecution would not be brought as things are today. It cannot be right that the prosecution should shoulder a duty not to prosecute in doubtful cases on the ground that it knows that the court will not give the accused a fair trial, but will exclude vital evidence in his favour.

I use the words machinery of justice, because the question how far a court will admit evidence and what weight it will give to it is part of the judicial process. It is the method of extracting the truth to which the law is to be applied and it cannot be considered *in vacuo* without regard to social conditions. The main argument against any change in principles of law is not applicable to the method of ascertaining the truth. When principles of law are disturbed, many persons who have ordered their affairs on the basis of existing legal authority may suffer injustice. There may be unforeseen repercussions in other branches of the law which may lead to confusion and injustices. The admission of records such as those in question can produce no such effect and lead to no injustice.

Either the total admission of hearsay or its total exclusion would lead to injustice and inefficiency in the search for truth. Professor Wigmore, in his book on *Evidence* (3rd ed. vol. 5, p. 27, quoted in Cross, 2nd ed., p. 383) was of opinion that the rule has been over-enforced and abused and concluded that "the problem for the coming generation is to preserve the fundamental value of the rule, while allowing the amplest exceptions to it and abstaining from petty meticulous exceptions."

There is not now and never has been a rule for the *total* exclusion of hearsay without exception. Originally hearsay was usual and admissible. Through the sixteenth and the earlier part of the seventeenth centuries there was no objection to it. But in the later seventeenth century objections to it grew and by the early eighteenth century there was a general exclusion of hearsay evidence, with certain exceptions. There was a transitional period when such evidence was accepted as confirmatory though not as sufficient by itself. And during the eighteenth century some hearsay, namely, evidence of prior statements by a witness, might be accepted to confirm the testimony of that witness. The courts were gradually working out their own compromises to obtain satisfactory machinery for handling evidence and ascertaining the truth. They were adopting the hearsay rule in general with such adaptations and exceptions as would make it work and conduce to just decisions.

This process of improvement and evolution was carried out by the inherent power of the courts to conduct its process so as to prevent abuse and secure justice. I see no reason why at some stage the courts should decide that evolution was now complete and that thereafter no further change must occur, however great the absurdity or injustice.

[Lord Pearce considered some American and English cases, and continued:]

I find it impossible to accept that there is any "dangerous uncertainty" caused by obvious and sensible improvements in the means by which the court arrives at the truth. One is entitled to choose between the individual conflicting *obiter dicta* of two great judges and I prefer that of Jessel MR. His dictum was as follows, *Sugden v. Lord St. Leonards*, (1876) 1 PD 154, 241:

> Now I take it the principle which underlies all these exceptions is the same. In the first place, the case must be one in which it is difficult to obtain other evidence, for no doubt the ground for admitting the exceptions was that very difficulty. In the next place the declarant must be disinterested; that is, disinterested in the sense that the declaration was not made in favour of his interest. And, thirdly, the declaration must be made before dispute or litigation, so that it was made without bias on account of the existence of a dispute or litigation which the declarant might be supposed to favour. Lastly, and this appears to me one of the strongest

reasons for admitting it, the declarant must have had peculiar means of knowledge not possessed in ordinary cases.

On that expression of principle he admitted the extension which has been acted on ever
since in the Probate Division.

That, I respectfully think, is the correct method of approach, particularly to a problem
that deals with the court's method of ascertaining truth. As new situations arise it adapts
its practice to deal with the situation in accordance with the basic and established principles which lie beneath the practice. To exalt the practice above the principle would be
to surrender to formalism. Since this branch of the law is so untidy, there is but little
appeal in "the demon of formalism which tempts the intellect with the lure of scientific
order."

· · ·

If your Lordships accept the appellant's argument in this case and thus, for the first
time, establish by direct authority that such records may not be admitted, it will fasten
the shackles of rigidity and formalism more firmly on this branch of the law of evidence
and repress the practice which has been developed by the good sense of the judges. Surely
"the better course is to recognise the existence of a residual exception as an umbrella
under which there can be collected evidence of all those facts which, from their very
nature, can only be established in a court of law if the hearsay rule is violated. The requisite conditions of admissibility can surely be left to the good sense of the judges." (*Cross
on Evidence*, 2nd ed., p. 457.)

· · ·

There are on balance strong grounds for admitting the evidence in this case. The evidence is clear and cogent on a vital issue in the case. It is the *best* evidence. There is no
authority directed to this point which binds your lordships to exclude it. The basic principles which have found expression in other sets of circumstances clearly justify it and
demand expression in this class of case also. The admission of this evidence is in accordance with a certain degree of practice which is fair and sensible. Its admission cannot
disturb or offend any existing legal principles. In so far as the admission throws up by
contract some exclusion in some other class of case as being anomalous, that is no disadvantage. The development of this branch of the law has always been sporadic.

In my opinion, where the person, who from his own knowledge made business records,
cannot be found, and where a business produces by some proper servant, who can speak
with knowledge to the method and system of record-keeping, its records reliably kept in
the ordinary way of business, they should be admitted as *prima facie* evidence. I say reliably kept because the judge must clearly have a discretion to exclude from a jury (as he
would reject from his own mind in adjudicating) records so ill-kept as not to be worthy
of credit. If any question arose about that, he could hear evidence or argument about it
in the absence of the jury, as is done for instance in the case of confessions.

· · ·

[Lord Morris of Borth-y-Gest and Lord Hodson agreed with Lord Reid in separate
speeches. Lord Donovan agreed with Lord Pearce. The majority of the House thus held
that the evidence should have been excluded. Nonetheless, the House unanimously agreed
with Lord Reid's application of the proviso, and dismissed Myers's appeal.]

QUESTIONS

1. Would the evidence excluded here be admissible in Canada under s 30 of the *Canada Evidence Act*? Would it make a difference if the records were stored in a computer database?

2. What effect would the adoption of Lord Pearce's proposed approach have on the law of hearsay?

Ares v Venner
[1970] SCR 608, 14 DLR (3d) 4
Abbott, Martland, Ritchie, Hall, and Spence JJ (28 April 1970)

HALL J: The appellant who was 21 years of age at the time and a student of Arts at St. John's College, Edmonton, was skiing in Jasper Park on the afternoon of February 21, 1965. At about 4:00 p.m. that afternoon he fell and sustained a severe comminuted fracture of both the tibia and fibula of his right leg some five or six inches below the knee. The Ski Patrol came to his assistance, and after applying a pneumatic splint took him to the Seton Hospital in Jasper. This hospital was being operated by the Sisters of Charity of St. Vincent de Paul.

On being admitted to the hospital, he came under the care of the respondent, Dr. Albert Venner, a specialist in internal medicine who was in general medical practice in Jasper at that time. The appellant was taken to an operating room and while under a general anesthetic the fracture was reduced by Dr. Venner and a plaster cast applied by him which extended from the toes to the upper thigh. This procedure was completed by about 6:00 p.m.

The learned trial judge summarized the events of the next four days as follows:

On Monday morning, the plaintiff was visited by Dr. Venner. The nurse's record indicates that at 8:00 p.m. the cast was split approximately eight inches and that the plaintiff's toes were numb, swollen and blue and that there was no movement in the toes. The plaintiff experienced the usual pain attributable to a fracture. He advised both the doctor and nurses on Monday evening that he had no feeling in his foot, he could not move his toes nor could he feel pinpricks or pinching. He said his leg was in pain and his toes were swollen and blue.

Dr. Venner in splitting the cast at eight o'clock did so for the purpose of examining the plaintiff's foot. The plaintiff's condition continued the same on Tuesday except that in addition to the other symptoms I have mentioned, his toes were cool.

On Wednesday, Dr. Venner split the cast to the knee and examined the plaintiff's leg. The plaintiff's condition was somewhat the same as previously, at best. On Wednesday evening, the cast was split its entire length. During the night, Dr. Venner visited the plaintiff on two occasions. He decided to send the plaintiff to Edmonton and this was done on Thursday, February 25th.

During the plaintiff's time in hospital his condition, to say the least, had not improved from Monday.

[Hall J reviewed the evidence concerning the treatment given to the plaintiff in Edmonton. The plaintiff's leg was amputated below the knee on 5 April 1965. Hall J continued:]

The appellant took action against Dr. Venner, Seton Hospital and the Sisters of Charity of St. Vincent de Paul claiming negligence on the part of Dr. Venner, the hospital and the Sisters of Charity as operators of the hospital. The action was tried by O'Byrne J who found Dr. Venner negligent and gave judgment against him for $29,407.13. The action against the hospital and the Sisters of Charity was dismissed. An appeal was taken to the Appellate Division of the Supreme Court of Alberta by Dr. Venner. The appellant cross-appealed against the hospital. The Appellate Division allowed the appeal and set aside the judgment of O'Byrne J and directed a new trial as to Dr. Venner. The cross-appeal against the hospital was dismissed. The appellant has appealed to this court against the order for the new trial. The respondent Venner has cross-appealed, claiming dismissal of the action rather than a new trial as ordered by the Appellate Division. Neither the hospital nor the Sisters of Charity are now parties to this appeal.

[The trial judge found that "the classic signs or symptoms of circulatory impairment manifested themselves clearly and early" and that Dr. Venner's treatment of the fracture was negligent.]

The main issue in the Appellate Division was as to the admissibility of notes made by the nurses who attended the appellant while he was in Seton Hospital. These notes were tendered in evidence as part of Dr. Venner's discovery evidence which was being read into the record on behalf of the appellant at the trial. Counsel for Dr. Venner objected to the notes being received in evidence, but they were admitted by O'Byrne J as being an exception to the hearsay rule. In receiving the evidence, O'Byrne J said:

> Well, I understand now your (defendant's counsel) objection but it strikes me at this time without having read the authorities that if you are not satisfied with the contents of this hospital record that it's up to you to call such evidence as you may wish to call to correct, amplify or amplify as you determine. It seems to me that what Mr. Veale was seeking to do is clearly within the authorities that he has quoted to me and I admit the records as Exhibit 6.

[A]nd in his judgment he said:

> I note that the nurses from the Seton Hospital were here during the three days of trial. No one called them. They were available to all. They were brought here at the plaintiff's expense. This impresses me, and strengthens my reception of the notes as being "generally trustwor-thy" to use the term from *Wigmore on Evidence*, cited by plaintiff's counsel on the first day of trial.

[The Appellate Division held that the nurses' notes were inadmissible hearsay and ordered a new trial.]

[Hall J reviewed the speeches from *Myers*, extracted above, and continued:]

Although the views of Lords Donovan and Pearce are those of the minority in *Myers*, I am of opinion that this court should adopt and follow the minority view rather than resort to saying in effect: "This judge-made law needs to be restated to meet modern conditions, but we must leave it to Parliament and the ten legislatures to do the job."

Hospital records, including nurses' notes, made contemporaneously by someone having a personal knowledge of the matters then being recorded and under a duty to make the entry or record should be received in evidence as *prima facie* proof of the facts stated therein. This should, in no way, preclude a party wishing to challenge the accuracy of the records or entries from doing so. Had the respondent here wanted to challenge the accuracy of the nurses' notes, the nurses were present in court and available to be called as witnesses if the respondent had so wished.

I would, accordingly, allow the appeal and restore the judgment of O'Byrne J with costs here and in the Appellate Division. The cross-appeal should be dismissed with costs.

NOTES AND QUESTIONS

The following sample of the nurses' notes at issue in *Ares v Venner* is taken from the Appellate Division's decision (1969), 70 WWR 96 at 104 (Alta SCAD):

Date & Hour	Medicines & Nourishment	Treatment and Remarks
Feb 24/65		
11-7		Awake on initial rounds Circ'n (R) toes checked. Toes cool to touch. Sole of foot blue. Still unable to wiggle toes. Swelling still apparent but toes blanching well. Routine night care given pt'n. Slept well most of night.
		J. Westman
Feb 25/65		
11-7	12 M	(R) Toes cold & greyish-white. Foot cool. Dr. Venner notified and visited. Foot lowered. Circulation improved. Color returning to toes, blanching slowly. 1 a.m. Toes remain cold. Color bluish pink. Blanching. 2 a.m. Circulation (R) foot & toes improving.
		J. Westman

1. Is there an argument to be made that the notes were not hearsay at all?

2. What is the precise ratio of *Ares v Venner*? Does the court adopt Lord Pearce's reasoning from *Myers*, or is the case decided on a narrower basis?

3. Since the burden of proof was on the plaintiff, why should the onus have been on the defendant to call the nurses as witnesses for the purpose of challenging their notes?

B. The Supreme Court's Revolution

R v Khan

[1990] 2 SCR 531, 59 CCC (3d) 92

Lamer CJ and Wilson, Sopinka, Gonthier, and McLachlin JJ (13 September 1990)

McLACHLIN J: ...

[For the facts of this case, see Chapter 2, Section I.C.]

2. Did the Trial Judge Err in Rejecting the Mother's Statement of What the Child Told Her After the Incident?

Fifteen minutes after leaving Dr. Khan's office, in response to her mother's query, "So you were talking to Dr. Khan, were you?," T. told her mother about the sexual act the doctor had performed on her. The issue is whether the mother's statement of what she was told is admissible in evidence. The trial judge rejected the statement, holding that it was hearsay and did not fall within any of the established exceptions to the hearsay rule, and in particular the spontaneous declaration exception. The Court of Appeal held that the statement should have been received on the ground that the inherent reliability of the child's statement was such that the usual requirements for spontaneous declarations of contemporaneity and intensity or pressure should be relaxed.

I am satisfied that applying the traditional tests for spontaneous declarations, the trial judge correctly rejected the mother's statement. The statement was not contemporaneous, being made 15 minutes after leaving the doctor's office and probably one-half hour after the offence was committed. Nor was it made under pressure or emotional intensity which would give the guarantee of reliability upon which the spontaneous declaration rule has traditionally rested. The question then is the extent to which, if at all, the strictures of the hearsay rule should be relaxed in the case of children's testimony. The issue is one of great importance in view of the increasing number of prosecutions for sexual offences against children and the hardships that often attend requiring children to retell and relive the frequently traumatic events surrounding the episode in a long series of encounters with parents, social workers, police and finally different levels of courts.

The hearsay rule has traditionally been regarded as an absolute rule, subject to various categories of exceptions, such as admissions, dying declarations, declarations against interest and spontaneous declarations. While this approach has provided a degree of certainty to the law on hearsay, it has frequently proved unduly inflexible in dealing with new situations and new needs in the law. This has resulted in courts in recent years on occasion adopting a more flexible approach, rooted in the principle and the policy underlying the hearsay rule rather than the strictures of traditional exceptions.

[McLachlin J referred to *Myers v Director of Public Prosecutions*, [1965] AC 1001 (HL) and *Ares v Venner*, [1970] SCR 608, and continued:]

Lord Pearce's four tests may be resumed in two general requirements: necessity and reliability. The child's statement to the mother in this case meets both these general requirements as well as the more specific tests. Necessity was present, other evidence of the event, as the trial judge found, being inadmissible. The situation was one where, to borrow Lord Pearce's phrase, it was difficult to obtain other evidence. The evidence also bore strong *indicia* of reliability. T. was disinterested, in the sense that her declaration was not made in favour of her interest. She made the declaration before any suggestion of litigation. And beyond doubt she possessed peculiar means of knowledge of the event of which she told her mother. Moreover, the evidence of a child of tender years on such matters may bear its own special stamp of reliability. As Robins JA stated in the Court of Appeal (at p. 210):

> Where the declarant is a child of tender years and the alleged event involves a sexual offence, special considerations come into play in determining the admissibility of the child's statement. This is so because young children of the age with which we are concerned here are generally not adept at reasoned reflection or at fabricating tales of sexual perversion. They, manifestly, are unlikely to use their reflective powers to concoct a deliberate untruth, and particularly one about a sexual act which in all probability is beyond their ken.

Because of the frequent difficulty of obtaining other evidence and because of the lack of reason to doubt many statements children make on sexual abuse to others, courts in the United States have moved toward relaxing the requirements of admissibility for such statements. This has been done in the context of the doctrine of spontaneous declarations. In *McCormick on Evidence*, 3rd ed. (1984), at p. 859 the authors refer to this development as the "tender years" exception to the general rule, and describe it as follows:

> A tendency is apparent in cases of sex offences against children of tender years to be less strict with regard to permissible time lapse and to the fact that the statement was in response to inquiry.

Similarly, *Wharton's Criminal Evidence*, 13th ed. (1972), at p. 84, states that while "[t]he *res gestae* rule in sex crimes is the same as in other criminal actions," the rule "should be applied more liberally in the case of children." In an attempt to analyze the many authorities in this area and arrive at some general "rule of thumb" with respect to the generally permissible time lapse between the alleged sexual assault and the spontaneous declaration, the author notes that declarations made up to an hour following the assault will generally be admissible, whereas such declarations "will not ordinarily be regarded as part of the *res gestae* where the time interval between the crime and the declaration is more than one hour" (at p. 90).

These developments underline the need for increased flexibility in the interpretation of the hearsay rule to permit the admission in evidence of statements made by children to others about sexual abuse. In so far as they are tied to the exception to the hearsay rule of spontaneous declarations, however, they suffer from certain defects. There is no requirement that resort to the hearsay evidence be necessary. Even where the evidence of the child might easily be obtained without undue trauma, the Crown would be able to use hearsay evidence. Nor is there any requirement that the reliability of the evidence in the particular be established; hence inherently unreliable evidence might be admitted. Finally, the rule being of an absolute "in-or-out" character, there is no means by which a trial judge could attach conditions on the reception of a particular statement which the judge might deem prudent in a particular case, as for example, the right to cross-examine the deponent referred to in *Ares v. Venner*. In addition to these objections, it can be argued that to extend the spontaneous declaration rule as far as these cases would extend it, is to deform it beyond recognition and is conceptually undesirable.

[McLachlin J referred to some Canadian cases where the hearsay evidence of children had been admitted, and continued:]

These cases point the way in the correct direction. Despite the need for caution, hearsay evidence of a child's statement may be received where the requirements of *Ares v. Venner* are met. The general approach is summed up in the comment of Wilson J in *R v. B. (G.)*, [1990] 2 SCR 30, at p. 55:

> In recent years we have adopted a much more benign attitude to children's evidence, lessen-ing the strict standards of oath taking and corroboration, and I believe that this is a desirable development.

The first question should be whether reception of the hearsay statement is necessary. Necessity for these purposes must be interpreted as "reasonably necessary." The inadmis-sibility of the child's evidence might be one basis for a finding of necessity. But sound evidence based on psychological assessments that testimony in court might be traumatic for the child or harm the child might also serve. There may be other examples of circum-stances which could establish the requirement of necessity.

The next question should be whether the evidence is reliable. Many considerations such as timing, demeanour, the personality of the child, the intelligence and understand-ing of the child, and the absence of any reason to expect fabrication in the statement may be relevant on the issue of reliability. I would not wish to draw up a strict list of consider-ations for reliability, nor to suggest that certain categories of evidence (for example the evidence of young children on sexual encounters) should be always regarded as reliable. The matters relevant to reliability will vary with the child and with the circumstances, and are best left to the trial judge.

In determining the admissibility of the evidence, the judge must have regard to the need to safeguard the interests of the accused. In most cases a right of cross-examination, such as that alluded to in *Ares v. Venner*, would not be available. If the child's direct evi-dence-in-chief is not admissible, it follows that his or her cross-examination would not be admissible either. Where trauma to the child is at issue, there would be little point in sparing the child the need to testify in chief, only to have him or her grilled in cross-examination. While there may be cases where, as a condition of admission, the trial judge thinks it possible and fair in all the circumstances to permit cross-examination of the child as the condition of the reception of a hearsay statement, in most cases the concerns of the accused as to credibility will remain to be addressed by submissions as to the weight to be accorded to the evidence, and submissions as to the quality of any corroborating evidence.

I add that I do not understand *Ares v. Venner* to hold that the hearsay evidence there at issue was admissible where necessity and reliability are established only where cross-examination is available. First, the court adopted the views of the dissenting judges in *Myers v. Director of Public Prosecutions* which do not make admissibility dependent on the right to cross-examine. Second, the cross-examination referred to in *Ares v. Venner* was of limited value. The nurses were present in court at the trial, but in the absence of some way of connecting particular nurses with particular entries, meaningful cross-examination on the accuracy of specific observations would have been difficult indeed.

I conclude that hearsay evidence of a child's statement on crimes committed against the child should be received, provided that the guarantees of necessity and reliability are met, subject to such safeguards as the judge may consider necessary and subject always to considerations affecting the weight that should be accorded to such evidence. This does not make out-of-court statements by children generally admissible; in particular the requirement of necessity will probably mean that in most cases children will still be called to give *viva voce* evidence.

I conclude that the mother's statement in the case at bar should have been received. It was necessary, the child's *viva voce* evidence having been rejected. It was also reliable. The child had no motive to falsify her story, which emerged naturally and without prompting. Moreover, the fact that she could not be expected to have knowledge of such sexual acts imbues her statement with its own peculiar stamp of reliability. Finally, her statement was corroborated by real evidence. Having said this, I note that it may not be necessary to enter the statement on a new trial, if the child's *viva voce* evidence can be received as suggested in the first part of my reasons.

Conclusion

I would dismiss the appeal and direct a new trial.

In the aftermath of *Khan*, there was some debate as to whether the Supreme Court had articulated a new approach to hearsay or had merely created an exception to the rule against hearsay for certain statements by children. Some of the doubts about the scope of *Khan* were resolved by *Smith*.

R v Smith
[1992] 2 SCR 915, 75 CCC (3d) 257
Lamer CJ and La Forest, Sopinka, Gonthier, Cory, McLachlin, and Iacobucci JJ
(27 August 1992)

LAMER CJ: The principal issue raised by this appeal is the admissibility of hearsay evidence as part of the Crown's case in a murder trial, when the declarant is dead.

The Facts

The respondent was convicted of the murder of Aritha Monalisa King and was sentenced to imprisonment for life with no parole eligibility for 13 years. Both the respondent and Ms. King were American citizens, ordinarily resident in Detroit. At the respondent's trial, the evidence showed that on August 6, 1986, the respondent picked up Ms. King at her mother's house in Detroit. Together, they drove across the border to Canada. The respondent spent the weekend of August 9th and 10th with Ms. King in a hotel in London, Ontario. Ms. King's body was subsequently discovered at approximately 1:30 a.m. on August 11th, near a service station at Beechville, Ontario. The body was found lying on a sheet which may have come from the hotel where Ms. King and the respondent had spent the night. Certain fibres found on the sheet matched fibres from the clothing of the respondent and Ms. King. The body's arms had been cut off, and were never found.

The theory of the Crown was that the respondent was a drug smuggler who had travelled to Canada with Ms. King in order to obtain cocaine. The Crown hypothesized that the respondent had asked Ms. King to take the cocaine back to the United States concealed in her body, but that she had refused. According to the Crown, he then abandoned her at the hotel in London. However, he later returned to pick her up, and drove her to a place where he strangled her, cut off her arms to impede identification, and dumped her body.

In support of this theory, the Crown relied upon evidence of four telephone calls made by the deceased to her mother in Detroit at 10:21 p.m., 11:21 p.m., 11:54 p.m. and 12:41 p.m. on the night between August 10 and 11, 1986. The first two telephone calls were traced to the telephone in Ms. King's room at the hotel in London. Ms. King's mother testified that in the first telephone call, her daughter said that Larry (the respondent) had abandoned her at the hotel in London and that she wanted a ride home. In the second call, Ms. King told her mother that Larry had still not returned. Her mother testified that she then telephoned from Detroit to a taxi company in London to attempt to arrange a ride home for her daughter. A taxi did arrive at the hotel, but refused to take Ms. King because the credit card that she had been using had been confiscated at the hotel.

The third call was traced to a pay telephone in the hotel lobby. Ms. King's mother testified that in this call her daughter told her that Larry had come back for her, and that she would not need a ride home after all. The fourth telephone call was traced to a pay telephone at the service station near which Ms. King's body was found. Ms. King's mother testified that in this call her daughter told her that she was "on her way."

In addition to these calls, there was evidence that a further telephone call had been made shortly after 1:00 a.m. on August 11th from a pay telephone at the service station near which Ms. King's body was later found. This call was traced to the respondent's residence in Detroit. There was no direct evidence as to who made this telephone call, or what was said. However, a witness at the service station testified that he had seen the respondent near the pay telephones at the service station around this time.

· · ·

The respondent did not testify at his trial, but set up a defence of alibi supported by the evidence of various witnesses who placed him in Windsor or Detroit at or around the time of the murder. Defence counsel did not object to the testimony by Ms. King's mother as to what her daughter told her in the first three telephone calls. Indeed, it was apparently the theory of the defence that the respondent actually did abandon Ms. King at the hotel in London, a hypothesis supported by the evidence of what Ms. King said in the first two telephone calls to her mother. However, the defence contended that after leaving Ms. King, the respondent returned to Detroit and did not return to the hotel, and therefore could not have been with her when she was murdered.

· · ·

Analysis

(1) Hearsay Evidence

[Lamer CJ held that the deceased's statements were not admissible under the traditional "present intentions" or "state of mind" exceptions to the rule against hearsay.]

This, however, is not fatal to the appellant's case. This court has not taken the position that the hearsay rule precludes the reception of hearsay evidence unless it falls within established categories of exceptions, such as "present intentions" or "state of mind." Indeed, in our recent decision in *R v. Khan*, [1990] 2 SCR 531, we indicated that the categorical approach to exceptions to the hearsay rule has the potential to undermine, rather than further, the policy of avoiding the frailties of certain types of evidence which the hearsay rule was originally fashioned to avoid.

It has long been recognized that the principles which underlie the hearsay rule are the same as that underlie the exceptions to it. Indeed, *Wigmore on Evidence* (2nd ed. 1923), Vol. III, described the rule and its exceptions at §1420 in the following terms:

> The purpose and reason of the Hearsay rule is the key to the exceptions to it. The theory of the Hearsay rule is that the many possible sources of inaccuracy and untrustworthiness which may lie underneath the bare untested assertion of a witness can best be brought to light and exposed, if they exist, by the test of cross-examination. But this test or security may in a given instance be superfluous; it may be sufficiently clear, in that instance, that the statement offered is free from the risk of inaccuracy and untrustworthiness, so that the test of cross-examination would be a work of supererogation. Moreover, the test may be impossible of employment—for example, by reason of the death of the declarant—, so that, if his testimony is to be used at all, there is a necessity for taking it in the untested shape. These two considerations—a Circumstantial Guarantee of Trustworthiness, and a Necessity, for the Evidence—may be examined more closely. ...

Of the criterion of necessity, Wigmore stated:

> Where the test of cross-examination is *impossible for application*, by reason of the declarant's death or some other cause rendering him now unavailable as a witness on the stand, we are faced with the alternatives of receiving his statements without that test, or of leaving his knowledge altogether unutilized. The question arises whether the interests of truth would suffer more by adopting the latter or the former alternative. ... [I]t is clear at least that, so far as in a given instance some substitute for cross-examination is found to have been present, there is ground for making an exception. [Emphasis in original.]

And of the companion principle of reliability—the circumstantial guarantee of trustworthiness—the following:

> There are many situations in which it can be easily seen that such a required test [i.e., cross-examination] would add little as a security, because its purposes had been already substantially accomplished. If a statement has been made under such circumstances that even a sceptical caution would look upon it as trustworthy (in the ordinary instance), in a high degree of probability, it would be pedantic to insist on a test whose chief object is already secured.

Well before the decision of this court in *Khan*, therefore, it was understood that the circumstances under which the declarant makes a statement may be such as to guarantee its reliability, irrespective of the availability of cross-examination. "Guarantee," as the word is used in the phrase "circumstantial guarantee of trustworthiness," does not require that reliability be established with absolute certainty. Rather, it suggests that where the circumstances are not such as to give rise to the apprehensions traditionally associated with hearsay evidence, such evidence should be admissible even if cross-examination is impossible. According to Wigmore, while it was not possible to generalize as to all cases in which other circumstances would provide a functional substitute for testing by cross-examination, certain broad categories could be identified:

> §1422 ... Though no judicial generalizations have been made, there is ample authority in judicial utterances for naming the following different classes of reasons underlying the exceptions:
>
> a. Where the circumstances are such that a sincere and accurate statement would naturally be uttered, and no plan of falsification be formed;
>
> b. Where, even though a desire to falsify might present itself, other considerations, such as the danger of easy detection or the fear of punishment, would probably counteract its force;
>
> c. Where the statement was made under such conditions of publicity that an error, if it had occurred, would probably have been detected and corrected.

The principled basis of the hearsay rule, and its exceptions, was thus understood by commentators on the common law of evidence early in this century. The decision of this court in *Khan*, therefore, should be understood as the triumph of a principled analysis over a set of ossified judicially created categories.

[Lamer CJ reviewed *Khan* and continued:]

It is no accident that the criteria identified by McLachlin J in *Khan* bear a close resemblance to the principle of necessity, and the circumstantial guarantee of reliability, referred to by Wigmore. Clearly, the facts of *Khan* are not similar to the facts on the present appeal. *Khan* was a case of hearsay evidence of statements made by a child, alleged to have been sexually assaulted, who was found to be insufficiently mature to be a competent witness. In the present case, the declarant would have been a competent witness had she been available to give evidence, but she is dead. However, *Khan* should not be understood as turning on its particular facts, but, instead, must be seen as a particular expression of the fundamental principles that underlie the hearsay rule and the exceptions to it. What is important, in my view, is the departure signalled by *Khan* from a view of hearsay characterized by a general prohibition on the reception of such evidence, subject to a limited number of defined categorical exceptions, and a movement towards an approach governed by the principles which underlie the rule and its exceptions alike. The movement towards a flexible approach was motivated by the realization that, as a general rule, reliable evidence ought not to be excluded simply because it cannot be tested by cross-examination. The preliminary determination of reliability is to be made exclusively by the trial judge before the evidence is admitted.

This court's decision in *Khan*, therefore, signalled an end to the old categorical approach to the admission of hearsay evidence. Hearsay evidence is now admissible on a principled basis, the governing principles being the reliability of the evidence, and its necessity. A few words about these criteria are in order.

The criterion of "reliability"—or, in Wigmore's terminology, the circumstantial guarantee of trustworthiness—is a function of the circumstances under which the statement in question was made. If a statement sought to be adduced by way of hearsay evidence is made under circumstances which substantially negate the possibility that the declarant was untruthful or mistaken, the hearsay evidence may be said to be "reliable," i.e., a circumstantial guarantee of trustworthiness is established. The evidence of the infant complainant in *Khan* was found to be reliable on this basis.

The companion criterion of "necessity" refers to the necessity of the hearsay evidence to prove a fact in issue. Thus, in *Khan*, the infant complainant was found by the trial judge not to be competent to testify herself. In this sense, hearsay evidence of her statements was necessary, in that what she said to her mother could not be adduced through her. It was her inability to testify that governed the situation.

The criterion of necessity, however, does not have the sense of "necessary to the prosecution's case." If this were the case, uncorroborated hearsay evidence which satisfied the criterion of reliability would be admissible if uncorroborated, but might no longer be "necessary" to the prosecution's case if corroborated by other independent evidence. Such an interpretation of the criterion of "necessity" would thus produce the illogical result that uncorroborated hearsay evidence would be admissible, but could become inadmissible if corroborated. This is not what was intended by this court's decision in *Khan*.

As indicated above, the criterion of necessity must be given a flexible definition, capable of encompassing diverse situations. What these situations will have in common is that the relevant direct evidence is not, for a variety of reasons, available. Necessity of this nature may arise in a number of situations. Wigmore, while not attempting an exhaustive enumeration, suggested at §1421 the following categories:

> (1) The person whose assertion is offered may now be dead, or out of the jurisdiction, or insane, or otherwise unavailable for the purpose of testing [by cross-examination]. This is the commoner and more palpable reason ...
>
> (2) The assertion may be such that we cannot expect, again or at this time, to get evidence of the same value from the same or other sources ... The necessity is not so great; perhaps hardly a necessity, only an expediency or convenience, can be predicated. But the principle is the same.

Clearly the categories of necessity are not closed. In *Khan*, for instance, this court recognized the necessity of receiving hearsay evidence of a child's statements when the child was not herself a competent witness. We also suggested that such hearsay evidence might become necessary when the emotional trauma that would result to the child if forced to give *viva voce* testimony would be great. Whether a necessity of this kind arises, however, is a question of law for determination by the trial judge.

It is now necessary to apply these principles to the evidence in question in this case. In my opinion, the hearsay evidence of what Ms. King said to her mother in the first two telephone conversations on the night of her murder satisfied the criteria of necessity and reliability set out by this court in *Khan*. In my view, this evidence falls within the same principles. Ms. King is dead, and will never be able to testify as to what happened on the night of August 10 to August 11, 1986. The relevant direct evidence is therefore unavailable. Ms. King's mother's evidence as to what her daughter told her on the telephone that night was clearly necessary, in the sense that there was no possibility that evidence of what was said could be adduced through the declarant.

Moreover, in respect of the first two telephone conversations, there is no reason to doubt Ms. King's veracity. She had no known reason to lie. In my view, the hearsay evidence relating to the first two telephone conversations between Ms. King and her mother could reasonably be relied upon by the jury, as the traditional dangers associated with hearsay evidence—perception, memory and credibility—were not present to any significant degree.

In my view, it would be neither sensible nor just to deprive the jury of this highly relevant evidence on the basis of an arcane rule against hearsay, founded on a lack of faith in the capacity of the trier of fact properly to evaluate evidence of a statement, made under circumstances which do not give rise to apprehensions about its reliability, simply because the declarant is unavailable for cross-examination. Where the criteria of necessity and reliability are satisfied, the lack of testing by cross-examination goes to weight, not admissibility, and a properly cautioned jury should be able to evaluate the evidence on that basis.

However, I arrive at a different conclusion in respect of the contents of the third telephone conversation ("Larry has come back and I no longer need a ride"). While, as in the case of the first two telephone conversations, the unavailability of the declarant to testify satisfies the criterion of necessity, the conditions under which the statement was made do not, in my view, provide that circumstantial guarantee of trustworthiness that would justify its admission without the possibility of cross-examination. On the evidence, I cannot say that I am without apprehensions that Ms. King may have been mistaken, or, indeed, might have intended to deceive her mother on this account.

The evidence at trial disclosed that after making the second telephone call to her mother, Ms. King was observed to leave the hotel and get into a taxi that her mother had arranged to pick her up. She attempted to negotiate a fare to Detroit, but the taxi would not take her because, at this stage, she no longer had a credit card. She was then observed to leave the taxi and proceed immediately to the telephone booth from which she made the third telephone call. It is not, therefore, unreasonable, to ask whether she actually had time to observe the respondent's return. It is at least possible that she was mistaken, and had simply observed a car which resembled the respondent's car. In any case, it does seem somewhat curious that she would make the statement, "Larry has come back and I no longer need a ride" before having spoken to the respondent to ascertain whether he proposed to allow her to continue to travel with him.

In my view, it is highly significant that it was suggested in the course of the previous telephone conversations that one Philip come to pick up Ms. King and drive her back to Detroit. She was vehemently opposed to this suggestion, and there was some evidence that Philip had assaulted her on a previous occasion. When faced with the choice between a ride home with a person for whom she apparently had a great dislike, and of whom she was quite possibly frightened, on the one hand, and with telling her mother that Larry would take her home, on the other, Ms. King might well have preferred the latter alternative.

Moreover, with all due respect, it must be recalled that Ms. King was travelling under an assumed name and using a credit card which she knew was either stolen or forged.

She was, therefore, at least capable of deceit. It may have been that she decided to lie to her mother to conceal some aspect of her activities or circumstances, or, indeed, simply to allay her mother's fears.

I wish to emphasize that I do not advance these alternative hypotheses as accurate reconstructions of what occurred on the night of Ms. King's murder. I engage in such speculation only for the purpose of showing that the circumstances under which Ms. King made the third telephone call to her mother were not such as to provide that circumstantial guarantee of trustworthiness that would justify the admission of its contents by way of hearsay evidence, without the possibility of cross-examination. Indeed, at the highest, it can only be said that hearsay evidence of the third telephone call is equally consistent with the accuracy of Ms. King's statements, and also with a number of other hypotheses. I cannot say that this evidence could not reasonably have been expected to have changed significantly had Ms. King been available to give evidence in person and subjected to cross-examination. I conclude, therefore, that the hearsay evidence of the contents of the third telephone conversation did not satisfy the criterion of reliability set out in *Khan*, and therefore were not admissible on that basis.

To conclude, as this court has made clear in its decisions in *Ares v. Venner, supra*, and *R v. Khan, supra*, the approach that excludes hearsay evidence, even when highly probative, out of the fear that the trier of fact will not understand how to deal with such evidence, is no longer appropriate. In my opinion, hearsay evidence of statements made by persons who are not available to give evidence at trial ought generally to be admissible, where the circumstances under which the statements were made satisfy the criteria of necessity and reliability set out in *Khan*, and subject to the residual discretion of the trial judge to exclude the evidence when its probative value is slight and undue prejudice might result to the accused. Properly cautioned by the trial judge, juries are perfectly capable of determining what weight ought to be attached to such evidence, and of drawing reasonable inferences therefrom.

In the result, therefore, I conclude that the hearsay evidence of what Ms. King told her mother in the first two telephone calls satisfied the criteria of necessity and reliability set out in *Khan*, and was properly admissible on that basis. While the contents of the third telephone call satisfied the criterion of necessity as well, the events surrounding the making of that call were not sufficient to provide that circumstantial guarantee of trustworthiness which would justify their admission without the test of cross-examination. The Crown did not appeal in respect of the fourth telephone conversation, and therefore I make no comment as to the admissibility of hearsay evidence of its contents, other than to say that, in the event of a new trial, it will be governed by the same principles.

NOTES AND QUESTIONS

On the retrial, the accused, Smith, was acquitted. The jury during their deliberations asked the judge why it was they could hear the contents of the first two calls but not the third!

(Ronald J Delisle, *Evidence in a Nutshell* (Scarborough, Ont: Carswell, 1996) at 89.)

Do you agree with Lamer CJ that the third phone call was so much less reliable than the first two that it should not have been admitted?

It is not uncommon for a witness's testimony to differ from an earlier statement that he or she made. The traditional rule was that the prior inconsistent statement was admissible not for its truth because that would be hearsay; the prior inconsistent statement was admissible only for the non-hearsay purpose of undermining the witness's credibility. See *R v Deacon*, [1947] SCR 531 and Chapter 6, below. (The prior inconsistent statement was admissible for its truth if the witness adopted it.) In *B (KG)*, the court considered the application of the principled approach to this situation.

R v B (KG)
[1993] 1 SCR 740, 79 CCC (3d) 257
Lamer CJ and L'Heureux-Dubé, Sopinka, Gonthier, Cory, McLachlin, and
Iacobucci JJ (25 February 1993)

LAMER CJ (Sopinka, Gonthier, McLachlin, and Iacobucci JJ concurring): The issue in this appeal is the substantive admissibility of prior inconsistent statements by a witness other than an accused. The Crown asks this court to reconsider the common law rule which limits the use of such statements to impeaching the credibility of the witness. In my opinion, the time has come for the orthodox rule to be replaced by a new rule recognizing the changed means and methods of proof in modern society.

I—The Facts

On April 24, 1988, Joseph Wright and his brother Steven got off a bus at an intersection in Scarborough, Ontario. The brothers crossed the street and began walking home. At about the same time, the respondent and three other young men were driving past the same intersection. An argument started between the group in the car and the two men on the street and shortly thereafter a fight occurred. The brothers were unarmed. In the course of the fight one of the four persons from the vehicle pulled a knife, slashing twice at Joseph's face and then stabbing him in the chest. The stab wound to the chest penetrated Joseph's heart and killed him. The four young men then fled the scene.

About two weeks later, the three young men involved with the respondent in the incident were interviewed separately by the police. While the appellant states that the three witnesses approached the police to make their statements, the respondent notes that two of the witnesses testified that they approached the police only after the police came to their homes in connection with the police investigation of the killing, and the third witness testified that it was his mother's idea that he give a statement to the police. Each was accompanied by a parent and in one case by a lawyer and each was advised of his right to counsel. It was also made clear that they were under no obligation to answer questions put to them by the police, and while the police told the witnesses that they were not charged with any offence, the interviewers also added the qualification "at this time" in two of the interviews. With the youths' consent the interviews were videotaped.

In their statements, the three young men told the police that the respondent had made statements to them in which he acknowledged that he thought he had, or had, caused the death of the deceased by the use of a knife. The respondent was charged with second degree murder and he entered a plea of not guilty. Following an unsuccessful attempt by the Crown to have the case transferred to adult court, the respondent's trial commenced before Judge MacDonnell in youth court on November 14, 1989.

When called at trial by the Crown, the three young men refused to adopt their earlier statements respecting the admissions made by the respondent. The trial judge allowed the Crown to cross-examine them on their prior statements pursuant to s. 9 of the *Canada Evidence Act*, RSC 1985, c. C-5. They admitted they had made the statements to the police but said that they had lied to the police and that the respondent had not in fact made the incriminating statements that they had previously attributed to him. Their explanation for having lied to the police was that they did so to exculpate themselves from possible involvement. They claimed to have either forgotten what occurred when the respondent was alleged to have made his inculpatory statements, or to have not heard the respondent.

The trial judge held that the only use that could be made of the prior inconsistent statements of the three witnesses was with respect to their credibility, and that the prior inconsistent statements could not be used as evidence of the truth of the matters stated therein; that is, they could not be tendered as proof that the respondent actually made the admissions. The only other evidence of the identity of the assailant was identification evidence provided by the victim's brother, who identified the accused at trial (in a "dock" identification with little evidential value) and testified as to the appearance of the deceased's assailant. The trial judge found that the dock identification was "naked opinion given 19 months after the event," and that the brother had only a poor opportunity to observe his brother's attacker. Doubts also existed in connection with his latter evidence because of several inconsistencies between elements of his description of the attacker shortly after the incident and elements of his description at trial, including the type of jacket and pants worn by the assailant, the clothing of the other youths, and the height and weight of the assailant relative to the other youths. At trial, the respondent argues, several other elements of the brother's description did not match the respondent's characteristics, including the colour of the respondent's skin relative to the other youths, the fact that the assailant held the knife in his right hand while the respondent was described as left-handed by two of the recanting witnesses, whether the assailant wore jewellery, and the colour of the assailant's hair.

As a result of the doubt which existed with respect to the issue of identification, and in the absence of other admissible evidence, the trial judge acquitted the respondent.

The appellant appealed the acquittal to the Court of Appeal for Ontario, which stated that it was bound by the decisions of this court, and accordingly dismissed the appeal.

Between the filing of the parties' facta and the hearing of this appeal, the three witnesses pleaded guilty to perjury. The Crown brought a motion on the day of oral argument in this appeal to adduce this new evidence which it asserted was relevant to two issues: (i) whether the operation of a revised rule would tend to enhance or detract from the public's perception of and respect for the administration of justice, and (ii) whether the application of the orthodox rule had caused a miscarriage of justice in this case. Counsel for the respondent consented to the admission of this fresh evidence on this basis and for this purpose alone, and not as evidence of the respondent's innocence or guilt. Counsel for the Crown agreed to this limitation.

· · ·

IV—Analysis

[Lamer CJ considered the traditional or "orthodox" rule that the prior inconsistent statement of a witness is not admissible for its truth unless the witness adopts it. He reviewed some academic and judicial criticism of the orthodox rule, including Estey J's concurrence in *McInroy and Rouse v R*, [1979] 1 SCR 588. Finally, he held that this was a proper case for the court to exercise its power to modify the common law.]

V—The New Admissibility Rule

A. Requirements and the Hearsay Dangers

I am of the view that evidence of prior inconsistent statements of a witness other than an accused should be substantively admissible on a principled basis, following this court's decisions in *Khan* [*R v Khan*, [1990] 2 SCR 531] and *Smith* [*R v Smith*, [1992] 2 SCR 915]. However, it is clear that the factors identified in those cases—reliability and necessity—must be adapted and refined in this particular context, given the particular problems raised by the nature of such statements. Furthermore, there must be a *voir dire* before such statements are put before the jury as substantive evidence, in which the trial judge satisfies him or herself that the statement was made in circumstances which do not negate its reliability.

As a threshold matter, before discussing the specific requirements of the reformed rule, I would adopt the requirement embodied in the provision proposed by the Law Reform Commission of Canada, and in the English *Civil Evidence Act, 1968*, that prior inconsistent statements will only be admissible if they would have been admissible as the witness's sole testimony. That is, if the witness could not have made the statement at trial during his or her examination-in-chief or cross-examination, for whatever reason, it cannot be made admissible through the back door, as it were, under the reformed prior inconsistent statement rule.

There are two situations which provide examples of this requirement. First, it may be that the content of the prior inconsistent statement would not normally be admissible because it is hearsay. If the witness makes a prior statement relating direct evidence about a material fact ("I saw Y fire the gun"), there will be no barrier to admitting the prior statement. Such direct evidence would have been subject to no exclusionary rule of evidence.

However, if the witness's prior statement merely repeated the direct evidence of another person ("X said he saw Y fire the gun"), such a statement, even when made with circumstantial guarantees of reliability, will not be substantively admissible for the truth of the evidence of that other person: because the statement is naked hearsay if offered to prove the fact that Y fired the gun, it would not have been admissible to prove that fact (absent a hearsay exception) as direct evidence from the testifying witness, and it does not become admissible evidence to prove that fact through the operation of the reformed rule. The only use that can be made of such prior statements is as proof that the statement was made to the witness, but not, obviously, as proof that Y fired the gun. This is no more than the hearsay rule applied to the prior statement as if it was evidence tendered at trial.

The final possibility in this category is the present case ("Y told me he fired the gun"), in which the statement relates hearsay which is admissible under an established hearsay exception: while the statement repeats the evidence of another person, as in the second example, the hearsay exception applicable to the reported statement because it is an admission applies to the prior statement, again, as if the prior statement itself had been the witness's sole testimony. Because of the circumstantial guarantees of reliability attaching to admissions (on the assumption that an accused would not falsely incriminate himself), the hearsay statement may be admitted to prove the fact that Y fired the gun. But it is crucial that the matters in the prior statement would have been admissible if offered as the witness's sole testimony.

. . .

(1) Reliability

The reliability of prior inconsistent statements is clearly a key concern for law reformers and courts which have reformed the orthodox rule, and, as I have outlined, this concern is centred on the hearsay dangers: the absence of an oath, presence, and contemporaneous cross-examination. The reliability concern is sharpened in the case of prior inconsistent statements because the trier of fact is asked to choose between two statements from the same witness, as opposed to other forms of hearsay in which only one account from the declarant is tendered. In other words, the focus of the inquiry in the case of prior inconsistent statements is on the comparative reliability of the prior statement and the testimony offered at trial, and so additional *indicia* and guarantees of reliability to those outlined in *Khan* and *Smith* must be secured in order to bring the prior statement to a comparable standard of reliability before such statements are admitted as substantive evidence.

In my opinion, and as my discussion of these dangers above indicates, only the first two of these dangers present real concerns in this context, and if these two dangers are addressed, a sufficient degree of reliability has been established to allow the trier of fact to weigh the statement against evidence tendered at trial by the same witness. The ultimate reliability of the statement and the weight to be attached to it remain, as with all evidence, determinations for the trier of fact. What the reliability component of the principled approach to hearsay exceptions addresses is a threshold of reliability, rather than ultimate or certain reliability.

The history of the common law exceptions to the hearsay rule suggests that for a hearsay statement to be received, there must be some other fact or circumstance which compensates for, or stands in the stead of the oath, presence and cross-examination. Where the safeguards associated with non-hearsay evidence are absent, there must be some substitute factor to demonstrate sufficient reliability to make it safe to admit the evidence.

I turn now to a consideration of what "substitute" *indicia* of trustworthiness might suffice to permit reception of prior inconsistent statements, bearing in mind that the question of reliability is a matter for the trial judge, to be decided on the particular circumstances of the case.

(i) The Oath

It is undeniable that the significance of the oath has drastically changed since its introduction. Originally the oath was grounded upon a belief that divine retribution would visit those who lied under oath. Accordingly, witnesses were required to believe in this retribution if they were to be properly sworn and their evidence admissible. In *Omychund v. Barker* (1744), 1 Atk. 21, 26 ER 15, Willes LCJ stated, at p. 31 ER:

Though I have shewn that an Infidel in general cannot be excluded from being a witness, and though I am of the opinion that infidels who believe a God, and future rewards and punishments in the other world, may be witnesses; yet I am as clearly of opinion, that if they do not believe a God, or future rewards and punishments, they ought not to be admitted as witnesses.

Similarly, Lord Hardwicke LC referred (at p. 32 ER) to the oath as "an appeal to the Supreme Being, as thinking him the rewarder of truth, and avenger of falsehood." The difference between sworn and unsworn evidence was therefore crucial, and the absence of an oath when the prior statement was made was an important obstacle to admitting prior inconsistent statements for their truth.

We no longer require this belief in divine retribution; in *Reference re Regina v. Truscott*, [1967] SCR 309, at p. 368, this court stated in the context of child witnesses that the witness need only understand "the moral obligation of telling the truth." In this sense the oath can be said to have a changed significance, and if critics of the oath suggest only that its original supernatural force has disappeared, I agree with that observation.

It is also true, as Cory J notes, that sanctions attach to statements not made under oath. A witness who tells one story to the police and another at trial is currently exposed to prosecution under ss. 139 (obstructing justice) and 140 (public mischief) of the *Criminal Code*, RSC 1985, c. C-46. Furthermore, with the court's decision in this case, prior statements which satisfy the criteria of admissibility will be used as substantive evidence in a subsequent trial; as a result, a witness who makes a false statement will also be liable to prosecution under s. 137 (fabricating evidence), once he or she is informed that the statement can, and indeed *will*, be used at trial if he or she recants. Finally, it may well be that, in light of this decision, Parliament will wish to extend other criminal sanctions (such as the offence of perjury, for example) to one who lies under oath, solemn affirmation or solemn declaration in the course of a criminal investigation.

However, there remain compelling reasons to prefer statements made under oath, solemn affirmation or solemn declaration. While the oath will not motivate all witnesses to tell the truth (as is indicated by the witnesses' perjury in this case), its administration may serve to impress on more honest witnesses the seriousness and significance of their statements, especially where they incriminate another person in a criminal investigation.

In addition to this positive effect on the declarant, the presence of an oath, solemn affirmation or solemn declaration will increase the evidentiary value of the statement when it is admitted at trial. First, it will mean that the trier of fact will not be asked to accept unsworn testimony over sworn testimony; instead, the trier will have the opportunity to choose between two sworn statements, and the trier's ultimate decision will not be made on the basis of unsworn or unaffirmed testimony. Similarly, should the prior statement be decisive, there is no danger of the accused being convicted solely on the basis of unsworn testimony.

Second, the presence of the oath during the making of the prior statement eliminates the explanation offered by many recanting witnesses, including one of the witnesses in this case: when confronted with the prior inconsistent statement, witnesses explain that it was not made under oath, and assert that the oath they took at trial persuaded them to tell the truth. This naturally privileges the trial testimony in the mind of the trier of fact. If both statements were made under oath, such an explanation can no longer be employed. Furthermore, since both statements cannot be true, the trier of fact has an indication of the low regard in which the witness holds the oath. Therefore, while it is true that the oath in itself has no power to ensure truthfulness in some witnesses, the fact that both statements were made under oath removes resort to the absence of an oath as an *indicium* of the alleged unreliability of the prior inconsistent statement.

The presence of an oath, solemn affirmation or solemn declaration will have yet another positive effect on the declarant's truthfulness and the administration of justice. A sworn prior statement will be highly persuasive evidence in any prosecution against the declarant related to false testimony (whether in the statement or at trial), and the knowledge that this evidence exists for this purpose should weigh heavily on the mind of one who considers lying in a statement, or recanting his or her prior statement to lie at trial.

Of course, the incentives provided by the declarant's exposure to prosecution under ss. 137, 139 and 140 in relation to the first statement, and his or her fear of a perjury prosecution in relation to testimony given at trial, will only be effective if these sanctions are made known to the declarant. For this reason, the witness should be warned by the person taking the statement that the statement may be used as evidence at a subsequent trial if the witness recants (thereby engaging s. 137), and also that severe criminal sanctions will accompany the making of a false statement. This warning should refer specifically to ss. 137, 139 and 140 of the *Criminal Code*, and repeat the elements of and sanctions for those offences. As does the formal swearing of the witness in the trial process, this warning and the administration of the oath should serve to bring home to the witness the gravity of the situation and his duty to tell the truth.

Therefore, the best *indicium* of reliability on the principled approach of *Smith* in the case of prior inconsistent statements is that the statement, to be substantively admissible, has been made (i) under oath, solemn affirmation, or solemn declaration, and (ii) following the administration of an explicit warning to the witness of his or her amenability to prosecution if it is discovered that he or she has lied. This *indicium* satisfies the first hearsay danger entirely: in no case will the trier of fact be asked to accept unsworn testimony over sworn testimony, verdicts will not be based on unsworn testimony, and the circumstances which promote truthful trial testimony will have been recreated as fully as is possible.

Were the oath an absolute requirement for a finding of reliability, the only prior inconsistent statements which could be received would be statements made in circumstances where the person receiving the statement is authorized to administer the warning and the oath or affirmation. Thus, statements made to family members or friends would generally not comply, unless the witness then repeats the statement for appropriately authorized persons. In the case of police interviews, this would likely present no real difficulty, since each police station will usually have a justice of the peace present or readily available for interim release hearings. The justice could then administer the warning before the statement is made, and the oath after the statement is made. Similarly, police officers on duty as the officer in charge could be made commissioners for the taking of oaths in the province, and administer the warning and oath in the justice's absence.

However, I do not wish to create technical categorical requirements duplicating those of the old approach to hearsay evidence. It follows from *Smith* that there may be situations in which the trial judge concludes that an appropriate substitute for the oath is established and that notwithstanding the absence of an oath the statement is reliable. Other circumstances may serve to impress upon the witness the importance of telling the truth, and in so doing provide a high degree of reliability to the statement. While these occasions may not be frequent, I do not foreclose the possibility that they might arise under the principled approach to hearsay evidence.

(ii) Presence

Proponents of the orthodox rule emphasize the many verbal and non-verbal cues which triers of fact rely upon in order to assess credibility. When the witness is on the stand, the trier can observe the witness's reaction to questions, hesitation, degree of commitment to the statement being made, etc. Most importantly, and subsuming all of these factors, the trier can assess the relationship between the interviewer and the witness to observe the extent to which the testimony of the witness is the product of the investigator's questioning. Such subtle observations and cues cannot be gleaned from a transcript, read in court in counsel's monotone, where the atmosphere of the exchange is entirely lost.

All of these *indicia* of credibility, and therefore reliability, are available to the trier of fact when the witness's prior statement is videotaped. During the course of the hearing, counsel for the appellant screened a brief excerpt from the videotape of one of the interviews. In the main portion of the television screen is a medium-length shot of the witness facing the camera and seated across a table from the interviewing officer, showing the physical relationship between the two people. In one upper corner is a close-up of the witness's face as he or she speaks, capturing nuances of expression lost in the main view. Along the bottom of the screen is a line showing the date and a time-counter, with the seconds ticking off, ensuring that the continuity and integrity of the record is maintained. The audio-visual medium captures other elements of the statement lost in a transcript, such as actions or distinctive motions which the witness demonstrates (as in this case), or answers given by nodding or shaking the head. In other words, the experience of being in the room with the witness and the interviewing officer is recreated as fully as possible for the viewer. Not only does the trier of fact have access to the full range of non-verbal *indicia* of credibility, but there is also a reproduction of the statement which is fully accurate, eliminating the danger of inaccurate recounting which motivates the rule against hearsay evidence. In a very real sense, the evidence ceases to be hearsay in this important respect, since the hearsay declarant is brought before the trier of fact.

Of course, the police would not resort to this precaution in every case; it may well be reserved for cases such as this, where a major crime such as murder is being investigated, the testimony of the witnesses is important to the Crown's case, and the character of the witnesses suggests that such precautions would be advisable. It is quite possible that such equipment would be available to police of given forces at a central location, and that such crucial though unstable witnesses will be taken to such locations to make their statements, or, where the statements have already been made, to repeat them in a form which may be substantively admissible should the witness recant.

In addition to an oath or solemn affirmation and warning, then, a complete videotape record of the type described above, or one which duplicates the experience of observing a witness in the court-room to the same extent, is another of the other important *indicia* of reliability which will satisfy the principled basis for the admission of hearsay evidence.

Again, it may be possible that the testimony of an independent third party who observes the making of the statement in its entirety could, in exceptional circumstances, also provide the requisite reliability with respect to demeanour evidence. I would only note at this point that there are many persons who could serve this function: police stations will have justices of the peace present or available, the witness may have his or her own lawyer present, and s. 56(2)(c) and (d) of the *Young Offenders Act*, RSC 1985, c. Y-1, provide that a young person making a statement has a right of access to counsel, parents, or adult relatives. It will be a matter for the trial judge to determine whether or not a sufficient substitute for a videotape record has been provided to allow the trier of fact access to sufficient demeanour evidence to make the statement admissible.

(iii) Cross-Examination

The final hearsay danger is the lack of contemporaneous cross-examination when the statement is made. The appellant is correct to concede that this is the most important of the hearsay dangers. However, in the case of prior inconsistent statements, it is also the most easily remedied by the opportunity to cross-examine at trial. This is a feature of prior inconsistent statements that conclusively distinguishes them from other forms of hearsay. As the United States Supreme Court noted in *California v. Green* [399 US 149 (1970)], at p. 159:

> … the inability to cross-examine the witness at the time he made his prior statement cannot easily be shown to be of crucial significance as long as the defendant is assured of full and effective cross-examination at the time of trial. The most successful cross-examination at the time the prior statement was made could hardly hope to accomplish more than has already been accomplished by the fact that the witness is now telling a different, inconsistent story and—in this case—one that is favorable to the defendant.

Furthermore, unlike the oath and presence, it is the hearsay danger which is impossible to address outside of judicial or *quasi-judicial* processes. Whereas the police can easily administer a warning and oath, and videotape a statement in the course of a witness interview, it would restrict the operation of a reformed rule to judicial or quasi-judicial proceedings to require contemporaneous cross-examination, and thereby severely restrict the impact of a reformed rule. Consider the facts of the present case: when the three witnesses were interviewed by the police, no one had yet been charged with an offence. Who could have cross-examined the witnesses at that point? How could cross-examination have been effective before the case to be met was known? These and other practical difficulties in requiring contemporaneous cross-examination tip the balance in favour of allowing cross-examination at trial to serve as a substitute. Again, we must remember that the question is not whether it would have been preferable to have had the benefit of contemporaneous cross-examination, but whether the absence of such cross-examination is a sufficient reason to keep the statement from the jury as substantive evidence. Given the other guarantees of trustworthiness, I do not think that it should be allowed to be a barrier to substantive admissibility. Of course, it will be an important consideration for the trier of fact in deciding what weight to attach to the prior inconsistent statement, and it is likely that opposing counsel will stress the absence of such cross-examination to the trier of fact.

Therefore, the requirement of reliability will be satisfied when the circumstances in which the prior statement was made provide sufficient guarantees of its trustworthiness with respect to the two hearsay dangers a reformed rule can realistically address: if (i) the statement is made under oath or solemn affirmation following a warning as to the existence of sanctions and the significance of the oath or affirmation, (ii) the statement is videotaped in its entirety, and (iii) the opposing party, whether the Crown or the defence, has a full opportunity to cross-examine the witness respecting the statement, there will be sufficient circumstantial guarantees of reliability to allow the jury to make substantive use of the statement. Alternatively, other circumstantial guarantees of reliability may suffice to render such statements substantively admissible, provided that the judge is satisfied that the circumstances provide adequate assurances of reliability in place of those which the hearsay rule traditionally requires.

(2) Necessity

Prior inconsistent statements present vexing problems for the necessity criterion. The necessity criterion has usually been satisfied by the unavailable witness: in *Khan*, the child declarant who could not be sworn, and in *Smith*, the dead declarant. By definition, the declarant in the case of prior inconsistent statements is available at trial; it is his or her prior statement that is unavailable because of the recantation.

However, it is important to remember that the necessity criterion "must be given a flexible definition, capable of encompassing diverse situations" (*Smith*, at pp. 933-34). Wigmore, vol. 5 (Chadbourn rev. 1974), §1421, at p. 253, referred to two classes of necessity:

(1) The person whose assertion is offered may now be *dead*, or out of the jurisdiction, or insane, or *otherwise unavailable* for the purpose of testing. This is the commoner and more palpable reason. …

(2) The assertion may be such that we cannot expect, again, or at this time, to get *evidence of the same value* from the same or other sources. … The necessity is not so great; perhaps hardly a necessity, only an expediency or convenience, can be predicated. But the principle is the same. [Emphasis in original.]

As an example of the second type of necessity, many established hearsay exceptions do not rely on the unavailability of the witness. Some examples include admissions, present sense impressions and business records. This is because there are very high circumstantial guarantees of reliability attached to such statements, offsetting that fact that only expediency or convenience militate in favour of admitting the evidence.

• • •

The precise limits of the necessity criterion remain to be established in the context of specific cases. It may be that in some circumstances, the availability of the witness will mean that hearsay evidence of that witness's prior *consistent* (the kind of statement at issue in *Khan*) statements will not be admissible. However, I am not prepared, at this point, to adhere to a strict interpretation that makes unavailability an indispensable condition of necessity.

In the case of prior *inconsistent* statements, it is patent that we cannot expect to get evidence of the same value from the recanting witness or other sources: as counsel for the appellant claimed, the recanting witness holds the prior statement, and thus the relevant evidence, "hostage." The different "value" of the evidence is found in the fact that something has radically changed between the time when the statement was made and the trial and, assuming that there is a sufficient degree of reliability established under the first criterion, the trier of fact should be allowed to weigh both statements in light of the witness's explanation of the change.

B. The Voir Dire

Pursuant to the circumstantial guarantees of reliability described above, prior statements may be used as substantive evidence of their contents by the jury. The two-stage process by which this may be done must now be described. After the calling party invokes s. 9 of the *Canada Evidence Act*, and fulfils its requirements in the *voir dire* held under that section, the party must then state its intention in tendering the statement. If the party indicates that it wishes to use the statement only to impeach the credibility of the witness, that is the end of the matter as regards the reformed rule: the trial proceeds as it did under the orthodox rule, with the judge instructing the jury accordingly. If, however, the party gives notice that it will seek to make substantive use of the statement, the trial judge must continue the *voir dire* to satisfy him or herself on the appropriate measure (which I will discuss below) that these *indicia* of reliability, or acceptable substitutes, are present: the oath, affirmation, or solemn declaration will be proved, the person who administered the oath, affirmation, or solemn declaration will testify that he or she also administered the warning (or perhaps this could be incorporated into the oath, affirmation, or solemn declaration), and the videotape will be tendered into evidence, its authenticity sworn to, and, if the trial judge wishes, screened to ensure its veracity and integrity.

With respect to the burden of proof in the *voir dire*, ordinarily the trial judge should be satisfied that these *indicia* of reliability are established on the balance of probabilities, the normal burden resting upon a party seeking to admit evidence. This is no more than a corollary of the requirement that the prior statements must relate evidence which would have been admissible as the witness' sole testimony had he or she not recanted.

A different situation might exist where the prior statement reports an admission made by the accused. If the statement is not made to a person in authority no special burden is required, since the ordinary burden for the admission of evidence would have applied to the witness's testimony at trial had he or she not recanted. However, if the prior statement reports an admission of the accused made to a person in authority, the higher burden associated with the law relating to confessions may well apply. Such incidents will be rare, since persons in authority who receive statements in the course of their duties from accused persons will not often recant. Additionally, if an agent of the state elicits a statement from a detained accused, the case-law developed under the Charter in this respect would have to be considered with respect to the burden during the *voir dire*.

As neither of these issues arise in this case (since the recanting witnesses were clearly neither persons in authority in relation to the accused, nor were they agents of the state when the accused made his admissions to them, nor was the accused detained), I would leave those rare and theoretical situations to be addressed when and if they arise.

However, I would incorporate another aspect of the rule relating to confessions in the *voir dire*. Even where there has been a warning and oath administered, and the statement videotaped, or sufficient substitutes established, the trial judge will still have the discretion to refuse to allow the jury to make substantive use of the statement. Prior statements share many characteristics with confessions, especially where police investigators are involved. Proponents of the orthodox rule voice the concern that malign influences on the witness by police may precede the making of the statement and shape its content, in the same way that confessions may be suspect if coerced by police investigators. That is, it still may be the case that the oath and videotape, and the acknowledgement of the warning, were made under circumstances that make them suspect. For this reason, the test developed by this court for the admission of confessions is well suited to making a threshold determination of whether the circumstances under which the statement was made undermine the veracity of the *indicia* of reliability.

The classic statement of the first part of the confession rule appears in *Ibrahim v. The King*, [1914] AC 599 at p. 609 (PC):

> It has long been established as a positive rule of English criminal law, that no statement by an accused is admissible in evidence against him unless it is shewn by the prosecution to have been a voluntary statement, in the sense that it has not been obtained from him either by fear of prejudice or hope of advantage exercised or held out by a person in authority.

Ibrahim was first adopted by this court in *Prosko v. The King* (1922), 63 SCR 226, and was extended in decisions such as *Horvath v. The Queen*, [1979] 2 SCR 376, in which Beetz J wrote (at pp. 424-25):

> Furthermore, the principle which inspires the rule remains a positive one; it is the principle of voluntariness. The principle always governs and may justify an extension of the rule to situations where involuntariness has been caused or otherwise than by promises, threats, hope or fear, if it is felt that other causes are as coercive as promises or threats, hope or fear and serious enough to bring the principle into play.

I would apply this test to prior statements. The trial judge must satisfy him or herself (again, in the majority of cases on the balance of probabilities) on the *voir dire* that the statement was not the product of coercion of any form, whether it involves threats, promises, excessively leading questions by the investigator or other person in a position of authority, or other forms of investigatory misconduct.

[The Crown's appeal was allowed and a new trial ordered, at which the admissibility of the Crown witness's videotaped statements would be decided, if necessary, under the new approach.]

[Cory J (L'Heureux-Dubé J concurring) concurred in the result, but took a different view of the criteria for admitting previous inconsistent statements for their truth and of the procedure to be followed on the *voir dire*. He held that the absence of an oath or a warning when the statement was taken was not fatal to admissibility for truth, and that videotaping would not be necessary "where a complete and comprehensive record ... of the statement together with satisfactory evidence of the circumstances of the interview and the demeanour of the witness" were available. He also held that the trial judge in the *voir dire* should be "satisfied beyond a reasonable doubt that the conditions for admitting the prior inconsistent statement have been fulfilled." He held that the trial judge should consider the following conditions in determining admissibility:]

(1) That the evidence contained in the prior statement is such that it would be admissible if given in court.

(2) That the statement has been made voluntarily by the witness and is not the result of any undue pressure, threats or inducements.

(3) That the statement was made in circumstances, which viewed objectively would bring home to the witness the importance of telling the truth.

(4) That the statement is reliable in that it has been fully and accurately transcribed or recorded.

(5) That the statement was made in circumstances that the witness would be liable to criminal prosecution for giving a deliberately false statement.

NOTES AND QUESTIONS

1. At the second trial, the witnesses M.T., P.L., and P.M. testified in accordance with their original statements to the police, so a *B (KG)* application was not required. K.G.B. was convicted of manslaughter, and his appeal from conviction was dismissed: see *R v B (KG)* (1998), 125 CCC (3d) 61 (Ont CA).

2. How do the indicia of reliability in *B (KG)* compare with those in *Smith*? Which are more demanding, and why?

3. Do you agree with Lamer CJ's suggestion that the parties might be able to call witnesses to testify as to the demeanour of the witness whose prior inconsistent statement has been put before the trier of fact? (You may want to revisit this question after considering the material in Chapter 6.)

In the following cases, should the out-of-court statement have been admitted according to the approach in *B (KG)*? After reading *Khelawon* (below), you may wish to revisit these problems and consider whether the court's reformulation of the principled approach would make any difference.

PROBLEM 1

The 12-year-old complainant alleged that she had had anal and oral sex with the accused, her father, over a period of almost a year, and that the accused had physically assaulted her. She gave a statement to Constable C, who attempted to tape record the statement; C testified later that the recorder had malfunctioned and nothing had been recorded. C prepared a summary of the complainant's statement, based on his notes and his recollection of the interview. Constables C and M then interviewed the accused. He admitted to having anal and oral sex with the complainant and to striking her twice. This interview was not recorded, and the accused refused to sign a written version of his statement. The accused was then charged with various sexual offences under ss 151, 155, and 159 of the *Criminal Code*. The trial judge found that the accused's statement to the police was admissible. The complainant was called as a Crown witness. She testified as to instances of non-sexual assault but retracted her allegations of sexual assault. The Crown obtained permission to cross-examine her on the statement given to the police, under s 9 of the *Canada Evidence Act*. The accused also testified at trial. He said that his confession was false. Should the jury have been allowed to consider the complainant's statement to the police for its truth? See *R v U (FJ)*, [1995] 3 SCR 764, 101 CCC (3d) 97, aff'g (1994), 90 CCC (3d) 541 (Ont CA).

PROBLEM 2

The 15-year-old complainant told her mother that the accused, her brother, had had intercourse with her when she was eight. A police officer audiotaped a statement from the complainant making the same allegation. There was no evidence of what the complainant was told regarding the importance of telling the truth. Her mother was present when the statement was audiotaped but was too drunk to recall the circumstances. The police officer believed the complainant was truthful. Immediately after the accused was arrested and charged, the complainant retracted her statement and accused her father. At trial, the complainant maintained that her father, not the accused, was the person who had had intercourse with her. The Crown obtained permission to cross-examine the complainant under s 9 of the *Canada Evidence Act*. Was the audiotaped statement admissible for its truth under the principles expressed in *B (KG)*? See *R v C (JR)* (1996), 110 CCC (3d) 373 (Sask CA).

PROBLEM 3

The victim, Gisele Pelzmann, was found dead on September 9, 1993. It appeared that she had been beaten to death with a rock. There was evidence that the victim had been a prostitute and that the accused, Doris Eisenhauer, had been her pimp. The theory of the Crown was that "the accused was angry and jealous about losing the deceased's services." The theory of the defence was that Pelzmann had been killed by someone else. Eisenhauer stated that she had been asleep on a couch, following a party, during the early morning of September 9.

The Crown's case rested in part on the eyewitness testimony of Claudette Chisholm, who testified that "she and the accused met the deceased in the early morning hours of September 9, that the accused began to punch, slap and kick the deceased as they moved along [the road] and that the assault culminated on the golf course when the accused got a large rock and struck the deceased with it while she was lying on the ground, crying." She stated that she and the accused had been at the party but that the accused had not been asleep at any time. But on November 3, Chisholm had been arrested, cautioned, and advised of her right to counsel. She had then given a long statement to the police in which she had said, *inter alia*, that Eisenhauer had been asleep for "an hour or two" before 3:30 a.m. on September 9. This statement was not recorded verbatim, but the interviewing officers had kept detailed notes, which, they testified, "fairly reflected the conversation." Should this statement have been admitted for its truth? See *R v Eisenhauer* (1998), 123 CCC (3d) 37 (NSCA), leave to appeal refused, 126 CCC (3d) vi (SCC).

PROBLEM 4

The two accused were charged with second-degree murder in the beating death of an elderly man. The victim was killed on December 7, 1994. The witness Jardine lived in the same apartment building as the two accused and frequently partied with them. On December 8, he gave a statement to the police in which he said he knew nothing about the killing. On

December 11, he gave a second statement to the police that implicated the two accused in the killing. The second statement was transcribed but not sworn, and Jardine refused to be videotaped. At trial, Jardine testified that he could not remember having given either statement to the police and did not know whether the content of the second statement was true. Was the second statement admissible for its truth? Would it be admissible if it had been made under oath and had been videotaped? See *R v Conway* (1997), 36 OR (3d) 579, 121 CCC (3d) 397 (CA).

PROBLEM 5

The complainant was assaulted and robbed in a hotel room. The complainant and his friend Cindy Pawliw, who was present during the assault, gave statements to the police, identifying the accused, Devine, as the assailant. Pawliw's statement was taken in compliance with the approach suggested in *B (KG)*. At trial, the complainant and Pawliw were called as Crown witnesses, but both recanted their identification, and both were cross-examined on the prior inconsistent statements. Pawliw testified that someone (though she could not remember who) had suggested that she use the accused's name in her statement. The Crown applied for leave to introduce Pawliw's statement to the police for the truth of its contents. The defence argued that the *B (KG)* statement was inadmissible because it was itself based on inadmissible hearsay (that is, someone had told Pawliw that Devine was the assailant, and she merely repeated that identification in her statement). How should the trial judge determine the admissibility of Pawliw's statement? See *R v Devine*, 2008 SCC 36, [2008] 2 SCR 283.

R v Hawkins
[1996] 3 SCR 1043, 111 CCC (3d) 129
Lamer CJ and La Forest, L'Heureux-Dubé, Sopinka, Gonthier, Cory, McLachlin, Iacobucci, and Major JJ (28 November 1996)

[The accused, Hawkins, a police officer, was charged with conspiring to obstruct justice, and other offences. The Crown's principal witness at the preliminary inquiry was Graham, Hawkins's girlfriend. After the preliminary inquiry but before the trial, Hawkins and Graham married. The trial judge held, and the Supreme Court agreed, that Graham was incompetent for the Crown (see Chapter 2, Section I) and that her testimony from the preliminary hearing was not admissible under s 715 of the *Criminal Code* (see Section II.C, above). The Crown then submitted that Graham's earlier testimony should be admitted under the principled approach. The Supreme Court was divided on this issue.]

LAMER CJC and IACOBUCCI J (Gonthier and Cory JJ concurring):

· · ·

C. *May Graham's Testimony Before the Preliminary Inquiry Be Read into Evidence at Trial Through a Principled Exception to the Hearsay Rule?*

· · ·

1. Necessity

[71] Under this Court's principled framework, hearsay evidence will be necessary in circumstances where the declarant is unavailable to testify at trial and where the party is unable to obtain evidence of a similar quality from another source: *B. (K.G.) [R v B (KG)*, [1993] 1 SCR 740], at p. 796. Consistent with a flexible definition of the necessity criterion, there is no reason why the unavailability of the declarant should be limited to [a] closed, enumerated list of causes. As Wigmore articulated the necessity criterion (*Wigmore on Evidence*, ... [(McNaughton rev 1961), vol 8], at §1421):

> (1) The person whose assertion is offered may now be *dead*, or out of the jurisdiction, or insane, <u>or otherwise unavailable</u> for the purpose of testing. [Italics in original; underlining added.]

But as this Court indicated in *B. (K.G.)*, at pp. 797-98, the statement of a declarant may still meet the necessity criterion in limited circumstances where the declarant is not unavailable in the strict physical sense. See, e.g., *R v. Rockey*, [1996] 3 SCR 829, at para. 20, *per* McLachlin J.

[72] For the purposes of these appeals, it will suffice to hold that the preliminary inquiry testimony of a witness will satisfy the criterion of necessity where the witness is generally unavailable to testify at trial. Without restricting the precise content of "unavailability," the categories of absence recognized under s. 715, specifically death, illness, and insanity, offer a helpful guide to the types of circumstances under which it will be sufficiently necessary to consider the admission of the witness's former testimony.

[73] In this instance, we are satisfied that Graham was unavailable to testify on behalf of the Crown for the purposes of the necessity criterion. The prosecution could not call upon Graham to testify as a result of her spousal incompetency, and there was no other means of presenting evidence of a similar value before the court. In both *Khan* [*R v Khan*, [1990] 2 SCR 531], at p. 548, and *Rockey, supra*, at para. 20, the Court similarly found that the necessity criterion would be met in circumstances where a child declarant was legally incompetent to give *viva voce* evidence at trial.

2. Reliability

[74] The requirement of reliability will be satisfied where the hearsay statement was made in circumstances which provide sufficient guarantees of its trustworthiness. In particular, the circumstances must counteract the traditional evidentiary dangers associated with hearsay. As the Court explained in *B. (K.G.)*, at p. 787:

> The history of the common law exceptions to the hearsay rule suggests that for a hearsay statement to be received, there must be some other fact or circumstance which compensates for, or stands in the stead of the oath, presence and cross-examination.

[75] The criterion of reliability is concerned with threshold reliability, not ultimate reliability. The function of the trial judge is limited to determining whether the particular hearsay statement exhibits sufficient indicia of reliability so as to afford the trier of fact a satisfactory basis for evaluating the truth of the statement. More specifically, the judge must identify the specific hearsay dangers raised by the statement, and then determine whether the facts surrounding the utterance of the statement offer sufficient circumstantial guarantees

of trustworthiness to compensate for those dangers. The ultimate reliability of the statement, and the weight to be attached to it, remain determinations for the trier of fact.

[76] We are persuaded that a witness's testimony before a preliminary inquiry will generally satisfy this threshold test of reliability since there are sufficient guarantees of trustworthiness. A preliminary inquiry will involve precisely the same issues and the same parties as the trial. The hearsay dangers associated with testimony in such an adjudicative proceeding are minimal. Preliminary inquiry testimony is given under oath, and is also subject to the adverse party's right to contemporaneous cross-examination. It is *only* tainted by the lack of the declarant's presence before the trier of fact. As this Court previously stressed in *B. (K.G.)*, at p. 792, the inability to observe the declarant's demeanour on the stand can handicap the trier of fact's ability to assess the credibility of the declarant:

> When the witness is on the stand, the trier can observe the witness's reaction to questions, hesitation, degree of commitment to the statement being made, etc. Most importantly, and subsuming all of these factors, the trier can assess the relationship between the interviewer and the witness to observe the extent to which the testimony of the witness is the product of the investigator's questioning. Such subtle observations and cues cannot be gleaned from a transcript, read in court in counsel's monotone, where the atmosphere of the exchange is entirely lost.

[77] However, the existence of this sole danger is not fatal to the threshold reliability of prior testimony. In both *Smith* [*R v Smith*, [1992] 2 SCR 915] and *Khan*, the trier of fact was unable to observe the demeanour of the declarant, but this Court nonetheless found that surrounding indicia of reliability compensated for this disadvantage. Indeed, under many of the recognized exceptions to the hearsay rule, the trier of fact will not enjoy the opportunity to observe the declarant on the stand. See, e.g., *Ares v. Venner*, … [[1970] SCR 608] (business records exception). In our view, this limited danger is more than compensated by the circumstantial guarantees of trustworthiness inherent in the adversarial, adjudicative process of a preliminary inquiry. A declarant's statements before an inquiry are given under oath or affirmation before the adverse party, and the accuracy of the statement is certified by a written transcript which is signed by the judge. Most importantly, the statement is subject to contemporaneous cross-examination and, as Arbour JA noted, the party against whom the hearsay evidence is tendered has the power, at trial, to call the witness whose out-of-court statement is being offered. Indeed, it is difficult to imagine more reliable circumstances for a declarant to utter an out-of-court statement which is then tendered into evidence.

[78] In this regard, it is worth repeating that the early common law was prepared to admit former testimony under certain circumstances, thus implicitly accepting the general reliability of former testimony notwithstanding the lack of the declarant's presence. In both the United States and Great Britain, legislators have concluded that testimony in preliminary hearings is sufficiently reliable to permit its substantive reception at trial. In Great Britain, Parliament has effectively codified the historical position of the common law through a number of statutes. See *Cross and Tapper on Evidence* [(8th ed 1995)], at p. 721. In the US, Rule 804(b)(1) of the *Federal Rules of Evidence* permits the use of the prior testimony of an unavailable witness through an exception to the hearsay rule where the adverse party had the opportunity to cross-examine the declarant. The US Supreme Court has underscored the "guarantees of trustworthiness in the accoutrements of the preliminary hearing itself": *Ohio v. Roberts*, 448 US 56 (1980), at p. 73. McCormick stated

that "few [hearsay] exceptions measure up in terms of the reliability of statements under former testimony": *McCormick on Evidence* [(4th ed 1992), vol 2], at p. 322.

[79] For these reasons, we find that a witness's recorded testimony before a preliminary inquiry bears sufficient hallmarks of trustworthiness to permit the trier of fact to make substantive use of such statements at trial. The surrounding circumstances of such testimony, particularly the presence of an oath or affirmation and the opportunity for contemporaneous cross-examination, more than adequately compensate for the trier of fact's inability to observe the demeanour of the witness in court. The absence of the witness at trial goes to the weight of such testimony, not to its admissibility.

[80] In this instance, the statements of Graham were made under oath before a properly constituted preliminary inquiry, and they were subject to the opportunity of contemporaneous cross-examination by counsel for both Hawkins and Morin (an opportunity which appears to have been vigorously exercised in this instance). As well, the statements of Graham were transcribed under circumstances which support their authenticity. Accordingly, we find that the statements of Graham before the inquiry satisfy the criterion of reliability.

[81] The trial judge held that Graham's testimony before the preliminary inquiry was so inherently unreliable that it failed to pass the test of threshold reliability set out in *Khan*, *Smith* and *B. (K.G.)*. In his view, the value of her testimony was permanently corrupted as a result of its internal contradictions, and as a result of her exposure to numerous threats and inducements during the inquiry. We disagree with the trial judge's application of the principled framework. These considerations relate to the actual probative value of Graham's testimony, and thus relate to the question of "ultimate reliability" rather than "threshold reliability." As stressed previously, the test of threshold reliability is limited to an examination of the surrounding circumstances of the prior statements to determine whether there are sufficient guarantees of trustworthiness to counteract the traditional hearsay dangers. However, considerations of the weight and probative value of a declarant's statements may be relevant to the exercise of the trial judge's residual discretion to exclude evidence. Thus, we shall defer our analysis of the judge's conclusions on the inherent plausibility of Graham's testimony to our discussion of the court's residual discretion.

3. Initial Conclusions

[82] In cases where the testimony of a witness before a preliminary inquiry is not rendered admissible by s. 715 of the *Code*, the testimony may still be substantively admissible at the ensuing trial under a principled exception to the hearsay rule if the witness's prior statements meet the dual requirements of "necessity" and "reliability." In our view, statements before the inquiry will generally be necessary at trial where the witness is no longer available to testify. Such prior statements will also generally be reliable where they were delivered under oath and subject to the opportunity of cross-examination within a larger adjudicative proceeding which promotes the search for truth. Accordingly, under the *Khan*, *Smith* and *B. (K.G.)* framework, a trial judge may permit the trier of fact to consider such statements for the truth of their contents if the witness could have offered such statements into evidence as a competent and available witness at trial according to the ordinary rules governing the admissibility of evidence. Where necessary, the trial judge should properly caution the jury in relation to the proper weight to be attached to

such statements given the witness's lack of presence in court. The trial judge, of course, continues to be vested with the residual discretion to exclude such statements where their probative value is outweighed by their risk of prejudice.

[83] For the purposes of these appeals, we are not called upon to decide whether testimony given in a prior adjudicative proceeding other than a preliminary inquiry may be similarly received into evidence at a criminal trial under a principled exception to the hearsay rule. See, e.g., *R v. Finta*, [1994] 1 SCR 701, at pp. 852-55, *per* Cory J (admissibility of prior deposition in absence of cross-examination in context of war crime prosecution). Similarly, it is unnecessary to determine whether testimony delivered before a preliminary inquiry in one criminal proceeding may be read into evidence at a criminal trial in a separate criminal proceeding (i.e., a trial involving a different charge, or a different accused). Finally, we have not considered whether and under what circumstances a witness's preliminary inquiry testimony may be admitted for its substantive use as a prior inconsistent statement in accordance with the principles of *B. (K.G.)* and *U. (F.J.)*. See *R v. Clarke* (1993), 82 CCC (3d) 377 (Ont. Ct. (Gen. Div.)), aff'd. (1994), 95 CCC (3d) 275 (Ont. CA), leave to appeal refused [1995] 3 SCR vi.

[84] In this instance, we are persuaded that Graham's statements before the inquiry on September 7 and 8, 1988, and January 19 and February 20, 1989, are sufficiently necessary and reliable to permit the Crown to make substantive use of such statements at trial under a principled exception to the hearsay rule. We also hold that the body of Graham's statements was properly admissible as direct testimony before the preliminary inquiry. The substance of her incriminating statements represented party admissions (i.e., "Hawkins told me X"), which fall under a recognized exception to the hearsay rule. To the extent that some of her statements may have been improperly received before the inquiry under the ordinary rules governing the admissibility of evidence, they should not then be admitted at trial under the principled hearsay framework. Thus, it will be open to the co-appellants to object to the reception of specific statements on this basis during their new trial.

4. The Trial Judge's Residual Discretion

[Lamer CJ and Iacobucci J held that the trial judge would have the residual discretion to exclude the transcript of Graham's evidence on the basis that its probative value was outweighed by its prejudicial effect, including its effects on Hawkins and Graham's marital harmony. However, the court held that the prejudice and unfairness of the evidence did not outweigh its probative value.]

(c) Conclusion

[97] In the balance of considerations, and notwithstanding considerations of "unfairness" to the accused in his marital relationship, the risk of prejudice arising from the admission of Graham's preliminary inquiry testimony did not significantly exceed the potential probative value of such evidence at trial. The trial judge should not have exercised his residual discretion to exclude her testimony, and the transcripts ought to have been put to the trier of fact, subject to appropriate safeguards and instructions. The Crown, of course, would be obliged to present Graham's preliminary inquiry testimony before the trier of fact in its entirety (i.e., both of her appearances). We reiterate that the credibility

of Graham at various points during the inquiry and the ultimate weight to be attached to her evidence remain within the province of the trier of fact.

[L'Heureux-Dubé J, La Forest J concurring, concurred with Lamer CJ and Iacobucci J on this issue.

Major J, McLachlin and Sopinka JJ concurring, dissented. In his view, the majority's decision to admit Graham's testimony from the preliminary inquiry undermined the majority's decision regarding spousal incompetence.

The appeal was dismissed, and the Court of Appeal's decision ordering a new trial was affirmed.]

NOTES AND QUESTIONS

1. Did the result in *Hawkins* undermine the former rule of spousal incompetency (see Chapter 2, Section II.A, above) or the regime created by s 715 of the *Criminal Code*?

2. In 1997, all the charges against Hawkins were withdrawn. He later brought an action for malicious prosecution against a number of police officers and Crown attorneys: see *Hawkins v Attorney General*, 2010 ONSC 303, 98 OR (3d) 321.

3. In *R v Couture*, 2007 SCC 28, [2007] 2 SCR 517, the accused was charged with two counts of second-degree murder. The victims, one of whom had been dating the accused, were killed in 1986. In 1989, while the accused was imprisoned for another offence, he met a prison counsellor named Darlene Schwab. The accused and Schwab married in 1996, but in 1997 Schwab alleged that the accused was abusing her. She gave an audio-recorded statement to the police, in which she both described the accused's alleged abuse and said that during a counselling session in 1989, the accused had confessed to the 1986 murders. Her statement to the police was audio-recorded. Despite difficulties in their marriage, the accused and Schwab were still married at the time of the trial in 2003; accordingly, Schwab was not a competent witness for the prosecution. Was her audiotaped statement from 1997 admissible under the principled approach? What additional information would you like to have, if any, in answering this question?

4. In *R v Wilcox*, 2001 NSCA 45, 152 CCC (3d) 157, the accused were charged with multiple violations of the *Fisheries Act*, RSC 1985, c F-14, and in particular with catching more than their quota of snow crab. Central to the Crown's case was a "crab book" in which the witness Kimm kept track of the catch. The trial judge found that the accused were unaware of the "crab book." Was the "crab book" admissible under any statutory or common law exception for business records (see Section II.G, above)? If not, how might the Crown argue for its admissibility under the principled approach?

5. In *Khan*, *Smith*, *B (KG)*, and *Hawkins*, the court used the principled approach to admit hearsay that would have been inadmissible under the traditional approach. Should the principled approach be used to *restrict* the admission of hearsay? That is, if a hearsay statement admissible under a traditional exception is unreliable or unnecessary, can the principled approach be applied to exclude it? In *Starr*, the Supreme Court considered that question.

R v Starr
2000 SCC 40, [2000] 2 SCR 144, 147 CCC (3d) 449
McLachlin CJ and L'Heureux-Dubé, Gonthier, Iacobucci, Major, Bastarache,
Binnie, Arbour, and LeBel JJ (29 September 2000)

IACOBUCCI J (Major, Binnie, Arbour, and LeBel JJ concurring):

I. Introduction and Summary

[103]   The appellant, Robert Starr, was convicted at trial before a judge and jury of two counts of first degree murder. He had been accused of killing Bernard (Bo) Cook and Darlene Weselowski by shooting them by the side of a provincial highway on the outskirts of Winnipeg in the early morning hours of August 21, 1994.

· · ·

[106]   In the result, I conclude that the Court of Appeal erred in admitting the statement in question under the "present intentions" exception to the hearsay rule. However, *Khan*, ... [*R v Khan*, [1990] 2 SCR 531] and subsequent cases have established that hearsay that does not fit within a traditional exception may nonetheless be admissible if it meets the twin criteria of reliability and necessity. This case therefore requires that we determine the admissibility of evidence under the principled approach, and more particularly, the interaction between the principled approach and the traditional exceptions. In so doing, I conclude that hearsay that *does* fit within a traditional hearsay exception, as currently understood, may still be inadmissible if it is not sufficiently reliable and necessary. The traditional exception must therefore yield to comply with the principled approach.

· · ·

II. Factual Background

[108]   Bernard Cook and Darlene Weselowski were drinking with the appellant at the Westbrook Hotel in the north end of Winnipeg during the late evening and early morning of August 20-21, 1994. Cook had been released from prison the previous day. A witness, Janet Daly, testified that at around 1:50 a.m., the appellant stood up and told Cook: "If we are going to get this done, we better get this done now." Cook, Weselowski, and the appellant then left the hotel.

[109]   Cook and Weselowski parted ways with the appellant. Outside, Cook and Weselowski offered a couple named Cheryl and Daniel Ball a ride home in Weselowski's station wagon to the Balls' residence in St. Norbert, a 20 to 30 minute drive away. Cook and Weselowski were intoxicated. Cook's blood-alcohol content at the time of his death, around 3:00 a.m., was .250. Weselowski's was .140. By Cheryl Ball's account at trial, the Balls were also "really, really drunk."

[110]   Weselowski drove, and the group first stopped at an adjacent Mohawk gas station, where Jodie Giesbrecht, a sometime girlfriend of Cook, approached the station wagon and had a conversation with Cook. During the conversation, Giesbrecht observed a car beside the Mohawk gas station, and saw the appellant in the car. She could not determine whether anyone else was in the car with the appellant. A day or two later, Giesbrecht saw a picture in the newspaper of what she believed was the car in which she had seen the appellant. The car had been found at the scene of the murder. After seeing the picture,

Giesbrecht phoned the police and told them she had seen the car on the night of August 20-21, 1994 at the Mohawk gas station, with the appellant in it.

[111] Giesbrecht had spent part of the previous evening with Cook, just after his release from prison. She had been sitting with Cook and the appellant at the Westbrook Hotel about 45 minutes before Cook left the hotel with Weselowski. Giesbrecht testified that she attempted to avoid being seen by Cook as she approached the car, because she did not want Cook "to take off on me while he was with Darlene [Weselowski]." In their discussion beside the station wagon, Cook told Giesbrecht that he was driving the Balls home with Weselowski. Giesbrecht became angry with Cook because he was out with Weselowski rather than her, and she walked away from the car. Cook got out of the car and followed Giesbrecht into a laneway, where they had a further conversation. Giesbrecht asked Cook why he would not come home with her. According to Giesbrecht, Cook replied that he had to "go and do an Autopac scam with Robert." Giesbrecht understood "Robert" to be the appellant. Cook said he was to receive $500 for his involvement in wrecking a car for insurance purposes. Giesbrecht testified that it was strange for Cook to discuss business matters like this with her.

[112] At trial, the defence unsuccessfully sought to exclude as hearsay Giesbrecht's testimony regarding Cook's stated intent to participate in an Autopac scam with the appellant.

[113] Weselowski, Cook, and the Balls drove to Le Maire Street in St. Norbert, where the Balls got out of the car. Shortly after exiting the station wagon, Cheryl Ball looked back and observed a smaller car alongside the station wagon. Cheryl Ball had seen the smaller car follow them as they turned onto Le Maire Street. She could not recall the colour or make of the smaller car. She could not see how many people were in the smaller car. She could not hear any voices coming from either of the two cars. Cheryl Ball then turned away and continued to walk home with her husband.

[114] Around 3:00 a.m., Albert and Darlene Turski were awakened by their dog barking and by the sound of spinning tires outside their bedroom window. The Turskis lived on a farm bordering on provincial highway 247, several kilometres from where the Balls had been dropped off.

[115] Albert Turski testified that he looked out the window and saw on the road the lights of two cars. One car seemed to be larger than the other, judging by the sound of its engine. He could not see the vehicles clearly, other than their lights. The road was 50 to 75 yards away. The smaller car was driving along a ditch and its tires sounded like they were spinning in the grass. The larger car approached the smaller car but did not come right up to it. The smaller car got stuck but then emerged from the ditch. The lights on the larger car turned off. Albert Turski heard mumbling from people talking for about 10 to 15 seconds. He could not determine whether it was two people talking, or more than two. He then heard two "pops," and about five seconds later the smaller car drove across the road into the ditch again and back out, weaving, while the larger car turned its lights on and drove off down the highway at a normal speed. Albert Turski went back to bed.

[116] Darlene Turski's testimony was largely similar to that of her husband. However, she heard the mumbling of people talking for what she considered to be one or two minutes, and she testified that the talking sounded as though it involved "more than two" people. Right after the conversation ended, she heard two "pops." About fifteen seconds later, she said, the two cars pulled away and she and her husband lay back down in bed. Albert fell asleep immediately, but Darlene Turski stayed awake for a period of time. She

then heard more "pops" in a fast series, which sounded as if they were further away from the house.

[117] At 4:26 a.m., a young couple drove by the Turskis' house on provincial highway 247 and discovered the body of Darlene Weselowski on the side of the road outside the house, and the body of Bernard Cook lying 400 metres up the road. Weselowski had been shot twice in the head. Cook had been shot three times in the head and three times in the chest. Both victims had been shot with the same 9mm Glock semi-automatic pistol. A damaged car was found driven into a telephone pole in the ditch near Cook's body.

[118] Four days later, on August 25, 1994, the Weselowski station wagon was found parked on Buchanan Street, a block and a half from the home of the appellant's brother William on Risbey Street. There were blood spatters all over the front passenger side of the car, and several shell casings were found in the car. The blood was determined to be Cook's. Some of the appellant's scalp hairs were found on the floor of the driver's side of the vehicle.

[119] On August 22, 1994, the day after the murders, the appellant and his common law wife Shelley Letexier checked into a room at the Downs Hotel. After they left the hotel at 3:28 a.m. on August 25, 1994, they drove to the home of the appellant's brother, William, on Risbey Street. After their departure, a leather jacket in good condition was found in a dumpster at the back of the hotel. A search of the appellant's home resulted in the seizure of a purchase receipt from the Sidney I. Robinson store for 9mm ammunition capable of being loaded into a 9mm Glock semi-automatic pistol such as that which killed Weselowski and Cook. Store records from the purchase bore the appellant's name.

• • •

[128] Finally, the trial judge called Constable Robert Young of the Winnipeg police to testify regarding his interactions with Cook on August 20, 1994, several hours before the murders. Young testified that Cook was the "sergeant at arms" of the Manitoba Warriors gang, meaning he was the person responsible for all of the gang's criminal matters. Young stated that he and Cook had had meetings previous to August 20, 1994, at which Cook had expressed his desire to dissociate himself from the Manitoba Warriors. Young stated that he met with Cook on August 20, 1994 at about 6:00 p.m. Cook told Young about a break-in that had occurred earlier that day at the Sidney I. Robinson store, in which guns had been stolen. Cook said that he was to meet with members of the Los Bravos gang later that night at the Westbrook Hotel to purchase some of these guns, and that he had been told by Joseph Flett, the President of the Manitoba Warriors, to wear his gang colours. Cook expressed a concern as to why he was being asked to wear gang colours. Cook told Young that if he purchased guns he would turn one over to Young, and that he would alert Young of success in the purchase by calling Young at around 1:00 a.m. Young never received the anticipated telephone call from Cook. When Cook's body was found, he was wearing the gang colours of the Manitoba Warriors.

[129] The theory of the Crown at trial was that the killing of Cook was a gang-related execution perpetrated by the appellant. Weselowski was an unfortunate witness who was killed simply because she was in the wrong place at the wrong time. The theory was that the appellant had used an Autopac scam as a pretext to get Cook out into the countryside. Outside the Turskis' home, Cook got into the smaller car and drove it into the ditch, hitting telephone poles in an effort to damage the car. The appellant shot Weselowski twice in the head, then drove Weselowski's station wagon up the road to where Cook had

stopped the smaller car in the ditch. When Cook entered the station wagon on the passenger side, the appellant shot him from the driver's seat three times in the head and three times in the chest. He then pushed Cook's body out of the vehicle and drove away, parking near his brother's house, where the appellant abandoned the station wagon.

[130] The defence theory focussed on the issue of identity. The defence argued that the circumstantial evidence adduced by the Crown had failed to prove that the appellant actually shot the victims, and had failed to dispel the real possibility that other gang-related individuals were the killers.

III. Judicial History

[The trial judge ruled that Giesbrecht's evidence that Cook told her that he had to "go and do an Autopac scam with Robert" was admissible under the "present intentions" or "state of mind" exception to the rule against hearsay. The accused was convicted as charged. His appeal to the Manitoba Court of Appeal was dismissed.]

V. Analysis

A. The Hearsay Issues

. . .

(3) Admissibility of Cook's Statement of Intention

(a) The Proposed Use of Cook's Statement

[164] Assuming the veracity of Jodie Giesbrecht's testimony at trial, approximately one hour before Cook was killed, he told Giesbrecht that he had to "go and do an Autopac scam with Robert," meaning the appellant.

[165] The first stage of the hearsay analysis is to ask whether Cook's out-of-court statement to Giesbrecht is sought to be adduced in order to prove the truth of its contents. The Crown acknowledged in the courts below that the purpose of adducing Cook's statement was to illustrate Cook's immediate intention, shortly prior to his death, to go with the appellant to wreck a car for insurance purposes. Cook's intended course of action on the night of his murder was relevant, the Crown argued, because the jury could infer from this evidence of intention that Cook followed through on his intention, thus shedding light upon the location of the murders and the presence of a wrecked car at the scene. The Crown submitted that the statement, if true, also linked the appellant to Cook, the car, and the scene. In short, the intention to "go and do an Autopac scam with Robert" is the content of Cook's statement, and the Crown sought to use the statement as proof of its contents.

[166] It is very important to note that the Crown's proposed use of Cook's statement to Giesbrecht went beyond proving just Cook's intentions. In his closing address to the jury, Crown counsel argued that Cook's statement proved that the appellant "proposed that [Autopac] scheme to Cook because it would isolate Cook if he followed along with it, without alarming him." Given the trial judge's instruction to the jury that it was "for [them] to decide whether the evidence of Cook's statement about the scam goes as far as the Crown would have [them] believe," it is apparent that the evidence was also admitted in order to prove the intentions, and subsequent actions in conformity therewith, of the

appellant. By permitting the Crown's argument to go to the jury, the trial judge expressly permitted the jury to infer the *appellant's* intentions and subsequent conduct based on *Cook's* statement of intention to Giesbrecht.

[167] In light of these proposed uses of the statement, Giesbrecht's testimony regarding Cook's statement to her is hearsay and would generally be inadmissible as such. It was an out-of-court statement, and it was offered by the Crown to prove the truth of the matter asserted; namely, that Cook intended to do an Autopac scam with Starr. The next stage of the hearsay analysis is to examine whether Giesbrecht's evidence is nonetheless admissible under the appropriate exception.

(b) The "State of Mind" or "Present Intentions" Exception to the Hearsay Rule

(I) SCOPE OF THE RULE

[168] The Crown argued that the "state of mind" or "present intentions" exception to the hearsay rule applied to render Cook's statement to Giesbrecht admissible. This exception was most recently discussed in detail by this Court in *Smith*, ... [*R v Smith*, [1992] 2 SCR 915], where it was recognized that an "exception to the hearsay rule arises when the declarant's statement is adduced in order to demonstrate the intentions, or state of mind, of the declarant at the time when the statement was made" (p. 925). Wigmore has argued that the present intentions exception also includes a requirement that a statement "be of a *present existing state of mind*, and must appear to have been made in a natural manner and not under circumstances of suspicion": *Wigmore on Evidence*, vol. 6 (Chadbourn rev. 1976), at §1725, p. 129 (emphasis in original). L'Heureux-Dubé J, at para. 63 of her reasons, denies that Wigmore's suggestion has ever been adopted in our jurisprudence. As I will discuss below, regardless of whether the present intentions requirement ever had such a requirement, the principled approach demands that it must have it now. I will therefore examine the admissibility of Cook's statement under the present intentions exception in light of that understanding.

[169] In *Smith*, Lamer CJ explained that the exception as it has developed in Canada permits the admission into evidence of statements of intent or of other mental states for the truth of their contents and also, in the case of statements of intention in particular, to support an inference that the declarant followed through on the intended course of action, provided it is reasonable on the evidence for the trier of fact to infer that the declarant did so. At the same time, there are certain inferences that may not permissibly be drawn from hearsay evidence of the out-of-court declarant's intentions. On this point, Lamer CJ cited with approval (at p. 927) from the judgment of Doherty J in *P. (R.)*, ... [*R v P(R)* (1990), 58 CCC (3d) 334 (Ont H Ct J)], at pp. 343-44, where the case law was summarized as follows:

> The evidence is not, however, admissible to show the state of mind of persons other than the deceased (unless they were aware of the statements), or to show that persons other than the deceased acted in accordance with the deceased's stated intentions, save perhaps cases where the act was a joint one involving the deceased and another person. The evidence is also not admissible to establish that past acts or events referred to in the utterances occurred.

[170] As noted by J. Sopinka, S.N. Lederman and A.W. Bryant, in *The Law of Evidence in Canada* (2nd ed. 1999), at §6.236, in *Smith* the Court adopted "the proposition that

the admissibility of statements of intention were to be limited to the declarant's state of mind and could not be used to prove the act or intention of any other person." It is important to emphasize that even in "cases where the act was a joint one involving the deceased and another person," the hearsay is not generally admissible to show the intentions of a third party. I draw this conclusion for two reasons.

[171] First, I can find no support in Canadian jurisprudence for the proposition that statements of intention are admissible against someone other than the declarant, apart from the one comment by Doherty J noted above. Any other interpretation focusses on the exception and ignores the rule. In support of the proposition quoted above, Doherty J cited three US cases. All three had held that statements about joint acts were only admissible to prove the state of mind of the declarant: see *Giles v. United States*, 432 A.2d 739 (DC App. 1981), at pp. 745-46; *United States v. Brown*, 490 F.2d 758 (DC Cir. 1973); *People v. Madson*, 638 P.2d 18 (Colo. 1981). See also *Shepard v. United States*, 290 US 96 (1933), at pp. 105-6; D. Kiesel, "One Person's Thoughts, Another Person's Acts: How the Federal Circuit Courts Interpret the Hillmon Doctrine" (1984), 33 *Cath. UL Rev.* 699, at pp. 738-39; and J.M. Maguire, "The Hillmon Case—Thirty-Three Years After" (1925), 38 *Harv. L Rev.* 709, at p. 721.

[172] Second, there are very good reasons behind the rule against allowing statements of present intention to be used to prove the state of mind of someone other than the declarant. As noted above, the central concern with hearsay is the inability of the trier of fact to test the reliability of the declarant's assertion. When the statement is tendered to prove the intentions of a third party, this danger is multiplied. If a declarant makes a statement about the intentions of a third party, there are three possible bases for this statement: first, it could be based on a prior conversation with the accused; second, it could be based on a prior conversation with a fourth party, who indicated the third party's intentions to the declarant; or third, it could be based on pure speculation on the part of the declarant. Under the first scenario, the statement is double hearsay. Since each level of double hearsay must fall within an exception, or be admissible under the principled approach, the mere fact that the declarant is making a statement of present intention is insufficient to render it admissible. The second level of hearsay must also be admissible.

[173] The other two scenarios also clearly require exclusion. If the statement about joint acts is based on a conversation with a fourth party, then the statement is triple hearsay, or worse. If, on the other hand, it is based on pure speculation, then it clearly is unreliable and does not fit within the rationale underlying the present intentions exception.

[174] In conclusion then, a statement of intention cannot be admitted to prove the intentions of someone other than the declarant, unless a hearsay exception can be established for each level of hearsay. One way to establish this would obviously be the co-conspirator exception: see *R v. Carter*, [1982] 1 SCR 938; Sopinka, Lederman and Bryant, *supra*, at pp. 303-7. This is no doubt what Doherty J was referring to in *P. (R.)*, *supra*, when he spoke of "cases where the act was a joint one involving the deceased and another person" (p. 344). Barring the applicability of this or some other exception to each level of hearsay involved, statements of joint intention are only admissible to prove the declarant's intentions.

(II) APPLICATION TO THIS APPEAL

[175] As noted above, the trial judge below admitted Cook's statement to Jodie Giesbrecht as admissible hearsay evidence of Cook's "state of mind to go with the accused," and as evidence from which the jury could infer that Cook acted in accordance with his stated intentions. He also admitted it as evidence from which the jury could conclude that the appellant "proposed that [Autopac] scheme to Cook because it would isolate Cook if he followed along with it, without alarming him." Therefore the evidence was admitted not only to prove the intentions of the declarant Cook, but also of a third party— the appellant-accused.

[176] All three judges in the Court of Appeal below accepted as a preliminary proposition that Cook's statement to Giesbrecht fell within the traditional "present intentions" or "state of mind" exception to the hearsay rule. Although Twaddle JA, dissenting, considered it inappropriate to admit Cook's statement, especially to show the intentions and subsequent course of conduct of the appellant, he would have excluded the statement through an application of the principled approach to hearsay admissibility, or alternatively pursuant to the court's residual discretion to exclude evidence where its prejudicial effect outweighs its probative force. Ordinarily, given our limited jurisdiction on appeals as of right, our scope of review would be limited to those issues raised by Twaddle JA's dissent. However, by ordering a re-hearing we expanded the scope of our review to include the question, answered unanimously in the affirmative below, of whether Cook's statement to Giesbrecht falls within the present intentions exception.

[177] With great respect to the Court of Appeal, I conclude that the trial judge erred in admitting Cook's statement to Giesbrecht under the present intentions exception and, having admitted it, in not limiting its use by the jury, for three reasons. First, the statement contained no indicia of reliability since it was made under circumstances of suspicion; second, the trial judge failed to instruct the jury that the statement was only admissible as evidence regarding the intentions of Cook, not the appellant; and third, even if it had been properly limited, the evidence was more prejudicial than probative.

[178] Turning first to the circumstances of suspicion, I agree with Twaddle JA that the statement lacked circumstantial guarantees of trustworthiness. As Twaddle JA noted, Cook and Giesbrecht had been romantically involved for almost two years. Cook had lived with Giesbrecht and her mother for a time, and had spent the night before his murder with Giesbrecht, after getting out of jail. Then, in the early morning hours of August 21, 1994, Giesbrecht observed Cook in the car of another woman, Darlene Weselowski. Giesbrecht testified that she thought Cook might try to "take off on her" if he saw Giesbrecht approaching the car, and she endeavoured not to be seen by Cook until she was close enough to talk to him. After an initial confrontation, Giesbrecht walked away into an alley behind the gas station, where Cook followed her. Their conversation ended in an argument because Cook was with Weselowski. She was angry at Cook for being with another woman, and asked him expressly why Cook would not come home with her rather than remain with Weselowski. It was at this point, and in this heated context, that Cook said he was going to engage in an Autopac scam with the appellant, who was sitting in a car nearby. Giesbrecht testified that it was unusual for Cook to discuss such business matters with her.

[179] Twaddle JA found that the circumstances surrounding the making of the statement cast serious doubt upon the reliability of the statement. The possibility that Cook was untruthful could not be said to have been substantially negated. Twaddle JA relied, in particular, upon the fact that Cook may have had a motive to lie in order to make it seem that he was not romantically involved with Weselowski, and upon the ease with which Cook could point to the appellant, who was sitting nearby in a car but out of earshot, as being the person with whom he was going to do a scam. In my view, Twaddle JA was correct in finding that these circumstances bring the reliability of Cook's statement into doubt. The statement was made under "circumstances of suspicion," and therefore does not fall within the present intentions exception. The statement should have been excluded.

[180] The statement was also inadmissible for the purpose tendered because it was a statement of joint intention. Even assuming, contrary to the foregoing, that the Court of Appeal was correct in concluding that Cook's statement was admissible with respect to his own intentions under the present intentions exception, we must remember that Cook's statement was at least double hearsay, if not worse. The Crown did not establish how Cook became qualified to comment on the appellant's intentions. The only hearsay exception that could conceivably apply is the co-conspirator exception. However, this exception was never raised at trial, and therefore the trial judge did not even attempt to comply with the strict requirements for this exception set out in *Carter, supra*.

[181] I should emphasize that statements of intention are not automatically inadmissible simply because they refer to joint acts. As Twaddle JA noted at p. 167 of his dissent, "[t]he controversy is not so much over whether such a statement can be admitted in evidence, but rather over the use to which it can be put." Therefore statements of intention, which refer to intentions of persons other than the declarant, may be admissible if the trial judge clearly restricts their use to proving the declarant's intentions, and if it is more probative than prejudicial.

· · ·

[187] Finally, I would exclude Cook's statement as more prejudicial than probative. The trial judge did not make a finding on the issue of reliability. His focus was upon the impermissible inferences that the jury might draw from otherwise admissible hearsay, and he regarded the primary prejudice to the appellant to be that the jury might infer that he was the type of person likely to commit insurance fraud. However, as noted above, this was not the primary source of prejudice.

[188] The trial judge erred by not considering whether "the prejudicial effect of the *prohibited* use of the evidence [i.e., the appellant's intentions] overbears its probative value on the *permitted* use [i.e., Cook's intentions]": *Watt's Manual of Criminal Evidence* (1999), at p. 281 (emphasis in original). The impermissible inferences that the jury might well have drawn from Cook's statement are that the appellant was in the car that followed Cook, that the appellant was alone in the car (since Cook referred only to the appellant), and that the appellant went with Cook as part of a plan to lure Cook to a secluded area and kill him. These were the specific impermissible inferences that the jury might have drawn *in this regard*—indeed, they are inferences that the Crown specifically invited the jury to draw—quite apart from the inferences that they might have drawn regarding his general criminality. In my view, Twaddle JA was correct in finding that the prejudicial

effect of the admission of Cook's statement accordingly outweighed the statement's probative value. The statement ought to have been excluded on this basis as well: see *R v. Sea-*
boyer, [1991] 2 SCR 577, at pp. 609-11, *per* McLachlin J.

[189] I have concluded that Cook's statement does not fall within the present intentions exception to the hearsay rule. Earlier, I recognized the conflict regarding the precise
scope of this exception, and noted that the principled approach requires adopting Wigmore's requirement that the statement not be made under circumstances of suspicion. I
turn now to this question of the relationship between the principled approach and the
traditional hearsay exceptions.

(c) Admissibility of Cook's Statement to Giesbrecht Under the Principled Approach

(I) WHY THE PRINCIPLED APPROACH SHOULD PREVAIL

· · ·

WHY THE EXCEPTIONS MUST BE RATIONALIZED

[199] As I have already discussed, a fundamental concern with reliability lies at the
heart of the hearsay rule. By excluding evidence that might produce unfair verdicts, and
by ensuring that litigants will generally have the opportunity to confront adverse witnesses, the hearsay rule serves as a cornerstone of a fair justice system.

[200] In *Khan*, *Smith*, and subsequent cases, this Court allowed the admission of
hearsay not fitting within an established exception where it was sufficiently reliable and
necessary to address the traditional hearsay dangers. However, this concern for reliability
and necessity should be no less present when the hearsay is sought to be introduced under
an established exception. This is particularly true in the criminal context given the "fundamental principle of justice, protected by the *Charter*, that the innocent must not be
convicted": *R v. Leipert*, [1997] 1 SCR 281, at para. 24, quoted in *R v. Mills*, [1999] 3 SCR
668, at para. 71. It would compromise trial fairness, and raise the spectre of wrongful
convictions, if the Crown is allowed to introduce unreliable hearsay against the accused,
regardless of whether it happens to fall within an existing exception.

[201] In addition to improving trial fairness, bringing the hearsay exceptions into line
with the principled approach will also improve the intellectual coherence of the law of
hearsay. It would seem anomalous to label an approach "principled" that applies only to
the admission of evidence, not its exclusion. Rationalizing the hearsay exceptions into the
principled approach shows that the former are simply specific manifestations of general
principles, rather than the isolated "pigeon-holes" referred to in *U. (F.J.)*, … [*R v U (FJ)*],
[1995] 3 SCR 764], at para. 20.

THE CONTINUING IMPORTANCE OF THE EXISTING EXCEPTIONS

[202] Having recognized the primacy of the principled approach, it is nevertheless
important for a court to exercise a certain degree of caution when reconsidering the
traditional exceptions. While the exceptions may need to be reexamined in light of the
principled approach, their complete abolition is not the answer. Rather, the exceptions
continue to play an important role under the principled approach. Our task therefore is
to reconcile the traditional exceptions with the principled approach.

[203] One important function that the hearsay exceptions have served has been to add predictability and certainty to the law of hearsay. In light of the exceptions, and regardless of how illogical or arbitrary they may be, litigants can be more or less certain when going into court of the types of issues that will be relevant in debating admissibility in a particular context, and of the likelihood that the evidence will indeed be admitted. This certainty has fostered greater efficiency in the use of court time both at trial and on appeal, and has facilitated the task of the too frequently overburdened trial judge who is called upon to rule on hearsay admissibility with speed and considerable regularity. As suggested by Rosenberg, ... [M. Rosenberg, "*B. (K.G.)*—Necessity and Reliability: The New Pigeon-holes" (1993), 19 CR (4th) 69], at p. 75, a complete abolition of the exceptions and their replacement by the principled approach standing alone would complicate the judicial task:

> [I]t is unfair to simply leave the decision as to the admission of hearsay completely open-ended, leaving the trial judges without any analytical tool for determining what is reasonably necessary. To simply define the test in terms of reliability and necessity is just too vague to be of any practical use. With all its rigidity and anomalies a hearsay rule consisting of a broad rule of exclusion with certain well-defined exceptions was *relatively* easy to apply. Taking away all of the rules and replacing them with necessity and reliability, while perhaps not inviting chaos, does make the role of the trial judge that much more difficult. [Emphasis in original.]

[204] Second, in addition to serving the utilitarian goals of providing greater certainty and fostering judicial efficiency, the exceptions have served an explanatory or educative function, instructing litigants and judges about the relevant factors to consider in determining whether to admit a *particular type* of hearsay evidence, or whether to admit hearsay in a *particular factual context*. Different hearsay scenarios by their nature raise different reliability concerns, and different issues of necessity. The specific requirements of the individual exceptions have had the useful effect of focussing attention upon the peculiar factors that make it desirable, or undesirable, to admit a particular form of out-of-court statement. This should be no surprise given Lamer CJ's statement in *Smith, supra*, that the principled approach is "governed by the principles which underlie the [hearsay] rule and its exceptions alike" (p. 932). Since the principled approach is implicit in most of the exceptions, they are likely to be strong evidence of necessity and reliability.

[205] It is true that there is guidance inherent in the principled approach itself, which directs a court to gauge whether a particular hearsay statement is reliable and whether its admission is necessary in the circumstances. However, the exceptions are more fact-specific and contextually sensitive. Properly modified to conform to the principled approach, the exceptions are practical manifestations of the principled approach in concrete and meaningful form. Indeed, it is precisely to illustrate the form of analysis under the principled approach that must occur in a particular factual context that this Court in its recent cases has outlined carefully the type of inquiry that must occur when dealing with a particular type of hearsay, whether it be the testimony of a child witness (*Khan, supra*), a prior inconsistent statement (*B. (K.G.), supra*, and *U. (F.J.), supra*), or prior testimony (*Hawkins*, ... [*R v Hawkins*, [1996] 3 SCR 1043]). Some commentators have suggested that the Court's recent hearsay jurisprudence may accordingly be seen as creating new hearsay exceptions to supplement the traditional exceptions: see, e.g., *Carter, supra*, at

p. 579. Perhaps a more accurate characterization is to say that all of the hearsay "exceptions" should be seen simply as concrete examples of the practical application of the purpose and principles of the hearsay rule in a particular context.

[206] A third important function played by the traditional hearsay exceptions is that they teach us about the historical and contemporary rationale for admitting certain forms of hearsay. It has quite properly been noted that some hearsay exceptions allow for the admission of evidence that is unreliable, unnecessary, or both. In the interest of fairness for the litigant against whom it is used, unreliable hearsay evidence should never be admitted. Apart from that, a review of the traditional exceptions reveals that there are reasons beyond "pure" necessity why a court might wish to admit reliable hearsay evidence. This point was addressed by Lamer CJ in *B. (K.G.)*, at pp. 796-97, where he explained that the need to permit the admission of certain forms of hearsay can stem not only from the unavailability of the out-of-court declarant, but also from the quality of the evidence itself. Lamer CJ cited Professor Wigmore's explanation (*Wigmore on Evidence*, vol. 5 (Chadbourn rev. 1974), at p. 253) that some hearsay evidence "may be such that we cannot expect, again, or at this time, to get *evidence of the same value* from the same or other sources" (emphasis in original). Such hearsay may be admitted, where appropriate, less on the basis of necessity and more on the basis of "expediency or convenience." The traditional exceptions are useful, therefore, because they are instructive as to the types of situations that may produce hearsay that is the best evidence in the circumstances.

[207] There are other important functions served by the traditional hearsay exceptions, but the issues I have referred to are sufficient to illustrate that it is neither desirable nor necessary to abolish these exceptions outright. The more appropriate approach is to seek to derive the benefits of certainty, efficiency, and guidance that the exceptions offer, while adding the benefits of fairness and logic that the principled approach provides. The task is to rid the exceptions of their arbitrary aspects, in order to avoid admitting hearsay evidence that should be excluded.

(II) IS COOK'S STATEMENT TO GIESBRECHT ADMISSIBLE UNDER THE PRINCIPLED
      APPROACH?

[208] For much the same reasons why the statement did not meet the requirements for admissibility under the present intentions exception, I conclude that the statement is not admissible under the principled approach either. This should not be particularly surprising—as I have discussed above, the traditional exceptions are based on the concepts of reliability and necessity. While occasionally, as in *Khan*, *supra*, a statement not falling within an existing exception will be admissible under the principled approach, this will likely be the exception, not the rule.

[209] The first requirement for admissibility under the principled approach is reliability. Given my conclusion above that Cook's statement was made under "circumstances of suspicion," it follows that the statement was not reliable. Nor are there any other circumstantial guarantees of trustworthiness that could render the statement reliable. Having found that the statement is unreliable, it is unnecessary to go on to ask whether it was necessary or not. I conclude that Cook's statement to Giesbrecht was inadmissible under the principled approach. Since it does not fall under an existing exception either, for all the reasons given above, the courts below erred in admitting this evidence. There being

no serious argument that the error was one that could be saved by the curative proviso, s. 686(1)(b)(iii) of the *Criminal Code*, RSC, 1985, c. C-46, the appeal must be allowed.

(d) Revisiting the Hearsay Exceptions in Future Cases

[210] While the foregoing is perhaps sufficient to dispose of this appeal, the majority of the arguments both in the court below and before this Court focussed on the relationship between the principled approach and the traditional exceptions. Given this, and the substantial controversy among both lower courts and commentators regarding the appropriate relationship between the principled approach and the traditional hearsay exceptions, I would like to offer some general remarks on this issue. I have no doubt that the lower courts will develop guidelines over time as circumstances warrant.

[211] I hope from the foregoing that it is clear that the existing exceptions are a long-standing and important aspect of our law of evidence. I am cognizant of their important role, and the need for caution in reforming them. Given their continuing importance, I would expect that in the clear majority of cases, the presence or absence of a traditional exception will be determinative of admissibility.

[212] While *Khan, supra*, and its progeny have set out the approach for evidence falling outside a traditional exception, I would note that evidence falling within a traditional exception is presumptively admissible. These exceptions traditionally incorporate an inherent reliability component. For example, testimony in former proceedings is admitted, at least in part, because many of the traditional dangers associated with hearsay are not present. As pointed out in Sopinka, Lederman and Bryant, *supra*, at pp. 278-79:

> … a statement which was earlier made under oath, subjected to cross-examination and admitted as testimony at a former proceeding is received in a subsequent trial *because the dangers underlying hearsay evidence are absent.* [Emphasis added.]

Other exceptions are based not on negating traditional hearsay dangers, but on the fact that the statement provides circumstantial guarantees of reliability. This approach is embodied in recognized exceptions such as dying declarations, spontaneous utterances, and statements against pecuniary interest.

[213] All this being said, it is also clear that the logic of the principled approach demands that it must prevail in situations where it is in conflict with an existing exception. For example, had there been any doubt in this appeal whether the present intentions exception required that the statement not be made under circumstances of suspicion, the principled approach would require holding that it does now. Hearsay evidence may only be admitted if it is necessary and reliable, and the traditional exceptions should be interpreted in a manner consistent with this requirement.

[214] In some rare cases, it may also be possible under the particular circumstances of a case for evidence clearly falling within an otherwise valid exception nonetheless not to meet the principled approach's requirements of necessity and reliability. In such a case, the evidence would have to be excluded. However, I wish to emphasize that these cases will no doubt be unusual, and that the party challenging the admissibility of evidence falling within a traditional exception will bear the burden of showing that the evidence should nevertheless be inadmissible. The trial judge will determine the procedure

(whether by *voir dire* or otherwise) to determine admissibility under the principled approach's requirements of reasonable necessity and reliability.

[215] In this connection, it is important when examining the reliability of a statement under the principled approach to distinguish between threshold and ultimate reliability. Only the former is relevant to admissibility: see *Hawkins, supra*, at p. 1084. Again, it is not appropriate in the circumstances of this appeal to provide an exhaustive catalogue of the factors that may influence threshold reliability. However, our jurisprudence does provide some guidance on this subject. Threshold reliability is concerned not with whether the statement is true or not; that is a question of ultimate reliability. Instead, it is concerned with whether or not the circumstances surrounding the statement itself provide circumstantial guarantees of trustworthiness. This could be because the declarant had no motive to lie (see *Khan, supra*; *Smith, supra*), or because there were safeguards in place such that a lie could be discovered (see *Hawkins, supra*; *U. (F.J.), supra*; *B. (K.G.), supra*).

[216] And indeed, lower courts have recognized that the absence of a motive to lie is a relevant factor in admitting evidence under the principled approach: see *R v. L. (J.W.)* (1994), 94 CCC (3d) 263 (Ont. CA); *R v. Tam* (1995), 100 CCC (3d) 196 (BCCA); *R v. Rose* (1998), 108 BCAC 221; see also B.P. Archibald, "The Canadian Hearsay Revolution: Is Half a Loaf Better Than No Loaf at All?" (1999), 25 *Queen's LJ* 1, at p. 34. Conversely, the presence of a motive to lie may be grounds for exclusion of evidence under the principled approach. Put another way, it is the role of the trial judge to determine threshold reliability by satisfying him- or herself that notwithstanding the absence of the declarant for cross-examination purposes, the statement possesses sufficient elements of reliability that it should be passed on to be considered by the trier of fact.

[217] At the stage of hearsay admissibility the trial judge should not consider the declarant's general reputation for truthfulness, nor any prior or subsequent statements, consistent or not. These factors do not concern the circumstances of the statement itself. Similarly, I would not consider the presence of corroborating or conflicting evidence. On this point, I agree with the Ontario Court of Appeal's decision in *R v. C. (B.)* (1993), 12 OR (3d) 608; see also *Idaho v. Wright*, 497 US 805 (1990). In summary, under the principled approach a court must not invade the province of the trier of fact and condition admissibility of hearsay on whether the evidence is ultimately reliable. However, it will need to examine whether the circumstances in which the statement was made lend sufficient credibility to allow a finding of threshold reliability.

. . .

VI. *Disposition*

[245] The appeal is allowed, the judgment of the Court of Appeal is set aside, and a new trial is directed.

[McLachlin CJ (Bastarache J concurring) (dissenting) agreed with Iacobucci J's reformulation of the "present intentions" exception to the rule against hearsay but held that there were no circumstances of suspicion making Cook's statement inadmissible. She held that Cook's statement could be considered, along with the other circumstantial evidence, to support "the inference that Starr was with the deceased later that night" and that the trial judge's instructions had made it clear that the jury should not "facilely jump from Cook's

statement to the conclusion that Cook and the accused actually met later that evening."
She would have dismissed the appeal.]

[L'Heureux-Dubé J (Gonthier J concurring) (dissenting) did not accept Iacobucci J's reformulation of the present intentions exception and would have held that Cook's statement was admissible for its truth and to support an inference that Cook had acted in accordance with it. She held further that, generally speaking, the principled approach should not be used to render hearsay inadmissible if it was admissible under a traditional exception.]

NOTES AND QUESTIONS ON STARR

1. Are any of the exceptions considered in Section II, above, likely targets for reformulation in the aftermath of *Starr*?

2. Consider Iacobucci J's statement in para 172 that Cook's statement of intention was double hearsay. Do you agree? If it was double hearsay, can you think of a further hearsay exception that would make it admissible?

3. What inference did the Crown want the jury to draw from Cook's statement? Did the drawing of that inference carry with it the dangers suggested by Iacobucci J?

4. In para 217 of his reasons, Iacobucci J states that in assessing the reliability of a hearsay statement, the judge should not consider "prior or subsequent statements, consistent or not [or] ... the presence of corroborating or conflicting evidence." What is the rationale for this limit? Is it consistent with the court's decisions in cases such as *Khan* and *U (FJ)*? Is it consistent with the ideas underlying the principled approach?

5. While in custody following his first trial, Starr gave a statement to corrections officials, admitting his presence at the scene of the crime but stating that someone else had shot the two victims. This statement was admitted at his second trial. He was convicted of one count of manslaughter, and was sentenced to six years' imprisonment in addition to one year on remand while awaiting trial and to six years in a penitentiary while his appeals were determined. See *R v Starr*, 2002 MBCA 97, 167 CCC (3d) 193.

6. In *R v Mapara*, 2005 SCC 23, [2005] 1 SCR 358, 195 CCC (3d) 225, McLachlin CJ for the majority explained the relationship between the traditional exceptions and the principled approach as follows:

(a) Hearsay evidence is presumptively inadmissible unless it falls under an exception to the hearsay rule. The traditional exceptions to the hearsay rule remain in place.

(b) A hearsay exception can be challenged to determine whether it is supported by *indicia* of necessity and reliability, required by the principled approach. The exception can be modified as necessary to bring it into compliance.

(c) In "rare cases," evidence falling within an existing exception may be excluded because the *indicia* of necessity and reliability are lacking in the particular circumstances of the case.

(d) If hearsay evidence does not fall under a hearsay exception, it may still be admitted if *indicia* of reliability and necessity are established on a *voir dire*.

How does this framework compare with the approach taken by Iacobucci J in *Starr*?

R v Khelawon
2006 SCC 57, [2006] 2 SCR 787
McLachlin CJ and Binnie, LeBel, Deschamps, Fish, Abella, and Charron JJ
(14 December 2006)

CHARRON J:

. . .

2. Background

[9] Mr. Khelawon was charged with aggravated assault on Teofil Skupien and threat-ening to cause him death. He was also charged with aggravated assault and assault with a weapon on Atillio Dinino, and assault causing bodily harm on three other complainants. The offences were alleged to have occurred during the month of May 1999 and, at the time, all the complainants were residents at the Bloor West Village Retirement Home. Mr. Khelawon was the manager of the retirement home and his mother was the owner. As indicated earlier, none of the complainants was available to testify at trial. Hence, the central issue concerned the admissibility of their hearsay statements made to various people. There were 10 statements in total, four of which consisted of videotaped statements made to the police. The trial, held before Grossi J without a jury, proceeded essentially as a *voir dire* into the admissibility of the evidence, with counsel agreeing that it would not be necessary to repeat the evidence about any statements later ruled admissible. None of the statements fit within any traditional exception to the hearsay rule. Their admissibility, rather, was contingent upon the Crown meeting the twin requirements of necessity and reliability under the principled approach to the hearsay rule, as established in *Khan* [R v Khan*, [1990] 2 SCR 531], *Smith* [R v Smith*, [1992] 2 SCR 915] and, later, *Starr* [R v Starr*, 2000 SCC 40, [2000] 2 SCR 144].

[10] The charges concerning Mr. Skupien are the only matters before this Court. I will therefore summarize the evidence concerning Mr. Skupien's statements in more detail. I will also describe the circumstances surrounding the taking of the statements from the other complainants to the extent that it is relevant to dispose of this appeal. The Crown sought to introduce three statements made by Mr. Skupien: the first to an employee of the retirement home, the second to the doctor who treated him for his injuries, and the third to the police. Only the latter was admitted at trial. I will describe each statement in turn.

2.1 Mr. Skupien's Statement to Ms. Stangrat

[11] Mr. Skupien was 81 years old and, at the time of the events in question, he had lived at the Bloor West Village Retirement Home for four years. Mr. Skupien's initial complaint was made to one of the employees at the retirement home, Joanna Stangrat. Ms. Stangrat, also known under several other names, was a cook who had been working at the retirement home for a few months. She had come to know Mr. Skupien because he would often visit the kitchen and would sometimes walk her to the subway at the end of her shifts. Ms. Stangrat played a prominent role in the case concerning Mr. Skupien. In part, it was the theory of the defence at trial that she had influenced Mr. Skupien and the other complainants in making their complaints out of spite because Mr. Khelawon had given her a notice of termination a few weeks earlier.

[12] On May 8, 1999, Ms. Stangrat noticed that Mr. Skupien did not come to breakfast. She went to check on him in his room and found him lying on his bed. His face was red and there was blood around his mouth. When she got closer to him she saw bruising on his eye and nose. His eyes were swollen. When Mr. Skupien saw her, he asked her to come in and close the door. He appeared to be in shock and very shaky. Ms. Stangrat noticed two full green garbage bags on the floor. She closed the door and asked him what had happened and what was in the green garbage bags. Mr. Skupien told her what had happened the previous evening. He also showed her bruises on his upper left chest area.

[13] Mr. Skupien told Ms. Stangrat that he had to leave before twelve o'clock that day because "Tony," the name Mr. Khelawon went by, would come back and kill him. Mr. Skupien described to Ms. Stangrat how Mr. Khelawon had come into his room in anger at about 8:00 p.m. the previous evening, and had punched him repeatedly in the face and ribs. After beating him up, Mr. Khelawon had packed the clothes into the green garbage bags and left them on the floor. Ms. Stangrat asked Mr. Skupien why Mr. Khelawon would attack him in this way. He told her that Tony was angry because Mr. Skupien had been going to the kitchen when he had no reason to go there. When the assault ended, Mr. Khelawon threatened Mr. Skupien that either he moved out of the home by twelve noon the next day or he would return and kill him. Mr. Skupien asked her what he should do. Ms. Stangrat told him she would phone her daughter to come and get him and that he should stay in his room until she was finished her duties for the day.

[14] Ms. Stangrat arranged for Mr. Skupien to stay at her daughter's home later that day, and then to her apartment. Mr. Skupien was in pain but he was scared and did not want to see a doctor at that time. Ms. Stangrat kept Mr. Skupien at her apartment where she and a friend of hers alternated caring for him. A few days later, Mr. Skupien agreed to go to the doctor. Ms. Stangrat and her friend took him to see Dr. Pietraszek.

2.2 Mr. Skupien's Statement to the Treating Physician

[15] On May 12, 1999, Dr. Pietraszek examined Mr. Skupien. He found visible bruising to Mr. Skupien's face as well as bruises to his back and on the left side of his chest and noted that Mr. Skupien appeared to be in pain while breathing. X-rays revealed that he had suffered fractures to three ribs. Dr. Pietraszek testified that Mr. Skupien told him he had been hit in the face and body with something that was either a cane or a pipe. He denied any suggestion that Ms. Stangrat had related the story but acknowledged that she was present and may have helped him in describing what had happened. Dr. Pietraszek considered that the injuries were consistent with Mr. Skupien's account of how they were caused. He also testified that the injuries could have resulted from a fall.

2.3 Mr. Skupien's Videotaped Statement to the Police

[16] The following day, on May 13, 1999, Ms. Stangrat took Mr. Skupien to the police. Detective Karpow took his complaint. He observed bruising to the left side of Skupien's face, in the eye area. He arranged for Mr. Skupien to give a videotaped statement. Both Detective Karpow and Cst. John Birrell were present. The statement was not given under oath; however, Mr. Skupien was asked if he understood that it was very important that he tell the truth and that if he did not tell the truth "[he] could be charged with that." Mr. Skupien answered "Yes" to both questions. After a few other preliminary questions,

he was asked what his complaint was. Mr. Skupien described how, on May 7, 1999, Tony came to his room and said: "enough is enough." He then began beating him by slapping and punching him in the face, the ribs and all over, telling him not to go into the kitchen. He said that if he did not leave, he would come by 12 o'clock the next day and shoot him. Mr. Skupien then went on at some length to make several complaints about the general management of the retirement home until Detective Karpow brought him back to the matter at hand by asking him further questions about the incident and the events that followed. Mr. Skupien was generally responsive to the officer's questions.

[17] After the interview was completed, Mr. Khelawon was arrested.

2.4 Further Investigation

[18] Ms. Stangrat gave the police a list of other people that she thought they should speak to at the retirement home. The next day, on May 14, 1999, several police officers attended the home to seek these people out. Because there were no markings on the doors, the police had to search through the residence, speaking to residents and nursing staff. When some of the people were located, they were found to be "unresponsive" and no meaningful interviews could be conducted with them. Others, however, were able and willing to speak. The police would identify themselves as police, then ask the residents how things were going at the home and if anything had happened to them that they wanted to talk about. The police arranged to take videotaped statements from those who wanted to speak to them. These included three of the other complainants, Mr. Dinino, Ms. Poliszak and Mr. Grocholska. The fourth complainant, Mr. Peiszterer, could not communicate with the police; however, his son provided a videotaped statement.

2.5 Medical Records

[19] On May 15, 1999, Det. Karpow attended at the retirement home and met with Dr. Michalski, a physician who attended regularly at the home to see the residents. On May 18, 1999, the police returned to the home and seized the medical records and a journal containing nursing notes.

[20] Documentation from Mr. Skupien's file revealed that he had been living in an apartment before suffering a stroke in February 1995. He was transferred to the retirement home in April 1995. A report dated April 13, 1995 noted his condition after the stroke. He suffered occasional periods of confusion, could not go outside on his own, needed help with meal preparation and banking, and had to be reminded to take his medication, but was able to perform all self-care tasks.

[21] Dr. Michalski's file noted frequent contact with Mr. Skupien during his stay at the retirement home. From time to time, he was described as "depressed," "aggressive," "angry," and "paranoid." A diagnosis of paranoid psychoses was made in June 1998 and medication was prescribed. In July 1998, "some improvement in paranoia" was noted. In August 1998, he was described as "angry, hostile" and his dosage was increased. In August 1998, he was described as "confused." The possibility of dementia was first noted. In September 1998, he was diagnosed with "depression" and prescribed medication. In September 1998, improvement with the depression was noted, and although apparently "eliminated" in January 1999, depression was again noted in February 1999. The notes also reflect a number of complaints of fatigue, weakness and dizziness.

2.6 Expert Evidence on the Voir Dire

[22] Dr. Susan Lieff, a geriatric psychiatrist, was qualified to provide opinion evidence on the *voir dire* with respect to Mr. Skupien's capacity to understand the importance of telling the truth and communicate evidence. She also provided an opinion with respect to Mr. Dinino. Her opinion was based solely on her review of the videotaped interviews and medical records. With regard to Mr. Skupien, Dr. Lieff testified that the videotape did not reveal any impaired judgment, delusions or hallucinations, or intellectual pathology. He seemed to comprehend what was asked and responded appropriately. In Dr. Lieff's view, Mr. Skupien's affirmative answer "Yes," when advised of the need to be truthful, reflected a clear understanding. Dr. Lieff did not consult with Dr. Michalski but took issue with his diagnosis of "dementia." In her opinion, the symptoms observed by Dr. Michalski were more likely side-effects of the anti-psychotic medication he was taking at the time. Dr. Lieff concluded that Mr. Skupien understood that it was important to tell the truth and that he had the capacity to communicate evidence.

[The trial judge ruled that Skupien's videotaped statement to the police was admissible. The accused was convicted at trial. His appeal to the Ontario Court of Appeal was allowed, and an acquittal was entered. The Crown appealed to the Supreme Court of Canada.]

5. Rule Against Hearsay

5.1 General Exclusionary Rule

[34] The basic rule of evidence is that all relevant evidence is admissible. There are a number of exceptions to this basic rule. One of the main exceptions is the rule against hearsay: absent an exception, hearsay evidence is *not* admissible. Hearsay evidence is not excluded because it is irrelevant—there is no need for a special rule to exclude irrelevant evidence. Rather, as we shall see, it is the difficulty of testing hearsay evidence that underlies the exclusionary rule and, generally, the alleviation of this difficulty that forms the basis of the exceptions to the rule. Although hearsay evidence includes communications expressed by conduct, I will generally refer to hearsay statements only.

5.2 Definition of Hearsay

[35] At the outset, it is important to determine what is and what is not hearsay. The difficulties in defining hearsay encountered by courts and learned authors have been canvassed before and need not be repeated here: see *R v. Abbey*, [1982] 2 SCR 24, at pp. 40-41, *per* Dickson J. It is sufficient to note, as this Court did in *Starr*, at para. 159, that the more recent definitions of hearsay are focussed on the central concern underlying the hearsay rule: the difficulty of testing the reliability of the declarant's assertion. See, for example, *R v. O'Brien*, [1978] 1 SCR 591, at pp. 593-94. Our adversary system puts a premium on the calling of witnesses, who testify under oath or solemn affirmation, whose demeanour can be observed by the trier of fact, and whose testimony can be tested by cross-examination. We regard this process as the optimal way of testing testimonial evidence. Because hearsay evidence comes in a different form, it raises particular concerns. The general exclusionary rule is a recognition of the difficulty for a trier of fact to assess what weight, if any, is to be given to a statement made by a person who has not been seen

or heard, and who has not been subject to the test of cross-examination. The fear is that untested hearsay evidence may be afforded more weight than it deserves. The essential defining features of hearsay are therefore the following: (1) the fact that the statement is adduced to prove the truth of its contents and (2) the absence of a contemporaneous opportunity to cross-examine the declarant.

. . .

5.4 Constitutional Dimension: Trial Fairness

[47] Prior to admitting hearsay statements under the principled exception to the hearsay rule, the trial judge must determine on a *voir dire* that necessity and reliability have been established. The onus is on the person who seeks to adduce the evidence to establish these criteria on a balance of probabilities. In a criminal context, the inquiry may take on a constitutional dimension, because difficulties in testing the evidence, or conversely the inability to present reliable evidence, may impact on an accused's ability to make full answer and defence, a right protected by s. 7 of the *Canadian Charter of Rights and Freedoms: Dersch v. Canada (Attorney General)*, [1990] 2 SCR 1505. The right to make full answer and defence in turn is linked to another principle of fundamental justice, the right to a fair trial: *R v. Rose*, [1998] 3 SCR 262. The concern over trial fairness is one of the paramount reasons for rationalizing the traditional hearsay exceptions in accordance with the principled approach. As stated by Iacobucci J in *Starr*, at para. 200, in respect of Crown evidence: "It would compromise trial fairness, and raise the spectre of wrongful convictions, if the Crown is allowed to introduce unreliable hearsay against the accused, regardless of whether it happens to fall within an existing exception."

[48] As indicated earlier, our adversary system is based on the assumption that sources of untrustworthiness or inaccuracy can best be brought to light under the test of cross-examination. It is mainly because of the inability to put hearsay evidence to that test, that it is presumptively inadmissible. However, the constitutional right guaranteed under s. 7 of the *Charter* is not the right to confront or cross-examine adverse witnesses in itself. The adversarial trial process, which includes cross-examination, is but the means to achieve the end. Trial fairness, as a principle of fundamental justice, is the end that must be achieved. Trial fairness embraces more than the rights of the accused. While it undoubtedly includes the right to make full answer and defence, the fairness of the trial must also be assessed in the light of broader societal concerns: see *R v. Mills*, [1999] 3 SCR 668, at paras. 69-76. In the context of an admissibility inquiry, society's interest in having the trial process arrive at the truth is one such concern.

[49] The broader spectrum of interests encompassed in trial fairness is reflected in the twin principles of necessity and reliability. The criterion of necessity is founded on society's interest in getting at the truth. Because it is not always possible to meet the optimal test of contemporaneous cross-examination, rather than simply losing the value of the evidence, it becomes necessary in the interests of justice to consider whether it should nonetheless be admitted in its hearsay form. The criterion of reliability is about ensuring the integrity of the trial process. The evidence, although needed, is not admissible unless it is sufficiently reliable to overcome the dangers arising from the difficulty of testing it. As we shall see, the reliability requirement will generally be met on the basis of two different grounds, neither of which excludes consideration of the other. In some cases, because of

the circumstances in which it came about, the contents of the hearsay statement may be so reliable that contemporaneous cross-examination of the declarant would add little if anything to the process. In other cases, the evidence may not be so cogent but the circumstances will allow for sufficient testing of evidence by means other than contemporaneous cross-examination. In these circumstances, the admission of the evidence will rarely undermine trial fairness. However, because trial fairness may encompass factors beyond the strict inquiry into necessity and reliability, even if the two criteria are met, the trial judge has the discretion to exclude hearsay evidence where its probative value is outweighed by its prejudicial effect.

6. The Admissibility Inquiry

6.1 Distinction Between Threshold and Ultimate Reliability: A Source of Confusion

[50] As stated earlier, the trial judge only decides whether hearsay evidence is admissible. Whether the hearsay statement will or will not be ultimately relied upon in deciding the issues in the case is a matter for the trier of fact to determine at the conclusion of the trial based on a consideration of the statement in the context of the entirety of the evidence. It is important that the trier of fact's domain not be encroached upon at the admissibility stage. If the trial is before a judge and jury, it is crucial that questions of ultimate reliability be left for the jury—in a criminal trial, it is constitutionally imperative. If the judge sits without a jury, it is equally important that he or she not prejudge the ultimate reliability of the evidence before having heard all of the evidence in the case. Hence, a distinction must be made between "ultimate reliability" and "threshold reliability." Only the latter is inquired into on the admissibility *voir dire*.

[Charron J quoted paras 215 and 217 of *Starr* and noted some of the criticisms of Iacobucci J's holding that a trial judge should not consider "corroborating or conflicting evidence" in determining threshold reliability. She continued:]

6.2 Identifying the Relevant Factors: A Functional Approach

6.2.1 Recognizing Hearsay

[56] The first matter to determine before embarking on a hearsay admissibility inquiry, of course, is whether the proposed evidence is hearsay. This may seem to be a rather obvious matter, but it is an important first step. Misguided objections to the admissibility of an out-of-court statement based on a misunderstanding of what constitutes hearsay are not uncommon. As discussed earlier, not all out-of-court statements will constitute hearsay. Recall the defining features of hearsay. An out-of-court statement will be hearsay when: (1) it is adduced to prove the truth of its contents *and* (2) there is no opportunity for a contemporaneous cross-examination of the declarant.

[57] Putting one's mind to the defining features of hearsay at the outset serves to better focus the admissibility inquiry. As we have seen, the first identifying feature of hearsay calls for an inquiry into the purpose for which it is adduced. Only when the evidence is being tendered for its truth will it constitute hearsay. The fact that the out-of-court statement is adduced for its *truth* should be considered in the context of the issues in the case

so that the court may better assess the potential impact of introducing the evidence in its hearsay form.

[58] Second, by putting one's mind, at the outset, to the second defining feature of hearsay—the absence of an opportunity for contemporaneous cross-examination of the declarant, the admissibility inquiry is immediately focussed on the dangers of admitting hearsay evidence. Iacobucci J in *Starr* identified the inability to test the evidence as the "central concern" underlying the hearsay rule. Lamer CJ in *U. (F.J.)* [*R v U (FJ)*, [1995] 3 SCR 764] expressed the same view but put it more directly by stating: "Hearsay is inadmissible as evidence because its reliability cannot be tested" (para. 22).

6.2.2 Presumptive Inadmissibility of Hearsay Evidence

[59] Once the proposed evidence is identified as hearsay, it is presumptively *inadmissible*. I stress the nature of the hearsay rule as a general exclusionary rule because the increased flexibility introduced in the Canadian law of evidence in the past few decades has sometimes tended to blur the distinction between admissibility and weight. Modifications have been made to a number of rules, including the rule against hearsay, to bring them up to date and to ensure that they facilitate rather than impede the goals of truth seeking, judicial efficiency and fairness in the adversarial process. However, the traditional rules of evidence reflect considerable wisdom and judicial experience. The modern approach has built upon their underlying rationale, not discarded it. In *Starr* itself, where this Court recognized the primacy of the principled approach to hearsay exceptions, the presumptive exclusion of hearsay evidence was reaffirmed in strong terms. Iacobucci J stated as follows (at para. 199):

> By excluding evidence that might produce unfair verdicts, and by ensuring that litigants will generally have the opportunity to confront adverse witnesses, the hearsay rule serves as a cornerstone of a fair justice system.

6.2.3 Traditional Exceptions

[60] The Court in *Starr* also reaffirmed the continuing relevance of the traditional exceptions to the hearsay rule. More recently, this Court in *Mapara* [*R v Mapara*, 2005 SCC 23, [2005] 1 SCR 358] reiterated the continued application of the traditional exceptions in setting out the governing analytical framework, as noted in para. 42 above. Therefore, if the trial judge determines that the evidence falls within one of the traditional common law exceptions, this finding is conclusive and the evidence is ruled admissible, unless, in a rare case, the exception itself is challenged as described in both those decisions.

6.2.4 Principled Approach: Overcoming the Hearsay Dangers

[61] Since the central underlying concern is the inability to test hearsay evidence, it follows that under the principled approach the reliability requirement is aimed at identifying those cases where this difficulty is sufficiently overcome to justify receiving the evidence as an exception to the general exclusionary rule. As some courts and commentators have expressly noted, the reliability requirement is usually met in two different ways: see, for example, *R v. Wilcox* (2001), 152 CCC (3d) 157, 2001 NSCA 45; *R v. Czibulka* (2004), 189 CCC (3d) 199 (Ont. CA); D.M. Paciocco, "The Hearsay Exceptions: A Game of 'Rock,

Paper, Scissors,'" in *Special Lectures of the Law Society of Upper Canada 2003: The Law of Evidence* (2004), 17, at p. 29.

[62] One way is to show that there is no real concern about whether the statement is true or not because of the circumstances in which it came about. Common sense dictates that if we can put sufficient trust in the truth and accuracy of the statement, it should be considered by the fact finder regardless of its hearsay form. Wigmore explained it this way:

> There are many situations in which it can be easily seen that such a required test [i.e., cross-examination] would add little as a security, because its purposes had been already substantially accomplished. If a statement has been made under such circumstances that even a sceptical caution would look upon it as trustworthy (in the ordinary instance), in a high degree of probability, it would be pedantic to insist on a test whose chief object is already secured. [§1420, p. 154]

[63] Another way of fulfilling the reliability requirement is to show that no real concern arises from the fact that the statement is presented in hearsay form because, in the circumstances, its truth and accuracy can nonetheless be sufficiently tested. Recall that the optimal way of testing evidence adopted by our adversarial system is to have the declarant state the evidence in court, under oath, and under the scrutiny of contemporaneous cross-examination. This preferred method is not just a vestige of past traditions. It remains a tried and true method, particularly when credibility issues must be resolved. It is one thing for a person to make a damaging statement about another in a context where it may not really matter. It is quite another for that person to repeat the statement in the course of formal proceedings where he or she must commit to its truth and accuracy, be observed and heard, and be called upon to explain or defend it. The latter situation, in addition to providing an accurate record of what was actually said by the witness, gives us a much higher degree of comfort in the statement's trustworthiness. However, in some cases it is not possible to put the evidence to the optimal test, but the circumstances are such that the trier of fact will nonetheless be able to sufficiently test its truth and accuracy. Again, common sense tells us that we should not lose the benefit of the evidence when there are adequate substitutes for testing the evidence.

[64] These two principal ways of satisfying the reliability requirement can also be discerned in respect of the traditional exceptions to the hearsay rule. Iacobucci J notes this distinction in *Starr*, stating as follows:

> For example, testimony in former proceedings is admitted, at least in part, because many of the traditional dangers associated with hearsay are not present. As pointed out in Sopinka, Lederman and Bryant, *supra*, at pp. 278-79:
>
>> ... a statement which was earlier made under oath, subjected to cross-examination and admitted as testimony at a former proceeding is received in a subsequent trial *because the dangers underlying hearsay evidence are absent.*
>
> Other exceptions are based not on negating traditional hearsay dangers, but on the fact that the statement provides circumstantial guarantees of reliability. This approach is embodied in recognized exceptions such as dying declarations, spontaneous utterances, and statements against pecuniary interest. [Emphasis in original; para. 212.]

[65] Some of the traditional exceptions stand on a different footing, such as admissions from parties (confessions in the criminal context) and co-conspirators' statements: see *Mapara*, at para. 21. In those cases, concerns about reliability are based on considerations other than the party's inability to test the accuracy of his or her own statement or that of his or her co-conspirators. Hence, the criteria for admissibility are not established in the same way. However, in cases where the exclusionary rule is based on the usual hearsay dangers, this distinction between the two principal ways of satisfying the reliability requirement, although not by any means one that creates mutually exclusive categories, may assist in identifying what factors need to be considered on the admissibility inquiry.

[66] *Khan* is an example where the reliability requirement was met because the circumstances in which the statement came about provided sufficient comfort in its truth and accuracy. Similarly in *Smith*, the focus of the admissibility inquiry was also on those circumstances that tended to show that the statement was true. On the other hand, the admissibility of the hearsay statement in *B. (K.G.)* [*R v B (KG)*, [1993] 1 SCR 740] and *Hawkins* [*R v Hawkins*, [1996] 3 SCR 1043] was based on the presence of adequate substitutes for testing the evidence. As we shall see, the availability of the declarant for cross-examination goes a long way to satisfying the requirement for adequate substitutes. In *U. (F.J.)*, the Court considered both those circumstances tending to show that the statement was true and the presence of adequate substitutes for testing the evidence. *U. (F.J.)* underscores the heightened concern over reliability in the case of prior inconsistent statements where the trier of fact is invited to accept an out-of-court statement over the sworn testimony from the same declarant. I will briefly review how the analysis of the Court in each of those cases was focussed on overcoming the particular hearsay dangers raised by the evidence.

[Charron J reviewed *Khan*, *Smith*, *B (KG)*, *U (FJ)*, and *Hawkins*. She continued:]

6.3 Revisiting Paragraphs 215 and 217 in Starr

[93] As I trust it has become apparent from the preceding discussion, whether certain factors will go only to ultimate reliability will depend on the context. Hence, some of the comments at paras. 215 and 217 in *Starr* should no longer be followed. Relevant factors should not be categorized in terms of threshold and ultimate reliability. Rather, the court should adopt a more functional approach as discussed above and focus on the particular dangers raised by the hearsay evidence sought to be introduced and on those attributes or circumstances relied upon by the proponent to overcome those dangers. In addition, the trial judge must remain mindful of the limited role that he or she plays in determining admissibility—it is crucial to the integrity of the fact-finding process that the question of ultimate reliability not be pre-determined on the admissibility *voir dire*.

[94] I want to say a few words on one factor identified in *Starr*, namely "the presence of corroborating or conflicting evidence" since it is that comment that appears to have raised the most controversy. I repeat it here for convenience:

> Similarly, I would not consider the presence of corroborating or conflicting evidence. On this point, I agree with the Ontario Court of Appeal's decision in *R v. C. (B.)* (1993), 12 OR (3d) 608; see also *Idaho v. Wright*, 497 US 805 (1990). [para. 217]

[95] I will briefly review the two cases relied upon in support of this statement. The first does not really provide assistance on this question and the second, in my respectful view, should not be followed.

[96] In *R v. C. (B.)* (1993), 12 OR (3d) 608 (CA), the trial judge, in convicting the accused, had used a co-accused's statement as evidence in support of the complainant's testimony. The Court of Appeal held that this constituted an error. While a statement made by a co-accused was admissible for its truth against the co-accused, it remained hearsay as against the accused. The co-accused had recanted his statement at trial. His statement was not shown to be reliable so as to be admitted as an exception to the hearsay rule against the accused. Therefore, this case is of no assistance on the question of whether supporting evidence should be considered or not in determining hearsay admissibility. It simply reaffirms the well-established rule that an accused's statement is only admissible against its maker, not the co-accused.

[97] *Idaho v. Wright*, 497 US 805 (1990), is more on point. In that case, five of the nine justices of the United States Supreme Court were not persuaded that "evidence corroborating the truth of a hearsay statement may properly support a finding that the statement bears 'particularized guarantees of trustworthiness'" (p. 822). In the majority's view, the use of corroborating evidence for that purpose "would permit admission of a presumptively unreliable statement by bootstrapping on the trustworthiness of other evidence at trial, a result we think at odds with the requirement that hearsay evidence admitted under the Confrontation Clause be so trustworthy that cross-examination of the declarant would be of marginal utility" (p. 823). By way of example, the majority observed that a statement made under duress may happen to be true, but evidence tending to corroborate the truth of the statement would be no substitute for cross-examination of the declarant at trial. The majority also raised the concern, arising mostly in child sexual abuse cases, that a jury may rely on the partial corroboration provided by medical evidence to mistakenly infer the trustworthiness of the entire allegation.

[98] In his dissenting opinion, Kennedy J, with whom the remaining three justices concurred, strongly disagreed with the position of the majority on the potential use of supporting or conflicting evidence. In my view, his reasons echo much of the criticism that has been voiced about this Court's position in *Starr*. He said the following:

> I see no constitutional justification for this decision to prescind corroborating evidence from consideration of the question whether a child's statements are reliable. It is a matter of common sense for most people that one of the best ways to determine whether what someone says is trustworthy is to see if it is corroborated by other evidence. In the context of child abuse, for example, if part of the child's hearsay statement is that the assailant tied her wrists or had a scar on his lower abdomen, and there is physical evidence or testimony to corroborate the child's statement, evidence which the child could not have fabricated, we are more likely to believe that what the child says is true. Conversely, one can imagine a situation in which a child makes a statement which is spontaneous or is otherwise made under circumstances indicating that it is reliable, but which also contains undisputed factual inaccuracies so great that the credibility of the child's statements is substantially undermined. Under the Court's analysis, the statement would satisfy the requirements of the Confrontation Clause despite substantial doubt about its reliability. [pp. 828-29]

[99] Kennedy J also strongly disagreed with the majority's view that only circumstances surrounding the making of the statement should be considered:

The [majority] does not offer any justification for barring the consideration of corroborating evidence, other than the suggestion that corroborating evidence does not bolster the "inherent trustworthiness" of the statements. But for purposes of determining the reliability of the statements, I can discern no difference between the factors that the Court believes indicate "inherent trustworthiness" and those, like corroborating evidence, that apparently do not. Even the factors endorsed by the Court will involve consideration of the very evidence the Court purports to exclude from the reliability analysis. The Court notes that one test of reliability is whether the child "use[d] … terminology unexpected of a child of similar age." But making this determination requires consideration of the child's vocabulary skills and past opportunity, or lack thereof, to learn the terminology at issue. And, when all of the extrinsic circumstances of a case are considered, it may be shown that use of a particular word or vocabulary in fact supports the inference of prolonged contact with the defendant, who was known to use the vocabulary in question. As a further example, the Court notes that motive to fabricate is an index of reliability. But if the suspect charges that a third person concocted a false case against him and coached the child, surely it is relevant to show that the third person had no contact with the child or no opportunity to suggest false testimony. Given the contradictions inherent in the Court's test when measured against its own examples, I expect its holding will soon prove to be as unworkable as it is illogical.

The short of the matter is that both the circumstances existing at the time the child makes the statements and the existence of corroborating evidence indicate, to a greater or lesser degree, whether the statements are reliable. If the Court means to suggest that the circumstances surrounding the making of a statement are the best indicators of reliability, I doubt this is so in every instance. And, if it were true in a particular case, that does not warrant ignoring other indicators of reliability such as corroborating evidence, absent some other reason for excluding it. If anything, I should think that corroborating evidence in the form of testimony or physical evidence, apart from the narrow circumstances in which the statement was made, would be a preferred means of determining a statement's reliability for purposes of the Confrontation Clause, for the simple reason that, unlike other indicators of trustworthiness, corroborating evidence can be addressed by the defendant and assessed by the trial court in an objective and critical way. [References omitted; pp. 833-34.]

[100] In my view, the opinion of Kennedy J better reflects the Canadian experience on this question. It has proven difficult and at times counterintuitive to limit the inquiry to the circumstances surrounding the making of the statement. This Court itself has not always followed this restrictive approach. Further, I do not find the majority's concern over the "bootstrapping" nature of corroborating evidence convincing. On this point, I agree with Professor Paciocco who commented on the reasoning of the majority in *Idaho v. Wright* as follows (at p. 36):

The final rationale offered is that it would involve "bootstrapping" to admit evidence simply because it is shown by other evidence to be reliable. In fact, the "bootstrapping" label is usually reserved to circular arguments in which a questionable piece of evidence "picks itself up by its own bootstraps" to fit within an exception. For example, a party claims it can rely on a hearsay statement because the statement was made under such pressure or involvement that the prospect of concoction can fairly be disregarded, but then relies on the contents of the hearsay statement to prove the existence of that pressure or involvement: *Ratten v. The Queen*, [1972] AC 378. Or, a party claims it can rely on the truth of the contents of a statement because it was a statement made by an opposing party litigant, but then relies on the contents of the statement to prove it was made by an opposing party litigant: see *R v. Evans*, [1991] 1 SCR 869. Looking to *other* evidence to confirm the reliability of evidence, the thing *Idaho v. Wright* purports to prevent, is the very antithesis of "bootstrapping."

7. Application to This Case

[101] Mr. Skupien's statements to the cook, Ms. Stangrat, to the doctor and to the police constituted hearsay. The Crown sought to introduce the statements for the truth of their contents. In the context of this trial, the evidence was very important—indeed the two charges against Mr. Khelawon in respect of this complainant were entirely based on the truthfulness of the allegations contained in his statements.

[102] Mr. Skupien's hearsay statements were presumptively inadmissible. None of the traditional hearsay exceptions could assist the Crown in proving its case. The evidence could only be admitted under the principled exception to the hearsay rule.

[103] Mr. Skupien's death before the trial made it necessary for the Crown to resort to Mr. Skupien's evidence in its hearsay form. It was conceded throughout that the necessity requirement had been met. The case therefore turned on whether the evidence was sufficiently reliable to warrant admission.

[104] Since Mr. Skupien had died before the trial, he was no longer available to be seen, heard and cross-examined in court. There was no opportunity for contemporaneous cross-examination. Nor had there been an opportunity for cross-examination at any other hearing. Although Mr. Skupien was elderly and frail at the time he made the allegations, there is no evidence that the Crown attempted to preserve his evidence by application under ss. 709 to 714 of the *Criminal Code*. He did not testify at the preliminary hearing. The record does not disclose if he had died by that time. In making these comments, I don't question the fact that it was necessary for the Crown to resort to Mr. Skupien's evidence in hearsay form. Necessity is conceded. However, in an appropriate case, the court in deciding the question of necessity may well question whether the proponent of the evidence made all reasonable efforts to secure the evidence of the declarant in a manner that also preserves the rights of the other party. That issue is not raised here.

[105] The fact remains however that the absence of any opportunity to cross-examine Mr. Skupien has a bearing on the question of reliability. The central concern arising from the hearsay nature of the evidence is the inability to test his allegations in the usual way. The evidence is not admissible unless there is a sufficient substitute basis for testing the evidence or the contents of the statement are sufficiently trustworthy.

[106] Obviously, there was no case to be made here on the presence of adequate substitutes for testing the evidence. This is not a *Hawkins* situation where the difficulties presented by the unavailability of the declarant were easily overcome by the availability of the preliminary hearing transcript where there had been an opportunity to cross-examine the complainant in a hearing that dealt with essentially the same issues. Nor is this a *B. (K.G.)* situation where the presence of an oath and a video were coupled with the availability of the declarant at trial. There are no adequate substitutes here for testing the evidence. There

is the police video—nothing more. The principled exception to the hearsay rule does not provide a vehicle for founding a conviction on the basis of a police statement, videotaped or otherwise, without more. In order to meet the reliability requirement in this case, the Crown could only rely on the inherent trustworthiness of the statement.

[107]   In my respectful view, there was no case to be made on that basis either. This was not a situation as in *Khan* where the cogency of the evidence was such that, in the words of Wigmore, it would be "pedantic to insist on a test whose chief object is already secured" (— 1420, at p. 154). To the contrary, much as in the case of the third statement ruled inadmissible in *Smith*, the circumstances raised a number of serious issues such that it would be impossible to say that the evidence was unlikely to change under cross-examination. Mr. Skupien was elderly and frail. His mental capacity was at issue—the medical records contained repeated diagnoses of paranoia and dementia. There was also the possibility that his injuries were caused by a fall rather than an assault—the medical records revealed a number of complaints of fatigue, weakness and dizziness and the examining physician, Dr. Pietraszek, testified that the injuries could have resulted from a fall (AR, vol. 2, at p. 259). The evidence of the garbage bags filled with Mr. Skupien's possessions provided little assistance in assessing the likely truth of his statement—he could have filled those bags himself. Ms. Stangrat's obvious motive to discredit Mr. Khelawon presented further difficulties. The initial allegations were made to her—Dr. Pietraszek acknowledged in his evidence that when he saw Mr. Skupien, Ms. Stangrat was present and may have helped him by giving some indication of what happened. The extent to which Mr. Skupien may have been influenced in making his statement by this disgruntled employee was a live issue. Mr. Skupien had issues of his own with the way the retirement home was managed. This is apparent from his rambling complaints on the police video itself. The absence of an oath and the simple "yes" in answer to the police officer's question as to whether he understood that it was important to tell the truth do not give much insight on whether he truly understood the consequences for Mr. Khelawon of making his statement. In these circumstances, Mr. Skupien's unavailability for cross-examination posed significant limitations on the accused's ability to test the evidence and, in turn, on the trier of fact's ability to properly assess its worth.

[108]   As indicated earlier, the crux of the trial judge's finding that the evidence was sufficiently trustworthy was based on the "striking similarities" between the statements of the five complainants. As Rosenberg JA, I too would not reject the possibility that the presence of a striking similarity between statements from different complainants could well provide sufficient cogency to warrant the admission of hearsay evidence in an appropriate case. However, the statements made by the other complainants in this case posed even greater difficulties and could not be substantively admitted to assist in assessing the reliability of Mr. Skupien's allegations. For example, the videotaped interview with Mr. Dinino which formed the basis of the second conviction against Mr. Khelawon was nine minutes in length. It was preceded by a 30-minute interview with the police. The police officer had no notes of the initial interview. Cst Pietroniro acknowledged that it "was very difficult" to get Mr. Dinino to answer questions and that much of the videotape is inaudible. Cst Pietroniro would generally put to Mr. Dinino what he thought Mr. Dinino was saying and Mr. Dinino would respond "yes" or "yeah." Cst Pietroniro agreed that he was making an educated guess as to what Mr. Dinino was saying and that there were some things said by Mr. Dinino that he did not understand. Quite apart from these difficulties,

it is also far from clear on the record on precisely what features the trial judge based his finding that there was a "striking similarity" between the various statements. However, I do not find it necessary to elaborate on this point. The admissibility of the other statements is no longer in issue. The Court of Appeal unanimously ruled them inadmissible.

[109] I conclude that the evidence did not meet the reliability requirement. The majority of the Court of Appeal was correct to rule it inadmissible.

8. Conclusion

[110] For these reasons, I would dismiss the appeal.

QUESTIONS ON THE PRINCIPLED APPROACH

1. How would you apply the principled approach to each of the following pieces of hearsay evidence? As a trial judge in a *voir dire*, what additional information, if any, would you like to have before making a decision on admissibility?

(a) The accused was charged with second-degree murder, following a stabbing on board a ship. Before dying, the victim made two statements identifying the accused as his assailant. The doctors who treated the victim were of the opinion that he was conscious and understood the questions that were asked of him. See *R v Kharsekin* (1994), 88 CCC (3d) 193 (Nfld CA).

(b) The accused was charged with first-degree murder. The offender shot the victim in broad daylight and fled on a motorcycle. A police officer testified that the accused took a ramp onto Highway 20 and drove in the direction of Montreal; but at the scene, the officer radioed a colleague that the accused was on the highway. The accused was apprehended on a motorcycle after a wild police chase. He testified that he had nothing to do with the shooting but was driving on the highway when the police began to pursue him. He said that he fled from the police because he had a bad driving record and to amuse himself. He wished to offer the officer's statement at the scene for its truth, to support his position that he had been on the highway the whole time and was therefore not the shooter. See *R v Bisson* (1997), 114 CCC (3d) 154 (Qc CA), rev'd on other grounds [1998] 1 SCR 306, 121 CCC (3d) 449.

(c) A father and mother were charged with murder in the death of their infant daughter. The Crown wished to put into evidence three videotaped statements of the victim's sister that described the father's mistreatment of the infant and which were made soon after the infant's death. The sister was eight years old when the tapes were made and ten years old at the trial. On the *voir dire*, the trial judge found that the sister was "petrified" of her parents, that she promised to tell the truth on the tapes, that she told her story through "incremental disclosure," and that there was no evidence that she had been "coached or prepped on or off camera." See *R v Olsen* (1999), 131 CCC (3d) 355 (Ont CA).

(d) The accused was charged with second-degree murder in the death of his wife. The theory of the Crown was that the accused had beaten the victim to death in a jealous rage. The theory of the defence was that the murder was committed by an unknown third party; there was also some evidentiary basis for the defences of intoxication and provocation. About three months before she was killed, the victim had written "a very disturbing letter" to her cousin, who lived in California. The letter stated that "he" (presumably, the accused) had "ripped out my hair ... trampled on my face ... beat me with the fist, kicked me." The letter also described other violent, jealous, and abusive behaviour by the accused, and stated that he was becoming "more dangerous." There was no evidence as to the circumstances under which the letter was written. Was the letter admissible to support the Crown's theory of the case? See *R v Czibulka* (2004), 189 CCC (3d) 199 (Ont CA).

(e) The accused was charged with first-degree murder in the shooting death of the victim Ellison. The shooting occurred in April 2001. The Crown's theory of the case was that the shooting was revenge for an incident in July 2000 in which Ellison had stabbed the accused. The Crown sought to show that in a previous attempt at revenge, the accused's brother had shot and injured Ellison in February 2001. Ellison had refused to discuss this incident with the police, but he had told his mother that the person who shot him was the brother of the person he had stabbed and that that person had not reported him to the police. How would you determine the reliability of Ellison's mother's hearsay evidence under the principled approach? See *R v Blackman*, 2008 SCC 37, [2008] 2 SCR 298.

2. Section 715.1 of the *Criminal Code* reads:

715.1(1) In any proceeding against an accused in which a victim or other witness was under the age of eighteen years at the time the offence is alleged to have been committed, a video recording made within a reasonable time after the alleged offence, in which the victim or witness describes the acts complained of, is admissible in evidence if the victim or witness, while testifying, adopts the contents of the video recording, unless the presiding judge or justice is of the opinion that admission of the video recording in evidence would interfere with the proper administration of justice.

(2) The presiding judge or justice may prohibit any other use of a video recording referred to in subsection (1).

Does this section create a hearsay exception? To what extent would your answer depend on the meaning of the word "adopts"? Does the section offend any principle of fundamental justice? See *R v L (DO)*, [1993] 4 SCR 419, 85 CCC (3d) 289 and *R v F (CC)*, [1997] 3 SCR 1183, 120 CCC (3d) 225.

3. The accused was charged with sexually assaulting a young child. The child gave a videotaped statement to the police. At the trial, the child was 6½ years old. The Crown sought to introduce the videotape pursuant to s 715.1 of the *Criminal Code*. The child refused to answer any questions in the *voir dire* and so did not "adopt" the contents of the videotape; it was therefore not admissible under s 715.1. The Crown offered no evidence as to why the child would not testify. Should the videotape have been admissible pursuant to the principled approach? See *R v F (WJ)*, [1999] 3 SCR 569, 138 CCC (3d) 1.

4. After *Khelawon*, how should a trial judge limit the inquiry into reliability in the *voir dire*? Since corroborating or conflicting evidence may now be considered, what is to stop a party from putting in its entire case—or asking the other party to put in its entire case—on the *voir dire*? See *Blackman*, above, at paras 53-57.

5. How does the principled approach compare with the "residual discretion" proposed by Lord Pearce in *Myers v Director of Public Prosecutions*, [1965] AC 1001 (HL), in Section III.A, above, or with the residual exception created by r 807 of the United States *Federal Rules of Evidence*? Which is preferable, in light of the general rationale for the exclusion of hearsay?

PROBLEM: OUT-OF-COURT STATEMENTS IN R v GALLOWAY

At Martin's trial there are a number of out-of-court statements that both sides attempt to introduce into evidence.

1. The Crown wishes to introduce a statement reportedly made by Angela to her mother during a telephone conversation in March 2016. Angela told her mother, "Martin and I aren't getting along, it seems like we're fighting all the time, and I am worried about the effect it's having on the kids." Is this statement admissible?

2. The Crown also wishes to call the Galloways' neighbour from next door. He will testify that on the evening of Sunday, March 27, 2016, at approximately 10:30 p.m., as he was lying in bed trying to fall asleep, he heard a shrill scream, which sounded almost like someone yelling "no," coming from the direction of the Galloways' home. He investigated by looking out his window, but saw nothing unusual and went back to bed. He was awakened shortly after 11:10 p.m. by the sound of sirens. Is what the neighbour overheard admissible?

3. The Crown wants to elicit testimony from Margaret Jenkins regarding a telephone conversation she had with Martin Galloway on Monday, April 5, 2016. During this call, Martin told Margaret that his wife had been murdered. Margaret will testify that she immediately responded: "You didn't kill her, did you, Martin? Please tell me you didn't kill her to be with me." To which Martin responded, after a very long pause, "You're not serious, are you?" Is Margaret's testimony about this telephone conversation admissible?

4. During the testimony of the officer in charge of the case, the defence wishes to elicit from him the substance of Martin Galloway's exculpatory statements to police during the course of his three police interviews on April 5 and then again on April 18 and June 2, 2016. Is this evidence admissible?

FURTHER READING

For discussions of the principled approach, see the following publications.

Archibald, Bruce P. "The Canadian Hearsay Revolution: Is Half a Loaf Better Than No Loaf at All?" (1999) 25 Queen's LJ 1.

Paciocco, David M. "The Hearsay Exceptions: A Game of 'Rock, Paper, Scissors'" in *Special Lectures of the Law Society of Upper Canada 2003: The Law of Evidence* (Toronto: Irwin Law, 2004) 17.

Rosenberg, Marc. "*B.(K.G.)*—Necessity and Reliability: The New Pigeon-Holes" (1993) 19 CR (4th) 69

Stewart, Hamish. "Hearsay After Starr" (2001) 7 Can Crim L Rev 1.

Stewart, Hamish. "Khelawon: The Principled Approach to Hearsay Revisited" (2007) 12 Can Crim L Rev 95.

Stewart, Hamish. "A Rationale for the Rejection of Extrinsic Evidence in Assessing the Reliability of Hearsay" (2005) 30 CR (6th) 306.

Stuesser, Lee. "R v. Starr and Reform of Hearsay Exceptions" (2001) 7 Can Crim L Rev 55.

Tanovich, David M. "Starr Gazing: Looking into the Future of Hearsay in Canada" (2003) 28 Queen's LJ 371.

CHAPTER FIVE

Opinion Evidence

I. THE EXCLUSIONARY RULE AND TWO EXCEPTIONS

The presumptive inadmissibility of opinion evidence was explained by Cromwell J on behalf of the court in *White Burgess Langille Inman v Abbott & Haliburton Co*, 2015 SCC 23, [2015] 2 SCR 182 at para 14, as follows:

> To the modern general rule that all relevant evidence is admissible there are many qualifications. One of them relates to opinion evidence, which is the subject of a complicated exclusionary rule. Witnesses are to testify as to the facts which they perceived, not as to the inferences—that is, the opinions—that they drew from them. As one great evidence scholar put it long ago, it is "for the jury to form opinions, and draw inferences and conclusions, and not for the witness": J.B. Thayer, *A Preliminary Treatise on Evidence at the Common Law* (1898; reprinted 1969), at p. 524 … . While various rationales have been offered for this exclusionary rule, the most convincing is probably that these ready-formed inferences are not helpful to the trier of fact and might even be misleading: [citations omitted].

In *R v K (A)* (1999), 45 OR (3d) 641, 137 CCC (3d) 225 at para 72 (CA), Charron JA (as she then was) explained the importance of drawing a clear distinction between evidence that is based on a witness's observations (which is evidence of facts) and opinion evidence:

> The line between fact and opinion must therefore be kept clearly in mind. A witness, who is an expert In a particular field, may be called simply to give evidence on the facts he or she has observed without offering an opinion based on those facts. To that extent, and if otherwise admissible, this evidence is not subject to the opinion rule. This would be the case, for example, where

a treating physician is called to describe the injuries he or she observed on a patient without offering any opinion on the matter. It is only when a witness purports to give an opinion on certain facts that the opinion rule comes into play. If, in our example, the treating physician goes on to say that it is usual or unusual, as the case may be, to observe this kind of injury in a patient who alleges that sexual intercourse has taken place, the witness is offering opinion evidence and the evidence will be subject to the general rule of exclusion. It will only be admissible if certain established criteria are met.

There are two types of exception to the rule excluding opinion evidence. First, ordinary witnesses may be permitted to communicate their perceptions in the form of an opinion on matters that are (1) within common knowledge and (2) based on multiple perceptions that can best be communicated in a compendious format. Thus, ordinary witnesses may testify in the form of an opinion on matters such as age, speed, identity, or physical and emotional state. Second, where the trier of fact requires assistance in order to understand the significance of the evidence, or requires assistance to determine what inferences can properly be drawn from the evidence, an expert may be permitted to provide assistance in the form of opinion evidence.

II. THE EXCEPTION FOR LAY OPINION

R v Graat
[1982] 2 SCR 819
Ritchie, Dickson, Beetz, Estey, McIntyre, Chouinard, and Wilson JJ
(21 December 1982)

DICKSON J: This appeal raises the issue whether on a charge of driving while impaired the Court may admit opinion evidence on the very question to be decided, namely, was the accused's ability to drive impaired by alcohol at the time and place stated in the charge.

. . .

At approximately 2:15 a.m. on the date in question, Constables Case and McMullen of the London City Police observed Mr. Graat's vehicle travelling at a high rate of speed. The constables followed for several blocks. They observed Mr. Graat's car weaving in the southbound lane, crossing the centre line on two occasions and driving onto the shoulder of the road on another occasion. When the vehicle turned left it straddled the centre line.

Both constables testified they noticed the smell of alcohol on the appellant's breath; both said Mr. Graat was unsteady on his feet, he staggered as he walked, and had blood-shot eyes.

At the police station Mr. Graat was observed by a Sergeant Spoelstra. The sergeant testified he smelled alcohol on the appellant's breath, the top part of his body was swaying, and his walk was "kind of wavy."

Mr. Graat complained of chest pains. He told the police he suffered from a heart condition and asked to be taken to a hospital. The police complied. By the time Mr. Graat returned to the police station it was too late to take two breath samples because the two-hour time limit for the taking of such samples had expired or was about to expire.

Mr. Graat testified he had had two drinks of gin between the hours of 3:00 p.m. and 7:00 p.m., and two glasses of wine with his dinner about 11:00 p.m. He said he and two friends, George Wilson and Vincent O'Donovan, were returning from a sailing party; he became tired. Wilson drove the car while he dozed in the back seat. The appellant resumed driving after Wilson had driven O'Donovan and himself home. Wilson testified that if he had thought Mr. Graat was not in a fit condition to drive he would have asked him to stay at his, Wilson's, house.

At trial Constable Case was asked the following questions and gave the following answers:

> Q. All right, now what, if any, opinion having made those observations, what if any opinion did you form regarding the accused man's ability to drive a motor vehicle?
>
> A. I formed the opinion that the accused's ability was impaired.
>
> Q. By?
>
> A. By alcohol.
>
> Q. You said the accused man's ability to what?
>
> A. To drive a motor vehicle was impaired by alcohol.

Constable McMullen was asked the following question:

> Q. Now officer when you were at the scene and having made the observations of the driving of the accused man, having observed him, having smelled the alcoholic beverage on his breath and observed him walk and observed him standing, observed him speaking to you what, if any, conclusion did you come to regarding his ability to drive a motor vehicle?
>
> A. It was in my opinion that the accused's ability to operate a motor vehicle was impaired by alcohol beverage.

Sergeant Spoelstra, the desk sergeant, gave similar evidence:

> Q. … You saw him standing and you saw him walking. What, if any opinion, did you form regarding his ability to drive a motor vehicle?
>
> A. In my opinion the accused's ability was impaired by the use of alcohol to drive a motor vehicle.

No objection was taken at trial to the admission of any of this evidence.

• • •

The trial judge preferred the evidence of the police witnesses to the evidence of Mr. Graat and Mr. Wilson. In particular, the judge relied on the evidence of Constable McMullen and Sergeant Spoelstra, policemen for 8 and 17 years respectively. Constable Case had only been a police officer for a few months, and had only charged two or three persons with impaired driving. The judge said he accepted the opinions of officers McMullen and Spoelstra in reaching his conclusion that the accused's ability to drive was impaired:

> I'm of the view that I'm entitled to accept and I do accept the opinions of those two police officers on the issue of impairment as part of the totality of the evidence.

[Dickson J reviewed case law from Canada, England, Eire, Northern Ireland, Australia, and New Zealand; considered the views of Cross and Wigmore; reviewed the recommendations of the Law Reform Commission of Canada and the Ontario Law Reform Commission; and discussed the proposed Uniform Evidence Act. He continued:]

… The subjects upon which the non-expert witness is allowed to give opinion evidence is a lengthy one. The list mentioned in *Sherrard v. Jacob*, … [[1965] NILR 151] is by no means exhaustive: (i) the identification of handwriting, persons and things; (ii) apparent age; (iii) the bodily plight or condition of a person, including death and illness; (iv) the emotional state of a person—e.g. whether distressed, angry, aggressive, affectionate or depressed; (v) the condition of things—e.g. worn, shabby, used or new; (vi) certain questions of value; and (vii) estimates of speed and distance.

Except for the sake of convenience there is little, if any, virtue in any distinction resting on the tenuous, and frequently false, antithesis between fact and opinion. The line between "fact" and "opinion" is not clear.

To resolve the question before the Court, I would like to return to broad principles. Admissibility is determined, first, by asking whether the evidence sought to be admitted is relevant. This is a matter of applying logic and experience to the circumstances of the particular case. The question which must then be asked is whether, though probative, the evidence must be excluded by a clear ground of policy or of law.

There is a direct and logical relevance between (i) the evidence offered here, namely, the opinion of a police officer (based on perceived facts as to the manner of driving, and indicia of intoxication of the driver) that the person's ability to drive was impaired by alcohol, and (ii) the ultimate probandum in the case. The probative value of the evidence is not outweighed by such policy considerations as danger of confusing the issues or misleading the jury. It does not unfairly surprise a party who had not had reasonable ground to anticipate that such evidence will be offered, and the adducing of the evidence does not necessitate undue consumption of time. …

• • •

… I can see no reason in principle or in common sense why a lay witness should not be permitted to testify in the form of an opinion if, by doing so, he is able more accurately to express the facts he perceived.

I accept the following passage from Cross [*Cross on Evidence*, 5th ed, 1979] as a good statement of the law as to the cases in which non-expert opinion is admissible.

> When, in the words of an American judge, "the facts from which a witness received an impression were too evanescent in their nature to be recollected, or too complicated to be separately and distinctly narrated," a witness may state his opinion or impression. He was better equipped than the jury to form it, and it is impossible for him to convey an adequate idea of the premises on which he acted to the jury:
>
> > "Unless opinions, estimates and inferences which men in their daily lives reach without conscious ratiocination as a result of what they have perceived with their physical senses were treated in the law of evidence as if they were mere statements of fact, witnesses would find themselves unable to communicate to the judge an accurate impression of the events they were seeking to describe."

There is nothing in the nature of a closed list of cases in which non-expert opinion evidence is admissible. Typical instances are provided by questions concerning age, speed, weather, handwriting and identity in general [at p. 448].

Before this Court counsel for the appellant took the position that although opinion evidence by non-experts may be admissible where it is "necessary" the opinions of the police officers in this case were superfluous, irrelevant and inadmissible. I disagree. It is well established that a non-expert witness may give evidence that someone was intoxicated, just as he may give evidence of age, speed, identity or emotional state. This is because it may be difficult for the witness to narrate his factual observations individually. Drinking alcohol to the extent that one's ability to drive is impaired is a degree of intoxication, and it is yet more difficult for a witness to narrate separately the individual facts that justify the inference, in either the witness or the trier of fact, that someone was intoxicated to some particular extent. If a witness is to be allowed to sum up concisely his observations by saying that someone was intoxicated, it is all the more necessary that he be permitted to aid the court further by saying that someone was intoxicated to a particular degree. I agree with the comment of Lord MacDermott LCJ in his dissent in *Sherrard v. Jacob, supra*:

I can find no good reason for allowing the non-expert to give his opinion of the driver's observable condition and then denying him the right to state an opinion on the consequences of that observed condition so far as driving is concerned [at p. 162].

Nor is this a case for the exclusion of non-expert testimony because the matter calls for a specialist. It has long been accepted in our law that intoxication is not such an exceptional condition as would require a medical expert to diagnose it. An ordinary witness may give evidence of his opinion as to whether a person is drunk. This is not a matter where scientific, technical, or specialized testimony is necessary in order that the tribunal properly understands the relevant facts. Intoxication and impairment of driving ability are matters which the modern jury can intelligently resolve on the basis of common ordinary knowledge and experience. The guidance of an expert is unnecessary.

If that be so it seems illogical to deny the court the help it could get from a witness' opinion as to the degree of intoxication, that is to say whether the person's ability to drive was impaired by alcohol. If non-expert evidence is excluded the defence may be seriously hampered. If an accused is to be denied the right to call persons who were in his company at the time to testify that in their opinion his ability to drive was by no means impaired, the cause of justice would suffer.

Whether or not the evidence given by police or other non-expert witnesses is accepted is another matter. The weight of the evidence is entirely a matter for the judge or judge and jury. The value of opinion will depend on the view the court takes in all the circumstances.

· · ·

A non-expert witness cannot, of course, give opinion evidence on a legal issue as, for example, whether or not a person was negligent. That is because such an opinion would not qualify as an abbreviated version of the witnesses [*sic*] factual observations. An opinion that someone was negligent is partly factual, but it also involves the application of legal standards. On the other hand, whether a person's ability to drive is impaired by alcohol is a question of fact, not of law. It does not involve the application of any legal standard. It is akin to an opinion that someone is too drunk to climb a ladder or to go swimming, and the fact that a witness' opinion, as here, may be expressed in the exact words of the *Criminal Code* does not change a factual matter into a question of law. It only reflects the fact that the draftsmen of the *Code* employed the ordinary English phrase: "his ability to drive … is impaired by alcohol" (s. 234).

In short, I know of no clear ground of policy or of law which would require the exclusion of opinion evidence tendered by the Crown or the defence as to Mr. Graat's impairment.

I conclude with two caveats. First, in every case, in determining whether an opinion is admissible, the trial judge must necessarily exercise a large measure of discretion. Second, there may be a tendency for judges and juries to let the opinion of police witnesses overwhelm the opinion evidence of other witnesses. Since the opinion is admitted under the "compendious statement of facts" exception, rather than under the "expert witness" exception, there is no special reason for preferring the police evidence over the "opinion" of other witnesses. As always, the trier of fact must decide in each case what weight to give what evidence. The "opinion" of the police officer is entitled to no special regard. Ordinary people with ordinary experience are able to know as a matter of fact that someone is too drunk to perform certain tasks, such as driving a car. If the witness lacks the relevant experience, or is otherwise limited in his testimonial capacity, or if the witness is not sure whether the person was intoxicated to the point of impairment, that can be brought out in cross-examination. But the fact that a police witness has seen more impaired drivers than a non-police witness is not a reason in itself to prefer the evidence of the police officer. Constable McMullen and Sergeant Spoelstra were not testifying as experts based on their extensive experience as police officers.

. . .

Mr. Wilson does not need any special qualifications. Nor were the police officers relying on any special qualifications when they gave their opinions. Both police and non-police witnesses are merely giving a compendious statement of facts that are too subtle and too complicated to be narrated separately and distinctly. Trial judges should bear in mind that this is non-expert opinion evidence, and that the opinion of police officers is not entitled to preference just because they may have extensive experience with impaired drivers. The credit and accuracy of the police must be viewed in the same manner as that of other witnesses and in the light of all the evidence in the case. If the police and traffic officers have been closely associated with the prosecution, such association may affect the weight to be given to such evidence.

The trial judge was correct in admitting the opinions of the three police officers and Mr. Wilson.

For the foregoing reasons, as well as for the reasons given by Chief Justice Howland, I would dismiss the appeal.

NOTES AND QUESTIONS

1. Do you agree that a police officer who is experienced in investigating impaired driving cases is in no better position than an ordinary lay person to assess whether a suspect is sufficiently intoxicated that her ability to drive a vehicle is impaired? Is it possible to identify separately the factors on which one relies in concluding that another person is intoxicated? If so, to what extent is it necessary to testify in the form of an opinion?

2. When a witness identifies the accused as the person who committed the crime, can the witness identify all the factors that he has taken into account in making that identification? Is the process of identification intuitive, comprehensive, and difficult to analyze? Even though a lay witness may be permitted to testify in the form of an opinion on conditions or phenomena that are within common knowledge and involve multiple perceptions, would it nonetheless be strategic to elicit from the witness the individual perceptions that are summarized in the opinion? Is the jury likely to give more weight to an opinion when they can assess the perceptions on which it is based?

3. In 1993, Detective David Spicer of the Ottawa Police had 15 to 20 telephone conversations and 10 to 12 personal conversations with one Theodore Williams. The following year, the police were investigating suspected drug dealing in a certain Ottawa neighbourhood. During this investigation, Spicer carried out several undercover transactions with a man going by the name "Digital," and received a CrimeStoppers tip stating that two males, Digital and "Theodore," were dealing crack cocaine at a certain apartment. The description of Theodore and the address matched that of Williams. On July 5, 1994, Spicer and other officers attempted to arrange a further undercover purchase from Digital. During the negotiations, a male identifying himself as "Brad" called Spicer from a second apartment and gave him instructions. Spicer identified Brad's voice as that of Theodore Williams. Digital later stated that Brad's role was "checking Spicer out." The negotiations did not lead to a transaction and, later that day, Spicer and other officers executed a search warrant at the second apartment. During the search, Williams entered the room and spoke to Spicer. Spicer placed him under arrest for trafficking in a narcotic. At trial, Spicer stated that he recognized the accused's voice as that belonging to Brad. The trial judge accepted this identification and convicted the accused. Fact or opinion? Does it matter? See *R v Williams* (1995), 23 OR (3d) 122 (CA), leave to appeal refused, (1995), 42 CR (4th) 409 (SCC).

III. THE EXCEPTION FOR EXPERT OPINION: BASIC PRINCIPLES

The second exception to the rule against opinion evidence arises when it is necessary for the trier of fact to have expert assistance in order to draw the proper inferences from the facts. Expert evidence presents unique difficulties to courts. By definition, expert evidence is needed because ordinary people would be unable to reach an appropriate conclusion without that evidence. However, the special training and skills that presumably equip expert witnesses to do their work also present a barrier to courts when seeking to guard against misleading or unreliable expert testimony. Expert testimony has been implicated in wrongful convictions in Canada and elsewhere: see the discussion of the Goudge Commission report in Section III.C, below, as well as Brandon L Garrett, *Convicting the Innocent* (Cambridge, Mass: Harvard University Press, 2011) ch 4. The trend in this area is therefore to exhort trial judges to exercise greater vigilance when reviewing admissibility. In this part, we introduce the test for admissibility of expert evidence as first laid out in *R v Mohan*, [1994] 2 SCR 9 and reformulated in *R v Abbey*, 2009 ONCA 624, 97 OR (3d) 330. Section III.B in this chapter elaborates on the "preconditions to admissibility" and Section III.C offers a more complete discussion of the task of assessing the benefits and costs of expert evidence, with a particular focus on the core principle of reliability.

A. Requirements for Admissibility

R v Mohan
[1994] 2 SCR 9, 89 CCC (3d) 402
Lamer CJ and La Forest, L'Heureux-Dubé, Sopinka, Gonthier, Cory, McLachlin,
Iacobucci, and Major JJ (5 May 1994)

SOPINKA J: ...

[For the facts of this case, see Chapter 7, Section II.B.4. The portion of the case reproduced here deals only with the general principles governing the admissibility of expert evidence.]

(1) Expert Opinion Evidence

Admission of expert evidence depends on the application of the following criteria:

(a)   relevance;

(b)   necessity in assisting the trier of fact;

(c)   the absence of any exclusionary rule;

(d)   a properly qualified expert.

(a) Relevance

Relevance is a threshold requirement for the admission of expert evidence as with all other evidence. Relevance is a matter to be decided by a judge as question of law. Although *prima facie* admissible if so related to a fact in issue that it tends to establish it, that does not end the inquiry. This merely determines the logical relevance of the evidence. Other considerations enter into the decision as to admissibility. This further inquiry may be described as a cost–benefit analysis, that is "whether its value is worth what it costs." See *McCormick on Evidence* (3rd ed. 1984), at p. 544. Cost in this context is not used in its traditional economic sense but rather in terms of its impact on the trial process. Evidence that is otherwise logically relevant may be excluded on this basis, if its probative value is overborne by its prejudicial effect, if it involves an inordinate amount of time which is not commensurate with its value or if it is misleading in the sense that its effect on the trier of fact, particularly a jury, is out of proportion to its reliability. While frequently considered as an aspect of legal relevance, the exclusion of logically relevant evidence on these grounds is more properly regarded as a general exclusionary rule: see *R v. Morris*, [1983] 2 SCR 190. Whether it is treated as an aspect of relevance or an exclusionary rule, the effect is the same. The reliability versus effect factor has special significance in assessing the admissibility of expert evidence.

There is a danger that expert evidence will be misused and will distort the fact-finding process. Dressed up in scientific language which the jury does not easily understand and submitted through a witness of impressive antecedents, this evidence is apt to be accepted by the jury as being virtually infallible and as having more weight than it deserves. ...

• • •

(b) Necessity in Assisting the Trier of Fact

In *R v. Abbey*, … [[1982] 2 SCR 24], Dickson J, as he then was, stated at p. 42:

> With respect to matters calling for special knowledge an expert in the field may draw infer-
> ences and state his opinion. An expert's function is precisely this: to provide the judge and
> jury with a ready-made inference which the judge and jury, due to the technical nature of
> the facts, are unable to formulate. "An expert's opinion is admissible to furnish the court with
> scientific information which is likely to be outside the experience and knowledge of a judge
> or jury. If on the proven facts a judge or jury can form their own conclusions without help
> then the opinion of the expert is unnecessary": *R v. Turner* (1974), 60 Cr. App. R 80, at p. 83,
> *per* Lawton LJ).

This precondition is often expressed in terms as to whether the evidence would be
helpful to the trier of fact. The word "helpful" is not quite appropriate and sets too low a
standard. However, I would not judge necessity by too strict a standard. What is required
is that the opinion be necessary in the sense that it provide information "which is likely to
be outside the experience and knowledge of a Judge or Jury": as quoted by Dickson J in *R v.
Abbey, supra*. As stated by Dickson J, the evidence must be necessary to enable the trier
of fact to appreciate the matters in issue due to their technical nature. In *Kelliher (Village)
v. Smith*, [1931] SCR 672, at p. 684, this court, quoting from *Beven on Negligence* (4th ed.
1928), at p. 141 stated that in order for expert evidence to be admissible, "[t]he subject-
matter of the inquiry must be such that ordinary people are unlikely to form a correct
judgment about it, if unassisted by persons with special knowledge." More recently, in
Lavallee, … [*R v Lavallee*, [1990] 1 SCR 852], the above passages from *Kelliher* and *Abbey*
were applied to admit expert evidence as to the state of mind of a "battered" woman. The
judgment stressed that this was an area that is not understood by the average person.

. . .

(c) The Absence of Any Exclusionary Rule

Compliance with criteria (a), (b) and (d) will not ensure the admissibility of expert evidence if it falls afoul of an exclusionary rule of evidence separate and apart from the
opinion rule itself. For example, in *R v. Morin* (1988), 44 CCC (3d) 193, [1988] 2 SCR
345, evidence elicited by the Crown in cross-examination of the psychiatrist called by the
accused was inadmissible because it was not shown to be relevant other than as to the
disposition to commit the crime charged. Notwithstanding, therefore, that the evidence
otherwise complied with the criteria for the admission of expert evidence it was excluded
by reason of the rule that prevents the Crown from adducing evidence of the accused's
disposition unless the latter has placed his or her character in issue. The extent of the
restriction when such evidence is tendered by the accused lies at the heart of this case
and will be discussed hereunder.

(d) A Properly Qualified Expert

Finally the evidence must be given by a witness who is shown to have acquired special or
peculiar knowledge through study or experience in respect of the matters on which he
or she undertakes to testify.

In summary, therefore, it appears from the foregoing that expert evidence which advances a novel scientific theory or technique is subjected to special scrutiny to determine whether it meets a basic threshold of reliability and whether it is essential in the sense that the trier of fact will be unable to come to a satisfactory conclusion without the assistance of the expert. The closer the evidence approaches an opinion on an ultimate issue, the stricter the application of this principle.

In *R v Abbey*, 2009 ONCA 624, 97 OR (3d) 330, 246 CCC (3d) 301, Doherty JA suggested that the *Mohan* factors could be reorganized as set out in the following extract:

[74] The current approach to the admissibility of expert opinion evidence was articulated by Sopinka J in *Mohan*. Broadly speaking, *Mohan* replaced what had been a somewhat *laissez faire* attitude toward the admissibility of expert opinion evidence with a principled approach that required closer judicial scrutiny of the proffered evidence. After *Mohan*, trial judges were required to assess the potential value of the evidence to the trial process against the potential harm to that process flowing from admission.

[75] The four criteria controlling the admissibility of expert opinion evidence identified in *Mohan* have achieved an almost canonical status in the law of evidence. No judgment on the topic seems complete without reference to them. The four criteria are:

- relevance;
- necessity in assisting the trier of fact;
- the absence of any exclusionary rule; and
- a properly qualified expert.

[76] Using these criteria, I suggest a two-step process for determining admissibility. First, the party proffering the evidence must demonstrate the existence of certain preconditions to the admissibility of expert evidence. For example, that party must show that the proposed witness is qualified to give the relevant opinion. Second, the trial judge must decide whether expert evidence that meets the preconditions to admissibility is sufficiently beneficial to the trial process to warrant its admission despite the potential harm to the trial process that may flow from the admission of the expert evidence. This "gatekeeper" component of the admissibility inquiry lies at the heart of the present evidentiary regime governing the admissibility of expert opinion evidence: see *Mohan*; *R. v. D.D.*, 2000 SCC 43, [2000] 2 SCR 275; *J.-L.J.* [*R v J (J)*], 2000 SCC 51, [2000] 2 SCR 600]; *R. v. Trochym*, 2007 SCC 6, [2007] 1 SCR 239; *K. (A.)* [*R v K (A)* (1999), 45 OR (3d) 641 (CA)]; *Ranger* [*R v Ranger* (2003), 67 OR (3d) 1 (CA)]; *R. v. Osmar*, 2007 ONCA 50, (2007), 84 OR (3d) 321 (CA), leave to appeal to SCC refused, (2007), 85 OR (3d) xviii.

[77] I appreciate that *Mohan* does not describe the admissibility inquiry as a two-step process. It does not distinguish between what I refer to as the preconditions to admissibility and the trial judge's exercise of the "gatekeeper" function. My description of the process as involving two distinct phases does not alter the substance of the analysis required by *Mohan*. In suggesting a two-step approach, I mean only to facilitate the admissibility analysis and the application of the *Mohan* criteria.

[78] It is helpful to distinguish between what I describe as the preconditions to admissibility of expert opinion evidence and the performance of the "gatekeeper" function because the two are very different. The inquiry into compliance with the preconditions to admissibility is a rules-

based analysis that will yield "yes" or "no" answers. Evidence that does not meet all of the precon-ditions to admissibility must be excluded and the trial judge need not address the more difficult and subtle considerations that arise in the "gatekeeper" phase of the admissibility inquiry.

[79] The "gatekeeper" inquiry does not involve the application of bright line rules, but instead requires an exercise of judicial discretion. The trial judge must identify and weigh competing considerations to decide whether on balance those considerations favour the admissibility of the evidence. This cost–benefit analysis is case-specific and, unlike the first phase of the admissibility inquiry, often does not admit of a straightforward "yes" or "no" answer. Different trial judges, properly applying the relevant principles in the exercise of their discretion, could in some situa-tions come to different conclusions on admissibility.

[80] In what I refer to as the first phase, four preconditions to admissibility must be estab-lished, none of which were in dispute at trial:

- the proposed opinion must relate to a subject matter that is properly the subject of expert opinion evidence;
- the witness must be qualified to give the opinion;
- the proposed opinion must not run afoul of any exclusionary rule apart entirely from the expert opinion rule; and
- the proposed opinion must be logically relevant to a material issue.

. . .

[86] As indicated above, it was not argued that Dr. Totten's evidence did not meet the precon-ditions to admissibility. Nor is it suggested that it was not logically relevant to identity, a fact in issue. The battle over the admissibility of his evidence was fought at the "gatekeeper" stage of the analysis. At that stage, the trial judge engages in a case-specific cost–benefit analysis.

. . .

[93] The cost–benefit analysis demands a consideration of the extent to which the proffered opinion evidence is necessary to a proper adjudication of the fact(s) to which that evidence is directed. In *Mohan*, Sopinka J describes necessity as a separate criterion governing admissibility. I see the necessity analysis as a part of the larger cost–benefit analysis performed by the trial judge. In relocating the necessity analysis, I do not, however, depart from the role assigned to necessity by the *Mohan* criteria.

[94] It seems self-evident that an expert opinion on an issue that the jury is fully equipped to decide without that opinion is unnecessary and should register a "zero" on the "benefit" side of the cost–benefit scale. Inevitably, expert opinion evidence that brings no added benefit to the process will be excluded: see, for example, *R v. Batista*, 2008 ONCA 804 (2008), 238 CCC (3d) 97 (Ont. CA), at paras. 45-47; *R v. Nahar*, 2004 BCCA 77 (2004), 181 CCC (3d) 449 (BCCA), at paras. 20-21. Opinion evidence that is essential to a jury's ability to understand and evaluate material evi-dence will register high on the "benefit" side of the scale. However, the ultimate admissibility of the opinion, even where it is essential, will depend on not only its potential benefit, but on the potential prejudice to the trial process associated with its admission.

[95] In many cases, the proffered opinion evidence will fall somewhere between the essential and the unhelpful. In those cases, the trial judge's assessment of the extent to which the evi-dence could assist the jury will be one of the factors to be weighed in deciding whether the benefits flowing from admission are sufficiently strong to overcome the costs associated with admission. In addressing the extent to which the opinion evidence is necessary, the trial judge

will have regard to other facets of the trial process—such as the jury instruction—that may provide the jury with the tools necessary to adjudicate properly on the fact in issue without the assistance of expert evidence: *D.D.*, at para. 33; *R v. Bonisteel*, 2008 BCCA 344, (2008), 236 CCC (3d) 170 (BCCA), at para. 69.

Doherty JA's approach to determining the admissibility of expert testimony was adopted with minor modification by the Supreme Court of Canada in *White Burgess Langille Inman v Abbott & Haliburton Co*, 2015 SCC 23, [2015] 2 SCR 182 at para 22 (and had in the meantime been adopted by almost every provincial court of appeal).

B. Preconditions to Admissibility

In *R v Abbey*, Doherty JA held that a trial judge must first define the nature and scope of the expert opinion evidence. Having conducted this exercise, a trial judge must consider the following matters as threshold questions:

- the proposed opinion must relate to a subject matter that is properly the subject of expert opinion evidence;
- the witness must be qualified to give the opinion;
- the proposed opinion must not run afoul of any exclusionary rule apart entirely from the expert opinion rule; and
- the proposed opinion must be logically relevant to a material issue.

In *White Burgess Langille Inman v Abbott & Haliburton Co*, Cromwell J adopted this formulation but added "I would retain necessity as a threshold requirement." This section therefore incorporates necessity as a precondition to admissibility, combining that requirement with Doherty JA's principle that the expert opinion must relate to a subject that is properly the subject of expert opinion evidence. In keeping with our practice elsewhere in the book, we begin this section with an extract from *Abbey* regarding logical relevance.

1. *Logical Relevance and Materiality*

In *R v Abbey*, Doherty JA identified logical relevance as a precondition to admissibility. In doing so, he distinguished his use of the term "relevance" from the more expansive meaning given to that term by Sopinka J in *R v Mohan*:

[81] For the purpose of explaining the analytic distinction I draw between the preconditions to admissibility and the "gatekeeper" function, I need not address the first three preconditions. The relevance criterion, however, does require some explanation. Relevance is one of the four *Mohan* criteria. However, I use the word differently than Sopinka J. used it in *Mohan*.

[82] Relevance can have two very different meanings in the evidentiary context. Relevance can refer to logical relevance, a requirement that the evidence have a tendency as a matter of human experience and logic to make the existence or non-existence of a fact in issue more or less likely than it would be without that evidence: *J.(J.)*, at para. 47. Given this meaning, relevance sets a low threshold for admissibility and reflects the inclusionary bias of our evidentiary rules: see *R. v. Clarke*, [1998] O.J. No. 3521, 129 C.C.C. (3d) 1 (C.A.), at p. 12 C.C.C. Relevance can also refer to a requirement that evidence be not only logically relevant to a fact in issue, but also sufficiently probative to justify its admission despite the prejudice that may flow from its admission.

This meaning of relevance is described as legal relevance and involves a limited weighing of the costs and benefits associated with admitting evidence that is undoubtedly logically relevant: see Paciocco & Stuesser [*The Law of Evidence*, 5th ed (Toronto: Irwin Law, 2008)], at pp. 30-35.

[83] The relevance criterion for admissibility identified in *Mohan* refers to legal relevance. To be relevant, the evidence must not only be logically relevant but must be sufficiently probative to justify admission: see *Mohan*, at pp. 20-21 S.C.R.; *K.(A.)* [*R v K (A)* (1999), 45 OR (3d) 641 (CA)], at paras. 77-89; Paciocco & Stuesser, at pp. 198-99.

[84] When I speak of relevance as one of the preconditions to admissibility, I refer to logical relevance. I think the evaluation of the probative value of the evidence mandated by the broader concept of legal relevance is best reserved for the "gatekeeper" phase of the admissibility analysis. Evidence that is relevant in the sense that it is logically relevant to a fact in issue survives to the "gatekeeper" phase where the probative value can be assessed as part of a holistic consideration of the costs and benefits associated with admitting the evidence. Evidence that does not meet the logical relevance criterion is excluded at the first stage of the inquiry: see, e.g., *R. v. Dimitrov* (2003), 68 O.R. (3d) 641, [2003] O.J. No. 5243 (C.A.), at para. 48, leave to appeal to S.C.C. refused (2004), 70 O.R. (3d) xvii, [2004] S.C.C.A. No. 59.

[85] My separation of logical relevance from the cost–benefit analysis associated with legal relevance does not alter the criteria for admissibility set down in *Mohan* or the underlying principles governing the admissibility inquiry. I separate logical from legal relevance simply to provide an approach which focuses first on the essential prerequisites to admissibility and second, on all of the factors relevant to the exercise of the trial judge's discretion in determining whether evidence that meets those preconditions should be received.

Doherty JA listed logical relevance as the last of his preconditions to admissibility. However, a clear articulation of relevance and materiality is foundational to all analyses of the admissibility, risks, and benefits of evidence. Accordingly, we recommend beginning with this question.

2. Defining the Nature and Scope of the Evidence

R v Abbey

2009 ONCA 624, 97 OR (3d) 330

Doherty, MacPherson, and Lang JJA (27 August 2009)

DOHERTY JA:

[62] The admissibility inquiry is not conducted in a vacuum. Before deciding admissibility, a trial judge must determine the nature and scope of the proposed expert evidence. In doing so, the trial judge sets not only the boundaries of the proposed expert evidence but also, if necessary, the language in which the expert's opinion may be proffered so as to minimize any potential harm to the trial process. A cautious delineation of the scope of the proposed expert evidence and strict adherence to those boundaries, if the evidence is admitted, are essential. The case law demonstrates that overreaching by expert witnesses is probably the most common fault leading to reversals on appeal: ...

[63] A determination of the scope of the proposed expert opinion evidence and the manner in which it may be presented to the jury if admissible will be made after a voir dire. The procedures to be followed on that voir dire are for the trial judge to decide.

Sometimes the expert must be examined and cross-examined on the voir dire to ensure that the proposed evidence is properly understood. At the conclusion of the voir dire, the trial judge must identify with exactitude the scope of the proposed opinion that may be admissible. He or she will also decide whether certain terminology used by the expert is unnecessary to the opinion and potentially misleading ... The trial judge may admit part of the proffered testimony, modify the nature or scope of the proposed opinion, or edit the language used to frame that opinion: ... .

[64] The importance of properly defining the limits and nature of proposed expert opinion evidence and the language to be used by the expert is one of the valuable lessons learned from the Inquiry into Pediatric Forensic Pathology in Ontario [Ontario, Inquiry into Pediatric Forensic Pathology in Ontario, *Report: Policy and Recommendations*, vol. 3 (Toronto: Queen's Printer, 2008)]. That inquiry examined the forensic work of Dr. Charles Smith, who at the time was considered to be a leading pediatric pathologist in Ontario. The inquiry determined that, among other failings, Dr. Smith often went beyond the limits of his expertise when offering opinions in his testimony. His excesses were sometimes not caught by the court or counsel and, along with other shortcomings, led to several miscarriages of justice. Goudge J.A., the Commissioner, stressed the trial judge's obligation to take an active role in framing the scope and the language of the proposed expert opinion evidence. He observed, at pp. 499-500:

> A final outcome from the admissibility process is a clear definition of the scope of the expertise that a particular witness is qualified to give. As discussed in the earlier part of this chapter, *it will be beneficial to define the range of expertise with as much precision as possible so that all the parties and the witness are alerted to areas where the witness has not been qualified to give evidence. ... As I earlier recommended, the trial judge should take steps at the outset to define clearly the proposed subject area of the witness's expertise. At the conclusion of the voir dire, the trial judge will be well situated to rule with precision on what the witness can and cannot say.* These steps will help to ensure that the witness's testimony, when given, can be confined to permissible areas and that it meets the requirement of threshold reliability. (Emphasis added)

[65] The present case affords an example of the problem that can ensue when the proffered expert opinion evidence is not properly circumscribed. In its primary position, the Crown contended that Dr. Totten's opinion could be put before the jury in the form of a hypothetical, which, as the trial judge accurately observed, was "tantamount to a confession" (at para. 92). The Crown's proposed formulation of Dr. Totten's evidence drew a straight and powerful line between the jury's acceptance of his opinion and the conviction of the respondent on a charge of first degree murder. As advanced by the Crown in its primary position, Dr. Totten's evidence reads less like the opinion of a sociologist on the meaning of a symbol used in a certain culture and more like evidence from a factual witness offering identification testimony: see *United States of America v. Mejia*, 545 F.3d 179 (2nd Cir. 2008), at pp. 195-96.

· · ·

[68] The Crown's attempt to link directly Dr. Totten's opinion to the identity of the respondent as the killer misconceived the true nature of Dr. Totten's opinion and the role he could legitimately play in assisting the jury. His report and his evidence made it clear that he could not speak to the reason the respondent placed a teardrop tattoo on his face.

Dr. Totten could speak to the culture within urban street gangs in Canada and specifically the potential meanings to be taken from the inscription of a teardrop tattoo on the face of a young male member of that culture. Dr. Totten's evidence was directed to the potential meanings attributed to that symbol within a given culture and not to the reason any particular individual placed a tattoo on his face. Properly understood, Dr. Totten's opinion provided context within which to assess other evidence that the jury would hear, thereby assisting the jury in making its own assessment as to the meaning, if any, to be given to the respondent's teardrop tattoo: … .

[69] The Crown's secondary position on the voir dire was described by the trial judge in these terms, at para. 28:

> … Dr. Totten's evidence could be limited to the introduction alone of the possible meanings for the tattoo without providing his analysis of the specific meaning attributable to Mr. Abbey's tattoo.

[70] This secondary position reflects the proper limits of the opinion that Dr. Totten could properly advance. Phrased in this manner, his opinion did not go directly to the ultimate issue of identity and did not invite the jury to move directly from acceptance of the opinion to a finding of guilt. Dr. Totten's opinion, as properly delineated, would form part of a larger evidentiary picture to be evaluated as a whole by the jury.

3. Necessity and Propriety of Hearing Expert Opinion Evidence

There are at least two dimensions to the proposition that one must assess whether proferred evidence is the proper subject of expert testimony. First, that evidence must be necessary according to the judicial definitions of necessity set out in *R v DD* and *R v K (A)* (extracted below). Second, an expert cannot offer an opinion on a pure question of domestic law (see e.g. *Parizeau v Lafrance*, [1999] RJQ 2399; and *Andersen v St Jude Medical, Inc*, 2011 ONSC 2178). This subsection focuses on the first dimension, as applying this dimension has caused considerable difficulty in practice.

R v DD

2000 SCC 43, [2000] 2 SCR 275

McLachlin CJ and L'Heureux-Dubé, Gonthier, Iacobucci, Major, Binnie and Arbour JJ (5 October 2000)

[1] McLACHLIN CJ [L'Heureux-Dubé and Gonthier JJ dissenting on the merits]: …

• • •

[3] The prosecution's case is that the accused, who was living with the complainant's mother, sexually assaulted the complainant by making her touch his penis on numerous occasions in 1991 and 1992 when she was 5 to 6 years old. The complainant told no one about these events for two and a half years. In January 1995, the complainant had a conversation with a school friend about "gross" things, some of which were true and some of which were false. During the conversation, the complainant told her friend about the assaults. The friend reported the complainant's disclosure to a teacher, and the matter was referred to the Children's Aid Society. A Society worker interviewed the complainant in

the presence of a police officer. The complainant first said that she could not remember any sexual touching, but later revealed incidents involving the accused. The accused categorically denies the allegations.

[4] Charges were laid and the matter proceeded to trial. At the time of the trial the complainant was 10 years old. Defence counsel cross-examined the complainant on why she had waited so long to report the incidents and suggested that she had fabricated the story to "one up" the stories told by her friend. In response, the Crown sought to call child psychologist Dr. Peter Marshall to rebut defence counsel's submission that the lateness of the complainant's disclosure supported an inference that she was not telling the truth when she said that the accused had sexually assaulted her. The trial judge called a *voir dire* on the admissibility of Dr. Marshall's evidence on this point.

· · ·

B. Necessity

[21] When it comes to necessity, the question is whether the expert will provide information which is likely to be outside the ordinary experience and knowledge of the trier of fact: *Burns*, … [*R v Burns*, [1994] 1 SCR 656]; *Mohan*, … [*R v Mohan*, [1994] 2 SCR 9]; *R. v. Lavallee*, [1990] 1 S.C.R. 852; *R. v. Abbey*, [1982] 2 S.C.R. 24; *Kelliher (Village of) v. Smith*, [1931] S.C.R. 672. "Necessity" means that the evidence must be more than merely "helpful," but necessity need not be judged "by too strict a standard": *Mohan, supra*, at p. 23. Absolute necessity is not required.

[22] The trial judge concluded that the evidence of delayed disclosure was outside the knowledge and expertise of the jury, citing the statement in *Marquard*, … [*R v Marquard*, [1993] 4 SCR 223], that such evidence has been properly received in the past. (As mentioned earlier, if the trial judge was bypassing a thorough examination of necessity on the basis that it could be inferred as a matter of law, he proceeded contrary to the case-by-case method *Mohan* prescribes. However, the question before us is whether his conclusion was justified, not how he arrived at it.) By contrast, the Court of Appeal held that the question of what inferences could be drawn from delay in disclosure was a matter within the knowledge and expertise of the jury, on which they required no expert help.

[23] The issue again may be put in simple terms: was there a sufficient basis for the trial judge to conclude that the issue of the child's delay in disclosure might involve matters beyond the ordinary knowledge and expertise of the jury? Was the evidence necessary to enable the trier of fact to properly dispose of the credibility issue? In answering this question, we must bear in mind that the trial judge is in the best position of determining the level of the jurors' understanding and what may assist them.

[24] In my view, there was an ample foundation for the trial judge's conclusion that Dr. Marshall's evidence went beyond the ordinary knowledge and expertise of the jury. Based on his knowledge of the relevant scientific literature, Dr. Marshall was able to present insights into why a child might not report incidents of sexual abuse promptly. Those insights might not be within the knowledge of the ordinary juror. Appellate courts have upheld numerous decisions in which trial judges have admitted expert evidence on delayed disclosure to assist the trier of fact in child sexual abuse cases: see, e.g., *C. (G.)*, … [*R v C (G)* (1996), 110 CCC (3d) 233 (Nfld CA)] ; *R. v. Mair* (1998), 122 C.C.C. (3d) 563 (Ont. C.A.); *R. v. T. (D.B.)* (1994), 89 C.C.C. (3d) 466 (Ont. C.A.); *R. v. C. (R.A.)*

(1990), 57 C.C.C. (3d) 522 (B.C.C.A.). These decisions indicate that there is still a significant perceived need for explanation of children's reactions to abuse, as it may be outside the knowledge and experience of ordinary people.

[25] Dr. Marshall testified, in essence, that contrary to what the ordinary juror might assume, there is no "normal" child response. Some abused children complain immediately, others wait for a period of time, and some never disclose the abuse. Thus the timing of the complaint, he testified, does not help to diagnose whether it is true or fabricated. He also outlined the factors that may lead to delay in disclosure, such as fear of reprisal, lack of understanding, fear of disrupting the family, the nature of the child's relationship with the abuser, and the nature of the abuse. Some of these explanations might have occurred to ordinary jurors as a matter of experience and common sense, but some might not have been apparent to them without expert assistance. Having heard on the *voir dire* what Dr. Marshall proposed to say, it was open to the trial judge to conclude that his evidence would assist the jurors by giving them an understanding of the issue of delay in reporting that their ordinary knowledge and experience might not provide.

[26] The accused raises three arguments against the finding that Dr. Marshall's evidence met the criterion of necessity. First, he argues that in the area of behavioural science, normal human behaviour should not require expert explanation. Only abnormal behaviour should satisfy the necessity requirement. Since the factors that might explain a delay in disclosure—fear, embarrassment, lack of understanding—are all normal human reactions and by implication within the ken of the jury, he submits that the necessity requirement is not met.

[27] I am reluctant to depart from the flexibility of the *Mohan* approach by adumbrating the necessity criterion with sub-rules relating to the type of science at issue. It seems to me that the wisest course is to retain the present approach. The trial judge must determine necessity in each individual case judged simply by whether the expert testifies on matters beyond the ordinary juror's knowledge and experience. Laying down category-based rules for the admissibility of expert evidence would contradict the principled approach of *Mohan*. I see no reason to judge social sciences by a different standard than other sciences. The *Mohan* criteria already require a qualified expert and permit scrutiny of the newness or validity of the science on which the proposed evidence is based.

[28] Moreover, a rule that expert evidence can be called only on abnormal behaviour would raise problems. It might be difficult to accurately distinguish between "normal" and "abnormal" human behaviour: see *Mohan, supra*, at pp. 35-36 (thus raising the spectre of ancillary expert evidence on what is normal and abnormal). Another problem is that the proposed rule rests on a questionable assumption—that ordinary jurors will invariably know all they need to know about "normal" behaviour in order to do justice in all cases. Judges and jurors are human, but their knowledge of a particular aspect of human behaviour may not equal that of an expert. As Wilson J. wrote in *Lavallee*, ... [*R v Lavallee*, [1990] 1 SCR 852], at pp. 870-71:

> The longstanding recognition that psychiatric or psychological testimony also falls within the realm of expert evidence is predicated on the realization that in some circumstances the average person may not have sufficient knowledge of or experience with human behaviour to draw an appropriate inference from the facts before him or her.

In such cases, expert testimony may be necessary to assist the trier of fact in resolving an issue. This does not mean, of course, that expert evidence is required in all cases in which the issue of delayed disclosure arises. It is for the parties to assess, and ultimately the trial judge to decide, whether the facts of a particular case establish a need to put expert evidence before the trier of fact: *R. v. T.E.M.* (1996), 187 A.R. 273 (C.A.).

[29] The accused's second argument against necessity is that the expert evidence on reasons for delay was not required because the child herself explained why she had not reported the incident more promptly. The fact that the complainant testifies does not preclude the trial judge from admitting other evidence on the issue. The defence having put the reason for delay in question by suggesting that it showed that the incidents had not occurred, it was open to the trial judge to permit the prosecution to respond with evidence of other possibilities. In so far as the expert provided information and insights that went beyond the complainant's testimony and the ordinary juror's knowledge, it might well have been required to assist the jury in properly assessing her credibility. Dr. Marshall's evidence did not simply repeat the complainant's evidence. He went further, positing that such explanations are common among child abuse victims. Furthermore, the current scientific consensus is that the truth or falsity of such an allegation cannot be determined on the basis of its timing. This was a subject that the child could not and did not attempt to address.

[30] The accused's third argument on necessity is that to the extent there was something the jury might not know from their own experience, the trial judge could have relayed this instruction to the jury in his charge. I agree that a trial judge considering the need to call expert evidence can ask whether the same thing could be accomplished by a warning to the jury. To the extent it can, the need to call the expert evidence may be diminished. However, before concluding that a jury direction renders expert evidence unnecessary, the trial judge must be satisfied that the jury instruction will achieve the same purpose as the expert evidence. If not, the expert evidence may still remain necessary.

· · ·

[33] Given the additional assistance that Dr. Marshall's testimony may have provided to the jury, I cannot conclude that the trial judge erred by failing to find that it was un-necessary because he could have given a jury warning. ..:

· · ·

[44] MAJOR J [Iacobucci, Binnie, and Arbour JJ]: This appeal raises the question of whether expert evidence may be admitted to inform the jury that children who have suffered sexual abuse respond in different ways with respect to disclosing the abuse. The expert here did not interview the child, so his evidence was not specific to this complainant but was a general explanation applicable to all children.

· · ·

[46] The second requirement of the *Mohan* analysis exists to ensure that the dangers associated with expert evidence are not lightly tolerated. Mere relevance or "helpfulness" is not enough. The evidence must also be *necessary*.

[47] I agree with the Chief Justice that some degree of deference is owed to the trial judge's discretionary determination of whether the *Mohan* requirements have been met on the facts of a particular case, but that discretion cannot be used erroneously to dilute the requirement of necessity. *Mohan* expressly states that mere helpfulness is too low a standard to warrant accepting the dangers inherent in the admission of expert evidence.

A fortiori, a finding that some aspects of the evidence "might reasonably have assisted the jury" is not enough. As stated by J. Sopinka, S. N. Lederman and A. W. Bryant,

> expert evidence must be necessary in order to allow the fact finder: (1) to appreciate the facts due to their technical nature, or; (2) to form a correct judgment on a matter if ordinary persons are unlikely to do so without the assistance of persons with special knowledge.

(*The Law of Evidence in Canada* (2nd ed. 1999), at p. 620, citing *Mohan, supra*, at p. 23.)

. . .

[58] In my view, the content of the expert evidence admitted in this case was not unique or scientifically puzzling but was rather the proper subject for a simple jury instruction. This being the case, its admission was not necessary.

[59] Distilling the probative elements of Dr. Marshall's testimony from its superfluous and prejudicial elements, one bald statement of principle emerges. In diagnosing cases of child sexual abuse, the timing of the disclosure, standing alone, signifies nothing. Not all victims of child sexual abuse will disclose the abuse immediately. It depends upon the circumstances of the particular victim. I find surprising the suggestion that a Canadian jury or judge alone would be incapable of understanding this simple fact. I cannot identify any technical quality to this evidence that necessitates expert opinion.

. . .

[64] Given that the statement of principle expressed by Dr. Marshall reflects the current state of Canadian law, it could have and should have been included in the trial judge's instructions to the jury. As this would have effectively dispelled the possibility that the jury might engage in stereotypical reasoning, it was not necessary to inject the dangers of expert evidence into the trial.

[65] A trial judge should recognize and so instruct a jury that there is no inviolable rule on how people who are the victims of trauma like a sexual assault will behave. Some will make an immediate complaint, some will delay in disclosing the abuse, while some will never disclose the abuse. Reasons for delay are many and at least include embarrassment, fear, guilt, or a lack of understanding and knowledge. In assessing the credibility of a complainant, the timing of the complaint is simply one circumstance to consider in the factual mosaic of a particular case. A delay in disclosure, standing alone, will never give rise to an adverse inference against the credibility of the complainant.

R v K (A)
(1999), 45 OR (3d) 641 (CA)
McMurtry CJO, Charron and Moldaver JJA (13 September 1999)

[K (A) and N (K) were charged with sexually assaulting children in their family. The Crown sought to introduce expert opinion evidence from a social worker for two purposes: (1) to show that the complainants exhibited behavioural patterns during childhood that were consistent with sexual abuse; and (2) to explain that certain behaviours by the complainants (such as delayed disclosure after a period of denial of the abuse) were not unusual for victims of sexual abuse.]

CHARRON JA (McMURTRY CJO concurring):

[90] The proposed expert opinion evidence must not only be relevant and worth receiving as discussed above, it must be necessary to assist the trier of fact. If the trier of fact can form his or her own conclusions on the facts without help, the opinion of an expert, even though it may be relevant, is unnecessary and inadmissible.

[91] As indicated in *Mohan* [*R v Mohan*, [1994] 2 SCR 9, 89 CCC (3d) 402], the evidence must be more than just helpful to meet this criterion. On the other hand, necessity cannot be judged by too high a standard. The test is formulated in different ways in *Mohan* (at p. 23 S.C.R., p. 413 C.C.C.):

- The "evidence must be necessary to enable the trier of fact to appreciate the matters in issue due to their technical nature."
- The "opinion must be necessary in the sense that it provides information 'which is likely to be outside the experience and knowledge of a judge or jury'."
- The "subject-matter of the inquiry must be such that ordinary people are unlikely to form a correct judgment about it, if unassisted by persons with special knowledge."

[92] Therefore, the following alternative questions should be asked:

(a) Will the proposed expert opinion evidence enable the trier of fact to appreciate the technicalities of a matter in issue?

(b) Will it provide information which is likely to be outside the experience of the trier of fact?

(c) Is the trier of fact unlikely to form a correct judgment about a matter in issue if unassisted by the expert opinion evidence?

. . .

[95] In cases of sexual abuse such as this one, the proposed expert evidence often touches upon matters of credibility. This presents an even more difficult task for the trial judge in the application of the criterion of necessity. In determining whether expert opinion is necessary to assist the trier of fact in arriving at his or her own conclusions, it becomes particularly important to keep in mind that the credibility of witnesses is a question that is reserved to the trier of fact. The Supreme Court, in *R. v. Marquard*, [1993] 4 S.C.R. 223 at p. 248, 85 C.C.C. (3d) 193 at p. 228, held it to be "a fundamental axiom of our trial process that the ultimate conclusion as to the credibility or truthfulness of a particular witness is for the trier of fact, and is not the proper subject of expert opinion."

[96] The difficulty lies in the fact that a distinction is drawn between evidence about credibility, which is inadmissible, and evidence about a feature of a witness's behaviour or testimony that may be admissible even though it will likely have some bearing on the trier of fact's ultimate determination of the question of credibility. For example, evidence tendered to show that it is not unusual for sexual offence complainants to delay reporting incidents of abuse may be admissible, if it meets the admissibility requirements for expert opinion evidence in the particular case, even though it may have some bearing on the ultimate determination of the complainant's credibility. However, any evidence tendered to show either directly or indirectly that the complainant is more or less likely to be telling the truth because she delayed reporting the abuse is not the proper subject-matter of expert testimony and is inadmissible. It is strictly up to the trier of fact to determine what

effect any delay in reporting may have on the credibility of the complainant without any expert assistance on this ultimate issue of credibility.

[In the result, the court ordered a new trial because (1) the trial judge and the lawyers failed to confine the expert witness to his scope of expertise and (2) the trial judge failed to supply appropriate limiting instructions. Charron JA expressed concern that the manner in which the expert's testimony was led would have encouraged the jury to conclude (incorrectly) that they could not discredit the complainants' testimony based on the behavioural patterns discussed by the expert (see para 130).

Moldaver JA (as he then was) concurred on this issue and in the result.]

NOTES AND QUESTIONS

1. How would you reconcile the majority's reasoning in *DD* with the case-by-case approach to the admissibility of expert opinion evidence? Do you think that Major J's observation that the proposition that some children delay reporting sexual abuse is "not unique or scientifically puzzling" effectively bars such evidence from admission in the future?

2. For the most part, trial judges seem to have interpreted Doherty JA's precondition that the expert opinion be a matter which is properly the subject of expert evidence as a reformulation of the proposition that it must be necessary for the trier of fact to hear the relevant information from an expert—or, putting the matter differently, that the trier of fact would be unable to come to a proper decision in the absence of the expert opinion evidence (see e.g. *R v Hersi*, 2014 ONSC 1258; *R v Shafia*, 2012 ONSC 1538, *Rees v Toronto District School Board*, 2010 ONSC 6677). In *Kelliher (Village of) v Smith*, [1931] SCR 672 at 684, [1931] 4 DLR 102 at 116, the Supreme Court of Canada adopted the principle that in order for expert evidence to be admissible "the subject-matter of the inquiry must be such that ordinary people are unlikely to form a correct judgment about it, if unassisted by persons with special knowledge."

3. In *R v Lavallee*, [1990] 1 SCR 852, Wilson J expanded upon the principle from *Kelliher (Village of) v Smith*. She held on behalf of a majority that:

> Where expert evidence is tendered in such fields as engineering or pathology, the paucity of the lay person's knowledge is uncontentious. The long-standing recognition that psychiatric or psychological testimony also falls within the realm of expert evidence is predicated on the realization that in some circumstances the average person may not have sufficient knowledge of or experience with human behaviour to draw an appropriate inference from the facts before him or her. An example may be found in *R v. Lyons*, [1987] 2 SCR 309, in which this court approved the use of psychiatric testimony in dangerous offender applications. At p. 366 La Forest J remarks that "psychiatric evidence is clearly relevant to the issue whether a person is likely to behave in a certain way and, indeed, is probably relatively superior in this regard to the evidence of other clinicians and lay persons." The need for expert evidence in these areas can, however, be obfuscated by the belief that judges and juries are thoroughly knowledgeable about "human nature" and that no more is needed. They are, so to speak, their own experts on human behaviour. This, in effect, was the primary submission of the Crown to this court.
>
> The bare facts of this case, which I think are amply supported by the evidence, are that the appellant was repeatedly abused by the deceased but did not leave him (although she twice pointed a gun at him), and ultimately shot him in the back of the head as he was leaving her room. The Crown submits that these facts disclose all the information a jury needs in order to

decide whether or not the appellant acted in self-defence. I have no hesitation in rejecting the Crown's submission.

Expert evidence on the psychological effect of battering on wives and common law partners must, it seems to me, be both relevant and necessary in the context of the present case. How can the mental state of the appellant be appreciated without it? The average member of the public (or of the jury) can be forgiven for asking: Why would a woman put up with this kind of treatment? Why should she continue to live with such a man? How could she love a partner who beat her to the point of requiring hospitalization? We would expect the woman to pack her bags and go. Where is her self-respect? Why does she not cut loose and make a new life for herself? Such is the reaction of the average person confronted with the so-called "battered wife syndrome." We need help to understand it and help is available from trained professionals.

· · ·

Expert testimony on the psychological effects of battering have [sic] been admitted in American courts in recent years. In *State v. Kelly*, 478 A.2d 364 at p. 378 (1984), the New Jersey Supreme Court commended the value of expert testimony in these terms:

It is aimed at an area where the purported common knowledge of the jury may be very much mistaken, an area where jurors' logic, drawn from their own experience, may lead to a wholly incorrect conclusion, an area where expert knowledge would enable the jurors to disregard their prior conclusions as being common myths rather than common knowledge.

The court concludes at p. 379 that the battering relationship is "subject to a large group of myths and stereotypes." As such, it is "beyond the ken of the average juror and thus is suitable for explanation through expert testimony." I share that view.

· · ·

Where evidence exists that an accused is in a battering relationship, expert testimony can assist the jury in determining whether the accused had a "reasonable" apprehension of death when she acted by explaining the heightened sensitivity of a battered woman to her partner's acts. Without such testimony I am skeptical that the average fact-finder would be capable of appreciating why her subjective fear may have been reasonable in the context of the relationship. After all, the hypothetical "reasonable man" observing only the final incident may have been unlikely to recognize the batterer's threat as potentially lethal. Using the case at bar as an example the "reasonable man" might have thought, as the majority of the Court of Appeal seemed to, that it was unlikely that Rust would make good on his threat to kill the appellant that night because they had guests staying overnight.

· · ·

In light of the foregoing discussion I would summarize as follows the principles upon which expert testimony is properly admitted in cases such as this:

1. Expert testimony is admissible to assist the fact-finder in drawing inferences in areas where the expert has relevant knowledge or experience beyond that of the lay person.

2. It is difficult for the lay person to comprehend the battered-wife syndrome. It is commonly thought that battered women are not really beaten as badly as they claim; otherwise they would have left the relationship. Alternatively, some believe that women enjoy being beaten, that they have a masochistic strain in them. Each of these stereotypes may adversely affect consideration of a battered woman's claim to have acted in self-defence in killing her mate.

3. Expert evidence can assist the jury in dispelling these myths.

4. Expert testimony relating to the ability of an accused to perceive danger from her mate may go to the issue of whether she "reasonably apprehended" death or grievous bodily harm on a particular occasion.

5. Expert testimony pertaining to why an accused remained in the battering relationship may be relevant in assessing the nature and extent of the alleged abuse.

6. By providing an explanation as to why an accused did not flee when she perceived her life to be in danger, expert testimony may also assist the jury in assessing the reasonableness of her belief that killing her batterer was the only way to save her own life.

. . .

Ultimately, it is up to the jury to decide whether, *in fact*, the accused's perceptions and actions were reasonable. Expert evidence does not and cannot usurp that function of the jury. The jury is not compelled to accept the opinions proffered by the expert about the effects of battering on the mental state of victims generally or on the mental state of the accused in particular. But fairness and the integrity of the trial process demand that the jury have the opportunity to hear them.

[The accused's appeal was allowed and the acquittal was restored.]

4. Qualifications

In *R v Mohan*, [1994] 2 SCR 9 at 25, Sopinka J held that an expert witness must be "shown to have acquired special or peculiar knowledge through study or experience in respect of the matters on which he or she undertakes to testify." This criterion has tended to be interpreted leniently by courts, and few expert witnesses fail to meet this threshold (although experts are frequently found to be unqualified in respect of some part of their evidence—see the discussion on defining the nature and scope of the evidence, in Section III.B.2, above). The recent Supreme Court of Canada decision in *White Burgess Langille Inman v Abbott & Haliburton Co* largely maintains this modest standard for qualifications. Concerns about the quality of an expert's qualifications should be incorporated into an assessment of the benefits and costs of the evidence (see Section 3.C, below).

White Burgess Langille Inman v Abbott & Haliburton Co
2015 SCC 23, [2015] 2 SCR 182
McLachlin CJ and Abella, Rothstein, Cromwell, Moldaver, Wagner, and
Gascon JJ (30 April 2015)

CROMWELL J [McLachlin CJ and Abella, Rothstein, Moldaver, Wagner, and Gascon JJ agreeing]:

. . .

D. *The Expert's Duty to the Court or Tribunal*

[26] There is little controversy about the broad outlines of the expert witness's duty to the court. As Anderson writes, "[t]he duty to provide independent assistance to the

Court by way of objective unbiased opinion has been stated many times by common law courts around the world": [G.R. Anderson, *Expert Evidence* (3rd ed 2014)] p. 227. I would add that a similar duty exists in the civil law of Quebec: J.-C. Royer and S. Lavallée, *La preuve civile* (4th ed. 2008), at para. 468; D. Béchard with the collaboration of J. Béchard, *L'expert* (2011) ch. 9; *An Act to establish the new Code of Civil Procedure*, S.Q. 2014, c. 1, art. 22 (not yet in force); L. Chamberland, *Le nouveau Code de procédure civile commenté* (2014), at pp. 14 and 121.

. . .

[28] Many provinces and territories have provided explicit guidance related to the duty of expert witnesses. In Nova Scotia, for example, the Civil Procedure Rules require that an expert's report be signed by the expert who must make (among others) the following representations to the court: that the expert is providing an objective opinion for the assistance of the court; that the expert is prepared to apply independent judgment when assisting the court; and that the report includes everything the expert regards as relevant to the expressed opinion and draws attention to anything that could reasonably lead to a different conclusion (r. 55.04(1)(a), (b) and (c)). While these requirements do not affect the rules of evidence by which expert opinion is determined to be admissible or inadmissible, they provide a convenient summary of a fairly broadly shared sense of the duties of an expert witness to the court.

[29] There are similar descriptions of the expert's duty in the civil procedure rules in other Canadian jurisdictions: Anderson, at p. 227; *The Queen's Bench Rules* (Saskatchewan), r. 5-37; Supreme Court Civil Rules, B.C. Reg. 168/2009, r. 11-2(1); Rules of Civil Procedure, R.R.O. 1990, Reg. 194, r. 4.1.01(1); Rules of Court, Y.O.I.C. 2009/65, r. 34(23); *An Act to establish the new Code of Civil Procedure*, art. 22. Moreover, the rules in Saskatchewan, British Columbia, Ontario, Nova Scotia, Prince Edward Island, Quebec and the Federal Courts require experts to certify that they are aware of and will comply with their duty to the court: Anderson, at p. 228; Saskatchewan *Queen's Bench Rules*, r. 5-37(3); British Columbia Supreme Court Civil Rules, r. 11-2(2); Ontario Rules of Civil Procedure, r. 53.03(2.1); Nova Scotia Civil Procedure Rules, r. 55.04(1)(a); Prince Edward Island *Rules of Civil Procedure*, r. 53.03(3)(g); *An Act to establish the new Code of Civil Procedure*, art. 235 (not yet in force); Federal Courts Rules, SOR/98-106, r. 52.2(1)(c).

[30] The formulation in the Ontario Rules of Civil Procedure is perhaps the most succinct and complete statement of the expert's duty to the court: to provide opinion evidence that is fair, objective and non-partisan: r. 4.1.01(1)(a). The Rules are also explicit that this duty to the court prevails over any obligation owed by the expert to a party: r. 4.1.01(2). Likewise, the newly adopted *Act to establish the new Code of Civil Procedure* of Quebec explicitly provides, as a guiding principle, that the expert's duty to the court overrides the parties' interests, and that the expert must fulfill his or her primary duty to the court "objectively, impartially and thoroughly": art. 22; Chamberland, at pp. 14 and 121.

. . .

[45] Following what I take to be the dominant view in the Canadian cases, I would hold that an expert's lack of independence and impartiality goes to the admissibility of the evidence in addition to being considered in relation to the weight to be given to the evidence if admitted. That approach seems to me to be more in line with the basic structure of our law relating to expert evidence and with the importance our jurisprudence has attached to the gatekeeping role of trial judges. Binnie J. summed up the Canadian

approach well in *J.-L.J.* [*R v J-LJ*, 2000 SCC 51, [2000] 2 SCR 600]: "The admissibility of the expert evidence should be scrutinized at the time it is proffered, and not allowed too easy an entry on the basis that all of the frailties could go at the end of the day to weight rather than admissibility" (para. 28).

. . .

[53] In my opinion, concerns related to the expert's duty to the court and his or her willingness and capacity to comply with it are best addressed initially in the "qualified expert" element of the *Mohan* framework [citations omitted]. A proposed expert witness who is unable or unwilling to fulfill this duty to the court is not properly qualified to perform the role of an expert. Situating this concern in the "properly qualified expert" ensures that the courts will focus expressly on the important risks associated with biased experts: [citations omitted].

NOTE

In *R v McIntosh* (1997), 35 OR (3d) 97 (CA), Finlayson JA signalled that he considered the qualification standard may be too low. In that case, the Crown had not contested the qualifications of a psychologist tendered by the defence to give evidence on the frailties of eyewitness evidence. Finlayson JA observed:

> In the light of the limited argument before this court on the matter, it is evident that this is not the case to engage in a full-scale analysis as to whether the type of evidence proffered by Dr. Yarmey is admissible in any circumstance. However, I do not intend to leave the subject without raising some warning flags. In my respectful opinion, the courts are overly eager to abdicate their fact-finding responsibilities to "experts" in the field of the behavioural sciences. We are too quick to say that a particular witness possesses special knowledge and experience going beyond that of the trier of fact without engaging in an analysis of the subject-matter of that expertise. I do not want to be taken as denigrating the integrity of Dr. Yarmey's research or of his expertise in the field of psychology, clearly one of the learned sciences, but simply because a person has lectured and written extensively on a subject that is of interest to him or her does not constitute him or her an expert for the purposes of testifying in a court of law on the subject of that specialty.

Finlayson JA's observations were made prior to the reformulation of the admissibility test by Doherty JA in *R v Abbey*. To what extent do you think his concerns are addressed elsewhere in the reformulated approach?

5. *Other Exclusionary Rules*

In general terms, exclusionary rules operate independently in the sense that where more than one exclusionary rule applies to a given piece of evidence, exceptions to each applicable rule must be found in order to admit the evidence. This rule holds with respect to expert opinion evidence; however, it is relaxed in respect of the interaction between hearsay and expert opinion evidence.

R v Abbey
[1982] 2 SCR 24, 68 CCC (2d) 394
Laskin CJ and Martland, Ritchie, Dickson, Beetz, Estey, McIntyre, Chouinard,
and Lamer JJ (22 July 1982)

DICKSON J:　Robert Mark Abbey was tried by a judge sitting alone on two charges (i) importing cocaine into Canada and (ii) unlawful possession of cocaine for the purpose of trafficking. His sole defence was that he was insane at the material time. The trial judge gave effect to that defence. He found Abbey not guilty on account of insanity and the Court of Appeal of British Columbia dismissed a Crown appeal. The matter has now, by leave, reached this Court.

The Facts and History of the Case

[The accused was arrested at Vancouver International Airport when found carrying 5.5 ounces of white powder, which was 50 percent cocaine. He did not testify at his eventual trial. Crown witnesses including customs officers and RCMP officers testified that Abbey seemed "normal" upon arrest and questioning. A psychiatrist called by Abbey testified that the accused was suffering from a disease of the mind called hypomania. A rebuttal expert called by the Crown testified that hypomania would not render Abbey incapable of appreciating the nature and quality of his actions or of knowing that his actions were wrong. The Crown appealed on the basis that the trial judge had erred in treating hearsay evidence conveyed by the psychiatric witnesses as proof of the truth of the relevant statements.]

. . .

Hearsay Evidence

[T]he Crown contends that the trial judge misdirected himself with respect to the use which could be made of hearsay evidence introduced during the testimony of the psychiatrists who were called as witnesses.

　Dr. Vallance testified that during the course of his interviews Abbey told him of various delusions, visions, hallucinations and sensations which he had experienced in the six months preceding his arrest. Dr. Vallance also testified that Abbey had described certain symptoms of the disease to his mother several months prior to the commission of the offence. In his testimony, Dr. Vallance recounted several incidents of bizarre and unstable conduct by Abbey both before his departure for Peru and during his stay. Abbey had told him, Dr. Vallance testified, that four days prior to his actual departure for Peru he had missed a flight and, in a rage, kicked in a window at Vancouver airport. Dr. Vallance was also told by Abbey of certain experiences in Peru: "he could see lights and follow the lights and would interpret those phenomenon with ideas that there was some power outside of him that was communicating with him. He would do strange things, like run out into the fields. He was licking the wetness from trees." The Crown submits that the trial judge accepted and treated as factual much of this hearsay evidence related by Dr. Vallance in the course of giving his opinion. The point is well taken.

　A general principle of evidence is that all relevant evidence is admissible. The law of evidence, however, reposes on a few general principles riddled by innumerable exceptions.

Two major exceptions to this general principle are hearsay evidence and opinion evidence. There are also exceptions to the exceptions: "expert witnesses may testify to their opinion on matters involving their expertise" (*Cross on Evidence*, 5th ed. (1979), p. 20) and may also, incidentally, base their opinions upon hearsay.

. . .

Opinion Evidence

Witnesses testify as to facts. The judge or jury draws inferences from the facts. "In the law of evidence 'opinion' means any inference from observed fact, and the law on the subject derives from the general rule that witnesses must speak only to that which was directly observed by them" (*Cross on Evidence*, p. 442). Where it is possible to separate fact from inference the witness may only testify as to fact. It is not always possible, however, to do so and the "law makes allowances for these borderline cases by permitting witnesses to state their opinion with regard to matters not calling for special knowledge whenever it would be virtually impossible for them to separate their inferences from the facts on which those inferences are based" (*ibid.*).

With respect to matters calling for special knowledge, an expert in the field may draw inferences and state his opinion. An expert's function is precisely this: to provide the judge and jury with a ready-made inference which the judge and jury, due to the technical nature of the facts, are unable to formulate. "An expert's opinion is admissible to furnish the Court with scientific information which is likely to be outside the experience and knowledge of a judge or jury. If on the proven facts a judge or jury can form their own conclusions without help, then the opinion of the expert is unnecessary": (*R v. Turner* (1974), 60 Cr. App. R 80 at p. 83, *per* Lawton LJ).

An expert witness, like any other witness, may testify as to the veracity of facts of which he has first-hand experience, but this is not the main purpose of his or her testimony. An expert is there to give an opinion. And the opinion more often than not will be based on second-hand evidence. This is especially true of the opinions of psychiatrists.

[Dickson J considered *Wilband v R*, [1967] SCR 14, and continued:]

Thus an expert opinion based on second-hand evidence is admissible, if relevant. The problem arose in *R v. Dietrich* (1970), 1 CCC (2d) 49 (Ont. CA), as to second-hand evidence itself which formed the basis of the opinion. Gale CJO reached the conclusion that (at p. 65): "Put shortly, if an expert is permitted to give his opinion, he ought to be permitted to give the circumstances upon which that opinion is based." Testimony as to circumstances upon which the opinion is based is not introduced, and cannot be introduced, in order to establish the veracity of the second-hand evidence. It is thus not hearsay evidence. Jessup JA correctly stated the law in *R v. Rosik* (1970), 2 CCC (2d) 351 (at pp. 388-9):

> In my view, a psychiatrist expressing an opinion as to a mental or emotional condition of an accused can relate in evidence, as Dr. Gray did, that he had been told by the accused *when such information is a basis of his opinion.*
>
> . . .
>
> The hearsay rule does not operate to exclude such evidence because it is not admitted to prove the fact of what the expert has been told: see *Wigmore on Evidence*, 3rd ed., vol. VI,

s. 1720, p. 70, approved by Gale, CJO, in the *Dietrich* case. The trial judge should have so instructed the jury, and it would have been proper for him also to point out that there was no sworn evidence that the accused ingested drugs or consumed the quantity of alcohol integral to Dr. Gray's opinion … .

(Emphasis added.) Jessup JA's view was recently confirmed by this court in *Phillion v. The Queen*, [1978] 1 SCR 18. After citing the excerpt from *Subramaniam v. Public Prosecutor* [[1956] 1 WLR 965 (PC)], which is quoted above with respect to hearsay evidence, Ritchie J went on to say (at p. 24):

> Statements made to psychiatrists and psychologists are sometimes admitted in criminal cases and when this is so it is because they have qualified as experts in diagnosing the behavioural symptoms of individuals and have formed an opinion which the trial Judge deems to be relevant to the case, but the statements on which such opinions are based are not admissible in proof of their truth but rather as indicating the basis upon which the medical opinion was formed in accordance with recognized professional procedures.

The danger, of course, in admitting such testimony is the ever present possibility, here exemplified, that the judge or jury, without more, will accept the evidence as going to the truth of the facts stated in it. The danger is real and lies at the heart of this case. Once such testimony is admitted, a careful charge to the jury by the judge or direction to himself is essential. …

In the present case Abbey did not testify. Dr. Vallance testified, in the course of his opinion, as to many events and experiences related to him during several interviews. This testimony, while admissible in the context of the opinion, was not in any way evidence of the factual basis of these events and experiences. The trial judge in his decision fell into the error of accepting as evidence of these facts, testimony which if taken to be evidence of their existence would violate the hearsay rule. There was no admissible evidence properly before the court with respect to: the delusions experienced by the accused; the accused having described the symptoms of his disease to his mother some six months prior to the commission of the offence; the accused having seen a psychiatrist before leaving for Peru; the accused's unstable conduct at the airport some days prior to leaving for Peru or his bizarre behaviour in Peru.

In my view, the trial judge erred in law in treating as factual the hearsay evidence upon which the opinions of the psychiatrist were based.

… While it is not questioned that medical experts are entitled to take into consideration all possible information in forming their opinions, this in no way removes from the party tendering such evidence the obligation of establishing, through properly admissible evidence, the factual basis on which such opinions are based. Before any weight can be given to an expert's opinion, the facts upon which the opinion is based must be found to exist.

R v Lavallee
[1990] 1 SCR 852, 55 CCC (3d) 97
Dickson CJ and Lamer, Wilson, L'Heureux-Dubé, Sopinka, Gonthier, and
McLachlin JJ (3 May 1990)

WILSON J (Dickson CJ and Lamer, L'Heureux-Dubé, Gonthier, and McLachlin JJ concurring): …

(iii) Adequacy of trial judge's charge to the jury

The second issue raised in this case is the adequacy of the trial judge's charge to the jury with respect to the expert evidence furnished by Dr. Shane. It appears that Dr. Shane relied on various sources in formulating his opinion—his series of interviews with the appellant, an interview with her mother, a police report of the incident (including information regarding her statement to the police), and hospital records documenting eight of her visits to emergency departments between 1983 and 1986. Neither the appellant nor her mother testified at trial. The contents of their statements to Dr. Shane were hearsay.

[Wilson J considered *R v Abbey*, [1982] 2 SCR 24, and continued:]

For present purposes I think the ratio of *Abbey* can be distilled into the following propositions:

1. An expert opinion is admissible if relevant, even if it is based on second-hand evidence.

2. This second-hand evidence (hearsay) is admissible to show the information on which the expert opinion is based, not as evidence going to the existence of the facts on which the opinion is based.

3. Where the psychiatric evidence is comprised of hearsay evidence, the problem is the weight to be attributed to the opinion.

4. Before any weight can be given to an expert's opinion, the facts upon which the opinion is based must be found to exist.

In the case at bar the trial judge was clearly of the view that Dr. Shane's evidence was relevant. He would not have admitted it otherwise. As I stated above, in light of the evidence of the battering relationship which subsisted between the appellant and the deceased, the trial judge was correct in so doing.

· · ·

The trial judge's instructions regarding the weight attributable to Dr. Shane's opinion also emphasize his distinction between admissible evidence and hearsay:

If the premises upon which the information is substantially based has not been proven in evidence, it is up to you to conclude that it is not safe to attach a great deal of weight to the opinion. An opinion of an expert depends, to a large extent, on the validity of the facts assumed by the evidence of the expert.

If there are some errors and the factual assumptions aren't too important to the eventual opinion, that's one thing. *If there are errors or matters not in evidence and those matters are substantial, in your view, in terms of the impact on the expert's opinion, then you will want to look at the value and weight of that expert's opinion very carefully.* It depends on how important you think the matters were that Dr. Shane relied on that are not in evidence.

(Emphasis added.)

I agree with Huband JA that these instructions with respect to weight conform to this court's judgment in *Abbey*. ...

• • •

The fourth proposition I have extracted from *Abbey* is that there must be admissible evidence to support the facts on which the expert relies before any weight can be attributed to the opinion. The majority of the Manitoba Court of Appeal appears to interpret this as a requirement that each and every fact relied upon by the expert must be independently proven and admitted into evidence before the entire opinion can be given any weight.

Dr. Shane referred in his testimony to various facts for which there was no admissible evidence. The information was elicited from his interviews with the appellant. It included the smoking of marijuana prior to the killing, the deterioration of the intimate relationship between the appellant and Rust, past episodes of physical and psychological abuse followed by intervals of contrition, the apparent denial of homicidal fantasies on the appellant's part, and her remorse after killing Rust.

If the majority of the Court of Appeal is suggesting that each of these specific facts must be proven in evidence before any weight could be given to Dr. Shane's opinion about the accused's mental state, I must respectfully disagree. *Abbey* does not, in my view, provide any authority for that proposition. The court's conclusion in that case was that the trial judge erred in treating as proven the facts upon which the psychiatrist relied in formulating his opinion. The solution was an appropriate charge to the jury, not an effective withdrawal of the evidence. In my view, as long as there is some admissible evidence to establish the foundation for the expert's opinion, the trial judge cannot subsequently instruct the jury to completely ignore the testimony. The judge must, of course, warn the jury that the more the expert relies on facts not proved in evidence the less weight the jury may attribute to the opinion.

• • •

Where the factual basis of an expert's opinion is a melange of admissible and inadmissible evidence the duty of the trial judge is to caution the jury that the weight attributable to the expert testimony is directly related to the amount and quality of admissible evidence on which it relies. The trial judge openly acknowledged to counsel the inherent difficulty in discharging such a duty in the case at bar. In my view, the trial judge performed his task adequately in this regard. A new trial is not warranted on the basis of the trial judge's charge to the jury.

I would accordingly allow the appeal, set aside the order of the Court of Appeal, and restore the acquittal.

SOPINKA J: I have read the reasons of my colleague Justice Wilson, and I agree in the result that this appeal must be allowed. I find it necessary, however, to add a few words concerning the interpretation of this Court's decision in *R v. Abbey*, [1982] 2 SCR 24.

Abbey has been roundly criticized: see, *e.g.*, Schiff, *Evidence in the Litigation Process*, 3rd ed., vol. I (1988), pp. 473-6, and Delisle, *Evidence: Principles and Problems*, 2nd ed. (1989), pp. 477-9. The essence of the criticism is that *Abbey* sets out more restrictive conditions for the use of expert evidence than did previous decisions of this court: *i.e.*, *City of St. John v. Irving Oil Co. Ltd.*, [1966] SCR 581; *Wilband v. The Queen*, [1967] SCR 14; and *R v. Lupien*, [1970] SCR 263. Upon reflection, it seems to me that the very special facts in *Abbey*, and the decision required on those facts, have contributed to the development of a principle concerning the admissibility and weight of expert opinion evidence that is self-contradictory. The contradiction is apparent in the four principles set out by Wilson J in the present case … .

The combined effect of Nos. 1, 3 and 4 is that an expert opinion relevant in the abstract to a material issue in a trial but based entirely on unproven hearsay (*e.g.*, from the mouth of the accused, as in *Abbey*) is admissible but entitled to no weight whatsoever. The question that arises is how any evidence can be admissible and yet entitled to no weight. As one commentator has pointed out, an expert opinion based entirely on unproven hearsay must, if anything, be inadmissible by reason of irrelevance, since the facts underlying the expert opinion are the only connection between the opinion and the case: see Wardle, "*R v. Abbey* and Psychiatric Opinion Evidence: Requiring the Accused to Testify" (1984), 17 *Ottawa L Rev.* 116, at pp. 122-23.

The resolution of the contradiction inherent in *Abbey*, and the answer to the criticism *Abbey* has drawn, is to be found in the practical distinction between evidence that an expert obtains and acts upon within the scope of his or her expertise (as in *City of St. John*), and evidence that an expert obtains from a party to litigation touching a matter directly in issue (as in *Abbey*).

In the former instance, an expert arrives at an opinion on the basis of forms of enquiry and practice that are accepted means of decision within that expertise. A physician, for example, daily determines questions of immense importance on the basis of the observations of colleagues, often in the form of second or third-hand hearsay. For a court to accord no weight to, or to exclude, this sort of professional judgment, arrived at in accordance with sound medical practices, would be to ignore the strong circumstantial guarantees of trustworthiness that surround it, and would be, in my view, contrary to the approach this court has taken to the analysis of hearsay evidence in general, exemplified in *Ares v. Venner*, [1970] SCR 608. In *R v. Jordan* (1984), 11 CCC (3d) 565 (BC CA), a case concerning an expert's evaluation of the chemical composition of an alleged heroin specimen, Anderson JA held, and I respectfully agree, that *Abbey* does not apply in such circumstances: see also *R v. Zundel* (1987), 31 CCC (3d) 97 at p. 146 (Ont. CA), where the court recognized an expert opinion based upon evidence "… of a general nature which is widely used and acknowledged as reliable by experts in that field."

Where, however, the information upon which an expert forms his or her opinion comes from the mouth of a party to the litigation, or from any other source that is inherently suspect, a court ought to require independent proof of that information. The lack of such proof will, consistent with *Abbey*, have a direct effect on the weight to be given to the opinions perhaps to the vanishing point. But it must be recognized that it will only be very rarely that an expert's opinion is entirely based upon such information, with no independent proof of any of it. Where an expert's opinion is based in part upon suspect information and in part upon either admitted facts or facts sought to be proved, the matter is purely one of weight. In this respect, I agree with the statement of Wilson J *ante*, p. 130, as applied to circumstances such as those in the present case:

> … as long as there is some admissible evidence to establish the foundation for the expert's opinion, the trial judge cannot subsequently instruct the jury to completely ignore the testimony. The judge must, of course, warn the jury that the more the expert relies on facts not proved in evidence the less weight the jury may attribute to the opinion.

As Wilson J holds, the trial judge's charge to the jury was adequate, and the appeal ought therefore to be allowed.

In *R v DD*, 2000 SCC 43, [2000] 2 SCR 275 and *R v K (A)* (1999), 45 OR (3d) 641 (CA) (see Section III.B.3, above) as well as *Lavallee*, we saw judges navigate a fine line between expert evidence that is necessary to assist the trier of fact to understand human behaviour and expert evidence that operates primarily to bolster a witness's credibility. Credibility is discussed at greater length in Chapter 6, but for now it is appropriate to note that a range of exclusionary rules limit the admissibility of evidence that might otherwise bolster a witness's credibility. The Supreme Court of Canada also considered the interplay between expert opinion evidence and rules regarding credibility in a case in which it assessed the admissibility of evidence about the results of a polygraph (lie detection) test.

R v Béland
[1987] 2 SCR 398, 60 CR (3d) 1
Dickson CJ and Beetz, McIntyre, Lamer, Wilson, Le Dain, and La Forest JJ
(15 October 1987)

McINTYRE J [Dickson CJ and Beetz and Le Dain JJ concurring]: This appeal involves the question of the admissibility in evidence in a criminal trial of the results of a polygraph examination of an accused person.

The respondents, Béland and Phillips, were charged with conspiracy to commit a robbery. The Crown led evidence to the effect that the respondents had conspired with one Grenier and one Filippone to rob an armoured truck. No robbery took place, because Grenier disclosed the conspiracy to the police. He later gave evidence for the Crown, and his testimony was the only evidence which directly implicated the respondents in the conspiracy. The respondents gave evidence on their own behalf, denying any participation in the conspiracy and saying that the evidence of Grenier was false. Each respondent during his testimony said that he was prepared to undergo a polygraph examination. After completion of the evidence at trial the respondents made an application to the trial judge to reopen their defence, in order to permit each of them to take a polygraph examination and submit the results in evidence. This motion was refused by the trial judge, who held that the results of such an examination were inadmissible in evidence, in accordance with *Phillion v. R*, [1978] 1 SCR 18. The respondents were convicted. An appeal to the Court of Appeal by the respondents succeeded. By a majority, the Court of Appeal granted an order reopening the trial and directing that the results of the polygraph examination be submitted to the trial judge for a ruling as to their admissibility in light of all the circumstances revealed in the evidence. The Crown appeals to this court as of right under s. 621(1)(a) of the *Criminal Code*. The parties agree that the sole issue in this appeal is whether evidence of the results of a polygraph examination is admissible in light of the particular facts of this case.

[McIntyre J briefly reviewed *Phillion*. He then held that the polygraph evidence would offend the rule that evidence may not be led for the sole purpose of bolstering a witness's credibility and the rule against leading the prior consistent statements of a witness. He held further that the polygraph evidence amounted to a form of inadmissible evidence of good character. He continued:]

Expert Evidence

It was also argued that the polygraph evidence was receivable as expert evidence. The polygraph operator, as an expert, was trained and qualified to give his opinion as to the veracity of the witness, based solely on his interpretation of the significance of the responses made by the witness to the questions put on the examination.

. . .

Here, the sole issue upon which the polygraph evidence is adduced is the credibility of the accused, an issue well within the experience of judges and juries and one in which no expert evidence is required. It is a basic tenet of our legal system that judges and juries are capable of assessing credibility and reliability of evidence.

. . .

In conclusion, it is my opinion, based upon a consideration of rules of evidence long established and applied in our courts, that the polygraph has no place in the judicial process where it is employed as a tool to determine or to test the credibility of witnesses. It is frequently argued that the polygraph represents an application of modern scientific knowledge and experience to the task of determining the veracity of human utterances. It is said that the courts should welcome this device and not cling to the imperfect methods of the past in such an important task. This argument has a superficial appeal but, in my view, it cannot prevail in the face of the realities of court procedures.

I would say at once that this view is not based on a fear of the inaccuracies of the polygraph. On that question we were not supplied with sufficient evidence to reach a conclusion. However, it may be said that even the finding of a significant percentage of error in its results would not by itself be sufficient ground to exclude it as an instrument for use in the courts. Error is inherent in human affairs, scientific or unscientific. It exists within our established court procedures and must always be guarded against. The compelling reason, in my view, for the exclusion of the evidence of polygraph results in judicial proceedings is twofold. First, the admission of polygraph evidence would run counter to the well-established rules of evidence which have been referred to. Second, while there is no reason why the rules of evidence should not be modified where improvement will result, it is my view that the admission of polygraph evidence will serve no purpose which is not already served. It will disrupt proceedings, cause delays, and lead to numerous complications which will result in no greater degree of certainty in the process than that which already exists.

. . .

For the above reasons, and following *Phillion*, *supra*, I would allow the Crown's appeal. I would set aside the order of the Court of Appeal and confirm the conviction recorded at trial.

[Wilson J rejected McIntyre J's reasoning concerning bolstering credibility, prior consistent statements, and character evidence. On the question of expert evidence, she said:]

WILSON J (Lamer J concurring) (dissenting on the merits): ...

(4) The Expert Evidence Rule

. . .

In my respectful view, the polygraph operator does not give an opinion on the credibility of the witness. Rather, she interprets the physiological data and gives an opinion as to whether the data pattern conforms to that of a person who is telling the truth. The operator will also testify as to the nature and accuracy of the device itself. The jury will consider this evidence along with the other evidence going to the issue of credibility in order to reach their final conclusion. Thus, the polygraph operator provides an expert opinion on the interpretation of the polygraph results. This evidence is relevant to, but not determinative of, the credibility issue.

. . .

Conclusion

The polygraph evidence is clearly relevant. I am not persuaded that it falls within any of the exclusionary rules advanced by the Crown.

. . .

[La Forest J concurred in the result with McIntyre J. He said: "I prefer ... to base my decision solely on the following factors ... , namely, human fallibility cloaked under the mystique of science, and the inadvisability of expending time on collateral-issues."]

QUESTIONS

After reading Chapter 6, Credibility, you may want to consider whether the evidence proffered in *Béland* really was a prior consistent statement or a form of character evidence. If not, are McIntyre J's remaining concerns about polygraph evidence nonetheless sufficient to justify its exclusion? Consider the willingness of Wilson J to rely on the jury to assess the reliability of the evidence for the purpose of determining its weight. How important is it that the trial judge determine whether expert evidence meets the threshold tests of admissibility now outlined in *R v Mohan*, [1994] 2 SCR 9, above?

C. Assessing the Benefits and Costs of the Evidence

Doherty JA described the process of assessing the benefits and costs of expert opinion evidence in *R v Abbey*, 2009 ONCA 624, 97 OR (3d) 330 as follows:

[87] The "benefit" side of the cost–benefit evaluation requires a consideration of the probative potential of the evidence and the significance of the issue to which the evidence is directed. When one looks to potential probative value, one must consider the reliability of the evidence. Reliability concerns reach not only the subject matter of the evidence, but also the methodology used by the proposed expert in arriving at his or her opinion, the expert's expertise and the extent to which the expert is shown to be impartial and objective.

[88] Assessment of the reliability of proffered expert evidence has become the focus of much judicial attention, particularly where the expert advances what is purported to be scientific opinion: see, for example, *Daubert v. Merrell Dow Pharmaceuticals Inc.*, 509 US 579 (1993); *J.-L.J.* [*R v J-LJ*, 2000 SCC 51, [2000] 2 SCR 600] at paras. 33-37; S. Casey Hill *et al.* [*McWilliams' Canadian Criminal Evidence*, 4th ed (Aurora, Ont: Canada Law Book, 2009) (loose-leaf)] at para. 12:30.20.30; Bruce D. Sales & Daniel W. Shuman, *Experts in Court Reconciling Law, Science, and Professional Knowledge* (Washington, DC: American Psychological Association, 2005).

[89] In assessing the potential benefit to the trial process flowing from the admission of the evidence, the trial judge must intrude into territory customarily the exclusive domain of the jury in a criminal jury trial. The trial judge's evaluation is not, however, the same as the jury's ultimate assessment. The trial judge is deciding only whether the evidence is worthy of being heard by the jury and not the ultimate question of whether the evidence should be accepted and acted upon.

[90] The "cost" side of the ledger addresses the various risks inherent in the admissibility of expert opinion evidence, described succinctly by Binnie J in *J.-L.J.* at para. 47 as "consumption of time, prejudice and confusion." Clearly, the most important risk is the danger that a jury will be unable to make an effective and critical assessment of the evidence. The complexity of the material underlying the opinion, the expert's impressive credentials, the impenetrable jargon in which the opinion is wrapped and the cross-examiner's inability to expose the opinion's shortcomings may prevent an effective evaluation of the evidence by the jury. There is a risk that a jury faced with a well presented firm opinion may abdicate its fact-finding role on the understandable assumption that a person labelled as an expert by the trial judge knows more about his or her area of expertise than do the individual members of the jury: *J.-L.J.* at para. 25.

[91] In addition to the risk that the jury will yield its fact finding function, expert opinion evidence can also compromise the trial process by unduly protracting and complicating proceedings. Unnecessary and excessive resort to expert evidence can also give a distinct advantage to the party with the resources to hire the most and best experts—often the Crown in a criminal proceeding.

[92] All of the risks described above will not inevitably arise in every case where expert evidence is offered. Nor will the risks have the same force in every case. For example, in this case, I doubt that the jury would have difficulty critically evaluating Dr. Totten's opinion. There was nothing complex or obscure about his methodology, the material he relied on in forming his opinion or the language in which he framed and explained his opinion. As when measuring the benefits flowing from the admission of expert evidence, the trial judge as "gatekeeper" must go beyond truisms about the risks inherent in expert evidence and come to grips with those risks as they apply to the particular circumstances of the individual case.

As is apparent from this extract, an assessment of the reliability of the expert opinion lies at the heart of the assessment of benefits and costs of the proposed evidence.

1. *Reliability*

a. Scientific Evidence

In *R v K (A)* (1999), 45 OR (3d) 641, 137 CCC (3d) 225 (CA), under the general heading of reliability of expert opinion evidence, Charron JA said the following:

> [85] … As indicated in *Mohan* [*R v. Mohan*, [1994] 2 SCR 9], any "novel scientific theory or technique" must be "subjected to special scrutiny to determine whether it meets a basic threshold of reliability" before it is admitted. In some cases, it may be obvious that a novel theory or technique is sought to be advanced. This was the case for example when polygraph evidence was sought to be admitted or when DNA evidence was first introduced. In other cases, the theory or the technique sought to be advanced may form part of a recognized field of expertise such as psychiatry or psychology and, for that reason, it may be more difficult to readily recognize that the theory or technique is novel within its field. It must nonetheless be scrutinized. *Mohan* itself provides an example where a psychiatrist's evidence of psychosexual profiles was held to be insufficiently reliable or helpful to be admitted in evidence. …
>
> [86] The same principle applies in the field of the behavioural sciences. Although psychology or sociology are certainly recognized fields of expertise, some theories advanced in courtrooms in recent years within those fields are entirely novel. Further, as indicated earlier, the state of scientific knowledge is fluid. The fact that a particular theory may have been accepted in the past does not necessarily end the inquiry. This case provides an example where the evidence showed that the Child Sexual Abuse Accommodation Syndrome, a theory that has been accepted in certain courts in the past, was not reliable as a diagnostic tool. Hence the basis for [the expert's] theory that certain of the complainants' behavioural symptoms were consistent with sexual abuse did not withstand scrutiny. The proposed evidence was insufficiently reliable to warrant admission.
>
> [87] This court's decision in *R v. McIntosh* (1997), 117 CCC (3d) 385 (Ont. CA), provides some guidance on the requirement of scrutinizing the subject matter of the proposed expert testimony to determine whether it meets a threshold of reliability. I also find the following comments by Hill J in *R v. T.(E.)*, [1994] OJ No. 43067 (QL) (Gen. Div.) to be helpful (at para. 75):
>
> > Needless to say there is a continuum of reliability in matters of science from near certainty in physical sciences to the far end of the spectrum inhabited by junk science and opinion akin to sorcery or magic. Whether the technique can be demonstrably tested, the existence of peer review for the theory or technique, the existence of publication, the testing or validation employing control and error measurement, and some recognition or acceptance in the relevant scientific field all contribute to an assessment of the reliability of the opinion and hence its capacity to outweigh the prejudicial impact of imposing on the jury highly suspect opinion evidence masquerading as science: *Daubert v. Merrell Dow Pharmaceuticals Inc.*, … [509 US 579, 113 S Ct 2786 (1993)], at 2795-2797 *per* Blackmun J; Gold, Alan, *Expert Evidence—Admissibility* (1994), 37 *CLQ* 16 at 21-30.

In *R v McIntosh* (1997), 35 OR (3d) 97, 117 CCC (3d) 385 (CA), the defence sought to challenge the reliability of eyewitness identification evidence through an expert witness who would testify to its frailties, particularly where the identification is cross-racial. Finlayson JA, for the court, held that the trial judge had properly excluded the evidence and had properly instructed the jury on the frailties of the identification evidence. He noted that in the United States, where judges do not instruct the jury and review the evidence for the jury, there may be more need for expert evidence to assist the jury. In this case, he held, the jury did not need expert assistance to confirm normal experience. Moreover, he questioned the reliability of the expertise. He held that expertise on identification could not be considered reliable unless "any expert in that field can evaluate the reliability of the identification made by a particular witness in a given case." He cautioned that courts should not abdicate fact-finding responsibilities to experts in behavioural sciences.

In *R v Melaragni* (1992), 73 CCC (3d) 348 (Ont Gen Div), cited in *R v Mohan*, Moldaver J (as he then was) held:

> When the Crown seeks to tender evidence which involves a new scientific technique or body of scientific knowledge, it must, of course, establish that the evidence is relevant and that it passes a minimum threshold test of reliability. As well, the evidence must be outside the experience and knowledge of the trier of fact, and it may only be tendered through a properly qualified expert.

He then listed a number of factors that should be considered in determining whether the evidence should be admitted, including the following factors relating to reliability and fairness in evaluating the evidence:

- Are there a sufficient number of experts available so that the defence can retain its own expert if desired?
- Has the scientific technique destroyed the evidence upon which the conclusions have been based, or has the evidence been preserved for defence analysis if requested?

When expert witnesses testify, counsel must take care not to elicit from them opinions on matters that go beyond their expertise or beyond the issues on which the trial judge has determined expert evidence is both necessary and reliable. Thus, in *R v Ranger* (2003), 67 OR (3d) 1, 178 CCC (3d) 375 (CA), an expert on the staging of crime scenes exceeded her expertise when she gave an opinion about the motivation of the perpetrator in staging the scene and the likelihood that the perpetrator had a particular interest in the victim. These opinions constituted evidence of criminal profiling, which is a novel field of expertise, the reliability of which had not been established at trial.

The case which first established a more rigorous approach to assessing the reliability of expert scientific evidence was the US Supreme Court decision in *Daubert v Merrell Dow Pharmaceuticals, Inc*. In the following extract from the majority's reasons in that decision, Blackmun J articulates the criteria by which the reliability of scientific evidence should be assessed.

Daubert v Merrell Dow Pharmaceuticals, Inc
509 US 579, 113 S Ct 2786 (1993) (footnotes and cross-references omitted)
Rehnquist CJ and White, Blackmun, Stevens, O'Connor, Scalia, Kennedy, Souter, and Thomas JJ (28 June 1993)

BLACKMUN J: In this case we are called upon to determine the standard for admitting expert scientific testimony in a federal trial.

I

Petitioners Jason Daubert and Eric Schuller are minor children born with serious birth defects. They and their parents sued respondent in California state court, alleging that the birth defects had been caused by the mothers' ingestion of Bendectin, a prescription anti-nausea drug marketed by respondent. Respondent removed the suits to federal court on diversity grounds.

After extensive discovery, respondent moved for summary judgment, contending that Bendectin does not cause birth defects in humans and that petitioners would be unable to come forward with any admissible evidence that it does. In support of its motion, respondent submitted an affidavit of Steven H. Lamm, physician and epidemiologist, who is a well-credentialed expert on the risks from exposure to various chemical substances. Doctor Lamm stated that he had reviewed all the literature on Bendectin and human birth defects—more than 30 published studies involving over 130,000 patients. No study had found Bendectin to be a human teratogen (i.e., a substance capable of causing malformations in fetuses). On the basis of this review, Doctor Lamm concluded that maternal use of Bendectin during the first trimester of pregnancy has not been shown to be a risk factor for human birth defects.

Petitioners did not (and do not) contest this characterization of the published record regarding Bendectin. Instead, they responded to respondent's motion with the testimony of eight experts of their own, each of whom also possessed impressive credentials. These experts had concluded that Bendectin can cause birth defects. Their conclusions were based upon "in vitro" (test tube) and "in vivo" (live) animal studies that found a link between Bendectin and malformations; pharmacological studies of the chemical structure of Bendectin that purported to show similarities between the structure of the drug and that of other substances known to cause birth defects; and the "reanalysis" of previously published epidemiological (human statistical) studies.

The District Court granted respondent's motion for summary judgment. The court stated that scientific evidence is admissible only if the principle upon which it is based is "'sufficiently established to have general acceptance in the field to which it belongs.'" 727 F Supp. 570, 572 (SD Cal. 1989), quoting *United States v. Kilgus*, 571 F.2d 508, 510 (CA9 1978). The court concluded that petitioners' evidence did not meet this standard. Given the vast body of epidemiological data concerning Bendectin, the court held, expert opinion which is not based on epidemiological evidence is not admissible to establish causation. 727 F Supp., at 575. Thus, the animal-cell studies, live-animal studies, and chemical-structure analyses on which petitioners had relied could not raise by themselves a reasonably disputable jury issue regarding causation. *Ibid.* Petitioners' epidemiological analyses, based as they were on recalculations of data in previously published studies that had found no causal link between the drug and birth defects, were ruled to be inadmissible because they had not been published or subjected to peer review. *Ibid.*

[The District Court's decision was affirmed by the Ninth Circuit Court of Appeals: see 951 F (2d) 1128 (1991). The Supreme Court granted *certiorari* "in light of sharp divisions among the courts regarding the proper standard for the admission of expert testimony."]

II

A

[Blackmun J held that *Frye v United States*, 54 App D C 46, 47, 293 F 1013 (DC Cir 1923) had been superseded by r 702 of the *Federal Rules of Evidence*, which reads as follows:]

> If scientific, technical, or other specialized knowledge will assist the trier of fact to understand the evidence or to determine a fact in issue, a witness qualified as an expert by knowledge, skill, experience, training, or education, may testify thereto in the form of an opinion or otherwise.

. . .

B

That the *Frye* test was displaced by the Rules of Evidence does not mean, however, that the Rules themselves place no limits on the admissibility of purportedly scientific evidence. Nor is the trial judge disabled from screening such evidence. To the contrary, under the Rules the trial judge must ensure that any and all scientific testimony or evidence admitted is not only relevant, but reliable.

The primary locus of this obligation is Rule 702, which clearly contemplates some degree of regulation of the subjects and theories about which an expert may testify. "*If scientific*, technical, or other specialized *knowledge will assist the trier of fact* to understand the evidence or to determine a fact in issue" an expert "may testify *thereto*." The subject of an expert's testimony must be "scientific ... knowledge." The adjective "scientific" implies a grounding in the methods and procedures of science. Similarly, the word "knowledge" connotes more than subjective belief or unsupported speculation. ... The term "applies to any body of known facts or to any body of ideas inferred from such facts or accepted as truths on good grounds." ... Of course, it would be unreasonable to conclude that the subject of scientific testimony must be "known" to a certainty; arguably, there are no certainties in science. ... But, in order to qualify as "scientific knowledge," an inference or assertion must [be] derived by the scientific method. Proposed testimony must be supported by appropriate validation—i.e., "good grounds," based on what is known. In short, the requirement that an expert's testimony pertain to "scientific knowledge" establishes a standard of evidentiary reliability.

Rule 702 further requires that the evidence or testimony "assist the trier of fact to understand the evidence or to determine a fact in issue." ... The consideration has been aptly described by Judge Becker as one of "fit." *Ibid.* "Fit" is not always obvious and scientific validity for one purpose is not necessarily scientific validity for other, unrelated purposes. See Starrs, "*Frye v. United States* Restructured and Revitalized: A Proposal to Amend Federal Evidence Rule 702," 26 *Jurimetrics J* 249, 258 (1986). The study of the phases of the moon, for example, may provide valid scientific "knowledge" about whether a certain night was dark, and if darkness is a fact in issue, the knowledge will assist the trier of fact. However (absent creditable grounds supporting such a link), evidence that the moon was full on a certain night will not assist the trier of fact in determining whether an individual was unusually likely to have behaved irrationally on that night. Rule 702's "helpfulness" standard requires a valid scientific connection to the pertinent inquiry as a precondition to admissibility.

That these requirements are embodied in Rule 702 is not surprising. Unlike an ordinary witness, ... , an expert is permitted wide latitude to offer opinions, including those that are not based on first-hand knowledge or observation. ... Presumably, this relaxation of the usual requirement of first-hand knowledge ... is premised on an assumption that the expert's opinion will have a reliable basis in the knowledge and experience of his discipline.

C

Faced with a proffer of expert scientific testimony, then, the trial judge must determine at the outset, pursuant to Rule 104(a), whether the expert is proposing to testify to (1) scientific knowledge that (2) will assist the trier of fact to understand or determine a fact in issue. This entails a preliminary assessment of whether the reasoning or methodology underlying the testimony is scientifically valid and of whether that reasoning or methodology properly can be applied to the facts in issue. We are confident that federal judges possess the capacity to undertake this review.

Many factors will bear on the inquiry, and we do not presume to set out a definitive checklist or test. But some general observations are appropriate.

Ordinarily, a key question to be answered in determining whether a theory or technique is scientific knowledge that will assist the trier of fact will be whether it can be (and has been) tested. "Scientific methodology today is based on generating hypotheses and testing them to see if they can be falsified; indeed, this methodology is what distinguishes science from other fields of human inquiry," Green, at 645. ...

Another pertinent consideration is whether the theory or technique has been subjected to peer review and publication. Publication (which is but one element of peer review) is not a *sine qua non* of admissibility; it does not necessarily correlate with reliability, see S. Jasanoff, *The Fifth Branch: Science Advisors as Policymakers* 61-76 (1990), and in some instances well-grounded but innovative theories will not have been published, see Horrobin, "The Philosophical Basis of Peer Review and the Suppression of Innovation," 263 *J Am. Med. Assn.* 1438 (1990). Some propositions, moreover, are too particular, too new, or of too limited interest to be published. But submission to the scrutiny of the scientific community is a component of "good science," in part because it increases the likelihood that substantive flaws in methodology will be detected. See J. Ziman, *Reliable Knowledge: An Exploration of the Grounds for Belief in Science* 130-133 (1978); Relman and Angell, "How Good Is Peer Review?" 321 *New Eng. J Med.* 827 (1989). The fact of publication (or lack thereof) in a peer-reviewed journal thus will be a relevant, though not dispositive, consideration in assessing the scientific validity of a particular technique or methodology on which an opinion is premised.

Additionally, in the case of a particular scientific technique, the court ordinarily should consider the known or potential rate of error, see, *e.g., United States v. Smith*, 869 F.2d 348, 353-354 (CA7 1989) (surveying studies of the error rate of spectrographic voice identification technique), and the existence and maintenance of standards controlling the technique's operation. See *United States v. Williams*, 583 F.2d 1194, 1198 (CA2 1978) (noting professional organization's standard governing spectrographic analysis), cert. denied, 439 US 1117, 59 L Ed. 2d 77, 99 S Ct. 1025 (1979).

Finally, "general acceptance" can yet have a bearing on the inquiry. A "reliability assessment does not require, although it does permit, explicit identification of a relevant scientific community and an express determination of a particular degree of acceptance within that community." *United States v. Downing*, 753 F.2d, at 1238. See also 3 Weinstein & Berger §702, pp. 702-41 to 702-42. Widespread acceptance can be an important factor in ruling particular evidence admissible, and "a known technique that has been able to attract only minimal support within the community," *Downing, supra*, at 1238, may properly be viewed with skepticism.

The inquiry envisioned by Rule 702 is, we emphasize, a flexible one. Its overarching subject is the scientific validity—and thus the evidentiary relevance and reliability—of the principles that underlie a proposed submission. The focus, of course, must be solely on principles and methodology, not on the conclusions that they generate. ...

III

We conclude by briefly addressing what appear to be two underlying concerns of the parties and *amici* in this case. Respondent expresses apprehension that abandonment of "general acceptance" as the exclusive requirement for admission will result in a "free-for-all" in which befuddled juries are confounded by absurd and irrational pseudoscientific assertions.

In this regard respondent seems to us to be overly pessimistic about the capabilities of the jury, and of the adversary system generally. Vigorous cross-examination, presentation of contrary evidence, and careful instruction on the burden of proof are the traditional and appropriate means of attacking shaky but admissible evidence. See *Rock v. Arkansas*, 483 US 44, 61, 97 L Ed. 2d 37, 107 S Ct. 2704 (1987). ...

Petitioners and, to a greater extent, their *amici* exhibit a different concern. They suggest that recognition of a screening role for the judge that allows for the exclusion of "invalid" evidence will sanction a stifling and repressive scientific orthodoxy and will be inimical to the search for truth. See, *e.g.*, Brief for Ronald Bayer et al. as *Amici Curiae*. It is true that open debate is an essential part of both legal and scientific analyses. Yet there are important differences between the quest for truth in the courtroom and the quest for truth in the laboratory. Scientific conclusions are subject to perpetual revision. Law, on the other hand, must resolve disputes finally and quickly. The scientific project is advanced by broad and wide-ranging consideration of a multitude of hypotheses, for those that are incorrect will eventually be shown to be so, and that in itself is an advance. Conjectures that are probably wrong are of little use, however, in the project of reaching a quick, final, and binding legal judgment—often of great consequence—about a particular set of events in the past. We recognize that in practice, a gatekeeping role for the judge, no matter how flexible, inevitably on occasion will prevent the jury from learning of authentic insights and innovations. That, nevertheless, is the balance that is struck by Rules of Evidence designed not for the exhaustive search for cosmic understanding but for the particularized resolution of legal disputes.

[All members of the court joined parts I and IIA of Blackmun J's opinion, and White, O'Connor, Scalia, Kennedy, Souter, and Thomas JJ joined in parts IIB, IIC, III, and IV. Rehnquist CJ, joined by Stevens J, dissented from these parts of the opinion.]

NOTE

In *R v J-LJ*, 2000 SCC 51, [2000] 2 SCR 600, Binnie J commented on *Daubert* in the following terms:

> [33] *Mohan* kept the door open to novel science, rejecting the "general acceptance" test formulated in the United States in *Frye v. United States*, 293 F 1013 (DC Cir. 1923), and moving in parallel with its replacement, the "reliable foundation" test more recently laid down by the US Supreme Court in *Daubert v. Merrell Dow Pharmaceuticals, Inc.*, 509 US 579 (1993). While *Daubert* must be read in light of the specific text of the *Federal Rules of Evidence*, which differs from our own procedures, the US Supreme Court did list a number of factors that could be helpful in evaluating the soundness of novel science ... .

This framing gives rise to the question of whether the *Daubert* factors should be used only by courts tasked with assessing novel scientific evidence.

b. Novel Scientific Evidence: An Unsettled Question?

In *R v Mohan*, [1994] 2 SCR 9, above, Sopinka J states (at 25) that "expert evidence which advances a novel scientific theory or technique is subjected to special scrutiny to determine whether it meets a basic threshold of reliability." This sentence of Sopinka J's decision gave rise to some uncertainty in the wake of *R v Mohan*, as commentators were unsure whether reliability was required only in respect of novel scientific evidence. (Elsewhere in his judgment, Sopinka J appeared to suggest that reliability is more generally applicable. For example (at 21): "Evidence that is otherwise logically relevant may be excluded ... if it is misleading in the sense that its effect on the trier of fact, particularly a jury, is out of proportion to its reliability. ... The reliability versus effect factor has special significance in assessing the admissibility of expert evidence.").

In *R v J-LJ*, 2000 SCC 51, [2000] 2 SCR 600, Binnie J held on behalf of a unanimous court that the criteria set out in *Daubert v Merrell Dow Pharmaceuticals, Inc*, 509 US 579 (1993) could assist a trial judge when assessing the reliability of novel scientific evidence. In *J-LJ*, Binnie J held (at para 35) that a technique used by an expert witness was novel, even though it was not new: "While the techniques he employed are not novel, he is using them for a novel purpose. A level of reliability that is quite useful in therapy because it yields some information about a course of treatment is not necessarily sufficiently reliable to be used in a court of law to identify or exclude the accused as a potential perpetrator of an offence." This judgment seems to suggest that expert opinion evidence will be treated as novel if it constitutes a new application of pre-existing techniques.

The ambiguity presented by Sopinka J's reference to reliability as a condition of admissibility for novel scientific evidence is reflected in the court's division over the proper approach to post-hypnosis evidence in *R v Trochym*, 2007 SCC 6, [2007] 1 SCR 239. In this case, the court was presented with evidence that had been elicited from a witness after she had undergone hypnosis.

R v Trochym
2007 SCC 6, [2007] 1 SCR 239
McLachlin CJ and Bastarache, Binnie, LeBel, Deschamps, Fish, Abella,
Charron, and Rothstein JJ (1 February 2007)

[Trochym was charged with the second-degree murder of his girlfriend. The victim was killed in her apartment on the night of October 13-14, 1992. On the afternoon of October 14, someone entered the apartment and repositioned the body. A neighbour told the police that she saw the accused arrive at the apartment on the afternoon of the October 15. The police asked the neighbour to undergo hypnosis to improve her memory. Under hypnosis, she stated that the accused had arrived at the apartment on October 14. The trial judge ruled that the witness could testify in accordance with her hypnotically enhanced recollection. The Crown and the defence then agreed that, in return for defence not cross-examining the witness on her prior inconsistent statement, the Crown would not lead any evidence concerning the hypnosis. Accordingly, the witness testified that she had seen the accused on October 14. The accused was convicted as charged.]

DESCHAMPS J (McLachlin CJ and Binnie, LeBel, and Fish JJ concurring): ...

(b) The Court's Approach to Evidence Involving Science

[31] Not all scientific evidence, or evidence that results from the use of a scientific technique, must be screened before being introduced into evidence. In some cases, the science in question is so well established that judges can rely on the fact that the admissibility of evidence based on it has been clearly recognized by the courts in the past. Other cases may not be so clear. Like the legal community, the scientific community continues to challenge and improve upon its existing base of knowledge. As a result, the admissibility of scientific evidence is not frozen in time.

[32] While some forms of scientific evidence become more reliable over time, others may become less so as further studies reveal concerns. Thus, a technique that was once admissible may subsequently be found to be inadmissible. An example of the first situation, where, upon further refinement and study, a scientific technique becomes sufficiently reliable to be used in criminal trials, is DNA matching evidence, which this Court recognized in *R. v. Terceira*, [1999] 3 S.C.R. 866. An example of the second situation, where a technique that has been employed for some time comes to be questioned, is so-called "dock," or in-court, identification evidence. In *R. v. Hibbert*, [2002] 2 S.C.R. 445, 2002 SCC 39, at para. 50, Arbour J., writing for the majority, stated that despite its long-standing use, dock identification is almost totally unreliable. Therefore, even if it has received judicial recognition in the past, a technique or science whose underlying assumptions are challenged should not be admitted in evidence without first confirming the validity of those assumptions.

[33] The concerns raised in *Taillefer* [*R v Taillefer* (1995), 100 CCC (3d) 1 (Qc CA)] and *Moore* [*State v Moore*, 902 A (2d) 1212 (NJ 2006)] are thus relevant to the instant case and coincide with a more general issue recently considered by this Court. Since *Clark* [*R v Clark* (1984), 13 CCC (3d) 117 (Alta QB)], this Court has had the opportunity to consider the admission of novel science in courtrooms. In *J.-L.J.* [*R v J-LJ*, 2000 SCC 51,

[2000] 2 SCR 600], it built on *Mohan* [*R v Mohan*, [1994] 2 SCR 9] to develop the test governing the admissibility of such evidence. Under this test, a party wishing to rely on novel scientific evidence must first establish that the underlying science is sufficiently reliable to be admitted in a court of law. This is particularly important where, as here, an accused person's liberty is at stake. Even though the use of expert testimony was not in itself at issue in the present case—this appeal concerns the application of a scientific technique to the testimony of a lay witness—the threshold reliability of the technique, and its impact on the testimony, remains crucial to the fairness of the trial.

[34] The central concern in *Mohan* was that scientific evidence be carefully scrutinized because, in Sopinka J.'s words, "[d]ressed up in scientific language which the jury does not easily understand and submitted through a witness of impressive antecedents, this evidence is apt to be accepted by the jury as being virtually infallible and as having more weight than it deserves" (p. 21). The situation in the case at bar is similar in that the evidence reveals a risk that post-hypnotic memories may be given more weight than they should. In *J.-L.J.*, the Court went a step further, establishing a framework for assessing the reliability of novel science and, consequently, its admissibility in court.

[35] In the instant case, the appellant questioned the admissibility of the post-hypnosis testimony, and several experts gave evidence of differences of opinion on the use of hypnosis in the judicial context. The technique therefore needs to be assessed based on the existing legal standards for criminal trials.

[36] In *J.-L.J.*, Binnie J. explained that Canadian courts require a "reliable foundation" for novel science to be admissible as evidence at trial. Drawing on the American case of *Daubert v. Merrell Dow Pharmaceuticals, Inc.*, 509 U.S. 579 (1993), he observed that reliability can be evaluated on the basis of four factors (*J.-L.J.*, at para. 33):

(1) whether the ... technique can be and has been tested[;]

· · ·

(2) whether the ... technique has been subjected to peer review and publication[;]

· · ·

(3) the known or potential rate of error ... ; and,

(4) whether the theory or technique used has been generally accepted ... .

[37] These factors can be used to determine the reliability of post-hypnosis evidence. *J.-L.J.* is particularly helpful for the purpose of drawing a distinction between the efficacy of hypnosis as a therapeutic tool and its utility as a forensic tool. As Binnie J. observed, techniques that are sufficiently reliable for therapeutic purposes are not necessarily sufficiently reliable for use as evidence in a court of law where an accused's liberty is at stake (para. 35). Ironically, it appears that one of the very characteristics that make the use of hypnosis reliable in a therapeutic context—the fact that both mental and physical perceptions are highly malleable under hypnosis—is a source of concern where hypnosis is used for evidentiary purposes and accordingly renders its use for forensic purposes suspect.

· · ·

(c) The Gap Between Clark and J.-L.J.

[55] When the factors set out in *J.-L.J.* are applied to hypnosis, it becomes evident that this technique and its impact on human memory are not understood well enough for

post-hypnosis testimony to be sufficiently reliable to be used in a court of law. Although hypnosis has been the subject of numerous studies, these studies are either inconclusive or draw attention to the fact that hypnosis can, in certain circumstances, result in the distortion of memory. Perhaps most troubling is the potential rate of error in the additional information obtained through hypnosis when it is used for forensic purposes. At the present time, there is no way of knowing whether such information will be accurate or inaccurate. Such uncertainty is unacceptable in a court of law. Furthermore, while the *Clark* guidelines aid significantly in ensuring that the hypnotist and police make as few involuntary suggestions as possible, they afford no protection against external sources of influence or against the other problems associated with hypnosis, such as confabulation out of a desire to compensate for a lack of actual memory, an increase in detail without sufficient assurances that this new information will be accurate, and memory hardening.

• • •

[61] In sum, it is evident, based on the scientific evidence on record, that post-hypnosis testimony does not satisfy the test for admissibility set out in *J.-L.J.* While hypnosis has been the subject of extensive study and peer review, much of the literature is inconclusive or highly contradictory regarding the reliability of the science in the judicial context. Unless a litigant reverses the presumption on the basis of the factors set out in *J.-L.J.*, post-hypnosis testimony should not be admitted in evidence.

[Charron J agreed with Deschamps J in respect of the concerns about the reliability of post-hypnosis testimony and the application of *J-LJ* to that evidence. However, she would have adopted a somewhat different approach to determining the admissibility of testimony given by a witness who has undergone hypnosis.]

• • •

BASTARACHE J (dissenting) (Abella and Rothstein JJ agreeing): …

3.1 Hypnotically Refreshed Evidence

[115] My concerns with the approach to hypnotically refreshed evidence that Deschamps J. advocates relate not only to her views on the admissibility of such evidence, but on the implications her decision will have on the admissibility of scientific evidence in future cases. In my view, the precedent set by permitting the appellant to succeed on this ground without his having adduced a sufficient evidentiary foundation for this challenge is, to say the least, troubling.

3.1.2 Hypnosis Is Not "Novel Science"

[131] Characterizing hypnosis as "novel science" by applying *R. v. J.-L.J.*, [2000] 2 S.C.R. 600, 2000 SCC 51, my colleague finds that hypnotically refreshed memories are, at least for now, presumptively inadmissible (para. 61).

[132] This ignores the fact that the technique has been used in Canada for almost 30 years, and has been employed in Canadian criminal investigations to assist in memory retrieval of both Crown and defence witnesses for a similar amount of time. The earliest Canadian cases where this technique is reported are *R. v. Pitt*, [1968] 3 C.C.C. 342 (B.C.S.C.), and *R. v. K.*, [1979] 5 W.W.R. 105 (Man. Prov. Ct.). Many more cases emerged

in the 1980s and 1990s. As well, as early as 1979, this Court specifically acknowledged the use of forensic hypnosis by police forces and by defence counsel: see *Horvath v. The Queen*, [1979] 2 S.C.R. 376, at pp. 433-34, *per* Beetz J. These cases stand for the proposition that hypnosis is in no way a novel science.

[133]   A scientific technique or knowledge will be considered "novel" in two situations: when it is new, or when the application of recognized scientific knowledge or technique is new (see *J.-L.J.*, at para. 35). In *J.-L.J.*, the expert in issue was characterized as a "pioneer in Canada" in trying to use a generally recognized therapeutic tool, penile plethysmograph, as a forensic tool in order to determine common traits or characteristics of sexual deviants (para. 35). This is what made the science in that case "novel". Hypnosis is not new science, nor is its use in forensic investigation new.

[134]   Deschamps J. maintains that the use of hypnosis in criminal investigation is not frozen in time and subject to judicial scrutiny when questioned. I agree. The question is how this process is to be undertaken and what is its object. One important question is the determination of the basis for the new query. As always, context is important. It is important to note, with regard to this, that very few Canadian courts have admitted hypnosis evidence without a *voir dire* as to its admissibility. This is contrary to some U.S. states that have adopted a *per se* admissibility rule (i.e., admission without a *voir dire*): see *State v. Brown*, 337 N.W.2d 138 (N.D. 1983); *State v. Jorgensen*, 492 P.2d 312 (Or. Ct. App. 1971); *State v. Glebock*, 616 S.W.2d 897 (Tenn. Crim. App. 1981); and *Prime v. State*, 767 P.2d 149 (Wyo. 1989). This illustrates the difficulty in applying foreign precedents without paying attention to differences in approaches. In Canada, the trend has always been to hold a *voir dire* examining the entire factual context surrounding the hypnosis evidence, with experts called to discuss the science of hypnosis and give their opinion as to whether the evidence in issue is sufficiently reliable to be admitted. [Citations omitted.] I fail to see how this is not "judicial assessment" of forensic hypnosis evidence. Clearly, the use of hypnosis evidence has been put to judicial scrutiny.

· · ·

[138]   The test for assessing the reliability of scientific evidence set out in *J.-L.J.* is not "new law" requiring that scientific methods, previously accepted as legitimate by our courts, must now be resubmitted for scrutiny under the *J.-L.J.* test. Many earlier cases cautioned for scrutiny of evidence based on new scientific methods and set out factors upon which trial judges may rely upon when assessing the reliability of such evidence: [citations omitted]. Thus, neither *R. v. Mohan*, [1994] 2 S.C.R. 9, nor *J.-L.J.* introduced the concept of probing scientific evidence. In fact, it was specifically rejected in *Terceira* (Ont. C.A.) [*R v Terceira* (1998), 38 OR (3d) 175 (CA)], that *Mohan* introduced a new standard for the assessment of novel science: "the rules laid down by Sopinka J. in *R. v. Mohan, supra*, do not signify a departure from the common law rules relating to the admission of opinion evidence in a criminal trial, nor do they purport to do so" (p. 185).

[139]   The point of both *Mohan* and *J.-L.J.* was to emphasize the need for courts to give special scrutiny to novel science or the new application of a recognized science, through a case-by-case evaluation, in light of the changing nature of our scientific knowledge (see *J.-L.J.*, at para. 34). See also S.C. Hill et al., *McWilliams' Canadian Criminal Evidence* (4th ed. (loose-leaf)), vol. 1, at p. 12-34:

Although the suggestion has been made that opinion testimony involving a novel field of expertise requires "a higher threshold of reliability" than attaches to other expert opinion testimony, this is not the prescription of *Mohan*. *Closer scrutiny means a more searching investigation or examination than normal into the reliability and validity of the science but not raising the bar of reliability to a higher standard than the admission entry point for non-novel science.* [Emphasis added.]

J.-L.J. was not intended, as my colleague appears to suggest, to set down a rigid formula where the results must be proved beyond a reasonable doubt before scientific evidence can be admitted. The factors from *Daubert v. Merrell Dow Pharmaceuticals, Inc.*, 509 U.S. 579 (1993), adopted in *J.-L.J.* were designed to be flexible and non-exclusive. As noted above, similar factors to assist courts in assessing the reliability of scientific evidence have existed at common law long before *J.-L.J.* was decided. Well-established scientific methods accepted by our courts do not need to be systematically reassessed under *J.-L.J.* While my colleague suggests that not all previously accepted scientific techniques will have to be reassessed under *J.-L.J.*, her guidance that science which is "so well established" (at para. 31) need not be reassessed is so vague that it opens the door to most if not all previously accepted techniques being subject to challenge under *J.-L.J.*, without establishing a serious basis for the inquiry.

[140] A further concern I have about Deschamps J.'s approach to *J.-L.J.* is that although she states that the standard it requires is "sufficient reliability" (para. 33), her reasoning really reflects a standard of total consensus by members of the scientific community. She acknowledges that hypnosis has been the subject of significant study and peer review, as well as testing, yet, because there is not unanimity in the scientific community on the reliability of hypnotically refreshed memories, she would find this evidence inadmissible. In my view, this standard is more akin to the "general acceptance" test that this Court specifically rejected in *Mohan* in favour of the *Daubert* "reliable foundation" test, as stated in *J.-L.J.*, at para. 33:

> *Mohan* kept the door open to novel science, rejecting the "general acceptance" test formulated in the United States in *Frye v. United States*, 293 F. 1013 (D.C. Cir. 1923), and moving in parallel with its replacement, the "reliable foundation" test more recently laid down by the U.S. Supreme Court in *Daubert v. Merrell Dow Pharmaceuticals, Inc.*, 509 U.S. 579 (1993).

In the test set out in *Frye v. United States*, 293 F. 1013 (D.C. Cir. 1923), demonstrating "general acceptance" of a theory or technique within a scientific community was *the* requirement to be met, while under the *Daubert* test adopted in *J.-L.J.*, "general acceptance" is weighed as only one of several factors to be considered. The problem with the mandatory "general acceptance" standard in *Frye* has been summarized as follows:

> The test does not specify what proportion of experts constitute general acceptance. Courts have never required unanimity, and anything less than full consensus in science can quickly resemble substantial disagreement. In fact, the most rigorous fields with the healthiest scientific discourse might fail the *Frye* test with the greatest frequency.

> (D.L. Faigman et al., Modern Scientific Evidence: The Law and Science of Expert Testimony (2005), vol. 1, at p. 9)

As this passage demonstrates, total unanimity is impossible to obtain and therefore completely unrealistic to expect. I fear that the high standard of reliability my colleague champions will result in the exclusion of far too much relevant and probative evidence.

[At the new trial, Trochym pleaded guilty to manslaughter. Having already served more than seven years in jail before and after his first trial, he was sentenced to one additional day in jail and three years' probation.]

NOTE

In *R v Abbey*, 2009 ONCA 624, 97 OR (3d) 330, Doherty JA criticized the trial judge for approaching Dr Totten's evidence as if it were novel scientific evidence. According to Doherty JA, the evidence was neither novel nor scientific. In *R v Aitken*, 2012 BCCA 134, the BC Court of Appeal considered an argument that "forensic gait analysis" evidence given by a clinical podiatrist was novel scientific evidence and that the *J-LJ* criteria (set out in the above extract from *Trochym*) should therefore guide the admissibility of this evidence.

R v Aitken
2012 BCCA 134
Finch CJBC, Hall and Hinkson JJA (2 April 2012)

[Aitken was charged with first-degree murder. The victim was shot at his apartment building in Victoria on December 28, 2004. The shooting was recorded by a security camera positioned in the building. However, the shooter's face was concealed. Other evidence found at or near the scene was linked by police to Aitken and his business partner. At trial, the Crown relied on the evidence of Haydn Kelly, podiatrist, who testified that both Aitken and the shooter captured in the security footage exhibited certain unusual gait patterns.]

HALL JA [Finch CJBC and Hinkson JA agreeing]:

· · ·

[66] The appellant challenges the admissibility of Mr. Kelly's evidence on the ground that it lacks the requisite level of reliability for novel science, which must be subjected to special scrutiny after *R. v. Mohan*, [1994] 2 S.C.R. 9 at 25. It is submitted that the forensic gait analysis provided by Mr. Kelly could be properly considered "novel" because this is the first time that such evidence has been advanced in a Canadian court. The relationship between podiatry, clinical gait analysis and forensic gait analysis was described by the trial judge as follows:

[9] Podiatry is the study, diagnosis and management of conditions affecting the foot. The field of study is an ancient one, stretching back a thousand years. Gait analysis is the analysis of the style or manner in which a person walks, sometimes because of symptoms or troubling pathology. …

[10] Forensic gait analysis is the term used to describe the application of gait analysis knowledge to legal problems. …

[67] The appellant challenges the reliability of Mr. Kelly's evidence on the following grounds: he has not performed blind testing or established an error rate for his conclusions; his opinions on gait comparison have not been peer reviewed and do not employ a scientific method; and there is no scientific basis for the six-point qualitative scale employed. As part of this last point, the appellant emphasizes that there was no way for Mr. Kelly to establish the prevalence of the identified podiatric features in the Canadian population at the time of the shooting.

[68] As observed by the respondent, the appellant is essentially arguing that Mr. Kelly's evidence fails to satisfy the factors outlined in *Daubert v. Merrell Dow Pharmaceuticals Inc.*, 509 U.S. 579 (1993), which Binnie J., writing for the Court in *R. v. J.-L.J.*, 2000 SCC 51, [2000] 2 S.C.R. 600, acknowledged could be "helpful in evaluating the soundness of novel science" (para. 33). These factors are: 1) whether the theory or technique can be and has been tested; 2) whether the theory or technique has been subjected to peer review and publication; 3) the known or potential rate of error or the existence of standards; and 4) whether the theory or technique has been generally accepted by the relevant scientific community.

. . .

[74] In evaluating Mr. Kelly's qualifications as an expert witness, the trial judge rejected the argument that his evidence was novel science. She observed, "Podiatry has been in existence for a thousand years and the expertise of a podiatrist to analyze an individual's gait has long been accepted and practiced in a clinical setting" (para. 34). Implicit in this conclusion is a determination that forensic applications of podiatry and gait analysis do not render the practice "novel" for the purposes of the *Mohan* test. In my respectful opinion, the trial judge did not err in so holding.

The decision in *R v Aitken* exemplifies the confusion caused by the adoption of a stiffened reliability analysis for novel scientific evidence. To what extent do you think the BC Court of Appeal's approach to forensic gait analysis is in keeping with that of the majority in *R v Trochym* and that of the court in *R v J-LJ*? In our respectful view, the BC Court of Appeal's approach is out of step with these decisions. See further Emma Cunliffe & Gary Edmond, "Gaitkeeping in Canada: Missteps in Assessing the Reliability of Expert Testimony" (2014) 92 Can Bar Rev 327.

c. Non-Scientific Expert Opinion Evidence

As you have seen, the US Supreme Court emphasized in *Daubert v Merrell Dow Pharmaceuticals, Inc*, 509 US 579 (1993), that it intended to establish a "flexible" approach to assessing reliability. In *Kumho Tire Co v Carmichael*, 526 US 137 (1999), the US Supreme Court held that a trial judge considering non-scientific expert evidence must still consider the reliability of that evidence. He or she may consider one or more of the *Daubert* factors in the course of assessing reliability, but the list supplied in *Daubert* is not a definitive checklist or test. In *R v Abbey*, 2009 ONCA 624, 97 OR (3d) 330, Doherty JA criticized the trial judge for relying upon the *Daubert* factors to assess the reliability of Dr Totten's evidence, finding that these factors were inappropriate to evidence that was plainly not scientific. Doherty JA offered a list of factors that may help a trial judge to assess the reliability of qualitative evidence:

[118] In holding that the trial judge improperly attempted to use the specific *Daubert* factors in assessing the reliability of Dr. Totten's evidence, I do not suggest that the Crown was not required to demonstrate threshold reliability. That reliability had to be determined, however, using tools appropriate to the nature of the opinion advanced by Dr. Totten.

[119] As with scientifically based opinion evidence, there is no closed list of the factors relevant to the reliability of an opinion like that offered by Dr. Totten. I would suggest, however, that the following are some questions that may be relevant to the reliability inquiry where an opinion like that offered by Dr. Totten is put forward:

- To what extent is the field in which the opinion is offered a recognized discipline, profession or area of specialized training?
- To what extent is the work within that field subject to quality assurance measures and appropriate independent review by others in the field?
- What are the particular expert's qualifications within that discipline, profession or area of specialized training?
- To the extent that the opinion rests on data accumulated through various means such as interviews, is the data accurately recorded, stored and available?
- To what extent are the reasoning processes underlying the opinion and the methods used to gather the relevant information clearly explained by the witness and susceptible to critical examination by a jury?
- To what extent has the expert arrived at his or her opinion using methodologies accepted by those working in the particular field in which the opinion is advanced?
- To what extent do the accepted methodologies promote and enhance the reliability of the information gathered and relied on by the expert?
- To what extent has the witness, in advancing the opinion, honoured the boundaries and limits of the discipline from which his or her expertise arises?
- To what extent is the proffered opinion based on data and other information gathered independently of the specific case or, more broadly, the litigation process?

In *Truscott (Re)*, 2007 ONCA 575, the Ontario Court of Appeal was invited to consider the evolution that had occurred in medicine, and particularly forensic pathology between 1959 and 2007. It accepted testimony from Dr Michael Pollanen, the Chief Forensic Pathologist for Ontario, to the following effect:

[169] In his report and in his testimony before us, Dr. Pollanen described a shift in approach in forensic medicine and in other branches of medicine more generally. Traditionally, expert opinions were largely based on authoritative experience and anecdotal case reports. In the past few decades, and particularly in the last ten years, an alternative model has developed called the "evidence-based approach". This approach requires a critical analysis of peer-reviewed literature and attention to primary reviewable evidence from the postmortem examination.

Based in part on this testimony, the Ontario Court of Appeal acquitted Stephen Truscott of the 1959 murder of Lynn Harper. Truscott was 14 years old when Harper died, and upon conviction in 1966 was sentenced to hang. His sentence was commuted to life imprisonment and he was paroled in 1969. However, he was not exonerated until the 2007 decision of the Ontario Court of Appeal.

Unreliable medical testimony is implicated in a number of Canadian wrongful convictions, including several child homicide cases that were prosecuted in Ontario between 1991 and

2003. Justice Stephen Goudge was commissioned by the Ontario government to investigate these wrongful convictions. His report contains a comprehensive discussion of reliability. Specifically in relation to medical evidence, he made the following observations:

> Forensic pathology provides a good example of a discipline that has not traditionally engaged in random testing or determining rates of error. The reasons are obvious: testing and reproducibility cannot be used to verify a cause of death. The forensic pathologist's opinion must instead rely on specialized training, accepted standards and protocols within the forensic pathology community, accurate gathering of empirical evidence, attention to the limits of the discipline and the possibility of alternative explanations or error, knowledge derived from established peer-reviewed medical literature, and sound professional judgment.

> Although it will often not be possible to look to testing and error rates, there are other tools that judges can use to determine the threshold reliability of interpretative sciences such as forensic pathology. Professor Edmond has provided a very useful inventory. Our systemic review also suggests a number of tools that are germane in assessing the threshold reliability of a forensic pathology opinion.

> First, it is important that the factors on which a sound forensic pathology opinion rests, and which I described earlier in this Report, be scrutinized to ensure that they have been adhered to in the particular case. Is the empirical evidence accurately recorded? Is the reasoning process clearly explained and logical? And, based on this foundation, does the opinion stated appear to be justifiable?

> As the evidence at the Inquiry made clear, the presence or absence of a system of quality assurance and meaningful peer review of post-mortem reports in the work environment from which the opinion comes is also important. So too is whether the expert witness has the training and experience to offer the particular opinion, or whether the witness is stepping beyond the limits of his or her expertise.

> In addition, because forensic pathology is an interpretive science, it is important to examine the language in which the expert opinion is expressed. As is often the case in fields where testing and error rates may not be available, the limits placed by the science on the precision or certainty with which a conclusion can be drawn from empirical evidence must be observed. Purported precision or certainty beyond that permitted by the empirical evidence may be a telltale sign of unreliability. This caution is one of the important lessons learned from our systemic review.

> We also learned that failure to acknowledge that a proffered opinion is located in an area of particular controversy within the science can matter for threshold reliability. So, too, can the failure to consider and provide reasoned rejection of alternative conclusions that might arguably be drawn from the data.

> Thus, like all expert scientific evidence, forensic pathology opinions can be tested for threshold reliability. The challenge for the trial judge as gatekeeper is to access the tools germane to the task when applying the element of judgment necessary to determine threshold reliability in a reasoned and transparent way.

> · · ·

> … I recognize that simply reciting a laundry list of factors or questions is of limited utility. It may be helpful to distinguish between those questions that focus on the reliability of the witness and of the relevant scientific field in general and those that focus on the reliability of the particular opinion that the witness proposes to provide. Although some expert evidence can be excluded on the basis that the witness or the discipline, or both, are not sufficiently reliable to justify admission, expert evidence should not be admitted solely on the basis that the witness has impressive

credentials and comes from a recognized discipline. In every case, the trial judge should drill down and determine whether the actual evidence to be given by the witness satisfies a standard of threshold reliability.

In determining that threshold reliability, the trial judge should focus on factors related to

1   the reliability of the witness, including whether the witness is testifying outside his or her expertise;

2   the reliability of the scientific theory or technique on which the opinion draws, including whether it is generally accepted and whether there are meaningful peer review, professional standards, and quality assurance processes;

3   whether the expert can relate his or her particular opinion in the case to a theory or technique that has been or can be tested, including substitutes for testing that are tailored to the particular discipline;

4   whether there is serious dispute or uncertainty about the science and, if so, whether the trier of fact will be reliably informed about the existence of that dispute or uncertainty;

5   whether the expert has adequately considered alternative explanations or interpretation of the data and whether the underlying evidence is available for others to challenge the expert's interpretation;

6   whether the language that the expert proposes to use to express his or her conclusions is appropriate, given the degree of controversy or certainty in the underlying science; and

7   whether the expert can express the opinion in a manner such that the trier of fact will be able to reach an independent opinion as to the reliability of the expert's opinion.

These factors obviously do not require the trial judge to be convinced that the proposed opinion is correct. That is a question of ultimate reliability for the trier of fact. The trial judge is to assess whether the particular conclusions and opinions offered by the expert are supportable by a body of specialized knowledge familiar to the expert, and whether the manner in which the expert proposes to present his or her testimony accurately reflects the science and any relevant controversies or uncertainties in it. This full disclosure of the limits and controversies of the science in a way that the trier of fact can understand is especially important in fields such as pediatric forensic pathology.

(The Hon Stephen T Goudge, *Inquiry into Pediatric Forensic Pathology in Ontario Report* (Toronto: Ontario Ministry of the Attorney General, 2008) at 493-95)

D. The Ultimate Issue

The "ultimate issue" rule is the proposition that an expert witness may not offer testimony that touches upon the ultimate question that must be decided by the trier of fact. The rule is discussed, and rejected in *R v Graat* ([1982] 2 SCR 819), *R v Mohan* ([1994] 2 SCR 9, 89 CCC (3d) 402), and *R v Lavallee* ([1990] 1 SCR 852, 55 CCC (3d) 97), above. It is no longer an objection to expert evidence that it addresses the ultimate issue to be decided by the jury. Nonetheless, the concern behind the "rule" (that is, that the expert evidence may unduly influence the jury's decision on the ultimate issue) remains significant. Accordingly, as the court states in *R v Mohan*, the closer the expert evidence is to the ultimate issue, the more strictly the tests of necessity and reliability will be applied. Moreover, an expert must not give an opinion on issues of mixed fact and law, such as guilt, negligence, etc. Whenever the trier of fact receives expert assistance, the trial judge must instruct that the final determination is for the trier of fact to make.

NOTE ON EXAMINING AND CROSS-EXAMINING EXPERT WITNESSES

In determining what weight to give to expert opinion evidence, the trier of fact must determine the extent to which the facts on which it is based have been proved in evidence. If the witness is giving an opinion on the basis of his own observations, he may be questioned on those observations and asked for his opinion. If the facts are established through the testimony of other witnesses and are not in dispute, the examining counsel may state the facts to the witness and elicit his opinion. If, however, the facts are in dispute, or the expert has taken into account facts that have not been proved in evidence, then the expert's opinion must be elicited on the basis of hypothetical facts. Sopinka, Lederman, and Bryant, *The Law of Evidence in Canada*, 2nd ed (Markham, Ont: Butterworths, 1999) explain at paras 12.47-48:

> Without a hypothetical question in which the expert is asked to assume that certain disputed facts given in evidence are true, there is the hazard that the premise upon which the opinion is based will be accepted by the jury as conclusive or alternatively, the jury's view of the evidence which the jury must weigh will be affected by the expert's acceptance of a particular version of the facts.
>
> The expert, in the absence of a hypothesis, would be placed in the untenable position of having to weigh evidence, assess credibility and choose among witnesses in order to determine the premise upon which the opinion is expressed. These matters are determined by the trier of fact and are not the responsibility or the proper role of the expert witness. ... If the trier of fact ultimately rejects the factual premises on which the opinion was based, then, of course, the expert's opinion must be rejected as well.

It is common practice to cross-examine an expert witness by posing to the witness contradictory opinions cited in authoritative works. In *R v Marquard*, [1993] 4 SCR 223, the majority (per McLachlin J) held that to avoid unfairness to the expert witness the technique can be used only if the witness acknowledges that he or she is familiar with the work cited and confirms that the work is authoritative. L'Heureux-Dubé J, dissenting, preferred a more flexible approach so that the expert witness would not be able to avoid "an inquiry into the breadth or depth of his knowledge simply by refusing to acknowledge a study."

PROBLEM (R v GALLOWAY)

We continue to deal with the case of Martin Galloway, who is charged with first-degree murder with respect to the death of his wife, Angela. Angela was killed on March 27, 2016. You will remember that *the issue* at trial is the identity of the killer.

Remember that in his statements to police Martin describes finding his wife's lifeless body on the floor of the drive shed situated on their isolated rural property. Angela had suffered serious blunt force trauma that caused her death. Martin denies playing any role in this homicide.

The police believe that Martin is the perpetrator and that he "staged" the crime scene to make it look like there had been a break-in. At the trial, the Crown wants to call Special Agent

Smith as an expert witness to give opinion evidence regarding the likelihood that the crime scene had been "staged." The following evidence has been heard on a *voir dire*:

Special Agent Smith has worked for the FBI for 17 years. He has been trained in and become an expert in what he described as criminal investigation analysis. Agent Smith testified that criminal investigation analysis is an umbrella designation referring to a number of investigative services offered to police agencies to assist them in their investigations and sometimes offered to the courts as expert evidence. These investigative services include profiling and crime scene analysis. Agent Smith testified that when performing a crime scene analysis, he is always concerned with whether the scene has been staged or manipulated to create a misleading impression. He defined staging as

> the intentional alteration or manipulation of the crime scene by the offender to divert attention away from that individual as a logical suspect and/or to divert attention away from the most logical motive.

Agent Smith opined that the scene in the drive shed had been staged to make it appear as though there had been a break-in. He emphasized that his opinion was based on the combined consideration of many circumstances and not on any one factor. He testified that there were many "behavioural, forensic, and investigative contradictions" that told him there had not been a real break-in, but rather an attempt to make it appear as though there had been a break-in.

The factors referred to by Agent Smith can be grouped into five categories. First, he opined that the drive shed was a "high risk" target for a break-in (in the sense that the risk to a burglar of being caught was substantial), and not one likely to be selected by a burglar. This statement of the risk posed to a burglar was based on many considerations, including the ample lighting around the drive shed, the locks on the doors, the alarm system, the presence of dogs in the home, the activity in the area of the home on that evening, the presence of Martin's family in the home that evening, the close proximity of neighbours, the relative unlikelihood that there would be valuable, easily portable property in the drive shed, and the availability of easier targets in the vicinity.

Second, Agent Smith described Angela as at a very low risk to be the victim of crime. She was security conscious, lived in a good neighbourhood, and did not engage in any activities—for example, drug dealing—that would make it more likely that she would become a victim of crime.

Third, based on a statistical review of break and enters in the county where the Galloways lived for the five-year period preceding the homicide on March 27, 2016, Agent Smith concluded that confrontations between the burglar and the victim were rare and, in those rare cases where a confrontation occurred, there was seldom any violence directed at the victim. Smith testified that his review of the five years for which he had statistics of break and enters in the area of the home in this case revealed no other case where a break and enter had resulted in a homicide.

Fourth, Smith considered the nature of the violence inflicted on Angela, the absence of any evidence of sexual assault or theft from her person, and the indication that the perpetrator had quickly gained control over Angela in a confined area as contraindicative of homicide by an unknown intruder.

Fifth, Agent Smith focused on the window that was the apparent point of entry by the burglar. In Smith's view, a burglar would not have entered the drive shed through that window. The window was in plain view and there were other, less exposed windows in the drive shed. The cutting of the screen on the window also, according to Agent Smith, seemed unnecessary to gain entry through the window because the screen could be easily removed. Agent Smith viewed the location of the cut on the screen and the manner in which the cut was made as inconsistent with the screen having been cut by someone who was trying to gain entry through the window. Finally, Smith found it significant that the window had been left open. In his opinion, a burglar would close the window after gaining entry to avoid the risk that the open window would attract someone's attention.

Is Agent Smith's proposed evidence that this crime scene was "staged" admissible?

Credibility

As you learned in Chapter 2, the witness sits at the heart of the common law trial. In general, all evidence must be admitted through the testimony of a competent and duly sworn witness. But how should such evidence be weighed? Otherwise put, how much reliance should a finder of fact place on relevant, admissible evidence offered by a witness on the stand? The assessment of credibility is central to answering these questions. If witnesses are the key players in the common law trial, the assessment of their credibility is the engine that drives the evaluation of their evidence. Credibility assessments are an important part of evaluating the probative value of evidence; they help the finder of fact to decide how much "stock" to put in a witness's testimony.

The term "credibility" is directed at the decision as to whether the witness's testimony is believable and, hence, safe to rely on. One may be tempted to conflate the ideas of "believability" and "honesty," but it is important to bear in mind that the credibility of a witness could be affected by two different kinds of concerns. One might worry that a witness is *dishonest* or *untruthful*—for example, a witness might have a motive to lie or mislead. Alternatively, one might worry that a witness who is being honest and sincere is nevertheless simply *mistaken*; here, a witness's flawed memory, perception, or capacity to communicate might have affected his or her testimony. Sometimes courts and commentators signal this distinction by using the term "credibility" to refer to the honesty of a witness, and the term "reliability" to capture the accuracy of that witness's testimony. The crucial point is to remember that credibility is not solely concerned with whether an accused might be lying, but also with whether a witness might be mistaken. Indeed, in most assessments of credibility, the chief concern is not that one might have a dishonest witness but that a witness might be sincere and honest, but mistaken.

An important example of this phenomenon is eyewitness identification evidence. A growing body of reports, scholarship, and judicial pronouncements has shown the frailties of eyewitness identification evidence. In *R v Hanemaayer*, 2008 ONCA 580 at para 29, Rosenberg JA of the Court of Appeal for Ontario cautioned that "[m]istaken eyewitness identification is the overwhelming factor leading to wrongful convictions. A study in the United States of DNA exonerations shows that mistaken eyewitness identification was a factor in over 80 percent of the cases: see [*The Inquiry Regarding Thomas Sophonow: The Investigation, Prosecution and Consideration of Entitlement to Compensation* (Winnipeg: Manitoba Justice, 2001)] at p. 27." In the earlier case of *R v Quercia* (1990), 75 OR (2d) 463, 60 CCC (3d) 380 at 389 (CA), Doherty JA observed as follows: "The spectre of erroneous convictions based on honest and convincing, but mistaken, eyewitness identification haunts the criminal law."

The starting point is this: any witness who takes the stand thereby puts his or her credibility in issue. The credibility of that witness, and with it the weight to be given to his or her evidence, must be determined, with all of the testimonial factors discussed in Chapter 2 kept in mind: the witness's (1) use of language, (2) sincerity, (3) memory, and (4) perception. The finder of fact, whether a jury or a judge sitting alone, is responsible for assessing credibility. In Section I of this chapter, we will consider the general principles governing this assessment of credibility, including the role of demeanour, special considerations regarding the credibility of child witnesses, and the deference that appellate courts give to the trier of fact's assessments of credibility.

Credibility determinations arise out of the normal process of the direct examination of one's own witness, cross-examination by the opposing party, and re-examination to clarify and address any issues that have emerged. In the unfolding of this process, certain rules guide what evidence can be used, and how, to influence the assessment of the credibility of a witness. In Section II we consider when and how you can adduce evidence to support the credibility of your own witness. Section III addresses the rules governing the impeachment of an opposing party's witness. In Section IV we turn to the special situation of when you seek to challenge the credibility of your own witness. The chapter concludes, in Section V, with a look at the law of corroboration: circumstances in which the trier of fact should be warned to take particular care and caution before giving weight to a witness's testimony.

I. ASSESSING CREDIBILITY

A. Assessing Credibility in the Context of All of the Evidence

In *R v Gagnon*, 2006 SCC 17, [2006] 1 SCR 621, Bastarache and Abella JJ explained that "[a]ssessing credibility is not a science. It is very difficult for a trial judge to articulate with precision the complex intermingling of impressions that emerge after watching and listening to witnesses and attempting to reconcile the various versions of events" (at para 20). The many factors relevant to assessing the credibility of a witness were discussed in *White v R*, [1947] SCR 268 at 272, Estey J, (cited with approval in *R v Norman* (1993), 16 OR (3d) 295, 87 CCC (3d) 153 (CA), Finlayson JA):

> [Credibility] is a matter in which so many human characteristics, both the strong and the weak, must be taken into consideration. The general integrity and intelligence of the witness, his powers to observe, his capacity to remember and his accuracy in statement are important. It is also important to determine whether he is honestly endeavouring to tell the truth, whether he is sincere and frank or whether he is biased, reticent and evasive. All these questions and others may be answered from the observation of the witness's general conduct and demeanour in determining the question of credibility.

An important principle is that the credibility of a witness must be assessed not just in light of these features and observations of the witness himself or herself, but in view of the overall context of the evidence adduced in the trial. In *R v Norman*, cited above, Finlayson JA adopted the statement of O'Halloran JA, for the BC Court of Appeal, in *Faryna v Chorny*, [1952] 2 DLR 354 at 357:

> [t]he real test of the truth of the story of a witness ... must be its harmony with the preponderance of the probabilities which a practical and informed person would readily recognize as reasonable in that place and in those conditions.

That overall process of assessing the credibility of a witness's testimony—evaluating all of these testimonial factors as well as the context of the evidence as a whole—is shaped by the various means of establishing and testing credibility that are discussed in the remainder of this chapter.

B. The Demeanour of the Witness

The final line in the extract from *White v R*, above, referenced the use of "observation of the witness's general conduct and demeanour" as helpful in determining credibility. Our trial system assumes that direct observation of the witness is an important piece in the assessment of credibility. Indeed, as you learned in Chapter 4, one of the reasons why hearsay evidence is *prima facie* inadmissible is because when the declarant's statement is reported to the court by another witness, the trier of fact is deprived of the opportunity to observe the declarant making the statement (see Chapter 4). In *R v B (KG)*, [1993] 1 SCR 740, Lamer CJ, for the majority, identified the advantage of assessing a statement made by the witness in court rather than a statement that is reported to the court:

> When the witness is on the stand, the trier can observe the witness's reaction to questions, hesitation, degree of commitment to the statement being made, etc. Most importantly, and subsi

all of these factors, the trier can assess the relationship between the interviewer and the witness to observe the extent to which the testimony of the witness is the product of the investigator's questioning. Such subtle observations and cues cannot be gleaned from a transcript, read in court in counsel's monotone, where the atmosphere of the exchange is entirely lost.

Yet the utility and reliability of demeanour as a guide to credibility has come into question in recent years. The assessment of demeanour can be affected by cultural assumptions and stereotypes. Thus, for example, directness of speech and eye contact may connote honesty in one culture but rudeness in another. Moreover, recall that credibility is just as concerned with mistakenness as with honesty. A witness might be extremely confident about evidence that turns out to be inaccurate. Is demeanour a helpful guide in such a situation?

The debate over the value of demeanour in the assessment of credibility recently emerged at the Supreme Court of Canada in the very interesting context of the following case.

R v NS

2012 SCC 72, [2012] 3 SCR 726

McLachlin CJ and LeBel, Deschamps, Fish, Abella, Rothstein, and Cromwell JJ

(20 December 2012)

McLACHLIN CJ (Deschamps, Fish, and Cromwell JJ concurring):

[Two accused (M-d S. and M-l S., the complainant's cousin and uncle) were charged with having sexually assaulted N.S. At the preliminary inquiry, the Crown called N.S. as a witness. N.S. wished to testify wearing her niqab but the two accused objected and sought an order requiring her to remove it. N.S. testified that her religious beliefs required her to wear the niqab in this public setting. The preliminary inquiry judge ordered her to remove the niqab. On review of this ruling, a superior court judge held that N.S. should be permitted to wear the niqab, but the Ontario Court of Appeal held that a more detailed balancing was required and sent the matter back to the preliminary inquiry judge to re-assess. N.S. appealed to the Supreme Court of Canada, seeking an order directing that she be permitted to wear the niqab.]

I. *Introduction*

[1] How should the state respond to a witness whose sincerely held religious belief requires her to wear a niqab that covers her face, except for her eyes, while testifying in a criminal proceeding? One response is to say she must always remove her niqab on the ground that the courtroom is a neutral space where religion has no place. Another response is to say the justice system should respect the witness's freedom of religion and always permit her to testify with the niqab on. In my view, both of these extremes must be rejected in favour of a third option: allowing the witness to testify with her face covered unless this unjustifiably impinges on the accused's fair trial rights.

[2] A secular response that requires witnesses to park their religion at the courtroom door is inconsistent with the jurisprudence and Canadian tradition, and limits freedom of religion where no limit can be justified. On the other hand, a response that says a witness can always testify with her face covered may render a trial unfair and lead to wrongful

conviction. What is required is an approach that balances the vital rights protecting freedom of religion and trial fairness when they conflict. The long-standing practice in Canadian courts is to respect and accommodate the religious convictions of witnesses, unless they pose a significant or serious risk to a fair trial. The *Canadian Charter of Rights and Freedoms*, which protects both freedom of religion and trial fairness, demands no less.

[3] For the reasons that follow, I conclude that a witness who for sincere religious reasons wishes to wear the niqab while testifying in a criminal proceeding will be required to remove it if:

> (a) requiring the witness to remove the niqab is necessary to prevent a serious risk to the fairness of the trial, because reasonably available alternative measures will not prevent the risk; *and*
>
> (b) the salutary effects of requiring her to remove the niqab, including the effects on trial fairness, outweigh the deleterious effects of doing so, including the effects on freedom of religion.

[As you can see, McLachlin CJ and the majority of the court favoured a case-by-case balancing of whether a witness should be required to remove the niqab. That balancing would ultimately turn on considerations like the harm that would be suffered by the witness, broader societal harms involved in requiring a witness to remove the niqab in order to testify, the nature of the proceeding, and the nature and importance of the evidence to be given by the witness. Nevertheless, she concluded, at para 44, that "it may be ventured that where the liberty of the accused is at stake, the witness's evidence is central to the case and her credibility vital, the possibility of a wrongful conviction must weigh heavily in the balance, favouring removal of the niqab." But even before arriving at this balancing exercise, the court had to address the question of whether wearing a niqab presented a risk to trial fairness, a question that squarely raised the utility of demeanour in the assessment of credibility:]

V. Would Permitting the Witness to Wear the Niqab While Testifying Create a Serious Risk to Trial Fairness?

[15] M-d S. submits that permitting N.S. to wear the niqab while testifying would infringe his fair trial rights. Both ss. 7 and 11(d) of the *Charter* protect an accused's right to a fair trial and to make full answer and defence. ... The right to a fair trial in s. 11(d) encompasses a right to make full answer and defence: *R. v. Mills*, [1999] 3 S.C.R. 668, at para. 69. More broadly, s. 7 of the *Charter* provides that a person cannot be deprived of his liberty except "in accordance with the principles of fundamental justice." Those principles include the right to a fair trial and to make full answer and defence. The principles of fundamental justice in s. 7 and the requirements of s. 11(d) are "inextricably intertwined": *R. v. Rose*, [1998] 3 S.C.R. 262, at para. 95, citing *R. v. Seaboyer*, [1991] 2 S.C.R. 577, at p. 603.

[16] M-d S. argues that allowing N.S. to testify with her face covered by a niqab denies his fair trial rights in two ways: first, by preventing effective cross-examination; and second, by interfering with the ability of the trier of fact (judge or jury) to assess N.S.'s credibility.

[17]   We have no expert evidence in this case on the importance of seeing a witness's face to effective cross-examination and accurate assessment of a witness's credibility. All we have are arguments and several legal and social science articles submitted by the parties as authorities.

[18]   M-d S. and the Crown argue that the link is clear. Communication involves not only words, but facial cues. A facial gesture may reveal uncertainty or deception. The cross-examiner may pick up on non-verbal cues and use them to uncover the truth. Credibility assessment is equally dependent not only on what a witness says, but on how she says it. Effective cross-examination and accurate credibility assessment are central to a fair trial. It follows, they argue, that permitting a witness to wear a niqab while testifying may deny an accused's fair trial rights.

[19]   N.S. and supporting interveners, on the other hand, argue that the importance of seeing a witness's face has been greatly exaggerated. They submit that untrained individuals cannot use facial expressions to detect deception. Moreover, to the extent that non-verbal cues are useful at all, a niqab-wearing witness's eyes, tone of voice and cadence of speech remain available to the cross-examiner and trier of fact.

[20]   The record sheds little light on the question of whether seeing a witness's face is important to effective cross-examination and credibility assessment and hence to trial fairness. The only evidence in the record is a four-page unpublished review article suggesting that untrained individuals cannot accurately detect lies based on the speaker's facial cues. This material was not tendered through an expert available for cross-examination. Interveners have submitted articles arguing for and against a connection, but they are not part of the record and not supported by expert witnesses, and so are more rhetorical than factual.

[21]   This much, however, can be said. The common law, supported by provisions of the *Criminal Code*, R.S.C. 1985, c. C-46, and judicial pronouncements, proceeds on the basis that the ability to see a witness's face is an important feature of a fair trial. While not conclusive, in the absence of negating evidence this common law assumption cannot be disregarded lightly.

[22]   As a general rule, witnesses in common law criminal courts are required to testify in open court, with their faces visible to counsel, the judge and the jury. Face-to-face confrontation is the norm, although not an independent constitutional right: *R. v. Levogiannis* (1990), 1 O.R. (3d) 351 (C.A.), at pp. 366-67, aff'd [1993] 4 S.C.R. 475. To be sure, long-standing assumptions of the common law can be displaced, if shown to be erroneous or based on groundless prejudice—thus the reforms to eliminate the many myths that once skewed the law of sexual assault. But the record before us has not shown the long-standing assumptions of the common law regarding the importance of a witness's facial expressions to cross-examination and credibility assessment to be unfounded or erroneous.

[23]   In recent years, Parliament and this Court have confirmed the common law assumption that the accused, the judge and the jury should be able to see the witness as she testifies. To protect child witnesses from trauma, Parliament has passed legislation permitting children to testify via closed-circuit television or from behind a screen so that they cannot see the accused: *Criminal Code*, s. 486.2(1). This Court has upheld these testimonial aids, relying on the fact that they do not prevent the accused from seeing the witness: *R. v. J.Z.S.*, 2010 SCC 1, [2010] 1 S.C.R. 3, aff'g 2008 BCCA 401, 261 B.C.A.C. 52. Before a witness is permitted to testify by audio link, the *Criminal Code* expressly requires that

the judge consider "any potential prejudice to either of the parties caused by the fact that the witness would not be seen by them": ss. 714.3(d) and 714.4(b). This, too, suggests that not seeing a witness's face during testimony may limit the fairness of a trial.

[24] Covering the face of a witness may impede cross-examination ... . Effective cross-examination is integral to the conduct of a fair trial and a meaningful application of the presumption of innocence: see *R. v. Osolin*, [1993] 4 S.C.R. 595, at pp. 663-65; *Mills*, at para. 69. Unwarranted constraints may undermine the fairness of the trial:

> ... the right of an accused to cross-examine witnesses for the prosecution—*without significant and unwarranted constraint—is an essential component of the right to make full answer and defence.* [Emphasis added.]

(*R. v. Lyttle*, 2004 SCC 5, [2004] 1 S.C.R. 193, at para. 2)

Non-verbal communication can provide the cross-examiner with valuable insights that may uncover uncertainty or deception, and assist in getting at the truth.

[25] Covering a witness's face may also impede credibility assessment by the trier of fact, be it judge or jury. It is a settled axiom of appellate review that deference should be shown to the trier of fact on issues of credibility because trial judges (and juries) have the "overwhelming advantage" of seeing and hearing the witness—an advantage that a written transcript cannot replicate: *Housen v. Nikolaisen*, 2002 SCC 33, [2002] 2 S.C.R. 235, at para. 24; see also *White v. The King*, [1947] S.C.R. 268, at p. 272; *R. v. W. (R.)*, [1992] 2 S.C.R. 122, at p. 131. This advantage is described as stemming from the ability to assess the demeanour of the witness, that is, to *see* how the witness gives her evidence and responds to cross-examination.

[26] Changes in a witness's demeanour can be highly instructive; in *Police v. Razamjoo*, [2005] D.C.R. 408, a New Zealand judge asked to decide whether witnesses could testify wearing burkas commented:

> ... there are types of situations ... in which the demeanour of a witness undergoes a quite dramatic change in the course of his evidence. The look which says "I hoped not to be asked that question," sometimes even a look of downright hatred at counsel by a witness who obviously senses he is getting trapped, can be expressive. So too can abrupt changes in mode of speaking, facial expression or body language. The witness who moves from expressing himself calmly to an excited gabble; the witness who from speaking clearly with good eye contact becomes hesitant and starts looking at his feet; the witness who at a particular point becomes flustered and sweaty, all provide examples of circumstances which, despite cultural and language barriers, convey, at least in part by his facial expression, a message touching credibility. [para. 78]

[27] On the record before us, I conclude that there is a strong connection between the ability to see the face of a witness and a fair trial. Being able to see the face of a witness is not the only—or indeed perhaps the most important—factor in cross-examination or accurate credibility assessment. But its importance is too deeply rooted in our criminal justice system to be set aside absent compelling evidence.

[28] However, whether the ability to observe a witness's face impacts trial fairness in any particular case will depend on the evidence that the witness is to provide. Where evidence is uncontested, credibility assessment and cross-examination are not in issue;

therefore, being unable to see the witness's face will not impinge on the accused's fair trial rights … .

[29]   If wearing the niqab poses no serious risk to trial fairness, a witness who wishes to wear it for sincere religious reasons may do so.

[Having set out this balancing approach to analyzing the question of whether a witness should be required to remove her niqab, McLachlin CJ dismissed the appeal and sent the matter back to be decided in accordance with her reasons. LeBel J (Rothstein J concurring) would have favoured a "clear rule that niqabs may not be worn," a rule that, he reasoned, "would be consistent with the principle of openness of the trial process and would safeguard the integrity of that process as one of communication" (at para 78). Abella J dissented, her dissent very much based on a different view of the utility of demeanour evidence:]

ABELLA J (dissenting):

. . .

[82]   I concede without reservation that seeing more of a witness' facial expressions is better than seeing less. What I am not willing to concede, however, is that seeing less is so impairing of a judge's or an accused's ability to assess the credibility of a witness, that the complainant will have to choose between her religious rights and her ability to bear witness against an alleged aggressor. This also has the potential to impair the rights of an accused, who may find herself having to choose between her religious rights and giving evidence in her own defence. The court system has many examples of accepting evidence from witnesses who are unable to testify under ideal circumstances because of visual, oral, or aural impediments. I am unable to see why witnesses who wear niqabs should be treated any differently.

[83]   I would, however, make an exception in cases where the accused can demonstrate that the witness' face is directly relevant to the case, such as where the witness' identity is in issue. In such cases, seeing the witness' face is central to the issues at trial, rather than merely being a part of the assessment of demeanour.

. . .

[86]   The crux of this case … is whether the impact of not having full access to the usual "demeanour assessment package" can be said to so materially harm trial fairness that the religious right must yield. In my view, with very limited exceptions, the harm to a complainant of requiring her to remove her niqab while testifying will generally outweigh any harm to trial fairness.

. . .

[97]   … The right to a fair trial is crucial to the presumption of innocence and maintaining confidence in the criminal justice system. While I agree that witnesses generally and ideally testify with their faces uncovered in open court, abridgements of this "ideal" often occur in practice yet are almost always tolerated.

[98]   "Demeanour" has been broadly described as "every visible or audible form of self-expression manifested by a witness whether fixed or variable, voluntary or involuntary, simple or complex": Barry R. Morrison, Laura L. Porter and Ian H. Fraser, "The Role of Demeanour in Assessing the Credibility of Witnesses" (2007), 33 *Advocates' Q.* 170, at

p. 179. Trial judges often rely on many indicators *other than* facial cues in finding a witness credible, including

> certitude in speaking, dignity while on the stand, exhibition of disability, exhibition of anger, exhibition of frustration, articulate speaking, thoughtful presentation, enthusiastic language, direct non-evasive answering, non-glib answering, exhibition of modesty, exhibition of flexibility, normal (as in as expected) body movement, cheerful attitude, kind manner, normal exhalation, normal inhalation. ...

(Morrison, at p. 189)

[99] Moreover, while the ability to assess a witness' demeanour is an important component of trial fairness, many courts have noted its limitations for drawing accurate inferences about credibility. In *Faryna v. Chorny*, [1952] 2 D.L.R. 354, for example, the British Columbia Court of Appeal held that relying on the "appearance of sincerity [would lead to] a purely arbitrary finding and justice would then depend upon the best actors in the witness box" (p. 356). According to the court, demeanour "is but one of the elements that enter into the credibility ... of a witness," with other factors including the witness' opportunity for knowledge, powers of observation, judgment, memory and ability to describe clearly what he or she has seen and heard (pp. 356-57).

[100] The Court of Appeal for Alberta similarly urged caution in relying on demeanour in *R. v. Pelletier* (1995), 165 A.R. 138:

> I question whether the respect given to our findings of fact based on the demeanour of the witnesses is always deserved. I doubt my own ability, and sometimes that of other judges, to discern from a witness's demeanour, or the tone of his voice, whether he is telling the truth. He speaks hesitantly. Is it the mark of a cautious man, whose statements are for that reason to be respected, or is he taking time to fabricate? Is the emphatic witness putting on an act to deceive me, or is he speaking from the fullness of his heart, knowing that he is right? Is he likely to be more truthful if he looks me straight in the face than if he casts his eyes on the ground, perhaps from shyness or a natural timidity? For my part I rely on these considerations as little as I can help.
>
> ... I judge a witness to be unreliable if his evidence is, in any serious respect, inconsistent with these undisputed or indisputable facts, or of course if he contradicts himself on important points. I rely as little as possible on such deceptive matters as his demeanour. [para. 18]

(Citing a 1973 paper by Justice MacKenna and approvingly quoted in P. Devlin, *The Judge* (1979), at p. 63.)

See also *R. v. Levert* (2001), 159 C.C.C. (3d) 71, at p. 81.

[101] The Canadian Judicial Council's model jury instructions also acknowledge the inherent limitations in relying on demeanour:

> What was the witness's manner when he or she testified? Do not jump to conclusions, however, based entirely on the witness's manner. Looks can be deceiving. Giving evidence in a trial is not a common experience for many witnesses. People react and appear differently. Witnesses come from different backgrounds. They have different intellects, abilities, values, and life experiences. There are simply too many variables to make the manner in which a witness testifies the only or the most important factor in your decision.

(Model Jury Instructions, Part I, Preliminary Instructions, 4.11 Assessing Testimony (online))

[102] And courts regularly accept the testimony of witnesses whose demeanour can only be partially observed. Section 14 of the *Charter*, for example, states that a witness who cannot hear, or who does not understand or speak the language used in the proceedings, has the right to the assistance of an interpreter. In such cases, "the trial judge ha[s] to make credibility findings through the filters of the interpreters": *R. v. A.F.* (2005), 376 A.R. 124 (C.A.), at para. 3; see also *R. v. R.S.M.*, 1999 BCCA 218 (CanLII), at paras. 12-14. The use of an interpreter may well have an impact on how the witness' demeanour is understood, but it is beyond dispute that interpreters render the assessment of demeanour neither impossible nor impracticable. ...

[103] A witness may also have physical or medical limitations that affect a judge's or lawyer's ability to assess demeanour. A stroke may interfere with facial expressions; an illness may affect body movements; and a speech impairment may affect the manner of speaking. All of these are departures from the demeanour ideal, yet none has ever been held to disqualify the witness from giving his or her evidence on the grounds that the accused's fair trial rights are thereby impaired.

[104] There are other situations where we accept a witness' evidence without being able to assess demeanour at all. The *Criminal Code*, R.S.C. 1985, c. C-46, permits a judge to order and admit a transcript of evidence by a witness who is unable to attend the trial because of a disability, even when the accused's counsel is not present for the taking of the evidence: ss. 709 and 713. Courts also allow witnesses, including material witnesses, to give evidence and be cross-examined by telephone: *Criminal Code*, s. 714.3; see also *R. v. Chapdelaine*, 2004 ABQB 39 (CanLII); *R. v. Butt* (2008), 280 Nfld. & P.E.I.R. 129 (NL Prov. Ct.).

[105] Exceptions to hearsay evidence are another example where the trier of fact is completely unable to assess the demeanour of the person whose statement is being admitted as evidence. In *R. v. Khan*, [1990] 2 S.C.R. 531, McLachlin J. developed a principled exception to the hearsay rule where the statement met the requirements of necessity and reliability (p. 542), with the result that the Court in a sexual assault case admitted the statement of a three-year-old child to her mother because it was unrealistic to require the child to testify and undergo cross-examination. The Court noted that "in most cases the concerns of the accused as to credibility [can] be addressed by submissions as to the weight to be accorded to the evidence" (p. 547).

[106] Wearing a niqab presents only a partial obstacle to the assessment of demeanour. A witness wearing a niqab may still express herself through her eyes, body language, and gestures. Moreover, the niqab has no effect on the witness' verbal testimony, including the tone and inflection of her voice, the cadence of her speech, or, most significantly, the substance of the answers she gives. Unlike out-of-court statements, defence counsel still has the opportunity to rigorously cross-examine N.S. on the witness stand.

[107] It is clear from all of this that trial fairness cannot reasonably expect ideal testimony from an ideal witness in every case, and that demeanour itself represents only one factor in the assessment of a witness' credibility. ...

[108] And since, realistically, not being able to see a witness' whole face is only a partial interference with what is, in any event, only one part of an imprecise measuring tool of

credibility, we are left to wonder why we demand full "demeanour access" where religious belief prevents it.

[109] In my view, therefore, the harmful effects of requiring a witness to remove her niqab, with the result that she will likely not testify, bring charges in the first place, or, if she is the accused, be unable to testify in her own defence, is a significantly more harmful consequence than not being able to see a witness' whole face.

[110] Since, in my view, N.S's sincerity has been established, I see no reason to require her to remove her niqab. I would therefore allow the appeal and remit the matter to the preliminary inquiry for continuation, directing that N.S. be permitted to wear her niqab throughout both the preliminary inquiry and any trial that may follow.

Appeal dismissed, ABELLA J *dissenting.*

[When the preliminary inquiry continued, the judge applied the majority's balancing test and ruled that N.S. would be required to remove her *niqab*. N.S. agreed to comply, with the public excluded from the courtroom, but the Crown withdrew the charges before trial.]

In *R v Rhayel*, 2015 ONCA 377, the Court of Appeal for Ontario set aside the accused's conviction for sexual assault and threatening the death of the complainant, a sex worker. She had given statements to the police, including a videotaped statement, and testified at the preliminary inquiry, but died before the trial took place. In allowing the accused's appeal, the Ontario Court of Appeal found a number of errors in the trial judge's reasons, including the fact that the videotaped statement had been improperly admitted under the principled exception to the hearsay rule. Among those errors, the court concluded that "the trial judge took an overly confident view of his ability to assess the complainant's credibility by reference to her demeanour" in her videotaped statement (at para 93). In arriving at this conclusion, Epstein JA, writing for the court, made the following comments on the value of demeanour in assessing credibility:

> [85] Cases in which demeanour evidence has been relied upon reflect a growing understanding of the fallibility of evaluating credibility based on the demeanour of witnesses: see *Law Society of Upper Canada v. Neinstein* (2010), 99 O.R. (3d) 1 (C.A.), at para. 66; *R. v. G. (P.)*, 2012 ONSC 4646, 104 W.C.B. (2d) 390, at paras. 31-33; *9129-9321 Quebec Inc. v. R.*, 2007 TCC 2, [2007] T.C.J. No. 23, at para. 31; *R. v. Powell*, [2007] O.J. No. 555, at paras. 9-10. It is now acknowledged that demeanour is of limited value because it can be affected by many factors including the culture of the witness, stereotypical attitudes, and the artificiality of and pressures associated with a courtroom. One of the dangers is that sincerity can be and often is misinterpreted as indicating truthfulness.
>
> [86] In *R. v. G.(M.)* (1994), 93 C.C.C. (3d) 347 (C.A.), at p. 355, this court quoted with approval the following passage from *Faryna v. Chorny*, [1952] 2 D.L.R. 354 (B.C.C.A.), at pp. 356-57:
>
>> If a trial judge's finding of credibility is to depend solely on which person he thinks made the better appearance of sincerity in the witness box, we are left with a purely arbitrary finding and justice would then depend upon the best actors in the witness box. On reflection it becomes almost axiomatic that the appearance of telling the truth is but one of the elements that enter into the credibility of the evidence of a witness.

For a trial judge to say "I believe him because I judge him to be telling the truth," is to come to a conclusion on consideration of only half the problem. In truth it may easily be self-direction of a dangerous kind.

· · ·

[88] A powerfully-worded and thoroughly-researched analysis of reliance on demeanour evidence can be found in the decision of the High Court of Australia in *State Rail Authority of New South Wales v. Earthline Constructions Pty. Ltd.* (1999), 160 A.L.R. 588. At para. 88, the Court says:

> There is growing understanding, both by trial judges and appellate courts, of the fallibility of judicial evaluation of credibility from the appearance and demeanour of witnesses in the somewhat artificial and sometimes stressful circumstances of the courtroom. Scepticism about the supposed judicial capacity in deciding credibility from the appearance and demeanour of a witness is not new. In *Societe D'Avances Commerciales (Societe Anonyme Egyptienne) v Merchants' Marine Insurance Co (The "Palitana")*, Atkin LJ remarked that "an ounce of intrinsic merit or demerit in the evidence, that is to say, the value of the comparison of evidence with known facts, is worth pounds of demeanour." To some extent, the faith in the judicial power to discern credibility from appearance was probably, at first, a consideration which the judiciary assumed that it inherited from juries. It was natural enough that trial judges, accustomed to presiding over jury trials, would claim, and appellate judges would accord, the same "infallible" capacity to tell truth from falsehood as had historically been attributed to the jury. Nowadays, most judges are aware of the scientific studies which cast doubt on the correctness of this assumption.

[89] I agree with the suggestion contained at the conclusion of the Court's analysis in the *State Rail Authority* decision that it is important for trial judges to bear in mind that, to the extent possible, they should try to decide cases that require assessing credibility without undue reliance on such fallible considerations as demeanour evidence.

Is the Court of Appeal's position on the value of demeanour consistent with the reasons of the majority of the Supreme Court of Canada in *R v NS*? What is your view of the value of such evidence in assessing credibility?

C. Assessing the Credibility of Child Witnesses

In *R v W (R)*, [1992] 2 SCR 122, McLachlin J, for the court, discussed "the general question of how courts should approach the evidence of young children" (at 133-34):

> [There is] a new appreciation that it may be wrong to apply adult tests for credibility to the evidence of children. One finds emerging a new sensitivity to the peculiar perspectives of children. Since children may experience the world differently from adults, it is hardly surprising that details important to adults, like time and place, may be missing from their recollection. Wilson J recognized this in *R v. B.(G.)*, [1990] 2 SCR 30, at pp. 54-55, when, in referring to submissions regarding the court of appeal judge's treatment of the evidence of the complainant, she said that:
>
> > [I]t seems to me that he was simply suggesting that the judiciary should take a common sense approach when dealing with the testimony of young children and not impose the same exacting standard on them as it does on adults. However, this is not to say that the courts should not carefully assess the credibility of child witnesses and I do not read his

reasons as suggesting that the standard of proof must be lowered when dealing with children as the appellants submit. Rather, he was expressing concern that a flaw, such as a contradiction, in a child's testimony should not be given the same effect as a similar flaw in the testimony of an adult. I think his concern is well-founded and his comments entirely appropriate. While children may not be able to recount precise details and communicate the when and where of an event with exactitude, this does not mean that they have misconceived what happened to them and who did it. In recent years we have adopted a much more benign attitude to children's evidence, lessening the strict standards of oath taking and corroboration and I believe that this is a desirable development. The credibility of every witness who testifies before the courts must, of course, be carefully assessed but the standard of the "reasonable adult" is not necessarily appropriate in assessing the credibility of young children.

As Wilson J emphasized in *B.(G.)*, these changes in the way the courts look at the evidence of children do not mean that the evidence of children should not be subject to the same standard of proof as the evidence of adult witnesses in criminal cases. Protecting the liberty of the accused and guarding against the injustice of the conviction of an innocent person require a solid foundation for a verdict of guilt, whether the complainant be an adult or a child. What the changes do mean is that we approach the evidence of children not from the perspective of rigid stereotypes, but on what Wilson J called a "common sense" basis, taking into account the strengths and weaknesses which characterize the evidence offered in the particular case.

It is neither desirable nor possible to state hard and fast rules as to when a witness's evidence should be assessed by reference to "adult" or "child" standards—to do so would be to create anew stereotypes potentially as rigid and unjust as those which the recent developments in the law's approach to children's evidence have been designed to dispel. Every person giving testimony in court, of whatever age, is an individual, whose credibility and evidence must be assessed by reference to criteria appropriate to her mental development, understanding and ability to communicate. But I would add this. In general, where an adult is testifying as to events which occurred when she was a child, her credibility should be assessed according to criteria applicable to her as an adult witness. Yet with regard to her evidence pertaining to events which occurred in childhood, the presence of inconsistencies, particularly as to peripheral matters such as time and location, should be considered in the context of the age of the witness at the time of the events to which she is testifying.

D. Deference of Appellate Courts to Findings of Credibility at Trial

In *R v Buhay*, 2003 SCC 30, [2003] 1 SCR 631, Arbour J, for the court, adopted the statement of Iacobucci J (dissenting in part) in *R v Belnavis*, [1997] 3 SCR 341 at para 76, explaining why appellate courts defer to the credibility findings of trial judges:

The reasons for this principle of deference are apparent and compelling. Trial judges hear witnesses directly. They observe their demeanour on the witness stand and hear the tone of their responses. They therefore acquire a great deal of information which is not necessarily evident from a written transcript, no matter how complete. Even if it were logistically possible for appellate courts to re-hear witnesses on a regular basis in order to get at this information, they would not do so; the sifting and weighing of this kind of evidence is the particular expertise of the trial court. The further up the appellate chain one goes, the more of this institutional expertise is lost and the greater the risk of a decision which does not reflect the realities of the situation.

Nonetheless, in *R v W (R)*, [1992] 2 SCR 122, McLachlin J, for the majority, confirmed that an appellate court can overturn a verdict based on findings of credibility where it concludes, following a review of the evidence and with appropriate deference to the trier of fact, that the findings are unreasonable (at 133-34):

> It is thus clear that a court of appeal, in determining whether the trier of fact could reasonably have reached the conclusion that the accused is guilty beyond a reasonable doubt, must re-examine, and to some extent at least, reweigh and consider the effect of the evidence. The only question remaining is whether this rule applies to verdicts based on findings of credibility. In my opinion, it does. The test remains the same: could a jury or judge properly instructed and acting reasonably have convicted? That said, in applying the test the court of appeal should show great deference to findings of credibility made at trial. This Court has repeatedly affirmed the import-ance of taking into account the special position of the trier of fact on matters of credibility: *White v. The King*, [1947] SCR 268, at p. 272; *R v. M.(S.H.)*, [1989] 2 SCR 446, at pp. 465-66. The trial judge has the advantage, denied to the appellate court, of seeing and hearing the evidence of wit-nesses. However, as a matter of law it remains open to an appellate court to overturn a verdict based on findings of credibility where, after considering all the evidence and having due regard to the advantages afforded to the trial judge, it concludes that the verdict is unreasonable.

In light of the discussion above about the value of demeanour as a test of credibility, are there circumstances in which it will it be inappropriate for an appellate court to defer to the trial judge's findings?

II. SUPPORTING THE CREDIBILITY OF YOUR OWN WITNESS

A. The General Rule Against Oath-Helping

Counsel often begins the examination of his or her witness with questions designed to "ac-credit" the witness as a person generally worthy of belief, focusing, for example, on the wit-ness's employment, length of residence in the community, credentials, etc. These accrediting questions put to the witness are permissible (see *R v Clarke* (1998), 129 CCC (3d) 1 at para 21 (Ont CA)). But to what extent can counsel call evidence from other witnesses, the sole pur-pose of which is to enhance the credibility of that witness?

Generally speaking, a party may not lead evidence as part of its case where the relevance of the evidence is limited to showing that his or her witness is credible. This type of evidence is sometimes called "oath-helping." Until a witness's credibility is challenged, it is assumed that the witness is trustworthy. Accordingly, the evidence of others that the witness is a truthful person, or that the witness has made consistent statements on previous occasions, is superfluous, and the time spent to adduce it would be unwarranted. This is the "rule against oath-helping," sometimes referred to as the "rule against self-serving evidence," which prohibits "adducing evidence solely for the purpose of bolstering a witness's credibility" (*R v Béland*, [1987] 2 SCR 398 at 408).

In this section, we will examine a number of exceptions to the rule against oath-helping. First, and most significantly, there are several situations in which a witness's prior consistent statement will be admissible to support some aspect of his or her testimony or to rebut an explicit or implicit allegation of recent fabrication. In addition, the fact that the statement was made may be admissible where it forms part of the witness's "narrative" and is important to understanding the witness's account of the events. Second, expert evidence may be admissible to equip the trier of fact to assess the credibility of a witness where the assessment requires knowledge or information that goes beyond common experience. However, as will be seen from *R v Marquard*, below, the conditions for admissibility of this type of evidence are quite stringent. Third, the defence in a criminal case may lead evidence of the accused's reputation for veracity, along with other evidence of the accused's good character.

While reading the cases that establish these exceptions, consider whether they are dependent on the witness's credibility having been questioned or attacked by the opposing party.

B. Prior Consistent Statements

1. The General Rule Against Prior Consistent Statements

As a general rule, a prior consistent statement of a witness—a statement made at some point in the past that is consistent with her testimony at trial—is not admissible to enhance that witness's credibility. The traditional rationale for this limitation is threefold. First, the mere fact that a witness has previously given a statement consistent with his or her testimony is not probative of its truth: the witness might be a consistent liar or consistently mistaken. Second, even if the prior consistent statement had some probative value, that probative value is minimal and does not justify the time required for the statement to be presented and tested by cross-examination. Third, such statements are hearsay if offered for the finder of fact to rely on as true (see *R v Dinardo*, 2008 SCC 24 at para 36, [2008] 1 SCR 788).

There are, however, several exceptions to the rule against prior consistent statements. First, a witness's prior consistent statement will be admissible to support his or her identification at trial of the accused or another person. Second, where it is suggested, explicitly or implicitly, that the witness has fabricated the statement, counsel can lead evidence of a prior consistent statement to rebut the suggestion. The special considerations regarding application of this rule to the complainant in a case of sexual assault will be considered separately below. Third, in certain circumstances, the law permits the introduction of the prior consistent statements of an accused, even absent an allegation of recent fabrication. Fourth, even when the contents of a prior statement are not admissible under one of these exceptions, the fact that the statement was made may nevertheless be admissible where it forms part of the "narrative."

2. Prior Identification

It is well established that, when a witness identifies the accused in court, evidence that the witness previously identified the accused is admissible to permit both parties to explore the reliability of the identification. In *R v Tat* (1997), 35 OR (3d) 641, 117 CCC (3d) 481 (CA), Doherty JA explained the rationale for this exception in the following terms:

> [35] [P]rior statements identifying or describing the accused are admissible where the identifying witness identifies the accused at trial. The identifying witness can testify to prior descriptions

given and prior identifications made. Others who heard the description and saw the identification may also be allowed to testify to the descriptions given and the identifications made by the identifying witness. ...

[36] Clearly, the evidence of the prior descriptions given and the prior identifications made by the identifying witness constitute prior consistent statements made by that witness. Generally speaking, evidence that a witness made prior consistent statements is excluded as irrelevant and self-serving. However, where identification evidence is involved, it is the in-court identification of the accused which has little or no probative value standing alone. The probative force of identification evidence is best measured by a consideration of the entire identification process which culminates with an in-court identification ... . The central importance of the pre-trial identification process in the assessment of the weight to be given to identification evidence is apparent upon a review of cases which have considered the reasonableness of verdicts based upon identification evidence: e.g. see *R. v. Miaponoose* (1996), 110 C.C.C. (3d) 445 (Ont. C.A.).

[37] If a witness identifies an accused at trial, evidence of previous identifications made and descriptions given is admissible to allow the trier of fact to make an informed determination of the probative value of the purported identification. The trier of fact will consider the entirety of the identification process as revealed by the evidence before deciding what weight should be given to the identification made by the identifying witness. Evidence of the circumstances surrounding any prior identifications and the details of prior descriptions given will be central to that assessment.

Is this use of a prior consistent statement hearsay or non-hearsay? What if the witness repudiates the earlier identification or can no longer identify the accused? See Chapter 4, Section I.

3. Recent Fabrication

The principal exception to the rule against prior consistent statements is that such statements are admissible to rebut an express or implied "allegation of recent fabrication." When one party suggests that the other party's witness came up with his or her story at some point between the events at issue and the giving of testimony, the witness's prior consistent statement is admissible to rebut that allegation. The prior consistent statement shows that the witness has consistently maintained the position reflected in his or her testimony—at least for a longer period than opposing counsel suggests.

In *R v Ellard*, 2009 SCC 27, [2009] 2 SCR 19, Abella J summarized the recent fabrication exception to the rule against prior consistent statements as follows:

[32] Certain exceptions have nevertheless developed in the jurisprudence. In particular, where a party has made an allegation of recent fabrication, the opposing party can rebut the allegation by introducing prior statements made *before* the alleged fabrication arose, that are consistent with the testimony at trial. The allegation need not be express. It is enough if "in light of the circumstances of the case and the conduct of the trial, the apparent position of the opposing party is that there has been a prior contrivance" (*Evans* [*R v Evans*, [1993] 2 SCR 629], at p. 643; see also *R v. Simpson*, [1988] 1 SCR 3, at p. 24).

[33] To be "recent," the fabrication need only have been made after the event testified about (*R v. Stirling*, 2008 SCC 10, at para. 5). A mere contradiction in the evidence is not enough to engage the recent fabrication exception. However, a "fabrication" can include being influenced by outside sources (*R v. B. (A.J.)*, [1995] 2 SCR 413). To rebut an allegation of recent fabrication, it

is necessary to identify statements made prior to the existence of a motive or of circumstances leading to fabrication. In all cases, the timing of the prior consistent statements will be central to whether they are admissible.

In cross-examination, defence counsel suggested to a Crown witness that her memory of the events in question had been influenced by and constructed on the basis of things she had heard from others over time. The trial judge allowed the Crown to re-examine a witness about certain prior consistent statements to rebut this suggestion. The Supreme Court held that the prior consistent statements were not admissible for the following reason:

> [34] In this case, the statements put to Ms. Bowles on re-examination were not made prior to the atmosphere of rumour and speculation that the defence claimed had led to her changed memory. As a result, their timing prevented them from being capable of rebutting an allegation of recent fabrication. The trial judge therefore erred in ruling that the re-examination was permissible on the basis of this exception.

As you can see, the term "recent fabrication" can be somewhat misleading. The allegation need not be that the witness intentionally concocted the statement because of some motive to lie; it could be, for example, that the witness was influenced by hearing other accounts of the events or that the witness simply became confused over time. The allegation is only one of "fabrication" in the sense of having come up with an inaccurate story. Equally, the fabrication is only "recent" in the sense that it took place at some point after the events being described. What is the evidentiary or probative value of prior consistent statements admitted under this exception? Consider the following case.

R v Stirling
2008 SCC 10, [2008] 1 SCR 272
McLachlin CJ and Bastarache, Binnie, LeBel, Deschamps, Fish, Abella, Charron, and Rothstein JJ (14 March 2008)

BASTARACHE J:

[1] The appellant, Mr. Stirling, appeals his convictions on two counts of criminal negligence causing death and one count of criminal negligence causing bodily harm. The convictions arose out of a single-vehicle accident in which two of the car's occupants were killed and two others, including Mr. Stirling, were seriously injured. The primary issue before the trial judge was whether the Crown had established that the appellant, and not the other survivor of the accident, Mr. Harding, was driving the vehicle when the crash occurred. The trial judge ultimately concluded that Mr. Stirling was the driver. He based this finding on a number of pieces of evidence, including the testimony of Mr. Harding, who stated that Mr. Stirling had been driving.

[2] During the cross-examination of Mr. Harding, counsel for the appellant questioned the witness about a pending civil claim he had launched against Mr. Stirling as the driver of the vehicle and about several drug-related charges against Mr. Harding which had recently been dropped. All parties agreed that this line of questioning raised the possibility that Mr. Harding had motive to fabricate his testimony and, following a *voir dire*, the judge admitted several prior consistent statements which served to rebut that suggestion.

[3] The appellant argues on appeal that although the trial judge was correct in admitting the prior consistent statements for the purpose of refuting the suggestion of recent fabrication, he erroneously considered them for the truth of their contents. ...

[4] In my view, this appeal ought to be dismissed. Although [passages from the reasons for judgment] contain some ambiguous comments about the use the trial judge made of the prior consistent statements, these remarks must be read in the context of the reasons as a whole. It is clear from this judgment that the trial judge was very aware of the limited use of the prior consistent statements, and he correctly instructed himself on this point repeatedly.

Analysis

[5] It is well established that prior consistent statements are generally inadmissible (*R. v. Evans*, [1993] 2 S.C.R. 629; *R. v. Simpson*, [1988] 1 S.C.R. 3; *R. v. Béland*, [1987] 2 S.C.R. 398). This is because such statements are usually viewed as lacking probative value and being self-serving (*Evans*, at p. 643). There are, however, several exceptions to this general exclusionary rule, and one of these exceptions is that prior consistent statements can be admitted where it has been suggested that a witness has recently fabricated portions of his or her evidence (*Evans*, at p. 643; *Simpson*, at pp. 22-23). Admission on the basis of this exception does not require that an allegation of recent fabrication be expressly made—it is sufficient that the circumstances of the case reveal that the "apparent position of the opposing party is that there has been a prior contrivance" (*Evans*, at p. 643). It is also not necessary that a fabrication be particularly "recent," as the issue is not the recency of the fabrication but rather whether the witness made up a false story at some point after the event that is the subject of his or her testimony actually occurred (*R. v. O'Connor* (1995), 100 C.C.C. (3d) 285 (Ont. C.A.), at pp. 294-95). Prior consistent statements have probative value in this context where they can illustrate that the witness's story was the same even before a motivation to fabricate arose.

[6] In this case, the parties do not dispute that the trial judge was correct to admit Mr. Harding's prior consistent statements. The cross-examination of this witness included questions about both a civil lawsuit he had pending against Mr. Stirling as the driver of the vehicle and the relationship between his testimony and criminal charges against him which had recently been dropped. Given these questions, it was appropriate for the judge to admit statements made prior to the launching of the civil suit and prior to the dropping of the charges because these statements, if consistent with the in-court testimony, could demonstrate that Mr. Harding's evidence was not motivated by either of these factors.

[7] However, a prior consistent statement that is admitted to rebut the suggestion of recent fabrication continues to lack any probative value beyond showing that the witness's story did not change as a result of a new motive to fabricate. Importantly, it is impermissible to assume that because a witness has made the same statement in the past, he or she is more likely to be telling the truth, and any admitted prior consistent statements should not be assessed for the truth of their contents. As was noted in *R. v. Divitaris* (2004), 188 C.C.C. (3d) 390 (Ont. C.A.), at para. 28, "a concocted statement, repeated on more than one occasion, remains concocted"; see also J. Sopinka, S.N. Lederman and A.W. Bryant, *The Law of Evidence in Canada* (2nd ed. 1999), at p. 313. This case illustrates the importance of this point. The fact that Mr. Harding reported that the appellant was driving on

the night of the crash before he launched the civil suit or had charges against him dropped does not in any way confirm that that evidence is not fabricated. All it tells us is that it wasn't fabricated *as a result of* the civil suit or the dropping of the criminal charges. There thus remains the very real possibility that the evidence was fabricated immediately after the accident when, as the trial judge found, "any reasonable person would recognize there was huge liability facing the driver" (Ruling on *voir dire*, June 21, 2005, at para. 24). The reality is that even when Mr. Harding made his very first comments about who was driving when the accident occurred, he already had a visible motive to fabricate—to avoid the clear consequences which faced the driver of the vehicle—and this potential motive is not in any way rebutted by the consistency of his story. It was therefore necessary for the trial judge to avoid using Mr. Harding's prior statements for the truth of their contents.

[8] It is clear from the reasons of the trial judge that he was aware of the limited value of Mr. Harding's prior statements. Not only did he acknowledge that this witness had a motive to fabricate immediately after the accident occurred (and thus before any statements were made about who was driving), but he also stated explicitly, on several occasions, that he had not considered the statements for the truth of their contents ... .

. . .

[10] In my view, the submission that the trial judge erroneously used the prior consistent statements to bolster Harding's "general" credibility must fail. As has been discussed, prior consistent statements have the impact of removing a potential motive to lie, and the trial judge is entitled to consider removal of this motive when assessing the witness's credibility.

. . .

[17] For the reasons above, I would dismiss this appeal.

As you read in the extracts from *Ellard*, above, an allegation of recent fabrication is often made expressly in cross-examination, but it can also be implicit. It is sufficient if "in light of the circumstances of the case and the conduct of the trial, the apparent position of the opposing party is that there has been a prior contrivance" (*R v Evans*, [1993] 2 SCR 629 at 643). For examples of cases involving an implied allegation of recent fabrication sufficient to trigger this exception, see *R v Giraldi* (1975), 28 CCC (2d) 248 (BCCA); and *R v B (AJ)*, [1995] 2 SCR 413.

PRIOR CONSISTENT STATEMENTS AND "RECENT COMPLAINT" IN SEXUAL OFFENCES

Historically, in cases involving sexual offences, the Crown was permitted, *even in the absence of an allegation of recent fabrication*, to adduce evidence that the complainant had made a swift and early complaint. Why were such prior consistent statements so easily admissible? In *Kribs v R*, [1960] SCR 400 at 405-6, Fauteaux J gave the following account of the underlying rationale for this practice:

> The principle is one of necessity. It is founded on factual presumptions which, in the normal course of events, naturally attach to the subsequent conduct of the prosecutrix shortly after the occurrence of the alleged acts of violence. One of these presumptions is that she is expected to complain upon the first reasonable opportunity, and the other, consequential thereto, is that if

she fails to do so, her silence may naturally be taken as a virtual self-contradiction of her story. In Hawkins' Pleas of the Crown, quoted by Hawkins J. in the *Lillyman* case ... [*R v Lillyman* (1869), 2 QB 167], at page 170, it is said:

> It is a strong, but not a conclusive, presumption against a woman that she made no complaint in a reasonable time after the fact.
>
> ...
>
> Thus it appears that by giving evidence of her conduct shortly after the alleged occurrence, the prosecutrix does not, in a sense, enhance or confirm her story any more than she does in reciting all that she did in resistance to the assault, but she rebuts a presumption and, in doing so, adds, for all practical purposes, a virtually essential complement to her story.

In essence, the common law presumed that a woman who did not, at the first opportunity, complain of a sexual assault was not credible. According to this doctrine of "recent complaint," if no such complaint could be shown, trial judges were required to instruct the jury to draw an adverse inference regarding the veracity of the complainant's story. In *R v Boyce* (1975), 7 OR (2d) 561, 23 CCC (2d) 16 at 33-34 (CA), Martin JA explained as follows:

> Since it is universally conceded that the failure to complain at the first reasonable opportunity is a circumstance which tells against the truthfulness of the complainant's evidence, it follows logically that the jury should be instructed as to the inference they may draw from the complainant's failure to so complain ... .

This presumption dictated that the Crown be permitted to lead evidence of the complainant's prior consistent statement, made immediately following the alleged attack. At the same time, the common law definition of a recent complaint was quite restrictive, so that not all statements made after a rape or indecent assault would be admissible under this exception.

In 1983, the *Criminal Code* was amended to provide, in s 275, that "[t]he rules relating to evidence of recent complaint in [specified sexual assault offences] are hereby abrogated." The ambiguity of this provision generated uncertainty. Did the provision merely preclude the Crown from leading evidence of recent complaint in anticipation that the defence would allege recent fabrication? Did the provision preclude the trier of fact from drawing an adverse inference from a complainant's delay in making a complaint? Or did it mean that evidence of the timing of a complaint would never be admissible?

In *R v DD*, 2000 SCC 43, [2000] 2 SCR 275, Major J, writing for the majority of the court, reviewed the rationales for the doctrine of recent complaint found in the early common law, including the court's decision in *Kribs*, cited above, and explained the impact of s 275. He concluded as follows:

> [62] Today and for some time, the rationale in *Kribs* has been repeatedly subjected to criticism, is not followed, and has been overruled. The *Report of the Federal/Provincial Task Force on Uniform Rules of Evidence* (1982), at p. 301, as cited by Sopinka, Lederman and Bryant ... [*The Law of Evidence in Canada* (2nd ed 1999)], at p. 322, states:
>
> > The expectations of medieval England as to the reaction of an innocent victim of a sexual attack are no longer relevant. A victim may have a genuine complaint but delay making it because of such legitimate concerns as the prospect of embarrassment and humiliation, or the destruction of domestic or personal relationships. The delay may also be attributable to the youth or lack of knowledge of the complainant or to threats of reprisal from

the accused. In contemporary society, there is no longer a logical connection between the genuineness of a complaint and the promptness with which it is made.

In response to this criticism, Parliament chose to abrogate the authority of *Kribs* and *Timm* [*Timm v R*, [1981] 2 SCR 315] by statute (see s. 275 of the *Criminal Code*, R.S.C., 1985, c. C-46).

[63] Application of the mistake reflected in the early common law now constitutes reversible error. See *R. v. W. (R.)*, [1992] 2 S.C.R. 122, *per* McLachlin J. (as she then was) at p. 136:

> Finally, the Court of Appeal relied on the fact that neither of the older children was "aware or concerned that anything untoward occurred which is really the best test of the quality of the acts." This reference reveals reliance on the stereotypical but suspect view that the victims of sexual aggression are likely to report the acts, a stereotype which found expression in the now discounted doctrine of recent complaint. In fact, the literature suggests the converse may be true; victims of abuse often in fact do not disclose it, and if they do, it may not be until a substantial length of time has passed.

The significance of the complainant's failure to make a timely complaint *must not* be the subject of any presumptive adverse inference based upon now rejected stereotypical assumptions of how persons (particularly children) react to acts of sexual abuse: *R. v. M. (P.S.)* (1992), 77 C.C.C. (3d) 402 (Ont. C.A.), at pp. 408-9; *R. v. T.E.M.* (1996), 187 A.R. 273 (C.A.).

• • •

[65] A trial judge should recognize and so instruct a jury that there is no inviolable rule on how people who are the victims of trauma like a sexual assault will behave. Some will make an immediate complaint, some will delay in disclosing the abuse, while some will never disclose the abuse. Reasons for delay are many and at least include embarrassment, fear, guilt, or a lack of understanding and knowledge. In assessing the credibility of a complainant, the timing of the complaint is simply one circumstance to consider in the factual mosaic of a particular case. A delay in disclosure, standing alone, will never give rise to an adverse inference against the credibility of the complainant.

Accordingly, no presumptive adverse inference arises solely by virtue of the failure of a complainant to make an early complaint. The timing of a complaint is relevant, but merely as one consideration to be taken into account when assessing the credibility of a complainant, and that assessment must be done free of stereotypical assumptions. Moreover, consistent with principles discussed earlier in this section, evidence of a "recent complaint" will still be admissible in the form of a prior consistent statement if the defence alleges recent fabrication (*R v O'Connor* (1995), 25 OR (3d) 19, 100 CCC (3d) 285 (CA); *R v Owens* (1986), 55 CR (3d) 386 (Ont CA)).

4. *Prior Consistent Statements of the Accused*

It is clear that if the accused testifies and the Crown implicitly or explicitly alleges that his or her testimony is recently fabricated, the accused's prior consistent statement is admissible, just as it would be for any other witness: see e.g. *R v Giraldi* (1975), 28 CCC (2d) 248 (BCCA) (where the statement was admitted); *R v Campbell* (1977), 17 OR (2d) 673 (CA) (where the statement was excluded). But what if the Crown does not allege recent fabrication? To what extent, and under what conditions, is a statement of the accused, protesting his or her innocence or offering an explanation, admissible as a prior consistent statement? And what is the probative value of such statements? In considering these questions, it is important to bear in mind that the Crown may, if it chooses, put these statements into evidence as party admissions (see Chapter 4), subject to the common law confessions rule and the Charter (see Chapter 8). But if the Crown chooses not to do so, are such statements admissible at the instance of the defence?

For many years, there has been authority from the Supreme Court of Canada indicating that statements made by an accused when found in possession of stolen goods or illegal drugs were admissible, though they take the form of self-serving prior consistent statements. In *R v Graham*, [1974] SCR 206, a case involving possession of stolen property, Ritchie J held at 213-14 as follows:

> [T]he respondent's verbal statement made when the attaché case was found, that he had never seen it before in his life, being one which was immediately connected with the initial discovery of the stolen goods, was properly admitted in evidence. Explanatory statements made by an accused upon his first being found "in possession" constitute a part of the *res gestae* and are necessarily admissible in any description of the circumstances under which the crime was committed ... .

The court confirmed this approach, admitting explanatory statements made by the accused when he was found in possession of narcotics, in *R v Risby*, [1978] 2 SCR 139. One understanding of this rule is that these statements are permitted as a response to a tacit allegation of recent fabrication: one fears that a finder of fact might expect an innocent accused to immediately offer an explanation if the possession is, in fact, innocent; if the defence can point to the explanatory statements made by the accused immediately upon being found in possession, he should be permitted to offer those to rebut this natural inference. And yet the court did not appear to limit the use of these statements to rebutting such an inference— these statements seemed to be admissible for the proof of their contents.

In the following case, the Ontario Court of Appeal took a fresh look at prior consistent statements made by an accused, and crafted a new, general exception.

R v Edgar
2010 ONCA 529, 101 OR (3d) 161
Feldman, Sharpe, and Gillese JJA (23 July 2010)

SHARPE JA:

[1] The appellant was convicted in 1996 of second degree murder in the stabbing death of his girlfriend, Tracey Kelsh. In January 2000, this court allowed his appeal from that conviction and ordered a new trial: (2000), 142 C.C.C. (3d) 401. In October 2001, after a three-week jury trial, the appellant was acquitted of murder but convicted of manslaughter. The Crown initiated a dangerous offender proceeding and, after a lengthy hearing, the trial judge designated the appellant a dangerous offender and sentenced him to indeterminate custody.

[2] The appellant appeals both the conviction and the dangerous offender designation. The central issue on the appeal from conviction is whether the trial judge erred by refusing to admit, in their entirety, out-of-court statements made by the appellant shortly after his arrest. ...

. . .

[24] For the following reasons, I conclude that the spontaneous exculpatory statements made by an accused person upon or shortly after arrest may be admitted as an exception to the general rule excluding prior consistent statements for the purpose of showing the reaction of the accused when first confronted with the accusation, provided the accused testifies and thereby exposes himself or herself to cross-examination.

(d) Rationale for the Traditional Exclusionary Rule

[25] An inculpatory statement of an accused person made outside of court is admissible against the accused as a confession (an admission against interest), provided that that it is compliant with the *Canadian Charter of Rights and Freedoms* and voluntary when made to a person in authority.

[26] Conversely, exculpatory out-of-court statements made by an accused person are generally considered inadmissible, although this rule is subject to many exceptions.

[Sharpe JA reviewed the rationales for this traditional exclusionary rule, including that "[e]xclusion of the prior consistent statements of the accused is ... viewed as a product of the rule against oath-helping or adducing evidence solely for the purpose of bolstering a witness's credibility" (para 34).]

(e) Exceptions to the Traditional Rule

[35] It is well recognized, however, that the prior consistent statements of an accused are not always excluded. Two established exceptions have already been mentioned. First, where an accused's prior consistent statement is relevant to his or her state of mind at the time the offence was committed, it may be admitted. Second, where the Crown alleges recent fabrication, the accused may adduce evidence of a prior consistent statement to rebut the allegation. A third exception is made for "mixed" statements that are partly inculpatory and partly exculpatory. Where the Crown seeks to adduce evidence of such a statement, the inculpatory portion is admissible as an admission against interest and, as a matter of fairness to the accused, the Crown is required to tender the entire statement, with the exculpatory portion being substantively admissible in favour of the accused: *Rojas* [*R v Rojas*, [2008] 3 SCR 111], at para. 37. A fourth exception is that the prior statement will be admitted where it forms part of the *res gestae*, in other words, where the statement itself forms part of the incident that gives rise to the charge: see *Graham* [*R v Graham*, [1974] SCR 206]; *R. v. Risby*, [1978] 2 S.C.R. 139.

[36] This list of exceptions is not exhaustive. In *Simpson* [*R v Simpson*, [1988] 1 SCR 3], the Supreme Court of Canada stated, at p. 22, that general exclusion of the prior consistent statements of an accused person is "not an inflexible rule, and in proper circumstances such statements may be admissible."

[37] In view of what the Supreme Court stated in *Simpson*, I approach the issue of whether the law does or should recognize the admissibility exception being advocated in this case on the basis of both existing authority and the general propositions advanced in *Seaboyer* [*R v Seaboyer; R v Gayme*, [1991] 2 SCR 577], at pp. 609-10. If the statements are relevant and probative, they should be admitted: "everything which is probative should be received, unless its exclusion can be justified on some other ground." Rules of evidence that prevent the trier of fact from getting at the truth "[run] afoul of our fundamental

conceptions of justice and what constitutes a fair trial," unless they can be justified on "a clear ground of policy or law."

[38] This was the approach taken in *R. v. B. (S.C.)* (1997), 36 O.R. (3d) 516 (Ont. C.A.), at p. 525, where in a jointly written judgment, Doherty and Rosenberg JJ.A. referred to the general rule that an accused's prior consistent statement is inadmissible "because it has very limited, if any, probative value and serves to expand unnecessarily the ambit of the trial inquiry." However, they went on to hold, at p. 526, that

> [t]he admissibility of after-the-fact conduct by an accused to support an inference that the accused did not commit the crime alleged should be approached on a principled basis. If the evidence is relevant, its probative value is not substantially outweighed by its prejudicial effect and it is not excluded by some policy-driven exclusionary rule, the evidence should be received when proffered by the defence.

[39] Application of this principle led them to conclude that evidence should be admitted that upon arrest the accused had, before consulting counsel, done several things from which innocence might be inferred. Knowing he faced an allegation of sexual assault, the accused volunteered to take a polygraph test (an act explicitly held to be inadmissible into evidence, on its own), provided samples of his clothing and his blood, scalp hair and pubic hair, scrapings from his fingernails, all while knowing that these samples would be forensically tested. Doherty and Rosenberg JJ.A. concluded, at p. 527, that "[a]s a matter of logic and human experience, a trier of fact could conclude that the [accused's] conduct after his arrest was inconsistent with that of a person who had committed the crime alleged." ...

[40] In my view, applying the *Seaboyer* and *B. (S.C.)* approach to the present case, the admissibility of the statements made by the appellant at the time of his arrest is supportable. It is also my view that, upon a fair reading, existing authorities support that result.

(f) Statements Made by an Accused When First Confronted with an Accusation

[41] The proposition that spontaneous exculpatory statements made by an accused person when first confronted by the police with an accusation, or upon arrest, are probative and should, therefore, be admitted enjoys considerable support in the case law.

[Sharpe JA then reviewed a number of English and Canadian authorities in support of this proposition, arriving at the following conclusion:]

• • •

[66] If a statement has probative value, it should only be excluded if there are sound reasons of law or policy to do so. In my view, the various rationales offered for exclusion simply do not warrant the imposition of a blanket exclusionary rule.

[67] The rule against oath-helping does no more than re-state the need for evidence to have probative value. If evidence fails to add anything new, repetition is less than helpful. However, where an accused makes a spontaneous statement in the face of an accusation or arrest for a crime, something is added. The reaction of the accused in such circumstances may yield persuasive evidence of innocence, which has quite a different quality than the accused's testimony given months or years later in the formal proceedings of the courtroom.

[68] I find the cases cited above entirely persuasive on the point that the hearsay rationale for exclusion of a prior consistent statement evaporates where the accused takes the stand and exposes himself or herself to cross-examination.

[69] I am also of the opinion that too much is easily made of the risk of fabrication. To assert blindly that all statements made by an accused person upon arrest are fatally tainted with self-interest and the motivation to lie assumes guilt and runs counter to the presumption of innocence: see James H. Chadbourn, *Wigmore on Evidence*, vol. 2, rev. ed. (Toronto: Little, Brown & Co., 1979), at §293, cited in S. Casey Hill et al. [*McWilliams' Canadian Criminal Evidence*, vol 1, 4th ed (Aurora, Ont: Canada Law Book, 2003) (loose-leaf)], at paras. 11:40.40.30. As discussed below at para. 97 of these reasons, this assertion is also contrary to the discouragement of jury directions counselling caution with respect to the evidence of an accused because of self-interest and motivation to say what it takes to secure an acquittal. The risk of fabrication can be dealt with more directly and precisely through cross-examination and by looking to the degree of spontaneity the proffered statement exhibits. Statements that are lacking in spontaneity may be either excluded or, in the case of doubt, made the subject of an instruction to the jury as to weight by the trial judge.

[70] Trial efficiency is an important factor generally but rarely, if ever, will it justify the exclusion of relevant, probative evidence that could lead the trier of fact to acquit.

[71] In my view, it is time to abandon what David Tanovich has described as the "myth" that exculpatory statements made upon arrest are inadmissible except to the extent that they bear upon state of mind or rebut an allegation of recent fabrication: "In the Name of Innocence: Using Supreme Court of Canada Evidence Jurisprudence to Protect Against Wrongful Convictions" (Paper presented to the Ontario Criminal Lawyers' Association Criminal Law in a Changing World Conference, Toronto, 8 November 2003) [unpublished].

[72] I conclude, therefore, that it is open to a trial judge to admit an accused's spontaneous out-of-court statements made upon arrest or when first confronted with an accusation as an exception to the general rule excluding prior consistent statements as evidence of the reaction of the accused to the accusation and as proof of consistency, provided the accused takes the stand and exposes himself or herself to cross-examination. As the English cases cited above hold, the statement of the accused is not strictly evidence of the truth of what was said (subject to being admissible under the principled approach to hearsay evidence) but is evidence of the reaction of the accused, which is relevant to the credibility of the accused and as circumstantial evidence that may have a bearing on guilt or innocence.

[Because Edgar had asked the trial judge to admit these statements before he took the stand, and given the low probative value of these statements on the facts of this case, Sharpe JA dismissed the appeal.]

What is the probative value of statements led under the *Edgar* approach? As you can see, this new and broad exception to the rule prohibiting prior consistent statements depends on two conditions: (1) that the accused "takes the stand and exposes himself or herself to cross-examination"; and (2) that the accused's statements were "spontaneous." Why are these two conditions important?

In *R v Badhwar*, 2011 ONCA 266, Moldaver JA confirmed this new exception as articulated by Sharpe JA in *Edgar*, but declined to apply it on the facts of the case because the prior consistent statement of the accused lacked spontaneity. The accused had been involved in a fatal street racing accident. It was only five hours later that he was contacted by the police, attended at the police station, and gave his explanatory statement. Given this delay the accused had time to "think things out" and talk with his friends before speaking with the police (at para 21).

For an analysis of the *Edgar* decision and the exception that it created, see Benjamin L Berger, "Reasoning with Inferences: Themes from Prior Consistent Statements and Trace Evidence" (2012) 92 CR (6th) 254.

5. Narrative

In some instances, the unfolding of events will simply not cohere or make sense without reference to prior statements made by a witness. Though these statements are prior consistent statements, their necessity in allowing the finder of fact to understand and evaluate the story allows their admission under the "narrative" exception. *R v George* (1985), 23 CCC (3d) 42 (BCCA) provides a helpful example. In that case, the Crown was permitted to lead evidence that the complainant had told her grandmother and parents that her cousin had sexually assaulted her. Though a prior consistent statement, and though it did not fit any of the exceptions that we have considered, it was admissible because it was necessary in order to understand why the parents had confronted the accused, leading to his admission. Without the prior consistent statement of the complainant, the unfolding and sequence of events would not have made sense. The prior consistent statement was, accordingly, admitted as part of the narrative.

In the context of a child sexual assault case, in *R v F (JE)* (1993), 16 OR (3d) 1, 85 CCC (3d) 457 at 472-76 (CA), Finlayson JA explained this exception, and the permissible uses of such narrative statements, as follows:

> It seems to me that the court should look to narrative as an exception to the rule against the admission of previous consistent statements for a more hopeful approach to this vexing problem of the evidence of children in sexual assault cases. It must be a part of the narrative in the sense that it advances the story from offence to prosecution or explains why so little was done to terminate the abuse or bring the perpetrator to justice. Specifically, it appears to me to be part of the narrative of a complainant's testimony when she recounts the assaults, how they came to be terminated, and how the matter came to the attention of the police.

> • • •

> [T]he admission of the previous consistent statements in this case takes into account the rationale for the rule prohibiting the admissibility of such statements. First, as noted in *R v. George* (1985), 23 CCC (3d) 42, the complaints are not admissible for the truth of their contents, but only for the fact of their existence. In those circumstances, it is not necessary for the jury's understanding of the unfolding of events that it be apprised of the content of the statements made although it is always open to the defence to explore the content if it feels that this will be to the

advantage of the accused. Unless the nature of the complaint becomes controversial at the instance of the defence, it is not what the complainant says that is important, but the fact that she said it. Since these out-of-court statements are not admissible to prove the truth of their contents, they are not considered hearsay and the first aspect of the rationale for the inadmissibility of out-of-court statements does not apply.

The second aspect of the rationale for the rule against admitting previous consistent statements is that such evidence has little, if any, probative value. However, narrative is justified as providing background to the story—to provide chronological cohesion and eliminate gaps which would divert the mind of the listener from the central issue. It may be supportive of the central allegation in the sense of creating a logical framework for its presentation—but it cannot be used, and the jury must be warned of this, as confirmation of the truthfulness of the sworn allegation.

. . .

To summarize ... To qualify as narrative, the witness must recount relevant and essential facts which describe and explain his or her experience as a victim of the crime alleged so that the trier of fact will be in a position to understand what happened and how the matter came to the attention of the proper authorities. In all cases where evidence is admitted under the rubric of prior consistent statements, the trial judge is obliged to instruct the jury as to the limited value of the evidence. The fact that the statements were made is admissible to assist the jury as to the sequence of events from the alleged offence to the prosecution so that they can understand the conduct of the complainant and assess her truthfulness. However, the jury must be instructed that they are not to look to the content of the statements as proof that a crime has been committed.

In *R v Dinardo*, 2008 SCC 24, [2008] 1 SCR 788, the accused was charged with sexual assault and sexual exploitation of a person with a disability. The complainant, who was mentally challenged, alleged that the accused, a taxi driver, had touched her sexually several times during a taxi ride from her residence to a *Maison des jeunes*. There were some serious frailties in the complainant's evidence; at one point, she testified that she may have made up the allegation. The Crown also called four witnesses who testified about the statements that the complainant had made around the time of the alleged assault. The trial judge convicted the accused. Charron J summarized the trial judge's use of the complainant's prior consistent statements as follows:

> [17] The trial judge then considered the complainant's credibility. He did not refer to the evidence that the complainant, by her own admission, had a tendency to lie. Rather, he observed only that [TRANSLATION] "[w]hen cross-examined by counsel for the accused, she never contradicted herself on important facts, only on certain details that the Court does not consider important enough for the contradictions to affect her credibility" (para. 70). He placed significant emphasis on the fact that the complainant's version of the events was consistent, noting that [TRANSLATION] "in this case, there is a form of corroboration in the facts and statements of the victim, who never contradicted herself" (para. 68). He also noted that the complainant's statement was made spontaneously upon her arrival at the Maison des jeunes. The accused was convicted of both offences.

The accused's appeal to the Quebec Court of Appeal was dismissed. His further appeal to the Supreme Court of Canada was allowed and a new trial ordered. Charron J, for a unanimous court, held that the trial judge's use of the complainant's prior consistent statements was an error requiring a new trial:

[36] As a general rule, prior consistent statements are inadmissible (*R v. Stirling*, [2008] 1 SCR 272, 2008 SCC 10). There are two primary justifications for the exclusion of such statements: first, they lack probative value (*Stirling*, at para. 5), and second, they constitute hearsay when adduced for the truth of their contents.

[37] In some circumstances, prior consistent statements may be admissible as part of the narrative. Once admitted, the statements may be used for the limited purpose of helping the trier of fact to understand how the complainant's story was initially disclosed. The challenge is to distinguish between "using narrative evidence for the impermissible purpose of 'confirm[ing] the truthfulness of the sworn allegation'" and "using narrative evidence for the permissible purpose of showing the fact and timing of a complaint, which may then *assist the trier of fact in the assessment* of truthfulness or credibility": *McWilliams's Canadian Criminal Evidence* (4th ed. (loose-leaf)), at pp. 11-44 and 11-45 (emphasis in original); see also *R v. F. (J.E.)* (1993), 85 C.C.C. (3d) 457 (Ont. C.A.), at p. 476).

[38] In *R v. G.C.*, [2006] OJ No. 2245 (QL), the Ontario Court of Appeal noted that the prior consistent statements of a complainant may assist the court in assessing the complainant's likely truthfulness, particularly in cases involving allegations of sexual assault against children. As Rouleau JA explained, for a unanimous court:

> Although properly admitted at trial, the evidence of prior complaint cannot be used as a form of self-corroboration to prove that the incident in fact occurred. It cannot be used as evidence of the truth of its contents. However, the evidence can "*be supportive of the central allegation in the sense of creating a logical framework for its presentation*," as set out above, *and can be used in assessing the truthfulness of the complainant*. As set out in *R v. F. (J.E.)* at p. 476:
>
> > The fact that the statements were made is admissible to assist the jury as to the sequence of events from the alleged offence to the prosecution so that they can understand the conduct of the complainant and assess her truthfulness. However, the jury must be instructed that they are not to look to the content of the statements as proof that a crime has been committed.
>
> . . .

[39] The Ontario Court of Appeal's reasoning in *G.C.* applies equally to the facts of this case. The complainant's prior consistent statements were not admissible under any of the traditional hearsay exceptions. Thus, the statements could not be used to confirm her in-court testimony. However, in light of the evidence that the complainant had difficulty situating events in time, was easily confused, and lied on occasion, the spontaneous nature of the initial complaint and the complainant's repetition of the essential elements of the allegations provide important context for assessing her credibility.

[40] The Court of Appeal correctly concluded that the trial judge erred when he considered the contents of the complainant's prior consistent statements to corroborate her testimony at trial, noting in his judgment that [TRANSLATION] "there is a form of corroboration in the facts and statements of the victim, who never contradicted herself" (para. 68). I am unable to agree with the majority, however, that the accused suffered no prejudice from the trial judge's improper use of the statements. The trial judge relied heavily on the corroborative value of the complainant's

prior statements in convicting Mr. Dinardo. He was clearly of the view that the complainant's consistency in recounting the allegations made her story more credible. Accordingly, I would also allow the appeal on this basis.

As you can see, statements admitted under the narrative exception cannot be used for their truth, thereby confirming a witness's in-court testimony; however, inasmuch that they clarify and help to present the unfolding of events, they can assist in the assessment of credibility. Do you think that this distinction is sustainable and supportable in practice?

Though potentially broad, there are limits to the reach of the narrative exception. Consider the following case.

R v Murphy
2014 YKCA 7
Bauman CJYT, Donald and Cooper JJA (11 June 2014)

DONALD JA:

Introduction

[1] Evangeline Billy died by drowning in the Yukon River at Whitehorse on 21 June 2008. Alicia Ann Murphy, the appellant, was charged with her second degree murder. On 27 October 2009, a jury at Whitehorse found her guilty as charged.

[2] She appeals from her conviction and seeks a new trial on several grounds, including that the prosecution engaged in oath-helping two key witnesses and led inadmissible evidence of the police investigation. I would give effect to these allegations, allow the appeal, and order a new trial.

. . .

Discussion

Ground B—Oath-Helping

[5] The problems arising from this ground ... result from an approach taken by the prosecution at trial that enlarged the notion of "narrative" as a basis for admissibility of evidence of the police investigation. How the police took the evidence of the key admission witnesses, their impressions of the witnesses' statements, the lead investigator's methodology in conducting the investigation overall, and his working theories as to the crime scene and cause of death, were not led in response to any challenge to the integrity of the investigation by the defence, but out of a desire to enhance the Crown's case.

[6] This is an impermissible strategy. The respondent's stated purpose for calling evidence surrounding the taking of statements from Tanya Murphy and Rae Lynne Gartner was to make their testimony more reliable. The evidence of their initial dealings with the police was not only irrelevant, in the sense that there was no fact in issue, but it violated the rule against oath-helping.

[7] As to the prosecution's purpose, this is what the prosecutor said in his closing address to the jury about Tanya Murphy's evidence:

Consider the timing of Tanya Murphy's statement to the police. First of all, she didn't go to the police with this. The police came to Tanya Murphy after the fact, after they had heard from Rae Lynne Gartner. This was another part of their investigation, to go to Tanya Murphy and find out if she knew anything about this. And so it was a statement which was given by Tanya Murphy to the police very shortly after the meeting between her and her sister. She was at the detachment. You heard Constable Corbett testify about what Tanya Murphy's demeanour was as she was providing that information to the police. It was very difficult for Tanya Murphy. This wasn't some sort of lark or anything of that nature.

and as to Rae Lynne Gartner's evidence:

Rae Lynne talked about how she hung around for a period of time, didn't want to attract attention to herself, just was trying to figure out how do I get myself away from this woman. And that eventually she left and immediately went, called her friend, asked to be picked up. Rae Lynne said she was hysterical at that time. And wouldn't she be? She then talked about call [*sic*] 9-1-1 and speaking with Constable Thur, about being extremely emotional. And again, wouldn't she be?

   And that was corroborated by Constable Thur in his testimony. He said that when he first talked to her on the telephone she was extremely emotional, and that she continued to be that way during his initial interview of her, and then later, when they were speaking to her some more, she calmed down. *But all of that evidence offered by Constable Thur, and the reason for those questions to Rae Lynne Gartner about how she was feeling at the time of this, are—were asked because that's all part of the narrative. That's part of the story.* And when you're looking at what she says Alicia has said to her, you can look at the way that the story came out, in *assessing whether Rae Lynne Gartner's evidence is reliable. And I say that, because of the way that the story was told, it's clearly reliable.*

[Emphasis added.]

[8]   The "story" to which counsel referred had no probative value. Had the defence raised police misconduct, such as bullying or other oppressive conduct, then the inter-action of the witnesses with the police would have had some relevance; but in any event it could not have been used to bolster the Crown's case, only to answer some point taken by the defence. No such allegation arose. What the witnesses said to the police, their demeanour, emotional condition and cooperativeness, should have had nothing to do with their testimony at trial, yet it was used to make the evidence more reliable.

NOTES AND QUESTIONS

Read ss 715.1 and 715.2 of the *Criminal Code* (see "Questions on the Principled Approach" in Chapter 4, Section III.B). These provisions allow a judge to admit into evidence "a video recording made within a reasonable time after the alleged offence, in which the victim or witness describes the acts complained of" if a victim or witness under the age of 18, or a wit-ness with a mental or physical disability, takes the stand and simply adopts the contents of that video statement. Under what conditions would these sections operate as a statutory exception to the rule against prior consistent statements?

C. Expert Evidence

It is for the trier of fact to assess the credibility of witnesses, but the trier (whether judge or jury) may require expert assistance to evaluate the credibility of a witness to whom common principles of credibility assessment may not apply. If that expert opinion evidence meets the requirements set out in Chapter 5, it might be admissible as an exception to the general rule against oath-helping. In such circumstances, there is concern that the expert should not be asked to express an opinion on the credibility of the particular witness, but only to explain the special phenomena that the trier of fact should take into account in making the assessment.

The following cases explore the boundaries of this exception, while also explaining the general rule against oath-helping.

R v Kyselka

[1962] OWN 164 (CA)

Porter CJO, Kelly, and McLennan JJA (30 May 1962)

[The three accused were charged with raping a young girl, who was described by the court as "16 years of age and mentally retarded." The only issue was whether the complainant had consented; she testified that she had not.]

PORTER CJO: ... Objection was taken by counsel for the accused on this appeal that certain evidence given by Dr. Cardwell was inadmissible. Dr. Cardwell is a qualified psychiatrist, who has worked for the Department of Health in mental hospitals for 31 years, and is now retired. He was called as a witness by the Crown immediately after the complainant gave her evidence. He had examined the complainant as to her mental capacity. The relevant portions of his evidence are as follows:

A. The first time I saw Margaret was on September 7th at my home. A constable brought her, accompanied by her mother. Her mother and she and I sat and talked together. Q. Did you form any opinion, or make any tests at that time? A. Well, this girl reached Grade 6 at fifteen after having repeated a number of grades up to Grade 6, so that she landed at Grade 6, which is about her ability. She was sixteen last June 10th. As far as I know, she has lived at home, and helped her mother with the work and has never gone out to work. Q. Did you determine her IQ? A. I would give her an IQ of under 60. Q. That is .6? A. With a mental age of between ten and eleven, nearer ten than eleven. Q. I see. What is your experience with these type of people? You say you have spent most of your life working, with your work, with them. What is your experience with respect to them, and the situation you have seen her go through, that is, giving testimony? A. Well, from my experience, and in asking the mother some questions, my experience has been that these children—that is all they are—are honest, easily led, and they can tell us a story in their simple way without elaborating very much. And I listened to Margaret tell her story this morning, and I thought she did remarkably well. Q. What about the ability to fabricate stories with these persons? A. In this type of case, with that degree of intelligence, they are not imaginative enough to concoct stories. Q. They lack imagination? A. They lack imagination. MR. BURBIDGE: Would you think an ordinary individual dealing with Margaret would quickly come to realize her disability? A. I think it was quite apparent in the witness box today.

The purpose of such evidence was clearly to suggest that the witness was because of her mental classification, likely to be a truthful person. The Crown relied upon the case of *Fisher v. The Queen*, 130 CCC 1, [1961] SCR 525. In that case the Supreme Court of Canada held, affirming the judgment of the Court of Appeal, that it was open to the Crown in a prosecution for murder where drunkenness negativing the intent to kill was the main defence to adduce evidence from a psychiatrist to show that the accused had the capacity to form the specific intent to kill. The accused had made a statement to the police which was admitted in evidence. The statement was the accused's version of his course of conduct and actions throughout the evening of the murder. The incidents described in this statement were put to the witness in the form of a hypothetical question. In answer to this question the witness stated that in his opinion, on the assumed state of facts contained in the question, that the accused was capable of forming the intent to kill.

The *Fisher* case is clearly distinguishable from the case at bar. In the former the evidence was introduced by Crown with reference to the accused and was directed to the proof of capacity to form at the material time the intent which was an essential ingredient of the crime charged. In the case at bar the evidence was led by the Crown with reference to the Crown's *own* witness and while based upon capacity, its primary and only function was to bolster up the credibility of the witness by evidence that she was or was likely to be a truthful person. It was not directed to an issue in the crime charged as it was in the *Fisher* case but only to the weight to be attached to the witness's evidence.

While the credit of any witness may be *impeached* by the *opposite party*: *R v. Gunewardene*, [1951] 2 All ER 290 at p. 294, there is no warrant or authority for such oath-helping as occurred in the circumstances of this case, reminiscent as it is of the method before the Norman Conquest by which a defendant in a civil suit or an accused person proved his case by calling witnesses to swear that the oath of the party was true. If this sort of evidence were admissible in the case of either party no limit could be placed on the number of witnesses who could be called to testify about the credibility of witnesses as to facts. It would tend to produce, regardless of the number of such character witnesses who were called, undue confusion in the minds of the jury by directing their attention away from the real issues and the controversy would become so intricate that truth would be more likely to remain hidden than be discovered. For these reasons this evidence was not admissible.

R v Marquard
[1993] 4 SCR 223, 108 DLR (4th) 47
Lamer CJ and La Forest, L'Heureux-Dubé, Sopinka, Gonthier, Cory, McLachlin, Iacobucci, and Major JJ (21 October 1993)

[The facts of this case are given in Chapter 2.]

McLACHLIN J (Lamer CJ and Sopinka, Cory, Iacobucci, and Major JJ concurring): …

. . .

5. *Expert Comment on the Credibility of the Child*

The defence called Dr. Mian to prove that the child, upon arriving at Sick Children's Hospital, told the staff that she had burned herself with a lighter. The Crown, in cross-examination, elicited from Dr. Mian the opinion that the child was lying when she told her that she had burned herself with a cigarette lighter. She testified that it is quite common that children "will initially ... give the accidental explanation and later on will give us a story that is more consistent with her injury which is then put in a more convincing [manner] which we believe is the first disclosure of what actually happened." She also testified that even if the child's burn had looked like a lighter burn, she would have been suspicious of the child's story "because of the way the child used it. ...".

Dr. Mian went on to buttress her view that the child's actual explanation was a lie by reference to the behaviour of abused children:

> There's another reason [why children initially lie] which is that children who have been abused often feel that they are responsible for the behaviour that was done to them, for the injury that was inflicted on them. ... Therefore if the care taker then takes them to the hospital and they're feeling that they did something wrong to elicit this punishment, they're certainly not going to want to tell the hospital staff that they did something wrong because they feel if my mom or whoever did this to me because of what I did, I wonder what these people who are strangers are going to do to me because of what I did.

The purport of this evidence was clear. Dr. Mian was of the view that the child was lying when she told the hospital staff that she had burned herself with a lighter, and that the child's second story—the one she told at trial—was the truth.

It is a fundamental axiom of our trial process that the ultimate conclusion as to the credibility or truthfulness of a particular witness is for the trier of fact, and is not the proper subject of expert opinion. This court affirmed that proposition in *R v. Béland*, [1987] 2 SCR 398, in rejecting the use of polygraph examinations as a tool to determine the credibility of witnesses:

> From the foregoing comments, it will be seen that the rule against oath-helping, that is, adducing evidence solely for the purpose of bolstering a witness's credibility, is well grounded in authority.

A judge or jury who simply accepts an expert's opinion on the credibility of a witness would be abandoning its duty to itself determine the credibility of the witness. Credibility must always be the product of the judge or jury's view of the diverse ingredients it has perceived at trial, combined with experience, logic and an intuitive sense of the matter. See *R v. B.(G.)* (1988), 65 Sask. R 134 at p. 149 (CA), *per* Wakeling JA; affirmed [1990] 2 SCR 3. Credibility is a matter within the competence of lay people. Ordinary people draw conclusions about whether someone is lying or telling the truth on a daily basis. The expert who testifies on credibility is not sworn to the heavy duty of a judge or juror. Moreover, the expert's opinion may be founded on factors which are not in the evidence upon which the judge and juror are duty-bound to render a true verdict. Finally, credibility is a notoriously difficult problem, and the expert's opinion may be all too readily accepted by a frustrated jury as a convenient basis upon which to resolve its difficulties. All these considerations have contributed to the wise policy of the law in rejecting expert evidence on the truthfulness of witnesses.

On the other hand, there may be features of a witness's evidence which go beyond the ability of a lay person to understand, and hence which may justify expert evidence. This is particularly the case in the evidence of children. For example, the ordinary inference from failure to complain promptly about a sexual assault might be that the story is a fabricated afterthought, born of malice or some other calculated stratagem. Expert evidence has been properly led to explain the reasons why young victims of sexual abuse often do not complain immediately. Such evidence is helpful; indeed it may be essential to a just verdict.

For this reason, there is a growing consensus that while expert evidence on the ultimate credibility of a witness is not admissible, expert evidence on human conduct and the psychological and physical factors which may lead to certain behaviour relevant to credibility, is admissible, provided the testimony goes beyond the ordinary experience of the trier of fact. Professor A. Mewett describes the permissible use of this sort of evidence as "putting that witness' testimony in its proper context." He states in "Editorial—Credibility and Consistency" (1991), 33 CLQ 385 at p. 386:

> The relevance of his testimony is to assist—no more—the jury in determining whether there is an explanation for what might otherwise be regarded as conduct that is inconsistent with that of a truthful witness. It does, of course, bolster the credibility of that witness, but it is evidence of how certain people react to certain experiences. Its relevance lies not in testimony that the prior witness is telling the truth but in testimony as to human behaviour.
>
> • • •
>
> There are concerns. As the court stated in *R v. J.(F.E.)*, [(1990), 53 C.C.C. (3d) 94, 74 C.R. (3d) 269, 36 O.A.C. 348 (C.A.)], and *R v. C.(R.A.)* (1990), 57 CCC (3d) 522, 78 CR (3d) 390, the court must require that the witness be an expert in the particular area of human conduct in question; the evidence must be of the sort that the jury needs because the problem is beyond their ordinary experience; and the jury must be carefully instructed as to its function and duty in making the final decision without being unduly influenced by the expert nature of the evidence.

The conditions set out by Professor Mewett, reflecting the observations of various appellate courts which have considered the matter, recommend themselves as sound. To accept this approach is not to open the floodgates to expert testimony on whether witnesses are lying or telling the truth. It is rather to recognize that certain aspects of human behaviour which are important to the judge or jury's assessment of credibility may not be understood by the lay person and hence require elucidation by experts in human behaviour.

Had Dr. Mian confined her comments to expert evidence explaining why children may lie to hospital staff about the cause of their injuries, there could have been no objection to her evidence. She was an expert in child behaviour, and the evidence would arguably have been evidence needed by a lay jury to understand fully the implications of the witness's change in story. However, Dr. Mian went further. She clearly indicated that she personally did not believe the first story of the child, preferring the second version which the child told at trial. In so doing, she crossed the line between expert testimony on human behaviour and assessment of credibility of the witness herself. Moreover, the trial judge failed to instruct the jury that it was their duty to decide on the child's credibility without being unduly influenced by the expert evidence. In fact, the trial judge's statement that Dr. Mian gave "evidence as an expert in child abuse and relating to the truthfulness of the testimony of small children" actually reinforced the effect of the inadmissible evidence.

In my view, this error, considered with the others, requires that a new trial be directed.

. . .

L'HEUREUX-DUBÉ J (dissenting): ...

My colleague has recommended that the three conditions set out by Professor Mewett ... be adopted in cases such as this ... . I agree and find that they have been respected in this case. My colleague, however, goes on to conclude that Dr. Mian's evidence crossed the boundary of permissible expert opinion and usurped the function of the jury in determining the credibility of Debbie-Ann. Here I must disagree.

It is important here to set out the sequence of events that led to the comments that the appellant now claims are prejudicial. Although Dr. Mian was a Crown witness, the defence itself called Dr. Mian to testify as to Debbie-Ann's statement that she had burned herself while playing with a lighter since, by the time of the trial, the child herself could not recall having given such a statement. Given the introduction of the statement to undermine Debbie-Ann's credibility, the Crown, then, was entitled to call evidence to rehabilitate the witness's credibility.

At that point, on cross-examination, Dr. Mian testified that children who are abused will often, particularly close to the time of their admission to hospital, go along with the "official story" and give an explanation that the injury was caused by an accident. Later on, they will give a story in a more convincing manner that is more consistent with the injury. Dr. Mian explained several possible reasons for this behaviour. ...

[T]his information was admissible as expert opinion relating to the characteristics of abused children. It was vitally important background which set the context to understand Debbie-Ann's behaviour, including her prior inconsistent statement. It is information which illustrates why a child might initially after an incident of abuse recount a version of events which is at variance with what actually happened. In a sense it is information which can be compared to such well-recognized phenomena among victims of sexual abuse or domestic violence as recantation of the reported assaults and delay in reporting which also, if weighed without knowledge of the particular context in which they occur, reflect negatively on the credibility of the witness.

In my view, Dr. Mian's evidence bears no comparison with the polygraph evidence that this court held should be excluded in *Béland*, *supra*, or the statistical evidence that children tend not to lie about abuse that was at issue in *Taylor*, ... [*R v Taylor* (1986), 18 OAC 219]. Dr. Mian's evidence was not tendered for the sole purpose of providing the jury with the answer to the question they had to decide. Rather, the information was tendered for the larger purpose of assisting the jury in understanding why a child *might* react in a certain way if he or she were abused. The jury, as trier of fact, was left with the ultimate assessment of the credibility of both of Debbie-Ann's statements.

Dr. Mian did not, at any point, state that she thought Debbie-Ann was lying, nor did she, contrary to my colleague's assertion comment at all as to whether Debbie-Ann's contradictory statement at trial was true. She merely said that she was "suspicious," "surprised" and "concerned" about Debbie-Ann's initial response in the circumstances. In short, she stated that Debbie-Ann's reactions alerted her. She reported that Debbie-Ann was unusually co-operative, her conversation was extremely flat without affect, feeling or concern. When she proceeded to ask her if anyone had hurt her, Debbie-Ann shut her out, repeating "nobody, nobody." Moreover, Dr. Mian found the burn inconsistent with the story. She stated that, based on these reactions, even without the questions raised by the physical evidence of the burn, she would have been "somewhat … concerned if not suspicious."

Issues such as denial, protection of the abusing parent and untimely or incomplete disclosure, which are intimately related to questions of credibility, lie at the heart of child abuse. In fact, as they often form the core reactions to abuse, credibility will often be the very issue to be decided. The difficulty in this case arises because, not only was Dr. Mian an expert on child abuse, testifying about its general characteristics, but she was also Debbie-Ann's examining physician. This made it difficult, if not impossible, for her to avoid testifying in a manner that touched, however slightly, on Debbie-Ann's credibility. However, the relevance of her testimony does not lie in whether or not Dr. Mian thought Debbie-Ann was lying, but rather in her knowledge of the characteristics of abused children, which led her to the conclusion that Debbie-Ann may not have been disclosing the truth about her injury.

The jury was explicitly instructed by the trial judge that it remained the sole judge as to the credibility of Debbie-Ann's statement. Moreover, the trial judge instructed the jury that they were entitled to draw an inference adverse to the Crown from Debbie-Ann's prior inconsistent statement: …

Although I acknowledge that it was an error to instruct the jury that it *was* Dr. Mian's opinion that Debbie-Ann was an abused child, since Dr. Mian did not, in fact, make such a statement, this error must be considered in light of the entire charge to the jury and the specific direction the trial judge gave to the jury not to decide the case in terms of child abuse, but to focus on the assault under consideration. …

· · ·

Considering the totality of the charge to the jury, as one must, in my view the jury cannot have been mistaken about the nature of the issue before them or their responsibility as triers of fact for the ultimate decision about the credibility of the witnesses in the case. This ground must accordingly fail.

[Gonthier J, La Forest J concurring, agreed with McLachlin J on this issue.]

QUESTIONS

1. Do the majority and the minority disagree on the relevant principles or on the application of those principles to Dr. Mian's evidence?

2. How would the approach in *Marquard* apply to *Kyselka*?

D. Good Reputation for Veracity

The defence in a criminal trial is permitted to lead reputation evidence to establish the good character of the accused for the purpose of raising a reasonable doubt that he or she committed the crime (see Chapter 7, Section II.B). Moreover, the defence can lead evidence of the accused's reputation for veracity for the purpose of enhancing his or her credibility, in the event that the accused testifies. Such evidence must take the form of a witness testifying as to the accused's general reputation for truthfulness in the community, not the witness's own view of whether the accused should be believed. As Rosenberg JA explained in *R v Clarke* (1998), 129 CCC (3d) 1 at para 24 (Ont CA), "while the defence may lead evidence of the accused's reputation in the community, including the accused's reputation for truthfulness and veracity, it may not ask those witnesses for their opinion whether they would believe the accused under oath." If the defence adduces evidence of the accused's good reputation for veracity, however, this opens the door for the Crown to respond with cross-examination and to call evidence of the accused's bad reputation for truthfulness or other character evidence bearing on the acccused's credibility.

With respect to witnesses other than the accused, the party tendering its evidence cannot lead evidence of the witness's good reputation for veracity unless and until that witness's general credibility is attacked. Evidence of a witness's general reputation for veracity is of limited probative value and is adduced infrequently.

III. IMPEACHING THE CREDIBILITY OF AN OPPOSING PARTY'S WITNESS

In this section we consider specific means by which the credibility of an opposing party's witnesses can be impeached. It is important to bear in mind that the principal means of challenging the credibility of a witness is through the normal process of cross-examination: asking relevant questions designed to draw out frailties, inconsistencies, and defects in the testimony of opposing witnesses.

In Chapter 2, Section IV, you learned certain principles governing the conduct of cross-examination. The rule in *Browne v Dunn* (1893), 6 R 67 (HL), for example, requires a party who wishes to contradict a witness to put that contradiction to the witness and allow him or her an opportunity to address it. *R v Lyttle*, 2004 SCC 5, [2004] 1 SCR 193, addressed the necessary foundation for cross-examination, explaining that the latitude for asking questions is wide, requiring only that counsel have a "good faith basis for putting [a] question" (at para 47) to a witness. This section begins with another rule governing the permissible scope of cross-examination, the collateral facts rule. The collateral facts rule limits when a cross-examining lawyer can adduce independent evidence to contradict the answers of an opposing witness.

Beyond the normal questioning involved in cross-examination, however, are certain specific means by which the credibility of an opposing witness can be impeached. The first technique that we will consider in this section is the cross-examination of an opposing witness on a prior inconsistent statement. A second means of impeachment is the cross-examination of a witness on his or her criminal record, pursuant to s 12 of the *Canada Evidence Act* or its provincial equivalents. As you will learn, given the special situation of an accused, s 12 operates differently when the Crown wishes to impeach the accused by using his or her criminal record, requiring a balancing of the probative value of the criminal record in relation to credibility against its prejudicial character effect. A third, and rather limited, technique is the leading of expert opinion evidence to show the testimonial unreliability of a witness. The final impeachment technique covered in this section is the leading of evidence of the witness's bad reputation for veracity.

A. A Limit on Impeachment: The Collateral Facts Rule

In the course of cross-examination, counsel will pose questions relevant to facts essential to deciding the case. However, a cross-examining lawyer will also pursue lines of questioning not designed to directly explore such "substantive" or "material" issues but, rather, aimed solely at impeaching the credibility of the witness. Subject to the principles set out in *Lyttle*, addressed in Chapter 2, and the general discretion of the trial judge, counsel is free to ask both kinds of questions.

But what if the witness provides an answer that the cross-examining lawyer wishes to contradict? Specifically, what if the witness provides an answer but the lawyer has independent or "extrinsic" evidence that would contradict the witness's answer? May counsel go about proving the contradiction by adducing this evidence? When that contradiction is on a material point at issue in the case, this would seem extremely helpful and worthwhile, indeed. A concern arises, however, when counsel wishes to adduce evidence to prove an inconsistency or contradiction solely directed at impeaching credibility. The worry is that doing so may distract the finder of fact from the main issues, could unnecessarily consume time and trial resources, and might even be unfair to the witness who does not expect to be examined on such points. The collateral facts rule responds to that worry by imposing a limit on the circumstances in which extrinsic evidence can be adduced to contradict a witness's testimony.

The classic articulation of this rule came in *Attorney-General v Hitchcock* (1847), 1 Ex 91, 154 ER 38. The accused was charged with illegal use of a cistern in the manufacture of malt. One of the Crown's witnesses was Spooner, who testified that he had seen the accused use the cistern. In cross-examination, accused's counsel asked Spooner whether he had, in the past, stated that officers of the Crown had offered him a bribe to testify against Hitchcock. He denied making such a statement. The accused then proposed to call Cook, who would have testified that he had heard Spooner say that he had been offered a bribe to testify against Hitchcock. The trial judge, Pollock CB, rejected the proposed evidence of Cook, on the ground that it was collateral. On appeal, his ruling was upheld. In attempting to define what "collateral" is, Pollock CB said:

> [M]y view, I say, has always been, that the test, whether the matter is collateral or not, is this: if the answer of a witness is a matter which you would be allowed on your part to prove in evidence—if it have such a connection with the issue, that you would be allowed to give it in evidence—then it is a matter on which you may contradict him. ... [The matter] must be connected with the issue as a matter capable of being distinctly given in evidence, or it must be so far connected with it as to be a matter which, if answered in a particular way, would contradict a part of the witness's testimony; and if it is neither the one nor the other of these, it is collateral to [*sic*], though in some sense it may be considered as connected with, the subject of the inquiry.
>
> A distinction should be observed between those matters which may be given in evidence by way of contradiction, as directly affecting the story of the witness touching the issue before the jury, and those matters which affect the motives, temper, and character of the witness, not with

respect to his credit, but with reference to his feelings towards one party or the other. ... It is certainly allowable to ask a witness in what manner he stands affected towards the opposite party in the cause, and whether he does not stand in such a relation to that person as is likely to affect him, and prevent him from having an unprejudiced state of mind, and whether he has not used expressions importing that he would be revenged on some one, or that he would give such evidence as might dispose of the cause in one way or the other. If he denies that, you may give evidence as to what he has said, not with the view of having a direct effect on the issue, but to show what is the state of mind of that witness, in order that the jury may exercise their opinion as to how far he is to be believed.

Alderson B explained as follows:

Now the question is this, can you ask a witness as to what he is supposed to have said on the previous occasion? You may ask him as to any fact material to the issue, and if he denies it, you may prove that fact, as you are at liberty to prove any fact material to the issue; and in that case, though it may not be thought necessary to put the question previously to the witness, yet it would be but just to do so. The witness may also be asked as to his state of equal mind, or impartiality, between the two contending parties, questions which would have a tendency to show that the whole of his statement is to be taken with a qualification, and that such a statement ought really to be laid out of the case, for want of impartiality. ...

But, with these exceptions, I am not aware that you can with propriety permit a witness to be examined first, and contradicted afterwards, on a point which is merely and purely collateral, as for instance as to his personal character, and as to his having committed any particular act. The inadmissibility of such a contradiction depends, indeed, upon another principle altogether. Perhaps it ought to be received, but for the inconvenience that would arise from the witness being called upon to answer to particular acts of his life, which he might have been able to explain, if he had had reasonable notice to do so, and to have shown that all the acts of his life had been perfectly correct and pure, although other witnesses were called to prove the contrary. The reason why a party is obliged to take the answer of a witness is, that if he were permitted to go into it, it is only justice to allow the witness to call other evidence in support of the testimony he has given, as those witnesses might be cross-examined as to their conduct, such a course would be productive of endless collateral issues. ...

Cook's evidence was that he had heard Spooner say that he had been offered a bribe; based on the reasoning in *Hitchcock*, do you think that the ruling would have been different had the statement been that he had *accepted* a bribe?

The Supreme Court of Canada's touchstone articulation of the collateral facts rule came in *R v Krause*, [1986] 2 SCR 466. McIntyre J cast the rule in the following terms (at 474-75):

... Crown counsel in cross-examining an accused are not limited to subjects which are strictly relevant to the essential issues in a case. Counsel are accorded a wide freedom in cross-examination which enable them to test and question the testimony of the witnesses and their credibility. Where something new emerges in cross-examination, which is new in the sense that the Crown had no chance to deal with it in its case-in-chief (i.e., there was no reason for the Crown to anticipate that the matter would arise), and where the matter is concerned with the merits of the case (i.e. it concerns an issue essential for the determination of the case) then the Crown may be allowed to call evidence in rebuttal. Where, however, the new matter is collateral, that is, not determinative of an issue arising in the pleadings or indictment or not relevant to matters which must be proved for the determination of the case, no rebuttal will be allowed. An early expres-sion of this proposition is to be found in *Attorney-General v. Hitchcock*, [1847] 1 Ex. 91, 154 E.R. 38, and examples of the application of the principle may be found in *R. v. Cargill*, [1913] 2 K.B. 271 (Ct. Crim. App.); *R. v. Hrechuk* (1951), 58 Man. R. 489 (C.A.); *R. v. Rafael* [1972] 3 O.R. 238 (Ont. C.A.); and *Latour v. The Queen*, [1978] 1 S.C.R. 361. This is known as the rule against rebuttal on collateral issues. Where it applies, Crown counsel may cross-examine the accused on the matters raised, but the Crown is bound by the answers given. This is not to say that the Crown or the trier of fact is bound to accept the answers as true. The answer is binding or final only in the sense that rebut-tal evidence may not be called in contradiction.

The heart of the collateral facts rule itself is relatively easy to state: it prohibits the calling of evidence to contradict a witness's answer on a merely collateral matter. The underlying rationale for the rule is also clear: although such contradictions are relevant to credibility—which is at issue for any witness who takes the stand—their limited probative value is over-whelmed by concerns about trial efficiency, confusion, and fairness. The principal point of difficulty in understanding the collateral facts rule is in defining what counts as a "merely collateral matter," such that extrinsic proof of a contradiction on that point in a witness's testi-mony is prohibited.

This definitional task is notoriously perplexing, and a variety of approaches and formula-tions of the rule have been offered. It is common ground that substantive issues or facts that must be resolved in the case—like alibi, identity, and evidence of negligence—are not col-lateral. Those are the heart of the case and justify the time and effort involved in proving contradictions. But what about the second group of questions discussed above—those not directed at a material fact in issue, but solely at exploring the credibility of the witness?

One approach defines all such credibility matters as "collateral." This formulation was adopted by the evidence scholar Phipson and finds support in the Supreme Court of Can-ada's articulation of the rule in *Krause*, above, which seemed to define a "collateral matter" as one that is "not determinative of an issue arising in the pleadings or indictment or not rel-evant to matters which must be proved for the determination of the case … ." Yet there are certain credibility points that seem so significant or important that proof of a contradiction would be sensible. That is why proponents of this approach have always recognized certain exceptions related to issues of bias, interest in the case, corruption, and a set of other cat-egories. If a matter falls into one of these stated exceptions, a witness's answer on those col-lateral issues can nevertheless be contradicted with extrinsic proof. The risk of this approach is that it depends on the categorization of forms of evidence and, if applied too strictly, could result in the exclusion of helpful credibility evidence.

Another more permissive and flexible approach to defining "collateral matters" draws in-spiration from certain formulations found in *Hitchcock*. This approach, advanced by Wigmore, asks, "Could the fact, as to which error is predicated, have been shown in evidence for any purpose independently of the contradiction?": JH Wigmore, *Evidence*, vol 3A, ed by James H Chadbourn (Boston: Little, Brown, 1970) at §1003, emphasis removed. This would include material facts in the case, as well as facts that would impugn the witness's testimonial qual-ities, such as ability to observe, bias, and motive to lie. On this approach, none of these matters are collateral, and extrinsic proof of a contradiction is therefore permitted. McCormick added the following "linchpin" scenario to Wigmore's two categories of permissible contradiction:

A witness has told a story of a transaction crucial to the controversy. To prove him wrong in some trivial detail of time, place or circumstance is 'collateral.' But to prove untrue some fact recited by the witness that if he were really there and saw what he claims to have seen, he could not have been mistaken about, is a convincing kind of impeachment that the courts must make place for, despite the fact that it does not meet the test of admissibility apart from the contradiction. To disprove such a fact is to pull out the linchpin of the story. So we may recognize this third type of allowable contradiction, namely, the contradiction of any part of the witness's account of the background and circumstances of a material transaction, which as a matter of human experience he would not have been mistaken about if his story were true. This test is of necessity a vague one because it must meet an indefinite variety of situations, and consequently in its application a reasonable latitude of discretionary judgment must be accorded to the trial judge. [Charles T McCormick, *Evidence* (St Paul, Minn: West, 1954) at 102.]

In effect, this second approach distinguishes between substantive matters and "major" credibility issues—neither of which are collateral—and all other minor credibility matters, which are "merely collateral."

Ultimately, it might be most helpful to understand a "collateral matter" simply in terms of its importance and usefulness to the finder of fact. Given that the rule is based primarily on efficiency concerns, if the probative value of the contradiction is enough—if it bears on a material fact or a major credibility issue—then the matter is not collateral, and extrinsic evidence to prove the contradiction should be permitted. In *The Law of Evidence*, 7th ed (Toronto: Irwin Law, 2015) at 478, Paciocco and Steusser propose a sensible and principled test: "Is the evidence offered of sufficient value and of sufficient importance to the issues before the court that we ought to hear it having regard to the necessary court time required, potential confusion of issues, and any unfairness and prejudice to the witness?" If the answer is "yes," proof of a contradiction is not barred by the collateral facts rule.

In light of this discussion, consider the following two cases applying the collateral facts rule. What formulation of the rule does each seem to apply? Do you agree with the outcome?

R v Melnichuk
(1995), 104 CCC (3d) 160 (Ont CA)
Griffiths, Doherty, and Weiler JJA (19 December 1995)

[The accused was convicted of fraud. The Court of Appeal, per Griffiths JA, Weiler JA concurring, dismissed his appeal. Doherty JA, dissenting, would have allowed the appeal and ordered a new trial. He held that the trial judge had erred in two respects in ruling that the Crown could lead reply evidence. One of those errors was as follows: The Crown led evidence that the accused had forged a mortgage document in order to obtain funds from the complainant Hobson and had falsely told Hobson that he would register the mortgage against the title of the property in question. The accused testified and denied any dishonesty in obtaining the funds.]

DOHERTY JA (dissenting):

· · ·

[48] ... In cross-examination, Crown counsel asked the appellant whether he had ever held himself out to be a chartered accountant. The appellant, who did refer to himself as an accountant, denied that he had ever said that he was a chartered accountant. Crown counsel then produced a document prepared for one of the appellant's clients. That document referred to the appellant as a chartered accountant. The appellant said that the document had not been prepared by him and that someone had "altered" the document to refer to him as a chartered accountant.

[49] Over the objection of the defence, the Crown was allowed to call Mrs. Mills in reply. She testified that she had retrieved the document put to the appellant in cross-examination from her former husband's office located in the matrimonial home. The defence then called two witnesses in surrebuttal. Both testified that they operated the company which had employed the appellant to prepare certain financial records. They had prepared the document showing the appellant as a chartered accountant on the "assumption" that he was a chartered accountant. They further testified that when the appellant saw the document, he told them that he was not a chartered accountant and refused to sign the document.

[50] In convicting the appellant, the trial judge totally rejected his evidence. He said: "In many ways, the accused is a stranger to truth."

[51] The trial judge referred to the document describing the appellant as a chartered accountant and said that he found the appellant's explanation for that representation to be "glib and unconvincing." Clearly, the trial judge found that the appellant had misrepresented himself as a chartered accountant and used that finding in determining that the appellant was not worthy of belief.

[52] It was no part of the Crown's case that the appellant had represented to Mrs. Hobson or her daughter that he was a chartered accountant, or that any such misrepresentation figured in the loan made to the appellant by Mrs. Hobson. The question of whether or not the appellant had ever misrepresented himself to be a chartered accountant was, therefore, relevant only to his credibility. In my view, it was a collateral matter. In the circumstances of this case, the Crown was entitled to ask the appellant whether he had ever held himself out to be a chartered accountant and to put a document to the appellant suggesting that he had, but the Crown was not entitled to contradict the appellant's answers on a collateral matter with reply evidence: *R v. Krause*, (1986), 29 CCC (3d) 385 (SCC).

[The accused's appeal to the Supreme Court of Canada was allowed and a new trial was ordered. Sopinka J, Lamer CJ, and Major J concurring, agreed with Doherty JA that Mills's reply evidence violated the collateral facts bar. Iacobucci J agreed in separate reasons. L'Heureux-Dubé J, dissenting, would have dismissed the appeal.]

The following case involves the application of the collateral facts rule to the issue of a witness's possible bias or partiality in a case.

R v McDonald
2007 ABCA 53, 219 CCC (3d) 369
Côté, Paperny, and Slatter JJA (22 February 2007)

THE COURT:

[1] The Crown appealed the respondent's acquittal on charges of confinement and sexual assault, allegedly committed on his former common-law partner. The appeal was based on the trial judge's refusal to allow the Crown to call rebuttal evidence. That evidence was intended to show bias on the part of one of the witnesses called by the respondent, the respondent's sister. The appeal was allowed after the hearing, with these reasons to follow.

Facts

[2] At some time in the past the respondent and his sister had been involved in a fight during which the respondent was stabbed and the sister received a broken jaw. As a result they were each charged with aggravated assault of the other. The sister initially gave a detailed statement to the police about what happened at the time. However, at the preliminary inquiry she testified that she was drunk and could not remember anything.

[3] Constable Palfy testified that a few months later the sister admitted that she did remember what had happened at the time of the alleged aggravated assaults. She explained that she had been under a lot of family pressure not to testify against her brother. She also indicated that she would not testify in a negative way against her brother out of loyalty to him.

[4] The present charges arise out of an alleged assault by the respondent on the complainant, who was a former common-law partner of his. The complainant testified to forced sexual intercourse. The respondent admitted the sexual intercourse, but testified that the complainant consented. The sister testified to certain conduct by the respondent and the complainant immediately prior to the events which were arguably consistent with consent and the respondent's version of events.

[5] During the cross-examination of the sister, the Crown put to her her previous statements to Constable Palfy, to the effect that she would not testify against her brother. She denied the accuracy of Constable Palfy's notes, and essentially denied having made the statements attributed to her.

[The Crown then proved her prior inconsistent oral statement under section 11 of the *Canada Evidence Act*, a point considered later in this chapter.]

[8] At the close of the defence case the Crown applied to enter rebuttal evidence. The proposed evidence included a transcript of the preliminary inquiry concerning the aggravated assaults, and certified copies of the Informations and endorsements relating to those assaults. In addition, the Crown sought to call Constable Palfy to testify as to the conversation he had with the sister.

[9] The defence objected to the rebuttal evidence, arguing that it was "collateral." ...

. . .

Rebuttal Evidence

[11] There is a wide ranging right to cross-examine a witness under our adversarial system. However, when questions are asked on "collateral" issues, the questioner is usually stuck with the answer. Rebuttal evidence is not permitted to contradict answers given to "collateral questions": *R. v. Krause*, [1986] 2 S.C.R. 466; *Marthaller v. Lansdowne Equity Venture Ltd.* (1997), 52 Alta. L.R. (3d) 329 (C.A.) at paras. 40-41.

[12] The trial judge was correct in suggesting that many questions going to the credibility of the witness might well be collateral within this rule. Bias of the witness is, however, always relevant, and is not collateral. The collateral evidence rule was recited in *Attorney General v. Hitchcock* (1847), 1 Ex. 91, 16 L.J. Ex. 259, 154 E.R. 38, but the partiality of a witness was excepted:

> There is, however, a distinction between contradicting a witness in particulars stated by him, and those which have reference to his motives, temper, character and feelings. ... A witness may be asked how he stands affected towards one of the parties; and if his relation towards them is such as to prejudice his mind, and to fill him with sentiments of revenge or other feelings of a similar kind, and if he denies the fact, evidence may be given to shew the state of his mind and feelings.

The ability to prove bias of a witness in rebuttal was confirmed in *R. v. Finnessey* (1906), 11 O.L.R. 338, 10 C.C.C. 347 at pp. 351-2; *R. v. S.(A.)* (2002), 159 O.A.C. 89, 165 C.C.C. (3d) 426 (C.A.) at paras. 28-32; *R. v. Mohammed* (1991), 72 Man. R. (2d) 39 (Q.B.), aff'd (1992), 83 Man. R. (2d) 162 (C.A.); *Anderson v. Harding* (1985), 3 C.P.C. (2d) 87 (Ont. Dist. Ct.); and *R. v. R. (D.)*, [1996] 2 S.C.R. 291, at para. 43. This exception to the collateral evidence rule was not brought to the attention of the trial judge.

[13] This was not a situation where the Crown was attempting to prove particular facts that occurred at the time of the aggravated assault charges to show that the substance of the witness's answers were inaccurate. Such evidence would be collateral. The Crown was not interested in "what happened at other trials," as the trial judge put it, but rather was attempting to prove the mental state or motivations of a witness in this trial, at this point in time. What the Crown wanted to prove was that the witness was either pressured by her family or biased towards her brother. The Crown was entitled to call this evidence to show the bias of the sister.

[14] That does not mean that all the evidence tendered by the Crown was admissible. The transcript of the preliminary inquiry of the aggravated assaults was not necessarily relevant. The details of how those assaults occurred, and the differences between the sister's statements to the police and her evidence on the stand, were probably collateral to the issues. The transcript was admissible to prove that the sister had testified that she could not remember any of the events because of drunkenness. That however had been admitted by the sister on the stand, and no rebuttal evidence was needed.

[15] The Crown conceded on appeal that the Informations and endorsements from the aggravated assault charges were not relevant to the issue of witness bias.

[16] The evidence of Constable Palfy was relevant: he would testify to admissions by the witness that she had been pressured and was biased. That evidence was already on the record in the s. 11 application. There was arguably no need to call Constable Palfy again to testify to exactly the same things, but the Crown was entitled to have the evidence considered on the issue of bias.

[The court allowed the Crown's appeal and ordered a new trial.]

PROBLEMS ON COLLATERAL FACTS

1. The accused (GP) was charged with the sexual assault of an 11-year-old girl, the daughter of CP, a friend. GP denied that the assault had occurred, and advanced two "somewhat inconsistent" theories to explain the false allegation. The first was that the complainant had made the allegation to destroy the relationship between GP and CP The second, advanced during cross-examination of CP and during examination in chief of GP, was that CP had encouraged the complainant to fabricate the complaint because CP was angry with GP for not pursuing a physical relationship with her. GP testified that his relationship with CP was "essentially platonic." In cross-examination, Crown counsel asked him if he had ever told VM, a friend, that he had had sexual intercourse or oral sex with CP He denied that he had. The Crown was permitted to call VM in reply to testify that GP had told her that he had spent the night with CP more than once, that he had been seeing her for about five months, and that he was going to ask her to marry him. Should VM's evidence have been barred by the rule against collateral facts? See *R v P (G)* (1996), 31 OR (3d) 504, 112 CCC (3d) 263 (CA).

2. Brown was charged with the murder of Hogan. Sherrick had previously been tried and acquitted of the murder of Hogan. The Crown's principal witness was Ellen McGillock, who testified that on December 1, 1859, she saw Brown and Sherrick throw Hogan into the Don River, and the next day she saw Brown and Sherrick cut away a bloody mark from the hand rail of the bridge at the spot where they had thrown Hogan over. In cross-examination and in re-examination, she repeated her testimony that Sherrick had been at the scene. The defence called Sherrick, who testified that he had not been at the scene of the crime. The defence also proposed to call Dolan, who would have testified that on December 1, 1859, Sherrick had been at his place, which was about 50 miles from the scene of the crime. The trial judge rejected Dolan's evidence on the ground that it was collateral, and Brown was convicted. Was the judge's ruling correct? See *R v Brown* (1861), 21 UCQB 330.

3. Carter, a Crown eyewitness, has identified the accused Smith as the shooter in a murder case. She says that she saw Smith and Cooper talking to the victim, and that Smith pulled a small pistol out of his pocket and shot the victim. She could not hear what they were saying. She says that Jones, whom the accused alleges was the killer, was not at the scene. She is acquainted with Smith, Cooper, Jones, and the victim; they all live nearby, and she has often seen them around the neighbourhood. Defence counsel cross-examines her as follows:

Q: I put it to you that it was Jones and not Smith who fired the fatal shot.

A: No, I'm sure it was Smith. I saw him and Cooper—they couldn't have been more than 20 feet away.

Q: Isn't it true, witness, that the shooting occurred in broad daylight?

A: Yes.

Q: The sun was shining very brightly?

A: Yes.

Q: Hadn't you just been to see your eye doctor?

A: Yes, I had.

Q: And he put some drops in your eyes to dilate your pupils, isn't that right?

By Crown Counsel:
I object, your honour. The witness is not an expert on ophthalmology.

The Court:
I agree. Defence counsel, ask your question a different way.

By Defence Counsel:
Q: The eye doctor did put some drops in your eyes?
A: Yes, he did.
Q: And what effect did these have on your vision?
A: None, really.
Q: I suggest to you that after visiting your eye doctor, you could not see well in the bright sunlight.
A: No, that's not true. I could see fine.
Q: I put it to you that you only saw one person talking to the victim.
A: No, that's not true. I'm sure Cooper was there as well.
Q: Are you sure? I can get Cooper in here to tell the jury that he was at home when Jones shot the victim.
A: Well, if he says that, he's lying. And it was Smith, not Jones.
Q: You said in your answer to Crown counsel's questions that you were convicted of fraud in 1996, isn't that right?
A: Yes, but I wasn't guilty. My lawyer told me to plead guilty, so I did.
Q: Oh, really? I suggest to you that the fraud charge was based on your participation in a scheme to steal books from your employer.
A: That's not true.
Q: Well, you worked for the Magenta bookstore at the time?
A: Yes, I did.
Q: And you had an arrangement with your friend Baker whereby you would falsify the price of books that she purchased.
A: No, that's not true. It was all her fault—she was switching price stickers—I had nothing to do with it.
Q: So it was just a coincidence that you were the only cashier Baker ever dealt with?
A: I wouldn't know about that.

Which of the following defence evidence is barred by (which formulation of) the collateral facts bar? In light of the rationale for the bar, which evidence should be barred?

     a. Miller, another witness, will testify that he saw Jones shoot the victim.

     b. Miller will testify that Jones, and only Jones, was talking to the victim before the shooting.

     c. Cooper will testify that he was at home at the time of the shooting.

     d. Dr. Augen will testify that Carter had visited him for a routine eye examination just before the shooting, that he had put drops in her eyes to dilate her pupils for better examination, and that patients who receive such drops usually have difficulty seeing in bright light for up to two hours.

     e. Baker will testify that Carter was her accomplice in a scheme to defraud Magenta.

B. Prior Inconsistent Statements

Counsel might impeach an opposing witness by cross-examining the witness about having made a prior statement inconsistent with his or her testimony at trial. This is a potent form of impeachment. The common law once imposed certain rules and strictures around cross-examination on such prior inconsistent statements, but legislation now governs. These legislative provisions are aimed at ensuring that the impeachment proceeds fairly, providing the witness with an opportunity to admit or explain the contradiction. In this sense, these provisions reflect a rationale similar to that which informs the rule in *Browne v Dunn*, discussed in Chapter 2. Federally, ss 10 and 11 of the *Canada Evidence Act* set out the rules applicable to cross-examination on prior inconsistent statements:

> 10(1) On any trial a witness may be cross-examined as to previous statements that the witness made in writing, or that have been reduced to writing, or recorded on audio tape or video tape or otherwise, relative to the subject-matter of the case, without the writing being shown to the witness or the witness being given the opportunity to listen to the audio tape or view the video tape or otherwise take cognizance of the statements, but, if it is intended to contradict the witness, the witness' attention must, before the contradictory proof can be given, be called to those parts of the statement that are to be used for the purpose of so contradicting the witness, and the judge, at any time during the trial, may require the production of the writing or tape or other medium for inspection, and thereupon make such use of it for the purposes of the trial as the judge thinks fit.
>
> . . .
>
> 11. Where a witness, on cross-examination as to a former statement made by him relative to the subject-matter of the case and inconsistent with his present testimony, does not distinctly admit that he did make the statement, proof may be given that he did in fact make it, but before that proof can be given the circumstances of the supposed statement, sufficient to designate the particular occasion, shall be mentioned to the witness, and he shall be asked whether or not he did make the statement.

Section 10 sets out the procedure for impeachment on prior inconsistent written or otherwise recorded statements, whereas s 11 applies to prior inconsistent oral statements. The heart of these provisions is that, before using the prior inconsistent statement to impeach the witness's testimony, counsel must draw the witness's attention to the prior contradictory statement. If a witness denies having made it, counsel may prove the statement. Impeachment using a prior consistent statement must be "relative to the subject matter of the case," a clause that reflects that such impeachments cannot be on collateral matters.

Similar provisions are found in provincial evidence acts: see e.g. *Alberta Evidence Act*, RSA 2000, c A-18, ss 22-23; *Evidence Act*, RSBC 1996, c 124, ss 13-14; *Manitoba Evidence Act*, CCSM c E150, ss 20-21; *Evidence Act*, RSNB 1973, c E-11, ss 18-19; *Evidence Act*, RSNL 1990, c E-16, ss 11-12; *Evidence Act*, RSNS 1989, c 154, ss 56-57; *Evidence Act*, RSO 1990, c E-23, ss 20-21; *Evidence Act*, RSPEI 1988, c E-11, ss 16-17; and *Evidence Act*, SS 2006, c E-11.2, s 19.

It is important to note that, once a prior inconsistent statement has been proven, it can only be used to assess the credibility of the witness; it cannot be used for its truth unless the witness adopts the statement as true, or the statement is otherwise admissible under a hearsay exception, such as the exception created in *R v B (KG)*, [1993] 1 SCR 740, 79 CCC (3d) 257, discussed in Chapter 4, Section III.B. Given the admissions exception to the hearsay rule, prior inconsistent statements made by an accused or a party to the litigation are admissible for their substantive truth without that witness adopting the statement. For further discussion of the applicability of s 11 of the *Canada Evidence Act* to the accused, see *R v P (G)* (1996), 31 OR (3d) 504, 112 CCC (3d) 263 at 276-87 (CA). If a prior inconsistent statement is introduced before a jury, the jury must be informed of the permissible use of the statement.

Finally, what constitutes an "inconsistent" statement? Clear contradictions between the testimony and the content of the prior statement certainly suffice. But what if the witness simply tells his or her story in a slightly different way or simply disavows any knowledge of the facts contained in the prior statement? Courts have tended to adopt a liberal interpretation of "inconsistent" (see e.g. *R v Moore* (1979), 36 NSR (2d) 228 (CA)). McCormick offers a helpful and principled test: "Could the jury reasonably find that a witness who believed the truth of the facts testified to would have been unlikely to make a prior statement of this tenor?" (Kenneth S Broud, ed, *McCormick on Evidence*, 7th ed (St Paul, Minn: Thomson Reuters, 2013) §34 at 211). If the answer is "yes," cross-examination on the prior statement, consistent with the governing legislative provisions, should be permitted.

C. Prior Convictions

Once a witness takes the stand, and thereby puts his or her credibility at issue, cross-examining counsel are permitted to seek to discredit the witness by adducing evidence of prior convictions. Prior convictions bear on credibility based on the theory that the fact that someone has been convicted of an offence suggests that he or she is less reputable and, hence, less trustworthy. Historically, cross-examination on prior convictions was permitted at common law, but statutory provisions now govern. Section 12 of the *Canada Evidence Act* states:

> 12(1) A witness may be questioned as to whether the witness has been convicted of any offence, excluding any offence designated as a contravention under the *Contraventions Act*, but including such an offence where the conviction was entered after a trial on an indictment.
>
> (1.1) If the witness either denies the fact or refuses to answer, the opposite party may prove the conviction.
>
> (2) A conviction may be proved by producing
>
> (a) a certificate containing the substance and effect only, omitting the formal part, of the indictment and conviction, if it is for an indictable offence, or a copy of the summary conviction, if it is for an offence punishable on summary conviction, purporting to be signed by the clerk of the court or other officer having the custody of the records of the court in which the conviction, if on indictment, was had, or to which the conviction, if summary, was returned; and
>
> (b) proof of identity.

Note that the effect of s 12(1.1) is to confirm that, though only relevant to the credibility of the witness, the existence of a prior conviction is not a merely collateral matter.

Provincial and territorial evidence acts contain similar provisions, governing impeachment with prior convictions in civil cases. See *Alberta Evidence Act*, RSA 2000, c A-18, s 24; *Evidence Act*, RSBC 1996, c 124, s 15; *Manitoba Evidence Act*, CCSM c E150, s 22; *Evidence Act*, RSNB 1973, c E-11, s 20; *Evidence Act*, RSNL 1990, c E-16, s 13; *Evidence Act*, RSNS 1989, c 154, s 58; *Evidence Act*, RSO 1990, c E.23, ss 22 and 22.1; *Evidence Act*, RSPEI 1988, c E-11, s 18; *Evidence Act*, SS 2006, c E-11.2, s 18; *Evidence Act*, RSNWT 1988, c E-8, s 29; and *Evidence Act*, RSY 2002, c 78, s 27.

What counts as a "conviction" for the purposes of these provisions? It is clear that any *Criminal Code* conviction may be the subject of cross-examination and it is equally settled that an absolute or conditional discharge following a finding of guilt cannot be used for impeachment under s 12 of the *Canada Evidence Act* (see *R v Danson* (1982), 35 OR (2d) 777, 66 CCC (2d) 369 (CA) and *R v Lynch* (1990), 77 CR (3d) 142 (Qc Sup Ct), although non-accused witnesses can be impeached on prior discreditable conduct outside the ambit of s 12 (*R v Cullen*, (1989), 52 CCC (3d) 459 (Ont CA)). There is also authority that a witness cannot be cross-examined under s 12 on the basis of a conviction for which he or she has been pardoned (*R v Paterson* (1998), 122 CCC (3d) 254 (BCCA)). Despite an older, divided decision of the Supreme Court holding that s 12 allowed impeachment using an offence for which an accused was found guilty under the *Juvenile Delinquents Act* (*R v Morris*, [1979] 1 SCR 405), courts now differ on the question of whether counsel can cross-examine a witness on his or her youth convictions: see e.g. *R v Upton*, 2008 NSSC 338 (permitting); *R v Sheik-Qasim* (2007), 230 CCC (3d) 531 (Ont Sup Ct J); and *R v Kanhai*, 2010 ONSC 3776 (prohibiting). Whether a witness can be impeached using a conviction for a provincial offence is also unclear: compare *Clarke v Holdsworth* (1967), 62 WWR 1 (BCSC) (permitting) and *Street v Guelph (City)*, [1964] 2 OR 421, 45 DLR (2d) 652 (H Ct J) (prohibiting).

Section 12 refers generally to "a witness." The historical precursor to this provision predated the competency of the accused, which was fully established in Canadian law in 1893. With time, it became clear that "a witness" includes an accused who chooses to testify. The trier of fact is entitled to infer that an accused with a criminal record, like any other witness with a criminal record, is, for that reason, less credible than a witness without a criminal record. And yet special considerations arise when one seeks to cross-examine an accused regarding his or her criminal record. Although prior convictions are thought to have some bearing on credibility, they are also evidence of prior bad acts. With respect to a non-accused witness, it is not that troubling for a finder of fact to learn, through impeachment, that the witness has a history of discreditable conduct. For an accused, however, the concern is that this evidence might be used not only to assess credibility, but to make the "prohibited character inference" that the accused is the type of person more likely to have committed the offence with which he is now charged. As you will learn in Chapter 7, such character evidence is generally inadmissible on the grounds that its prejudicial impact outweighs its probative value—it can lead to an unfair trial. An accused who takes the stand has something of a dual status: that accused is now both a witness and also the only person whose liberty is at issue. Evidence of prior convictions thus also has a dual nature for the accused: it is helpful credibility evidence, but it is also dangerous character or "propensity" evidence.

Accordingly, special limitations have been applied to the Crown's ability to impeach the accused pursuant to s 12 of the *Canada Evidence Act*. For example, unlike a non-accused witness, an accused witness cannot be asked about the conduct or facts that led to the prior conviction. As Houlden and Morden JJA stated in *R v Laurier* (1983), 1 OAC 128 (CA):

> In cross-examining an accused about his prior criminal record, Crown counsel is entitled to ask for the name of the crime, the substance and effect of the indictment, the place of the conviction and the penalty, but he is not entitled to cross-examine the accused about the details of the offences.

Moreover, if an accused was impeached on his or her criminal record, jurors were to be instructed to use the record only for the purpose of assessing credibility, and not for the purpose of assessing propensity. With the introduction of the Charter, questions soon arose: can the prejudice be overcome with this kind of instruction? If jurors cannot make such a distinction, what are the implications for our system of evidence law? If jurors cannot make the distinction, does s 12 infringe the accused's right to a fair trial pursuant to s 11(d) of the Charter? Does s 12 authorize the trial judge to edit the accused's record of convictions? Does the trial judge have a general discretion to edit the accused's record and thus relieve against the operation of s 12? If so, is the discretion derived from the application of the Charter or from some other source of authority? These important issues were considered by the Supreme Court in *Corbett*. As you read this decision, consider also the judges' comments on the role of the jury and the nature of jury reasoning.

R v Corbett

[1988] 1 SCR 670

Dickson CJ and Beetz, Estey, McIntyre, Lamer, Le Dain, and La Forest JJ

(26 May 1988)

[The accused was convicted of the first-degree murder of an associate in the cocaine trade. He appealed on the ground that he had been deprived of his right to a fair hearing. At trial, he had sought a ruling that, if he were called to testify, s 12 of the *Canada Evidence Act* would not apply to him and he could not be cross-examined on his prior criminal record. When the trial judge denied the motion, defence counsel elicited the previous convictions during examination in chief of the accused. The accused admitted that he had been convicted, in the 1950s, of armed robbery, receiving stolen property, breaking, entering and theft, escaping custody, and auto theft, and that, in 1971, he had been convicted of non-capital murder. The trial judge properly instructed the jury that the convictions could be taken into account only in assessing the accused's credibility as a witness, and not in determining whether the Crown has proven beyond a reasonable doubt that the accused committed the offence.]

DICKSON CJ (Lamer J concurring):

. . .

The case clearly turned on credibility and on whether the jury believed [the Crown witnesses] or the accused. After deliberating for some 27 hours, the jury returned a verdict of guilty of second degree murder.

. . .

V

Purpose and Effect of the Canada Evidence Act, s. 12

... What lies behind s. 12 is a legislative judgment that prior convictions do bear upon the credibility of a witness. In deciding whether or not to believe someone who takes the stand, the jury will quite naturally take a variety of factors into account. They will observe the demeanour of the witness as he or she testifies, the witness' appearance, tone of voice, and general manner. Similarly, the jury will take into account any information it has relating to the witness's habits or mode of life. There can surely be little argument that a prior criminal record is a fact which, to some extent at least, bears upon the credibility of a witness. Of course, the mere fact that a witness was previously convicted of an offence does not mean that he or she necessarily should not be believed, but it is a fact which a jury might take into account in assessing credibility.

. . .

Charter of Rights and Freedoms

. . .

Does s. 12 of the *Canada Evidence Act* violate the guarantee contained in s. 11(d) of the *Charter*? ...

The essence of the *Charter* argument is that in light of the evidentiary rules restricting the admissibility of similar fact evidence and evidence relating to bad character, evidence of prior convictions against an accused person would ordinarily be inadmissible. Section 12 purports to make such evidence admissible on the issue of credibility only, but it is contended that the trier of fact will be incapable of restricting the use of such evidence to the issue of credibility. It is argued that permitting cross-examination on prior convictions unfairly prejudices an accused in the sense that it presents the trier of fact with evidence, not otherwise admissible, which the trier of fact will inevitably take into account not only on the issue of credibility but also on the ultimate issue of guilt or innocence. It is argued that when presented with such information, the jury will inevitably tend to conclude that the accused is a person of bad character or a person who has a propensity to commit criminal offences and hence draw an inference it is not legally entitled to draw.

. . .

The issue to be faced, therefore, is whether the risk that the jury will use the evidence of prior convictions for an improper purpose is so great that Parliament is not entitled to provide, as it has in s. 12 of the *Canada Evidence Act*, that a witness, specifically in this case an accused, may be cross-examined as to prior criminal convictions.

. . .

It is my view that on the facts of the present case, a serious imbalance would have arisen had the jury not been apprised of Corbett's criminal record. Counsel for Corbett vigorously attacked the credibility of the Crown witnesses and much was made of [their] prior criminal records .... What impression would the jury have had if Corbett had given his evidence under a regime whereby the Crown was precluded from bringing to the jury's attention the fact that Corbett had a serious criminal record? It would be impossible to explain to the jury that one set of rules applies to ordinary witnesses, while another applies to the accused, for the very fact of such an explanation would undermine the purpose of the exclusionary rule. Had Corbett's criminal record not been revealed, the jury would have been left with the quite incorrect impression that while all the Crown witnesses were hardened criminals, the accused had an unblemished past. It cannot be the case that nothing short of this entirely misleading situation is required to satisfy the accused's right to a fair trial.

There is perhaps a risk that if told of the fact that the accused has a criminal record, the jury will make more than it should of that fact. But concealing the prior criminal record of an accused who testifies deprives the jury of information relevant to credibility, and creates a serious risk that the jury will be presented with a misleading picture.

In my view, the best way to balance and alleviate these risks is to give the jury all the information, but at the same time give a clear direction as to the limited use they are to make of such information. Rules which put blinders over the eyes of the trier of fact should be avoided except as a last resort. It is preferable to trust the good sense of the jury and to give the jury all relevant information, so long as it is accompanied by a clear instruction in law from the trial judge regarding the extent of its probative value.

· · ·

In my view, it would be quite wrong to make too much of the risk that the jury *might* use the evidence for an improper purpose. This line of thinking could seriously undermine the entire jury system. The very strength of the jury is that the ultimate issue of guilt or innocence is determined by a group of ordinary citizens who are not legal specialists and who bring to the legal process a healthy measure of common sense. The jury is, of course, bound to follow the law as it is explained by the trial judge. Jury directions are often long and difficult, but the experience of trial judges is that juries do perform their duty according to the law. We should regard with grave suspicion arguments which assert that depriving the jury of all relevant information is preferable to giving them everything, with a careful explanation as to any limitations on the use to which they may put that information. So long as the jury is given a clear instruction as to how it may and how it may not use evidence of prior convictions put to an accused on cross-examination, it can be argued that the risk of improper use is outweighed by the much more serious risk of error should the jury be forced to decide the issue in the dark.

It is of course, entirely possible to construct an argument disputing the theory of trial by jury. Juries are capable of egregious mistakes and they may at times seem to be ill-adapted to the exigencies of an increasingly complicated and refined criminal law. But until the paradigm is altered by Parliament, the court should not be heard to call into question the capacity of juries to do the job assigned to them. The ramifications of any such statement could be enormous. Moreover, the fundamental *right* to a jury trial has recently been underscored by s. 11(f) of the *Charter*. If that right is so important, it is logically incoherent to hold that juries are incapable of following the explicit instructions of a judge. Yet it is just this holding that is urged upon this court by the appellant, for it is only this holding that can justify the conclusion that when s. 12(1) of the *Canada Evidence Act* is employed against an accused, the section infringes the accused's right to a "fair hearing."

· · ·

There are many situations where the jury is permitted to hear and use evidence relevant to one issue, but not to another. In these situations, all that is required is a clear direction to the jury indicating what is permissible use and what is not. [Dickson CJ referred to limits on the use of similar fact evidence, the confession of a co-accused, and prior inconsistent statements.]

· · ·

If risk that the jury might misuse evidence were enough to render such evidence inadmissible in all cases, then in each of the situations just identified, the evidence would have to be excluded. Yet the risk of error inherent in depriving the jury of such information is so strong that the balance is struck by allowing the evidence to be received, subject to the trial judge's discretion, but at the same time insisting on a careful direction from the trial judge as to the permissible conclusion or inferences which may be drawn. As it was put in an American decision (*State v. Anderson*, 641 P.2d 728 at p. 731 (1982 Wash. Ct. App.), *per* Durham J): "If we are to continue in our belief that a trial by a jury of 12 peers offers the fairest determination of guilt or innocence, then we must credit the jury with the intelligence and conscience to consider evidence of prior convictions only to impeach the credibility of the defendant if it is so instructed." Similarly, in *State v. Ruzicka* ... [570 P (2d) 1208 (Wash 1977)], at p. 1214, Hamilton J stated: "We are not convinced that juries either cannot or willfully do not follow the court's instructions to use evidence of a defendant's prior criminal record only in weighing the defendant's veracity on the witness stand."

It is worth noting as well that it would be quite wrong to view this aspect of s. 12 and evidence in relation to prior convictions in isolation. Judicial decisions have carefully circumscribed the extent to which the Crown may use prior convictions. It has been held, for example, that the accused may be examined only as to the fact of the conviction itself and not concerning the conduct which led to that conviction: *R v. Stratton* ... [(1978), 42 CCC (2d) 449 (Ont CA)], at p. 467; *R v. Laurier* (1983), 1 OAC 128; *Koufis v. The King* ... [[1941] SCR 481]. Similarly, it has been held that an accused cannot be cross-examined as to whether he testified on the prior occasion when convicted in order to show that he is one who was not believed by a jury on a previous occasion: *R v. Geddes* (1979), 52 CCC (2d) 230, 2 Man. R (2d) 339 (Man. CA). The Crown is not entitled to go beyond prior convictions to cross-examine an accused as to discreditable conduct or association with disreputable individuals to attack his credibility: *R v. Waite* (1980), 57 CCC (9d) 34 at pp. 45-6, 42 NSR (2d) 546 (NSSCAD); *R v. Davison, DeRosie and MacArthur* ... [(1974), 20 CCC (2d) 424 (Ont CA)], at p. 444; *R v. MacDonald* (1939), 72 CCC 182 at p. 197, [1939] 4 DLR 60 at p. 73, [1939] OR 606 (Ont. CA). Unless the accused takes the stand, the Crown is not permitted to adduce evidence of prior convictions, even if the accused has launched an attack on the character of Crown witnesses: *R v. Butterwasser*, [1948] 1 KB 4 (CCA). It has been held that an accused may be cross-examined only as to "convictions" strictly construed and that there can be no cross-examination where the accused was found guilty and granted a conditional discharge, conditions subsequently having been fulfilled: *R v. Danson* (1982), 66 CCC (2d) 369, 35 OR (2d) 777 (Ont. CA).

These limitations on the use of prior convictions, together with the discretion recognized by the reasons of La Forest J, demonstrate a marked solicitude for the right of the accused to a fair trial and indicate that the law relating to the use of prior convictions strives to avoid the risk of prejudicing an accused's trial by introduction of evidence of prior misdeeds. Taken as a whole, this body of law is entirely protective of the right of the accused not to be convicted except on evidence directly relevant to the charge in question. Within this context, it cannot be said that s. 12 of the *Canada Evidence Act* operates in such a way as to deprive the accused of the right to a fair trial.

VII

Does a Trial Judge Have the Discretion to Preclude Cross-Examinations as to Prior Convictions?

I agree with my colleague, Justice La Forest, that basic principles of the law of evidence embody an inclusionary policy which would permit into evidence everything logically probative of some fact in issue, subject to the recognized rules of exclusion and exceptions thereto. Thereafter the question is one of weight. The evidence may carry much weight, little weight, or no weight at all. If error is to be made it should be on the side of inclusion rather than exclusion and our efforts in my opinion, consistent with the ever-increasing openness of our society, should be toward admissibility unless a very clear ground of policy or law dictates exclusion.

[Dickson CJ agreed with La Forest J's holding that a trial judge has a discretion to exclude overly prejudicial evidence of prior convictions, and adopted his list of factors that are useful in making this decision. He disagreed, however, on the application of these factors to the facts of this case. Dickson CJ would have put more weight on the fact that the accused had strongly attacked the credibility of Crown witnesses. In his view, admitting the evidence of the accused's prior conviction was necessary and would not be unduly prejudicial.

Beetz J, concurring with Dickson CJ, held that s 12 "would not conform with ss 7 and 11(d) of the *Canadian Charter of Rights and Freedoms* unless it be construed as leaving room for the trial judge's discretion to disallow the cross-examination of an accused as to prior convictions if the convictions are of tenuous probative value in assessing credibility and their disclosure would be highly prejudicial to the accused."

McIntyre J, Le Dain J concurring, held that there was no judicial discretion in s 12 and that the section did not offend the Charter.]

LA FOREST J (dissenting): ...

. . .

The Nature of the Prejudice

Simply put, the appellant's submissions are twofold: first, that the admission into evidence of an accused's previous convictions harbours the potential to prejudice profoundly the fairness of the accused's trial, and secondly, that some means (constitutional or otherwise) must exist to negate that potential.

For the reasons that follow, and in the face of a resoundingly uniform body of judicial and academic opinion, as well as empirical evidence to the effect that the section's actual or putative operation is capable of causing manifold prejudice to the interests of the accused (and, for that matter, of the public) in a fair trial, one cannot help but concede the force of the appellant's submissions regarding prejudice. By prejudice is meant, of course, that the acceptance of such evidence could operate unfairly and unjustly, and not merely unfortunately to the accused: see *Wray* ... [*R v Wray*, [1971] SCR 272], per Martland J at p. 293; *DPP v. Boardman*, [1970] AC 421 (HL).

The most obvious way in which this prejudice manifests itself arises from the fact that the operation of s. 12 significantly, and often invidiously, circumvents the complex of rules that precludes, in general, the introduction by the Crown of evidence of an accused's "bad character," or disposition for criminal activity or discreditable acts not related to the charge. ...

. . .

[B]y assimilating an accused to the position of an ordinary witness, s. 12 places the trier of fact in the unenviable position of entertaining at once two highly, and often impossibly dissonant trains of thought. As Ratushny points out, [Edward Ratushny, *Self-Incrimination in the Canadian Criminal Process* (Toronto: Carswell, 1979)] the trier of fact is entitled to infer that because the accused committed criminal acts in the past he or she is now more likely to lie, but that same trier of fact is not entitled to infer therefrom that the accused is also more likely to have committed the evil act for which he is now on trial (*ibid.*, pp. 336-7). Ironically, however, as a matter of logic and human experience which are, after all, our touchstones in the present inquiry, the probative value of such evidence to the latter question (of guilt) appears to be far more prepossessing.

This perception, as Hutcheon JA demonstrated in the Court of Appeal, is shared by academics, practitioners and judges alike: see, for example, M.L. Friedland, "Cross-Examination on Previous Convictions in Canada" ... [(1969) 47 Can Bar Rev 656], especially p. 658; Eric Teed, "The Effect of s. 12 of the Canada Evidence Act Upon an Accused" (1970-71), 13 *Crim. LQ* 70, especially pp. 75-6. Indeed, with respect to evidence of crimes similar to that for which the accused is being tried, it is, to say the least, ironic that the carefully considered judicial criteria that require similar fact evidence to be rejected unless it reaches such a high level of probative value as to outweigh any prejudice that may arise from its admission, should, by virtue of s. 12, automatically cease to obtain. This starkly highlights the fact that the prejudice explicitly recognized by the law does not cease to obtain merely because of the accused's decision to testify.

I agree with Professor Friedland, loc. cit., that the law's sedulously fostered position, that the character of an accused may not be considered unless he first raises the issue or unless the Crown meets the criteria of similar fact evidence, ought not easily yield to what a Law Reform Commission of Canada paper has described as "the fallacy [in s. 12] that it is rational to treat the accused like an ordinary non-party witness" (Evidence, Study Paper No. 3: *Credibility* (1972), p. 8). Furthermore, I think it self-evident that the law cannot profess to learn from common sense and experience and yet selectively ignore such lessons. I also think it significant that I have not unearthed any academic or empirical evidence tending to undermine these observations. Indeed, quite the contrary is true: see Wissler and Saks, "On the Inefficacy of Limiting Instructions: When Jurors Use Prior Conviction Evidence to Decide on Guilt" (1985), 9 *Law and Human Behavior* 37; Ratushny, op. cit.; Friedland, loc. cit.

Nor, in my opinion, ought the law simply to assert away this problem by reflexively invoking the virtues of the jury system, and in particular the time-honoured and obviously practical and necessary assumption that jurors are eminently capable of following a judge's limiting instructions respecting the uses to which evidence may be put, as seems to be done in some cases; ...

It seems to me that it is specious to say that to recognize what we know from experience to be the limitations of the human reasoning process is simultaneously to discredit the general utility of the jury as an instrument of justice. Indeed, an appreciation of human limitations can only redound to the benefit of the system as a whole by ensuring that these are accounted for and protected against. We deceive ourselves if we expect the jury to reason in ways that we, as lawyers and judges, know from experience to be often unrealistic, if not impossible.

. . .

… Having satisfied myself that the risk of prejudice is by no means speculative or illusory, I now turn to the question whether s. 12 admits of a discretion in the trial judge to prevent such prejudice materializing.

[La Forest J held that the word "may" in s 12 preserved the trial judge's common law discretion to exclude evidence where the prejudicial effect of the evidence outweighed its probative value. He continued:]

Factors to Be Considered

. . .

It is impossible to provide an exhaustive catalogue of the factors that are relevant in assessing the probative value or potential prejudice of such evidence, but among the most important are the nature of the previous conviction and its remoteness or nearness to the present charge.

Clearly, the probative value and prejudicial effect of a previous conviction are directly affected by the nature of that conviction. As the Court of Appeals, DC Circuit stated, in *Gordon v. US*, 383 F.2d 936 at p. 940 (1967):

> In considering how the District Court is to exercise the discretionary power we granted, we must look to the legitimate purpose of impeachment which is, of course, not to show that the accused who takes the stand is a "bad" person but rather to show background facts which bear directly on whether jurors ought to believe him rather than other and conflicting witnesses. In common human experience acts of deceit, fraud, cheating, or stealing, for example, are universally regarded as conduct which reflects adversely on a man's honesty and integrity. Acts of violence on the other hand, which may result from a short temper, a combative nature, extreme provocation, or other causes, generally have little or no direct bearing on honesty and veracity.

Clearly, too, the more similar the offence to which the previous conviction relates to the conduct for which the accused is on trial, the greater the prejudice harboured by its admission. I agree fully with the opinion of the court in *Gordon*, *supra*, at p. 940, that:

> A special and even more difficult problem arises when the prior conviction is for the same or substantially the same conduct for which the accused is on trial. Where multiple convictions of various kinds can be shown, strong reasons arise for excluding those which are for the same crime because of the inevitable pressure on lay jurors to believe that "if he did it before he probably did so this time." *As a general guide those convictions which are for the same crime should be admitted sparingly; one solution might well be that discretion be exercised to limit the impeachment by way of a similar crime to a single conviction and then only when the circumstances indicate strong reasons for disclosure and where the conviction directly relates to veracity.* [Emphasis added.]

I think that a court should be very chary of admitting evidence of a previous conviction for a similar crime, especially when the rationale for the stringent test for admitting "similar fact" evidence is kept in mind.

The remoteness or nearness of the previous conviction is also, as the court in *Gordon*, *supra*, stated, "a factor of no small importance" (at p. 940). Combined with this factor are the circumstances of the accused. As the court in that case put it, at p. 940: "Even [a conviction] involving fraud or stealing, for example, if it occurred long before and has been followed by a legally blameless life, should generally be excluded on the ground of remoteness."

One further, and to my mind, problematic factor that often surfaces in the case-law of both countries (as it does in the present case) is whether it is fair not only to the accused but to the prosecution to prohibit cross-examination respecting previous convictions, especially when a deliberate attack has been made upon the credibility of a Crown witness and where the resolution of the case boils down to a credibility contest between the accused and that witness … .

The rationale for permitting cross-examination in such circumstances clearly is that the jury ought to have before it the record of the person attacking the credibility of the Crown witness' character in order to determine whether he is any more worthy of belief than the person attacked.

· · ·

My own view is that there may be cases where the interests of not presenting a distorted picture to the jury might require permitting such cross-examination, but I do not think this factor can override the concern for a fair trial. Indeed, cross-examination should only be permitted on the foregoing basis where to do so would render the trial more, and not less, fair; … .

It must be remembered that prejudicial potential and probative value are not abstract qualities. They exist in the context of a concrete case and are determined with reference to the circumstances of the case. I turn now to briefly consider the *Charter*.

Section 12 and the Charter

It may be argued that even the recognition of a discretion to exclude after consideration of the factors outlined earlier in this judgment does not ensure that s. 12, as it applies to an accused person, satisfies the constitutional mandates of the *Charter*. Indeed, while the appellant's main argument was that such a discretion must exist, as a minimum, to validate s. 12 under the *Charter*, he also appears to have attacked more generally the application of s. 12 to accused persons under any circumstances.

In so far as his argument questions the fairness of the trial or the impartiality of the triers of fact (s. 11(d)) on the ground that s. 12 admits evidence irrelevant to the issue of credibility, I reiterate my view that such evidence is relevant and *prima facie* admissible. Evidence of previous convictions advances, to a greater or lesser extent, a fact in issue, *i.e.*, the credibility of an accused who testifies, and is therefore relevant. In my view, admitting relevant evidence, in the absence of a valid reason for excluding it, accords with the principles of fundamental justice, as does the exclusion of irrelevant evidence. Thus this general or first principle of the law of evidence, the principle of relevancy, helps to ensure that the trial is conducted fairly and that justice is done.

If the appellant's broader argument is based on the notion that, to ensure a fair trial and impartial jurors, evidence of the previous convictions of an accused should always, as a matter of law, be excluded because of their prejudicial effect and in spite of their probative value, I cannot agree. It is true that s. 11 of the *Charter* constitutionalizes the right of an accused and not that of the state to a fair trial before an impartial tribunal. But "fairness" implies, and in my view demands, consideration also of the interests of the state as representing the public. Likewise the principles of fundamental justice operate to protect the integrity of the system itself, recognizing the legitimate interest not only of the accused but also of the accuser. To accept the appellant's argument would be to ignore those considerations.

In my view, the recognition of a discretion to exclude evidence when its probative value is overshadowed by prejudicial effect ensures that the legitimate interests of both the public and the accused are taken into account. Justice and fairness demand no less and expect no more. The factors that should be considered in exercising this discretion, which I have earlier set out, ensure that this occurs. Each of them assists in focusing the inquiry on whether the probative value of any previous convictions the Crown seeks to introduce into evidence is sufficient to counterbalance the unjustified prejudice to the accused that would result, thus securing fairness to both. Indeed, as I earlier noted, the touchstone of all these factors is the fairness of the proceedings.

The recognition and proper exercise of this discretion, therefore, ensures that s. 12 is constitutionally valid. Of course if it is improperly exercised, or if, as is the case here, the trial judge fails to recognize that such a discretion is vested in him, then an appellate court may review the matter and order a new trial, find there has not been a miscarriage of justice and confirm the conviction or, in appropriate circumstances, exercise its own discretion in the matter: see *R v. Watts* ... [(1983), 77 Cr App R 126 (CA)].

I would stress, however, that, as is the case when an appellate court undertakes to review a trial judge's decision which is based at least in part on the unique circumstances of the case before him and his own first hand view of the proceedings, restraint ought to be exercised in interfering with a trial judge's exercise of discretion. More specifically, an appellate court should never, in the absence of clear error, simply substitute its own view of how that discretion ought to have been exercised for that of the trial judge.

I turn now to consider whether, in the circumstances of the present case, the trial judge, had he considered himself to have a discretion to exclude, ought to have excluded the previous conviction for non-capital murder, and if so whether the conviction entered against the appellant can now stand.

Disposition

· · ·

As I indicated in my earlier comments respecting the admission into evidence of previous convictions for offences similar to that for which the accused is on trial, I think it self-evident that the prejudicial potential harboured by the admission at a trial for murder of a previous conviction for non-capital murder is manifestly profound. Furthermore, the probative value of this item of evidence in relation to credibility (which is the only use to which it legitimately could be put) is, at best, trifling, certainly in this case. The foregoing alone appears to satisfy a narrow reading of the test in *Wray, supra*.

However, as I mentioned earlier, discretion cannot be judicially exercised in a vacuum; it is only with reference to the circumstances of the case that its exercise becomes meaningful. The circumstances of the present case, however, rather than "indicat[ing] strong reasons for disclosure" (*Gordon, supra,* at p. 940), militate strenuously for exclusion. It is true that the appellant had assailed the credibility of Crown witnesses and, indeed, that credibility was the vital issue at trial. However, the circumstances of the case itself, indicating a violation by the appellant of his parole conditions, and the substance of the appellant's defence, indicating clearly the appellant's involvement in cocaine transactions, would have served to bring home to the jury the unsavoury criminal character of the appellant and, on the theory that such evidence affects credibility, this objective would have been fulfilled. This, along with the evidence of the appellant's previous convictions for theft and breaking and entering, amply served the purpose of impeaching his credibility. Indeed, the convictions for theft and breaking and entering, though quite remote in time, would appear far more probative of a disposition for dishonesty than a conviction for murder. The latter, in the circumstances of the case, added very little, if anything, to the jury's perception of the appellant's character for veracity; on the other hand, in the words of Hutcheon JA in the court below, "it might well be that the fact that he had been convicted some years before of a similar offence might have been the last ounce which turned the scales against him." The jury's actions at trial in this case in no way diminish this possibility.

Conclusion

I conclude, therefore, that s. 12 of the *Canada Evidence Act,* when read in conjunction with the salutary common law discretion to exclude prejudicial evidence, does not violate an accused's right to a fair trial nor deprive him of his liberty except in accordance with the principles of fundamental justice. Here, the trial judge erred in law in failing to recognize the existence of the exclusionary discretion described above and, consequently, in admitting into evidence the previous conviction for murder. Given my belief that the introduction of this evidence was, in the circumstances of the case, unjustifiably prejudicial to the fairness of the appellant's trial, I am unable to conclude that no substantial wrong or miscarriage of justice was occasioned thereby. I would, therefore, allow the appeal, quash the conviction and order a new trial pursuant to s. 613(9)(b) of the *Criminal Code.*

[Estey J took no part in the judgment.]

As a result of the ruling in *Corbett,* the defence may now make a "*Corbett* application" to determine what portions of the accused's criminal record may be the subject of cross-examination pursuant to s 12 of the *Canada Evidence Act.* A *voir dire* is held in which the trial judge considers the factors outlined by La Forest J in *Corbett,* in light of the accused's criminal record, the nature of the case, and the evidence that the defence intends to call, all in order to weigh the probative value of the prior convictions in relation to their potential for prejudice. In *R v Underwood,* [1998] 1 SCR 77, the Supreme Court of Canada explained that—as part of the "case-to-meet" principle protected by s 7 of the Charter—the defence is entitled to know whether the Crown will be permitted to cross-examine on the accused's criminal record before calling evidence and deciding whether the accused will take the stand. Accordingly, the defence should make a *Corbett* application after the Crown closes its case.

In *R v St Pierre* (1974), 3 OR (2d) 642, 17 CCC (2d) 489 (CA), the Ontario Court of Appeal held that it was permissible for the accused's counsel to question him in chief as to his prior convictions:

> In the absence of [s 12], except in cases where the accused has put his good character in issue, and unless the question comes within other specific exceptions, Crown counsel would not be permitted to cross-examine the accused as to whether he has in the past been found guilty of other criminal offences. There has been a long-established practice in this Province wherein counsel for the accused has been permitted to examine the accused in chief on these same matters. Although in a technical sense it may be said that at that stage of the trial where the accused is not otherwise putting his character in issue the evidence is inadmissible, it has been permitted to be asked on the basis of its fairness. Where an accused with a criminal record does testify, his failure to disclose his criminal record in chief, and his admission of it only when being confronted with it on his cross-examination, may lead the jury to conclude that he had been less than frank and may have been concealing his record from the jury.

If the result of a *Corbett* application is that the Crown will be entitled to cross-examine on the accused's criminal record, introducing that information in direct examination is a wise way to "soften the blow" of the impeachment.

As you can see, the decision on a *Corbett* application is highly discretionary, asking a judge to weigh a range of factors, none of which alone is dispositive. Moreover, the law is clear that appellate courts should give a high degree of deference to such rulings (*R v NAP* (2002), 171 CCC (3d) 70 (Ont CA); *R v Simpson*, 2004 ABCA 146). The mix of this wide discretion and deference has produced significant variance in the outcomes of *Corbett* applications: see Peter Sankoff, "The Search for a Better Understanding of Discretionary Power in Evidence Law" (2007) 32 Queen's LJ 487.

Although *Corbett* applications arose in the criminal realm, where the liberty of the accused is at issue, they may have some role in civil proceedings, in which substantial concerns about the prejudicial effect of a prior criminal record can also arise. In *Hutton v Way* (1997), 105 OAC 361 (CA), a personal injury case heard before a jury, the defendant was permitted to cross-examine the plaintiff with respect to convictions for sexual assault, dangerous driving, and possession of marijuana, all committed when he was a teenager. Finlayson JA, writing for the court, noted that "the stale dated criminal record of the appellant did not relate to offences involving fraud or dishonesty" and found that "[w]hile *prima facie* admissible under the Ontario *Evidence Act*, these convictions should have been excluded on the *Corbett* application brought by the appellant" (at para 5).

PROBLEMS: APPLYING CORBETT

1. The accused was charged with sexual assault and incest with his daughter. His defence was denial. His criminal record included two convictions for rape in 1976 and two convictions for wounding with intent. The complainant had no criminal record. Before the accused

testified, defence counsel applied to have the record excluded, or in the alternative, edited to exclude cross-examination on the rape convictions. As trial judge, would you (a) exclude the record entirely, (b) edit the record to prevent cross-examination on the rape convictions, (c) permit cross-examination on the entire record, but instruct the jury on the difference between crimes of dishonesty and crimes of violence, or (d) permit cross-examination on the entire record, and instruct the jury that the convictions were relevant only to the accused's credibility, not to his guilt? See *R v T (DB)* (1994), 89 CCC (3d) 466 (Ont CA).

2. The accused was charged with trafficking in cocaine. The Crown witnesses were all police officers. Identity was in issue; in particular, although the officers picked him out of a photo line-up of known offenders, the accused had distinctive scars on his face which were not mentioned by the officers in their descriptions of the offender. The accused had a lengthy criminal record which included offences of dishonesty as well as three prior convictions for narcotics offences. He sought to have the three narcotics convictions excluded pursuant to *Corbett*. As trial judge, would you (a) exclude the narcotics convictions, or (b) permit cross-examination on the entire record, but instruct the jury on the difference between crimes of dishonesty and crimes relating to narcotics? See *R v Brand* (1995), 98 CCC (3d) 477 (Ont CA).

3. The accused was charged with sexual assault. His defence was consent. He had a lengthy criminal record culminating in two convictions for sexual assault in 1989. The complainant had no criminal record. The trial judge refused to exclude the last two convictions and instructed the jury that they were relevant to the accused's credibility. He was convicted. On appeal, McFayden JA, Perras J concurring, held that the convictions were properly admitted as relevant to credibility in that a person who disregards society's rules is more likely to lie. Kerans JA, dissenting, would have excluded the last two convictions because of the great danger that the jury would use them improperly to conclude that the accused liked non-consensual sex and was therefore more likely to have committed the offence charged. The accused has appealed as of right to the Supreme Court. You are a judge of that court. Do you agree with the majority's rationale for allowing cross-examination on the entire record? If you do, what will you say about its consistency with *Corbett*? See *R v Charland* (1996), 110 CCC (3d) 300 (Alta CA), aff'd [1997] 3 SCR 1006.

4. The accused is charged with sexual assault. He has a criminal record that includes recent convictions for sexual assault. His *Corbett* application is unsuccessful. He chooses not to testify and is convicted. On appeal, he submits that the *Corbett* ruling was erroneous, and that it precluded him from testifying in his own defence. The Crown submits that, since the accused chose not to testify, it is impossible to assess the extent to which he was prejudiced, and that the correctness of the *Corbett* ruling should therefore not be considered. You are a justice of appeal. How do you rule on the threshold question of whether the *Corbett* ruling is reviewable on appeal? See *R v Grant* (1996), 110 CCC (3d) 287 (Man CA), leave to appeal refused, [1996] SCCA No 602 (QL).

D. Expert Evidence

A party may impeach a witness by calling expert opinion evidence that discloses a physical or mental defect affecting the witness's capacity to observe, remember, and communicate—a fault in that witness's testimonial capacities. Any such evidence would have to satisfy the criteria for the admission of expert opinion evidence, canvassed in Chapter 5, including the requirement for necessity. Accordingly, when the trier of fact would be able to assess the witness's credibility without expert assistance, expert's evidence impeaching credibility would be inadmissible. Thus a psychiatrist will not be permitted to testify regarding the reliability of a witness where he has based his assessment primarily on his observation of her testimony, and acknowledges that her character flaws would be evident to, and assessable by, the trier of fact (see *R v French* (1977), 37 CCC (2d) 201 (Ont CA)). Consider the following case on the admission of such expert evidence to impeach credibility.

Toohey v Metropolitan Police Commissioner
[1965] 1 All ER 506, [1965] AC 595 (HL)
Lord Reid, Lord Morris of Borth-y-Gest, Lord Hodson, Lord Pearce,
and Lord Donovan (1 February 1965)

LORD PEARCE: My Lords, the appellant and two other men were convicted on indictment of together assaulting Madden, a youth of seventeen, with intent to rob him. The episode took place in the dark in an alleyway beside and behind a cinema. The main evidence for the prosecution was that of Madden. There was also evidence from two police officers who saw two men standing in the shadows outside the cinema, and, being suspicious, turned their car. A faint crying noise directed them to the alleyway where they found Madden with his back to the wall and the three accused standing round him. The appellant was holding his arm. Madden's face was tear-stained; he was in a very distressed and hysterical condition, and his clothes were dishevelled. The accused claimed that they had done nothing wrong to him and were going to take him home. The boy said that he was going to the police station. He attempted to run away from the police officers, but they caught him and took him to the police station where he was examined by the divisional police surgeon. At the trial Madden gave evidence that he was dragged into the dark alleyway, that the appellant hit him in the stomach and on the head until he "saw sparks"; and that one of the accused searched him but took nothing since he did not find the 10s. note which was in an inside pocket.

The defence was that Madden appeared to have been drinking and was behaving strangely, laughing and joking, and apparently incapable of taking care of himself. The three accused men were going to take him home, but one of them wanted to make water; so they went down the alleyway behind the cinema. While the appellant was relieving himself, Madden bumped into him from behind, banged himself against a wall, and became hysterical, saying that someone had hit him and that they were after his money. They held his arm and took him up the alleyway to calm him down and get him home. They claimed that his account was an hysterical invention.

The police surgeon gave evidence for the defence to the effect that no bruises or signs of injury were found on Madden; that there was a definite smell of alcohol on his breath; that throughout the examination he was weeping and in a state of acute hysteria; that he was unable to reply sensibly to any question; and that at the end of the examination he just "flopped down" on the floor. The doctor was, however, prevented by a ruling of the learned commissioner from giving certain further evidence. That exclusion is the ground of the present appeal.

. . .

[Lord Pearce first addressed the question as to whether the evidence of the police surgeon was admissible as relevant to the facts at issue in the trial, apart from its use in showing a defect in Mr. Madden's testimonial abilities. On this first question, he ruled that this evidence was admissible because, quite apart from its possible use in generally discrediting the witness, it was relevant to help establish what had happened in the alleyway. He then turned to the key point in the appeal:]

The second question, whether it was permissible to impeach the credibility of Madden, *qua* witness, by medical evidence of his hysterical and unstable nature, raises a wider and more important problem which applies to evidence in criminal and civil cases.

The Court of Criminal Appeal held that such evidence was not admissible, since they were bound by the case of *Gunewardene* [*R v Gunewardene*, [1951] 2 All ER 290 (KB)]. Undoubtedly they were right in thinking that on this point the present case is not distinguishable from it. In *Gunewardene*'s case the appellant (to quote the words of Lord Goddard)

> wished to call [Doctor Leigh] to say that he … had examined the witness and had come to
> the conclusion that the man was suffering from a disease of the mind, and that, therefore,
> he regarded his testimony as unreliable. In our opinion, that is exactly what the cases show
> cannot be done.

. . .

From olden times it has been the practice to allow evidence of bad reputation to discredit a witness's testimony. It is perhaps not very logical and not very useful to allow such evidence founded on hearsay. None of your lordships, and none of the counsel before you, could remember being concerned in a case where such evidence was called; but the rule has been sanctified through the centuries in legal examinations and text books and in some rare cases, and it does not create injustice.

. . .

There seems little point, however, for present purposes in exploring these archaic niceties. The old cases are concerned with lying as an aspect of bad character, and are of little help in establishing any principle that will deal with modern scientific knowledge of mental disease and its effect on the reliability of a witness. I accept all of the judgment in *Gunewardene*'s case in so far as it deals with the older cases and the topic with which they were concerned; but, in my opinion, the court erred in using it as a guide to the admissibility of medical evidence concerning illness or abnormality affecting the mind of a witness and reducing his capacity to give reliable evidence. This unreliability may have two aspects either separate from one another or acting jointly to create confusion. The witness may, through his mental trouble, derive a fanciful or untrue picture from events while they are actually occurring, or he may have a fanciful or untrue recollection of them which distorts his evidence at the time when he is giving it.

. . .

If a witness purported to give evidence of something which he believed that he had seen at a distance of fifty yards, it must surely be possible to call the evidence of an oculist to the effect that the witness could not possibly see anything at a greater distance than twenty yards, or the evidence of a surgeon who had removed a cataract from which the witness was suffering at the material time and which would have prevented him from seeing what he thought he saw. So, too, must it be allowable to call medical evidence of mental illness which makes a witness incapable of giving reliable evidence, whether through the existence of delusions or otherwise.

It is obviously in the interest of justice that such evidence should be available. The only argument that I can see against its admission is that there might be a conflict between the doctors and that there would then be a trial within a trial; but such cases would be rare. And if they arose, they would not create any insuperable difficulty, since there are many cases in practice where a trial within a trial is achieved without difficulty. And in such a case as this (unlike the issues relating to confessions) there would not be the inconvenience of having to exclude the jury, since the dispute would be for their use and their instruction.

. . .

Gunewardene's case was, in my opinion, wrongly decided. Medical evidence is admissible to show that a witness suffers from some disease or defect or abnormality of mind that affects the reliability of his evidence. Such evidence is not confined to a general opinion of the unreliability of the witness, but may give all the matters necessary to show not only the foundation of and reasons for the diagnosis but also the extent to which the credibility of the witness is affected.

I would therefore allow the appeal.

What is the difference between the test for the admissibility of expert evidence to attack credibility and to enhance credibility? What is the rationale for the difference?

E. Bad Reputation for Veracity

As you learned in the section on supporting the credibility of your own witness, the defence in a criminal trial is permitted to call a witness to testify to the accused's good reputation for veracity. Although an uncommon practice, the law also permits the calling of a witness who will testify to another witness's bad reputation for veracity. The rationale is to prevent a jury from unwittingly relying on the testimony of a witness known to be an inveterate liar. And yet this practice presents the risk of distraction and inefficiency, not to mention the apparently low probative value of this kind of evidence.

In *R v Gonzague* (1983), 4 CCC (3d) 505 at 512 (Ont CA), Martin JA listed the following questions that could be asked of a defence witness called to give evidence about a Crown witness's reputation for veracity:

1. Do you know the reputation of the witness as to truth and veracity in the community in which the witness resides?
   If the answer is "yes" the questioning proceeds.
2. Is that reputation good or bad?
   If the answer is "bad" a final question is permitted.
3. From that reputation, would you believe the witness on oath?

The ability to call such evidence was described by Rosenberg JA in *R v Clarke* (1998), 129 CCC (3d) 1 at para 1 (Ont CA), as "one of the more anomalous rules" of evidence. In *Clarke*, Rosenberg JA reconsidered this practice of an accused calling a witness to testify to the bad reputation for veracity of a Crown witness. He explained that certain developments in the law since *Gonzague* put this practice into question:

[45] The most important development in the law of evidence since the decisions of this court is the recognition by McLachlin J. in [*R v Seaboyer; R v Gayme*, [1991] 2 SCR 577] that relevant defence evidence is subject to the balancing of probative value against prejudicial effect. The test for exclusion of relevant defence evidence is strict, but it exists.

He also explained that the Supreme Court of Canada's decision in *R v Béland*, [1987] 2 SCR 398 (discussed earlier in this chapter), was an important development in its strong disapproval of the practice of oath-helping, risking as it did "a return to the method of pre-Norman trials where parties relied heavily upon oath-helpers who swore to their veracity" (at 418). Although *Béland* was concerned with oath-helping, Rosenberg JA found that such concerns were equally applicable to the practice of oath-attacking evidence. In light of these considerations, Rosenberg JA looked back at the three questions permitted by *Gonzague* and concluded as follows:

[49] In my view, the prejudicial effect of the answer to the third question will almost invariably substantially outweigh its probative value. The form in which the evidence is presented tends to usurp the function of the jury ... .

[50] ... While the defence witnesses may know the Crown witness' reputation for telling the truth in everyday affairs, for the reasons expressed earlier, their ability to predict the witness' behaviour in court is limited and entitled to no special deference.

[51] Where the outcome of the case depends upon the evidence of a single witness, an expression of opinion as to that witness' veracity is a comment on the ultimate issue. There is the risk that in some cases the jury will simply defer to the opinion of the character witness rather than embarking on the difficult task of examining the evidence and measuring it against the standard of proof beyond a reasonable doubt, on the theory that the character witness obviously knows the Crown witness and is in a much better position to determine the outcome of the case. Put another way, the ability of a character witness, who has not heard the evidence in the case, to predict whether another witness has told the truth under oath is very limited. The jury may, however, overvalue that opinion because the character witness knows the witness.

[52] Accordingly, I would hold that the accused does not have the absolute right to ask the third question and that in most cases the trial judge would be justified in refusing to permit that question to be asked. I would adopt the holding by Cumming J.A. in *Masztalar v. Wiens* (1992), 10 B.C.A.C. 19 (B.C. C.A.), at 23 to the effect that while the rule need not be absolutely abolished it should be retained "to be sparingly applied only in the rare case where the interests of justice require it." To the extent that the decisions of this court in Gonzague and *Taylor* [*R v Taylor* (1986), 55 CR (3d) 321 (Ont CA)] hold to the contrary, they should no longer be followed.

With respect to the first two questions, Rosenberg JA held that the trial judge also has the discretion to refuse to allow that evidence, though "it would be an extremely rare case where a trial judge would be warranted in excluding the evidence" (at para 53). Those first two questions do not carry the same risk of usurpation, distraction, or the proliferation of side issues, he reasoned. As to the risk of the undue consumption of time, he explained that a trial judge has the discretion to limit the number of such witnesses called by the defence, though he warned that "[t]he judge will, however, wish to keep in mind that the Supreme Court in *Seaboyer* has held that the discretion to exclude relevant evidence must be exercised with extreme caution and that in most cases the better course would be to permit the defence to call all of those witnesses" (at para 54).

Finally, Rosenberg JA held that when evidence of bad reputation for veracity of a witness is admitted, a trial judge should cover at least two points in a charge to the jury:

> [55] ... First, whatever the witness' reputation for veracity in the community, testifying in court under oath is a very different circumstance and the jury will want to bear this in mind. Second, the character witnesses have not heard all the evidence, and are not sworn to the heavy duty of the juror to render a true verdict. The jury may find the reputation evidence helpful in determining the credibility of the witnesses, but they should not automatically defer to that evidence. ...

Once a witness's credibility is impeached by evidence of that witness's bad reputation for veracity, a party may respond with rebuttal evidence, including evidence of that witness's good reputation for truthfulness (*Clarke*, at para 22).

QUESTIONS

1. Do you agree with the distinction that Rosenberg JA draws between the first two questions and the third question? Note that, with respect to expert opinion evidence, the concern that it addresses the "ultimate issue" is no longer considered a bar to admissibility (see Chapter 5, Section III.D). Nonetheless, is there a rationale for limiting the testimony of one witness regarding his or her opinion of the reliability of another witness?

2. If the first two questions are asked, what factors might justify a trial judge's exercise of discretion to permit the third question?

3. Does Rosenberg JA's reasoning support any distinction between evidence of good reputation for veracity offered to support the credibility of a defence witness and evidence of bad reputation offered to attack the credibility of a Crown witness? Can the Crown lead this type of evidence to support the credibility of its witnesses and attack the credibility of the defence witnesses?

IV. CHALLENGING THE CREDIBILITY OF YOUR OWN WITNESS

So far, this chapter has proceeded on the assumption that a party will seek to support the credibility of its own witnesses, called in its case in chief, and aims to impeach the credibility of the opposing party's witnesses through cross-examination. However, what if counsel calls a witness for direct examination and that witness fails to provide the evidence hoped for or anticipated? If the witness claims not to remember the past events in question, counsel may attempt to refresh that witness's memory, as discussed in Chapter 2, Section III.C, or, with leave of the court, may ask leading questions: see *R v Coffin*, [1956] SCR 191 at 211. But what if the problem is greater than simply a matter of forgetfulness, capable of being addressed with these techniques? What if a party's own witness provides evidence that is inconsistent with past statements or that counsel believes to be false? Counsel cannot generally cross-examine her own witness and yet in this situation she will want to go about impeaching her witness's testimony, including by proving past inconsistent statements and cross-examining on those statements and, perhaps, beyond.

This section introduces the rules applicable to this situation, exploring the common law and statutory means by which counsel can be given leave to prove prior inconsistent statements and impeach their own witness through cross-examination. The section begins by examining the common law rule that allows one's own witness to be declared "hostile," and the scope of impeachment that flows from that declaration. The section then turns to a complex set of statutory provisions focused on findings that a witness is "adverse," provisions that augment or, on some interpretations, functionally replace the common law hostility test. For an excellent treatment of these issues, see David M Paciocco, "Confronting Disappointing, Hostile and Adverse Witnesses in Criminal Cases" (2012) 59 Crim LQ 301.

As you proceed through this section, bear in mind that, whatever permission to impeach one's own witness might be granted through the common law or statutory schemes, counsel are never permitted to engage in general attacks on the character of their own witness for trustworthiness, for example, by calling general bad reputation evidence for veracity or discrediting their witness on the basis of prior convictions or other past discreditable conduct. This boundary on impeachment of one's own witness flows from the theory—perhaps somewhat dated and open to question—that one has tacitly "vouched for" a witness that one has called.

A. "Hostility" at Common Law

At common law, counsel could apply to have their own witness declared "hostile." In *R v Coffin*, cited above, the court described a hostile witness as one who is "not giving her evidence fairly and with a desire to tell the truth because of a hostile animus toward" (at 213) the party who called her. The reference to a *hostile animus* signals that the concern under this common law test is not just with the content of the witness's testimony, but with the motivations and attitudes evident in the witness's approach to providing her evidence. In deciding whether a witness is hostile, on this definition, a trial judge will consider "all and any evidence relevant to that issue" (*Wawanesa Mutual Insurance Co v Hanes*, [1961] OR 495, [1963] 1 CCC 176 at 222 (CA)), including the substance of the witness's evidence, as well as the witness's demeanour and attitude on the stand.

The consequence of a finding of hostility at common law is that counsel is entitled to cross-examine that witness "at large." "At large" means that counsel is not limited to cross-examining the witness on prior inconsistent statements; rather, the witness "is subject to a general cross-examination as to all matters in issue" (*Wawanesa*, at 220). Subject to the prohibition on general attacks on the character of one's own witness, counsel may impeach the reliability of the witness's testimony and may even seek, through cross-examination, to obtain helpful evidence from this now "hostile" witness.

B. "Adversity" Under Statute

Statutory provisions, at both the federal and provincial levels, offer another means of impeaching one's own witness, one that turns on a party's witness proving "adverse." On the face of these provisions, they appear to be concerned with providing a procedure by which counsel can prove prior inconsistent statements made by their own witness. As you will see, however, as a product of expansive judicial interpretation, the reach and effect of these provisions is far greater. The federal statutory provision, s 9(1) of the *Canada Evidence Act*, reads as follows:

9(1) A party producing a witness shall not be allowed to impeach his credit by general evidence of bad character, but if the witness, in the opinion of the court, proves adverse, the party may contradict him by other evidence, or, by leave of the court, may prove that the witness made at other times a statement inconsistent with his present testimony, but before the last mentioned proof can be given the circumstances of the supposed statement, sufficient to designate the particular occasion, shall be mentioned to the witness, and he shall be asked whether or not he did make the statement.

The text of this provision, and the provincial provisions that mirror it, does not reflect the way that this area of law operates in practice. Indeed, the statute is afflicted by a drafting error: s 9(1) suggests that a finding of "adversity" is a precondition to a party contradicting its witness "by other evidence." This is not the case: see *Greenough v Eccles* (1859), 5 CB (NS) 786, 141 ER 315, and *Wawanesa*, cited above. Counsel are always permitted to "contradict" the evidence of one of their own witnesses by calling another witness who will provide different and, counsel will urge, preferable testimony.

Through judicial consideration, two issues regarding the interpretation and effect of this provision have emerged. The first is the meaning of "adversity." Although some courts have expressed the view that "adverse" means the same thing as "hostile" at common law, meaning that it would require that a witness display a hostile animus towards the party who called him, the prevailing view is that adversity is a broader concept than hostility. Interpreting the predecessor to the current s 23 of the Ontario *Evidence Act*, in *Wawanesa*, at 187-91, Porter CJO explained as follows, also setting out the procedure for determining if a witness has proven "adverse":

If it had been intended that a witness must be shown to be hostile in mind before the statement could be admitted, the statute could have said so. The word "adverse" is a more comprehensive expression than "hostile." It includes the concept of hostility of mind, but also includes what may be merely opposed in interest or unfavourable in the sense of opposite in position. As defined in the *Shorter Oxford English Dictionary*, the word is given the following meanings: "1. Acting in opposition to, actively hostile. 2. Opposing anyone's interests; hence, unfavourable, injurious, calamitous. 3. Opposite in position." At common law, in some cases it was attempted to draw a distinction between the use of a prior inconsistent statement for the purpose solely of impeaching the credit of a witness and cases in which it was introduced for other purposes, although it might consequentially impeach the credit of a witness. By the section the prior inconsistent statement even though its only effect is to impeach the credibility of the witness, may be put to the witness. I also think that the argument which was rejected in the *Greenough* case is persuasive. It is summarized by Williams J at p. 803, and in part is as follows:

The fetter thus imposed, it is further said, would be harmless in its operation, if "adverse" be construed "unfavourable," but most oppressive if it means "hostile"; because the party producing the witness would be fixed with his evidence, when it proved pernicious in case the judge did not think the witness "hostile," which might often happen; whereas, he could not in such a case fail to think him "unfavorable."

That is precisely the situation in the case at bar. The prior inconsistent statements were submitted for the purpose of impeaching the credit of the witnesses. The learned Judge refused to declare the witnesses hostile. Consequently, by reason of his ruling that "adverse" meant "hostile," the learned Judge did not consider whether the witness, although not hostile, was adverse in the broader sense and therefore did not exercise any discretion as to the admission of the alleged statement.

. . .

I am of the opinion that s. 24 of the *Evidence Act* covers the whole field of prior inconsistent statements made by a witness of a party producing him. It embraces inconsistent prior state-ments made by a hostile witness, and by one who though not hostile is unfavourable in the sense of assuming by his testimony a position opposite to that of the party calling him.

In cases where application is made to introduce a prior inconsistent statement under the Act, the Judge should to determine whether a witness is adverse, consider the testimony of the wit-ness, and the statement, and satisfy himself upon any relevant material presented to him that the witness made the statement. He should consider the relative importance of the statement, and whether it is substantially inconsistent. I think the Judge is entitled to consider all surrounding circumstances that may assist him in forming his opinion as to whether the witness is adverse. It would be proper and the safer course, if such an enquiry becomes necessary, to conduct it in the absence of the jury, if the case is being tried by a jury. If after due enquiry the Judge is satisfied that the witness is adverse, he may consider whether under all the circumstances, and bearing in mind the possible dangers of admitting such a statement, the ends of justice would be best attained by admitting it. The section does not contemplate the indiscriminate admission of statements of this kind. If he exercises this discretion in favour of giving leave, he should in the presence of the Jury, direct that the circumstances of the making of the statement be put to the witness and that he be asked whether he made the statement. Then, in the presence of the jury, he should allow the statement to be proved but he should instruct the jury that the prior statement is not evi-dence of the facts contained therein, but is for the purpose of showing that the sworn testimony given at the trial could not be regarded as of importance: *R v. Duckworth*, 26 Can. CC at p. 351, 37 OLR at p. 234, *per* Masten J and *R v. Harris* ... [(1927), 20 Cr App R 144]. It is for the jury, upon all the evidence before them, to decide whether the prior statement had in fact been made by the witness, and if so whether it did affect the credibility of the evidence given at the trial. ...

As such, an adverse witness is not necessarily "hostile." As confirmed in *R v Cassibo* (1982), 39 OR (2d) 288, 70 CCC (2d) 498 at 514 (CA), an adverse witness is simply one who is "unfavourable in the sense of assuming by his testimony a position opposite to that of the party calling him." In determining whether a party's witness is adverse, a judge may look at a wide range of factors, including the content of the witness's evidence, any inconsistencies in the witness's testimony, and the tenor and manner of the witness's testimony. No hostile animus is necessary.

But what is the consequence of a finding of adversity? This is the second issue that has arisen in the judicial interpretation of s 9(1) and equivalent provincial statutes. It is clear that, upon a finding of adversity, a party may, with leave of the court, prove that its witness made a prior inconsistent statement. Like s 11 of the *Canada Evidence Act*, the provision requires that counsel first draw the witness's attention to the prior statement and ask the witness whether he or she made that statement. Although the provision makes no explicit mention of cross-examination, courts agree that a finding of adversity also entitles counsel to cross-examine and impeach the witness on the basis of that prior inconsistent statement.

The issue is whether the finding of adversity permits counsel to go further, cross-examining more broadly. One view, accepted by some courts and commentators, is that, on a finding of adversity, a party may cross-examine a witness "at large"—as permitted on a finding of hostil-ity at common law—going beyond exploring the prior inconsistent statement to impeach more generally, even seeking to obtain useful information or a more helpful version of events: see e.g. *R v T (TE)* (1991), 3 BCAC 29 (CA); and David M Paciocco & Lee Steusser, *The Law of Evidence*, 7th ed (Toronto: Irwin Law, 2015) at 551. On this view, given the expansive definition of adversity accepted by the courts, these statutory provisions render the common law hostility test obsolete. This interpretation is appealing for a number of reasons, including that it contributes to the ease with which useful and important evidence can be produced at the trial.

Some courts, however, have taken a more restrictive view on the scope of cross-examination permitted after a finding of adversity, limiting a party to cross-examining on the prior inconsistent statement and thereby preserving a role for the common law hostility test. Consider the following case, reflecting the position in Ontario:

R v Figliola
2011 ONCA 457, 105 OR (3d) 641
Rosenberg, Goudge, and Blair JJA (17 June 2011)

BY THE COURT:

[1] The appellants, Maria Figliola and Daniele Di Trapani, appeal from their convictions for first degree murder by a court composed of C. Raymond Harris J. and a jury. The Crown alleged that Ms. Figliola hired Mr. Di Trapani to kill Frank Figliola, Ms. Figliola's husband. While the appellants raised a number of grounds of appeal, we have found it necessary to deal with two: Ms. Figliola's submission concerning the cross-examination by Crown counsel of his own witness, Teresa Pignatelli, and Mr. Di Trapani's submission that the trial judge erred in refusing to grant his application for severance. For the following reasons, the appeals are allowed and separate new trials are ordered.

The Facts

[The court reviewed the events leading to the killing and the evidence adduced at trial before focusing on the evidence that raised the issue of s 9(1) of the *Canada Evidence Act*:]

Teresa Pignatelli's Evidence

[30] Crown counsel called Ms. Pignatelli to testify. She testified that she had seen Mr. Di Trapani twice on August 6, 2001. Around 9:30 p.m., while walking to a store, she saw him in the parking lot of the social club that he operated. A few minutes later, she saw him drive by her esthetics shop with Luigi Latorre. She called him on his cellphone and spoke to him for a little over two minutes at 9:31 p.m. She spoke to him again at 10:21 p.m. for four seconds. She testified that she probably called him at this time when she was going home.

[31] Ms. Pignatelli also testified to financial transactions with Ms. Figliola in November and December 2001. She received a $1,000 cheque from Ms. Figliola on November 26, 2001, which was partial repayment of a loan Ms. Pignatelli had given Ms. Figliola for her son's school tuition. Ms. Figliola gave her a cheque for $22,000 on December 10, 2001 to complete repayment of the loan and help Ms. Pignatelli retire a line of credit for which the bank was demanding repayment. Ms. Figliola confirmed this version of events.

[32] Ms. Pignatelli testified that she and Mr. Di Trapani were good friends in 2001. They had a falling out in 2002 as a result of a dispute between him and her husband. They reconciled in December of that year.

[33] Following a *voir dire*, the trial judge permitted Crown counsel to cross-examine Ms. Pignatelli as an adverse witness under s. 9(1) of the *Canada Evidence Act*, R.S.C. 1985, c. C-5. This turned into an extensive cross-examination and is the subject of a ground of appeal by Ms. Figliola. We will provide further details when dealing with this ground of appeal. In short, during this cross-examination Ms. Pignatelli was cross-examined on when she learned of Ms. Figliola's relationship with Mr. Gonsalves, the amount of money Ms. Figliola had given her, a supposed gap in telephone contact with Ms. Figliola in the week prior to the murder and allegedly inconsistent statements she had given about talking to Mr. Di Trapani on August 6, 2001 and the number of times she saw him that night. Crown counsel suggested to Ms. Pignatelli that she was covering for the appellants and was prepared to say anything on the witness stand.

The Grounds of Appeal

[34] Each of the appellants raises a number of grounds of appeal. While Ms. Figliola argues that the trial judge erred in admitting certain evidence and misdirected the jury in some respects, we only find it necessary to deal with the one ground of appeal—permitting Crown counsel to cross-examine Teresa Pignatelli as an adverse witness under s. 9(1) of the *Canada Evidence Act*.

. . .

Analysis

Cross-Examination of Ms. Pignatelli as an Adverse Witness

. . .

[37] Ms. Figliola attacks the trial judge's ruling declaring the witness, Teresa Pignatelli, an adverse witness pursuant to s. 9(1), and the Crown's cross-examination following that ruling. She submits the trial judge erroneously permitted the Crown to cross-examine its own witness for the sole purpose of demonstrating the witness was a liar attempting to cover up for the two accused and thus impermissibly tarring the appellants with the same credibility brush—all contrary to this court's decision in *R. v. Soobrian* (1994), 21 O.R. (3d) 603, [1994] O.J. No. 2836 (C.A.).

. . .

[44] Ms. Pignatelli was a close friend of both Ms. Figliola and Mr. Di Trapani. She spoke to each on a regular basis, sometimes more than once daily by telephone. She was able to give evidence with respect to (a) the relationship between the various principals, particularly of the relationship between Ms. Figliola and Mr. Gonsalves and between Ms. Figliola and Mr. Di Trapani; (b) the fact that Ms. Figliola agreed to provide a cellphone to Mr. Di Trapani through her work at her own expense; (c) the fact that she had seen Mr. Di Trapani at around 9:00 p.m. on the night of the murder in an area not far from the scene of the murder; and (d) that she had seen him in the company of the witness Louis Latorre, thus corroborating the testimony of Mr. Latorre at least insofar as they were together in the same car on the night in question.

[45] The Crown was thus justified in calling—and, indeed, may have had little choice but to call—Ms. Pignatelli as a witness. We are not able to conclude on the basis of this record that the Crown initially, and deliberately, called her for the purpose of impeaching her testimony through prior inconsistent statements and then, having obtained a s. 9(1) order and permission to cross-examine her at large, showing that she was an inveterate liar who was covering up for, and collaborating with, the two accused—thereby tarnishing their credibility as well and enhancing the likelihood of a finding of guilt. It is that type of purpose on the part of the Crown that is forbidden by *Soobrian*.

[46] That said, however, the cross-examination of Ms. Pignatelli became problematic as it evolved.

[47] The Crown cannot be faulted for seeking an adversity ruling under s. 9(1), nor do we think there is any basis for interfering with the trial judge's discretionary decision to grant that order in the circumstances. He concluded after a *voir dire*—correctly, in our view—that Ms. Pignatelli had made a number of prior statements to the police and at the preliminary hearing that were inconsistent with her testimony at trial; that she adopted a position in her testimony opposite to the Crown's position; and that she had a motive to protect her friends. There was ample support on the record for those findings and for the decision based on them.

[48] The Crown sought an order under s. 9(1) declaring Ms. Pignatelli an *adverse* witness. The trial judge made an order declaring Ms. Pignatelli an *adverse* witness. The Crown did not seek, nor did the trial judge grant, an order declaring her a *hostile* witness, and, contrary to Ms. Pignatelli's submission, the trial judge did not make an order granting the Crown leave to cross-examine Ms. Pignatelli at large. Perilously, though, everyone appears to have assumed that such an order had been made. The Crown proceeded to cross-examine the witness forcefully in a wide-ranging fashion—and with considerable success—with no intervention by the trial judge and no objection from defence counsel (not counsel on the appeal) or request for a limiting instruction to the jury.

[49] However, this seamless move to a cross-examination at large was misguided. In Ontario, a ruling that a witness is "adverse" pursuant to s. 9(1) of the *Canada Evidence Act* is not the equivalent of a common law declaration of "hostility" entitling the beneficiary of the ruling to cross-examine the witness at large. This court has held that adversity and hostility are not synonymous for these purposes: *Wawanesa Mutual Insurance Co. v. Hanes*, [1961] O.R. 495, [1961] O.J. No. 562 (C.A.); *R. v. Cassibo* (1982), 39 O.R. (2d) 288, [1982] O.J. No. 3511 (C.A.). ...

[50] This jurisprudence confirms that an "adverse" witness is one who is opposed in interest or unfavourable in the sense of opposite in position to the party calling that witness, whereas a "hostile" witness is one who demonstrates an antagonistic attitude or hostile mind toward the party calling him or her. In *R. v. Coffin*, [1956] S.C.R. 191, [1956] S.C.J. No. 1, 114 C.C.C. 1, at p. 213 S.C.R., p. 24 C.C.C., Kellock J. described a hostile witness as one who does not give his or her evidence fairly and with a desire to tell the truth because of a hostile *animus* towards the prosecution.

[51] The common law right of a party to cross-examine his or her own witness at large with leave of the trial judge, if in the judge's opinion the witness is "hostile," is not affected by s. 9(1) of the *Canada Evidence Act*: *Cassibo*, *per* Martin J.A., at p. 302 O.R. Section 9 makes no reference to a witness "proving *hostile*" and contains no suggestion of a right to cross-examine at large. As Porter C.J.O. pointed out in *Wawanesa*, a declaration of

hostility and its consequences are something that arise "in addition [to]" a finding of adversity. At pp. 507-508 O.R., after reviewing the steps to be taken by a judge in deciding whether to make a declaration of adversity and the factors to be considered, he stated that "[t]he Judge, *if he declared the witness hostile*, might, *in addition* permit him to be cross-examined" (emphasis added). It follows that a declaration of adversity pursuant to s. 9(1) was not, itself, sufficient to trigger a right in the Crown to cross-examine Ms. Pignatelli generally as to all matters in issue.

[52] Ill-advisedly, however, that is what happened. The Crown cross-examined the witness about inconsistencies between her evidence at trial and statements she had made to the police during interviews on three occasions (October 2, 2002, January 14, 2003 and January 22, 2003) as well as between her evidence at trial and at the preliminary hearing. These inconsistencies related to such things as when she knew [that] Ms. Figliola was in a relationship with Mr. Gonsalves (at trial she acknowledged suspecting they were involved at the time of the murder, but in October she told the police she did not know); the amount of money Ms. Figliola had given her; and a number of details about the evening of August 6, 2001 (in her October statement she did not tell the police she had seen Mr. Di Trapani that night; in both January statements she said she twice saw Mr. Di Trapani and Mr. Latorre drive by her shop, where she was having an ice cream with Ms. Figliola's cousin, Bruna; at trial she said they drove by once).

[53] As Ms. Pignatelli's cross-examination by the Crown developed, however, it is apparent that these questions were simply a springboard to a much broader attack on her credibility. The "cover up" theory emerged.

[54] In this respect, the Crown cross-examined Ms. Pignatelli on an intercepted phone conversation in which she had offered to "cover" for Ms. Figliola so that she could conceal from her children the fact that she had spent the night with Mr. Gonsalves at his home, thus suggesting she was "covering" for the appellant with her testimony as well.

[55] Intercepted phone calls were also the theme around which the Crown's attack on the witness' denial that she knew that Ms. Figliola's relationship with Mr. Gonsalves was intimate before the murder was built. The Crown put to Ms. Pignatelli a large number of interceptions showing Ms. Figliola's cellphone moving from the Stoney Creek area to the Scarborough area, where Mr. Gonsalves lived, over a lengthy period of time, interspersed with calls to one of Ms. Figliola's phones at or about the same time. ...

[56] During the October 2, 2002 interview, Ms. Pignatelli made no mention of Mr. Di Trapani. When questioned about Mr. Di Trapani's cellphone number, Ms. Pignatelli denied that she recognized it. Phone records showed that Ms. Pignatelli had called that number on many, many occasions. At the time of this interview, Mr. Di Trapani had not been interviewed by the police and it is not clear that he was then a suspect. The Crown used this exchange to make the point that the witness was withholding information from the police in order to deceive them, because she knew "if [she] mentioned [that the phone number was Mr. Di Trapani's] ... the logical result would be that the police would go speak to Mr. Di Trapani." Twice, Crown counsel put directly to Ms. Pignatelli that she did not identify the owner of the phone number because she was protecting Mr. Di Trapani, adding once that she was doing so "just like [she] protected Maria Figliola."

[57] Two other aspects of the Crown's cross-examination of Ms. Pignatelli bear mentioning.

[58] First, the Crown's take on the "drive-by" testimony appears to shift. In examination-in-chief, and before the adverse witness ruling, Crown counsel elicited evidence from the witness about the fact that she had seen Mr. Di Trapani and Mr. Latorre drive by her esthetics shop at around 9:30 p.m. on the night of the murder while she and Bruna Di Iorio were sitting out in front eating ice cream. She said she called Mr. Di Trapani on his cellphone (phone records show a call at 9:31 p.m. lasted two minutes and 57 seconds). This evidence was capable of corroborating the testimony of Mr. Latorre, who said he and Mr. Di Trapani were together that night and that Mr. Di Trapani had requested him to drive him to a point near the site of the murder. Indeed, this is one of the purposes, as noted above, that Crown counsel on appeal submits entitled the Crown to call Ms. Pignatelli as a witness.

[59] Following the ruling, however, and during the robust cross-examination at large, the Crown appears to use the testimony in a different fashion—to show that it was false and designed to provide an alibi for Mr. Di Trapani. Building on a discrepancy between Ms. Pignatelli's evidence-in-chief that Mr. Latorre was driving the vehicle and earlier statements to the police that she didn't know who was driving, Crown counsel suggested that the reason why she couldn't remember was that the event never happened. Near the close of cross-examination, the subject was revisited. Ms. Pignatelli had made no mention of Mr. Di Trapani in her October 2, 2002 statement to the police. The Crown extracted an admission that she had talked to Mr. Di Trapani prior to her statements to the police on January 14 and 22, 2003, and was aware that he had been interviewed as well. The Crown then suggested that "lo and behold [she now] came up with this story that [she] saw Mr. Di Trapani with Mr. Latorre." She then gave Mr. Latorre's name to the police during the January interviews, suggested the Crown, "because he was part of a plan to provide an alibi for Danny Di Trapani on the night of the murder."

[60] Lastly, the Crown established through Ms. Pignatelli that she had visited Mr. Di Trapani while he was in jail awaiting his bail hearing following his arrest and that, in August 2004, she and her husband had accosted Mr. Latorre in a bar in Toronto. The suggestion was that they were trying to intimidate a potential Crown witness in order to protect Mr. Di Trapani.

[61] The Crown's s. 9(1) cross-examination was very effective. However, that is not the point. It is the problem. In our view, by taking the tack it did, the Crown—inadvertently or otherwise—strayed into impermissible *Soobrian* territory. Even without any initial intent to do so, the ultimate effect of the cross-examination was to create the very scenario that *Soobrian* envisages: the effect of the cross-examination was to shred the credibility of the Crown's own witness and to create a factual matrix in which the jury might well conclude that Ms. Pignatelli was not only a liar, but was a witness lying for the very purpose of covering up for the appellants' wrongful deeds and that the appellants were therefore liars themselves, and guilty too.

[62] Following the s. 9(1) ruling, the Crown should have been restricted to cross-examining on the prior inconsistent statements and the circumstances surrounding them. Once the cross-examination at large evolved, however, without any objection from defence counsel for either accused, the jury was in the same position as the jury in *Soobrian*. The jurors needed to understand clearly that if they found Ms. Pignatelli not to be credible, they could not use that finding to conclude that either or both of the appellants were not

credible either. Nor could they use such a finding to so support a conclusion that either or both of the appellants were guilty. ...

[63] In our view, a specific instruction relating to Ms. Pignatelli was required in these circumstances. ...

. . .

[65] We would therefore allow the appeal, set aside Ms. Figliola's conviction and order a new trial.

[Di Trapani's appeal was also allowed. The court ordered new, separate, trials for each accused.]

Which interpretation of the scope of cross-examination permitted on a finding of adversity do you prefer?

Provincial evidence acts include provisions that mimic s 9 of the *Canada Evidence Act* in most respects. Certain of those provisions explicitly provide that a court may permit counsel to cross-examine her own witness on a finding of adversity: see *Manitoba Evidence Act*, CCSM c E150, s 19; *Evidence Act*, RSNWT 1988, c E-8, s 30 (also applying in Nunavut); *Evidence Act*, RSY 2002, c 78, s 29. Others mirror the *Canada Evidence Act* in this respect: *Alberta Evidence Act*, RSA 2000, c A-18, s 25; *Evidence Act*, RSPEI 1988, c E-11, s 15; *Evidence Act*, RSBC 1996, c 124, s 16; *Evidence Act*, RSNB 1973, c E-11, s 17; *Evidence Act*, RSNS 1989, c 154, s 55; *Evidence Act*, SS 2006, c E-11.2, ss 19(7), (8); *Evidence Act*, RSNL 1990, c E-16, s 10. Note that the Quebec *Code of Civil Procedure*, s 310, does not specify a requirement of adversity for proof of the witness's prior inconsistent statement. Despite small differences in the wording of these provisions, their effect is equivalent to s 9(1), as interpreted by the courts.

The *Canada Evidence Act* provides another mechanism, not found in provincial evidence acts, to impeach the credibility of one's own witness. Section 9(2) reads as follows:

> 9(2) Where the party producing a witness alleges that the witness made at other times a statement in writing, reduced to writing, or recorded on audio tape or video tape or otherwise, inconsistent with the witness' present testimony, the court may, without proof that the witness is adverse, grant leave to that party to cross-examine the witness as to the statement and the court may consider the cross-examination in determining whether in the opinion of the court the witness is adverse.

Notice that, although it also addresses prior inconsistent statements made by a witness called by a party, unlike s 9(1), which would apply to oral statements, s 9(2) applies only to statements that have been recorded in some manner.

Again, the effect of generous judicial interpretation means that the language of this provision is not entirely reflective of its true effect and functioning. The subsection was introduced in 1969 to clarify and confirm that prior inconsistent recorded statements could be used in determining whether a witness is adverse for the purposes of s 9(1). In *McInroy and Rouse v R*, [1979] 1 SCR 588, however, the Supreme Court gave the provision a more expansive interpretation by which s 9(2) provides an independent means of cross-examining one's own witness on a prior inconsistent recorded statement. A Crown witness, St. Germaine, had given the police a detailed written statement implicating the accused in a murder. At trial, she testified that she could not recall her conversation with the accused. The Crown was permitted to cross-examine her on the earlier statement before the jury, which was instructed not to use the earlier statement for its truth but only to test her credibility. The accused were convicted, and argued on appeal that the Crown should not have been permitted to cross-examine St. Germaine because her testimony was not "adverse" to the Crown. The Supreme Court, upholding the convictions, said:

> The procedure to be followed in respect of an application under s. 9(2) has been recommended by Culliton CJS in *R v. Milgaard* (1971), 2 CCC (2d) 206, leave to appeal refused 4 CCC (2d) 566n:
>
> (1) Counsel should advise the court that he desires to make an application under s. 9(2) of the *Canada Evidence Act*.
>
> (2) When the court is so advised, the court should direct the jury to retire.
>
> (3) Upon retirement of the jury, counsel should advise the learned trial judge of the particulars of the application and produce for him the alleged statement in writing, or the writing to which the statement has been reduced.
>
> (4) The learned trial judge should read the statement, or writing, and determine whether, in fact, there is an inconsistency between such statement or writing and the evidence the witness has given in court. If the learned trial judge decides there is no inconsistency, then that ends the matter. If he finds there is an inconsistency, he should call upon counsel to prove the statement or writing.
>
> (5) Counsel should then prove the statement or writing. This may be done by producing the statement or writing to the witness. If the witness admits the statement, or the statement reduced to writing, such proof would be sufficient. If the witness does not so admit, counsel then could provide the necessary proof by other evidence.
>
> (6) If the witness admits making the statements, counsel for the opposing party should have the right to cross-examine as to the circumstances under which the statement was made. A similar right to cross-examine should be granted if the statement is proved by other witnesses. It may be that he will be able to establish that there were circumstances which would render it improper for the learned trial judge to permit the cross-examination, notwithstanding the apparent inconsistencies. The opposing counsel, too, should have the right to call evidence as to factors relevant to obtaining the statement, for the purpose of attempting to show that cross-examination should not be permitted.
>
> (7) The learned trial judge should then decide whether or not he will permit the cross-examination. If so, the jury should be recalled.
>
> . . .
>
> Section 9(2) is not concerned with the cross-examination of an adverse witness. That subsection confers a discretion on a trial judge where the party producing a witness alleges that the witness has made, at another time, a written statement inconsistent with the evidence being given at the trial. The discretion is to permit, without proof that the witness is adverse, cross-examination as to the statement.

The task of the trial judge was to determine whether Mrs. St. Germaine's testimony was inconsistent with her statement to the police. In my opinion he was properly entitled to conclude that it was. At trial Mrs. St. Germaine swore that she could not recall any part of the conversation with McInroy in the kitchen of her house on the night of the killing, although only some seven months earlier she had given to the police, in her written statement, the details of that conversation, including McInroy's admission that he was the murderer. If her statement at trial as to her recollection was true, inconsistency would not arise, but the trial judge saw Mrs. St. Germaine and heard her evidence on the *voir dire*. It was quite open to him to conclude that she was lying about her recollection and to form his own conclusions as to why she was refusing to testify as to her true recollection. Farris CJBC says in terms that "the trial judge clearly did not believe her when she said she had a lack of recall." This being so there was evidence of an inconsistency between what she said at the trial, i.e., that she had no recollection of a conversation, and what was contained in her written statement, i.e., a detailed recollection of it.

In effect, s 9(2) creates a kind of shortcut for impeachment of one's own witness using a prior inconsistent recorded statement. Without having to obtain a ruling that a witness is adverse under s 9(1), counsel may (following the procedure from *R v Milgaard* set out in *McInroy and Rouse v R*, above) seek leave from a judge to cross-examine their own witness on a prior inconsistent recorded statement. As under s 9(1), the test governing a judge's discretion to grant leave to do so is "whether the ends of justice would be best attained" by permitting cross-examination and proof of the prior inconsistent statement: *R v Carpenter* (1982), 1 CCC (3d) 49 (Ont CA). If leave is granted, counsel may then cross-examine on the statement and, if necessary, prove it (see *Cassibo*, cited above); this cross-examination may then be used should counsel wish to seek a finding of adversity under s 9(1).

In criminal cases, sworn statements made by the witness to the police or testimony by the witness at a preliminary hearing are useful sources of prior inconsistent statements. In civil cases, the transcript of the party's examination for discovery is similarly useful. Prior inconsistent statements made under oath or affirmation are particularly effective in impugning the witness's credibility by establishing that the witness has told two different stories, both under oath. If the prior inconsistent statement was not under oath, the witness may take the position that he or she is now under oath and telling the truth.

It is important to bear in mind that, as in all cases of impeachment on a prior inconsistent statement, unless the witness adopts the prior statement, it is hearsay and can only be used for credibility purposes, not for the truth of its contents. If a prior inconsistent statement is introduced under s 9(1) or 9(2), the jury should be instructed about this limited use. In s 9(2) situations involving a recorded prior inconsistent statement, an important hearsay exception is the one established in *R v B (KG)*, [1993] 1 SCR 740 (discussed in Chapter 4, Section III.B), in which the court held that if the statement is necessary and has adequate indicia of reliability to overcome the hearsay dangers, it can also be admitted to prove the truth of its contents. Indeed, there is some authority that a prior inconsistent recorded statement can be admitted under the authority of *B (KG)* without resort to s 9 of the *Canada Evidence Act*: see *R v Glowatski*, 2001 BCCA 678.

Given the complex and sometimes misleading statutory provisions, and divergent judicial interpretations of the sections, the law governing s 9 of the *Canada Evidence Act* and the interaction of ss 9(1) and 9(2), is widely regarded as being in need of reconsideration and reform.

PROBLEM

Assume that you are the prosecutor in a case of spousal assault. Following the assault, the victim gave detailed sworn statements to the police, which were videotaped. At the preliminary hearing, the victim also testified to the assault under oath. Prior to the trial she advises you that she is no longer willing to participate in the prosecution of her husband. She is concerned that, if he is convicted of assaulting her, he will lose his job, be imprisoned, and will no longer be able to support his family financially. She tells you that, if you call her as a witness, she will deny that she has any recollection of the assault and deny that it happened. Advise her of the risks she will take in pursuing this course of action.

V. CORROBORATION

The word "corroboration" means two quite different things, even in judicial reasoning. Sometimes "corroboration" refers to the common sense idea that a witness's evidence is easier to accept if there is other admissible evidence supporting it. There are no special rules about this common sense idea of "corroboration." Sometimes, however, "corroboration" refers to a highly technical doctrine that once loomed large in the law of evidence. Corroboration, in this sense, was required in relation to certain kinds of offences, as well as to support the testimony of certain classes or categories of witnesses whose evidence was viewed as intrinsically unsafe. Although statutory and common law changes have virtually eliminated the old, technical form of this doctrine from Canadian law, it is still useful to examine its main outlines, reflected in the following case about corroboration for a particular category of witnesses—accomplices.

R v Baskerville

[1916] 2 KB 658 (Crim App)

Lord Reading CJ and Scrutton, Avory, Rowlatt, and Atkin JJ (31 July 1916)

LORD READING CJ: The appellant was convicted of having committed offences under s. 11 of the Criminal Law Amendment Act, 1885, with two boys. He appeals to this Court on the ground that there was no such corroborative evidence as is required by law of the testimony of the boys who were called for the prosecution at the trial and were accomplices in the crime. There is no statutory provision requiring corroboration applicable to these offences.

[Lord Reading CJ reviewed the evidence, and explained as follows:]

We entertained no doubt that this evidence afforded ample corroboration of the boys' testimony, even if we assumed that the corroboration required was corroboration "in some material particular implicating the accused." The learned Recorder directed the jury that they must not convict upon the testimony of the accomplices unless they were satisfied that there was "corroboration in some material particular affecting the accused." We were of opinion that in any event this direction gave no cause of complaint to the appellant. The warning by the Recorder to the jury was sufficient, if indeed not more than sufficient. We, therefore, intimated that the appeal would be dismissed.

Having regard, however, to the arguments addressed to the Court, and to the difficulty of reconciling all the opinions expressed in the cases cited, and to the general importance of reviewing and restating the law applicable to corroboration of the evidence of accomplices, we took time to consider our judgment.

There is no doubt that the uncorroborated evidence of an accomplice is admissible in law: see *Rex v. Atwood*. But it has long been a rule of practice at common law for the judge to warn the jury of the danger of convicting a prisoner on the uncorroborated testimony of an accomplice or accomplices, and, in the discretion of the judge, to advise them not to convict upon such evidence; but the judge should point out to the jury that it is within their legal province to convict upon such unconfirmed evidence: *Reg. v. Stubbs; In re Meunier*.

· · ·

We hold that evidence in corroboration must be independent testimony which affects the accused by connecting or tending to connect him with the crime. In other words, it must be evidence which implicates him, that is, which confirms in some material particular not only the evidence that the crime has been committed, but also that the prisoner committed it. The test applicable to determine the nature and extent of the corroboration is thus the same whether the case falls within the rule of practice at common law or within that class of offences for which corroboration is required by statute. The language of the statute, "implicates the accused," compendiously incorporates the test applicable at common law in the rule of practice. The nature of the corroboration will necessarily vary according to the particular circumstances of the offence charged. It would be in high degree dangerous to attempt to formulate the kind of evidence which would be regarded as corroboration, except to say that corroborative evidence is evidence which shows or tends to show that the story of the accomplice that the accused committed the crime is true, not merely that the crime has been committed, but that it was committed by the accused.

The corroboration need not be direct evidence that the accused committed the crime; it is sufficient if it is merely circumstantial evidence of his connection with the crime. ...

· · ·

The appeal stands dismissed.

The *Baskerville* formula for corroboration was embodied in both the common law of Canada and in the *Criminal Code*. Section 142 of the *Criminal Code*, RSC 1970, c C-34, for example, required judges in cases involving rape and other sexual offences against women to instruct the jury that it was unsafe to convict the accused if the only evidence against him was the testimony of the complainant and if that testimony was "not corroborated by a material particular by evidence that implicates the accused." This section was only one of many evidentiary obstacles to obtaining convictions for sexual offences. For an example of a rape conviction based on very credible evidence being set aside because of errors in the trial judge's instruction as to what amounted to corroboration, see *R v Ethier*, [1959] OR 533 (CA).

Most of the historical requirements for formal corroboration in respect of certain offences have been removed from our *Criminal Code*. The requirement for corroboration to convict of forgery has been abrogated and s 274 states that, in respect of sexual offences, "no corroboration is required for a conviction and the judge shall not instruct the jury that it is unsafe to find the accused guilty in the absence of corroboration." The strict *Baskerville* formula for corroboration is still required only for very few offences, including high treason (s 47), perjury (s 133), and procuring a feigned marriage (s 292).

Certain rules of corroboration regarding particular classes of witnesses have also been removed. For example, s 659 of the *Criminal Code*, enacted in 1993, states that "[a]ny requirement whereby it is mandatory for a court to give the jury a warning about convicting an accused on the evidence of a child is abrogated." Yet common law requirements for corroboration for other categories of witnesses thought to be inherently unreliable—such as accomplices—persisted. The strict *Baskerville* formulation for corroboration, combined with this categorical approach to the types of witnesses that called for corroboration, created an extremely complicated and cumbersome area of evidence law.

The next case concerns the common law requirement that the evidence of an accomplice be corroborated; in this case, the Supreme Court of Canada establishes a new, more functional approach to the need for caution in assessing the evidence of some witnesses.

Vetrovec v R; Gaja v R
[1982] 1 SCR 811, 67 CCC (2d) 1
Laskin CJ and Martland, Ritchie, Dickson, Beetz, Estey, McIntyre, Chouinard,
and Lamer JJ (31 May 1982)

[Vetrovec and Gaja were charged with conspiracy to traffic in heroin. Langvand, an accomplice, testified for the Crown. In accordance with the common law rule described in *Baskerville*, the trial judge instructed the jury that it was dangerous to convict on Langvand's testimony unless they found that it was corroborated, and that certain pieces of evidence were capable of corroborating Langvand's testimony. The accused were convicted. On appeal, they argued that the trial judge's instruction concerning the evidence that was capable of corroborating Langvand's testimony was erroneous.]

DICKSON J: ... The objection of the appellants is framed in the following manner. The testimony of Langvand, the accomplice, related to a trip to Hong Kong for the purpose of importing heroin between May 11 and 16, 1975. None of the evidence outlined by the trial judge, with the exception of the customs declarations and Gaja's passport, relates directly to this specific trip. It tends to connect the appellants with drug trafficking generally, but not necessarily with the trip described by Langvand. Therefore, according to the appellants, it cannot be regarded as corroborative. It does not relate to the "overt act" testified to by Langvand. Putting the objection another way, the supporting evidence is said to be "too remote" to have corroborative effect.

. . .

Let me say at the outset that I agree with the majority of the Court of Appeal that both appeals should be dismissed.

Before elaborating, however, I would like to review and reassess general principles relating to the law of corroboration of accomplices. This is one of the most complicated and technical areas of the law of evidence. It is also in need of reform. Both the Law Reform Commission of Canada (Report on Evidence, s. 88(b) of the proposed Code) and the English Criminal Law Revision Committee (11th Report on Evidence 1972,

Cmnd 4991, paras. 183-5), have recently recommended a drastic overhaul of the law of corroboration. The Evidence Code proposed by the Law Reform Commission of Canada would contain the following provision:

> 88. For greater certainty it is hereby provided that
>
> . . .
>
> (b) Every rule of law that requires the corroboration of evidence as a basis for a conviction or that requires that the jury be warned of the danger of convicting on the basis of uncorroborated evidence is abrogated.

Professor Heydon states that ("The Corroboration of Accomplices," [1973] *Crim. LR* 264 at p. 281):

> ... it is at least difficult to deny that the current English law on accomplice evidence has become both too wide and too narrow for the mischief it is attempting to control. It is too wide in applying to accomplices who are in fact trustworthy; it is too narrow in applying only to participants in exactly the same crime as that charged against the accused.

Professor Wakeling questions the necessity for the rules and wonders whether "the rules will impede justice as often as promote it" (*Corroboration in Canadian Law* (1977), at p. 103), although she favours a non-discretionary warning with respect to accomplice evidence (*ibid.* at pp. 112-3).

. . .

In the case of a jury charge in which a witness who might be regarded as an accomplice testifies, it has become not merely a rule of practice but a rule of law for the trial judge to warn the jury that it is dangerous to found a conviction on the evidence of an accomplice unless that evidence is corroborated in a material particular implicating the accused. The jury may convict in such circumstances but it is dangerous to do so. The judge must determine as a matter of law whether the witness might be an accomplice for the purposes of the rule. The jury must then decide whether he is in fact an accomplice. The judge explains the legal definition of "corroboration" with heavy reliance upon what was said by Lord Reading in *R v. Baskerville* ... [extracted above]. The judge lists for the jury the pieces of evidence which are in his view capable of amounting to corroboration. Finally, they are told that it is for the jury to decide whether the evidence to which their attention has been directed does amount to corroboration. As the study paper of the Law Reform Commission of Canada "Evidence: Paper Study 11 Corroboration" dryly observes an "enormous superstructure ... has been erected on the original basic proposition that the evidence of some witnesses should be approached with caution" (at p. 7).

The accused is in the unhappy position of hearing the judge draw particular attention to the evidence which tends to confirm the testimony the accomplice has given. Cogent prejudicial testimony is thus repeated and highlighted. For the jury this part of the charge can only be, in the words of Lord Diplock in *Director of Public Prosecutions v. Hester*, [1972] 3 All ER 1056 at p. 1075, "a frequent source of bewilderment." The task of a trial judge seeking to identify the evidence capable of amounting to corroboration is unenviable. Lord Reading in the *Baskerville* case said that it would be in high degree dangerous to attempt to formulate the kind of evidence which could be regarded as corroboration. It is also often a difficult and dangerous exercise identifying what pieces of evidence are capable of being corroborative. To take a simple example. In a rape case, to what degree must the appearance of the complainant be dishevelled, or a garment torn, in order to constitute evidence capable of amounting to corroboration as to non-consent?

Two circumstances in particular make it appropriate, as it seems to me, to pause and reassess the law as it affects corroboration, with particular reference to accomplice evidence. The first such circumstance is the increasing length and complexity of criminal trials, particularly in cases of so-called "white collar" crime. I think of the case of *Kirsch and Rosenthal v. The Queen*, [1981] 1 SCR 440, which came to the court recently. After a trial extending over some weeks and a guilty verdict, the whole process started afresh after this court found that the Crown prosecutor was in error in telling the jury that two pieces of evidence were capable of corroborative effect and the trial judge had failed to correct the error. I think of the case of *R v. McNamara et al.* (1981), 56 CCC (2d) 193 (Ont. CA), another trial that extended over months. At the end, the trial judge charged the jury that there were some 42 pieces of evidence, each of which the judge referred to, as being capable of corroborating certain accomplice testimony. I think of the instant case and the task facing the trial judge in sifting through over 9,000 pages of transcript in a search for evidence capable of corroborative effect.

The second circumstance is the apparent trend in the English courts to cast aside the technical impedimenta with which the idea of corroboration has increasingly been loaded and return to the conceptual basics. I refer in particular to *Director of Public Prosecutions v. Hester, supra* (HL), and *Director of Public Prosecutions v. Kilbourne*, [1973] 1 All ER 440 (HL). The House of Lords has never specifically approved the definition of corroboration set out in *Baskerville*. The same antipathy to the detailed *Baskerville* doctrine can be discerned in two recent cases in this court: *Warkentin, Hanson and Brown v. The Queen*, [1977] 2 SCR 355, and *Murphy and Butt v. The Queen*, [1977] 2 SCR 603.

The common law, rejecting the "numerical criterion" common to some legal systems, has traditionally held that the testimony of a single witness is a sufficient basis for a criminal conviction. The general rule applied equally in the case of accomplices: where the testimony of an accomplice was admissible, it could justify a verdict of guilty. But while the common law (after some initial doubts) recognized an accomplice as a competent witness, it continued to harbour some suspicions as to the trustworthiness of his testimony. There appeared to be something unsavoury about a self-confessed knave, often for reward, accusing his companions in crime. Thus the practice arose in the 18th century of warning the jury that, while they might legally convict on the basis of the testimony of an accomplice, it would be dangerous to do so unless the testimony were supported or "corroborated" by other unimpeachable evidence. This warning was for many years a matter for the discretion of the trial judge but in 1916, the English Court of Criminal Appeal declared that the practice had become "virtually equivalent to a rule of law": *R v. Baskerville, supra*, at p. 663. ...

• • •

In evaluating the adequacy of the law in this area, the first question which must be answered is a basic one: why have a special rule for accomplices at all? Credibility of witnesses and the weight of the evidence is, in general, a matter for the trier of fact. Identification evidence, for example, is notoriously weak, and yet the trial judge is not automatically required, as a matter of law, to instruct the jury on this point. Similarly, the trial judge is not required in all cases to warn the jury with respect to testimony of other witnesses with disreputable and untrustworthy backgrounds. Why, then, should we automatically require a warning when an accomplice takes the stand?

[Dickson J then reviewed a series of "oft-repeated justifications" for this categorical and automatic rule, including that an accomplice might be seeking to save himself from punishment or transfer blame to another, might be seeking to protect his friends, or should not be believed because "he is a self-confessed criminal and is 'morally guilty.'" Dickson J found these rationales wanting:]

None of these arguments can justify a fixed and invariable rule regarding all accomplices. All that can be established is that the testimony of some accomplices may be untrustworthy. But this can be said of many other categories of witness. There is nothing inherent in the evidence of an accomplice which automatically renders him untrustworthy. To construct a universal rule singling out accomplices, then, is to fasten upon this branch of the law of evidence a blind and empty formalism. Rather than attempting to pigeon-hole a witness into a category and then recite a ritualistic incantation, the trial judge might better direct his mind to the facts of the case, and thoroughly examine all the factors which might impair the worth of a particular witness. If, in his judgment, the credit of the witness is such that the jury should be cautioned, then he may instruct accordingly. If, on the other hand, he believes the witness to be trustworthy, then, regardless of whether the witness is technically an "accomplice" no warning is necessary.

. . .

There are at least three difficulties associated with the *Baskerville* definition. The first is that it tends to obscure and, indeed, confuse the reason behind the "accomplice warning." As noted, the reason for the warning is that the accomplice is potentially untrustworthy, and we therefore desire other evidence which will accredit his testimony. After *Baskerville* courts began to frame the issue in terms of whether the corroborative evidence conformed to Lord Reading's definition, and ignored the real issue, whether there was evidence that bolstered the credibility of the accomplice. The result was, in effect, that in due course "corroboration" became virtually divorced from the issue of the credibility of the accomplice. Evidence which strengthened credibility was at the same time characterized as not corroborative "in law." Corroboration became a legal term of art, wholly unconnected with the original reason for the accomplice warning.

The second difficulty associated with *Baskerville* is related to the first. Once it is decided that corroboration is a legal term of art, the law in the area becomes increasingly complex and technical. It immediately becomes necessary for the trial judge to define for the jury the legal meaning of corroboration. Moreover, the issue of whether there is any evidence which may be corroborative, according to that definition, becomes a matter of law. The trial judge must therefore examine the evidence to determine that question. The next step is to require the trial judge to specify for the jury those items of evidence which, in his opinion may be corroborative. ...

Since the judge's instructions on this issue involve questions of law, numerous technical appeals are taken on the issue of whether a particular item of evidence is "capable" of constituting corroboration. The body of case-law is so complex that it has in turn produced a massive periodical literature: see bibliography in Wakeling, *Corroboration in Canadian Law* (1977), at pp. 149-51. Moreover, the cases are difficult to reconcile. The

Law Reform Commission of Canada has described the case-law in the area as full of "subtleties, variations, inconsistencies and great complexities": study paper 11, *supra*, at p. 7. The result is that what was originally a simple, common-sense proposition—an accomplice's testimony should be viewed with caution—becomes transformed into a difficult and highly technical area of law. Whether this "enormous superstructure" (to use the description of the Law Reform Commission) has any meaningful relationship with the task performed by the jury is unknown.

The third and perhaps most serious difficulty associated with the *Baskerville* definition is that the definition itself seems unsound in principle. Prior to the judgment of Lord Reading, there had been controversy over whether corroborative evidence must implicate the accused, or whether it was sufficient if it simply strengthened the credibility of the accomplice. Lord Reading settled the controversy in favour of the former view.

With great respect, on principle Lord Reading's approach seems perhaps over-cautious. The reason for requiring corroboration is that we believe the witness has good reason to lie. We therefore want some other piece of evidence which tends to convince us that he is telling the truth. Evidence which implicates the accused does indeed serve to accomplish that purpose but it cannot be said that this is the only sort of evidence which will accredit the accomplice. This is because, as Wigmore said, the matter of credibility is an entire thing, not a separable one (*ibid.*, p. 424):

> [W]hatever restores our trust in him personally restores it as a whole; if we find that he is desiring and intending to tell a true story, we shall believe one part of his story as well as another; whenever, then, by any means, that trust is restored, our object is accomplished, and it cannot matter whether the efficient circumstance related to the accused's identity or to any other matter. The important thing is, not *how* our trust is restored, but whether it is restored at all.

· · ·

It is, I think, unfortunate that the word "corroboration" ever became part of the legal lexicon. It is not a word of common parlance. When explained to juries it is given a technical definition, the exact content of which is still a matter giving rise to difference of opinion among jurists. ...

· · ·

This court has in the past declared its willingness to depart from its own prior decisions as well as decisions of the Privy Council and the House of Lords: *Reference re Agricultural Products Marketing Act and two other Acts*, [1978] 2 SCR 1198; *A.V.G. Management Science Ltd. v. Barwell Developments Ltd. et al.*, [1979] 2 SCR 43. The present case is an appropriate occasion to exercise this discretion. The law of corroboration is unduly and unnecessarily complex and technical.

I would hold that there is no special category for "accomplices." An accomplice is to be treated like any other witness testifying at a criminal trial and the judge's conduct, if he chooses to give his opinion, is governed by the general rules.

I would only like to add one or two observations concerning the proper practice to be followed in the trial court where as a matter of common sense something in the nature of confirmatory evidence should be found before the finder of fact relies upon the evidence of a witness whose testimony occupies a central position in the purported demonstration of guilt and yet may be suspect by reason of the witness being an accomplice or complainant or of disreputable character. There are great advantages to be gained by simplifying the instruction to juries on the question as to when a prudent juror will seek some confirmation of the story of such a witness, before concluding that the story is true and adopting it in the process of finding guilt in the accused as charged. It does not, however, always follow that the presiding justice may always simply turn the jury loose upon the evidence without any assisting analysis as to whether or not a prudent finder of fact can find confirmation somewhere in the mass of evidence of the evidence of a witness. Because of the infinite range of circumstance which will arise in the criminal trial process it is not sensible to attempt to compress into a rule, a formula or a direction the concept of the need for prudent scrutiny of the testimony of any witness. What may be appropriate, however, in some circumstances, is a clear and sharp warning to attract the attention of the juror to the risks of adopting, without more, the evidence of the witness. There is no magic in the word corroboration, or indeed in any other comparable expression such as confirmation and support. The idea implied in those words may, however, in an appropriate case, be effectively and efficiently transmitted to the mind of the trier of fact. This may entail some illustration from the evidence of the particular case of the type of evidence, documentary or testimonial, which might be drawn upon by the juror in confirmation of the witness's testimony or some important part thereof. I do not wish to be taken as saying that such illustration must be carried to exhaustion. However, there is, in some circumstances, particularly in lengthy trials, the need for helpful direction on the question of sifting the evidence where guilt or innocence might, and probably will, turn on the acceptance or rejection, belief or disbelief, of the evidence of one or more witnesses. All of this applies equally in the case of an accomplice, or a disreputable witness of demonstrated moral lack, as, for example, a witness with a record of perjury. All this takes one back to the beginning and that is the search for the impossible: a rule which embodies and codifies common sense in the realm of the process of determining guilt or innocence of an accused on the basis of a record which includes evidence from potentially unreliable sources such as an accomplice.

I would point out that my comments have been limited to situations in which corroboration is required as a matter of common law. The *Criminal Code* specifies a number of instances in which corroboration is required, and defines the nature of the corroboration which must be supplied: see, for example, ss. 139 and 195. The statutory requirements would, of course, be controlling in cases coming under any of those sections.

II

I return to the facts of the present case. In light of my earlier comments, it would have been sufficient for the trial judge simply to have instructed the jury that they should view the testimony of Langvand with great caution, and that it would be wise to look for other supporting evidence before convicting the appellants. However, since the trial judge outlined for the jury items of evidence he considered capable of corroborating Langvand's testimony, it is necessary to examine this evidence to ensure that the appellants were not prejudiced by the instruction. The question that must be kept in mind is: does this supporting evidence strengthen our belief that Langvand is telling the truth?

The answer to this question can only be in the affirmative. Langvand had testified as to a trip to Hong Kong in 1975 for the purpose of purchasing and importing heroin. The supporting evidence strongly implicated the accused in illegal drug trafficking. As Mr. Justice Seaton noted in the court below, the supporting evidence against Gaja would, considered alone, have been sufficient to support his conviction on the charge. As for the appellant Vetrovec, the material found in his apartment all pointed to his participation in illegal drug trafficking (see the evidence on this point of Sergeant Domansky, at trial). The items of evidence were, to use the phrase of Mr. Justice Seaton, "badges of membership in this conspiracy." All of this incriminating evidence, when considered together, strongly strengthens the belief that Langvand was telling the truth regarding the participation of Vetrovec and Gaja. It rebuts any suggestion that he is falsely implicating innocent individuals. The fact that this supporting evidence does not directly relate to the other overt acts testified to by Langvand is irrelevant. The evidence is capable of inducing a rational belief that Langvand is telling the truth and is for that reason corroborative. ...

In the result, the instructions by the trial judge did not prejudice the appellants. The appeals should be dismissed.

After *Vetrovec*, trial judges were ready simply to deliver "a clear and sharp warning to attract the attention of the juror to the risks of adopting, without more, the evidence of the witness" when the Crown's case depended upon the credibility of a witness whose veracity might be seen as particularly questionable. The use of a "*Vetrovec* warning" would not be confined to accomplices or particular categories of witnesses but, rather, to all such "unsavoury witnesses." How does this warning differ from the common law corroboration requirement abolished in *Vetrovec*? The adequacy of an unsavoury witness warning, or the trial judge's decision not to give one, is a frequent ground of appeal from conviction. See, among many other cases, *R v Wang* (2001), 153 CCC (3d) 321 (Ont CA).

Although the court described the *Vetrovec* warning as discretionary, in the years after *Vetrovec*, the question emerged as to whether such a warning should ever be mandatory. In *R v Brooks*, 2000 SCC 11, [2000] 1 SCR 237, the court addressed this question in the context of testimony provided by jailhouse informants. Bastarache J held that whether a *Vetrovec* warning would be required would depend on "the credibility of the witness and the importance of the evidence to the Crown's case" (at para 4). "In other words," he explained, "the greater the concern over the credibility of the witness and the more important the evidence, the more likely the *Vetrovec* caution will be mandatory" (at para 4). Applying these principles, a majority of the court in *Brooks* held that a warning to the jury about the use of the testimony of a jailhouse informant was required. In arriving at this conclusion, Major J referred to "the extreme dangers of relying on the use of 'jailhouse informers' as witnesses in criminal prosecutions" (at para 81) and cited the *Report of the Commission on Proceedings Involving Guy Paul Morin* (Toronto: Ontario Ministry of the Attorney General, 1998) at 638 as follows:

> The evidence at this Inquiry demonstrates the inherent unreliability of in-custody informer testimony, its contribution to miscarriages of justice and the substantial risk that the dangers may not be fully appreciated by the jury. In my view, the present law has developed to the point that a cautionary instruction is virtually mandated in cases where the in-custody informer's testimony is contested: see *R. v. Simmons*, [[1998] OJ No 152 (QL) (CA)]; *R. v. Bevan*, [(1993), 82 CCC (3d) 310].

Does *Brooks* present the possibility of reintroducing, post-*Vetrovec*, categories of witnesses for whom a corroboration warning is required? For a case applying the criteria from

Brooks for determining whether a *Vetrovec* caution was mandatory, see *R v McCarroll*, 2008 ONCA 715.

In the years following *Vetrovec*, another question that arose was what forms of evidence were capable of providing the kind of trust-restoring confirmation described in *Vetrovec*: see e.g. *R v Dhillon* (2002), 166 CCC (3d) 262 (Ont CA); *R v Kehler*, 2004 SCC 11, [2004] 1 SCR 328. In the following case, the Supreme Court of Canada addressed this point.

R v Khela
2009 SCC 4, [2009] 1 SCR 104 (footnotes omitted)
Binnie, LeBel, Deschamps, Fish, Abella, Charron, and Rothstein JJ
(29 January 2009)

FISH J (Binnie, LeBel, Abella, Charron, and Rothstein JJ concurring):

I

[1] Legal systems far separated in time and place have long recognized that it is dangerous to rest a criminal conviction on the testimony of a single witness, or on a single piece of evidence. This concern is at least as old as Deuteronomy. It arises because witnesses can lie deliberately or mislead inadvertently, documents can be forged, and other items of evidence can be tampered with or planted: P. Roberts and A. Zuckerman, *Criminal Evidence* (2004), at p. 466.

[2] The evidence of a single witness is nonetheless sufficient in Canada to support a conviction for any offence other than treason, perjury or procuring a feigned marriage. Many serious crimes might otherwise go unpunished. But where the guilt of the accused is made to rest exclusively or substantially on the testimony of a single witness of doubtful credit or veracity, the danger of a wrongful conviction is particularly acute.

[3] It is therefore of the utmost importance, in a trial by judge and jury, for the jury to understand *when* and *why* it is unsafe to find an accused guilty on the unsupported evidence of witnesses who are "unsavoury," "untrustworthy," "unreliable," or "tainted." For present purposes, I use these terms interchangeably. And I mean to include all witnesses who, because of their amoral character, criminal lifestyle, past dishonesty or interest in the outcome of the trial, cannot be trusted to tell the truth—even when they have expressly undertaken by oath or affirmation to do so.

[4] I hasten to add that a specific instruction is sometimes required in this regard not because jurors are thought to be unintelligent, but rather because they might otherwise be uninformed. It is meant to bring home to lay jurors the accumulated wisdom of the law's experience with unsavoury witnesses. Judges are alert to the concern that unsavoury witnesses are prone to favour personal advantage over public duty. And we know from recent experience that unsavoury witnesses, especially but not only "jailhouse informants," can be convincing liars and can effectively conceal their true motives for testifying as they have: see *R. v. Sauvé* (2004), 182 C.C.C. (3d) 321 (Ont. C.A.), at para. 76.

[5] Without a cautionary instruction, however, jurors may appreciate neither the need nor the reasons for skepticism and particular scrutiny in dealing with witnesses of this sort. Essentially for that reason, trial judges may—and in some cases *must*—include in

their charges "a clear and sharp warning to attract the attention of the juror[s] to the risks of adopting, without more, the evidence of the witness" (*Vetrovec v. The Queen*, [1982] 1 S.C.R. 811, at p. 831).

[6] In *Vetrovec*, the Court held that no particular category of witness requires this warning. And the Court held as well that the caution, where it is found to be necessary or appropriate, need not be framed in technical or formulaic language. Nor must the judge include in the caution any legal definition of "corroboration" in explaining to the jury the type of evidence that is capable of supporting the testimony of the tainted witness.

[7] *Vetrovec* thus stripped the traditional cautionary instruction of its archaic and technical content and packaging. But it was not intended to deprive an accused of the protection that the warning has historically been meant to provide. As Major J. (dissenting on other grounds) explained in *R. v. Brooks*, 2000 SCC 11, [2000] 1 S.C.R. 237, at para. 69, once a *Vetrovec* caution had been given, "the jury could view that evidence with more ease but not less scepticism than previously required."

· · ·

[11] The central purpose of a *Vetrovec* warning is to alert the jury to the danger of relying on the unsupported evidence of unsavoury witnesses and to explain the reasons for special scrutiny of their testimony. In appropriate cases, the trial judge should also draw the attention of the jurors to evidence capable of confirming or supporting the material parts of the otherwise untrustworthy evidence.

[12] Since the decision of this Court in *Vetrovec*, the very real dangers of relying in criminal prosecutions on the unsupported evidence of unsavoury witnesses, particularly "jailhouse informers," has been highlighted more than once by commissions of inquiry into wrongful convictions (see, for example, *The Commission on Proceedings Involving Guy Paul Morin: Report* (1998) and *The Inquiry Regarding Thomas Sophonow* (2001)). The danger of a miscarriage of justice is to be borne in mind in crafting and in evaluating the adequacy of a caution.

· · ·

[14] No single formula can be expected to produce an appropriate instruction for every foreseeable—let alone *unforeseeable*—situation at trial. That is why we vest in trial judges the discretion they must have in fashioning cautionary instructions responsive to the circumstances of the case. Trial judges nonetheless seek, and are entitled to expect, guidance from this Court as to the general characteristics of a sufficient warning. I shall later outline in broad brushstrokes a proposed template which, while not at all mandatory, will in my view be of assistance to trial judges without unduly fettering their discretion, and will reduce the number of appeals attributable to the present uncertainty regarding the governing principles.

[15] Read as a whole, and in the context of the trial, the charge to the jury in this case was adequate. Any shortcomings in the *Vetrovec* caution itself were compensated for in the remainder of the charge. I am satisfied that the jury would have understood that it could not convict the appellants on the basis of the evidence of the impugned witnesses unless they found elsewhere in the [evidence] sufficient comfort that those witnesses were telling the truth.

[16] Accordingly, I would dismiss the appeals.

II

[Fish J then set out the facts of the case: Khela and his co-accused were charged with and convicted of first-degree murder in the shooting death of the victim, Sidhu. The Crown's theory was that Khela had paid the shooters to kill Sidhu, seemingly as part of some form of blood feud. Although there was other evidence implicating Khela, the case against him turned on the evidence of two witnesses, Sandoval and Stein. Both had lengthy criminal records and, along with one of the shooters, were members of a prison gang. Khela denied any involvement in the murder.]

[23] Sandoval and Stein were the subject of a *Vetrovec* warning. ... In relation to Sandoval's and Stein's evidence, the trial judge instructed the jury as follows:

• • •

Unsavoury Witness

In respect to two of the Crown's witnesses I am going to give you a special instruction.

This instruction relates only to Mr. Sandoval and Mr. Stein. Given their admitted lifestyles and criminal background, common sense tells you that there is good reason to look at their evidence with the greatest care and caution. You should look for some confirmation of their evidence from somebody or something other than what they have to say before relying upon it in deciding whether Crown has proved its case against any accused beyond a reasonable doubt. To put it another way, it is dangerous to convict on the evidence of Sandoval or Stein unless it is confirmed or supported by other evidence.

You may find that there is some other evidence in this case that confirms or supports some parts of either Sandoval or Stein's evidence. It is for you to say whether this, or any evidence, confirms or supports their testimony and how that affects whether or how much of it you believe or rely upon in deciding this case. In this respect you should look at the evidence of the girlfriends and female associates, remembering of course the defence have labelled them as liars. Of course, you must look at all the other evidence as well that might bear upon this aspect, including the admissions, the intercepts, the expert Mr. Hall [firearms], the testimony of the Sidhu [victim's] family, and the exhibits. [Appellant's Record, No. 31933, at pp. 1760-61]

[24] The appellants argue that the trial judge's warning about the evidence of Stein and Sandoval was insufficient because it failed to instruct the jury that to be confirmatory, evidence supporting Stein and Sandoval's testimony must be independent and material. Given the central place of this evidence in the case against them, the appellants submitted that the alleged error caused them serious prejudice.

• • •

IV

[31] This Court, in *Vetrovec*, changed the law in relation to unsavoury witness warnings in two important ways. First, the Court held that trial judges, rather than attempting to "pigeonhole" witnesses as an "accomplices" [*sic*], ought instead to consider all of the factors that might impair their credibility and decide on that basis whether a special instruction is necessary. Second, the Court relieved triers of fact from applying the technical

definition of corroboration and directed them instead simply to determine whether the "evidence properly weighed overcame its suspicious roots" (*Brooks*, at para. 69). Dickson J. held that there was no magic in the word corroboration, "or indeed in any other comparable expression such as confirmation and support" (*Vetrovec*, at p. 831).

[32] Dickson J. adopted this "common sense" approach having found the law of corroboration "unduly and unnecessarily complex and technical" (p. 830). This approach, while unburdening judges and juries of the technical requirements of corroboration, was not meant to imply that any and all evidence is capable of confirming the testimony of a potentially untrustworthy witness. ...

[33] The relaxation of the corroboration rules in *Vetrovec* was not a signal that juries should be set "loose upon the evidence without any assisting analysis as to whether or not a prudent finder of fact can find confirmation somewhere in the mass of evidence" (*Vetrovec*, at p. 831). The trial judge retains the role of providing the jury with "the proper framework within which that credibility can be evaluated" (*Brooks*, at para. 130, *per* Binnie J.).

[34] Since *Vetrovec*, this Court and several appellate courts have provided guidance on the appropriate form and content of the "clear, sharp warning." In *Brooks*, Justice Major wrote (at para. 94) that while no particular language is required, "[a]t a minimum," the caution must

> focus the jury's attention specifically on the inherently unreliable evidence. It should refer to the characteristics of the witness that bring the credibility of his or her evidence into serious question. It should plainly emphasize the dangers inherent in convicting an accused on the basis of such evidence unless confirmed by independent evidence.

. . .

[37] In *Sauvé*, at para. 82, the Ontario Court of Appeal set out a principled framework that will assist trial judges in constructing *Vetrovec* warnings appropriate to the circumstances of each case. That proposed framework, which I adopt and amplify here, is composed of four main foundation elements: (1) drawing the attention of the jury to the testimonial evidence requiring special scrutiny; (2) explaining *why* this evidence is subject to special scrutiny; (3) cautioning the jury that it is dangerous to convict on unconfirmed evidence of this sort, though the jury is entitled to do so if satisfied that the evidence is true; and (4) that the jury, in determining the veracity of the suspect evidence, should look for evidence from another source tending to show that the untrustworthy witness is telling the truth as to the guilt of the accused (*R. v. Kehler*, 2004 SCC 11, [2004] 1 S.C.R. 328, at paras. 17-19).

[38] While this summary should not be applied in a rigid and formulaic fashion, it accurately captures the elements that should guide trial judges in crafting their instructions on potentially untrustworthy witnesses. The fourth component, of particular interest on this appeal, provides guidance on the kind of evidence that is capable of confirming the suspect testimony of an impugned witness.

[39] Common sense dictates that not all evidence presented at trial is capable of confirming the testimony of an impugned witness. The attribute of independence defines the kind of evidence that can provide comfort to the trier of fact that the witness is telling the truth. Where evidence is "tainted" by connection to the *Vetrovec* witness it can not serve to confirm his or her testimony (N. Harris, "*Vetrovec* Cautions and Confirmatory

Evidence: A Necessarily Complex Relationship" (2005), 31 C.R. (6th) 216, at p. 225; *R. v. Sanderson*, 2003 MBCA 109, 180 C.C.C. (3d) 53, at para. 61).

[40] Materiality is a more difficult concept. In *Vetrovec*, the Court did away with the requirement that corroborating evidence implicate the accused. As Dickson J. noted, such evidence is not the only type capable of convincing a jury that a witness is telling the truth. In *Kehler*, the Court confirmed that evidence, to be considered confirmatory, does not have to implicate the accused. We maintain that position here.

[41] Individual items of confirmatory evidence need not implicate the accused. ...

[42] However, when looked at in the context of the case as a whole, the items of confirmatory evidence should give comfort to the jury that the witness can be trusted in his or her assertion that the accused is the person who committed the offence. ...

· · ·

V

[44] I agree with the Ontario Court of Appeal in *Sauvé* that a *Vetrovec* warning should address, in terms appropriate to the circumstances of each case, the four elements outlined above. Where the caution has these characteristics, an appellate court, in the absence of some other flaw in the instructions, will generally be expected to find the caution adequate. I emphasize, however, that failure to include any of the components in the terms outlined above may not prove fatal where, as in this case, the judge's charge read as a whole otherwise serves the purposes of a *Vetrovec* warning.

[45] As the Ontario Court of Appeal found in *Zebedee* [*R v Zebedee* (2006), 211 CCC (3d) 199 (Ont CA)], "*Vetrovec* was like a breath of fresh air. It put a premium on common sense and it recognized that juries were intelligent and they could be trusted to do the right thing. ... Elaborate instruction, the Court said, was not needed" (para. 81). No benefit comes from a return to the overly rigid pre-*Vetrovec* era.

[46] That said, the absence or presence of confirmatory evidence plays a key role in determining whether it is safe to rely on the testimony of an impugned witness (Harris, at p. 222). Accordingly, the instruction to the jury must make clear the type of evidence capable of offering support. It is not sufficient to simply tell the jury to look for whatever it feels confirms the truth of a witness' testimony (see *R. v. Chenier* (2006), 205 C.C.C. (3d) 333 (Ont. C.A.), at para. 34).

[47] It is not "overly formalistic" to ensure that triers of fact attain the appropriate level of comfort before convicting an accused on the basis of what has for centuries been considered unreliable evidence. A truly functional approach must take into account the dual purpose of the *Vetrovec* warning: first, to alert the jury to the danger of relying on the unsupported evidence of unsavoury witnesses and to explain the reasons for special scrutiny of their testimony; and second, in appropriate cases, to give the jury the tools necessary to identify evidence capable of enhancing the trustworthiness of those witnesses.

[48] Acknowledging this second function of the caution does not represent a departure from the Court's judgment in *Vetrovec*. Dickson J. recognized that in some circumstances, particularly in lengthy trials, there is a "need for helpful direction on the question of sifting the evidence where guilt or innocence might, and probably will turn on the

acceptance or rejection, belief or disbelief, of the evidence of one or more witnesses"
(pp. 831-32).

· · ·

VII

[51] With respect, I would not characterize the trial judge's *Vetrovec* caution as a model
to be followed in other cases. In my view, however, it adequately conveyed to the jury the
degree of special scrutiny to be applied in weighing the testimony of Sandoval and Stein.

[52] In the context of this case, where allegations of corroboration and collusion
between the impugned witnesses and others were made, the trial judge's warning should
have better explained the need for confirmatory evidence to be independent and relate
to an important and relevant aspect of the impugned testimony. However, any deficiencies
in the *Vetrovec* caution itself were compensated for in other portions of the charge. Read
as a whole, and in the context of the trial, I am satisfied that the charge to the jury was
adequate.

· · ·

[65] DESCHAMPS J: The law of evidence needs more common sense, not a new technical rule. My colleague Fish J., writing for the majority, believes that there is a middle
position between micromanagement and functional analysis by courts of appeals of
warnings given to jurors as to the reliability of unsavoury witnesses' testimony (para. 29).
I disagree.

[66] The majority's opinion is part of an incremental return to the formalism of *R. v.
Baskerville*, [1916] 2 K.B. 658 (C.C.A.). In the judgment appealed from in the instant case,
Donald J.A. correctly pointed out (at para. 20) that *R. v. Chenier* (2006), 205 C.C.C. (3d)
333 (Ont. C.A.), is symptomatic of this phenomenon. I would add that *R. v. Sauvé* (2004),
182 C.C.C. (3d) 321 (Ont. C.A.), a case heavily relied on by the majority, is part of the
same trend.

[67] ... The majority is taking the wind out of *Vetrovec*'s sails by imposing requirements regarding the content of warnings given to jurors. I take specific issue with the
requirement that jurors be told to look for "material" and "independent" corroboration
of an unsavoury witness's testimony. While superficially attractive, such criteria detract
from what jurors should really be doing: assessing the witness's credibility in a rational
and flexible manner.

[68] While I agree with the majority's disposition of this appeal, for the reasons that
follow I believe that a functional approach to *Vetrovec* warnings is preferable and that this
Court should preserve the legacy of that case ... .

[Deschamps J set out the framework from *Sauvé*, endorsed by Fish J for the majority (at
para 37), indicating that she agreed with the first three elements, but disagreed with the
fourth, which she viewed as "both unnecessary and unworkable" (at para 73). She explained that requirements for independence and materiality are "intractable concepts"
(at para 78), extremely difficult to define, and engage courts in "a futile line-drawing
exercise" (at para 85). She concluded as follows:]

[99] There has been a general trend in the law of evidence towards more flexible rules, as trial judges and juries are shown the trust they need to perform their fact-finding duties properly. The majority's decision in this case is a step back from that trend. ...

[100] Despite statements by the majority that it does not wish to depart from *Vetrovec*, the proposed framework does exactly that. Although the majority says that its intention is to provide guidance to trial judges (para. 14), the framework and the requirements thereof can only be seen as mandatory. It is foreseeable that courts of appeal will from now on use the four elements of the *Sauvé* framework as review checklists. Technical appeals are likely to flourish.

[101] Finally, I am troubled by the reference my colleague makes, in his opening paragraph, to Deuteronomy19:15. Many centuries ago, religion, myths and the criminal law coalesced to produce rules and penalties that would not be tolerated today. Courts are now neutral and the criminal law does not need support from religion.

NOTES AND QUESTIONS

1. Do you agree with Fish J that the requirements for independence and materiality are sensible aspects of a *Vetrovec* warning, necessary to providing appropriate protection to an accused? Or do you think, like Deschamps J, that the majority's decision in *Khela* represents an undesirable incremental return to the technical *Baskerville* approach to corroboration abandoned in *Vetrovec*?

2. It is well established that a *Vetrovec* warning should not be given in respect of defence witnesses or an accused who chooses to testify: see *R v Tzimopoulos* (1986), 29 CCC (3d) 304 (Ont CA); *R v Hoilett* (1991), 3 OR (3d) 449 (CA); *R v Lavallee*, 2001 SKCA 43, 153 CCC (3d) 120. What justifies this rule?

3. An interesting question that has arisen is whether the reasoning in *Vetrovec* should have any impact on remaining statutory corroboration provisions that impose the strict *Baskerville* formulation requiring that testimony be "corroborated in a material particular by evidence that implicates the accused." In *R v B (G)*, [1990] 2 SCR 3, Wilson J considered the now-abrogated requirement for corroboration of the unsworn testimony of a child, and interpreted the strict, traditional formulation flexibly, drawing inspiration from *Vetrovec*. In *R v Neveu* (2004), 184 CCC (3d) 18 (Qc CA), considering the corroboration requirement still found in respect of the offence of perjury (s 133 of the *Criminal Code*), the court found that "the *Vetrovec* decision did not modify the state of the law in cases where, as in perjury, corroboration is required by a legislative provision" (at para 9). Nevertheless, the court narrowly construed the applicability of the corroboration requirement in s 133, holding that it "is inapplicable in the case of circumstantial evidence because it requires corroboration only when an accused can be found guilty of perjury on the evidence of *only one witness*" (at para 19). Paciocco and Steusser summarize the law on this point by stating that "[w]hile statutory language cannot be ignored, it is clear that the trend is to construe corroboration requirements into near oblivion" (*The Law of Evidence*, 7th ed (Toronto: Irwin Law, 2015) at 570).

PROBLEM (R v GALLOWAY)

Consider each of the following questions separately:

1. As noted in Chapter 2, the Crown witness Margaret was originally a suspect, but co-operated with the police after being given a promise of immunity from prosecution. Is Margaret a witness who warrants a *Vetrovec* warning?

2. Imagine that Martin intends to testify as part of the defence case. As it happens, he was convicted of possession of a large quantity of marijuana when he was 21 (while he was at university). Martin had a trial on that charge (he was charged along with his two roommates). At that trial, he testified that he knew nothing about the drugs, which were located in a common area of the home. Martin and his two roommates were each convicted. Martin was fined $500 and placed on probation for a year. At trial, is the Crown permitted to cross-examine Martin regarding the details with respect to his prior conviction? Can the Crown elicit from Martin the fact that he had testified at his earlier trial and had nevertheless been convicted? Is there anything the defence can do in an effort to preclude the Crown from delving into this conviction when Martin is cross-examined?

3. Refer to the summary of Margaret Jenkins's evidence in Chapter 2, and consider the following questions:

   a. Imagine that Amanda is prepared to testify that Margaret said to her: "Martin is a no good SOB. After he was arrested I found out that he was also sleeping with his kids' nanny!" Could the defence call Amanda to give this evidence as part of its case?

   b. In cross-examination, Margaret denies making the statement that Amanda is alleged to have heard. Now imagine that Amanda denies that Margaret ever made such a statement to her. Is the Crown entitled to call Amanda to confirm Margaret's denial?

Character

In the law of evidence, a person's "character" is understood as his or her propensity or disposition to behave in a certain way. Evidence of character seeks to establish that an individual is the *kind of person* more or less likely to engage in particular conduct. For example, character evidence tendered by the Crown in a criminal case may be offered to show that, given past discreditable acts, reputation in the community, psychiatric traits, or other facts about the accused, he or she is more likely to have committed the offence in question. Character evidence thus invites the trier of fact to infer that a person behaved in a certain way at a certain time because that behaviour would be consistent with that person's good or bad character or disposition. It is therefore sometimes referred to as "propensity" or "disposition" evidence.

This reasoning from general good or bad disposition to the likelihood of behaving in a particular way is what distinguishes character evidence from evidence of habit. For example, the time at which an individual routinely goes to bed would be considered a matter of habit, not character. Equally, the fact that an individual habitually smokes a particular brand of cigarette might be useful in predicting whether he or she was smoking that brand of cigarette on another occasion. Such evidence says nothing about whether the individual is of reputable or disreputable general character, and therefore does not engage the policy concerns that generate the rules that carefully regulate the admission and use of character evidence; it is "mere" habit and is admissible if relevant and not subject to other exclusionary rules. If, however, the evidence of "habit" reflects more broadly on the kind of person the accused is—if it creates the impression of an accused as a good or bad kind of person more likely to have behaved in a certain way—that evidence engages character reasoning and should be assessed using the rules discussed in this chapter. For example, evidence that an accused has a tendency to get into violent altercations, offered to suggest that he is more likely to have assaulted another—or, alternatively, evidence that an accused has a habit of returning lost goods, which suggests that he is not the sort of person to have committed theft—is the kind of propensity or disposition evidence with which the law of character is concerned. The essence of character evidence is that it colours one's sense of the kind of person the individual is and seeks to draw an inference about behaviour from that good or bad disposition.

The law's concern with character evidence stems from a number of sources.

First, although it might be true that people tend to behave in keeping with their general character, we also know that this is not always so. Moreover, the fact that someone who has stolen in the past might be more likely to steal in the future does not mean that he was the thief on this particular occasion. Character evidence thus presents the risk of judging an individual on the basis of his or her general disposition or propensities rather than on evidence that proves whether the individual actually committed the act in question on the occasion in question. This is called the "prohibited character inference"; as Justice Binnie wrote in the leading Canadian case on similar fact evidence, *R v Handy*, 2002 SCC 56 at para 139, [2002] 2 SCR 908, "[t]he forbidden chain of reasoning is to infer guilt from *general* disposition or propensity." As you will read in this chapter, the risk of reasoning based on stigmatizing the individual in question is referred to as "moral prejudice." As Justice Binnie wrote in *Handy* at para 72, speaking of the criminal context, "[b]ad character is not an offence known to the law. Discreditable disposition or character evidence, at large, creates nothing but 'moral prejudice' and the Crown is not entitled to ease its burden by stigmatizing the accused as a bad person."

Second, the law of evidence is concerned that adducing character evidence will distract a finder of fact, and consume time and resources at trial out of proportion to the probative value of the evidence, and that a finder of fact might overvalue such evidence. These concerns are referred to as "reasoning prejudice." Given the risk of moral prejudice and reasoning prejudice, the law of evidence has traditionally placed strict limitations on the admissibility and use of character evidence.

As you can see, evidentiary limits on the use of character evidence are not based on character being irrelevant. The relevance of character evidence is accepted—as a matter of logic and human experience, the fact that a person has a disposition or propensity to behave in a certain way may increase or decrease the likelihood that he or she acted in that way on the occasion in question. Rather, rules limiting the admissibility and use of character evidence are based on the potential prejudicial effect of such evidence outweighing its legal usefulness. Again, Justice Binnie captured the essential idea well in *Handy*, above:

> [39] It is, of course, common human experience that people generally act consistently with their known character. We make everyday judgments about the reliability or honesty of particular individuals based on what we know of their track record. If the jurors in this case had been the respondent's inquisitive neighbours, instead of sitting in judgment in a court of law, they would undoubtedly have wanted to know everything about his character and related activities. His ex-wife's anecdotal evidence would have been of great interest. Perhaps too great, as pointed out by Sopinka J. in *B. (C.R.)*, *supra*, at p. 744:
>
>> The principal reason for the exclusionary rule relating to propensity is that there is a natural human tendency to judge a person's action on the basis of character. Particularly with

juries there would be a strong inclination to conclude that a thief has stolen, a violent man has assaulted and a pedophile has engaged in pedophilic acts. Yet the policy of the law is wholly against this process of reasoning.

[40] The policy of the law recognizes the difficulty of containing the effects of such information which, once dropped like poison in the juror's ear, "swift as quicksilver it courses through the natural gates and alleys of the body": *Hamlet*, Act I, Scene v, ll. 66-67.

As such, the field of character evidence is an expression of the general exclusionary principle (examined in Chapter 3, Section II) that relevant evidence whose probative value is outweighed by its potential for prejudice should not be admitted. Equally, as you will see as the chapter unfolds, when the probative value of such evidence is strong enough to overcome these concerns, character evidence will be admitted.

The material in this chapter is concerned largely with the common law limits on proof of character, whether good or bad, as circumstantial evidence. This chapter begins, in Section I, with a brief word about the uncommon situation in which character is directly in issue in a trial. Section II goes on to consider when, despite the general prohibition on the Crown adducing evidence of the accused's bad character, such evidence might nevertheless be admissible. As you will read, the two principal situations in which character evidence might be introduced against an accused are (1) to rebut an accused's assertion that he or she is of good character, having thereby put character in issue, and (2) when the Crown is able to satisfy the strict test to introduce "similar fact evidence." Section III takes up the situation of an accused who, in his or her trial, seeks to call character evidence against other persons, such as third-party suspects or complainants. The chapter ends, in Section IV, by examining the use of character evidence in civil cases.

I. CHARACTER DIRECTLY IN ISSUE

On occasion, a person's character is something that a party may or must prove as an element of the cause of action. For example, where the Crown applies under s 753 of the *Criminal Code* to have someone declared a dangerous offender, the person's dangerousness is the issue in the application, and character evidence is admissible on this point: *Criminal Code*, s 757. (See also *R v Currie*, [1997] 2 SCR 260, which illustrates this point, though it does not deal with the admissibility of evidence.) In a defamation case in which the defendant has made a general attack on a character trait such as the plaintiff's honesty, the defendant's claim of justification puts the plaintiff's character squarely in issue. For a discussion of the use of character evidence in defamation actions, see *Plato Films Ltd v Speidel*, [1961] AC 1090 (HL). When character is directly in issue, there are no special rules governing the admissibility of character evidence.

More commonly, evidence of a person's character is circumstantial evidence—that is, the trier of fact is asked to infer that, because the person has a certain character trait or propensity, he or she is more likely to have behaved in the manner alleged. For example, a person accused of theft might offer evidence of his honesty to suggest that he would not have taken the goods in question; or an accused charged with murder, where identity is in issue, might point to the violent disposition of another person connected to the victim in order to raise a reasonable doubt that the accused is the killer. Before the reforms now embodied in s 276 of the *Criminal Code*, persons accused of sexual offences commonly pointed to the complainant's "poor character" for chastity to suggest that she was likely to have consented to the sexual activity in question. In each case, the structure of the argument is the same: the person is more likely to have done a certain thing on the occasion in question because he or she has a disposition—in other words, it's in his or her "character"—to behave in that way. The rest of this chapter is primarily concerned with the limits on the use of character evidence in this way—that is, as circumstantial evidence.

II. CHARACTER OF THE ACCUSED

The general principle is that the Crown is prohibited from adducing evidence "simply to show that the accused is the sort of person likely to commit the offence charged": *R v Johnson*, 2010 ONCA 646 at para 83. As explained above, although relevant, the probative value of such character evidence is generally outweighed by its potential for prejudice. Nevertheless, there are certain circumstances in which the Crown might be permitted to adduce what would otherwise be inadmissible character evidence. This part examines three such situations: (1) when character evidence is not being offered for propensity purposes; (2) when the accused puts his or her character in issue; and (3) when the Crown is permitted to adduce evidence of prior discreditable conduct pursuant to the similar fact evidence rule.

A. "Character" Evidence Not Offered for Propensity Purposes

Before turning to cases in which character evidence is offered as circumstantial evidence of the accused's conduct, it is important to recognize that sometimes the Crown will seek to introduce evidence that appears to reflect poorly on the character of the accused, but is not offered for propensity purposes. Given that such evidence does not rely on the prohibited character inference, its admissibility will turn simply on relevance and the normal weighing of the probative value of the evidence against its potential for prejudice.

For example, in a drug-related prosecution or the trial of an offence related to a criminal organization, setting out the facts and context surrounding the alleged offence may necessarily involve introducing evidence that could be highly discreditable to the accused. In such cases, the Crown is not offering such evidence for propensity purposes; rather, that "character" evidence is inextricably linked to the unfolding of events and a finder of fact's appreciation of the context and narrative. Consider the case of *R v Boucher* (2000), 149 CCC (3d) 429 (Qc CA), leave to appeal to SCC refused, [2001] 1 SCR vii. The accused was charged with the first degree murder of two prison guards and the attempted murder of another guard. The Crown's theory of the case was that the accused was the head of a violent, highly structured criminal organization, that he was the direct supervisor of those involved in the killings, and that he had ordered them to commit the murders for the ends and purposes of the organization. The Quebec Court of Appeal ruled that evidence of the accused's status in the criminal organization was admissible because it was necessary for the jury to assess the case, but that the trial judge was right to warn the jury not to engage in prohibited propensity reasoning. See also *R v Aitken*, 2012 BCCA 134 at paras 56-62, 289 CCC (3d) 79, leave to appeal to SCC refused, [2012] SCCA No 481; *R v Lamirande*, 2002 MBCA 41. Care must be taken when evidence of this sort is offered on the basis that it is necessary to establish the context, background, or narrative of the case; if the evidence engages propensity reasoning and invites the prohibited inference, it falls within the general bar on the Crown introducing evidence of bad character and is subject to the rules explored below.

Evidence relevant to credibility is another example of evidence that might appear to reflect on the accused's character but is not offered for propensity purposes, and therefore does not fall within the general prohibition against the Crown introducing evidence of bad character. As Martin JA explained in *R v Davison* (1974), 20 CCC (2d) 424 at 444 (Ont CA), "[c]ross-examination ... which is directly relevant to prove the falsity of the accused's evidence does not fall within the ban, notwithstanding that it may incidentally reflect upon the accused's character by disclosing discreditable conduct on his part." Martin JA provided a hypothetical example (at 444):

> Thus, if an accused found in possession of goods recently stolen were to give evidence that he had purchased them from X in good faith without knowing that they were stolen, it would not seem open to doubt that he could be cross-examined for the purpose of showing, if such were the fact, that he had been associated with X in the commission of prior thefts. Such cross-examination would be permissible as being directly relevant to the veracity of the accused's explanation.

The admission of the criminal record of an accused who chooses to take the stand is also an instance of evidence relevant to credibility but not offered for propensity purposes, though it reveals discreditable conduct on the part of the accused. As discussed in Chapter 6, Section III.C, this evidence is admissible under s 12 of the *Canada Evidence Act*, subject to the Supreme Court's decision in *R v Corbett*, [1988] 1 SCR 670. Such evidence is admissible if its probative value in relation to the accused's credibility as a witness outweighs its potential for prejudice; and in such instances the jury must be warned not to use it for prohibited character purposes.

The remainder of this section considers the two principal exceptions to the rule prohibiting the introduction of character evidence against the accused.

B. The Accused's Character Put in Issue

1. Putting Character in Issue

In a criminal prosecution, the Crown will often have information about the accused's bad character, perhaps in the form of a criminal record or other complaints about the accused's criminal activity, or in the form of non-criminal conduct that nonetheless casts the accused in a bad light. It has been repeatedly held in Anglo-Canadian law that the Crown may not lead such evidence to support an inference about the accused's character unless the accused "puts his character in issue"—that is, unless the accused himself has led evidence to suggest that he was unlikely to have committed the offence by virtue of a character trait. The rationale for this limitation was expressed by Willes J (dissenting on other grounds) in *R v Rowton* (1865), 169 ER 1497 at 1506:

> Such evidence is admissible, because it renders less probable that what the prosecution has averred is true. It is strictly relevant to the issue; but it is not admissible on the part of the prosecution, because ... if the prosecution were allowed to go into such evidence, we should have the whole life of the prisoner ripped up, and, as has been witnessed elsewhere, upon a trial for murder you might begin by shewing that when a boy at school the prisoner had robbed an orchard,

and so on through the whole of his life; and the result would be that the man on his trial would be overwhelmed by prejudice, instead of being convicted on that affirmative evidence which the law of this country requires. The evidence is relevant, but it is excluded for reasons of policy and humanity; because, although by admitting it you might arrive at justice in one case out of a hundred, you would probably do injustice in the other ninety-nine.

What does an accused person have to do to "put his character in issue" and thereby open the door to bad character evidence being offered in response? Consider the following case.

R v McNamara (No 1)
(1981), 56 CCC (2d) 193 (Ont CA)
Martin, Lacourcière, Houlden, Weatherston, and Goodman JJA
(15 January 1981)

[In this case, 13 individuals and corporations appealed from their convictions for offences of conspiracy to defraud. The charges arose out of the alleged rigging of bids submitted on tenders for dredging contracts. The Ontario Court of Appeal dealt with several issues in a lengthy judgment. One of the appellants argued that the trial judge erred in permitting Crown counsel to cross-examine him with respect to a previous transaction, referred to in the case as the "Marine Building transaction." The appellant had pleaded guilty to a charge of income tax evasion in connection with that transaction.]

BY THE COURT: … One of the principal grounds of appeal advanced on behalf of the appellant Jean Simard was that the trial judge erred in permitting Crown counsel to cross-examine Jean Simard with respect to his involvement in the Marine Building transaction. A brief outline of the transaction has been given under the heading "Jean Simard: Corroboration."

Mr. Robinette contended that the cross-examination of the appellant with respect to the Marine Building transaction violated the general rule that the Crown may not initially introduce evidence which shows that the accused is a person of bad character and that the cross-examination could not be justified under any of the exceptions to the general rule. The trial judge ruled that the evidence was admissible on two grounds:

1. That the appellant had given evidence of good character.

2. That the evidence was directly relevant to prove the falsity of the appellant's evidence, even though it incidentally reflected on his character.

The trial judge in ruling that the cross-examination was permissible said in part:

> The Crown submits that there are two grounds for admissibility; one as a response to evidence of good character; and two to prove the falsity of the accused's evidence-in-chief.
>
> On the first point I am satisfied that the evidence called for Mr. Simard, and the evidence of Mr. Simard, has been much more than a denial of the Crown evidence. The only implication from the evidence is that Jean Simard, as a director of family's companies, stands for legality in the operation of such companies, and is, therefore, a man of good character.

The *Phillip Morris* case indicates that character can be put in issue in more than one way, and I think the accused has put his character in issue.

For reasons which will subsequently be developed, we are of the opinion that the trial judge did not err in ruling that the appellant had put his character in issue, and that the evidence was admissible. We will later discuss the limited purpose for which this evidence could be used.

The appellant testified in his examination-in-chief that his training had been in the field of financial management, that he was a member of the board of directors of a number of public companies in which the Simard family owned shares, and that he was not involved in the day-to-day operation of the Simard family companies. He said that the Simard policy was to leave the day-to-day operations of the Simard companies to professional managers.

In reply to a question put by his counsel as to the mandate he had given Rindress, the appellant gave the following answer:

Q. Mr. Rindress in giving his evidence has told us that what he considered his mandate was in connection with the operation of the Porter Company and the Richelieu Company, what did you consider was the mandate of Mr. Rindress in connection with operating the company?

A. The mandate that Mr. Rindress had is to run the company like a company should be run, legally.

Q. I am sorry?

A. Like any company should be run, legally.

Q. Prior to you coming on the Board of Directors of the Porter Company in December, '63, did you have any knowledge of any bid-rigging or other illegal activity in the dredging industry?

A. No, sir.

Q. After you came on the Board of Directors of J.P. Porter in December of 1963, did you become aware of any bid-rigging or other illegal activity in the dredging industry prior to late 1973, early 1974?

A. No, sir.

Q. Prior to December of 1973 after the RCMP began their investigation, did you have any knowledge that Rindress was involved in bid-rigging or other illegal activities in connection with the J.P. Porter Company?

A. No, sir.

The appellant, in response to a question by his counsel whether he had any position of influence with Jean Marchand, made the following lengthy statement which is of sufficient importance to reproduce in full:

Q. Have you ever had any position of special influence with Marchand?

A. No. I never discussed business with Mr. Marchand, but if you, if I may have a minute I would like to explain. The position in a situation like mine, Mr. Marchand is a minister, and if ever I had—I never did—but if ever, ever I had to talk to Mr. Marchand at the ministerial level I would have gone. And one example I can give you if ever it had happened I would have done it; if instead in the dredging industry of what we learned today try to keep that industry alive going by through bid-rigging from the managers and all that. If our people would had report to us that if we want to survive that industry we need subsidies, that would be in my position to go and discuss at ministerial level that this industry needs subsidies. It has been done in the shipping industry. My uncle has been at ministerial level to discuss subsidies so that the shipbuilding industry can survive in Canada. But I think that in a situation each one has his own level, and me I rate myself at the ministerial level. If I had to talk to them, but I never did. I never had this subject, and I had a thing that was at that level. On the second level is the people that runs the business. The people that runs the business they hit in the political places in Ottawa, I would call them from deputy minister down. Those people are there to keep industry going, so you go at their level. So Mr. Rindress if he had something to do in Ottawa he has to go to the deputy minister down to the engineers at the Department of Transport to discuss, not favours, but to discuss business. There is certain etiquette in life for businessmen, and in my situation if I am not trained for that I would never be where I am today. I will give you one example. I am a director for many years of Consolidated Bathurst. Consolidated Bathurst has operations all around, over Canada, lumber camps, all kinds. They use I am sure thousands and thousands of propane gas cylinders. We are the manufacturer of all the propane gas in Canada.

Q. What do you mean by we?

A. I am talking about Engineering Products.

Q. One of the Simard family companies?

A. We have Sorel Industries that makes the best of the paper machines in the industry. To me as a director of Consolidated Bathurst, if they need to buy paper machines we have people in the sales department, and it is the man that runs Sorel who has to go to Consolidated Bathurst and sell the machine. And always, and this is the way the man should operate. If they start a directors' meeting, and sometimes they probably kind of forget that I have some interest in the Sorel Industries. Before they even attack … attack, excuse me for using the expression. They touch the subject right away. I would say I am sorry I have to declare my interest because I am a shareholder of Sorel Industries, and here I am sitting here as a director of Consolidated Bathurst. I am not sitting here as shareholder of Sorel Industries. So this is where the levels are. If I am there, I am sitting at Consolidated Bathurst, the man sitting right next to me is the chairman of the board of the Bank of Montreal. Do I go to take this opportunity as a director of Consolidated Bathurst to have a talk with the chairman of the board of the Bank of Montreal, because I know that one of our industries or even a friend of mine, and this and that, is having a loan at the bank. That's not done. So there is an etiquette to be respected, and this is the same for the Government, and all the ministers that I know, and Mr. Marchand, that I said [was] a friend and acquaintance, if ever it had a thing on our level I would have talked to Mr. Marchand, but he didn't have it. But some people have in their minds as political contributions, it is like they give money and expect to receive something in favours out of it. They think that when they subscribe is like going to Woodbine Race Track. I give five dollars and expect 35 out of it. That is not the way we think. As politics of our family it is a responsibility that the family has towards democracy. We believe in two parties. And if we were not doing the contribution like we did, that we have to put what we think is the people that have to be named as the head of the country to run it, where would we be in the Province of Quebec if we were not there and to fight it. Let the terrorists take over? We have to defend that. If we don't subscribe, who would subscribe, Russia? We have to defend democracy. This is that level, not to get favours. I don't need favours. In our situation people are asking us all the time all kinds of things. We know what it is that people come and ask us all the time. In that position you don't go and ask somebody else. I am sorry if I elaborate too much, but this is ...

Q. Mr. Simard, I want to bring you back to the July 1972 memorandum referred to.

A. Yes.

Mr. Robinette contended that the appellant's answers were not made with a view to establishing that the appellant was a man of good character, but constituted only a denial of the allegations made against him. Further, he contended that it was an essential part of the appellant's defence that the appellant's role as overseer of the Simard family investments involved his being a director of numerous public and other companies and that he was thus removed from the day-to-day operation of the various Simard companies.

Mr. McLeod, on the other hand, contended that the appellant clearly asserted that he was a man of integrity and of an honest moral disposition, and hence, had put his character in issue. Manifestly, an accused does not put his character in issue by denying his guilt and repudiating the allegations made against him, nor by giving an explanation of matters which are essential to his defence. An accused is not entitled, however, under the guise of repudiating the allegations against him to assert expressly or impliedly that he would not have done the things alleged against him because he is a person of good character, if he does, he puts his character in issue.

The difficult question is whether the appellant crossed over the line of permissible repudiation of the charge and asserted that he was an honest man.

. . .

It is also accepted in Canada that, within limits at any rate, introductory questions put to the accused as to his place of residence, his marital status and his employment, do not put his character in issue: see Kenneth L. Chasse: *Exclusions of Certain Circumstantial Evidence: Character and Other Exclusionary Rules*, 18 OHLJ 446 (1980). In *Morris v. The Queen* (1978), 43 CCC (2d) 129, [1979] 1 SCR 405, the Supreme Court of Canada held, however, that an accused had given evidence of good character when he stated that he had never been convicted nor arrested. Pratte J, delivering the majority judgment of the court, said at p. 156 CCC, p. 438 SCR:

> [T]hese statements were nothing but an attempt on his part to lead evidence of good character. By projecting the image of a law-abiding citizen, the appellant's purpose could only have been to show that because of his character he was not likely to have committed the offence with which he was charged.

In that case, of course, it was more obvious that the accused had put his character in issue. Pratte J in his reasons referred, with apparent approval, to two English cases. The first of these cases was *R v. Baker* (1912), 7 Cr. App. R 252, in which the English Court of Criminal Appeal held that the appellant's evidence that he had been earning an honest living for four years was evidence of good character which laid him open to cross-examination as to character. The second of the cases referred to by Pratte J was *R v. Samuel* (1956), 40 Cr. App. R 8. In that case the appellant had been charged with larceny by finding.

He testified that on two previous occasions he had found property and handed it over to the police. Lord Goddard said: "Of course, if a man has done that, it is an indication that he is an honest person" (p. 10). Lord Goddard said at p. 11: "… the only object of those questions could be to induce the jury to say: 'This man is one of those people who, if he finds property, gives it up; in other words, he is an honest man.'"

The appellant Jean Simard in response to his counsel's question as to the scope of Rindress' mandate did not confine himself to saying that the mandate was to run the company legally. The appellant said that Rindress' mandate was to run the company like a company should be run, legally. He followed that answer by repeating that Rindress' mandate was to run the company "like any company should be run, legally." The appellant's evidence is consistent only with his intention to assert that he would not knowingly permit a Simard company to be operated other than legally. If there were any doubt whether the appellant, by these answers, intended to project the image of a law-abiding citizen, these answers, when taken together with his subsequent evidence, make it clear that the appellant intended to project the image of a man of integrity and of an ethical businessman.

The appellant was, of course, entitled to repudiate Rindress' evidence that the appellant had claimed to have influence with Jean Marchand. He was also entitled to explain that political contributions were proper and that any such contributions by the Simard family or their companies were not made with any improper motives or to purchase favours. Such evidence would not have put his character in issue.

Even making all due allowance for the emotional stress that an accused is under in a criminal trial for a serious offence, the appellant, none the less, went far beyond repudiation and explanation. He compared the principles of some people in making political contributions with his own: he said that the Simard family, unlike some people, did not expect favours in return for political contributions. He illustrated his sense of propriety by stating that he would immediately declare his interest if, at a meeting of the board of directors of Consolidated Bathurst, a purchase of machinery from Sorel Industries fell to be considered. He also gratuitously said he would not exploit, in connection with a loan, the fact that a fellow director was also chairman of the board of a bank. Surely, those statements could only have been made to induce the jury to think he was an upright man, whose character was such that it was unlikely that he would commit the offence charged. In our view, the trial judge was entitled to hold that the appellant had put his character in issue.

[The court's discussion of the propriety of the Crown's cross-examination of Simard on the "Marine Building transaction" is reproduced below.]

As *McNamara* indicates, the accused does not put his or her character in issue simply by denying guilt or repudiating the allegations against him or her. Rather, the test is whether the accused, through the evidence offered, suggested that he or she is not the kind of person likely to commit the offence; in the words of the court in *McNamara*, an accused puts his character in issue by "assert[ing] expressly or impliedly that he would not have done the things alleged against him because he is a person of good character." It is generally accepted that there are three ways that an accused person can put his character in issue: (1) by adducing evidence of good reputation (as in *Rowton*, discussed below); (2) by testifying as to his own good character (as in *McNamara*); or (3) by calling expert evidence of propensity or disposition (see Section II.B.4, below).

If an accused chooses to put his or her good character in issue in any of these ways, the trial judge must instruct the jury that they are entitled to use that evidence both to infer that the accused is less likely to have committed the offence and to support the credibility of the accused, if the accused chooses to take the stand: see *R v H (ED)*, 2000 BCCA 523; *R v Millar* (1989), 49 CCC 3d 193 (Ont CA); *R v Logiacco* (1984), 11 CCC (3d) 374 (Ont CA). As discussed above, with the accused's character now in issue, the Crown may rebut the assertion that the accused is of good character with evidence that this is not so—that the accused is not of good character. However, the use to which such rebuttal evidence may be put is not symmetrical: the trier of fact may not use that evidence of bad character to infer that the accused is the kind of person more likely to have committed the offence. That is the prohibited character inference. Rather, the theory is that this rebuttal bad character evidence simply refutes the assertion of good character, and a jury must be instructed as to this limited use. As the BC Court of Appeal put it in *H (ED)*, above at para 19, "the evidence may be used to refute the assertion of good character and on the issue of the accused's credibility, but it may not be used as a basis for determining guilt or innocence." Whether this theory matches reality in the mind of the trier of fact is another question.

Determining whether an accused has put his good character in issue can sometimes be a difficult matter for the trial judge. Consider the case of *R v Castaneda* 2001 BCCA 599, 160 CCC (3d) 218. In 1994, the accused was charged with sexual assault. In 1995, he went to Guatemala (his country of origin) and was drafted into the army. He served two years in the Guatemalan army and returned to Canada in 1997. His trial took place in 2000. Concerned that the jury might infer consciousness of guilt from the accused's absence from Canada, defence counsel questioned him regarding his visit to Guatemala and his army service. During this testimony the accused stated that he had wanted to come back to Canada "to clear his name." Did this testimony have the effect of putting his character in issue so as to entitle the Crown to neutralize its effect by introducing bad character evidence? Although the trial judge permitted the Crown to cross-examine the accused on his character, Hall JA, writing for the BC Court of Appeal, stated at para 9, "I am gravely doubtful that what the appellant said about coming back to Canada to face charges in the circumstances of this case put his character in issue."

The Crown cannot put the accused's character in issue, whether through cross-examination of the accused or of other defence witnesses: see *R v A (WA)* (1996), 112 CCC (3d) 83 (Man CA). In *R v Bricker* (1994), 90 CCC (3d) 268 at 278 (Ont CA), Laskin JA said:

> The prosecutor cannot compel an accused to put his character in issue and, therefore, a prosecutor cannot by his cross-examination adduce good character evidence in order to provide a basis for questioning an accused on his criminal record.

Can you think of the rationale for this holding?

We now turn to consider the three limited methods of proving character and how those methods can be used by both the accused and by the Crown in response.

2. Reputation

The first means by which an accused may adduce evidence of his or her good character is by calling witnesses who will testify to the accused's general good reputation in the community.

In *R v Rowton* (1865), 169 ER 1497, the accused, a schoolmaster, was charged with indecent assault. He called several witnesses who, in the trial judge's words, "gave him an excellent character, as a moral and well-conducted man" (at 1499). In reply, the Crown called a witness who stated that he and his brothers had been students at Rowton's school, and "my opinion, and the opinion of my brothers ... is that his character is that of a man capable of the grossest indecency and the most flagrant immorality" (at 1499). Rowton was convicted. On appeal, he argued that the Crown was not entitled to reply to his evidence of good character, and in the alternative that the answer given by the Crown's rebuttal witness was improper. Cockburn CJ, for the majority, held on the first issue that if the accused raised the issue of his character, the Crown was entitled to reply: "[N]othing could be more unjust than that he should have the advantage of a character which, in point of fact, may be the very reverse of that which he really deserves" (at 1502). On the second issue, he held that, in proving character, the accused and the Crown were confined to evidence of general reputation (at 1502-3):

> Now, in determining this point, it is necessary to consider what is the meaning of evidence of character. Does it mean evidence of general reputation or evidence of disposition? I am of opinion that it means evidence of general reputation. What you want to get at is the tendency and disposition of the man's mind towards committing or abstaining from committing the class of crime with which he stands charged ... .
>
> • • •
>
> It is quite clear that, as the law now stands, the prisoner cannot give evidence of particular facts, although one fact would weigh more than the opinion of all his friends and neighbours. So too, evidence of antecedent bad conduct would form equally good ground for inferring the prisoner's guilt, yet it is quite clear evidence of that kind is inadmissible. The allowing evidence of good character has arisen from the fairness of our laws, and is an anomalous exception to the general rule. It is quite true that evidence of character is most cogent, when it is preceded by a statement shewing that the witness has had opportunities of acquiring information upon the subject beyond what the man's neighbours in general would have; and in practice the admission of such statements is often carried beyond the letter of the law in favour of the prisoner. It is, moreover, most essential that a witness who comes forward to give a man a good character should himself have a good opinion of him; for otherwise he would only be deceiving the jury; and so the strict rule is often exceeded. But when we consider what, in the strict interpretation of the law, is the limit of such evidence, in my judgment it must be restricted to the man's general reputation, and must not extend to the individual opinion of the witness.
>
> • • •
>
> If that be the true doctrine as to the admissibility of evidence to character in favour of the prisoner, the next question is, within what limits must the rebutting evidence be confined? I think that that evidence must be of the same character and confined within the same limits— that, as the prisoner can only give evidence of general good character, so the evidence called to rebut it must be evidence of the same general description shewing that the evidence which has been given in favour of the prisoner is not true, but that the man's general reputation is bad.

Rowton's conviction was quashed.

From what community should the accused's reputation derive? The next case considers that question.

R v Levasseur
1987 ABCA 70, 35 CCC (3d) 136
Haddad, Harradence, and Kerans JJA (26 March 1987)

HARRADENCE JA (Kerans JA concurring):

[1] The Appellant, Janice Levasseur, was charged with breaking and entering and theft. The objects allegedly stolen were a truck and an automobile. The premises in question were owned by the Appellant's employer, Femco Financial, but were leased to Union Tractor. The Appellant's defence was that she removed the vehicles at the request of her employer and therefore had colour of right. Her defence included evidence of her good character which her counsel sought to introduce through testimony by Alec Dabisza, a subsequent employer of the Appellant. Defence counsel attempted to qualify him as a character witness by proving that Dabisza had discussed the Appellant's general reputation with about 15 of their business acquaintances. The learned trial judge held that Dabisza's testimony was inadmissible, stating):

> He cannot give evidence of what the community thinks of her. We have heard his evidence of what he thinks of her; he cannot give evidence of what he feels the community in which he lives thinks of her character. (A.B., p. 173, 1, 19-23)

[2] The Appellant appeals from her conviction on the ground that the trial judge erred in not admitting Dabisza's evidence because he could not state her reputation in her residential community. The issue is whether evidence of general reputation as to character is confined to reputation in the residential community of the party whose credibility is under attack.

[3] The answer to this can only be that such a restriction has no place in modern society. *Wigmore on Evidence*, Chadbourn revision vol. V, (1974), §1616, at pp. 591-2, agrees that this restriction is archaic:

> In that type of community where the ordinary person's home is under the same roof as his store or workshop, or where the stores, workshops, offices, and homes are all collected within a small village or town group, and one's working associates are equally the neighbors of one's home, there is but one community for the purpose of forming public opinion, and there is but a single capacity in which the ordinary person can exhibit his character to the community. In other words, there he can have but one reputation. But in the conditions of life today, especially in large cities, a man may have one reputation in the suburb of his residence and another in the office or the factory at his place of work; or he may have one reputation in his place of technical domicile in New York and another in the region of the mines of Michigan or the steel mills of Ohio where his investments call him for supervision for portions of time. There may be distinct circles of persons, each circle having no relation to the other, and yet each having a reputation based on constant and intimate personal observation of the man.
>
> There is every reason why the law should recognize this. Time has produced new conditions for reputations. The traditional requirement about "neighbourhood" reputation was appropriate to the conditions of the time; but it should not be taken as imposing arbitrary limitations not appropriate in other times. Alia tempora, alii mores. *What the law, then as now, desired was a trustworthy reputation; if that is to be found among a circle of persons other than the circle of dwellers about a sleeping-place, it should be received.*

(Emphasis added.)

[4] Restricting character witnesses to neighbours may be traced back to the 19th century. For example, Cockburn J, in *R v. Rowton* (1865), Le. & Ca. 520 at p. 530, 169 ER 1497 at p. 1502, stated:

> The only way of getting at it is by giving evidence of his general character founded on his general reputation in the neighbourhood in which he lives. That, in my opinion, is the sense in which the word "character" is to be taken, when evidence of character is spoken of.

However, *Phipson on Evidence*, 13th ed. (1982), p. 214, notes that *Rowton* has not been subject "to critical scrutiny by a modern appellate court."

[5] Scrutiny by a modern appellate court can only result in the conclusion that the neighbourhood requirement is no longer justifiable. While it may have been appropriate in the days of the redoubtable Duke of Wellington, who regretted the advent of the British railroad system because it would allow the lower classes to move about, it is not appropriate to a society which has supersonic transport available to it.

[6] The laws of evidence must not continue to reflect this parochial attitude; as Lord Ellenborough pointed out, "[t]he rules of evidence must expand according to the exigencies of society" (*Pritt v. Fairclough* (1812), 3 Camp. 305 at p. 307, 170 ER 1392).

. . .

[10] There is no reason for sustaining this archaic rule in Canadian evidence law. No purpose is served by denying an accused the opportunity of providing witnesses who can report on his reputation in his work environment rather than in his residential community. The rule must reflect the modern metropolitan reality in which neighbours' names frequently are not even known, let alone their general reputations. To sustain this restriction would be to deny individuals whose lives do not centre on their residential communities the opportunity to offer witnesses of their good character. Instead, the rule should seek to provide for the best qualified witnesses, and if these witnesses should happen to be business associates rather than residential neighbours, what rational reason is there for excluding their testimony?

[11] I emphasize that the issue is not about the weight to be given evidence of general reputation but rather, whether it is admissible. The evidence was admissible.

[Kerans JA held that s 613(1)(b)(iii) (the curative proviso), now s 686(1)(b)(iii) of the *Criminal Code*, was not applicable because the excluded evidence might have affected the jury's assessment of the accused's credibility. The accused's appeal was allowed and a new trial ordered. Haddad JA dissented. Although he did not disagree with the legal principles stated by the majority, he was of the view that this was an appropriate case to apply the curative proviso.]

In a footnote to *R v Clarke* (1998), 129 CCC (3d) 1 (Ont CA), Rosenberg JA said:

> I should point out that, in my view, the trial judge was in error in holding that the character witnesses could only give evidence about reputation if they were aware of the accused's or complainant's reputation in a particular city or town where they lived, such as Trenton. With the increasing urbanization of society, a person's community will not necessarily coincide with a particular

geographic location. Thus, in this case, it would seem to me that it was open to the defence to lead evidence of the respondent's reputation in the Caribbean community in the area. In *R v. Levasseur* (1987), 35 CCC (3d) 136 (Alta. CA), the court held that the accused should have been permitted to call a witness to testify as to the accused's reputation at her place of work even though the witness knew nothing of the accused's reputation in the community where she resided.

How useful will the kind of character evidence contemplated in these cases be to a trier of fact? The next case concerns the weight to be attached to general reputation evidence of good character in a situation in which the accused was charged with sexual offences against children.

R v Profit
(1992), 11 OR (3d) 98 (Ont CA)
Blair, Goodman, and Griffiths JJA (27 October 1992)

GOODMAN JA (Blair JA concurring): The appellant, a 57-year-old school principal, appeals from his conviction in the District Court of Ontario at Newmarket on June 18, 1990 by His Honour District Court Judge E.B. Fedak on two counts in an indictment charging that during the months of October 1977 to February 1978, he did indecently assault one Guy Davis contrary to the provisions of s. 156 of the *Criminal Code*, RSC 1985, c. C-46, and further that he did during the month of March 1978 indecently assault Guy Davis.

On the same day the appellant was acquitted of an assault against Davis alleged to have occurred between May and June 1978. He was also acquitted of one count of sexual exploitation and four counts of sexual interference alleged to have occurred between September 1988 and January 1989. The five counts last mentioned related to Grade 8 students at Holland Landing Public School of which the appellant was the principal at the time of the alleged offences. The offences relating to Davis were said to have occurred when Davis was a Grade 8 student at Rogers Public School of which the appellant was the principal at the relevant times.

The appellant was acquitted on the third count relating to Davis on the ground that the evidence failed to prove that the acts alleged took place in the time frame within which the offence was alleged to have taken place.

The trial judge acquitted the appellant of the charges set forth in the five counts relating to the Holland Landing Public School students on the ground that he was not satisfied that the acts complained of were sexual in nature.

The complaints of Davis with respect to the offences of which the appellant was convicted consisted in each case of an allegation that the appellant had arranged to see him in places where they were alone in the school and had on each occasion cupped his genitals on the outside of his trousers for a period said to have lasted a few moments and thirty seconds respectively. He was 14 or 15 years of age at the time of the offences. The trial judge sentenced the appellant to a term of 90 days to be served intermittently and placed him on probation for two years. The Crown appeals this sentence.

[Goodman JA concluded that there was no merit in the first three grounds of appeal, and continued:]

Ground 4: The trial judge failed to properly consider the dual significance of the evidence of good character as it related both to the appellant's testimonial trustworthiness and the likelihood that he may have committed the offences alleged

Twenty-two character witnesses testified on behalf of the appellant. Fifteen were colleagues or school board employees who had worked either for or with the appellant. Three were associated with the appellant through volunteer or church organizations. Two were independent businessmen from the appellant's community and two were personal friends. Some of them had, as children, attended camps where the appellant was a director and in later years had acted as counsellors in the camp under the appellant's supervision. All of these witnesses had seemingly impeccable backgrounds and were well qualified to give evidence with respect to the reputation of the appellant in the community with respect to honesty, integrity and morality.

A fair résumé of their evidence with respect to their personal knowledge was that they had never seen the appellant conduct himself in a sexually inappropriate manner, nor had they ever heard the appellant make a statement that they would consider sexually inappropriate. None of them had ever received a complaint about the appellant's conduct.

Although this evidence is not admissible as character evidence in the sense of being evidence of general reputation in the community, it is indicative of the fact that the attention of the various witnesses had been directed towards the matter of the accused's sexual morality before they were asked the question as to his general reputation in the community for honesty and morality. It provides grounds for a reasonable inference that the character witnesses, in responding to the general question with respect to morality were referring to reputation as to sexual moral behaviour specifically as well as to reputation as to honesty in the sense of truth telling and other types of behaviour.

. . .

The trial judge, however, made no reference whatsoever to the use of character evidence as a basis of an inference that the appellant was unlikely to have committed the crime charged. In that respect he failed to give any recognition to the dual significance of such evidence. Although a trial judge need not in his reasons specifically refer to each principle of law upon which he relies, there are cases where the reasons given are such as to create at the very least a reasonable doubt as to whether such judge has misdirected himself or has failed to direct himself as to the proper principle of law applicable to a particular issue in the case. In the case at bar the trial judge dealt specifically in his reasons with the use that he made of the character evidence which had been adduced. In view of his failure to refer to its admissibility as the basis for an inference that the appellant was unlikely to have committed the crime charged, it is a matter of considerable doubt as to whether he was aware of its admissibility for that purpose or whether he directed his attention to its use for such purpose.

[Goodman JA referred next to cases where courts had noted that good character evidence relating to an accused's reputation for honesty and integrity was of limited value where an offence involving sexual misconduct is alleged, but distinguished those decisions because they did not involve character evidence relating to the accused's reputation for *morality*.]

In my opinion, however, where the character witnesses have given evidence as to the moral behaviour of an accused with respect to children in cases alleging sexual offences against children and have given evidence with respect to the general reputation of an accused for not only honesty and integrity but also morality, in the broader sense, such evidence has the same degree of relevance and weight to establish the improbability that the accused committed the offence, as evidence of general reputation with respect to honesty has in the case of an alleged offence involving a theft or a fraudulent transaction. In each case it is only one part of the evidence to be considered by the finder of fact along with all other evidence in determining the culpability of an accused and its weight will no doubt vary with the circumstances of each case. As noted above the character evidence in the case at bar dealt specifically with the appellant's behaviour with his students and his general reputation with respect to morality.

· · ·

It is not apparent from the reasons of the trial judge that he considered the character evidence as a basis for drawing an inference with respect to the probability of the appellant having committed the offence. The reasons would appear to indicate that he did not do so and in my opinion, in not doing so, he fell into error.

[Goodman JA held that the trial judge's error required a new trial.]

GRIFFITHS JA (dissenting):

· · ·

Traditionally, good character evidence has been limited to testimony of the witness' knowledge of the accused's reputation in the community. Generally speaking, good character evidence is not admissible where it merely consists of an expression of the witness' own opinions of the accused's character, nor is the witness entitled to testify to observations he made of certain conduct of the accused tending to show good character: see Sopinka, Lederman and Bryant, *The Law of Evidence in Canada* (Toronto: Butterworths, 1992), p. 446; *R v. Grosse* (1983), 9 CCC (3d) 465, at pp. 473-74. On this traditional view of good character evidence, the following summary of the evidence by Goodman JA ... in my respectful view, would not be admissible as character evidence and would not be relevant to the issue of whether the appellant is likely to have committed the offence in question:

> A fair résumé of their evidence with respect to their personal knowledge was that they had never seen the appellant conduct himself in a sexually inappropriate manner, nor had they ever heard the appellant make a statement that they would consider sexually inappropriate. None of them had ever received a complaint about the appellant's conduct.

However, I accept the position that there was some testimony offered that met the requirements of character evidence, that is, evidence of the reputation for good character enjoyed by the appellant in the community. In my opinion, however, while such evidence may be relevant in cases involving crimes of commercial dishonesty, it has little probative value in cases involving sexual misconduct against children by persons in positions of trust or control.

Recently there have been a number of cases involving persons who enjoyed impeccable reputations in the community for honesty, integrity and morality, such as teachers, scout leaders, priests and others who, in breach of their positions of trust, have committed acts of sexual assault. In these cases, the sexual assaults were generally shrouded in secrecy, and the flaw in the character of the offender frequently did not come to light until he had been charged and convicted: see, for example, the following cases concerning teachers: *R v. Pilgrim* (1981), 64 CCC (2d) 523, 35 Nfld. & PEIR 30 (Nfld. CA); *R v. Owens* (1986), 33 CCC (3d) 275, 55 CR (3d) 386 (Ont. CA); *R v. Horne*, [1987] NWTR 168 (SC); *R v. Stewart* (1988), 3 YR 107 (SC); *R v. Lysack* (1988), 26 OAC 338 (CA). For the case of a scout leader see *R v. Robertson* (1979), 46 CCC (2d) 573, 10 CR (3d) S-46 (Ont. CA), and a parish priest, *R v. Hoskins* (1987), 63 Nfld. & PEIR 119 (Nfld. SC).

I note with interest that the Task Force on Sexual Abuse of Patients, in its final report dated November 25, 1991, commissioned by the College of Physicians & Surgeons of Ontario, recommended that the discipline tribunal of the college place little or no emphasis on the use of character evidence as an indication that an accused doctor is unlikely to have committed the offence of sexual abuse. The report says, c. 10, p. 40:

> Recommendation 44 may effectively counter the first use of character evidence identified in *Millar* [*R v Millar* (1989), 49 CCC (3d) 193 (Ont CA)], i.e. the use of good character evidence as an indication of a lack of propensity for the accused to commit the offence in question. The Task Force indicated that there is data to show that evidence of good character does not have any bearing in the propensity of an individual to abuse patients sexually. Indeed, there is evidence to suggest that abusers often build good character profiles to camouflage their abuse.

The recommendations of the Task Force simply confirm what in my view is a commonsense conclusion, and that is that character evidence should be given little weight when considering the propensity of persons in positions of trust or control to sexually abuse.

• • •

Assuming, in this case, that the trial judge overlooked the additional consideration to be given to good character evidence, I am not persuaded that this omission was of such significance and seriousness as to warrant a new trial.

In the alternative, I am not satisfied that the trial judge necessarily overlooked the relevance of good reputation to the improbability of the offences being committed, or that this factor would necessarily have changed his decision, having regard to his findings of credibility. As I have mentioned earlier, the trial judge was apparently satisfied beyond a reasonable doubt that the complainant was telling the truth and that the appellant was not. I find it somewhat unreal to expect that the trial judge, having made those findings of credibility, might have acquitted the appellant on the basis of the second consideration to be given to good character evidence.

In the passage from the reasons of the trial judge referred to by Goodman JA ... , the trial judge, after referring to the evidence of "highly distinguished people," said:

> Their evidence of good character of the accused was just one of the factors that I had to consider in determining the credibility of any of the witnesses.

In my view, the passage in his reasons, which immediately follows the above statement, indicates that the trial judge recognized that those who testified to the good character of the appellant would unlikely be aware of the flaws in his character and propensity for sexual misconduct and therefore little weight should be given to their opinions in assessing the likelihood that the appellant committed the offences in question. The trial judge said:

This case as well I hope, has demonstrated to all those who showed interest in its progress, that these were very serious charges which, because of their very nature, occur usually in private between people who have some close type of relationship, be it in the nature of family authority or with people in authority such as this.

The abused are very often in such circumstances reluctant to report because of being afraid of getting someone into trouble, sometimes because they are just plain embarrassed, and in other situations, they simply want to block out the events from their minds.

. . .

The trial judge simply did not believe the appellant and, in my view, his failure to specifically refer to the second purpose of good character evidence did not amount to a misdirection or non-direction.

I would dismiss the appeal.

R v Profit

[1993] 3 SCR 637

Lamer CJC and L'Heureux-Dubé, Sopinka, McLachlin, and Iacobucci JJ

(7 October 1993)

SOPINKA J: We agree with the conclusion of Griffiths JA in his dissenting reasons. When the reasons of the trial judge are considered as a whole, we are satisfied that he dealt with the character evidence tendered in this case adequately. The reasons of the trial judge must be viewed in light of the fact that as a matter of common sense, but not as a principle of law, a trial judge may take into account that in sexual assault cases involving children, sexual misconduct occurs in private and in most cases will not be reflected in the reputation in the community of the accused for morality. As a matter of weight, the trial judge is entitled to find that the propensity value of character evidence as to morality is diminished in such cases.

Accordingly, the appeal is allowed and the convictions restored.

What exactly is the effect of *Profit*? Does it establish any legal rule? Is its reasoning applicable to other types of cases?

As *Rowton* established, once the accused has put his or her character in issue, one method that the Crown has at its disposal to rebut good character evidence is by calling witnesses who will testify to the bad reputation of the accused, but such rebuttal evidence must conform to the same strictures that bind good reputation evidence—that is, the witness may not give a personal opinion as to the character of the accused, but, rather, can testify only to the general reputation of the accused in the relevant community. It is important to note that the Crown might also seek to rebut good reputation evidence simply by cross-examining the witness who provided the evidence. As David M Paciocco and Lee Steusser state in *The Law of Evidence*, 7th ed (Toronto: Irwin Law, 2015) at 96, this kind of cross-examination "is particularly dangerous for the accused." They explain:

Since reputation is the product of what is said about another, It Is, by its very nature, hearsay information. Hearsay can therefore be used to rebut it. In particular, the reputation witness can be asked whether he has heard rumours involving the accused, ostensibly to test his familiarity with the reputation of the accused or his judgment about the quality of that reputation.

Given the risks of such cross-examination, the potentially low probative value of good reputation evidence, and the risks involved in putting one's character in issue, the instances in which it is strategically appealing to adduce good character evidence by means of reputation witnesses may well be narrow.

3. Specific Acts

The Crown may not lead evidence of specific bad acts of the accused that are not the subject matter of the charges before the court (subject to the "similar fact" rule discussed in Section II.C, below), nor may the accused call witnesses to testify as to his prior good acts. But, as we saw in the excerpt from *McNamara*, above, if the accused himself chooses to testify, not only may he assert his good character but he may also give evidence of specific instances of his own good conduct. Once he has done that, and has thereby put his character in issue, what should be the permissible scope of the Crown's rebuttal evidence?

R v McNamara (No 1)
(1981), 56 CCC (2d) 193 (Ont CA)
Martin, Lacourcière, Houlden, Weatherston, and Goodman JJA
(15 January 1981)

Character Evidence

[Having held that the accused had put his character in issue, the court considered the propriety of Crown counsel's cross-examination of the accused concerning the "Marine Building transaction." The accused had been a director of the Marine Building Company at the relevant time, and the company and one of the accused's relatives had pleaded guilty to tax evasion in relation to this transaction.]

BY THE COURT: ... Mr. Robinette also argued that character means general reputation and that the accused can only put his character in issue by adducing evidence of general reputation. With respect, we do not agree. The common law rule was that evidence of good character could only be given by evidence of reputation, and could only be rebutted by evidence of reputation and not by specific acts of bad conduct: *R v. Rowton* (1865), Le & Ca. 520, 169 ER 1497. That rule was, however, established at a time when the accused could not himself give evidence. A long series of cases in England (two of which were cited with approval in *Morris v. The Queen, supra*) have held that an accused may put his character in issue by testifying as to his good character. The word "character" in the *Criminal Evidence Act, 1898* has uniformly been held to mean not only reputation, but actual moral disposition: *Cross on Evidence*, 4th ed. (1974), p. 426; *Phipson on Evidence*, 12th ed. (1976), p. 218. It is true that when the accused wishes to adduce extrinsic evidence of good character by calling witnesses, such evidence is confined to evidence of general reputation, but that has no application where the accused himself gives the evidence.

It was also contended on behalf of the appellant that where evidence of good character, in whatever form, is introduced by the prisoner (whether it be extrinsic evidence or by his own testimony) it cannot be rebutted by evidence of specific acts of bad conduct: rather, the Crown is confined to rebutting the evidence of good character by evidence of general reputation or by proof of a previous conviction pursuant to s. 593 of the *Criminal Code* [now s 666, reproduced below]. Counsel for the appellant argued that the provisions in s. 593 constitute the only exception to the common law rule that evidence of good character can only be rebutted by evidence of bad reputation. There is at least one additional exception, namely, *the Crown may adduce similar fact evidence in rebuttal of evidence of good character*. In *Guay v. The Queen* (1978), 42 CCC (2d) 536, Pigeon J, delivering the judgment of the Supreme Court of Canada, said at p. 547:

> On the admissibility of similar fact evidence, I think it should be said that it is essentially in the discretion of the trial judge. In exercising this discretion, he must have regard to the general principles established by the cases. There is no closed list of the sort of cases where such evidence is admissible. It is, however, well established that it may be admitted to rebut a defence of legitimate association for honest purposes, *as well as to rebut evidence of good character*. Where the evidence is admissible on the first mentioned basis, it may be admitted as part of the case for the prosecution. [Emphasis added.]

Whatever the limitations may be on the use of *extrinsic* evidence (i.e., evidence of other witnesses) to rebut evidence of good character, we are satisfied that those limitations did not preclude the cross-examination of the appellant with respect to the Marine Building transaction. It is not necessary to decide the difficult question whether an accused who testifies to his good character (moral disposition) for honesty, thereby lays himself open to be cross-examined on every phase of his character, such as, for example, his sexual morality, nor to consider the extent of the judge's discretion where the alleged bad conduct has not resulted in a conviction. Here the appellant had asserted a good disposition in relation to honesty and integrity. The cross-examination on the Marine Building transaction related to that particular moral disposition and was highly relevant to rebut the appellant's assertion of good character.

The learned trial judge also permitted the cross-examination of the appellant with respect to the Marine Building transaction because it was directly relevant to show that the appellant had lied in examination-in-chief. Mr. Robinette forcefully argued that the cross-examination could not be justified on the ground that it *directly* proved that the appellant had lied in his examination-in-chief, since the appellant had not testified about the Marine Building transaction in chief and hence the cross-examination could not prove that anything the appellant said in his examination-in-chief was false. We are disposed to think that, but for the fact that the accused had put his character in issue by testifying that he conducted his business affairs in an ethical manner, the cross-examination would not have been admissible on the ground that it showed directly that the appellant had lied. Where, however, an accused puts his character in issue, thereby opening the door to cross-examination on his past conduct, the proof of the previous bad conduct may have a double effect: it not only rebuts his claim to a good character, but it directly proves that he lied in the witness-box if he has impliedly asserted that he is a law-abiding citizen. For example, if an accused puts his character in issue by saying: "I have been honestly employed all my life," and the prosecution proves that he has knowingly been engaged in unlawful activities, the prosecution has not only rebutted his evidence of good character, but at the same time has proved that he lied.

In *Morris v. The Queen* (1978), 43 CCC (2d) 129, [1979] 1 SCR 405, Pratte J clearly pointed out the distinction between (a) cross-examination on previous convictions to permit an inference that because the accused is of bad disposition, he is testimonially untrustworthy, which permits a further inference that his testimony on the witness stand is suspect, and (b) cross-examination to prove *directly* that the accused lied in the witness-box. If an accused who had a criminal record were so foolish, however, as to say in examination-in-chief that he had never been convicted, the proof of his criminal record would not only give rise to the usual inference of untrustworthiness but would also directly show that he had lied. The ordinary witness may be cross-examined as to past misconduct and discreditable associations for the purpose of showing that his moral disposition is such that his oath should not be relied upon. An accused who testifies in his own defence, unlike the ordinary witness, provided he does not put his character in issue, is protected against that type of cross-examination unless, of course, the previous conduct has resulted in a conviction, or unless the cross-examination can be justified under some other exception to the general rule, e.g., similar facts.

[The court quoted at length from *Morris* and continued:]

When Jean Simard asserted, as we have held, that he was a man of integrity, his cross-examination on the Marine Building transaction was directly relevant to show that his assertion was untrue.

We are unable to accept the submission that this evidence was so prejudicial in relation to its probative value that the trial judge should have exercised his discretion to exclude it. We are of the opinion that it had substantial relevance on the issue of credibility. We do not wish to be taken, however, as holding that a trial judge would not have a discretion, even when an accused had put his character in issue, to exclude cross-examination on previous conduct, not resulting in a conviction, that was remote in time, or of little probative value on the issue of credibility and that was gravely prejudicial.

Counsel for the appellant also contended that even if the evidence of the Marine Building transaction was admissible, the trial judge should have charged the jury that it could only be used on the issue of Jean Simard's credibility, and must not be used to show propensity. Instead of giving this instruction to the jury, the trial judge erred by charging the jury that the Marine Building transaction could be used as evidence of guilt.

Where the only avenue of admissibility of evidence of bad character is to rebut the accused's evidence of good character, the evidence has a limited use. Wigmore says:

> After a defendant has attempted to show his good character in his own aid, *prosecution may in rebuttal* offer as evidence his bad character. The true reason for this seems to be, not any relaxation of the principle just mentioned, i.e. not a permission to show the defendant's bad character, but a liberty to refute his claim that he has a good one. Otherwise a defendant, secure from refutation, would have too clear a license unscrupulously to impose a false character upon the tribunal.

(*Wigmore on Evidence*, 3rd ed., vol. 1 (1940), pp. 457-8.)

Thus, the evidence of bad character cannot be used to show that the person was likely from his character to have committed the offence. The evidence does, however, have a bearing on the general credibility of the accused. In theory, what the jury is asked to do is to reject the accused's evidence as unreliable: see *R v. Samuel* (1956), 40 Cr. App. R 8. Different considerations, of course, apply where the evidence adduced to rebut good character evidence is similar fact evidence, or other evidence which may have probative value in its own right on the issue of guilt. Where the accused in the course of cross-examination as to character, makes admissions having probative value on the issue of guilt, these may, of course, be used against him.

[Simard's appeal was allowed on other grounds, and a new trial was ordered; leave to appeal to SCC refused, [1981] 1 SCR xi.]

As *McNamara* shows, if an accused takes the stand and testifies as to his or her good character, the Crown may cross-examine in a manner that seeks to show that the accused is not of good character, including by questioning the accused about prior specific bad acts. For example, in *R v O (D)* (2001), 156 CCC (3d) 369 (Ont CA), the accused was charged with the sexual abuse of his stepdaughter. The accused took the stand and testified at length about his good parenting of his children and stepchildren. Since the accused had put his character as a parent in issue, the Crown was entitled to cross-examine him about specific features of his parenting, including whether (1) he took good care of his son, (2) he demonstrated concern about his own daughter, and (3) he had allowed his stepdaughter to move in with her mother knowing that she was not properly caring for the children.

Once the accused has put his or her character in issue, the Crown may also adduce evidence of certain specific bad acts of the accused by invoking s 666 of the *Criminal Code*:

> 666. Where, at trial, the accused adduces evidence of his good character, the prosecutor may, in answer thereto, before a verdict is returned, adduce evidence of the previous conviction of the accused for any offences, including any previous conviction by reason of which a greater punishment may be imposed.

Section 666 entitles the Crown to go further than what is allowed under s 12 of the *Canada Evidence Act* (discussed in Chapter 6, Section III.C). In *R v P (NA)* (2002), 171 CCC (3d) 70 (Ont CA), Doherty JA explained the difference:

> If an accused puts his or her character in issue during examination-in-chief, the scope of cross-examination on the criminal record permitted by s. 666 goes beyond that allowed under s. 12 of the *Canada Evidence Act*. Since the cross-examination under s. 666 is predicated on the accused having put his or her character in issue, the accused may also be questioned about the specifics underlying the criminal convictions.

Can you offer a rationale to justify the difference between what the Crown is authorized to do under s 12 of the *Canada Evidence Act* as compared to s 666 of the *Criminal Code*?

4. Psychiatric Evidence of Disposition

The cases recognize that, although such instances are rare, character evidence may also come in the form of expert psychiatric opinion evidence.

R v Robertson
(1975), 29 CRNS 141, 21 CCC (2d) 385 (Ont CA)
Gale CJO and Dubin and Martin JJA (18 February 1975)

[The accused was charged with the murder of a nine-year-old girl.]

MARTIN JA: … The appellant's fourth ground of appeal is:

> The learned Trial Judge erred in rejecting the evidence of expert witnesses tendered by the defence that the appellant did not show any violent or aggressive tendencies as character traits or in his psychiatric make-up.

Defence counsel at the trial stated that he proposed to call expert witnesses to give opinion evidence "that the accused lacked any aggressive or violent tendencies." He elaborated on the purpose for which he proposed to adduce expert evidence by stating:

> … but basically the sole opinion which I will request is that he did not show any aggressive—perhaps there are two opinions—that he did not show any violent or aggressive tendencies as character traits or psychiatric makeup and the type of individual who would commit this type of offence is likely one who would show these characteristics, My Lord.

> . . .

It will be observed that counsel for the accused at the trial initially submitted that the evidence of psychiatrists was admissible to show that a propensity for violence was not a part of the appellant's psychological makeup, and that such a propensity was part of the psychological makeup of the perpetrator of the crime.

> . . .

Evidence that the offence had distinctive features which identified the perpetrator as a person possessing unusual personality traits constituting him a member of an unusual and limited class of persons would render admissible evidence that the accused did not possess the personality characteristics of the class of persons to which the perpetrator of the crime belonged.

[Martin JA then referred to *R v Glynn* (1972), 5 CCC (3d) 364 (Ont CA), and to *R v Lupien*, [1970] SCR 263. In the latter case, the majority of the Supreme Court had held that an accused charged with "gross indecency," an offence that was made out on proof that an accused had engaged in homosexual sex, was entitled to adduce psychiatric opinion evidence that he would react violently against any homosexual behaviour. Martin JA then continued:]

While the judgment of Ritchie J [in *Lupien*] deals only with the admissibility of psychiatric evidence with respect to disposition in offences involving homosexuality, there would appear to be no logical reason why such evidence should not be admitted on the same principle in other cases where there is evidence tending to show that, by reason of the nature of the offence, or its distinctive features, its perpetrator was a person who, in the language of Lord Sumner, was a member of "a specialized and extraordinary class," and whose psychological characteristics fall within the expertise of the psychiatrist, for the purpose of showing that the accused did not possess the psychological characteristics of persons of that class. Obviously, where such evidence is adduced by the accused, the prosecution is entitled to call psychiatric evidence in order to rebut the evidence introduced by the defence.

In my view, however, the judgment of Ritchie J in *Lupien* provides no support for a conclusion that, in the case of ordinary crimes of violence, psychiatric evidence is admissible to prove that the accused's psychological makeup does not include a tendency or disposition for violence. Martland J, with whom Judson J concurred, said at p. 169:

> If such evidence is held to be admissible in a case of this kind, then there would seem to be no reason why, on a charge of murder, psychiatric evidence could not be led as to the innate abhorrence of the accused in respect of physical violence, or on a charge of theft, of the innate respect of the accused for private property rights.

Indeed, counsel at the trial took the position that *Lupien* had very little bearing on the submission he was making with respect to the admissibility of psychiatric evidence.

. . .

In my view psychiatric evidence with respect to disposition or its absence is admissible on behalf of the defence, if relevant to an issue in the case, where the disposition in question constitutes a characteristic feature of an abnormal group falling within the range of study of the psychiatrist, and from whom the jury can, therefore, receive appreciable assistance with respect to a matter outside the knowledge of persons who have not made a special study of the subject. A *mere* disposition for violence, however, is not so uncommon as to constitute a feature characteristic of an abnormal group falling within the special field of study of the psychiatrist and permitting psychiatric evidence to be given of the absence of such disposition in the accused.

Mr. Maloney in this court submitted that the proposed evidence was admissible on a somewhat different basis than that advanced by counsel at the trial. He said that the extreme brutality displayed by the perpetrator of the crime here under consideration indicated that the perpetrator was a "psychopath" and psychiatric evidence was admissible to show that the appellant did not have the psychological makeup of the perpetrator of the crime and that he lacked capacity to commit an act of such brutality.

In this case the evidence shows no more than that the young deceased was killed by an act of great brutality. It cannot be said that such an act would only be committed by a person with recognizable personality characteristics or traits. In these circumstances, I am not persuaded that the evidence in the present case justifies us in holding that the killing of the deceased was marked by features which identify its perpetrator as a member of a special class more readily identifiable than the ordinary criminal, which I consider to be a condition of the admissibility of psychiatric evidence of absence of disposition or behavioural incapacity when it is tendered on the basis advanced before us.

Accordingly, I would not give effect to this ground of appeal.

[Gale CJO concurred with Martin JA in a brief judgment. Dubin JA concurred on this issue but dissented on another. The appeal was allowed on another ground, and a new trial was ordered. Leave to appeal to SCC refused, [1975] 1 SCR xi.]

R v Mohan
[1994] 2 SCR 9, 89 CCC (3d) 402
Lamer CJC and La Forest, L'Heureux-Dubé, Sopinka, Gonthier, Cory, McLachlin,
Iacobucci, and Major JJ (5 May 1994)

SOPINKA J: In this appeal we are required to determine under what circumstances expert
evidence is admissible to show that character traits of an accused person do not fit the
psychological profile of the putative perpetrator of the offences charged. Resolution of
this issue involves an examination of the rules relating to expert and character evidence.

I. Facts

A. The Events

The respondent, a practising paediatrician in North Bay, was charged with four counts of
sexual assault on four of his female patients, aged 13 to 16 at the relevant time. The alleged
sexual assaults were perpetrated during the course of medical examinations of the patients
conducted in the respondent's office. The complainants had been referred to the respondent for conditions which were, in part, psychosomatic in nature.

Evidence relating to each complaint was admitted as similar fact evidence with respect
to the others. The complainants did not know one another. Three of them came forth
independently. Following a mistrial, which was publicized, the fourth victim came forward, having heard about the other charges. Three of the four complainants had been
victims of prior sexual abuse. With respect to two of them, the respondent knew about
their sexual abuse at the hands of others. The alleged assaults consisted of fondling of the
girls' breasts and digital penetration and stimulation of their vaginal areas, accompanied
by intrusive questioning of them as to their sexual activities. All of the complainants testified that the respondent did not wear gloves while examining them internally. The respondent, who testified in his own defence, denied the complainants' evidence.

At the conclusion of the respondent's examination-in-chief, counsel for the respondent
indicated that he intended to call a psychiatrist who would testify that the perpetrator of
the offences alleged to have been committed would be part of a limited and unusual group
of individuals and that the respondent did not fall within that narrow class because he
did not possess the characteristics belonging to that group. The Crown sought a ruling
on the admissibility of that evidence. The trial judge held a *voir dire* and ruled that the
evidence tendered on the *voir dire* would not be admitted.

The jury found the respondent guilty as charged on November 16, 1990. He was sentenced to nine months' imprisonment on each of the four counts, to be served concurrently, and to two years' probation. The respondent appealed his convictions and the
Crown appealed the sentence. The Court of Appeal allowed the respondent's appeal,
quashed the convictions and ordered a new trial. Accordingly, the Court of Appeal found
it was not necessary to deal with the Crown's sentence appeal and refused the Crown leave
to appeal.

. . .

B. The Excluded Evidence

In the *voir dire*, Dr. Hill, the expert, began his testimony by explaining that there are three general personality groups that have unusual personality traits in terms of their psycho-sexual profile perspective. The first group encompasses the psychosexual who suffers from major mental illnesses (e.g., schizophrenia) and engages in inappropriate sexual behaviour occasionally. The second and largest group contains the sexual deviation types. This group of individuals shows distinct abnormalities in terms of the choice of individuals with whom they report sexual excitement and with whom they would like to engage in some type of sexual activity. The third group is that of the sexual psychopaths. These individuals have a callous disregard for people around them, including a disregard for the consequences of their sexual behaviour towards other individuals. Another group would include paedophiles who gain sexual excitement from young adolescents, probably pubertal or post-pubertal.

Dr. Hill identified paedophiles and sexual psychopaths as examples of members of unusual and limited classes of persons. In response to questions hypothetically encompassing the allegations of the four complainants, the expert stated that the psychological profile of the perpetrator of the first three complaints would likely be that of a paedophile, while the profile of the perpetrator of the fourth complaint would likely be that of a sexual psychopath. Dr. Hill also testified that, if but one perpetrator was involved in all four complaints described in the hypothetical questions, he would uniquely categorize that perpetrator as a sexual psychopath. He added that such a person would belong to a very small, behaviourally distinct category of persons. Dr. Hill was asked whether a physician who acted in the manner described in the hypothetical questions would be a member of a distinct group of aberrant persons. His answer was that such behaviours could only flow from a significant abnormality of character and would be part of an unusual and limited class. In cross-examination, Dr. Hill said: "You bring an extra abnormal, extra component for the abnormality when you talk about a physician in his or her office." According to Dr. Hill, physicians who were also sexual offenders would be a small group because not only would they be breaking the usual norms of society, but they would also be breaking out against the norms of the medical profession which are very strict given the intimate contact necessary to treat patients. It was contemplated that Dr. Hill would go on to testify "to the effect that Doctor Mohan does not have the characteristics attributable to any of the three groups in which most sex offenders fall."

II. Judgments Below

A. High Court of Justice (Ruling on Voir Dire, Bernstein J)

[The trial judge held that Dr. Hill's evidence was inadmissible. In his ruling on the *voir dire*, he said, among other things:]

> Doctor Hill is of the opinion that sexual assault is a crime committed by a distinguishable group. As I read the cases, I came to the conclusion that it is the size and the degree of distinctiveness of the "unusual and limited class of persons" which determines whether expert opinion will be helpful in defining the class and categorizing accused persons within or without the group. These days it is trite to say that a large number of men from all walks of life commit sexual offences on young women. While all may have some type of character

disorder, I doubt that expert evidence regarding the normality of any given accused would be of assistance to a trier of fact absent some more distinguishing within the wide spectrum of sexual assault.

The evidence of Doctor Hill is not sufficient, I believe, to establish that doctors who commit sexual assaults on patients are in a significantly more limited group in psychiatric terms than are other members of society. There is no scientific data available to warrant that conclusion. A sample of three offenders is not a sufficient basis for such a conclusion. Even the allegations of the fourth complainant ... are not so unusual, as sex offenders go, to warrant a conclusion that the perpetrator must have belonged to a sufficiently narrow class.

I conclude that if the evidence was received as proposed, it would merely be character evidence of a type that is inadmissible as going beyond evidence of general reputation, and does not fall within the proper sphere of expert evidence.

B. Ontario Court of Appeal

[The Court of Appeal allowed the accused's appeal. Finlayson JA held that Dr. Hill's evidence was admissible to show "that the offences alleged were unlikely to have been committed by the same person" and "that paedophiles and sexual psychopaths are members of special and extraordinary classes."]

III. Analysis

The admissibility of the rejected evidence was analyzed in argument under two exclusionary rules of evidence: (1) expert opinion evidence, and (2) character evidence. I have concluded that, on the basis of the principles relating to exceptions to the character evidence rule and under the principles governing the admissibility of expert evidence, the limitations on the use of this type of evidence require that the evidence in this case be excluded.

. . .

(2) Expert Evidence as to Disposition

[Sopinka J referred to *R v Morin*, [1988] 2 SCR 345, in which the Crown sought to adduce expert evidence to identify the accused as the person who had committed the crime. The court in *Morin* held that if the Crown wishes to lead psychiatric evidence for that purpose, it must satisfy the similar fact evidence test, discussed in Section II.C, below, and that "if the evidence's *sole* relevance or *primary* relevance is to show disposition, then the evidence must be excluded" (at 370).]

When, however, the evidence is tendered by the accused, other considerations apply. The accused is permitted to adduce evidence as to disposition both in his or her own evidence or by calling witnesses. The general rule is that evidence as to character is limited to evidence of the accused's reputation in the community with respect to the relevant trait or traits. The accused in his or her own testimony, however, may rely on specific acts of good conduct: see *R v. Canadian Dredge & Dock Co. Ltd.* (1981), 56 CCC (2d) 193 at p. 348; leave to appeal refused CCC *loc. cit.*, [1981] 1 SCR xi. Evidence of an expert witness that the accused, by reason of his or her mental make-up or condition of the mind, would be incapable of committing or disposed to commit the crime does not fit either of these categories. A further exception, however, has developed that is limited in scope. I propose to examine the extent of this exception.

[Sopinka J reviewed *Lupien*, *McMillan* (excerpted in Section III.C, below), and *Robertson* (excerpted above), as well as some English cases and scholarly commentary that used the terms "abnormal" and "normal" to explain the sorts of psychiatric characteristics that might be the subject of expert evidence, before continuing:]

In my opinion, the term "distinctive" more aptly defines the behavioural characteristics which are a pre-condition to the admission of this kind of evidence.

How should the criteria for the admission of this type of evidence be applied? I find the following statement of Professor Mewett [Alan W Mewett, "Character as a Fact in Issue in Criminal Cases" (1984) 27 Crim LQ 29], at p. 36, to be an apt characterization of the nature of the decision which the trial judge must make:

> The categorization of crimes into the "ordinary" and the "extraordinary" is therefore a legal question to be determined by the judge, as is the "normality" or "abnormality" of the accused—to the despair, no doubt, of psychiatrists. But admissibility of evidence is a legal question and depends primarily upon relevance, that is, upon its assistance to the trier of fact in his inference-drawing process, and this is governed, not by expertise, but by common sense and experience; words like "ordinary," "extraordinary" or "abnormal" are not meant to be scientific expressions but assessments of relevance and are thus clearly within the domain of the judge.

Before an expert's opinion is admitted as evidence, the trial judge must be satisfied, as a matter of law, that either the perpetrator of the crime or the accused has distinctive behavioural characteristics such that a comparison of one with the other will be of material assistance in determining innocence or guilt. Although this decision is made on the basis of common sense and experience, as Professor Mewett suggests, it is not made in a vacuum. The trial judge should consider the opinion of the expert and whether the expert is merely expressing a personal opinion or whether the behavioural profile which the expert is putting forward is in common use as a reliable indicator of membership in a distinctive group. Put another way: Has the scientific community developed a standard profile for the offender who commits this type of crime? An affirmative finding on this basis will satisfy the criteria of relevance and necessity. Not only will the expert evidence tend to prove a fact in issue but it will also provide the trier of fact with assistance that is needed. Such evidence will have passed the threshold test of reliability which will generally ensure that the trier of fact does not give it more weight than it deserves. The evidence will qualify as an exception to the exclusionary rule relating to character evidence provided, of course, that the trial judge is satisfied that the proposed opinion is within the field of expertise of the expert witness.

(3) Application to This Case

I take the findings of the trial judge to be that a person who committed sexual assaults on young women could not be said to belong to a group possessing behavioural characteristics that are sufficiently distinctive to be of assistance in identifying the perpetrator of the offences charged. Moreover, the fact that the alleged perpetrator was a physician did not advance the matter because there is no acceptable body of evidence that doctors who commit sexual assaults fall into a distinctive class with identifiable characteristics. Notwithstanding the opinion of Dr. Hill, the trial judge was also not satisfied that the characteristics associated with the fourth complaint identified the perpetrator as a member of a distinctive group. He was not prepared to accept that the characteristics of that complaint were such that only a psychopath could have committed the act. There was nothing to indicate any general acceptance of this theory. Moreover, there was no material in the record to support a finding that the profile of a paedophile or psychopath has been standardized to the extent that it could be said that it matched the supposed profile of the offender depicted in the charges. The expert's group profiles were not seen as sufficiently reliable to be considered helpful. In the absence of these *indicia* of reliability, it cannot be said that the evidence would be necessary in the sense of usefully clarifying a matter otherwise unaccessible, or that any value it may have had would not be outweighed by its potential for misleading or diverting the jury. Given these findings and applying the principles referred to above, I must conclude that the trial judge was right in deciding as a matter of law that the evidence was inadmissible.

· · ·

I would allow the appeal, set aside the judgment of the Court of Appeal, restore the convictions and remit the matter to the Court of Appeal for disposition of the sentence appeal.

Given the preconditions that must be satisfied before an accused will be permitted to introduce expert psychiatric evidence regarding his or her character, it should come as no surprise that examples of this sort of evidence being admitted are difficult to come by.

In both *Robertson* and *Mohan*, extracted above, the accused sought to lead expert evidence of his disposition not to commit the offence. May the Crown lead expert evidence of the accused's disposition to commit the offence?

As noted in the extract from *Mohan*, above, the Supreme Court held in *Morin* that if the Crown wishes to introduce psychiatric evidence for the purpose of establishing the identity of the accused as the perpetrator, it would have to meet the strict similar fact evidence test, discussed below. If offered solely to show the disposition of the accused, such evidence would not be admissible. But *Morin* was not a case in which the accused had put his character in issue. If the accused puts his character in issue—be it with reputation evidence, by testifying as to his own good character, or with psychiatric evidence—should the Crown be allowed to respond with expert evidence of propensity?

This issue arose in *R v Tierney* (1982), 70 CCC (2d) 481 (Ont CA). The accused was charged with sexual assault of his ex-girlfriend after she rejected him. As part of his defence, the accused called a number of witnesses who testified that Tierney "was a person of good character, particularly with respect to decency and the absence of violence" (at 484). The Crown sought to reply with evidence of the accused's bad character, including evidence of the accused's psychiatric makeup. That evidence would be offered by the accused's psychiatrist, who would testify that the accused had an "ongoing hostile conflict with women" (at 487), including a particular vulnerability to separation from women and propensity to react with anger and violence. The trial judge ruled that this evidence was inadmissible. In holding that this evidence should have been admitted and ordering a new trial, Justice Zuber, writing for the court, explained at 487-88:

> Ordinarily, evidence which shows nothing more than a disposition toward crime is not admissible. In this case, however, the ambit of admissibility has been enlarged by the respondent. The respondent, by adducing evidence of good character in this case, asserts to the jury that he is a man that has no tendency or disposition to commit an act of violence or indecency. In an earlier era this proposition could be rebutted by the Crown only by evidence as to the respondent's general reputation. It is now clear that character evidence in the sense of disposition may be given by a psychiatrist. In *R. v. Lupien*, [1970] 2 C.C.C. 193 at p. 202, 9 D.L.R. (3d) 1, 9 C.R.N.S. 165 at p. 176, Ritchie J. observed:
>
> > This was not a question of adducing character evidence in the sense of reputation, and I think that the rule laid down in 1865 by Cockburn C.J., in *R. v. Rowton*, 10 Cox C.C. 25 at 29 (C.C.R.), to the effect that evidence of character can only be introduced by seeking evidence of the accused's general reputation in the neighbourhood to which he belongs, is singularly inappropriate to the introduction of evidence from psychiatrists as to the accused's disposition.
> >
> > The *Rowton* case was decided many years before the development of psychiatry as an accepted branch of medicine and we were not referred to any case in which the rule there stated was applied so as to exclude such evidence.
> >
> > . . .
>
> The *Lupien* case does not go so far as to say that psychiatric evidence of all dispositions or disinclinations should be admitted, but it appears that the presence or absence of abnormal dispositions may be adduced as character evidence. Further, the disposition must be one which falls within the expertise of a psychiatrist. Here the accused sought psychiatric assistance from Dr. Kerr and the disposition in question was diagnosed as a part of his psychiatric make-up. The thrust of Dr. Kerr's evidence is to demonstrate an abnormal disposition on the part of the respondent to react violently to separation from women, and should be admitted to rebut his evidence of good character, particularly his peaceable nature.

Justice Zuber went on to underscore that "the evidence of Dr. Kerr respecting the respondent's abnormal disposition is admissible only to rebut evidence of good character and not to prove guilt" (at 489).

C. Similar Fact Evidence

In the prior section, you saw that the Crown is generally limited to introducing evidence of the bad character of the accused in reply to the accused having adduced evidence of his or her good character. In such circumstances, the Crown's bad character evidence can only be used to refute the accused's suggestion of good character; it cannot be used to infer the guilt of the accused.

Similar fact evidence does not depend on the accused having first put character in issue, nor is its use so narrowly circumscribed. The similar fact evidence rule allows the Crown to adduce, in its own case, evidence of the accused's discreditable conduct in an effort to prove the guilt of the accused. As currently understood, the similar fact evidence rule thus allows the Crown to lead propensity evidence to establish that the accused committed the offence with which he is charged. Although referred to as "similar fact" evidence, this label is somewhat misleading because the evidence (1) need not be "similar" to be admissible, and (2) may not be admissible even if "similar." As Justice Charron explained in her judgment in *R v Mahalingan*, 2008 SCC 63 at para 160, [2008] 3 SCR 316, "the rule also extends to criminal or otherwise discreditable acts that bear no similarity to the offence with which the accused is charged." As such, the rules developed in the cases that follow apply whenever, in seeking to support an inference of guilt, the Crown wants to introduce evidence of acts of the accused that would reflect adversely on his or her character and that are not the subject matter of the charge(s).

What permits the Crown to adduce such evidence? Recall that the rationale for the general rule prohibiting bad character evidence introduced by the Crown is not that such evidence is irrelevant; rather, the assumption is that the probative value of such evidence will normally be outweighed by its potential for prejudice. But what if the evidence is so compelling, so persuasive in the circumstances of the case, that its probative value is high enough to overcome its potential for prejudice? What if, in terms used in the jurisprudence, the evidence is so probative that its exclusion would be "an affront to common sense?" Should it not then be admitted? As you will see in the cases that follow, that is precisely the circumstance to which the similar fact evidence rule responds.

Before turning to the modern Canadian law, consider the following three cases that reflect this underlying principle animating the similar fact evidence rule.

Makin v Attorney-General for New South Wales
[1894] AC 57 (PC)
Lord Herschell LC and Lord Watson, Lord Halsbury, Lord Ashbourne,
Lord Macnaghten, Lord Morris, and Lord Shand (12 December 1893)

[John and Sarah Makin were convicted of the murders of Horace Amber Murray and an unidentified male infant.]

The special case contained the following statement: "On the 9th of November some constables found the remains of four infants in the back yard of 109, George Street, among which was the body of a male child, from two to nine weeks old. It was clothed with a long white baby's gown and underneath a baby's small white shirt, both of which were identified as being the gown and shirt in which Murray's baby had been dressed. A minute portion of the infant's hair resembled the hair of Murray's child. Previous to the finding of the four infants in George Street, Redfern (on the 9th of November), two bodies of infants had been discovered, one on the 11th and the other on the 12th of October, on the premises in Burren Street, McDonaldtown, where the prisoners had, it appears, resided from the end of June until about the middle of August. During the adjournment of an inquest on one of those bodies held in October, the prisoner Sarah came to her former residence in George Street, Redfern, and said to witness, then residing there, that she had called to see about those people that had lived there before her, that she was a great friend of theirs, and asked if the police had dug the yard up, and further asked if any bodies had been found in the yard. At this inquest both prisoners were examined, no charge at that time having been made against them. They both swore that the only child that they had ever received to nurse was the one which they had in Burren Street, and which was given them after they arrived there. The prisoner Sarah swore that none but her own family had removed from George Street, to Burren Street. On the 2nd of November one, and on the 3rd four more bodies were discovered buried in Burren Street, and on the 3rd of November the prisoners were arrested. On the night of that day prisoner John was placed in a cell with a witness, who deposed that prisoner said to him that he (Makin) was there for baby-farming, that there were seven found and there was another to be found, and when that was found he would never see daylight any more; that is what a man gets for obliging people, and that he could do nothing outside as they were watching the ground too close; that there was no doctor could prove that he ever gave them anything, that he did not care for himself, but that his children were innocent. On the 12th of November the bodies of two infants, bones only, were found on the premises of Levy Street, Chippendale, where prisoners had resided some time previous to their residence in Kettle Street." The prisoners had moved from Kettle Street to George Street, and thence to Burren Street.

LORD HERSCHELL LC: … There can be no doubt, in their Lordships' opinion, that there was ample evidence to go to the jury that the infant was murdered. Indeed, that point was scarcely contested in the argument of the learned counsel for the appellants. The question which their Lordships had to determine was the admissibility of the evidence relating to the finding of other bodies, and to the fact that other children had been entrusted to the appellants.

In their Lordships' opinion the principles which must govern the decision of the case are clear, though the application of them is by no means free from difficulty. It is undoubtedly not competent for the prosecution to adduce evidence tending to shew that the accused has been guilty of criminal acts other than those covered by the indictment, for the purpose of leading to the conclusion that the accused is a person likely from his criminal conduct or character to have committed the offence for which he is being tried. On the other hand, the mere fact that the evidence adduced tends to shew the commission of other crimes does not render it inadmissible if it be relevant to an issue before the jury, and it may be so relevant if it bears upon the question whether the acts alleged to constitute the crime charged in the indictment were designed or accidental, or to rebut a defence which would otherwise be open to the accused. The statement of these general principles is easy, but it is obvious that it may often be very difficult to draw the line and to decide whether a particular piece of evidence is on the one side or the other.

· · ·

Their Lordships do not think it necessary to enter upon a detailed examination of the evidence in the present case. The prisoners had alleged that they had received only one child to nurse; that they had received 10s. a week whilst it was under their care, and that after a few weeks it was given back to the parents. When the infant with whose murder the appellants were charged was received from the mother she stated that she had a child for them to adopt. Mrs. Makin said that she would take the child, and Makin said that they would bring it up as their own and educate it, and that he would take it because Mrs. Makin had lost a child of her own two years old. Makin said that he did not want any clothing; they had plenty of their own. The mother said that she did not mind his getting £3 premium so long as he took care of the child. The representation was that the prisoners were willing to take the child on payment of the small sum of £3, inasmuch as they desired to adopt it as their own.

Under these circumstances their Lordships cannot see that it was irrelevant to the issue to be tried by the jury that several other infants had been received from their mothers on like representations, and upon payment of a sum inadequate for the support of the child for more than a very limited period, or that the bodies of infants had been found buried in a similar manner in the gardens of several houses occupied by the prisoners.

[The Makins' appeal was dismissed.]

R v Smith
(1915), 11 Cr App R 229
Reading LCJ and Darling and Lush JJ (29 July 1915)

[Smith had gone through a form of marriage with three women, Bessie Munday, Alice Burnham, and Margaret Lofty. Each of the three women was found dead in her bath. Smith stood to benefit financially from each woman's death. He was charged with the murder of Munday. He did not testify, but the theory of the defence was that Munday had drowned accidentally.]

THE LORD CHIEF JUSTICE: The appellant was charged with the murder of Bessie Munday; evidence was admitted to show that he murdered two other women at a later date. The first question raised is that the judge was wrong in admitting evidence of the deaths of Alice Burnham and Margaret Lofty. Whether the evidence was admissible or not depends on principles of law which have been considered by this Court many times, and which depend in the main on the statement of the law by Lord Herschell in *Makin v. Attorney-General for New South Wales*.

. . .

Now in this case the prosecution tendered the evidence, and it was admitted by the judge on the ground that it tended to shew that the act charged had been committed, that is, had been designed. A question has been raised on which we have heard valuable arguments, but it is a matter which we need not, and do not intend to decide in this case. It is undesirable that we should decide the point unless it has been fully argued. It is sufficient to say that it is not disputed, and could not be disputed, that if as a matter of law there was *prima facie* evidence that the appellant committed the act charged, evidence of similar acts became admissible, and the other point does not arise for the reason that we have come to the conclusion that there was undoubtedly, as a matter of law, *prima facie* evidence that the appellant committed the act charged apart altogether from the other cases. Viewing the case put forward with regard to Bessie Munday only, we are of opinion that there was a case which the judge was bound in strict law to put to the jury. The case was reinforced by the evidence admitted with reference to the other two cases for the purpose of shewing the design of the appellant. We think that that evidence was properly admitted, and the judge was very careful to point out to the jury the use they could properly make of the evidence. He directed them more than once that they must not allow their minds to be confused and think that they were deciding whether the murders of Burnham and

Lofty had been committed; they were trying the appellant for the murder of Munday. We are of opinion therefore that the first point fails.

The second point taken is that even assuming that evidence of the death of the two women was admissible, the prosecution ought only to have been allowed to prove that the women were found dead in their baths. For the reasons already given in dealing with the first point, it is apparent that to cut short the evidence there would have been of no assistance to the case. In our opinion it was open to the prosecution to give, and the judge was right in admitting, evidence of the facts surrounding the deaths of the two women.

[Smith's appeal was dismissed.]

R v Straffen
[1952] 2 QB 911, [1952] 2 All ER 657 (CA)
Slade, Devlin, and Gorman JJ (20 August 1952)

[The accused was convicted of murdering a young girl. He appealed on two grounds, one of which is not relevant here.]

SLADE J: … The other ground of appeal raises a far more serious point, but one on which the members of this court have reached a clear conclusion. On Apr. 29, 1952, the appellant escaped from Broadmoor and was at large from 2.40 to 6.40 p.m. on that day. At about 6 a.m. on Apr. 30 the dead body of Linda Bowyer was found in the village of Little Farley and her bicycle was found some two hundred yards away from the body. She had died from manual strangulation, and the medical evidence showed that her death had taken place some twelve to fifteen hours previously, which would come within the period during which the appellant was at large. Miss Saxby, who was called as a witness for the prosecution, was the last person to see Linda Bowyer alive. She said that she had seen her shortly after 5.30 p.m. The appellant's movements were more or less accounted for except for a period between 5.30 and 6 p.m., and having regard to the distances involved there is no doubt that that time provided him with ample opportunity to commit the crime had he been so minded.

[Slade J discussed the appellant's statement to the police and continued:]

The defence of the appellant was that he did not kill Linda Bowyer. He pleaded Not Guilty, and it was for the prosecution to prove their case. To do that the prosecution were entitled to call any evidence which was admissible in law. At an early stage, in the absence of the jury, they sought the judge's permission to admit evidence of the deaths of Brenda Goddard and Cicely Batstone, and they came prepared with evidence which amounted to a confession by the appellant that he murdered those two little girls. Indeed, one of the answers made by the appellant to the police officers in the case of Linda Bowyer was: "I know I killed two little children, but I did not kill the little girl." Unquestionably the two little children to whom he was there referring were Brenda Goddard and Cicely Batstone. The learned judge, after hearing legal argument, admitted the evidence. The question here is whether that evidence was properly admitted. The ground on which it was admitted was that it was material to establish the identity of the murderer of Linda Bowyer.

The general rule is that evidence should be excluded which tends to show that the accused has been guilty of criminal acts other than those covered by the indictment, and it is an irrefragable rule that evidence of the commission of criminal offences not covered by the indictment shall not be admitted for the purpose of proving that the accused is a person of criminal disposition, or even that he has a propensity for committing the particular type of crime with which he is charged. But, apart from statute, there are certain recognised exceptions to the general rule under which evidence is admissible of other crimes committed by the accused, the reason for its admission being that it tends to prove, not that he is a man who has criminal propensities, but that he was the man who committed the particular offence charged.

[Slade J quoted from *Makin*, above, and continued:]

In dealing with *Makin*'s case recently in the House of Lords in *Harris v. Director of Public Prosecutions*, [1952] 1 All ER 1044, Viscount Simon said: "In my opinion, the principle laid down by Lord Herschell, LC, in *Makin*'s case remains the proper principle to apply, and I see no reason for modifying it. ... It is, I think, an error to attempt to draw up a closed list of the sort of cases in which the principle operates. Such a list only provides instances of its general application, whereas what really matters is the principle itself and its proper application to the particular circumstances of the charge that is being tried. It is the application that may sometimes be difficult, and the particular case now before the House illustrates that difficulty." Further on Viscount Simon said (*ibid.*, 1047): "The substance of the matter appears to me to be that the prosecution may adduce all proper evidence which tends to prove the charge." After dealing with *Thompson v. R*, [1918] AC 221, he said (*ibid.*, 1048): "It is the fact that [the accused] was involved in the other occurrences which may negative the inference of accident or establish his *mens rea* by showing 'system,' or, again, the other occurrences may sometimes assist to prove his identity, as, for instance, in *Perkins v. Jeffery*, [1915] 2 KB 702. But evidence of other occurrences which merely tend to deepen suspicion does not go to prove guilt."

That being the law, the question is whether the evidence in the present case falls within the category of admissibility as being relevant to prove the crime charged by showing that it was the appellant who committed it. The grounds on which the admissibility of the evidence was urged by the Solicitor-General in the court below was the similarity of the deaths and of the circumstances surrounding them in the case of the two murders at Bath, on the one hand, with the circumstances of the murder at Little Farley, on the other. He stated the similarities to be, first, that each of the victims was a young girl; secondly, that each of the young girls was killed by manual strangulation; thirdly, that in each case there was no attempt at sexual interference or any apparent motive for the crime; fourthly, that in none of the three cases was there any evidence of a struggle; and, fifthly, that in none of the three cases was any attempt made to conceal the body although the body could have been easily concealed.

[In support of these similarities, Slade J quoted from the evidence of two physicians.]

The evidence with regard to the deaths of Brenda Goddard and Cicely Batstone was admitted to show that the person who manually strangled those two little girls also manually strangled Linda Bowyer in similar circumstances. In the opinion of the court, that evidence was rightly admitted, not to show, to use the words of counsel for the appellant, that the appellant was a professional strangler, but to show that he strangled Linda Bowyer—in other words, to identify the murderer of Linda Bowyer as being the same person as the person who had murdered the other two little girls in precisely the same way. I see no distinction in principle between this case and *Thompson v. R*, [1918] AC 221, and, indeed, I think one cannot distinguish abnormal propensities from identification. Abnormal propensity is a means of identification. In *Thompson*'s case the offence charged was committed on Mar. 16, 1917, and the evidence was that on that day an appointment was made by the man who committed the offences with the boys to meet those boys again on Mar. 19. It was common ground that it was the accused who went to the appointed place on Mar. 19, and he found the police waiting for him. When he was arrested there were found on him powder puffs, and at his lodgings there were found indecent photographs of boys. Evidence was admitted of the powder puffs and of the photographs that were found on the 19th to prove that the accused committed the offence on the 16th, the boys having identified him as being the person who committed that offence and he having set up an alibi. It was admitted to prove his identity by showing that he was one of those persons who suffer from the abnormal propensity of homosexuality. In the present case it is an abnormal propensity to strangle young girls without any apparent motive, without any attempt at sexual interference, and to leave their dead bodies where they can be seen and where presumably their deaths would be rapidly detected. In the judgment of the court, this evidence was admissible because it tended to identify the person who had murdered Linda Bowyer with the person who had confessed in his statements to having murdered in similar circumstances a year before Brenda Goddard and Cicely Batstone.

Counsel for the appellant asked: How far, then, does the admissibility of such evidence go? Does it apply in the case of a burglar, housebreaker, thief, and so on? Lord Sumner, in *Thompson*'s case, pointed out (at 235) that such persons were merely examples of those who fell within the genus of dishonest persons, but, speaking for myself, if the question of identity arose in a case of housebreaking and it were possible to adduce evidence that there was some peculiarity in relation to earlier housebreakings which was apparent also in the case of the housebreaking charged so as to stamp the accused man not only with the housebreaking charged but with the earlier housebreakings, and there was a confession or other evidence that he had committed the earlier housebreakings, that evidence would fall within the same principle of admissibility, not to prove his propensity for housebreaking, but to prove that he was the person who committed the housebreaking charged. Counsel for the appellant has conceded that, if the evidence was admissible, the discretion of the learned judge to admit it at the trial and not to reject it on the ground that its prejudicial effect was disproportionate to its probative value was judicially exercised, and, therefore, this appeal is dismissed.

In light of cases like *Makin*, *Smith*, and *Straffen*, it was often held that similar fact evidence was not admissible unless it was relevant to one of a limited set of issues: "to prove intent, to prove a system, to prove a plan, to show malice, to rebut the defence of accident or mistake, to prove identity, to rebut the defence of innocent association" (McIntyre J in *Sweitzer*, below).

In *DPP v Boardman*, [1975] AC 421, [1974] 3 All ER 887 (HL), the House of Lords turned away from this categorical approach, in favour of a more principled rule that admits evidence of an accused's prior misconduct when its probative value in relation to a fact in issue outweighs its inevitable prejudicial effects. As we shall see in *Sweitzer* and in *R v B (CR)*, below, this development was quickly followed in Canada. The challenge since then, however, has been to articulate the precise basis for the admission of similar fact evidence under this principled approach. Several of the remaining cases in this section attempt to come to grips with this problem, culminating in the Supreme Court of Canada's leading case on similar fact evidence, *R v Handy*, 2002 SCC 56, [2002] 2 SCR 908.

Sweitzer v R

[1982] 1 SCR 949, 68 CCC (2d) 193

Laskin CJC and Martland, Ritchie, Dickson, Beetz, Estey, McIntyre,
Chouinard, and Lamer JJ (23 June 1982)

McINTYRE J: This appeal raises the question of the admissibility of evidence of "similar facts" involving an accused, tendered in proof of the allegations in the indictment upon which he is tried.

Between April 11, 1974, and October 19, 1978, an interval of about four and a half years, the police investigated a series of 15 sexual attacks which took place in Calgary against various women. On October 18, 1978, the appellant was apprehended in a woman's apartment at about 5:50 a.m. She had been alone and was awakened by the appellant's entry into her apartment. She raised an alarm and after a brief struggle the police arrived and arrested him. In January, 1979, a preliminary hearing was held and as a result the appellant was committed for trial upon 15 charges, one arising out of each of the 15 assaults. The indictment which was drawn for presentment at trial contained 15 counts which included charges of rape, indecent assault and breaking and entry with intent to commit an indictable offence. Prior to trial a motion was made to Moshansky J by the appellant which led to an order severing the various counts. The Crown then elected to proceed on count 1 ... .

At the commencement of the trial, because the Crown wished to adduce in evidence the particulars and circumstances of the 14 other offences referred to in the indictment, the jury was excused and a *voir dire* was held to determine whether evidence of the other assaults and attempts was properly admissible as evidence of similar facts. The entire evidence in the trial was led on the *voir dire*, including all the evidence the Crown tendered relating to the other 14 episodes. All the evidence so adduced was found by the trial judge to be admissible and thereafter the jury was recalled and it was repeated in their presence.

The evidence led in respect of the offence referred to in count 1 established that the complainant ... was awakened early in the morning of April 12, 1974, in her apartment by a voice which told her not to scream or cry out or she and her infant daughter would be hurt. She felt an arm over her head and something sharp at her back. She was taken out of bed, her hands were held behind her back and she was pushed into the bathroom where the assailant forced her to have intercourse with him. She was blindfolded with a towel in the bathroom and then taken to the living-room where she was put upon the floor and an attempt was made at anal penetration and an attempt made to force her to perform *fellatio* upon the intruder. Her assailant left her after about an hour. She was unable to identify him and could give no evidence upon which an identification could be based. It is evident that her evidence, if believed, would have justified a conviction of rape save for the fact that there was nothing in it from which the appellant could be identified as the attacker. The Crown was thus compelled in order to remedy this deficiency to rely on the evidence of the other episodes and the evidence of Detective Ogg who on one occasion saw a man whom he identified as the accused looking in a window at the rear of a motel at which certain of these events had occurred.

The allegedly similar facts fall for the purpose of this discussion into two groups. First, there are those forming the basis of counts 2, 4, 5, 6, 7, 8, 9, 10, 12, 13 and 14. In these 11 episodes there is no evidence of identification of the appellant save for the alleged similarity in the conduct of the assailant to the conduct attributed to the appellant in the four episodes referred to hereafter. The second group comprises allegations in counts 3, 11 and 15 and the evidence of Detective Ogg. In these four episodes there is some direct evidence of the identification of the appellant as the assailant. In counts 3 and 11 the victims of the assault swore to his identity, in count 15 he was apprehended by the police at the scene, and Detective Ogg swore he was the man seen to be peering in a window at the rear of a motel who fled when the police came upon him. Detective Ogg's observations were made on an occasion separate in time from any of the attacks forming the subject of any of the counts. It is the admission of all of this evidence which was approved in the Court of Appeal that forms the basis of this appeal.

The question of the admissibility of similar fact evidence has been the subject of much legal writing to be found in the decided cases and textbooks and in the academic articles and commentaries. The general principle stated by Lord Herschell LC in *Makin and Makin v. A-G for New South Wales*, [1894] AC 57 at p. 65, has been largely accepted as the basis for the admission of this evidence.

[McIntyre J quoted from *Makin*, above, and continued.]

Over the years in seeking to apply this principle judges have tended to create a list of categories or types of cases in which similar fact evidence could be admitted, generally by reference to the purpose for which the evidence was adduced. Evidence of similar facts has been adduced to prove intent, to prove a system, to prove a plan, to show malice, to rebut the defence of accident or mistake, to prove identity, to rebut the defence of innocent association and for other similar and related purposes. That list is not complete.

This approach has been useful because similar fact evidence by its nature is frequently adduced for its relevance to a single issue in the case under trial. It has however involved, in my opinion, a tendency to overlook the true basis upon which evidence of similar facts is admissible. The general principle described by Lord Herschell may and should be applied in all cases where similar fact evidence is tendered and its admissibility will depend upon the probative effect of the evidence balanced against the prejudice caused to the accused by its admission whatever the purpose of its admission. This approach finds support in

Boardman v. Director of Public Prosecutions, [1974] 3 All ER 887, and is implicit in the words of Lord Herschell in the *Makin* case. ...

[McIntyre J quoted with approval from Lord Morris's speech in *Makin*, and continued.]

The general principle enunciated in the *Makin* case by Lord Herschell, should be borne in mind in approaching this problem. The categories, while sometimes useful, remain only as illustrations of the application of that general rule.

Before evidence may be admitted as evidence of similar facts, there must be a link between the allegedly similar facts and the accused. In other words there must be some evidence upon which the trier of fact can make a proper finding that the similar facts to be relied upon were in fact the acts of the accused for it is clear that if they were not his own but those of another they have no relevance to the matters at issue under the indictment. ...

* * *

Dealing with the 11 episodes I say at once that in my view evidence relating to them was inadmissible and ought not to have been admitted. I put that proposition simply upon the footing that they afford no evidence of identification of the appellant, because, despite the existence of varying degrees of similarity between the acts revealed in the evidence and the facts of the case under trial, there is no evidence which connects the appellant with any of those episodes. They are not shown to be connected with him and cannot therefore be relevant as evidence against him. It was the similarity between the 11 incidents and the four incidents which led the learned chief justice to consider that evidence of the 11 incidents was admissible. McGillivray CJA in his reasons, speaking for a unanimous Court of Appeal, said:

> We are all of the view that the only link with the accused in 12 cases [the 11 cases referred to above and the count in count 1] was the similarity of his technique; but there is sufficient similarity in technique to that in the three cases where the accused was identified, in our opinion, to permit the findings to be admissible as a matter of identifying the accused as being the attacker in the Page case. We are, therefore, of the opinion that the appeal on the ground of admissibility of what is said to be similar fact evidence, fails.

In my view, this approach seems to proceed on the basis that, while the 11 episodes themselves are not shown to be connected with the accused, they are made admissible because of the similarity to the four incidents in respect of which there had been a testimonial connection with the appellant. They should therefore be admitted into evidence, as it were, upon the coat-tails of the four episodes. In my view, this is to cast the net too wide in a search for evidence. This line of reasoning could make evidence of any nocturnal rape committed in Calgary in a period of four and a half years, where some similarity could be shown, receivable in evidence against the appellant. I would confine the admission of such evidence to cases where there is some evidentiary link, direct or circumstantial, with the accused.

It is my opinion that the error which was made by the admission into evidence of the 11 episodes was so highly prejudicial that the only remedy open is a new trial. Because there is to be a new trial, I make no comment in respect of the relevancy of the four episodes involving some evidentiary connection with the appellant because I do not wish to embarrass the trial judge in his approach to the matter. The question of the admissibility of that evidence I leave to be resolved on the new trial. I would, accordingly, allow the appeal and direct a new trial.

As you saw, an important principle enunciated in *Sweitzer* is that before similar fact evidence can be introduced against an accused, there must be some evidence establishing a link between the discreditable acts and the accused. The issue of the requisite link between an accused and the prior acts arises again in *R v Arp*, extracted below.

Since the decision in *Boardman*, similar fact evidence has often been tendered in cases involving allegations of sexual abuse. In these cases, unlike older cases such as *Makin* or *Straffen*, identity is typically not in issue. What is the rationale for admitting the evidence in such cases? The following case, while continuing the move to a more principled and less categorical approach to similar fact evidence, addresses this question of the relevance of such evidence.

R v B (CR)
[1990] 1 SCR 717, 76 CR (3d) 1
Dickson CJC and Lamer, Wilson, L'Heureux-Dubé, Sopinka, Gonthier,
and McLachlin JJ (12 April 1990)

McLACHLIN J (Dickson CJC and Wilson, L'Heureux-Dubé, and Gonthier JJ concurring): The accused was charged with sexual offences against a young child, his natural daughter. The issue was not who had committed the offences but whether they had occurred at all. The main Crown evidence was that of the child. The question was whether she should be believed.

In support of the child's testimony, the Crown sought to introduce evidence that the accused had previously had sexual relations with an older girl, the daughter of his common law wife, with whom he had enjoyed a father-daughter relationship. The trial judge admitted the evidence and convicted the accused. Although the judge appears to have applied the correct test, a comment suggesting that the similar fact evidence related to the issue of identity was in error. The Court of Appeal, Harradence JA dissenting, held that the similar fact evidence was properly admitted and upheld the conviction: 39 CCC (3d) 230.

The question before us is whether the majority of the Court of Appeal was correct in holding that the evidence was admissible, notwithstanding the trial judge's reference to identity and the distinctions relied on by the accused between the case alleged against him and the similar fact evidence.

The Test for Similar Fact Evidence

The common law has traditionally taken a strict view of similar fact evidence, regarding it with suspicion. In recent years, the courts have moved to loosen the formalistic strictures which had come to encumber the rule. The old category approach determining what types of similar fact evidence is admissible has given way to a more general test which balances the probative value of the evidence against its prejudice.

Despite the apparent simplicity of the modern rule for the admission of similar fact evidence, the rule remains one of considerable difficulty in application. The problems stem in part from a tendency to view the modern formulation of the rule in isolation from the historical context from whence it springs. While the contemporary formulation may permit a more flexible, less restricted analysis, the dangers which it addresses and the principles upon which it rests remain unchanged.

· · ·

The Canadian Jurisprudence

The Canadian jurisprudence since *Boardman* is generally consistent with the approach advocated in that case. It has followed *Boardman* in rejecting the categorical approach to the admission of similar fact evidence. At the same time, cases in Canada have on the whole maintained an emphasis on the general rule that evidence of mere propensity is inadmissible, and have continued to emphasize the necessity that such evidence possess high probative value in relation to its potential prejudice.

· · ·

While our courts have affirmed the general exclusionary rule for evidence of disposition and propensity, they have for the most part cast it in terms of *Boardman* rather than *Makin*. It is no longer necessary to hang the evidence tendered on the peg of some issue other than disposition. While the language of some of the assertions of the exclusionary rule admittedly might be taken to suggest that mere disposition evidence can *never* be admissible, the preponderant view prevailing in Canada is the view taken by the majority in *Boardman*—evidence of propensity, while generally inadmissible, may exceptionally be admitted where the probative value of the evidence in relation to an issue in question is so high that it displaces the heavy prejudice which will inevitably inure to the accused where evidence of prior immoral or illegal acts is presented to the jury.

The second characteristic of Canadian treatment of the similar fact rule since *Boardman* is a rejection of the categorical approach in favour of one of general principle. In *Guay v. R*, [1979] 1 SCR 18, 42 CCC (2d) 536, the Court, per Pigeon J, held that the admissibility of similar fact evidence is based on "general principles" and that there is discretionary power in the trial judge to exclude such evidence (p. 32). Citing *Boardman* with approval, he rejected a mechanical, categorical approach, holding that there is "no closed list of the sort of cases where such evidence is admissible," but that it is "well established that it may be admitted to rebut a defence of legitimate association for honest purposes, as well as to rebut evidence of good character" (p. 547).

· · ·

Catchwords have gone the same way as categories. Just as English courts have expressed doubts about the necessity of showing "striking similarity" (see *R v. Rance*, supra; *R v. Mansfield* (1977), 65 *Crim. L Rev.* 276; *R v. Scarrott*, [1978] QB 1016, [1978] 1 All ER 672), so in *Robertson* Wilson J rejected the validity of this phrase as a legal test.

A third feature of this Court's treatment of the similar fact rule since *Boardman* is the tendency to accord a high degree of respect to the decision of the trial judge, who is charged with the delicate process of balancing the probative value of the evidence against its prejudicial effect. In *Morris*, the Court affirmed that the task of determining whether the evidence possesses sufficient probative value is that of the trial judge. Similarly, in *Guay, Robertson, Morin*, and *D. (L.E.)*, this Court affirmed the decision of the trial judge with respect to similar fact evidence. This deference to the trial judge may in part be seen as a function of the broader, more discretionary nature of the modern rule at the stage where the probative value of the evidence must be weighed against its prejudicial effect. As a consequence of the rejection of the category approach, the admissibility of similar fact evidence since *Boardman* is a matter which effectively involves a certain amount of discretion. As pointed out in *Morris*, the weight to be given to evidence is a question for the trier of fact. Generally, where the law accords a large degree of discretion to a trial judge, courts of appeal are reluctant to interfere with the exercise of that discretion in the absence of demonstrated error of law or jurisdiction.

. . .

This review of the jurisprudence leads me to the following conclusions as to the law of similar fact evidence as it now stands in Canada. The analysis of whether the evidence in question is admissible must begin with the recognition of the general exclusionary rule against evidence going merely to disposition. As affirmed in *Boardman* and reiterated by this Court in *Guay, Cloutier, Morris, Morin* and *D. (L.E.)*, evidence which is adduced solely to show that the accused is the sort of person likely to have committed an offence is, as a rule, inadmissible. Whether the evidence in question constitutes an exception to this general rule depends on whether the probative value of the proposed evidence outweighs its prejudicial effect. In a case such as the present, where the similar fact evidence sought to be adduced is prosecution evidence of a morally repugnant act committed by the accused, the potential prejudice is great and the probative value of the evidence must be high indeed to permit its reception. The judge must consider such factors as the degree of distinctiveness or uniqueness between the similar fact evidence and the offences alleged against the accused, as well as the connection, if any, of the evidence to issues other than propensity, to the end of determining whether, in the context of the case before him, the probative value of the evidence outweighs its potential prejudice and justifies its reception.

Against this background, I turn to the facts in this case and the ruling of the trial judge.

Application of the Test for Similar Fact Evidence to This Case

. . .

Did the trial judge err in admitting the evidence of MHS? In the reasons for his ruling, he stated the correct test. He clearly proceeded on the assumption that the evidence was *prima facie* inadmissible, going on to note that its reception "depend[s] upon the probative effect of [the] evidence balanced against the prejudice caused the accused by its admission, whatever the purpose of its admission." However, he erred in later stating that the appropriate test for the probative effect of the evidence was "whether the similarities are sufficient to show that the accused had common characteristics in the methods he used in the sexual acts with [the two girls] and that it is likely that they are one and the same man." While the trial judge's concern with the degree of similarity between the two stories was proper, he appears to have viewed the similar fact evidence as going to the identity of the perpetrator, which was not in issue. As Hetherington JA, writing for the majority of the Court of Appeal, pointed out, "the admissibility of the evidence of MHS depended on whether its probative value *with respect to the credibility of ALB* [the alleged victim] outweighed its prejudicial effect." [Emphasis added.]

. . .

As noted earlier, the probative value of similar fact evidence must be assessed in the context of other evidence in the case. In cases such as the present, which pit the word of the child alleged to have been sexually assaulted against the word of the accused, similar fact evidence must be useful on the central issue of credibility.

Against that background, I turn to the similarities between the evidence of the complainant and the similar fact evidence of MHS. The main similarity is that in each case the accused, shortly after establishing a father-daughter relationship with the victim, is alleged to have engaged her in a sexual relationship. Additionally, the trial judge detailed similarities relating to the place and manner in which the relations occurred in the two situations. The age of the girls was different; one was sexually mature, the other only a child when the acts began. One girl was a blood relation, the other was not. While many of the acts were the same, there is no suggestion of urination with MHS. And there is a considerable lapse of time between the two alleged relationships.

That said, it cannot be concluded that the evidence necessarily fails the test indicated by the authorities to which I earlier referred. The fact that in each case the accused established a father-daughter relationship with the girl before the sexual violations began might be argued to go to showing, if not a system or design, a pattern of similar behaviour suggesting that the complainant's story is true. The question then is whether the probative value of the evidence outweighs its prejudicial effect. While I may have found this case to have been a borderline case of admissibility if I had been the trial judge, I am not prepared to interfere with the conclusion of the trial judge, who was charged with the task of weighing the probative value of the evidence against the prejudicial effect in the context of the case as a whole.

I would dismiss the appeal and affirm the conviction.

SOPINKA J (dissenting) (Lamer J concurring): I have read the reasons for judgment of Madam Justice McLachlin and I regret that I am unable to agree with her conclusion. My disagreement is both with the application of the principles relating to similar fact evidence and the admission of the evidence in the case.

Similar Fact Evidence

. . .

To have probative value the evidence must be susceptible of an inference relevant to the issues in the case other than the inference that the accused committed the offence because he or she has a disposition to the type of conduct charged: *Morris v. R*, supra, per Lamer J, at p. 203. In that case the evidence was admitted because the majority, although agreeing with the observation of Lamer J with respect to relevance, disagreed "with his characterization of the newspaper clipping in this case as evidence indicating *only* a disposition on the part of the appellant" (per McIntyre J, at p. 191 (emphasis added)). The law excludes this logically relevant evidence because "its logically probative significance is considered to be grossly outweighed by its prejudice to the accused, so that a fair trial is endangered if it is admitted" (per Lord Simon in *Kilbourne* [*Director of Public Prosecutions v Kilbourne*, [1973] AC 729], at p. 757). As in the case of relevance, evidence can be logically probative but not legally probative. When the term "probative value" is employed in the cases, reference is made to legally probative value.

The principal reason for the exclusionary rule relating to propensity is that there is a natural human tendency to judge a person's action on the basis of character. Particularly with juries there would be a strong inclination to conclude that a thief has stolen, a violent man has assaulted and a pedophile has engaged in pedophilic acts. Yet the policy of the law is wholly against this process of reasoning. This policy is reflected not only in similar acts cases, but as well in the rule excluding evidence of the character of the accused unless placed in issue by him. The stronger the evidence of propensity, the more likely it is that the forbidden inference will be drawn and, therefore, the greater the prejudice.

I am unable therefore to subscribe to the theory that in exceptional cases propensity alone can be the basis for admissibility. To say that propensity may have probative value in a sufficiently high degree to be admissible is a contradiction in terms. It is tantamount to saying that when the danger of the application of the forbidden line of reasoning is the strongest, the evidence can go in. ...

. . .

Application to This Case

Although my colleague and I differ somewhat on the interpretation of *Boardman*, the test for admission is stated by her to be as follows:

> [E]vidence of propensity, while generally inadmissible, may exceptionally be admitted where the probative value of the evidence in relation to an issue in question is so high that it displaces the heavy prejudice which will inevitably inure to the accused where evidence of prior immoral or illegal acts is presented to the jury.

Her reasons also refer to the rejection of the category approach to which I have alluded and to the tendency "to accord a high degree of respect to the decision of the trial judge." The probative value of the evidence is stated to be its relevance to the "issue of whether the complainant should be believed" and corroboration. Probative value apparently is used in the sense to which I have referred above.

I agree with my colleague's statement that it is important for the trial judge to spell out the relevance of the evidence and the issue to which it relates. This the trial judge did not do. Indeed, at two separate stages of the trial he misstated its relevance. In his reasons on the *voir dire*, he stated:

> In my view the admissibility of the evidence depends on whether the similarities are sufficient to show that the accused had common characteristics in the methods he used in the sexual acts with [the complainant and MHS] and that it is likely that they are one and the same man.

This was repeated at the trial. Nowhere in the reasons is there any assessment of the prejudicial effect versus the probative value. It is pure speculation, then, to say that he treated the evidence as relevant to the issue of the credibility of the complainant. Having twice expressly stated it was relevant to an issue which is conceded to be in error, one would need to have some indication in the language in the reasons that the error had been corrected. I can find nothing.

Nevertheless, assuming his statement accepting the evidence of the complainant can be construed as relating the similar fact evidence to that issue, in my opinion that is an insufficient identification of relevance to an issue. The Crown's case was based almost entirely on the evidence of the complainant. The defence was a denial of the complaint.

Any relevant evidence having the tendency to show guilt could be said to be relevant to the issue of credibility of the complainant. The credibility of the complainant is co-extensive with the issue of innocence or guilt. To say that evidence supports the credibility of the complainant is to say no more than that the evidence supports guilt. That could equally be said if the evidence was admitted for the purpose of showing that the appellant was guilty because he engaged in similar conduct on a prior occasion. More specific identification is required. ...

In considering the admissibility of the evidence in this case, I observe that no attempt appears to have been made to negative the possibility of collaboration. No questions were directed to Crown witnesses to determine whether this possibility existed. The Crown, who must persuade the trial judge that the evidence has probative value, has the burden of proof. ...

In my view, the Crown must negative conspiracy or collaboration in accordance with the criminal standard. This is a requirement that applies whenever a preliminary finding of fact is a precondition to the admissibility of evidence tendered by the Crown. ...

There is then the further question of coincidence. Are the common characteristics in the evidence of the two girls so unusual that it would be against common sense to conclude that they are not both telling the truth? In this connection, the observation of Lord Cross in *Boardman*, quoted above, is helpful. We have only two instances and should proceed with caution. They are separated by a considerable passage of time and as well there are material differences which are detailed in the reasons of Harradence JA in the Court of Appeal. McLachlin J stresses that in each case the appellant established a father relationship. As her statement of the facts indicates, the appellant was the father of one child and he enjoyed a father-daughter relationship with the other. These are not unusual facts and indeed are neutral. In any case, where it is alleged that a father has had an incestuous relationship with two of his children, this fact will be common to both. If one or both girls are not telling the truth, is it unlikely that they would both have said that the appellant established a father relationship with them? Obviously not, because that happened irrespective of whether the balance of their evidence is true.

In *Boardman*, Lord Wilberforce expressed the fear that the case, "if regarded as an example, may be setting the standard of 'striking similarity' too low" (p. 445). While it is unfashionable to compare the facts of different cases, I fear that if this evidence is admitted, we are setting it so low as to be virtually non-existent.

Notwithstanding the rejection of the evidence, the trial judge could have accepted the evidence of the complainant and rejected the evidence of the appellant. If the evidence excluded all reasonable doubt, the appellant would be convicted. I am unable to say what would have occurred if the similar fact evidence had been rejected by the trial judge. Accordingly, I would direct a new trial. The appeal is therefore allowed and a new trial directed.

Can you articulate the heart of the disagreement between Justice Sopinka and the majority in *B (CR)*?

In *R v Arp*, [1998] 3 SCR 339, 166 DLR (4th) 296, the accused was charged with and convicted of two counts of first degree murder. The charges related to two separate incidents. In 1989, the first victim got into a vehicle and was not seen again. Three weeks later, a cross-country skier discovered her body in a clearing. Although the clinical cause of death could not be determined, a forensic pathologist testified that "the death was the result of homicidal violence." The accused's vehicle matched the description of the vehicle in which the victim had last been seen; in addition, one of the victim's rings and fibres matching her sweater were found in the vehicle. The second victim disappeared in 1993. Her body was discovered on a snowbank the next day. She had been physically assaulted and strangled. DNA obtained from semen in her vagina was matched to the accused. The trial judge permitted the jury to consider the evidence on each charge as similar fact evidence going to the issue of identity on the other charge. In writing for the court, Cory J said the following about the general principles governing the admissibility of similar fact evidence:

[38] The rule allowing for the admissibility of similar fact evidence is perhaps best viewed as an "exception to an exception" to the basic rule that all *relevant* evidence is admissible. Relevance depends directly on the facts in issue in any particular case. The facts in issue are in turn determined by the charge in the indictment and the defence, if any, raised by the accused. See *Koufis v. The King*, [1941] SCR 481, at p. 490. To be logically relevant, an item of evidence does not have to firmly establish, on any standard, the truth or falsity of a fact in issue. The evidence must simply tend to "increase or diminish the probability of the existence of a fact in issue." See Sir Richard Eggleton, *Evidence, Proof and Probability* (2nd ed. 1978), at p. 83. As a consequence, there is no minimum probative value required for evidence to be relevant. See *R v. Morris*, [1983] 2 SCR 190, at pp. 199-200.

[39] Evidence of propensity or disposition (e.g., evidence of prior bad acts) is relevant to the ultimate issue of guilt, in so far as the fact that a person has acted in a particular way in the past tends to support the inference that he or she has acted that way again. Though this evidence may often have little probative value, it is difficult to say it is not relevant. In this regard, I disagree in part with Lord Hailsham's judgment in *Director of Public Prosecutions v. Boardman*, [1975] AC 421. He wrote, at p. 451 that "[w]hen there is nothing to connect the accused with a particular crime except bad character or similar crimes committed in the past, the probative value of the evidence is nil and the evidence is rejected on that ground." I think this statement may go too far, and find the approach taken by Lamer J, as he then was, in *Morris, supra*, is more accurate. He stated, at p. 203:

Disposition the nature of which is of no relevance to the crime committed has no probative value and ... for that reason excluded. But if relevant to the crime, even though there is nothing else connecting the accused to that crime, it is of some probative value, be it slight, and should be *excluded as inadmissible not as irrelevant*. [Emphasis added.]

[40] Thus evidence of propensity or disposition may be relevant to the crime charged, but it is usually inadmissible because its slight probative value is ultimately outweighed by its highly prejudicial effect. ...

. . .

[41] However, as Lord Hailsham stated in *Boardman, supra*, "what is *not* to be admitted is a chain of reasoning and not necessarily a state of facts" (emphasis added). That is, disposition evidence which is adduced *solely* to invite the jury to find the accused guilty because of his or her past immoral conduct is inadmissible. However, evidence of similar past misconduct may exceptionally be admitted where the prohibited line of reasoning may be avoided.

Cory J cited from McLachlin J's reasons in *B (CR)*, but did *not* quote her statement that "[i]t is no longer necessary to hang the evidence tendered on the peg of some issue other than disposition," and continued:

[42] It can be seen that in considering whether similar fact evidence should be admitted the basic and fundamental question that must be determined is whether the probative value of the evidence outweighs its prejudicial effect. As well it must be remembered that a high degree of deference must be given to the decision of a trial judge on this issue. See *B. (C.R.)*, *supra*, at pp. 732-33.

[43] It follows that where identity is at issue in a criminal case and the accused is shown to have committed acts which bear a striking similarity to the alleged crime, the jury is not asked to infer from the accused's habits or disposition that *he is the type of person* who would commit the crime. Instead, the jury is asked to infer from the degree of distinctiveness or uniqueness that exists between the commission of the crime and the similar act that *the accused is the very person* who committed the crime. This inference is made possible only if the high degree of similarity between the acts renders the likelihood of coincidence objectively improbable. See *Hoch v. The Queen* (1988), 165 CLR 292 (Aust. HC). That is, there is always a possibility that by coincidence the perpetrator of the crime and the accused share certain predilections or that the accused may become implicated in crimes for which he is not responsible. However, where the evidence shows a distinct pattern to the acts in question, the possibility that the accused would repeatedly be implicated in strikingly similar offences purely as a matter of coincidence is greatly reduced. ...

[44] Because similar fact evidence is admitted on the basis of an objective improbability of coincidence, the evidence necessarily derives its probative value from the degree of similarity between the acts under consideration. The probative value must, of course, significantly outweigh the prejudice to the accused for the evidence to be admissible. See *B. (C.R.)*, *supra*. However, the majority in *B. (C.R.)*, at pp. 732-33, rejected the proposition that the evidence must show a "striking similarity" between the acts in question in order for the evidence to have the requisite probative value. I agree that the requirement of "striking similarity" needs to be qualified. ...

[45] Instead, a principled approach to the admission of similar fact evidence will in all cases rest on the finding that the accused's involvement in the alleged similar acts or counts is unlikely to be the product of coincidence. This conclusion ensures that the evidence has sufficient probative force to be admitted, and will involve different considerations in different contexts. Where, as here, similar fact evidence is adduced on the issue of identity, there must be a high degree of similarity between the acts for the evidence to be admitted. For example, a unique trademark or signature will automatically render the alleged acts "strikingly similar" and therefore highly probative and admissible. In the same way, a number of significant similarities, taken together, may be such that by their cumulative effect, they warrant admission of the evidence. Where identity is at issue ordinarily, the trial judge should review the manner in which the similar acts were committed—that is to say, whether the similar acts involve a unique trademark or reveal a number of significant similarities. This review will enable him or her to decide whether the alleged similar acts were all committed by the same person. This preliminary determination establishes the objective improbability that the accused's involvement in the alleged acts is the product of coincidence and thereby gives the evidence the requisite probative force. Thus, where the similar fact evidence is adduced to prove identity, once this preliminary determination is made, the evidence related to the similar act (or count, in a multi-count indictment) may be admitted to prove the commission of another act (or count).

On the issue of linking the similar facts to the accused, Cory J stated the following:

[53] Where the similar fact evidence adduced to prove identity suggests that the same person committed the similar acts, then logically this finding makes the evidence linking the accused to each similar act relevant to the issue of identity for the offence being tried. Similarly, in a multi-count indictment, the link between the accused and any one count will be relevant to the issue of identity on the other counts which disclose a striking similarity in the manner in which those offences were committed.

[54] A link between the accused and the alleged similar acts is, however, also a precondition to admissibility. This requirement was set forth in *R. v. Sweitzer*, [1982] 1 S.C.R. 949 at 954 ... .

[55] Should the trial judge be required to conclude *not only* that the evidence suggests that the acts are the work of one person with sufficient force to outweigh the prejudicial effect of the evidence, but that they also are likely the acts of the accused? This is the approach advocated by Professor R. Mahoney in "Similar Fact Evidence and the Standard of Proof," [1993] Crim. L.R. 185, at pp. 196-97, and is implicitly favoured by those courts which have endorsed the "anchor" or "sequential" approach to similar fact evidence. See, e.g., *R. v. Ross*, [1980] 5 W.W.R. 261 (B.C. C.A.); *R. v. J.T.S.*, [1997] A.J. No. 125 (QL) (C.A.).

[56] The suggestion that the evidence linking the accused to the similar acts must also link the acts to the accused goes too far. Once the trial judge has concluded that the similar acts were likely the work of one person and that there is some evidence linking the accused to the alleged similar acts, it is not necessary to conclude that the similar acts were likely committed by the accused. The answer to this question may well determine guilt or innocence. This is the very question which the trier of fact must determine on the basis of all the evidence related to the similar acts, including of course the accused's involvement in each act. The standard set out in *Sweitzer* should be maintained. This only requires that the trial judge be satisfied that there is some evidence which links the accused to the similar acts.

If the trial judge decides that the jury should be permitted to use the evidence with respect to one count to establish guilt on the other, and vice versa, a special jury instruction becomes necessary. Cory J said the following about what the jury needs to be told:

[80] In summary, where similar fact evidence is admitted to prove identity in a multi-count indictment situation, a proper charge to the jury should include the following factors considered by Martin JA in *Simpson* [(1981), 58 CCC (2d) 122, 20 CR (3d) 36 (Ont CA)], and by this Court in *Sweitzer, supra*, and *D. (L.E.)*, [[1989] 2 SCR 111].

(1) The trial judge should instruct the jury that they may find from the evidence, though they are not required to do so, that the manner of the commission of the offences is so similar that it is likely they were committed by the same person.

(2) The judge should then review the similarities between the offences.

(3) The jury should then be instructed that if they conclude it is likely the same person committed more than one of the offences, then the evidence on each of those counts may assist them in deciding whether the accused committed the other similar count or counts.

(4) The trial judge must instruct the jury that if it accepts the evidence of the similar acts, it is relevant for the limited purpose for which it was admitted.

(5) The jury must be warned that they are not to use the evidence on one count to infer that the accused is a person whose character or disposition is such that he or she is likely to have committed the offence or offences charged in the other count or counts.

(6) If they do not conclude that it is likely the same person committed the similar offences, they must reach their verdict by considering the evidence related to each count separately, and put out of their minds the evidence on any other count or counts.

(7) Finally, the trial judge must of course make it clear that the accused must not be convicted on any count unless the jury are satisfied beyond a reasonable doubt that he or she is guilty of that offence.

The trial judge's decision to admit the evidence and his instructions to the jury were upheld, and Arp's appeal was dismissed.

The following case drew together the complex developing jurisprudence and offered the court's leading statement of the analytical framework governing the admissibility of similar fact evidence.

R v Handy
2002 SCC 56, [2002] 2 SCR 908
McLachlin CJC and L'Heureux-Dubé, Gonthier, Iacobucci, Major, Bastarache, Binnie, Arbour, and LeBel JJ (21 June 2002)

BINNIE J (for the court):

[1] The principal issues in this case are (i) the test for the admissibility of discreditable similar fact evidence where the credibility of the complainant (as distinguished from the identification of the accused) is the issue, and (ii) the impact of potential collusion on the admissibility of such evidence.

[2] The respondent was charged with sexual assault causing bodily harm. The complainant, a casual acquaintance, says that consensual vaginal sex following a drinking session at a bar turned into hurtful non-consensual vaginal and subsequently anal sex accompanied by physical abuse. At the respondent's trial, the Crown sought to introduce the evidence of his ex-wife about seven allegedly "similar fact" incidents (or "similar acts") that occurred during their seven-year, abusive and sometimes violent cohabitation (interrupted by his incarceration for unrelated sexual assaults) which produced three children. The trial judge admitted the evidence and the jury convicted the respondent of the lesser offence of sexual assault.

[3] The respondent says that the jury ought not to have considered evidence of alleged misconduct which was outside the subject matter of the charge in the indictment, and that evidence of his allegedly brutal disposition, or alleged propensity for hurtful sex, was highly prejudicial to a fair trial. Moreover, he says, the "similar" facts are not similar and in any event the complainant and his ex-wife colluded. The Ontario Court of Appeal ruled that the similar fact evidence was wrongly admitted and ordered a new trial. I agree and would dismiss the appeal.

I. Facts

[4] The complainant's evidence was that on the evening of December 6, 1996, she went out drinking with some friends. The respondent, whom she had met six months earlier, was also at the bar. The two spent the evening drinking and flirting with one another. After leaving the bar, they went to the home of one of the complainant's friends to smoke marijuana. The respondent and the complainant left the house together and drove to a nearby motel intending to have sex. In the course of vaginal intercourse, she became upset because the respondent was hurting her, forcing himself into her. She told him that it was painful but he continued. He then brusquely switched to anal intercourse. She said, "Stop that, it hurts." She tried to get him off her or to make him stop but he would not. She slapped his face. She says he hit her on the chest, he grabbed her arms, squeezed her stomach and choked her, and he punched her. She says she was pleading and crying. She had consented to vaginal sex but she did not consent to and did not want anal sex. After the incident, she told the respondent that he had made her bleed. He allegedly responded to her by saying, "What the hell am I doing here? Why does this kee[p] happening to me?"

[5] A number of witnesses testified that they had seen bruises on her throat, chest and arms in the days following the incident. The complainant was diagnosed with post-traumatic stress.

A. The Similar Fact Evidence

[6] The respondent's defence was that the sex was consensual. The issue thus came down to credibility on the consent issue. The Crown sought to introduce similar fact evidence from the respondent's former wife to the effect that the respondent has a propensity to inflict painful sex and when aroused will not take no for an answer. It was thus tendered to explain why the complainant should be believed when she testified that the assault proceeded despite her protest.

(1) Incident One

[7] In March 1990, a few weeks after their first child was born, the ex-wife says the respondent wanted to have sexual intercourse with her to "see what it would feel like." She did not want to do so because she thought that it would be painful. The respondent insisted that they have vaginal intercourse. Once they started she told the respondent that she was in pain but he did not stop.

(2) Incident Two

[8] Five or six months later she and the respondent visited her sister and brother-in-law in their mobile trailer. After everyone went to bed, the respondent wanted to have sexual intercourse. She told the respondent that she did not want to have sex because her sister and her husband were at the other end of the trailer. She tried to move away from him. The respondent told her to shut up and had vaginal intercourse with her anyway.

(3) Incident Three

[9] She returned home one day to find that the respondent had invited a number of people to their apartment for a party. After seeing the respondent tickle two women on the couch, she got angry and told everyone to leave. After most of the guests departed, she went into the bedroom. The respondent followed her. He was upset that she had broken up his party. He tried to have intercourse with her. She tried to get away but he blocked the door with a dresser. She then attempted to flee through the second floor bedroom window, but he pulled her back in. He then forced her to have vaginal intercourse and passed out.

(4) Incident Four

[10] Sometime early in 1992, the respondent came home drunk and wanted to have anal intercourse. She told him that she did not want to do so because it had hurt her on previous occasions. The respondent initiated anal intercourse nonetheless. She kept moving and tried to get away. Eventually, he grabbed a bottle of baby oil from underneath the bed and applied the oil to his penis and her anus. He initiated anal intercourse. They were interrupted by a crying baby, and she used the distraction to escape to the basement but the respondent followed her. He told her that if she did not stop running, he would tie her up with a rope. She ran naked from the house and over to the neighbour's house. The police were called but she did not lay charges.

(5) Incident Five

[11] The respondent was imprisoned from 1992 until 1995 for sexual assaults on two other women (although the fact they were "other" women was withheld from the jury by agreement of counsel). In that period he placed a threatening phone call to his then wife, which precipitated their divorce. They resumed living together soon after he was released. Shortly thereafter, she became upset because the respondent had gone out with a woman he had once dated. The respondent became angry, grabbed her by the throat, threw her around, pinned her against the wall and broke their glass coffee table. He did not, however, sexually assault her on that occasion.

(6) Incident Six

[12] One night during the summer of 1996, she and the respondent were returning home after dropping off their friends. The respondent told her that instead of going home, they were going to a gravel pit where she "was going to get it up the ass." She testified that he had forced her to have sex with him at the gravel pit in the past. She told him that she was willing to do anything other than anal intercourse because it hurt too much. The respondent, however, insisted on anal intercourse. Once at the gravel pit he attempted anal intercourse, but was unsuccessful because there was insufficient room in the back seat of the car. The respondent took her out of his car and put her face down on the hood. He attempted anal intercourse again. He eventually turned her over onto her back and had vaginal intercourse.

(7) Incident Seven

[13] In October 1996, her grandfather passed away. She and the respondent were alone in her mother's home. She was crying and upset. She testified that her crying "turned [the respondent] on" and that he wanted to have sexual intercourse on her mother's new couch. She told him that she did not want to. The respondent put her on the couch and commenced vaginal intercourse. She cried. While they were having intercourse, he punched her a number of times in the stomach to make her cry louder.

B. The Respondent's Testimony

[14] The respondent denied committing any of the alleged assaults on his ex-wife. With respect to the complainant's allegations, he testified that he met her at the bar, that they were both intoxicated and that they left the bar together. Eventually they went to a motel room. He testified that once inside the room, the complainant straddled him while he lay on his back and they engaged in approximately 15 to 20 minutes of vaginal intercourse. He denied that she had complained or told him to stop. He also denied hitting her and choking her. He testified that she drove him home at approximately 6:40 a.m. He did not see her again.

C. The Evidence of Collusion

[15] The ex-wife testified that she had met the complainant a few months before the alleged sexual assault took place. She had told the complainant at that time about the respondent's criminal record and her allegations of his abuse of her during their marriage. The ex-wife told the complainant that she had received $16,500 from the Criminal Injuries Compensation Board and agreed when it was put to her in cross-examination that "[a]ll you had to do [to get the money] was say that you were abused." The ex-wife's cross-examination was, in part, as follows:

Q. You knew [the complainant]?

A. Yes, I did.

Q. You had met her in the summer of '96?

A. That's correct.

Q. She had come over and visited with you, right?

A. That's correct.

Q. At one point, she actually said to you that she thought that [the respondent] loved you very much?

A. Yes, she did.

Q. And you straightened her out?

A. That's correct.

Q. And you told her that he had been to jail?

A. Yes, I did.

Q. You told her that he abused you?

A. Yes, I did.

Q. *And you told her that you collected $16,500 from the government. All you had to do was say that you were abused.*

A. *Yes.*

Q. So she knew all of that before December of 1996?

A. Yes. [Emphasis added.]

[16] Subsequently, on December 6, 1996, the complainant met up with the respondent at the bar and, after sharing some marijuana, agreed to accompany him to a motel for sex.

II. Judicial History

A. Ontario Court (General Division) Jennings J

[17] At the conclusion of the *voir dire*, the trial judge admitted the "similar fact" evidence on the basis that:

(i) the ex-wife's proposed evidence might assist the jury in determining how he had acted with the complainant;

(ii) the evidence was discreditable to the respondent and could only be admitted if its probative value outweighed its prejudicial effect;

(iii) the issue for the jury was the credibility of the complainant's allegation that sex continued in a violent manner in the face of attempts to refuse sex and not simply whether a withdrawal of consent had been communicated; and

(iv) the similar fact evidence, if believed, "establishe[d] a pattern of using an initially consensual situation to escalate into violent, painful sexual connection, with both vaginal and anal penetration." It would show a pattern of behaviour and confirm the credibility of the complainant, both of which the trial judge described as legitimate purposes for the reception of the evidence. This showed more than a mere propensity to commit the acts based upon bad character. The cogency was derived from the overriding similarity of the conversion of an occasion when consensual sex may be anticipated, into one of continuing vaginal sex after complaint, pain and request to stop, accompanied by physical attack, and of initiating and continuing anal sex without consent, persuades me the proposed evidence has the substantial probative value required, and as was the case in *R v. B. (L.)* [[1997] 35 OR (3d) 35] the proposed evidence is relevant to an important issue, the credibility of [the complainant].

[18] The trial judge ruled that it was not for him to resolve the possibility of collusion between the former wife and the complainant.

There is no direct evidence of collusion between [the ex-wife and the complainant], although the former told the latter of the assaults upon her. *Regardless, this is a decision for the trier of fact to make.* [Emphasis added.]

B. Ontario Court of Appeal (2000), 48 OR (3d) 257

[19] Charron JA for the court held that the trial judge had identified the correct test for admitting similar fact evidence but he had erred in its application. In her opinion, the

evidence should not have been admitted at trial since the probative value of the evidence was outweighed by its potential prejudicial effect.

[20] The strength of the evidence was weakened by the fact that the respondent had denied the incidents and that they formed the subject matter of other proceedings in which they were as yet unproven.

[21] The alleged similar acts were quite disparate in nature and, despite sharing certain characteristics, it was difficult to fit them into any pattern specific enough to bolster the complainant's credibility. Charron JA further held that there were non-superficial dissimilarities. While the acts alleged by the ex-wife took place during a conjugal, long-term relationship, the acts alleged by the complainant took place during a short, casual affair that had began with her consent.

[22] Charron JA also held that there had been a potential for collusion that further weakened any probative value that could be derived from the former wife's testimony. She held that potential for collusion "is always a serious consideration in the assessment of the strength of this kind of evidence" (para. 41) since collusion between witnesses may deprive similar fact evidence of most of its probative value. The prospect of collusion is "not a matter that can simply be left for the jury to determine without giving it due consideration in the assessment of the probative value of the evidence" (para. 41).

[23] The credibility of the ex-wife was problematic. She had considerably delayed reporting any of the incidents. The eventual timing of her complaints raised issues with respect to her motives. The complaint with respect to four incidents had first been made in support of an uncontested application for compensation before the Criminal Injuries Compensation Board when the respondent was in prison. The rest of the complaints had been made after her final separation from the respondent and shortly after she had learned of the charges laid in this case.

III. Analysis

. . .

A. The Disputed Inferences

[26] The ex-wife's testimony relates to incidents removed in time, place and circumstances from the charge. It is thus only circumstantial evidence of the matters the jury was called on to decide and, as with any circumstantial evidence, its usefulness rests entirely on the validity of the inferences it is said to support with respect to the matters in issue. The argument for admitting this circumstantial evidence is that the jury may infer firstly that the respondent is an individual who derives pleasure from sex that is painful to his partner, and will not take no for an answer, and secondly, that his character or propensity thus established gives rise to the further inference that he proceeded wilfully in this case knowing the complainant did not consent. As stated by Wilson J in *R v. Robertson*, [1987] 1 SCR 918, at p. 943:

> In discussing the probative value we must consider the degree of relevance to the facts in issue and the strength of the inference that can be drawn.

. . .

[27] The contest over the admissibility of similar fact evidence is all about inferences, i.e., when do they arise? What are they intended to prove? By what process of reasoning

do they prove it? How strong is the proof they provide? When are they so unfair as to be excluded on the grounds of judicial policy and the presumption of innocence? The answers to these questions have proven so controversial as to create what Lord Hailsham described as a "pitted battlefield": *Director of Public Prosecutions v. Boardman*, [1975] AC 421 (HL), at p. 445.

. . .

B. The General Exclusionary Rule

[31] The respondent is clearly correct in saying that evidence of misconduct beyond what is alleged in the indictment which does no more than blacken his character is inadmissible. Nobody is charged with having a "general" disposition or propensity for theft or violence or whatever. The exclusion thus generally prohibits character evidence to be used as circumstantial proof of conduct, i.e., to allow an inference from the "similar facts" that the accused has the propensity or disposition to do the type of acts charged and is therefore guilty of the offence. The danger is that the jury might be confused by the multiplicity of incidents and put more weight than is logically justified on the ex-wife's testimony ("reasoning prejudice") or by convicting based on bad personhood ("moral prejudice"): Great Britain Law Commission, Consultation Paper No. 141, *Evidence in Criminal Proceedings: Previous Misconduct of a Defendant* (1996), at § 7.2.

[32] This is a very old rule of the common law. Reference may be made to seventeenth-century trials in which the prosecution was scolded for raising prior felonious conduct, as for example to Lord Holt CJ in *Harrison's Trial* (1692), 12 How. St. Tr. 833 (Old Bailey (London)), at p. 864: "Are you going to arraign his whole life? Away, Away, that ought not to be; that is nothing to the matter."

[The court then quoted Lord Herschell's formulation of the general rule from *Makin*; see above.]

[35] The dangers of propensity reasoning are well recognized. Not only can people change their ways but they are not robotic. While juries in fourteenth-century England were expected to determine facts based on their personal knowledge of the character of the participants, it is now said that to infer guilt from a knowledge of the mere character of the accused is a "forbidden type of reasoning": *Boardman, supra*, at p. 453, *per* Lord Hailsham.

[36] The exclusion of evidence of general propensity or disposition has been repeatedly affirmed in this Court and is not controversial. See *Morris v. The Queen*, [1983] 2 SCR 190; *R v. Morin*, [1988] 2 SCR 345; *R v. B. (C.R.)*, [1990] 1 SCR 717; *R v. Arp*, [1998] 3 SCR 339.

Policy Basis for the Exclusion

[37] The policy basis for the exclusion is that while in some cases propensity inferred from similar facts may be relevant, it may also capture the attention of the trier of fact to an unwarranted degree. Its potential for prejudice, distraction and time consumption is very great and these disadvantages will almost always outweigh its probative value. It ought, in general, to form no part of the case which the accused is called on to answer. It is excluded notwithstanding the general rule that all relevant evidence is admissible: *Arp*,

supra, at para. 38; *Robertson, supra*, at p. 941; *Morris, supra*, at pp. 201-2; *R v. Seaboyer*, [1991] 2 SCR 577

[38] If propensity evidence were routinely admitted, it might encourage the police simply to "round up the usual suspects" instead of making a proper unblinkered investigation of each particular case. One of the objectives of the criminal justice system is the rehabilitation of offenders. Achievement of this objective is undermined to the extent the law doubts the "usual suspects" are capable of turning the page and starting a new life.

[39] It is, of course, common human experience that people generally act consistently with their known character. We make everyday judgments about the reliability or honesty of particular individuals based on what we know of their track record. If the jurors in this case had been the respondent's inquisitive neighbours, instead of sitting in judgment in a court of law, they would undoubtedly have wanted to know everything about his character and related activities. His ex-wife's anecdotal evidence would have been of great interest. Perhaps too great, as pointed out by Sopinka J in *B. (C.R.), supra*, at p. 744:

> The principal reason for the exclusionary rule relating to propensity is that there is a natural human tendency to judge a person's action on the basis of character. Particularly with juries there would be a strong inclination to conclude that a thief has stolen, a violent man has assaulted and a pedophile has engaged in pedophilic acts. Yet the policy of the law is wholly against this process of reasoning.

[40] The policy of the law recognizes the difficulty of containing the effects of such information which, once dropped like poison in the juror's ear, "swift as quicksilver it courses through the natural gates and alleys of the body": *Hamlet*, Act I, Scene v, ll. 66-67.

C. The Narrow Exception of Admissibility

[41] While emphasizing the general rule of exclusion, courts have recognized that an issue may arise in the trial of the offence charged to which evidence of previous misconduct may be so highly relevant and cogent that its probative value in the search for truth outweighs any potential for misuse, *per* Sopinka J, dissenting, in *B. (C.R.), supra*, at p. 751:

> The fact that the alleged similar facts had common characteristics with the acts charged, could render them admissible, and, therefore, supportive of the evidence of the complainant. In order to be admissible, however, it would be necessary to conclude that the similarities were such that absent collaboration, *it would be an affront to common sense to suggest that the similarities were due to coincidence* ... . [Emphasis added.]

[42] The "common sense" condemnation of exclusion of what may be seen as highly relevant evidence has prompted much judicial agonizing, particularly in cases of alleged sexual abuse of children and adolescents, whose word was sometimes unfairly discounted when opposed to that of ostensibly upstanding adults. The denial of the adult, misleadingly persuasive on first impression, would melt under the history of so many prior incidents as to defy innocent explanation. That said, there is no special rule for sexual abuse cases. In *any* case, the strength of the similar fact evidence must be such as to outweigh "reasoning prejudice" and "moral prejudice." The inferences sought to be drawn must accord with common sense, intuitive notions of probability and the unlikelihood of coincidence. Although an element of "moral prejudice" may be introduced, it must be

concluded by the trial judge on a balance of probabilities that the probative value of the sound inferences exceeds any prejudice likely to be created.

· · ·

Policy Basis for the Exception

[47] The policy basis for the exception is that the deficit of probative value weighed against prejudice on which the original exclusionary rule is predicated is reversed. Probative value exceeds prejudice, because the force of similar circumstances defies coincidence or other innocent explanation.

[48] Canadian case law recognizes that as the "similar facts" become more focussed and specific to circumstances similar to the charge (i.e., more situation specific), the probative value of propensity, thus circumscribed, becomes more cogent. As the differences and variables that distinguish the earlier "similar facts" from the subject matter of the charge in this type of case are reduced, the cogency of the desired inferences is thought to increase. Ultimately the policy premise of the general exclusionary rule (prejudice exceeds probative value) ceases to be true.

D. The Test of Admissibility

· · ·

[The court then reviewed those cases that established the contemporary principled approach, quoting from *Sweitzer*, above; *B (CR)*, above; *R v C (MH)*, [1991] 1 SCR 763; and *Arp*, above, before continuing.]

[54] ... The *B. (C.R.)* test can thus be taken as stating the law in Canada.

[55] Similar fact evidence is thus presumptively inadmissible. The onus is on the prosecution to satisfy the trial judge on a balance of probabilities that in the context of the particular case the probative value of the evidence in relation to a particular issue outweighs its potential prejudice and thereby justifies its reception.

Difficulties in the Application of the Test

[56] It has been recognized since Lord Herschell LC's time that it is one thing to talk about so general a test as balancing probative value against prejudice, and a different and much more difficult thing to apply the test in a practical way (*Makin*, *supra*, at p. 65). What are the manageable criteria? How "probative" must the evidence be to get over the admissibility hurdle? How much prejudice is too much? How do we calibrate the scales that balance probative value against prejudice?

[57] In an attempt to provide more precise guidance, Canadian appellate courts have from time to time advocated, amongst others, a "categories" approach, a multi-step "purpose" approach and a "conclusiveness" approach. Each of these attempts, helpful as they were in practice, were ultimately thought to obfuscate and detract from the principled approach eventually adopted in *Sweitzer*, *B. (C.R.)* and *Arp*. ...

[58] Nevertheless, *Sweitzer*, *B. (C.R.)* and *Arp* did not advocate a free-wheeling approach. They fully recognized the potentially poisonous nature of propensity evidence, and sharply circumscribed the circumstances in which it can be introduced.

(1) Propensity Evidence by Any Other Name Is Still Propensity Evidence

[59] It is occasionally suggested that once the similar fact evidence is related to an issue other than "mere" propensity or "general" disposition, it somehow ceases to be propensity evidence. I do not think this is true.

[60] One of the virtues of *B. (C.R.)* is its candid acknowledgment that "evidence of propensity, while generally inadmissible, may exceptionally be admitted" (p. 732) to help establish that the accused did or did not do the act in question (at pp. 731-32):

> While the language of some of the assertions of the exclusionary rule admittedly might be taken to suggest that mere disposition evidence can *never* be admissible, the preponderant view prevailing in Canada is the view taken by the majority in *Boardman*—evidence of propensity, while generally inadmissible, may exceptionally be admitted where the probative value of the evidence in relation to an issue in question is so high that it displaces the heavy prejudice which will inevitably inure to the accused where evidence of prior immoral or illegal acts is presented to the jury. [Emphasis in original.]

[61] In other words, while identification of the issue defines the precise purpose for which the evidence is proffered, it does not (and cannot) change the inherent nature of the propensity evidence, which must be recognized for what it is. By affirming its true character, in my view, the Court keeps front and centre its dangerous potential.

[62] I refer again to *Arp, supra*, where Cory J, for the Court, reaffirmed the proposition that in exceptional circumstances propensity evidence *is* admissible, at para. 40:

> Thus evidence of propensity or disposition may be relevant to the crime charged, but it is *usually* inadmissible because its slight probative value is ultimately outweighed by its highly prejudicial effect. [Emphasis added.]

[63] While Cory J rested admissibility on the improbability of coincidence (paras. 43 and 45), this does not in my view detract from his recognition that the underlying reasoning was through propensity. When similar facts are attributed to an accused acting "in character," it is the inferred continuity of character and nothing else that displaces what might otherwise be explained innocently as mere "coincidence."

[64] I emphasize the reference in *Arp* to "usually inadmissible." Cory J recognized, as did McLachlin J in *B. (C.R.), supra*, that disposition evidence could *unusually* and exceptionally be admitted if it survives the rigours of balancing probative value against prejudice.

• • •

(2) Identification of the "Issue in Question" Is an Important Control

• • •

[71] This Court has frequently gone out of its way to emphasize that the general disposition of the accused does not qualify as "an issue in question." As stated, the similar fact evidence may be admissible if, *but only if*, it goes beyond showing general propensity (moral prejudice) and is more probative than prejudicial in relation to an issue in the crime now charged. I accept as correct the dictum of Lord Goddard CJ in *R v. Sims*, [1946] 1 All ER 697 (CCA), at p. 700, that "[e]vidence is not to be excluded merely because it tends to show the accused to be of a bad disposition, but only if it shows nothing more,"

provided the "something more" is taken to refer to an excess of probative value over prejudice. ...

[72] Proof of *general* disposition is a prohibited purpose. Bad character is not an offence known to the law. Discreditable disposition or character evidence, at large, creates nothing but "moral prejudice" and the Crown is not entitled to ease its burden by stigmatizing the accused as a bad person. The defence of "innocent association" in *B. (F.F.)* was simply another way of expressing the denial by an accused of an element of the offence. The evidence of his prior discreditable conduct of a distinctive and particular nature, was considered to be strongly probative of specific issues in the case. Thus read, *B. (F.F.)* is quite consistent with *B. (C.R.)*, and should not be interpreted as a rival "two-step" variant of the test.

[73] The requirement to identify the material issue "in question" (i.e., the purpose for which the similar fact evidence is proffered) does not detract from the probative value/ prejudice balance, but is in fact essential to it. Probative value cannot be assessed in the abstract. The utility of the evidence lies precisely in its ability to advance or refute a live issue pending before the trier of fact.

[74] The issues in question derive from the facts alleged in the charge and the defences advanced or reasonably anticipated. It is therefore incumbent on the Crown to identify the live issue in the trial to which the evidence of disposition is said to relate. If the issue has ceased to be in dispute, as for example when the fact is admitted by the accused, then the evidence is irrelevant and it must be excluded ... . The relative importance of the issue in the particular trial may also have a bearing on the weighing up of factors for and against admissibility. Similar fact evidence that is virtually conclusive of a minor issue may still be excluded for reasons of overall prejudice.

[75] The "issues in question" are not, it should be emphasized, categories of admissibility. Their identification is simply an element of the admissibility analysis which, as stated, turns on weighing probative value against prejudice.

(3) Identification of the Required Degree of Similarity

[76] The principal driver of probative value in a case such as this is the connectedness (or nexus) that is established between the similar fact evidence and the offences alleged, particularly where the connections reveal a "degree of distinctiveness or uniqueness" (*B. (C.R.)*, *supra*, at p. 735). As stated by Cory J in *Arp*, *supra*, at para. 48:

> [W]here similar fact evidence is adduced to prove a fact in issue, in order to be admissible, the trial judge should evaluate the degree of similarity of the alleged acts and decide whether the objective improbability of coincidence has been established. Only then will the evidence have sufficient probative value to be admitted.

[77] Thus in *Arp*, where the issue was identification, Cory J cited at para. 43 *R v. Scopelliti* (1981), 63 CCC (2d) 481 (Ont. CA), where Martin JA observed that evidence of propensity on the issue of identification is not admissible "unless the propensity is so highly distinctive or unique as to constitute a signature" (p. 496). ...

· · ·

[78] The issue in the present case is not identification but the *actus reus* of the offence. The point is not that the degree of similarity in such a case must be *higher* or *lower* than

in an identification case. The point is that the issue is *different*, and the drivers of cogency in relation to the desired inferences will therefore not be the same. ...

[79] If, for example, the complainant in this case had not been able to identify the respondent as the perpetrator of the alleged offence, the conduct described by the ex-wife was not so "peculiar and distinctive" as to amount to a "signature" or "fingerprints at the scene of the crime" that would safely differentiate him from other possible assailants.

[80] On the other hand, in a case where the issue is the *animus* of the accused towards the deceased, a prior incident of the accused stabbing the victim may be admissible even though the victim was ultimately shot—the accused says accidentally (Rosenberg, *supra*, at p. 8). The acts could be said to be dissimilar but the inference on the "issue in question" would nonetheless be compelling.

(4) Identification of Connecting Factors—Is the Similar Fact Evidence Appropriately Connected to the Facts Alleged in the Charge?

[81] The decided cases suggest the need to pay close attention to similarities in character, proximity in time and frequency of occurrence. ... Similarity in this respect does not necessarily require a strong peculiarity or unusual distinctiveness underlying the events being compared, although similar facts manifesting a singular trait (such as necrophilia) would likely be a powerful tool in the hands of the prosecution.

[82] The trial judge was called on to consider the cogency of the proffered similar fact evidence in relation to the inferences sought to be drawn, as well as the strength of the proof of the similar facts themselves. Factors connecting the similar facts to the circumstances set out in the charge include:

(1) proximity in time of the similar acts: *D. (L.E.)*, *supra*, at p. 125; *R v. Simpson* (1977), 35 CCC (2d) 337 (Ont. CA), at p. 345; *R v. Huot* (1993), 16 OR (3d) 214 (CA), at p. 220;

(2) extent to which the other acts are similar in detail to the charged conduct: *Huot*, *supra*, at p. 218; *R v. Rulli* (1999), 134 CCC (3d) 465 (Ont. CA), at p. 471; *C.(M.H.)*, *supra*, at p. 772;

(3) number of occurrences of the similar acts: *Batte* [*R v Batte* (2000), 34 CR (5th) 197], at pp. 227-28;

(4) circumstances surrounding or relating to the similar acts (*Litchfield* [*R v Litchfield*, [1993] 4 SCR 333], at p. 358);

(5) any distinctive feature(s) unifying the incidents: *Arp*, *supra*, at paras. 43-45; *R v. Fleming* (1999), 171 Nfld. & PEIR 183 (Nfld. CA), at paras. 104-5; *Rulli*, *supra*, at p. 472;

(6) intervening events: *R v. Dupras*, [2000] BCJ No. 1513 (QL) (SC), at para. 12;

(7) any other factor which would tend to support or rebut the underlying unity of the similar acts.

[83] On the other hand, countervailing factors which have been found helpful in assessing prejudice include the inflammatory nature of the similar acts (*D. (L.E.)*, at p. 124)

and whether the Crown can prove its point with less prejudicial evidence. In addition, as stated, the court was required to take into account the potential distraction of the trier of fact from its proper focus on the facts charged, and the potential for undue time consumption. These were collectively described earlier as moral prejudice and reasoning prejudice.

[84] This list is intended to be helpful rather than exhaustive. Not all factors will exist (or be necessary) in every case. ...

(5) Differentiating Admissible from Inadmissible Propensity Evidence

[85] Part of the conceptual problem with similar fact evidence is that words like "disposition" or "propensity" are apt to describe a whole spectrum of human character and behaviour of varying degrees of potential relevance. At the vague end of the spectrum, it might be said that the respondent has a general disposition or propensity "for violence." This, by itself, proved nothing of value in this trial. The respondent was not charged with having a brutal personality, and his general character was, in that sense, irrelevant.

[86] At a more specific level, it is alleged here that the propensity to violence emerges in this respondent in a desire for hurtful sex. This formulation provides more context, but the definition of so general a propensity is still of little real use, particularly when it is sought to use "propensity" not to predict future conduct in a general way, but to conclude that the respondent is guilty of acting in the specific way under the specific circumstances on December 6, 1996 alleged by this complainant.

[87] Cogency increases as the fact situation moves further to the specific end of the spectrum. ...

• • •

[90] On the facts of B. (C.R.), the majority concluded that the accused was shown to have a situation specific propensity to abuse sexually children to whom he stood in parental relationship, and there was a close match between the "distinct and particular" propensity demonstrated in the similar fact evidence and the misconduct alleged in the charge, although even the majority considered the admissibility to be "borderline" (p. 739). Similar fact evidence is sometimes said to demonstrate a "system" or "modus operandi," but in essence the idea of "modus operandi" or "system" is simply the observed pattern of propensity operating in a closely defined and circumscribed context.

[91] References to "calling cards" or "signatures" or "hallmarks" or "fingerprints" similarly describe propensity at the admissible end of the spectrum precisely because the pattern of circumstances in which an accused is disposed to act in a certain way are so clearly linked to the offence charged that the possibility of mere coincidence, or mistaken identity or a mistake in the character of the act, is so slight as to justify consideration of the similar fact evidence by the trier of fact. The issue at that stage is no longer "pure" propensity or "general disposition" but repeated conduct in a particular and highly specific type of situation. At that point, the evidence of similar facts provides a compelling inference that may fill a remaining gap in the jigsaw puzzle of proof, depending on the view ultimately taken (in this case) by the jury.

• • •

(6) Similar Fact Evidence Need Not Be Conclusive

[94] Some authorities urge adoption of a further refinement that has been accepted in some common law jurisdictions in the balancing of prejudice against probative value, namely that similar fact evidence should only be admitted if its probative value is so great as to be virtually conclusive of guilt. As Lord Cross put it in *Boardman, supra*, at p. 457:

> The question must always be whether the similar fact evidence taken together with the other evidence would do no more than raise or strengthen a suspicion that the accused committed the offence with which he is charged or would point so strongly to his guilt that only an ultra-cautious jury … would acquit in face of it.

> • • •

[96] The test is a variant of the rule generally applicable to circumstantial evidence laid down in *Hodge's Case* (1838), 2 Lewin 227, 168 ER 1136, i.e., that the circumstances must be consistent with the conclusion of guilt and inconsistent with any other rational conclusion. The difference, of course, is that we are dealing here with admissibility, not adjudication. The conclusiveness test does not sit well with the balancing model set out in *B. (C.R.)*. If the evidence were truly "conclusive," its probative value would *ex hypothesi* outweigh its prejudice: [*Pfennig v R* (1995), 127 ALR 99], at p. 138.

[97] In my view, the "conclusiveness" test takes the trial judge's "gatekeeper" function too far into the domain of the trier of fact.

F. Application of the Test to the Facts of This Case

[98] I proceed to apply the test for similar fact evidence to the facts of this case under the following headings:

(1) The Probative Value of the Evidence

[99] Under this heading it is necessary first to determine the precise *"issue in question"* for which the Crown seeks to adduce the similar fact evidence. I will then address the *cogency* of the similar fact evidence in relation to that particular question. This will require consideration of the various *connecting factors* which the Crown considers persuasive, together with those factors which the defence regards as fatally weakening the inferences desired by the prosecution. An important element of the probative weight analysis is the issue of potential *collusion* between the complainant and the ex-wife. I agree with the respondent that it was part of the trial judge's "gatekeeper" function to consider this issue because collusion, if established to the satisfaction of the trial judge on a balance of probabilities, would be destructive of the very basis on which the similar fact evidence was sought to be admitted, namely the improbability that two women would independently concoct stories with so many (as the Crown contends) similar features.

(2) Assessment of the Prejudice

[100] Under this heading, it is necessary to evaluate both moral prejudice (i.e., the potential stigma of "bad personhood") and reasoning prejudice (including potential confusion and distraction of the jury from the actual charge against the respondent). Of importance in this respect is the inflammatory nature of the sexual and domestic abuse

alleged by the ex-wife, and the need for the jury to keep separate consideration of the seven "similar fact" incidents from the only charge they were asked to decide, the sexual assault alleged by the complainant.

(3) *Weighing Up Probative Value Versus Prejudice*

[101] The starting point, of course, is that the similar fact evidence is presumptively inadmissible. It is for the Crown to establish on a balance of probabilities that the likely probative value will outweigh the potential prejudice.

· · ·

(a) *The Potential for Collusion*

[104] I mention this issue at the outset because if collusion is present, it destroys the foundation on which admissibility is sought, namely that the events described by the ex-wife and the complainant, testifying independently of one another, are too similar to be credibly explained by coincidence. ...

· · ·

[111] Charron JA found, and I agree, that there was an issue of potential collusion between the complainant and the ex-wife. The evidence went beyond mere "opportunity," which will be a feature in many cases alleging sexual abuse with multiple complainants. The issue is concoction or collaboration, not contact. If the evidence amounts to no more than opportunity, it will usually best be left to the jury. Here there *is* something more. It is the whiff of profit. The ex-wife acknowledged that she had told the complainant of the $16,500 she received from the Criminal Injuries Compensation Board on the basis, she agreed, that "[a]ll you had to do was say that you were abused." A few days later the complainant, armed with this information, meets the respondent and goes off with him to have sex in a motel room.

[112] The Court in *Arp, supra*, concluded that the test for the admission of similar fact evidence is based on probability rather than reasonable doubt (paras. 65, 66 and 72). Accordingly where, as here, there is some evidence of actual collusion, or at least an "air of reality" to the allegations, the Crown is required to satisfy the trial judge, on a balance of probabilities, that the evidence of similar facts is not tainted with collusion. That much would gain admission. It would then be for the jury to make the ultimate determination of its worth.

[113] Here it was not sufficient for the Crown simply to proffer dicey evidence that *if* believed *would* have probative value. It was not incumbent on the defence to prove collusion. It was a condition precedent to admissibility that the probative value of the proffered evidence outweigh its prejudicial effect and the onus was on the Crown to satisfy that condition. The trial judge erred in law in deferring the whole issue of collusion to the jury.

[114] While that error of law is sufficient to affirm the need for a new trial as ordered by the Court of Appeal, I proceed to examine the other elements of the test previously described.

(b) Identification of "the Issue in Question"

[115] The Crown says the issue generally is "the credibility of the complainant" and more specifically "that the accused has a strong disposition to do the very act alleged in the charges against him," but this requires some refinement. Care must be taken not to allow too broad a gateway for the admission of propensity evidence or, as it is sometimes put, to allow it to bear too much of the burden of the Crown's case (Sopinka, Lederman and Bryant, *supra*, at § 11.26). Credibility is an issue that pervades most trials, and at its broadest may amount to a decision on guilt or innocence.

[116] Anything that blackens the character of an accused may, as a by-product, enhance the credibility of a complainant. Identification of credibility as the "issue in question" may, unless circumscribed, risk the admission of evidence of nothing more than general disposition ("bad personhood").

[117] Moreover, broadly speaking, the non-consent of the ex-wife on the different occasions described in her evidence is of no relevance to whether the complainant here consented or not: *Clermont, supra*, at p. 135. Because complainant A refused consent in 1992 scarcely establishes that complainant B refused consent in 1996.

[118] A conviction for sexual assault requires proof beyond reasonable doubt of two basic elements, that the accused committed the *actus reus* and that he had the necessary *mens rea*. The *actus reus* of assault is unwanted sexual touching. The *mens rea* is the intention to touch, knowing of, or being reckless of, or wilfully blind to, a lack of consent: *R v. Ewanchuk* [1999] 1 SCR 330, at para. 23.

[119] The respondent admits that sexual touching took place and that he intended it. He denies that it was unwanted. He therefore puts in issue the consent element of the *actus reus*: *Ewanchuk, supra*, at para. 27. Is he to be believed when he says consent was never withdrawn, or is the prosecution correct that he has a demonstrated situation-specific propensity to proceed regardless, indeed to derive heightened pleasure from being rejected and forcing sex on his sex partner? If so, was it manifested in this case?

[120] If the jury could legitimately infer sexual intransigence in closely comparable circumstances from the respondent's past behaviour and refusal to take his wife's no for an answer, the present complainant's testimony that intercourse occurred despite her lack of consent gains in credibility. The issue broadly framed is credibility, but more accurately and precisely framed, the "issue in question" in this trial was the consent component of the *actus reus* and in relation to that issue the respondent's alleged propensity to refuse to take no for an answer.

*(c) Similarities and Dissimilarities Between the Facts Charged and the
     Similar Fact Evidence*

[121] I propose to assess the evidence in light of the relevant "connecting factors" listed above at para. 82. I repeat that not every factor is useful in every case, and that cogency also depends on the other evidence.

(i) Proximity in Time of the Similar Acts

[122] Lapse of time opens up a greater possibility of character reform or "maturing out" personality change, and would tend to undermine the premise of continuity of character or disposition. Remoteness in time may also affect relevance and reliability. The charge against the respondent relates to December 6, 1996. The ex-wife's seven alleged incidents occurred between March 1990 and October 1996, interrupted by the respondent's incarceration from 1992 to 1995. The evidence of the respondent's inability to take no for an answer gains cogency both from its repetition over many years and its most recent manifestation a couple of months before the offence charged.

(ii) Extent to Which the Other Acts Are Similar in Detail to the Charged Conduct

[123] In this case, in my view, with respect, the learned trial judge paid insufficient attention to the dissimilarities.

[124] At least one of the incidents is largely irrelevant. Incident five involved choking, did not demonstrate sexual misconduct and was not remotely connected to the factual allegations in the charge. While the Crown can legitimately argue for the *cumulative* effect of a string of "similar" facts, I think an incident so remote from the charge could do nothing but blacken the respondent's character in a general way. Conduct that is so dissimilar or equivocal does not raise an inference capable of overcoming the prejudice.

[125] There are other important dissimilarities. None of the incidents described by the ex-wife began as consensual, then allegedly became non-consensual. Each of the incidents recounted by the ex-wife were bound up with the intimacy of a long-term relationship. Incident one relates to premature sex after birth of their child. Incident five arose out of expressions of jealousy by one *conjointe* to another. Incident seven followed a death in the family. The dynamic of these situations is not the same as the motel scene, although it is true that they all did lead (apart from incident five) to the respondent's refusal to accept his ex-wife's rejection of his sexual demands.

[126] Incident two (where the ex-wife's initial concern was based on being in close proximity to her sister and brother-in-law in a trailer) bears no obvious similarities, although again, the respondent's aggression seemed to be heightened by his ex-wife's resistance.

[127] It should be repeated that the search for similarities is a question of degree (*Boardman, supra,* at p. 442, *per* Lord Wilberforce). Sexual activity may not show much diversity or distinctiveness. Not every dissimilarity is fatal, but for the reasons already mentioned, substantial dissimilarities may dilute probative strength and, by compounding the confusion and distraction, aggravate the prejudice.

(iii) Number of Occurrences of the Similar Acts

[128] An alleged pattern of conduct may gain strength in the number of instances that compose it. The cogency of the similar act evidence in the "brides in the bathtub" case undoubtedly gathered strength from the fact the charge related to the third victim who had died under identical circumstances to her two predecessors: *R v. Smith* (1915), 84 LJKB 2153 (CCA). The ex-wife's evidence here, if believed, established a pattern over many years that the jury might think showed that the respondent's pleasure in not taking no for an answer in sexual encounters was a predictable characteristic of general application.

(iv) Circumstances Surrounding or Relating to the Similar Acts

[129] Perhaps the most important dissimilarity, as Charron JA points out, lies not in the acts themselves but in the broader context. The "similar fact" evidence occurred in the course of a long-term dysfunctional marriage whereas the charge relates to a one-night stand following a chance meeting of casual acquaintances in a bar.

[130] The ex-wife admitted in her testimony that, as one would expect, there were numerous periods of consensual sex during their relationship. They produced three children. She testified that the alleged abuse did not begin until after she and the respondent were married, at which time their relationship demonstrated many complexities that have no parallel with the situation in which the complainant found herself. To what extent was the respondent's behaviour with his ex-wife an incident of a particular conjugal relationship and to what extent did it reflect a propensity to deal in a certain way with casual sex partners, including the complainant? To what extent can "common sense" be safely relied upon to answer this question? With what confidence can the necessary inferences be drawn? There is no satisfactory answer to these basic questions in this record.

(v) Any Distinctive Feature(s) Unifying the Incidents

[131] It is not alleged that the sex acts themselves or the surrounding circumstances were highly distinctive. Cogency was said to derive from repetition rather than distinctiveness.

(vi) Intervening Events

[132] If the similar facts were sufficient to raise the inferences suggested by the Crown, there were no "intervening events" as such to undermine their probative value. An example (not applicable here) might be evidence of supervening physical incapacity: *R v. Minhas* (1986), 29 CCC (3d) 193 (Ont. CA), at p. 219.

(d) Strength of the Evidence That the Similar Acts Actually Occurred

[133] The respondent did not admit the prior misconduct, and (quite apart from the issue of collusion) a vigorous attack was made in cross-examination on the ex-wife's credibility. The evidence relating to incident six, for example, was said to be confused and contradictory. The ex-wife initially told the police that the alleged assault only involved vaginal sex. Her evidence on this incident subsequently varied. At the preliminary hearing, she testified that there was anal intercourse but did not mention vaginal intercourse. (An incomplete trial with respect to her allegations was held in April 1998 where she repeated her allegations of anal sex but, contrary to the initial testimony, did not mention vaginal sex.) At both the *voir dire* and the trial in this case, she testified that the respondent assaulted her vaginally *and* anally.

[134] In the usual course, frailties in the evidence would be left to the trier of fact, in this case the jury. However, where admissibility is bound up with, and dependent upon, probative value, the credibility of the similar fact evidence is a factor that the trial judge, exercising his or her gatekeeper function is, in my view, entitled to take into consideration. Where the ultimate assessment of credibility was for the jury and not the judge to make,

this evidence was potentially too prejudicial to be admitted unless the judge was of the view that it met the threshold of being reasonably *capable* of belief.

[135] I conclude that the similar fact evidence, if admitted, is certainly capable of raising the first inference, namely that the respondent derived pleasure from sex that was painful to his ex-wife and would not take no for an answer. The second inference (that he proceeded wilfully in *this* case knowing the complainant did not consent) is a good deal more problematic, for the reasons mentioned.

[136] If the proffered similar fact evidence is not properly capable of supporting the inferences sought by the Crown, the analysis generally need go no further. In this case, the issues were fully argued and I therefore go on to the next stage.

(2) Assessment of the Prejudice

[137] The principal wellsprings of prejudice flowing from propensity evidence were described above in outlining its presumptive exclusion, and there is no need to repeat those worries here.

[138] The poisonous potential of similar fact evidence cannot be doubted. Sopinka, Lederman and Bryant, *supra*, at § 11.173, refer to the observations of an English barrister who has written of that jurisdiction:

> Similar fact evidence poses enormous problems for Judges, jurors and magistrates alike. The reason for this is the headlong conflict between probative force and prejudicial effect. Often, in the Crown Court, *it is as close as a Judge comes to singlehandedly deciding the outcome of a case*. [Emphasis added.]

> (G. Durston, "Similar Fact Evidence: A Guide for the Perplexed in the Light of Recent Cases" (1996), 160 *Justice of the Peace & Local Government Law* 359, at p. 359)

Canadian trial lawyers take the same view.

(a) Moral Prejudice

[139] It is frequently mentioned that "prejudice" in this context is not the risk of conviction. It is, more properly, the risk of an unfocussed trial and a *wrongful* conviction. The forbidden chain of reasoning is to infer guilt from *general* disposition or propensity. The evidence, if believed, shows that an accused has discreditable tendencies. In the end, the verdict may be based on prejudice rather than proof, thereby undermining the presumption of innocence enshrined in ss. 7 and 11(d) of the *Canadian Charter of Rights and Freedoms*.

[140] The inflammatory nature of the ex-wife's evidence in this case cannot be doubted. It is, to the extent these things can be ranked, more reprehensible than the actual charge before the court. The jury would likely be more appalled by the pattern of domestic sexual abuse than by the alleged misconduct of an inebriated lout in a motel room on an isolated occasion. It may be noted that s. 718.2 of the *Criminal Code*, RSC 1985, c. C-46, reflects society's denunciation of spousal abuse by making such abuse an aggravating factor for the purposes of sentencing.

[141] Some model studies of jury behaviour have put into question the effectiveness of the trial judge's instruction as to the limited use that may be made of propensity evidence: R.L. Wissler and M.J. Saks, "On the Inefficacy of Limiting Instructions: When Jurors Use

Prior Conviction Evidence to Decide on Guilt" (1985), 9 *Law & Hum. Behav.* 37, at p. 43; S. Lloyd-Bostock, "The Effects on Juries of Hearing About the Defendant's Previous Criminal Record: A Simulation Study," [2000] *Crim. LR* 734, at p. 742; and K.L. Pickel, "Inducing Jurors to Disregard Inadmissible Evidence: A Legal Explanation Does Not Help" (1995), 19 *Law & Hum. Behav.* 407. This is not to undermine our belief in the ability of the jury to do its job, but it underlines the poisonous nature of propensity evidence, and the need to maintain a high awareness of its potentially prejudicial effect.

[142] To some extent, the prejudice could be contained by limiting the extent and nature of the ex-wife's evidence, even if some of it were admitted, by a process analogous to that followed in *R v. Corbett* [1988] 1 SCR 670, with respect to criminal convictions. That approach was adopted here only to the limited extent that the fact of the respondent's jail time for two sexual assaults on other parties was suppressed by agreement of counsel.

[143] I conclude that this evidence has a serious potential for moral prejudice.

(b) Reasoning Prejudice

[144] The major issue here is the distraction of members of the jury from their proper focus on the charge itself aggravated by the consumption of time in dealing with allegations of multiple incidents involving two victims in divergent circumstances rather than the single offence charged.

[145] Distraction can take different forms. In *R v. D. (L.E.)* (1987), 20 BCLR (2d) 384 (CA), McLachlin JA (as she then was) observed at p. 399 that the similar facts may induce

in the minds of the jury sentiments of revulsion and condemnation which might well deflect them from the rational, dispassionate analysis upon which the criminal process should rest.

[146] Further, there is a risk, evident in this case, that where the "similar facts" are denied by the accused, the court will be caught in a conflict between seeking to admit what appears to be cogent evidence bearing on a material issue and the need to avoid unfairness to the right of the accused to respond. The accused has a limited opportunity to respond. Logistical problems may be compounded by the lapse of time, surprise, and the collateral issue rule, which will prevent (in the interest of effective use of court resources) trials within trials on the similar facts. Nor is the accused allowed to counter evidence of discreditable conduct with similar fact evidence in support of his or her credibility (as discussed in Sopinka, Lederman and Bryant, *supra*, at § 11.74). Thus the practical realities of the trial process reinforce the prejudice inherent in the poisonous nature of the propensity evidence itself.

[147] In my view, the evidence of the ex-wife had the potential to create, in addition to moral prejudice, significant reasoning prejudice at the respondent's trial.

(3) Weighing Up Probative Value Versus Prejudice

[148] One of the difficulties, as McHugh J pointed out in *Pfennig*, *supra*, at p. 147, is the absence of a common basis of measurement: "The probative value of the evidence goes to proof of an issue, the prejudicial effect to the fairness of the trial." The two variables do not operate on the same plane.

[149] As probative value advances, prejudice does not necessarily recede. On the contrary, the two weighing pans on the scales of justice may rise and fall together. Nevertheless,

probative value and prejudice pull in opposite directions on the admissibility issue and their conflicting demands must be resolved.

[150] In *Director of Public Prosecutions v. P.*, [1991] 2 AC 447 (HL), at p. 460, Lord Mackay suggested that similar fact evidence should be admitted when its probative value is "sufficiently great to make it just to admit the evidence," notwithstanding its prejudicial value. Lord Wilberforce in *Boardman*, at p. 442, also referred to "the interests of justice." See also *Pfennig*, *supra*, at pp. 147-48. Justice is achieved when relevant evidence whose prejudice outweighs any probative value is excluded (*R v. Marquard* [1993] 4 SCR 223, at p. 246) and where evidence whose probative value exceeds its prejudice (albeit an exceptional circumstance) is admitted. Justice includes society's interest in getting to the truth of the charges as well as the interest of both society and the accused in a fair process. A criminal justice system that has suffered some serious wrongful convictions in part because of misconceived notions of character and propensity should not (and does not) take lightly the dangers of misapplied propensity evidence.

[151] In this case, the similar fact evidence was *prima facie* inadmissible and I agree with Charron JA that the Crown did not discharge the onus of establishing on a balance of probabilities that its probative value outweighed its undoubted prejudice. The probative value of the evidence, especially with respect to potential collusion, was not properly evaluated. The potential of such evidence for distraction and prejudice was understated. The threshold for admission of this sort of evidence was set too low.

[152] Consent, or the lack of it, and the complainant's credibility in relation thereto, was *the* crucial issue at the trial. It can hardly be doubted that the jury, listening to the ex-wife's evidence, would form a very low opinion of the respondent as an individual who behaved abominably towards his wife, and be readier on that account to believe the worst of him in his conduct towards the complainant. This is precisely the sort of general disposition reasoning (moral prejudice) that the similar fact exclusion rule was designed to prevent.

G. Review of the Trial Judge's Decision

[153] A trial judge has no discretion to admit similar fact evidence whose prejudicial effect outweighs its probative value. Nevertheless, a trial judge's decision to admit similar fact evidence is entitled to substantial deference: *B. (C.R.)*, *supra*, at p. 739; and *Arp*, *supra*, at para. 42. In this case, however, quite apart from the other frailties of the similar fact evidence previously discussed, the trial judge's refusal to resolve the issue of collusion as a condition precedent to admissibility was an error of law. A new trial is required.

IV. Conclusion

[154] The Crown's appeal is dismissed.

Do you think an application of the criteria identified in *Handy* for assessing probative value and prejudicial effect would have led to the same or a different result in *B (CR)*?

A significant issue in the *Handy* case was the spectre of collusion between the complainant and Handy's ex-wife. The court soon had occasion to again address the issue of collusion when it applied its newly minted *Handy* test in the case of *R v Shearing*, 2002 SCC 58, [2002] 3 SCR 33. Shearing was the leader of a cult, the Kabalarians, who preached that sexual experience was a way to progress to higher levels of consciousness and that he, as cult leader, could help young girls to reach higher levels through sexual and spiritual contact. He was charged with 20 counts of sexual offences over a 24-year period. Of the 11 complainants, 9 were members of the cult, and two were non-members who lived with the accused while teenagers. The counts were tried together and the trial judge admitted each as similar fact evidence for the others. Applying the framework that he set out in *Handy*, Justice Binnie began by assessing the probative value of the evidence and made the following statements regarding the issue of collusion:

[39] As the test of admissibility weighs probative value against prejudice, a question that quickly emerges is whether the Crown is able to lead cogent evidence of the alleged similar acts. In this case, the similar acts are all the subject of distinct charges. They are therefore, in any event, before the jury for a verdict. Apart from the usual issues of credibility, the appellant says there is evidence of collusion.

[40] The theory of similar fact evidence turns largely on the improbability of coincidence. Collusion, by offering an alternative explanation for the "coincidence" of evidence emanating from different witnesses, destroys its probative value, and therefore the basis for its admissibility.

[41] In *Handy*, we held that where there is an air of reality to the allegation of collusion, the trial judge, in assessing the admissibility of the similar fact evidence, must be satisfied on a balance of probabilities that the evidence is not the product of concoction. This is inherent in deciding whether, as a matter of law, the evidence has sufficient probative value to overcome the prejudice.

[42] If this threshold test is passed, the jury must determine for itself what weight, if any, to assign to the similar fact evidence.

[43] There was evidence of some communication among the complainants. With respect to the G sisters, this was almost inevitable. They had also kept in touch with JV. Other complainants were in touch with each other prior to trial. Civil proceedings had been commenced by the G sisters for compensation and to close down the Kabalarians. KWG expressed the hope that the appellant would "rot in hell."

[44] The evidence here is far more speculative than in *Handy*. In that case, there was consultation between the complainant and the similar fact witness *prior* to the alleged offence about the prospect of financial profit. Here, there is some evidence of opportunity for collusion or collaboration and motive, but nothing sufficiently persuasive to trigger the trial judge's gatekeeper function. There is no reason here to interfere with the trial judge's decision to let the collusion issue go to the jury. He instructed the jury to consider "all of the circumstances which affect the reliability of that evidence including the possibility of collusion or collaboration between the complainants." He defined collusion as the possibility that the complainants in sharing their stories with one another, intentionally or accidentally allowed themselves to change or modify their stories in order that their testimony would seem more similar or more convincing. It was for the jury to make the ultimate determination whether the evidence was "reliable despite the opportunity for collaboration" or that "less weight or no weight should be given to evidence which may have been influenced by the sharing of information."

[45] While the trial judge did not specifically link the potential of collusion to the issue of admissibility, he appears to have thought collusion (as distinguished from contact) was not a serious danger. The evidence supports his decision. He was justified in letting the collusion issue go to the jury with an appropriate warning.

With respect to the other factors outlined in *Handy* that influence probative value, Justice Binnie found that although the sexual acts themselves were not particularly distinctive, "the underlying unity lies in the alleged abuse of a cult leader's authority. It is the fantastic sales pitch and rationale developed by the appellant that could be considered 'particular and distinctive'" (at para 50). The incidents overlapped in time, showing an extended consistency in behaviour. There were, if believed, hundreds of incidents and all occurred in similar circumstances involving the use of distinctive spiritual claims and the "abuse of power to obtain sexual gratification at the expense of adolescent girls who were to a greater or lesser extent in his charge over a period of 24 years" (at para 57). Although the appellant pointed to certain dissimilarities among the acts, particularly as between those involving the member and non-member adolescents, Justice Binnie explained as follows:

> [60] In my view, this objection advocates an excessively mechanical approach. The judge's task is not to add up similarities and dissimilarities and then, like an accountant, derive a net balance. At microscopic levels of detail, dissimilarities can always be exaggerated and multiplied. This may result in distortion: *Litchfield* [*R v Litchfield*, [1993] 4 SCR 333]. At an excessively macroscopic level of generality, on the other hand, the drawing of similarities may be too facile. Where to draw the balance is a matter of judgment. In this case, for the reasons already given, the "differences" urged by the appellant do not the importance he asserts. The defence, as discussed earlier, wants to compartmentalize the appellant into roles. I do not think this is realistic. The Kabalarian cult created a closed domestic and "spiritual" system under the appellant's authority to which all of the complainants, to a greater or lesser extent, were subject.

Justice Binnie reviewed the potential moral and reasoning prejudice and concluded as follows:

> [71] In my view, the similar act evidence has significant potential to create moral prejudice. The appellant's defence to the non-G complainants (religiously inspired consent) becomes more delicate when the jury is told that he also had sexual relations with two sisters from the age of 13 years old who were not Kabalarian disciples but simply residents of his Kabalarian household. The atmosphere of the case is redolent of quack spiritualism and this would clearly disturb a Canadian jury. Similarly, the appellant's denial of abuse of the G sisters may lose much of its force in light of the admitted sexual touching of other adolescent girls, to which the only defence is consent (vitiated, so the jury must have found, by the abuse of authority).

Justice Binnie emphasized that "[i]n the weighing up of probative value *versus* prejudice, a good deal of deference is inevitably paid to the view of the trial judge" (at para 73) and concluded that there was no reason to disturb the trial judge's conclusion that, although both the probative value and potential for prejudice were high in this case, "in the end the probative value prevailed" (at para 74). The court dismissed the appeal on the similar fact evidence ground.

What if the prior bad acts aren't exclusively those of the accused but of a gang that he routinely joined with in committing crimes? This issue arose in the case of *R v Perrier*, 2004 SCC 56, [2004] 3 SCR 228. The accused was charged with several offences arising from three separate home invasions that were committed by a gang and occurred in the same area over a four-week period. The accused's link to one of the robberies was strong, and he was convicted of it in a separate trial. The accused then faced trial for his alleged role in the two other home invasions. The issue before the court was whether the evidence implicating the accused in each of the robberies could be used to establish his guilt with respect to the others and vice versa. The gang used the same *modus operandi* in each home invasion. After the victim, in each case an Asian female, opened the door, accomplices who were standing out of sight would force their way inside. The victim was tied up while the gang members searched for valuables. In each incident the victims gave inconsistent descriptions of the assailants and their number (between five and six). The Crown conceded that the same gang members did not always attend every robbery, and that different members had played different roles in executing each of the crimes. Nevertheless, the Crown maintained that the accused was involved in all three incidents. Beyond the similar fact evidence that the Crown wanted to adduce, the evidence linking the accused to the other two incidents was tenuous. Some of the property stolen during one of the robberies was found in an apartment that the accused shared with another gang member. In addition, cellular phone records showed that the accused had been in telephone contact with some of the other gang members before and after each robbery. Applying both *Arp* and *Handy*, above, do you think the proposed similar fact evidence is admissible?

As established in *Arp*, if similar fact evidence is admitted against an accused, the jury must be instructed as to its limited and proper use. Most importantly, a trial judge must instruct the jury that they may not rely on the prohibited character inference, inferring generally that the accused is the kind of person more likely to have committed the offence. In *R v B (C)* (2003), 171 CCC (3d) 159 (Ont CA), the Ontario Court of Appeal held that "when cautioning the jury about the misuse of similar fact evidence, we think it would be preferable for trial judges to give the jury the double warning: (1) that they may not use the similar fact evidence to reason from general disposition or character to guilt, and (2) nor may they use it to punish the accused for past misconduct by finding the accused guilty of the offence or offences charged" (at para 35). Moreover, a trial judge must describe to the jury the permissible use of the similar fact evidence; as Justice Binnie explained in *Handy*, above at para 70, "[a]n indication of the importance of identifying 'the issue in question' is that the trial judge is required to instruct the jury that they may use the evidence in relation to that issue and not otherwise." A jury should be reminded that "they must first be satisfied that the similar acts occurred before any use can be made of them" (*B (C)* at para 29) and any frailties in the similar fact evidence should be drawn to the attention of the jury: see *R v Anderson* (2003), 179 CCC (3d) 11 at paras 28-29 (Ont CA).

III. CHARACTER OF NON-ACCUSED PERSONS IN CRIMINAL CASES

Although the Crown's use of character evidence will be focused on the accused, the accused may, in certain circumstances, wish to offer evidence of the bad character of some other person. When an accused seeks to do so, the law does not impose the same strictures that it does on the Crown's use of character evidence. Recall that the general exclusionary rule that limits Crown offers of character evidence is based largely on the concern that a finder of fact will infer that the accused is the kind of person likely to have committed the offence. When the focus shifts to a non-accused person, that worry does not exist—the accused is the only person on trial. Accordingly, the "moral prejudice" associated with character evidence is far less of a concern in the case of non-accused persons. Moreover, the accused enjoys the presumption of innocence and the right to full answer and defence; accordingly, as you have learned, the law is slow to exclude defence offers of evidence. For all of these reasons, the rules governing the accused's use of character evidence are far more relaxed: see *R v Arcangioli*, [1994] 1 SCR 129 at 139; *R v Grant*, 2013 MBCA 95, 302 CCC (3d) 491. The general principle is that the accused may adduce evidence of a third party's bad character when it is relevant to an issue at trial and when its probative value is not substantially outweighed by its potential for prejudice.

This is not to say, however, that the accused's ability to adduce bad character evidence about others is without restriction. You will see that the law places certain limits on when the defence may introduce such evidence. In particular, as we will explore below, Parliament has enacted special rules governing the introduction of character evidence regarding complainants in sexual assault cases, given the substantial history of, and ongoing potential for, abuse and distortion arising from the use of this kind of evidence.

A. The Character of Third-Party Suspects and Victims

If the general rule is that an accused is entitled to adduce evidence of the bad character of a third party when it is relevant to an issue at trial, the question becomes "when will such evidence be relevant?" When might an accused wish to offer evidence that another person is the kind of person likely to have behaved in a particular way? One situation in which this can arise is when an accused's defence is that some other person is the likely perpetrator. As you read the following case, consider what limits the law places on how far an accused may go in attempting to raise a reasonable doubt by calling character evidence with respect to a third party.

R v McMillan

(1975), 23 CCC (2d) 160, 29 CRNS 191 (Ont CA)

Gale CJO and Kelly and Martin JJA (14 February 1975)

MARTIN JA: The Crown appeals, pursuant to the provisions of s. 605 of the *Criminal Code*, RSC 1970, c. C-34, from the acquittal of the respondent on a charge that on or about 22nd March 1973 he murdered Mary McMillan.

The deceased was the infant daughter of the respondent and his wife Roberta Gale McMillan. The deceased infant was about 2½ weeks old at the time of her death. She was brought to the Scarborough General Hospital shortly after midnight on the morning of 23rd March 1973, by the respondent and his wife, and died at 2:30 a.m. that morning.

· · ·

Dr. Cooper, a psychiatrist, testified that Mrs. McMillan suffered from a psychopathic personality disorder and that a person suffering from such a personality disorder would be a danger to her child. The learned trial judge ruled, however, that Crown counsel was not entitled to cross-examine Dr. Cooper with respect to his diagnosis of the respondent as a psychopath or to call evidence in reply as to the "mental state or mental condition" of the respondent. The learned trial judge held that such evidence was in the nature of character evidence and that the evidence of good character introduced by the respondent could only be rebutted by evidence of general reputation.

The grounds of appeal are:

1. That the learned trial judge erred in admitting evidence with respect to the mental makeup of Mrs. McMillan.

2. That, if the evidence with respect to the mental makeup of Mrs. McMillan was admissible, the learned trial judge erred in denying Crown counsel the right to cross-examine the defence witnesses with respect to the respondent's mental makeup and to call psychiatric evidence in reply on that issue.

Mr. Manning in his able argument first contended that the evidence with respect to the mental makeup or disposition of Mrs. McMillan was inadmissible because it was not relevant to any issue between the Crown and the accused.

The admissibility of the impugned evidence raises a question of some novelty with respect to which there appears to be no direct authority and it must be determined by the application of the general principles of the law of evidence in the light of modern knowledge in relation to human behaviour.

I take it to be self-evident that if A is charged with the murder of X, then A is entitled, by way of defence, to adduce evidence to prove that B, not A, murdered X: see *Wigmore on Evidence*, 3rd ed., vol. 1, p. 139. A may prove that B murdered X either by direct or circumstantial evidence.

Evidence that a third person had a motive to commit the murder with which the accused is charged, or had made threats against the deceased, is commonly admitted on this principle. Evidence directed to prove that the crime was committed by a third person, rather than the accused, must, of course, meet the test of relevancy and must have sufficient probative value to justify its reception. Consequently, the courts have shown a disinclination to admit such evidence unless the third person is sufficiently connected by other circumstances with the crime charged to give the proffered evidence some probative value: see Wigmore at pp. 573-76.

The tendency or disposition of a person to do a certain act is relevant to indicate the probability of his doing or not doing the act.

. . .

When the law of evidence excludes evidence of character, in the sense of disposition, it frequently does so not on the ground of lack of probative value but on policy grounds, because it may cause undue prejudice in relation to its probative value, create unfair surprise, may unduly distract from the issues, or be too time-consuming in relation to its probative value. Thus, the prosecution is not permitted to introduce evidence for the purpose of proving that the accused is a person who by reason of his criminal character or propensity is likely to have committed the crime charged. The relevance of evidence with respect to the accused's character is conceded, however, by the rule of evidence which permits an accused to offer evidence of his good character as the basis of an inference that he is unlikely to have committed the crime charged.

It follows that evidence of the disposition of a third person to commit the crime in question, like other circumstantial evidence, is admissible, if relevant, to prove that the crime was committed by the third person.

"Where the character is that of a *third person, not a party* to the cause, the reasons of policy (noted ante, …) for exclusion seem to disappear or become inconsiderable; hence, if there is any relevancy in the fact of character, i.e. if some act is involved upon the probability of which a moral trait can throw light, the character may well be received": Wigmore at p. 488.

Obviously, unless the third person is connected with the crime under consideration by other circumstances, evidence of such person's disposition to commit the offence is inadmissible on the grounds of lack of probative value. For example, if A is charged with murdering X, in the absence of some nexus with the alleged offence, evidence that B has a propensity or disposition for violence, by itself, is inadmissible to prove B is the murderer because standing alone it has no probative value with respect to the probability of B having committed the offence. If, however, it is proved that A, B and X all lived in the same house when X was killed, and that B had a motive to kill X, then evidence that B had a propensity for violence may have probative value on the issue whether B, and not A, killed X, and is accordingly admissible.

In the case at bar there is some evidence of opportunity on the part of Mrs. McMillan to cause the injuries to the baby which caused her death. The respondent testified that he and his wife were together in the same room during Thursday, 22nd March, except for a period of about an hour in the afternoon, when he was alone with the baby, and that his wife was alone with the baby for about 10 or 15 minutes in the evening. There was, in addition, other evidence of opportunity on the part of the wife fit for the consideration of the jury. There was also evidence that Mrs. McMillan had a motive to injure the baby, in that a neighbour, Mrs. McMullen, testified that after the death of the baby, Mrs. McMillan said to Mrs. McMullen's child that the "baby had gone away, and 'I didn't want the baby anyways.'" There was also other evidence that initially, at any rate, she did not want the baby. I am consequently of the view that Mrs. McMillan's disposition was relevant in relation to whether it was more probable that she inflicted the injuries which caused the child's death than that her husband caused them.

Once it is accepted that, in the above circumstances, Mrs. McMillan's disposition or tendency for violence is relevant and admissible, the only question that remains is the means by which such disposition or tendency may be proved.

In general, and subject to exceptions, the tendency or disposition of *an accused* to do an act of a certain kind, or its absence, when relevant and admissible, can only be proved by evidence of general reputation.

· · ·

One of the exceptions to the general rule that the character of the accused, in the sense of disposition, when admissible, can only be evidenced by general reputation, relates to the admissibility of psychiatric evidence where the particular disposition or tendency in issue is characteristic of an abnormal group, the characteristics of which fall within the expertise of the psychiatrist. … There is no logical reason why the same reasoning should not apply *a fortiori* to the manner in which the disposition of a third person may be proved when that disposition is relevant to an issue in the case.

As previously stated, Dr. Cooper diagnosed Mrs. McMillan as having a psychopathic personality disturbance with brain damage. He expressed the opinion that, while she was not insane within the meaning of s. 16 of the Code, she had a disease of the mind or mental illness. The psychopathic personality disturbance from which Mrs. McMillan suffered was manifested by a "cluster" of characteristics which are diagnostic of the psychopathic personality from which she suffers. Dr. Cooper found that she was immature, impulsive, had a poor appreciation of the difference between right and wrong, and poor ability for empathy with other people. Her impulsiveness was manifested by the fact that her anger could be "focused" very quickly from one person to another. Her mood could fluctuate rapidly from cheerfulness to anger. She had a bad temper and a "short fuse." He considered that she was a danger to the child. In my view, the sum of Mrs. McMillan's personality traits constituted a disposition of a kind which, in the circumstances of this case, was relevant to the issue as to whether it was more probable that she had inflicted the injuries to the child, than that her husband had inflicted them. The "cluster" of characteristics exhibited by Mrs. McMillan was diagnostic of an abnormal group and as such was capable of being proved by the expert evidence of a psychiatrist.

· · ·

It is also contended by counsel for the Crown that the injuries were not of such a character that they could only have been inflicted by the person with a special or abnormal propensity, and hence psychiatric evidence of the wife's mental makeup was not admissible.

I do not consider that, because the crime under consideration was not one that could only be committed by a person with a special or abnormal propensity, psychiatric evidence with respect to Mrs. McMillan's disposition was therefore inadmissible in the circumstances of this case.

All evidence to be admissible must, of course, be relevant to some issue in the case. Psychiatric evidence with respect to the personality traits or disposition of a person, whether of the accused or another, may be admissible for different purposes. While those purposes are not mutually exclusive, evidence which is relevant for one purpose may not be for another.

Psychiatric evidence with respect to the personality traits or disposition of an accused, or another, is admissible provided: (a) the evidence is relevant to some issue in the case; (b) the evidence is not excluded by a policy rule; (c) the evidence falls within the proper sphere of expert evidence.

One of the purposes for which psychiatric evidence may be admitted is to prove identity when that is an issue in the case, since psychical as well as physical characteristics may be relevant to identify the perpetrator of the crime.

Where the offence is of a kind [that] is committed only by members of an abnormal group, for example, offences involving homosexuality, psychiatric evidence that the accused did or did not possess the distinguishing characteristics of that abnormal group is relevant either to bring him within, or to exclude him from, the special class of which the perpetrator of the crime is a member. In order for psychiatric evidence to be relevant for that purpose, the offence must be one which indicates that it was committed by a person with an abnormal propensity or disposition which stamps him as a member of a special and extraordinary class.

Psychiatric evidence with respect to the personality traits or disposition of the accused, or another, if it meets the three conditions of admissibility above set out, is also admissible, however, as bearing on the *probability* of the accused, or another, having committed the offence.

· · ·

The question here presented involves the admissibility of psychiatric evidence with respect to the character, in the sense of the personality traits or disposition, of a third person, as throwing light on the probability that the acts in question were committed by such person rather than the accused.

As I have already indicated, Mrs. McMillan's disposition was relevant, in the circumstances of this case, as bearing on the probability that the acts in question were committed by her rather than her husband. Since her personality traits were characteristic, indeed diagnostic, of the abnormal personality disturbance from which she suffered, their existence and description fell within the proper sphere of the psychiatrist. Moreover, there is no policy rule which required the exclusion of the evidence as to Mrs. McMillan's personality traits or disposition when tendered by the accused. All the conditions of the admissibility of such evidence have accordingly been met.

· · ·

I turn now to the other ground of appeal advanced, namely, that if the evidence with respect to Mrs. McMillan's mental makeup was admissible, the learned trial judge erred in ruling that Crown counsel was not entitled to cross-examine Dr. Cooper with respect to the respondent's mental makeup or to call psychiatric evidence in reply with respect thereto. The position taken by defence counsel in his address to the jury was that there were two people in the house in which the child received the injuries from which she died. One of those persons, the wife, was a psychopathic personality with a disposition or tendency toward violence. The other occupant of the house, the respondent, was a person of good reputation for honesty and responsibility, and of a gentle nature. In those circumstances, the jury was asked to say whether it was more probable that the wife inflicted the injuries or that the respondent had inflicted them. It was implicit in the defence advanced that there were two people in the house who could have inflicted the injuries which caused the baby's death; one was a psychopath (the wife), the other was a normal person of good character (the respondent). In my view, the entire nature of the defence involved an assertion that the respondent was a person of normal mental makeup. In those circumstances, Crown counsel was entitled to show, if he could, that there were two persons present in the house who were psychopaths, not one. Any other conclusion would permit an accused to present an entirely distorted picture to the jury. The respondent, having introduced psychiatric evidence to show that it was more probable that his wife had caused the injuries to the child than that he had caused them, because he lacked her dangerous characteristics, lost his protection, in the circumstances of this case, against having his own mental makeup revealed to the jury.

Dr. Cooper, on the *voir dire*, testified that the respondent is a psychopath. However, he said that there are different categories of psychopathic personalities. Dr. Cooper's evidence in cross-examination on the *voir dire* was that the respondent fell within the category of the inadequate psychopath and that he was not physically dangerous. It seems obvious that the right to cross-examine Dr. Cooper before the jury on this issue, which was wrongly denied to the Crown, was unlikely to have affected the verdict.

There remains the error in refusing the Crown the right to call psychiatric evidence in reply.

At the request of both counsel the Court has examined a report dated April 13, 1973, by Dr. Common, consultant psychiatrist, Toronto Jail, to Provincial Court Judge McMahon, following a remand by that Judge of the accused on March 24, 1973, for a mental assessment in connection with the charge of manslaughter then pending against the accused, arising out of the death of the deceased baby. The report states that the appellant is mentally fit to stand trial and makes some reference to his personality traits. The report, however, being directed to the fitness of the accused to stand trial, cannot be regarded as other than inconclusive as to whether the respondent is a psychopath with personality characteristics that are relevant to the issue whether it is more probable that the deceased baby was killed by one rather than the other of the parents.

Although the report of Dr. Common is inconclusive, it does not follow, having regard to the limited purpose for which the report was made, that the refusal of the trial Judge to permit the Crown to call psychiatric evidence in reply did not result in a miscarriage of justice within the meaning of that term in relation to appeals by the Crown from acquittals. It cannot be assumed that the psychiatric evidence available to the Crown was limited to the facts contained in Dr. Common's report.

I would, therefore, allow the appeal, set aside the acquittal and direct a new trial.

[This decision was affirmed, [1977] 2 SCR 824.]

In your view, did the Crown's expert evidence in *McMillan* meet the standard for the admission of psychiatric evidence of character discussed earlier in this chapter? If not, on the basis of the facts of *McMillan*, is there nonetheless an argument for its admissibility?

As you have read, before the accused will be entitled to adduce evidence of the character or propensity of a third party in order to suggest that this person committed the offence, there must be some evidence linking that third party to the offence. For a more recent Supreme Court of Canada decision confirming that requirement, see *R v Grandinetti*, 2005 SCC 5, [2005] 1 SCR 27. For another case involving an accused adducing propensity evidence of a third party to suggest that the third party was the perpetrator, see *R v Arcangioli*, [1994] 1 SCR 129. In *Arcangioli*, the accused was charged with aggravated assault in connection with a stabbing. He adduced evidence that another person, Semester, who was also at the scene of the crime, was involved in a stabbing earlier that night. Moreover, Semester had a criminal record that included a conviction for a robbery in which a knife and gun were used. The Supreme Court ruled that the jury should have been instructed that this evidence could be used to support the defence's suggestion that it was Semester, not Arcangioli, who stabbed the victim.

Another circumstance in which the character of a third party might be relevant is when the accused is advancing a claim of self-defence. In that situation, an accused may wish to adduce evidence of the victim's propensity for violence or aggression to support the defence. The following case addresses precisely that situation.

R v Scopelliti
(1981), 63 CCC (2d) 481 (Ont CA)
Martin, Zuber, and Weatherston JJA (9 November 1981)

MARTIN JA: Antonio Scopelliti, following a trial by jury presided over by Mr. Justice Saunders, was acquitted on two counts of second degree murder. Count 1 charged him with murdering David B. Sutton, and count 2 charged him with murdering Michael J. McRae. As the counts arose out of the same transaction, they were properly tried together.

The two deceased were killed by shots fired by the respondent from a Baretta semi-automatic hand-gun. The principal defence advanced was self-defence although the trial judge also left with the jury the qualified defences of provocation and excessive force in self-defence.

The Attorney-General for Ontario now appeals against the acquittal. This appeal raises, among other questions, the important question as to the admissibility for prior acts of violence by the deceased, not known to the accused, towards other persons, where the defence advanced by the accused is self-defence.

The Facts

[The accused operated a variety store and gas pump in Orillia, Ontario. He shot the two victims in his store shortly before 10:00 p.m. on January 22, 1979.]

The respondent was taken to the Orillia police station where he was lodged in the cells. At 12:36 a.m. he was taken to Staff-Sergeant Smith's office. He was cautioned, and asked by Sergeant Hough if he could tell him what had occurred. The respondent's version as to what occurred, as elicited by questions, was, in substance, that shortly before 10:00 p.m., which was closing time, two men entered the store. One of the men (Sutton), tried to "hit [him] slap [him]," but the respondent ducked back and the blow missed him. He told them that they had better go and Sutton replied "We don't want to go, you'll have to make us." The other man (McRae), at this time had his foot on the chocolate bar display rack. The respondent asked McRae three times to move, and he went and got a magazine. Sutton "tried to open the till" and the respondent told him to "get away." The respondent reached under the counter where the gun was. He said he "shot the one in blue [Sutton] first." The other youth (McRae), called him a "son-of-a-bitch and a bastard, [and he] shot him too." When asked by Sergeant Hough if the other youth had tried to "get him at all," the respondent replied no. When asked if they had indicated they were going to rob him, the respondent said that they had not but that he did not know if they were or if they were "horsing around." He said that he was not certain how many shots he had fired; that the gun was not fully loaded; and that he did not know how many bullets the clip held. The trial judge ruled all the respondent's conversations with the police voluntary and admissible in evidence.

Both the deceased died of gun shot wounds. David Sutton sustained three bullet wounds and two bullet creases. The wound which in the opinion of the pathologist was, in all likelihood, the wound causing death was an entry wound on the left side of the back of the chest with a corresponding exit wound at the front of the chest. Another bullet entered the left side of the back below the shoulder and exited at the front of the body. A third bullet wound was found in the upper part of the right side of the back just below the shoulder. The bullet had travelled in a straight, slightly upwards path across the body, lodging in the opposite shoulder.

Michael McRae had been shot twice in the head. One bullet had entered just below the right eye and the other bullet had entered above the right ear and passed through the vital portions of the brain to rest on the left side of the head. Either wound would have been fatal.

The pathologist testified that it was not possible to determine the sequence in which the shots were fired, the position of the deceased when shot, or whether they were standing when shot, since he could not say if the impact of the bullet would cause the body to move in a particular way.

A firearms examiner testified that the semi-automatic Baretta had no tendency to discharge accidentally and that each time a shot is fired the trigger must be pulled. The magazine holds eight cartridges and is inserted in the grip or butt. The expert witness said that he fired four shots at two separate targets in seven and a half seconds, taking aim each time he pulled the trigger. However, if the weapon were fired rapidly without aiming, the clip could be emptied in two and a half seconds. A bullet hole in the back of Sutton's jacket had powder residue around it, indicating that the muzzle of the weapon was six to 15 inches away from the deceased when it was fired.

The deceased McRae lived with his parents whose home is across the street from the Gold Star Trailer Park. The deceased Sutton also lived with his parents whose home is about three-quarters of a mile from the trailer park.

On January 22, 1979, Sutton had been at the home of a friend, one Langley, from morning until late afternoon during which time Sutton consumed approximately 12 bottles of beer. After going home for dinner, Sutton returned to Langley's home and they again began drinking. McRae arrived shortly after 7:00 p.m. During the evening Sutton drank a further eight bottles of beer and McRae had four bottles. They left together around 9:30 p.m. It is 2.6 miles from the Langley home to the Gold Star Trailer Park. Staff-Sergeant Smith testified that he could detect an odour of alcohol emanating from the bodies of the deceased. A blood sample taken from McRae contained 54 mg of alcohol per 100 cubic centimetres of blood, representing approximately the equivalent of two bottles of beer remaining in his system at the time of death. The blood sample taken from Sutton contained 133 mg of alcohol per 100 cubic centimetres of blood, the equivalent of six bottles of beer at the time of death. About an ounce of marijuana was found in McRae's pocket and both the deceased had on their persons devices used for smoking marijuana.

The respondent testified in his own defence. He said that he had purchased the Baretta hand-gun in 1964, and brought it with him when he came to Canada in 1968. He said that while he and his family lived at the store, he kept the pistol in the bedroom, hidden away from the children. After he purchased the house in August, 1978, he was alone in the store at night, and when his wife and children left the store each night after having dinner with him, he would put the pistol on the shelf beneath the cash register.

The respondent had had some previous difficulties with the deceased of a rather minor nature. On one occasion in 1977 or 1978, they had purchased two bottles of Coca Cola, gargled with it and spit it on the floor. He called the police and the officer told them that if they ever did that again the police would see that they cleaned up the store. On another occasion they broke the light above the door which illuminates the store window by throwing snowballs at it. In January, 1978, as a result of what a child told him, the respondent went outside and saw Sutton carrying a five-gallon container. He called him, went to the pump and found five gallons of gasoline were missing. He telephoned the police who followed footprints in the snow to the McRae home, but Mrs. McRae said that there were no young men there.

The respondent testified that just before closing time on the evening of January 22, 1979, Sutton and McRae entered the store. McRae put his foot on the chocolate display rack. The respondent said he told McRae to take his boot off the display rack and that McRae, from the look that he gave the respondent, did not like what the respondent said to him. The respondent said that he began to get nervous and frightened. When Sutton purchased two packages of "gumballs," he threw a dime at the respondent, and it went on the floor. The respondent said he picked the dime off the floor and put it on the counter, but did not open the cash register because he was afraid. While the respondent was bending down to pick up the dime, Sutton put the gum in his mouth, chewed it, removed it from his mouth and threw it in the respondent's face. The physical findings at the scene tend to confirm this part of the respondent's evidence. Sutton said the gum was no good. The respondent took the dime from the counter and said "Take your dime and leave, please, I want to close." The respondent said that Sutton swung with his closed fist at the respondent's face, but missed when he ducked back. The respondent said that he was frightened. He told Sutton to go away, and that he was going to call the police. Sutton put his hand in his pocket and at the same time asked the respondent "for the money." Sutton said he would kill him before he called the police. The respondent said he heard the words "son-of-a-bitch" and "bastard," but did not know who said them. When Sutton asked for the money, he put out his hand towards the cash register "to open the cash register." The respondent testified that when Sutton put his hand in his pocket, he believed Sutton wanted "to steal, rob the place and in order to do so they would kill [him]." He thought they would kill him and he was very frightened. The respondent said he grabbed the pistol and fired. He did not know exactly how many times he fired. He said he did not mean to kill either of the deceased, but he believed that if he had not used the gun, he would "be the one that was dead."

. . .

I turn now to the grounds of appeal.

Whether the Trial Judge Erred in Admitting Evidence of Specific Acts of the Deceased Which Were Not Known to the Respondent

Mr. Hunt for the Crown contended that the trial judge erred in holding that certain specific acts of the deceased which were not known to the respondent were admissible as corroborative of the respondent's evidence with respect to the events in question.

The learned trial judge, after hearing argument on the question, permitted counsel for the respondent to adduce evidence with respect to prior acts of violence or threats of violence, not known to the respondent, by Sutton and McRae directed at other persons. The defence then adduced evidence with respect to the following occurrences.

[Justice Martin then reviewed three prior incidents, unknown to the accused at the time of the shooting, in which Sutton and McRae engaged in unprovoked acts of aggression and violence—the pursuit and assault of a motorist, a dangerous car chase, and the unprovoked assault of a pedestrian.]

It is well established that where self-defence is raised, evidence not only of previous assaults by the deceased, known to the accused, towards third persons, is admissible to show the accused's reasonable apprehension of violence from the deceased. Evidence of the deceased's reputation for violence, known to the accused, is admissible on the same principle: see *R v. Drouin* (1909), 15 CCC 205 and commentary at p. 207; *R v. Scott* (1910), 15 CCC 442; *Wigmore on Evidence*, 3rd ed., vol. II (1940), pp. 44-52; *Phipson on Evidence*, 12th ed. (1976), pp. 188, 228.

Obviously, evidence of previous acts of violence by the deceased, not known to the accused, is not relevant to show the reasonableness of the accused's apprehension of an impending attack. However, there is impressive support for the proposition that, where self-defence is raised, evidence of the deceased's character (i.e., disposition) for violence is admissible to show the probability of the deceased having been the aggressor and to support the accused's evidence that he was attacked by the deceased.

. . .

Dean Wigmore would require as a condition of the admissibility of evidence with respect to the uncommunicated character of the deceased for violence, where self-defence is an issue, the existence of some other appreciable evidence of the deceased's aggression on the occasion in question; otherwise, the deceased's bad character may be put forward improperly as a mere excuse for the killing under the pretext of evidencing his aggression (*ibid.*, pp. 469-70). I would agree with this limitation. The additional evidence of the deceased's aggression may, in my view, however, emanate from the accused.

We were not referred by counsel to any Canadian or Commonwealth decision on the question of the admissibility of evidence of the deceased's character (disposition) for violence, not known to the accused, as evidence of the probability of the deceased's aggression where self-defence is raised as an issue. However the admission of such evidence accords in principle with the view expressed by this Court that the disposition of a person to do a certain act is relevant to indicate the probability of his having done or not having done the act. The law prohibits the prosecution from introducing evidence for the purpose of showing that the *accused* is a person who by reason of his criminal character (disposition) is likely to have committed the crime charged, on policy grounds, not because of lack of relevance. There is, however, no rule of policy which excludes evidence of the disposition of a third person for violence where that disposition has probative value on some issue before the jury: see *R v. McMillan* (1975), 23 CCC (2d) 160 at p. 167; affirmed, 33 CCC (2d) 360; *R v. Schell and Paquette* (1977), 33 CCC (2d) 422 at p. 426.

. . .

To sum up, the disposition of a third person, if relevant and otherwise admissible, may be proved: (a) by evidence of reputation; (b) by proof of specific acts, and (c) by psychiatric evidence if the disposition in question falls within the proper sphere of expert evidence.

In the present case, since the disposition of the deceased for violence was not sought to be proved by psychiatric evidence, the admissibility of the impugned evidence did not depend upon the disposition for violence being a characteristic feature of an abnormal class of persons.

It is not a condition of the admissibility of previous acts of violence by the deceased, where self-defence is an issue, that the proffered evidence meet the test for the introduction of similar fact evidence against an accused. Evidence of prior acts of bad conduct of an accused which has no probative value other than to permit an inference that the *accused* is a person who by reason of his criminal conduct or character is likely to have committed the offence charged is excluded by a rule of policy. Thus, the admission of

similar fact evidence against an accused is exceptional, being allowed only if it has substantial probative value on some issue, otherwise than as proof of propensity (unless the
propensity is so highly distinctive or unique as to constitute a signature). No such policy
rule operates to exclude evidence of propensity with respect to a person other than the
accused where that person's propensity to act in a particular way is relevant to an issue in
the case.

I agree, of course, that evidence of previous acts of violence by the deceased, not known
to the accused, must be confined to evidence of previous acts of violence which may
legitimately and reasonably assist the jury in arriving at a just verdict with respect to the
accused's claim of self-defence. To exclude, however, evidence offered by the accused
which is relevant to prove his innocence would not, in my view, be in the interests of
justice.

Since evidence of prior acts of violence by the deceased is likely to arouse feelings of
hostility against the deceased, there must inevitably be some element of discretion in the
determination whether the proffered evidence has sufficient probative value for the purpose for which it is tendered to justify its admission. Moreover, great care must be taken
to ensure that such evidence, if admitted, is not misused.

In the present case, the impugned evidence discloses serious acts of unprovoked violence and intimidation by both the deceased, acting together, on three occasions which
were reasonably proximate in time to the occurrence in question, and, in my view, such
evidence had significant probative value on the issue whether the deceased attacked the
respondent in the manner that he alleged on the occasion in question.

· · ·

There is one further observation I would make with respect to the following statement
in the reasons given by the trial judge for admitting evidence of previous acts of violence
by the deceased:

> While the matter has not been argued it would seem to me that the Crown can introduce
> evidence in rebuttal which would contradict the proposed evidence as to the disposition of
> the victims, but cannot offer evidence as to the disposition of the accused that would not
> have been admissible as part of its case.

The learned trial judge was clearly right in stating that the respondent having introduced
evidence that the deceased were of violent disposition, the Crown was entitled to refute
this evidence by calling evidence that the deceased were of peaceable disposition. Moreover, the respondent having introduced evidence that he was a person of peaceable
character it was also open to the Crown to call evidence to rebut such evidence of peaceable character. I would wish, however, to guard myself against being taken to hold that,
even if the respondent had not adduced evidence of his peaceable character, it would not
have been open to the Crown, to adduce evidence in reply with respect to the respondent's
disposition for violence, if such were the case, as the trial judge's reasons seem to imply.
It may be that by introducing evidence of the deceased's character for violence, an accused
impliedly puts his own character for violence in issue. See *Wigmore on Evidence*, 3rd ed.,
vol. I (1940) at p. 472. However, I set aside this question until it requires to be decided.

· · ·

It may appear to one detached from the events and assessing those events only in light
of the transcript that the force used by the respondent was excessive. It is rarely possible,

however, to capture the atmosphere of a trial by a reading of the transcript. The jury, representing a cross-section of the community, and having the advantage of hearing and seeing the witnesses including the respondent, were in a much better position than any appellate court to judge whether the respondent in the particular circumstances was acting under a *reasonable* apprehension of death or grievous bodily harm and believed on *reasonable* and probable grounds that he could not preserve himself from death or grievous bodily harm otherwise than by doing what he did. The jury resolved those questions in favour of the respondent.

For the reasons given, I would dismiss the appeal.

Can you think of other defences to which the propensity for violence or bad character of the victim or another third party might be relevant?

In *R v Khan* (2004), 189 CCC (3d) 49 (Ont Sup Ct J), the accused alleged that he had been the victim of racial profiling and sought to introduce evidence that the same officers who had arrested him had, on another instance, engaged in racial profiling. Applying some of the factors set out in *Handy*, Molloy J refused to admit the evidence in this case on the basis that it had insufficient probative value; however, she accepted that such evidence could be admissible in other circumstances.

As you have seen in both *McMillan* and *Scopelliti*, an accused who introduces evidence of another person's general propensity for violence or bad acts as part of his or her defence does so at some risk. In so doing, the accused may put his or her character in issue, opening the door to the Crown introducing rebuttal evidence of the accused's bad character. This is justified on the basis that preventing the Crown from adducing such evidence once the accused has painted a picture of the bad character of a third party might give the jury a distorted picture of the facts, leaving the incorrect impression that the accused is of good or unblemished character: see *R v Parsons* (1993), 84 CCC (3d) 226 at 237-38 (Ont CA); *R v Williams*, 2008 ONCA 413, 233 CCC (3d) 40. Of course, the introduction of such evidence is subject to the judge's residual discretion, and if the Crown is permitted to introduce evidence of the bad character of the accused, that evidence may only be used to refute any implicit suggestion that the accused is—in comparison to the third party—not the kind of person likely to have committed the offence.

B. Complainants in Sexual Assault Cases

At common law, in a trial of a sexual offence, an accused could adduce evidence of the complainant's past sexual history and of her poor reputation for chastity. Such evidence was thought to be relevant to both consent and credibility. A woman who had shown a "propensity" to consent could be viewed as more likely to have consented in the case at hand; moreover, at a time when sexual experience was viewed as a reflection of a woman's bad character, this evidence was said to establish that she was less worthy of belief. Now called the "twin myths," these inferences from past sexual conduct to a higher likelihood to consent and lower general credibility were manifestly based on sexist and prejudicial assumptions about women and how they ought to behave.

Concerns about the effects of these inferences on the equality, dignity, and privacy of complainants, as well as about the chronic underreporting of sexual offences, led Parliament to enact strict statutory limits on the use of such evidence. In Chapter 3, Section II, you read *R v Seaboyer*, [1991] 2 SCR 577, in which a majority of the court ruled that s 276 was unconstitutional because it unduly limited an accused's ss 7 and 11(d) fair trial rights. However, the court upheld s 277, finding that it did not exclude any evidence that an accused was constitutionally entitled to lead. You may wish to review this decision.

Parliament responded to *Seaboyer* and the court's guidance in that case with the following provisions of the *Criminal Code*, which now govern the use of sexual history evidence in trials of sexual offences:

> 276(1) In proceedings in respect of an offence under section 151, 152, 153, 153.1, 155 or 159, subsection 160(2) or (3) or section 170, 171, 172, 173, 271, 272 or 273, evidence that the complainant has engaged in sexual activity, whether with the accused or with any other person, is not admissible to support an inference that, by reason of the sexual nature of that activity, the complainant

> > (a)   is more likely to have consented to the sexual activity that forms the subject-matter of the charge; or

> > (b)   is less worthy of belief.

> (2) In proceedings in respect of an offence referred to in subsection (1), no evidence shall be adduced by or on behalf of the accused that the complainant has engaged in sexual activity other than the sexual activity that forms the subject-matter of the charge, whether with the accused or with any other person, unless the judge, provincial court judge or justice determines, in accordance with the procedures set out in sections 276.1 and 276.2, that the evidence

> > (a)   is of specific instances of sexual activity;

> > (b)   is relevant to an issue at trial; and

> > (c)   has significant probative value that is not substantially outweighed by the danger of prejudice to the proper administration of justice.

> (3) In determining whether evidence is admissible under subsection (2), the judge, provincial court judge or justice shall take into account

> > (a)   the interests of justice, including the right of the accused to make a full answer and defence;

> > (b)   society's interest in encouraging the reporting of sexual assault offences;

> > (c)   whether there is a reasonable prospect that the evidence will assist in arriving at a just determination in the case;

> > (d)   the need to remove from the fact-finding process any discriminatory belief or bias;

> > (e)   the risk that the evidence may unduly arouse sentiments of prejudice, sympathy or hostility in the jury;

> > (f)   the potential prejudice to the complainant's personal dignity and right of privacy;

> > (g)   the right of the complainant and of every individual to personal security and to the full protection and benefit of the law; and

> > (h)   any other factor that the judge, provincial court judge or justice considers relevant.

> · · ·

277. In proceedings in respect of an offence under section 151, 152, 153, 153.1, 155 or 159, subsection 160(2) or (3) or section 170, 171, 172, 173, 271, 272 or 273, evidence of sexual reputation, whether general or specific, is not admissible for the purpose of challenging or supporting the credibility of the complainant.

In the following case, the Supreme Court of Canada explained and upheld the constitutionality of the revised version of s 276.

R v Darrach

2000 SCC 46, [2000] 2 SCR 443

McLachlin CJC and L'Heureux-Dubé, Gonthier, Iacobucci, Major, Bastarache, Binnie, Arbour, LeBel JJ (12 October 2000)

GONTHIER J:

I. Introduction

[1] The proper use of a complainant's sexual history in sexual offence prosecutions was last before this Court in *R. v. Seaboyer*, [1991] 2 S.C.R. 577. There the Court struck down an earlier version of s. 276 of the *Criminal Code*, R.S.C. 1985, c. C-46, because it excluded all evidence about a complainant's sexual history from the judicial process, subject to three exceptions. The majority found that s. 276 could potentially exclude evidence of critical relevance (at p. 616). Parliament then enacted the current s. 276 in Bill C-49 in 1992 (now S.C. 1992, c. 38). It essentially codifies the decision in *Seaboyer* and provides a mechanism for the trial judge to determine the admissibility of evidence of prior sexual activity.

[2] The current s. 276 categorically prohibits evidence of a complainant's sexual history only when it is used to support one of two general inferences. These are that a person is more likely to have consented to the alleged assault and that she is less credible as a witness by virtue of her prior sexual experience. Evidence of sexual activity may be admissible, however, to substantiate other inferences. Sections 276.1 and 276.2 provide a procedure to determine the admissibility of such evidence. In brief, the defence must file a written affidavit; if the judge finds that it discloses relevant evidence capable of being admissible under s. 276(2), the judge will hold a *voir dire* to determine the admissibility of the evidence the defence seeks to adduce.

[3] The accused challenges the constitutionality of parts of s. 276 under the *Canadian Charter of Rights and Freedoms* and the way in which they were interpreted by the trial judge. In my view, his challenge fails. The current version of s. 276 is carefully crafted to comport with the principles of fundamental justice. It protects the integrity of the judicial process while at the same time respecting the rights of the people involved. The complainant's privacy and dignity are protected by a procedure that also vindicates the accused's right to make full answer and defence. The procedure does not violate the accused's s. 7 *Charter* right to a fair trial nor his s. 11(c) right not to testify against himself or his s. 11(d) right to a fair hearing. For the reasons below, I find that the impugned sections of the law are constitutional and that their application by the trial judge was beyond reproach.

· · ·

VI. Analysis

[20] The current version of s. 276 is in essence a codification by Parliament of the Court's guidelines in *Seaboyer*. It contains substantive sections that prevent evidence of a complainant's past sexual activity from being used for improper purposes and procedural sections that enforce this rule. ...

. . .

A. The Approach to Sections 7, 11(c) and 11(d) of the Charter

. . .

[24] [T]he Court's jurisprudence ... has consistently held that the principles of fundamental justice enshrined in s. 7 protect more than the rights of the accused. ... One of the implications of this analysis is that while the right to make full answer and defence and the principle against self-incrimination are certainly core principles of fundamental justice, they can be respected without the accused being entitled to "the most favourable procedures that could possibly be imagined" (*R. v. Lyons*, [1987] 2 S.C.R. 309, at p. 362; cited in *Mills*, ... [*R v Mills*, [1999] 3 SCR 668] at para. 72). Nor is the accused entitled to have procedures crafted that take only his interests into account. Still less is he entitled to procedures that would distort the truth-seeking function of a trial by permitting irrelevant and prejudicial material at trial.

[25] In *Seaboyer*, the Court found that the principles of fundamental justice include the three purposes of s. 276 identified above: protecting the integrity of the trial by excluding evidence that is misleading, protecting the rights of the accused, as well as encouraging the reporting of sexual violence and protecting "the security and privacy of the witnesses" (p. 606). This was affirmed in *Mills*, *supra*, at para. 72. The Court crafted its guidelines in *Seaboyer* in accordance with these principles, and it is in relation to these principles that the effects of s. 276 on the accused must be evaluated.

[26] The Court in *Mills* upheld the constitutionality of the provisions in the *Criminal Code* that control the use of personal and therapeutic records in trials of sexual offences. The use of these records in evidence is analogous in many ways to the use of evidence of prior sexual activity, and the protections in the *Criminal Code* surrounding the use of records at trial are motivated by similar policy considerations. L'Heureux-Dubé J. has warned that therapeutic records should not become a tool for circumventing s. 276: "[w]e must not allow the defence to do indirectly what it cannot do directly" (*R. v. O'Connor*, [1995] 4 S.C.R. 411, at para. 122, and *R. v. Osolin*, [1993] 4 S.C.R. 595, at p. 624). Academic commentators have observed that the use of therapeutic records increased with the enactment of s. 276 nonetheless (see K. Kelly, " 'You must be crazy if you think you were raped': Reflections on the Use of Complainants' Personal and Therapy Records in Sexual Assault Trials" (1997), 9 *C.J.W.L.* 178, at p. 181)

. . .

[31] In the case at bar, I affirm the reasons in *Seaboyer* and find that none of the accused's rights are infringed by s. 276 as he alleges. *Seaboyer* provides a basic justification for the legislative scheme in s. 276, including the determination of relevance as well as the prejudicial and probative value of the evidence. *Mills* and *White* show how the impact of s. 276 on the principles of fundamental justice relied on by the accused should be assessed in light of the other principles of fundamental justice that s. 276 was designed to protect.

The reasons in *Mills* are apposite because they demonstrate how the same principles of equality, privacy and fairness can be reconciled. I shall show below how the procedure created by s. 276 to protect the trial process from distortion and to protect complainants is consistent with the principles of fundamental justice. It is fair to the accused and properly reconciles the divergent interests at play, as the Court suggested in *Seaboyer*.

B. The Substantive Sections

(1) Section 276(1): The Exclusionary Rule

[32] The accused objects to the exclusionary rule itself in s. 276(1) on the grounds that it is a "blanket exclusion" that prevents him from adducing evidence necessary to make full answer and defence, as guaranteed by ss. 7 and 11(d) of the *Charter*. He is mistaken in his characterization of the rule. Far from being a "blanket exclusion," s. 276(1) only prohibits the use of evidence of past sexual activity when it is offered to support two specific, illegitimate inferences. These are known as the "twin myths," namely that a complainant is more likely to have consented or that she is less worthy of belief "by reason of the sexual nature of the activity" she once engaged in.

[33] This section gives effect to McLachlin J.'s finding in *Seaboyer* that the "twin myths" are simply not relevant at trial. They are not probative of consent or credibility and can severely distort the trial process. Section 276(1) also clarifies *Seaboyer* in several respects. Section 276 applies to all sexual activity, whether with the accused or with someone else. It also applies to non-consensual as well as consensual sexual activity, as this Court found implicitly in *R. v. Crosby*, [1995] 2 S.C.R. 912, at para. 17. Although the *Seaboyer* guidelines referred to "consensual sexual conduct" (pp. 634-35), Parliament enacted the new version of s. 276 without the word "consensual." Evidence of non-consensual sexual acts can equally defeat the purposes of s. 276 by distorting the trial process when it is used to evoke stereotypes such as that women who have been assaulted must have deserved it and that they are unreliable witnesses, as well as by deterring people from reporting assault by humiliating them in court. The admissibility of evidence of non-consensual sexual activity is determined by the procedures in s. 276. Section 276 also settles any ambiguity about whether the "twin myths" are limited to inferences about "unchaste" women in particular; they are not (as discussed by C. Boyle and M. MacCrimmon, "The Constitutionality of Bill C-49: Analyzing Sexual Assault As If Equality Really Mattered" (1998), 41 *Crim. L.Q.* 198, at pp. 231-32).

[34] The *Criminal Code* excludes all discriminatory generalizations about a complainant's disposition to consent or about her credibility based on the *sexual nature* of her past sexual activity on the grounds that these are improper lines of reasoning. This was the import of the Court's findings in *Seaboyer* about how sexist beliefs about women distort the trial process. The text of the exclusionary rule in s. 276(1) diverges very little from the guidelines in *Seaboyer*. The mere fact that the wording differs between the Court's guidelines and Parliament's enactment is itself immaterial. ...

[35] The phrase "by reason of the sexual nature of the activity" in s. 276 is a clarification by Parliament that it is inferences from the *sexual nature* of the activity, as opposed to inferences from other potentially relevant features of the activity, that are prohibited. If evidence of sexual activity is proffered for its non-sexual features, such as to show a pattern of conduct or a prior inconsistent statement, it may be permitted. The phrase "by

reason of the sexual nature of the activity" has the same effect as the qualification "solely to support the inference" in *Seaboyer* in that it limits the exclusion of evidence to that used to invoke the "twin myths" (p. 635).

[36] This Court has already had occasion to admit evidence of prior sexual activity under the current version of s. 276. In *Crosby, supra*, such evidence was admissible because it was inextricably linked to a prior inconsistent statement that was relevant to the complainant's credibility (at para. 14). This case itself demonstrates that s. 276 does not function in practice as a blanket exclusion, as alleged by the accused. On the contrary, s. 276 controls the admissibility of evidence of sexual activity by providing judges with criteria and procedures to help them exercise their discretion to admit it. I explain below why the procedure to assess relevance is constitutional. Suffice it here to say that it is this procedure that makes the *Seaboyer* guidelines and the current version of s. 276 constitutional where the earlier version of s. 276 was not.

[37] An accused has never had a right to adduce irrelevant evidence. Nor does he have the right to adduce misleading evidence to support illegitimate inferences: "the accused is not permitted to distort the truth-seeking function of the trial process" (*Mills, supra*, at para. 74). Because s. 276(1) is an evidentiary rule that only excludes material that is not relevant, it cannot infringe the accused's right to make full answer and defence. Section 276(2) is more complicated, and I turn to it now.

(2) Section 276(2)(c): "Significant Probative Value"

[38] If evidence is not barred by s. 276(1) because it is tendered to support a permitted inference, the judge must still weigh its probative value against its prejudicial effect to determine its admissibility. This essentially mirrors the common law guidelines in *Seaboyer* which contained this balancing test (at p. 635). The accused takes issue with the fact that s. 276(2)(c) specifically requires that the evidence have "significant probative value." The word "significant" was added by Parliament but it does not render the provision unconstitutional by raising the threshold for the admissibility of evidence to the point that it is unfair to the accused.

[39] It may be noted that the word "significant" is not found in the French text; the law speaks simply of "*valeur probante.*" The rule of equal authenticity and the rule against unconstitutional interpretation require that the two versions be reconciled where possible. The interpretation of "significant" by the Ontario Court of Appeal satisfies this requirement: Morden A.C.J.O found that "the evidence is not to be so trifling as to be incapable, in the context of all the evidence, of raising a reasonable doubt" (p. 16). At the same time, Morden A.C.J.O. agrees with *R. v. Santocono* (1996), 91 O.A.C. 26 (C.A.), at p. 29, where s. 276(2)(c) was interpreted to mean that "it was not necessary for the appellant to demonstrate 'strong and compelling' reasons for admission of the evidence." This standard is not a departure from the conventional rules of evidence. I agree with the Court of Appeal that the word "significant," on a textual level, is reasonably capable of being read in accordance with ss. 7 and 11(d) and the fair trial they protect.

[40] The context of the word "significant" in the provision in which it occurs substantiates this interpretation. Section 276(2)(c) allows a judge to admit evidence of "*significant probative value that is not substantially* outweighed by the danger of prejudice to the proper administration of justice" (emphasis added). The adverb "substantially" serves to protect the accused by raising the standard for the judge to exclude evidence once the

accused has shown it to have significant probative value. In a sense, both sides of the equation are heightened in this test, which serves to direct judges to the serious ramifications of the use of evidence of prior sexual activity for all parties in these cases.

[41] In light of the purposes of s. 276, the use of the word "significant" is consistent with both the majority and the minority reasons in *Seaboyer*. Section 276 is designed to prevent the use of evidence of prior sexual activity for improper purposes. The requirement of "significant probative value" serves to exclude evidence of trifling relevance that, even though not used to support the two forbidden inferences, would still endanger the "proper administration of justice." The Court has recognized that there are inherent "damages and disadvantages presented by the admission of such evidence" (*Seaboyer, supra,* at p. 634). As Morden A.C.J.O. puts it, evidence of sexual activity must be significantly probative if it is to overcome its prejudicial effect. The *Criminal Code* codifies this reality.

[42] By excluding misleading evidence while allowing the accused to adduce evidence that meets the criteria of s. 276(2), s. 276 enhances the fairness of trials of sexual offences. Section 11(d) guarantees a fair trial. Fairness under s. 11(d) is determined in the context of the trial process as a whole (*R. v. Stoddart* (1987), 37 C.C.C. (3d) 351 (Ont. C.A.), at pp. 365-66). As L'Heureux-Dubé J. wrote in *Crosby, supra,* at para. 11, "[s]ection 276 cannot be interpreted so as to deprive a person of a fair defence." At the same time, the accused's right to make full answer and defence, as was held in *Mills, supra,* at para. 75, is not "automatically breached where he or she is deprived of relevant information." Nor is it necessarily breached when the accused is not permitted to adduce relevant information that is not "significantly" probative, under a rule of evidence that protects the trial from the distorting effects of evidence of prior sexual activity.

[43] When the trial judge determines the admissibility of evidence under s. 276(2), she is to take into account the multiple factors in s. 276(3), which include "the right of the accused to make a full answer and defence" in s. 276(3)(a). Section 276 is designed to exclude irrelevant information and only that relevant information that is more prejudicial to the administration of justice than it is probative. The accused's right to a fair trial is, of course, of fundamental concern to the administration of justice. ... Thus the threshold criteria that evidence be of "significant" probative value does not prevent an accused from making full answer and defence to the charges against him. Consequently his *Charter* rights under ss. 7 and 11(d) are not infringed by s. 276(2)(c).

[Justice Gonthier then considered and upheld the constitutionality of the associated procedural provisions, before concluding.]

VII. *Conclusion*

[71] On the basis of this Court's decision in *Seaboyer*, Parliament gave the trial judge the role of deciding whether a complainant's sexual history is relevant in the trial of a sexual offence. She is to exercise her discretion within the structure of a procedure created by s. 276. The legislation lists factors to take into account, similar to those upheld by this Court's decision in *Mills, supra,* which prominently include the accused's right to make full answer and defence in s. 276(3)(a). This discretion, of course, cannot be exercised in an unconstitutional manner. The accused's constitutional rights are protected by this legislation.

. . .

[73] The appeal is dismissed.

Section 277 establishes a complete bar to the admissibility of sexual reputation evidence on the issue of the complainant's credibility. As the court explained in *Darrach*, s 276 only imposes an absolute prohibition on evidence of specific instances of sexual activity offered to advance, on the basis of *the sexual nature of that activity*, one of the two prohibited inferences. If evidence is not offered for its sexual nature or does not support one or both of the "twin myths," its admissibility is assessed pursuant to s 276(2), informed by the factors listed in s 276(3). As such, and as acknowledged in *Darrach*, some evidence of the prior sexual activity of a complainant might still be admitted at a trial on a sexual offence.

Consider, for example, the case of *R v Butts*, 2012 ONCA 24. The accused was charged with sexual assault of the complainant. In the course of the trial, the Crown suggested that the complainant would not have consented to sex with the accused because she was loyal to her boyfriend and because she was too upset at the time in question to have consensual sex at all. The Court of Appeal held that the defence should have been permitted to establish that, very shortly after the alleged assault, the complainant had sex with another man. The court explained that, on its own, this evidence would be excluded pursuant to s 276(1); however, "given the manner in which the Crown chose to present its case, the excluded evidence acquired significant probative value" (at para 24) that warranted its admission.

IV. CHARACTER IN CIVIL CASES

As noted above in Section I, when a person's character is directly in issue in a civil case, there are no special rules governing the admissibility of character evidence. But beyond this uncommon circumstance, what principles guide the use of character evidence in civil cases?

A. Evidence of Good Character

Evidence of good character is not generally admissible in civil proceedings. This rule was classically stated in *Attorney-General v Radloff* (1854), 156 ER 366 at 371 (Ex Ct), in which the rationale given was that, whereas "there is a fair and just presumption that a person of good character would not commit a crime," no similar inference from character to propensity to commit a civil wrong could be made. In essence, on this explanation, such evidence is excluded on grounds of irrelevance: see *Deep v Wood* (1983), 143 DLR (3d) 246 at 250 (Ont CA). Whether or not this is a convincing rationale, this general rule can be supported on the basis that we allow the accused to offer evidence of his or her good character as a matter of full answer and defence and in light of the presumption of innocence; in civil proceedings, in which those principles are inapplicable and no liberty interests are engaged, the introduction of good character evidence is simply inefficient, distracting from the main issues at trial, and may be unfair to the opposing party. There is authority, however, that if the civil matter involves claims about conduct that is criminal in character, a party should be allowed to introduce evidence of his or her own good character: see *Plester v Wawanesa Mutual Insurance Co* (2006), 269 DLR (4th) 624 at paras 41-44 (Ont CA).

B. Evidence of Bad Character: Similar Facts

Similarly, given the priority on efficiency and fairness as between the parties in civil litigation, evidence of the bad character of one of the parties is admissible in civil cases only if it satisfies the similar fact evidence rule. There is some authority that the test for the admission of similar fact evidence in civil cases should be the same as that used in criminal cases: see *Statton v Johnson*, 1999 BCCA 170, 172 DLR (4th) 535 at para 45. Yet given that the presumption of innocence and concerns about wrongful conviction are not at play in civil cases, it would seem that the "moral prejudice" at issue in offers of similar fact evidence is much diminished in a civil setting; the prohibited character inference that shapes the strict approach to similar fact evidence in criminal cases is not similarly applicable. Accordingly, courts generally apply a somewhat relaxed form of the similar fact analysis that should not begin with a presumption of inadmissibility. Consider, for example, the following case decided by Lord Denning.

Mood Music Publishing Co Ltd v De Wolfe Ltd
[1976] 1 All ER 763 (CA)
Lord Denning MR and Orr and Browne LJJ (28 October 1975)

LORD DENNING MR: The plaintiffs, Mood Music Publishing Co Ltd, keep a library consisting of records of musical works. They own the copyright in the works and supply them to television producers, who use them for background music for their productions. One of the works in the plaintiffs' library is a musical work called "Sogno Nostalgico." It was composed by an Italian, Mr. Sciascia, in 1963. The copyright of it was assigned to the plaintiffs in 1964. A record was made of it in Italy. One of the records was brought to England and kept in the plaintiffs' library here. After 1967 copies were made here and were available in the library.

Mr. de Wolfe is in the same line of business. In 1967 he had in his library a musical work called "Girl in the Dark." He supplied it to television producers for use in a play called "Magnum for Schneider." Someone in the plaintiffs' employment saw that play and heard the music. He thought that "Girl in the Dark" was very like "Sogno Nostalgico" and might have been copied from it. So on 10th March 1967 the plaintiffs wrote to Mr. de Wolfe complaining that "Girl in the Dark" was an infringement of "Sogno Nostalgico."

On 23rd March 1967 the solicitors for Mr. de Wolfe replied in these terms:

Girl in the Dark

It appears from your letter that you have in your library a musical work entitled "Sogno Nostalgico" which apparently bears some resemblance to the above work which is included in our Clients' Music Library and in which they own the copyright. Our Clients' work was composed by J. Trombey who resides in Holland and from whom they took an assignment of copyright in 1966. The fact that your work [i.e., Sogno Nostalgico] was composed prior to our Clients' work is not really relevant in the circumstances as, of course, mere similarity between two musical works does not constitute any infringement. Infringement only occurs where there has been an actual copying of a copyright work by another person without the owner's consent. It would appear therefore that the similarity between the works is coincidental, in which event neither work infringes the other.

That letter shows that Mr. de Wolfe recognised that the two works were very similar. Also, that the plaintiffs' work was produced prior to his own. But that his answer to the claim was that the similarity had arisen by sheer coincidence without any copying from the plaintiffs' work.

[The plaintiffs sought to introduce similar fact evidence. The trial judge ruled the evidence admissible, and the defendants brought an interlocutory appeal to the Court of Appeal.]

In order to appreciate the point, I must state the nature of the evidence which is sought to be admitted. One matter relates to a "trap order" which was given by or on behalf of the plaintiffs. It was arranged in this way. The plaintiffs made a record of a distinctive piece of music called "Fixed Idea." The copyright undoubtedly belonged to the plaintiffs. They wrote on the record "Taken off air U.S.A." That was not true. It was not taken from a piece which had been broadcast in the United States. It had been made by the plaintiffs from their own copyright. Those words "Taken off air U.S.A." would lead anyone to believe that it was copyright, though not in the plaintiffs. The plaintiffs then got Mr. Shillingford, an agent provocateur, to take it to the defendants and ask them to make a new record from that piece of music. Mr. Shillingford saw a Mr. Chambers and arranged that, in return for a sum altogether of £250, the defendants would make a new record from that piece of music. Now this is where the defendants fell into the trap. They made the new record, but they called it a de Wolfe work. They called it "Visions." They said the composer was Mr. Reg Tilsley, the defendants were the publishers and £250 had been paid for it.

The plaintiffs say that the work "Visions" is a copy of their own "Fixed Idea," which was their copyright. No doubt they invited it, they asked for it, they paid for it; but here were the defendants copying their music and putting it out to the world as if it was their own publication of a work by a different composer altogether.

The plaintiffs gave notice to the defendants some time ago of their intention to put those matters in evidence relating to the "trap order."

There are two other matters which the plaintiffs desire to give in evidence. They have only been discovered in the last week or so. It appears that records have been made by other publishers of music by Sibelius and Elgar. Both of them are the subject of copyright. We have had them played before us. The plaintiffs say that de Wolfe has recorded music which bears a close resemblance to those copyright airs. They were also played before us. There is indeed a very close resemblance so that one may well think that the defendants may well have copied them from the copyright works.

The plaintiffs wish to give those matters in evidence. They say that they go to show that, in other cases, Mr. de Wolfe has been reproducing musical works which are subject to copyright; and so he may have done the same in regard to the work "Sogno Nostalgico." Counsel for the defendants says that those matters are not admissible.

The admissibility of evidence as to "similar facts" has been much considered in the criminal law. Some of them have reached the highest tribunal, the latest being *Boardman v. Director of Public Prosecutions*, [1974] 3 All ER 887. The criminal courts have been very careful not to admit such evidence unless its probative value is so strong that it should be received in the interests of justice: and its admission will not operate unfairly to the accused. In civil cases the courts have followed a similar line but have not been so chary of admitting it. In civil cases the courts will admit evidence of similar facts if it is logically probative, that is if it is logically relevant in determining the matter which is in issue; provided that it was not oppressive or unfair to the other side; and also that the other side has fair notice of it and is able to deal with it. Instances are: *Brown v. Eastern & Midlands Railway Co* (1889), 22 QBD 391, *Moore v. Ransome's Dock Committee* (1898), 14 TLR 539, *Hales v. Kerr*, [1908] 2 KB 601.

The matter in issue in the present case is whether the resemblances which "Girl in the Dark" bears to "Sogno Nostalgico" are mere coincidences or are due to copying. On that issue it is very relevant to know that there are other cases of musical works which are undoubtedly the subject of copyright, but yet the defendants have produced musical works bearing close resemblance to them. Whereas it might be due to mere coincidence in one case, it is very unlikely that there would be coincidences in four cases. It is rather like *R v. Sims*, [1946] 1 All ER 698 at 701, where it was said: "The probative force of all the acts together is much greater than one alone." So the probative force of four resemblances together is much better than one alone.

Counsel for the defendants urges that this is virtually a charge of fraud; and fraud is not pleaded. But in infringement of copyright fraud is not an essential ingredient. Reproduction without the owner's consent is enough. Even subconscious copying is an infringement. And even if there were a charge of fraud, it would not mean that evidence of similar fraud should be excluded. It might be very relevant to prove the fraud.

It seems to me the judge was right. He said the evidence of these three matters is of sufficient probative weight to be relevant to this issue and should be admitted. Incidentally, he rejected evidence of other matters which was not of sufficient probative value. I would dismiss the appeal.

[Orr and James LJJ agreed.]

How does the test for the admissibility of similar fact evidence in civil cases outlined by Lord Denning MR differ from the test for admissibility in criminal cases? Was the evidence of the defendants' other acts of copying relevant in any way, apart from showing that the defendants had a propensity to copy other publishers' music? Would it matter whether the defendants claimed that all four cases were coincidences?

For examples of civil cases in which courts admitted evidence using a relaxed form of the similar fact test, see *RCMS v GMK*, 2005 SKQB 296; *JG v Tyhurst* (2003), 226 DLR (4th) 447 (BCCA). In *Tyhurst*, the court explicitly used the factors and analytical structure set out in *Handy* to inform its assessment of admissibility. Given the reduced concern about moral prejudice, similar fact analysis in civil cases will turn on a normal balancing of probative value and potential for prejudice, emphasizing issues of reasoning prejudice particularly germane to the civil context, such as fairness as between the parties and concerns about efficiency, confusion, and distraction from the central issues in the case.

PROBLEM (R v GALLOWAY)

To prove its case, the Crown wishes to call evidence regarding certain matters that will undoubtedly serve to portray Martin Galloway in a less than positive light. In addition, the defence is hoping to elicit evidence at the trial to demonstrate that some third party was the likely perpetrator of the murder in the course of a burglary gone wrong.

The Crown wishes to introduce the following evidence at trial:

1. Testimony from Margaret Jenkins. She will describe how she met Martin at a conference in December 2015, and how the two of them thereafter began a passionate but secret love affair that continued throughout 2016, up until Martin's arrest in early December of that year. According to Margaret, she saw Martin two days after Angela's murder. At that time, he expressed concern for the impact of the murder on his children, but did not voice any specific concern for his wife. Rather, it was during this meeting that Martin first mentioned to Margaret the possibility of the two of them moving in together in the near future, a topic he returned to during their conversations throughout 2016 up until the time of his arrest. Is this evidence admissible?

2. Testimony from Stella Smith, Martin's girlfriend for three years while the two of them attended university (1997 to 2000). She will testify about the couple's acrimonious breakup at the end of university, and how Martin seemed to "turn on her" when he decided to end the relationship. She will testify that she took the breakup badly and continued to contact Martin in its aftermath in an effort to make sense of his decision. Martin responded to these overtures with anger and hostility. At one point, Martin said: "Stop calling me, you're starting to make me angry and you don't want to see what I am capable of when I am angry!" Stella will testify that this comment terrified her and that she never called Martin again. Is this evidence admissible?

The defence wishes to cross-examine the lead detective during the investigation regarding the following:

1. At one point during their lengthy investigation, the police had focused their attention on an individual named Kevin Grey. Grey, who is 28 years old, lives with his parents on a rural property about 3 kilometres from the Galloways. Grey has an extensive criminal record dating back to his teenage years, mostly relating to drug offences. That record includes three prior convictions for breaking and entering, as well as two prior convictions for simple assault and one conviction for assault causing bodily harm. With respect to the prior break-ins, they all related to rural properties within a 10-kilometre radius of the Galloways' home. In each case, Grey burglarized barns and garages, never homes, stealing tools, gardening equipment, ATVs, and snowmobiles. During their investigation, police interviewed Grey. He readily acknowledged his earlier crimes, but reports that he has been clean and sober since the fall of 2015 and has not been involved in crime since then. He denied involvement in the Galloway homicide and insisted that he was at home, with his parents, on the evening of Sunday, March 27, 2016. His parents corroborated his alibi. The latent partial palm print on the snow blower was compared to Grey's known prints and eliminated. Grey was asked to produce the shoes he was wearing in April 2016, but was unable to do so.

He claimed that he spilt paint on the shoes and had thrown them out. During his last encounter with the criminal justice system (in July 2015) Grey was still suffering from the effects of severe drug use, which resulted in concerns about his fitness to stand trial. A court-ordered assessment was undertaken. Although Grey was found fit, the psychiatrist who evaluated Grey diagnosed him as a psychopath, opining that he "is completely lacking in empathy and therefore poses a significant danger to others." Assuming that both the detective and the psychiatrist are available to testify, is this evidence regarding Kevin Grey admissible at Martin Galloway's trial?

PART III

Exclusionary Rules Based on Policy

CHAPTER EIGHT

Statements of an Accused and Illegally Obtained Evidence

A number of exclusionary rules are designed to limit the state's ability to obtain and use an accused's self-incriminating statements, and in the case of s 24 of the Charter, any type of illegally obtained evidence. These rules serve to balance the state's need to obtain and use evidence of wrongdoing against individuals' interests in liberty, privacy, and the like. In some cases, the balance between these interests is a zero-sum game: exclusion serves to vindicate individual rights at the expense of truth-seeking. But in others, exclusion may further the search for truth, by either preventing reliance on unreliable evidence or giving witnesses an incentive to testify truthfully.

This chapter examines three sources of these exclusionary rules: the common law, s 24 of the *Canadian Charter of Rights and Freedoms*, Part I of the *Constitution Act, 1982*, being Schedule B to the *Canada Act 1982* (UK), 1982, c 11 [Charter], and ss 13 and 7 of the Charter. The common law precludes the admission of three types of statements made by an accused: (1) involuntary statements made to a "person in authority"; (2) statements obtained in a manner that would "shock the community"; and (3) statements made during undercover sting operations that: (a) are more prejudicial than probative; or (b) were acquired through abusive methods. Section 24(2) of the Charter permits judges to exclude any evidence "obtained in a manner" that violated the Charter if admitting it could "bring the administration of justice into disrepute." Sections 13 and 7 of the Charter provide various kinds of protection to persons compelled to make self-incriminating statements. In this chapter we limit our focus to the rules emanating from these provisions that limit the state's ability to use an accused's previous testimony (or evidence derived therefrom).

I. COMMON LAW

A. The Confessions Rule

Recall from Chapter 4, Section II.F, that hearsay statements by parties are admissible when offered by the opposing party. This exception to the rule against hearsay applies to statements by accused persons offered by the Crown. Where the statement is made to a person not in authority, there are ordinarily no special rules regarding its admissibility: it is simply a party admission. But, according to the common law "confessions rule," an accused person's statement made to a person in authority is not admissible in the Crown's case unless the Crown proves beyond a reasonable doubt that the statement was made voluntarily. This rule raises the following questions: Who is a person in authority? What are the rules governing the *voir dire* concerning the admissibility of the statement? On what grounds may a statement be found involuntary? And what is the status of the common law confessions rule under the Charter?

1. Who Is a Person in Authority?

R v Hodgson
[1998] 2 SCR 449, 127 CCC (3d) 449
Lamer CJ and L'Heureux-Dubé, Gonthier, Cory, McLachlin, Iacobucci, Major,
Bastarache, and Binnie JJ (24 September 1998)

CORY J (Lamer CJ and Gonthier, McLachlin, Iacobucci, Major, and Binnie JJ concurring):
    [1] The same issues must be resolved in both this appeal and that of *R v. Wells*, [1998] 2 SCR 517.
    [2] In both cases, defence counsel did not request a *voir dire* to test the voluntariness of certain out-of-court statements allegedly made by the accused and, as a result, the statements were admitted into evidence. The appellants contend that the trial judge erred in failing to direct a *voir dire* of his own motion to determine whether the statements were given to a person in authority and if so, whether they were made voluntarily.
    [3] In order to determine whether the trial judge erred it is necessary to consider several subsidiary issues. First, does the onus always rest with the defence to request a *voir dire* to test the voluntariness of an accused's out-of-court statements? If not, when and under what circumstances should a trial judge hold a *voir dire* of his or her own motion? Further, is the trial judge's obligation to hold a *voir dire* triggered only where the receiver of the statement is a "conventional" person in authority, or should the obligation

be construed more broadly? Lastly, to what extent should the "person in authority" requirement remain part of the confessions rule?

I. Factual Background

[4] The appellant was a friend of the complainant's family and occasionally babysat the complainant and her siblings. The complainant, who was sixteen years old at the time of trial, testified that commencing when she was approximately seven or eight years of age and continuing until she was approximately eleven years of age, the appellant sexually assaulted her on several occasions. The complainant testified that she never told anyone about the incidents because she was afraid and because the appellant told her that she would get in trouble if she did.

[5] The complainant testified that in 1993, she finally told her mother about these incidents. When the allegations were revealed, the complainant, her mother, her father, and her stepfather went to the appellant's place of employment and confronted him. They all testified that the appellant confessed to having sexually assaulted the complainant on several occasions, that the appellant had said he was sorry, and that he had said he "knew it would catch up with him." The complainant's mother went to call the police, and when she returned she struck the appellant. At some point, the complainant's father pulled out a knife and held it to the appellant's back. The father, stepfather and mother testified that the father pulled the knife after the appellant confessed in order to prevent the appellant from leaving before the police arrived.

[6] At trial, the appellant testified that he was confronted at work by the complainant and her family about the sexual assaults, but he denied making a confession. He stated that he was stunned, shocked and upset by the confrontation and did not want the situation to get blown out of proportion, but that he was neither frightened nor threatened during the confrontation.

[7] At trial, the appellant raised no objection to the admission of the confession evidence. The trial judge relied on this evidence and convicted the appellant.

· · ·

III. Analysis

[12] It "can now be taken to be clearly established in Canada that no statement made out of court by an accused to a person in authority can be admitted into evidence against him unless the prosecution shows, to the satisfaction of the trial judge, that the statement was made freely and voluntarily." See *Erven v. The Queen*, [1979] 1 SCR 926, at p. 931, *per* Dickson J, as he then was. This, of course, is the confessions rule.

[13] The basic issue in this appeal is whether the trial judge erred in failing to hold a *voir dire* of his own motion to test the voluntariness of certain out-of-court statements made by the accused before admitting them. In order to resolve this issue, it is appropriate to consider whether the confessions rule should continue to apply only to statements made to persons in authority, or whether it should be expanded so as to capture the out-of-court statements made by the accused in this case. It will therefore be helpful to begin by examining the history of the confessions rule generally, and the person in authority requirement in particular, in order to understand the purpose and function of the rule in the criminal law.

A. The Confessions Rule and Its Relation to the Person in Authority Requirement

[14] Evidence of a confession has always been accorded great weight by triers of fact. This is a natural manifestation of human experience. It is because of the tremendous significance attributed to confessions and the innate realization that they could be obtained by improper means that the circumstances surrounding a confession have for centuries been carefully scrutinized to determine whether it should be admitted. A confession is not excluded, however, simply because of the risk that a conviction may result, but because of the greater risk that the conviction will be unfairly obtained and unjust. The unfairness of admitting a confession has historically been addressed by a consideration of two factors. First, the voluntariness of the statement; and second, the status of the receiver of the statement, that is to say, whether the receiver was a person in authority.

[15] As to the first factor, a statement is said to be voluntary when it is made without "fear of prejudice or hope of advantage": see *Ibrahim v. The King*, [1914] AC 599 (PC), at p. 609, adopted in Canada in *Prosko v. The King* (1922), 63 SCR 226. In *Boudreau v. The King*, [1949] SCR 262, at p. 269, Rand J explained that "the rule is directed against the danger of improperly instigated or induced or coerced admissions." Voluntariness also requires that the statement must be the product of an operating mind: see *Ward v. The Queen*, [1979] 2 SCR 30, at p. 40, *per* Spence J and *Horvath v. The Queen*, [1979] 2 SCR 376, at p. 425, *per* Beetz J. Voluntariness is determined by a careful investigation of the circumstances surrounding the statement of the accused, and involves a consideration of both objective and subjective factors.

[16] Second, the person in authority requirement generally refers to anyone formally engaged in "the arrest, detention, examination or prosecution of the accused": see, e.g., *A.B.* [(1986), 26 CCC (3d) 17 (Ont CA)], at p. 26. This definition may be enlarged to encompass persons who are deemed to be persons in authority as a result of the circumstances surrounding the making of the statement. For the moment, however, let us consider the purpose of each of these factors as they pertain to the admissibility of statements of the accused.

[17] Historically the insistence that a confession must be voluntary related to concerns about the reliability of the evidence. Indeed, the basis for the admission of a statement of the accused as an exception to the rule against hearsay is that what people freely say which is contrary to their interest is probably true. However, where a statement is prompted by a threat or inducement held out by a person in authority, it can no longer be presumed to be true. Initially when considering the admissibility of confessions some judges focused exclusively on reliability concerns as the sole rationale for the confessions rule. This is made readily apparent in the case of *R v. Warickshall* (1783), 1 Leach 263, 168 ER 234, at p. 263 and at pp. 234-35, respectively:

> It is a mistaken notion, that the evidence of confessions and facts which have been obtained from prisoners by promises or threats, is to be rejected from a regard to public faith: no such rule ever prevailed. The idea is novel in theory, and would be as dangerous in practice as it is repugnant to the general principles of criminal law. *Confessions are received in evidence, or rejected as inadmissible, under a consideration whether they are or are not intitled (sic) to credit.* A free and voluntary confession is deserving of the highest credit, because it is presumed to flow from the strongest sense of guilt. ... [Emphasis added.]

[18] There is also strong historical precedent for the proposition that the confessions rule is rooted in a concern for the administration of justice and fundamental principles of fairness, in particular the principle against self-incrimination. In a treatise on the law of evidence written by Lord Chief Baron Gilbert and published in 1754, the author makes the following comment:

> [T]he voluntary Confession of the Party in Interest is reckoned the best Evidence; for if a Man's swearing for his Interest can give no Credit, he must certainly give most Credit when he swears against it; *but then this Confession must be voluntary and without Compulsion; for our Law differs from the Civil Law, that it will not force any Man to accuse himself; and in this we do certainly follow the Law of Nature, which commands every Man to endeavor his own Preservation*; and therefore Pain and Force may compel Men to confess what is not the Truth of Facts, and consequently such extorted confessions are not to be depended upon. [Emphasis added.]

See Lawrence Herman, "The Unexplored Relationship Between the Privilege Against Compulsory Self-Incrimination and the Involuntary Confession Rule (Part I)" (1992), 53 *Ohio St. LJ* 101, at p. 153, citing Sir Geoffrey Gilbert, *The Law of Evidence* (1769). Thus, it is apparent that from its very inception, the confessions rule was designed not only to ensure the reliability of the confession, but also to guarantee fundamental fairness in the criminal process.

[19] Of particular significance is the relationship between these two concerns of reliability and fairness. It must be recognized that the purpose of the confessions rule is to exclude putatively unreliable statements, not actually unreliable statements. In other words, the confessions rule excludes statements obtained by force, threat or promises as somehow inherently unreliable, but does not inquire into the actual truth or falsity of the statement. If the concern of the confessions rule were truly the reliability of the statement, then the court's inquiry would focus on objective corroboration of the confession evidence; if additional evidence confirmed the confession was accurate, it should be admitted under a reliability rationale.

[20] Instead, the confessions rule asks only if the statement was voluntary, not if the statement is true. *DeClercq v. The Queen*, [1968] SCR 902. This focus on voluntariness allows a court to analyse the circumstances surrounding the statement and effectively acts as a check on the abuse of state power. In other words, if the state were left with the option of simply corroborating forced confessions, there would be little incentive to refrain from reprehensible investigative measures. That is why the confessions rule automatically excludes involuntary statements, regardless of their veracity. As stated by Professor Mark Berger in "The Exclusionary Rule and Confession Evidence: Some Perspectives on Evolving Practices and Policies in the United States and England and Wales" (1991), 20 *Anglo-Am. L Rev.* 63, at p. 71:

> [I]t is inescapable that the decision to reject all involuntary confessions incorporates policies that find fault with the use of coercive tactics to extract statements, independent of their impact on reliability. In short, the exclusion of involuntary confessions, at least as practised in the United States and formerly in England, is designed as a response to improper police interrogation tactics as much as, if not more than, it is aimed at ensuring evidence reliability.

This aspect of the confessions rule—which focuses on voluntariness over truth—indicates that the rule is not concerned solely with accuracy or reliability.

[21] This approach to the rule determining the admissibility of a statement of the accused also accords with the view that the quality, weight or reliability of evidence is a matter for the jury, and that the admission of evidence which may be unreliable does not *per se* render a trial unfair: see, e.g., *R v. Buric* (1996), 28 OR (3d) 737 (CA), aff'd [1997] 1 SCR 535, and *R v. Charemski*, [1998] 1 SCR 679. The confessions rule does not force a trial judge to exclude "unreliable" evidence that is highly probative of guilt. Rather it focuses on putative reliability, by analysing the circumstances surrounding the statement and their effect on the accused, regardless of the statement's accuracy. Thus the "reliability" rationale and the "fairness" rationale for the confessions rule blend together, so as to ensure fair treatment to the accused in the criminal process by deterring coercive state tactics.

[22] Indeed, when considering this notion of fairness, several courts have found that the confessions rule is based upon the principle against self-incrimination. Two decisions of the House of Lords, *Commissioners of Customs and Excise v. Harz*, [1967] 1 AC 760, and *R v. Sang*, [1979] 2 All ER 1222, suggest that this is the modern basis for the rule. The relationship between the principle against self-incrimination and the confessions rule has also been noted in *dicta* in a number of Canadian decisions. See, e.g., *DeClercq, supra*, at p. 923, *per* Hall J (dissenting); *Piché v. The Queen*, [1971] SCR 23, at p. 26, *per* Cartwright CJ; *Rothman v. The Queen*, [1981] 1 SCR 640, at pp. 653-54, *per* Estey J (dissenting). More recently, McLachlin J in *R v. Hebert*, [1990] 2 SCR 151, at p. 173 specifically linked the confessions rule to fundamental notions of fairness and the principle that accused persons should not be conscripted to provide evidence against themselves. She put it in this way:

> [O]ne of the themes running through the jurisprudence on confessions is the idea that a person in the power of the state's criminal process has the right to freely choose whether or not to make a statement to the police. This idea is accompanied by a correlative concern with the repute and integrity of the judicial process. This theme has not always been ascendant. Yet, its importance cannot be denied. It persists, both in Canadian jurisprudence and in the rules governing the rights of suspects in other countries.

[23] I recognize, as did McLachlin J in *Hebert*, supra, at p. 173, Iacobucci J in *R v. S.(R.J.)*, [1995] 1 SCR 451, at pp. 500-501, and Sopinka J in *R v. Whittle*, [1994] 2 SCR 914, at p. 932, that the self-incrimination basis for the confessions rule "must be historically qualified" (*S.(R.J.)*, at p. 499) and that "[i]n Canada, a rationale for the confessions rule extending beyond trustworthiness has not always been easy to locate" (*S.(R.J.)*, at p. 500). Nevertheless, I must recognize, as did my colleagues, that in a modern sense, the confessions rule has clearly been associated with these ideas. Indeed, in the *Report of the Federal/Provincial Task Force on Uniform Rules of Evidence* (1982), the Task Force concluded at p. 175 that "the clear common law principle that the Crown must establish its case without the assistance of the accused ... is the primary rationale of the Confessions Rule today."

[24] For this reason, the person in authority requirement is properly seen as an integral component of the confessions rule. The emphasis on voluntariness has two main effects: it both avoids the unfairness of a conviction based on a confession that might be unreliable, and has a deterrent effect on the use of coercive tactics. This deterrent effect is properly focused upon the prosecutorial authority of the state, not the personal authority of private individuals. It cannot be forgotten that it is the nature of the authority exerted

by the state that might prompt an involuntary statement. As Estey J stated in *Rothman*, *supra*, at pp. 650-51, "*their very authority* might, by promise or threat, express or implied, produce a statement whether or not the accused was truly willing to speak" (emphasis added). In other words, it is the fear of reprisal or hope of leniency that persons in authority may hold out and which is associated with their official status that may render a statement involuntary. The rule is generally not concerned with conversations between private citizens that might indicate guilt, as these conversations would not be influenced or affected by the coercive power of the state. This limitation is appropriate since most criminal investigations are undertaken by the state, and it is then that an accused is most vulnerable to state coercion.

[25] On a practical level, the Crown would obviously face an overwhelming burden if it had to establish the voluntariness of every statement against interest made by an accused to any person. See the Law Reform Commission of Canada, *Report on Evidence* (1975), at p. 62. In particular, as the intervener the Attorney General of Canada notes, the elimination of the person in authority requirement would have serious consequences for undercover police work and for the admissibility of wiretap evidence, where the identity of the receiver of the accused's statement is often unknown. For example, if the Crown were to intercept a phone call between an accused and a confederate who is senior to him in a criminal hierarchy, the Crown would obviously have difficulty tendering the requisite evidence if it were forced to prove beyond a reasonable doubt that the statements were made without "fear of prejudice or hope of advantage." Moreover, all statements to undercover police officers would become subject to the confessions rule, even though the accused was completely unaware of their status and, at the time he made the statement, would never have considered the undercover officers to be persons in authority.

[Cory J suggested that the concern about the "great unfairness suffered by the accused when an involuntary confession obtained as a result of violence or credible threats of imminent violence by a private individual is admitted into evidence" might be dealt with by legislative reform of the common law of evidence. He continued:]

[30] In the meantime I would suggest that in circumstances where a statement of the accused is obtained by a person who is not a person in authority by means of degrading treatment such as violence or threats of violence, a clear direction should be given to the jury as to the dangers of relying upon it. The direction might include words such as these: "A statement obtained as a result of inhuman or degrading treatment or the use of violence or threats of violence may not be the manifestation of the exercise of a free will to confess. Rather, it may result solely from the oppressive treatment or fear of such treatment. If it does, the statement may very well be either unreliable or untrue. Therefore, if you conclude that the statement was obtained by such oppression very little if any weight should be attached to it." However, if a private individual resorts to violence or threatens violence after the statement has been made, this conduct will not as a general rule be a factor affecting the voluntariness of the statement and the suggested direction will not be needed.

B. Limits of the Person in Authority Requirement

[31] It has been seen that the person in authority requirement is grounded in the underlying rationales for the confessions rule, and as a result it should remain part of the rule. Consideration must now be given as to who should come within the designation "person in authority."

[32] "Person in authority" typically refers to those persons formally engaged in the arrest, detention, examination or prosecution of the accused: see *A.B.*, *supra*, at p. 26. However, it may take on a broader meaning. Canadian courts first considered the meaning of "person in authority" in *R v. Todd* (1901), 4 CCC 514 (Man. KB). In that case, the accused made a statement to two men he believed to be fellow prisoners, but who were in fact acting as agents of the police. It was held, at pp. 526-27, that:

> A person in authority means, generally speaking, anyone who has authority or control over the accused or over the proceedings or the prosecution against him. ... [T]he authority that the accused *knows such persons to possess* may well be supposed in the majority of instances both to animate his hopes of favour on the one hand and on the other to inspire him with awe, and so in some degree to overcome the powers of his mind. ... [Emphasis added.]

Thus, from its earliest inception in Canadian law, the question as to who should be considered as a person in authority depended on the extent to which the accused believed the person could influence or control the proceedings against him or her. The question is therefore approached from the viewpoint of the accused. See also *R v. Roadhouse* (1933), 61 CCC 191 (BC CA), at p. 192.

[33] The subjective approach to the person in authority requirement has been adopted in this Court. See *Rothman*, *supra*, at p. 663. The approach adopted by McIntyre JA (as he then was) in *R v. Berger* (1975), 27 CCC (2d) 357 (BC CA), at pp. 385-86 is, in my view, a clear statement of the law:

> The law is settled that a person in authority is a person concerned with the prosecution who, in the opinion of the accused, can influence the course of the prosecution. The test to be applied in deciding whether statements made to persons connected in such a way with the prosecution are voluntary is subjective. In other words what did the accused think? Whom did he think he was talking to? ... Was he under the impression that the failure to speak to this person, because of his power to influence the prosecution, would result in prejudice or did he think that a statement would draw some benefit or reward? If his mind was free of such impressions the person receiving this statement would not be considered a person in authority and the statement would be admissible.

[34] However, to this statement I would add that the accused's belief that he is speaking to a person in authority must also be reasonable, in the context of the circumstances surrounding the making of the statement. If the accused were delusional or had no reasonable basis for the belief that the receiver of the statement could affect the course of the prosecution against him, the receiver should not be considered a person in authority. Since the person in authority requirement is aimed at controlling coercive state conduct, the test for a person in authority should not include those whom the accused unreasonably believes to be acting on behalf of the state. Thus, where the accused speaks out of fear of reprisal or hope of advantage because he reasonably believes the person receiving

the statement is acting as an agent of the police or prosecuting authorities and could therefore influence or control the proceedings against him or her, then the receiver of the statement is properly considered a person in authority. In other words, the evidence must disclose not only that the accused subjectively believed the receiver of the statement to be in a position to control the proceedings against the accused, but must also establish an objectively reasonable basis for that belief. For example, if the evidence discloses a relationship of agency or close collaboration between the receiver of the statement and the police or prosecution, and that relationship was known to the accused, the receiver of the statement may be considered a person in authority. In those circumstances the Crown must prove beyond a reasonable doubt that the statement was made voluntarily.

[35] Over the years, the courts have determined when and in what circumstances a person will be deemed a person in authority for the purposes of the confessions rule. See, e.g., *R v. Trenholme* (1920), 35 CCC 341 (Que. KB) (complainant's father was held to be a person in authority where he has control over the prosecution of the accused); *R v. Wilband*, [1967] SCR 14 (psychiatrist is not a person in authority where he cannot control or influence the course of the proceedings); *R v. Downey* (1976), 32 CCC (2d) 511 (NS SC AD) (victim is a person in authority if the accused believed that the victim had control over the proceedings); *A.B.*, *supra* (a parent is not, in law, a person in authority if there is no close connection between the decision to call the authorities and the inducement to a child to make a statement); *R v. Sweryda* (1987), 34 CCC (3d) 325 (Alta. CA) (a social worker is a person in authority if the accused knew the social worker was investigating allegations of child abuse and believed it could lead to his arrest). These cases have not departed from the governing rule that defines a person in authority in relation to the accused's perception of the receiver's involvement with the investigation or prosecution of the crime nor have these decisions defined a person in authority solely in terms of the personal authority that a person might wield in relation to the accused. Moreover, in concluding that the receiver of the statement was a person in authority, the courts have consistently found the accused believed the receiver was allied with the state authorities and could influence the investigation or prosecution against the accused.

[36] The important factor to note in all of these cases is that there is no catalogue of persons, beyond a peace officer or prison guard, who are automatically considered a person in authority solely by virtue of their status. A parent, doctor, teacher or employer all may be found to be a person in authority if the circumstances warrant, but their status, or the mere fact that they may wield some personal authority over the accused, is not sufficient to establish them as persons in authority for the purposes of the confessions rule. As the intervener the Attorney General of Canada observed, the person in authority requirement has evolved in a manner that avoids a formalistic or legalistic approach to the interactions between ordinary citizens. Instead, it requires a case-by-case consideration of the accused's belief as to the ability of the receiver of the statement to influence the prosecution or investigation of the crime. That is to say, the trial judge must determine whether the accused reasonably believed the receiver of the statement was acting on behalf of the police or prosecuting authorities. This view of the person in authority requirement remains unchanged.

[Cory J held that an accused had an evidentiary burden to raise the issue of whether the receiver of a statement was a person in authority, and that if this burden was met, the onus shifted "to the Crown to establish beyond a reasonable doubt either that the receiver is not a person in authority, or … that the statement was made voluntarily." He held further that a trial judge would have to hold a *voir dire* on this issue on his or her own motion "only where the evidence makes the need for a *voir dire* clear."]

IV. Summary

[48]   Perhaps it may be of some assistance to set out in summary form the applicable principles pertaining to the admission of statements made by the accused to persons in authority and some of the factors to be taken into consideration with regard to them.

1.   The rule which is still applicable in determining the admissibility of a statement made by an accused to a person in authority is that it must have been made voluntarily and must be the product of an operating mind.

2.   The rule is based upon two fundamentally important concepts: the need to ensure the reliability of the statement and the need to ensure fairness by guarding against improper coercion by the state. This results in the requirement that the admission must *not* be obtained by either threats or inducements.

3.   The rule is applicable when the accused makes a statement to a person in authority. Though no absolute definition of "person in authority" is necessary or desirable, it typically refers to those formally engaged in the arrest, detention, examination or prosecution of the accused. Thus, it would apply to persons such as police officers and prison officials or guards. When the statement of the accused is made to a police officer or prison guard a *voir dire* should be held to determine its admissibility as a voluntary statement, unless the *voir dire* is waived by counsel for the accused.

4.   Those persons whom the accused reasonably believes are acting on behalf of the police or prosecuting authorities and could therefore influence or control the proceedings against him or her may also be persons in authority. That question will have to be determined on a case-by-case basis.

5.   The issue as to who is a person in authority must be resolved by considering it subjectively from the viewpoint of the accused. There must, however, be a reasonable basis for the accused's belief that the person hearing the statement was a person in authority.

6.   The issue will not normally arise in relation to undercover police officers. This is because the issue must be approached from the viewpoint of the accused. On that basis, undercover police officers will not usually be viewed by the accused as persons in authority.

7.   If it is contended that the recipient of the statement was a person in authority in the eyes of the accused then the defence must raise the issue with the trial judge. This is appropriate for it is only the accused who can know that the statement was made to someone regarded by the accused as a person in authority.

8. On the ensuing *voir dire* the accused will have the evidential burden of demonstrating that there is a valid issue for consideration. If the accused meets the burden, the Crown will then have the persuasive burden of demonstrating beyond a reasonable doubt that the receiver of the statement was not a person in authority or if it is found that he or she was a person in authority, that the statement of the accused was made voluntarily.

9. In extremely rare cases the evidence adduced during a trial may be such that it should alert the trial judge that the issue as to whether the receiver of a statement made by an accused was a person in authority should be explored by way of *voir dire*. In those cases, which must be extremely rare in light of the obligation of the accused to raise the issue, the trial judge must of his or her own motion direct a *voir dire*, subject, of course, to waiver of the *voir dire* by counsel for the accused.

10. The duty of the trial judge to hold a *voir dire* of his or her own motion will only arise in those rare cases where the evidence, viewed objectively, is sufficient to alert the trial judge of the need to hold a *voir dire* to determine if the receiver of the statement of the accused was, in the circumstances, a person in authority.

11. If the trial judge is satisfied that the receiver of the statement was not a person in authority but that the statement of the accused was obtained by reprehensible coercive tactics, such as violence or credible threats of violence, then a direction should be given to the jury. The jury should be instructed that if they conclude that the statement was obtained by coercion, they should be cautious about accepting it, and that little if any weight should be attached to it.

V. Application to This Appeal

[49] The appellant contends that the fact that the confession was made to the complainant and her immediate family should have alerted the trial judge to the need for a *voir dire* since they are capable of being persons in authority for the purpose of the confessions rule. It is true the complainant and her family members are capable of being persons in authority. Indeed, anyone is capable of being a person in authority where a person becomes sufficiently involved with the arrest, detention, examination or prosecution of an accused, and the accused believes that the person may influence the process against him or her. It does not follow that simply because it has been held, in the circumstances presented in other cases, that a family member was a person in authority, that the trial judge should have been alerted to the need for a *voir dire*. Virtually any category of person—parents of the accused, parents of the complainant, teachers, psychiatrists, physicians—may, in light of the particular evidence adduced, be considered to be a person in authority. As the respondent observed, to hold that the trial judge committed an error on the basis that the receiver of the confession is merely capable of being a person in authority is to require a *voir dire* (or waiver) for every statement against interest made by every accused person to anyone. It cannot be forgotten that it is the accused who is in the best position to demonstrate that the receiver of the statement was in his or her eyes a person in authority.

[50] In this case, the evidence at trial did not disclose any evidence that was sufficient to trigger the trial judge's obligation to hold a *voir dire*. The confrontation at the appellant's

workplace was first described by the complainant. She testified as to the events leading up to the confrontation. She stated (1) that her mother questioned her about whether she was pregnant and whether she had had intercourse; (2) that in the course of that conversation, she told her mother that the appellant had sexually assaulted her; (3) that her mother telephoned her father; (4) that she and her mother visited a walk-in clinic in Mississauga where it was confirmed that the complainant was pregnant (her boyfriend at the time was the father); (5) that the complainant, together with her mother, father, stepfather and cousin went to confront the appellant. The complainant then related, without objection by the defence, the statements made by the appellant. Thus, when the statements were admitted into evidence, there was nothing to suggest that the complainant or her family members had spoken to the police or anyone else in authority or were even considering making a complaint. Similarly, there was nothing to suggest that the appellant subjectively believed the complainant's family to have control over criminal proceedings. In those circumstances, the trial judge cannot be said to have committed an error by failing to hold a *voir dire* on his own motion.

[The concurring judgment of L'Heureux-Dubé J, Bastarache J concurring, is omitted.]

NOTE ON R v WELLS

In *R v Wells*, [1998] 2 SCR 517, 127 CCC (3d) 500, the accused was charged with sexually assaulting three children. After the children reported the alleged assaults to their parents, two of them consulted the RCMP and attempted to obtain an admission from the accused by a trick. When this was not entirely successful, GD, one of the fathers, proceeded as follows:

> G.D. confronted the respondent with the allegations, and he denied them. G.D. then grabbed the respondent by the hair and held a bread knife to his throat. He said he could kill the respondent for what he had done to his children. The respondent replied, "I wish you would. I don't know what's wrong with me." G.D. then dropped the knife and punched the respondent once, cutting him above the eye. G.D. also forced the respondent to apologize to the children. The respondent told the children, "I never meant to hurt you and I was wrong for touching you. I'm sorry." G.D. took the children to see the RCMP the next day and the day after that, the respondent was arrested.

The statement was admitted and Wells was convicted. Applying the principles from *Hodgson*, Cory J held that the trial judge should have held a *voir dire* to determine whether GD was a person in authority:

> Thus G.D. testified that he had contacted the police and informed them of the situation, and that he and S.T. were planning, by means of a trick, to obtain an admission from the respondent. The content of the conversation with the RCMP was not revealed. It is significant that the complainants' parents visited and spoke to the police and, after that visit, planned to obtain an admission from the respondent by a trick. In light of the evidence, it is reasonable to conclude that the trial judge should have inquired of defence counsel whether or not he was willing to waive a *voir dire* in relation to statements against interest made by the respondent to G.D. It does appear that there was sufficient evidence before the judge to constitute this one of those "rare cases." The testimony was such that it required the trial judge make [*sic*] an inquiry as to whether there

should be a *voir dire* to determine if the parents were persons in authority for the purposes of the confessions rule.

A new trial was ordered. L'Heureux-Dubé J (Bastarache J concurring), dissenting, held that there was no "reasonable possibility that the [fathers] were acting as agents for the RCMP, or that either had any control over prospective proceedings."

NOTE ON R v SGT

In *R v SGT*, 2010 SCC 20, [2010] 1 SCR 688, the accused was charged with sexually assaulting his adopted daughter, A. After being interviewed by police, he wrote an apology to A (which was found inadmissible at trial because of an improper inducement). Subsequent to the apology, A's mother sent him an email requesting permission to travel out of the country. He made incriminating statements in his response that the prosecution wished to adduce at trial. The court had this to say on the issue of whether the mother could be considered a person in authority for the purposes of the confessions rule:

[24] In this case, the recipient of the e-mail, A's mother, was not a conventional person in authority. Further, S.G.T. did not raise the issue at trial. While A's mother may, as a parent of a minor complainant in a criminal trial, be a person in authority, her status alone is not sufficient to render her a person in authority ... . In those cases where parents have been held to be persons in authority, there has generally been some type of interaction between the parents and the police. For example, in *R. v. Trenholme* (1920), 30 B.R. 232, the victim's father was held to be person in authority on the basis that he actually "laid the charge" and "had authority and control over the prosecution against the accused" (pp. 249 and 243). More recently, in *R. v. Wells*, [1998] 2 S.C.R. 517, this Court held that a *voir dire* was required into whether a parent was a person in authority where the parent had previously spoken to the police about his intention to trick the accused into making a statement. It was on that basis that *Wells* was one of those "rare cases" where a *voir dire* was required for an individual who was not a clear person in authority (para. 16). By contrast, in *Hodgson*, the mere fact that the parents of a young girl confronted the accused about sexually assaulting their daughter did not serve to turn them into persons in authority. ...

[25] The question then becomes whether clear evidence existed in the record which should have alerted the trial judge to the need for a *voir dire*. The relevant circumstances are the following.

[26] S.G.T. did not testify that he believed that A's mother could influence or control the proceedings. Even if he had testified to that effect, any subjective belief has to be reasonably based in fact. There is no evidence that A's mother had any control over the prosecution of S.G.T., or that she was operating on behalf of the investigating authorities. Rather, the record suggests quite the contrary. While A's mother called the police after A disclosed the incidents to her in 2003, she was told to call back later, as the relevant department was not open at that time. She never called back, as she was concerned about the effect that any complaint might have on her son, B. The police only began investigating S.G.T. in 2004 after A disclosed the matter to authorities at her school ... . In these circumstances, there was nothing on the record to indicate to the trial judge that A's mother may have been anything other than an ordinary witness in the proceedings. I therefore conclude that the trial judge did not err by failing to hold a *voir dire* on the question whether A's mother was a person in authority.

QUESTIONS

1. Given the reasoning and outcomes in *Hodgson*, *Wells*, and *SGT*, how likely is it that private citizens could be found to be persons in authority?

2. On the retrial, Wells's statement was admitted and he was convicted. His appeal to the British Columbia Court of Appeal was dismissed: *R v Wells*, 2003 BCCA 242, 174 CCC (3d) 301. However, the court suggested at para 65 of its reasons that it would have been "open to the trial judge to exclude the appellant's statements obtained in circumstances of violence and threats of violence on the basis that the potential prejudicial effect of the evidence outweighed its probative value." Would that be a satisfactory approach to the situation that arose in *Hodgson*, *Wells*, or *Grandinetti* (described below)? See also *R v Hart*, 2014 SCC 52, [2014] 2 SCR 544.

3. The accused Cory Grandinetti was charged with the murder of his aunt. There was some circumstantial evidence against him, but the police were anxious to obtain a confession:

> [7] In July 1997, with few leads to investigate but suspicious that Cory Grandinetti was involved, the RCMP began an undercover operation, Project Kilometer, in an attempt to obtain additional evidence against him. Several police officers posed as members of a criminal organization and worked at winning Cory Grandinetti's confidence. Mr. Grandinetti thought the criminal enterprise he was dealing with was a large international organization involved in drug trafficking and money laundering. He was led to believe that this organization was moving to Calgary, that he had been chosen as its Calgary contact, and that he could potentially make hundreds of thousands of dollars by participating in the organization's criminal activities.
>
> [8] As part of Project Kilometer, the police engaged Mr. Grandinetti in criminal activities, including money laundering, theft, receiving illegal firearms, and selling drugs. A number of police officers were involved in this operation, including Cst. Keith Pearce, known to the appellant as "Mac," Cpl. Gordon Rennick, known as "Dan," and Cst. Robert Johnston, known as "Zeus." "Mac" posed as the head of the criminal organization. At no time was the appellant aware of the true identity of the undercover officers.
>
> [9] From the beginning, the undercover officers encouraged Mr. Grandinetti to talk about his aunt's murder, but he consistently refused to do so. By late October, the undercover officers decided a new tactic was necessary. They began trying to convince the appellant that they had contacts in the police department who were prepared to act unlawfully, and that they had been able to use those contacts in the past to influence an investigation. On October 30, 1997, the undercover officers convinced Mr. Grandinetti that they had managed to have a murder charge against "Dan" reduced to aggravated assault by using their police connections to relocate a witness and retrieve incriminating photos. They reinforced the perception that they had corrupt police contacts on November 13, 1997, when "Mac" told Mr. Grandinetti that he had easily learned the name of the investigator on the Connie Grandinetti murder investigation.
>
> [10] To further encourage Mr. Grandinetti to talk about Connie Grandinetti's murder, the undercover officers suggested to him that they could use their corrupt police contacts to steer the Connie Grandinetti murder investigation away from him. When he continued to balk at talking about the murder, they told him that he might be a liability to their organization because of the ongoing murder investigation. They forcefully suggested he "come clean" with them to protect the organization from possible police interference.
>
> [11] This led Mr. Grandinetti to confess his involvement in the murder, provide details to the undercover officers, and take them to the location where Connie Grandinetti was killed. The

confessions were recorded. On the basis of his confessions to the undercover officers, Mr. Grandinetti was arrested on December 9, 1997.

In these circumstances, were the undercover police officers persons in authority for the purpose of the confessions rule? See *R v Grandinetti*, 2005 SCC 5, [2005] 1 SCR 27, 191 CCC (3d) 449. See also *R v Hart*, 2014 SCC 52 at para 174, [2014] 2 SCR 544.

2. The Voir Dire

Where the Crown offers in evidence the statement of an accused given to a person in authority, the Crown must establish the voluntariness of the statement beyond a reasonable doubt before using it for any purpose, including impeaching the accused's credibility: *Monette v R*, [1956] SCR 400; *R v G (B)*, [1999] 2 SCR 475. It does not matter whether the statement is in substance inculpatory or exculpatory: *Piché v R*, [1971] SCR 23. If voluntariness is not conceded, there must be a *voir dire*: *Erven v R*, [1979] 1 SCR 926. The accused will often be a witness on the *voir dire*; if so, his testimony may not be used in the Crown's case in chief in the main trial: *R v Magdish, Bennett, and Sweet* (1978), 41 CCC (2d) 449 (Ont H Ct J). To take an extreme example, if in the *voir dire* the accused does admit the offence charged, the admission may not be used against him in the main trial: *R v Brophy*, [1981] 2 All ER 705 (HL). Furthermore, the evidence from the *voir dire* cannot be brought into the main trial without the consent of both parties: *R v Gauthier*, [1977] 1 SCR 441.

In *Magdish*, Grange J left open the question whether the accused's credibility may be impeached in the main trial if his testimony in the *voir dire* is inconsistent with his testimony in the main trial. How would you resolve this question? Would it matter whether, in the *voir dire*, the trial judge found the statement to be voluntary or involuntary? How, if at all, would s 7 or s 13 of the Charter (see Section III of this chapter) affect the answer?

The issue on the *voir dire* is the voluntariness and not the truth of the statement. But in *DeClercq v R*, [1968] SCR 902, it was held that, during the *voir dire*, the accused may be asked whether the statement is true. How might the answer to that question be relevant to the issue in the *voir dire*? In *R v Tessier*, 2001 NBCA 34 at para 56, 153 CCC (3d) 361, rev'd on other grounds, 2002 SCC 6, [2002] 1 SCR 144, 162 CCC (3d) 478, the majority held that the trial judge had erred in considering the truth or falsity of the accused's statement in the *voir dire*. The majority refused to follow *DeClercq* on the ground that in *Wong Kam-Ming v R*, [1980] AC 247, the Privy Council had overruled its earlier decision in *R v Hammond* (1941), 28 Cr App R 84, which was "the jurisprudential underpinning for the decision in *DeClercq*." Should a provincial Court of Appeal refuse to follow a decision of the Supreme Court of Canada on this ground?

3. Voluntariness

In most confessions rule cases, the question in dispute is whether the statement made by the accused to a person in authority was "voluntary." Initially, the voluntariness determination turned on whether police used improper inducements to gain a confession.

In *Ibrahim v The King*, [1914] AC 599, the Privy Council, per Lord Sumner, summarized the confessions rule in the following terms:

It has long been established as a positive rule of English criminal law, that no statement by an accused is admissible in evidence against him unless it is shewn by the prosecution to have been a voluntary statement, in the sense that it has not been obtained from him either by fear of prejudice or hope of advantage exercised or held out by a person in authority. The principle is as old as Lord Hale. The burden of proof in the matter has been decided by high authority in recent times in *Reg. v. Thompson*, [1893] 2 QB 12, a case which, it is important to observe, was considered by the trial judge before he admitted the evidence. There was, in the present case, Major Barrett's affirmative evidence that the prisoner was not subjected to the pressure of either fear or hope in the sense mentioned. There was no evidence to the contrary. With *Reg. v. Thompson* before him, the learned judge must be taken to have been satisfied with the prosecution's evidence that the prisoner's statement was not so induced either by hope or fear, and, as is laid down in the same case, the decision of this question, albeit one of fact, rests with the trial judge. Their Lordships are clearly of opinion that the admission of this evidence was no breach of the aforesaid rule.

The appellant's objection … rested on the two bare facts that the statement was preceded by and made in answer to a question, and that the question was put by a person in authority and the answer given by a man in his custody. This ground, in so far as it is a ground at all, is a more modern one. With the growth of a police force of the modern type, the point has frequently arisen, whether, if a policeman questions a prisoner in his custody at all, the prisoner's answers are evidence against him, apart altogether from fear of prejudice or hope of advantage inspired by a person in authority.

It is to be observed that logically these objections all go to the weight and not to the admissibility of the evidence. What a person having knowledge about the matter in issue says of it is itself relevant to the issue as evidence against him. That he made the statement under circumstances of hope, fear, interest or otherwise strictly goes only to its weight. In an action of tort evidence of this kind could not be excluded when tendered against a tortfeasor, though a jury might well be told as prudent men to think little of it. Even the rule which excludes evidence of statements made by a prisoner, when they are induced by hope held out, or fear inspired, by a person in authority, is a rule of policy. "A confession forced from the mind by the flattery of hope or by the torture of fear comes in so questionable a shape, when it is to be considered as evidence of guilt, that no credit ought to be given to it": *Rex v. Warwickshall*. It is not that the law presumes such statements to be untrue, but from the danger of receiving such evidence judges have thought it better to reject it for the due administration of justice: *Reg. v. Baldry*. Accordingly, when hope or fear was not in question, such statements were long regularly admitted as relevant, though with some reluctance and subject to strong warnings as to their weight.

Over time, voluntariness came to encompass two additional concepts: "operating mind" and "oppression." And in the following decision, the Supreme Court of Canada set out the modern framework for assessing voluntariness.

R v Oickle
2000 SCC 38, [2000] 2 SCR 3, 147 CCC (3d) 321
L'Heureux-Dubé, McLachlin, Iacobucci, Major, Bastarache, Binnie, and Arbour JJ
(29 September 2000)

IACOBUCCI J (L'Heureux-Dubé, McLachlin, Major, Bastarache, and Binnie JJ concurring):

I. Introduction

[1] This appeal requires this Court to rule on the common law limits on police interrogation. Specifically, we are asked to decide whether the police improperly induced the respondent's confessions through threats or promises, an atmosphere of oppression, or any other tactics that could raise a reasonable doubt as to the voluntariness of his confessions. I conclude that they did not. The trial judge's determination that the confessions at stake in this appeal were voluntarily given should not have been disturbed on appeal, and accordingly the appeal should be allowed.

[2] In this case, the police conducted a proper interrogation. Their questioning, while persistent and often accusatorial, was never hostile, aggressive, or intimidating. They repeatedly offered the accused food and drink. They allowed him to use the bathroom upon request. Before his first confession and subsequent arrest, they repeatedly told him that he could leave at any time. In this context, the alleged inducements offered by the police do not raise a reasonable doubt as to the confessions' voluntariness. Nor do I find any fault with the role played by the polygraph test in this case. While the police admittedly exaggerated the reliability of such devices, the tactic of inflating the reliability of incriminating evidence is a common, and generally unobjectionable one. Whether standing alone, or in combination with the other mild inducements used in this appeal, it does not render the confessions involuntary.

II. Facts

[3] The facts surrounding the respondent's interrogation are obviously central to the resolution of this appeal, and I will refer to them throughout my legal analysis. At this point, I will simply give an overview.

[4] Between February 5, 1994 and April 4, 1995, a series of eight fires involving four buildings and two motor vehicles occurred in and around the community of Waterville, Nova Scotia. Most of the incidents occurred between 1:00 a.m. and 4:00 a.m. The vehicle fires involved a van belonging to the respondent's father, and a car belonging to the respondent's fiancée, Tanya Kilcup. The building fires occurred relatively close to where the respondent had lived when the various fires occurred. The fires appeared to have been deliberately set, with the possible exception of Ms. Kilcup's vehicle. The respondent was a member of the Waterville Volunteer Fire Brigade, and had responded to each of the fires in that capacity.

[5] The last fire involved Ms. Kilcup's vehicle. The car was parked in the driveway of the apartment building where the respondent and Ms. Kilcup lived. The fire was discovered by a passerby who extinguished it. The Fire Marshall investigated the fire and concluded that since the car was subject to a prior recall for a possible faulty ignition switch, the fire may have been accidental owing to an electrical fault.

[6] The police also conducted an extensive investigation of the fires. To help narrow the list of possible suspects, they asked a total of seven or eight individuals to submit to polygraph tests. Five or six individuals did so, passed the test, and were effectively removed from the list of suspects. Another person had agreed to take a polygraph, but was not examined after the respondent confessed to the crimes. The respondent, after initial doubts, agreed to submit to a test. Around 3:00 p.m. on April 26, 1995, the respondent went to the Wandlyn Motel for the test, according to a prior arrangement. The police

audiotaped the events at the motel. Sergeant Taker administered the polygraph test. The respondent was fully advised of his rights to silence, to a lawyer (including the availability of Legal Aid), and to leave at any time. Sergeant Taker also advised him that while Sergeant Taker's interpretation of the polygraph results was not admissible, anything said by the respondent was admissible. The respondent was given a pamphlet to review, which discussed the polygraph procedures, and he signed a consent form.

[7] Before conducting the test itself, Sergeant Taker conducted a lengthy "pre-test" interview, which involved a variety of questions, many of them personal in nature. This interview was designed to provide a basis for the polygraph test itself, to help Sergeant Taker compose "control questions" for the polygraph exam, and to foster a sense of intimacy between examiner and subject. An exculpatory statement, which formed the basis for the polygraph test itself, was taken at the conclusion of the pre-test. Sergeant Taker then conducted the polygraph exam, which lasted only a matter of minutes. During the test Sergeant Taker did not ask about any specific fire, but instead asked if the respondent's earlier statement had been truthful. At the conclusion of the test, around 5:00 p.m., Taker checked the charts and informed the respondent that he had failed the test. He reminded the respondent that his rights were still in effect, and proceeded to question him for approximately one hour. At one point the respondent asked "What if I admit to the car? … Then I can walk out of here and it's over." Though Sergeant Taker replied "You can walk out at any time," the respondent did not leave.

[8] At 6:30 p.m. Sergeant Taker was relieved by Corporal Deveau, who reminded the respondent of his right to counsel. After 30 to 40 minutes, the respondent confessed to setting fire to his fiancée's car. He appeared emotionally distraught at this time. After a recitation of his rights, and an acknowledgement that he understood them, the police took a written statement, in which he continued to deny any involvement in the other fires. The respondent was arrested, warned of his right to counsel, given the secondary police warning, and driven to the police station at 8:15 p.m. En route he was very upset and was crying. He was placed in an interview room equipped with videotaping facilities, which recorded the subsequent interrogation where Corporal Deveau questioned him about the other fires. Around 8:30 p.m. and 9:15 p.m. the respondent indicated that he was tired, and wanted to go home to bed. He was informed that he was under arrest, and he could call a lawyer if he wanted, but that he could not go home. Questioning did not cease.

[9] Constable Bogle took over the interrogation at 9:52 p.m., after giving the respondent the secondary police warning. Constable Bogle questioned the respondent until about 11:00 p.m., at which time the respondent confessed to setting seven of the eight fires. He denied any involvement in the fire in his father's van. At this time, Constable Bogle left the room, and the respondent was seen crying with his head in his hands. Constable Bogle returned with Corporal Deveau, and took a written statement. The respondent's *Charter* rights and the police warning were on the statement, and were acknowledged by the respondent. The police warning stated that "[y]ou need not say anything. You have nothing to hope from any promise or favour and nothing to fear from any threat whether or not you do say anything. Anything you do say may be used as evidence." The statement concluded at 1:10 a.m. on April 27. After the police attended to various administrative tasks, the respondent was placed in a cell to sleep at 2:45 a.m. At 6:00 a.m., Corporal Deveau noticed that the respondent was awake and asked whether he would agree to a re-enactment. On the tape of the re-enactment, the respondent was given a *Charter* warning, the

secondary warning, and was advised that he could stop the re-enactment at any time. The police drove the respondent around Waterville to the various fire scenes, where he described how he had set each fire. The respondent was charged with seven counts of arson.

[10] At trial, the trial judge held a *voir dire* to determine the admissibility of the respondent's statements, including the video re-enactment. The trial judge ruled that the statements were voluntary and admissible, and subsequently convicted him on all counts. However, the Nova Scotia Court of Appeal found that the statements were involuntary and thus inadmissible, and allowed the respondent's appeal. The Court of Appeal excluded the confessions, overturned the convictions, and entered acquittals.

. . .

IV. Analysis

. . .

C. The Confessions Rule Today

[32] As previously mentioned, this Court has not recently addressed the precise scope of the confessions rule. Instead, we have refined several elements of the rule, without ever integrating them into a coherent whole. I believe it is important to restate the rule for two reasons. First is the continuing diversity of approaches as evidenced by the courts below in this appeal. Second, and perhaps more important, is our growing understanding of the problem of false confessions. As I will discuss below, the confessions rule is concerned with voluntariness, broadly defined. One of the predominant reasons for this concern is that involuntary confessions are more likely to be unreliable. The confessions rule should recognize which interrogation techniques commonly produce false confessions so as to avoid miscarriages of justice.

[33] In defining the confessions rule, it is important to keep in mind its twin goals of protecting the rights of the accused without unduly limiting society's need to investigate and solve crimes. Martin JA accurately delineated this tension in *R v. Precourt* (1976), 18 OR (2d) 714 (CA), at p. 721:

> Although improper police questioning may in some circumstances infringe the governing [confessions] rule it is essential to bear in mind that the police are unable to investigate crime without putting questions to persons, whether or not such persons are suspected of having committed the crime being investigated. Properly conducted police questioning is a legitimate and effective aid to criminal investigation. ... On the other hand, statements made as the result of intimidating questions, or questioning which is oppressive and calculated to overcome the freedom of will of the suspect for the purpose of extracting a confession are inadmissible. ...

All who are involved in the administration of justice, but particularly courts applying the confessions rule, must never lose sight of either of these objectives.

1. The Problem of False Confessions

[34] The history of police interrogations is not without its unsavoury chapters. Physical abuse, if not routine, was certainly not unknown. Today such practices are much less common. In this context, it may seem counterintuitive that people would confess to a

crime that they did not commit. And indeed, research with mock juries indicates that people find it difficult to believe that someone would confess falsely. See S.M. Kassin and L.S. Wrightsman, "Coerced Confessions, Judicial Instructions, and Mock Juror Verdicts" (1981), 11 *J Applied Soc. Psychol.* 489.

[35] However, this intuition is not always correct. A large body of literature has developed documenting hundreds of cases where confessions have been proven false by DNA evidence, subsequent confessions by the true perpetrator, and other such independent sources of evidence. See, e.g., R.A. Leo and R.J. Ofshe, "The Consequences of False Confessions: Deprivations of Liberty and Miscarriages of Justice in the Age of Psychological Interrogation" (1998), 88 *J Crim. L & Criminology* 429 (hereinafter Leo & Ofshe (1998)); R.J. Ofshe and R.A. Leo, "The Social Psychology of Police Interrogation: The Theory and Classification of True and False Confessions" (1997), 16 *Stud. L Pol. & Soc.* 189 (hereinafter Ofshe & Leo (1997)); R.J. Ofshe and R.A. Leo, "The Decision to Confess Falsely: Rational Choice and Irrational Action" (1997), 74 *Dénv. UL Rev.* 979 (hereinafter Ofshe & Leo (1997a)); W.S. White, "False Confessions and the Constitution: Safeguards Against Untrustworthy Confessions" (1997), 32 *Harv. CR-CL L Rev.* 105; G.H. Gudjonsson and J.A.C. MacKeith, "A Proven Case of False Confession: Psychological Aspects of the Coerced-Compliant Type" (1990), 30 *Med. Sci. & L* 329 (hereinafter Gudjonsson & MacKeith (1990)); G.H. Gudjonsson and J.A.C. MacKeith, "Retracted Confessions: Legal, Psychological and Psychiatric Aspects" (1988), 28 *Med. Sci. & L* 187 (hereinafter Gudjonsson & MacKeith (1988)); H.A. Bedau and M.L. Radelet, "Miscarriages of Justice in Potentially Capital Cases" (1987), 40 *Stan. L Rev.* 21.

[36] One of the overriding concerns of the criminal justice system is that the innocent must not be convicted: see, e.g., *R v. Mills*, [1999] 3 SCR 668, at para. 71; *R v. Leipert*, [1997] 1 SCR 281, at para. 4. Given the important role of false confessions in convicting the innocent, the confessions rule must understand why false confessions occur. Without suggesting that any confession involving elements discussed below should automatically be excluded, I hope to provide a background for my synthesis of the confessions rule in the next section.

[37] Ofshe & Leo (1997), *supra*, at p. 210, provide a useful taxonomy of false confessions. They suggest that there are five basic kinds: voluntary, stress-compliant, coerced-compliant, non-coerced-persuaded, and coerced-persuaded. Voluntary confessions *ex hypothesi* are not the product of police interrogation. It is therefore the other four types of false confessions that are of interest.

[38] According to Ofshe & Leo (1997), *supra*, at p. 211, stress-compliant confessions occur "when the aversive interpersonal pressures of interrogation become so intolerable that [suspects] comply in order to terminate questioning." They are elicited by "exceptionally strong use of the aversive stressors typically present in interrogations," and are "given knowingly *in order to escape* the punishing experience of interrogation" (emphasis in original). See also Gudjonsson & MacKeith (1990), *supra*. Another important factor is confronting the suspect with fabricated evidence in order to convince him that protestations of innocence are futile: see *ibid.*; Ofshe & Leo (1997a), *supra*, at p. 1040.

[39] Somewhat different are coerced-compliant confessions. These confessions are the product of "the classically coercive influence techniques (e.g., threats and promises)," with which the *Ibrahim* [*Ibrahim v The King*, [1914] AC 599 (PC)] rule is concerned: Ofshe & Leo (1997), *supra*, at p. 214. As Gudjonsson & MacKeith (1988), *supra*, suggest

at p. 191, "most cases of false confession that come before the courts are of the compliant-coerced type." See also White, *supra*, at p. 131.

[40] A third kind of false confession is the non-coerced-persuaded confession. In this scenario, police tactics cause the innocent person to "become confused, doubt his memory, be temporarily persuaded of his guilt and confess to a crime he did not commit": Ofshe & Leo (1997), *supra*, at p. 215. For an example, see *Reilly v. State*, 355 A.2d 324 (Conn. Super. Ct. 1976); Ofshe & Leo (1997), *supra*, at pp. 231-34. The use of fabricated evidence can also help convince an innocent suspect of his or her own guilt. ·

[41] A final type of false confession is the coerced-persuaded confession. This is like the non-coerced-persuaded, except that the interrogation also involves the classically coercive aspects of the coerced-compliant confession: see Ofshe & Leo (1997), *supra*, at p. 219.

[42] From this discussion, several themes emerge. One is the need to be sensitive to the particularities of the individual suspect. For example, White, *supra*, at p. 120, notes the following:

> False confessions are particularly likely when the police interrogate particular types of suspects, including suspects who are especially vulnerable as a result of their background, special characteristics, or situation, suspects who have compliant personalities, and, in rare instances, suspects whose personalities make them prone to accept and believe police suggestions made during the course of the interrogation.

And indeed, this is consistent with the reasons of Rand J in *Fitton* ... [*R v Fitton*, [1956] SCR 958], at p. 962:

> The strength of mind and will of the accused, the influence of custody or its surroundings, the effect of questions or of conversation, all call for delicacy in appreciation of the part they have played behind the admission, and to enable a Court to decide whether what was said was freely and voluntarily said, that is, was free from the influence of hope or fear aroused by them.

Ward ... [*Ward v R*, [1979] 2 SCR 30], and *Horvath* ... [*Horvath v R*, [1979] 2 SCR 376], similarly recognized the particular circumstances of the suspects that rendered them unable to confess voluntarily: in *Ward*, the accused's state of shock, and in *Horvath*, the psychological fragility that precipitated his hypnosis and "complete emotional disintegration" (p. 400).

[43] Another theme is the danger of using non-existent evidence. Presenting a suspect with entirely fabricated evidence has the potential either to persuade the susceptible suspect that he did indeed commit the crime, or at least to convince the suspect that any protestations of innocence are futile.

[44] Finally, the literature bears out the common law confessions rule's emphasis on threats and promises. Coerced-compliant confessions are the most common type of false confessions. These are classically the product of threats or promises that convince a suspect that in spite of the long-term ramifications, it is in his or her best interest in the short- and intermediate-term to confess.

[45] Fortunately, false confessions are rarely the product of proper police techniques. As Leo & Ofshe (1998), *supra*, point out at p. 492, false confession cases almost always involve "shoddy police practice and/or police criminality." Similarly, in Ofshe & Leo

(1997), *supra*, at pp. 193-96, they argue that in most cases, "eliciting a false confession takes strong incentives, intense pressure and prolonged questioning. ... Only under the rarest of circumstances do an interrogator's ploys persuade an innocent suspect that he is in fact guilty and has been caught."

[46]   Before turning to how the confessions rule responds to these dangers, I would like to comment briefly on the growing practice of recording police interrogations, preferably by videotape. As pointed out by J.J. Furedy and J. Liss in "Countering Confessions Induced by the Polygraph: Of Confessionals and Psychological Rubber Hoses" (1986), 29 *Crim. LQ* 91, at p. 104, even if "notes were accurate concerning the *content* of what was said ... , the notes cannot reflect the *tone* of what was said and any body language that may have been employed" (emphasis in original). White, *supra*, at pp. 153-54, similarly offers four reasons why videotaping is important:

> First, it provides a means by which courts can monitor interrogation practices and thereby enforce the other safeguards. Second, it deters the police from employing interrogation methods likely to lead to untrustworthy confessions. Third, it enables courts to make more informed judgments about whether interrogation practices were likely to lead to an untrustworthy confession. Finally, mandating this safeguard accords with sound public policy because the safeguard will have additional salutary effects besides reducing untrustworthy confessions, including more net benefits for law enforcement.

This is not to suggest that non-recorded interrogations are inherently suspect; it is simply to make the obvious point that when a recording is made, it can greatly assist the trier of fact in assessing the confession.

2. The Contemporary Confessions Rule

[47]   The common law confessions rule is well-suited to protect against false confessions. While its overriding concern is with voluntariness, this concept overlaps with reliability. A confession that is not voluntary will often (though not always) be unreliable. The application of the rule will by necessity be contextual. Hard and fast rules simply cannot account for the variety of circumstances that vitiate the voluntariness of a confession, and would inevitably result in a rule that would be both over- and under-inclusive. A trial judge should therefore consider all the relevant factors when reviewing a confession.

[Iacobucci J reviewed three branches of the confessions rule—"threats or promises," "oppression," and "operating mind"—and continued:]

(e) Summary

[68]   While the foregoing might suggest that the confessions rule involves a panoply of different considerations and tests, in reality the basic idea is quite simple. First of all, because of the criminal justice system's overriding concern not to convict the innocent, a confession will not be admissible if it is made under circumstances that raise a reasonable doubt as to voluntariness. Both the traditional, narrow *Ibrahim* rule and the oppression doctrine recognize this danger. If the police interrogators subject the suspect to utterly intolerable conditions, or if they offer inducements strong enough to produce an unreliable confession, the trial judge should exclude it. Between these two extremes, oppressive

conditions and inducements can operate together to exclude confessions. Trial judges must be alert to the entire circumstances surrounding a confession in making this decision.

[69] The doctrines of oppression and inducements are primarily concerned with reliability. However, as the operating mind doctrine and Lamer J's concurrence in *Rothman* ... [*Rothman v R*, [1981] 1 SCR 640], both demonstrate, the confessions rule also extends to protect a broader conception of voluntariness "that focuses on the protection of the accused's rights and fairness in the criminal process": J. Sopinka, S.N. Lederman and A.W. Bryant, *The Law of Evidence in Canada* (2nd ed. 1999), at p. 339. Voluntariness is the touchstone of the confessions rule. Whether the concern is threats or promises, the lack of an operating mind, or police trickery that unfairly denies the accused's right to silence, this Court's jurisprudence has consistently protected the accused from having involuntary confessions introduced into evidence. If a confession is involuntary for any of these reasons, it is inadmissible.

[70] Wigmore perhaps summed up the point best when he said that voluntariness is "shorthand for a complex of values": *Wigmore on Evidence* (Chadbourn rev. 1970), vol. 3, §826, at p. 351. I also agree with Warren CJ of the United States Supreme Court, who made a similar point in *Blackburn v. Alabama*, 361 US 199 (1960), at p. 207:

> [N]either the likelihood that the confession is untrue nor the preservation of the individual's freedom of will is the sole interest at stake. As we said just last Term, "The abhorrence of society to the use of involuntary confessions ... also turns on the deep-rooted feeling that the police must obey the law while enforcing the law; that in the end life and liberty can be as much endangered from illegal methods used to convict those thought to be criminals as from the actual criminals themselves." ... Thus a complex of values underlies the stricture against use by the state of confessions which, by way of convenient shorthand, this Court terms involuntary, and the role played by each in any situation varies according to the particular circumstances of the case.

See *Hebert* ... [*R v Hebert*, [1990] 2 SCR 151]. While the "complex of values" relevant to voluntariness in Canada is obviously not identical to that in the United States, I agree with Warren CJ that "voluntariness" is a useful term to describe the various rationales underlying the confessions rule that I have addressed above.

[71] Again, I would also like to emphasize that the analysis under the confessions rule must be a contextual one. In the past, courts have excluded confessions made as a result of relatively minor inducements. At the same time, the law ignored intolerable police conduct if it did not give rise to an "inducement" as it was understood by the narrow *Ibrahim* formulation. Both results are incorrect. Instead, a court should strive to understand the circumstances surrounding the confession and ask if it gives rise to a reasonable doubt as to the confession's voluntariness, taking into account all the aspects of the rule discussed above. Therefore a relatively minor inducement, such as a tissue to wipe one's nose and warmer clothes, may amount to an impermissible inducement if the suspect is deprived of sleep, heat, and clothes for several hours in the middle of the night during an interrogation: see *Hoilett* ... [*R v Hoilett* (1999), 136 CCC (3d) 449 (Ont CA)]. On the other hand, where the suspect is treated properly, it will take a stronger inducement to render the confession involuntary. If a trial court properly considers all the relevant circumstances, then a finding regarding voluntariness is essentially a factual one, and should only be overturned for "some *palpable and overriding* error which affected [the trial

judge's] assessment of the facts": *Schwartz v. Canada*, [1996] 1 SCR 254, at p. 279 (quoting *Stein v. The Ship "Kathy K"*, [1976] 2 SCR 802, at p. 808) (emphasis in *Schwartz*).

D. Application to the Present Appeal

[72] Applying the foregoing law to the facts of this appeal, and having viewed the relevant video—and audiotapes, I find no fault with the trial judge's conclusion that the respondent's confession was voluntary and reliable. The respondent was fully apprised of his rights at all times; he was never subjected to harsh, aggressive, or overbearing interrogation; he was not deprived of sleep, food, or drink; and he was never offered any improper inducements that undermined the reliability of the confessions. As the Court of Appeal reached a contrary conclusion with respect to a number of these issues, I will address them in turn.

1. Minimizing the Seriousness of the Crimes

[73] The Court of Appeal concluded that the police improperly offered leniency to the respondent by minimizing the seriousness of his offences and suggesting "that the same punishment would likely be given whether he confessed to one or a number of fires" (para. 156). This, in their opinion, was an improper inducement (at para. 126):

> In the beginning, it was suggested that "there isn't much in a car fire." Once the admission relating to the car was obtained, then the suggestion was made—and on several occasions— that the accused was not really a criminal and that the police did not want to treat him as a criminal. In addition, it was stated to the accused—again more than once—that there was little difference between being found guilty of one fire as compared to 10.

[74] Insofar as the police simply downplayed the moral culpability of the offence, their actions were not problematic. As even the Court of Appeal recognized (at para. 126), "minimizing the moral significance of the offence is a common and usually unobjectionable feature of police interrogation." Instead, the real concern is whether the police suggested that "confession will result in the legal consequences being minimal" (para. 126). As discussed above, this is inappropriate.

[75] However, and with the greatest respect to the Court of Appeal, I believe they have mischaracterized the police interrogators' words. The offending passages are well represented by the following excerpt (AR at p. 552), made shortly after the respondent arrived at the police station subsequent to his initial confession:

> If you done the other ones this—or some of the other ones this is the time—this is the time to just get them off your chest. This is the perfect opportunity because of what you've already told us, okay. And everybody can see this, that it's—You didn't do one fire and then years down the road you did—this is a series of fires we've been having in Waterville. *So we can look at it—we look at it as a one-package type of thing.* Okay. And it's—if you had a problem, I don't know what it is yet. Maybe we'll find out what it is, maybe you can help us on this. It's not unrealistic that you would set some more things on fire especially when you would do your girlfriend's vehicle, your fiancee's vehicle but you don't know why. So there's something that—there's something that triggers you into setting that fire. [Emphasis added.]

[76] The Court of Appeal focused on the [italicized] passage to suggest that the police were offering a "package deal," whereby the respondent would not be charged with multiple crimes if he confessed to them all. However, as the rest of the passage makes clear, the police were doing nothing of the sort. Instead, they were simply pointing out their reasons for believing that he was responsible for all the fires, not just one: namely, that it was a series of fires in issue, not isolated incidents. The police therefore treated the fires as a "package," all of which were likely set by the same person.

[77] This interpretation is confirmed by the police's consistent refusal to accept Oickle's own suggestions of a "package deal." Shortly before confessing to the vehicle fire, the following exchange took place between the respondent and Corporal Deveau (AR at pp. 519-20):

A: No, hang on, hang on. If [I] admit to her car and are the other ones looked at too?

Q: Richard, all I can tell you now is I want the truth out. I don't want—you said, "If I admit to her car," which leads me to believe that maybe you're involved in that.

A: Um.

Q: Well, if you're involved in it, tell me the truth and then we'll look—you know, if—I don't think for one minute that you're involved in everything. Okay? But if you did the car, Richard, tell me you did the car. And if I believe that's it, if we believe that you did not do the other one, I mean, we're—remember I said, we're not here to trick you into anything?

A: I trust you.

Q: I'm not here to bring everything down on you. The last thing I want to do, Richard. You've been good to me and I'm trying to be good to you.

A: Uh-huh.

Q: And I want you to tell me the truth. So if you did the car, tell me you did the car. *But I want the truth. I just don't want you to say, "I did the car, so I'm free from all the others."* Okay? That's why it's important here that—

A: Uh-huh.

Q: It's the truth that we want. [Emphasis added.]

As this passage reveals, it was the respondent, not the police, who was seeking a "package deal"—a deal Corporal Deveau squarely rejected. While the police did minimize the moral significance of the crimes, there was never any suggestion by the police that a confession would minimize the *legal* consequences of the respondent's crimes.

2. Offers of Psychiatric Help

[78] The Court of Appeal also found that the police improperly offered psychiatric help in return for a confession. For example, at para. 121, the Court of Appeal noted passages wherein the police told the respondent "I think you need help," and "[m]aybe you need professional help." See also paras. 108 (pp. 363-64) and 122 (pp. 371-72). However, at no point did the police ever suggest that the respondent could only get help if he confessed. The distinction here is between the police suggesting the potential benefits of

confession, and making offers that are conditional upon receiving a confession. The former is entirely appropriate—it is not an inducement because there is no *quid pro quo*. The latter is improper. However, the police made no such offer in the course of their interrogation of the respondent.

3. "It Would Be Better"

[79] The transcripts are indeed rife with these sorts of comments. The police suggested that a confession would make the respondent feel better, that his fiancée and members of the community would respect him for admitting his problem (para. 120) and that he could better address his apparent pyromania if he confessed (para. 122). However, read in context, none of these statements contained an implied threat or promise. Instead, they were merely moral inducements suggesting to the respondent that he would feel better if he confessed and began addressing his problems. And indeed, after his confession, Corporal Deveau asked him "[s]o how do you feel now, Richard?" His answer was "[b]etter."

[80] To hold that the police officers' frequent suggestions that things would be better if the respondent confessed amounted to an improper threat or inducement would be to engage in empty formalism. The tapes of the transcript clearly reveal that there could be no implied threat in these words. The respondent was never mistreated. Nor was there any implied promise. The police may have suggested possible benefits of confession, but there was never any insinuation of a *quid pro quo*. I therefore respectfully disagree with the Court of Appeal that these comments undermined the confessions' voluntariness.

4. Alleged Threats Against the Respondent's Fiancée

[81] As discussed in connection with *Jackson* [*R v Jackson* (1977), 34 CCC (2d) 35 (BCCA)], a threat or promise with respect to a third person could be an improper inducement. The Court of Appeal stated, at para. 128, that the police effectively told the respondent that "If he confessed, it would not be necessary to continue the investigation or put his fiancé [*sic*] through extensive interrogation."

[82] The majority of references during the interrogation to the respondent's fiancée, Tanya Kilcup, centered on the respondent's reliance on her as an alibi witness: see, e.g., AR at p. 570. However, the Court of Appeal is correct that there were moments when the police intimated that it might be necessary to question Ms. Kilcup to make sure she was not involved in the fires at all, either alone or in collaboration with the respondent:

> Q. You know, this whole thing is—we might even ask Tanya if she would take a polygraph on this because we don't know where she stands, okay.
>
> A. Do I have to sit here for that?
>
> Q. Oh, no, no, not until she takes the polygraph. She's not going to take the polygraph tonight. But if you can tell us anything—[AR at p. 574]
>
> • • •
>
> Q. Do you realize the other reason is that we—that you've got to come clean with everything with us is for Tanya.
>
> A. Um.

Q. We don't want to put Tanya through any—I mean she's going to be going through enough trying to—we don't want to—and I'm sure you don't want her to get—to go through half or what you went through today. It's no fun.

A. No, no.

Q. It won't be any fun for her. But in order for her to—in order for us to be one hundred percent we have to do it. So if there's anything that you can tell us that can put her—that we say, okay, we don't need you, Tanya, we have it here, you know, and we have some stuff. But we're not convinced on everything else. So don't put Tanya through that if there's something you can tell me, okay. [AR at pp. 603-4]

[83] The relationship the respondent had with Ms. Kilcup was, in my opinion, strong enough potentially to induce a false confession were she threatened with harm. However, I do not believe any such threat ever occurred. There were no pending charges against Ms. Kilcup that the police were offering to drop; they never threatened to bring charges against her; indeed, the police never seriously suggested her as a suspect. The most they did was promise not to polygraph her if the respondent confessed. Given the entire context, the most likely reason to polygraph her was not as a suspect, but as an alibi witness. In my opinion, this is not a strong enough inducement to raise a reasonable doubt as to the voluntariness of the respondent's confessions.

[84] Moreover, the timing of the comments regarding Ms. Kilcup suggests that there was no causal connection between the police inducements and the subsequent confession. After the statements quoted above, Corporal Deveau left the room, and told the respondent that he intended to speak to Tanya. Therefore the respondent's actual confession was approximately two hours after he thought the police were already speaking to Tanya. Moreover, soon after Constable Bogle took over the interrogation, the respondent himself made it clear that he thought the police were only talking to Ms. Kilcup in order to verify his alibi (AR at p. 611):

Q. Okay. I mean we have to go and—we asked Cst. Taker to talk to Tanya, okay. (Inaudible).

A. But I didn't tell her.

Q. What?

A. I didn't tell her.

Q. Yeah.

A. Totally by myself.

The "inducements" regarding the respondent's fiancée lacked both the strength and causal connection necessary to warrant exclusion.

5. Abuse of Trust

[85] The Court of Appeal suggests at para. 129 that the police in general, and Corporal Deveau in particular, improperly abused the respondent's trust to obtain a confession. With respect, I cannot agree. In essence, the court criticizes the police for questioning the respondent in such a gentle, reassuring manner that they gained his trust. This does not

render a confession inadmissible. To hold otherwise would send the perverse message to police that they should engage in adversarial, aggressive questioning to ensure they never gain the suspect's trust, lest an ensuing confession be excluded.

6. Atmosphere of Oppression

[86] To hold that the police conduct in this interrogation was oppressive would leave little scope for police interrogation, and ignore Lamer J's reminder in *Rothman*, *supra*, at p. 697, that "the investigation of crime and the detection of criminals is not a game to be governed by the Marquess of Queensbury rules." Quite simply, the police acted in a proper manner. Viewing the videotapes and listening to the audiotapes reveal that at all times the police were courteous; they did not deprive the respondent of food, sleep, or water (at para. 119); they never denied him access to the bathroom; and they fully apprised him of his rights at all times (see, e.g., AR at pp. 370, 497 and 650). They did not fabricate evidence in an attempt to convince him denials were futile. They comforted him, with apparent sincerity, when he broke down in tears upon confessing. While the re-enactment was admittedly done at a time when the respondent had had little sleep, he was already awake when they approached him, and was told that he could stop at any time. And indeed, the Court of Appeal did not directly claim that the police created an atmosphere of oppression sufficient to exclude the statements.

[87] The absence of oppression is important not only in its own right, but also because it affects the overall voluntariness analysis. In the preceding sections, I have concluded that the police offered the respondent, at best, extremely mild inducements. In particular, they suggested that "it would be better" if he confessed, and suggested that his girlfriend could be spared questioning if he confessed. However, given the entirely non-oppressive atmosphere maintained by the police, I do not believe that any of the alleged inducements are sufficient to render the confessions involuntary.

E. The Relevance of the Polygraph Test

[88] In addition to the issues addressed above, the Court of Appeal found the police use of a polygraph particularly problematic. Because of the growing frequency with which police are using the polygraph as an investigative tool, and the absence of any direction thus far from this Court regarding the proper use of polygraphs in interrogations, I will now briefly discuss how polygraphs fit into the analytical framework set out above. The Court of Appeal identified several problems with the police's use of a polygraph in this appeal. I will address each in turn.

1. Informing the Suspect of the Uses to Which the Polygraph Test Can Be Put

[Iacobucci J agreed with the trial judge's finding that the accused was not confused about the admissibility of the results of the polygraph test.]

Exaggerating the Polygraph's Validity

[94] The Court of Appeal also noted, correctly in my opinion, that the police made "repeated assertions to the accused that the polygraph was an infallible determiner of truth" (para. 156). Throughout the interrogation that produced the respondent's initial

admission that he set Ms. Kilcup's vehicle on fire, both Sergeant Taker and Constable Deveau emphasized that the polygraph did not make mistakes, and that if Sergeant Taker interpreted it to indicate deception, then the respondent must have lied. For example, the Court of Appeal cited the following passage (at paras. 141-42):

[Oickle:] But if you read the chart and it says they are lying, then they are.

[Taker:] That's right. That's right.

. . .

Deveau: *There's no doubt in anybody's mind now that you are involved in some of these fires.*

Oickle: Because I failed that ...

Deveau: Yes, very simple Richard ... and when asked the question about these eight fires, the polygraph says that you are not truthful ... *the machine does not lie.* You found that out today. [Emphasis added.]

[95] I agree that the police exaggerated the accuracy of the polygraph. As many sources have demonstrated, polygraphs are far from infallible: see, e.g., D.T. Lykken, *A Tremor in the Blood: Uses and Abuses of the Lie Detector* (1998); J.J. Furedy, "The 'control' question 'test' (CQT) polygrapher's dilemma: logico-ethical considerations for psycho-physiological practitioners and researchers" (1993), 15 *Int. J. Psychophysiology* 263; C.J. Patrick and W.G. Iacono, "Validity of the Control Question Polygraph Test: The Problem of Sampling Bias" (1991), 76 *J. App. Psych.* 229. ...

[Iacobucci J distinguished *R v Amyot* (1990), 58 CCC (3d) 312 (Qc CA), where the accused's statement had been excluded after police told him that a polygraph was infallible, on the ground that Oickle, unlike Amyot, "was not overwhelmed by the polygraph results."]

[99] Granted that the police misled the respondent with regards to the accuracy of the polygraph, the question remains whether, in light of the entire circumstances of the interrogation, this rendered the confessions inadmissible. In my opinion it did not. As discussed above, there was no emotional disintegration in this case. The mere fact that a suspect begins to cry when he or she finally confesses, as the respondent did, is not evidence of "complete emotional disintegration"; tears are to be expected when someone finally divulges that they committed a crime—particularly when the suspect is a generally law-abiding and upstanding citizen like the respondent.

[100] Nor, as discussed above, do I believe that the police created an oppressive atmosphere. Simply confronting the suspect with adverse evidence, like a polygraph test, is not grounds for exclusion: see *Fitton, supra.* This holds true even for inadmissible evidence: see *Alexis* [*R v Alexis* (1994), 35 CR (4th) 117 (Ont Ct (Gen Div))]. Nor does the fact that the police exaggerate the evidence's reliability or importance necessarily render a confession inadmissible. Eyewitness accounts are by no means infallible; yet in *Fitton*, this Court ruled admissible a statement taken after the police told a suspect they did not believe his denials because several eyewitnesses had come forward against him. In short, merely confronting a suspect with adverse evidence—even exaggerating its accuracy and reliability—will not, standing alone, render a confession involuntary.

3. *Misleading the Accused Regarding the Duration of the Interview*

[101] The final ground on which the Court of Appeal challenged the use of the polygraph, at para. 156, was the police's

> misleading the accused about the expected duration of the test procedure, particularly concerning the interrogation to follow and immediately commencing intense questioning upon informing the accused that he had "failed" the test ... .

A similar argument was made in *Nugent* [R v *Nugent* (1988), 84 NSR (2d) 191 (CA)]. Since this Court has ruled that polygraph results are not admissible in evidence, *Béland* [R v *Béland*, [1987] 2 SCR 398], "then the administering of a test must be clearly separated from questioning for the purpose of obtaining statements" (*Nugent, supra*, at p. 212). According to the Court of Appeal, a statement directly following a polygraph should not be admissible because the defence cannot adequately explain the context of the statement—which it might wish to do in order to attack the weight of the statement before the jury—without notifying the jury that the accused failed a polygraph test.

[102] Drawing on these arguments, the intervener, the Criminal Lawyer's Association, argued that the police have only two options when using polygraphs. One is to ensure that the suspect has consulted with counsel before consenting to the test. The other is to "clearly separate any post-test interrogation from the test itself." I do not believe that it is necessary to limit the police's discretion in this manner. It is true that the police procedures present the defence with the unpalatable choice of either trying to explain away the confession without using the polygraph, or admitting that the accused failed the test. However, this is true any time a suspect confesses after being confronted with inadmissible evidence, and it does not necessarily render the confession involuntary. Tactical disadvantage to the defence is not relevant to the voluntariness of the defendant's confession; instead, if anything, it simply suggests prejudicial effect. However, given the immense probative value of a voluntary confession, I cannot agree that exclusion is appropriate.

[103] The final argument in favour of separating the interrogation from the polygraph test is related to the alleged "abuse of trust" addressed above. It is submitted that the intimacy fostered during the pre-test interview improperly carries over to the post-test interrogation. Whether this is true or not, I do not believe it would be grounds to exclude the confession. On this point, I agree with the Ontario Court of Appeal in *R v. Barton* (1993), 81 CCC (3d) 574 at p. 575:

> There is no question that the procedure is intrusive and purports to use expertise in psychology to create a relationship between the interviewer and the candidate which is conducive to making the technical analysis more accurate. It is also true that the appearance of intimacy carries over into the third stage when, in this case, the inculpatory statement was made. Yet, all police interrogations may include these features in one form or another. The "good cop, bad cop" routine is the best known.

Moreover, in this appeal the respondent did not confess until Corporal Deveau took over the questioning from Sergeant Taker. Therefore any intimacy created by the pre-test interview could not have precipitated the respondent's confessions.

F. Summary on Voluntariness

[104] In summary, there were several aspects of the police's interrogation of the respondent that could potentially be relevant to the voluntariness of his confessions. These include the comments regarding Ms. Kilcup; the suggestions that "it would be better" for the respondent to confess; and the exaggeration of the polygraph's accuracy. These are certainly relevant considerations when determining voluntariness. However, I agree with the trial judge that neither standing alone, nor in combination with each other and the rest of the circumstances surrounding the respondent's confessions, do these factors raise a reasonable doubt about the voluntariness of the respondent's confessions. The respondent was never mistreated, he was questioned in an extremely friendly, benign tone, and he was not offered any inducements strong enough to raise a reasonable doubt as to voluntariness in the absence of any mistreatment or oppression. As I find no error in the trial judge's reasons, the Court of Appeal should not have disturbed her findings.

[Arbour J dissented on two grounds: first, that the interrogation contained "improper inducements" and, second, that the use of the polygraph put the accused "in the unfair position of having to lead prejudicial, unreliable and inadmissible evidence against himself in order to impeach the veracity of the statements obtained."]

[The Crown's appeal was allowed and the convictions were restored.]

a. Inducements

It is difficult to generalize about what sort of police conduct will be found to have induced a statement through fear of prejudice or hope of advantage. As discussed by the Supreme Court in *Oickle*, above, the determination will be very fact-specific and depend on the trial judge's assessment of the credibility of the accused and the police officers. The following examples should be read with this in mind.

In *R v Spencer*, 2007 SCC 11, [2007] 1 SCR 500, the accused was charged with 18 robberies, some of which involved his girlfriend's vehicle. After his arrest, police interviewed him for close to nine hours. He repeatedly expressed a desire to visit his girlfriend, who had been arrested for one of the robberies. Police told him that he would not be able to do so until he offered at least a "partial" confession. Writing for the majority, Deschamps J stated as follows:

> With respect to promises, which are at issue in the present appeal, this Court has recognized that they "need not be aimed directly at the suspect ... to have a coercive effect" (*Oickle*, at para. 51). While Iacobucci J. recognized in *Oickle* that the existence of a *quid pro quo* is the "most important consideration" when an inducement is alleged to have been offered by a person in authority, he did not hold it to be an exclusive factor, or one determinative of voluntariness. ... Furthermore, *Oickle* does not state that any *quid pro quo* held out by a person in authority, regardless of its significance, will necessarily render a statement by an accused involuntary. ...
>
> ⋅ ⋅ ⋅
>
> Therefore, while a *quid pro quo* is an important factor in establishing the existence of a threat or promise, it is the strength of the inducement, having regard to the particular individual and his or her circumstances, that is to be considered in the overall contextual analysis into the voluntariness of the accused's statement.

. . .

In my view, the trial judge made no error of law in concluding that no offer of leniency was made in respect of Ms. Harrison and that the withholding of a visit to her until at least a partial confession was made was an inducement that was not strong enough to render the accused's statements inadmissible. It was a relevant factor that the accused had not "lost control of the interview to the point where he and Cst. Parker [were] no longer playing on a level field" (*voir dire*, at para. 35). ...

It was also relevant to the particularities of the respondent that, according to the trial judge, he was aggressive and a "mature and savvy participant," and that he unsuccessfully attempted many times to secure "deals" with the police. While none of these factors are determinative, it was not an error for the trial judge to consider them in his contextual analysis.

In his dissenting reasons, Fish J stressed that the inducements branch of the confessions rule is distinct from the concept of an operating mind. In his view, in cases, like *Spencer*, where the result turns on the former, "the will of the detainee has not been 'overborne' in the sense that he or she 'has lost any meaningfu[l] independent ability to choose to remain silent' ... ; rather, the will of the detainee is said to have been 'overborne' only in the sense that he or she would not otherwise have given a statement but was persuaded to do so in order to achieve an expected result—to avoid threatened pain or achieve promised gain. A statement thus given is the result of a calculated decision by an operating mind; it is nonetheless considered 'involuntary' for the reasons set out in both *Ibrahim* and *Oickle*." Fish J characterized the actions of police and their effect on the respondent very differently than the majority:

> The uncontradicted evidence on the *voir dire* discloses what I would characterize as a compound *quid pro quo*—an implicit but unmistakable threat accompanied by an implicit but unmistakable promise that rendered inadmissible the respondent's inculpatory statements to the police. At the very least, they raise a reasonable doubt whether the statements were improperly induced and therefore involuntary under both *Ibrahim* and *Oickle*.
>
> The threat and the promise were both directed at the respondent's girlfriend and it appears plain from the record that their relationship was "strong enough to raise a reasonable doubt about whether the will of the [respondent] ha[d] been overborne." ...

. . .

In the present case, the respondent's relationship with his girlfriend, Tanya, was likewise strong enough to induce a false confession were she threatened with harm. And unlike *Oickle*, there *was* such a threat—accompanied, as I have mentioned, by Constable Parker's promise of advantageous intervention with the Crown and with other police officers on Tanya's behalf.

The depth of the respondent's concern with Tanya's welfare and his determination to save her from being charged were apparent throughout his interrogation. He referred repeatedly to his wish that Tanya be "kept out of it"; he inquired about the potential consequences for Tanya's child if Tanya were charged; he offered to confess to 30-40 robberies if Tanya were "ke[pt] ... out of everything."

Constable Parker himself acknowledged the respondent's vulnerability with regard to Tanya, as well as the strength of their relationship. "Tanya's the center of your world," he asked the respondent rhetorically, "is [that] what you're telling me?"

Constable Parker clearly indicated to the respondent that he would recommend to the Crown that Tanya not be charged if the respondent confessed ... . No less subtly, Constable Parker threatened that Tanya would be charged *unless* the respondent confessed ... .

In short, unlike *Oickle*, the interrogating officer in this case did threaten to bring charges against the respondent's girlfriend and, to lend added weight to the threat, referred to the evidence implicating her as the driver of the getaway car used in the robberies. Constable Parker suggested that she was more than a mere suspect. And, again unlike *Oickle*, the respondent confessed *immediately after being told once more that Tanya would be charged unless he confessed.*

At the end of his interrogation, Constable Parker asked the respondent why he had confessed. The respondent's spontaneous reply was short and eloquent: "For my girl," he said. This confirms to me that, on the uncontradicted evidence before us, there is a real likelihood that the respondent was induced to confess by the compound *quid pro quo* held out to him by Constable Parker.

In *R v Leblanc* (1972), 8 CCC (2d) 562 (BCCA), an accused charged with theft testified in the *voir dire* that the police had in effect stated "until we get some sort of answers where the stuff come from ... we just can't get no bail." The officers did not contradict the accused on this point. The Court of Appeal held that the accused's subsequent statement was involuntary.

In *R v Letendre* (1979), 46 CCC (2d) 398 (BCCA), an accused charged with various offences in relation to stolen stereo equipment was interrogated by two police officers and denied involvement. One officer stated, "Well, I'm getting mad," and the other stated that he did not like to see his partner get mad. The accused "got scared" and stated, "I stole the stuff myself, okay," and made further admissions. The Court of Appeal held that the statement was involuntary.

In *R v Parsons* (1979), 48 CCC (2d) 476 (Nfld CA), an accused charged with a narcotics offence made an inculpatory statement after he was told that if the matter was not cleared up soon, he would be held in custody over the weekend. The statement was involuntary.

In *R v Hayes*, 1982 ABCA 30, 65 CCC (2d) 294, the police told an accused that it would be better for him to answer questions and "It wouldn't be very good if you're telling us a story now, and it turns out that you're lying." The accused's subsequent statement was held to be voluntary in the circumstances.

In *R v Reyat* (1993), 80 CCC (3d) 210 (BCCA), an accused was charged with manslaughter resulting from a notorious terrorist bombing. At several points during a lengthy interrogation, a police officer referred to the accused's family. For example:

> You have to admit to me, you can't ... deny the fact that you haven't told me the truth quite a few times when we've been talking here. ... Reyat ah let me say again, look I know your position here in the community an I know the type a person you are. I know your family, like—like your family is—is—they're beautiful people. Look at your little kids how nice they are. Okay they're—they're nice. I don't wan—I—I just hate to see something come out in my investigation that—that shows, like my investigation shows a certain thing. An I'm—an I'm saying geez if it's not like that way then tell me the truth about the way it is.

A significant admission was obtained in this interrogation. While recognizing that "some of the statements made by the officers could be construed as oblique promises or threats," the Court of Appeal held that the trial judge had not erred in admitting the accused's statements.

In *R v S (SL)*, 1999 ABCA 41, 132 CCC (3d) 146, an accused was charged with a sexual offence. A police officer stated that "the only way you can get better is by telling me the truth," and the accused's denials of the allegations were met with statements like "you're not on the right track." A majority of the Court of Appeal held that the statement was involuntary because it was induced by planting in the accused's mind the notion that the path to rehabilitation had to begin with a statement to the officer that demonstrated that he was on the right track. See also *R v MSM*, 2014 ONCA 441.

b. Operating Mind

The operating mind issue typically arises when there is an allegation that the accused was suffering from some kind of cognitive deficiency when making the statement. The leading decision is *R v Whittle*, [1994] 2 SCR 914, 92 CCC (3d) 11. In that case, an accused suffering from schizophrenia was charged with murder. The victim had died in circumstances that the police regarded as accidental, but suspicious. The accused and others were interviewed at the time, but no charges were laid. Several weeks later, the accused was taken into custody on another matter. He made several statements concerning his involvement in the death of the victim, including statements that led the police to physical evidence connected with the crime. The Supreme Court described the circumstances surrounding these statements as follows:

> The appellant told the officers that he had sawed the axe in half and thrown it in a field near Brock St. and Highway 401. The appellant then accompanied [Detective Constables] Orban and Gillespie to the location which he described where they met with two other officers from DRPF. During the 15-minute car trip to that location, the appellant "talked continuously" about the Windsor offences and the occurrence in Whitby. Although the search was unsuccessful at that point, the axe handle was located during a subsequent search of that area. On the return trip from the area, the appellant continued to disclose details relating to the murder, including the fact that he had disposed of his shoes after the incident and took precautions to avoid leaving fingerprints at the scene. Interspersed with this running discussion by the appellant were a series of two or three incidents in which the appellant stopped talking and made reference to someone being in his brain or having fog in his head. After this, he would continue talking about the incidents in question, as if these digressions had never occurred. Detective Constable Orban testified that it was more what the appellant said than how he said it which indicated to him that certain of the appellant's statements were divorced from reality.
>
> • • •
>
> … Gillespie contacted a defence attorney, Robert Nuttall, on behalf of the appellant. Gillespie spoke first with Nuttall and told him that the appellant had confessed to several serious crimes. Nuttall agreed to speak with the appellant and testified that he had advised the appellant to "keep his mouth shut." He also testified that the appellant had told him that he had voices in his head, that he had to talk, that he had a pain in his head and that he could see dead babies' faces in cement. The appellant told Nuttall that he needed to talk to the police in order to stop the voices. After speaking with the appellant, Nuttall was convinced that the appellant would speak with authorities against his advice. When the appellant turned the phone over to Gillespie, Nuttall indicated that he agreed with Gillespie's characterization of the appellant as a "loon" or a "nutbar" and that he was sure that the appellant would speak with the authorities, in spite of Nuttall's advice to the contrary. Nuttall also told Gillespie that any other officers who wished to speak with the appellant should contact Nuttall before doing so.
>
> As predicted by Nuttall, the appellant indicated that he still wished to continue with the video statement. In the result, a second video statement was initiated at 12:21 a.m. on February 7, 1990. This statement lasted approximately one hour. At the outset, the appellant stated that he had not

committed the offences described in the committal warrants and alleged "somebody has used my name." He described his reason for coming to the police as the result of "crackin' in [his] mind" and his resulting inability to live in society any longer. When reminded of the exercise of his right to counsel, the appellant acknowledged that he was informed that he had the right not to speak with the police, but that he wanted to talk to them anyway. Further, he indicated that he understood that it would be up to a judge whether or not his statements would be used in making a decision about him. After some prompting by Gillespie, the appellant repeated the details relating to the death of Frank Dowson which he had relayed earlier. Throughout the video statement the appellant made comments such as "I'm just ah, feel like I got snow in my head," "I feel like I got [other people's] brains on me ... So they're always tryin' a' think out a' me ... And every time I say somethin', unless I been asked a question, I can't think above them ... we're both bein' punished," and "I managed to, ah, come up with this idea to walk backwards to New Brunswick ... That would exercise me back to normal." When asked whether he had been forced to say anything, the appellant indicated that he was uncertain whether he had been manipulated into it in that "somebody maybe plotted murder in this life and they picked me to do it for them, right?". The appellant also stated that he had always wanted to die, but that he had never been able to and that he intended to stay on his tippy-toes regardless of whether anyone liked it.

The accused was found to be fit to stand trial. The psychiatrists who assessed him testified on the *voir dire* to determine the admissibility of his statements. The Supreme Court summarized these opinions as follows:

Perhaps the most central testimony came from Dr. Malcolm, who testified for the defence, and Dr. McDonald, who testified for the Crown. Dr. McDonald is a forensic psychiatrist with METFORS who examined the appellant during his 30-day psychiatric assessment in February and March 1990. Dr. Malcolm is also a forensic psychiatrist. Both gave the opinion that the appellant suffers from schizophrenia and that a common symptom of this illness is auditory hallucination. However, Dr. Malcolm testified that the appellant's condition would have been florid at the time of the video statement and that although the appellant may have been rationally aware of the consequences of giving the statement, he was driven to make the statements by the voices in his head. In contrast, Dr. McDonald testified that it was possible that the appellant had been experiencing auditory hallucinations at the time of the video statement, but that there was no specific evidence of that in the tape itself.

On the legal test for an "operating mind," the Supreme Court, per Sopinka J, said:

The operating mind test ... requires that the accused possess a limited degree of cognitive ability to understand what he or she is saying and to comprehend that the evidence may be used in proceedings against the accused. Indeed it would be hard to imagine what an operating mind is if it does not possess this limited amount of cognitive ability. In determining the requisite capacity to make an active choice, the relevant test is: Did the accused possess an operating mind? It goes no further and no inquiry is necessary as to whether the accused is capable of making a good or wise choice or one that is in his or her interest.

. . .

The operating mind test, which is an aspect of the confessions rule, includes a limited mental component which requires that the accused have sufficient cognitive capacity to understand what he or she is saying and what is said. This includes the ability to understand a caution that the evidence can be used against the accused.

On the question of whether the statements were the product of the accused's operating mind, the court reviewed Dr. Malcolm's testimony and said:

> In summary, the evidence of Dr. Malcolm was that the appellant was aware of what he was saying and what was said to him and of the court process. He was fit to instruct counsel but, because of the voices that were telling him to unburden himself, he did not care about the consequences.
>
> On the basis of evidence which the trial judge accepted, the appellant's mental condition satisfied the operating mind test including the subjective element to which I have referred above. There was no obligation on the Crown to establish that the appellant possessed a higher degree of cognitive capacity. To the extent that the inner voices prompted the appellant to speak in apparent disregard of the advice of his counsel and to his detriment, because he did not care about the consequences or felt that he could not resist the urging of the voices, they cannot be the basis for exclusion. Inner compulsion, due to conscience or otherwise, cannot displace the finding of an operating mind unless, in combination with conduct of a person in authority, a statement is found to be involuntary.

The accused's statements were therefore held to be the product of his operating mind and were admissible under the common law confessions rule.

c. Oppression

In *Oickle*, the Supreme Court succinctly defined oppression as an interrogation conducted under "inhumane conditions." In *R v Prager*, [1972] 1 All ER 1114, the Court of Appeal considered the meaning of the word "oppression" in the Judges' Rules:

> The only reported judicial consideration of "oppression" in the Judges' Rules of which we are aware is that of Sachs J in *R v Priestley*, [1965] 51 Cr App 1 where he said
>
> > "[T]o my mind, this word in the context of the principles under consideration imports something which tends to sap, and has sapped, that free will which must exist before a confession is voluntary. ... Whether or not there is oppression in an individual case depends upon many elements. I am not going into all of them. They include such things as the length of time of any individual period of questioning, the length of time intervening between periods of questioning, whether the accused person has been given proper refreshment or not, and the characteristics of the person who makes the statement. What may be oppressive as regards a child, an invalid or an old man or somebody inexperienced in the ways of this world may turn out not to be oppressive when one finds that the accused person is of a tough character and an experienced man of the world."
>
> In an address to the Bentham Club in 1968 (See (1968) 21 *Current Legal Problems*, p 10), Lord MacDermott described "oppressive questioning" as—
>
> > Questioning which by its nature, duration or other attendant circumstances (including the fact of custody) excites hopes (such as the hope of release) or fears, or so affects the mind of the suspect that his will crumbles and he speaks when otherwise he would have stayed silent.
>
> We adopt these definitions or descriptions and apply them to the present case.

On the facts of the case, no oppression was found.

In *Hobbins v R*, [1982] 1 SCR 553, 66 CCC (2d) 289, Laskin CJ, speaking for the court, said:

> There is no doubt that the state of mind of the accused is relevant to the admissibility of a statement made by him to the police after interrogation, and even if he has been cautioned, as was the case here in respect of the second statement. An atmosphere of oppression may be created in the circumstances surrounding the taking of a statement, although there be no inducement held out of hope of advantage or fear of prejudice, and absent any threats of violence or actual violence. However, and counsel for the appellant accused conceded this, an accused's own timidity or subjective fear of the police will not avail to avoid the admissibility of a statement or confession unless there are external circumstances brought about by the conduct of the police that can be said to cast doubt on the voluntariness of a statement or confession by the accused or there are considerations affecting the accused, as in the *Ward* case [*Ward v R*, [1979] 2 SCR 30], ... which would justify doubt as to voluntariness. In this respect, it does not, of course, matter that the police did not commit any illegality if the circumstances of the interrogation, including time and place and length of interrogation, raise or should raise doubt in the trial judge whether the statement or confession was freely and voluntarily given.

How far do these comments go in recognizing oppression as a branch of the voluntariness rule independent of fear of prejudice or hope of advantage? Do Laskin CJ's comments about the accused's state of mind refer to "voluntariness" in the sense of fear of prejudice or hope of advantage, to oppression, or to both? *Hobbins* seems to reject a purely subjective standard; but what standard is adopted? Must the "external circumstances" be intended by the police to obtain a statement, or is it enough that they had the effect of producing a statement? Would you favour a purely objective test (a reasonable person would have perceived the police's conduct as creating a fear of prejudice, etc.) or a mixed standard (the police's conduct in the circumstances could have caused a reasonable person to fear, etc., and the accused did fear, etc.)? See also *R v Griffin* (1981), 59 CCC (2d) 503 (Ont H Ct J); *R v Hoilett* (1999), 136 CCC (3d) 449 (Ont CA); *R v Serack*, [1974] 2 WWR 377 (BCSC).

4. Evidence Derived from Involuntary Confessions

Though involuntary statements are not admissible, they may lead to the discovery of other evidence. There are two lines of authority dealing with this situation: one for subsequent statements and one for physical evidence.

a. The Derived Confession Rule

Refer again to the facts of *R v SGT*, 2010 SCC 20, [2010] 1 SCR 688 (Section I.A.1, above). In addition to deciding whether the mother was a "person in authority," the court also had to determine whether the email sent to her by the accused constituted an inadmissible "derived confession." Writing for the majority, Charron J stated as follows:

> [28] The leading case on the derived confessions rule is *R. v. I.(L.R.) and T.(E.)*, [1993] 4 S.C.R. 504. In brief, the derived confessions rule serves to exclude statements which, despite not appearing to be involuntary when considered alone, are sufficiently connected to an earlier involuntary confession as to be rendered involuntary and hence inadmissible. For example, in that

case, a young offender was charged with second degree murder and gave an inculpatory statement to the police. The next day, after meeting with his lawyer, the accused came to the police,
wishing to modify the statement that he had given the previous day. The trial judge excluded the
first statement but admitted the second, and the accused was convicted by a jury. The accused
appealed the conviction on the basis that the second statement should not have been admitted.
His appeal was ultimately successful in this Court.

[29] In outlining the principles applicable to derived confessions, the Court articulated a contextual and fact-based approach to determining whether a subsequent statement is sufficiently
connected to a prior, inadmissible confession to also be excluded. In assessing the degree of
connection, the Court outlined a number of factors to be considered, including "the time span
between the statements, advertence to the previous statement during questioning, the discovery of additional incriminating evidence subsequent to the first statement, the presence of the
same police officers at both interrogations and other similarities between the two circumstances"
(p. 526). The Court then held:

> In applying these factors, a subsequent confession would be involuntary if either the
> tainting features which disqualified the first confession continued to be present or if the
> fact that the first statement was made was a substantial factor contributing to the making
> of the second statement. [p. 526]

The Court was clear in adding that "[n]o general rule excluded subsequent statements on the
ground that they were tainted irrespective of the degree of connection to the initial admissible
statement" (p. 526).

[30] It is plain from the above principles that the "derived confessions rule" emanates from
the common law confessions rule. As such, like its parent, it is clear that it applies to secondary
confessions, that is, statements made to a person in authority that are sufficiently connected to a
previous involuntary confession to be deemed also involuntary. Whether the derived confessions
rule also applies in respect of subsequent admissions made to persons not in authority, however,
is not so clear.

· · ·

[32] I respectfully disagree with Fish J. that "[a]s a matter of principle and logic" it is clear that
"derived confessions need not be made to a person in authority in order to be found inadmissible" (para. 85). As a matter of principle, this broad assertion ignores the distinction between
confessions and admissions discussed earlier. As for logic, much will depend on the facts of the
particular case. Logic may have compelled the conclusion reached in *G.(B.)* where the later statement, which actually contained the earlier tainted confession given to the police, was made to a
psychiatrist during the course of a court-ordered examination into his mental condition. It may
not be so compelling in a case where, for example, the accused repeats the contents of the
tainted confession to a personal friend who has no connection to the prosecution.

[33] It is not necessary, nor would it be appropriate on this record, to decide whether the
derived confessions rule extends to admissions made to ordinary persons. It suffices for our purposes to assume that, given an appropriate evidentiary basis connecting the police inducement
and the later e-mail, it would at least be arguable that the subsequent statement could be excluded, if not on the basis of the common law derived confessions rule, perhaps on a *Charter*
basis. The distinction between the two possible bases for exclusion remains important as the
application of the common law "derived confessions rule" would result in the automatic exclusion

of the tainted statement, whereas under the *Canadian Charter of Rights and Freedoms* the question of exclusion would fall to be determined under s. 24(2). However, the defence did not raise the argument concerning the derived confessions rule at trial, nor did S.G.T. bring a *Charter* application seeking the exclusion of the e-mail. For example, it would have been an opportune time to raise the argument during the course of the *voir dire* into the admissibility of the police confession if the defence contended that there was some connection between the police confession and the e-mail. Again, no issue was raised when the trial judge specifically asked whether the defence contested the admissibility of the e-mail at the time the evidence was presented. Quite to the contrary, in answer to the trial judge's inquiry, the defence expressly *consented* to its admission.

· · ·

[38] On the facts, it is difficult to find evidence of a connection between the two statements which should have alerted the trial judge to the need to conduct a *voir dire* and to question the wisdom of counsel. In terms of the time span between the statements, the initial apology was made on May 27, 2004, while the e-mail was sent over five weeks later on July 5, 2004. The inducement held out by the police, as found by the trial judge on the *voir dire*, was the suggestion that S.G.T. may not be charged if he apologized. However, by the time S.G.T. sent the e-mail, he had been charged notwithstanding his apology in the police statement. It is therefore far from obvious on what basis the inducement could still be operative in the accused's mind. Additionally, there was no advertence to the previous inadmissible statement in the e-mail to A's mother. Finally, the two statements were made to different persons in entirely different circumstances. The first statement was made to a police officer in the context of a custodial interrogation, while the second was made to A's mother in an e-mail exchange relating to A's mother's attempt to secure S.G.T.'s permission to allow A and B to travel to California with her. But, more importantly, as the accused's later testimony in the trial revealed, it was his contention that the apology in the e-mail concerned a completely *unrelated* incident. This exemplifies why trial judges should generally defer to the tactical decisions of counsel who generally know more about the case. Given that the accused's own version was contrary to any theory of a potential connection between the e-mail and the earlier confession, it is difficult to see on what basis counsel's consent to the admissibility of the e-mail could be faulted.

[39] Based on this record, with respect, it is my view that the Court of Appeal erred in overturning the conviction on the basis that it did.

[Fish J (with Binnie J, concurring), dissented. He would have held, first, that the trial judge should have held a *voir dire* to decide whether there was a sufficient connection between the two statements, and second, that a derived confession need not be made to a person in authority to be excluded.]

b. Confession Confirmed by Subsequent Fact

Suppose the police obtain a confession from the accused, and then discover further evidence that confirms the confession in whole or in part. At trial, the confession is found to be involuntary. At common law, the further evidence is nonetheless admissible (see Section II, below). Should the fact that the further evidence confirms the confession have any effect on the admissibility of the confession itself?

Rex v St Lawrence
[1949] OR 215, 93 CCC 376 (Sup Ct)
McRuer CJHC (1-2 February 1949)

McRUER CJHC (orally): The witness Parrington has given evidence that on Saturday
night, October 9th, he saw the accused run across his path as he approached the place
where he found the deceased man lying in a dying condition.

· · ·

Following Parrington's statement to the police the accused was taken into custody and
on being questioned he made a statement under circumstances that would render it inadmissible in evidence. In the statement the accused gave an account of the disposition
of a "twitch" and the deceased man's wallet, together with an admission that he had given
a sum of money to one Pete Hylinsky on the night in question with the request to lock it
up for him. As a result of these admissions he was taken to a point not far distant from
the scene of the crime where a high wire fence separated the Woodbine Race-track
grounds from a marsh covered with underbrush. Here he pointed out where he had
thrown the twitch and the wallet. On searching the locality a twitch similar to one used
in the stables where the accused was employed, and a wallet similar to that carried by the
deceased, together with a liquor permit bearing his name, were found. The theory of the
Crown is that the accused used the twitch to beat the deceased to death, that he subsequently robbed him, and that to avoid detection he threw the twitch, wallet and liquor
permit into the marsh and gave the money to Hylinsky.

The matter involved in considering the admissibility of the evidence tendered by the
Crown is one of great difficulty, and one on which there is no unanimity of opinion among
judges or textbook writers.

Phipson on Evidence, 8th ed., p. 255, deals with it in this way: "Facts and documents
disclosed in consequence of inadmissible confessions are receivable if relevant. And where
property has been discovered or delivered up in this way so much of the confession as
strictly relates thereto will be admissible, for these portions at least cannot be untrue; but
independent statements not qualifying or explaining the fact, though made at the same
time, will be rejected."

The learned author does not make clear what he means by the phrase "where property
has been discovered or delivered up in this way, so much of the confession as strictly
relates thereto." I shall deal with this on an examination of the authorities relied upon by
the author.

After referring to *R v. Butcher* (1798), 1 Leach 265n, 168 ER 235; *R v. Griffin* (1809),
Russ. & Ry. 151, 168 ER 732; *R v. Harris*, cited in *Joy on Confessions*, p. 83; and *Reg. v.
Gould* (1840), 9 Car. & P 364, 173 ER 870, the author states: "The earlier rule admitted
the facts, but excluded the accompanying statements." In considering the authorities one
must have clearly in mind what follows: "If, however, the inadmissible confession be *not
confirmed* by the finding of the property, no proof either of the statements or acts can be
received; for the influence which produces a groundless confession may equally produce
groundless conduct." *R v. Jenkins* (1822), Russ. & Ry. 492, 168 ER 914, is relied on for this
statement.

Taylor on Evidence, 12th ed., para. 902, states the principle and, with respect I would
suggest, in more precise language: "When, *in consequence of information unduly obtained*

from the prisoner, the property stolen, or the instrument of the crime, or the body of the person murdered, or any other material fact, *has been discovered*, proof is admissible that such discovery was made conformably with the information so obtained. The prisoner's statement about his knowledge of the place where the property or other article was to be found, being thus confirmed by the fact, is shown to be true, and not to have been fabricated in consequences of any inducement."

I pause there for a moment to emphasize that what the learned author says is that "the prisoner's statement about his knowledge of the place where the property or other article was to be found, being thus confirmed by the fact, is shown to be true"; that is, that the finding of the article verifies the knowledge of the prisoner that the article was there, and that what he may have said with respect to his knowledge could not have been fabricated in consequence of the inducement. The learned author goes on: "It is, therefore, competent to prove that the prisoner stated that the thing would be found by searching a particular place, and that it was accordingly so found, *but it would not, in such a case of a confession improperly obtained, be competent to inquire whether he confessed that he had concealed it there*. So much of the confession as relates *distinctly* to the fact discovered by it may be given in evidence, as this part at least of the statement cannot have been false." (The italics are mine.)

. . .

After the most earnest consideration that I have been able to give the whole matter in the time at my disposal, I have come to the conclusion that my decision must rest on this fundamental principle:

Where the discovery of the fact confirms the confession—that is, where the confession must be taken to be true by reason of the discovery of the fact—then that part of the confession that is confirmed by the discovery of the fact is admissible, but further than that no part of the confession is admissible. Of all the authorities referred to, Taylor most nearly agrees with this view of the law.

It is therefore permissible to prove in this case the facts discovered as a result of the inadmissible confession, but not any accompanying statements which the discovery of the facts does not confirm. Anything done by the accused which indicates that he knew where the articles in question were is admissible to prove the *fact* that he knew the articles were there when that fact is confirmed by the finding of the articles; that is, the knowledge of the accused is a fact, the place where the articles were found is a fact. If he does or says something that indicates his knowledge of where the articles are located, and that is confirmed by the finding of the articles, then the fact of his knowledge is established. On the other hand, it is not admissible to show that the accused said he put the articles where they were found, as the finding of them does not confirm this statement. The finding of them is equally consistent with the accused's knowledge that some other person may have put them in the place where they were found.

I realize this is placing a limitation on the evidence … but I cannot rationalize the decisions in those cases with the underlying principle, i.e., that the finding of the article confirms the statement. If, for instance, the accused had said, and I am only using this as an illustration, "I threw the wallet over the fence," the finding of the wallet does not confirm that he threw it over the fence; it is equally consistent with his seeing some other person throw it over the fence. We are therefore driven back to an inadmissible confession for proof that he threw it over the fence. On the other hand, the finding of the wallet does confirm that he knew it was in the place where it was found.

I will now review the evidence tendered on the *voir dire* and apply these principles to it. It may be that in the light of my finding Crown counsel will desire to offer the evidence that is available, in conformity with my ruling. Det. Sgt. Keay's evidence may be conveniently dealt with as follows: "The accused was taken to the southeast portion of the racetrack." I think it would be admissible for Det. Sgt. Keay to say that as the result of information received the accused was taken by the officers to the southeast portion of the racetrack.

"He indicated the place on the map." That is admissible.

The witness says the accused said at that place, referring to the twitch, "I did not throw it; I just tossed it." In my view, that is not admissible.

"It should be about ten feet in." That is admissible.

"The different articles will be separated by a little distance." Up to that point, that is admissible. The remaining part—"I was just going along the fence as I tossed them over"—is not admissible.

Then Det. Sgt. Keay was asked again to detail the events, and I again deal with his evidence as it was repeated:

"After we got to the Woodbine the accused and I were standing opposite the wire fence." That is admissible.

"I asked him how far he threw the twitch. The accused replied, 'I didn't throw it; I just tossed it.'" That is not admissible.

"He indicated with his hand that he had just flipped it over." That is not admissible.

"I asked him if he threw the twitch and the pocket-book at the same time. He said, 'No, I threw them separately.'" That is not admissible.

"I took the handcuffs off, got a ladder and started to search." That is admissible.

"He said he would take us down and show us where he had thrown the twitch." That is not admissible.

"He indicated to us where to place the ladder. Do not recall how he had indicated." That is admissible.

Sgt. Bolton's evidence that the accused stated "So I took his money and also his wallet" is not admissible.

"I threw the twitch away" is not admissible.

"I threw the wallet into the bay at the same place as I threw the twitch." That is not admissible.

"I gave the money to Pete Hylinsky and said to him, 'Lock this up, Pete.'" That statement gives me much more concern, as the fact that he gave the money to Pete Hylinsky is confirmed by Hylinsky, but I am rejecting it because of the danger that the words "the money" raise in interpreting the statement. It might be interpreted as a confession that it was the money he took from the deceased's person. That would not be admissible. We already have the proof that a sum of money was given to Hylinsky, and I do not think the confession can be drawn on to amplify that proof as identifying it with money taken from the deceased.

"Det. Serg. Keay handed the accused over to Mace." That is admissible.

"Mace asked the accused where he threw the twitch and wallet and he indicated." That is not admissible in that way, but it would be admissible if it was tendered that the accused indicated to the officers where the twitch and wallet should be, but no statement that he put them there.

"On arrival at the Woodbine we turned east and came along the side of the restaurant." That is admissible.

"The accused said he threw the twitch over the fence." That portion, as I have stated, is not admissible, but the officer went on to say that he pointed out the place. The officer would be permitted to say that the accused did the physical act of pointing to a particular place and indicating what would be found there, but he must not give evidence that the accused said he put it there.

"The accused walked with Sergt. Mace. We stopped at the second place. He said he threw the wallet and liquor permit there." There again it would be permissible to give in evidence that the accused walked with Sgt. Mace and stopped at a certain point and indicated that the wallet and liquor permit would be found in that place, and they were found in that place. But not that the accused put them in that place.

"In a short time O'Driscoll placed the ladder where he said, 'You will find the twitch right here.'" That is admissible.

"He pointed to a section of the fence, he said, 'This is the place here.'" That is admissible.

And in cross-examination: "The accused pointed to the spot." That is admissible.

NOTES AND QUESTIONS

1. In *R v Wray*, [1971] SCR 272, 11 CRNS 235, eight of the nine judges of the Supreme Court held that *St Lawrence* was correctly decided. The case is excerpted on another issue in Section I.B, below.

2. Does the Charter have any implications for the rule in *St Lawrence*? See *R v Sweeney* (2000), 50 OR (3d) 321, 148 CCC (3d) 247 (CA).

5. *The Confessions Rule and the Charter*

The confessions rule is a very important and well-entrenched common law rule of evidence. It is therefore a plausible candidate for recognition as a principle of fundamental justice under s 7 of the *Canadian Charter of Rights and Freedoms*. But in *Oickle*, Iacobucci J urged caution in constitutionalizing the confessions rule:

[30] ... First, the confessions rule has a broader scope than the *Charter*. For example, the protections of s. 10 only apply "on arrest or detention." By contrast, the confessions rule applies whenever a person in authority questions a suspect. Second, the *Charter* applies a different burden and standard of proof from that under the confessions rule. Under the former, the burden is on the accused to show, on a balance of probabilities, a violation of constitutional rights. Under the latter, the burden is on the prosecution to show beyond a reasonable doubt that the confession was voluntary. Finally, the remedies are different. The *Charter* excludes evidence obtained in violation of its provisions under s. 24(2) only if admitting the evidence would bring the administration of justice into disrepute: see *R v. Stillman*, [1997] 1 SCR 607, *R v. Collins*, [1987] 1 SCR 265, and the related jurisprudence. By contrast, a violation of the confessions rule always warrants exclusion.

On other occasions, however, the Supreme Court of Canada has found the confessions rule to be incorporated in s 7 of the Charter. In *R v G (B)*, [1999] 2 SCR 475, the court used s 7 to read down a provision of the *Criminal Code* to exclude an involuntary statement from the accused's trial. And in *R v Singh*, 2007 SCC 48, [2007] 3 SCR 405, the court held that the common law confessions rule was closely related to the Charter right to silence arising upon detention:

[8] [I]n the context of a police interrogation of a person in detention, where the detainee knows he or she is speaking to a person in authority, the two tests are functionally equivalent. It follows that, where a statement has survived a thorough inquiry into voluntariness, the accused's *Charter* application alleging that the statement was obtained in violation of the pre-trial right to silence under s. 7 cannot succeed. Conversely, if circumstances are such that the accused can show on a balance of probabilities that the statement was obtained in violation of his or her constitutional right to remain silent, the Crown will be unable to prove voluntariness beyond a reasonable doubt.

On this approach, the obtaining of an involuntary statement is, at least under some circumstances, understood as a violation of the accused's right to silence.

How does this holding in *Singh* compare with paras 29-30 of *Oickle*?

For further discussion of these issues, see Hamish Stewart, "The Confessions Rule and the Charter" (2009) 54 McGill LJ 517.

B. Community Shock

At common law, apart from the confessions rule discussed above, illegal or improper behaviour by agents of the state had no effect on the admissibility of evidence in criminal proceedings. In *Kuruma v R*, [1955] AC 197 (PC), Lord Goddard said:

In their Lordships' opinion the test to be applied in considering whether evidence is admissible is whether it is relevant to the matters in issue. If it is, it is admissible and the court is not concerned with how the evidence was obtained. While this proposition may not have been stated in so many words in any English case there are decisions which support it, and in their Lordships' opinion it is plainly right in principle.

Twenty-five years later, in *R v Sang*, [1980] AC 402, Lord Diplock considered whether a trial judge had discretion to exclude evidence obtained through alleged police misconduct. He said:

A fair trial according to law involves, in the case of a trial upon indictment, that it should take place before a judge and a jury; that the case against the accused should be proved to the satisfaction of the jury beyond all reasonable doubt upon evidence that is admissible in law; and, as a corollary to this, that there should be excluded from the jury information about the accused which is likely to have an influence on their minds prejudicial to the accused which is out of proportion to the true probative value of admissible evidence conveying that information. If these conditions are fulfilled and the jury receive correct instructions from the judge as to the law applicable to the case, the requirement that the accused should have a fair trial according to law is, in my view, satisfied; for the fairness of a trial according to law is not all one-sided; it requires that those who are undoubtedly guilty should be convicted as well as that those about whose guilt there is any reasonable doubt should be acquitted. However much the judge may dislike the way in which a particular piece of evidence was obtained before proceedings were commenced, if it is admissible evidence probative of the accused's guilt it is no part of his judicial function to exclude it for this reason. If your Lordships so hold you will be reverting to the law as it was laid down by Lord Moulton in *Rex v. Christie*, [1914] AC 545, Lord du Parcq in *Noor Mohamed v. The King*, [1949] AC 182 and Viscount Simon in *Harris v. Director of Public Prosecutions*, [1952] AC 694 before the growth of what I believe to have been a misunderstanding of Lord Goddard's dictum in *Kuruma v. The Queen*, [1955] AC 197.

I would accordingly answer the question certified in terms which have been suggested by my noble and learned friend, Viscount Dilhorne, in the course of our deliberations on this case. (1) A trial judge in a criminal trial has always a discretion to refuse to admit evidence if in his opinion its prejudicial effect outweighs its probative value. (2) Save with regard to admissions and confessions and generally with regard to evidence obtained from the accused after commission of the offence, he has no discretion to refuse to admit relevant admissible evidence on the ground that it was obtained by improper or unfair means. The court is not concerned with how it was obtained. It is no ground for the exercise of discretion to exclude that the evidence was obtained as the result of the activities of an agent provocateur.

In *R v Wray*, [1971] SCR 272, 11 CRNS 235, a majority of the Supreme Court said:

I am not aware of any judicial authority in this country or in England which supports the proposition that a trial judge has a discretion to exclude admissible evidence because, in his opinion, its admission would be calculated to bring the administration of justice into disrepute.

· · ·

This development of the idea of a general discretion to exclude admissible evidence is not warranted by the authority on which it purports to be based. The dictum of Lord Goddard, in the *Kuruma* case, appears to be founded on *Noor Mohamed v. The King* ... [[1949] AC 182], and it has, I think, been unduly extended in some of the subsequent cases. It recognized a discretion to disallow evidence if the strict rules of admissibility would operate unfairly against the accused. Even if this statement be accepted, in the way in which it is phrased, the exercise of a discretion by the trial judge arises only if the admission of the evidence would operate unfairly. The allowance of admissible evidence relevant to the issue before the court and of substantial probative value may operate unfortunately for the accused, but not unfairly. It is only the allowance of evidence gravely prejudicial to the accused, the admissibility of which is tenuous, and whose probative force in relation to the main issue before the court is trifling, which can be said to operate unfairly.

In my opinion, the recognition of a discretion to exclude admissible evidence, beyond the limited scope in the *Noor Mohamed* case, is not warranted by authority, and would be undesirable. The admission of relevant admissible evidence of probative value should not be prevented, except within the very limited sphere recognized in that case. My view is that the trial judge's discretion does not extend beyond those limits and, accordingly, I think, with respect, that the definition of that discretion by the Court of Appeal in this case was wrong in law.

While Canadian courts have still not recognized a general discretion to exclude improperly obtained evidence at common law, they have developed new common law rules to exclude self-incriminating statements in particular circumstances. In *R v Oickle*, 2000 SCC 38,

[2000] 2 SCR 3, 147 CCC (3d) 321, Iacobucci J said that an accused's statements may be excluded where police used tactics that were "so appalling as to shock the community." Referring to Lamer J's concurring reasons in *Rothman v R*, [1981] 1 SCR 640, Iacobucci J listed examples of such trickery: "a police officer pretending to be a chaplain or a legal aid lawyer, or injecting truth serum into a diabetic under the pretense that it was insulin."

In the context of statements made to persons in authority, it is difficult to imagine police tactics that would shock the community but, nonetheless, elicit a voluntary confession, especially since under *Oickle* police deception "is a relevant factor in the overall voluntariness analysis." But lawyers have (almost always unsuccessfully) invoked the "community shock" principle in attempts to exclude confessions given to non-persons in authority, including undercover police: see e.g. *R v Welsh*, 2013 ONCA 190 at paras 93-106. The following section, however, excerpts a recent Supreme Court of Canada decision outlining a new rule, distinct from both voluntariness and community shock, to deal with these situations.

C. Undercover Stings

R v Hart
2014 SCC 52, [2014] 2 SCR 544 (footnotes omitted)
McLachlin CJ and LeBel, Abella, Cromwell, Moldaver, Karakatsanis,
and Wagner JJ (31 July 2014)

MOLDAVER J (McLachlin CJ and LeBel, Abella, and Wagner JJ, concurring):

I. Introduction

[1] When conventional investigations fail to solve serious crimes, police forces in Canada have sometimes used the "Mr. Big" technique. A Mr. Big operation begins with undercover officers luring their suspect into a fictitious criminal organization of their own making. Over the next several weeks or months, the suspect is befriended by the undercover officers. He is shown that working with the organization provides a pathway to financial rewards and close friendships. There is only one catch. The crime boss—known colloquially as "Mr. Big"—must approve the suspect's membership in the criminal organization.

[2] The operation culminates with an interview-like meeting between the suspect and Mr. Big. During the interview, Mr. Big brings up the crime the police are investigating and questions the suspect about it. Denials of guilt are dismissed, and Mr. Big presses the suspect for a confession. As Mr. Big's questioning continues, it becomes clear to the suspect that by confessing to the crime, the big prize—acceptance into the organization—awaits. If the suspect does confess, the fiction soon unravels and the suspect is arrested and charged.

[3] This case provides us with an opportunity to take an in-depth look at Mr. Big confessions and the principles that should govern their admissibility. While such operations have a long history in this country, courts have yet to create a legal framework that addresses the unique issues which accompany such confessions. As we undertake that task in this case, we must strive to achieve a just balance—one which guards against the risk of wrongful convictions that stem from false confessions but which ensures the police

are not deprived of the opportunity to use their skill and ingenuity in solving serious crimes.

[4] To be sure, the Mr. Big technique has proven to be an effective investigative tool. It has produced confessions and secured convictions in hundreds of cases that would otherwise have likely gone unsolved. The confessions elicited are often detailed and confirmed by other evidence. Manifestly, the technique has proved indispensible in the search for the truth.

[5] But the technique comes with a price. Suspects confess to Mr. Big during pointed interrogations in the face of powerful inducements and sometimes veiled threats—and this raises the spectre of unreliable confessions.

[6] Unreliable confessions present a unique danger. They provide compelling evidence of guilt and present a clear and straightforward path to conviction. Certainly in the case of conventional confessions, triers of fact have difficulty accepting that an innocent person would confess to a crime he did not commit. And yet our experience with wrongful convictions shows that innocent people can, and do, falsely confess. Unreliable confessions have been responsible for wrongful convictions—a fact we cannot ignore.

[7] The concern about Mr. Big confessions does not end there. The confessions are invariably accompanied by evidence that shows the accused willingly participated in "simulated crime" and was eager to join a criminal organization. This evidence sullies the accused's character and, in doing so, carries with it the risk of prejudice. It also creates credibility hurdles that may be difficult to overcome for an accused who chooses to testify.

[8] Experience in Canada and elsewhere teaches that wrongful convictions are often traceable to evidence that is either unreliable or prejudicial. When the two combine, they make for a potent mix—and the risk of a wrongful conviction increases accordingly. Wrongful convictions are a blight on our justice system and we must take reasonable steps to prevent them before they occur.

[9] Finally, Mr. Big operations run the risk of becoming abusive. Undercover officers provide their targets with inducements, including cash rewards, to encourage them to confess. They also cultivate an aura of violence by showing that those who betray the criminal organization are met with violence. Thought must be given to the kinds of police tactics we, as a society, are prepared to condone in pursuit of the truth.

[The respondent's twin three-year-old daughters drowned in a lake. He initially told police that after one daughter had fallen in from a dock, he panicked because he could not swim and drove back to get his wife, forgetting his other daughter. Police did not believe him, but he maintained that he did not drown his daughters, even after being interrogated for eight hours. Several weeks later, however, he contacted police and changed his story, telling them that he had had an epileptic seizure at the lake and that when he regained his faculties he saw that one daughter was in the water. He explained that he had lied in his first statement because he did not want to lose his driver's licence, which had been suspended on previous occasions because of his condition. Police remained unconvinced but did not have enough evidence to charge him.

Two years later, the police decided to target the respondent in a Mr. Big sting. Knowing that he was socially isolated and on welfare, undercover officers befriended him and began paying him to make truck deliveries for them. They also revealed that they were part of a criminal organization headed by a "boss." The respondent thereafter participated in a series of simulated criminal activities, delivering purportedly smuggled alcohol and stolen credit cards. He was paid substantial sums and travelled widely, staying in hotels paid for by the officers and dining with them frequently. He developed great affection for them, saying that he loved one of them and that they were like "brothers" to him.

A few months after the operation began, he was dining with one of the officers who told him that prostitutes working for the organization sometimes had to be assaulted if they were dishonest. He responded that he was comfortable getting his hands dirty and (according to police) confessed to drowning his daughters (this conversation was not recorded and the respondent denied making this confession at trial).

Over the next two months, the officers continued to stress the organization's expectations of trust, honesty, and loyalty for its members as well as the violent consequences for those who failed to meet them. They told the respondent that he had a chance to participate in a big transaction for the organization that would pay him between $20,000 and $25,000. The boss, however, would have to approve of his involvement after conducting a background check on him. They then revealed that this check had uncovered an issue that the boss would question him about. At the meeting, the boss told the respondent that there was "heat" coming from his daughters' deaths and asked him to explain why he had killed them. He replied that he had had a seizure and that the drownings had been accidental. After the boss told him that this was a lie, the respondent said that he had pushed them into the lake because he had feared they would be taken by child welfare. He later re-enacted the event for one of the officers at the lake. Police arrested the respondent soon after and allowed him to make a phone call. He made his first call to one of the officers, whom he still believed was his friend.

At trial, the confessions made by the respondent during the sting were admitted into evidence and he was convicted of two counts of first-degree murder.]

· · ·

B. The Admissibility of the Mr. Big Confessions

· · ·

(2) Do We Need a Test for Determining the Admissibility of Mr. Big Confessions?

[63] In cases where the Mr. Big technique has been used, the ensuing confessions have typically been received at trial. Under the existing case law, they have been admitted under the party admissions exception to the hearsay rule (see *R. v. Evans*, [1993] 3 S.C.R. 653, at p. 664; *R. v. Osmar*, 2007 ONCA 50, 84 O.R. (3d) 321, at para. 53). The admissibility of party admissions flows from the adversarial nature of our trial system, and the belief that "what a party has previously stated can be admitted against the party in whose mouth it does not lie to complain of the unreliability of his or her own statements" (*Evans*, at p. 664).

[64] Attempts to extend existing legal protections to Mr. Big operations have failed. This Court has held that Mr. Big operations do not engage the right to silence because the accused is not detained by the police at the time he or she confesses (see *R. v. McIntyre*, [1994] 2 S.C.R. 480; *R. v. Hebert*, [1990] 2 S.C.R. 151). And the confessions rule—which requires the Crown to prove an accused's statement to a person in authority is "voluntary"—is inoperative because the accused does not know that Mr. Big is a police officer when he confesses (see *R. v. Grandinetti*, 2005 SCC 5, [2005] 1 S.C.R. 27).

[65] Under existing law, it appears that defence counsel have only two options for challenging the admissibility of these confessions: under the doctrine of abuse of process, or under a trial judge's overriding discretion to exclude evidence that is more prejudicial than probative. Trial judges have only rarely excluded Mr. Big confessions under either of these doctrines. Indeed, the parties could find no case in which a Mr. Big confession was excluded as an abuse of process, and only one case in which a confession was excluded on the basis that its prejudicial effect exceeded its probative value (see *R. v. Creek*, 1998 CanLII 3209 (B.C.S.C.)).

[66] A threshold issue raised by this appeal is whether the existing framework adequately protects the rights of those subject to Mr. Big investigations. The Crown contends that no further protections are needed and that the law as it stands strikes a proper balance between the accused's rights and the need for effective policing. By contrast, the respondent and *amicus curiae* submit that Mr. Big confessions present unique dangers that must be addressed by placing a filter on their admissibility.

[67] I agree with the respondent and *amicus curiae*. In my view, the law as it stands today provides insufficient protection to accused persons who confess during Mr. Big operations. Three concerns lead me to this conclusion.

(a) The Danger of Unreliable Confessions

[68] First, because of the nature of Mr. Big operations, concerns arise as to the reliability of the confessions they produce. The purpose of these operations is to induce confessions, and they are carefully calibrated to achieve that end. Over a period of weeks or months, suspects are made to believe that the fictitious criminal organization for which they work can provide them with financial security, social acceptance, and friendship. Suspects also come to learn that violence is a necessary part of the organization's business model, and that a past history of violence is a boast-worthy accomplishment. And during the final meeting with Mr. Big—which involves a skillful interrogation conducted by an experienced police officer—suspects learn that confessing to the crime under investigation provides a consequence-free ticket into the organization and all of the rewards it provides.

[69] It seems a matter of common sense that the potential for a false confession increases in proportion to the nature and extent of the inducements held out to the accused. Unsurprisingly, this view is supported by academic literature (see *R. v. Oickle*, 2000 SCC 38, [2000] 2 S.C.R. 3, at paras. 39 and 44; S.M. Kassin et al., "Police-Induced Confessions: Risk Factors and Recommendations" (2010), 34 *Law & Hum. Behav.* 3, at pp. 14-15).

[70] The common law confessions rule serves to illustrate the importance of a trial judge's role in assessing reliability. The confessions rule has long concerned itself with the dangers posed by unreliable confessions (see, e.g., G.A. Martin, "The Admissibility of Confessions and Statements" (1963), 5 *Crim. L.Q.* 35, at p. 35). Under the confessions rule, we recognize that unreliable confessions made by an accused pose particular dangers, as juries often attach great weight to the accused's own words. When an accused falsely confesses to a crime, the risk of a wrongful conviction becomes acute. This Court recognized as much in *Oickle*, when it noted that false confessions have played an "important role" in cases where wrongful convictions have occurred (para. 36). Subsequent research has confirmed that risk. In 40 of the first 250 DNA exonerations in the United States, for example, the accused was found to have falsely confessed to the crime (see B.L. Garrett, "The Substance of False Confessions" (2010), 62 *Stan. L. Rev.* 1051).

[71] The confessions rule thus guards against the danger of unreliable confessions by requiring the Crown to prove to a judge beyond a reasonable doubt that an accused's statement was voluntarily made. Where the Crown is unable to do so, the accused's statement is rendered inadmissible.

[72] But as the law stands today, unlike our approach with the confessions rule, we have failed to adopt a consistent approach to assessing the reliability of Mr. Big confessions before they go to the jury. This is so despite the obvious nature of the inducements these operations create. In my view, it would be dangerous and unwise to assume that we do not need to be concerned about the reliability of Mr. Big confessions simply because the suspect does not know that the person pressuring him to confess is a police officer. And although it will be easier for a jury to understand why an accused would falsely confess to Mr. Big than to the police during a conventional interrogation (because of the more obvious nature of the inducements and the accused's belief that it is in his self-interest to confess), this does not provide a complete answer to the reliability concerns raised by these confessions. Under the confessions rule, we do not abandon our concern for reliability in cases where a confession is the product of clear threats or inducements, on the assumption that the jury will have an easier time understanding why it is unreliable.

(b) The Prejudicial Effect of Mr. Big Confessions

[73] The second concern with Mr. Big confessions—and one that distinguishes them from confessions made in other contexts—is that they are invariably accompanied by prejudicial facts regarding the accused's character. Putting these confessions into evidence requires showing the jury that the accused wanted to join a criminal organization and that he participated in "simulated" crimes that he believed were real. The absence of a consistent approach in assessing the admissibility of these confessions sits uneasily with the general rule that bad character evidence is presumptively inadmissible for the Crown. This centuries-old rule prohibits the Crown from leading evidence of misconduct engaged in by the accused that is unrelated to the charges before the court, unless it can demonstrate that its probative value outweighs its prejudicial effect (see *R. v. Handy*, 2002 SCC 56, [2002] 2 S.C.R. 908).

[74] Bad character evidence causes two kinds of prejudice. It causes "moral prejudice" by marring the character of the accused in the eyes of the jury, thereby creating a risk that the jury will reason from the accused's general disposition to the conclusion that he is guilty of the crime charged, or that he is deserving of punishment in any event (*Handy*, at para. 31). And it causes "reasoning prejudice" by distracting the jury's focus away from the offence charged, toward the accused's extraneous acts of misconduct (*ibid.*). As this Court held in *Handy*, the "poisonous potential" of bad character evidence cannot be doubted (para. 138).

[75] When a Mr. Big confession is admitted, the character evidence that accompanies it places the accused in a difficult situation. In these cases, the accused is often obliged, as a tactical necessity, to testify in order to explain why he falsely confessed to Mr. Big. The character evidence that has already been admitted is damaging in this context because it shrouds the accused with an aura of distrust before he or she steps into the witness box. This distrust is compounded when the accused asks the jury to disregard his confession

because he was lying when he gave it. And all of this furnishes the Crown with ample fodder for a forceful attack on the accused's credibility in cross-examination.

[76] Despite the well-established presumption that bad character evidence is inadmissible, it is routinely admitted in Mr. Big cases because it provides the relevant context needed to understand how the accused's pivotal confession came about. Indeed, even the accused comes to depend on this evidence in order to show the nature of the inducements he faced and the reason his confession should not be believed.

[77] In my view, the prejudicial effect of Mr. Big confessions is a substantial concern, especially since these confessions may also be unreliable. Putting evidence before a jury that is both unreliable and prejudicial invites a miscarriage of justice. The law must respond to these dangers. The fact that there are no proven wrongful convictions in cases involving Mr. Big confessions provides little comfort. The criminal justice system cannot afford to wait for miscarriages of justice before taking reasonable steps to prevent them.

(c) Police Misconduct

[78] Finally, Mr. Big operations create a risk that the police will resort to unacceptable tactics in their pursuit of a confession. As mentioned, in conducting these operations, undercover officers often cultivate an aura of violence in order to stress the importance of trust and loyalty within the organization. This can involve—as it did in this case— threats or acts of violence perpetrated in the presence of the accused. In these circumstances, it is easy to see a risk that the police will go too far, resorting to tactics which may impact on the reliability of a confession, or in some instances amount to an abuse of process.

[79] At present, however, these operations are conducted in a legal vacuum. The legal protections afforded to accused persons, which are often intended at least in part to place limits on the conduct of the police in their investigation and interrogation of accused people, have no application to Mr. Big operations. The confessions rule, for example, is intended not only to guard against the risk of unreliable confessions, but also to prevent abusive state conduct (see *R. v. Hodgson*, [1998] 2 S.C.R. 449, at para. 20). Yet its protection does not apply because the accused does not know the person he is speaking to is a person in authority. Other protections—like the right to counsel under s. 10(b) of the *Charter*—are rendered inapplicable because the accused is not "det[ained]" by the police while the operation is ongoing. And the doctrine of abuse of process—intended to protect against abusive state conduct—appears to be somewhat of a paper tiger. To date, it has never operated to exclude a Mr. Big confession, nor has it ever led to the stay of charges arising from one of these operations.

[80] In my view, the lack of an effective mechanism for monitoring the conduct of the undercover officers who engage in these operations is problematic. The law must enable trial judges to respond effectively to police misconduct in this context.

(3) How Should the Law Respond to the Problems Posed by Mr. Big Confessions?

[81] Having determined that the law must respond to the risks inherent in Mr. Big confessions, the more difficult question is what form that response should take. Mr. Big operations raise three distinct concerns—reliability, prejudice, and the potential for police

misconduct—and we must ensure that trial judges have the tools they need to address all three of these issues.

. . .

[83] In searching for a response to the concerns these operations raise, we must proceed cautiously. To be sure, Mr. Big operations can become abusive, and they can produce confessions that are unreliable and prejudicial. We must seek a legal framework that protects accused persons, and the justice system as a whole, against these dangers. On the other hand, Mr. Big operations are not necessarily abusive, and are capable of producing valuable evidence, the admission of which furthers the interests of justice. We ought not forget that the Mr. Big technique is almost always used in cold cases involving the most serious crimes. Put simply, in responding to the dangers posed by Mr. Big confessions, we should be wary about allowing serious crimes to go unpunished.

(a) Summary of a Proposed Solution

[84] In this section, I propose a solution that, in my view, strikes the best balance between guarding against the dangers posed by Mr. Big operations, while ensuring the police have the tools they need to investigate serious crime. This solution involves a two-pronged approach that (1) recognizes a new common law rule of evidence, and (2) relies on a more robust conception of the doctrine of abuse of process to deal with the problem of police misconduct.

[85] The first prong recognizes a new common law rule of evidence for assessing the admissibility of these confessions. The rule operates as follows: Where the state recruits an accused into a fictitious criminal organization of its own making and seeks to elicit a confession from him, any confession made by the accused to the state during the operation should be treated as presumptively inadmissible. This presumption of inadmissibility is overcome where the Crown can establish, on a balance of probabilities, that the probative value of the confession outweighs its prejudicial effect. In this context, the confession's probative value turns on an assessment of its reliability. Its prejudicial effect flows from the bad character evidence that must be admitted in order to put the operation and the confession in context. If the Crown is unable to demonstrate that the accused's confession is admissible, the rest of the evidence surrounding the Mr. Big operation becomes irrelevant and thus inadmissible. This rule, like the confessions rule in the case of conventional police interrogations, operates as a specific qualification to the party admissions exception to the hearsay rule.

[86] As regard [sic] the second prong, I would rely on the doctrine of abuse of process to deal with the problem of police misconduct. I recognize that the doctrine has thus far proved less than effective in this context. While the problem is not an easy one, I propose to provide some guidance on how to determine if a Mr. Big operation crosses the line from skillful police work to an abuse of process.

[87] The purposes of this two-pronged approach are to protect an accused's right to a fair trial under the *Charter*, and to preserve the integrity of the justice system. Those are the ends that must ultimately be achieved. This approach strives to reach them by ensuring that only those confessions that are more probative than prejudicial, and which do not result from abuse, are admitted into evidence.

[88] However, it must be remembered that trial judges always retain a discretion to exclude evidence where its admission would compromise trial fairness (see *R. v. Harrer*, [1995] 3 S.C.R. 562). This is because "the general principle that an accused is entitled to a fair trial cannot be entirely reduced to specific rules" (*ibid.*, at para. 23). It is impossible to predict every factual scenario that could present itself. As such, I do not foreclose the possibility that, in an exceptional case, trial fairness may require that a Mr. Big confession be excluded even where the specific rules I have proposed would see the confession admitted.

[89] In practice, this two-pronged approach will necessitate that a *voir dire* be held to determine the admissibility of Mr. Big confessions. The Crown will bear the burden of establishing that, on balance, the probative value of the confession outweighs its prejudicial effect, and it will be for the defence to establish an abuse of process. Trial judges may prefer to begin their analysis by assessing whether there has been an abuse of process. A finding of abuse makes weighing the probative value and prejudicial effect of the evidence unnecessary.

[90] Against this backdrop, I will now elaborate on the main features of this two-pronged solution.

. . .

[102] Confessions derive their persuasive force from the fact that they are against the accused's self-interest. People do not normally confess to crimes they have not committed (*Hodgson*, at para. 60). But the circumstances in which Mr. Big confessions are elicited can undermine that supposition. Thus, the first step in assessing the reliability of a Mr. Big confession is to examine those circumstances and assess the extent to which they call into question the reliability of the confession. These circumstances include—but are not strictly limited to—the length of the operation, the number of interactions between the police and the accused, the nature of the relationship between the undercover officers and the accused, the nature and extent of the inducements offered, the presence of any threats, the conduct of the interrogation itself, and the personality of the accused, including his or her age, sophistication, and mental health.

[103] Special note should be taken of the mental health and age of the accused. In the United States, where empirical data on false confessions is more plentiful, researchers have found that those with mental illnesses or disabilities, and youth, present a much greater risk of falsely confessing (Garrett, at p. 1064). A confession arising from a Mr. Big operation that comes from a young person or someone suffering from a mental illness or disability will raise greater reliability concerns.

[104] In listing these factors, I do not mean to suggest that trial judges are to consider them mechanically and check a box when they apply. That is not the purpose of the exercise. Instead, trial judges must examine all the circumstances leading to and surrounding the making of the confession—with these factors in mind—and assess whether and to what extent the reliability of the confession is called into doubt.

[105] After considering the circumstances in which the confession was made, the court should look to the confession itself for markers of reliability. Trial judges should consider the level of detail contained in the confession, whether it leads to the discovery of additional evidence, whether it identifies any elements of the crime that had not been made public (e.g., the murder weapon), or whether it accurately describes mundane details of the crime the accused would not likely have known had he not committed it (e.g., the presence or absence of particular objects at the crime scene). Confirmatory

evidence is not a hard and fast requirement, but where it exists, it can provide a powerful guarantee of reliability. The greater the concerns raised by the circumstances in which the confession was made, the more important it will be to find markers of reliability in the confession itself or the surrounding evidence.

(d) How Is Prejudicial Effect Measured?

[106] Weighing the prejudicial effect of a Mr. Big confession is a more straightforward and familiar exercise. Trial judges must be aware of the dangers presented by these confessions. Admitting these confessions raises the spectre of moral and reasoning prejudice. Commencing with moral prejudice, the jury learns that the accused wanted to join a criminal organization and committed a host of "simulated crimes" that he believed were real. In the end, the accused is forced to argue to the jury that he lied to Mr. Big when he boasted about committing a very serious crime because his desire to join the gang was so strong. Moral prejudice may increase with operations that involve the accused in simulated crimes of violence, or that demonstrate the accused has a past history of violence. As for reasoning prejudice—defined as the risk that the jury's focus will be distracted away from the charges before the court—it too can pose a problem depending on the length of the operation, the amount of time that must be spent detailing it, and any controversy as to whether a particular event or conversation occurred.

[107] On the other hand, the risk of prejudice can be mitigated by excluding certain pieces of particularly prejudicial evidence that are unessential to the narrative. Moreover, trial judges must bear in mind that limiting instructions to the jury may be capable of attenuating the prejudicial effect of this evidence.

· · ·

(f) What Is the Role of the Doctrine of Abuse of Process?

[111] The rule of evidence I have proposed goes a long way toward addressing all three of the concerns raised by Mr. Big operations. It squarely tackles the problems they raise with reliability and prejudice. And it takes significant account of the concern regarding police misconduct both by placing the admissibility onus on the Crown, and by factoring the conduct of the police into the assessment of a Mr. Big confession's probative value.

[112] I should not, however, be taken as suggesting that police misconduct will be forgiven so long as a demonstrably reliable confession is ultimately secured. That state of affairs would be unacceptable, as this Court has long recognized that there are "inherent limits" on the power of the state to "manipulate people and events for the purpose of ... obtaining convictions" (*R. v. Mack*, [1988] 2 S.C.R. 903, at p. 941).

[113] In my view, this is where the doctrine of abuse of process must serve its purpose. After all, the doctrine is intended to guard against state conduct that society finds unacceptable, and which threatens the integrity of the justice system (*R. v. Babos*, 2014 SCC 16, [2014] 1 S.C.R. 309, at para. 35). Moreover, the doctrine provides trial judges with a wide discretion to issue a remedy—including the exclusion of evidence or a stay of proceedings—where doing so is necessary to preserve the integrity of the justice system or the fairness of the trial (*ibid.*, at para. 32). The onus lies on the accused to establish that an abuse of process has occurred.

[114] I acknowledge that, thus far, the doctrine has provided little protection in the context of Mr. Big operations. This may be due in part to this Court's decision in *R. v. Fliss*, 2002 SCC 16, [2002] 1 S.C.R. 535, where Binnie J., writing for the majority, described the Mr. Big technique as "skillful police work" (para. 21). But the solution, in my view, is to reinvigorate the doctrine in this context, not to search for an alternative framework to guard against the very same problem. The first step toward restoring the doctrine as an effective guard against police misconduct in this context is to remind trial judges that these operations can become abusive, and that they must carefully scrutinize how the police conduct them.

[115] It is of course impossible to set out a precise formula for determining when a Mr. Big operation will become abusive. These operations are too varied for a bright-line rule to apply. But there is one guideline that can be suggested. Mr. Big operations are designed to induce confessions. The mere presence of inducements is not problematic (*Oickle*, at para. 57). But police conduct, including inducements and threats, becomes problematic in this context when it approximates coercion. In conducting these operations, the police cannot be permitted to overcome the will of the accused and coerce a confession. This would almost certainly amount to an abuse of process.

[116] Physical violence or threats of violence provide examples of coercive police tactics. A confession derived from physical violence or threats of violence against an accused will not be admissible—no matter how reliable—because this, quite simply, is something the community will not tolerate (see, e g , *R. v. Singh*, 2013 ONCA 750, 118 O.R. (3d) 253).

[117] Violence and threats of violence are two forms of unacceptable coercion. But Mr. Big operations can become coercive in other ways as well. Operations that prey on an accused's vulnerabilities—like mental health problems, substance addictions, or youthfulness—are also highly problematic (see *Mack*, at p. 963). Taking advantage of these vulnerabilities threatens trial fairness and the integrity of the justice system. As this Court has said on many occasions, misconduct that offends the community's sense of fair play and decency will amount to an abuse of process and warrant the exclusion of the statement.

[118] While coercion is an important factor to consider, I do not foreclose the possibility that Mr. Big operations can become abusive in other ways. The factors that I have outlined, while not identical, are similar to those outlined in *Mack*, with which trial judges are well-familiar (p. 966). At the end of the day, there is only so much guidance that can be provided. Our trial judges have long been entrusted with the task of identifying abuses of process and I have no reason to doubt their ability to do the same in this context.

. . .

(4) Application to the Facts

(a) The Admissibility of the Respondent's Confessions

. . .

[133] Turning first to the circumstances in which these confessions were made, I am of the view that the circumstances cast serious doubt on the reliability of the respondent's confessions. At the time the Mr. Big operation began, the respondent was socially isolated, unemployed, and living on welfare. Over the next four months, the Mr. Big operation transformed the respondent's life, becoming its focal point. ...

· · ·

[136] At least as enticing as the financial inducements held out to the respondent was the promise of friendship that came with working for the criminal organization. The undercover officers—aware of the respondent's social isolation—sought to become his "best friend." At the outset of the operation, the officers plotted to separate the respondent from his wife, telling him that she was not allowed to accompany him as he traveled across the country working for the organization.

· · ·

[138] The depth of the respondent's commitment to the organization and the under-cover officers can hardly be exaggerated. The respondent would constantly call his friends—Jim and Paul—looking for work, and he would anxiously await their planned meetings. He told the officers he was planning to leave Newfoundland so he could work for the organization full time. He even purported a willingness to leave his wife if that is what it would take to join the organization. And when he was finally arrested on June 13, the respondent's first call for help was naturally placed to Jim.

[139] It was in these circumstances that the respondent confessed to Mr. Big and participated in the re-enactment. When he entered their June 9 meeting, the respondent knew that his ticket out of poverty and social isolation was at stake. Jim implored him to be "honest" with the boss. Early on in the interrogation, Mr. Big drove home the import-ance of honesty, telling the respondent that "the minute the trust is gone ... everything is gone." The conversation quickly turned to the death of the respondent's daughters, and Mr. Big immediately asserted that the respondent had killed them. When the respondent denied it and claimed to have had a seizure, Mr. Big perfunctorily dismissed this explan-ation as a lie: "No don't lie to me ... don't go with the seizure stuff ... [y]ou're lying to me on this okay."

[140] The circumstances left the respondent with a stark choice: confess to Mr. Big or be deemed a liar by the man in charge of the organization he so desperately wanted to join. In my view, these circumstances, considered as a whole, presented the respondent with an overwhelming incentive to confess—either truthfully or falsely.

[141] Having determined that the circumstances in which these confessions were made cast serious doubt on the reliability of the respondent's confessions, the next question is whether these confessions contain any indicators of reliability. In my view, they do not.

[142] In the first place, the respondent's description of how the crime was committed is somewhat inconsistent. In his meeting with Mr. Big, the respondent started off by denying that he killed his daughters. Later, he said that they "fell" into the water. After further pressing by Mr. Big, the respondent claimed that he pushed his daughters into the water by striking them with his shoulder. But when he participated in the re-enactment with Jim two days later, his explanation changed again. When Jim knelt down next to the respondent and asked him to demonstrate how he pushed his daughters, the respondent nudged him with his knee. He had to use his knee because Jim, kneeling down, was not tall enough for the respondent to shove with his shoulder. The same would undoubtedly have been true for his small children.

[143] More important than these inconsistencies is the complete lack of confirmatory evidence. Given the peculiar circumstances of the case, this is unsurprising. The issue has always been whether the respondent's daughters drowned accidentally or were murdered. There was never any question that the respondent was present when his daughters entered

the water. All of the objectively verifiable details of the respondent's confession (e.g., his knowledge of the location of the drowning) flow from his acknowledged presence at the time the drowning occurred.

[144] When the circumstances in which the respondent's confessions were made are considered alongside their internal inconsistencies and the lack of any confirmatory evidence, their reliability is left in serious doubt, and I am forced to conclude that their probative value is low.

[145] On the other hand, these confessions—like all Mr. Big confessions—carried with them an obvious potential for prejudice. The jury heard extensive evidence that—for four months—the respondent devoted his entire life to trying to join a criminal gang. They heard that he repeatedly participated in what he thought were criminal acts, including transporting stolen property and smuggling alcohol. On one occasion, he and Jim, wearing balaclavas, broke into a car to steal a package from it. The jury was repeatedly told that the respondent had described himself as having "no limits," and that he would do anything "as long as the trust was there." And it is easy to see how the jury could come to view the respondent with disdain. Here was a man who bragged about killing his three-year-old daughters to gain the approval of a group of criminals. The potential for moral prejudice in these circumstances was significant.

[146] Comparing the probative value and prejudicial effect of these confessions leads me to conclude that their limited probative value is outweighed by their prejudicial effect. Put simply, these confessions are not worth the risk they pose. In my view, it would be unsafe to rest a conviction on this evidence.

. . .

(b) Abuse of Process

[148] Given my conclusion that the respondent's confessions must be excluded under the common law, it is not necessary to consider whether the police conduct in this case amounted to an abuse of process. But there is no denying that this was an extremely intensive Mr. Big operation, and one that preyed upon the respondent's poverty and social isolation. In addition, the respondent had a seizure in front of an undercover officer. The respondent's past seizures had caused his licence to be suspended to protect against the risk that a seizure would cause him to have an accident while driving. However, the operation continued after this seizure, and undercover officers continued to send the respondent long distances over public roads in order to make deliveries for the fictitious criminal organization. The respondent submits that this placed his and the public's safety at risk, and that this conduct warrants excluding the confessions.

[149] Without question, the police conduct in this case raises significant concerns, and might well amount to an abuse of process. However, this is not how the issue was presented at trial. At trial, the respondent took issue with the threatening and intimidating conduct of the officers, and the trial judge rejected those arguments. Given this, and the fact that there is no need to decide the matter, I do not believe this is an appropriate case to decide whether an abuse of process has been established.

[Moldaver J accordingly concluded that the respondent's confessions should have been excluded, and upheld the Court of Appeal's order for a new trial. Cromwell J, concurring, agreed with the legal principles set out by Moldaver J but would have left the question of determining the admissibility of the confessions to the judge at the new trial. Karakatsanis J agreed that the confessions should have been excluded, but on the basis that police had violated the self-incrimination principle inhering in s 7 of the Charter and that admitting the evidence would bring the administration of justice into disrepute under s 24(2). After the Supreme Court's decision, the Crown withdrew the charges.]

NOTE ON R v MACK

Just a few months after *Hart*, the court revisited the Mr. Big tactic in *R v Mack*, 2014 SCC 58, [2014] 3 SCR 3. There it concluded that the accused's confession was admissible. Writing for a unanimous court, Moldaver J explained as follows:

[33] To begin with, the probative value of the appellant's confessions is high. The inducements provided by the undercover officers were modest—the appellant was paid approximately $5,000 over a four-month period, at a time when well-paying, legitimate work was readily available to him. He was not threatened by the officers. And he was told, in his first meeting with Liam, that he could decline to say anything and remain on the organization's "third line"—an option he initially accepted.

[34] Moreover, there was an abundance of evidence that was potentially confirmatory. First, the appellant's purported confessions to Mr. Argueta and Mr. Love described the same motive for killing Mr. Levoir as his confessions to the undercover officers. They also made reference to burning Mr. Levoir's body. Second, immediately after confessing to Ben, the appellant led him to the firepit in which Mr. Levoir's remains lay undiscovered. And third, shell casings fired from a gun found in the appellant's apartment were found in the same firepit. All of this made for a confession that was highly probative.

[35] On the other hand, while the confessions were accompanied by bad character evidence, the prejudice was limited. The appellant was not involved in any scenarios that involved violence, nor did the operation reveal prejudicial facts about the appellant's past history. The appellant's involvement with the organization was primarily limited to assisting with repossessing vehicles and delivering packages. In my view, any prejudicial effect arising from the Mr. Big confessions is easily outweighed by their probative value.

[36] Nor did the undercover officers engage in any improper conduct which could ground an application for abuse of process. The appellant was not presented with overwhelming inducements. He had prospects for legitimate work that would have paid even more than the undercover officers were offering. Nor did the officers threaten the appellant with violence if he would not confess. The most that can be said is that the officers created an air of intimidation by referring to violent acts committed by members of the organization. But the appellant was not coerced into confessing. This much is evidenced by the appellant's initial refusal to speak with Ben and Liam about Mr. Levoir's disappearance. Indeed, the undercover officers explicitly made clear to the appellant that he did not have to speak with them about Mr. Levoir, and that he could remain in his current role within the organization. None of the undercover officers' conduct approaches abuse.

· · ·

[44] The common law rule of evidence that was set out in *Hart* was intended to respond to the evidentiary concerns raised by Mr. Big operations. However, while this rule responds to these two evidentiary concerns, it does not erase them. The focus of the rule is to determine whether

a Mr. Big confession should be admitted into evidence. It does not decide the ultimate question of whether the confession is reliable, nor does it eliminate the prejudicial character evidence that accompanies its admission. Thus, even in cases where Mr. Big confessions are admitted into evidence, concerns with their reliability and prejudice will persist. It then falls to the trial judge to adequately instruct the jury on how to approach these confessions in light of these concerns.

• • •

[50] ... In my view, there is no magical incantation that must be read to juries by trial judges in all Mr. Big cases. Instead, trial judges are required to provide juries with the tools they need to address the concerns about reliability and prejudice that arise from these confessions. The nature and extent of the instructions required will vary from case to case.

[51] However, there is some guidance—short of a prescriptive formula—that can be provided to trial judges who must instruct juries in cases where a Mr. Big confession has been admitted into evidence.

[52] With respect to the reliability concerns raised by a Mr. Big confession, the trial judge should tell the jury that the reliability of the accused's confession is a question for them. The trial judge should then review with the jury the factors relevant to the confessions and the evidence surrounding it. As explained in *Hart*, the reliability of a Mr. Big confession is affected by the circumstances in which the confession was made and by the details contained in the confession itself. Thus, the trial judge should alert the jury to "the length of the operation, the number of interactions between the police and the accused, the nature of the relationship between the undercover officers and the accused, the nature and extent of the inducements offered, the presence of any threats, the conduct of the interrogation itself, and the personality of the accused"— all of which play a role in assessing the confession's reliability (see *Hart*, at para. 102).

[53] Moreover, the trial judge should discuss the fact that the confession itself may contain markers of reliability (or unreliability). Jurors should be told to consider the level of detail in the confession, whether it led to the discovery of additional evidence, whether it identified any elements of the crime that had not been made public, or whether it accurately described mundane details of the crime the accused would not likely have known had he not committed it (see *Hart*, at para. 105).

• • •

[55] With respect to the bad character evidence that accompanies a Mr. Big confession, the challenge is a more familiar one. The trial judge must instruct the jury that this sort of evidence has been admitted for the limited purpose of providing context for the confession. The jury should be instructed that it cannot rely on that evidence in determining whether the accused is guilty. Moreover, the trial judge should remind the jury that the simulated criminal activity— even that which the accused may have eagerly participated in—was fabricated and encouraged by agents of the state.

QUESTIONS

1. Does the probative value versus prejudice test in Mr. Big cases differ in any way from courts' general discretion to exclude evidence that is more prejudicial than probative?

2. Do the principles outlined in *Hart*, and applied in *Hart* and *Mack*, provide sufficient guidance to police in deciding whether and how to mount a Mr. Big sting?

3. Should the Mr. Big rules apply to any statement made by an accused to an undercover police outside detention, or should they be confined to the elaborate, long-term operations used in *Hart* and *Mack* (however those might be defined)?

4. Should Parliament set out detailed rules for Mr. Big stings, including requiring police to obtain prior judicial authorization (as they must for many other kinds of intrusive surveillance)?

5. Should the Mr. Big rules be extended to statements made during a Mr. Big sting by a *non-accused* person? What other exclusionary rule (and exception) might apply to this situation? See *R v Campeau*, 2015 ABCA 210; *R v Tingle*, 2015 SKQB 184.

II. EXCLUSION OF EVIDENCE UNDER SECTION 24 OF THE CHARTER

As we have seen, at common law, evidence obtained illegally by the state was admissible. The enactment of s 24(2) of the Charter dramatically changed this state of affairs. Section 24 reads:

24(1) Anyone whose rights or freedoms, as guaranteed by this Charter, have been infringed or denied may apply to a court of competent jurisdiction to obtain such remedy as the court considers appropriate and just in the circumstances.

(2) Where, in proceedings under subsection (1), a court concludes that evidence was obtained in a manner that infringed or denied any rights or freedoms guaranteed by this Charter, the evidence shall be excluded if it is established that, having regard to all the circumstances, the admission of it in the proceedings would bring the administration of justice into disrepute.

In this section, we consider four issues arising under s 24(2):

- What are the prerequisites for a s 24(2) application?
- What does "obtained in a manner" mean?
- When does the admission of unconstitutionally obtained evidence bring the administration of justice into disrepute?
- Does a change in circumstances during the trial ever justify revisiting a s 24(2) ruling?

A. Prerequisites

An application to exclude evidence under s 24(2) of the Charter must be made to a "court of competent jurisdiction." In criminal trials, s 24(2) applications are made before the trial court, which is always a court of competent jurisdiction. Courts trying regulatory offences and extradition judges are also courts of competent jurisdiction. Though the superior courts are always courts of competent jurisdiction, when not acting as the trial court they will decline to exercise that jurisdiction for s 24(2) purposes. Judicial officers (other than the trial judge) presiding at pre-trial hearings such as arraignments, preliminary inquiries, and bail hearings are not courts of competent jurisdiction. Administrative tribunals will be considered courts of competent jurisdiction if they have the power to decide questions of law. But they may not award a particular type of remedy, such as the exclusion of evidence, unless it is contemplated by their statutory mandate. See *R v Mills*, [1986] 1 SCR 863, 58 OR (2d) 543; *Mooring v Canada (National Parole Board)*, [1996] 1 SCR 75; *R v 974649 Ontario Inc*, 2001 SCC 81, [2001] 3 SCR 575; *R v Hynes*, 2001 SCC 82, [2001] 3 SCR 623; *United States of America v Cobb*, 2001 SCC 19, [2001] 1 SCR 587; *R v Conway*, 2010 SCC 22, [2010] 1 SCR 765.

If the application is before a court of competent jurisdiction, the applicant (usually a person charged with an offence) must next prove that at least one of his or her own Charter rights were violated. The Charter provisions that arise most often in the investigative process are ss 7, 8, 9, 10(a), and 10(b).

The case law interpreting and applying these rights is voluminous and typically studied in a course on criminal procedure. Very briefly, these rights place limits on the ways in which police and other governmental authorities investigate and collect evidence of criminal and regulatory offences. Section 8 limits the police's ability to intrude onto people's reasonable expectations of privacy, often by first requiring them to obtain a warrant based on reasonable grounds to believe that the search will uncover evidence of an offence.

Section 9 limits the police's ability to intrude onto people's physical and mental liberty. This typically requires them to have objectively justifiable reasons to suspect that someone has committed an offence before imposing significant restraints on liberty.

Persons subject to such restraints are also protected by ss 10(a) and 10(b), which oblige police to impart certain information to detainees, including the reasons for their detention, their right to talk to a lawyer, and information about how to contact one. In addition, if a detainee expresses a desire to talk to a lawyer, police must facilitate access to one and refrain from eliciting self-incriminating evidence until the detainee has had a reasonable opportunity to consult with counsel.

The Supreme Court of Canada has interpreted s 7 as giving detainees a "right to silence"— that is, a freedom to choose whether to speak to police. As mentioned in Section I.A.5, above, when a detainee is questioned by a "person in authority," this constitutional protection largely dovetails with the common law confessions rule. Section 7 supplements the confessions rule, however, by prohibiting police from using undercover agents to actively elicit confessions from persons in custody. See *R v Hebert*, [1990] 2 SCR 151; *R v Broyles*, [1991] 3 SCR 595.

We must also mention s 1, which subjects all Charter rights to "such reasonable limits prescribed by law as can be demonstrably justified in a free and democratic society." Statutes authorizing infringements of ss 9 and 10(b), for example, have sometimes been upheld under s 1, especially in the context of detention and search powers used in impaired driving investigations. See e.g. *R v Orbanski; R v Elias*, 2005 SCC 37, [2005] 2 SCR 3.

The issue addressed in the case below is whether an accused may apply under s 24(2) to exclude evidence based on a breach of someone else's Charter rights.

R v Edwards
[1996] 1 SCR 128, 26 OR (3d) 736, 104 CCC (3d) 136
Lamer CJ and La Forest, L'Heureux-Dubé, Sopinka, Gonthier, McLachlin,
Iacobucci, and Major JJ (8 February 1996)

CORY J (Lamer CJ, Sopinka, McLachlin, Iacobucci, and Major JJ, concurring):

[1] What rights does an accused person have to challenge the admission of evidence obtained as a result of a search of a third party's premises? That is the question that must be resolved on this appeal.

Factual Background

[2] As a result of receiving information that the appellant was a drug trafficker operating out of his car using a cellular phone and a pager, the police placed him under surveillance. They were told that he had drugs either on his person, at his residence or at the apartment occupied by his girlfriend, Shelly Evers. At the time, Ms. Evers was an 18-year-old student in grade 11 who lived alone.

[3] On the day of his arrest, the police observed the appellant drive Ms. Evers' vehicle from a residence to her apartment. The appellant entered the apartment and stayed there for a brief period of time. Shortly after he left, he was stopped by the police. They knew his driver's licence was under suspension and that a person driving while his or her licence is under suspension may be arrested without a warrant (pursuant to the provisions of the *Highway Traffic Act*, RSO 1990, c. H.8, s. 217(2)).

[4] The police saw the appellant speaking on the cellular phone in the car. When they approached the vehicle, they saw the appellant swallow an object wrapped in cellophane about half the size of a golf ball. The car doors were locked, and the appellant did not unlock them until he had swallowed the object. He was arrested for driving while his licence was under suspension and taken into custody. Evers' car was then towed to the vehicle pound.

[5] It was conceded that the usual practice upon arresting a person for driving while under suspension was to impound the car and give the individual a ticket. It was unusual to take someone into custody and it was acknowledged that this procedure was adopted in order to facilitate the drug investigation.

[6] The police suspected that there might be crack cocaine in Ms. Evers' apartment, but they did not consider that they had sufficient evidence to obtain a search warrant. After taking the appellant into custody, two police officers attended at the apartment. They made a number of statements to Evers, some of which were lies and others half-truths, in order to obtain her cooperation. They advised her: (1) that the appellant had told them there were drugs in the apartment; (2) that if she did not cooperate, a police officer would stay in her apartment until they were able to get a search warrant; (3) that it would be inconvenient for them to get a search warrant because of the paperwork involved; and (4) that one of the officers would be going on vacation the following day and regardless of what they found in her apartment, she along with the appellant would not be charged.

[7] There is conflicting evidence as to whether these statements were made before or after the officers were admitted to the apartment. Nonetheless, once inside, Ms. Evers directed them to a couch in her living room where she thought she had seen the appellant replacing a cushion a few days earlier. The cushion was removed, revealing a plastic bag containing six baggies of crack cocaine with a value of between $11,000 and $23,000. These were seized by the police. Twenty minutes later, they returned and arrested Ms. Evers. This they had been instructed to do by a superior officer after he had consulted a Crown Attorney. At no time prior to being taken into custody was Ms. Evers advised of her right to refuse entry to the police or of her right to counsel.

[8] At the police station, Ms. Evers was questioned and in response, she gave a statement naming the appellant as the person who placed the drugs under the cushion of the couch in her apartment. She and the appellant were jointly charged under s. 4(2) of the

Narcotic Control Act, RSC, 1985, c. N-1, with possession of crack cocaine for the purpose of trafficking. Ms. Evers was then released. Charges against her were eventually dropped on the morning her trial was scheduled to begin.

[9] On the evening of the arrest, the police attended at the vehicle pound and without a search warrant seized the cellular phone and pager used by the appellant. Then for several hours, they intercepted a number of calls from people ordering small amounts of crack cocaine from the appellant.

[10] At the conclusion of the trial, the appellant was found guilty as charged. His appeal from conviction was dismissed by the Court of Appeal of Ontario, with Abella JA dissenting on the issue of the appellant's standing to assert his rights under s. 8 of the *Canadian Charter of Rights and Freedoms* in relation to the search of his girlfriend's apartment. The appeal to this Court is limited to that issue.

. . .

Analysis

. . .

[34] In any determination of a s. 8 challenge, it is of fundamental importance to remember that the privacy right allegedly infringed must, as a general rule, be that of the accused person who makes the challenge. This has been stressed by the United States Supreme Court in several cases dealing with searches that allegedly violated the Fourth Amendment guarantee. In *Alderman v. United States*, 394 US 165 (1969), for example, White J, delivering the judgment of the majority, stated at pp. 171-72 that:

> ... [the] suppression of the product of a Fourth Amendment violation can be successfully urged *only by those whose rights were violated by the search itself, not by those who are aggrieved solely by the introduction of damaging evidence.* [Emphasis added.]

[35] This principle was adopted and applied in *Rakas v. Illinois*, 439 US 128 (1978), at p. 133, and *United States v. Salvucci*, 448 US 83 (1980), at p. 86. The view expressed in these cases is persuasive and should be applied when s. 8 challenges are considered.

[36] The intrusion on the privacy rights of a third party may however be relevant in the second stage of the s. 8 analysis, namely whether the search was conducted in a reasonable manner. The reasons in *R v. Thompson*, [1990] 2 SCR 1111, considered this question. At issue was a wiretap authorization which allowed the police to eavesdrop on several public pay telephones that were often used by the appellant as well as other members of the public. The appellants argued that the failure of the authorizing judge to limit the intrusion on those third-party users rendered the search unreasonable. Sopinka J agreed and stated at p. 1143:

> In my view, the extent of invasion into the privacy of these third parties is constitutionally relevant to the issue of whether there has been an "unreasonable" search or seizure. To hold otherwise would be to ignore the purpose of s. 8 of the *Charter* which is to restrain invasion of privacy within reasonable limits. A potentially massive invasion of the privacy of persons not involved in the activity being investigated cannot be ignored simply because it is not brought to the attention of the court by one of those persons. Since those persons are unlikely to know of the invasion of their privacy, such invasions would escape scrutiny, and s. 8 would not fulfil its purpose.

[37] It is important to observe that Sopinka J was careful to point out that the invasion of third-party privacy rights is not determinative of the reasonableness of the search. He put it in this way at pp. 1143-44:

> In any authorization there is the possibility of invasion of privacy of innocent third parties. For instance a wiretap placed on the home telephone of a target will record communications by other members of the household. This is an unfortunate cost of electronic surveillance. But it is one which Parliament has obviously judged is justified in appropriate circumstances in the investigation of serious crime.

[38] In what may be somewhat rare circumstances, the extent of the invasion of privacy may be constitutionally relevant. This was the case in *Thompson, supra*, where the actions of the police were judged at p. 1143 as a "potentially massive invasion of ... privacy" of members of the general public who were not involved in the suspected criminal activity.

[39] In the case at bar, there is no need to consider the reasonableness of the search since the appellant has not established the requisite expectation of privacy. Even if it were necessary to consider the invasion of the privacy of Ms. Evers, I would conclude that there was neither a potentially massive invasion of property nor a flagrant abuse of individual's right to privacy.

· · ·

[51] Since no personal right of the appellant was affected by the police conduct at the apartment, the appellant could not contest the admissibility of the evidence pursuant to s. 24(2) of the *Charter*. It is therefore not necessary to consider either this aspect of the case or whether Ms. Evers did in fact consent to the search of her apartment. This is, in itself, a sufficient basis for dismissing the appeal.

[52] However, the appellant has argued that automatic standing should be granted to challenge the search of a third party's premises in those circumstances where the Crown alleges that the accused is in possession of the property which was discovered and seized. The United States Supreme Court has resiled from its earlier position on this issue. See *Jones v. United States*, 362 US 257 (1960). In *Salvucci, supra*, and in *Rawlings*, ... [*Rawlings v Kentucky*, 448 US 98 (1980)], it was determined that the correct approach to asserting Fourth Amendment rights was to satisfy the "legitimate expectation of privacy test."

[53] Not only has the United States Supreme Court rejected the automatic standing rule, but so too have the great majority of state courts. As one author writes, "they have done so not because they are required to, but rather, because they agree with the policy underlying the Supreme Court decisions." See David A. Macdonald, Jr., "Standing to Challenge Searches and Seizures: A Small Group of States Chart Their Own Course" (1990), 63 *Temp. L Rev.* 559, at pp. 571-72 and 576.

[54] Further, the adaptation of the automatic standing rule would seem to fly in the face of the wording of s. 24 of the *Charter*. It provides:

> 24.(1) *Anyone whose rights or freedoms, as guaranteed by this Charter, have been infringed or denied may apply to a court of competent jurisdiction to obtain such remedy as the court considers appropriate and just in the circumstances.*
>
> (2) Where, in proceedings under subsection (1), a court concludes that evidence was obtained in a manner that infringed or denied any rights or freedoms guaranteed by this

Charter, the evidence shall be excluded if it is established that, having regard to all the circumstances, the admission of it in the proceedings would bring the administration of justice into disrepute. [Emphasis added.]

[55] As I noted earlier, s. 24(2) provides remedies only to applicants whose *own* *Charter* rights have been infringed. This position was adopted by Wilson J in *Rahey* … [*R v Rahey*, [1987] 1 SCR 588], at p. 619, when she stated:

> … I want to stress the following. An application for relief under s. 24(1) can only be made by a person whose right under s. 11(b) has been infringed. This is clear from the opening words of s. 24(1).

[56] The reasonable expectation of privacy concept has worked well in Canada. It has proved to be reasonable, flexible, and viable. I can see no reason for abandoning it in favour of the discredited rule of automatic standing.

Disposition

[57] In the result, I would dismiss the appeal and confirm the order of the Court of Appeal upholding the conviction of the appellant.

[LA FOREST J concurred in the result because, in his view, Abella JA's dissent in the court below did not raise a question of law. But he said: "I am deeply concerned with the implications of [the majority's] reasons which, I think, result in a drastic diminution of the protection to the public s. 8 of the *Canadian Charter of Rights and Freedoms* was intended to ensure." He continued:]

[59] As I see it, the protection accorded by s. 8 is not in its terms limited to searches of premises over which an accused has a personal right to privacy in the sense of some direct control or property. Rather the provision is intended to afford protection to all of us to be secure against intrusion by the state or its agents by unreasonable searches or seizures, and is not solely for the protection of criminals even though the most effective remedy will inevitably protect the criminal as the price of liberty for all. The section, it must be remembered, reads: "*Everyone* has the right *to be secure* against unreasonable search or seizure" (emphasis added). It is a right enuring to all the public. It applies to *everyone*, an expression that unlike many of the other *Charter* provisions is not qualified by express circumstances, such as, for example, s. 9, which protects everyone arbitrarily detained or imprisoned, s. 10, which applies to a everyone arrested or detained, and s. 11, which is limited to a person charged with an offence. Moreover, s. 8 does not merely prohibit unreasonable searches or seizures, but also guarantees to everyone the right to be *secure* against such unjustified state action; see *R v. Dyment*, [1988] 2 SCR 417, at p. 427. It draws a line between the rights of the state and the rights of the citizen, and not just those of an accused. It is a public right, enjoyed by all of us. It is important for everyone, not only an accused, that police (or what is even more dangerous for the public, other agents of the state) do not break into private premises without warrant.

[L'Heureux-Dubé J and Gonthier J agreed with La Forest J that the issue of standing was not properly before the court. L'Heureux-Dubé J expressed substantial agreement with Cory J, while Gonthier J expressly declined to comment on standing.]

QUESTIONS

1. After *Edwards*, is there any remedy at all for the breach of a third party's rights? Could evidence obtained in such cases be excluded on the basis of any of the doctrines mentioned in Section II.B, below?
2. Could a third party whose rights had been infringed be granted standing in a criminal trial to argue for exclusion?

B. "Obtained in a Manner"

An accused seeking the exclusion of evidence under s 24(2) of the Charter must also show that the evidence was "obtained in a manner that infringed or denied any rights or freedoms guaranteed by this Charter." What kind of link between the infringement and the evidence does this phrase contemplate?

R v Strachan

[1988] 2 SCR 980, 46 CCC (3d) 479

Dickson CJ and Beetz, Estey, McIntyre, Lamer, Wilson, Le Dain, La Forest, and
L'Heureux-Dubé JJ (15 December 1988)

DICKSON CJ (Beetz, McIntyre, La Forest, and L'Heureux-Dubé JJ concurring): The appellant, Joseph Colin Strachan, was charged with unlawfully having in his possession a narcotic, to wit, cannabis (marijuana) for the purpose of trafficking contrary to s. 4(2) of the *Narcotic Control Act*, RSC 1970, c. N-1. He was acquitted at trial. The trial verdict was reversed on appeal. The appellant now appeals as of right to this court.

This case involves evidence seized during a search of a dwelling-house under a search warrant issued under s. 10(2) of the *Narcotic Control Act*. The appellant argues that the search was unreasonable and therefore contrary to s. 8 of the *Canadian Charter of Rights and Freedoms*. He further submits that his right to counsel under s. 10(b) of the *Charter* was denied. He contends that the evidence of the drugs and drug-related paraphernalia found in the dwelling was properly excluded by the trial judge under s. 24(2) of the *Charter*.

. . .

II The Facts

On 9th September 1983 Constable Bisceglia was the officer in charge of the Drug Section of the Royal Canadian Mounted Police (RCMP) Detachment in Campbell River, British Columbia. That day, a confidential source told him that the appellant had a quantity of marijuana at his apartment. Two other sources had given Constable Bisceglia the same tip within the previous few days. Early in the afternoon, Constable Bisceglia appeared before a justice of the peace and applied under s. 10 of the *Narcotic Control Act* for a warrant to search a dwelling for narcotics. The justice of the peace issued the search warrant. In compliance with s. 10(2) of the Act, the warrant named Constables Bisceglia, Arseneault, Clark and Underhill, all of the RCMP, as the peace officers authorized to enter and search the dwelling. The warrant was valid between 3:00 p.m. and 7:00 p.m. of that day.

The officers went to the appellant's apartment at 4:00 p.m. but no one was home. They did not attempt to enter but went about other duties. At approximately 6:00 p.m., Constable Arseneault learned that the appellant was at home, but was leaving shortly for Vancouver, and would not be back for two or three days. Constable Bisceglia decided to execute the warrant immediately, but Constables Clark and Underhill were about to go off duty. Constable Bisceglia telephoned the justice of the peace who had issued the search warrant, explained the circumstances, and asked if it would be possible to substitute two other officers. The justice of the peace authorized the substitution and the officers went to the appellant's apartment, arriving there around 6:20 p.m. All four were dressed in civilian clothes.

The police officers knocked on the door. The appellant answered. Two other men were in the apartment, in the living room. Constable Bisceglia gave the appellant a copy of the search warrant, showed his identification and arrested the appellant for possession of marijuana. He then read the standard police warning, including the right to counsel guaranteed by the *Charter*. The appellant immediately picked up the phone and said he was going to call his lawyer, but Constable Bisceglia told him that he could not telephone until the police had "matters under control." Constable Bisceglia then asked the appellant for his full name, address and age, and for some identification. He also asked the appellant some questions concerning his marijuana usage. Constable Bisceglia then asked the other two men for their names. Approximately 40 minutes after the police entered the apartment, the two men left. While Constable Bisceglia interviewed the appellant and the two men, the other officers searched the apartment. After the two men left, Constable Bisceglia assisted in the search. Constable Vanschaik and Corporal McBratney, the two substituted officers, did not seize items they discovered in the search, but pointed them out to Constables Bisceglia and Arseneault to seize. Constables Bisceglia and Arseneault together seized about 300 gm of "green plant-like material," a set of scales, plastic bags, a "hook up" (*sic*) pipe, and a "huge number" of bills totalling $3,193. After the conclusion of the search, the police took the accused to the police station, arriving there around 8:00 p.m. He was then allowed to telephone his lawyer.

At the *voir dire* on the admission of the evidence, Constable Bisceglia was asked to explain what he had meant when he told the appellant that he could not telephone his lawyer until the officers had matters under control. Constable Bisceglia explained that he wanted to find out who were the two additional occupants of the apartment. He was also aware that the appellant had two restricted firearms at the apartment, for which the appellant had the appropriate registration certificates. Constable Bisceglia explained that he wanted to locate the two revolvers.

After his initial attempt to contact counsel, the appellant made no further request to use the telephone. The police officers did not advise him again of his right to retain counsel after the initial warnings.

· · ·

V The Validity of the Search Warrant

[Dickson J held that the substitution of two unnamed officers for two officers named in the warrant did not infringe s 8 because the search was carried out by two officers who were named in the warrant and who were entitled to rely on the assistance of unnamed officers. He also noted that in attempting to get judicial authorization for the substitution, "Constable Bisceglia showed respect for the spirit of s. 8 of the *Charter* and awareness of the limitations on police search powers."]

VI Section 10(b) and the Right to Counsel

The respondent has conceded in this court and in the Court of Appeal that the police violated the appellant's right to counsel when they refused to allow him to telephone a lawyer until after he was taken to the police station. Because of that concession, it is not necessary to consider the violation of the right to counsel in depth in this case, but it is nevertheless opportune to comment on one aspect.

The trial judge rejected the argument that Constable Bisceglia needed to get the situation "under control" before allowing any telephone calls and held that the violation of the right to counsel occurred as soon as the constable refused to let the appellant telephone his lawyer. Esson JA disagreed with the trial judge on this point and held that Constable Bisceglia's concern to stabilize the situation was a proper one. Although it is not necessary to decide the point in this case, I would be inclined to agree with Esson JA. The combination of an arrest in the accused's home, the presence of two unknown people, and the knowledge that two restricted weapons were in the apartment, was a potentially volatile situation. It is true the accused had the proper registration permits for the weapons, but, notwithstanding, the possibility of their use was a serious matter for a police officer to consider while taking a person into custody. In my opinion, Constable Bisceglia was justified in preventing any new factors from entering the situation until some of the unknowns had been clarified. Thus I would say that the violation of s. 10(b) did not occur when Constable Bisceglia initially prevented the appellant from telephoning his counsel. But once the accused had been arrested, the weapons located and the other two people had left, the police were clearly in control and there was no reason why they should not have allowed the appellant to telephone a lawyer. I would hold that the denial of counsel began from that point.

VII Section 24 and the Exclusion of Evidence

Counsel for the Crown submitted that the narcotics should not be excluded under s. 24(2). The respondent advanced two arguments for this submission. First, the Crown contended that there was no direct relationship between the breach of the accused's right to counsel and the discovery of the drugs. Absent a causal connection, the evidence could not be said to have been obtained in a manner that infringed the *Charter*, and therefore s. 24(2) could not be invoked to exclude the evidence in question. Second, and in the alternative, the respondent submitted that, on the test enunciated in *R v. Collins*, [1987] 1 SCR 265, 33 CCC (3d) 1, 38 DLR (4th) 508, for exclusion under s. 24(2), the evidence ought not to be excluded. I will consider each of these arguments in turn.

A. Was the Evidence Obtained in a Manner That Infringed the Charter?

The respondent's first argument rests on a restrictive interpretation of the scope of s. 24(2). Section 24(2) is a special remedial provision. It is set apart from s. 24(1), the general remedial section of the *Charter*. Section 24(2) sets out the conditions in which the exclusion of evidence may be granted in an application for a remedy under s. 24(1). In *R v. Therens* [[1985] 1 SCR 613] and *R v. Collins*, majorities of the court held that s. 24(2) provides the sole basis for the exclusion of evidence; evidence cannot be excluded under s. 24(1) alone. The wording of s. 24(2) suggests that two conditions must be met before evidence will be excluded: (i) the evidence must be "obtained in a manner that infringed or denied any rights or freedoms guaranteed" by the *Charter* and (ii) the admission of the evidence in the proceedings "would bring the administration of justice into disrepute." In Crown counsel's submission, there must be a causal connection between the *Charter* breach and the evidence sought to be excluded. Evidence does not clear the first hurdle in s. 24(2) unless it is the product of, or derived from the exploitation of, a *Charter* violation.

This court has discussed the meaning of the phrase "obtained in a manner that infringed or denied rights and freedoms guaranteed by this Charter" on only one occasion. In *R v. Therens*, Le Dain and Lamer JJ each considered the first requirement of s. 24(2). Le Dain J, speaking for himself and McIntyre J in dissent, suggested that the first branch of s. 24(2) generally requires only a temporal connection. He rejected a more stringent interpretation calling for a causal connection between the *Charter* violation and the discovery of the evidence (at p. 649):

> In my opinion the words "obtained in a manner that infringed or denied any rights or freedoms guaranteed by this Charter" particularly when they are read with the French version, *obtenues dans des conditions qui portent atteinte aux droits et libertés garantis par la présente charte*, do not connote or require a relationship of causation. It is sufficient if the infringement or denial of the right or freedom has preceded, or occurred in the course of, the obtaining of the evidence. It is not necessary to establish that the evidence would not have been obtained but for the violation of the *Charter*. Such a view gives adequate recognition to the intrinsic harm that is caused by a violation of a *Charter* right or freedom, apart from its bearing on the obtaining of evidence. I recognize, however, that in the case of derivative evidence, which is not what is in issue here, some consideration may have to be given in particular cases to the question of relative remoteness.

Lamer J disagreed with the view that a temporal link is sufficient for the purposes of the first branch of s. 24(2). He was of the view that there must be some additional nexus between the *Charter* violation and the evidence, but he did not elaborate on what this requirement might be. Justice Estey, speaking for himself and Beetz, Chouinard and Wilson JJ, did not address the question but applied s. 24(2) to exclude breathalyzer readings taken in violation of the accused's right to counsel.

In the present appeal, Esson JA rejected the Crown's submission that s. 24(2) requires a causal link between the *Charter* infringement and the discovery of the evidence. He considered *Therens* and held that it did not stand for the proposition that s. 24(2) requires a causal nexus. In his view, the language of s. 24(2) militated against such an interpretation. If present, a causal link was one factor to take into account in the later s. 24(2) determination whether admission of the evidence would bring the administration of justice into disrepute. Esson JA concluded that the evidence was obtained in a manner that infringed the *Charter*.

I am inclined to agree with Esson JA and to reject the approach to the first requirement of s. 24(2) advanced by the Crown. In my view, reading the phrase "obtained in a manner" as imposing a causation requirement creates a host of difficulties. A strict causal nexus would place the courts in the position of having to speculate whether the evidence would have been discovered had the *Charter* violation not occurred. Speculation on what might have happened is a highly artificial task. Isolating the events that caused the evidence to be discovered from those that did not is an exercise in sophistry. Events are complex and dynamic. It will never be possible to state with certainty what would have taken place had a *Charter* violation not occurred. Speculation of this sort is not, in my view, an appropriate inquiry for the courts.

A causation requirement also leads to a narrow view of the relationship between a *Charter* violation and the discovery of evidence. Requiring a causal link will tend to distort the analysis of the conduct that led to the discovery of evidence. The inquiry will tend to focus narrowly on the actions most directly responsible for the discovery of evidence rather than on the entire course of events leading to its discovery. This will almost inevitably lead to an intellectual endeavour essentially amounting to "splitting hairs" between conduct that violated the *Charter* and that which did not.

· · ·

Imposing a causation requirement in s. 24(2) would generally have the effect of excluding from consideration under that section much of the real evidence obtained following a violation of the right to counsel. Violations of the right to counsel may frequently occur in the course of a valid arrest or, as in the present appeal, in the execution of a valid search power. In these situations, real evidence discovered on the person of the accused or in the course of the search will not, subject to one exception, have a direct causal relationship with the denial of the right to counsel. Derivative evidence, obtained as a direct result of a statement or other indication made by the accused, is the only type of real evidence that may be said to be causally connected to violations of the right to counsel in these situations. With the exception of derivative evidence, infringements of the right to counsel occurring in the course of arrest or execution of a search warrant can only be causally connected to self-incriminating evidence. *R v. Manninen*, [1987] 1 SCR 1233, 34 CCC (3d) 385, is a case in point. A strict causal requirement would tend to preclude real evidence discovered after a violation of s. 10(b) from being considered under s. 24(2) of the *Charter*.

In situations other than valid arrest or reasonable execution of a search warrant, it may be possible to argue that the presence of counsel might have prevented the discovery of real evidence. This could be the case, for example, under the personal search provisions of the *Customs Act*, RSC 1970, c. C-40, considered in *R v. Simmons* (1988), 66 CCC (3d) 297, or under the provisions of the new *Customs Act*, SC 1986, c. 1. These provisions permit a person about to be searched to request a second authorization before the search is conducted. Persons who are not given the opportunity to consult counsel in this situation may be unaware of their right to request a second opinion and the search may proceed without further authorization. It would be possible to argue that had the person been informed of the right to counsel, counsel would have advised the person to demand a second opinion and this might have been that a search should not be conducted. Imposing a causal requirement would result in treating violations of s. 10(b) differently depending on the role counsel could have performed and would invite idle speculation on what might have happened if the accused had exercised the right to counsel.

In my view, it is not useful to create a requirement in the first stage of s. 24(2) that would separate violations of s. 10(b) into two categories based on the role of counsel. Nor is it fruitful to read into the first stage a condition that would limit the scope of s. 24(2) to self-incriminating or derivative evidence for certain s. 10(b) violations. Ordinarily only a few *Charter* rights, ss. 8, 9 and 10, will be relevant to the gathering of evidence and therefore to the remedy of exclusion under s. 24(2). So long as a violation of one of these rights precedes the discovery of evidence, for the purposes of the first stage of s. 24(2) it makes little sense to draw distinctions based on the circumstances surrounding the violation or the type of evidence recovered. A better approach, in my view, would be to consider all evidence gathered following a violation of a *Charter* right, including the right to counsel, as within the scope of s. 24(2).

In my view, all of the pitfalls of causation may be avoided by adopting an approach that focuses on the entire chain of events during which the *Charter* violation occurred and the evidence was obtained. Accordingly, the first inquiry under s. 24(2) would be to determine whether a *Charter* violation occurred in the course of obtaining the evidence. A temporal link between the infringement of the *Charter* and the discovery of the evidence figures prominently in this assessment, particularly where the *Charter* violation and the discovery of the evidence occur in the course of a single transaction. The presence of a temporal connection is not, however, determinative. Situations will arise where evidence, though obtained following the breach of a *Charter* right, will be too remote from the violation to be "obtained in a manner" that infringed the *Charter*. In my view, these situations should be dealt with on a case-by-case basis. There can be no hard and fast rule for determining when evidence obtained following the infringement of a *Charter* right becomes too remote.

If a *Charter* violation has occurred in the course of obtaining the evidence, the analysis will proceed to the second, and in my view the more important, branch of s. 24(2), whether the admission of the evidence would bring the administration of justice into disrepute. In *R v. Collins* the court articulated a comprehensive test for the second branch of s. 24(2). Lamer J, for the majority, identified three groups of factors to be considered in the course of this inquiry. The first group concerns the fairness of the trial. The nature of the evidence, whether it is real evidence or self-incriminating evidence produced by the accused, will be relevant to this determination. The second group relates to the seriousness of the *Charter* violation. Consideration will focus on the relative seriousness of the violation, whether the violation was committed in good faith or was of a merely technical nature or whether it was wilful, deliberate and flagrant, whether the violation was motivated by circumstances of urgency or necessity, and whether other investigatory techniques that would not have infringed the *Charter* were available. The final set of factors relates to the disrepute that would arise from exclusion of the evidence. In my view, the three groups of factors encompass aspects of the relationship between the *Charter* violation and the evidence at issue, thereby permitting some examination of the relationship in the course of the core inquiry under s. 24(2). The presence of a causal link will be a factor for consideration under the second branch of s. 24(2).

I conclude that the narcotics in this appeal were obtained in a manner that infringed the *Charter*. During the execution of a search of his apartment, the appellant was denied his right to consult counsel. Marijuana was discovered during the course of the search. In my view, this chain of events is sufficient to clear the first branch of s. 24(2). I therefore turn to consider the second branch, whether admission of the evidence would bring the administration of justice into disrepute.

[Dickson CJ held that the evidence was admissible under s 24(2) because it was real evidence; the breach of s 10(b) did not "appear to have been part of a larger pattern of disregard for Charter rights"; and, in these circumstances, "exclusion of the evidence rather than its admission would tend to bring the administration of justice into disrepute." The appeal was therefore dismissed.]

[Lamer J concurred in brief separate reasons. Wilson J concurred in the result. She held that s 10(b) had been violated when Constable Bisceglia refused to allow Strachan to use the phone, but she agreed with Dickson CJ that the evidence should have been admitted under s 24(2).]

R v Goldhart
[1996] 2 SCR 463, 107 CCC (3d) 481
Lamer CJ and La Forest, L'Heureux-Dubé, Sopinka, Gonthier, Cory, McLachlin,
Iacobucci, and Major JJ (4 July 1996)

SOPINKA J (Lamer CJ, L'Heureux-Dubé, Gonthier, Cory, McLachlin, Iacobucci, and Major JJ concurring):

[1] This appeal concerns the question of when evidence can be said to have been obtained in a manner that infringes a right or freedom of the *Canadian Charter of Rights and Freedoms* so as to attract the provisions of s. 24(2) of the *Charter*. Specifically, the Court must determine whether the *viva voce* evidence of a witness who was arrested following an illegal search is subject to a s. 24(2) analysis. I have determined that s. 24(2) has no application in that there is no temporal connection between the *viva voce* evidence and the breach of the *Charter* and that any causal connection is too remote.

I. Facts

[2] William Goldhart was convicted for the possession and cultivation of narcotics for his involvement in a marijuana-growing operation. On appeal to the Ontario Court of Appeal (1995), 25 OR (3d) 72, Goldhart's convictions were overturned on the grounds that the *viva voce* evidence of the Crown's only witness (Gerald Mayer) had been obtained through a breach of the *Charter*. According to the majority of the Ontario Court of Appeal, the admission of Mayer's evidence at trial would have brought the administration of justice into disrepute. The Court of Appeal accordingly ordered the exclusion of the evidence under s. 24(2) of the *Charter*. As a result of this decision, Goldhart's convictions were set aside and replaced with a verdict of acquittal. The Crown now appeals to this Court.

[3] In assessing the merits of the Crown's appeal, it is necessary to review the circumstances in which the evidence at issue (i.e., the oral evidence given by Gerald Mayer) came to be "obtained" by the Crown. Only if this evidence was "obtained in a manner"

that violated the *Charter* within the meaning of s. 24(2) can the evidence be excluded under that section. If the evidence should not have been excluded under the *Charter*, the evidence must be admitted and the appeal must be allowed.

[4] The investigation that ultimately led to Goldhart's arrest commenced in February 1991. At that time, the Peterborough Police received a tip that narcotics were being cultivated by the occupants of a converted schoolhouse near Ennismore, Ontario. According to information that had been given to the police, an individual named "Willie" was operating a hydroponic marijuana garden in the building. The property on which the converted schoolhouse was located was registered to Mr. Robert Spence, and a vehicle belonging to William Goldhart (the respondent) had been sighted on the property in question.

[5] Constable Robert Campbell of the Peterborough Police kept the converted schoolhouse under surveillance, but found little information that could further the investigation. At one point in the course of the police investigation, Constable Campbell and a colleague had knocked on the doors of the schoolhouse in order to meet with the occupants of the building. Unfortunately for the officers conducting the investigation, no one ever answered the schoolhouse door.

[6] Constable Campbell and his colleagues left the converted schoolhouse, and concocted a plan to further their largely fruitless investigation. Constable Campbell decided to approach the schoolhouse again and knock on the door a second time, this time masquerading as the grandson of the building's former owner. According to Constable Campbell, the purpose of this ruse was to make contact with the occupants of the building, and to ascertain whether there were narcotics within the structure. The police returned to the schoolhouse and Constable Campbell attempted to carry out his plan.

[7] Upon arriving at the schoolhouse, Constable Campbell circled the building and approached the back door, still hoping to knock on the door and confront the residents. As Constable Campbell approached the door, however, he detected the strong odour of marijuana.

[8] Constable Campbell asked several of his colleagues to confirm that the odour in question was the scent of marijuana. The other officers confirmed Constable Campbell's observations and suspected that the odour came from a vent in the building's gable. The officers further noted that the windows of the schoolhouse had been "blacked out," making it impossible to see the structure's interior. After taking note of their sensory observations, the officers left the building without attempting to enter.

[9] Using the results of their "olfactory surveillance," the police obtained a warrant and returned to search the building. In the basement of the schoolhouse, the police discovered and seized a hydroponic garden which included approximately 3,000 marijuana plants. The occupants of the schoolhouse were identified as Judith Slippoy, Gerald Mayer and William Goldhart, each of whom was arrested for the possession and cultivation of narcotics.

[10] On June 13, 1991, one of the occupants of the schoolhouse (Gerald Mayer) attended court for the purposes of a preliminary hearing. Mayer had been advised that the propriety of the search was being questioned, and that the evidence obtained through the search could be excluded under s. 24(2) of the *Charter*. Against the advice of his counsel, however, Mayer pleaded guilty to the offence of cultivating narcotics, notwithstanding his counsel's suggestion that he could have been acquitted. According to Mayer, a recent religious conversion had led him to enter the plea of guilty, as he wanted "to get something out of [his] heart."

[11] The trial of the respondent Goldhart began on October 19, 1992. At the commencement of the trial, Goldhart's counsel challenged the admissibility of the marijuana plants that had been seized in the search of the converted schoolhouse. Murphy J of the Ontario Court, General Division held a *voir dire* in order to determine whether the relevant evidence was admissible under s. 24(2) of the *Charter*. Relying on the decision of this Court in *R v. Kokesch*, [1990] 3 SCR 3, Murphy J determined that the search had been unreasonable and that "the evidence obtained as a result of the search warrant should be excluded." Murphy J rejected the officers' claim that they had attended at Goldhart's home for the purpose of identifying the occupants of the schoolhouse. According to the trial judge, the police were engaged in a search, and the purpose of that search was to gather evidence that could provide the police with sufficient grounds for a warrant.

[12] At the conclusion of the *voir dire* concerning the marijuana plants, the Crown was granted an adjournment to reconsider its position. When Goldhart's trial finally resumed, the Crown advised the court that it intended to call Gerald Mayer to give *viva voce* evidence against the accused. Counsel for Goldhart applied to have Mayer's testimony excluded under s. 24(2) on the ground that Mayer's evidence had been derived from the unreasonable search and seizure.

[13] Murphy J held a second *voir dire* in order to determine whether Mayer's evidence should be excluded under s. 24(2). After reviewing the relevant cases, Murphy J determined that the evidence was admissible as its admission would not adversely affect the fairness of Goldhart's trial. The evidence was admitted, and Goldhart was convicted on the strength of Mayer's evidence. Goldhart appealed his convictions to the Ontario Court of Appeal, where a majority of the court allowed the appeal on the grounds that the evidence given by Mayer should have been excluded under s. 24(2). As a result of this decision, the Court of Appeal quashed Goldhart's convictions and entered a verdict of acquittal. The Crown now appeals that decision to this Court.

[14] For the purposes of this appeal, the Crown has made several important concessions. First, the Crown admits that the warrant used to search the converted schoolhouse was obtained on the strength of unlawfully garnered evidence. The Crown has properly admitted that, without the information gleaned from the unlawful perimeter search of the old schoolhouse, the warrant that was relied on in this case could not have issued. As a result, the Crown concedes that the search conducted under the warrant was unreasonable within the meaning of s. 8 of the *Charter*.

. . .

III. *Judgments in Appeal*

(a) *Ontario Court, General Division (Voir Dire), Murphy J*

[16] Murphy J began by reviewing the judgment of the Ontario Court (General Division) in *R v. Church of Scientology of Toronto (No. 2)* (1992), 74 CCC (3d) 341, which dealt with issues similar to the ones raised in this case. In *Church of Scientology*, the court had been asked to exclude the evidence of five former scientologists who were discovered by the Crown through a search which violated the *Charter*. According to the court, at p. 344:

> The first question to be decided is whether the obtaining of the secondary evidence is sufficiently connected with the breach of the Charter. If so, the second question under s. 24(2)

of the Charter is whether the admission of the secondary evidence would bring the administration of justice into disrepute.

The court in *Church of Scientology* found a causal connection between the search and the *viva voce* evidence given by the scientologists, and accordingly concluded that the evidence triggered the application of s. 24(2) of the *Charter*. According to Goldhart's counsel in this case, *Church of Scientology* was analogous to the facts of the case at bar, leading to the conclusion that Mayer's *viva voce* evidence, like that of the scientologists, was subject to exclusion under the *Charter*.

[17] Murphy J considered the presence or absence of a connection between the evidence given by Mayer and the unreasonable search and seizure in this case. In Murphy J's opinion:

> There is a possibility that the police might have approached [Mayer] without the aid of the search. There was certainly ample time for the police to make a contact with [Mayer] as they were aware of the presence of [Mayer's] vehicle some considerable time before the search occurred.

However, Murphy J went on to state that:

> [T]he applicants have satisfied me on the balance of probabilities that there is a causal connection between the seizure of the marijuana plants in violation of the Charter and the evidence obtained from Mr. [Mayer].
> I am not able to say that Mr. [Mayer] would have come forward had he not been arrested. The arrest was causally connected with the Charter breach.

According to Murphy J, this led to the conclusion that Mayer's evidence had been "obtained in a manner" that breached the *Charter*, thereby engaging the application of s. 24(2). As a result, if the admission of the evidence would bring the administration of justice into disrepute, the evidence could be excluded under s. 24(2).

[18] In regard to s. 24(2), Murphy J found it useful to consider how Mayer had come forward. Murphy J stated:

> Mr. [Mayer], at his preliminary inquiry, gave evidence that he did not wish to testify but he would, and because of his religion he would tell the truth. In his evidence on the voir dire Mr. [Mayer] indicated a strong willingness to testify. He indicated he decided to plead guilty in order to get the matter off his chest. He entered the plea despite the advice from his counsel. He was told that there might be a defence based on a Charter application. He was told that the other two accused were going to mount such an attack and that he could sit in the bushes and see if they were successful in their attack. There is no evidence that he was offered any consideration for his plea and testimony.

[19] After reviewing the relevant factors, Murphy J ruled in favour of the admission of the evidence. He concluded as follows:

> I have found the evidence of [Mayer] to be causally connected to the Charter breach, but as my judgment it is still open to me to consider the willingness of Mr. [Mayer] to testify as one of the factors to consider on the issue of s. 24(2), and particularly as it relates to the disrepute if the evidence is excluded. I am satisfied that Mr. [Mayer] is now expressing his own free will when he told the Court that he wishes to testify. It is not related to any favour or inducements.

Mr. [Mayer] is a born-again Christian and one is always suspicious of the timing of such a conversion when it is so closely connected to a plea of guilty on a serious charge. I am satisfied that Mr. [Mayer's] decision is truly the product of a detached reflection and the expression of a sincere desire to co-operate.

Applying the principles that I have reviewed that there should be greater reluctance to exclude live evidence from witnesses, I therefore dismiss the application because to exclude the evidence of a live witness on a trial of this nature would, in my judgment, bring the administration of justice into disrepute in the eyes of a reasonable man dispassionate and fully appraised [*sic*] of the circumstances of this case.

(b) Ontario Court of Appeal (1995), 25 OR (3d) 72

[The Court of Appeal, Brooke JA dissenting, allowed the accused's appeal and entered an acquittal.]

V. Analysis

[31] I conclude in these reasons that the answer to the question raised in the first issue should be in the negative. It is therefore unnecessary to deal with the second issue.

[32] Section 24(2) of the *Charter* makes it clear that only evidence that was "obtained in a manner" that breached the *Charter* can be subject to exclusion under that section. In the Crown's submission, the evidence given by Mayer is not sufficiently connected to the breach of s. 8 to warrant the invocation of s. 24(2). In other words, the Crown contends that the evidence given by Mayer was not "obtained in a manner" that breached the *Charter*.

[33] When can evidence be said to have been "obtained in a manner" that breached the *Charter*? The proper method of determining whether s. 24(2) of the *Charter* is engaged was developed by this Court in *R v. Therens*, [1985] 1 SCR 613, and *Strachan* … [*R v Strachan*, [1988] 2 SCR 980]. In both cases, the Court rejected the strict application of the form of "causal analysis" relied on by the courts below in the instant case.

· · ·

[36] In these judgments of our Court, causation was rejected as the sole touchstone of the application of s. 24(2) of the *Charter* by reason of the pitfalls that are inherent in the concept. Its use in other areas of the law has been characterized by attempts to place limits on its reach. The happening of an event can be traced to a whole range of causes along a spectrum of diminishing connections to the event. The common law of torts has grappled with the problem of causation. In order to inject some degree of restraint on the potential reach of causation, the concepts of proximate cause and remoteness were developed. These concepts place limits on the extent of liability in order to implement the sound policy of the law that there exists a substantial connection between the tortious conduct and the injury for which compensation is claimed. On the other hand, causation need not be proved with scientific precision. See *Snell v. Farrell*, [1990] 2 SCR 311.

[37] Causation has also played an important role in other *Charter* jurisprudence. It is the basis for exclusion of evidence that would not have been discovered "but for" the existence of compelled testimony. See *R v. S.(R.J.)*, [1995] 1 SCR 451; *British Columbia Securities Commission v. Branch*, [1995] 2 SCR 3. It is also a factor in the application of s. 24(2) as the underpinning of the principle of discoverability. See *Collins* … [*R v Collins*, [1987] 1 SCR 265], and *R v. Burlingham*, [1995] 2 SCR 206.

· · ·

[40] Although *Therens* and *Strachan* warned against over-reliance on causation and advocated an examination of the entire relationship between the *Charter* breach and the impugned evidence, causation was not entirely discarded. Accordingly, while a temporal link will often suffice, it is not always determinative. It will not be determinative if the connection between the securing of the evidence and the breach is *remote*. I take remote to mean that the connection is tenuous. The concept of remoteness relates not only to the temporal connection but to the causal connection as well. It follows that the mere presence of a temporal link is not necessarily sufficient. In obedience to the instruction that the whole of the relationship between the breach and the evidence be examined, it is appropriate for the court to consider the strength of the causal relationship. If both the temporal connection and the causal connection are tenuous, the court may very well conclude that the evidence was not obtained in a manner that infringes a right or freedom under the *Charter*. On the other hand, the temporal connection may be so strong that the *Charter* breach is an integral part of a single transaction. In that case, a causal connection that is weak or even absent will be of no importance. Once the principles of law are defined, the strength of the connection between the evidence obtained and the *Charter* breach is a question of fact. Accordingly, the applicability of s. 24(2) will be decided on a case-by-case basis as suggested by Dickson CJ in *Strachan*.

[41] In concluding that s. 24(2) applied in this case, the trial judge relied exclusively on his finding that there was a causal connection between the *Charter* breach and the *viva voce* evidence of Mayer. For convenience, I repeat that finding:

> … the applicants have satisfied me on the balance of probabilities that *there is a causal connection between the seizure of the marijuana plants in violation of the Charter and the evidence obtained from Mr. [Mayer].*
>
> I am not able to say that Mr. [Mayer] would have come forward had he not been arrested. The arrest was causally connected with the Charter breach. [Emphasis added.]

[42] Applying the principles in *Church of Scientology, supra*, the trial judge concluded that s. 24(2) applied. With respect, the learned trial judge erred in concluding that the existence of a causal connection was sufficient to attract the provisions of s. 24(2). By focusing on the causal connection the trial judge failed to examine the entire relationship between the evidence and the illegal search and seizure. In particular, he failed to consider whether there existed a temporal link. He also failed to evaluate the strength of the connection between the impugned evidence and the breach. To the extent that the *Church of Scientology* decision supports this approach, it should not be followed. I note, however, that in that case the trial judge expressly found that the illegally seized documents incriminated the witnesses and were a key factor in the decisions of the witnesses to come forward and testify. Here, the trial judge, although he found a causal connection, went on to make the further finding that the *viva voce* evidence of Mayer was an expression of his own free will, a product of detached reflection and a sincere desire to cooperate, largely brought about by his recent conversion as a born-again Christian. A proper evaluation of these findings in relation to the causal connection might well have led the trial judge to the conclusion that the causal connection was tenuous.

[43] In order to assess properly the relationship between the breach and the impugned evidence, it is important to bear in mind that it is the *viva voce* evidence of Mayer that is

said to have been obtained in a manner that breaches the *Charter*. A distinction must be made between discovery of a person who is arrested and charged with an offence and the evidence subsequently volunteered by that person. The discovery of the person cannot simply be equated with securing evidence from that person which is favourable to the Crown. The person charged has the right to remain silent and in practice will usually exercise it on the advice of counsel. The prosecution has no assurance, therefore, that the person will provide any information let alone sworn testimony that is favourable to the Crown. In this regard it has been rightly observed that testimony cannot be treated in the same manner as an inanimate object. As Brooke JA observed in his dissenting opinion, at p. 85:

> Testimony is the product of a person's mind and known only if and when that person discloses it. It cannot be obtained or discovered in any other way. Testimony which is heard for the first time some months after a search cannot be equated with or analogized to evidence of an inanimate thing found or seized when an illegal search is carried out.

[44] Similarly, Rehnquist J, as he then was, in *United States v. Ceccolini*, 435 US 268 (1978), explained the difference as follows, at pp. 276-77:

> Witnesses are not like guns or documents which remain hidden from view until one turns over a sofa or opens a filing cabinet. Witnesses can, and often do, come forward and offer evidence entirely of their own volition. And evaluated properly, the degree of free will necessary to dissipate the taint will very likely be found more often in the case of live-witness testimony than other kinds of evidence.

[45] When the evidence is appropriately characterized as indicated above, the application of the relevant factors yields a different result from that reached by the trial judge and the majority of the Court of Appeal. In order to find a temporal link the pertinent event is the decision of Mayer to cooperate with the Crown and testify, and not his arrest. Indeed the existence of a temporal link between the illegal search and the arrest of Mayer is of virtually no consequence. Moreover, any temporal link between the illegal search and the testimony is greatly weakened by the intervening events of Mayer's voluntary decision to cooperate with the police, to plead guilty and to testify. The application of the causal connection factor is to the same effect. The connection between the illegal search and the decision by Mayer to give evidence is extremely tenuous. Having regard, therefore, to the entire chain of events, I am of the opinion that the nexus between the impugned evidence and the *Charter* breach is remote. In this regard I agree with Brooke JA when he states, at pp. 85-86:

> Clearly, the testimony of Mayer cannot be said to be derivative of the breach as was the case of the testimony of Hall in *R v. Burlingham* ... . There may be some link to the evidence of the finding of the marijuana, but this is surely not a basis on which to say the testimony was discovered or obtained by the breach of the appellant's rights. There must be a point at which a chain connecting the breach and the testimony is sufficiently weakened as to render the testimony untainted or too remote from the original breach. If this is not so, the ramifications may be far-reaching with respect to the exclusion of testimony of a co-accused where the Crown seeks to take advantage of it. In my opinion, the link between the breach and Mayer's testimony does not survive an analysis of remoteness or attenuation.

[46] For the foregoing reasons, the relationship between the infringement of s. 8 of the *Charter* and the *viva voce* evidence of Mayer does not lead me to conclude that the latter was obtained in a manner that infringes or denies a *Charter* right or freedom. Section 24(2) of the *Charter* is, therefore, not engaged and is not available to exclude the evidence. The evidence is relevant and was properly admitted at trial. The majority of the Court of Appeal was in error in setting aside the conviction.

[47] In the result the appeal is allowed, the judgment of the Court of Appeal is set aside and the convictions are restored.

[La Forest J dissented. In his view, a causal connection between the breach and the evidence, though not necessary, was sufficient to engage s 24(2).]

R v Wittwer

2008 SCC 33, [2008] 2 SCR 235

McLachlin CJ and Binnie, LeBel, Deschamps, Fish, Abella, and Charron JJ

(5 June 2008)

FISH J (McLachlin CJ and Binnie, LeBel, Deschamps, Abella, and Charron JJ concurring):

. . .

[6] Dieter Helmut Wittwer, who was 71 years old at the time of trial, stands convicted of three counts of sexual interference, contrary to s. 151 of the *Criminal Code*, RSC 1985, c. C-46. The offences are alleged to have been committed between January 1, 1998 and July 14, 2003. Each count alleges a different victim: SLR, who was between two and six at the time; CMF, who was between six and seven; and SMF, who was between five and six.

[7] As mentioned earlier, the appellant gave three statements to the police. There is no dispute that the appellant's first and second statements were both obtained in a manner that infringed his constitutional rights. ...

[8] Mr. Wittwer appeals on the ground that his third statement, given while he was in custody on another charge, was likewise obtained in violation of his right to counsel and should have been excluded under s. 24(2) of the *Charter*.

[9] Mr. Wittwer was first questioned, by Constable Samuel Ghadban, on July 29, 2003, at the Kamloops Regional Correctional Centre where he was then detained on an unrelated charge. The interview lasted 1 h 40 min. In the course of that interview, the appellant recounted an incident that was said to have occurred three or four months earlier—an incident described in the courts below as a "bizarre" sexual encounter involving two of the three complainants.

[10] Shortly thereafter, the Crown realized that Constable Ghadban had failed to properly inform the appellant of his right to counsel and that the statement might for that reason be inadmissible at trial. After some discussion, the police decided to again question the appellant.

[11] The second interview was conducted by Constable David Helgason, who informed Mr. Wittwer properly of his right to counsel but hindered its exercise by making no effort to enable the appellant to contact his lawyer. The interview was not videotaped and the audio recording was of poor quality. Recognizing that the appellant's second

statement was therefore of doubtful admissibility, the police decided to question him once again—for the third time.

[12] The third interview, which is our concern here, was conducted by Sergeant Cary Skrine. That interview lasted almost five hours. Sergeant Skrine began by informing Mr. Wittwer of his right to counsel. Sergeant Skrine also told Mr. Wittwer that his decision whether to answer his questions should not be influenced by anything he had previously said to other police officers. Sergeant Skrine did not inform Mr. Wittwer that his prior statements might be inadmissible against him at his trial. And he claimed, as a matter of strategic misinformation, that he had no knowledge of the content of those statements.

[13] Sergeant Skrine questioned the appellant about the sexual encounter he had described in the first two interviews. The appellant, however, repeatedly told Sergeant Skrine to "talk to 'Sam' [Constable Ghadban]," and persisted for more than four hours in his refusal to discuss the matter with Sergeant Skrine.

[14] Sergeant Skrine testified that he and the appellant remained "at loggerheads." He felt that the only way to get the appellant to incriminate himself was to acknowledge that he knew about the sexual encounter described by the appellant in the first two interviews. Sergeant Skrine concluded that there was only one way he could get the appellant "to talk." In the officer's words:

> ... I felt that if he were going to make admissions with regard to those assaults, that he would only do it if he knew that I knew about his conversation with Constable Ghadban [who had taken the appellant's first statement]. [A.R., at p. 157]

[15] Sergeant Skrine's conclusion proved correct. On his return to the interview room after leaving briefly to consult with Constable Ghadban, Sergeant Skrine informed the appellant that he now knew what the appellant had told Constable Ghadban. Only then did the "gates ope[n]": The appellant proceeded immediately to give the statement that he had until then resolutely refused to provide (A.R., p. 12, judgment on the *voir dire*, at para. 27).

[16] The trial judge found that Sergeant Skrine's purpose was to obtain "an independent statement, independent, that is, of the two earlier statements given to Constable Helgason and Constable Ghadban" (A.R., p. 6, judgment on the *voir dire*, at para. 10). The appellant persisted, however, in declining to say what the officer wanted to hear—until Sergeant Skrine told him, for the first time, that he knew what the appellant had already told Constable Ghadban.

[17] The trial judge nonetheless concluded that there was a "significant temporal separation" between the impugned statement and the statement given to Constable Ghadban some five months earlier. The judge found, moreover, that the causal connection between the two statements was relatively weak; that the statement taken by Sergeant Skrine was not tainted by any defect in the initial statement; and that it was therefore admissible against Mr. Wittwer. And he convicted Mr. Wittwer on all three counts of sexual interference, contrary to s. 151 of the *Criminal Code*.

[18] The British Columbia Court of Appeal agreed substantially with the trial judge and upheld the appellant's convictions: (2007), 219 CCC (3d) 449, 2007 BCCA 275.

· · ·

[20] The decisive question on this appeal is whether the appellant's third statement was tainted by the *Charter* breaches that marred the appellant's earlier statements relating to the same charges.

[21] In considering whether a statement is tainted by an earlier *Charter* breach, the courts have adopted a purposive and generous approach. It is unnecessary to establish a strict causal relationship between the breach and the subsequent statement. The statement will be tainted if the breach and the impugned statement can be said to be part of the same transaction or course of conduct: *Strachan* [*R v Strachan*, [1988] 2 SCR 980], at p. 1005. The required connection between the breach and the subsequent statement may be "temporal, contextual, causal or a combination of the three": *R v. Plaha* (2004), 189 OAC 376, at para. 45. A connection that is merely "remote" or "tenuous" will not suffice: *R v. Goldhart*, [1996] 2 SCR 463, at para. 40; *Plaha*, at para. 45.

[22] In this case, I am satisfied that the connection is *temporal*, in the sense that mention of the first inadmissible statement (the "Ghadban statement") was followed *immediately* by the appellant's statement to Sergeant Skrine. The connection is *causal* as well, in the sense that the impugned statement was elicited after more than four hours of resistance by the appellant and—as the interrogator expected—as a result of the interrogator's reference to the Ghadban statement. In this regard, I again reproduce Sergeant Skrine's prescient observation: "I felt," he testified, "that if he were going to make admissions with regard to those assaults, that he would only do it if he knew that I knew about his conversation with Constable Ghadban." Finally, I am satisfied that the connection between the impugned statement and its inadmissible predecessors is to some extent *contextual*, in that any prior gap between the two was intentionally and explicitly bridged by Sergeant Skrine's association of one with the other in the course of his interrogation of the appellant with Constable Ghadban's watchful assistance. On any view of the matter, the connection required under *Goldhart* and *Plaha* has plainly been established.

[23] In this regard, I consider particularly apt the observations of Sopinka J, speaking for a unanimous Court in *R v. I.(L.R.) and T.(E.)*, [1993] 4 SCR 504, at pp. 526-27:

> Under the rules relating to confessions at common law, the admissibility of a confession which had been preceded by an involuntary confession involved a factual determination based on factors designed to ascertain the degree of connection between the two statements. These included the time span between the statements, advertence to the previous statement during questioning, the discovery of additional incriminating evidence subsequent to the first statement, the presence of the same police officers at both interrogations and other similarities between the two circumstances. ...
>
> In applying these factors, a subsequent confession would be involuntary if either the tainting features which disqualified the first confession continued to be present *or if the fact that the first statement was made was a substantial factor contributing to the making of the second statement.* ...
>
> In these cases the fact that a caution or warning had been given or that the advice of counsel had been obtained between the two statements was a factor to be considered but it was by no means determinative. While such an occurrence went a long way to dissipate elements of compulsion or inducement resulting from the conduct of the interrogators, it might have *little or no effect in circumstances in which the second statement is induced by the fact of the first.* [Emphasis added.]

[24] Justice Sopinka found in that case that the existence of the first statement was a substantial factor in the making of the second statement and, accordingly, that the latter statement was inadmissible on the common law test. Justice Sopinka took care to add

that, had it been necessary, he would also have excluded the second statement under s. 24(2) (p. 532).

[25] I would do so here. In my view, the required connection between the first statement and the third statement is direct and obvious. If Sergeant Skrine had not acknowledged that he was already aware of what the appellant had told Constable Ghadban, the appellant would not have reiterated the same incriminating admissions. What we have here, then, is not a suspect's change of heart but an interrogator's fatal change in strategy.

[26] With a view to obtaining these incriminating admissions from the accused, the police knowingly and deliberately made use of an earlier statement that they themselves had obtained from the appellant in a manner that infringed his constitutional rights under the *Charter*. This alone is sufficient to taint the subsequent statement and to cry out for its exclusion under the principles set out in *Strachan*. To hold otherwise is to invite the perception that the police are legally entitled to reap the benefit of their own infringements of a suspect's constitutional rights. And this, in my view, would bring the administration of justice into disrepute.

[27] For all of these reasons, I would allow the appeal, set aside the appellant's convictions, and order a new trial. ...

PROBLEMS

1. The accused was arrested for impaired driving. He was taken to a police station and strip-searched according to a policy that should not have applied to his case. The police then obtained a sample of the accused's breath and charged him with impaired driving and "over 80." The strip-search was found to be a flagrant violation of the accused's s 8 rights. Was the breath sample "obtained in a manner" for the purpose of s 24(2)? See *R v Flintoff* (1998), 126 CCC (3d) 321 (Ont CA).

2. The police failed to inform the accused of his right to retain and instruct counsel when he was initially detained. He did not say anything. Later, the police properly warned him of his s 10 rights and the accused subsequently confessed. Assuming that the initial failure to caution violated s 10(b), was the confession "obtained in a manner" for the purpose of s 24(2)? See *R v Upston*, [1988] 1 SCR 1083. Now assume that the accused had made an inculpatory statement *before* receiving the s 10(b) caution and then made a full confession after. Would a court be more likely to find that the confession was "obtained in a manner"? See *R v Plaha* (2004), 188 CCC (3d) 289 (Ont CA).

3. The police used information obtained from an unconstitutional search of the perimeter of the accused's residence to obtain a warrant to search inside his home. In obtaining the warrant, the police presented other evidence that would have been sufficient to establish reasonable and probable grounds for the search in the absence of the tainted evidence. Was the evidence found inside the home "obtained in a manner" for the purpose of s 24(2)? See *R v Kokesch*, [1990] 3 SCR 3; *R v Grant*, [1993] 3 SCR 223.

4. Police conducting a "Mr. Big" sting obtained a wiretap authorization to intercept and record the accused's phone conversations. At trial, the prosecution conceded that the authorization should not have been issued and s 8 of the Charter had been violated. It did not therefore seek to admit the accused's intercepted statements. The defence argued, however, that confessions made to undercover officers during the Mr. Big sting should be excluded

under s 24(2) of the Charter because they had been obtained as part of the same transaction as the s 8 violation. See *R v Mack*, 2014 SCC 58 at paras 38-42, [2014] 3 SCR 3.

C. Bringing the Administration of Justice into Disrepute

The key question in most s 24(2) cases is whether the admission of evidence obtained in a manner that violated the Charter could "bring the administration of justice into disrepute"? The leading decision on that question appears below.

R v Grant

2009 SCC 32, [2009] 2 SCR 353

McLachlin CJ and Binnie, LeBel, Deschamps, Fish, Abella and Charron JJ

(17 July 2009)

McLACHLIN CJ and CHARRON J (LeBel, Fish, and Abella JJ concurring):

. . .

II. Facts

[4] The encounter at the centre of this appeal occurred at mid-day on November 17, 2003, in the Greenwood and Danforth area of Toronto. With four schools in the area and a history of student assaults, robberies, and drug offences occurring over the lunch hour, the three officers involved in the encounter were on patrol for the purposes of monitoring the area and maintaining a safe student environment. Two of the officers, Constables Worrell and Forde, were dressed in plainclothes and driving an unmarked car. Although on patrol, their primary task was to visit the various schools to determine if there were persons on school property who should not have been there—either non-students or students from another school. The third officer, Constable Gomes, was in uniform and driving a marked police car. On "directed patrol," he had been tasked with maintaining a visible police presence in the area in order to provide student reassurance and to deter crime during the high school lunch period.

[5] Mr. Grant, a young black man, was walking northbound on Greenwood Avenue when he came to the attention of Constables Worrell and Forde. As the two officers drove past, Cst. Worrell testified that the appellant "stared" at them in an unusually intense manner and continued to do so as they proceeded down the street, while at the same time "fidgeting" with his coat and pants in a way that aroused their suspicions. Given their purpose for being in the area and based on what he had just seen, Cst. Worrell decided that "maybe we should have a chat with this guy and see what's up with him." Cst. Worrell wanted to know whether Mr. Grant was a student at one of the schools they were assigned to monitor, and, if he was not, whether he was headed to one of the schools anyway. Noticing Cst. Gomes parked on the street ahead of Mr. Grant, and in light of his uniformed attire, the two plainclothes officers suggested to Cst. Gomes that he "have a chat" with the approaching appellant to determine if there was any need for concern.

[6] Cst. Gomes then got out of his car and initiated an exchange with Mr. Grant, while standing on the sidewalk directly in his intended path. The officer asked the appellant

"what was going on," and requested his name and address. In response, the appellant provided a provincial health card. At one point, the appellant, behaving nervously, adjusted his jacket, prompting the officer to ask him to "keep his hands in front of him." By this point, the two other officers had returned and parked on the side of the street.

[7] Cst. Worrell testified on cross-examination that he and Cst. Forde pulled up because he got a funny feeling based on Mr. Grant's way of looking over at them, looking around "all over the place," and adjusting himself. On direct examination he said that "[h]e still seemed to be, I don't know, looking a bit nervous the way he was looking around, looking at us, looking around when speaking to Officer Gomes. And at this time, I suggested to my partner, you know, I don't think it would hurt if we just go up to Officer Gomes and just stand by, just to make sure everything was okay." Thus, after a brief period observing the exchange from their car, the two officers approached the pair on the sidewalk, identified themselves to the appellant as police officers by flashing their badges, and took up positions behind Cst. Gomes, obstructing the way forward. The exchange between Cst. Gomes and Mr. Grant subsequent to the arrival of the two officers was as follows:

Q. Have you ever been arrested before?

A. I got into some trouble about three years ago.

Q. Do you have anything on you that you shouldn't?

A. No. (Pause.) Well, I got a small bag of weed.

Q. Where is it?

A. It's in my pocket.

Q. Is that it?

A. (Male puts his head down.) Yeah. Well, no.

Q. Do you have other drugs on you?

A. No, I just have the weed, that's it.

Q. Well, what is it that you have?

A. I have a firearm.

[8] At this point, the officers arrested and searched the appellant, seizing the marijuana and a loaded revolver. They then advised Mr. Grant of his right to counsel and took him to the police station.

[McLachlin CJ and Charron J concluded that the officers detained Mr. Grant when they told him to "keep his hands in front of him." Since they did not have reasonable suspicion to detain him for investigative purposes, the detention was unlawful and hence arbitrary under s 9 of the Charter. McLachlin CJ and Charron J also concluded that Mr. Grant's s 10(b) right to counsel was violated because the officers did not immediately advise him of his rights upon detention.]

[60] The test set out in s. 24(2)—what would bring the administration of justice into disrepute having regard to all the circumstances—is broad and imprecise. The question is what considerations enter into making this determination. In *Collins* [*R v Collins*, [1987]

1 SCR 265] and in *R v. Stillman*, [1997] 1 SCR 607, this Court endeavoured to answer this question. The *Collins/Stillman* framework, as interpreted and applied in subsequent decisions, has brought a measure of certainty to the s. 24(2) inquiry. Yet the analytical method it imposes and the results it sometimes produces have been criticized as inconsistent with the language and objectives of s. 24(2). In order to understand these criticisms, it is necessary to briefly review the holdings in *Collins* and *Stillman*.

[61] In *Collins*, the Court (*per* Lamer J, as he then was) proceeded by grouping the factors to be considered under s. 24(2) into three categories: (1) whether the evidence will undermine the fairness of the trial by effectively conscripting the accused against himself or herself; (2) the seriousness of the *Charter* breach; and (3) the effect of excluding the evidence on the long-term repute of the administration of justice. While Lamer J acknowledged that these categories were merely a "matter of personal preference" (p. 284), they quickly became formalized as the governing test for s. 24(2).

[62] *Collins* shed important light on the factors relevant to determining admissibility of *Charter*-violative evidence under s. 24(2). However, the concepts of trial fairness and conscription under the first branch of *Collins* introduced new problems of their own. Moreover, questions arose about what work (if any) remained to be done under the second and third categories, once conscription leading to trial unfairness had been found. Finally, issues arose as to how to measure the seriousness of the breach under the second branch and what weight, if any, should be put on the seriousness of the offence charged in deciding whether to admit evidence.

[63] The admission of physical or "real" evidence obtained from the body of the accused in breach of his or her *Charter* rights proved particularly problematic. Ten years after *Collins*, the Court revisited this question in *Stillman*. The majority held that evidence obtained in breach of the *Charter* should, at the outset of the s. 24(2) inquiry, be classified as either "conscriptive" or "non-conscriptive." Evidence would be classified as conscriptive where "an accused, in violation of his *Charter* rights, is compelled to incriminate himself at the behest of the state by means of a statement, the use of the body or the production of bodily samples": *Stillman*, at para. 80, *per* Cory J. The category of conscriptive evidence was also held to include real evidence discovered as a result of an unlawfully conscripted statement. This is known as derivative evidence.

[64] *Stillman* held that conscriptive evidence is generally inadmissible—because of its presumed impact on trial fairness—unless if it would have been independently discovered. Despite reminders that "all the circumstances" must always be considered under s. 24(2) (see *R v. Burlingham*, [1995] 2 SCR 206, *per* Sopinka J, *R v. Orbanski*, 2005 SCC 37, [2005] 2 SCR 3, *per* LeBel J), *Stillman* has generally been read as creating an all-but-automatic exclusionary rule for non-discoverable conscriptive evidence, broadening the category of conscriptive evidence and increasing its importance to the ultimate decision on admissibility.

[65] This general rule of inadmissibility of all non-discoverable conscriptive evidence, whether intended by *Stillman* or not, seems to go against the requirement of s. 24(2) that the court determining admissibility must consider "all the circumstances." The underlying assumption that the use of conscriptive evidence always, or almost always, renders the trial unfair is also open to challenge. In other contexts, this Court has recognized that a fair trial "is one which satisfies the public interest in getting at the truth, while preserving basic procedural fairness to the accused": *R v. Harrer*, [1995] 3 SCR 562, at para. 45. It is

difficult to reconcile trial fairness as a multifaceted and contextual concept with a near-automatic presumption that admission of a broad class of evidence will render a trial unfair, regardless of the circumstances in which it was obtained. In our view, trial fairness is better conceived as an overarching systemic goal than as a distinct stage of the s. 24(2) analysis.

[66] This brief review of the impact of *Collins* and *Stillman* brings us to the heart of our inquiry on this appeal: clarification of the criteria relevant to determining when, in "all the circumstances," admission of evidence obtained by a *Charter* breach "would bring the administration of justice into disrepute."

2. Overview of a Revised Approach to Section 24(2)

[67] The words of s. 24(2) capture its purpose: to maintain the good repute of the administration of justice. The term "administration of justice" is often used to indicate the processes by which those who break the law are investigated, charged and tried. More broadly, however, the term embraces maintaining the rule of law and upholding *Charter* rights in the justice system as a whole.

[68] The phrase "bring the administration of justice into disrepute" must be understood in the long-term sense of maintaining the integrity of, and public confidence in, the justice system. Exclusion of evidence resulting in an acquittal may provoke immediate criticism. But s. 24(2) does not focus on immediate reaction to the individual case. Rather, it looks to whether the overall repute of the justice system, viewed in the long term, will be adversely affected by admission of the evidence. The inquiry is objective. It asks whether a reasonable person, informed of all relevant circumstances and the values underlying the *Charter*, would conclude that the admission of the evidence would bring the administration of justice into disrepute.

[69] Section 24(2)'s focus is not only long-term, but prospective. The fact of the *Charter* breach means damage has already been done to the administration of justice. Section 24(2) starts from that proposition and seeks to ensure that evidence obtained through that breach does not do further damage to the repute of the justice system.

[70] Finally, s. 24(2)'s focus is societal. Section 24(2) is not aimed at punishing the police or providing compensation to the accused, but rather at systemic concerns. The s. 24(2) focus is on the broad impact of admission of the evidence on the long-term repute of the justice system.

[71] A review of the authorities suggests that whether the admission of evidence obtained in breach of the *Charter* would bring the administration of justice into disrepute engages three avenues of inquiry, each rooted in the public interests engaged by s. 24(2), viewed in a long-term, forward-looking and societal perspective. When faced with an application for exclusion under s. 24(2), a court must assess and balance the effect of admitting the evidence on society's confidence in the justice system having regard to: (1) the seriousness of the *Charter*-infringing state conduct (admission may send the message the justice system condones serious state misconduct), (2) the impact of the breach on the *Charter*-protected interests of the accused (admission may send the message that individual rights count for little), and (3) society's interest in the adjudication of the case on its merits. The court's role on a s. 24(2) application is to balance the assessments under each of these lines of inquiry to determine whether, considering all the circumstances, admission of the evidence would bring the administration of justice into disrepute. These

concerns, while not precisely tracking the categories of considerations set out in *Collins*, capture the factors relevant to the s. 24(2) determination as enunciated in *Collins* and subsequent jurisprudence.

(a) Seriousness of the Charter-Infringing State Conduct

[72] The first line of inquiry relevant to the s. 24(2) analysis requires a court to assess whether the admission of the evidence would bring the administration of justice into disrepute by sending a message to the public that the courts, as institutions responsible for the administration of justice, effectively condone state deviation from the rule of law by failing to dissociate themselves from the fruits of that unlawful conduct. The more severe or deliberate the state conduct that led to the *Charter* violation, the greater the need for the courts to dissociate themselves from that conduct, by excluding evidence linked to that conduct, in order to preserve public confidence in and ensure state adherence to the rule of law.

[73] This inquiry therefore necessitates an evaluation of the seriousness of the state conduct that led to the breach. The concern of this inquiry is not to punish the police or to deter *Charter* breaches, although deterrence of *Charter* breaches may be a happy consequence. The main concern is to preserve public confidence in the rule of law and its processes. In order to determine the effect of admission of the evidence on public confidence in the justice system, the court on a s. 24(2) application must consider the seriousness of the violation, viewed in terms of the gravity of the offending conduct by state authorities whom the rule of law requires to uphold the rights guaranteed by the *Charter*.

[74] State conduct resulting in *Charter* violations varies in seriousness. At one end of the spectrum, admission of evidence obtained through inadvertent or minor violations of the *Charter* may minimally undermine public confidence in the rule of law. At the other end of the spectrum, admitting evidence obtained through a wilful or reckless disregard of *Charter* rights will inevitably have a negative effect on the public confidence in the rule of law, and risk bringing the administration of justice into disrepute.

[75] Extenuating circumstances, such as the need to prevent the disappearance of evidence, may attenuate the seriousness of police conduct that results in a *Charter* breach: *R v. Silveira*, [1995] 2 SCR 297, *per* Cory J. "Good faith" on the part of the police will also reduce the need for the court to disassociate itself from the police conduct. However, ignorance of *Charter* standards must not be rewarded or encouraged and negligence or wilful blindness cannot be equated with good faith: *R v. Genest*, [1989] 1 SCR 59, at p. 87, *per* Dickson CJ; *R v. Kokesch*, [1990] 3 SCR 3, at pp. 32-33, *per* Sopinka J; *R v. Buhay*, 2003 SCC 30, [2003] 1 SCR 631, at para. 59. Wilful or flagrant disregard of the *Charter* by those very persons who are charged with upholding the right in question may require that the court dissociate itself from such conduct. It follows that deliberate police conduct in violation of established *Charter* standards tends to support exclusion of the evidence. It should also be kept in mind that for every *Charter* breach that comes before the courts, many others may go unidentified and unredressed because they did not turn up relevant evidence leading to a criminal charge. In recognition of the need for courts to distance themselves from this behaviour, therefore, evidence that the *Charter*-infringing conduct was part of a pattern of abuse tends to support exclusion.

(b) Impact on the Charter-Protected Interests of the Accused

[76] This inquiry focuses on the seriousness of the impact of the *Charter* breach on the *Charter*-protected interests of the accused. It calls for an evaluation of the extent to which the breach actually undermined the interests protected by the right infringed. The impact of a *Charter* breach may range from fleeting and technical to profoundly intrusive. The more serious the impact on the accused's protected interests, the greater the risk that admission of the evidence may signal to the public that *Charter* rights, however high-sounding, are of little actual avail to the citizen, breeding public cynicism and bringing the administration of justice into disrepute.

[77] To determine the seriousness of the infringement from this perspective, we look to the interests engaged by the infringed right and examine the degree to which the violation impacted on those interests. For example, the interests engaged in the case of a statement to the authorities obtained in breach of the *Charter* include the s. 7 right to silence, or to choose whether or not to speak to authorities (*Hebert* [*R v Hebert*, [1990] 2 SCR 151])—all stemming from the principle against self-incrimination: *R v. White*, [1999] 2 SCR 417, at para. 44. The more serious the incursion on these interests, the greater the risk that admission of the evidence would bring the administration of justice into disrepute.

[78] Similarly, an unreasonable search contrary to s. 8 of the *Charter* may impact on the protected interests of privacy, and more broadly, human dignity. An unreasonable search that intrudes on an area in which the individual reasonably enjoys a high expectation of privacy, or that demeans his or her dignity, is more serious than one that does not.

(c) Society's Interest in an Adjudication on the Merits

[79] Society generally expects that a criminal allegation will be adjudicated on its merits. Accordingly, the third line of inquiry relevant to the s. 24(2) analysis asks whether the truth-seeking function of the criminal trial process would be better served by admission of the evidence, or by its exclusion. This inquiry reflects society's "collective interest in ensuring that those who transgress the law are brought to trial and dealt with according to the law": *R v. Askov*, [1990] 2 SCR 1199, at pp. 1219-20. Thus the Court suggested in *Collins* that a judge on a s. 24(2) application should consider not only the negative impact of admission of the evidence on the repute of the administration of justice, but the impact of *failing to admit* the evidence.

[80] The concern for truth-seeking is only one of the considerations under a s. 24(2) application. The view that reliable evidence is admissible regardless of how it was obtained (see *R v. Wray*, [1971] SCR 272) is inconsistent with the *Charter*'s affirmation of rights. More specifically, it is inconsistent with the wording of s. 24(2), which mandates a broad inquiry into all the circumstances, not just the reliability of the evidence.

[81] This said, public interest in truth-finding remains a relevant consideration under the s. 24(2) analysis. The reliability of the evidence is an important factor in this line of inquiry. If a breach (such as one that effectively compels the suspect to talk) undermines the reliability of the evidence, this points in the direction of exclusion of the evidence. The admission of unreliable evidence serves neither the accused's interest in a fair trial nor the public interest in uncovering the truth. Conversely, exclusion of relevant and reliable evidence may undermine the truth-seeking function of the justice system and render

the trial unfair from the public perspective, thus bringing the administration of justice into disrepute.

[82] The fact that the evidence obtained in breach of the *Charter* may facilitate the discovery of the truth and the adjudication of a case on its merits must therefore be weighed against factors pointing to exclusion, in order to "balance the interests of truth with the integrity of the justice system": *Mann* [R v *Mann*, 2004 SCC 52, [2004] 3 SCR 59], at para. 57, *per* Iacobucci J. The court must ask "whether the vindication of the specific *Charter* violation through the exclusion of evidence extracts too great a toll on the truth-seeking goal of the criminal trial": R v. *Kitaitchik* (2002), 166 CCC (3d) 14 (Ont. CA), at para. 47, *per* Doherty JA.

[83] The importance of the evidence to the prosecution's case is another factor that may be considered in this line of inquiry. Like Deschamps J, we view this factor as corollary to the inquiry into reliability, in the following limited sense. The admission of evidence of questionable reliability is more likely to bring the administration of justice into disrepute where it forms the entirety of the case against the accused. Conversely, the exclusion of highly reliable evidence may impact more negatively on the repute of the administration of justice where the remedy effectively guts the prosecution.

[84] It has been suggested that the judge should also, under this line of inquiry, consider the seriousness of the offence at issue. Indeed, Deschamps J views this factor as very important, arguing that the more serious the offence, the greater society's interest in its prosecution (para. 226). In our view, while the seriousness of the alleged offence may be a valid consideration, it has the potential to cut both ways. Failure to effectively prosecute a serious charge due to excluded evidence may have an immediate impact on how people view the justice system. Yet, as discussed, it is the long-term repute of the justice system that is s. 24(2)'s focus. As pointed out in *Burlingham,* the goals furthered by s. 24(2) "operate independently of the type of crime for which the individual stands accused" (para. 51). And as Lamer J observed in *Collins*, "[t]he *Charter* is designed to protect the accused from the majority, so the enforcement of the *Charter* must not be left to that majority" (p. 282). The short-term public clamour for a conviction in a particular case must not deafen the s. 24(2) judge to the longer-term repute of the administration of justice. Moreover, while the public has a heightened interest in seeing a determination on the merits where the offence charged is serious, it also has a vital interest in having a justice system that is above reproach, particularly where the penal stakes for the accused are high.

[85] To review, the three lines of inquiry identified above—the seriousness of the *Charter*-infringing state conduct, the impact of the breach on the *Charter*-protected interests of the accused, and the societal interest in an adjudication on the merits—reflect what the s. 24(2) judge must consider in assessing the effect of admission of the evidence on the repute of the administration of justice. Having made these inquiries, which encapsulate consideration of "all the circumstances" of the case, the judge must then determine whether, on balance, the admission of the evidence obtained by *Charter* breach would bring the administration of justice into disrepute.

[86] In all cases, it is the task of the trial judge to weigh the various indications. No overarching rule governs how the balance is to be struck. Mathematical precision is obviously not possible. However, the preceding analysis creates a decision tree, albeit more flexible than the *Stillman* self-incrimination test. We believe this to be required by the words of s. 24(2). We also take comfort in the fact that patterns emerge with respect to

particular types of evidence. These patterns serve as guides to judges faced with s. 24(2) applications in future cases. In this way, a measure of certainty is achieved. Where the trial judge has considered the proper factors, appellate courts should accord considerable deference to his or her ultimate determination.

3. Application to Different Kinds of Evidence

[87] We have seen that a trial judge on a s. 24(2) application for exclusion of evidence obtained in breach of the *Charter* must consider whether admission would bring the administration of justice into disrepute, having regard to the results of the three lines of inquiry identified above.

[88] We now turn to some of the types of evidence the cases have considered.

(a) Statements by the Accused

[89] Statements by the accused engage the principle against self-incrimination, "one of the cornerstones of our criminal law": *R v. Henry*, 2005 SCC 76, [2005] 3 SCR 609, at para. 2. This Court in *White*, at para. 44, *per* Iacobucci J, described the principle against self-incrimination as "an overarching principle within our criminal justice system, from which a number of specific common law and *Charter* rules emanate, such as the confessions rule, and the right to silence." The principle also informs "more specific procedural protections such as, for example, the right to counsel in s. 10(b), the right to non-compellability in s. 11(c), and the right to use immunity set out in s. 13." Residual protection for the principle against self-incrimination is derived from s. 7.

[90] This case concerns s. 24(2). However, it is important to note at the outset that the common law confessions rule, quite apart from s. 24(2), provides a significant safeguard against the improper use of a statement against its maker. Where a statement is made to a recognized person in authority, regardless of whether its maker is detained at the time, it is inadmissible unless the Crown can establish beyond a reasonable doubt that it was made voluntarily. Only if such a statement survives scrutiny under the confessions rule and is found to be voluntary, does the s. 24(2) remedy of exclusion arise. Most commonly, this will occur because of added protections under s. 10(b) of the *Charter*.

[91] There is no absolute rule of exclusion of *Charter*-infringing statements under s. 24(2), as there is for involuntary confessions at common law. However, as a matter of practice, courts have tended to exclude statements obtained in breach of the *Charter*, on the ground that admission on balance would bring the administration of justice into disrepute.

[92] The three lines of inquiry described above support the presumptive general, although not automatic, exclusion of statements obtained in breach of the *Charter*.

[93] The first inquiry focusses on whether admission of the evidence would harm the repute of justice by associating the courts with illegal police conduct. Police conduct in obtaining statements has long been strongly constrained. The preservation of public confidence in the justice system requires that the police adhere to the *Charter* in obtaining statements from a detained accused.

[94] The negative impact on the justice system of admitting evidence obtained through police misconduct varies with the seriousness of the violation. The impression that courts

condone serious police misconduct is more harmful to the repute of the justice system than the acceptance of minor or inadvertent slips.

[95] The second inquiry considers the extent to which the breach actually undermined the interests protected by the right infringed. Again, the potential to harm the repute of the justice system varies with the seriousness of the impingement on the individual's protected interests. As noted, the right violated by unlawfully obtained statements is often the right to counsel under s. 10(b). The failure to advise of the right to counsel undermines the detainee's right to make a meaningful and informed choice whether to speak, the related right to silence, and, most fundamentally, the protection against testimonial self-incrimination. These rights protect the individual's interest in liberty and autonomy. Violation of these fundamental rights tends to militate in favour of excluding the statement.

[96] This said, particular circumstances may attenuate the impact of a *Charter* breach on the protected interests of the accused from whom a statement is obtained in breach of the *Charter*. For instance, if an individual is clearly informed of his or her choice to speak to the police, but compliance with s. 10(b) was technically defective at either the informational or implementational stage, the impact on the liberty and autonomy interests of the accused in making an informed choice may be reduced. Likewise, when a statement is made spontaneously following a *Charter* breach, or in the exceptional circumstances where it can confidently be said that the statement in question would have been made notwithstanding the *Charter* breach (see *R v. Harper*, [1994] 3 SCR 343), the impact of the breach on the accused's protected interest in informed choice may be less. Absent such circumstances, the analysis under this line of inquiry supports the general exclusion of statements taken in breach of the *Charter*.

[97] The third inquiry focusses on the public interest in having the case tried fairly on its merits. This may lead to consideration of the reliability of the evidence. Just as involuntary confessions are suspect on grounds of reliability, so may, on occasion, be statements taken in contravention of the *Charter*. Detained by the police and without a lawyer, a suspect may make statements that are based more on a misconceived idea of how to get out of his or her predicament than on the truth. This danger, where present, undercuts the argument that the illegally obtained statement is necessary for a trial of the merits.

[98] In summary, the heightened concern with proper police conduct in obtaining statements from suspects and the centrality of the protected interests affected will in most cases favour exclusion of statements taken in breach of the *Charter*, while the third factor, obtaining a decision on the merits, may be attenuated by lack of reliability. This, together with the common law's historic tendency to treat statements of the accused differently from other evidence, explains why such statements tend to be excluded under s. 24(2).

(b) Bodily Evidence

[99] Bodily evidence is evidence taken from the body of the accused, such as DNA evidence and breath samples. Section 8 of the *Charter* protects against unreasonable search and seizure, and hence precludes the state from obtaining such evidence in a manner that is unreasonable.

[100] The majority in *Stillman*, applying a capacious definition of conscription, held that bodily evidence is "conscriptive" and that its admission would affect trial fairness.

This resulted in a near-automatic exclusionary rule for bodily evidence obtained contrary to the *Charter*.

[101] *Stillman* has been criticized for casting the flexible "in all the circumstances" test prescribed by s. 24(2) into a straitjacket that determines admissibility solely on the basis of the evidence's conscriptive character rather than all the circumstances; for inappropriately erasing distinctions between testimonial and real evidence; and for producing anomalous results in some situations: see, e.g., *Burlingham*, *per* L'Heureux-Dubé J; *R v. Schedel* (2003), 175 CCC (3d) 193 (BCCA), at paras. 67-72, *per* Esson JA; D.M. Paciocco, "*Stillman*, Disproportion and the Fair Trial Dichotomy under Section 24(2)" (1997), 2 *Can. Crim. LR* 163; R. Mahoney, "Problems with the Current Approach to s. 24(2) of the Charter: An Inevitable Discovery" (1999), 42 *Crim. LQ* 443; S. Penney, "Taking Deterrence Seriously: Excluding Unconstitutionally Obtained Evidence Under Section 24(2) of the *Charter*" (2004), 49 *McGill LJ* 105; D. Stuart, *Charter Justice in Canadian Criminal Law* (4th ed. 2005), at p. 581. We will briefly review each of these criticisms.

[102] The first criticism is that the *Stillman* approach transforms the flexible "all the circumstances" test mandated by s. 24(2) into a categorical conscriptive evidence test. Section 24(2) mandates a broad contextual approach rather than an automatic exclusionary rule: D.M. Paciocco, "The Judicial Repeal of s. 24(2) and the Development of the Canadian Exclusionary Rule" (1989-90), 32 *Crim. LQ* 326; A. McLellan and B.P. Elman, "The Enforcement of the Canadian Charter of Rights and Freedoms: An Analysis of Section 24" (1983), 21 *Alta. L Rev.* 205, at pp. 205-8; *Orbanski*, at para. 93. As stated in *Orbanski*, *per* LeBel J, the inquiry under s. 24(2) "amounts to finding a proper balance between competing interests and values at stake in the criminal trial, between the search for truth and the integrity of the trial ... All the *Collins* factors remain relevant throughout this delicate and nuanced inquiry" (para. 94).

[103] A flexible, multi-factored approach to the admissibility of the evidence is required, not only by the wording of s. 24(2) but by the wide variation between different kinds of bodily evidence. The seriousness of the police conduct and the impact on the accused's rights of taking the bodily evidence, may vary greatly. Plucking a hair from the suspect's head may not be intrusive, and the accused's privacy interest in the evidence may be relatively slight. On the other hand, a body cavity or strip search may be intrusive, demeaning and objectionable. A one-size-fits-all conscription test is incapable of dealing with such differences in a way that addresses the point of the s. 24(2) inquiry—to determine if the admission of the evidence will bring the administration of justice into disrepute.

[104] Recent decisions suggest a growing consensus that the admissibility of bodily samples should not depend solely on whether the evidence is conscriptive: *R v. Richfield* (2003), 178 CCC (3d) 23 (Ont. CA), *per* Weiler JA; *R v. Dolynchuk* (2004), 184 CCC (3d) 214 (Man. CA), *per* Steel JA; *R v. Banman*, 2008 MBCA 103, 236 CCC (3d) 547, *per* MacInnes JA. This Court in *R v. S.A.B.*, 2003 SCC 60, [2003] 2 SCR 678, dealing with the constitutionality of DNA warrant provisions in the *Criminal Code*, acknowledged that the *Charter* concerns raised by the gathering of non-testimonial evidence are better addressed by reference to the interests of privacy, bodily integrity and human dignity, than by a blanket rule that by analogy to compelled statements, such evidence is always inadmissible. See also: L. Stuesser, "*R v. S.A.B.*: Putting 'Self-Incrimination' in Context" (2004), 42 *Alta. L Rev.* 543.

[105] The second and related objection to a simple conscription test for the admissibility of bodily evidence under s. 24(2) is that it wrongly equates bodily evidence with statements taken from the accused. In most situations, statements and bodily samples raise very different considerations from the point of view of the administration of justice. Equating them under the umbrella of conscription risks erasing relevant distinctions and compromising the ultimate analysis of systemic disrepute. As Professor Paciocco has observed, "in equating intimate bodily substances with testimony we are not so much reacting to the compelled participation of the accused as we are to the violation of the privacy and dignity of the person that obtaining such evidence involves" ("*Stillman*, Disproportion and the Fair Trial Dichotomy under Section 24(2)," at p. 170). Nor does the taking of a bodily sample trench on the accused's autonomy in the same way as may the unlawful taking of a statement. The pre-trial right to silence under s. 7, the right against testimonial self-incrimination in s. 11(c), and the right against subsequent use of self-incriminating evidence in s. 13 have informed the treatment of statements under s. 24(2). These concepts do not apply coherently to bodily samples, which are not communicative in nature, weakening self-incrimination as the sole criterion for determining their admissibility.

[106] A third criticism of the conscription test for admissibility of bodily evidence under s. 24(2) is that from a practical perspective, the conscriptive test has sometimes produced anomalous results, leading to exclusion of evidence that should, in principle and policy, be admitted: see *Dolynchuk*; *R v. Shepherd*, 2007 SKCA 29, 218 CCC (3d) 113, *per* Smith JA dissenting, aff'd 2009 SCC 35 (released concurrently); and *R v. Padavattan* (2007), 223 CCC (3d) 221 (Ont. SCJ), *per* Ducharme J. Notably, breath sample evidence tendered on impaired driving charges has often suffered the fate of automatic exclusion even where the breach in question was minor and would not realistically bring the administration of justice into disrepute. More serious breaches in other kinds of cases—for instance, those involving seizures of illegal drugs in breach of s. 8—have resulted in admission on the grounds that the evidence in question was non-conscriptive. This apparent incongruity has justifiably raised concern.

[107] We conclude that the approach to admissibility of bodily evidence under s. 24(2) that asks simply whether the evidence was conscripted should be replaced by a flexible test based on all the circumstances, as the wording of s. 24(2) requires. As for other types of evidence, admissibility should be determined by inquiring into the effect admission may have on the repute of the justice system, having regard to the seriousness of the police conduct, the impact of the *Charter* breach on the protected interests of the accused, and the value of a trial on the merits.

[108] The first inquiry informing the s. 24(2) analysis—the seriousness of the *Charter*-infringing conduct—is fact-specific. Admission of evidence obtained by deliberate and egregious police conduct that disregards the rights of the accused may lead the public to conclude that the court implicitly condones such conduct, undermining respect for the administration of justice. On the other hand, where the breach was committed in good faith, admission of the evidence may have little adverse effect on the repute of the court process.

[109] The second inquiry assesses the danger that admitting the evidence may suggest that *Charter* rights do not count, thereby negatively impacting on the repute of the system of justice. This requires the judge to look at the seriousness of the breach on the accused's protected interests. In the context of bodily evidence obtained in violation of s. 8, this

inquiry requires the court to examine the degree to which the search and seizure intruded upon the privacy, bodily integrity and human dignity of the accused. The seriousness of the intrusion on the accused may vary greatly. At one end of the spectrum, one finds the forcible taking of blood samples or dental impressions (as in *Stillman*). At the other end of the spectrum lie relatively innocuous procedures such as fingerprinting or iris-recognition technology. The greater the intrusion on these interests, the more important it is that a court exclude the evidence in order to substantiate the *Charter* rights of the accused.

[110] The third line of inquiry—the effect of admitting the evidence on the public interest in having a case adjudicated on its merits—will usually favour admission in cases involving bodily samples. Unlike compelled statements, evidence obtained from the accused's body is generally reliable, and the risk of error inherent in depriving the trier of fact of the evidence may well tip the balance in favour of admission.

[111] While each case must be considered on its own facts, it may be ventured in general that where an intrusion on bodily integrity is deliberately inflicted and the impact on the accused's privacy, bodily integrity and dignity is high, bodily evidence will be excluded, notwithstanding its relevance and reliability. On the other hand, where the violation is less egregious and the intrusion is less severe in terms of privacy, bodily integrity and dignity, reliable evidence obtained from the accused's body may be admitted. For example, this will often be the case with breath sample evidence, whose method of collection is relatively non-intrusive.

(c) Non-Bodily Physical Evidence

[112] The three inquiries under s. 24(2) will proceed largely as explained above. Again, under the first inquiry, the seriousness of the *Charter*-infringing conduct will be a fact-specific determination. The degree to which this inquiry militates in favour of excluding the bodily evidence will depend on the extent to which the conduct can be characterized as deliberate or egregious.

[113] With respect to the second inquiry, the *Charter* breach most often associated with non-bodily physical evidence is the s. 8 protection against unreasonable search and seizure: see, e.g., *Buhay*. Privacy is the principal interest involved in such cases. The jurisprudence offers guidance in evaluating the extent to which the accused's reasonable expectation of privacy was infringed. For example, a dwelling house attracts a higher expectation of privacy than a place of business or an automobile. An illegal search of a house will therefore be seen as more serious at this stage of the analysis.

[114] Other interests, such as human dignity, may also be affected by search and seizure of such evidence. The question is how seriously the *Charter* breach impacted on these interests. For instance, an unjustified strip search or body cavity search is demeaning to the suspect's human dignity and will be viewed as extremely serious on that account: *R v. Simmons*, [1988] 2 SCR 495, at pp. 516-17, *per* Dickson CJ; *R v. Golden*, 2001 SCC 83, [2001] 3 SCR 679. The fact that the evidence thereby obtained is not itself a bodily sample cannot be seen to diminish the seriousness of the intrusion.

[115] The third inquiry, whether the admission of the evidence would serve society's interest in having a case adjudicated on its merits, like the others, engages the facts of the particular case. Reliability issues with physical evidence will not generally be related to the *Charter* breach. Therefore, this consideration tends to weigh in favour of admission.

(d) Derivative Evidence

[116] The class of evidence that presents the greatest difficulty is evidence that combines aspects of both statements and physical evidence—physical evidence discovered as a result of an unlawfully obtained statement. The cases refer to this evidence as derivative evidence. This is the type of evidence at issue in this case.

[117] We earlier saw that at common law, involuntary confessions are inadmissible. The common law's automatic exclusion of involuntary statements is based on a sense that it is unfair to conscript a person against himself or herself and, most importantly, on a concern about the unreliability of compelled statements. However, the common law drew the line of automatic inadmissibility at the statements themselves and not the physical or "real" evidence found as a result of information garnered from such statements. Because reliability was traditionally the dominant focus of the confessions rule, the public interest in getting at the truth through reliable evidence was seen to outweigh concerns related to self-incrimination: *Wray* and *R v. St. Lawrence*, [1949] OR 215 (HCJ).

[118] Section 24(2) of the *Charter* implicitly overruled the common law practice of always admitting reliable derivative evidence. Instead, the judge is required to consider whether admission of derivative evidence obtained through a *Charter* breach would bring the administration of justice into disrepute.

[119] The s. 24(2) jurisprudence on derivative physical evidence has thus far been dominated by two related concepts—conscription and discoverability. Physical evidence that would not have been discovered but for an inadmissible statement has been considered conscriptive and hence is inadmissible: *R v. Feeney*, [1997] 2 SCR 13, and *Burlingham*. The doctrine of "discoverability" has been developed in order to distinguish those cases in which the accused's conscription was necessary to the collection of the evidence, from those cases where the evidence would have been obtained in any event. In the former cases, exclusion was the rule, while in the latter, admission was more likely.

[120] The conscription-discoverability doctrine has been justifiably criticized as overly speculative and capable of producing anomalous results: D. Stuart, "Questioning the Discoverability Doctrine in Section 24(2) Rulings" (1996), 48 CR (4th) 351; Hogg [PW Hogg, *Constitutional Law of Canada*, 5th ed supp, vol 2 (Scarborough, Ont: Thomson/Carswell, 2007)], at section 41.8(d). In practice, it has proved difficult to apply because of its hypothetical nature and because of the fine-grained distinctions between the tests for determining whether evidence is "derivative" and whether it is "discoverable": see *Feeney*, at paras. 69-71.

[121] The existing rules on derivative evidence and discoverability were developed under the *Collins* trial fairness rationale. They gave effect to the insight that if evidence would have been discovered in any event, the accused's conscription did not truly *cause* the evidence to become available. The discoverability doctrine acquired even greater importance under *Stillman* where the category of conscriptive evidence was considerably enlarged. Since we have concluded that this underlying rationale should no longer hold and that "trial fairness" in the *Collins/Stillman* sense is no longer a determinative criterion for the s. 24(2) inquiry, discoverability should likewise not be determinative of admissibility.

[122] Discoverability retains a useful role, however, in assessing the actual impact of the breach on the protected interests of the accused. It allows the court to assess the strength of the causal connection between the *Charter*-infringing self-incrimination and

the resultant evidence. The more likely it is that the evidence would have been obtained even without the statement, the lesser the impact of the breach on the accused's underlying interest against self-incrimination. The converse, of course, is also true. On the other hand, in cases where it cannot be determined with any confidence whether evidence would have been discovered in absence of the statement, discoverability will have no impact on the s. 24(2) inquiry.

[123] To determine whether the admission of derivative evidence would bring the administration of justice into disrepute under s. 24(2), courts must pursue the usual three lines of inquiry outlined in these reasons, taking into account the self-incriminatory origin of the evidence in an improperly obtained statement as well as its status as real evidence.

[124] The first inquiry concerns the police conduct in obtaining the statement that led to the real evidence. Once again, the extent to which this inquiry favours exclusion will depend on the factual circumstances of the breach: the more serious the state conduct, the more the admission of the evidence derived from it tends to undermine public confidence in the rule of law. Were the police deliberately and systematically flouting the accused's *Charter* rights? Or were the officers acting in good faith, pursuant to what they thought were legitimate policing policies?

[125] The second inquiry focuses on the impact of the breach on the *Charter*-protected interests of the accused. Where a statement is unconstitutionally obtained, in many cases the *Charter* right breached is the s. 10(b) right to counsel, which protects the accused's interest in making an informed choice whether or not to speak to authorities. The relevant consideration at this stage will be the extent to which the *Charter* breach impinged upon that interest in a free and informed choice. Where that interest was significantly compromised by the breach, this factor will strongly favour exclusion. In determining the impact of the breach, the discoverability of the derivative evidence may also be important as a factor strengthening or attenuating the self-incriminatory character of the evidence. If the derivative evidence was independently discoverable, the impact of the breach on the accused is lessened and admission is more likely.

[126] The third inquiry in determining whether admission of the derivative evidence would bring the administration into disrepute relates to society's interest in having the case adjudicated on its merits. Since evidence in this category is real or physical, there is usually less concern as to the reliability of the evidence. Thus, the public interest in having a trial adjudicated on its merits will usually favour admission of the derivative evidence.

[127] The weighing process and balancing of these concerns is one for the trial judge in each case. Provided the judge has considered the correct factors, considerable deference should be accorded to his or her decision. As a general rule, however, it can be ventured that where reliable evidence is discovered as a result of a good faith infringement that did not greatly undermine the accused's protected interests, the trial judge may conclude that it should be admitted under s. 24(2). On the other hand, deliberate and egregious police conduct that severely impacted the accused's protected interests may result in exclusion, notwithstanding that the evidence may be reliable.

[128] The s. 24(2) judge must remain sensitive to the concern that a more flexible rule may encourage police to improperly obtain statements that they know will be inadmissible, in order to find derivative evidence which they believe may be admissible. The judge should refuse to admit evidence where there is reason to believe the police deliberately abused their power to obtain a statement which might lead them to such evidence. Where

derivative evidence is obtained by way of a deliberate or flagrant *Charter* breach, its admission would bring the administration of justice into further disrepute and the evidence should be excluded.

4. Application to This Case

[129] The issue is whether the gun produced by Mr. Grant after Toronto police stopped and questioned him should be excluded from the evidence at his trial. The trial judge held that had a *Charter* breach been established, he would not have excluded the evidence. While the trial judge's s. 24(2) conclusion may not command deference where an appellate court reaches a different conclusion on the breach itself (see *R v. Grant*, [1993] 3 SCR 223, at pp. 256-57, *per* Sopinka J; *R v. Harris*, 2007 ONCA 574, 225 CCC (3d) 193, at p. 212), the trial judge's underlying factual findings must be respected, absent palpable and overriding error.

[130] Here, the admissibility of Mr. Grant's incriminatory statements is not in issue, the statements having no independent evidentiary value. The only issue is the admission or exclusion of the gun. This falls to be determined in accordance with the inquiries described earlier.

[131] At the outset, it is necessary to consider whether the gun was "obtained in a manner" that violated Mr. Grant's *Charter* rights: see *R v. Strachan*, [1988] 2 SCR 980, and *R v. Goldhart*, [1996] 2 SCR 463. As explained above, we have concluded that Mr. Grant's rights under ss. 9 and 10(b) of the *Charter* were breached. The discovery of the gun was both temporally and causally connected to these infringements. It follows that the gun was obtained as a result of a *Charter* breach.

[132] Because the gun was discovered as a result of statements taken in breach of the *Charter*, it is derivative evidence. The question, as always, is whether its admission would bring the administration of justice into disrepute. To answer this question, it is necessary to consider the concerns that underlie the s. 24(2) analysis, as discussed above, in "all the circumstances" of the case, including the arbitrary detention and the breach of the right to counsel.

[133] We consider first the seriousness of the improper police conduct that led to the discovery of the gun. The police conduct here, while not in conformity with the *Charter*, was not abusive. There was no suggestion that Mr. Grant was the target of racial profiling or other discriminatory police practices. The officers went too far in detaining the accused and asking him questions. However, the point at which an encounter becomes a detention is not always clear, and is something with which courts have struggled. Though we have concluded that the police were in error in detaining the appellant when they did, the mistake is an understandable one. Having been under a mistaken view that they had not detained the appellant, the officers' failure to advise him of his right to counsel was similarly erroneous but understandable. It therefore cannot be characterized as having been in bad faith. Given that the police conduct in committing the *Charter* breach was neither deliberate nor egregious, we conclude that the effect of admitting the evidence would not greatly undermine public confidence in the rule of law. We add that the Court's decision in this case will be to render similar conduct less justifiable going forward. While police are not expected to engage in judicial reflection on conflicting precedents, they are rightly expected to know what the law is.

[134] The second inquiry under the s. 24(2) analysis focuses on whether the admission of the evidence would bring the administration of justice into disrepute from the perspective of society's interest in respect for *Charter* rights. This inquiry focuses on the impact of the breach on the accused's protected interests. Because the two infringed *Charter* rights protect different interests, it is necessary to consider them separately at this stage.

[135] The initial *Charter* violation was arbitrary detention under s. 9 of the *Charter*, curtailing Mr. Grant's liberty interest. This interaction, beginning as a casual conversation, quickly developed into a subtly coercive situation that deprived Mr. Grant of his freedom to make an informed choice as to how to respond. This is so, notwithstanding the fact that the detention did not involve any physical coercion and was not carried out in an abusive manner. We therefore conclude that the impact of this breach, while not severe, was more than minimal.

[136] The second *Charter* violation was breach of Mr. Grant's s. 10(b) right to counsel. Cst. Gomes, by his own admission, was probing for answers that would give him grounds for search or arrest. Far from being spontaneous utterances, the appellant's incriminating statements were prompted directly by Cst. Gomes' pointed questioning. The appellant, in need of legal advice, was not told he could consult counsel.

[137] As discussed, discoverability remains a factor in assessing the impact of *Charter* breaches on *Charter* rights. The investigating officers testified that they would not have searched or arrested Mr. Grant but for his self-incriminatory statements. Nor would they have had any legal grounds to do so. Accordingly, the fact that the evidence was non-discoverable aggravates the impact of the breach on Mr. Grant's interest in being able to make an informed choice to talk to the police. He was in "immediate need of legal advice" (*Brydges* [*R v Brydges*, [1990] 1 SCR 190], at p. 206) and had no opportunity to seek it.

[138] Considering all these matters, we conclude that the impact of the infringement of Mr. Grant's rights under ss. 9 and 10(b) of the *Charter* was significant.

[139] The third and final concern is the effect of admitting the gun on the public interest in having a case adjudicated on its merits. The gun is highly reliable evidence. It is essential to a determination on the merits. The Crown also argues that the seriousness of the offence weighs in favour of admitting the evidence of the gun, so that the matter may be decided on its merits, asserting that gun crime is a societal scourge, that offences of this nature raise major public safety concerns and that the gun is the main evidence in the case. On the other hand, Mr. Grant argues that the seriousness of the offence makes it all the more important that his rights be respected. In the result, we do not find this factor to be of much assistance.

[140] To sum up, the police conduct was not egregious. The impact of the *Charter* breach on the accused's protected interests was significant, although not at the most serious end of the scale. Finally, the value of the evidence is considerable. These effects must be balanced in determining whether admitting the gun would put the administration of justice into disrepute. We agree with Laskin JA that this is a close case. The balancing mandated by s. 24(2) is qualitative in nature and therefore not capable of mathematical precision. However, weighing all these concerns, in our opinion the courts below did not err in concluding that the admission of the gun into evidence would not, on balance, bring the administration of justice into disrepute. The significant impact of the breach on Mr. Grant's *Charter*-protected rights weighs strongly in favour of excluding the gun, while the public interest in the adjudication of the case on its merits weighs strongly in favour

of its admission. Unlike the situation in *R v. Harrison*, 2009 SCC 34, the police officers here were operating in circumstances of considerable legal uncertainty. In our view, this tips the balance in favour of admission, suggesting that the repute of the justice system would not suffer from allowing the gun to be admitted in evidence against the appellant.

[Binnie J wrote separate concurring reasons relating to the meaning of detention under ss 9 and 10 of the Charter. He agreed with the majority's approach to s 24(2). Deschamps J also wrote concurring reasons, disagreeing with the majority's approach to both detention and the exclusion of unconstitutionally obtained evidence.]

R v Harrison

2009 SCC 34, [2009] 2 SCR 494, 97 OR (3d) 560
McLachlin CJ and Binnie, LeBel, Deschamps, Fish, Abella, and Charron JJ
(17 July 2009)

McLACHLIN CJ (Binnie, LeBel, Fish, Abella, and Charron JJ concurring):

[1] The sole issue on this appeal is whether 35 kg of cocaine, discovered as a result of an unconstitutional detention and search, should have been admitted into evidence against the appellant at trial. The trial judge admitted the evidence and convicted the appellant of trafficking in cocaine. The Court of Appeal majority upheld the conviction, Cronk JA dissenting.

. . .

[4] On October 24, 2004, the appellant and his friend Sean Friesen were driving a Dodge Durango S.U.V. near Kirkland Lake, Ontario. They had rented the vehicle at Vancouver International Airport two days earlier and were on their way from Vancouver to Toronto. Although they had been sharing driving duties, the appellant was at the wheel on this occasion.

[5] Cst. Bertoncello of the Ontario Provincial Police was on highway patrol when he saw the Durango approaching from the opposite direction, traveling at the speed limit of 90 km per hour with a line of eight or nine other vehicles directly behind it. Cst. Bertoncello noticed that the S.U.V. had no front licence plate, which for a car registered in Ontario would constitute an offence. Only after turning around to follow the Durango and activating his roof lights to pull it over did he realize that, because it was registered in Alberta, the vehicle did not require a front licence plate. Cst. Bertoncello was informed by radio dispatch that the vehicle had been rented at the Vancouver airport. Even though he had no grounds to believe that any offence was being committed, the officer testified that he decided to pull the Durango over anyway because abandoning the detention may have affected the integrity of the police in the eyes of observers.

[6] Cst. Bertoncello's suspicions seem to have been aroused from the beginning of this encounter. He observed that the car was littered with food and drink containers and had a "lived-in look," suggesting to him that the appellant and Friesen had been traveling straight through from Vancouver. He knew that rental cars are often used to courier drugs because of the risk that the car could be confiscated by the state if apprehended. Additionally, in the officer's experience, it was rare for someone to be driving that stretch of

highway at exactly the speed limit, as the appellant had been. Questioned separately, the appellant and Friesen gave stories that seemed to be contradictory.

[7] The appellant identified himself accurately and produced the vehicle's registration, insurance, and rental agreement. He was, however, unable to find his driver's licence, explaining that he might have left it in Vancouver. Cst. Bertoncello ran computer checks on both occupants of the S.U.V. and learned that the appellant's licence was under suspension. He therefore arrested the appellant for driving while suspended.

[8] With the appellant under arrest, Cst. Bertoncello asked him and Friesen whether there were any drugs or weapons in the vehicle. They both answered in the negative. Other officers soon arrived on the scene. Cst. Bertoncello proceeded to search the S.U.V. "incident to arrest," ostensibly for the appellant's missing driver's licence, even though its whereabouts was irrelevant to the charge of driving while suspended. He began his search in the rear cargo area, which contained (among other things) two cardboard boxes which were taped shut. When asked, Friesen claimed that the boxes contained dishes and books for his mother. However, according to Cst. Bertoncello, the look and feel of the boxes belied this explanation. When asked again whether there were any drugs or weapons in the box, Friesen looked very nervous and said "yeah," then said he did not know.

[9] One of the boxes was opened and found to contain bricks of a white substance, which turned out to be cocaine. Friesen was arrested, and the appellant was held on the drug charge as well. In all, 35 kg of cocaine was discovered in the S.U.V.

[10] The appellant's conviction or acquittal hinged primarily on the admissibility of the cocaine.

. . .

[20] The *Charter* breaches in this case are clear. It is common ground that the appellant's rights under ss. 8 and 9 of the *Charter* were violated by the detention and search, as found by the trial judge. Given that the officer recognized prior to the detention that the appellant's S.U.V. did not require a front licence plate, he should not have made the initial stop. A vague concern for the "integrity" of the police, even if genuine, was clearly an inadequate reason to follow through with the detention. The subsequent search of the S.U.V. was not incidental to the appellant's arrest for driving under a suspension and was likewise in breach of the *Charter*. While an officer's "hunch" is a valuable investigative tool—indeed, here it proved highly accurate—it is no substitute for proper *Charter* standards when interfering with a suspect's liberty.

[21] Breaches of the *Charter* established, the question is whether the evidence thereby obtained should be excluded under s. 24(2) of the *Charter*. The test set out in s. 24(2) is simply stated: would the admission of the evidence bring the administration of justice into disrepute? *Grant* [*R v Grant*, 2009 SCC 32, [2009] 2 SCR 353] identifies three lines of inquiry relevant to this determination. Once again, they are: (1) the seriousness of the *Charter*-infringing state conduct, (2) the impact of the breach on the *Charter*-protected interests of the accused, and (3) society's interest in the adjudication of the case on its merits. I will discuss each of these in turn.

(a) Seriousness of the Charter-Infringing State Conduct

[22] At this stage the court considers the nature of the police conduct that infringed the *Charter* and led to the discovery of the evidence. Did it involve misconduct from

which the court should be concerned to dissociate itself? This will be the case where the departure from *Charter* standards was major in degree, or where the police knew (or should have known) that their conduct was not *Charter*-compliant. On the other hand, where the breach was of a merely technical nature or the result of an understandable mistake, dissociation is much less of a concern.

[23] The trial judge found that the police officer's conduct in this case was "brazen," "flagrant" and "very serious." The metaphor of a spectrum used in *R v. Kitaitchik* (2002), 166 CCC (3d) 14 (Ont. CA), *per* Doherty JA, may assist in characterizing police conduct for purposes of this s. 24(2) factor:

> Police conduct can run the gamut from blameless conduct, through negligent conduct, to conduct demonstrating a blatant disregard for *Charter* rights ... . What is important is the proper placement of the police conduct along that fault line, not the legal label attached to the conduct. [Citation omitted; para. 41.]

[24] Here, it is clear that the trial judge considered the *Charter* breaches to be at the serious end of the spectrum. On the facts found by him, this conclusion was a reasonable one. The officer's determination to turn up incriminating evidence blinded him to constitutional requirements of reasonable grounds. While the violations may not have been "deliberate," in the sense of setting out to breach the *Charter*, they were reckless and showed an insufficient regard for *Charter* rights. Exacerbating the situation, the departure from *Charter* standards was major in degree, since reasonable grounds for the initial stop were entirely non-existent.

[25] As pointed out by the majority of the Court of Appeal, there was no evidence of systemic or institutional abuse. However, while evidence of a systemic problem can properly aggravate the seriousness of the breach and weigh in favour of exclusion, the absence of such a problem is hardly a mitigating factor.

[26] I note that the trial judge found the officer's in-court testimony to be misleading. While not part of the *Charter* breach itself, this is properly a factor to consider as part of the first inquiry under the s. 24(2) analysis given the need for a court to dissociate itself from such behaviour. As Cronk JA observed, "the integrity of the judicial system and the truth-seeking function of the courts lie at the heart of the admissibility inquiry envisaged under s. 24(2) of the *Charter*. Few actions more directly undermine both of these goals than misleading testimony in court from persons in authority" (para. 160).

[27] In sum, the conduct of the police that led to the *Charter* breaches in this case represented a blatant disregard for *Charter* rights. This disregard for *Charter* rights was aggravated by the officer's misleading testimony at trial. The police conduct was serious, and not lightly to be condoned.

(b) Impact on the Charter-Protected Interests of the Accused

[28] This factor looks at the seriousness of the infringement from the perspective of the accused. Did the breach seriously compromise the interests underlying the right(s) infringed? Or was the breach merely transient or trivial in its impact? These are among the questions that fall for consideration in this inquiry.

[29] In this case, the detention and the search had an impact on the appellant's liberty and privacy interests. The question is how that impact should be characterized.

[30] The majority of the Court of Appeal emphasized the relatively brief duration of the detention and the appellant's low expectation of privacy in the S.U.V., and concluded that the effect of the breach on the appellant was relatively minor. It is true that motorists have a lower expectation of privacy in their vehicles than they do in their homes. As participants in a highly regulated activity, they know that they may be stopped for reasons pertaining to highway safety—as in a drinking-and-driving roadblock, for instance. Had it not turned up incriminating evidence, the detention would have been brief. In these respects, the intrusion on liberty and privacy represented by the detention is less severe than it would be in the case of a pedestrian. Further, nothing in the encounter was demeaning to the dignity of the appellant.

[31] This said, being stopped and subjected to a search by the police without justification impacts on the motorist's rightful expectation of liberty and privacy in a way that is much more than trivial. As Iacobucci J observed in *Mann* [*R v Mann*, 2004 SCC 52, [2004] 3 SCR 59], the relatively non-intrusive nature of the detention and search "must be weighed against the absence of *any* reasonable basis for justification" (para. 56 (emphasis in original)). A person in the appellant's position has every expectation of being left alone—subject, as already noted, to valid highway traffic stops.

[32] I conclude that the deprivation of liberty and privacy represented by the unconstitutional detention and search was therefore a significant, although not egregious, intrusion on the appellant's *Charter*-protected interests.

(c) Society's Interest in an Adjudication on the Merits

[33] At this stage, the court considers factors such as the reliability of the evidence and its importance to the Crown's case.

[34] The evidence of the drugs obtained as a consequence of the *Charter* breaches was highly reliable. It was critical evidence, virtually conclusive of guilt on the offence charged. The evidence cannot be said to operate unfairly having regard to the truth-seeking function of the trial. While the charged offence is serious, this factor must not take on disproportionate significance. As noted in *Grant*, while the public has a heightened interest in seeing a determination on the merits where the offence charged is serious, the public also has a vital interest in a justice system that is beyond reproach, particularly where the penal stakes for the accused are high. With that caveat in mind, the third line of inquiry under the s. 24(2) analysis favours the admission of the evidence as to do so would promote the public's interest in having the case adjudicated on its merits.

(d) Balancing the Factors

[35] I begin by summarizing my findings on the three factors in *Grant*. The police conduct in stopping and searching the appellant's vehicle without any semblance of reasonable grounds was reprehensible, and was aggravated by the officer's misleading testimony in court. The *Charter* infringements had a significant, although not egregious, impact on the *Charter*-protected interests of the appellant. These factors favour exclusion, the former more strongly than the latter. On the other hand, the drugs seized constitute highly reliable evidence tendered on a very serious charge, albeit not one of the most serious known to our criminal law. This factor weighs in favour of admission.

[36] The balancing exercise mandated by s. 24(2) is a qualitative one, not capable of mathematical precision. It is not simply a question of whether the majority of the relevant factors favour exclusion in a particular case. The evidence on each line of inquiry must be weighed in the balance, to determine whether, having regard to all the circumstances, admission of the evidence would bring the administration of justice into disrepute. Dissociation of the justice system from police misconduct does not always trump the truth-seeking interests of the criminal justice system. Nor is the converse true. In all cases, it is the long-term repute of the administration of justice that must be assessed.

[37] In my view, when examined through the lens of the s. 24(2) analysis set out in *Grant*, the trial judge's reasoning in this case placed undue emphasis on the third line of inquiry while neglecting the importance of the other inquiries, particularly the need to dissociate the justice system from flagrant breaches of *Charter* rights. Effectively, he transformed the s. 24(2) analysis into a simple contest between the degree of the police misconduct and the seriousness of the offence.

[38] The trial judge placed great reliance on the Ontario Court of Appeal's decision in *Puskas* [*R v Puskas* (1997), 120 CCC (3d) 548 (Ont CA)]. However, the impact of the breach on the accused's interests and the seriousness of the police conduct were not at issue in *Puskas*; Moldaver JA opined that *if* there was a breach of s. 8, it was "considerably less serious than the trial judge perceived it to be," the police having fallen "minimally" short of the constitutional mark (para. 16). In those circumstances, the public interest in truth-seeking rightly became determinative.

[39] This case is very different. The police misconduct was serious; indeed, the trial judge found that it represented a "brazen and flagrant" disregard of the *Charter*. To appear to condone wilful and flagrant *Charter* breaches that constituted a significant incursion on the appellant's rights does not enhance the long-term repute of the administration of justice; on the contrary, it undermines it. In this case, the seriousness of the offence and the reliability of the evidence, while important, do not outweigh the factors pointing to exclusion.

[40] As Cronk JA put it, allowing the seriousness of the offence and the reliability of the evidence to overwhelm the s. 24(2) analysis "would deprive those charged with serious crimes of the protection of the individual freedoms afforded to all Canadians under the *Charter* and, in effect, declare that in the administration of the criminal law 'the ends justify the means'" (para. 150). *Charter* protections must be construed so as to apply to everyone, even those alleged to have committed the most serious criminal offences. In relying on *Puskas* in these circumstances, the trial judge seemed to imply that where the evidence is reliable and the charge is serious, admission will always be the result. As *Grant* makes clear, this is not the law.

[41] Additionally, the trial judge's observation that the *Charter* breaches "pale in comparison to the criminality involved" in drug trafficking risked the appearance of turning the s. 24(2) inquiry into a contest between the misdeeds of the police and those of the accused. The fact that a *Charter* breach is less heinous than the offence charged does not advance the inquiry mandated by s. 24(2). We expect police to adhere to higher standards than alleged criminals.

[42] In summary, the price paid by society for an acquittal in these circumstances is outweighed by the importance of maintaining *Charter* standards. That being the case, the

admission of the cocaine into evidence would bring the administration of justice into disrepute. It should have been excluded.

4. *Conclusion*

[43] I would allow the appeal. Because the evidence in question was essential to the Crown's case, rather than order a new trial I would enter an acquittal.

[Deschamps J dissented, concluding that the impact of the breach on the accused's Charter rights was minimal; the officer did not act with malice or bad faith; and the evidence was reliable and important to the adjudication of a very serious offence.]

NOTES AND QUESTIONS

1. After *Grant*, what if anything remains of the *Collins/Stillman* approach to evidence affecting the "fairness of the trial"? In *Grant*, the majority stated that there is a "presumptive general, although not automatic, exclusion of statements obtained in breach of the *Charter*." This presumption is justified, it reasoned, by the centrality of the "principle against self-incrimination." Why should this interest (which is most likely to be affected by violations of s 10(b) of the Charter) be privileged over others, such as the liberty and privacy interests protected by ss 8 and 9? Notably, in the cases decided since *Grant* to date, physical evidence has been excluded almost as frequently (69 percent) as statements (74 percent). See Mike Madden, "Empirical Data on Section 24(2) Under R v Grant" (2010) 78 CR (6th) 278.

2. Should "good faith" be interpreted to include the actions of *all* state authorities whose conduct contributes to a constitutional violation? Suppose that a senior Crown prosecutor incorrectly and unreasonably advised the police that a particular investigative method is constitutional. Assuming that the police's reliance on this advice was reasonable, is this an example of "good faith" that would lessen the seriousness of the violation? What if police reasonably rely on a search warrant issued by a judge who has made an unreasonable error in granting it?

3. In *Grant*, the court confirmed that Charter violations are less serious when committed in situations of urgency or necessity, as when police act to prevent the loss or destruction of evidence. How is this rule likely to affect police behaviour, keeping in mind that exceptions for exigent circumstances are already built into many constitutional procedural rules, such as those relating to warrantless searches and warrantless residential arrests?

4. In *Grant*, the court concluded (in contrast to its previous jurisprudence) that the seriousness of the offence "has the potential to cut both ways," noting that society has a "vital interest in having a justice system that is above reproach, particularly where the penal stakes for the accused are high." Absent concerns about the reliability of the evidence, why should the seriousness of the offence heighten the importance of compliance with the Charter? As Deschamps J pointed out in dissent (at para 218), this approach appears to "place value in the benefit derived by the accused from the exclusion of reliable evidence." That said, what would be the likely effect on Charter compliance of a rule dictating that evidence of serious crimes should generally be admitted? See also *R v Spencer*, 2014 SCC 43 at paras 79-80, [2014] 2 SCR 212.

5. In *Grant*, the court held that evidence derived from unconstitutionally obtained statements is more likely to be admitted if it can be shown that it would have been discovered notwithstanding the Charter violation. The court did not say whether this principle applied to other kinds of evidence. In *R v Côté*, 2011 SCC 46, [2011] 3 SCR 215, it found that it did. There, the court found that the impact of a violation on an accused's Charter-protected interests is mitigated if the prosecution shows that evidence (including physical evidence) would have been discovered without the violation. Cromwell J explained as follows:

[71] I turn to the first branch of the *Grant* test which is concerned with the seriousness of the *Charter*-infringing state conduct. If the police officers could have conducted the search legally but failed to turn their minds to obtaining a warrant or proceeded under the view that they could not have demonstrated to a judicial officer that they had reasonable and probable grounds, the seriousness of the state conduct is heightened. As in *Buhay* [*R v Buhay*, 2003 SCC 30, [2003] 1 SCR 631], a casual attitude towards, or a deliberate flouting of, *Charter* rights will generally aggravate the seriousness of the *Charter*-infringing state conduct. On the other hand, the facts that the police exhibited good faith and/or had a legitimate reason for not seeking prior judicial authorization of the search will likely lessen the seriousness of the *Charter*-infringing state conduct.

[72] We come now to the effect of discoverability on the second branch of the *Grant* test—the impact on the *Charter*-protected interests of the accused. Section 8 of the *Charter* protects an individual's reasonable expectation of privacy. That reasonable expectation of privacy must take account of the fact that searches may occur when a judicial officer is satisfied that there are reasonable and probable grounds and authorizes the search before it is carried out. If the search could not have occurred legally, it is considerably more intrusive of the individual's reasonable expectation of privacy. On the other hand, the fact that the police could have demonstrated to a judicial officer that they had reasonable and probable grounds to believe that an offence had been committed and that there was evidence to be found at the place of the search will tend to lessen the impact of the illegal search on the accused's privacy and dignity interests protected by the *Charter*.

[73] This is not to say, however, that in such circumstances there is no infringement of an accused's privacy interests. A reasonable expectation of privacy protected under s. 8 of the *Charter* includes not only that proper grounds exist but also the requirement of prior judicial authorization. Thus the absence of a warrant when one was legally required constitutes an infringement of an accused's privacy. The intrusiveness of such an unauthorized search will be assessed according to the level of privacy that could have reasonably been expected in the given set of circumstances. The greater the expectation of privacy, the more intrusive the unauthorized search will have been. The seriousness of the impact on the accused's *Charter*-protected interests will not always mirror the seriousness of the breach, i.e. the *Charter*-infringing state conduct. For instance, where the police acted in good faith in obtaining a warrant that was found on review not to disclose reasonable and probable grounds to believe that a crime had been committed and that there was evidence to be found at the place of the search, the seriousness of the *Charter*-infringing state conduct is reduced but the impact of the search on the accused's *Charter*-protected interests is greater because the search could not have occurred legally.

[74] The lawful discoverability of evidence may thus be a relevant consideration when a court must determine whether to exclude evidence pursuant to s. 24(2) of the *Charter*. When relevant, courts should assess the effect of the discoverability of the evidence under the first and second *Grant* lines of inquiry in light of all of the circumstances.

See also *R v Nolet*, 2010 SCC 24, [2010] 1 SCR 851.

6. Should evidence be excluded under s 24(2) if police are found to have violated the Charter when the state of the law at the time of violation was uncertain? For example, if technological change makes it unclear whether there is reasonable expectation of privacy in a certain realm, should police be required to err on the side of caution to avoid Charter violations? Or should they be entitled to intrude until the courts firmly establish an expectation of privacy in a particular domain? See e.g. *R v Cole*, 2012 SCC 53 at paras 83-90, [2012] 3 SCR 34; *R v Spencer*, 2014 SCC 43 at para 77, [2014] 2 SCR 212; *R v Fearon*, 2014 SCC 77 at paras 91-95, [2014] 3 SCR 621.

D. Shifting Use of Unconstitutionally Obtained Evidence

Suppose that, at the outset of the trial, the accused successfully applies for exclusion of evidence under s 24(2). Is it possible for the "circumstances" to change as the trial proceeds so that admission would no longer "bring the administration of justice into disrepute?" In particular, may evidence excluded from the Crown's case in chief be used to impeach the accused's credibility?

R v Calder
[1996] 1 SCR 660, 27 OR (3d) 258, 105 CCC (3d) 1
La Forest, Sopinka, Gonthier, Cory, McLachlin, Iacobucci, and Major JJ
(21 March 1996)

LA FOREST J:

[1] I am in general agreement with Justice Sopinka except that I find it difficult to imagine any special circumstances to which he refers in para. 35 that would warrant departure from the approach he sets forth.

SOPINKA J (Gonthier, Cory, Iacobucci, and Major JJ concurring):

[2] This appeal involves the question whether the proposed purpose for the use of evidence has any bearing on its admissibility pursuant to s. 24(2) of the *Canadian Charter of Rights and Freedoms*. In this case, a statement was obtained from the respondent in violation of his right to counsel, and was excluded from the Crown's case in chief. The Crown later sought to have the statement admitted for the purpose of impeaching the testimony of the respondent at trial.

I. The Facts

[3] Murray Calder, a police officer, was charged with attempting to purchase the sexual services of a person under 18 years of age, extortion, and breach of trust. All of the charges arose out of a single incident involving Calder and Shelley Desrochers, a 17-year-old prostitute.

[4] Prior to being charged, Calder was interviewed by two investigating officers. He was cautioned as follows:

[W]e are investigating alleged sexual misconduct which could result in criminal charges or charges under the *Police Act*. You do not have to say anything unless you wish to do so, but whatever you do say may be given in evidence at the criminal trial or a trial under charges under the *Police Act*. Do you understand?

Calder answered that he did understand. He was then told that the complaint came from Shelley Desrochers, and he asked: "What's with the caution?" No answer was given, and Calder asked again: "Why the caution?" At this point, the investigating officer read the section of the *Criminal Code* dealing with procuring the sexual services of a person under 18. There was no further explanation given for the caution. The trial judge held that s. 10(b) of the *Charter* had been breached by the investigating officers.

[5] During the course of the interview, Calder denied having gone to the corner of Queen and Bathurst the previous night at the time allegedly appointed for a meeting with Desrochers. This statement was untrue, as was demonstrated by the evidence of an independent witness as well as that of the complainant, and of the respondent at trial. The Crown wished to use Calder's statement as substantive evidence of consciousness of guilt. The trial judge excluded the statement pursuant to s. 24(2) of the *Charter*.

[6] Calder's testimony in chief contradicted his earlier statement to the police respecting his whereabouts on the night in question. The trial judge refused to permit the Crown to use the previously excluded statement to impeach credibility during cross-examination. The Crown used other evidence to attempt to impeach credibility: Calder's notes, the police car computer records and police records from the night in question.

[7] A jury acquitted Calder of all charges. The Crown appealed to the Ontario Court of Appeal, submitting that the trial judge erred in excluding the evidence from the case for the Crown, and alternatively, that if the statement was properly excluded initially, the Crown should have been permitted to use the statement for impeachment purposes during cross-examination of the respondent. The Crown's appeal was dismissed, Doherty JA dissenting: (1994), 19 OR (3d) 643, 92 CCC (3d) 97. The appeal is before this Court as an appeal as of right.

· · ·

IV. Analysis

[19] The submission of the Crown which accords with the dissenting reasons of Doherty JA is that tender of the respondent's out-of-court statement for the purpose of cross-examination constituted a change of circumstances justifying a reconsideration of the trial judge's earlier ruling that admission of the evidence would bring the administration of justice into disrepute. The Crown submits that in light of the changed circumstances the trial judge should have held a further *voir dire* to reconsider the application of s. 24(2) of the *Charter* having regard to the change in the proposed use of the evidence. The Crown does not appeal from the decision of the trial judge which excluded the evidence when it was tendered during the Crown's case. In his dissent, Doherty JA agreed that the trial judge had been correct in respect of this ruling which was properly based on the factors in *Collins* … [*R v Collins*, [1987] 1 SCR 265], and concluded that the admission of the evidence would bring the administration of justice into disrepute. No leave having been granted on this point, no issue can be taken with that ruling here.

[20] Much reliance was placed on the decision of this Court in *Kuldip* [*R v Kuldip*, [1990] 3 SCR 618]. That decision, however, is not of immediate assistance to the Crown. *Kuldip* decided that the accused could be cross-examined on a statement made by him at a previous trial notwithstanding s. 13 of the *Charter* and s. 5(2) of the *Canada Evidence Act*. At bottom, the ratio of that decision is that the provisions referred to are to be interpreted as prohibiting use of prior inconsistent statements for the purposes of incrimination but not for the purpose of challenging credibility. *Kuldip* did not involve any previous determination that the statement was inadmissible. All that stood in the way of the Crown's use of the statement was the wording of ss. 13 and 5(2), which prohibited use of the statements for the purpose of incrimination. When that prohibition was interpreted to permit cross-examination on the statement for the purpose of challenging credibility, the Crown was free to use the statement accordingly. Here, we have a determination by the trial judge that admission of the evidence would bring the administration of justice into disrepute. The evidence was therefore rejected. The Crown properly conceded that use of the evidence for the limited purpose of cross-examination as to credibility was an "admission" of the evidence. The Crown must therefore establish a change of circumstances by reason of the proposed limited use of the evidence such that the decision to exclude the evidence should be varied. In this regard, the distinction made in *Kuldip* between the use of evidence for the purpose of incrimination and for the purpose of cross-examination as to credibility will have some relevance.

[21] In *R v. Adams*, [1995] 4 SCR 707, a recent decision of this Court, we set out the circumstances under which an order made at trial can be varied or revoked. At p. 722, in unanimous reasons for the Court, we stated:

> As a general rule, any order relating to the conduct of a trial can be varied or revoked if the circumstances that were present at the time the order was made have materially changed. In order to be material, the change must relate to a matter that justified the making of the order in the first place.

Earlier, at p. 722, we stated:

> For instance, if the order is a discretionary order pursuant to a common law rule, the precondition to its variation or revocation will be less formal. On the other hand, an order made under the authority of statute will attract more stringent conditions before it can be varied or revoked.

[22] The order here was made under the authority of a constitutional provision. The condition for its reconsideration must be at least as stringent as those that obtain with respect to an order made under the authority of a statute.

[23] The circumstances relied on by the Crown to justify a change of circumstances in this case were: (a) the fact that the accused testified at variance with his previous statement; and (b) the proposed limited use of the evidence. With respect to (a) I have difficulty accepting that when the Crown is in possession of a previous statement it does not foresee that the accused may testify in a manner that contradicts the statement. The Crown sought the introduction of the statement because it was in a position to prove from its own witnesses that it was false. In light of this, it would not have escaped the Crown that the accused would likely testify and that his testimony could contradict the statement. With respect to (b), tender of an admission as evidence generally constitutes tender of it for all

purposes unless it is tendered for a limited purpose. In this case, there was no indication that the admission was to be used only as part of the Crown's case in chief and not for the purpose of cross-examination. Indeed, if the statement had been admitted, can there be any doubt that it would have been used for both purposes? Accordingly, the proposed use was one of the two uses for which the evidence had been tendered and excluded. It was submitted, however, that the Crown's proposal that the evidence be admitted solely for the purpose of cross-examination was a change of circumstances which warranted reopening the issue. Whereas the tender of the evidence during the Crown's case was with a view to its admission generally, the more limited proposed use of the evidence was a circumstance that was not present when the evidence was originally excluded. The Crown argues, and the argument found favour with Doherty JA, that the change in the proposed use could have a significant effect on the balancing of the relevant factors in the application of s. 24(2) of the *Charter*.

[24] The distinction between admitting evidence generally for all purposes, including incrimination and credibility, on the one hand, and admitting evidence solely for the purposes of impeaching credibility on the other, is one that is well entrenched in the law of evidence. It has existed for years. The distinction is frequently made in connection with the use of prior inconsistent statements. See *Deacon v. The King*, [1947] SCR 531, and *McInroy v. The Queen*, [1979] 1 SCR 588. Most recently the distinction was made in *Kuldip* and *R v. Crawford*, [1995] 1 SCR 858. This distinction has, however, been eroded in certain limited circumstances by recent decisions of this Court. See *B.(K.G.)* [*R v B (KG)*, [1993] 1 SCR 740], and *R v. U.(F.J.)*, [1995] 3 SCR 764.

[25] The distinction draws a fine line. When a statement is admitted, generally it is available as positive evidence of innocence or guilt. The statement is evidence of the truth of its contents which may be incriminating. Moreover, the mere fact that a false exculpatory statement was made may be evidence of consciousness of guilt. On the other hand, a statement whose use is limited to a challenge of credibility can serve only to impeach the testimony of the witness. The most that can be achieved is the nullification of the witness's evidence. No matter how complete the impeachment, it does not constitute proof upon which the Crown can rely to establish its case beyond a reasonable doubt, although it may result in non-acceptance of a defence set up by the accused.

[26] Is the distinction between use of a statement for all purposes rather than for the limited purpose of impeaching credibility a valid one in the application of s. 24(2)? The respondent draws an analogy with the practice relating to confessions. An involuntary confession could not be used for any purpose. As stated by Fauteux J in *Monette v. The Queen*, [1956] SCR 400, at p. 402:

> As stated by Humphreys J delivering the judgment of the Court of Appeal in England, in *Rex v. Treacy* (1934), 60 TLR 544 at 545, a statement made by a prisoner under arrest is either admissible or not; if it is admissible, the proper course for the prosecution is to prove it, and, if it is not admissible, nothing more ought to be heard of it; and it is wrong to think that a document can be made admissible in evidence which is otherwise inadmissible simply because it is put to a person in cross-examination.

The authority of this case has not been questioned. Moreover, it is acknowledged by the appellant that involuntary statements may not be used by the Crown for any purpose. However, the appellant seeks to distinguish the factual context of this case from that situation by stating that the reason for the exclusion of involuntary statements is their inherent unreliability. Doherty JA, in the Ontario Court of Appeal, distinguished the voluntariness inquiry from that under s. 24(2), stating (at p. 659):

> Voluntariness is determined by reference to the circumstances surrounding the taking of the statement. Those circumstances are static and determinable at the outset of the trial. Nothing done in the context of the trial can alter those circumstances or otherwise affect the voluntariness of the statement. Similarly, the voluntariness of the statement cannot be affected by the purpose for which the Crown proposes to use that statement.

[27] In light of the recent jurisprudence of this Court, it is evident that while the rule against admission of involuntary statements was initially based primarily on reliability concerns, the law has evolved considerably since that time. In *R v. Whittle*, [1994] 2 SCR 914, this Court held, at p. 932, that:

> Although the confession rule in its traditional formulation had as its *raison d'être* the reliability of the confession, a strong undercurrent developed which also supported the rule in part on fairness in the criminal process.

[28] It is, therefore, not strictly accurate to distinguish the practices relating to confessions on the basis either that reliability was the sole touchstone of their admissibility or that the circumstances relating to admissibility remained static irrespective of the proposed use. The distinction to which I have referred between use for general purposes and use limited to impeachment is one that was recognized by this Court before *Monette* was decided. See *Deacon, supra*. If it is correct to suggest, as does the appellant, that use for the limited purpose of cross-examination has an effect on fairness that favours admissibility, presumably the same consideration would apply to some extent to confessions.

[29] The analogy to the confession rule, although of assistance, is not precise. The focus of s. 24(2) is somewhat different, the whole of the emphasis being on the effect on the repute of the administration of justice. The impact of admission of the evidence on the fairness of the trial plays a more significant role than in the case of the confession rule. I would not be prepared to rest my decision on this issue by reference to the practice relating to confessions.

· · ·

[34] The effect on the repute of the administration of justice is to be assessed by reference to the standard of the reasonable, well-informed citizen who represents community values. The effect of destroying the credibility of an accused who takes the stand in his or her defence using evidence obtained from the mouth of the accused in breach of his or her *Charter* rights will usually have the same effect as use of the same evidence when adduced by the Crown in its case in chief for the purpose of incrimination. The fact that a jury carefully instructed can apply the distinction does not mean that use for the purpose of impeachment will, in the eyes of the jury, have a less detrimental effect on the case of the accused. Moreover, in determining admissibility under s. 24(2), it is not the carefully instructed juror who is the arbiter of the effect on the administration of justice but rather the well-informed member of the community. This mythical person does not have the benefit of a careful instruction from the trial judge on the distinction. Not only will that person not tend to understand the distinction in theory, but, in any event, will regard the distinction as immaterial in assessing the effect on the repute of the administration of

justice. If use of the statement is seen to be unfair by reason of having been obtained in breach of an accused's *Charter* rights, it is not likely to be seen to be less unfair because it was only used to destroy credibility.

[35] In view of the foregoing, I conclude that it will only be in very limited circumstances that a change in use as proposed in this case will qualify as a material change of circumstances that would warrant reopening the issue once evidence has been excluded under s. 24(2). I would not, however, entirely rule out the possibility in some very special circumstances. To the extent that the Crown considers in a given case that restricting use of a statement to cross-examination will lighten its task in getting the statement admitted for this purpose under s. 24(2), it can seek a ruling to this effect either during its case or before cross-examining the accused. In either case, a *voir dire* will be necessary in which the trial judge will consider the admissibility of the statement for the limited purpose for which the Crown intends to use the statement. See *R v. Krause*, [1986] 2 SCR 466; *R v. Drake* (1970), 1 CCC (2d) 396 (Sask. QB); *R v. Levy* (1966), 50 Cr. App. R 198 (CCA).

Application to This Case

[36] As previously observed, the admission of the impugned statement was rejected by the trial judge when it was tendered during the Crown's case in chief. The trial judge found that its admission would bring the administration of justice into disrepute. This finding was confirmed by the Court of Appeal and is not challenged by the appellant. In rejecting the Crown's application to cross-examine on the statement, the trial judge found that this would be "grossly unfair."

[37] The evidence at trial developed into a contest of credibility between the complainant and the respondent. In acquitting the respondent, the jury no doubt considered that the evidence of the respondent was sufficiently credible at least to raise a reasonable doubt. In view of the potential effect on the credibility of the respondent and the findings of the trial judge, I conclude that the proposed use of the statement for impeachment of credibility was not a material change of circumstances which warranted a reconsideration of the finding that the admission of the statement would bring the administration of justice into disrepute.

[38] Accordingly, the appeal is dismissed.

McLACHLIN J (dissenting):

. . .

[45] The concern for getting at the truth may weigh against admitting a statement tendered as substantive evidence where there is fear that the *Charter* violation may have rendered it unreliable. The same concern for getting at the truth may weigh in favour of using the same statement in cross-examination to test the accused's credibility and uncover any inaccuracies or fabrications in his evidence in chief. From the perspective of the individual case, it is important to permit the jury to fairly judge the truthfulness of the witness. From the perspective of the trial process as a whole, it is equally important not to permit witnesses to take the stand and fabricate lies free from the fear that they may be cross-examined on earlier contradictory statements.

[46] The same applies to the interest of protecting the accused's right to a fair trial. It may be seen as unfair to tender against an accused as substantive evidence a statement

which the state obtained from him in violation of his *Charter* rights. However, where the accused chooses to take the stand and place his credibility in issue, vouching to the jury that what he is telling them is the whole truth and nothing but the truth, it is more difficult to say that it is unfair to permit the Crown to cross-examine him on his prior inconsistent statement and to put to him the vital question of which version is true. These are important considerations which must be weighed against any unfairness arising from the way the statement was taken, if the judge is to properly determine whether admission of the statement would bring the administration of justice into disrepute.

[47] The trial judge in the case at bar appears to have based his decision against permitting the statement to be used in cross-examination largely on the fact that he had earlier ruled the evidence to be inadmissible, although he alluded to fairness to the accused and the fact that to prevent the Crown from cross-examining Calder on his previous statement might result in evidence "that was not a true statement." While it is difficult to be sure of what the trial judge's precise reasoning was, I think it is fair to say, as did Doherty JA below, that "[t]he trial judge erred in law in holding that he could not reassess the admissibility of Calder's statement when it was offered for impeachment purposes during Calder's cross-examination" (p. 667). I also agree with Doherty JA that the record does not permit one to say with certainty that the statement should not have been admitted for cross-examination purposes and that had the statement been admitted, it could have changed the course of the trial. In these circumstances, Doherty JA correctly concluded that the Crown had met the heavy onus of demonstrating with a reasonable degree of certainty that the verdict would not necessarily have been the same had the error in law not been made.

QUESTIONS

1. In a situation where a statement obtained through a Charter violation is unreliable, how would it contribute to truth-finding to use the statement to cross-examine the accused?

2. In *R v Cook*, [1998] 2 SCR 597, 128 CCC (3d) 1, the Supreme Court revisited the issue raised in *Calder*. The majority reiterated the view from *Calder* that the circumstances allowing for reassessment of the *Collins* factors as the trial progressed would be "very rare indeed" and did not include impeachment of the accused's credibility. At para 76, Cory and Iacobucci JJ said: "we find there should be no difference, for the purposes of deciding whether to exclude the evidence under s. 24(2), between the admission of the evidence generally and admission for the limited purpose of challenging the credibility of the accused." In light of *Calder* and *Cook*, can you envision any circumstances in which evidence initially excluded under s 24(2) could be subsequently used for any purpose?

E. Excluding Evidence Where Admission Would Violate the Charter

Evidence may be excluded outside of s 24(2) when it is alleged that the state's *use* of it in legal proceedings (as opposed to the state's *acquisition* of it) would violate the Charter. This may occur in a variety of circumstances. For example, in *R v White*, [1999] 2 SCR 417 at paras 86-89, the court excluded the statements of the accused that were compelled under provincial driving legislation. Though the taking of the statements did not violate the Charter, it found that their use in a criminal prosecution would violate the s 7 self-incrimination principle. See also

R v Milne (1996), 28 OR (3d) 577, 48 CR (4th) 182 (CA); *R v Rivera*, 2011 ONCA 225, 104 OR (3d) 561. Similarly, the court has stated that it may sometimes violate the Charter to admit unfairly obtained evidence at trial in situations where the Charter did not apply, as when evidence is obtained outside Canada or by non-state actors. See *R v Harrer*, [1995] 3 SCR 562 at paras 21-24; *R v Terry*, [1996] 2 SCR 207 at para 25; *R v Buhay*, 2003 SCC 30 at para 40, [2003] 1 SCR 631; *R v Cook*, [1998] 2 SCR 597. See also *R v Hart*, 2014 SCC 52 at para 88, [2014] 2 SCR 544.

The Supreme Court has not been clear, however, on the precise route to exclusion. In *Harrer*, *Terry*, and *Buhay*, it suggested that exclusion could be grounded on the right to a fair trial guaranteed by ss 7 and 11(d) of the Charter (or perhaps even the common law). In *White*, in contrast, it found that while admission would violate the accused's s 7 right, the exclusionary remedy flows from s 24(1) of the Charter. See also *R v Bjelland*, 2009 SCC 38 at paras 3, 19, [2009] 2 SCR 651. Should such a remedy also be available in civil proceedings? See *P (D) v Wagg* (2004), 71 OR (3d) 229, 184 CCC (3d) 321 at paras 59-60 (CA); *Mooring v Canada (National Parole Board)*, [1996] 1 SCR 75.

III. SECTIONS 13 AND 7 OF THE CHARTER AND THE SELF-INCRIMINATION PRINCIPLE

At common law, a witness could refuse to give self-incriminating testimony. This "privilege" against self-incrimination was abrogated by s 5(1) of the *Canada Evidence Act*, which states that "[n]o witness shall be excused from answering any question on the ground that the answer to the question may tend to criminate him, or may tend to establish his liability to a civil proceeding at the instance of the Crown or of any person." In exchange for the loss of the privilege, however, Parliament gave witnesses the evidentiary immunity set out in s 5(2) of the Act, which states as follows:

> (2) Where with respect to any question a witness objects to answer on the ground that his answer may tend to criminate him, or may tend to establish his liability to a civil proceeding at the instance of the Crown or of any person, and if but for this Act, or the Act of any provincial legislature, the witness would therefore have been excused from answering the question, then although the witness is by reason of this Act or the provincial Act compelled to answer, the answer so given shall not be used or admissible in evidence against him in any criminal trial or other criminal proceeding against him thereafter taking place, other than a prosecution for perjury in the giving of that evidence or for the giving of contradictory evidence.

As will be seen below, while still in force, s 5(2) of the *Canada Evidence Act* has been largely overtaken by the evidentiary immunities granted by ss 13 and 7 of the Charter.

A. Section 13 of the Charter

Section 13 of the Charter states:

> A witness who testifies in any proceedings has the right not to have any incriminating evidence so given used to incriminate that witness in any other proceedings, except in a prosecution for perjury or for the giving of contradictory evidence.

After several years of confusing and conflicting jurisprudence, the Supreme Court of Canada clarified the meaning of this provision in the following two cases.

R v Henry

2005 SCC 76, [2005] 3 SCR 609

McLachlin CJ and Major, Bastarache, Binnie, LeBel, Deschamps, Fish,
Abella, and Charron JJ (15 December 2005)

BINNIE J (McLachlin CJ and Major, Bastarache, LeBel, Deschamps, Fish, Abella, and Charron JJ concurring):

[1] In their retrial on a charge of first degree murder the appellants told a different story under oath than they had five years earlier at their first trial on the same charge. They were cross-examined at the subsequent trial on these prior inconsistent statements. They were again convicted of first degree murder. They claim this use of prior statements violated their constitutional right against self-incrimination guaranteed by s. 13 of the *Canadian Charter of Rights and Freedoms*.

[2] The right against self-incrimination is of course one of the cornerstones of our criminal law. The right to stand silent before the accusations of the state has its historical roots in the general revulsion against the practices of the Star Chamber, and in modern times is intimately linked to our adversarial system of criminal justice and the presumption of innocence. Section 13 of the *Charter* gives constitutional protection to a more specific privilege against *testimonial* self-incrimination. In *Dubois v. The Queen*, [1985] 2 SCR 350, the Court stated at p. 358 that

> the purpose of s. 13, when the section is viewed in the context of s. 11(c) and (d), is to protect individuals from being indirectly *compelled* to incriminate themselves, to ensure that the Crown will not be able to do indirectly that which s. 11(c) prohibits. [Emphasis added.]

It seems a long stretch from the important purpose served by a right designed to protect against compelled self-incrimination to the proposition advanced by the appellants in the present case, namely that an accused can volunteer one story at his or her first trial, have it rejected by the jury, then after obtaining a retrial on an unrelated ground of appeal volunteer a different and contradictory story to a jury differently constituted in the hope of a better result because the second jury is kept in the dark about the inconsistencies.

[3] The protective policy of s. 13 must be considered in light of the countervailing concern that an accused, by tailoring his or her testimony at successive trials on the same indictment, may obtain through unexposed lies and contradictions an unjustified acquittal, thereby bringing into question the credibility of the trial process itself. Effective cross-examination lies at the core of a fair trial: *R v. Seaboyer*, [1991] 2 SCR 577, at p. 608; *R v. Osolin*, [1993] 4 SCR 595, at p. 663; *R v. Shearing*, [2002] 3 SCR 33, 2002 SCC 58, at para. 76; *R v. Lyttle*, [2004] 1 SCR 193, 2004 SCC 5, at para. 41. Catching a witness in self-contradictions is one of the staples of effective cross-examination.

[4] Having said that, there are observations in the Court's previous s. 13 jurisprudence that can fairly be said to fuel the appellants' argument (none of which escaped their counsel's skilful attention). It is therefore necessary to return to the foundational case of *Dubois* and trace the subsequent jurisprudence to clarify the role and function of s. 13,

and to explain why the appellants' interpretation of s. 13 overshoots its purpose, and why it must therefore be rejected. The appeals, in the result, will be dismissed.

I. *Introduction*

[5] The present case arises out of a botched "rip-off" of a marijuana-growing operation ("grow-op") at Port Coquitlam, British Columbia. The appellants admit they carried out the rip-off, stealing 170 marijuana plants, in the course of which the in-house caretaker of the grow-op was murdered. He was suffocated by 24 feet of duct tape being wound around his head, blocking the passage of air to his nose and mouth. The appellants admit their involvement. They accept culpability for manslaughter. At issue is whether the proper verdict is manslaughter or murder.

[6] The Crown's case rested on both physical evidence and out-of-court statements by both appellants to undercover police officers. In accordance with *Dubois*, the Crown did not attempt to file at the retrial as part of its case-in-chief the testimony of the appellants at their first trial.

[7] At the close of the Crown's case on the retrial, both appellants decided to testify. As he had at the first trial, Henry again claimed that he was intoxicated, but other than remembering being intoxicated he now admitted to no significant recollection of what happened. Riley testified in chief that while he had "on occasion" lied at the first trial he now had a clear recollection that he was not in the room when the fatal winding took place. He argued that his candour in admitting previous falsehoods was a badge of present truthfulness. Riley's defence strategy at the retrial thus incorporated his testimony at the previous trial. Henry's defence was more simple. Not only did he claim to recall less at the second trial than he testified to at the first trial, at times he seemed to suggest that he did not even recall that an earlier trial had taken place. The Crown took the view that it was entitled to cross-examine both appellants on the testimony given at the prior trial for the purpose of impeaching their credibility, and did so, relying in this respect on *R v. Kuldip*, [1990] 3 SCR 618. The defence says that such cross-examination even for the purpose of impeachment of credibility was unfair, but in any event that the distinction in these circumstances between the purposes of impeachment of credibility and incrimination is illusory. Reliance was placed on *R v. Noël*, [2002] 3 SCR 433, 2002 SCC 67, and *R v. Allen*, [2003] 1 SCR 223, 2003 SCC 18, to exclude the damaging inconsistencies. The Crown, for its part, says that the accused in volunteering their testimony at the second trial stepped outside the protection of s. 13, and that any observations to the contrary in the Court's previous s. 13 jurisprudence should be reconsidered. Thus issue was joined on the proper scope of s. 13.

[8] I pause at this juncture to observe that both parties view with scepticism the idea that the trier of fact can truly isolate the purpose of impeaching credibility from the purpose of incrimination. They agree on the problem but disagree about the solution. The appellants' solution, relying on *Noël*, is that unless the statements used to contradict the present testimony were innocuous when made at the first trial, and still innocuous at the second trial, they should be altogether excluded, i.e. even for the limited purpose of challenging credibility. They wish to see a roll-back of *Kuldip*. Otherwise, they fear, the contradictions may well be used by the trier of fact for the forbidden purpose of incrimination. The Crown also recognizes the troublesome nature of the distinction but, relying on *Kuldip*,

says that fair trial considerations absolutely require that the contradictions in the evidence of an accused be exposed. The Crown then goes further than *Kuldip* in saying that the trier of fact should be able to make of the contradictions what it wishes, including drawing an inference of guilt, and indeed that a realistic appraisal of the trial process permits no other conclusion, human nature being what it is.

[9] It has long been recognized that the distinction between credibility and incrimination in this particular context is "troublesome" (as Lamer CJ described it in *Kuldip*, at p. 635) and "difficult" (as Martin JA described it in *Kuldip* when the case was before the Ontario Court of Appeal ((1988), 40 CCC (3d) 11, at p. 23)). As both the defence lawyers and the prosecutors agree that a problem exists, the question is: what should be done about it, having regard to the 20 years of experience since *Dubois*?

II. Facts

[10] On October 17, 2001, a jury convicted the two appellants of the first degree murder of Timothy Langmead, who had operated a marijuana "grow-op" at Port Coquitlam, B.C. In the course of a "rip-off" of that operation by the appellants, Langmead was tied to a chair, had duct tape wound around his mouth and nose, and suffocated. At their first trial in 1996 the appellants admitted their involvement in the unlawful confinement that led up to his death, but they pleaded diminished responsibility because of intoxication.

[11] The appellant Riley and the victim Langmead were acquaintances. They had both done work over the years for the same marijuana dealer. In fact Riley had helped set up the marijuana grow-op in Port Coquitlam that was being tended by Langmead on the night Langmead was killed. Riley claimed that he was owed $5,000 to $10,000 by the drug dealer for wiring a bypass of the hydro meter and other services. On the night of June 8, 1994, he and two accomplices planned to help themselves to some marijuana plants by way of compensation.

[12] Riley and the appellant Henry knew each other from high school in the B.C. Interior. The two of them, along with another individual (Gabe Abbott, who was not charged) drove to Langmead's house. They said they expected that Langmead would not be home, but he was, or came home shortly after they entered the house. Riley knew that Langmead recognized him from their earlier dealings. Although the details are not clear, it seems there was some struggle between Riley and Langmead. Once subdued, Langmead was put in a chair and his arms secured by rope or duct tape. He began to yell. Tape was applied to his mouth. The question was whether Henry or Riley applied the fatal windings of 24 feet of duct tape to Langmead's mouth and nose, or whether it was both of them, and with what intent. After the killing, the three intruders stole marijuana plants, a guitar, a VCR and a van. They took Langmead's body with them. They drove a couple of hours to the Alexandra Bridge in the Fraser Canyon, threw the body into the river and rolled the van over a cliff. Nine days later, Langmead's body was found floating downstream. The duct tape was still wound around his head.

[13] The police mounted an undercover operation and obtained incriminating statements from both of the appellants boasting of responsibility for the death of Langmead. After Riley's arrest, he made some further admissions to the police.

[14] Both appellants were convicted of first degree murder, but in 1999 the British Columbia Court of Appeal held that the trial judge had failed to properly instruct the

jury on the defence of intoxication. A new trial was ordered: (1999), 117 BCAC 49, 1999 BCCA 22.

[15] At the second trial Henry continued to advance the defence of intoxication but Riley largely resiled from it, seeking instead to use his greater recollection of events to push the responsibility onto Henry. He testified to having assisted in securing Langmead's mouth with a few small pieces of tape only to stop him yelling, and said that thereafter Henry was alone with Langmead. Both men, through their counsel, again admitted criminal responsibility for manslaughter. The only live issue at the second trial, as at the first trial, was whether it was a case of murder.

[The trial judge, on the authority of *Kuldip*, permitted Crown counsel to cross-examine Henry and Riley on their inconsistent testimony from their first trial. Both accused were convicted of first-degree murder. Their appeal to the British Columbia Court of Appeal was dismissed. Southin JA and Newbury JA both held that s 13, as interpreted in *Noël*, did not prohibit the cross-examination in this case, though they had different reasons for reaching this conclusion. Hall JA, dissenting, held that the cross-examination was directed not just at undermining the accused's credibility but also at "incriminating" them, and therefore was prohibited by s 13 of the Charter as interpreted in *Noël*. On the strength of Hall JA's dissent, the accused appealed to the Supreme Court of Canada.]

III. Analysis

[22] The consistent theme in the s. 13 jurisprudence is that "the purpose of s. 13 ... is to protect individuals from being indirectly compelled to incriminate themselves" (*Dubois*, at p. 358, and reiterated in *Kuldip*, at p. 629). That same purpose was flagged in *Noël*, the Court's most recent examination of s. 13, by Arbour J, at para. 21:

> Section 13 reflects a long-standing form of statutory protection against *compulsory* self-incrimination in Canadian law, and is best understood by reference to s. 5 of the *Canada Evidence Act*. Like the statutory protection, the constitutional one represents what Fish JA called a *quid pro quo*: when a witness *who is compelled* to give evidence in a court proceeding is exposed to the risk of self-incrimination, the state offers protection against the subsequent use of that evidence against the witness in exchange for his or her full and frank testimony. [Emphasis added.]

[23] There is thus a consensus that s. 13 was intended to extend s. 5 of the *Canada Evidence Act* to give further and better effect to this purpose. As McIntyre J pointed out in *Dubois*, in reasons that dissented in the result but not on this point, s. 13 "does not depend on any objection made by the witness giving the evidence. It is applicable and effective without invocation, and even where the witness in question is unaware of his rights" (p. 377). Further, s. 13 "is not limited to a question in respect of which a witness would have been entitled to refuse to answer at common law and its prohibition against the use of incriminating evidence is not limited to criminal proceedings. It confers a right against incrimination by the use of evidence given in one proceeding in any other proceedings" (p. 377). *Noël*, our most recent pronouncement, also agreed that s. 13 was intimately linked (though not necessarily limited to) the role and function traditionally served by s. 5 of the *Canada Evidence Act*.

[24] Despite these broad areas of agreement, the Court's s. 13 jurisprudence bristles with observations that enable the appellants to argue with a measure of indignation that notwithstanding the fact they were not (and could not be) compelled to testify at their first trial, they ought nevertheless to have been protected as volunteers at their second trial from exposure of the contradictory testimony they gave at the first trial, despite the misleading impression with which such non-disclosure would have left the jury. The search for truth, they say, is limited by constitutional considerations. The appellants rely in particular on observations made in *Noël*, even though *Noël* did not involve the retrial of an accused on the same indictment, but the trial of an accused whose previous testimony had been compelled at the trial of somebody else on charges related to the same subject matter. *Noël* was a classic application of s. 5(2) of the *Canada Evidence Act*, which in fact had wisely been invoked on Noël's behalf at the earlier trial of that other person, who happened to be his brother. It is therefore desirable to retrace the essentials of the jurisprudence from *Dubois* to *Noël* to determine whether the appellants' position on s. 13 is well founded.

1. The Scope of Section 13 of the Charter

[25] Section 13 of the *Charter* precludes "incriminating evidence" given in one proceeding from being "used to incriminate that witness in any other proceedings." Incriminating evidence means "something 'from which a trier of fact may infer that an accused is guilty of the crime charged'": *Kuldip*, at p. 633. The meaning of this protection in the context of a retrial of an accused on the same charge was first considered in *Dubois*. The question was phrased in that case by Lamer J (as he then was): "When a new trial is ordered on the same charge or on an included offence by a court of appeal, can the Crown adduce *as evidence-in-chief* the testimony given by an accused at the former trial?" (p. 353 (emphasis added)). Dubois was charged with second degree murder. At his first trial he admitted that he had killed the deceased but alleged justification. He was convicted, but successfully appealed the conviction and was granted a new trial on grounds of a misdirection to the jury. At the retrial, as part of its case-in-chief, the Crown read in Dubois' testimony from the first trial over an objection by Dubois' counsel based on s. 13 of the *Charter*. Dubois chose not to testify nor did he call any evidence. He was again convicted. The majority of our Court agreed that the testimony of the accused at the first trial could not be used by the Crown as part of its "case to meet" to incriminate the accused at the retrial on the same charge.

[26] More specifically, *Dubois* concluded that the reference in s. 13 to "other proceedings" includes a retrial on the same indictment and that the term "witness" in s. 13 also applies to an accused testifying (voluntarily) in his or her own defence. Lamer J, for the majority, held that "given the nature and purpose of the [s. 13] right, which is essentially protection against self-incrimination, the issue of whether the testimony was compulsory or voluntary at the moment it was given is largely irrelevant. The focus of the right is on the second proceedings, the time at which the previous testimony is sought to be used, rather than the time at which it is given" (p. 361). At the second proceeding, however, Dubois was not a witness. He was exercising his absolute right not to testify at all. Therefore, as Lamer J pointed out at p. 365: "I do not see how the evidence given by the accused to meet the case as it was in the first trial could become part of the Crown's case against

the accused in the second trial, without being in violation of s. 11(d) [the presumption of innocence], and to a lesser extent of s. 11(c) [the right not to be compelled to be a witness]."

[27] In my view, the same result would have followed if at the retrial in the present case the appellants had chosen not to testify. Whether or not the appellants had been voluntary witnesses at the earlier trial would have been, in that respect, irrelevant. At the second trial the testimony, had the Crown been permitted to file it as part of the case-in-chief, would have been compelled, and its use, on a purposeful interpretation of s. 13, prohibited.

[28] *Dubois* was applied in *R v. Mannion*, [1986] 2 SCR 272, where, as in the present case, the Crown attempted to use prior inconsistent statements in the *cross-examination* of an accused at a retrial. The accused was charged with raping a woman in Edmonton. Shortly thereafter, but before an arrest could be made, he left Edmonton heading for British Columbia. Whether or not his departure could give rise to an inference of guilt depended in part on whether he knew of the rape investigation before he left. At the first trial he said that when he spoke to a police officer before his departure, he had been told that the officer wanted to see him concerning a rape. At the second trial, no doubt sensing the danger, he changed his story to say that while he knew the officer wanted to speak with him, he understood it was about his work as a police informant on unrelated matters, and he was afraid to speak to the officer because he had not lived up to certain obligations. At the second trial, the accused was cross-examined on the different explanation he gave at the first trial, which the Crown submitted for the truth of its content. McIntyre J, for the Court, held that the cross-examination was improper. In doing so, however, he focussed on the *purpose* of the cross-examination (incrimination), rather than the *purpose* of s. 13 (protection against *compelled* self-incrimination). McIntyre J, with the unanimous support of his colleagues, accepted that the result of the holding in *Dubois* (in which he had dissented) dictated the outcome in *Mannion*. The distinction between Dubois' status as a compelled witness at the second trial and Mannion's status as a volunteer at both trials was not commented upon.

[29] The Court returned to a purposive interpretation in *Kuldip*. The accused was charged with failing to remain at the scene of a car accident with the intent of escaping civil or criminal liability. At his first trial he volunteered that he had reported the accident to a constable at a police station in Toronto whom he identified as P.C. Brown. The Crown established that Brown was not on duty on the day in question. At the retrial, the accused again chose to testify, but changed his story to accommodate that awkward fact. Lamer CJ for the majority of the Court held that the accused was properly confronted with his prior inconsistent statement:

> An interpretation of s. 13 which insulates such an accused from having previous inconsistent statements put to him/her on cross-examination where the only purpose of doing so is to challenge that accused's credibility, would, in my view, "stack the deck" too highly in favour of the accused. [p. 636]

[30] In other respects, *Kuldip* followed where *Mannion* had led. Lamer CJ stated that the questions raised in the appeal were "identical to those examined by this Court in *Mannion*" (p. 628). The only difference in his view was that in *Mannion*, the purpose of the cross-examination was to incriminate, whereas in *Kuldip* it was to impeach credibility.

A successful impeachment would do no more than nullify the accused's testimony. The Crown could not obtain a conviction except on the basis of other evidence.

[31] Of interest in *Kuldip* is the example given by Lamer CJ, at p. 634, of a witness at a murder trial who testifies that the accused could not have murdered the victim in Ottawa because on the day in question they were both in Montreal doing a bank robbery. If the witness were later charged with the bank robbery in Montreal, and changed his story at his trial to say that in fact he was in Ottawa that day, Lamer CJ said it would not infringe s. 13 to impeach credibility using the earlier admission (despite the fact the statement was incriminating both when given at the earlier trial and when used at the later trial). However the trial judge must warn the jury "that it would not be open to it to conclude, on the basis of his previous statement, that the accused was in Montreal on the day of the alleged bank robbery nor to conclude that the accused did, in fact, commit the bank robbery" (pp. 634-35). As will be seen, the facts of the example anticipate, to some extent, the situation in *Noël*.

[32] *Kuldip* thus qualified *Mannion*. If the prior testimony is used at the retrial to incriminate, *Mannion* says s. 13 is violated. If the prior testimony is used to impeach credibility, and thereby to nullify the accused's retrial testimony, *Kuldip* says s. 13 permits it. As Lamer CJ's example of the bank robber shows, however, the distinction poses problems. There can be few triers of fact, whether judge or jurors, who would not have found the prior admission of the accused, that on the day in question he was in Montreal robbing a bank, probative on the issue of guilt of that offence.

[33] *Kuldip* was endorsed by *Noël*, which applied the s. 13 jurisprudence to the case of an accused who at the previous trial was not the accused but a mere witness at somebody else's trial (as in Lamer CJ's bank robbery example in *Kuldip*). The accused had testified as a compellable witness during his brother's trial about his complicity in the senseless strangulation of a nine-year-old boy. He was subsequently charged with the murder, but at his own trial he denied any such complicity. The Crown put to him statement after statement that he had made at the earlier trial, which he acknowledged having made, and which formed an important element (if it was not virtually conclusive) in establishing his guilt. In that context, and recognizing that when testifying as a witness at his brother's trial Noël had claimed the protection of s. 5 of the *Canada Evidence Act*, Arbour J emphasized the *quid pro quo* "when a witness *who is compelled* to give evidence in a court proceeding is exposed to the risk of self-incrimination" (emphasis added) and held that "the state offers protection against the subsequent use of that evidence against the witness in exchange for his or her full and frank testimony" (para. 21). The emphasis in *Noël* on the *quid pro quo* reinforces the link between s. 13 of the *Charter* and s. 5 of the *Canada Evidence Act* and the whole issue of compelled testimony. It must be recognized that a witness who was also the accused at the first trial is at *both* trials a voluntary rather than a compelled witness, and therefore does not offer the same *quid pro quo*. (The notion that an accused who volunteers testimony can simultaneously object to answering questions whose answers may tend to incriminate him or her is a difficult concept. The whole point of volunteering testimony is to respond to the prosecution's case. Even answers to his or her own counsel's questions may tend to incriminate.)

[34] Despite the difference between the trial of an accused who was a compelled witness in another "proceeding" and the retrial of an accused who volunteered evidence at

both the first and second trials, the appellants here rely on the observation of Arbour J at para. 4 of *Noël*:

> When an accused testifies at trial, he cannot be cross-examined on the basis of a prior testimony unless the trial judge is satisfied that there is no realistic danger that his prior testimony could be used to incriminate him. The danger of incrimination will vary with the nature of the prior evidence and the circumstances of the case including the efficacy of an adequate instruction to the jury.

The facts of *Noël* provide an interesting parallel to Lamer CJ's bank robbery example in *Kuldip*. In Lamer CJ's example, the prior testimony was considered admissible for impeachment, although it was undeniably incriminatory when given, and would almost certainly have been taken as incriminatory if allowed into evidence at the second trial. In *Noël*, the Crown's incriminatory purpose was unmistakable. Yet in both the bank robber example and in *Noël* itself the prior testimony was compelled, and its use thus posed a serious problem not only under the *Dubois* analysis of s. 13 but under s. 11(c) of the *Charter* and s. 5(2) of the *Canada Evidence Act*. (For present purposes, evidence of compellable witnesses should be treated as compelled even if their attendance was not enforced by a subpoena.)

[35] *Kuldip* can be seen as an attempt by the Court to put the brakes on *Mannion*, but in its unwillingness to reconsider its reasoning in *Mannion*, the Court was required to resort to reliance on the sometimes difficult distinction between the purposes of impeachment of credibility and incrimination. Although this distinction is well established in the law (see, e.g., *R v. Calder*, [1996] 1 SCR 660, at para. 25), its practicality in this particular context is frequently questioned. It is worth setting out in full what was said by Arthur Martin JA, writing in *Kuldip*, when it was before the Ontario Court of Appeal:

> Furthermore, in my view, where the prior evidence is used ostensibly to impeach the accused's credibility only, it nevertheless does assist the Crown in its case and, in a broad sense, may help to prove guilt. It is often difficult to draw a clear line between cross-examination on the accused's prior testimony for the purpose of incriminating him and such cross-examination for the purpose of impeaching his credibility. If the court concludes on the basis of the accused's contradictory statements that he deliberately lied on a material matter, that lie could give rise to an inference of guilt. [p. 23]

In Martin JA's view, successful invocation of s. 5(2) of the *Canada Evidence Act* ought to exclude the prior testimony of the witness for *any* purpose, including impeachment of credibility (p. 20). Arbour J, writing in *Noël* in the context of incriminating statements made by a current accused at the earlier trial of somebody else, agreed with this interpretation (paras. 31-33) except for her acceptance of *Kuldip* in the very limited case of statements innocuous when made at the first trial and still innocuous with respect to the issue of guilt at the second trial (paras. 30 and 45). This, she observed, is the only outcome consistent with the *quid pro quo* that "lies at the heart of s. 13" (para. 25), which should be interpreted in a manner "co-extensive with that of s. 5(2) of the *Canada Evidence Act*" (para. 34).

[36] The controversial aspect of *Noël* lies in its *obiter* extending to an accused at a retrial on the same indictment the identical protection enjoyed by witnesses who are compelled to testify at the trial of somebody else (or in another "proceeding"), and who

can therefore invoke both s. 13 of the *Charter* and s. 5(2) of the *Canada Evidence Act*. *Noël* decides that in both cases, the root of this protection lies "in the *quid pro quo*" (para. 22) under which as a matter of legislative policy, testimonial immunity at common law was exchanged in 1893 for a limited testimonial *use* immunity.

[37] *Noël* was subsequently applied by this Court in *Allen*. That too was a case of an accused being confronted with prior testimony he had given as a witness at the trial of somebody else for the same murder. The Newfoundland Court of Appeal, O'Neill JA dissenting, found that the cross-examination was directed to credibility, and was therefore authorized by *Kuldip*: (2002), 208 Nfld. & PEIR 250, 2002 NFCA 2. Some of the prior compelled testimony used "to impeach" included statements that the accused had killed or thought he had killed the victim. In a brief judgment, this Court without much discussion applied *Noël* to find a s. 13 violation.

[38] To recapitulate: *Dubois* was an attempt to compel testimony at a retrial; *Mannion* and *Kuldip* involved the use of prior voluntary testimony of an accused at the retrial; and *Noël* and *Allen*, were attempts by the Crown to use the compelled testimony of a witness at an earlier trial who had become the accused at the later trial. Despite this variation, in all of these cases except *Kuldip*, the prior testimony was excluded on the basis of s. 13 operating in combination with s. 11(c) of the *Charter* (and, in *Noël*, with s. 5(2) of the *Canada Evidence Act*). Clearly there has not been consistent adherence to the underlying purpose of s. 13, namely "to protect individuals from being indirectly *compelled* to incriminate themselves" (emphasis added) (*Dubois*, at p. 358; *Kuldip*, at p. 629; and *Noël*, at para. 21).

2. Should the Court Reconsider Dubois?

[39] The Attorney General of Canada submits that the Court should overrule *Dubois* and hold that s. 13 has no application to a retrial. The rationale underlying *Dubois* for extending s. 13 protection to an accused in a retrial, however, was because when a "new" trial is ordered the accused is entitled not to testify at all. Thus, to allow the Crown simply to file the testimony of the accused given at the prior trial (now overturned) would permit the Crown indirectly to compel the accused to testify at the retrial where s. 11(c) of the *Charter* would not permit such compelled self-incrimination directly. The Crown must prove its case without recruiting the accused to self-incriminate. As Lamer J pointed out,

> the accused is being *conscripted* to help the Crown in discharging its burden of *a case to meet*, and is thereby denied his or her right to stand mute until a case has been made out. [Emphasis in original; p. 365.]

[40] *Dubois*, to repeat, was an attempt to compel testimony. The result was correct and we should decline the invitation to revisit it.

3. Should the Court Reconsider Mannion?

[41] While *Mannion* followed *Dubois* on the textual point that the words "other proceedings" in s. 13 include a retrial of the same accused on the same indictment, it did not ask the further question whether excluding cross-examination on the prior volunteered testimony would further the *purpose* of s. 13 identified in *Dubois*, namely "to protect individuals from being indirectly *compelled* to incriminate themselves" (p. 358 (emphasis

added)). *Mannion* was under reserve at the same time as *Dubois* and, as stated, the Court seems to have concluded that the result in the latter dictated the outcome of the former.

[42] In my view, the crux of the problem is this. In *Dubois*, the prosecution sought to pre-empt the right of the accused not to testify. The filing of the earlier testimony was compelled self-incrimination. In *Mannion*, there was no such compulsion. The accused freely testified at his first trial and freely testified at his second trial. The compulsion, which lies at the root of the *quid pro quo* which in turn lies at the root of s. 13, was missing. Experience in the 20 years since *Dubois* and *Mannion* were decided shows that taking our eye off the underlying purpose of s. 13 has given rise to a number of distinctions and sub-distinctions that in the end have proven unworkable. Indeed in *Noël*, as Fish JA pointed out when the case was before the Quebec Court of Appeal, the jury asked a question which clearly demonstrated their failure (or unwillingness) to grasp the distinction between use of prior statements for the impeachment of credibility and use of prior statements for the purpose of incrimination (see (2001), 156 CCC (3d) 17, at paras. 169 and 173-74, and in this Court, at paras. 19-20).

[43] In my respectful view, notwithstanding the strong Court that decided *Mannion* and the cases that followed it, we should hold that s. 13 is *not* available to an accused who chooses to testify at his or her retrial on the same indictment.

[44] The Court's practice, of course, is against departing from its precedents unless there are compelling reasons to do so: *R v. Salituro*, [1991] 3 SCR 654; *R v. Chaulk*, [1990] 3 SCR 1303; *R v. B.(K.G.)*, [1993] 1 SCR 740, at pp. 777-83; and *R v. Robinson*, [1996] 1 SCR 683, at paras. 16-46. Nevertheless, while rare, departures do occur. In *Clark v. Canadian National Railway Co.*, [1988] 2 SCR 680, it was said that "[t]his Court has made it clear that constitutional decisions are not immutable, even in the absence of constitutional amendment" (p. 704), and in the *Charter* context the Court in *United States v. Burns*, [2001] 1 SCR 283, 2001 SCC 7, effectively overturned the result (if not the reasoning) in *Kindler v. Canada (Minister of Justice)*, [1991] 2 SCR 779, and *Reference re Ng Extradition (Can.)*, [1991] 2 SCR 858. In the area of human rights, important reappraisals were made in *Central Alberta Dairy Pool v. Alberta (Human Rights Commission)*, [1990] 2 SCR 489 (overturning the reasoning in *Bhinder v. Canadian National Railway Co.*, [1985] 2 SCR 561), and *Brooks v. Canada Safeway Ltd.*, [1989] 1 SCR 1219 (overturning *Bliss v. Attorney General of Canada*, [1979] 1 SCR 183). The Court should be particularly careful before reversing a precedent where the effect is to diminish *Charter* protection.

[45] I believe there are compelling reasons for declining to follow *Mannion*. The first, as discussed earlier, is that *Mannion* did not adopt an interpretation in line with the purpose of s. 13 spelled out in *Dubois*. Although *Dubois* had said that no distinction should be drawn between testimony that had been compelled or voluntary at the first trial, that comment was made in the context of an attempt to compel testimony at the second trial. The second reason is that the consequences of failing to return to the purpose of s. 13 have only emerged over time as the courts have struggled to work with the distinction between impeachment of credibility and incrimination in ways that, as the appellants' invocation of *Noël* illustrates in the present case, become "unduly and unnecessarily complex and technical": *R v. Bernard*, [1988] 2 SCR 833, at p. 859. In *Noël*, it will be recalled, the Court identified permissible cross-examination by reference to testimony "innocuous" when made at the initial trial and "innocuous" when used at the retrial, opening up consideration of various combinations and permutations of statements innocuous/incriminating,

incriminating/innocuous and incriminating/incriminating, an exercise in classification that when argued on a question by question basis can become both protracted and somewhat unpredictable, as an examination of the questions at issue in the present appeal illustrates.

[46] The third reason, and I think the most important, is that the insistence that s. 13 has the same application in a retrial of the same accused on the same indictment as it does in a trial where the accused was formerly not an accused but a compellable witness has led to an unfair dilution of the s. 13 protection in the latter situation. Thus in the bank robbery example in *Kuldip*, the compelled testimony given as a witness at somebody else's trial would virtually guarantee the bank robber's conviction in his own subsequent prosecution. This is contrary to sound principle. Even though the bank robber was a compelled witness who had given *quid pro quo* testimony (as in *Noël*) at somebody else's trial, he would receive no greater or lesser protection than an accused who had been under no such compulsion at the earlier trial (*Kuldip* and *Mannion*). The attempt to subject these very different situations to the same constitutional rule results in the end in a satisfactory solution for neither.

[47] In *Noël*, the Court saw the unfairness of putting *compelled* testimony to the accused and held that the Crown would be permitted to cross-examine an accused on prior testimony only

> when there is *no possibility* that the jury could use the content of the prior testimony to draw an inference of guilt, except to the limited extent that a finding that the accused has been untruthful under oath could be damaging to his defence. [Emphasis added; para. 54.]

The "no possibility" test significantly raises the bar set in *Kuldip*, yet one can readily see the need for such a stringent test on the facts of *Noël*, where the prior statements were made by a compelled witness who had invoked s. 5(2) of the *Canada Evidence Act*. However, the stringency of the "no possibility" test in *Noël* does not provide a satisfactory resolution in the case of a retrial of the accused who volunteers testimony at both trials and then seeks to shelter self-serving inconsistencies behind a *Charter* barrier. While the appellants argue (with some justification) that such an immunity flows from the *Mannion* line of cases, such a result is completely inconsistent with a purposive reading of s. 13. For these reasons, I believe *Mannion* should not be followed. Accused persons who testify at their first trial and then volunteer inconsistent testimony at the retrial on the same charge are in no need of protection "from being indirectly *compelled* to incriminate themselves" in any relevant sense of the word, and s. 13 protection should not be available to them.

4. Should the Court Reconsider Kuldip?

[48] Insofar as *Kuldip* permitted cross-examination of the accused on the inconsistent testimony he volunteered at his first trial, *Kuldip* should, of course, be affirmed. However, insofar as the Court felt compelled by *Mannion* to narrow the purpose of the cross-examination to the impeachment of credibility, and to deny the probative effect of the answers on the issue of guilt or innocence, it seems to me our decision today not to follow *Mannion* renders such restrictions no longer operative. If the contradiction reasonably

gives rise to an inference of guilt, s. 13 of the *Charter* does not preclude the trier of fact from drawing the common sense inference.

5. Should the Court Reconsider Noël?

[49] *Noël* is a classic example of prosecutorial abuse of the very "bargain" s. 13 was designed to enforce. Noël was not on trial at the time he gave the testimony subsequently relied upon by the Crown. He was a compellable witness who at common law could have refused to answer the Crown's questions that tended to show his guilt. He was compelled by s. 5(1) of the *Canada Evidence Act* to answer the incriminating questions, and in consequence he invoked the protection of s. 5(2). When s. 5(2) says "the answer so given shall not be used or admissible in evidence," it means not to be used for *any* purpose, including the impeachment of credibility. We should affirm the correctness of the result in *Noël* on its facts.

[50] I would go further. Even though s. 13 talks of precluding the use of prior evidence "to incriminate that witness," and thus implicitly leaves the door open to its use for purposes other than incrimination such as impeachment of credibility (as *Kuldip* accepted), experience has demonstrated the difficulty in practice of working with that distinction. If, as *Noël* held, and as Arthur Martin JA observed in *Kuldip*, the distinction is unrealistic in the context of s. 5(2) of the *Canada Evidence Act*, it must equally be unrealistic in the context of s. 13 of the *Charter*. Accordingly, by parity of reasoning, I conclude that the prior *compelled* evidence should, under s. 13 as under s. 5(2), be treated as inadmissible in evidence against the accused, even for the ostensible purpose of challenging his or her credibility, and be restricted (in the words of s. 13 itself) to "a prosecution for perjury or for the giving of contradictory evidence."

6. Should the Court Reconsider Allen?

[51] *Allen* was a straightforward application of *Noël* to an accused who was confronted with prior compelled testimony given at the trial of somebody else. He had given his *quid pro quo*. The decision was correct.

7. The Significance of Obiter Dicta in Noël

[Binnie J discussed the doctrine of *stare decisis* as applied to the *obiter dicta* of the Supreme Court of Canada. On this point, he concluded:]

[57] The issue in each case ... is what did the case decide? Beyond the *ratio decidendi* which, as the Earl of Halsbury LC pointed out, is generally rooted in the facts, the legal point decided by this Court may be as narrow as the jury instruction at issue in *Sellars* [*Sellars v R*, [1980] 1 SCR 527] or as broad as the *Oakes* test [*R v Oakes*, [1986] 1 SCR 103]. All *obiter* do not have, and are not intended to have, the same weight. The weight decreases as one moves from the dispositive *ratio decidendi* to a wider circle of analysis which is obviously intended for guidance and which should be accepted as authoritative. Beyond that, there will be commentary, examples or exposition that are intended to be helpful and may be found to be persuasive, but are certainly not "binding" in the sense the *Sellars* principle in its most exaggerated form would have it. The objective of the exercise is to

promote certainty in the law, not to stifle its growth and creativity. The notion that each phrase in a judgment of this Court should be treated as if enacted in a statute is not supported by the cases and is inconsistent with the basic fundamental principle that the common law develops by experience.

[58] These propositions may be illustrated by *Noël* itself. At paragraph 36 and following, Arbour J summarizes aspects of the jurisprudence under s. 5(2) of the *Canada Evidence Act*, including points not necessary to the *Noël* judgment itself. The discussion, while *obiter*, is (as the saying goes) learned *obiter*, and would quite properly be regarded in future cases as an authoritative summary. On the other hand, the "rare circumstances" comment that bothered the Attorney General of Ontario was not part of the analysis, and should not be taken as imposing a rule or norm or even a statistical hurdle limiting other courts.

[59] It is neither desirable nor practical to go through *Dubois*, *Mannion*, *Kuldip* and *Noël* to identify which of the *obiter* statements urged upon us by counsel at the hearing of this appeal should be regarded as authoritative. The present reasons endeavour to re-establish the core concept stated in *Dubois* that "the purpose of s. 13, when the section is viewed in the context of s. 11(c) and (d), is to protect individuals from being indirectly compelled to incriminate themselves" (p. 358). To the extent statements in the other cases are inconsistent with the rationale of compulsion (the "*quid pro quo*"), they should no longer be regarded as authoritative.

IV. Conclusion

[60] The result of a purposeful interpretation of s. 13 is that an accused will lose the *Mannion* advantage in relation to prior *volunteered* testimony but his or her protection against the use of prior *compelled* testimony will be strengthened. The two different situations will be treated differently instead of homogenized, and the unpredictability inherent in sorting out attacks on credibility from attempts at incrimination will be avoided.

[61] For the foregoing reasons, I conclude that the s. 13 *Charter* rights of the appellants (who were volunteers at both trials) were not violated by the Crown's cross-examination. Their appeals must therefore be dismissed.

R v Nedelcu
2012 SCC 59, [2012] 3 SCR 311
McLachlin CJ and LeBel, Deschamps, Fish, Abella, Rothstein, Cromwell, Moldaver, and Karakatsanis JJ (7 November 2012)

[The respondent took a co-worker for a ride on a motorcycle and crashed, severely injuring the co-worker. Examined for discovery at civil proceedings brought by the co-worker, the respondent stated that he had no memory of the accident. At his subsequent criminal trial, however, he gave a detailed account of the accident. The prosecution sought to cross-examine him on his discovery evidence to impeach his credibility. The defence objected on the basis that this cross-examination would violate s 13 of the Charter.]

MOLDAVER J (McLachlin CJ and Deschamps, Abella, Rothstein, and Karakatsanis JJ, concurring):

[1] I have had the privilege of reading Justice LeBel's reasons for judgment and I agree with him on the issue of compulsion. In particular, I accept his conclusion, at para. 109, that Mr. Nedelcu "was statutorily compellable, and therefore 'compelled' ... for the purposes of s. 13 [of the *Canadian Charter of Rights and Freedoms*]" to testify at his examination for discovery in the civil action.

[2] Where I part company with my colleague is on the interpretation of s. 13 and in particular, its application to the facts of this case. In my respectful view, s. 13 was never meant to apply to a case such as this—and I am convinced it does not. This Court's decision in *R. v. Henry*, 2005 SCC 76, [2005] 3 S.C.R. 609, does not provide otherwise.

[3] My colleague has canvassed *Henry* in detail and I see no need to retrace his steps. Fundamentally, as he observes at para. 81 of his reasons, the Court in *Henry* outlined "a unified approach to s. 13, one based on the historical rationale underlying s. 13—the *quid pro quo*." I take no issue with that observation.

[4] The difficulty I have with the present case is that there was no "*quid*" for there to be a "*quo*"—and hence, in my view, s. 13 was never engaged. I would accordingly allow the appeal.

[5] Section 13 of the *Charter* reads as follows:

> 13. A witness who testifies in any proceedings has the right not to have any incriminating evidence so given used to incriminate that witness in any other proceedings, except in a prosecution for perjury or for the giving of contradictory evidence.

[6] As I read the section, the "*quid*" that forms the critical first branch of the historical rationale, refers to "incriminating evidence" the witness has given at a prior proceeding in which the witness could not refuse to answer. The section does not refer to all manner of evidence the witness has given at the prior proceeding. It refers to "incriminating evidence" the witness has given under compulsion.

[7] The "*quo*" refers to the state's side of the bargain. In return for having compelled the witness to testify, to the extent the witness has provided "incriminating evidence," the state undertakes that it will not use *that* evidence to incriminate the witness in any other proceeding, except in a prosecution for perjury or for the giving of contradictory evidence.

[8] Thus, a party seeking to invoke s. 13 must first establish that he or she gave "incriminating evidence" under compulsion at the prior proceeding. If the party fails to meet these twin requirements, s. 13 is not engaged and that ends the matter.

[9] What then is "incriminating evidence"? The answer, I believe, should be straightforward. In my view, it can only mean evidence given by the witness at the prior proceeding that the Crown could use at the subsequent proceeding, if it were permitted to do so, to prove guilt, i.e., to prove or assist in proving one or more of the essential elements of the offence for which the witness is being tried.

. . .

[16] The law is clear and I accept it to be so, that the time for determining whether the evidence given at the prior proceeding may properly be characterized as "incriminating evidence" is the time when the Crown seeks to use it at the subsequent hearing. (See *Dubois v. The Queen*, [1985] 2 S.C.R. 350, at pp. 363-64.) That, however, does not detract from my contention that the evidence to which s. 13 is directed is not "any evidence" the

witness may have been compelled to give at the prior proceeding, but evidence that the Crown could use at the subsequent proceeding, if permitted to do so, to prove the witness's guilt on the charge for which he or she is being tried.

[17]   In so concluding, I recognize that there will be instances where evidence given at the prior proceeding, though seemingly innocuous or exculpatory at the time, may become "incriminating evidence" at the subsequent proceeding, thereby triggering the application of s. 13.

[18]   Take for example, the witness who, at the trial of a third party for robbery, admits to having been present at the scene of the crime but denies any involvement in it. If the witness is subsequently charged with the same robbery and testifies that he was not present when the robbery occurred, his evidence from the prior proceeding, though innocuous at the time, will have taken on new meaning. For purposes of s. 13, it would now be treated as "incriminating evidence" because it is evidence that the Crown could use at the witness's robbery trial, if permitted to do so, to prove the essential element of identity. And that is where s. 13 comes in. It precludes the Crown from introducing it for any purpose, whether as part of its case to prove identity or as a means of impeaching the witness's testimony.

[19]   Manifestly, I take a different view where the evidence given by the witness at the prior proceeding could not be used by the Crown at the subsequent proceeding to prove the witness's guilt on the charge for which he or she is being tried. In such circumstances, because the prior evidence is not "incriminating evidence," there can be no "*quid*" for purposes of s. 13—and because there is no "*quid*," no "*quo*" is owed in return. The case at hand provides a classic example of this.

[20]   On its own, Mr. Nedelcu's "I ... remember nothing" testimony from his discovery could not have been used by the Crown to prove or assist in proving one or more of the essential elements of the criminal charges he was facing—dangerous driving causing bodily harm and impaired driving causing bodily harm. I say "on its own" because in theory, if the Crown were able to prove that Mr. Nedelcu had concocted his discovery evidence with a view to deliberately misleading the court and obstructing the course of justice, that finding would constitute evidence of consciousness of guilt from which the trier of fact could, if it chose to, infer guilt.

[21]   But realistically, that scenario is one with which we need not be concerned. Any attempt on the Crown's part to convert Mr. Nedelcu's "non-incriminating" evidence from the discovery into potentially "incriminating evidence" at his criminal trial would trigger the application of s. 13 and the protection afforded by it. And that would be self-defeating. It would disentitle the Crown from being able to use Mr. Nedelcu's "non-incriminating" discovery evidence for impeachment purposes—the sole purpose of the exercise. In short, the Crown would know that it could not suggest in cross-examination that the prior evidence had been concocted, nor could it lead any evidence to that effect.

[22]   The mere possibility that evidence, which is otherwise "non-incriminating," can be converted into "incriminating" evidence if the Crown were to take the added steps needed to make it so, is not enough to trigger the application of s. 13. The use of Mr. Nedelcu's discovery evidence to test his credibility, and nothing else, could not convert his discovery evidence into incriminating evidence. The discovery evidence would retain its original characteristics and it would not become evidence from which the triers of fact could infer guilt.

· · ·

[24] In the present context, it would of course be incumbent on trial judges to provide juries with clear instructions as to the use they could make of the evidence given at the prior proceeding, similar to the instructions that trial judges have been providing in cases where an accused has given alibi evidence. Thus, in Mr. Nedelcu's case, unless he were to adopt his discovery evidence, the jury would be told that they could not use his discovery evidence for its truth, but only to test his credibility and for no other purpose. The jury would also be told that if they were to reject Mr. Nedelcu's trial evidence, they could not use that rejection to bolster the Crown's case. They would simply remove Mr. Nedelcu's evidence from their consideration. To convict, the jury would have to be satisfied, on the basis of the remaining evidence, that the Crown had proved its case beyond a reasonable doubt.

[25] In sum, I am satisfied that the use of Mr. Nedelcu's non-incriminating discovery evidence for impeachment purposes, and nothing else, could not and did not trigger the application of s. 13.

[26] In my respectful view, *Henry* could not have meant something different. In concluding that a witness's testimony from a prior proceeding could not be used to impeach that witness in a subsequent proceeding, the Court must have been referring to "incriminating evidence" being used for that purpose; it could not have been referring to "non-incriminating" evidence since s. 13 does not concern itself with that type of evidence.

[27] To take an obvious example, assume that at a prior proceeding, a witness has testified, as part of the narrative, that she got up at 10:00 a.m., had breakfast, went to the corner store for a paper and then returned home. Assume further that none of that information has any bearing on the crime of robbery she is alleged to have committed at 5:00 p.m. later that day. At her subsequent robbery trial, some three years later, she states in chief that she awoke at noon, had nothing to eat and stayed home until 3:00 p.m. As for the robbery itself, she admits to having been at the robbery scene but claims that she could not have been the robber because she was wearing a pink coat that day and all of the witnesses have described the robber as wearing a black coat.

[28] On that example, surely the Crown would not be precluded, on the basis of *Henry*, from cross-examining on the apparent inconsistencies relating to her morning activities, with a view to testing the witness's powers of recollection and hence, the overall credibility and reliability of her testimony—particularly as to her ability to remember what she was wearing at the time of the robbery. Using non-incriminating evidence for impeachment purposes does not engage s. 13. And I do not read *Henry* as holding otherwise, even though some of the language used could leave that impression. At para. 50, Binnie J. states: "… the prior *compelled* evidence [of the witness] should, under s. 13 … , be treated as inadmissible in evidence against the accused, even for the ostensible purpose of challenging his or her credibility, and be restricted (in the words of s. 13 itself) to 'a prosecution for perjury or for the giving of contradictory evidence'" (italics in original).

[29] While Justice Binnie speaks only of "prior compelled evidence," s. 13 is concerned with prior "incriminating evidence" that has been compelled. It should not be interpreted as referring to "compelled" evidence of *any* kind—and certainly not compelled evidence that was neither incriminating at the time it was given nor incriminating at the witness's subsequent trial. Using Justice Binnie's definition of "incriminating evidence" as "something 'from which a trier of fact may infer that an accused is guilty of the crime charged'" (*Henry*, para. 25), Mr. Nedelcu's discovery evidence fails to meet that test.

[30] In this case, the Crown sought to use Mr. Nedelcu's "non-incriminating" prior discovery evidence to impeach him. The use of his non-incriminating discovery evidence for that purpose did not convert it into incriminating evidence, i.e., evidence that the Crown could use, if permitted to do so, to prove or assist in proving one or more of the essential elements of the offences upon which Mr. Nedelcu was being tried. As such, s. 13 was not engaged. There was no "*quid*" and, therefore, no "*quo*" for the state to honour.

[31] My colleague, Justice LeBel, takes issue with my conclusion that s. 13 is not engaged here. He maintains that I have misconstrued *Henry* and misinterpreted s. 13. He predicts that the interpretation of s. 13 to which I ascribe will lead to confusion and unpredictability. Courts will be inundated with time-consuming *voir dires*; the scope of s. 13 will be rendered dubious in theory and uncertain in practice; and the objective of the *quid pro quo*, which is to encourage full and frank testimony, will be undermined.

[32] I propose to address each of these concerns in brief compass.

[33] But first, let me deal with the suggestion that the way in which I interpret s. 13 was not raised by any of the parties or interveners and that it is "entirely contrary to Crown counsel's submissions before this Court" (para. 127).

[34] At para. 56 of their factum, Ms. Fairburn and Mr. Schwartz, on behalf of the Crown, wrote:

> Mr. Nedelcu's discovery evidence would not even have the potential to incriminate. Properly conceptualized, his discovery evidence was non-evidence: *I remember nothing*. Query whether at common law he could have asserted his silence in relation to this non-evidence. What is incriminating about remembering nothing? Nothing. If the *Henry* interpretation of s. 13 extends even to non-evidence, through the conduit of compulsion, with great respect, this signals a need for change. [Italics in original; underlining added; footnote omitted.]

[35] My reasons address this very issue. They make clear that *Henry* did not extend the protection of s. 13 to non-incriminating evidence—and that those who believed it had were mistaken. While some might like to read the words "incriminating evidence" out of s. 13, the Court in *Henry* did no such thing.

[36] Turning to my colleague's prediction that the construction I place on s. 13 will lead to uncertainty and time-consuming *voir dires*, unlike my colleague, I expect that trial judges will have little trouble discerning whether evidence given by the accused as a witness in a prior proceeding is "incriminating" evidence—that is, evidence that the Crown could use, if permitted to do so, to prove guilt.

[37] Under the test I have proposed, trial judges are not given a discretion. The only added burden on the court will be to qualify the evidence as incriminating or not—hardly a difficult or time-consuming task. Where the evidence the Crown seeks to introduce could be used by the Crown, if it were permitted to do so, to prove guilt—i.e., to prove or assist in proving one or more of the essential elements of the offence for which the witness is being tried—it is not admissible under s. 13 for *any purpose* (other than a prosecution for perjury or giving contradictory evidence).

[38] In sum, far from opening the *voir dire* floodgates, I am confident that trial judges will have little difficulty deciding whether evidence put forward by the Crown meets the test for "incriminating" evidence as I have defined it.

[39] That brings me to the last of my colleague's concerns—that in construing s. 13 as I have, the objective of the *quid pro quo*, which is to encourage full and frank testimony, will be undermined.

[40] With respect, I do not agree. Full and frank testimony presupposes a witness who wants to tell the truth but is afraid to do so lest the evidence be used to incriminate him at a subsequent proceeding. It does not presuppose a witness who is bent on giving false testimony.

[41] Be that as it may, on my construction of s. 13, neither the truthful witness nor the perjurer need be concerned that any incriminating evidence given by them at a prior proceeding will be used against them, for any purpose, at a subsequent proceeding (the perjurer need only fear a prosecution for perjury or for giving contradictory evidence). Thus, the witness who sincerely wants to tell the truth—that is, make full and frank disclosure—need not fear any repercussions. He or she will gain the full protection of s. 13, and the bargain contemplated by s. 13 will have been fulfilled.

[42] I do not gainsay the possibility that construing s. 13 as I have may impinge ever so slightly on the clarity and predictability that my colleague considers all-important. Clarity and predictability are laudable goals, to be sure—but they should not be pursued at the expense of rewriting s. 13 to remove critical words that alter the meaning of the section and impermissibly extend its protection beyond its intended purpose.

[43] I would accordingly allow the appeal, set aside the order for a new trial and restore the guilty verdict on the charge of dangerous driving causing bodily harm.

[LeBel J, dissenting (Fish and Cromwell JJ, concurring) would have denied the appeal on the basis that *Henry* forbids the use of an accused's previous compellable testimony for impeachment purposes in all cases.]

NOTES AND QUESTIONS

1. Is it proper for counsel to cross-examine an opposing witness on his or her knowledge of the protection of s 13 of the Charter? See *R v Jabarianha*, 2001 SCC 75, [2001] 3 SCR 430.

2. Does s 13 protect against the admission of previous compellable testimony in non-criminal proceedings? See *Knutson v Saskatchewan Registered Nurses Assn* (1990), 46 Admin LR 234 (Sask CA); *Jaballah, Re*, 2010 FC 224, [2011] 3 FCR 155, 88 Imm LR (3d) 268.

3. Does s 13 protect against the admission of testimony by an accused made in a pre-trial hearing in the same prosecution, such as a bail hearing, preliminary inquiry, or *voir dire*? See *R v Ramsaran*, [2007] OJ No 5033 at para 49 (QL), 46 MVR (5th) 129, 41 CPC (6th) 357 (Sup Ct J); *R v Scully*, [2007] OJ No 2837 at paras 13-14 (QL) (Ct J); *R v Simpson*, 2012 NSSC 66.

4. Does s 13 permit the admission of an accused's allegedly false testimony only in prosecutions for perjury or for giving contradictory evidence, or does it also allow for admission in any case where the earlier testimony comprises the *actus reus* of the offence? See *R v Staranchuk* (1983), 8 CCC (3d) 150 (Sask CA), aff'd (*sub nom Staranchuk v R*) [1985] 1 SCR 439; *R v Schertzer*, 2015 ONCA 259.

For further discussion of s 13, see Peter Sankoff, "R. v. Nedelcu: The Role of Compulsion in Excluding Incriminating Prior Testimony Under Section 13 of the Charter" (2011) 83 CR (6th) 55; Hamish Stewart, "Henry in the Supreme Court of Canada: Reorienting the S. 13 Right Against Self-Incrimination" (2006) 34 CR (6th) 112; Steven Penney, "What's Wrong with Self-Incrimination?

The Wayward Path of Self-Incrimination Law in the Post-Charter Era, Part III: Compelled Communications, the Admissibility of Defendants' Previous Testimony, and Inferences from Defendants' Silence" (2004) 48 Crim LQ 474 at 509-16.

B. Section 7 of the Charter: Derivative Use and Exemption

As we have seen, while s 5(2) of the *Canada Evidence Act* and s 13 of the Charter prevent a witness's self-incriminating testimony from being used in future proceedings ("use immunity"), neither excuses witnesses from providing such testimony ("exemption") or immunizes evidence derived from it ("derivative use" immunity). The Supreme Court of Canada has interpreted s 7 of the Charter, however, as providing witnesses with these protections in limited circumstances. In *Application Under S 83.28 of the Criminal Code (Re)*, 2004 SCC 42, [2004] 2 SCR 248, the court explained how these three types of protection against self-incrimination function:

> [71] Use immunity serves to protect the individual from having the compelled incriminating testimony used directly against him or her in a subsequent proceeding. The derivative use protection insulates the individual from having compelled incriminating testimony used to obtain other evidence, unless that evidence is discoverable through alternative means. The constitutional exemption provides a form of complete immunity from testifying where proceedings are undertaken or predominately used to obtain evidence for the prosecution of the witness. Together these necessary safeguards provide the parameters within which self-incriminating testimony may be obtained. ...

How do courts decide whether evidence is "derived" from compelled testimony and therefore immune from subsequent use? In *R v S (RJ)*, [1995] 1 SCR 451, 96 CCC (3d) 1, Iacobucci J explained that this immunity extends to

> [191] ... derivative evidence which could not have been obtained, or the significance of which could not have been appreciated, but for the testimony of a witness, ought generally to be excluded under s. 7 of the *Charter* in the interests of trial fairness. Such evidence, although not *created* by the accused and thus not self-incriminatory by definition, is self-incriminatory nonetheless because the evidence could not otherwise have become part of the Crown's case. To this extent, the witness must be protected against assisting the Crown in creating a case to meet.
>
> • • •
>
> [195] ... I have expressed the test for exclusion as involving the question whether evidence could have been obtained but for a witness's testimony. I wish to emphasize that in using the word "could" in this context, I am proposing an inquiry into logical probabilities, not mere possibilities. At some level, all evidence which has independent existence *could* have been located by authorities. The important consideration, however, is whether the evidence, *practically speaking*, could have been located. That is, *would* the evidence, on the facts, have otherwise come to light? Logic must be applied to the facts of each case, not to the mere fact of independent existence.
>
> • • •
>
> [202] Finally, the burden of proof must be considered. In this regard, I see no reason to depart from the general *Charter* rule pursuant to which the party claiming a *Charter* breach must prove that breach on a balance of probabilities. Thus, it should fall to the accused to demonstrate that proposed evidence is derivative evidence deserving of the limited immunity protection I have described. In some circumstances, the disclosure of the Crown's case may help the accused to

realize that evidence was obtained independently, or it may seem obvious that derivative evidence could have been obtained by the Crown in any event: see *Stinchcombe* [*R v Stinchcombe*, [1991] 3 SCR 326].

[203] When this is not true, however, the accused can raise the issue with the trial judge by demonstrating a plausible connection between the proposed evidence and prior testimony. The role of the *voir dire* cannot be avoided. In respect of this burden on the accused, however, it must be recognized that the accused can do little more than point to the plausible connection. As a practical matter, the burden is likely to be borne by the Crown, since it is the Crown which can be expected to know how evidence was, or could have been, obtained. In this regard, the following statement from Sopinka, Lederman and Bryant ... [*The Law of Evidence in Canada* (Toronto: Butterworths, 1992)], at p. 397, regarding the burden under s. 24(2) is apposite:

> [T]he true burden is in practice bound to drift towards the Crown, since many factors in the equation are within the peculiar knowledge of the Crown (e.g., good faith, urgency, availability of other investigative techniques); and, perhaps more important, it is the Crown that is functionally responsible for the maintenance of the administration of justice.

In rare and limited circumstances, compelling testimony would in itself violate s 7. Though the Supreme Court has not been entirely clear on the matter, it is likely that s 7 of the Charter gives compelled witnesses a "constitutional exemption" from testifying when either (1) the predominant purpose of compulsion is to obtain self-incriminating evidence or (2) the compulsion would cause undue prejudice to the witness. Prejudice arises when compulsion would threaten the fairness of any subsequent trial. Though this is less clear, prejudice may also arise from any unjustified harassment, stigmatization, or other abuse that compulsion might create. See *Application Under S 83.28 of the Criminal Code (Re), supra,* at paras 47-54 and 71; *Phillips v Nova Scotia (Commission of Inquiry into the Westray Mine Tragedy),* [1995] 2 SCR 98 at paras 82-86, 98 CCC (3d) 20, per Cory J; *R v Jarvis,* 2002 SCC 73 at para 96, [2002] 3 SCR 757; *British Columbia Securities Commission v Branch,* [1995] 2 SCR 3, 97 CCC (3d) 505 at para 9, Cory J concurring; *Catalyst Fund General Partner I Inc v Hollinger Inc* (2005), 255 DLR (4th) 233 (Ont Sup Ct J), aff'd (2005), 79 OR (3d) 70, 261 DLR (4th) 591 (CA).

A finding of prejudice, however, will not always merit a constitutional exemption. In cases where the concern is adverse publicity, for example, courts most often award less drastic remedies, such as ordering a ban on publication to avoid influencing future jurors. See *Phillips, supra,* at paras 34-35, per L'Heureux-Dubé J, and at para 134, per Cory J. If a court finds, however, that a witness who has already been compelled to testify at previous proceedings should have been exempted from doing so, then ordinarily it will stay the proceedings. See *R v Liakas* (2000), 144 CCC (3d) 359 at para 42 (Qc CA); *R v Z (L)* (2001), 54 OR (3d) 97, 43 CR (5th) 133 at para 44, 155 CCC (3d) 152 (CA).

PROBLEM (R v GALLOWAY)

Evaluate the admissibility of the following items of evidence:

1. As noted previously, Martin Galloway is a chiropractor. He is employed by a company that owns a number of clinics that operate in retail malls. Within weeks of the homicide, police are very suspicious of Martin, but they lack solid evidence. Police are

desperate for hard evidence that they can then use to obtain a warrant to begin intercepting Martin's telephone conversations in order to begin building a case against him. To that end, they attend at his place of employment while he is off work. They speak with the manager of the location, as well as a chiropractor who is working that day and who shares an office with Martin. Both consent to the police looking through the desk that Martin shares. In a drawer that Martin uses, police locate a manila envelope. Inside it, they find a notebook. The book contains poetry in handwriting (the manager identifies the handwriting as Martin's). Many of the poems are flowery testaments to the writer's love for a woman named "Margaret." Is the poem book admissible at trial? (If you have taken a course on criminal procedure, consider whether the police conduct in obtaining the notebook violated Galloway's rights under s 8 of the Charter. If you have not taken a course on criminal procedure, you may assume a violation of the Charter.)

2. It will be remembered that Martin Galloway cooperated with the police and gave three separate statements, initially on April 5 and then again on April 18 and June 2, 2016. Although during the first two statements, police were clearly suspicious of Martin, it was still early and they had no hard evidence; at that point, they still did not know about the affair with Margaret Jenkins. By the third statement, however, the police knew about Margaret and had begun to focus their investigative efforts on securing evidence incriminating Martin in the hope of arresting him and charging him with murder in his wife's death. Despite this, when police interviewed Martin on June 2, 2016, they continued to actively represent to him that they were still looking for the perpetrator and gave no hint that, by that point in time, they firmly believed the perpetrator was Martin. Accordingly, the police did not give Martin any sort of caution before interviewing him on June 2, including not apprising Martin of his rights to remain silent and to retain and instruct counsel. At the end of that third and final interview, Martin was permitted to leave. He was arrested over six months later, in December 2016. Is Martin's June 2, 2016 statement admissible at his trial?

3. Imagine that at trial Martin chooses to testify. However, the jury, despite deliberating for five days, is unable to reach a verdict and a mistrial is declared. The Crown believes that Martin's evidence at the first trial actually harmed his case, and that he did not hold up well under cross-examination. At the retrial, is the Crown entitled to introduce into evidence a transcript of Martin's evidence from the first trial?

Privilege and Related Issues

Privilege protects information from disclosure in court, despite that information being relevant and probative. Privileges generally operate to enable people to speak and write with complete candour and openness in certain relationships, secure in the knowledge that the recipient of the communication cannot be compelled to disclose it even in legal proceedings. The classic example is the privilege associated with obtaining legal advice. The Supreme Court of Canada explained the rationale for this privilege in *R v Cunningham*, 2010 SCC 10, [2010] 1 SCR 331:

> [26] … It need hardly be said that solicitor–client privilege is a fundamental tenet of our legal system. The solicitor–client relationship is integral to the administration of justice; privilege encourages the free and full disclosure by the client required to ensure effective legal representation.

Unlike the many other rules of evidence designed to prevent error by excluding information that may be unreliable, the exclusion of privileged evidence represents an acknowledgement by the legal system that truth is not an absolute value; indeed, in the realm of privilege, the law asserts that the pursuit of truth in a specific case is less important than other interests. In this chapter we explore those "other interests" and the structure of analysis required any time a claim for privilege is made. It is vital to bear in mind that any privilege from disclosure operates as an exception to the primary and countervailing principle that "[t]he public has the right to every person's evidence. That is the general rule." (*R v National Post*, 2010 SCC 16, [2010] 1 SCR 477 at 1.)

There are several privileges in evidence law. We begin with the privilege between a lawyer and his or her client, which we refer to as *solicitor–client privilege*, or *legal advice privilege*. Despite its ancient pedigree and a settled understanding of when it attaches and when the client has waived it, there are several contemporary Supreme Court of Canada decisions. These cases have brought controversy and clarity. Most controversial is the court's steady march toward constitutional fortification of solicitor–client privilege. Further, the few permitted exceptions, explained below, are successfully invoked only in rare cases. With respect to clarity, the court provided welcome guidance on the distinction between solicitor–client privilege and *litigation privilege* (sometimes called *work product* or *lawyer's brief* privilege), a topic beset with confusion despite being critical to the day-to-day work of litigation counsel. We now know that litigation privilege serves different goals from solicitor–client privilege and has other crucial differences: it comes into existence only with the anticipation of litigation, it encompasses communication from persons other than the client, and, unlike solicitor–client privilege, it dies with the litigation. While litigation is in play, however, a given communication may be protected under both types of privilege and it is important to properly identify each.

Popular culture depictions notwithstanding, confidential communications between doctors and patients, journalists and sources, and religious advisers and those seeking solace are *not* presumptively inadmissible under common law rules of evidence. The starting point is quite the opposite: anyone with relevant information can be compelled to testify and to answer any relevant question. This makes eminent sense given the goal of ascertaining the truth. Privilege represents an extraordinary exception, and this chapter explores why the law accommodates it; we also look at why the law is more solicitous of the relationship between lawyers and clients than other relationships in which confidential information passes. Finally, despite dizzying overlap, the concepts of confidentiality and privilege are distinct. For example, while a lawyer is ethically bound to keep *all information* about his or her client confidential, regardless of how that information is obtained, only *communication* between a lawyer and client regarding legal advice attracts solicitor–client privilege.

The first step in analyzing a claim is to determine whether the type of communication is recognized as a "class" privilege or a "case-by-case" privilege. Class privilege is insensitive to the facts of the particular case (*National Post*, above, at 42), whereas case-by-case privilege is dependent on the particular facts. In this chapter we examine class privileges before we turn to case-by-case privileges. The Supreme Court of Canada distinguished the two types of privilege in *R v McClure*, 2001 SCC 14, [2001] 1 SCR 445 at paras 26-29:

> [26] The law recognizes a number of communications as worthy of confidentiality. The protection of these communications serves a public interest and they are generally referred to as privileged.
>
> [27] There are currently two recognized categories of privilege: relationships that are protected by a "class privilege" and relationships that are not protected by a class privilege but may still be protected on a "case-by-case" basis. See *R v. Gruenke*, [1991] 3 SCR 263, Lamer CJ, at p. 286, for a description of "class privilege":

The parties have tended to distinguish between two categories: a "blanket," *prima facie*, common law, or "class" privilege on the one hand, and a "case-by-case" privilege on the other. The first four terms are used to refer to a privilege which was recognized at common law and one for which there is a *prima facie* presumption of inadmissibility (once it has been established that the relationship fits within the class) unless the party urging admission can show why the communications should *not* be privileged (i.e., why they should be admitted into evidence as an exception to the general rule). Such communications are excluded not because the evidence is not relevant, but rather because, there are overriding policy reasons to exclude this relevant evidence. Solicitor–client communications appear to fall within this first category ... . [Emphasis in original.]

[28] For a relationship to be protected by a class privilege, thereby warranting a *prima facie* presumption of inadmissibility, the relationship must fall within a traditionally protected class. Solicitor–client privilege, because of its unique position in our legal fabric, is the most notable example of a class privilege. Other examples of class privileges are spousal privilege (now codified in s. 4(3) of the *Canada Evidence Act*, RSC 1985, c. C-5) and informer privilege (which is a subset of public interest immunity).

[29] Other confidential relationships are not protected by a class privilege, but may be protected on a case-by-case basis. Examples of such relationships include doctor–patient, psychologist–patient, journalist–informant and religious communications. The Wigmore test, containing four criteria, has come to govern the circumstances under which privilege is extended to certain communications that are not traditionally-recognized class privileges (Wigmore, [*Evidence In Trials at Common Law*, vol 8, McNaughton Revision (Toronto: Little, Brown, 1961)] at p. 527):

(1) The communications must originate in a confidence that they will not be disclosed.

(2) This element of confidentiality must be essential to the full and satisfactory maintenance of the relation between the parties.

(3) The relation must be one which in the opinion of the community ought to be sedulously fostered.

(4) The injury that would inure to the relation by the disclosure of the communications must be greater than the benefit thereby gained for the correct disposal of litigation. [Emphasis deleted.]

Sections I through VI of this chapter deal with several recognized privileges: solicitor–client privilege and its exceptions, litigation privilege, dispute settlement privilege, informer privilege, public interest immunity, and the privilege for matrimonial communications. Section VII examines the Supreme Court's approach to recognizing new claims of privilege and the application of the Wigmore criteria above. Section VIII considers a relatively new form of protection, less stringent than a privilege but similarly motivated, for records in which a third party to criminal proceedings has a privacy interest, typically the therapeutic records of a complainant witness in a sexual assault trial. The chapter concludes with an examination of the Supreme Court decision in *Juman v Doucette*, 2008 SCC 8, [2008] 1 SCR 157, which holds that parties in civil matters are *deemed* to undertake to keep confidential any information obtained during pre-trial or the discovery process until it is admitted into evidence in open court. There are limited exceptions to this "deemed undertaking rule" and codifications can be found in the rules of civil procedure in different jurisdictions.

I. SOLICITOR–CLIENT PRIVILEGE

A. Requirements of Solicitor–Client Privilege

Solicitor–client privilege is perhaps the highest and certainly the best-recognized privilege in the Anglo-American legal system. The requirements for this class privilege are from Wigmore, above, and are set out in *Solosky v R*, [1980] 1 SCR 821. The communication must: (1) be between a solicitor (this category includes the agents of a solicitor—for example, articling clerks or secretaries—who are not lawyers themselves) and client; (2) entail the seeking or giving of legal advice; and (3) be intended to be confidential (at 837). It is important to stress that the privilege is not merely for legal advice per se, but for all communications "engaged in for the purpose of enabling the client to communicate and obtain the necessary information or advice in relation to his or her conduct, decisions or representation in the courts" (*Maranda v Richer*, 2003 SCC 67, [2003] 3 SCR 193 at para 30). As stated by the court in *Pritchard v Ontario (Human Rights Commission)*, 2004 SCC 31, [2004] 1 SCR 809, excerpted below:

> [16] Generally, solicitor–client privilege will apply as long as the communication falls within the usual and ordinary scope of the professional relationship. The privilege, once established, is considerably broad and all-encompassing. In *Descôteaux v. Mierzwinski*, [1982] 1 S.C.R. 860, the scope of the privilege was described, at p. 893, as attaching "to all communications made within the framework of the solicitor–client relationship, which arises as soon as the potential client takes the first steps, and consequently even before the formal retainer is established." The scope of the privilege does not extend to communications: (1) where legal advice is not sought or offered; (2) where it is not intended to be confidential; or (3) that have the purpose of furthering unlawful conduct: see *Solosky*, *supra*, at p. 835.

The burden of establishing this privilege is on the claiming party. That said, if these conditions are met, privilege attaches, whether or not it is claimed: see *Lavallee, Rackel & Heintz v Canada (Attorney General)*, 2002 SCC 61, [2002] 3 SCR 209 at para 39. *Pritchard*, above, correctly notes that no privilege attaches to communications in furtherance of unlawful conduct. Cases, however, often refer to the unlawful conduct issue as an "exception" and we address it under Section I.D, after we have outlined the parameters of the privilege.

The Supreme Court has held that there is a presumption that lawyers' bills are *prima facie* privileged and the onus lies on the party seeking disclosure to prove that production would not violate the confidentiality of the relationship: *Maranda v Richer*, above, at para 33. However, non-payment of fees is not necessarily privileged. In *Cunningham*, above, the court explained:

> [29] Counsel seeking to withdraw for non-payment of legal fees is a decidedly different context from a police search of counsel's accounts and records. The most significant difference is the content of the information being disclosed. The only information revealed by counsel seeking to withdraw is the sliver of information that the accused has not paid or will not be paying fees. It has not been explained how, in this case, this sliver of information could be prejudicial to the accused. Indeed, it is hard to see how this simple fact alone could be used against the accused on the merits of the criminal proceeding: it is unrelated to the information given by the client to the lawyer, and unrelated to the advice given by the lawyer to the client. It would not be possible to infer from the bare fact of non-payment of fees any particular activities of the accused that pertain to the criminal charges against him.

[30] To be sure, this is the case where non-payment of fees is not linked to the merits of the matter and disclosure of non-payment will not cause prejudice to the accused. However, in other legal contexts, payment or non-payment of fees may be relevant to the merits of the case, for example, in a family law dispute where support payments are at issue and a client is alleging inability to pay. Or disclosure of non-payment of fees may cause prejudice to the client, for example, where the opposing party may be prompted to bring a motion for security for costs after finding out that the other party is unable to pay its legal fees. Where payment or non-payment of fees is relevant to the merits of the case, or disclosure of such information may cause prejudice to the client, solicitor–client privilege may attach.

[31] Disclosure of non-payment of fees in cases where it is unrelated to the merits and will not cause prejudice to the accused is not an exception to privilege, such as the innocence at stake or public safety exceptions … . Rather, non-payment of legal fees in this context does not attract the protection of solicitor–client privilege in the first place. However, nothing in these reasons, which address the application, or non-application, of solicitor–client privilege in disclosures to a court, should be taken as affecting counsel's ethical duty of confidentiality with respect to payment or non-payment of fees in other contexts.

B. Waiver

Evidence that meets the requirements of privilege is inadmissible (barring an exception), unless the holder of the privilege *waives* his or her right to non-disclosure of the communication. The burden of establishing waiver lies on the party asserting it. Waiver may be express or implied by conduct that is inconsistent with keeping a matter privileged. A client may wish to waive only part of a privileged communication, but this is subject to careful review; if fairness requires that the balance of related communication be disclosed, courts will order it.

Normally, sharing advice with a third party constitutes waiver, because it is inconsistent with the intention of keeping communication confidential. An important exception to the rules on waiver of solicitor–client privilege (and of litigation privilege, discussed in the next section) arises when the clients of two or more separate lawyers have a *common interest* in keeping shared advice on litigation or potential litigation confidential. Obviously, clients share information only when it is in their interest to do so. This takes place typically when the clients face a common adversary, with respect to whom they are confronting the same or a similar litigation issue. This exception to waiver was first recognized by Lord Denning in *Buttes Gas and Oil Co v Hammer (No 3)*, [1980] 3 All ER 475 (Eng CA). In his inimitable phrasing Lord Denning explained (at 483-84):

> There is a privilege which may be called a "common interest" privilege. That is a privilege in aid of anticipated litigation in which several persons have a common interest. It often happens in litigation that a plaintiff or defendant has other persons standing alongside him—who have the self-same interest as he—and who have consulted lawyers on the self-same points as he—but these others have not been made parties to the action. Maybe for economy or for simplicity or what you will. All exchange counsel's opinions. All collect information for the purpose of litigation. All make copies. All await the outcome with the same anxious anticipation—because it affects each as much as it does the others. Instances come readily to mind. Owners of adjoining houses complain of a nuisance which affects them both equally. Both take legal advice. Both exchange relevant documents. But only one is a plaintiff. An author writes a book and gets it published. It

is said to contain a libel or to be an infringement of copyright. Both author and publisher take legal advice. Both exchange documents. But only one is made a defendant.

In all such cases I think the courts should—for the purposes of discovery—treat all the persons interested as if they were partners in a single firm or departments in a single company. Each can avail himself of the privilege in aid of litigation. Each can collect information for the use of his or the other's legal adviser. Each can hold originals and each make copies. And so forth. All are the subject of the privilege in aid of anticipated litigation, even though it should transpire that, when the litigation is afterwards commenced, only one of them is made a party to it. No matter that one has the originals and the other has the copies. All are privileged.

Parties involved in litigation will often create a "common interest privilege agreement" to memorialize their intentions and govern their conduct regarding the sharing of information. While there is considerable appellate and trial case law on the topic of common interest privilege, there is no contemporary discussion by the Supreme Court of Canada, apart from a brief rejection of it applying to the facts in *Pritchard*, below. Professor Dodek has criticized the court's treatment of common interest privilege in *Pritchard* in *Solicitor–Client Privilege* (Markham, Ont: LexisNexis, 2014) at 247-50. He argues that the court confused this privilege with the concept of "joint privilege"; that is, the situation where two parties share one lawyer. As you read *Pritchard*, try to identify what might be wrong about the common interest exception to waiver discussion. Professor Dodek is also critical of emerging lower court cases that extend common interest privilege to the commercial transaction (that is, non-litigation) context in which parties to a deal may exchange legal opinions to support positions they take in negotiations (*Solicitor–Client Privilege*, above, at 250-53).

Inadvertent disclosure, once treated as constituting a "waiver" permitting subsequent use of the communication by a third party, is now more likely to be seen for the human error it is. The consequences of mistaken disclosure are the subject of debate, but before solicitor–client privileged communications will be admitted as evidence, a court will need to be satisfied that what is being sought to be proved by the communication is important to the outcome of the case, and that there is no reasonable alternative form of evidence that can serve the same purpose. Consider the detailed discussion and survey of the cases in *Metcalfe v Metcalfe*, 2001 MBCA 35, and the discussion of counsel's recklessness in *Canada (National Revenue) v Thornton*, 2012 FC 1313.

C. From Rule of Evidence to Substantive Law to Constitutional Protection

In a series of important cases, summarized and excerpted here, the Supreme Court of Canada defends a nearly absolute protection for solicitor–client privilege. Historically, this privilege was conceived as a rule of evidence. It has now evolved into a substantive principle of law, conceived as essential to the effective functioning of a constitutional democracy. As a rule of evidence, it is triggered only in a legal proceeding and precludes admission; as a substantive principle, it applies whenever it is threatened and, once cloaked in constitutional clothes as a principle of fundamental justice, triumphs over any lesser interest. The shift from rule of evidence to rule of substantive law was accomplished in *Descôteaux v Mierzwinski*, [1982] 1 SCR 860, in which the court held that the special status of solicitor–client privilege must be taken into account in interpreting legislation that might have an impact on the privilege (at 875):

It would, I think, be useful for us to formulate this substantive rule, as the judges formerly did with the rule of evidence; it could, in my view, be stated as follows:

1. The confidentiality of communications between solicitor and client may be raised in any circumstances where such communications are likely to be disclosed without the client's consent.

2. Unless the law provides otherwise, when and to the extent that the legitimate exercise of a right would interfere with another person's right to have his communications with his lawyer kept confidential, the resulting conflict should be resolved in favour of protecting the confidentiality.

3. When the law gives someone the authority to do something which, in the circumstances of the case, might interfere with that confidentiality, the decision to do so and the choice of means of exercising that authority should be determined with a view to not interfering with it except to the extent absolutely necessary in order to achieve the ends sought by the enabling legislation.

4. Acts providing otherwise in situations under paragraph 2 and enabling legislation referred to in paragraph 3 must be interpreted restrictively.

In *Foster Wheeler Power Co v Société intermunicipale de gestion et d'élimination des déchets (SIGED) inc*, 2004 SCC 18, [2004] 1 SCR 456, LeBel J explains why the substantive principle is critical to the effective operation of a just legal order, applicable to both criminal and civil matters, and in common and civil law jurisdictions:

[34] Although the relevant jurisprudence consists for the most part of criminal law cases, it still clearly establishes the fundamental importance of solicitor–client privilege as an evidentiary rule, a civil right of supreme importance and a principle of fundamental justice in Canadian law that serves to both protect the essential interests of clients and ensure the smooth operation of Canada's legal system ... . The lawyer's obligation of confidentiality is necessary to preserve the fundamental relationship of trust between lawyers and clients. Protecting the integrity of this relationship is itself recognized as indispensable to the continued existence and effective operation of Canada's legal system. It ensures that clients are represented effectively and that the legal information required for that purpose can be communicated in a full and frank manner ... .

In *McClure*, above, the court reaffirmed the centrality of solicitor–client privilege to the legal system, rejecting the claim that it is merely of instrumental value, and distinguishing it from other claims of confidentiality—for example, doctor–patient, psychologist–patient, journalist–informant, and religious communications relationships—and then continued:

[31] The foregoing privileges, such as communication between a doctor and his patient, do not occupy the unique position of solicitor–client privilege or resonate with the same concerns. This privilege, by itself, commands a unique status within the legal system. The important relationship between a client and his or her lawyer stretches beyond the parties and is integral to the workings of the legal system itself. The solicitor–client relationship is a part of that system, not ancillary to it. See *Gruenke*, [[1991] 3 SCR 263], *per* Lamer CJ, at p. 289:

The *prima facie* protection for solicitor–client communications is based on the fact that the relationship and the communications between solicitor and client are essential to the effective operation of the legal system. Such communications are inextricably linked with the very system which desires the disclosure of the communication (see: *Geffen v. Goodman Estate*, ... , and *Solosky v. The Queen*, [[1980] 1 SCR 821]). In my view, religious communications, notwithstanding their social importance, are not inextricably linked with the justice system in the way that solicitor–client communications surely are.

It is this distinctive status within the justice system that characterizes the solicitor–client privilege as a class privilege, and the protection is available to all who fall within the class. ...

[33] The importance of solicitor–client privilege to both the legal system and society as a whole assists in determining whether and in what circumstances the privilege should yield to an individual's right to make full answer and defence. The law is complex. Lawyers have a unique role. Free and candid communication between the lawyer and client protects the legal rights of the citizen. It is essential for the lawyer to know all of the facts of the client's position. The existence of a fundamental right to privilege between the two encourages disclosure within the confines of the relationship. The danger in eroding solicitor–client privilege is the potential to stifle communication between the lawyer and client. The need to protect the privilege determines its immunity to attack.

While acknowledging exceptions to the rule, explored below in Section I.D, the court stressed that these are narrowly defined (*McClure*, at para 35): "Solicitor–client privilege must be as close to absolute as possible to ensure public confidence and retain relevance. As such, it will only yield in certain clearly defined circumstances, and does not involve a balancing of interests on a case-by-case basis." The court refers to its prior holdings as "categorical jurisprudence" and stated "[a]bsolute necessity is as restrictive a test as may be formulated short of an absolute prohibition": *Goodis v Ontario (Ministry of Correctional Services)*, 2006 SCC 31, [2006] 2 SCR 32 at para 20. See also *Ontario (Public Safety and Security) v Criminal Lawyers' Association*, 2010 SCC 23, [2010] 1 SCR 815 at para 53: "[S]olicitor–client privilege ... has been held to be all but absolute in recognition of the high public interest in maintaining the confidentiality of the solicitor–client relationship."

A perfect illustration of this heightened commitment to privilege can be seen in decisions that show the Supreme Court of Canada's treatment of laws that permit searches of lawyers' offices. In 2002, in *Lavallee*, above, the court struck down s 488.1 of the *Criminal Code*, which created a procedure for the issuance of a warrant to search a lawyer's office and seize documents. Section 488.1 violated the requirement in s 8 of the Charter that search and seizures be reasonable because the provisions permitted loss of the privilege without the client's knowledge or authorization. Recall that only the client can waive privilege. The majority opinion explained that the criminal context of the matter was important in assessing whether the Charter was violated:

[23] In the context of a criminal investigation, the privilege acquires an additional dimension. The individual privilege holder is facing the state as a "singular antagonist" and for that reason requires an arsenal of constitutionally guaranteed rights (*Irwin Toy Ltd. v. Quebec (Attorney General)*, [1989] 1 S.C.R. 927, at p. 994). It is particularly when a person is the target of a criminal investigation that the need for the full protection of the privilege is activated. It is then not an abstract proposition but a live issue of ensuring that the privilege delivers on the promise of confidentiality that it holds.

[24] It is critical to emphasize here that all information protected by the solicitor–client privilege is out of reach for the state. It cannot be forcibly discovered or disclosed and it is inadmissible

in court. It is the privilege of the client and the lawyer acts as a gatekeeper, ethically bound to protect the privileged information that belongs to his or her client. Therefore, any privileged information acquired by the state without the consent of the privilege holder is information that the state is not entitled to as a rule of fundamental justice.

The majority then concluded that the provisions failed to pass constitutional muster because of the impact on solicitor–client privilege:

> [39] While I think it unnecessary to revisit the numerous statements of this Court on the nature and primacy of solicitor–client privilege in Canadian law, it bears repeating that the privilege belongs to the client and can only be asserted or waived by the client or through his or her informed consent … . In my view, the failings of s. 488.1 identified in numerous judicial decisions and described above all share one principal, fatal feature, namely, the potential breach of solicitor–client privilege without the client's knowledge, let alone consent. The fact that competent counsel will attempt to ascertain the whereabouts of their clients and will likely assert blanket privilege at the outset does not obviate the state's duty to ensure sufficient protection of the rights of the privilege holder. Privilege does not come into being by an assertion of a privilege claim; it exists independently. By the operation of s. 488.1, however, this constitutionally protected right can be violated by the mere failure of counsel to act, without instruction from or indeed communication with the client. Thus, s. 488.1 allows the solicitor–client confidentiality to be destroyed without the client's express and informed authorization, and even without the client's having an opportunity to be heard.
>
> [40] … [U]nder this statutory scheme, reasonable opportunity has to be provided to the privilege keeper, but not to the privilege holder, to ensure that the privileged information remains so. This positive obligation on counsel shifts the burden of guaranteeing the respect for *Charter* rights from the state to the lawyer. I stress here that I am making no adverse assumption about the competence, professionalism and integrity of lawyers. However, in the context of searches of law offices, it cannot simply be assumed that the lawyer is the *alter ego* of the client. The solicitor–client relationship may have been terminated long before the search. This of course does not displace the duty of loyalty owed by the solicitor to the client. But law office searches may place lawyers in a conflict of interest with their clients, or may place them in conflict regarding their ongoing duties to several present and former clients. I cannot see how s. 488.1(8), limited as it is, can raise this entire procedural scheme to a standard of constitutional reasonableness when it fails to address directly the entitlement that the privilege holder, the client, should have to ensure the adequate protection of his or her rights. Indeed, because of the complete lack of notification provisions within the s. 488.1 scheme, the client may not even be aware that his or her privilege is threatened.

In the absence of any new legislation to replace s 488.1, searches of law offices are now governed by detailed principles, set out at paragraph 49 of *Lavallee*:

1. No search warrant can be issued with regards to documents that are known to be protected by solicitor–client privilege.

2. Before searching a law office, the investigative authorities must satisfy the issuing justice that there exists no other reasonable alternative to the search.

3. When allowing a law office to be searched, the issuing justice must be rigorously demanding so to afford maximum protection of solicitor–client confidentiality.

4. Except when the warrant specifically authorizes the immediate examination, copying and seizure of an identified document, all documents in possession of a lawyer must be sealed before being examined or removed from the lawyer's possession.

5. Every effort must be made to contact the lawyer and the client at the time of the execution of the search warrant. Where the lawyer or the client cannot be contacted, a representative of the Bar should be allowed to oversee the sealing and seizure of documents.

6. The investigative officer executing the warrant should report to the justice of the peace the efforts made to contact all potential privilege holders, who should then be given a reasonable opportunity to assert a claim of privilege and, if that claim is contested, to have the issue judicially decided.

7. If notification of potential privilege holders is not possible, the lawyer who had custody of the documents seized, or another lawyer appointed either by the Law Society or by the court, should examine the documents to determine whether a claim of privilege should be asserted, and should be given a reasonable opportunity to do so.

8. The Attorney General may make submissions on the issue of privilege, but should not be permitted to inspect the documents beforehand. The prosecuting authority can only inspect the documents if and when it is determined by a judge that the documents are not privileged.

9. Where sealed documents are found not to be privileged, they may be used in the normal course of the investigation.

10. Where documents are found to be privileged, they are to be returned immediately to the holder of the privilege, or to a person designated by the court.

In 2015, the court returned to this issue in *Canada (Attorney General) v Federation of Law Societies of Canada*, 2015 SCC 7, [2015] 1 SCR 401 and applied the above common law principles to provisions of the *Proceeds of Crime (Money Laundering) and Terrorist Financing Act*, SC 2000, c 17 and accompanying regulations. The court found unjustifiable violations of both ss 7 and 8 of the Charter. The complex scheme of that Act required lawyers to collect, record, and retain material, including information verifying the identity of those on whose behalf they pay or receive money (excluding transactions such as fees and disbursements). This material could then be subject to search and seizure by the oversight agency, the Financial Transactions and Reports Analysis Centre of Canada (FINTRAC). Fines and penal sanctions could be imposed for non-compliance, triggering both ss 7 and 8 of the Charter. Unlike with *Lavallee*, however, the provisions were not in the *Criminal Code*. The issue was whether this made a difference. The court concluded that it did not, and in doing so extended further constitutional protection for solicitor–client privilege:

> [37] I accept, of course, that when a search provision is part of a regulatory scheme, the target's reasonable expectation of privacy may be reduced .... However, I do not accept the Attorney General's contention that this scheme may be properly characterized as "an administrative law regulatory compliance regime" .... Its purposes, as stated in the Act and indeed as described by the Attorney General in his submissions, are to detect and deter the criminal offences of money laundering and terrorist financing and to facilitate the investigation and prosecution of these

serious offences: s. 3(a). The regime imposes penal sanctions on lawyers for non-compliance. It therefore has a predominantly criminal law character and its regulatory aspects serve criminal law purposes.

[38] ... However, the reasonable expectation of privacy in relation to communications subject to solicitor–client privilege is invariably high, regardless of the context. The main driver of that elevated expectation of privacy is the specially protected nature of the solicitor–client relationship, not the context in which the state seeks to intrude into that specially protected zone. I do not accept the proposition that there is a reduced expectation of privacy in relation to solicitor–client privileged communication when a FINTRAC official searches a law office rather than when a police officer does so in the course of investigating a possible criminal offence. While Arbour J. placed her analysis in the context of criminal investigations (see, e.g., paras. 25 and 49), her reasons, as have many others before and since, strongly affirmed the fundamental importance of solicitor–client privilege. ...

[39] I see no basis for thinking that solicitor–client communications should be more vulnerable to non-consensual disclosure in the course of a search and seizure by FINTRAC officials than they would be in the course of any other search by other law enforcement authorities.

[40] The Attorney General submits that the information here is sought in aid of monitoring the lawyer's activities, not the client's and that there is protection against derivative use. But these factors are entitled to little weight here. ... The Act on its face purports to give the authorized person licence to troll through vast amounts of information in the possession of lawyers. As the intervener Criminal Lawyers' Association fairly put it, the Act gives authorized persons the power "to roam at large within law offices, and ... to examine and seize any record or data found therein" .... The exercise of these powers in relation to records in possession of lawyers creates a very high risk that solicitor–client privilege will be lost.

The law's failure to properly protect solicitor–client privilege drove the court's reasoning on both ss 7 and 8. The court was unanimous on the s 8 violation. A majority held that "the lawyer's duty of commitment to the client's cause" was a principle of fundamental justice under s 7 and that the Act violated that principle. With respect to this newly identified principle of fundamental justice, the majority stated:

[81] The duty of lawyers to avoid conflicting interests is at the heart of both the general legal framework defining the fiduciary duties of lawyers to their clients and of the ethical principles governing lawyers' professional conduct. This duty aims to avoid two types of risks of harm to clients: the risk of misuse of confidential information and the risk of impairment of the lawyer's representation of the client (see, e.g., *Canadian National Railway Co. v. McKercher LLP*, 2013 SCC 39, [2013] 2 S.C.R. 649, at para 23).

[82] The Court has recognized that aspects of these fiduciary and ethical duties have a constitutional dimension. I have already discussed at length one important example. The centrality to the administration of justice of preventing misuse of the client's confidential information, reflected in solicitor–client privilege, led the Court to conclude that the privilege required constitutional protection in the context of law office searches and seizures: see *Lavallee*. Solicitor–client privilege is "essential to the effective operation of the legal system": *R. v. Gruenke*, [1991] 3 S.C.R. 263, at p. 289. As Major J. put it in *R. v. McClure*, 2001 SCC 14, [2001] 1 S.C.R. 445, at para. 31: "The important relationship between a client and his or her lawyer stretches beyond the parties and is <u>integral to the workings of the legal system itself</u>" (emphasis added) [in the original].

[83] The question now is whether another central dimension of the solicitor–client relationship—the lawyer's duty of commitment to the client's cause—also requires some measure of constitutional protection against government intrusion. In my view it does, for many of the same reasons that support constitutional protection for solicitor–client privilege. "The law is a complex web of interests, relationships and rules. The integrity of the administration of justice depends upon the unique role of the solicitor who provides legal advice to clients within this complex system": *McClure*, at para. 2. These words, written in the context of solicitor–client privilege, are equally apt to describe the centrality to the administration of justice of the lawyer's duty of commitment" to the client's cause. A client must be able to place "unrestricted and unbounded confidence" in his or her lawyer; that confidence which is at the core of the solicitor–client relationship is a part of the legal system itself, not merely ancillary to it: *Smith v. Jones*, [1999] 1 S.C.R. 455, at para. 45, citing with approval, *Anderson v. Bank of British Columbia* (1876), 2 Ch. D. 644 (C.A.); *McClure*. The lawyer's duty of commitment to the client's cause, along with the protection of the client's confidences, is central to the lawyer's role in the administration of justice.

[84] We should, in my view, recognize as a principle of fundamental justice that the state cannot impose duties on lawyers that undermine their duty of commitment to their clients' causes. Subject to justification being established, it follows that the state cannot deprive someone of life, liberty or security of the person otherwise than in accordance with this principle.

In its four-paragraph opinion, the minority held that s 7 did not include such a duty, but did agree solicitor–client privilege is protected already in ss 7 and 8:

[120] [W]e are inclined to the view that the s. 7 analysis would be better resolved relying on the principle of fundamental justice which recognizes that the lawyer is required to keep the client's confidences—solicitor–client privilege. This duty, as our colleague explains in his discussion of s. 8, has already been recognized as a constitutional norm. We note that in applying the norm of commitment to the client's cause, our colleague relies on breach of solicitor–client privilege. In our view, breach of this principle is sufficient to establish that the potential deprivation of liberty would violate s. 7.

Two cases involving many of these same concerns, and with many of the same intervening organizations, are now before the Supreme Court of Canada, with decisions pending. They involve the search provisions of the *Income Tax Act* as applied to a lawyer's office: *Thompson v Canada (National Revenue)*, 2013 FCA 197, leave to appeal to SCC granted, 2014 CanLII 11038 and *Canada (Procureur général) v Chambre des notaires du Québec*, 2014 QCCA 552, leave to appeal to SCC granted, 2014 CanLII 76801.

In the above cases involving a search of a lawyer's office, any documents over which solicitor–client privilege is claimed must be sealed to preserve privilege until the issue is determined. Another context where sealing is required is when an *ex parte* court order, called an Anton Piller order, is issued by a court. This exceptional order allows one party to a litigation—called the moving party—to search the opposing party's business (or home), without notice, where a court is satisfied by the moving party that the search is required to prevent the destruction of material evidence. Such a surprise search might obviously jeopardize the confidentiality of any solicitor–client communications. The same concern can arise with respect to two other exceptional court orders: *Mareva* injunctions (preventing removal and transfer of assets) and *Norwich* orders (requiring a non-party to participate in aid of a moving party when necessary to the interests of justice). As a result, these orders typically contain protections for solicitor–client privilege. In *Celanese Canada Inc v Murray Demolition Corp*, 2006 SCC 36, [2006] 2 SCR 189, the court held that in the context of an Anton Piller order, if the moving party fails to ensure that privileged communication is protected from improper disclosure, a court has the ability to remove the law firm representing the moving party. Although the remedy of preventing a law firm from continuing to act is severe—it deprives the moving party of its lawyer of choice—it is justified on the basis that, otherwise, there is a risk that the moving party could benefit from the improper disclosure of the opposing party's solicitor-and-client communication.

The Supreme Court of Canada recently addressed a lawyer's obligations regarding solicitor–client privilege and confidentiality when faced with a *Mareva* order against the assets of a client in *Carey v Laiken*, 2015 SCC 17, [2015] 2 SCR 79. Carey, the lawyer, was convicted of contempt of a *Mareva* order obtained by Laiken, with whom Carey's client Sabourin was in a legal dispute. The *Mareva* order prohibited any transfer of Sabourin's assets. Carey was found in contempt for transferring assets to Sabourin after the order was issued. The assets were funds that Sabourin had previously sent to Carey, and that Carey placed in his trust account. Carey argued that the existence of Sabourin's funds in his trust account attracted solicitor–client privilege, and that made it impossible for him to comply with the *Mareva* order, or to seek advice from the court. The court held that Carey could have fulfilled both of his duties (to his client and to the court issuing the *Mareva* order) by simply leaving the funds in the trust account. The court criticized Carey's decision to act unilaterally: Carey could have moved on an *ex parte* and *in camera* basis to obtain a determination about whether the existence of the funds in trust was covered by solicitor–client privilege, and he could have sought a variation of the order or direction from the issuing court.

The case that follows illustrates how different aspects of the law on solicitor–client privilege are applied in a particular fact situation to specific documents and communications. Bear in mind that many lawyers work for public or private entities as government or in-house counsel rather than in the traditional legal setting of a law office, and regardless of where they work, many lawyers provide business or policy advice in addition to legal advice. As a result of this, an issue that arises is whether or not a particular lawyer's communication to a client–employer is "legal advice" or something else. When the communication does not entail the provision of legal advice, privilege does not attach.

Pritchard v Ontario (Human Rights Commission)
2004 SCC 31, [2004] 1 SCR 809
Iacobucci, Major, Bastarache, Binnie, LeBel, Deschamps, and Fish JJ
(14 May 2004)

MAJOR J:

I. Introduction

[1] The appellant, Ms. Colleen Pritchard, filed a human rights complaint with the respondent Ontario Human Rights Commission, against her former employer Sears Canada Inc., alleging gender discrimination, sexual harassment and reprisal. The Commission

decided, pursuant to s. 34(1)(b) of the Ontario *Human Rights Code*, RSO 1990, c. H.19 ("Code"), not to deal with her complaint. The appellant sought judicial review and brought a motion for production of all documents that were before the Commission when it made its decision, including a legal opinion provided to the Commission by in-house counsel.

. . .

V. *Issues*

[13]   The sole issue in this appeal is whether the Court of Appeal erred in overturning the decision of the motions judge ordering production of the legal opinion. The question is whether a legal opinion, prepared for the Ontario Human Rights Commission by its in-house counsel, is protected by solicitor–client privilege in the same way as it is privileged if prepared by outside counsel retained for that purpose.

VI. *Analysis*

A. *Solicitor–Client Privilege Defined*

[The court referred to the case law summarized above and then considered its application to the case at bar.]

[19]   Solicitor–client privilege has been held to arise when in-house government lawyers provide legal advice to their client, a government agency: see *R. v. Campbell*, [1999] 1 SCR 565, at para. 49. In *Campbell*, the appellant police officers sought access to the legal advice provided to the RCMP by the Department of Justice and on which the RCMP claimed to have placed good faith reliance. In identifying solicitor–client privilege as it applies to government lawyers, Binnie J compared the function of public lawyers in government agencies with corporate in-house counsel. He explained that where government lawyers give legal advice to a "client department" that traditionally would engage solicitor–client privilege, and the privilege would apply. However, like corporate lawyers who also may give advice in an executive or non-legal capacity, where government lawyers give policy advice outside the realm of their legal responsibilities, such advice is not protected by the privilege.

[20]   Owing to the nature of the work of in-house counsel, often having both legal and non-legal responsibilities, each situation must be assessed on a case-by-case basis to determine if the circumstances were such that the privilege arose. Whether or not the privilege will attach depends on the nature of the relationship, the subject matter of the advice, and the circumstances in which it is sought and rendered: *Campbell*, *supra*, at para. 50.

[21]   Where solicitor–client privilege is found, it applies to a broad range of communications between lawyer and client as outlined above. It will apply with equal force in the context of advice given to an administrative board by in-house counsel as it does to advice given in the realm of private law. If an in-house lawyer is conveying advice that would be characterized as privileged, the fact that he or she is "in-house" does not remove the privilege, or change its nature.

B. *The Common Interest Exception*

[22]   The appellant submitted that solicitor–client privilege does not attach to communications between a solicitor and client as against persons having a "joint interest"

with the client in the subject-matter of the communication. This "common interest," or "joint interest" exception does not apply to the Commission because it does not share an interest with the parties before it. The Commission is a disinterested gatekeeper for human rights complaints and, by definition, does not have a stake in the outcome of any claim.

[23] The common interest exception to solicitor–client privilege arose in the context of two parties jointly consulting one solicitor. See *R. v. Dunbar* (1982), 138 D.L.R. (3d) 221 (Ont. C.A.), *per* Martin J.A., at p. 245:

> The authorities are clear that where two or more persons, each having an interest in some matter, jointly consult a solicitor, their confidential communications with the solicitor, although known to each other, are privileged against the outside world. However, as between themselves, each party is expected to share in and be privy to all communications passing between each of them and their solicitor. Consequently, should any controversy or dispute arise between them, the privilege is inapplicable, and either party may demand disclosure of the communication … .

[24] The common interest exception originated in the context of parties sharing a common goal or seeking a common outcome, a "selfsame interest" as Lord Denning, M.R., described it in *Buttes Gas & Oil Co. v. Hammer (No. 3)*, [1980] 3 All E.R. 475 (C.A.), at p. 483. It has since been narrowly expanded to cover those situations in which a fiduciary or like duty has been found to exist between the parties so as to create common interest. These include trustee–beneficiary relations, fiduciary aspects of Crown–aboriginal relations and certain types of contractual or agency relations, none of which are at issue here.

[25] The Commission neither has a trust relationship with, nor owes a fiduciary duty to, the parties appearing before it. The Commission is a statutory decision-maker. The cases relied on by the appellant related to trusts, fiduciary duty, and contractual obligations. These cases are readily distinguishable and do not support the position advanced by the appellant. The common interest exception does not apply to an administrative board with respect to the parties before it.

· · ·

C. Application to the Case at Bar

[27] As stated, the communication between the Commission and its in-house counsel was protected by solicitor–client privilege.

[28] The opinion provided to the Commission by staff counsel was a *legal opinion*. It was provided to the Commission by in-house or "staff" counsel to be considered or not considered at their discretion. It is a communication that falls within the class of communications protected by solicitor–client privilege. The fact that it was provided by in-house counsel does not alter the nature of the communication or the privilege.

[29] There is no applicable exception that can remove the communication from the privileged class. There is no common interest between this Commission and the parties before it that could justify disclosure; nor is this Court prepared to create a new common law exception on these facts.

· · ·

[31] Procedural fairness does not require the disclosure of a privileged legal opinion. Procedural fairness is required both in the trial process and in the administrative law context. In neither area does it affect solicitor–client privilege; both may co-exist without

being at the expense of the other. In addition, the appellant was aware of the case to be met without production of the legal opinion. The concept of fairness permeates all aspects of the justice system, and important to it is the principle of solicitor–client privilege.

. . .

[33] Legislation purporting to limit or deny solicitor–client privilege will be interpreted restrictively: see *Lavallee*, [2002 SCC 61, [2002] 3 SCR 209], at para. 18. Solicitor–client privilege cannot be abrogated by inference. While administrative boards have the delegated authority to determine their own procedure, the exercise of that authority must be in accordance with natural justice and the common law.

[34] Where the legislature has mandated that the record must be provided in whole to the parties in respect of a proceeding within its legislative competence and it specifies that the "whole of the record" includes opinions provided to the administrative board, then privilege will not arise as there is no expectation of confidentiality. Beyond that, whether solicitor–client privilege can be violated by the express intention of the legislature is a controversial matter that does not arise in this appeal.

NOTES AND QUESTIONS

1. Is the solicitous regard for solicitor–client privilege a little much? Are there disadvantages to society that are not being acknowledged? Is there a danger with overprotection given that the legal profession is self-regulated? Does the privilege serve to insulate lawyers from ethical reflection with respect to their own or their client's conduct? Do you think this is in the public interest? For excellent and provocative analysis of these and related issues, see Adam M Dodek, "Reconceiving Solicitor–Client Privilege" (2010) 35 Queen's LJ 493 and "Solicitor–Client Privilege in Canada: Challenges for the 21st Century" (February 2011), A Discussion Paper for the Canadian Bar Association, online: <http://www.cba.org/CBA/activities/pdf/Dodek-English.pdf>.

2. *Canada (Privacy Commissioner) v Blood Tribe Department of Health*, 2008 SCC 44, [2008] 2 SCR 574 offers a further example of the principle, stated above, that privilege cannot be abrogated by statutory inference. In this case, the court rejected the assertion by the federal privacy commissioner that she had statutory authority to review a privileged document to decide whether the government's assertion of privilege was valid. The court held that the power to review a privileged document was derived from the power to adjudicate disputed claims over legal rights. That power was not within the mandate of the privacy commissioner, despite express statutory authority to compel production of any records "in the same manner and to the same extent as a superior court of record" and to "receive and accept any evidence and other information ... whether or not it is or would be admissible in a court of law." This language does *not* grant a statutory right to the administrative investigator to review documents even for the limited purpose of determining whether solicitor–client privilege is properly claimed. The reasoning in *Blood Tribe* is applicable to all statutory administrative investigators. It is oft-cited and debated. The *Blood Tribe ratio*, and its relationship to modern principles of interpretation, is before the Supreme Court of Canada in *University of Calgary v JR*, 2015 ABCA 118, leave to appeal to SCC granted, 2015 CanLII 69443.

3. *Ontario (Public Safety and Security) v Criminal Lawyers' Association*, 2010 SCC 23, [2010] 1 SCR 815 affords an example of the way in which legislation is interpreted so as to protect solicitor–client communications from disclosure, even in the face of a claim to freedom of

expression under s 2(b) of the Charter. The court held (at para 31, emphasis added): "We conclude that the scope of the s. 2(b) protection includes a right to access to documents only where access is necessary to permit meaningful discussion on a matter of public importance, *subject to privileges* and functional constraints." The interplay between the constitutional right to freedom of expression and the common law rules of privilege was explained:

> [39] Privileges are recognized as appropriate derogations from the scope of the protection offered by s. 2(b) of the Charter. The common law privileges, like solicitor–client privilege, gener-ally represent situations where the public interest in confidentiality outweighs the interests served by disclosure. This is also the rationale behind common law privileges that have been cast in statutory form, like the privilege relating to confidences of the Queen's Privy Council under s. 39 of the *Canada Evidence Act*, RSC 1985, c. C-5. Since the common law and statutes must conform to the Charter, assertions of particular categories of privilege are in principle open to constitu-tional challenge. However, in practice, the outlines of these privileges are likely to be well-settled, providing predictability and certainty to what must be produced and what remains protected.

4. The Supreme Court of Canada has yet to decide whether a statute can expressly limit solicitor–client privilege and survive *constitutional* attack. *Blood Tribe*, above, makes clear that it can do so as a matter of statutory power. Recall, however, that in *Pritchard*, excerpted above, the court stated (at para 34): "whether solicitor–client privilege can be violated by the express intention of the legislature is a controversial matter that does not arise in this appeal." The constitutional point may be determined soon, in one of the above-noted pending cases involving searches of lawyers' offices. That case arises under the *Income Tax Act*, sections of which define solicitor–client privilege more narrowly than the common law: *Canada (Procureur général) v Chambre des notaires du Québec*, 2014 QCCA 552, leave to appeal to SCC granted, 2014 CanLII 76801.

5. In the criminal system, Crown counsel decide whether to approve charges laid by the police. Is this decision one that attracts privilege? In *British Columbia (Attorney General v Davies)*, 2009 BCCA 337, the court decided that charging decisions made by Crown counsel are not covered by solicitor–client privilege—that is, they are not made within any solicitor–client relationship, but "as an officer of the Crown, independently exercising prosecutorial discretion."

6. The Supreme Court of Canada in *Pritchard*, above, referred to its earlier decision in *R v Campbell*, [1999] 1 SCR 565. *Campbell* illustrates neatly the concept of waiver. The accused argued that he had been entrapped by the police. If so, that could afford a defence to the charges. Counsel for the Crown asserted that the officers involved had good faith reliance on a legal opinion by Crown counsel before undertaking the reverse sting operation. The court readily concluded that solicitor–client privilege attached to the opinion of the Department of Justice lawyer, Mr. Leising, but found that the assertion of good faith reliance on the opin-ion in defence to a claim of entrapment constituted a waiver:

> [70] … [I]t is not always necessary for the client actually to disclose part of the contents of the advice in order to waive privilege to the relevant communications of which it forms a part. It was sufficient in this case for the RCMP to support its good faith argument by undisclosed advice from legal counsel in circumstances where, as here, the existence or non-existence of the as-serted good faith depended on the content of that legal advice. The clear implication sought to be conveyed to the court by the RCMP was that Mr. Leising's advice had assured the RCMP that the proposed reverse sting was legal.

7. For an example of a case where *Campbell* was distinguished on the facts, see *R v Ruti-gliano*, 2015 ONCA 452. In *Goodswimmer v Canada (Attorney General)*, 2015 ABCA 253, the court held that the position taken by the Indian Band plaintiff concerning a treaty agreement constituted an implied waiver over solicitor–client communications. Excellent discussion of the cases and complexity surrounding waiver and privilege, and the importance of clarifying the "legal" versus "business" roles of counsel in offering advice to clients, is afforded in Adam M Dodek, *Solicitor–Client Privilege* (Markham, Ont: LexisNexis, 2014) and Sheila Block & Lynn Iding, "Privilege in Civil Cases Revisited" in *Law Society of Upper Canada Special Lectures 2003: The Law of Evidence* (Toronto: Irwin Law, 2004) at 219-49. For a further example of waiver, see *Foster Wheeler*, above, at paras 48-49.

8. In *Foster Wheeler*, above, the Supreme Court of Canada considered the extensive legis-lative protection in Quebec for professional secrecy and the obligation of confidentiality that attaches to many professionals, including lawyers. It held that in resolving conflicts over solicitor–client privilege under Quebec law (and by analogy in other provinces) decision-makers begin with a rebuttable presumption that the communication is covered when there is a relationship between a solicitor and client. That said, it is also critical to understand that not every fact reported in a solicitor–client relationship falls under the rubric of a communi-cation in furtherance of legal advice; the lawyer is not a shield behind which the client's actions can be immune from reporting:

> [38] … It would be inaccurate to reduce the content of the obligation of confidentiality to opinions, advice or counsel given by lawyers to their clients. While this is, on many occasions, the main goal in creating a professional relationship with a lawyer, it is often the case that this rela-tionship can also entail some highly diverse activities, such as representing clients before various tribunals or administrative bodies, negotiating or drawing up contracts, preparing reports, filling out various forms and having discussions with members of governing bodies of public entities or private corporations. In the course of carrying out these mandates, lawyers receive and send out a wide range of information. Some of these activities, such as the filing of pleadings or rep-resenting a client in court, pose few difficulties because of their public nature. However, when the professional relationship arises out of a complex and prolonged mandate, as in the case at bar, the limits of the scope of application of the obligation of confidentiality can sometimes only be arrived at after the court has taken a close look at the relationship between the parties, includ-ing the nature and context of the professional services rendered.

> [39] Despite the intense nature of the obligation of confidentiality and the importance of professional secrecy, not all facts and events that lawyers deal with in the execution of their mandates are covered by professional secrecy, nor does the legal institution of professional secrecy exempt lawyers from testifying about facts involving their clients in all situations. To illustrate, let us take the case of a lawyer who holds discussions with a client while riding as a passenger in the client's car. In the event of an accident, the lawyer would not be competent to testify about the opinion he or she was giving the client at the time of the incident, but could be forced to answer questions regarding whether the car was travelling above the speed limit. We must use an analyti-cal method that upholds professional secrecy while allowing us to resolve difficulties of this sort.

> [40] It is unrealistic to expect that we could set absolutely clear and simple rules and tests that would leave trial courts with no margin of uncertainty or individual discretion in such matters. Solutions will vary and must be tailored to the circumstances of a case. In the case of an individ-ual professional act, the person claiming professional secrecy would without doubt need only

simple or summary evidence to show the confidentiality of the information sought and his or her right to immunity from disclosure. The burden of proof can thus be placed on the professional without compromising the exercise and integrity of the institution.

[41] In the case of complicated and prolonged mandates, the obligation of justifying each case as one where confidentiality and, by extension, immunity from judicial disclosure apply is poorly adapted to the nature of professional relationships and the safeguards required to maintain secrecy in an effective manner. ...

[42] In such cases, a different method would be preferable. It would be enough to have the party invoking professional secrecy establish that a general mandate had been given to a lawyer for the purpose of obtaining a range of services generally expected of a lawyer in his or her professional capacity. At this stage, there would be a presumption of fact, albeit a rebuttable one, to the effect that all communications between client and lawyer and the information they shared would be considered *prima facie* confidential in nature. ... The opposing party would then have to give a specific indication of the nature of the information sought and show that it is subject neither to the obligation of confidentiality nor to immunity from disclosure, or that this is a case where the law authorizes disclosure notwithstanding professional secrecy. This method would have procedural consequences. The opposing party would be obliged to ask precise and limited questions about the information sought. This sort of question would better take into account the sensitive nature of any line of questioning regarding professional relationships between clients and lawyers and the need to minimize violations of professional secrecy. This would prevent "fishing expeditions" in which lawyers, through the files they handle and reports they prepare for their clients, are used as a source of information for building cases against their own clients. One would also hope that every effort would first be made to obtain the information from available sources other than lawyers. A sound judicial policy, mindful of the social importance of lawyers' professional secrecy and the need to protect it, should certainly not attempt to facilitate this sort of questioning, but rather restrain it as much as possible.

D. Exceptions to Solicitor–Client Privilege

If the communication is protected by solicitor–client privilege, the next stage of analysis is to determine whether there is an exception that permits disclosure. Three exceptions predominate—(1) criminal purpose, (2) public safety, and (3) innocence at stake. The first is really not actually an exception because privilege does not attach to communications in service of crime or fraud, but it is convenient to discuss it here. The latter two are true exceptions: they apply even when, in Wigmore's words, "legal advice of any kind is sought from a professional legal adviser in his capacity as such" and confidentiality has been promised or expected.

1. Facilitating a Criminal Purpose

Legal advice must be "lawful" to attract protection: *R v McClure*, 2001 SCC 14, [2001] 1 SCR 445, 151 CCC (3d) 321 at para 37. If the client seeks legal advice to commit a crime or fraud, that same advice can be used against the client. The most frequently cited case on this point remains *Descôteaux v Mierzwinski*, above. The Supreme Court of Canada there held that where an individual lies about her financial state in order to obtain legal aid, she is committing a crime and therefore privilege cannot attach to statements that constitute the *actus reus* of the offence (at 881):

Confidential communications, whether they relate to financial means or to the legal problem it-self, lose that character if and to the extent that they were made for the purpose of obtaining legal advice to facilitate the commission of a crime.

The same is true *a fortiori* where, as in the case at bar, the communication itself is the material element (*actus reus*) of the crime; this is all the more evident where the victim of the crime is precisely the office of the lawyer to whom the communication was made.

The explanation for the exception in *R v Cox and Railton* (1884), 14 QBD 153 was cited with approval (*ibid*, emphasis added in *Descôteaux*):

The reason on which the rule is said to rest cannot include the case of communications, *criminal in themselves*, or intended to further any criminal purpose, for the protection of such communi-cations cannot possibly be otherwise than injurious to the interests of justice, and to those of the administration of justice. Nor do such communications fall within the terms of the rule.

In *R v Campbell*, above, Binnie J stated in *obiter* that had the privilege not been waived, he would have been inclined to order production of the legal opinion regarding entrapment on the basis that it may have counselled a criminal act:

[62] … In my view, destruction of the privilege takes more than evidence of the existence of a crime and proof of an anterior consultation with a lawyer. There must be something to suggest that the advice facilitated the crime or that the lawyer otherwise became a "dupe or conspirator." The evidence of Cpl. Reynolds does not establish such things, but the formal position of the Crown, with the support of the RCMP, goes beyond his evidence. The RCMP position before the Court was that the decision to proceed with the reverse sting had been taken with the participation and agreement of the Department of Justice. By adopting this position, the RCMP belatedly brought itself within the "future crimes" exception, and put in question the continued existence of its privilege.

[63] If there had been no waiver of privilege by the RCMP in this case, I would have taken the view that any papers documenting the legal advice (or, if there was no contemporaneous docu-mentation, an affidavit setting out the content of the relevant advice) ought to be provided in the first instance to the trial judge. If he or she were satisfied, either on the basis of the docu-ments themselves or on the basis of the documents supplemented by other evidence, that the documented advice could be fairly said in some way to have facilitated the crime, the documents would then be provided to the appellants. If the lawyer had merely advised about the legality of the operation, and thereby made himself neither dupe nor conspirator in the facilitation of a crime, the proper course would have been to return the papers to the RCMP.

QUESTION

Should the criminal-purpose exception be expanded to cases where the client seeks legal advice to facilitate the commission of a civil wrong, such as an intentional tort? See *Dublin v Montessori Jewish Day School of Toronto* (2007), 281 DLR (4th) 366 (Ont Sup Ct J); *Goldman, Sachs & Co v Sessions* (1999), 38 CPC (4th) 143 (BCSC); and the comprehensive discussion in Dodek, *Solicitor–Client Privilege*, above, at 54-64. What about a violation of the deemed undertaking rule (see Section IX, below)? Consider the discussion in *Brome Financial Corpor-ation Inc v Bank of Montreal*, 2013 ONSC 6834.

PROBLEM

An accused is charged with sexual assault. He hires a defence attorney. Prior to the trial for sexual assault, two acquaintances of the accused meet with the accused's defence attorney and they offer statements regarding the events on the night of the sexual assault. The defence attorney makes notes of those conversations. At the preliminary inquiry on the sexual assault, these two acquaintances testify that the accused pressured them into making false statements to the accused's defence attorney. The Crown charges the accused with obstruction of justice, and seeks production of the defence attorney's notes. Does the criminal purpose exception apply? See *R v Swearengan* (2003), 68 OR (3d) 24 (Sup Ct J).

2. Public Safety

Unlike the criminal-purpose exception, the public-safety exception aims at preventing a serious crime from happening by allowing a lawyer to warn an identifiable person about a specific threat posed by a client. This is a limited disclosure—the scope is determined by the threat itself. All law societies also address the right of a lawyer to disclose to protect against the imminent risk of death or serious bodily harm.

Smith v Jones
[1999] 1 SCR 455, 169 DLR (4th) 385
Lamer CJC and L'Heureux-Dubé, Gonthier, Cory, McLachlin, Iacobucci,
Major, Bastarache, and Binnie JJ (25 March 1999)

I. *Introduction*

MAJOR J (Lamer CJC and Binnie JJ concurring) (dissenting):

[1] I agree with Justice Cory's summation of the facts giving rise to this appeal and with his conclusion that the confidentiality of the solicitor–client privilege must, in exceptional circumstances of public safety, yield to the public good.

[2] The point of departure arises in the restriction each of us places on the scope of disclosure.

[3] In my opinion a limited exception which does not include conscriptive evidence against the accused would address the immediate concern for public safety in this appeal while respecting the importance of the privilege. I do not read Cory J's reasons as imposing that limitation.

[4] This approach will in my view foster a climate in which dangerous individuals are more likely to disclose their disorders, seek treatment and pose less danger to the public. ...

. . .

CORY J (L'Heureux-Dubé, Gonthier, McLachlin, Iacobucci, and Bastarache JJ concurring):

[35] The solicitor–client privilege permits a client to talk freely to his or her lawyer secure in the knowledge that the words and documents which fall within the scope of the

privilege will not be disclosed. It has long been recognized that this principle is of fundamental importance to the administration of justice and to the extent it is feasible, it should be maintained. Yet when public safety is involved and death or serious bodily harm is imminent, the privilege should be set aside. This appeal must determine what circumstances and factors should be considered and weighed in determining whether solicitor–client privilege should be set aside in the interest of protecting the safety of the public.

I. Factual Background

[36] Solicitor–client privilege is claimed for a doctor's report. Pending the resolution of that claim the names of the parties involved have been replaced by pseudonyms. The appellant, "James Jones," was charged with aggravated sexual assault of a prostitute. His counsel referred him to a psychiatrist, the respondent, "John Smith," for a forensic psychiatric assessment. It was hoped that it would be of assistance in the preparation of the defence or with submissions on sentencing in the event of a guilty plea. His counsel advised Mr. Jones that the consultation was privileged in the same way as a consultation with him would be. Dr. Smith interviewed Mr. Jones for 90 minutes on July 30, 1997. His findings are contained in an affidavit he submitted to the judge of first instance. They set out the basis for his belief that Mr. Jones poses a continuing danger to the public.

[37] Dr. Smith reported that Mr. Jones described in considerable detail his plan for the crime to which he subsequently pled guilty. It involved deliberately choosing as a victim a small prostitute who could be readily overwhelmed. He planned to have sex with her and then to kidnap her. He took duct tape and rope with him, as well as a small blue ball that he tried to force into the woman's mouth. Because he planned to kill her after the sexual assault he made no attempt to hide his identity.

[38] Mr. Jones planned to strangle the victim and to dispose of her body in the bush area near Hope, British Columbia. He was going to shoot the woman in the face before burying her to impede identification. He had arranged time off from his work and had carefully prepared his basement apartment to facilitate his planned sexual assault and murder. He had told people he would be going away on vacation so that no one would visit him and he had fixed dead bolts on all the doors so that a key alone would not open them.

[39] Mr. Jones told Dr. Smith that his first victim would be a "trial run" to see if he could "live with" what he had done. If he could, he planned to seek out similar victims. He stated that, by the time he had kidnapped his first victim, he expected that he would be "in so deep" that he would have no choice but to carry out his plans.

[40] On July 31, Dr. Smith telephoned Mr. Jones's counsel and informed him that in his opinion Mr. Jones was a dangerous individual who would, more likely than not, commit future offences unless he received sufficient treatment.

[41] On September 24, 1997, Mr. Jones pled guilty to aggravated assault and the matter was put over for sentencing. Sometime after November 19, Dr. Smith phoned Mr. Jones's counsel to inquire about the proceedings. On learning that the judge would not be advised of his concerns, Dr. Smith indicated that he intended to seek legal advice and shortly thereafter commenced this action.

[42] The *in camera* hearing took place in December 1997. Dr. Smith filed an affidavit describing his interview with Mr. Jones and his opinion based upon the interview. Mr. Jones

filed an affidavit in response. On December 12, 1997, Henderson J ruled that the public safety exception to the law of solicitor–client privilege and doctor-patient confidentiality released Dr. Smith from his duties of confidentiality. He went on to rule that Dr. Smith was under a duty to disclose to the police and the Crown both the statements made by Mr. Jones and his opinion based upon them. Henderson J ordered a stay of his order to allow for an appeal and Mr. Jones promptly appealed the decision.

[43] The Court of Appeal allowed the appeal but only to the extent that the mandatory order was changed to one permitting Dr. Smith to disclose the information to the Crown and police. The order was stayed to permit Mr. Jones to consider a further appeal. It also directed that pseudonyms be used, that proceedings be heard *in camera* and that the file remain sealed pending further order. This order is discussed in greater detail below. The sentencing of Mr. Jones on the aggravated assault charge was adjourned pending the outcome of this appeal.

II. Analysis

A. The Nature of the Solicitor–Client Privilege

[44] Both parties made their submissions on the basis that the psychiatrist's report was protected by solicitor–client privilege, and it should be considered on that basis. It is the highest privilege recognized by the courts. By necessary implication, if a public safety exception applies to solicitor–client privilege, it applies to all classifications of privileges and duties of confidentiality. It follows that, in these reasons, it is not necessary to consider any distinctions that may exist between a solicitor–client privilege and a litigation privilege.

[45] The solicitor–client privilege has long been regarded as fundamentally important to our judicial system. Well over a century ago in *Anderson v. Bank of British Columbia* (1876), 2 Ch. D 644 (CA), at p. 649, the importance of the rule was recognized:

> The object and meaning of the rule is this; that as, by reason of the complexity and difficulty of our law, litigation can only be properly conducted by professional men, it is absolutely necessary that a man, in order to prosecute his rights or to defend himself from an improper claim, should have recourse to the assistance of professional lawyers, ... to use a vulgar phrase, that he should be able to make a clean breast of it to the gentleman whom he consults with a view to the prosecution of his claim, or the substantiating of his defence ... that he should be able to place unrestricted and unbounded confidence in the professional agent, and that the communications he so makes to him should be kept secret, unless with his consent (for it is his privilege, and not the privilege of the confidential agent), that he should be enabled properly to conduct his litigation.

[46] Clients seeking advice must be able to speak freely to their lawyers secure in the knowledge that what they say will not be divulged without their consent. It cannot be forgotten that the privilege is that of the client, not the lawyer. The privilege is essential if sound legal advice is to be given in every field. It has a deep significance in almost every situation where legal advice is sought whether it be with regard to corporate and commercial transactions, to family relationships, to civil litigation or to criminal charges. Family secrets, company secrets, personal foibles and indiscretions all must on occasion be revealed to the lawyer by the client. Without this privilege clients could never be candid and furnish all the relevant information that must be provided to lawyers if they are to

properly advise their clients. It is an element that is both integral and extremely important to the functioning of the legal system. It is because of the fundamental importance of the privilege that the onus properly rests upon those seeking to set aside the privilege to justify taking such a significant step.

[Cory J briefly reviewed three limitations on solicitor–client privilege—innocence of the accused, criminal communications, and public safety—and continued:]

C. The Public Safety Exception and Solicitor–Client Privilege

[74] The foregoing review makes it clear that even the fundamentally important right to confidentiality is not absolute in doctor-patient relationships, and it cannot be absolute in solicitor–client relationships: *Solosky, supra*. When the interest in the protection of the innocent accused and the safety of members of the public is engaged, the privilege will have to be balanced against these other compelling public needs. In rare circumstances, these public interests may be so compelling that the privilege must be displaced. Yet the right to privacy in a solicitor–client relationship is so fundamentally important that only a compelling public interest may justify setting aside solicitor–client privilege.

[75] Danger to public safety can, in appropriate circumstances, provide the requisite justification. It is significant that public safety exceptions to the solicitor–client privilege are recognized by all professional legal bodies within Canada. See, for example, Chapter 5, s. 12, of the British Columbia *Professional Conduct Handbook*:

> **Disclosure to prevent a crime**
>
> 12. A lawyer may disclose information received as a result of a solicitor–client relation-
> ship if the lawyer has reasonable grounds to believe that the disclosure is necessary to prevent
> a crime involving death or serious bodily harm to any person.

See as well the even broader Rule 4.11 of the Law Society of Upper Canada's *Professional Conduct Handbook*.

[76] Quite simply society recognizes that the safety of the public is of such importance that in appropriate circumstances it will warrant setting aside solicitor–client privilege. What factors should be taken into consideration in determining whether that privilege should be displaced?

(1) Determining When Public Safety Outweighs Solicitor–Client Privilege

[77] There are three factors to be considered: First, is there a clear risk to an identifiable person or group of persons? Second, is there a risk of serious bodily harm or death? Third, is the danger imminent? Clearly if the risk is imminent, the danger is serious.

[78] These factors will often overlap and vary in their importance and significance. The weight to be attached to each will vary with the circumstances presented by each case, but they all must be considered. As well, each factor is composed of various aspects, and, like the factors themselves, these aspects may overlap and the weight to be given to them will vary depending on the circumstances of each case. Yet as a general rule, if the privilege is to be set aside the court must find that there is an imminent risk of serious bodily harm or death to an identifiable person or group.

(a) Clarity

[79] What should be considered in determining if there is a clear risk to an identifiable group or person? It will be appropriate and relevant to consider the answers a particular case may provide to the following questions: Is there evidence of long range planning? Has a method for effecting the specific attack been suggested? Is there a prior history of violence or threats of violence? Are the prior assaults or threats of violence similar to that which was planned? If there is a history of violence, has the violence increased in severity? Is the violence directed to an identifiable person or group of persons? This is not an all-encompassing list. It is important to note, however, that as a general rule a group or person must be ascertainable. The requisite specificity of that identification will vary depending on the other factors discussed here.

[80] The specific questions to be considered under this heading will vary with the particular circumstances of each case. Great significance might, in some situations, be given to the particularly clear identification of a particular individual or group of intended victims. Even if the group of intended victims is large considerable significance can be given to the threat if the identification of the group is clear and forceful. For example, a threat, put forward with chilling detail, to kill or seriously injure children five years of age and under would have to be given very careful consideration. In certain circumstances it might be that a threat of death directed toward single women living in apartment buildings could in combination with other factors be sufficient in the particular circumstances to justify setting aside the privilege. At the same time, a general threat of death or violence directed to everyone in a city or community, or anyone with whom the person may come into contact, may be too vague to warrant setting aside the privilege. However, if the threatened harm to the members of the public was particularly compelling, extremely serious and imminent, it might well be appropriate to lift the privilege. See in this regard *Egdell, supra.* All the surrounding circumstances will have to be taken into consideration in every case.

[81] In sum, the threatened group may be large but if it is clearly identifiable then it is a factor—indeed an essential factor—that must be considered together with others in determining whether the solicitor–client privilege should be set aside. A test that requires that the class of victim be ascertainable allows the trial judge sufficient flexibility to determine whether the public safety exception has been made out.

(b) Seriousness

[82] The "seriousness" factor requires that the threat be such that the intended victim is in danger of being killed or of suffering serious bodily harm. Many persons involved in criminal justice proceedings will have committed prior crimes or may be planning to commit crimes in the future. The disclosure of planned future crimes without an element of violence would be an insufficient reason to set aside solicitor–client privilege because of fears for public safety. For the public safety interest to be of sufficient importance to displace solicitor–client privilege, the threat must be to occasion serious bodily harm or death.

[83] It should be observed that serious psychological harm may constitute serious bodily harm, as this Court held in *R v. McCraw*, [1991] 3 SCR 72, at p. 81:

So long as the psychological harm substantially interferes with the health or well-being of the complainant, it properly comes within the scope of the phrase "serious bodily harm." There can be no doubt that psychological harm may often be more pervasive and permanent in its effect than any physical harm.

(c) Imminence

[84] The risk of serious bodily harm or death must be imminent if solicitor–client communications are to be disclosed. That is, the risk itself must be serious: a serious risk of serious bodily harm. The nature of the threat must be such that it creates a sense of urgency. This sense of urgency may be applicable to some time in the future. Depending on the seriousness and clarity of the threat, it will not always be necessary to impose a particular time limit on the risk. It is sufficient if there is a clear and imminent threat of serious bodily harm to an identifiable group, and if this threat is made in such a manner that a sense of urgency is created. A statement made in a fleeting fit of anger will usually be insufficient to disturb the solicitor–client privilege. On the other hand, imminence as a factor may be satisfied if a person makes a clear threat to kill someone that he vows to carry out three years hence when he is released from prison. If that threat is made with such chilling intensity and graphic detail that a reasonable bystander would be convinced that the killing would be carried out the threat could be considered to be imminent. Imminence, like the other two criteria, must be defined in the context of each situation.

[85] In summary, solicitor–client privilege should only be set aside in situations where the facts raise real concerns that an identifiable individual or group is in imminent danger of death or serious bodily harm. The facts must be carefully considered to determine whether the three factors of seriousness, clarity, and imminence indicate that the privilege cannot be maintained. Different weights will be given to each factor in any particular case. If after considering all appropriate factors it is determined that the threat to public safety outweighs the need to preserve solicitor–client privilege, then the privilege must be set aside. When it is, the disclosure should be limited so that it includes only the information necessary to protect public safety. See in this respect *Descôteaux, supra*, at p. 891.

(2) Extent of Disclosure

[86] The disclosure of the privileged communication should generally be limited as much as possible. The judge setting aside the solicitor–client privilege should strive to strictly limit disclosure to those aspects of the report or document which indicate that there is an imminent risk of serious bodily harm or death to an identifiable person or group. In undertaking this task consideration should be given to those portions of the report which refer to the risk of serious harm to an identifiable group; that the risk is serious in that it involves a danger of death or serious bodily harm; and that the serious risk is imminent in the sense given to that word in para. 84 above. The requirement that the disclosure be limited must be emphasized. For example, if a report contained references to criminal behaviour that did not have an imminent risk of serious bodily harm but disclosed, for example, the commission of crimes of fraud, counterfeiting or the sale of stolen goods, those references would necessarily be deleted.

D. Application of the Public Safety Exception to Solicitor–Client Privilege to the Case at Bar

(1) Clarity

[87] Would a reasonable observer, given all the facts for which solicitor–client privilege is sought, consider the potential danger posed by Mr. Jones to be clear, serious, and imminent? The answer must, I think, be in the affirmative. According to Dr. Smith's affidavit, the plan described by Mr. Jones demonstrated a number of the factors that should be considered in determining the clarity of the potential danger. They are the clear identification of the victim group, the specificity of method, the evidence of planning, and the prior attempted or actual acts that mirror the potential act of threatened future harm.

[88] It is apparent that Mr. Jones had planned in considerable detail attacks on prostitutes on Vancouver's Downtown Eastside. He had gathered materials together that he planned to use to achieve his ultimate goal of forcing a prostitute to become his "sex slave" before killing her. He had arranged for vacation time from his job and had modified his basement apartment to ensure that no one else could enter. Mr. Jones had proceeded so far as to take rope and duct tape with him and had planned to shoot the intended victim in the face to obliterate her identity. Perhaps most important, he had called the initial assault to which he pled guilty a "trial run." These factors should be considered together with Dr. Smith's diagnosis of Mr. Jones, namely that he suffered a paraphiliac disorder with multiple paraphilias (in particular, sexual sadism), personality disorder with mixed features, and some antisocial features and drug abuse difficulty. The original planning and the prior attack on a prostitute emphasize the potential risk of serious bodily harm or death to prostitutes in the Downtown Eastside of Vancouver.

[89] Although Mr. Jones attempted to explain his failure to seek treatment for fear of a longer sentence and the danger he would be exposed to in prison, this does not affect the gravity of the threatened attack on prostitutes. The combination of the factors referred to in the paragraph above meets the standard of clarity necessary to set aside solicitor–client privilege. The potential victim or group of victims is identifiable. Mr. Jones had already acted once in committing the crime for which he is waiting to be sentenced. It is clear that he intended to act again. The risk of serious bodily harm or death was readily apparent and the group of victims was readily identifiable. The harm potentially caused was of the utmost gravity.

(2) Seriousness

[90] The seriousness of the potential harm, a sexually sadistic murder, is clearly sufficient. The fact that Mr. Jones has after careful and detailed planning already committed an assault upon a prostitute supports the finding that the potential harm caused would be extremely serious.

(3) Imminence

[91] The most difficult issue to resolve is whether the risk of serious bodily harm can be termed "imminent." Mr. Jones was arrested on September 17, 1996, for the assault he had committed three days earlier. He consulted Dr. Smith on July 30, 1997. Dr. Smith

contacted Mr. Jones's counsel the following day to inform him that, in Dr. Smith's opinion, Mr. Jones was a dangerous individual. About three months later, some 14 months after Mr. Jones's arrest, Dr. Smith telephoned Mr. Jones's counsel again and learned that his (Dr. Smith's) concerns would not be addressed in the sentencing hearing. He then began these legal proceedings. Mr. Jones has been in custody since December 15, 1997, pursuant to the order of Henderson J. Mr. Jones was thus at liberty from September 14, 1996, to December 15, 1997, a period of almost 15 months. During that time he did not carry out his plan to attack and kill another prostitute. Moreover, Mr. Jones has not carried out a series of attacks over a period of time, which would lead to the conclusion that another attack was imminent. He has been charged and convicted of only one incident.

[92] No evidence was adduced as to whether Dr. Smith considered that a future attack was imminent. It is noteworthy that, first, he waited over three months to contact Mr. Jones's counsel. Second, there is no evidence that he believed it was probable Mr. Jones would commit a serious attack in the near future. Yet it must be remembered that Dr. Smith did take it upon himself to call Mr. Jones's counsel regarding the sentencing hearing. Even more significantly, Dr. Smith undertook these proceedings so that his report and opinion might be considered in the sentencing of Mr. Jones.

[93] There are two important factors that indicate that the threat of serious bodily harm was indeed imminent. First, Mr. Jones admitted that he had breached his bail conditions by continuing to visit the Downtown Eastside where he knew prostitutes could be found. Second, common sense would indicate that after Mr. Jones was arrested, and while he was awaiting sentence, he would have been acutely aware of the consequences of his actions. This is of particular significance in light of his fear of being attacked while he was in jail.

[94] Let us assume that the evidence as to imminence of the danger may not be as clear as might be desired. Nonetheless, there is some evidence of imminence. Furthermore, the other factors pertaining to clarity, the identifiable group of victims, and the chilling evidence of careful planning, when taken together, indicate that the solicitor–client privilege must be set aside for the protection of members of the public.

[95] The judge of first instance very properly limited disclosure of Dr. Smith's affidavit to those portions of it which indicated that there was an imminent risk of death or serious bodily harm to an identifiable group comprising prostitutes located in the Downtown Eastside of Vancouver. In light of these conclusions, the solicitor–client privilege attaching to Dr. Smith's report, to the extent provided by the order of Henderson J, must be set aside.

E. Appropriate Procedures to Adopt

[96] Dr. Smith chose to bring a legal action for a declaration that he was entitled to disclose the information he had in his possession in the interests of public safety. However, this is not the only manner in which experts may proceed. Although it is true that this procedure may protect the expert from legal consequences, there may not always be time for such an action. In whatever action is taken by the expert, care should be exercised that only that information which is necessary to alleviate the threat to public safety is revealed.

[97] It is not appropriate in these reasons to consider the precise steps an expert might take to prevent the harm to the public. It is sufficient to observe that it might be appropriate to notify the potential victim or the police or a Crown prosecutor, depending on the specific circumstances.

· · ·

III. Disposition

[105] The file will be unsealed and the ban on the publication of the contents of the file is removed, except for those parts of the affidavit of the doctor which do not fall within the public safety exception. Subject to this direction the order of the British Columbia Court of Appeal is affirmed and this appeal is dismissed without costs.

QUESTIONS

This exception has arisen in only one reported decision, *R v Butt*, 2012 ONSC 4326, a sexual assault sentencing appeal. The lawyer for the accused (who had pleaded guilty) relied on the exception to disclose to the Crown that her client had tested HIV-positive in order for the Crown to advise the parents of the 12-year-old victim so that he could be tested for the illness. The lawyer consulted with senior members of the bar before deciding to disclose. She was commended for "her appreciation of her ethical obligations in this difficult matter" (at para 5). What would you have done in these circumstances?

Should the public safety concerns at issue in *Smith v Jones* be treated as exceptions to the lawyer's duty of confidentiality rather than, or as well as, exceptions to solicitor–client privilege?

3. *Innocence at Stake*

In *R v McClure*, above, the Supreme Court of Canada held that no privilege is absolute; all privileges must give way in a case where there is a danger that an innocent person may be wrongfully convicted. This is called the "innocence at stake" exception and it is procedurally and substantively demanding. In *McClure*, the accused was charged with sexual assault against a number of his former students. The complainant read about the charges, went to a lawyer, then to the police, then to a therapist, and eventually filed a civil suit. The accused sought production of the complainant's litigation file, which of course included solicitor–client communications. The accused asserted that he needed access to the contents of the file "to determine the nature of the allegations first made by the appellant to his solicitor and to assess the extent of the appellant's motive to fabricate or exaggerate the incidents of abuse" (*McClure*, above, at para 8). The court held the claim could be made in principle, but it failed on the facts (at paras 64-65):

> [64] The first stage of the innocence at stake test for solicitor–client privilege was not met. There was no evidence that the information sought by the respondent McClure could raise a reasonable doubt as to his guilt. Even if the chronology of events in this case—i.e. lawyer, police, therapist, civil suit—was unusual, it does not justify overriding solicitor–client privilege. This "unusual" chronology does not rise to a level that demonstrates that the litigation file could raise a reasonable doubt as to guilt and so fails at the first stage.
>
> [65] In addition, the accused would be able to raise the issue of the complainant's motive to fabricate events for the sake of a civil action at trial from another source, simply by pointing out the sequence of events and the fact that a civil action was initiated.

The test set out in *McClure* has been refined and explained in the case that follows. Together, *McClure* and *Brown* make clear that this is an exceptionally difficult exception to establish.

R v Brown
2002 SCC 32, [2002] 2 SCR 185
McLachlin CJ and L'Heureux-Dubé, Gonthier, Iacobucci, Major,
Bastarache, Binnie, Arbour, and LeBel JJ (28 March 2002)

MAJOR J:

I. Introduction

[1] This appeal deals with the application of the test set out in *R v. McClure*, [2001] 1 SCR 445, 2001 SCC 14. It raises again the competing interests of solicitor–client privilege and an accused's right under s. 7 of the *Canadian Charter of Rights and Freedoms* to make full answer and defence. Both are fundamental tenets of our system of justice. In *McClure*, this Court recognized that solicitor–client privilege is not absolute and may, in rare circumstances, be required to yield in order to permit an accused to make full answer and defence to a criminal charge.

[2] While it is impossible to place either right higher on a hierarchy, as these reasons hope to explain, Canadians' abhorrence at the possibility of a faulty conviction tips the balance slightly in favour of innocence at stake over solicitor–client privilege. A similar decision on public policy has been made to protect the identity of informants.

[3] However, it was also emphasized in *McClure*, at para. 5, that "the occasions when the solicitor–client privilege yields are rare and the test to be met is a stringent one." While obvious, the Court reiterated that any erosion of the absolute nature of solicitor–client privilege would of necessity cause some damage to the solicitor–client relationship. *McClure* should be considered as determining that the appropriate test is one of innocence at stake, such that solicitor–client privilege "should be infringed only where core issues going to the guilt of the accused are involved and there is a genuine risk of wrongful conviction" (para. 47). It is intended to be a rare exception and used as a last resort.

[4] The *McClure* test comprises a threshold question and a two-stage innocence at stake test, which proceed as follows:

- To satisfy the threshold test, the accused must establish that:
  - the information he seeks from the solicitor–client communication is not available from any other source; and
  - he is otherwise unable to raise a reasonable doubt.
- If the threshold has been satisfied, the judge should proceed to the innocence at stake test, which has two stages.
  - Stage #1: The accused seeking production of the solicitor–client communication has to demonstrate an evidentiary basis to conclude that a communication exists that could raise a reasonable doubt as to his guilt.
  - Stage #2: If such an evidentiary basis exists, the trial judge should examine the communication to determine whether, in fact, it is likely to raise a reasonable doubt as to the guilt of the accused.
- It is important to distinguish that the burden in the second stage of the innocence at stake test (likely to raise a reasonable doubt) is stricter than that in the first stage (could raise a reasonable doubt).

- If the innocence at stake test is satisfied, the judge should order disclosure of the communications that are likely to raise a reasonable doubt, in accordance with the guiding principles discussed *infra*.

[5] In the present appeal, I respectfully conclude that the motions judge's decision to grant the accused access to materials protected by a third party's solicitor–client privilege was premature. It was not clear at the time that the privileged information was not available from another source. Nor was it clear that the privileged information was necessary for the accused to raise a reasonable doubt. Moreover, as there were indications that the privilege may have been waived by voluntary disclosure, that issue should have been resolved before an infringement of a valid privilege was contemplated. In short, the accused's innocence was not at stake, and the *McClure* application should not have been granted. The appeal is allowed.

II. Facts

[6] At approximately 4:00 a.m. on July 21, 1998, Shaun Baksh was discovered lying on the east side of Barrington Avenue in Toronto. He had been stabbed in the chest and died a short time later at St. Michael's Hospital. The subsequent autopsy confirmed that he had received a single knife wound to the heart.

[7] On August 12, 1998, Donna Robertson told two homicide detectives that her then boyfriend, the appellant, David Benson, had told her that he was the person who had killed Baksh. According to Robertson's account, Benson told her that he had gone out to the fire escape one night when he could not sleep. A man with an accent approached him and offered to sell him drugs. Benson declined, but he persisted and put his arm around Benson. Benson told the man to "back off" and, when he refused, Benson pulled a knife and stabbed him. The man then staggered away through the adjacent park and then west toward Barrington Avenue. Benson threw away the clothes that he was wearing, except for his shoes.

[8] Robertson also told the police that Benson told her that he had confessed to his lawyers, Edward Greenspan, and later Todd Ducharme and Peter Copeland. She said that she had gone with Benson to meet Mr. Copeland, and that he had provided them with business cards on which he wrote words that purported to invoke the right to silence in the face of police questioning. Robertson produced her card to the police.

[9] The police investigated Benson in relation to the homicide for a number of months. The investigation included a consent wiretap of Robertson's home telephone and the interception of her communications with Benson using a body pack. Armed with a search warrant, the police seized clothing, knives and footwear from Benson's residence. All items tested negative for the blood of the deceased. Benson has since denied killing Baksh. Benson was never charged with respect to the murder and the investigation against him was dropped.

[10] The respondent Jason Brown was seen looking for Baksh on the morning that Baksh was killed. Brown was also looking for a mountain bike that he had allegedly fronted to Baksh as part of a drug deal. Witnesses stated that Brown had in his possession a napkin, on which Baksh's pager number was written in red ink. A videotape showed Brown entering his own apartment building, located one block from the crime scene, at 4:47 a.m. on July 21, 1998, less than an hour after Baksh had been found stabbed.

[11] On July 29, 1998, under warrant, the police seized from Brown's apartment, among other things, a napkin with the deceased's pager number on it. Brown entered his apartment during the search and provided a statement to the police in which he denied knowing the deceased, denied knowing anything about a mountain bike, and said that he had been home on the night of the homicide.

[12] On July 31, 1998, with counsel present, Brown gave a second statement to the police. In this statement, he said that he had bought cocaine from the deceased three times on the night and early morning of the homicide. On the third such time, Brown said that he had no money and therefore fronted a stolen mountain bike for more cocaine. Brown wanted the bike back and said that he would bring money later for the cocaine. He denied killing Baksh.

[13] Brown was charged with Baksh's murder on November 1, 1999. Prior to that date, the police claimed to lack reasonable and probable grounds to charge either Benson or Brown with the homicide. Brown's charge came shortly after a jailhouse informant, who had shared a cell with Brown at the Toronto jail in November 1998, reported that he had overheard a conversation between Brown and a third inmate, McDoom. According to the informant, Brown told McDoom that he had purchased drugs from Baksh, stabbed him, and taken a bag of crack cocaine.

[14] Although the informant was called as a witness at the preliminary hearing, the prosecutor has not yet received the approval of the "In-Custody Informer Committee" within the office of the Attorney General to call the informant at trial. The Committee is waiting for the final determination of Brown's *McClure* application and a further determination of whether the Crown may review the material ordered disclosed to Brown in order to assess the reliability of the informant.

[The court held that there was a serious issue as to whether or not Benson waived solicitor–client privilege and that the issue should be decided before the *McClure* application, which is available only as a last resort (at paras 26-28). The court then continued in its analysis and application of *McClure* in this case.]

C. Application to the Case at Bar

(1) The Threshold Test

(a) Is the Information Available from Any Other Source?

· · ·

[32] In the present case, Brown became aware of Benson's alleged confession as a result of Robertson's statement to the police. Thus, strictly speaking, the "information" sought by Brown is available from another source, Robertson's statement. Benson submitted that, because Robertson's statement is known by Brown, the information is available even if it is not admissible at trial. This proposition cannot stand. Of necessity, any *McClure* application will be based on some "information" that a potentially exculpatory third party solicitor–client communication exists. It would be illogical to deny the accused access to the solicitor–client communication solely because he has access to "information" about its existence. The question at this point becomes whether there is alternative information as to the contents of the communication.

[33] Moreover, to jump ahead to the innocence at stake test, it is noteworthy that the first stage requires an accused to provide some evidentiary basis for believing that a privileged communication exists that could exculpate him. This evidentiary basis will invariably consist of information concerning the alleged communication that has come to the attention of the accused.

[34] *McClure* allows for the invasion of solicitor–client privilege when necessary to permit an accused to raise a reasonable doubt about his guilt. Necessity is to be considered in the context of a legal proceeding, and can be demonstrated when the information sought in the solicitor–client communication is not otherwise admissible at trial.

[35] It is clear that "information" in the context of the threshold question in a *McClure* application must mean more than simple knowledge of a fact. A *McClure* application should only succeed on the threshold question if the accused does not have access to other information that will be admissible at trial.

[36] Returning to the present appeal, the Court must determine whether the information sought in this case—Benson's alleged confession—is available from any other source. More specifically, did Brown have access to admissible evidence of Benson's confession from any other source?

[37] The record establishes that Brown had another source of information regarding Benson's confession in the form of Donna Robertson's testimony. However, Dambrot J [the motions judge who heard the application at the Ontario Superior Court of Justice] expressed serious concerns about the admissibility of such testimony and about whether, if admissible, it would be believed at trial. In particular, both Benson and Robertson had been drinking at the time of the alleged confession, and their stormy relationship was apparently coming to an end. Moreover, Benson subsequently denied confessing to Robertson. These factors led Dambrot J to believe that Robertson's testimony might not be admitted under an exception to the hearsay rule and that, even if admitted, there might be significant challenges to the credibility of her testimony.

[38] In contrast, the motions judge believed that Benson's alleged confession to his solicitors rested on better evidentiary footing. While Dambrot J. acknowledged that it was "legally in no different position than his confession to Robertson" ([2001] OJ no. 3408 (QL), at para. 10) in that it too was hearsay, he reasoned that it had a better chance of being admitted and believed due to its enhanced reliability. Benson's confession to his solicitors was not likely to be clouded to the same extent as his confession to Robertson, and the solicitors would have no personal reasons to implicate him in a murder. Moreover, Dambrot J reasonably thought that it would be unusual for a person to lie to his own solicitors by making a false murder confession.

[39] In the end, having interpreted "information" as meaning "potentially substantively usable and reliable evidence" (para. 10), Dambrot J concluded that the privileged information was not otherwise available.

[40] However, with respect, Dambrot J reached this conclusion prematurely. While there are undoubtedly some obstacles to the admission of Donna Robertson's evidence, it is not clear that it will be inadmissible. First, there is a significant degree of necessity to her testimony, in that, absent a successful *McClure* application, it is the only evidence of Benson's confession, which may exculpate the accused. Second, it may be considered sufficiently reliable to be admitted under an exception to the hearsay rule.

[41] Finally, there is some potential that the confession to Robertson may be admissible as a declaration against penal interest. ...

. . .

[43] In any event, these observations are not intended to comment on the validity of any of the above arguments regarding the admissibility of Donna Robertson's evidence. They are only raised to indicate that the inadmissibility of Robertson's testimony should not be considered a foregone conclusion.

[44] Indeed, if a trial judge allows a *McClure* application on the basis that another source of the requested information is *potentially* inadmissible at trial, she runs the risk of her conclusion being subsequently undermined if the alternative source is ultimately found to be admissible. The accused will then have gained access to solicitor–client privileged information in a situation where that information was, in fact, available from another source, and will have succeeded in unnecessarily destroying a solicitor–client privilege. Such a result directly conflicts with the stringent nature of the innocence at stake test, which seeks to maximize the protection for the privilege.

[45] In this case, Dambrot J ought to have held a *voir dire* to determine the admissibility of Donna Robertson's hearsay testimony before concluding that the requested information was not available from another source. If it is found to be admissible, then the *McClure* application should fail on the threshold question because the requested information is available from another source as admissible evidence. ... Only if Dambrot J. had concluded that there was no waiver *and* that Robertson's testimony was inadmissible should he have proceeded to the other elements of the *McClure* test.

(b) Can the Accused Raise a Reasonable Doubt as to His Guilt in Any Other Way?

[46] This second element of the threshold test raises significant procedural issues, particularly regarding the proper timing of a *McClure* application. These issues obviously troubled the motions judge (at paras. 12-13):

> It is of course indisputable that if the accused can raise a reasonable doubt without access to the solicitor–client file, then his or her innocence would not be at stake, and access to the file would be unnecessary. But how is a trial judge to assess whether or not the accused can raise a reasonable doubt in the minds of the jurors, without usurping the jury's function? Perhaps the matter should be left until the Crown's case is complete, so that the judge would be better able to assess the extent of the accuser's [*sic*] jeopardy. But the implications for the orderly conduct of the trial, and the avoidance of undue delay and disruption for the jurors should such a course be followed need hardly be mentioned. Moreover, even at the end of the Crown's case, the judge is not in a position to meaningfully predict the outcome of the trial.
>
> In the end, I conclude that what Major J was imposing on trial judges was simply an obligation to consider whether there is, in the particular circumstances of the case, a genuine danger of wrongful conviction. On the basis of the evidence before me, I can only conclude that in this case, there is.

[47] With respect, Dambrot J erred in reaching his conclusion on this issue. The test established in *McClure* was intended to carefully screen requests for access to solicitor–client communications and to allow such access only when the accused has shown that he has no other defence *and* that the requested communications would make a positive difference

in the strength of the defence case. As acknowledged in *McClure*, the solicitor–client privilege is fundamental to Canada's justice system and will yield only in rare circumstances.

[48] In every trial based on circumstantial evidence alone, there exists a "genuine danger of wrongful conviction." Based on Dambrot J's interpretation, the Crown's reliance on circumstantial evidence would thereby trigger the opportunity for the accused to infringe a third party's solicitor–client privilege. Obviously, this runs counter to the nature of the threshold test. The test stipulates that privilege should only be violated where the accused cannot raise a reasonable doubt in any other way. However, in a case based entirely on circumstantial evidence, it is more likely that the defence will be able to raise a reasonable doubt, and the risk of conviction will typically be less than in cases where there is direct evidence linking the accused to the crime. It would be illogical to weaken the threshold test in cases where the likelihood of conviction is weakest.

[49] With respect, Dambrot J erred in his application of the threshold test to the facts of this case. Although it is too early to decide the issue, I note that it may be possible for Brown to raise a reasonable doubt as to his guilt by other means. As indicated, absent the testimony of the jailhouse informant, the case against him is based primarily on circumstantial evidence. The evidence suggesting that Brown may have murdered Baksh is: (a) his statement that he had bought drugs from Baksh three times that evening and wanted to reclaim a mountain bike from him; (b) witness accounts that Brown had Baksh's pager number written on a napkin; (c) the napkin itself; and (d) a videotape of Brown entering his own apartment shortly after the murder. No witness saw Brown kill or even threaten Baksh, and neither Brown nor any of his possessions was found to have Baksh's blood on them. With only this evidence, it is speculative that the Crown could prove its case against Brown beyond a reasonable doubt.

[50] The only other evidence that may implicate Brown is that of the jailhouse informant who allegedly overheard Brown confessing to another inmate. To date, the In-Custody Informer Committee of the Attorney General's office has not made a ruling as to whether the informant will be called to give evidence. The Committee is waiting for a decision on the *McClure* application before it makes its final decision on the informant's testimony. This is an error. The Crown should decide early whether the informant's testimony will be introduced, and should not wait for a determination on the *McClure* application. The informant's testimony affects the strength of the Crown's case, and is important to the trial judge's assessment of whether the accused is able to raise a reasonable doubt. It may be that the informant's testimony will sufficiently strengthen the Crown's case to obtain a guilty verdict from a jury. However, I need not explain the pitfalls of relying on the testimony of a jailhouse informant who allegedly overheard a murder confession. See *R v. Brooks*, [2000] 1 SCR 237, 2000 SCC 11. A jury may well find such testimony suspect. At any rate, as there has yet been no decision to call the informant to testify, it would be premature to conclude that Brown will be unable to raise a reasonable doubt without invading Benson's solicitor–client privilege.

[51] The learned motions judge's premature decision highlights the problems that may arise with respect to the timing of a *McClure* application. Although the trial judge has discretion in every case as to when to hear the *McClure* application, it may be helpful to develop some guidance on this issue to avoid premature *McClure* applications and/or orders.

[The court held that it is preferable to wait until the end of the Crown's case to decide whether the Crown can succeed in proving the accused guilty beyond all reasonable doubt. If the Crown cannot meet that standard, there is no need for the *McClure* application. The trial judge is at this point merely assessing the case, not determining it and therefore not usurping the jury's function. If the Crown has made a strong case in chief but the trial judge believes the defence may be able to raise reasonable doubt, then the application can be postponed or denied and renewed as the evidence unfolds. The key is that the defence cannot raise a reasonable doubt without the privileged information, and thus "innocence is at stake." Defence counsel are permitted the latitude to bring the application as they see fit, as long as they do not abuse the availability of the application.]

[56] Finally, due to the stringent nature of the test, and because the accused must establish each element on a balance of probabilities, successful *McClure* applications will be difficult and likely rare. There is potential, in some instances, that an accused may fail on a *McClure* application and ultimately be convicted of the crime. At a later time, when the accused is out of the system, i.e., exhausted his appeals, he may then learn of the contents of the third-party's solicitor–client communication, and discover that it may have allowed him to raise a reasonable doubt. This raises a concern that a failed *McClure* application may precede a wrongful conviction.

[57] Such wrongful convictions ought to be addressed through the traditional procedure of appealing to royal prerogative, as codified in s. 690 of the *Criminal Code*, RSC 1985, c. C-46. They do not justify a relaxation of the *McClure* test. The test has been designed to balance solicitor–client privilege against the right to make full answer and defence. The invasion of solicitor–client privilege should be rare, and the burden of proof rests with the accused. On occasion, the process may lead to a decision that, upon obtaining complete knowledge of the facts, appears to have disadvantaged the accused. Nevertheless, it is for the accused to convince the court that the solicitor–client communications ought to be disclosed, and that burden cannot be altered simply because one gains the benefit of hindsight.

(3) The Innocence at Stake Test

(a) Stage #1: Is There an Evidentiary Basis for the Belief That a Solicitor–Client Communication Exists That Could Raise a Reasonable Doubt as to the Accused's Guilt?

[58] This stage of the innocence at stake test requires the accused to provide some evidentiary basis for his belief that a solicitor–client communication exists that could raise a reasonable doubt as to his guilt. In this case, Dambrot J found that such an evidentiary basis existed. Although he concluded that Donna Robertson's testimony may not be admissible to prove the truth of Benson's confession, Dambrot J found that it was reliable insofar as it indicates that Benson did, in fact, make the statements to her. In addition, Robertson had provided to police the business card on which Benson's solicitors wrote their instructions purporting to invoke the right to silence. Thus, I agree with Dambrot J that there was a sufficient evidentiary basis to find that some solicitor–client communications exist.

[59] Further, I agree with Dambrot J's conclusion that the solicitor–client communications, if they exist, are capable of raising a reasonable doubt as to Brown's guilt. A confession by a third party, if sufficiently credible, is capable of raising a reasonable doubt. Therefore, although Dambrot J allowed the *McClure* application prematurely, and should not have proceeded past the threshold issue, I believe that he applied the first stage of the innocence at stake test correctly.

(b) Can a Judge Require Amplification of the Record Between
Stages #1 and #2 of the Innocence at Stake Test?

· · ·

[64] That being said, I am mindful of the danger that requiring counsel to testify about the privileged communications may render the *McClure* application a fishing expedition akin to a discovery process. To avoid that, the amplification of the record should consist of an affidavit for the benefit of the trial judge. Its use at this stage is to assist the trial judge, not to provide additional or better evidence to the accused.

[65] When a judge orders a lawyer to produce his or her files relating to certain client communications, the judge, for his eyes only at this stage, may also request the lawyer to supply an affidavit stating either that the information contained in the files is a complete record of the communications in question or containing all other information necessary to complete the record. The judge will then be in a position to review the solicitor–client communications and to determine whether any part of the communications is likely to raise a reasonable doubt as to the guilt of the accused.

(c) Stage #2: Is There a Communication in the File That Is Likely to
Raise a Reasonable Doubt as to the Guilt of the Accused?

[66] In light of the fact that Dambrot J's ruling on the *McClure* application was premature, it is not necessary to decide whether a communication exists in the solicitors' files that is likely to raise a reasonable doubt as to Brown's guilt. Nevertheless, a general comment on Dambrot J's decision on this issue may prevent confusion in the future.

[67] When ordering particular items from the solicitors' files to be disclosed, Dambrot J noted that they included "brief notations that are meaningless on their own, but highly significant when viewed in the context of the other evidence led on the *voir dire*" (para. 7). Counsel for Benson had argued that the items were not likely to raise a reasonable doubt, and placed the accused no further ahead than with the information that was already available to him. To this submission, Dambrot J responded (at para. 8):

> While this argument certainly has some force, it ignores the significance of the source of the information, coming as it does from solicitors' files, and the potential cumulative effect of evidence coming from multiple sources. Viewed in this light, I consider the information to be far from marginal.

[68] This, with respect, is an erroneous interpretation of *McClure*. The ability to infringe solicitor–client privilege must be limited to cases where the accused's innocence is at stake, and where there is no other way to raise a reasonable doubt. Its purpose is not, as Dambrot J may appear to suggest, to strengthen the evidence the accused has already

tendered by imbuing it with the high degree of credibility we assume there to be in a privileged communication. He was in error in ordering production of the files on the basis that it would have a "cumulative effect."

[69] Cumulative effect might be a basis for allowing access to solicitor–client communications where the other evidence would not, in the absence of those solicitor–client communications, be able to raise a reasonable doubt. That is, cumulative effect should only be considered where, given their context, the solicitor–client communications help to make sense of the other evidence and thereby raise a reasonable doubt. A court may not allow these privileged communications to be admitted to breathe credibility into other evidence; it may do so only in order to breathe meaning into otherwise sterile facts.

[70] Moreover, Dambrot J's comments are contrary to the principles of the threshold test set out in *McClure*, namely, that the information sought by the accused "*is not available from any other source*" (para. 48 (emphasis added)). This requirement precludes any production order based on the accused's enhanced ability to raise evidence from "multiple sources." In addition, the words "any other source" simply refer to a source of admissible evidence, and are not qualified by the reliability of the source or the quality of his or her evidence.

[71] The *McClure* application cannot be used to invade solicitor–client privilege simply because a solicitor's file will provide evidence that is more likely to be believed than the evidence already available to the accused. The quality of the evidence is not a factor. It will likely always be the case that a solicitor's file will be seen as a more reliable and complete source of information, due to the nature of clients' communication to their counsel. However, it would be an unjustified affront to solicitor–client privilege to allow that frank and open manner, which is fostered by the confidential nature of the solicitor–client relationship, to become the basis for invading privilege. The very essence of the privilege would then become its own undoing.

[72] To reiterate, the disclosure of communications under stage #2 of *McClure* can only be ordered where the solicitor's file is the *only* way for the accused to raise a reasonable doubt as to his guilt. It cannot be ordered to bolster or corroborate evidence that is already available to the accused. Further, the trial judge should be satisfied that the communication sought to be entered is not otherwise inadmissible, such as being the expression of an opinion rather than a statement of fact. Other examples come to mind, but it should be left to the trial judge in the appropriate case to deal with them.

(d) Scope of Disclosure

[73] Once a trial judge has decided to allow a *McClure* application and order disclosure of certain privileged communications, the scope of that disclosure remains to be decided. ...

. . .

[77] ... The judge should order production of only those communications that are necessary to allow an accused, whose innocence is otherwise at stake, to raise a reasonable doubt as to his guilt. A thoughtful and close examination of the communications is required to serve the public interest in avoiding wrongful conviction, while at the same time protecting solicitor–client privilege to the greatest extent possible. For example, if the communications refer to other crimes committed by the privilege holder, those references ought to be omitted. Further, care should be taken to ensure that third parties who are

named in the privileged communications have their identities protected. In short, any portions of the communications that are not necessary to raise a reasonable doubt as to the guilt of the accused should not be disclosed under the *McClure* application.

[78] The second issue to be determined regarding the scope of disclosure is who should be entitled to disclosure of the privileged communications. The Attorney General of Ontario has submitted that any disclosure made to Brown ought also be made to the Crown. ...

· · ·

[84] In my view, the principles that apply in an ordinary criminal prosecution are not altered by a successful *McClure* application. The application provides for limited disclosure to an accused whose innocence is at stake, and who cannot raise a reasonable doubt in any other way. The disclosure is allowed for a specific, exceptional purpose. The Crown cannot "piggy back" onto this exceptional purpose to obtain disclosure of privileged material to which it would not have access in the ordinary case. This would allow the Crown to invade solicitor–client privilege without meeting the rigorous requirements set out in *McClure*.

[85] To avoid this result, the material produced to the accused pursuant to a *McClure* application should be subject to the normal disclosure provisions of a criminal trial. If the accused decides not to raise the privileged communications as evidence, then they will never come to the Crown's attention, and the privilege holder will not be jeopardized. Conversely, if the defence decides to rely on the privileged communications, whether at trial or during pre-trial negotiations, the Crown will gain access to those communications to the extent that the accused uses them.

[86] The Crown has raised the concern that the privileged communications might themselves be unreliable, and submitted that the public has an interest in ensuring that an accused's acquittal is not based on unreliable communications. While this is a legitimate concern, I think that it is adequately addressed by the procedures that have been suggested. If the accused decides not to rely on the privileged communications, then there is no danger that they will be the basis for any subsequent acquittal. Moreover, to the extent that the accused relies on the privileged communications, the Crown will have access to them. If the Crown doubts the reliability of the privileged statements, then it may challenge them according to the ordinary rules of evidence. This may include cross-examination of the solicitor at trial, if necessary, subject to the vigilance of the trial judge that invasion of the privilege is kept to its essentials. Thus, the Crown's concerns about "wrongful acquittals" can be adequately addressed without further incursions into solicitor–client privilege.

[87] In addition, the trial judge should use his or her discretion to protect the confidentiality of the disclosed communications *vis-à-vis* the participants in the trial and the public.

[The court then discussed issues surrounding the subsequent use of the communication against the privilege holder. It held that the privilege holder is entitled to immunity under s 7 of the Charter against the subsequent use of the communication against him, since that would be self-incriminating. The court also allowed the holder who becomes an accused to be protected against the use of the communications to obtain derivative evidence against him or to impeach his credibility at a trial. We address these issues in more detail in Chapter 8, Statements of an Accused and Illegally Obtained Evidence.

NOTES AND QUESTIONS

1. The court in *McClure* allows for defence counsel to bring several *McClure* applications at different points in the same trial. Normally, such an approach would be rejected as utterly unwieldy and if this were a common scenario (a third party confessing to their lawyer a crime that another is charged with), perhaps the court would not have been so accommodating. Is this sacrifice of efficiency legitimate?

2. For an example of an application of *McClure* in the context of charges for tax evasion, and a rejection of it on the basis that there was no claim of knowledge by the accused of the contents of the legal opinions prepared for the Crown, see *Chapelstone Developments Inc, Action Motors Ltd and Hamilton v R*, 2004 NBCA 96, 277 NBR (2d) 350. This case also deals with the issue of inadvertent disclosure and whether that constitutes a waiver of solicitor–client privilege.

3. An issue explicitly left unanswered in *R v Campbell*, [1999] 1 SCR 565, 133 CCC (3d) 257 at para 66 was whether solicitor–client privilege between the Crown and police can be lifted to permit the defence to prove abuse of process. The issue continues to be litigated. Recently, in *R v Rutigliano*, 2015 ONCA 452, the court declined to answer the question. The court held that a judge ought to first decide whether an abuse of process defence could be established without recourse to solicitor–client privileged documents. The motion judge had held the relevant solicitor–client communications could, in a material way, establish an abuse of process. He then decided that it was necessary for him to review the communications to determine whether, in fact, the communications were "likely to significantly advance the record as to the intention of the relevant state actors," and if the "communications [were] likely to substantiate proof of the existence of abuse of process" he would order disclosure (para 29). The appeal court found that this decision was "premature and unnecessary" and that it was not appropriate to decide "whether full answer and defence considerations may require disclosure of privileged communications in an abuse of process proceedings and, if so, in what circumstances" (para 47). In British Columbia, applications to stay proceedings based on an alleged abuse of process fall within the innocence at stake exception. For an illustrative example of a failed request for privileged documents on this basis, see *USA v Rogan*, 2014 BCSC 2228.

II. LITIGATION PRIVILEGE

Litigation privilege, sometimes called "work product privilege" or "lawyer's brief privilege," protects the work done by counsel from disclosure to other parties. Rather than protecting the relationship between the solicitor and the client, it protects the counsel's role in the litigation process.

The Supreme Court of Canada, in *Blank v Canada (Minister of Justice)*, 2006 SCC 39, [2006] 2 SCR 319, provided a thorough examination of litigation privilege and noted one more difference: unlike solicitor–client privilege, litigation privilege ends when the litigation does. While both privileges can attach to the same communication, solicitor–client privilege is permanent, whereas a communication protected by litigation privilege can be disclosed when the litigation is over. Because of this overlap, until *Blank*, lower courts and academics had debated whether litigation privilege and solicitor–client privilege were two branches of the same tree or two different trees. *Blank* answers that conclusively: they are "distinct conceptual animal[s]."

Blank v Canada (Minister of Justice)
2006 SCC 39, [2006] 2 SCR 319
McLachlin CJ and Binnie, Deschamps, Fish, and Abella JJ (8 September 2006)

FISH J:

I

[1] This appeal requires the Court, for the first time, to distinguish between two related but conceptually distinct exemptions from compelled disclosure: the solicitor–client privilege and the litigation privilege. They often co-exist and one is sometimes mistakenly called by the other's name, but they are not coterminous in space, time or meaning.

[2] More particularly, we are concerned in this case with the litigation privilege, with how it is born and when it must be laid to rest. And we need to consider that issue in the narrow context of the *Access to Information Act*, RSC 1985, c. A-1 ("*Access Act*"), but with prudent regard for its broader implications on the conduct of legal proceedings generally.

[3] This case has proceeded throughout on the basis that "solicitor–client privilege" was intended, in s. 23 of the *Access Act*, to include the litigation privilege which is not elsewhere mentioned in the Act. Both parties and the judges below have all assumed that it does.

[4] As a matter of statutory interpretation, I would proceed on the same basis. The Act was adopted nearly a quarter-century ago. It was not uncommon at the time to treat "solicitor–client privilege" as a compendious phrase that included both the legal advice privilege and litigation privilege. This best explains why the litigation privilege is not separately mentioned anywhere in the Act. And it explains as well why, despite the Act's silence in this regard, I agree with the parties and the courts below that the *Access Act* has not deprived the government of the protection previously afforded to it by the legal advice privilege and the litigation privilege: In interpreting and applying the Act, the phrase "solicitor–client privilege" in s. 23 should be taken as a reference to both privileges.

[5] In short, we are not asked in this case to decide whether the government can invoke litigation privilege. Quite properly, the parties agree that it can. Our task, rather, is to examine the defining characteristics of that privilege and, more particularly, to determine its lifespan.

[6] The Minister contends that the solicitor–client privilege has two "branches," one concerned with confidential communications between lawyers and their clients, the other relating to information and materials gathered or created in the litigation context. The first of these branches, as already indicated, is generally characterized as the "legal advice privilege"; the second, as the "litigation privilege."

[7] Bearing in mind their different scope, purpose and rationale, it would be preferable, in my view, to recognize that we are dealing here with distinct conceptual animals and not with two branches of the same tree. Accordingly, I shall refer in these reasons to the solicitor–client privilege as if it includes only the legal advice privilege, and shall indeed use the two phrases—solicitor–client privilege and legal advice privilege—synonymously and interchangeably, except where otherwise indicated.

[8]   As a matter of substance and not mere terminology, the distinction between litigation privilege and the solicitor–client privilege is decisive in this case. The former, unlike the latter, is of temporary duration. It expires with the litigation of which it was born. Characterizing litigation privilege as a "branch" of the solicitor–client privilege, as the Minister would, does not envelop it in a shared cloak of permanency.

[9]   The Minister's claim of litigation privilege fails in this case because the privilege claimed, by whatever name, has expired: The files to which the respondent seeks access relate to penal proceedings that have long terminated. By seeking civil redress for the manner in which those proceedings were conducted, the respondent has given them neither fresh life nor a posthumous and parallel existence.

[10]   I would therefore dismiss the appeal.

II

[11]   The respondent is a self-represented litigant who, though not trained in the law, is no stranger to the courts. He has accumulated more than ten years of legal experience first-hand, initially as a defendant and then as a petitioner and plaintiff. In his resourceful and persistent quest for information and redress, he has personally instituted and conducted a plethora of related proceedings, at first instance and on appeal, in federal and provincial courts alike.

[12]   This saga began in July 1995, when the Crown laid 13 charges against the respondent and Gateway Industries Ltd. ("Gateway") for regulatory offences under the *Fisheries Act*, RSC 1985, c. F-14, and the *Pulp and Paper Effluent Regulations*, SOR/92-269. The respondent was a director of Gateway. Five of the charges alleged pollution of the Red River and another eight alleged breaches of reporting requirements.

[13]   The counts relating to reporting requirements were quashed in 1997 and the pollution charges were quashed in 2001. In 2002, the Crown laid new charges by way of indictment—and stayed them prior to trial. The respondent and Gateway then sued the federal government in damages for fraud, conspiracy, perjury and abuse of its prosecutorial powers.

[14]   This appeal concerns the respondent's repeated attempts to obtain documents from the government. He succeeded only in part. His requests for information in the penal proceedings and under the *Access Act* were denied by the government on various grounds, including "solicitor–client privilege." The issue before us now relates solely to the *Access Act* proceedings. We have not been asked to decide whether the Crown properly fulfilled, in the criminal proceedings, its disclosure obligations under *R v. Stinchcombe*, [1991] 3 SCR 326. And in the record before us, we would in any event be unable to do so.

[15]   In October 1997, and again in May 1999, the respondent requested from the Access to Information and Privacy Office of the Department of Justice all records pertaining to his prosecution and the prosecution of Gateway. Only some of the requested documents were furnished.

[16]   Additional materials were released after the respondent lodged a complaint with the Information Commissioner. The Director of Investigation found that the vast majority of the remaining documents were properly exempted from disclosure under the solicitor–client privilege.

[17] The respondent pursued the matter further by way of an application for review pursuant to s. 41 of the *Access Act*. Although the appellant relied on various exemptions from disclosure in the *Access Act*, proceedings before the motions judge focussed on the appellant's claims of solicitor–client privilege in reliance on s. 23 of the *Access Act*.

[18] On the respondent's application, Campbell J held that documents excluded from disclosure pursuant to litigation privilege should be released if the litigation to which the record relates has ended (2003 CarswellNat 5040, 2003 FCT 462).

[19] On appeal, the Federal Court of Appeal divided on the duration of the privilege. Pelletier JA, for the majority on this point, found that litigation privilege, unlike legal advice privilege, expires with the end of the litigation that gave rise to the privilege, "subject to the possibility of defining … litigation … broadly" ([2005] 1 FCR 403, 2004 FCA 287, at para. 89). He therefore held that s. 23 of the *Access Act* did not apply to the documents for which a claim of litigation privilege is made in this case because the criminal prosecution had ended.

[20] Létourneau JA, dissenting on this point, found that the privilege did not necessarily end with the termination of the litigation that gave rise to it. He would have upheld the privilege in this case.

III

[21] Section 23 of the *Access Act* provides:

> **23.** The head of a government institution may refuse to disclose any record requested under this Act that contains information that is subject to solicitor–client privilege.

[22] The narrow issue before us is whether documents once subject to the litigation privilege remain privileged when the litigation ends.

[23] According to the appellant, this Court has determined that litigation privilege is a branch of the solicitor–client privilege and benefits from the same near-absolute protection, including permanency. But none of the cases relied on by the Crown support this assertion. The Court has addressed the solicitor–client privilege on numerous occasions and repeatedly underlined its paramount significance, but never yet considered the nature, scope or duration of the litigation privilege.

[24] Thus, the Court explained in *Descôteaux v. Mierzwinski*, [1982] 1 SCR 860, and has since then reiterated, that the solicitor–client privilege has over the years evolved from a rule of evidence to a rule of substantive law. And the Court has consistently emphasized the breadth and primacy of the solicitor–client privilege: see, for example, *Geffen v. Goodman Estate*, [1991] 2 SCR 353; *Smith v. Jones*, [1999] 1 SCR 455; *R v. McClure*, [2001] 1 SCR 445, 2001 SCC 14; *Lavallee, Rackel & Heintz v. Canada (Attorney General)*, [2002] 3 SCR 209, 2002 SCC 61; and *Goodis v. Ontario (Ministry of Correctional Services)*, 2006 SCC 31. In an oft-quoted passage, Major J, speaking for the Court, stated in *McClure* that "solicitor–client privilege must be as close to absolute as possible to ensure public confidence and retain relevance" (para. 35).

[25] It is evident from the text and the context of these decisions, however, that they relate only to the legal advice privilege, or solicitor–client privilege properly so called, and not to the litigation privilege as well.

[26] Much has been said in these cases, and others, regarding the origin and rationale of the solicitor–client privilege. The solicitor–client privilege has been firmly entrenched for centuries. It recognizes that the justice system depends for its vitality on full, free and frank communication between those who need legal advice and those who are best able to provide it. Society has entrusted to lawyers the task of advancing their clients' cases with the skill and expertise available only to those who are trained in the law. They alone can discharge these duties effectively, but only if those who depend on them for counsel may consult with them in confidence. The resulting confidential relationship between solicitor and client is a necessary and essential condition of the effective administration of justice.

[27] Litigation privilege, on the other hand, is not directed at, still less, restricted to, communications between solicitor and client. It contemplates, as well, communications between a solicitor and third parties or, in the case of an unrepresented litigant, between the litigant and third parties. Its object is to ensure the efficacy of the adversarial process and not to promote the solicitor–client relationship. And to achieve this purpose, parties to litigation, represented or not, must be left to prepare their contending positions in private, without adversarial interference and without fear of premature disclosure.

[28] R.J. Sharpe (now Sharpe JA) has explained particularly well the differences between litigation privilege and solicitor–client privilege:

> It is crucially important to distinguish litigation privilege from solicitor–client privilege. There are, I suggest, at least three important differences between the two. First, solicitor–client privilege applies only to confidential communications between the client and his solicitor. Litigation privilege, on the other hand, applies to communications of a non-confidential nature between the solicitor and third parties and even includes material of a non-communicative nature. Secondly, solicitor–client privilege exists any time a client seeks legal advice from his solicitor whether or not litigation is involved. Litigation privilege, on the other hand, applies only in the context of litigation itself. Thirdly, and most important, the rationale for solicitor–client privilege is very different from that which underlies litigation privilege. This difference merits close attention. The interest which underlies the protection accorded communications between a client and a solicitor from disclosure is the interest of all citizens to have full and ready access to legal advice. If an individual cannot confide in a solicitor knowing that what is said will not be revealed, it will be difficult, if not impossible, for that individual to obtain proper candid legal advice.
>
> Litigation privilege, on the other hand, is geared directly to the process of litigation. Its purpose is not explained adequately by the protection afforded lawyer–client communications deemed necessary to allow clients to obtain legal advice, the interest protected by solicitor–client privilege. Its purpose is more particularly related to the needs of the adversarial trial process. Litigation privilege is based upon the need for a protected area to facilitate investigation and preparation of a case for trial by the adversarial advocate. In other words, litigation privilege aims to facilitate a process (namely, the adversary process), while solicitor–client privilege aims to protect a relationship (namely, the confidential relationship between a lawyer and a client).

("Claiming Privilege in the Discovery Process," in *Special Lectures of the Law Society of Upper Canada* (1984), 163, at pp. 164-65)

[29] With the exception of *Hodgkinson v. Simms* (1988), 33 BCLR (2d) 129, a decision of the British Columbia Court of Appeal, the decisions of appellate courts in this country have

consistently found that litigation privilege is based on a different rationale than solicitor–client privilege: *Liquor Control Board of Ontario v. Lifford Wine Agencies Ltd.* (2005), 76 OR (3d) 401; *Ontario (Attorney General) v. Ontario (Information and Privacy Commission, Inquiry Officer)* (2002), 62 OR (3d) 167 ("*Big Canoe*"); *College of Physicians and Surgeons (British Columbia) v. British Columbia (Information and Privacy Commissioner)* (2002), 9 BCLR (4th) 1, 2002 BCCA 665; *Gower v. Tolko Manitoba Inc.* (2001), 196 DLR (4th) 716, 2001 MBCA 11; *Mitsui & Co. (Point Aconi) Ltd. v. Jones Power Co.* (2000), 188 NSR (2d) 173, 2000 NSCA 96; *General Accident Assurance Co. v. Chrusz* (1999), 45 OR (3d) 321.

[30] American and English authorities are to the same effect: ...

[31] Though conceptually distinct, litigation privilege and legal advice privilege serve a common cause: The secure and effective administration of justice according to law. And they are complementary and not competing in their operation. But treating litigation privilege and legal advice privilege as two branches of the same tree tends to obscure the true nature of both.

[32] Unlike the solicitor–client privilege, the litigation privilege arises and operates even in the absence of a solicitor–client relationship, and it applies indiscriminately to all litigants, whether or not they are represented by counsel: see *Alberta (Treasury Branches) v. Ghermezian* (1999), 242 AR 326, 1999 ABQB 407. A self-represented litigant is no less in need of, and therefore entitled to, a "zone" or "chamber" of privacy. Another important distinction leads to the same conclusion. Confidentiality, the *sine qua non* of the solicitor–client privilege, is not an essential component of the litigation privilege. In preparing for trial, lawyers as a matter of course obtain information from third parties who have no need nor any expectation of confidentiality; yet the litigation privilege attaches nonetheless.

[33] In short, the litigation privilege and the solicitor–client privilege are driven by different policy considerations and generate different legal consequences.

[34] The purpose of the litigation privilege, I repeat, is to create a "zone of privacy" in relation to pending or apprehended litigation. Once the litigation has ended, the privilege to which it gave rise has lost its specific and concrete purpose—and therefore its justification. But to borrow a phrase, the litigation is not over until it is over: It cannot be said to have "terminated," in any meaningful sense of that term, where litigants or related parties remain locked in what is essentially the same legal combat.

[35] Except where such related litigation persists, there is no need and no reason to protect from discovery anything that would have been subject to compellable disclosure but for the pending or apprehended proceedings which provided its shield. Where the litigation has indeed ended, there is little room for concern lest opposing counsel or their clients argue their case "on wits borrowed from the adversary," to use the language of the US Supreme Court in *Hickman*, at p. 516.

[36] I therefore agree with the majority in the Federal Court of Appeal and others who share their view that the common law litigation privilege comes to an end, absent closely related proceedings, upon the termination of the litigation that gave rise to the privilege: ... .

[37] Thus, the principle "once privileged, always privileged," so vital to the solicitor–client privilege, is foreign to the litigation privilege. The litigation privilege, unlike the solicitor–client privilege, is neither absolute in scope nor permanent in duration.

[38] As mentioned earlier, however, the privilege may retain its purpose—and, therefore, its effect—where the litigation that gave rise to the privilege has ended, but related

litigation remains pending or may reasonably be apprehended. In this regard, I agree with Pelletier JA regarding "the possibility of defining ... litigation more broadly than the particular proceeding which gave rise to the claim" (at para. 89): see *Ed Miller Sales & Rentals Ltd. v. Caterpillar Tractor Co.* (1988), 90 AR 323 (CA).

[39] At a minimum, it seems to me, this enlarged definition of "litigation" includes separate proceedings that involve the same or related parties and arise from the same or a related cause of action (or "juridical source"). Proceedings that raise issues common to the initial action and share its essential purpose would in my view qualify as well.

[40] As a matter of principle, the boundaries of this extended meaning of "litigation" are limited by the purpose for which litigation privilege is granted, namely, as mentioned, "the need for a protected area to facilitate investigation and preparation of a case for trial by the adversarial advocate" (Sharpe, p. 165). This purpose, in the context of s. 23 of the *Access Act* must take into account the nature of much government litigation. In the 1980s, for example, the federal government confronted litigation across Canada arising out of its urea formaldehyde insulation program. The parties were different and the specifics of each claim were different but the underlying liability issues were common across the country.

[41] In such a situation, the advocate's "protected area" would extend to work related to those underlying liability issues even after some but not all of the individual claims had been disposed of. There were common issues and the causes of action, in terms of the advocate's work product, were closely related. When the claims belonging to that particular group of causes of action had all been dealt with, however, litigation privilege would have been exhausted, even if subsequent disclosure of the files would reveal aspects of government operations or general litigation strategies that the government would prefer to keep from its former adversaries or other requesters under the *Access Act*. Similar issues may arise in the private sector, for example in the case of a manufacturer dealing with related product liability claims. In each case, the duration and extent of the litigation privilege are circumscribed by its underlying purpose, namely the protection essential to the proper operation of the adversarial process.

IV

[42] In this case, the respondent claims damages from the federal government for fraud, conspiracy, perjury and abuse of prosecutorial powers. Pursuant to the *Access Act*, he demands the disclosure to him of all documents relating to the Crown's conduct of its proceedings against him. The source of those proceedings is the alleged pollution and breach of reporting requirements by the respondent and his company.

[43] The Minister's claim of privilege thus concerns documents that were prepared for the dominant purpose of a criminal prosecution relating to environmental matters and reporting requirements. The respondent's action, on the other hand, seeks civil redress for the manner in which the government conducted that prosecution. It springs from a different juridical source and is in that sense unrelated to the litigation of which the privilege claimed was born.

[44] The litigation privilege would not in any event protect from disclosure evidence of the claimant party's abuse of process or similar blameworthy conduct. It is not a black hole from which evidence of one's own misconduct can never be exposed to the light of day.

[45] Even where the materials sought would otherwise be subject to litigation privilege, the party seeking their disclosure may be granted access to them upon a *prima facie* showing of actionable misconduct by the other party in relation to the proceedings with respect to which litigation privilege is claimed. Whether privilege is claimed in the originating or in related litigation, the court may review the materials to determine whether their disclosure should be ordered on this ground.

[46] Finally, in the Court of Appeal, Létourneau JA, dissenting on the cross-appeal, found that the government's status as a "recurring litigant" could justify a litigation privilege that outlives its common law equivalent. In his view, the "[a]utomatic and uncontrolled access to the government lawyer's brief, once the first litigation is over, may impede the possibility of effectively adopting and implementing [general policies and strategies]" (para. 42).

[47] I hesitate to characterize as "[a]utomatic and uncontrolled" access to the government lawyer's brief once the subject proceedings have ended. In my respectful view, access will in fact be neither automatic nor uncontrolled.

[48] First, as mentioned earlier, it will not be automatic because all subsequent litigation will remain subject to a claim of privilege if it involves the same or related parties and the same or related source. It will fall within the protective orbit of the same litigation defined broadly.

[49] Second, access will not be uncontrolled because many of the documents in the lawyer's brief will, in any event, remain exempt from disclosure by virtue of the legal advice privilege. In practice, a lawyer's brief normally includes materials covered by the solicitor–client privilege because of their evident connection to legal advice sought or given in the course of, or in relation to, the originating proceedings. The distinction between the solicitor–client privilege and the litigation privilege does not preclude their potential overlap in a litigation context.

[50] Commensurate with its importance, the solicitor–client privilege has over the years been broadly interpreted by this Court. In that light, anything in a litigation file that falls within the solicitor–client privilege will remain clearly and forever privileged.

[51] I hasten to add that the *Access Act* is a statutory scheme aimed at promoting the disclosure of information in the government's possession. Nothing in the Act suggests that Parliament intended by its adoption to extend the lifespan of the litigation privilege when a member of the public seeks access to government documents.

[52] The language of s. 23 is, moreover, permissive. It provides that the Minister may invoke the privilege. This permissive language promotes disclosure by encouraging the Minister to refrain from invoking the privilege unless it is thought necessary to do so in the public interest. And it thus supports an interpretation that favours more government disclosure, not less.

[53] The extended definition of litigation, as I indicated earlier, applies no less to the government than to private litigants. As a result of the *Access Act*, however, its protection may prove less effective in practice. The reason is this. Like private parties, the government may invoke the litigation privilege only when the original or extended proceedings are pending or apprehended. Unlike private parties, however, the government may be required under the terms of the *Access Act* to disclose information once the original proceedings have ended and related proceedings are neither pending nor apprehended.

A mere hypothetical possibility that related proceedings may in the future be instituted does not suffice. Should that possibility materialize—should related proceedings in fact later be instituted—the government may well have been required in the interim, in virtue of the *Access Act*, to disclose information that would have otherwise been privileged under the extended definition of litigation. This is a matter of legislative choice and not judicial policy. It flows inexorably from Parliament's decision to adopt the *Access Act*. Other provisions of the *Access Act* suggest, moreover, that Parliament has in fact recognized this consequence of the Act on the government as litigator, potential litigant and guardian of personal safety and public security.

[54] For example, pursuant to s. 16(1)(b) and (c), the government may refuse to disclose any record that contains information relating to investigative techniques or plans for specific lawful investigations or information the disclosure of which could reasonably be expected to be injurious to law enforcement or the conduct of lawful investigations. And, pursuant to s. 17, the government may refuse to disclose any information the disclosure of which could reasonably be expected to threaten the safety of individuals. The special status of the government as a "recurring litigant" is more properly addressed by these provisions and other legislated solutions. In addition, as mentioned earlier, the nature of government litigation may be relevant when determining the boundaries of related litigation where multiple proceedings involving the government relate to common issues with closely related causes of action. But a wholesale expansion of the litigation privilege is neither necessary nor desirable.

[55] Finally, we should not disregard the origins of this dispute between the respondent and the Minister. It arose in the context of a criminal prosecution by the Crown against the respondent. In criminal proceedings, the accused's right to discovery is constitutionally guaranteed. The prosecution is obliged under *Stinchcombe* to make available to the accused all relevant information if there is a "reasonable possibility that the withholding of information will impair the right of the accused to make full answer and defence" (p. 340). This added burden of disclosure is placed on the Crown in light of its overwhelming advantage in resources and the corresponding risk that the accused might otherwise be unfairly disadvantaged.

[56] I am not unmindful of the fact that *Stinchcombe* does not require the prosecution to disclose everything in its file, privileged or not. Materials that might in civil proceedings be covered by one privilege or another will nonetheless be subject, in the criminal context, to the "innocence at stake" exception—at the very least: see *McClure*. In criminal proceedings, as the Court noted in *Stinchcombe*:

> The trial judge might also, in certain circumstances, conclude that the recognition of an existing privilege does not constitute a reasonable limit on the constitutional right to make full answer and defence and thus require disclosure in spite of the law of privilege. [p. 340]

[57] On any view of the matter, I would think it incongruous if the litigation privilege were found in civil proceedings to insulate the Crown from the disclosure it was bound but failed to provide in criminal proceedings that have ended.

V

[58] The result in this case is dictated by a finding that the litigation privilege expires when the litigation ends. I wish nonetheless to add a few words regarding its birth.

[59] The question has arisen whether the litigation privilege should attach to documents created for the substantial purpose of litigation, the dominant purpose of litigation or the sole purpose of litigation. The dominant purpose test was chosen from this spectrum by the House of Lords in *Waugh v. British Railways Board*, [1979] 2 All ER 1169. It has been adopted in this country as well: *Davies v. Harrington* (1980), 115 DLR (3d) 347 (NSCA); *Voth Bros. Construction (1974) Ltd. v. North Vancouver S. Dist. No. 44 Board of School Trustees* (1981), 29 BCLR 114 (CA); *McCaig v. Trentowsky* (1983), 148 DLR (3d) 724 (NBCA); *Nova, an Alberta Corporation v. Guelph Engineering Co.* (1984), 5 DLR (4th) 755 (Alta. CA); *Ed Miller Sales & Rentals*; *Chrusz*; *Lifford*; *Mitsui*; *College of Physicians*; *Gower*.

[60] I see no reason to depart from the dominant purpose test. Though it provides narrower protection than would a substantial purpose test, the dominant purpose standard appears to me consistent with the notion that the litigation privilege should be viewed as a limited exception to the principle of full disclosure and not as an equal partner of the broadly interpreted solicitor–client privilege. The dominant purpose test is more compatible with the contemporary trend favouring increased disclosure. As Royer has noted, it is hardly surprising that modern legislation and case law

[TRANSLATION] which increasingly attenuate the purely accusatory and adversarial nature of the civil trial, tend to limit the scope of this privilege [that is, the litigation privilege]. [para. 1139]

Or, as Carthy JA stated in *Chrusz*:

The modern trend is in the direction of complete discovery and there is no apparent reason to inhibit that trend so long as counsel is left with sufficient flexibility to adequately serve the litigation client. [p. 331]

[61] While the solicitor–client privilege has been strengthened, reaffirmed and elevated in recent years, the litigation privilege has had, on the contrary, to weather the trend toward mutual and reciprocal disclosure which is the hallmark of the judicial process. In this context, it would be incongruous to reverse that trend and revert to a substantial purpose test.

[62] A related issue is whether the litigation privilege attaches to documents gathered or copied—but not created—for the purpose of litigation. This issue arose in *Hodgkinson*, where a majority of the British Columbia Court of Appeal, relying on *Lyell v. Kennedy* (1884), 27 Ch. D 1 (CA), concluded that copies of public documents gathered by a solicitor were privileged. McEachern CJBC stated:

It is my conclusion that the law has always been, and in my view, should continue to be, that in circumstances such as these, where a lawyer exercising legal knowledge, skill, judgment and industry has assembled a collection of relevant copy documents for his brief for the purpose of advising on or conducting anticipated or pending litigation he is entitled, indeed required, unless the client consents, to claim privilege for such collection and to refuse production. [p. 142]

[63] This approach was rejected by the majority of the Ontario Court of Appeal in *Chrusz*.

[64] The conflict of appellate opinion on this issue should be left to be resolved in a case where it is explicitly raised and fully argued. Extending the privilege to the gathering

of documents resulting from research or the exercise of skill and knowledge does appear to be more consistent with the rationale and purpose of the litigation privilege. That being said, I take care to mention that assigning such a broad scope to the litigation privilege is not intended to automatically exempt from disclosure anything that would have been subject to discovery if it had not been remitted to counsel or placed in one's own litigation files. Nor should it have that effect.

[Concurring reasons were delivered by Bastarache J (Charron J concurring), who provided an interpretation of s 23 of the *Access Act* and excluded a parallel application of the common law rule regarding litigation privilege in cases where the *Access Act* is invoked.]

QUESTIONS

1. The court left open the issue of "ingathered documents." In *Edgar v Auld*, [2000] NBJ No 69 (QL) (CA), the court firmly rejected the contention that the act of copying was enough to cloak a pre-existing document with litigation privilege. See also *Bennett v State Farm Fire and Casualty Co*, 2013 NBCA 4. Why do you think the Supreme Court decided to let the debate continue when it could have resolved an ongoing point of controversy?

Because *Blank* establishes the distinct nature of litigation privilege, it generated a line of cases addressing the statutory regulation of such privilege. As noted in many cases, solicitor–client privilege is carefully protected by interpretive doctrines: see *Blood Tribe*, above. Should litigation privilege generate the same regard? The Supreme Court of Canada will likely be deciding this issue in its pending decision in an appeal from *Lizotte c Aviva, compagnie d'assurances du Canada*, 2015 QCCA 152. The Quebec Court of Appeal held absent express statutory authorization that administrative decision-makers cannot access documents covered by litigation privilege. In *Llewellyn v Carter*, 2008 PESCAD 12, 278 Nfld & PEIR 96, the Prince Edward Island Court of Appeal held that litigation privilege can be limited by rules of court, whereas solicitor–client privilege, because it is a rule of substantive law, cannot be so limited. Can these cases be reconciled?

2. When does solicitor–client privilege extend to communications between a client or a solicitor and a non-lawyer third party retained to assist in litigation? In *General Accident Assurance Co v Chrusz* (1999), 45 OR (3d) 321, discussed in *Blank*, above, Doherty JA provides a lengthy analysis of this problem. Do you think the parties in *Smith v Jones*, above, Section I.D, were right to agree that Jones's communications with Smith were *prima facie* protected by solicitor–client privilege?

3. In *R v Trang*, 2002 ABQB 19, 1 Alta LR (4th) 247, the court accepted the argument that litigation privilege applied in criminal cases (at para 83), but rejected an argument in favour of a separate, police work-product privilege (at paras 84-95). As a result, Crown litigation privilege was used to protect from production, work produced by the police for the purpose of trial (at para 97). For another application of litigation privilege in a criminal context and its interplay with a *McClure* application (innocence at stake, above, Section I.D.2), see *R v Mann and Soomel*, 2003 BCSC 140. Given the differences between the two types of legal privilege, should it be easier to bring a *McClure* application when the material is covered by litigation privilege rather than solicitor–client privilege? In *USA v Rogan*, above, the court relied on paras 44 and 45 from *Blank*, above, to conclude that litigation privilege can be set aside more readily than solicitor–client privilege. Do you agree?

III. SETTLEMENT PRIVILEGE

It is well recognized that communications made during attempts to settle a litigious matter through negotiation or mediation are not admissible if negotiation or mediation fails and the matter is litigated. Such communications are often labelled "without prejudice" to indicate that the party making them is asserting the privilege, but the "without prejudice" label is not strictly necessary if it is clear from the circumstances that the communication was made with the intent that it not be disclosed in litigation.

The policy behind the privilege is to encourage settlement by encouraging the parties to speak and to negotiate freely without the fear that what they say could be used to their detriment in subsequent litigation. This has important consequences for access to justice: settlement privilege has been time-tested and keeps disputes out the vortex of the litigation system. This was noted by a unanimous court in *Sable Offshore Energy Inc v Ameron International Corp*, 2013 SCC 37, [2013] 2 SCR 623. In this case the court confirmed settlement privilege is a class privilege, and, as such, exceptions depend on the interests of justice. In particular, exceptions require proof of a countervailing interest, such as allegations of misrepresentation, fraud or undue influence, or prevention of overcompensation. Finally, and contrary cases notwithstanding, the court clarified that successful negotiations are as equally entitled as failed ones to protection under settlement privilege.

The next case involves complex commercial litigation under Quebec civil law and an established exception to settlement privilege that enables parties to produce evidence of confidential communications in order to prove the existence or scope of a settlement. The court made clear in the judgment that the law in Quebec and common law jurisdictions is the same on these points.

Union Carbide Canada Inc v Bombardier Inc
2014 SCC 35, [2014] 1 SCR 800
McLachlin CJ and LeBel, Rothstein, Cromwell, Moldaver, Karakatsanis, and Wagner JJ (8 May 2014)

WAGNER J (for the court):

I. Introduction

[1] This Court recently confirmed the vital importance of the role played by settlement privilege in promoting the settlement of disputes and improving access to justice: *Sable Offshore Energy Inc. v. Ameron International Corp.*, 2013 SCC 37, [2013] 2 S.C.R. 623. Settlement privilege is a common law evidentiary rule that applies to settlement negotiations regardless of whether the parties have expressly invoked it. This privilege is not the only tool available to parties, however, as parties like the appellants and the respondents in the case at bar often sign mediation agreements that provide for the confidentiality of communications made in the course of the mediation process.

[2] This case concerns the interaction between these two protections: confidentiality of communications provided for in a private mediation contract, and the common law settlement privilege. More specifically, it relates to a common law exception to settlement

privilege that applies where a party seeks to prove the existence or the scope of a settlement. At issue is whether a mediation contract with an absolute confidentiality clause displaces the common law settlement privilege, including this exception, thereby foreclosing parties from proving the terms of a settlement.

[3] Ironically, both the appellants and the respondents argue that the Court's answer could negatively affect the development of mediation in Canada, either by undermining its confidential nature or by frustrating its main objectives. I disagree. I reach this decision bearing in mind the overriding benefit to the public of promoting the out-of-court settlement of disputes regardless of the legal means employed to reach a given settlement. For the reasons that follow, I find that parties are at liberty to sign mediation contracts under which the protection of confidentiality is different from the common law protection. This enables parties to secure the safeguards they deem important and fosters the free and frank negotiation of settlements, thereby serving the same purpose as settlement privilege: the promotion of settlements. However, I reject the presumption that a confidentiality clause in a mediation agreement automatically displaces settlement privilege, and more specifically the exceptions to that privilege that exist at common law. The exceptions to settlement privilege have been developed for public policy reasons, and they exist to further the overall purpose of the privilege. A mediation contract will not deprive parties of the ability to prove the terms of a settlement by producing evidence of communications made in the mediation context unless a court finds, applying the appropriate rules of contractual interpretation, that that is the intended effect of the agreement.

[4] Because this dispute arose in Quebec, Quebec contract law applies. I find that although it was open to the parties to contract out of the exception to settlement privilege, they did not do so. They therefore retain their right to produce evidence of communications made in the mediation context in order to prove the terms of their settlement. I would affirm the Court of Appeal's decision, albeit for different reasons.

II. Facts

[5] The parties are entangled in a decades-long, multi-million dollar civil suit about defective gas tanks used on Sea-Doo personal watercraft. The appellants ... "Dow Chemical" ... manufacture and distribute gas tanks for personal watercraft. The respondent Bombardier Inc. manufactured and distributed Sea-Doo personal watercraft .... A dispute arose over the fitness of the gas tanks as a result of consumer complaints.

[Once the action was begun, the parties agreed to private mediation and signed a standard agreement with a confidentiality clause. The clause provided in part: "Nothing which transpires in the Mediation will be alleged, referred to or sought to be put into evidence in any proceeding." Bombardier accepted a settlement offer submitted by Dow Chemical for $7 million. Dow Chemical then advised Bombardier that it viewed the offer as a "global" settlement amount that encompassed any gas tank litigation brought against it, anywhere. Bombardier replied that the offer was for the Montreal litigation only and demanded payment. None was forthcoming. Bombardier then brought a motion for homologation (that is, for its claim for $7 million) and relied on evidence from the mediation sessions. Dow Chemical argued that this evidence was inadmissible.]

IV. Analysis

[27] In my view, there are two questions to answer in this appeal. The first is whether a confidentiality clause in a private mediation contract can override the exception to the common law settlement privilege that enables parties to produce evidence of confidential communications in order to prove the existence or the scope of a settlement. The second question, which arises only if the answer to the first is yes, is whether the confidentiality clause at issue in the case at bar displaces that exception. If it does, the information referred to in the impugned paragraphs cannot be disclosed. If it does not, that information may be disclosed if it meets the criteria of the exception.

. . .

A. Does a Confidentiality Clause Supersede the Exception to the Common Law Doctrine of Settlement Privilege?

. . .

(1) Settlement Privilege

[The Court reviewed *Sable Offshore*, above, and continued.]

[35] The exception to settlement privilege at issue in the case at bar is the rule that protected communications may be disclosed in order to prove the existence or scope of a settlement. This exception is explained by [AW Bryant, SN Lederman & MK Fuerst, *The Law of Evidence in Canada*, 3rd ed (Markham, Ont: LexisNexis, 2009)]:

> If the negotiations are successful and result in a consensual agreement, then the communications may be tendered in proof of the settlement where the existence or interpretation of the agreement is itself in issue. Such communications form the offer and acceptance of a binding contract, and thus may be given in evidence to establish the existence of a settlement agreement. [para. 14.340]

The rule is simple, and it is consistent with the goal of promoting settlements. A communication that has led to a settlement will cease to be privileged if disclosing it is necessary in order to prove the existence or the scope of the settlement. Once the parties have agreed on a settlement, the general interest of promoting settlements requires that they be able to prove the terms of their agreement. Far from outweighing the policy in favour of promoting settlements (*Sable Offshore*, at para. 30), the reason for the disclosure—to prove the terms of a settlement—tends to further it. The rule makes sense because it serves the same purpose as the privilege itself: to promote settlements.

[The court outlined the various reasons parties sign a confidentiality clause as part of mediation and continued.]

(3) Can a Confidentiality Clause in a Mediation Agreement Displace the Exception to Settlement Privilege That Applies Where a Party Seeks to Prove the Terms of a Settlement?

[45] The common law settlement privilege and confidentiality in the mediation context are often conflated. They do have a common purpose: facilitating out-of-court settlements.

But as we saw above, confidentiality clauses in mediation agreements can also have different purposes. In most cases involving such clauses, the status of the common law settlement privilege will not arise, because the two protections generally serve the same purpose, namely to foster negotiations by encouraging parties to be honest and forthright in reaching a settlement without fear that the information they disclose will be used against them at a later date. However, as I mentioned above, settlement privilege and a confidentiality clause are not the same, and they may in some circumstances conflict. One is a rule of evidence, while the other is a binding agreement; they do not afford the same protection, nor are the consequences for breaching them necessarily the same.

[46] The differences between these protections may be muddled in a case like this one in which both of them could apply, but to different parts of the sequence of events. The parties met for the mediation session on April 27, 2011, the day after they had signed an agreement with a confidentiality clause. The clause in question applied to discussions that took place in the course of the mediation session and prohibited the disclosure of information about those discussions at any time in the future. A settlement offer was made at the mediation session, was kept open for 30 days after that date, and was discussed by the parties' lawyers after the session. Any additional information that came up in the course of these subsequent discussions falls outside the protection of the confidentiality clause—however, since it formed part of negotiations aimed at reaching a settlement, it is protected by settlement privilege. As regards the timing of the communications, the scope of settlement privilege is broader, because it is not limited to the duration of the mediation session.

[47] On the other hand, there are recognized exceptions to settlement privilege at common law that limit the scope of its protection, but such exceptions may be lacking in the case of a confidentiality clause. The question is whether an absolute confidentiality clause in a mediation agreement displaces the common law exception, thereby preventing parties from producing evidence of communications made in the mediation process in order to prove the terms of a settlement.

[48] There is indeed a delicate balance to be struck. The concerns articulated by commentators about the uncertainty of confidentiality clauses in mediation contracts are legitimate. ...

[49] In my view, the inquiry in each case will begin with an interpretation of the contract. It must be asked whether the confidentiality clause actually conflicts with settlement privilege or with the recognized exceptions to that privilege. Where parties contract for greater confidentiality protection than is available at common law, the will of the parties should presumptively be upheld absent such concerns as fraud or illegality. ...

[50] But contracting out of the exception to settlement privilege that applies where a party seeks to prove the terms of a settlement is a different matter. As I mentioned above, a failure to apply this common law exception could frustrate the broader purpose of promoting settlements in that it might prevent parties from enforcing the terms of settlements they have negotiated. Thus, whereas contracting for broader protection than is afforded by the common law settlement privilege may further the overall purpose of that privilege in most circumstances, contracting out of the exceptions to the privilege might undermine that purpose. ...

[51] In my respectful opinion, the Court of Appeal did not devote adequate attention in its analysis to freedom of contract. It is open to contracting parties to create their own

rules with respect to confidentiality that entirely displace the common law settlement privilege. This furthers both freedom of contract and the likelihood of settlement, two important public purposes. However, the mere fact of signing a mediation agreement that contains a confidentiality clause does not automatically displace the privilege and the exceptions to it. As I mentioned above, these protections do not have the same scope. For instance, settlement privilege applies to all communications that lead up to a settlement, even after a mediation session has concluded. It cannot be argued that parties who agree to confidentiality in respect of a mediation session thereby deprive themselves of the application of settlement privilege after the conclusion of the mediation session. The protection afforded by the privilege does not evaporate the moment the parties contract for confidentiality with respect to the mediation process, unless that is the contract's intended effect.

[The court describes the approach taken in international trade law disputes, as well as in other civil and common law jurisdictions that acknowledge an exception to settlement privilege to prove the existence or the terms of a settlement.]

[54] Where an agreement could have the effect of preventing the application of a recognized exception to settlement privilege, its terms must be clear. ...

[55] I wish to emphasize that my analysis concerns one exception to the common law settlement privilege—the one that applies where a party seeks to prove the terms of a settlement. I have not discussed other exceptions, such as the one with respect to fraudulent or unlawful communications, as they are not at issue in this case. Nor will I consider whether the mediator could be compelled to testify in a situation such as this one. The evidence before this Court is limited to the impugned paragraphs of the motion for homologation, so I will not address the appropriate legal threshold for permitting or compelling direct testimony by the mediator. I will leave that question for another day.

[56] In my opinion, the information the respondents seek to disclose with the impugned paragraphs of their motion for homologation is protected by the confidentiality clause, and not solely by settlement privilege. It was open to the parties to displace settlement privilege, including the exceptions to it. The question is whether they did so.

[57] The mediation contract was signed and performed in Quebec. It must be interpreted in accordance with the *Civil Code of Québec* and with the law of obligations.

B. Does This Mediation Contract Permit the Parties to Use Confidential Information in Order to Prove the Terms of a Settlement?

. . .

[62] On its face, the mediation contract at issue in the case at bar shows a common intention on the part of the parties to be bound by confidentiality in respect of anything that might transpire in the course of the mediation. But the question to be answered is more specific and concerns an incidental aspect of the contract, for which the common intention of the parties is not immediately clear: Was the confidentiality clause intended to exceed the protection of the common law settlement privilege and, more specifically, to displace the exception to that privilege that applies where a party seeks to prove the existence or the scope of a settlement? I find that a review of the nature of the contract, of the circumstances in which it was formed and of the contract as a whole reveals that

the parties did not intend to disregard the usual rule that settlement privilege can be dispensed with in order to prove the terms of a settlement.

[The court concluded that in the absence of an express provision stating otherwise, parties who agree to mediation for the purpose of reaching a settlement do not renounce their right to prove the terms of the settlement.]

[66] I therefore find that the mediation contract does not preclude the parties from producing evidence of communications made in the course of the mediation process in order to prove the terms of a settlement. However, I would note that this exception is a narrow one. Parties may produce such evidence only insofar as it is necessary in order to prove the terms of the settlement. The judge who hears the motion for homologation will consider the impugned paragraphs of the motion individually to determine whether each of them is necessary for that purpose. If either party would prefer that potentially sensitive information tendered in support of those paragraphs not be made available to the public, an application can be made to the motion judge for a confidentiality order and to consider the evidence *in camera*, as long as the parties meet the test from *Sierra Club of Canada v. Canada (Minister of Finance)*, 2002 SCC 41, [2002] 2 S.C.R. 522.

NOTE

Settlement privilege is a mainstay in civil cases, but it also applies to plea deals in the criminal context. One issue is whether an allegation of abuse of process arising in a criminal case can operate as an exception to settlement privilege. In *R v Delchev*, 2015 ONCA 381, the court concluded that it can, although it stressed that the facts were "rare and exceptional." The settlement or plea offer in issue included the following term (at para 11): "the Crown indicated that if the [appellant] was to provide an induced statement in which he would admit that his evidence up to that point in the proceeding regarding duress was false, and that his counsel knew it to be false, the Crown would recommend a conditional sentence to the Crown Attorney for Scarborough as the Crown position on sentence upon the [appellant's] plea of guilty to certain charges." The trial judge denied a defence motion for a stay of proceedings for abuse of process. The judge decided that settlement privilege applied to the offer, there was no extrinsic evidence supporting an exception based on prosecutorial impropriety, and therefore the evidence of the discussion was inadmissible. The Court of Appeal disagreed, voicing serious concerns with the Crown making an offer to an accused that could negatively affect the accused's relationship with his counsel and, as a result, impair the administration of justice. On the issue of settlement privilege, the court held that the allegation at issue was analogous to the exceptions to settlement privilege identified in *Sable Offshore*: misrepresentation, fraud, and undue influence. All reflect wrongdoing that corrupts the fair process of law. The court concluded that the abuse of process claim was a countervailing public interest that outweighed the public interest in promoting settlement. The court also held that extrinsic evidence of prosecutorial misconduct was not required to establish an exception to settlement privilege, noting that the Supreme Court did not give any indication in *Sable Offshore* that extrinsic evidence was required and (at para 39): "[w]here the content of an offer itself is alleged to be the abuse, there will necessarily be no or limited extrinsic evidence to support the allegation." See also, for an application to a civil suit for malicious prosecution: *Singh v Montreal (City of)*, 2014 QCCA 307 (allowing evidence of a plea offer).

IV. INFORMER PRIVILEGE

Informer privilege is intended to guard the identity of police informers to protect them from retribution from criminals and to encourage informers to come forward. In *Leipert*, the Supreme Court of Canada considered several aspects of informer privilege, including the question of exceptions.

R v Leipert
[1997] 1 SCR 281, 112 CCC (3d) 385
Lamer CJC and La Forest, L'Heureux-Dubé, Sopinka, Gonthier,
Cory, McLachlin, Iacobucci, and Major JJ (6 February 1997)

McLACHLIN J (Lamer CJC and La Forest, Sopinka, Gonthier, Cory, Iacobucci, and Major JJ concurring):

[1] This appeal raises the issue of whether the defence is entitled to receive details of an informer telephone tip to Crime Stoppers, a public service organization working to combat crime. The appellant asserts that he is entitled to such details pursuant to his right under the *Canadian Charter of Rights and Freedoms* to make full answer and defence. The Crown argues that disclosure is barred by the common law rule that an informer's communications are privileged. For the reasons that follow, I am of the view that the information is privileged and need not be disclosed.

I. The Facts

[2] The police received a tip from the Greater Vancouver Crime Stoppers Association that the appellant, Richard Leipert, was growing marijuana in his basement. A police detective went to Leipert's residence accompanied by Bruno, a sniffer dog. On four different occasions the policeman and Bruno walked the street in front of Leipert's residence. Each time Bruno indicated the presence of drugs in Leipert's house. On one occasion, the policeman smelled the aroma of marijuana coming from Leipert's house. The officer also observed that the basement windows were covered and one window was barred shut. On the basis of these observations, the officer obtained a search warrant. The information filed in support of the application for the warrant disclosed that the officer had received a Crime Stoppers tip that drugs were being grown in Leipert's house. However, the main allegations raised in support of the warrant were the observations of the police officer at the site. When the search warrant was executed, evidence was seized and the appellant was charged with cultivation of marijuana and possession of marijuana for the purpose of trafficking.

II. Rulings

[3] At trial, the accused asked the officer if he had the Crime Stoppers document reporting the tip. The officer had the document, but the Crown refused disclosure on the ground of informer privilege. The trial judge viewed the document and attempted to edit out all references to the identity of the informer. He then ordered disclosure. The Crown

asked to rely on the warrant without reference to the tip. The trial judge refused this request because the accused did not consent. As a result, the Crown ceased to tender evidence, the defence elected to call no evidence, and the trial judge entered an acquittal.

[4] The Court of Appeal reversed the decision of the trial judge and ordered a new trial ... .

. . .

IV. Discussion

A. Did the Trial Judge Err in Ordering Production of the Edited Tip Sheet?

(1) The Argument on Informer Privilege

[6] The appellant relies on the principle that the Crown is under a general duty to disclose all information within its control unless it is clearly irrelevant or privileged: *R v. Stinchcombe*, [1991] 3 SCR 326, at p. 339. He argues that the Crown did not establish that the information in the tip sheet was clearly irrelevant. As for privilege, he asserts that there is no privilege in the edited document which the trial judge ordered disclosed, since it could not reveal the identity of the informer. It follows, he concludes, that the trial judge properly ordered production of the tip sheet to the defence.

[7] The Crown in reply asserts that the entire tip sheet is privileged, subject only to the "innocence at stake" exception. Since that exception is not proved, the tip sheet should not have been disclosed. The trial judge's approach of editing the privileged document to transform it into a non-privileged document is improper and risky, as seemingly innocuous details may be sufficient to identify an informant. This would, moreover, undermine Crime Stoppers' efficacy, which depends on being able to assure informants that they will not be identified.

[8] The trial judge was faced with two apparently conflicting rules. The first was the rule requiring disclosure to the defence of all information not clearly irrelevant or privileged. The second was the rule of informer privilege. The trial judge attempted to accommodate both rules by editing the tip sheet to remove information that could reveal the tipster's identity and ordering production of the balance of the tip sheet. I share the view of McEachern CJBC in the Court of Appeal that the trial judge's approach gave insufficient weight to both the importance of maintaining informer privilege and the danger of ordering disclosure of tip sheets containing details which, despite editing, may enable an accused person to identify the informant.

(a) The Importance of Informer Privilege

[9] A court considering this issue must begin from the proposition that informer privilege is an ancient and hallowed protection which plays a vital role in law enforcement. It is premised on the duty of all citizens to aid in enforcing the law. The discharge of this duty carries with it the risk of retribution from those involved in crime. The rule of informer privilege was developed to protect citizens who assist in law enforcement and to encourage others to do the same. As Cory JA (as he then was) stated in *R v. Hunter* (1987), 57 CR (3d) 1 (Ont. CA), at pp. 5-6:

> The rule against the non-disclosure of information which might identify an informer is one of long standing. It developed from an acceptance of the importance of the role of informers

in the solution of crimes and the apprehension of criminals. It was recognized that citizens have a duty to divulge to the police any information that they may have pertaining to the commission of a crime. It was also obvious to the courts from very early times that the identity of an informer would have to be concealed, both for his or her own protection and to encourage others to divulge to the authorities any information pertaining to crimes. It was in order to achieve these goals that the rule was developed.

[10] The rule is of fundamental importance to the workings of a criminal justice system. As described in *Bisaillon v. Keable*, [1983] 2 SCR 60, at p. 105:

> The rule gives a peace officer the power to promise his informers secrecy expressly or by implication, with a guarantee sanctioned by the law that this promise will be kept even in court, and to receive in exchange for this promise information without which it would be extremely difficult for him to carry out his duties and ensure that the criminal law is obeyed.

In *R v. Scott*, [1990] 3 SCR 979, at p. 994, Cory J stressed the heightened importance of the rule in the context of drug investigations:

> The value of informers to police investigations has long been recognized. As long as crimes have been committed, certainly as long as they have been prosecuted, informers have played an important role in their investigation. It may well be true that some informers act for compensation or for self-serving purposes. Whatever their motives, the position of informers is always precarious and their role is fraught with danger.
>
> The role of informers in drug-related cases is particularly important and dangerous. Informers often provide the only means for the police to gain some knowledge of the workings of drug trafficking operations and networks. ... The investigation often will be based upon a relationship of trust between the police officer and the informer, something that may take a long time to establish. The safety, indeed the lives, not only of informers but also of the undercover police officers will depend on that relationship of trust.

[11] In most cases, the identity of the informer is known to the police. However, in cases like the instant one, the identity of the informer is unknown to everyone including the Crime Stoppers' agent who received the call. The importance of the informer privilege rule in cases where the identity of the informer is anonymous was stressed by the California Court of Appeal in *People v. Callen*, 194 Cal. App. 3d 558 (1987). The court, in holding that the police have no duty to determine or disclose the identity of anonymous informers, stated at p. 587:

> Such an investigatory burden would not only be onerous and frequently futile, it would destroy programs such as Crimestoppers by removing the guarantee of anonymity. Anonymity is the key to such a program. It is the promise of anonymity which allays the fear of criminal retaliation which otherwise discourages citizen involvement in reporting crime. In turn, by guaranteeing anonymity, Crimestoppers provides law enforcement with information it might never otherwise obtain. We are satisfied the benefits of a Crimestoppers-type program—citizen involvement in reporting crime and criminals—far outweigh any speculative benefits to the defense arising from imposing a duty on law enforcement to gather and preserve evidence of the identity of informants who wish to remain anonymous.

[12] Informer privilege is of such importance that once found, courts are not entitled to balance the benefit enuring from the privilege against countervailing considerations,

as is the case, for example, with Crown privilege or privileges based on Wigmore's four-part test: J. Sopinka, S.N. Lederman and A.W. Bryant, *The Law of Evidence in Canada* (1992), at pp. 805-6. In *Bisaillon v. Keable, supra*, this Court contrasted informer privilege with Crown privilege in this regard. In Crown privilege, the judge may review the information and in the last resort revise the minister's decisions by weighing the two conflicting interests, that of maintaining secrecy and that of doing justice. The Court stated at pp. 97-98:

> This procedure, designed to implement Crown privilege, is pointless in the case of secrecy regarding a police informer. In this case, the law gives the Minister, and the Court after him, no power of weighing or evaluating various aspects of the public interest which are in conflict, since it has already resolved the conflict itself. It has decided once and for all, subject to the law being changed, that information regarding police informers' identity will be, because of its content, a class of information which it is in the public interest to keep secret, and that this interest will prevail over the need to ensure the highest possible standard of justice.

Accordingly, the common law has made secrecy regarding police informers subject to a special system with its own rules, which differ from those applicable to Crown privilege.

[13] The Court in *Bisaillon v. Keable* summed the matter up by asserting that the application of informer privilege "does not depend on the judge's discretion, as it is a legal rule of public order by which the judge is bound" (p. 93).

[14] In summary, informer privilege is of such importance that it cannot be balanced against other interests. Once established, neither the police nor the court possesses discretion to abridge it.

(b) Who May Claim Informer Privilege?

[15] The privilege belongs to the Crown: *Solicitor General of Canada v. Royal Commission of Inquiry (Ontario Health Records)*, [1981] 2 SCR 494. However, the Crown cannot, without the informer's consent, waive the privilege either expressly or by implication by not raising it: *Bisaillon v. Keable, supra*, at p. 94. In that sense, it also belongs to the informer. This follows from the purpose of the privilege, being the protection of those who provide information to the police and the encouragement of others to do the same. This is the second reason why the police and courts do not have a discretion to relieve against the privilege.

[16] The fact that the privilege also belongs to the informer raises special concerns in the case of anonymous informants, like those who provide telephone tips to Crime Stoppers. Since the informer whom the privilege is designed to protect and his or her circumstances are unknown, it is often difficult to predict with certainty what information might allow the accused to identify the informer. A detail as innocuous as the time of the telephone call may be sufficient to permit identification. In such circumstances, courts must exercise great care not to unwittingly deprive informers of the privilege which the law accords to them.

(c) The Scope of Informer Privilege

[17] Connected as it is to the essential effectiveness of the criminal law, informer privilege is broad in scope. While developed in criminal proceedings, it applies in civil proceedings as well: *Bisaillon v. Keable, supra*. It applies to a witness on the stand. Such a

person cannot be compelled to state whether he or she is a police informer: *Bisaillon v. Keable, supra*. And it applies to the undisclosed informant, the person who although never called as a witness, supplies information to the police. Subject only to the "innocence at stake" exception, the Crown and the court are bound not to reveal the undisclosed informant's identity.

[18] Informer privilege prevents not only disclosure of the name of the informant, but of any information which might implicitly reveal his or her identity. Courts have acknowledged that the smallest details may be sufficient to reveal identity. In *R v. Garofoli*, [1990] 2 SCR 1421, at p. 1460, Sopinka J suggested that trial judges, when editing a wiretap packet, consider:

> … whether the identities of confidential police informants, and consequently their lives and safety, may be compromised, bearing in mind that such disclosure may occur as much by reference to the nature of the information supplied by the confidential source as by the publication of his or her name;

This principle was also confirmed by the British Columbia Court of Appeal in *R v. Hardy* (1994), 45 BCAC 146, at p. 149:

> It is well recognized that information which might identify a confidential informant need not be disclosed to the Justice of the Peace or at trial.

Similarly, McEachern CJBC in the case at bar suggested (at para. 35) that an "accused may know that only some very small circle of persons, perhaps only one, may know an apparently innocuous fact that is mentioned in the document." He noted: "The privilege is a hallowed one, and it should be respected scrupulously."

[19] The jurisprudence therefore suggests that the Crown must claim privilege over information that reveals the identity of the informant or that may implicitly reveal identity. In many cases, the Crown will be able to contact the informer to determine the extent of information that can be released without jeopardizing the anonymity of the tipster. The informer is the only person who knows the potential danger of releasing those facts to the accused. The difficulty in this case is that the identity of the informer is unknown. Therefore, the Crown is not in a position to determine whether any part of the information could reveal his or her identity. This led the Crown in the case at bar to claim privilege for all of the information provided by the informer. The extension of privilege to all information that could identify an informant justifies this claim in the case of an anonymous informant.

(d) The "Innocence at Stake" Exception

[20] Informer privilege is subject only to one exception, known as the "innocence at stake" exception. Lord Esher MR, described this exception in *Marks v. Beyfus* (1890), 25 QBD 494 (CA), at p. 498:

> … if upon the trial of a prisoner the judge should be of opinion that the disclosure of the name of the informant is necessary or right in order to shew the prisoner's innocence, then one public policy is in conflict with another public policy, and that which says that an innocent man is not to be condemned when his innocence can be proved is the policy that must prevail.

In *Bisaillon v. Keable, supra,* this Court held (at p. 93):

> The rule is subject to only one exception, imposed by the need to demonstrate the innocence of an accused person.

As Cory J stated in *Scott, supra,* at pp. 995-96:

> In our system the right of an individual accused to establish his or her innocence by raising a reasonable doubt as to guilt has always remained paramount.

[21] In order to raise the "innocence at stake" exception to informer privilege, there must be a basis on the evidence for concluding that disclosure of the informer's identity is necessary to demonstrate the innocence of the accused: *R v. Chiarantano*, [1990] OJ no. 2603 (CA), *per* Brooke JA, aff'd. [1991] 1 SCR 906. In *Chiarantano*, the possibility that the information provided by the informer regarding the arrival at a residence of drugs later found in the possession of the accused might conflict with the evidence of the accused was held not to raise a basis for disclosure pursuant to the "innocence at stake" exception. The court held that the usefulness of the information was speculative and that mere speculation that the information might assist the defence is insufficient. If speculation sufficed to remove the privilege, little if anything would be left of the protection which the privilege purports to accord.

[22] On the other hand, circumstances may arise where the evidence establishes a basis for the exception, as where the informer is a material witness to the crime or acted as an *agent provocateur*: see *Scott, supra*. Where such a basis is established, the privilege must yield to the principle that a person is not to be condemned when his or her innocence can be proved.

(e) Informer Privilege and the Charter

[23] It has been suggested (although not by the appellant) that the *Canadian Charter of Rights and Freedoms*, as interpreted in *Stinchcombe, supra*, has introduced another exception to the informer privilege rule based on the right to full disclosure of documents in the Crown's possession in aid of the *Charter* guarantee of the right to make full answer and defence: D.M. Tanovich, "When Does *Stinchcombe* Demand that the Crown Reveal the Identity of a Police Informer?" (1995), 38 CR (4th) 202. According to this argument, "innocence at stake" would no longer be the only exception to the informer privilege rule.

[24] This argument rests on a right to disclosure broader than any which this Court has enunciated. In *Stinchcombe, supra*, the right to disclosure of Crown documents was expressly made subject to two conditions: relevance (to be interpreted generously as including all that is not clearly irrelevant) and privilege. The right to disclosure was not to trump privilege. Any doubt about its application to informer privilege was expressly negated (at p. 335):

> ... it is suggested that disclosure may put at risk the security and safety of persons who have provided the prosecution with information. No doubt measures must occasionally be taken to protect the identity of witnesses and informers. *Protection of the identity of informers is covered by the rules relating to informer privilege and exceptions thereto.* ... [Emphasis added.]

In *R v. O'Connor*, [1995] 4 SCR 411, and *A.(L.L.) v. B.(A.)*, [1995] 4 SCR 536, this Court in dealing with disclosure of third party medical and therapeutic records, did not suggest that the informer privilege rule had been altered by the requirement of Crown disclosure, under the *Charter*. Rather, it appears to have endorsed the common law rule: "so important is the societal interest in preventing a miscarriage of justice that our law requires the state to disclose the identity of an informer in certain circumstances, despite the fact that the revelation may jeopardize the informer's safety": *O'Connor, supra*, at para. 18, *per* Lamer CJ and Sopinka J. The comments of L'Heureux-Dubé J in *A.(L.L.) v. B.(A.), supra*, at paras. 37 and 69, are to the same effect. This Court has consistently affirmed that it is a fundamental principle of justice, protected by the *Charter*, that the innocent must not be convicted: *R v. Seaboyer*, [1991] 2 SCR 577, at p. 611; *Stinchcombe, supra*; *O'Connor, supra*. To the extent that rules and privileges stand in the way of an innocent person establishing his or her innocence, they must yield to the *Charter* guarantee of a fair trial. The common law rule of informer privilege, however, does not offend this principle. From its earliest days, the rule has affirmed the priority of the policy of the law "that an innocent man is not to be condemned when his innocence can be proved" by permitting an exception to the privilege where innocence is at stake: *Marks v. Beyfus, supra*. It is therefore not surprising that this Court has repeatedly referred to informer privilege as an example of the policy of the law that the innocent should not be convicted, rather than as a deviation from it.

[25] I find no inconsistency between the *Charter* right to disclosure of Crown documents affirmed in *Stinchcombe, supra*, and the common law rule of informer privilege.

(f) Informer Privilege and Challenges to Search Warrants

[26] Where the accused seeks to establish that a search warrant was not supported by reasonable grounds, the accused may be entitled to information which may reveal the identity of an informer notwithstanding informer privilege "in circumstances where it is absolutely essential": *Scott, supra*, at p. 996. "Essential" circumstances exist where the accused establishes the "innocence at stake" exception to informer privilege. Such a case might arise, for example, where there is evidence suggesting that the goods seized in execution of the warrant were planted. To establish that the informer planted the goods or had information as to how they came to be planted, the accused might properly seek disclosure of information that may incidentally reveal the identity of the informer.

[27] Absent a basis for concluding that disclosure of the information that may reveal the identity of the informer is necessary to establish the innocence of the accused, the information remains privileged and cannot be produced, whether on a hearing into the reasonableness of the search or on the trial proper.

(g) Judicial Editing

[28] The ultimate issue on this appeal is whether the trial judge erred in editing the tip sheet to remove references to the informer's identity and in ordering the edited sheet disclosed to the appellant. In addressing this question, I have regard to the following propositions, discussed above. Informer privilege is of great importance. Once established, the privilege cannot be diminished by or "balanced off against" other concerns relating to the administration of justice. The police and the court have no discretion to diminish it and are bound to uphold it. The only exception to the privilege is found where there is a basis to conclude that the information may be necessary to establish the innocence of the accused. The scope of the rule extends not only to the name of the informer, but to

any details which might reveal the informer's identity. It is virtually impossible for the court to know what details may reveal the identity of an anonymous informer. The same considerations apply on challenges to search warrants or wiretap authorizations.

[29] These considerations suggest that anonymous tip sheets should not be edited with a view to disclosing them to the defence unless the accused can bring himself within the innocence at stake exception. To do so runs the risk that the court will deprive the informer of the privilege which belongs to him or her absolutely, subject only to the "innocence at stake" exception. It also undermines the efficacy of programs such as Crimestoppers, which depend on guarantees of anonymity to those who volunteer information on crimes.

[30] The appellant relies on judicial editing of confidential material approved in challenges to wiretap authorizations. In *Garofoli*, *supra*, Sopinka J stated at p. 1458: "Editing ... is essential in cases in which confidential information is included in the affidavit filed in support of an authorization." He added, "In determining what to edit, the judge will have regard for the rule against disclosure of police informants." A similar conclusion was reached *per* Cory J in *Hunter*, *supra*.

[31] These cases are distinguishable from the case at bar on two grounds. First, the informants in those cases were not anonymous, enabling the court to make judgments on what details might or might not reveal the identity of the informers. Second, the defence was seeking to review the affidavit or "Information to Obtain" filed in support of the application for the authorization, as distinguished from background documents and information. In the case at bar, the appellant had disclosure of the "Information to Obtain." He knew the entire basis for the authorization. He wanted more—the details of the information given by the tipster. Those details, recorded by the police officer who received the call, were contained in a separate document. In *Hunter*, *Garofoli* and *Scott*, the combination of the known informant and the fact that what was at issue was the very document upon which the Crown relied to sustain the warrant or authorization, supported the approval for editing. The case here is quite different.

[32] There may be cases where the informer and his circumstances are known, in which the court can be certain that what remains of an informant document after editing will not reveal the informer's identity. When, however, as in the case at bar, it is impossible to determine which details of the information provided by an informer will or will not result in that person's identity being revealed, then none of those details should be disclosed, unless there is a basis to conclude that the innocence at stake exception applies.

(h) Procedure

[33] When an accused seeks disclosure of privileged informer information on the basis of the "innocence at stake" exception, the following procedure will apply. First, the accused must show some basis to conclude that without the disclosure sought his or her innocence is at stake. If such a basis is shown, the court may then review the information to determine whether, in fact, the information is necessary to prove the accused's innocence. If the court concludes that disclosure is necessary, the court should only reveal as much information as is essential to allow proof of innocence. Before disclosing the information to the accused, the Crown should be given the option of staying the proceedings. If the Crown chooses to proceed, disclosure of the information essential to establish innocence may be provided to the accused.

(i) Application to the Case at Bar

[34] The identity of the anonymous informer was protected by informer privilege. The police and the courts were bound to protect the identity of the informant from disclosure. Given the anonymous nature of the tip, it was impossible to conclude whether the disclosure of details remaining after editing might be sufficient to reveal the identity of the informer to the accused and others who might have been involved in this crime and seeking retribution. It follows that the statement should not have been edited and ordered disclosed to the defence. The informer's privilege required nothing short of total confidentiality. As it was not established that the identity was necessary to establish the innocence of the accused, the privilege continued in place.

NOTES AND QUESTIONS

1. The Supreme Court of Canada reaffirmed and applied the principles of *Leipert* in *Named Person v Vancouver Sun*, 2007 SCC 43, [2007] 3 SCR 253 and *R v Basi*, 2009 SCC 52, [2009] 3 SCR 389. In *Named Person*, the "informer" appeared before an extradition judge and during an *in camera* hearing identified himself as such. The judge, after seeking recommendations from a court-appointed *amicus curiae*, decided to allow certain media counsel access to a continued hearing into the claim of informer privilege, upon undertakings of confidentiality and non-disclosure to their clients. The Supreme Court of Canada condemned these decisions because they erroneously sought to balance the open-court principle with that of protecting informers. The court held that once informer status is asserted, the court must assume that privilege attaches until it is determined that it does not exist or there is an exception. This is done *in camera* at a "first stage" hearing, without any disclosure of even the existence of the claim to the privilege. Usually, only the putative informant and the Crown appear, although an *amicus curiae* may be appointed where the interests of the informant and the Crown are aligned. The court explained:

> [4] [I]nformer privilege must remain absolute. Information which might tend to identify a confidential informant cannot be revealed, except where the innocence of a criminal accused is at stake. Open courts are undoubtedly a vital part of our legal system and of our society, but their openness cannot be allowed to fundamentally compromise the criminal justice system.
>
> . . .
>
> [26] In addition to its absolute non-discretionary nature, the rule is extremely broad in its application. The rule applies to the identity of every informer: it applies when the informer is not present, where the informer is present, and even where the informer himself or herself is a witness. It applies to both documentary evidence and oral testimony: Sopinka, Lederman and Bryant, at pp. 882-83. It applies in criminal and civil trials. The duty imposed to keep an informer's identity confidential applies to the police, to the Crown, to attorneys and to judges: Hubbard, Magotiaux and Duncan, at p. 2-2. The rule's protection is also broad in its coverage. Any information which might tend to identify an informer is protected by the privilege. Thus the protection is not limited simply to the informer's name, but extends to any information that might lead to identification.
>
> [27] The informer privilege rule admits but one exception: it can be abridged if necessary to establish innocence in a criminal trial (there are no exceptions to the rule in civil proceedings). According to the innocence at stake exception, "there must be a basis on the evidence for

concluding that disclosure of the informer's identity is necessary to demonstrate the innocence of the accused": Leipert, at para. 21. It stands to be emphasized that the exception will apply only if there is an evidentiary basis for the conclusion; mere speculation will not suffice: Sopinka, Lederman and Bryant, at p. 884. The exception applies only where disclosure of the informer's identity is the only way that the accused can establish innocence: *R v. Brown*, [2002] 2 SCR 185, 2002 SCC 32, at para 4.

[28] In this Court's decision in *Leipert*, it was clearly established that innocence at stake is the only exception to the informer privilege rule. The rule does not allow an exception for the right to make full answer and defence. Nor does the rule allow an exception for disclosure under *R v. Stinchcombe*, [1991] 3 SCR 326. Indeed, the Court's decision in *Leipert* suggests, at para. 24, that an absolute informer privilege rule, subject only to the innocence at stake exception, is consistent with the Charter's provisions dealing with trial rights:

> To the extent that rules and privileges stand in the way of an innocent person establishing his or her innocence, they must yield to the Charter guarantee of a fair trial. The common law rule of informer privilege, however, does not offend this principle. From its earliest days, the rule has affirmed the priority of the policy of the law "that an innocent man is not to be condemned when his innocence can be proved" by permitting an exception to the privilege where innocence is at stake: *Marks v. Beyfus* [(1980), 25 QBD 494 (CA)]. It is therefore not surprising that this Court has repeatedly referred to informer privilege as an example of the policy of the law that the innocent should not be convicted, rather than as a deviation from it.

[29] For the sake of clarity, it is useful to pause here to explain the law regarding what were argued before us as some "other" exceptions to the informer privilege rule. As already noted, the only real exception to the informer privilege rule is the innocence at stake exception: *Leipert*. All other purported exceptions to the rule are either applications of the innocence at stake exception or else examples of situations in which the privilege does not actually apply.

Justice LeBel dissented in part, saying that "innocence at stake" isn't the only exception; he found that the trial judge has discretion to decide to weigh the underlying interests at issue.

In *Basi*, above, the trial judge allowed defence counsel to participate in an *in camera* hearing to determine whether informer privilege existed. The Supreme Court of Canada applied *Named Person* and said that the procedure was inappropriate, although it noted that, in some cases, the duty of fairness to an accused may require the trial judge to take measures to try to accommodate defence concerns in the *in camera* hearing, short of disclosing identifying information:

> [44] ... No one outside the circle of privilege may access information over which the privilege has been claimed until a judge has determined that the privilege does not exist or that an exception applies. It follows that the trial judge erred in permitting defence counsel to hear the testimony of an officer tending to reveal the identity of the putative informant at the "first stage" hearing.

2. In *Canada (Citizenship and Immigration) v Harkat*, 2014 SCC 37, [2014] 2 SCR 33, the court held that Canadian Security and Intelligence Services (CSIS) "human sources"—that is, individuals who secretly provided information to CSIS—are *not* covered by class privilege, and, in limited circumstances, may be cross-examined by special advocates (lawyers with security clearance permitted to participate in closed hearings on terrorism-related security

certificates issued against "named persons") to test the validity of the government's claim for privilege. Harkat was alleged to have come to Canada for the purpose of engaging in terrorism and was either detained or living under strict conditions for over a decade. His special advocates challenged the governing statute, the *Immigration and Refugee Protection Act*, SC 2001, c 27 (the "*IRPA* scheme") as unconstitutional because it provides insufficient disclosure to the named person, does not allow the special advocates to communicate freely with the named person, and allows for the admission of hearsay evidence. The court upheld the scheme. A majority rejected the government's claim that the CSIS "human sources" were protected by informer privilege. The majority reasoned:

(1) Does Privilege Attach to CSIS Human Sources?

[81] It is important to note at the outset that the *IRPA* scheme provides protection for the identity of sources and of information that tends to reveal that identity. Indeed, the starting point under the *IRPA* scheme is that all information whose disclosure would be injurious to national security or endanger the safety of a person is protected from disclosure to the named person and to the public: s. 83(1)(d). In most cases, the disclosure of the identity of human sources would both be injurious to national security and endanger the safety of those sources. Consequently, their identity will generally be protected from disclosure under the *IRPA* scheme.

[82] As a limited exception to this general principle of non-disclosure, the *IRPA* scheme provides that special advocates get full disclosure of all the evidence provided by the Minister to the judge: s. 85.4(1). The Minister has no obligation, however, to disclose privileged materials to anyone.

[83] It thus becomes necessary to determine whether the identities of CSIS human sources, and related information, are privileged. But it is important to bear in mind that even if they are not privileged, the judge under the *IRPA* scheme has the duty to prevent disclosure to the public and to the named person of this information if it would be injurious to national security or the safety of the sources. The information will thus generally remain within the confines of the closed circle formed by the designated judge, the special advocates—who, it bears repeating, are security-cleared lawyers—and the Minister's lawyers.

[84] Against this background, I come to the question: Are the identities of CSIS human sources and information that might reveal their identity protected by common law privilege?

[85] It is argued that police informer privilege attaches to CSIS human sources. I agree with the Federal Court of Appeal that it does not. Traditional police work involving informers, on the one hand, and the collection of security intelligence and information, on the other, are two different things. Indeed, Parliament created CSIS in recognition of this emerging distinction: *Charkaoui v. Canada (Citizenship and Immigration)*, 2008 SCC 38, [2008] 2 S.C.R. 326 ("*Charkaoui II*"), at paras. 21-22. Courts developed police informer privilege at a time when the police investigated crimes locally and collected evidence mainly for use in criminal trials. By contrast, the intelligence gathering conducted by CSIS takes place on a global scale and is geared towards prospectively preventing risks: K. Roach, "The eroding distinction between intelligence and evidence in terrorism investigations," in N. McGarrity, A. Lynch and G. Williams, eds., *Counter-Terrorism and Beyond: The Culture of Law and Justice after 9/11* (2010), 48. Police have an incentive not to promise confidentiality except where truly necessary, because doing so can make it harder to use an informer as a witness. CSIS, on the other hand, is not so constrained. It is concerned primarily with obtaining security intelligence, rather than finding evidence for use in court. While evidence gathered by the police was traditionally used in criminal trials that provide the accused with significant evidentiary

safeguards, the intelligence gathered by CSIS may be used to establish criminal conduct in proceedings that—as is the case here—have relaxed rules of evidence and allow for the admission
of hearsay evidence. The differences between traditional policing and modern intelligence gathering preclude automatically applying traditional police informer privilege to CSIS human
sources.

[86] I have found no persuasive authority for the proposition that police informer privilege
applies to CSIS human sources. In *R. v. Y.(N.)*, 2012 ONCA 745, 113 O.R. (3d) 347, cited as authority
by Abella and Cromwell JJ […]The court's reasons can be read as assuming that privilege would
attach to a CSIS informer, but that point was not squarely before the court and was not decided.

[87] Nor, in my view, should this Court create a new privilege for CSIS human sources. This
Court has stated that "[t]he law recognizes very few 'class privileges'" and that "[i]t is likely that in
future such 'class' privileges will be created, if at all, only by legislative action": *R. v. National Post*,
2010 SCC 16 [2010] 1 S.C.R. 477, at para. 42. The wisdom of this applies to the proposal that privilege be extended to CSIS human sources: *Canada (Attorney General) v. Almalki*, 2011 FCA 199,
[2012] 2 F.C.R. 594, at paras. 29-30, *per* Létourneau J.A. If Parliament deems it desirable that CSIS
human sources' identities and related information be privileged, whether to facilitate coordina-
tion between police forces and CSIS or to encourage sources to come forward to CSIS (see reasons
of Abella and Cromwell JJ.), it can enact the appropriate protections. Finally, the question arises
whether judges should have the power to shield the identity of human sources from special
advocates on a case-by-case basis where they conclude that public interests in non-disclosure
outweigh the benefits of disclosure. This question was not argued by the parties, and I offer no
comment on it, other than to note that the *IRPA* scheme already affords broad protection to human
sources by precluding the public disclosure of information that would injure national security or
endanger a person.

(2) Should the Special Advocates Be Authorized to Interview and Cross-Examine the Human Sources?

[88] The special advocates ask this Court to rule that they may interview and cross-examine
the CSIS human sources who have provided information used against Mr. Harkat. [Endnote omitted.] I have concluded that the identity of CSIS human sources is not privileged. However, it does
not follow from the absence of a privilege that special advocates have an unlimited ability to
interview and cross-examine human sources. As discussed above, the designated judge may
admit information provided by these sources as hearsay evidence, if he concludes that the evidence is "reliable and appropriate": s. 83(1)(h), *IRPA*. The Minister has no obligation to produce
CSIS human sources as witnesses, although the failure to do so may weaken the probative value
of his evidence.

[89] This said, the special advocates may "exercise, with the judge's authorization, any other
powers that are necessary to protect the interests" of the named person: s. 85.2(c), *IRPA*. The
designated judge has the discretion to allow the special advocates to interview and cross-
examine human sources in a closed hearing. This discretion should be exercised as a last resort.
The record before us establishes that a generalized practice of calling CSIS human sources before
a court, even if only in closed hearings, may have a chilling effect on potential sources and hinder
CSIS' ability to recruit new sources. In most cases, disclosure to the special advocates of the human
source files and other relevant information regarding the human sources will suffice to protect
the interests of the named person.

[90] The case at hand is not one of those rare cases in which it is necessary to give special advocates permission to interview and cross-examine CSIS human sources. The special advocates

contend that cross-examination is necessary in order to test the credibility of the human sources, to cross-examine them on Mr. Harkat's motives for coming to Canada in the mid-1990s, and to undermine the allegation that Mr. Harkat traveled to Afghanistan. In my view, Mr. Harkat and his special advocates have had sufficient opportunity to pursue those objectives, and the designated judge's weighing of the relevant evidence took into account the fact that it was hearsay. Indeed, the evidence on the record allowed the special advocates to undermine the credibility of one of the human sources and led Noël J. to rely on information originating from this source only when corroborated: see 2010 FC 1241, [2012] 3 F.C.R. 251, at footnote 1. Moreover, Mr. Harkat testified with respect to his motives for coming to Canada and denied the allegations that he visited Afghanistan. Noël J. made a strong adverse finding of credibility against Mr. Harkat on these issues: it is highly improbable that cross-examination of the human sources could have bolstered his credibility. There is therefore no need for this Court to authorize the exceptional measure of interviewing and cross-examining human sources.

The dissent opinion would have recognized human sources as entitled to informer privilege and it rejected the distinction between traditional police work and intelligence gathering by CSIS. As a result, it had to address whether the security certificate proceedings required an exception to be created to allow for the rights of those named in a security certificate.

[135] The final question relates to whether an exception to the privilege should apply in the security certificate context. Noël J. [of the Federal Court of Appeal below] was of the view that there was a "need to know" exception, analogous to the "innocence at stake" exception to the police informer privilege. This exception means that the privilege can be set aside in cases where maintaining it would undermine the accused's ability to raise a reasonable doubt. The "need to know" exception would similarly be engaged when abrogating the privilege is necessary to prevent a serious breach of procedural fairness that would impugn the administration of justice. On the facts before him, Noël J. held that the requirements of the "need to know" exception had not been met and therefore denied the special advocates' request.

[136] In our view, the "need to know exception" outlined by Noël J. is overly broad: 2009 FC 204, at para. 46. We agree with the ministers that this exception is broader than the "innocence at stake" exception because the latter applies only where there is a risk of an unjust outcome, whereas the "need to know" exception applies where there is an unjust procedure. It also appears to overlook the considerable procedural flexibility that is available to the reviewing judge and the particular role of the special advocate.

[137] But given the intensity of the interests at stake in the security certificate context, we acknowledge that it would be appropriate to recognize a limited exception specifically crafted for the security certificate process which would address only disclosure to the special advocate, not to the subject of the proceedings. Identity should be disclosed only if the reviewing judge is satisfied that other measures, including withdrawing the substance of the informant's evidence from consideration in support of the certificate, are not sufficient to ensure a just outcome. Noël J. ordered generous disclosure of material to the special advocates concerning the credibility of informers and the information they supplied. He allowed cross-examination of CSIS witnesses on the value, reliability and usefulness of informer information. In some circumstances, he relied on informer information only where it had been corroborated. If these measures are not considered adequate, the reviewing judge also has discretion under s. 83(1)(h) of *IRPA* to refuse to rely on evidence that he or she does not consider to be reliable and appropriate. Only if resort to these measures would not ensure a just outcome should identity be disclosed.

[138] Even when disclosure of identity is ordered, there should be no cross-examination of the source by the special advocate. Requiring a human source to testify will have a profound chilling effect on the willingness of other sources to come forward, and will undoubtedly damage the relationship between CSIS and the source compelled to testify. CSIS operatives must be able to provide confident assurances to their sources that their identities will not be revealed, not vague assurances hedged with qualifications. Moreover, the human sources themselves, who are not subject to the necessary security clearance, may learn sensitive material in the closed proceedings which CSIS will then be unable to control.

The federal government acted swiftly following the court's decision and passed the *Protection of Canada from Terrorists Act*, SC 2015, c 9, which is available at <http://laws-lois.justice .gc.ca/eng/AnnualStatutes/2015_9/page-1.html>. The relevant sections establish a strong statutory privilege. Which do you believe is preferable: the common law as outlined in the dissent, or the new statutory framework, below?

18.1(1) The purpose of this section is to ensure that the identity of human sources is kept confidential in order to protect their life and security and to encourage individuals to provide information to the Service.

(2) Subject to subsections (3) and (8), no person shall, in a proceeding before a court, person or body with jurisdiction to compel the production of information, disclose the identity of a human source or any information from which the identity of a human source could be inferred.

(3) The identity of a human source or information from which the identity of a human source could be inferred may be disclosed in a proceeding referred to in subsection (2) if the human source and the Director consent to the disclosure of that information.

(4) A party to a proceeding referred to in subsection (2), an *amicus curiae* who is appointed in respect of the proceeding or a person who is appointed to act as a special advocate if the proceeding is under the *Immigration and Refugee Protection Act* may apply to a judge for one of the following orders if it is relevant to the proceeding:

(a) an order declaring that an individual is not a human source or that information is not information from which the identity of a human source could be inferred; or

(b) if the proceeding is a prosecution of an offence, an order declaring that the disclosure of the identity of a human source or information from which the identity of a human source could be inferred is essential to establish the accused's innocence and that it may be disclosed in the proceeding.

(5) The application and the applicant's affidavit deposing to the facts relied on in support of the application shall be filed in the Registry of the Federal Court. The applicant shall, without delay after the application and affidavit are filed, serve a copy of them on the Attorney General of Canada.

(6) Once served, the Attorney General of Canada is deemed to be a party to the application.

(7) The hearing of the application shall be held in private and in the absence of the applicant and their counsel, unless the judge orders otherwise.

(8) If the judge grants an application made under paragraph (4)(b), the judge may order the disclosure that the judge considers appropriate subject to any conditions that the judge specifies.

(9) If the judge grants an application made under subsection (4), any order made by the judge does not take effect until the time provided to appeal the order has expired or, if the order

is appealed and is confirmed, until either the time provided to appeal the judgement confirming the order has expired or all rights of appeal have been exhausted.

(10) The judge shall ensure the confidentiality of the following:

(a) the identity of any human source and any information from which the identity of a human source could be inferred; and

(b) information and other evidence provided in respect of the application if, in the judge's opinion, its disclosure would be injurious to national security or endanger the safety of any person.

(11) In the case of an appeal, subsection (10) applies, with any necessary modifications, to the court to which the appeal is taken.

3. In light of the rationale for the informer privilege articulated in *Leipert*, would you uphold the claim of privilege in the following cases?

(a) The accused was charged with trafficking in narcotics and sought to raise a defence of entrapment. The accused believed that an individual named Ross was a police informer who would, if called, give evidence relevant to a defence of entrapment. As trial judge would you: (1) permit the accused's counsel to cross-examine a police officer about Ross's identity as the informant? (2) issue a material witness warrant for Ross? (3) permit the defence to call Ross as a witness when he unexpectedly appeared in court? See *R v Scott*, [1990] 3 SCR 979, 61 CCC (3d) 300.

(b) The accused were charged with offences arising out of a marijuana grow operation. The police relied on an informer in executing a search warrant. The accused sought a stay of proceedings on the basis that the Crown had failed to provide the name and address of an informant witness, which the accused claimed was necessary to their defence. The informant had told the police that one group of individuals was on the premises prior to 1999 and thereafter, presumably when the grow operation came into existence, a different group of persons occupied the premises. Counsel for the accused asserted before the chambers judge that the informant would be able to identify the individuals who were in possession after 1999, and if those individuals were not the parties charged, that would demonstrate the innocence of the accused. The chambers judge ordered the Crown to produce the informant, who would be examined by defence counsel in an *in camera* proceeding, and on defence counsel's undertaking not to disclose the identity of the informant to the accused. If you were reviewing this order on appeal, would you overturn it in light of the more recent holdings in *Named Person* and *Basi*? See *R v Ly*, 2004 BCCA 173.

(c) The Province of Ontario established a Commission of Inquiry into the Confidentiality of Health Records. One of the issues the Commission was concerned about was whether certain "physicians and hospital employees [had] divulged medical information to members of the RCMP without the patient's authorization." This issue was clearly within the Commission's terms of reference, but the RCMP and others objected to the Commission's asking RCMP officers about the identity of the relevant physicians and hospital employees, on the ground that they were police informants. Should the privilege be recognized in this context? If so, should an exception to the privilege be recognized in this context? See *Solicitor-General of Canada v Royal Commission (Health Records)*, [1981] 2 SCR 494, 62 CCC (2d) 193.

V. PUBLIC INTEREST IMMUNITY

A. National Security and Related Grounds

The doctrine of public interest immunity, sometimes called "Crown privilege," is concerned with situations in which a public official objects to disclosure of information on the ground that disclosure would be contrary to the public interest. For example, in *Duncan v Cammell, Laird & Co*, [1942] 1 All ER 587 (HL), a private action for negligence arising out of the sinking of a submarine, the Admiralty objected to disclosure of the design of the submarine on grounds of national security. In *Duncan*, the court accepted the claim at face value; but in *Conway v Rimmer*, [1968] 1 All ER 874, the House of Lords held that the court had a discretion to examine the information in question to determine whether in the circumstances the public interest in non-disclosure outweighed the public and private interests in disclosure.

Public interest immunity in proceedings under federal jurisdiction is now governed by ss 37 through 38.16 of the *Canada Evidence Act*, RSC 1985, c C-5, which were enacted in the fall of 2001 by Bill C-36. Federal Cabinet confidences can be claimed under a specific regime in s 39. Section 37 can also be used to address informer privilege. (Section 37 is used when the Crown seeks to immediately appeal an unfavourable ruling under common law in a criminal case because s 37.1 provides an immediate right of appeal despite the interlocutory nature of the order; see *Basi*, above.) *Canada (Justice) v Khadr*, 2008 SCC 28, [2008] 2 SCR 125 held that disclosure obligations in criminal cases are subject to resolution of claims of privilege on specified public interest grounds embodied in these provisions and at common law.

Section 37 provides, in part:

> 37(1) Subject to sections 38 to 38.16, a Minister of the Crown in right of Canada or other official may object to the disclosure of information before a court, person or body with jurisdiction to compel the production of information by certifying orally or in writing to the court, person or body that the information should not be disclosed on the grounds of a specified public interest.
>
> (1.1) If an objection is made under subsection (1), the court, person or body shall ensure that the information is not disclosed other than in accordance with this Act.
>
> (2) If an objection to the disclosure of information is made before a superior court, that court may determine the objection.
>
> (3) If an objection to the disclosure of information is made before a court, person or body other than a superior court, the objection may be determined, on application, by
>
>> (a) the Federal Court, in the case of a person or body vested with power to compel production by or under an Act of Parliament if the person or body is not a court established under a law of a province; or
>>
>> (b) the trial division or trial court of the superior court of the province within which the court, person or body exercises its jurisdiction, in any other case.
>
> • • •
>
> (4.1) Unless the court having jurisdiction to hear the application concludes that the disclosure of the information to which the objection was made under subsection (1) would encroach upon a specified public interest, the court may authorize by order the disclosure of the information.
>
> (5) If the court having jurisdiction to hear the application concludes that the disclosure of the information to which the objection was made under subsection (1) would encroach upon a specified public interest, but that the public interest in disclosure outweighs in importance the

specified public interest, the court may, by order, after considering both the public interest in disclosure and the form of and conditions to disclosure that are most likely to limit any encroachment upon the specified public interest resulting from disclosure, authorize the disclosure, subject to any conditions that the court considers appropriate, of all of the information, a part or summary of the information, or a written admission of facts relating to the information.

(6) If the court does not authorize disclosure under subsection (4.1) or (5), the court shall, by order, prohibit disclosure of the information.

Section 37 therefore preserves the common law position that the court has a discretion to examine the information in question and to weigh the competing interests involved; but s 37 is expressly made subject to the sections that follow it.

Sections 38 through 38.16 create a regime of public interest immunity to protect a wide range of information. This regime applies to "potentially injurious information," defined as "information of a type that, if it were disclosed to the public, could injure international relations or national defence or national security," and to "sensitive information," defined as "information relating to international relations or national defence or national security that is in the possession of the Government of Canada, whether originating from inside or outside Canada, and is of a type that the Government of Canada is taking measures to safeguard." Section 38.01 imposes an obligation on "participants" in proceedings to notify the federal Attorney General about possible disclosure of "potentially injurious" or "sensitive" information in proceedings, and s 38.04 provides for applications to a judge of the Federal Court for an order concerning disclosure of such information. Section 38.06 reads in part:

> 38.06(1) Unless the judge concludes that the disclosure of the information or facts referred to in subsection 38.02(1) would be injurious to international relations or national defence or national security, the judge may, by order, authorize the disclosure of the information or facts.
>
> (2) If the judge concludes that the disclosure of the information would be injurious to international relations or national defence or national security but that the public interest in disclosure outweighs in importance the public interest in non-disclosure, the judge may by order, after considering both the public interest in disclosure and the form of and conditions to disclosure that are most likely to limit any injury to international relations or national defence or national security resulting from disclosure, authorize the disclosure, subject to any conditions that the judge considers appropriate, of all of the information, a part or summary of the information, or a written admission of facts relating to the information.
>
> (3) If the judge does not authorize disclosure under subsection (1) or (2), the judge shall, by order, confirm the prohibition of disclosure.

What is the rationale for funnelling determinations of claims of public interest immunity made on grounds of national security or international relations to the Federal Court, rather than leaving them in the hands of the judges or other officials presiding over the proceedings in which they arise? The Supreme Court of Canada considered most of the s 38 regime in *R v Ahmad*, below, and held that it did not violate the Charter because it can be interpreted to ensure that the accused either receives a fair trial or is not tried at all.

R v Ahmad

2011 SCC 6, [2011] 1 SCR 110

McLachlin CJ and Binnie, LeBel, Deschamps, Fish, Abella,
Charron, Rothstein, and Cromwell JJ (10 February 2011)

[1] THE COURT: This appeal concerns the potential conflict between two fundamental obligations of the state under our system of government: first, to protect society by preventing the disclosure of information that could pose a threat to international relations, national defence, or national security; and second, to prosecute individuals accused of offences against our laws. In s. 38 of the *Canada Evidence Act*, RSC 1985, c. C-5 ("*CEA*"), Parliament has recognized that on occasion it may become necessary to choose between these objectives, but has laid out an elaborate framework to attempt, where possible, to reconcile them. At the heart of this appeal lies the respondents' challenge to the constitutional validity of this provision. In their view, the scheme violates s. 96 of the *Constitution Act, 1867* and s. 7 of the *Canadian Charter of Rights and Freedoms*.

[2] We acknowledge at the outset that in some situations, the prosecution's refusal to disclose relevant (if sensitive or potentially injurious) information in the course of a criminal trial may on the facts of a particular case prejudice the constitutional right of every accused to "a fair and public hearing" and the separately guaranteed right "to be tried within a reasonable time" (*Charter*, ss. 11(d) and (b), respectively). Where the conflict is irreconcilable, an unfair trial cannot be tolerated. Under the rule of law, the right of an accused person to make full answer and defence may not be compromised. However, s. 38, as we interpret it, preserves the full authority and independence of the judge presiding over the criminal trial to do justice between the parties, including, where he or she deems it necessary, to enter a stay of proceedings.

[3] In our view, for the reasons that follow, s. 38 itself (the text of which is attached hereto in the Appendix) provides enough flexibility to avoid the drastic result of a stay of proceedings in all but the most intractable of cases, as recently demonstrated in the *Air India* prosecution (*R v. Malik*, 2005 BCSC 350 (CanLII)). While the statutory scheme of s. 38, particularly its division of responsibilities between the Federal Court and the criminal courts of the provinces, raises numerous practical and legal difficulties, we are satisfied that s. 38, properly understood and applied, is constitutionally valid.

. . .

[7] As we stated in *Charkaoui v. Canada (Citizenship and Immigration)*, 2007 SCC 9, [2007] 1 SCR 350, the Court "has repeatedly recognized that national security considerations can limit the extent of disclosure of information to the affected individual" (para. 58). But we took care in *Charkaoui* to stress as well the importance of the principle of fundamental justice that "a person whose liberty is in jeopardy must be given an opportunity to know the case to meet, and an opportunity to meet the case" (para. 61). *Charkaoui* was an immigration case. In criminal cases, the court's vigilance to ensure fairness is all the more essential. Nevertheless, as we interpret s. 38, the net effect is that state secrecy will be protected where the Attorney General of Canada considers it vital to do so, but the result is that the accused will, if denied the means to make a full answer and defence, and if lesser measures will not suffice in the opinion of the presiding judge to ensure a fair trial, walk free. While we stress this critical protection of the accused's fair trial rights, we

also note that, notwithstanding serious criticisms of the operation of these provisions, they permit considerable flexibility as to how to reconcile the accused's rights and the state's need to prevent disclosure.

· · ·

[22] Central to the scheme of s. 38 are two ministerial powers exercised by the Attorney General of Canada, one in relation to the disclosure or non-disclosure of potentially injurious or sensitive information and the other with respect to the conduct of prosecutions.

[23] First, s. 38.13 empowers the federal Attorney General to personally issue a certificate that prohibits disclosure even of information whose disclosure has been authorized by the Federal Court judge. This certificate is only subject to judicial review by a single judge of the Federal Court of Appeal, and that judge may only vary or cancel the certificate on the ground that the material it contains is not "information obtained in confidence from, or in relation to, a foreign entity … or to national defence or national security" (ss. 38.13 and 38.131). In short, this narrow right of review provides no effective judicial means for challenging or correcting a debatable decision by the Attorney General in balancing the public interest in non-disclosure against the public and private interests in disclosure of the subject information.

[24] The validity of these powers has not been challenged in this case and, for present purposes, they must therefore be presumed to be constitutionally valid. That being so, we think it particularly difficult for the respondents to maintain that s. 38 is unconstitutional on the theory that disclosure decisions are inherently judicial in nature. As we will demonstrate, this is neither historically nor legally correct. The subset of this argument—that it is unconstitutional to allocate disclosure decisions to the Federal Court instead of to the judges in the criminal courts—is equally untenable, for the same reasons.

[25] As we will see, however, this authority of the Attorney General of Canada to disclose or withhold disclosure of potentially injurious or sensitive information, and on what terms, largely independently of the regular Federal Court channel, comes at a price: the potential collapse of the prosecution, whether initiated federally or provincially.

[26] Turning to the second power, the prosecutorial authority of the Attorney General is further reinforced by s. 38.15(1), which authorizes the Attorney General to assume by *fiat* exclusive control of any prosecution in connection with which sensitive or potentially injurious information may be disclosed—even where the proceedings were instituted by a provincial Attorney General.

D. A Practical Approach to Section 38

[27] The respondents' submissions, like the judgment below, have all assumed that because the judge presiding at a criminal trial has no right of access to potentially injurious or sensitive material, such access will not normally occur. The respondents further argue that it would be impossible for the defence to demonstrate prejudice without knowing the nature of the material and that it would be impossible for the trial judge to fashion a just and appropriate remedy under s. 38.14 or s. 24(1) of the *Charter*. Properly interpreted and applied, however, s. 38 does not command this result.

[28] This Court has repeated on numerous occasions that "the words of an Act are to be read in their entire context and in their grammatical and ordinary sense harmoniously with the scheme of the Act, the object of the Act, and the intention of Parliament":

E.A. Driedger in *Construction of Statutes* (2nd ed. 1983), at p. 87; *Rizzo & Rizzo Shoes Ltd. (Re)*, [1998] 1 SCR 27. Moreover, "Parliament is presumed to have intended to enact legislation in conformity with the *Charter*": *R v. Hamilton*, 2005 SCC 47, [2005] 2 SCR 432, at para. 75; *R v. Sharpe*, 2001 SCC 2, [2001] 1 SCR 45, at para. 33.

[29] We therefore begin from the proposition that, in the absence of clear and un-ambiguous statutory language to the contrary, the legislation must be understood not to contemplate that trial judges would determine the impact of non-disclosure on trial fair-ness in a manner that would result in granting unwarranted stays or declining to grant appropriate remedies. Parliament must have been aware of these potential injustices and cannot have intended either result.

[30] Lack of disclosure in this context cannot necessarily be equated with the denial of the right to make full answer and defence resulting in an unfair trial. There will be many instances in which non-disclosure of protected information will have no bearing at all on trial fairness or where alternatives to full disclosure may provide assurances that trial fairness has not been compromised by the absence of full disclosure. For example, in the *Air India* terrorism prosecution, the prosecution and the defence reached an agreement whereby the defence was allowed to inspect documents in the possession of CSIS after giving an undertaking not to disclose the contents to anyone without permission, includ-ing the accused. In a subsequently released report on the trial, lead prosecutor Robert Wright and defence counsel Michael Code reported that "in almost every instance defence counsel were able to conclude that the material was not relevant to the proceedings": see the Commission of Inquiry into the Investigation of the Bombing of Air India Flight 182, *Air India Flight 182: A Canadian Tragedy*. ("Air India Report") (2010), vol. 3, at p. 152.

[31] We must presume that Parliament was aware of the possibility that proceedings would be needlessly stayed if the trial judge was denied access to material that could not be disclosed for valid reasons of state secrecy. In light of the vast resources expended in investigating and prosecuting offences that implicate national security and the injustice to society that would result if such prosecutions were needlessly derailed, this cannot have been Parliament's intention.

[32] Nor can Parliament have intended that trial judges be presented with an inad-equate record or incomplete picture that could lead them to conclude, erroneously, that trial fairness will be unimpaired. As stated, Parliament is presumed to intend to enact *Charter*-compliant legislation. Even more significantly, in this case, the presumption of constitutionality is reinforced by the existence of s. 38.14, which expressly indicates that the fair trial rights of the accused must be protected—not sacrificed—in applying the other provisions of the scheme. This provision also suggests a recognition by Parliament that it is ultimately the trial judge, having experience with the criminal proceedings and having heard all of the evidence adduced, who will be best placed to make remedial deci-sions following a s. 38 non-disclosure order.

[33] However, the public interest will only be served if the trial judge in the criminal proceedings is able to exercise his or her discretion with an adequate understanding of the nature of the withheld information. In other words, the drastic nature of the potential remedies specified in s. 38.14 leads us to the conclusion that Parliament expected trial judges to be provided with a sufficient basis of relevant information on which to exercise their remedial powers judicially and to avoid, where possible (and appropriate), the col-lapse of the prosecution.

[34] Trial judges are under a duty to protect the accused's constitutional right to a full and fair defence quite apart from s. 38.14. The broad remedial discretion under s. 24(1) of the *Charter* already includes the power to order any of the remedies listed in s. 38.14 of the *CEA* to prevent an unfair trial. Yet Parliament has chosen to explicitly set out a number of statutory remedies that range from the finely tailored (i.e., dismissing specified counts of the indictment) to the very blunt (a complete stay of all proceedings). Dismissing a specified count of the indictment (or proceeding only on a lesser included offence) as suggested by the legislation, would generally require a thorough enough understanding of the s. 38 information to evaluate it against specific elements of the offences charged. Conversely, if the trial judge lacks that understanding, it will often be impossible to determine what charge, element or component of the defence that information might relate to. In such circumstances, the trial judge may have no choice but to enter a stay. This possibility was referred to in argument as putting the Attorney General and the trial courts in the dilemma of playing *constitutional chicken*, an outcome which a sensible interpretation of s. 38 will help to avoid.

[35] This leads us to the further observation that the stay of proceedings remedy in s. 38.14 is a statutory remedy to be considered and applied in its own context. It should not be burdened with the non-statutory "clearest of cases" test for a stay outlined in *R v. Jewitt*, [1985] 2 SCR 128; *R v. Keyowski*, [1988] 1 SCR 657; *R v. O'Connor*, [1995] 4 SCR 411; and *R v. Regan*, 2002 SCC 12, [2002] 1 SCR 297. The criminal court judge may be placed in a position of trying to determine an appropriate remedy where lack of disclosure has made it impossible to determine whether proceeding with a trial in its absence would truly violate "the community's sense of fair play and decency" (*Jewitt*, at p. 135). Nevertheless, the legislative compromise made in s. 38 will require a stay in such circumstances if the trial judge is simply unable to conclude affirmatively that the right to a fair trial, including the right of the accused to a full and fair defence, has not been compromised.

. . .

[76] We recognize that the legislative division of responsibilities does have the potential to cause delays and to pose serious challenges to the fair and expeditious trial of an accused, especially when the trial is by jury. While we do not find that this potential invalidates the legislative scheme, situations may well arise in which the division of responsibilities between courts will give rise to unreasonable trial delays, undue disruption to jurors and risk of juror contamination. These will have to be addressed on a case-by-case basis and the appropriate remedies issued to avoid an unfair trial.

[77] An important step the parties can take is attempting to identify potential national security issues during pre-trial proceedings. This would allow the disclosure arguments to take place at an early date. Section 38 encourages early-stage disclosure proceedings. In fact, it was amended in 2001 to allow the scheme to be engaged prior to the criminal trial and to "permit the government to take pro-active steps in the appropriate circumstances" (Department of Justice, "Amendments to the Canada Evidence Act," www.justice.gc.ca/antiter/sheetfiche/ceap2-lpcp2-eng.asp). Due diligence in this respect will work to minimize the risk of mistrials. Disclosure by the Crown in a series of stages over a period of time, each new stage of disclosure triggering additional s. 38 proceedings, will heighten the risk of resort by the trial judge to s. 38 remedies.

[78] As we have stated, co-operative arrangements between the prosecution and the defence are to be encouraged, as they have the potential to greatly facilitate complex trials

for all parties involved and to reduce the strain on judicial resources. However, the defence is under no obligation to cooperate with the prosecution and if the end result of non-disclosure by the Crown is that a fair trial cannot be had, then Parliament has determined that in the circumstances a stay of proceedings is the lesser evil compared with the disclosure of sensitive or potentially injurious information.

[79] We noted earlier that the exercise by the trial judge of the s. 38.14 statutory remedy is not constrained by the ordinary *Charter* jurisprudence concerning abuse of process. Neither is it constrained by the ordinary *Charter* jurisprudence in relation, for example, to trial within a reasonable time. If the trial process resulting from the application of the s. 38 scheme becomes unmanageable by virtue of excessive gaps between the hearing of the evidence or other such impediments, such that the right of the accused to a fair trial is compromised, the trial judge should not hesitate to use the broad authority Parliament has conferred under s. 38.14 to put an end to the prosecution.

[80] It will ultimately be for Parliament to determine with the benefit of experience whether the wisdom of the bifurcated scheme should be reconsidered. We conclude, however, that s. 38 as we have interpreted it passes constitutional muster. Trial unfairness will not be tolerated.

Note that s 38.13, which allows the Attorney General of Canada to issue a non-reviewable certificate prohibiting disclosure of information in service of national security or defence *after* a court has ordered disclosure, was not challenged in *Ahmad*, and thus was presumed constitutional. We discuss its vulnerability after "Cabinet Secrecy," next.

B. Cabinet Secrecy

At common law, a claim that the deliberations of Cabinet should not be disclosed in legal proceedings is governed by the same basic principles that govern other claims of public interest immunity: the objection must come from a proper official and the court has a discretion to examine the information in question and determine whether disclosure is warranted. See *Carey v Ontario*, [1986] 2 SCR 637, 30 CCC (3d) 498. But the deliberations of the federal Cabinet are protected by the following provision of the *Canada Evidence Act*:

> 39(1) Where a minister of the Crown or the Clerk of the Privy Council objects to the disclosure of information before a court, person or body with jurisdiction to compel the production of information by certifying in writing that the information constitutes a confidence of the Queen's Privy Council for Canada, disclosure of the information shall be refused without examination or hearing of the information by the court, person or body.
>
> (2) For the purpose of subsection (1), "a confidence of the Queen's Privy Council for Canada" includes, without restricting the generality thereof, information contained in
>
> > (a) a memorandum the purpose of which is to present proposals or recommendations to Council;
> >
> > (b) a discussion paper the purpose of which is to present background explanations, analyses of problems or policy options to Council for consideration by Council in making decisions;
> >
> > (c) an agendum of Council or a record recording deliberations or decisions of Council;

(d) a record used for or reflecting communications or discussions between ministers of the Crown on matters relating to the making of government decisions or the formulation of government policy;

(e) a record the purpose of which is to brief Ministers of the Crown in relation to matters that are brought before, or are proposed to be brought before, Council or that are the subject of communications or discussions referred to in paragraph (d); and

(f) draft legislation.

(3) For the purposes of subsection (2), "Council" means the Queen's Privy Council for Canada, committees of the Queen's Privy Council for Canada, Cabinet and committees of Cabinet.

(4) Subsection (1) does not apply in respect of

(a) a confidence of the Queen's Privy Council for Canada that has been in existence for more than twenty years; or

(b) a discussion paper described in paragraph (2)(b)

(i) if the decisions to which the discussion paper relates have been made public, or

(ii) where the decisions have not been made public, if four years have passed since the decisions were made.

In the next case, the plaintiffs challenged the constitutionality of s 39.

Babcock v Canada (Attorney General)
2002 SCC 57, [2002] 3 SCR 3
McLachlin CJ and L'Heureux-Dubé, Gonthier, Iacobucci, Major,
Bastarache, Binnie, Arbour, and LeBel JJ (11 July 2002)

McLACHLIN CJ:

[1] This case raises the issue of when, if ever, Cabinet confidences must be disclosed in litigation between the government and private citizens.

[2] On June 6, 1990, the Treasury Board of Canada set the pay of Department of Justice lawyers working in the Toronto Regional Office at a higher rate than that of lawyers working elsewhere. Vancouver staff lawyers brought an action in the Supreme Court of British Columbia, contending that by failing to pay them the same salaries as Toronto lawyers the government breached their contracts of employment and the fiduciary duty toward them.

[3] The action proceeded, and the parties exchanged lists of relevant documents in December 1996, as required by the BC Supreme Court Rules. A supplemental list of documents was delivered by the government in June 1997. The government listed a number of documents as producible.

[4] The government then brought a motion to have the action transferred from the Supreme Court of British Columbia to the Federal Court. In support of its application, it filed an affidavit by Joan McCoy, an officer of the Treasury Board Secretariat. The affidavit stated that the rationale for the Order-in-Council authorizing the pay raise for Toronto lawyers was that lawyers in Toronto generally commanded higher salaries than lawyers in other parts of the country. The affidavit also disclosed the date of the Treasury Board's decision.

[5] The government's motion to transfer the action was denied and the action continued in the Supreme Court of British Columbia. The government, nearly two years after it delivered the first list of documents, changed its position on disclosure of documents. It delivered a certificate of the Clerk of the Privy Council pursuant to s. 39(1) of the *Canada Evidence Act*, RSC 1985, c. C-5, objecting to the disclosure of 51 documents and any examination thereon, on the ground that they contain "information constituting confidences of the Queen's Privy Council for Canada." The certificate claimed protection for 12 government documents previously listed as producible (some of which had already been disclosed), for five documents in the control or possession of the plaintiffs, and for 34 government documents and information previously listed as not producible.

[6] The plaintiffs (respondents) brought an application to compel production of the documents for which the government claimed protection. The chambers judge, Edwards J, ruled against them, holding that s. 39 of the *Canada Evidence Act* was constitutional and clear. If the Clerk of the Privy Council filed a certificate, that was the end of the matter, and the courts had no power to set the certificate aside. A majority of the Court of Appeal reversed this decision and ordered production of the documents on the ground that the government had waived its right to claim confidentiality by listing some of the documents as producible and by disclosing selective information in the McCoy affidavit. The government appeals this decision to this Court.

I. Legislation

[The court reproduced s 39, above, reviewed the decisions below, and set up its analysis.]

. . .

[9] The majority of the Court of Appeal held that Edwards J erred in rejecting the claim that the government had waived protection to the documents and information. The Crown, as a public representative, must be able to waive privilege; otherwise, any litigant opposing the Crown would be in the untenable position of being unable to rely on the government's production of documents, regardless of how essential the documents were to their case or how late the Crown's application for immunity. While there might be a need for "extreme curtailment" of a litigant's rights to full discovery for documents concerned with sensitive matters like state defence, internal security or diplomatic relations, the government must be permitted to waive protection in appropriate cases.

[10] Applying this principle, the majority held that the government waived immunity for the 17 documents previously identified as producible. Protection was also waived for the information in the McCoy affidavit which outlined the government's rationale for the salary differential at the heart of the litigation. Any claim for privilege thereafter would be selective, requiring that claims for confidentiality on all related information be treated as waived. With respect to the remaining 34 documents, the majority held that s. 39 confers class immunity rather than selective immunity; it followed that waiver operates on a class basis. Thus, waiver of immunity for 17 of the documents covered by the s. 39 certificate waived the immunity for all of the relevant documents within the class. In view of this conclusion, it was not necessary to consider whether s. 39 was constitutional.

[11] Southin JA dissented. In her view, it is "not appropriate for the judiciary to intermeddle in the business of the Cabinet and its committees and it is not at all clear to me … that the judiciary must regain its control over this whole field of the law, a proposition

which to me has a distasteful ring of judicial arrogance" (para. 52). This said, s. 39 is limited to papers that are actually put before the Cabinet or a Cabinet committee and the Clerk must exercise her powers properly. She must properly describe the documents, bringing them within the ambit of the section, and if it can be shown, either from internal or external evidence, that the Clerk has exceeded the power conferred upon her, the court can require disclosure of all documents not within the section.

[12] Southin JA held that only an act of the Clerk or of a minister of the Crown can effect waiver. Otherwise, junior functionaries having no conception of the importance of Cabinet confidentiality would be able to waive it, to the detriment of the national interest.

[13] Newbury JA concurred with MacKenzie JA with respect to the waiver of privilege in this case. However, she went on to state that had waiver not occurred, she would have agreed with Southin JA's findings concerning the requirements of particularity on the part of the Clerk in claiming the privilege.

III. Issues

[14] 1. What is the nature of Cabinet confidentiality and the processes by which it may be claimed and relinquished? 2. Is s. 39 of the *Canada Evidence Act* constitutional?

IV. Discussion

A. The Principles

[15] Cabinet confidentiality is essential to good government. The right to pursue justice in the courts is also of primary importance in our society, as is the rule of law, accountability of the executive, and the principle that official actions must flow from statutory authority clearly granted and properly exercised. Yet sometimes these fundamental principles conflict. How are such conflicts to be resolved? That is the question posed by this appeal.

[16] The answer to the question lies in our understanding of Cabinet confidentiality. What is its purpose? What does it apply to? What is the process for claiming it? Once claimed, can it be relinquished or lost, and if so, how? These questions find their answers in an understanding of Cabinet confidentiality and the ambit and effect of s. 39 of the *Canada Evidence Act* that protects it.

(1) The Function of Section 39 of the Canada Evidence Act

[17] Sections 37, 38 and 39 of the *Canada Evidence Act* deal with objections to the disclosure of protected information held by the federal government. Section 37 relates to all claims for Crown privilege, except Cabinet confidences, or confidences of the Queen's Privy Council; s. 38 pertains to objections related to international relations or national defence; and s. 39 deals with Cabinet confidences. Under ss. 37 and 38, a judge balances the competing public interests in protection and disclosure of information. Under s. 39, by contrast, the Clerk or minister balances the competing interests. If the Clerk or minister validly certifies information as confidential, a judge or tribunal must refuse any application for disclosure, without examining the information.

[18] The British democratic tradition which informs the Canadian tradition has long affirmed the confidentiality of what is said in the Cabinet room, and documents and

papers prepared for Cabinet discussions. The reasons are obvious. Those charged with the heavy responsibility of making government decisions must be free to discuss all aspects of the problems that come before them and to express all manner of views, without fear that what they read, say or act on will later be subject to public scrutiny: see *Singh v. Canada (Attorney General)*, [2000] 3 FC 185 (CA), at paras. 21-22. If Cabinet members' statements were subject to disclosure, Cabinet members might censor their words, consciously or unconsciously. They might shy away from stating unpopular positions, or from making comments that might be considered politically incorrect. ... The process of democratic governance works best when Cabinet members charged with government policy and decision-making are free to express themselves around the Cabinet table unreservedly. In addition to ensuring candour in Cabinet discussions, this Court in *Carey v. Ontario*, [1986] 2 SCR 637, at p. 659, recognized another important reason for protecting Cabinet documents, namely to avoid "creat[ing] or fan[ning] ill-informed or captious public or political criticism." Thus, ministers undertake by oath as Privy Councillors to maintain the secrecy of Cabinet deliberations and the House of Commons and the courts respect the confidentiality of Cabinet decision-making.

[19]   At one time, the common law viewed Cabinet confidentiality as absolute. However, over time the common law has come to recognize that the public interest in Cabinet confidences must be balanced against the public interest in disclosure, to which it might sometimes be required to yield: see *Carey, supra*. Courts began to weigh the need to protect confidentiality in government against the public interest in disclosure, for example, preserving the integrity of the judicial system. It follows that there must be some way of determining that the information for which confidentiality is claimed truly relates to Cabinet deliberations and that it is properly withheld. At common law, the courts did this, applying a test that balanced the public interest in maintaining confidentiality against the public interest in disclosure: see *Carey, supra*.

[20]   In addition, many jurisdictions have enacted laws that modify the common law and provide a statutory process for determining what documents are protected and how claims to confidentiality may be challenged: see, for example, the *Ombudsman Act*, RSBC 1996, c. 340. The exercise of this statutory power is subject to the well-established rule that official actions must flow from statutory authority clearly granted and properly exercised: *Roncarelli v. Duplessis*, [1959] SCR 121. The courts have the power and the responsibility, when called upon, to determine whether the certifying official has exercised his or her statutory power in accordance with the law.

[21]   Section 39 of the *Canada Evidence Act* is Canada's response to the need to provide a mechanism for the responsible exercise of the power to claim Cabinet confidentiality in the context of judicial and quasi-judicial proceedings. It sets up a process for bringing information within the protection of the Act. Certification by the Clerk of the Privy Council or by a minister of the Crown, is the trigger by which information becomes protected. The Clerk must certify that the "information constitutes a confidence of the Queen's Privy Council for Canada." For more particularity, s. 39(2) sets out categories of information that falls within its scope.

[22]   Section 39(1) permits the Clerk to certify information as confidential. It does not restrain voluntary disclosure of confidential information. This is made clear from the French enactment of s. 39(1) which states that s. 39 protection arises only "*dans les cas où*" (in the cases where) the Clerk or minister opposes disclosure of information. Therefore,

the Clerk must answer two questions before certifying information: first, is it a Cabinet confidence within the meaning of ss. 39(1) and 39(2); and second, is it information which the government should protect taking into account the competing interests in disclosure and retaining confidentiality? If, and only if, the Clerk or minister answers these two questions positively and certifies the information, do the protections of s. 39(1) come into play. More particularly, the provision that "disclosure of the information shall be refused without examination or hearing of the information by the court, person or body" is only triggered when there is a valid certification.

[23] If the Clerk or minister *chooses* to certify a confidence, it gains the protection of s. 39. Once certified, information gains greater protection than at common law. If s. 39 is engaged, the "court, person or body with jurisdiction" hearing the matter *must* refuse disclosure; "disclosure of the information shall be refused." Moreover, this must be done "without examination or hearing of the information by the court, person or body." This absolute language goes beyond the common law approach of balancing the public interest in protecting confidentiality and disclosure on judicial review. Once information has been validly certified, the common law no longer applies to that information.

[24] This raises the issue of what constitutes valid certification. Two requirements are plain on the face of the legislation. First, it must be done by the Clerk of the Privy Council or a minister of the Crown. Second, the information must fall within the categories described in s. 39(2).

[25] A third requirement arises from the general principle applicable to all government acts, namely, that the power exercised must flow from the statute and must be issued for the *bona fide* purpose of protecting Cabinet confidences in the broader public interest. The function of the Clerk under the Act is to protect Cabinet confidences, and this alone. It is not to thwart public inquiry nor is it to gain tactical advantage in litigation. If it can be shown from the evidence or the circumstances that the power of certification was exercised for purposes outside those contemplated by s. 39, the certification may be set aside as an unauthorized exercise of executive power: see *Roncarelli, supra*.

[26] A fourth requirement for valid certification flows from the fact that s. 39 applies to *disclosure* of the documents. Where a document has already been disclosed, s. 39 no longer applies. ...

[27] On the basis of these principles, I conclude that certification is generally valid if: (1) it is done by the Clerk or minister; (2) it relates to information within s. 39(2); (3) it is done in a *bona fide* exercise of delegated power; (4) it is done to prevent disclosure of hitherto confidential information.

[28] It may be useful to comment on the formal aspects of certification. As noted, the Clerk must determine two things: (1) that the information is a Cabinet confidence within s. 39; and (2) that it is desirable that confidentiality be retained taking into account the competing interests in disclosure and retaining confidentiality. What formal certification requirements flow from this? The second, discretionary element may be taken as satisfied by the act of certification. However, the first element of the Clerk's decision requires that her certificate bring the information within the ambit of the Act. This means that the Clerk or minister must provide a description of the information sufficient to establish on its face that the information is a Cabinet confidence and that it falls within the categories of s. 39(2) or an analogous category; the possibility of analogous categories flows from the general language of the introductory portion of s. 39(2). This follows from the principle

that the Clerk or minister must exercise her statutory power properly in accordance with the statute. The kind of description required for claims of solicitor–client privilege under the civil rules of court will generally suffice. The date, title, author and recipient of the document containing the information should normally be disclosed. If confidentiality concerns prevent disclosure of any of these preliminary indicia of identification, then the onus falls on the government to establish this, should a challenge ensue. On the other hand, if the documents containing the information are properly identified, a person seeking production and the court must accept the Clerk's determination. The only argument that can be made is that, on the description, they do not fall within s. 39, or that the Clerk has otherwise exceeded the powers conferred upon her.

[29] As to the timing of certification, the only limits are those found in s. 39(4). Subject to these outer limits, it seems that information that falls within s. 39(2) may be certified long after the date the confidence existed or arose in Cabinet. At the same time, as discussed, if there has been disclosure, s. 39 no longer applies, since its only purpose is to prevent disclosure.

· · ·

(2) Waiver

[31] On the facts of this case, the concept of waiver in any ordinary sense of the term finds no place. As discussed, the Clerk or minister is not compelled to certify Cabinet confidences and invoke the protection of s. 39(1). However, if the Clerk or minister chooses to do so, the protection of s. 39 automatically follows. That protection continues indefinitely, unless: (i) the certificate is successfully challenged on the ground that it related to information that does not fall under s. 39; (ii) the power of certification of the Clerk or minister has otherwise been improperly exercised; (iii) s. 39(4) is engaged; or (iv) the Clerk or minister chooses to decertify the information. The clear language of s. 39(1) permits no other conclusion.

[32] This is consistent with the fact that waiver does not apply at common law. … If a certificate is not properly filed, and documents are released, the Crown is precluded from claiming s. 39 protection. However, by releasing some documents, the Crown has not waived its right to invoke s. 39 over other documents.

[33] It is argued that unless the broad power of waiver envisioned by the majority of the Court of Appeal is recognized, litigants opposing the Crown will be placed in the untenable position of being unable to rely on the Crown's production of documents, no matter how essential such documents are to their case or how late the Crown makes its claim to immunity. This concern is alleviated by the fact that s. 39(1) cannot be applied retroactively to documents that have already been produced in litigation; it applies only to compel disclosure.

[34] The conclusion that waiver does not apply here makes it unnecessary to consider the issue of class waiver—whether disclosure of one document removes protection from all documents in the same class. However, the related issue of class disclosure of information must be addressed.

[35] Section 39 protects "information" from disclosure. It may be that some information on a particular matter has been disclosed, while other information on the matter has not been disclosed. The language of s. 39(1) does not permit one to say that disclosure of some information removes s. 39 protection from other, non-disclosed information. If the

related information has been disclosed in other documents, then s. 39 does not apply and the documents containing the information must be produced. If the related information is contained in documents that have been properly certified under s. 39, the government is under no obligation to disclose the related information.

[36] This raises the concern that selective disclosure of documents or information may be used unfairly as a litigation tactic. The fear is that the Crown could choose to disclose only those documents which are favourable to its position and certify those documents which are detrimental. Selective disclosure designed to prevent getting at the truth would not be a proper exercise of the Clerk's or minister's s. 39 powers: *Roncarelli, supra*. Moreover, the ordinary rules of litigation offer protection from abuse. First, government witnesses may be cross-examined on the information produced. Second, the refusal to disclose information may permit a court to draw an adverse inference. For example, in *RJR-MacDonald Inc. v. Canada (Attorney General)*, [1995] 3 SCR 199, the Attorney General's refusal to disclose information relating to an advertising ban on tobacco, led to the inference that the results of the studies must undercut the government's claim that a less invasive ban would not have produced an equally salutary result (para. 166, *per* McLachlin J).

(3) Judicial Review

[37] Judicial review under s. 39 arises when "a court, person or body with jurisdiction to compel the production of information" is presented with an application to order disclosure of information which the Clerk or a minister has certified as a Cabinet confidence under s. 39(1). Section 39 is directed to whether a document is protected from disclosure.

[38] Section 39(1) leaves little scope for judicial review of a certification of Cabinet confidentiality. It states flatly that "disclosure of the information *shall* be refused" (emphasis added). Furthermore, it must be refused "without examination or hearing of the information by the court, person or body."

[39] As discussed, even language this draconian cannot oust the principle that official actions must flow from statutory authority clearly granted and properly exercised: *Roncarelli, supra*. It follows from this principle that the certification of the Clerk or minister under s. 39(1) may be challenged where the information for which immunity is claimed does not on its face fall within s. 39(1), or where it can be shown that the Clerk or minister has improperly exercised the discretion conferred by s. 39(1). "[T]he Court may entertain a proceeding for judicial review of the issuance of a certificate although it may not review the factual correctness of the certificate if it is otherwise in proper form": *Singh, supra*, at para. 43. The appropriate way to raise an argument that the Clerk has exercised her decision improperly is "by way of judicial review of the Clerk's certificate" (para. 50). The party challenging the decision may present evidence of "improper motives in the issue of the certificate" (para. 50), or otherwise present evidence to support the claim of improper issuance.

[40] The court, person or body reviewing the issuance of a s. 39 certificate works under the difficulty of not being able to examine the challenged information. A challenge on the basis that the information is not a Cabinet confidence within s. 39 thus will be generally confined to reviewing the sufficiency of the list and evidence of disclosure. A challenge based on wrongful exercise of power is similarly confined to information on the face of the certificate and such external evidence as the challenger may be able to provide. Doubtless

these limitations may have the practical effect of making it difficult to set aside a s. 39 certification.

[41] However, it does not follow from the fact that s. 39 makes it difficult to attack a certification that the procedure is unlawful. As pointed out in *Singh, supra*, at para. 50, the restrictions in s. 39(1) amount to a privative clause—an unusual privative clause perhaps, but one nevertheless open to Parliament to prescribe. Courts are not unfamiliar with privative clauses that preclude them from making certain findings of fact. Provided they are within Parliament's constitutional power, they will apply. This does not, however, prevent the tribunal from drawing inferences as to the motives of the Clerk or minister from all the surrounding evidence in determining whether the statutory power to certify has been properly exercised: see *Roncarelli, supra*, where the majority of the Court drew the inference of illegitimate exercise of power from circumstantial evidence.

[42] One issue remains: what tribunals are competent to decide whether a s. 39 certificate's claim to protection should be set aside on grounds that the information, as described, does not fall within s. 39 or that the certification power has been improperly exercised? The wording of s. 39(1) refers to "information before a court, person or body with jurisdiction to compel the production of information" and directs the relevant tribunal to refuse disclosure. It would seem to follow that the same bodies are competent to make orders for disclosure for improperly claimed s. 39 protection. This view is reinforced by the fact that s. 39(1) is essentially an evidentiary provision; questions of the admissibility of evidence normally fall to be decided by the tribunal seized of the matter in which the admissibility issue arises.

[43] The Federal Court of Appeal in *Singh, supra*, at para. 44, however, suggested that only judicial bodies, like the Federal Court, could review a s. 39 certificate: the RCMP Public Complaints Commission could not do so because it "is essentially an agency of the Executive and draws such powers as it has solely from an Act of the same Parliament that enacted the *Canada Evidence Act*." It is not apparent why this should be so, however. It seems open to Parliament to confer on a court, person or body with jurisdiction the power to determine whether acts of other public officials are valid. While the issue need not be decided in this case, I see no reason why all bodies expressly mentioned in s. 39 should not have the power to inquire into the validity of s. 39 claims for protection. The same would seem to apply for reviews at common law, given that the matter is essentially one of admissibility of evidence in a proceeding. The common law does not restrict review of claims for public immunity to superior courts.

[44] Against this may be put the concern that to permit a proliferation of tribunals to set aside s. 39 certificates risks undue disclosure of important Cabinet confidences. However, s. 39 review is limited by the condition that the tribunal cannot inspect the documents, undermining the concern of improvident disclosure. Moreover, the government may appeal the tribunal's decision. Ultimately, I am not persuaded that permitting tribunals other than superior courts to determine s. 39 issues will illegitimately undermine s. 39 claims to protection.

B. Application of the Principles

(1) The Documents

[45] The government issued a s. 39 certificate for 51 documents. Twelve of these had been identified in its list of documents under "Part I: Documents to which there is no objection to production." Of these 12, a number appear to have been not only listed, but

actually disclosed to the plaintiffs. The certificate also claimed confidentiality for five documents which were in the plaintiffs' possession or control and which the plaintiffs had listed as producible.

[46] On the record before us, s. 39 certification applies to the 34 documents listed as not producible.

[47] As discussed, s. 39 of the *Canada Evidence Act* does not apply to the government documents already disclosed. Nor does s. 39 apply to the five certified documents that were in the plaintiffs' possession or control. The documents were disclosed by the government in the context of litigation. The disclosure provisions of s. 39 therefore do not apply and these documents should be produced.

(2) Information in the McCoy Affidavit

[48] The government claims protection from disclosure for the information contained in the affidavit of Joan McCoy, which was filed in support of the government's unsuccessful motion to transfer the plaintiffs' case from the Supreme Court of British Columbia to the Federal Court.

[49] Of particular importance is Ms. McCoy's statement in para. 21 that: "The rationale for the Treasury Board's decision to increase rates for legal officers in the Toronto Regional Office was the rise in private sector salaries to levels well above those paid in the public sector during a period of rapid economic growth in the late 1980s." According to the McCoy affidavit, "[t]he escalation of external pay rates, matched to a large degree by increases for provincial lawyers as well, had impaired the ability of the Department of Justice to attract candidates for positions in the Law group in the Toronto Regional Office. It had also led to an increase in resignations from the federal Public Service as experienced legal officers, attracted by higher salaries, left for employment in the provincial government and the private sector in the Toronto area. The viability of the regional operation was imperilled by these losses and immediate action was required to stem the flow" (para. 21 of McCoy affidavit).

[50] The plaintiffs take issue with this rationale and seek to cross-examine Ms. McCoy on her statement. The government refuses to permit the statement to be used in evidence and denies the right to cross-examine on the information contained in it.

[51] When it filed the McCoy affidavit, the government chose to disclose the reason for the decision to pay the Toronto Law group more than other Law groups. The government disclosed that information to support the motion that the B.C. Supreme Court was not the appropriate forum for the case. Therefore, s. 39 cannot be invoked. The affidavit must be disclosed and Ms. McCoy may be cross-examined on its contents.

[52] As to related information, if it has been voluntarily disclosed in other documents, then s. 39 does not apply and the documents must be produced. By contrast, the government is under no obligation to disclose related information contained in documents that have been properly certified under s. 39, but runs the risk that refusal may permit the court to draw an adverse inference.

C. The Constitutionality of Section 39

[53] Because s. 39 applies to the undisclosed documents, it is necessary to consider the constitutional questions in this case. The respondents argue that s. 39 of the *Canada Evidence Act* is of no force or effect by reason of one or both of the preamble to the *Constitution Act, 1867* and s. 96 of the *Constitution Act, 1867*.

(1) The Preamble to the Constitution Act, 1867

[54] The respondents in this case challenge the constitutionality of s. 39 and argue that the provision is *ultra vires* Parliament because of the unwritten principles of the Canadian Constitution: the rule of law, the independence of the judiciary, and the separation of powers. Although the unwritten constitutional principles are capable of limiting government actions, I find that they do not do so in this case.

[55] The unwritten principles must be balanced against the principle of Parliamentary sovereignty. In *Commission des droits de la personne v. Attorney General of Canada*, [1982] 1 SCR 215, this Court upheld as constitutional s. 41(2) of the *Federal Court Act*, the predecessor to s. 39, which permitted the government to claim absolute privilege over a broader class of confidences.

[56] Recently, the Federal Court of Appeal considered the constitutional validity of s. 39 of the *Canada Evidence Act* in *Singh, supra*. On the basis of a thorough and compelling review of the principle of parliamentary sovereignty in the context of unwritten constitutional principles, Strayer JA held that federal Crown privilege is part of valid federal law over which Parliament had the power to legislate. Strayer JA concluded at para. 36:

> ... the rule of law cannot be taken to invalidate a statute which has the effect of allowing representatives of the Crown to identify certain documents as beyond disclosure: that is, the rule of law does not preclude a special law with a special result dealing with a special class of documents which, for long standing reasons based on constitutional principles such as responsible government, have been treated differently from private documents in a commercial law suit.

[57] I share the view of the Federal Court of Appeal that s. 39 does not offend the rule of law or the doctrines of separation of powers and the independence of the judiciary. It is well within the power of the legislature to enact laws, even laws which some would consider draconian, as long as it does not fundamentally alter or interfere with the relationship between the courts and the other branches of government.

. . .

[61] I therefore conclude that there is no basis upon which to find that s. 39 of the *Canada Evidence Act* is unconstitutional.

V. Conclusion

[62] I would allow the appeal in part, with costs to the respondents.

[63] On the record before us, the documents certified but disclosed, including the McCoy affidavit, are no longer protected and may be used in the litigation. The plaintiffs may cross-examine on the McCoy affidavit. The remaining documents are protected by s. 39 of the *Canada Evidence Act*. These conclusions are made without prejudice to future applications in this case.

L'HEUREUX-DUBÉ J:

[64] While I agree substantially with the reasons of the Chief Justice and the result she reaches, I cannot agree with her view as reflected in paras. 17, 22 and 28 of her reasons that "competing interests" in disclosure must be taken into account.

[65] In my view, the unequivocal language of the statute does not mandate consideration of the public interest in disclosure; I believe the Clerk or the minister must only answer two questions before certifying, namely, whether (1) the document is a Cabinet confidence; and (2) it is information that the government wishes to protect.

NOTES AND QUESTIONS

1. How meaningful is the possibility of challenging the *bona fides* of the exercise of power to refuse disclosure? How surprising is Justice L'Heureux-Dubé's disavowal of the possibility of any review beyond technical compliance? For a different view of the proper scope of a claim of privilege by the executive, see *United States v Nixon*, 418 US 683 (1974).

2. In *Slansky v Canada (Attorney General)*, 2013 FCA 199, the Canadian Judicial Council (CJC) dismissed a complaint by a lawyer (Slansky) against a judge. The CJC is established under the *Judges Act*, RSC 1985, c J-1 and empowered to investigate and discipline judges. Here, the CJC commissioned and relied on an investigative report from Martin Friedland, a criminal law professor. In his application for judicial review of the CJC's decision, Slansky sought production of this report. The CJC claimed that the report was protected by solicitor–client privilege and public interest privilege. A majority of the Federal Court of Appeal held that the CJC could refuse to disclose information gathered in the course of an examination into a judge's conduct, despite the lack of a statutory reference to either privilege (at para 146): "these privileges flow from the common law, and at least in the case of the public interest privilege, from the constitution itself which recognizes judicial independence as a fundamental concept." The dissent argued that the CJC's concern that the absence of confidentiality would hamper investigations was true of many professional disciplinary bodies, and yet courts review those bodies, using sealing orders as necessary to protect confidentiality concerns. It opined that judicial independence would be imperiled rather than secured by withholding the report from a reviewing court. Finally, it noted that if public interest privilege applies to the Friedland report, as a matter of logic, it applies to all such investigative reports in the future. Whose analysis do you find most persuasive? Leave to appeal to the Supreme Court of Canada was refused: 2014 CanLII 5977.

C. The Attorney General's Power to Prevent Disclosure

Enacted by Bill C-36, s 38.13 of the *Canada Evidence Act* provides the federal attorney general with a remarkable power:

> 38.13(1) The Attorney General of Canada may personally issue a certificate that prohibits the disclosure of information in connection with a proceeding for the purpose of protecting information obtained in confidence from, or in relation to, a foreign entity as defined in subsection 2(1) of the *Security of Information Act* or for the purpose of protecting national defence or national security. The certificate may only be issued after an order or decision that would result in the disclosure of the information to be subject to the certificate has been made under this or any other Act of Parliament.

A party to a proceeding may apply to a single judge of the Federal Court for an order "varying or cancelling a certificate issued" under s 38.13, and further appeals to any court are not possible (s 38.131(11)).

Given the existing doctrine of public interest immunity, are these provisions necessary to combat terrorism? Is it wise to grant the federal attorney general such a sweeping power? What is the rationale for preventing appeals to the Supreme Court of Canada in these matters? Consider the following critique in Hamish Stewart, "Public Interest Immunity After Bill C-36" (2003) 47 Crim LQ 249 at 255-56 (internal citations omitted):

(6) The Minister's New Power

Section 38.13 gives the federal Attorney General a new power to prevent disclosure of information in proceedings. It provides that he "may personally issue a certificate that prohibits the disclosure of information in connection with a proceeding for the purpose of protecting information obtained in confidence from, or in relation to, a foreign entity ... or for the purpose of protecting national defence or national security." This power permits the federal Attorney General to second-guess the result of any judicial determination concerning disclosure, including determinations made pursuant to s. 38.04. The decision is protected by a strongly worded privative clause (s. 38.13(8)). A party can apply to a single judge of the Federal Court of Appeal "for an order varying or cancelling a certificate" (s. 38.131(1)) on the ground that the information is not of the right kind (s. 38.131(8), (9), (10)). There is no further appeal from the judge's decision (s. 38.131(11)).

Section 38.13 as it appeared after first reading in the House of Commons would have provided the Attorney General with an effectively unreviewable power to conceal information. Sections 38.13 and 38.131 as enacted represent an improvement over the earlier version. But the right of appeal is still extremely limited, both institutionally and in the scope of the grounds. It is not the person presiding over the proceeding who makes the decision either to issue the certificate or to vary or cancel the certificate; indeed these sections apply only after the person presiding *and* a judge of the Federal Court, Trial Division have done whatever they can do. Furthermore, the new provisions still provide no mechanism for correcting any error by the Attorney General in assessing the balance between the interests in disclosure and the interests in non-disclosure. In short, under ss. 38.13 and 38.131 the Attorney General is permitted to second-guess the outcome of a proceeding to which he was a party.

It might be argued that these concerns about s. 38.13 are misplaced, in light of the undoubted power of a prosecutor, faced with an unfavourable ruling on an issue of public interest immunity, to stay a proceeding ... and to reinstate the proceedings before another judge. The Supreme Court has held that the exercise of this power, though it avoids normal appeal routes and may appear to permit judge-shopping, does not necessarily amount to an abuse of process [see *R v Scott*, [1990] 3 SCR 979]. Assuming that this holding is correct, we ought nonetheless to be cautious about expanding the ability of a party to a proceeding to second-guess the evidentiary rulings of the presiding officer. In my view, the only factor that makes this type of power constitutionally permissible is that, in criminal proceedings at least, the Crown is in a different position from any other party. In the frequently quoted words of Rand J [*Boucher v R*, [1955] SCR 16 at 23-24]:

> It cannot be over-emphasized that the purpose of a criminal prosecution is not to obtain a conviction; it is to lay before a jury what the Crown considers to be credible evidence relevant to what is alleged to be a crime ... The role of prosecutor excludes any notion of winning or losing; his function is a matter of public duty than which in civil life there can be none charged with greater personal responsibility. It is to be efficiently performed with an ingrained sense of the dignity, the seriousness and the justness of judicial proceedings.

These words were written in response to a Crown prosecutor's inflammatory and improper language in an address to a jury, but they flow from a larger sense of the proper role of the Attorney

General and his or her prosecutors. The Attorney General's new power, like his or her other powers, must only be exercised for a proper purpose, and not merely for tactical advantages in litigation or other improper purposes.

VI. MATRIMONIAL COMMUNICATIONS

Section 4(3) of the *Canada Evidence Act* provides:

> 4(3) No husband is compellable to disclose any communication made to him by his wife during their marriage, and no wife is compellable to disclose any communication made to her by her husband during their marriage.

Recall that, subject to certain statutory exceptions, the married spouse of an accused person was neither competent nor compellable as a witness for the Crown. Those provisions were amended recently, and married spouses are now treated as ordinary witnesses. The statutory provision for marital communication privilege has not, however, been removed. Charter equality guarantees still have to be considered because common law spouses do not have access to this privilege. Presumably, same-sex marriages would be included, as otherwise this would be contrary to the Charter. The following case of the Supreme Court of Canada provides a useful summary of the basic law that determines when this privilege can be invoked.

R v Couture
2007 SCC 28, [2007] 2 SCR 517
McLachlin CJ and Bastarache, Binnie, LeBel, Deschamps, Fish,
Abella, Charron, and Rothstein JJ (15 June 2007)

[The accused was convicted of second degree murder with respect to two adult victims. During a period of estrangement from the accused, his spouse told police that she had been the accused's Christian volunteer counsellor in prison where he was serving time on unrelated offences. In the early days of their relationship he confided in her that he had murdered two women. This confidence was shared before they were married. At the time of trial, the couple had reconciled. Because their marriage was valid and subsisting, the wife was not competent or compellable and the Crown sought to have her statements admitted to the police as necessary and reliable hearsay. The court rejected the statements on the basis that admitting them would undermine the law protecting legally married spouses from testifying against each other. In the course of the opinion, the court provided an overview of the law on marital spousal privilege at paras 37-48 (which was affirmed also by the dissent at para 105).]

3.1 The Law Respecting Spousal Testimony

. . .

[41] Section 4(3) creates a spousal privilege in respect of marital communications. The question of privilege was not really an issue at common law because spouses, with few exceptions, were not competent to testify. The concept of spousal privilege was therefore

created by statute after legislation in the 19th century made spouses competent witnesses. The privilege is testimonial in nature, giving a right to withhold evidence but the communications themselves are not privileged. The privilege belongs to the spouse receiving the communication and can be waived by him or her. See *Lloyd v. The Queen*, [1981] 2 SCR 645, at pp. 654-55. The question of privilege does not arise in this case with respect to the alleged confessions made by Mr. Couture to Darlene in 1989 since these communications were made prior to their marriage on February 14, 1996. It would arise in respect of any later communications made during the marriage. The question of spousal privilege must be kept in mind in considering broader implications that may result from any modification to the law respecting spousal testimony.

In *R v St-Jean* (1976), 34 CRNS 378, the accused was charged with incest. His wife, a competent and compellable witness pursuant to s 4(2) of the *Canada Evidence Act*, was called by the Crown. In re-examination, Crown counsel asked her whether she had discussed with her husband the testimony that she was going to give. The trial judge held that s 4(3) prevented the question from being asked. The accused was acquitted. On appeal by the Crown, the Quebec Court of Appeal held that the trial judge's ruling was erroneous: "in cases where a spouse is competent and compellable, he or she may testify about *all* aspects of the case, subject only to the ordinary rules of evidence." The court held that s 4(3) would still apply "where a spouse is called by the defence." A new trial was ordered.

In *R v Zylstra* (1995), 99 CCC (3d) 477 (Ont CA), the court rejected the reasoning in *St-Jean*:

Section 4(3) is unambiguous and can be given its plain meaning without making it subject to any other subsection. It says simply that where a wife or husband is otherwise compellable or competent to give evidence, there is no compulsion to divulge communications with a spouse.

With respect to the procedure for asserting the privilege, the court said:

We do agree that if the privilege was asserted, it should be done in the presence of the jury. To proceed otherwise might have left the jury in some confusion by the failure of Crown counsel to pursue obvious lines of inquiry in cross-examination because they were not aware that the privilege had been asserted. We agree with the Crown on appeal that openness in the trial process is to be preferred. The Supreme Court of Canada has elected for this option when dealing with problems of prior criminal convictions, *R v Corbett* (1988), 41 CCC (3d) 385, [1988] 1 SCR 670, and pre-trial publicity *Dagenais v. Canadian Broadcasting Corp.* (1994), 94 CCC (3d) 289, 120 DLR (4th) 12, [1994] 3 SCR 835. However, a special instruction is called for. We do not think that s. 4(6) has any application to a spouse who has testified. The Crown appears to concede this. It suggests the following in its factum:

The jury ought then to be instructed with respect to the following points:

(a) The privilege in s. 4(3) is a statutory privilege which all legally married witnesses are entitled to assert in a trial; and

(b) The privilege is one that belongs to the witness, not the accused person, and, as such, the decision whether to assert or waive the privilege lies with the witness, not the accused.

In our opinion, the above represents a minimum requirement for a proper jury instruction. Whether or not the jury should be instructed that they can draw an adverse inference from the assertion of the privilege, we leave to another day. The trial judge should have a discretion as to what instruction is appropriate and we are not prepared to lay down a hard and fast rule in a case where no testimony was given.

NOTES AND QUESTIONS

1. Do you agree with the holding in *St-Jean* that s 4(3) is not applicable where the spouse is called by the Crown? Is there any indication of this limitation in the wording of s 4 or in the rationale for the privilege?

2. Why should the decision to waive the privilege rest with the witness spouse rather than with the communicating spouse?

3. Is the matrimonial communication privilege limited to existing marriages? Do you think it should be amended to include any adult interdependent partnerships (see s 8 of the *Alberta Evidence Act*, RSA 2000, c A-18, as amended by SA 2002, c A-4.5, s 15)? What about common law relationships? In *R v Nero*, 2016 ONCA 160, the court found that the privilege did not apply on the facts, but in *obiter* suggested that it would have upheld the restriction to married couples, relying on *R v Nguyen*, 2015 ONCA 278, 125 OR (3d) 321, leave to appeal refused, 2016 CanLII 936 (SCC), which helpfully outlined applicable principles when considering a claim under s 4(3).

4. Do you agree with the holding in *Zylstra* that the privilege should be asserted before the jury? How do you think the question left open in the last paragraph of *Zylstra* should be answered? How would these questions be answered if another privilege, for example, solicitor–client privilege or informer privilege, were at stake?

5. For an example in the context of a prisoner–spouse relationship, see *R v Siniscalchi*, 2010 BCCA 354, mentioned in *Nero*, above. Here, the court held that the communication (over a prison phone that recorded all calls automatically) was not caught by s 4(3). This was followed in *R v Meer*, 2015 ABCA 141, in which the defence, Crown, and trial judge all failed to notice the spousal privilege issue. The Appeal Court held the accused and his wife knew their calls were being monitored, and thus no privilege applied. The opinion helpfully notes that confidence is critical to the privilege (at para 70): "[C]ommunications between the spouses at a busy dinner table, or otherwise within obvious earshot of other persons, are not privileged. If the spouses communicate in public, requiring them to repeat those conversations while testifying is not within the purpose of the privilege. Disclosing communications that are already public cannot reasonably affect the marital relationship. Once something is made public, it cannot thereafter be made secret."

VII. OTHER RELATIONSHIPS: PRIVILEGED OR MERELY CONFIDENTIAL?

Disclosure of information that is not protected by a recognized privilege has often been resisted on the ground that a new privilege or other protection should be recognized. The Supreme Court, relying heavily on Wigmore's analysis, has developed a framework for assessing such claims of privilege. A precedent setting decision in 1976, *Slavutych v Baker*, [1976] 1 SCR 254, 38 CR 306, paved the way forward. Slavutych was an associate professor at the University of Alberta. The University started proceedings to dismiss him, relying in part on a document entitled "tenure form sheet" that was marked "Confidential." It directed the writer to "state frankly your opinion on the advisability of tenure, given your *factual* knowledge of the case." Slavutych had filled out this form in offering his opinion of a candidate for tenure. He was informed by the head of the department that the information received would be kept strictly confidential until the tenure committee met and then the sheet would be destroyed. Slavutych included among his comments the statement that the relevant candidate "was highly dishonest, often unethical." Other comments were to similar effect. Slavutych objected to this document being admitted and used against him in the dismissal proceedings.

The Alberta Court of Appeal and the Supreme Court of Canada agreed with Slavutych. In finding for Slavutych, the judges adopted the framework from *Wigmore on Evidence*, 3rd ed, McNaughton Revision (Boston, Mass: Little, Brown, 1961) vol 8, para 2285, which outlines four fundamental conditions as necessary to the establishment of a case-by-case privilege against the disclosure of communications: "(1) The communications must originate in a *confidence* that they will not be disclosed. (2) This element of *confidentiality must be essential* to the full and satisfactory maintenance of the relation between the parties. (3) The *relation* must be one which in the opinion of the community ought to be sedulously *fostered*. (4) The *injury* that would inure to the relation by the disclosure of the communications must be *greater than the benefit* thereby gained for the correct disposal of litigation."

The next set of cases explains and illustrates the approach begun with *Slavutych v Baker*.

R v Gruenke
[1991] 3 SCR 263, 67 CCC (3d) 289
Lamer CJC and La Forest, L'Heureux-Dubé, Sopinka, Gonthier, Cory,
McLachlin, Stevenson, and Iacobucci JJ (24 October 1991)

LAMER CJC (La Forest, Sopinka, McLachlin, Stevenson, and Iacobucci JJ concurring): This case, an appeal from a jury conviction for first degree murder, involves the alleged inadmissibility of certain evidence: the testimony of a pastor and lay counsellor of the Victorious Faith Centre Church regarding communications made to them by the appellant regarding her involvement in the murder. The appellant argues that the communications were privileged, and therefore inadmissible, both on the basis of the common law and on the basis of s. 2(a) of the *Canadian Charter of Rights and Freedoms*. Two further issues, raised on appeal, relate to the fairness of the trial judge's charge to the jury.

The appellant and her co-accused, Mr. Fosty, were convicted at trial and appealed unsuccessfully to the Manitoba court of Appeal. Ms. Gruenke was granted leave to appeal to this court; Mr. Fosty is not in appeal to this court.

This case requires the court to consider whether a common law, *prima facie* privilege for religious communications should be recognized or whether claims of privilege for such communications should be dealt with on a case-by-case basis. The court has also been invited to consider how the constitutional guarantee of freedom of conscience and religion impacts on these questions.

The Facts

The appellant was (at the time of the incident) a 22-year-old woman, trained in reflexology (reflexology is a form of therapy like acupressure). The victim, Philip Barnett, was an

82-year-old client of Ms. Gruenke who had befriended both Ms. Gruenke and her mother (the appellant's father died of leukemia when she was 15). Mr. Barnett loaned money to Ms. Gruenke to start her own reflexology business and had provided her with a car and an allowance. In his will, Mr. Barnett had left a life interest in his estate to the appellant. Ms. Gruenke testified that she considered Mr. Barnett to be a "surrogate father." At one point, Ms. Gruenke and the victim had lived together in a platonic relationship; however, she moved back to her mother's home after Mr. Barnett began to express jealousy over her relationships with men and to make unwelcome sexual advances toward her. After she moved home, Mr. Barnett would telephone her and visit her from time to time and his requests for sex became more and more insistent. Ms. Gruenke testified that she had become frightened of Mr. Barnett and did not want to be alone with him.

About the time Ms. Gruenke moved back home, she began to feel very ill and tired. She became convinced that she had leukemia (like her father) and began attending the Victorious Faith Centre (a born-again Christian church) with the hope of receiving both physical and emotional healing. The church pastor, Ms. Harmony Thiessen, assigned a counsellor, Ms. Janine Frovich, to work with the appellant.

On November 28, 1986, Mr. Barnett telephoned Ms. Gruenke, again asking her to have sex with him, and insisted that he was coming over to see her. The appellant testified that she was frightened and asked her boyfriend (the co-accused) Mr. Fosty, to come over and wait outside in his car in case she needed him. Mr. Barnett arrived and Ms. Gruenke sat in his car and talked to him. According to Ms. Gruenke, Mr. Barnett suddenly pulled out of the driveway and drove off, saying that he had done a great deal for her and it was time for her to "repay his kindness." She said she attempted to jump out of the car while it was moving and a struggle ensued; eventually Mr. Barnett stopped the car. Ms. Gruenke testified that she struck Mr. Barnett with a piece of wood which was in the car and then the struggle continued outside with her and Mr. Barnett wrestling on the ground. She says then she saw Mr. Fosty's feet approaching, but could not recall much past this point, other than that she saw Mr. Barnett covered in blood before she and Mr. Fosty drove away. Later she remembered washing the car and going to a hotel with Mr. Fosty.

The testimony at trial revealed that the victim had been found in the front seat of his car which was in a ditch off the highway, not far from Ms. Gruenke's home. The victim's head had been severely battered with a heavy, blunt instrument consistent with a nail-puller which Mr. Fosty had owned and had sold on the evening the victim was murdered. There was other physical evidence connecting Mr. Fosty and the appellant to the murder. Mr. Fosty did not testify at the trial, but the theory of the defence was that Mr. Fosty had killed Mr. Barnett in the course of defending Ms. Gruenke and that she had had little or nothing to do with the victim's death. The theory of the Crown was that Ms. Gruenke had enlisted the aid of Mr. Fosty in planning and committing the murder of Mr. Barnett both to stop his sexual harassment of Ms. Gruenke and to benefit from the provisions of his will.

The evidence of Harmony Thiessen (the pastor) and Janine Frovich (the counsellor), which was ruled admissible by the trial judge, directly supported the Crown's theory. The communications between the appellant, Pastor Thiessen and Ms. Frovich took place two days after Mr. Barnett's death. Ms. Frovich went to visit the appellant at her home after hearing of Mr. Barnett's death. After the appellant began to speak of her involvement in the murder, she and Ms. Frovich moved to the Frovich home, where there was a more "peaceful atmosphere," and Ms. Frovich telephoned Pastor Thiessen. The appellant and

Ms. Frovich then met Pastor Thiessen at the church, where the discussion continued. Later, the appellant went home with Ms. Frovich and Mr. Fosty came by. ...

[Lamer CJC then quoted from the evidence of Pastor Thiessen and Ms. Frovich.]

...

Issues

1. Whether the Court of Appeal erred in failing to conclude that the conversations between the appellant and Pastor Thiessen and Janine Frovich, the church's lay counsellor, were protected by common law privilege such that disclosure ought not to have been compelled.

2. Alternatively, whether these conversations were confidential communications the disclosure of which ought not to have been compelled in accordance with the principles accepted in *Slavutych v. Baker*, [[1976] 1 SCR 254].

...

Analysis

...

The first two grounds of appeal (see above) require this court to consider four basic questions:

- whether there is a common law, *prima facie* privilege for religious communications which would cover the communications involved in this case;
- if not, whether such religious communications can be excluded in particular cases by applying the Wigmore criteria on a case-by-case basis;
- if so, whether the communications in this case should have been excluded on the Wigmore criteria;
- how the constitutional guarantee of freedom of religion affects the determination of the above questions.

1. *Common Law, Prima Facie Privilege*

The parties to this appeal have (understandably) urged conflicting interpretations of pre-Reformation history on this court, in order to support their respective positions on the existence of a common law, *prima facie* privilege for religious communications. In my opinion, the best that can be said of this material is that it is inconclusive with respect to this question. While the appellant may well be correct in pointing out that English and Canadian courts have not, as a matter of *practice*, compelled members of the clergy to disclose confidential religious communications, this does not answer the question of whether there is a *legal* common law privilege for religious communications. Furthermore, I cannot agree with the appellant that the existence of a limited *statutory* religious privilege in some jurisdictions (see Quebec's *Charter of Human Rights and Freedoms*, RSQ, c. C-12, s. 9, and Newfoundland's *Evidence Act*, RSN 1970, c. 115, s. 6) indicates that a common law privilege exists. If anything, the fact that there is a statutory privilege in some jurisdictions indicates that the common law did *not* protect religious communications—thus necessitating the statutory protection.

In the end, the question of whether a *prima facie* privilege exists for religious communications is essentially one of policy. ... As I have mentioned, a *prima facie* privilege for religious communications would constitute an exception to the general principle that all relevant evidence is admissible. Unless it can be said that the policy reasons to support a class privilege for religious communications are as compelling as the policy reasons which underlay the class privilege for solicitor–client communications, there is no basis for departing from the fundamental "first principle" that all relevant evidence is admissible until proven otherwise.

In my view, the policy reasons which underlay the treatment of solicitor–client communications as a separate class from most other confidential communications, are not equally applicable to religious communications. The *prima facie* protection for solicitor–client communications is based on the fact that the relationship and the communications between solicitor-and-client are essential to the effective operation of the legal system. Such communications are inextricably linked with the very system which desires the disclosure of the communication: see *Geffen v. Goodman Estate*, [[1991] 2 SCR 353], and *R v. Solosky*, [[1980] 1 SCR 821]. In my view, religious communications, notwithstanding their social importance, are not inextricably linked with the justice system in the way that solicitor–client communications surely are.

While the value of freedom of religion, embodied in s. 2(a), will become significant in particular cases, I cannot agree with the appellant that this value must necessarily be recognized in the form of a *prima facie* privilege in order to give full effect to the Charter guarantee. The extent (if any) to which disclosure of communications will infringe on an individual's freedom of religion will depend on the particular circumstances involved, for example: the nature of the communication, the purpose for which it was made, the manner in which it was made, and the parties to the communication.

Having found no common law, *prima facie* privilege for religious communications, I will consider whether such communications can be excluded in particular cases by applying the Wigmore criteria on a case-by-case basis.

2. Case-by-Case Privilege

In *R v. Church of Scientology*, [(1987), 31 CCC (3d) 449], the Ontario Court of Appeal recognized the existence of a "priest and penitent" privilege determined on a case-by-case basis, having regard to the Wigmore criteria. This approach is consistent with the approach taken by this court in *Slavutych v. Baker*, supra, and is, in my view, consistent with a principled approach to the question which properly takes into account the particular circumstances of each case. This is not to say that the Wigmore criteria are now "carved in stone," but rather that these considerations provide a general framework within which policy considerations and the requirements of fact-finding can be weighed and balanced on the basis of their relative importance in the particular case before the court. Nor does this preclude the identification of a new class on a principled basis.

Furthermore, a case-by-case analysis will allow courts to determine whether, in the particular circumstances, the individual's freedom of religion will be imperilled by the admission of the evidence. As was stated in *R v. Church of Scientology*, at p. 540:

> Chief Justice Dickson stated in *R v. Big M Drug Mart Ltd.* (1985), 18 CCC (3d) 385, 18 DLR
> (4th) 321, [1985] 1 SCR 295, that the fundamental freedom of conscience and religion now

enshrined in s. 2(a) of the Charter embraces not only the freedom of religious thought and belief but also "the right to manifest religious belief by worship and practice or by teaching and dissemination." This protection will no doubt strengthen the argument in favour of recognition of a priest-and-penitent privilege. The restrictive common law interpretation of the privilege may have to be reassessed to bring it in conformity with the constitutional freedom.

> *In our view, however, while s. 2 of the Charter enhances the claim that communications made in confidence to a priest or ordained minister should be afforded a privilege, its applicability must be determined on a case-by-case basis. The freedom is not absolute.* [Emphasis added.]

The Wigmore criteria will be informed both by the Charter guarantee of freedom of religion and by the general interpretative statement in s. 27 of the Charter:

> 27. This Charter shall be interpreted in a manner consistent with the preservation and enhancement of the multicultural heritage of Canadians.

> . . .

It is for this reason that I have, throughout these reasons, employed the general term "religious communications" in place of the more traditional term "priest-penitent communications." In applying the Wigmore criteria to particular cases, both s. 2(a) and s. 27 must be kept in mind. This means that the case-by-case analysis must begin with a "non-denominational" approach. The fact that the communications were not made to an ordained priest or minister or that they did not constitute a formal confession will not bar the possibility of the communications being excluded. All of the relevant circumstances must be considered and the Wigmore criteria applied in a manner which is sensitive to the fact of Canada's multicultural heritage. This will be most important at the second and third stages of the Wigmore inquiry. ...

Having found that religious communications can be excluded in particular cases where the Wigmore criteria are satisfied, I turn now to the question of whether the communications involved in this case satisfy the Wigmore criteria.

Application of the Wigmore Criteria

In my opinion, a consideration of the Wigmore criteria and the facts of this case reveals that the communications between the appellant, Pastor Thiessen and Janine Frovich were properly admitted at trial.

In my view, these communications do not even satisfy the first requirement; namely, that they originate in a confidence that they will not be disclosed. Leaving aside the other components of the Wigmore test, it is absolutely crucial that the communications originate with an expectation of confidentiality (in order for those communications to qualify as "privileged" and to thereby be excluded from evidence). Without this expectation of confidentiality, the raison d'être of the privilege is missing.

In the case at bar, there is evidence that Ms. Gruenke's communications to Pastor Thiessen and Ms. Frovich did not originate in a confidence that they would not be disclosed. The testimony of Pastor Thiessen and Janine Frovich indicates that they were unclear as to whether they were expected to keep confidential what Ms. Gruenke had told them about her involvement in the murder. As was stated by Twaddle JA in the Court of Appeal judgment at p. 463, "there was no evidence that the accused Gruenke made her admissions to them in the confident belief that they would be disclosed to no one." Ms. Gruenke did not approach Ms. Frovich and the pastor on the basis that the communications were to be confidential. In fact, Ms. Frovich initiated the meeting and Ms. Gruenke testified that she saw no harm in speaking to Janine Frovich because she had already made up her mind to turn herself in to the police and "take the blame." In my view, the Court of Appeal accurately described these communications as being made more to relieve Ms. Gruenke's emotional stress than for a religious or spiritual purpose. I note that my view is based on the parties' statements and behaviour in relation to the communication and not on the lack of a formal practice of "confession" in the Victorious Faith Centre Church. While the existence of a formal practice of "confession" may well be a strong indication that the parties expected the communication to be confidential, the lack of such a formal practice is not, in and of itself, determinative.

The communications in question do not satisfy the first Wigmore criterion and their admission into evidence does not infringe Ms. Gruenke's freedom of religion. As I have stated above, whether an individual's freedom of religion will be infringed by the admission of religious communications will depend on the particular facts of each case. In the case at bar, there is no such infringement.

[L'Heureux-Dubé J and Gonthier J, concurring, agreed with Lamer CJC "that, in the circumstances of this case, the communications did not originate in the confidence that they would not be disclosed." But she would have recognized a general religious communications privilege on the basis of the social value of religious communications, the Charter guarantee of freedom of religion, and the individual's privacy interest in "*spiritual* guidance and assistance." She reviewed statutory versions of the privilege in Newfoundland, Quebec, and other jurisdictions, and continued:]

L'HEUREUX-DUBÉ J: With these rationales and policy, and constitutional and historical considerations in mind, as well as the caselaw and the statutory provisions previously discussed, should this court recognize a particular category of privileges for religious communications? While it may be that Parliament or the provincial legislatures are at liberty to enact statutory provisions creating such a privilege besides those already existing in Quebec and Newfoundland, it is my view that there is a human need for a spiritual counsellor, a need which, in a system of religious freedom and freedom of thought and belief, must be recognized. While serving a number of other policy interests, the values to society of "the human need to disclose to a spiritual counsellor, in total and absolute confidence, what are believed to be flawed acts or thoughts and to receive priestly consolation and guidance in return" in the words of Berger CJ in *Trammel v. United States*, [445 US 40 (1980)], at p. 51, must supersede the truth-searching policy.

V. The Wigmore Approach and Religious Communications

• • •

In my view, it is more in line with the rationales identified earlier, the spirit of the Charter and the goal of assuring the certainty of the law, to recognize a pastor-penitent category of privilege in this country. If our society truly wishes to encourage the creation and development of spiritual relationships, individuals must have a certain amount of confidence that their religious confessions, given in confidence and for spiritual relief, will not be disclosed. Not knowing in advance whether his or her confession will be afforded any protection, a penitent may not confess, or may not confess as freely as he or she otherwise would. Both the number of confessions and their quality will be affected: see Mitchell at p. 763. The special relationship between clergy and parishioners may not develop, resulting in a chilling effect on the spiritual relationship within our society. In that case, the very rationale for the pastor-penitent privilege may be defeated. The lack of a recognized category also has ramifications for freedom of religion. Concerns about certainty apply as much to the development of specific religions as to spiritual practices in general.

Of course, this does not mean that every communication between pastor and penitent will be protected. The creation of the category simply acknowledges that our society recognizes that the relationship should be fostered, and that disclosure of communications will generally do more harm than good. Accordingly, the pastor-penitent relationship answers the third and fourth legs of the Wigmore test. But in any given case, the specific nature of the relationship must be examined to ensure it fits the category. Furthermore, the extent of the privilege will still be determined in accordance with the first and second legs of Wigmore's test.

M (A) v Ryan
[1997] 1 SCR 157
La Forest, L'Heureux-Dubé, Sopinka, Cory, McLachlin,
Iacobucci, and Major JJ (6 February 1997)

[The appellant was 17 years old when she underwent psychiatric treatment from Dr. Ryan. She brought a civil suit for damages against him for injuries sustained as a result of sexual relations and acts of gross indecency. Dr. Ryan admitted the conduct, pleaded consent, and denied causation. The appellant sought psychiatric treatment from Dr. Parfitt to deal with her difficulties and expressed concern that their communications remain confidential. She received the assurance from Dr. Parfitt that everything possible would be done to ensure that their discussions would remain confidential, and at one point Dr. Parfitt refrained from taking her usual notes. Civil suits require parties to produce all relevant documentation and to submit to discoveries. The issue was whether Dr. Parfitt's notes were protected by privilege from disclosure. Dr. Parfitt agreed to release her reports, but claimed privilege in relation to her notes. The British Columbia Court of Appeal ordered disclosure as limited by four conditions: that inspection be confined to Dr. Ryan's solicitors and expert witnesses, and that Dr. Ryan himself could not see them; that any person who saw the documents should not disclose their contents to anyone not entitled to inspect them; that the documents could be used only for the purposes of the litigation; and that only one copy of the notes was to be made by Dr. Ryan's solicitors, to be passed on as necessary to Dr. Ryan's expert witnesses. The Supreme Court of Canada, L'Heureux-Dubé J dissenting, dismissed the appeal.]

McLACHLIN J:
[1] After having been sexually assaulted by the respondent Dr. Ryan, the appellant sought counselling from a psychiatrist. The question on this appeal is whether the psychiatrist's notes and records containing statements the appellant made in the course of

treatment are protected from disclosure in a civil suit brought by the appellant against Dr. Ryan. Put in terms of principle, should a defendant's right to relevant material to the end of testing the plaintiff's case outweigh the plaintiff's expectation that communications between her and her psychiatrist will be kept in confidence?

. . .

IV. General Principles

. . .

[20]　While the circumstances giving rise to a privilege were once thought to be fixed by categories defined in previous centuries—categories that do not include communications between a psychiatrist and her patient—it is now accepted that the common law permits privilege in new situations where reason, experience and application of the principles that underlie the traditional privileges so dictate: *Slavutych v. Baker*, [1976] 1 SCR 254; *R v. Gruenke*, [1991] 3 SCR 263, at p. 286. The applicable principles are derived from those set forth in Wigmore on Evidence, vol. 8 (McNaughton rev. 1961), § 2285. First, the communication must originate in a confidence. Second, the confidence must be essential to the relationship in which the communication arises. Third, the relationship must be one which should be "sedulously fostered" in the public good. Finally, if all these requirements are met, the court must consider whether the interests served by protecting the communications from disclosure outweigh the interest in getting at the truth and disposing correctly of the litigation.

[21]　It follows that the law of privilege may evolve to reflect the social and legal realities of our time. One such reality is the law's increasing concern with the wrongs perpetrated by sexual abuse and the serious effect such abuse has on the health and productivity of the many members of our society it victimizes. Another modern reality is the extension of medical assistance from treatment of its physical effects to treatment of its mental and emotional aftermath through techniques such as psychiatric counselling. Yet another development of recent vintage which may be considered in connection with new claims for privilege is the Canadian *Charter* ... .

. . .

[23]　... Nevertheless, ensuring that the common law of privilege develops in accordance with "*Charter* values" requires that the existing rules be scrutinized to ensure that they reflect the values the *Charter* enshrines. This does not mean that the rules of privilege can be abrogated entirely and replaced with a new form of discretion governing disclosure. Rather, it means that the basic structure of the common law privilege analysis must remain intact, even if particular rules which are applied within that structure must be modified and updated to reflect emerging social realities.

V. Privilege for Communications Between Psychiatrist and Patient

[24]　The first requirement for privilege is that the communications at issue have originated in a confidence that they will not be disclosed. The Master held that this condition was not met because both the appellant and Dr. Parfitt had concerns that notwithstanding their desire for confidentiality, the records might someday be ordered disclosed in the course of litigation. With respect, I do not agree. The communications were made in confidence. The appellant stipulated that they should remain confidential and Dr. Parfitt

agreed that she would do everything possible to keep them confidential. The possibility that a court might order them disclosed at some future date over their objections does not change the fact that the communications were made in confidence. With the possible exception of communications falling in the traditional categories, there can never be an absolute guarantee of confidentiality; there is always the possibility that a court may order disclosure. Even for documents within the traditional categories, inadvertent disclosure is always a possibility. If the apprehended possibility of disclosure negated privilege, privilege would seldom if ever be found.

[25] The second requirement—that the element of confidentiality be essential to the full and satisfactory maintenance of the relation between the parties to the communication—is clearly satisfied in the case at bar. It is not disputed that Dr. Parfitt's practice in general and her ability to help the appellant in particular required that she hold her discussions with the appellant in confidence. Dr. Parfitt's evidence establishes that confidentiality is essential to the continued existence and effectiveness of the therapeutic relations between a psychiatrist and a patient seeking treatment for the psychiatric harm resulting from sexual abuse. Once psychiatrist–patient confidentiality is broken and the psychiatrist becomes involved in the patient's external world, the "frame" of the therapy is broken. At that point, it is Dr. Parfitt's practice to discontinue psychotherapy with the patient. The result is both confusing and damaging to the patient. At a time when she would normally find support in the therapeutic relationship, as during the trial, she finds herself without support. In the result, the patient's treatment may cease, her distrustfulness be exacerbated, and her personal and work relations be adversely affected.

[26] The appellant too sees confidentiality as essential to her relationship with Dr. Parfitt. She insisted from the first that her communications to Dr. Parfitt be held in confidence, suggesting that this was a condition of her entering and continuing treatment. The fact that she and Dr. Parfitt feared the possibility of court-ordered disclosure at some future date does not negate the fact that confidentiality was essential "to the full and satisfactory maintenance" of their relationship.

[27] The third requirement—that the relation must be one which in the opinion of the community ought to be sedulously fostered—is equally satisfied. Victims of sexual abuse often suffer serious trauma, which, left untreated, may mar their entire lives. It is widely accepted that it is in the interests of the victim and society that such help be obtained. The mental health of the citizenry, no less than its physical health, is a public good of great importance. Just as it is in the interest of the sexual abuse victim to be restored to full and healthy functioning, so is it in the interest of the public that she take her place as a healthy and productive member of society.

[28] It may thus be concluded that the first three conditions for privilege for communications between a psychiatrist and the victim of a sexual assault are met in the case at bar. The communications were confidential. Their confidence is essential to the psychiatrist–patient relationship. The relationship itself and the treatment it makes possible are of transcendent public importance.

[29] The fourth requirement is that the interests served by protecting the communications from disclosure outweigh the interest of pursuing the truth and disposing correctly of the litigation. This requires first an assessment of the interests served by protecting the communications from disclosure. These include injury to the appellant's ongoing relationship with Dr. Parfitt and her future treatment. They also include the effect that a finding of

no privilege would have on the ability of other persons suffering from similar trauma to obtain needed treatment and of psychiatrists to provide it. The interests served by non-disclosure must extend to any effect on society of the failure of individuals to obtain treatment restoring them to healthy and contributing members of society. Finally, the interests served by protection from disclosure must include the privacy interest of the person claiming privilege and inequalities which may be perpetuated by the absence of protection.

[30] As noted, the common law must develop in a way that reflects emerging *Charter* values. It follows that the factors balanced under the fourth part of the test for privilege should be updated to reflect relevant *Charter* values. One such value is the interest affirmed by s. 8 of the *Charter* of each person in privacy. Another is the right of every person embodied in s. 15 of the *Charter* to equal treatment and benefit of the law. A rule of privilege which fails to protect confidential doctor/patient communications in the context of an action arising out of sexual assault perpetuates the disadvantage felt by victims of sexual assault, often women. The intimate nature of sexual assault heightens the privacy concerns of the victim and may increase, if automatic disclosure is the rule, the difficulty of obtaining redress for the wrong. The victim of a sexual assault is thus placed in a disadvantaged position as compared with the victim of a different wrong. The result may be that the victim of sexual assault does not obtain the equal benefit of the law to which s. 15 of the *Charter* entitles her. She is doubly victimized, initially by the sexual assault and later by the price she must pay to claim redress—redress which in some cases may be part of her program of therapy. These are factors which may properly be considered in determining the interests served by an order for protection from disclosure of confidential patient-psychiatrist communications in sexual assault cases.

[31] These criteria, applied to the case at bar, demonstrate a compelling interest in protecting the communications at issue from disclosure. More, however, is required to establish privilege. For privilege to exist, it must be shown that the benefit that inures from privilege, however great it may seem, in fact outweighs the interest in the correct disposal of the litigation.

. . .

[33] It follows that if the court considering a claim for privilege determines that a particular document or class of documents must be produced to get at the truth and prevent an unjust verdict, it must permit production to the extent required to avoid that result. On the other hand, the need to get at the truth and avoid injustice does not automatically negate the possibility of protection from full disclosure. In some cases, the court may well decide that the truth permits of nothing less than full production. This said, I would venture to say that an order for partial privilege will more often be appropriate in civil cases where, as here, the privacy interest is compelling. Disclosure of a limited number of documents, editing by the court to remove non-essential material, and the imposition of conditions on who may see and copy the documents are techniques which may be used to ensure the highest degree of confidentiality and the least damage to the protected relationship, while guarding against the injustice of cloaking the truth.

[34] In taking this approach, I respectfully decline to follow the all-or-nothing approach adopted by the majority of the Supreme Court of the United States of endorsing an absolute privilege for all psychotherapeutic records ... .

[35] It must be conceded that a test for privilege which permits the court to occasionally reject an otherwise well-founded claim for privilege in the interests of getting at the

truth may not offer patients a guarantee that communications with their psychiatrists will never be disclosed. On the other hand, the assurance that disclosure will be ordered only where clearly necessary and then only to the extent necessary is likely to permit many to avail themselves of psychiatric counselling when certain disclosure might make them hesitate or decline. The facts in this case demonstrate as much. I am reinforced in this view by the fact, as Scalia J points out in his dissenting reasons in *Jaffee v. Redmond*, that of the 50 states and the District of Columbia which have enacted some form of psychotherapist privilege, none have adopted it in absolute form. All have found it necessary to specify circumstances in which it will not apply, usually related to the need to get at the truth in vital situations. Partial privilege, in the views of these legislators, can be effective.

[36] The view that privilege may exist where the interest in protecting the privacy of the records is compelling and the threat to proper disposition of the litigation either is not apparent or can be offset by partial or conditional discovery is consistent with this Court's view in *R v. O'Connor*, [1995] 4 SCR 411. The majority there did not deny that privilege in psychotherapeutic records may exist in appropriate circumstances. Without referring directly to privilege, it developed a test for production of third party therapeutic and other records which balances the competing interests by reference to a number of factors including the right of the accused to full answer and defence and the right of the complainant to privacy. Just as justice requires that the accused in a criminal case be permitted to answer the Crown's case, so justice requires that a defendant in a civil suit be permitted to answer the plaintiff's case. In deciding whether he or she is entitled to production of confidential documents, this requirement must be balanced against the privacy interest of the complainant. This said, the interest in disclosure of a defendant in a civil suit may be less compelling than the parallel interest of an accused charged with a crime. The defendant in a civil suit stands to lose money and repute; the accused in a criminal proceeding stands to lose his or her very liberty. As a consequence, the balance between the interest in disclosure and the complainant's interest in privacy may be struck at a different level in the civil and criminal case; documents produced in a criminal case may not always be producible in a civil case, where the privacy interest of the complainant may more easily outweigh the defendant's interest in production.

[37] My conclusion is that it is open to a judge to conclude that psychiatrist–patient records are privileged in appropriate circumstances. Once the first three requirements are met and a compelling prima facie case for protection is established, the focus will be on the balancing under the fourth head. A document relevant to a defence or claim may be required to be disclosed, notwithstanding the high interest of the plaintiff in keeping it confidential. On the other hand, documents of questionable relevance or which contain information available from other sources may be declared privileged. The result depends on the balance of the competing interests of disclosure and privacy in each case. It must be borne in mind that in most cases, the majority of the communications between a psychiatrist and her patient will have little or no bearing on the case at bar and can safely be excluded from production. Fishing expeditions are not appropriate where there is a compelling privacy interest at stake, even at the discovery stage. Finally, where justice requires that communications be disclosed, the court should consider qualifying the disclosure by imposing limits aimed at permitting the opponent to have the access justice requires while preserving the confidential nature of the documents to the greatest degree possible.

[38] It remains to consider the argument that by commencing the proceedings against the respondent Dr. Ryan, the appellant has forfeited her right to confidentiality. I accept that a litigant must accept such intrusions upon her privacy as are necessary to enable the judge or jury to get to the truth and render a just verdict. But I do not accept that by claiming such damages as the law allows, a litigant grants her opponent a licence to delve into private aspects of her life which need not be probed for the proper disposition of the litigation.

VI. Procedure for Ascertaining Privilege

[The court noted that a judge could proceed by examining every document or by reviewing affidavit summation of the documents and their relevance. While it is not essential that the judge examine every disputed document, the court may choose to do so if necessary to the inquiry. In this particular case, a "court might well consider it best to inspect the records individually to the end of weeding out those which were irrelevant to this defence" (at para 41), but the appeal was dismissed on the basis that the Court of Appeal's approach was not in error.]

QUESTIONS

1. If the Wigmore criteria do not support the creation of a *prima facie* privilege, how can they support the recognition of a privilege in particular cases? If the privilege in *Ryan*, above, is not a class privilege, what would qualify or is the list closed? The weakness of the case-by-case approach is obviously that it cannot generate certainty or predictability. In the context of civil suits, this inevitably encourages litigation, and in the context of criminal cases, delay. Would it have been better, in the long run, to simply protect privileges by class and accommodate the need to protect against injustice through recourse to exceptions?

2. Litigation has now resolved the issue of whether journalist–source privilege is a "class" or "case-by-case" claim. Unsurprisingly, the Supreme Court of Canada held in *R v National Post*, 2010 SCC 16, [2010] 1 SCR 477 that it merits case-by case protection only and expressly noted that, in this context (at para 58),

> [t]he fourth Wigmore criterion does most of the work. Having established the value to the public of the relationship in question, the court must weigh against its protection any countervailing public interest such as the investigation of a particular crime (or national security, or public safety or some other public good).

In *National Post*, a reporter investigated alleged conflict of interest by a former prime minister of Canada with regard to business dealings. The reporter promised his sources that he would keep their identities confidential. He also received an anonymous envelope containing a bank loan authorization that, if true, implicated the prime minister. The bank and the prime minister asserted that the document was a forgery. The police had reasonable grounds to believe so as well and sought investigatory warrants to obtain the envelope (and subject it to forensic testing) and the information contained in it and to compel the reporter to reveal his secret source. The court rejected a class-based privilege and an argument under freedom of expression, holding that (at para 41)

[t]he law needs to provide solid protection against the compelled disclosure of secret source identities in appropriate situations but the history of journalism in this country shows that the purpose of s. 2(b) can be fulfilled without the necessity of implying a constitutional immunity. Accordingly, a judicial order to compel disclosure of a secret source would not in general violate s. 2(b).

The Supreme Court concluded that the trial judge failed to adequately consider the interest of a journalist in protecting his source in *Globe and Mail v Canada (Attorney General)*, 2010 SCC 41, [2010] 2 SCR 592. This case also held that the Wigmore factors, despite originating at common law, apply to claims of privilege in Quebec.

1654776 Ltd v Stewart, 2013 ONCA 184 provides an example of where journalist source privilege was upheld on the basis that the public interest in securing compliance with the Ontario *Securities Act*, RSO 1990, c S.5 could be served without requiring disclosure of a journalist's confidential source.

3. Dupont was serving a penitentiary term for offences of rape and armed robbery. He was given hormonal treatments and was then subject to periodic assessments by Lacroix, a psychologist working for the National Parole Board, whose observations would be reported and used to determine whether Dupont's treatment should continue. During one such visit, the accused "told her that he had something to tell her; he asked her if she was bound by a duty of professional confidentiality. She answered in the affirmative." The accused then confessed to the murders of two children that had occurred some 14 years earlier and were unsolved. Lacroix was "bowled over" and reported the conversation to Dupont's case management officer, who in turn contacted the police. The investigation into the murders was reopened and Dupont was charged. The police obtained from him a signed, incriminating statement and "an authorization relieving Lucie Lacroix [and two other psychologists] of their duty of professional confidentiality." Dupont later testified that he had signed the statement and the authorization "after the police had promised him that his hormone treatment and his meetings with Lucie Lacroix would be continued." Should Dupont's statement to Lacroix or his subsequent statement to the police be admitted in his trial for the murder of the two children? See *R v Dupont* (1998), 129 CCC (3d) 77 (Qc CA), leave to appeal refused, (1999), 130 CCC (3d) vi (SCC).

4. A physician unsuccessfully applied for a staff position at a hospital. The chief of staff indicated that the physician's reference letters were "particularly negative." The physician was considering suing the authors of the letters for defamation, and asked the hospital to provide them to him. The hospital refused. The physician then applied for an order requiring the hospital to produce the letters. The hospital argued that the letters were privileged. Do you agree? See *Straka v Humber River Regional Hospital* (2000), 193 DLR (4th) 680 (Ont CA).

VIII. PROTECTING PRIVACY WITHOUT PRIVILEGE

When a woman has been sexually assaulted, she will often require treatment and counselling by medical professionals and others. Where a sexual assault is alleged, to what extent should the accused have access to the complainant's medical and other records? In *R v O'Connor*, [1995] 4 SCR 411, the Supreme Court held that in resolving this issue there must be sufficient protection for the privacy interests of third parties. The court treated the question of the production of records relating to third parties as a problem of balancing the accused's s 7 right to make full answer and defence against the third party's s 7 right to privacy and s 15 right to equal benefit of the law, bearing in mind that the third party in question will almost always be a complainant.

R v O'Connor

[1995] 4 SCR 411

Lamer CJC and La Forest, L'Heureux-Dubé, Sopinka, Gonthier, Cory, McLachlin, Iacobucci, and Major JJ (14 December 1995)

L'HEUREUX-DUBÉ J (La Forest and Gonthier JJ concurring):

· · ·

[99] The question of production of private records not in the possession of the Crown arises in a wide variety of contexts. Although many of these contexts involve medical and therapeutic records of complainants to sexual assault, it will become apparent that the principles and guidelines outlined herein are equally applicable to any record, in the hands of a third party, in which a reasonable expectation of privacy lies. Although the determination of when a reasonable expectation of privacy actually exists in a particular record (and, if so, to what extent it exists) is inherently fact-and context-sensitive, this may include records that are medical or therapeutic in nature, school records, private diaries, and activity logs prepared by social workers, to name just a few. For the sake of convenience, information that is generically of this nature shall hereafter be referred to as "private records held by third parties."

· · ·

(ii) The Competing Constitutional Rights at Issue

[106] In formulating an approach to govern production of private records held by third parties, it is important to appreciate fully the nature of the various interests at issue. I will describe briefly each of the three constitutional rights that I believe to be implicated in this analysis: (1) the right to full answer and defence; (2) the right to privacy; and (3) the right to equality without discrimination.

(a) The Right to a Fair Trial

[107] Much has been written about the right to a fair trial. An individual who is deprived of the ability to make full answer and defence is deprived of fundamental justice. However, full answer and defence, like any right, cannot be considered in the abstract. The principles of fundamental justice vary according to the context in which they are invoked. For this reason, certain procedural protections might be constitutionally mandated in one context but not in another: R v. Lyons, [1987] 2 SCR 309, at p. 361. Moreover, though the Constitution guarantees the accused a fair hearing, it does not guarantee the most favourable procedures imaginable: Lyons, supra, at p. 362. Finally, although fairness of the trial and, as a corollary, fairness in defining the limits of full answer and defence, must primarily be viewed from the point of view of the accused, both notions must nevertheless also be considered from the point of view of the community and the complainant:

E. (A.W.), [[1993] 3 SCR 155], at p. 198. There is no question that the right to make full answer and defence cannot be so broad as to grant the defence a fishing licence into the personal and private lives of others. The question is therefore not *whether* the defence can be limited in its attempts to obtain production of private records held by third parties, but *how* it can be limited in a manner that accords appropriate constitutional protection to all of the constitutional rights at issue.

[108] When the defence seeks production of third party records whose contents it is not aware of, the defence is obviously in a position of some difficulty. In assessing whether this difficulty poses a threat of constitutional proportions to the accused's ability to make fair answer and defence, however, one thing must be borne in mind. Given that these records are not in the possession of the Crown and have not constituted a basis for its investigations, they do not, by definition, constitute part of the state's "case to meet" against the accused. Unlike sealed wiretap packages, which represent the fruits of state investigation of the accused, private records in the hands of third parties are not subject to such a presumption of materiality.

[109] I would note, finally, that an important element of trial fairness is the need to remove discriminatory beliefs and bias from the fact-finding process: *Seaboyer*, [[1991] 2 SCR 577]. As I pointed out in *R v. Osolin*, [1993] 4 SCR 595, at pp. 622-23, for instance, the assumption that private therapeutic or counselling records are relevant to full answer and defence is often highly questionable, in that these records may very well have a greater potential to derail than to advance the truth-seeking process:

> *[M]edical records concerning statements made in the course of therapy are both hearsay and inherently problematic as regards reliability. A witness's concerns expressed in the course of therapy after the fact, even assuming they are correctly understood and reliably noted, cannot be equated with evidence given in the course of a trial.* Both the context in which the statements are made and the expectations of the parties are entirely different. In a trial, a witness is sworn to testify as to the particular events in issue. By contrast, in therapy an entire spectrum of factors such as personal history, thoughts, emotions as well as particular acts may inform the dialogue between therapist and patient. *Thus, there is serious risk that such statements could be taken piecemeal out of the context in which they were made to provide a foundation for entirely unwarranted inferences by the trier of fact.* [Emphasis added.]

(b) The Right to Privacy

[110] This Court has on many occasions recognized the great value of privacy in our society. It has expressed sympathy for the proposition that s. 7 of the *Charter* includes a right to privacy: *Beare, supra*, at p. 412; *B.(R.) v. Children's Aid Society of Metropolitan Toronto*, [1995] 1 SCR 315, at p. 369, per La Forest J. On numerous other occasions, it has spoken of privacy in terms of s. 8 of the *Charter*: see, e.g., *Hunter v. Southam Inc.*, [1984] 2 SCR 145; *R v. Pohoretsky*, [1987] 1 SCR 945; *R v. Dyment*, [1988] 2 SCR 417. On still other occasions, it has underlined the importance of privacy in the common law: *McInerney v. MacDonald*, [1992] 2 SCR 138, at pp. 148-49; *Hill v. Church of Scientology of Toronto*, [1995] 2 SCR 1130.

[111] On no occasion has the relationship between "liberty," "security of the person," and essential human dignity been more carefully canvassed by this Court than in the reasons of Wilson J in *R v. Morgentaler*, [1988] 1 SCR 30. In her judgment, she notes that

the *Charter* and the right to individual liberty guaranteed therein are tied inextricably to the concept of human dignity. She urges that both "liberty" and "security of the person" are capable of a broad range of meaning and that a purposive interpretation of the *Charter* requires that the right to liberty contained in s. 7 be read to "guarantee[] to every individual a degree of personal autonomy over important decisions intimately affecting their private lives" (p. 171). Concurring on this point with the majority, she notes, as well, that "security of the person" is sufficiently broad to include protection for the psychological integrity of the individual.

[112] Equally relevant, for our purposes, is Lamer J's recognition in *Mills*, [[1986] 1 SCR 863], at p. 920, that the right to security of the person encompasses the right to be protected against psychological trauma. In the context of his discussion of the effects on an individual of unreasonable delay contrary to s. 11(b) of the *Charter*, he noted that such trauma could take the form of

> stigmatization of the accused, loss of privacy, stress and anxiety resulting from a multitude of factors, including possible disruption of family, social life and work, legal costs, uncertainty as to the outcome and sanction.

If the word "complainant" were substituted for the word "accused" in the above extract, I think that we would have an excellent description of the psychological traumas potentially faced by sexual assault complainants. These people must contemplate the threat of disclosing to the very person accused of assaulting them in the first place, and quite possibly in open court, records containing intensely private aspects of their lives, possibly containing thoughts and statements which have never even been shared with the closest of friends or family.

[113] In the same way that this Court recognized in *Re BC Motor Vehicle Act*, [[1985] 2 SCR 486], that the "principles of fundamental justice" in s. 7 are informed by fundamental tenets of our common law system and by ss. 8 to 14 of the *Charter*, I think that the terms "liberty" and "security of the person" must, as essential aspects of a free and democratic society, be animated by the rights and values embodied in the common law, the civil law and the *Charter*. In my view, it is not without significance that one of those rights, s. 8, has been identified as having as its fundamental purpose "to protect individuals from unjustified state intrusions upon their privacy" (*Hunter*, *supra*, at p. 160). The right to be secure from unreasonable search and seizure plays a pivotal role in a document that purports to contain the blueprint of the Canadian vision of what constitutes a free and democratic society. Respect for individual privacy is an essential component of what it means to be "free." As a corollary, the infringement of this right undeniably impinges upon an individual's "liberty" in our free and democratic society.

[114] A similarly broad approach to the notion of liberty has been taken in the United States. In *Board of Regents of State Colleges v. Roth*, 408 US 564 (1972), at pp. 571-72, the United States Supreme Court affirmed that "liberty" was a "broad and majestic term" and that "[i]n a Constitution for a free people, there can be no doubt that the meaning of 'liberty' must be broad indeed." More significant for our purposes, the right to privacy was expressly found to reside in the term "liberty" in the Fourteenth Amendment in the landmark case of *Roe v. Wade*, 410 US 113 (1973). In a similar vein, the right to personal privacy has also received recognition in international documents such as Article 17 of the *International Covenant on Civil and Political Rights*, 999 UNTS 171, Article 12 of the

Universal Declaration of Human Rights, GA Res. 217 A (III), UN Doc. A/810, at 71 (1948), and Article 8 of the *European Convention for the Protection of Human Rights and Fundamental Freedoms*, 213 UNTS 221.

[L'Heureux-Dubé J discussed certain private law protections of the right of privacy, and continued:]

[117] It is apparent, however, that privacy can never be absolute. It must be balanced against legitimate societal needs. This Court has recognized that the essence of such a balancing process lies in assessing *reasonable expectation of privacy*, and balancing that expectation against the necessity of interference from the state: *Hunter, supra*, at pp. 159-60. Evidently, the greater the reasonable expectation of privacy and the more significant the deleterious effects flowing from its breach, the more compelling must be the state objective, and the salutary effects of that objective, in order to justify interference with this right. See *Dagenais*, [[1994] 3 SCR 835].

[118] In *R v. Plant*, [1993] 3 SCR 281, albeit in the context of a discussion of s. 8 of the *Charter*, a majority of this Court identified one context in which the right to privacy would generally arise in respect of documents and records (at p. 293):

> In fostering the underlying values of dignity, integrity and autonomy, it is fitting that s. 8 of the *Charter* should seek to protect a biographical core of personal information which individuals in a free and democratic society would wish to maintain and control from dissemination to the state. *This would include information which tends to reveal intimate details of the lifestyle and personal choices of the individual.* [Emphasis added.]

Although I prefer not to decide today whether this definition is exhaustive of the right to privacy in respect of all manners of documents and records, I am satisfied that the nature of the private records which are the subject matter of this appeal properly brings them within that rubric. Such items may consequently be viewed as disclosing a reasonable expectation of privacy which is worthy of protection under s. 7 of the *Charter*.

[119] The essence of privacy, however, is that once invaded, it can seldom be regained. For this reason, it is all the more important for reasonable expectations of privacy to be protected at the point of disclosure. As La Forest J observed in *Dyment, supra*, at p. 430:

> [I]f the privacy of the individual is to be protected, we cannot afford to wait to vindicate it only after it has been violated. This is inherent in the notion of being *secure* against unreasonable searches and seizures. *Invasions of privacy must be prevented, and where privacy is outweighed by other societal claims, there must be clear rules setting forth the conditions in which it can be violated.* [Emphasis in last sentence added.]

In the same way that our constitution generally requires that a search be premised upon a pre-authorization which is of a nature and manner that is proportionate to the reasonable expectation of privacy at issue (*Hunter, supra; Thomson Newspapers*, [[1990] 1 SCR 425]), s. 7 of the *Charter* requires a reasonable system of "pre-authorization" to justify court-sanctioned intrusions into the private records of witnesses in legal proceedings. Although it may appear trite to say so, I underline that when a private document or record is revealed and the reasonable expectation of privacy therein is thereby displaced, the invasion is not with respect to the particular document or record in question. Rather, it is an invasion of the dignity and self-worth of the individual, who enjoys the right to privacy as an essential aspect of his or her liberty in a free and democratic society.

(c) The Right to Equality Without Discrimination

[120] Unlike virtually every other offence in the *Criminal Code*, sexual assault is a crime which overwhelmingly affects women, children and the disabled. Ninety percent of all victims of sexual assault are female: *Osolin, supra*, at p. 669, per Cory J. Moreover, studies suggest that between 50 and 80 percent of women institutionalized for psychiatric disorders have prior histories of sexual abuse (T. Firsten, "An Exploration of the Role of Physical and Sexual Abuse for Psychiatrically Institutionalized Women" (1990), unpublished research paper, available from Ontario Women's Directorate). Children are most highly vulnerable (*Sexual Offences Against Children* (the Badgley Report), vol. 1 (1984)).

[121] It is a common phenomenon in this day and age for one who has been sexually victimized to seek counselling or therapy in relation to this occurrence. It therefore stands to reason that disclosure rules or practices which make mental health or medical records routinely accessible in sexual offence proceedings will have disproportionately invasive consequences for women, particularly those with disabilities, and children. In particular, in determining questions of disclosure of records of persons allegedly assaulted in institutions where they get psychiatric assistance, the courts must take care not to create a class of vulnerable victims who have to choose between accusing their attackers and maintaining the confidentiality of their records.

[122] This Court has recognized the pernicious role that past evidentiary rules in both the *Criminal Code* and the common law, now regarded as discriminatory, once played in our legal system: *Seaboyer, supra*. We must be careful not to permit such practices to reappear under the guise of extensive and unwarranted inquiries into the past histories and private lives of complainants of sexual assault. We must not allow the defence to do indirectly what it cannot do directly under s. 276 of the *Code*. This would close one discriminatory door only to open another.

[123] As I noted in *Osolin, supra*, at pp. 624-25, uninhibited disclosure of complainants' private lives indulges the discriminatory suspicion that women and children's reports of sexual victimization are uniquely likely to be fabricated. Put another way, if there were an explicit requirement in the *Code* requiring corroboration before women or children could bring sexual assault charges, such a provision would raise serious concerns under s. 15 of the *Charter*. In my view, a legal system which devalues the evidence of complainants to sexual assault by *de facto* presuming their uncreditworthiness would raise similar concerns. It would not reflect, far less promote, "a society in which all are secure in the knowledge that they are recognized at law as human beings equally deserving of concern, respect and consideration" (*Andrews v. Law Society of British Columbia*, [1989] 1 SCR 143, at p. 171).

[124] Routine insistence on the exposure of complainants' personal backgrounds has the potential to reflect a built-in bias in the criminal justice system against those most vulnerable to repeat victimization. Such requests, in essence, rest on the assumption that the personal and psychological backgrounds and profiles of complainants of sexual assault are relevant as to whether or not the complainant consented to the sexual contact, or whether the accused honestly believed that she consented. Although the defence must be free to *demonstrate*, without resort to stereotypical lines of reasoning, that such information

is actually relevant to a live issue at trial, it would mark the triumph of stereotype over logic if courts and lawyers were simply to *assume* such relevance to exist, without requiring any evidence to this effect whatsoever.

[125] It is revealing, for instance, to compare the approach often taken to private records in sexual assault trials with the approach taken in three decisions in which private files were sought by defence counsel in situations which did not involve sexual assaults. In *Gingras*, [(1992), 71 CCC (3d) 53 (Alta CA)], the defence in a murder case sought disclosure of the prison file of an important Crown witness, who was serving time in a penitentiary in another province. The credibility of the witness was invoked as being at issue. In addition to finding important irregularities in the disclosure order, the Court concluded that the disclosure request amounted to no more than a fishing expedition and therefore quashed the order, notwithstanding the seriousness of the charge against the accused.

[126] In both *R v. Gratton*, [1987] OJ no. 1984 (Prov. Ct.), and *R v. Callaghan*, [1993] OJ no. 2013 (Ont. Ct. (Prov. Div.)), an accused charged with assault of a police officer sought disclosure of the officer's personnel files and, in particular, any files relating to complaints or disciplinary actions taken against the officer. In both cases, the justification offered for this disclosure was to show that the officer had a propensity for violence. In both cases, in the absence of any evidence as to the likelihood that the records would contain evidence to the predisposition to violence or unreasonable use of force, the judge refused to give disclosure of those files. The contents of the files were characterized as hearsay, as potentially based on unfounded allegations, and as generally irrelevant. The only disclosure granted was of a file containing details of the *formal investigation* of the particular complaint filed by the accused in relation to activity which was the subject matter of the charges.

[127] I see no reason to treat a sexual assault complainant any differently, or to accord any less respect to her credibility or privacy, than that which was accorded police officers and convicted criminals in the above-mentioned cases.

[128] All of these factors, in my mind, justify concluding not only that a privacy analysis creates a presumption against ordering production of private records, but also that ample and meaningful consideration must be given to complainants' equality rights under the *Charter* when formulating an appropriate approach to the production of complainants' records. Consequently, I have great sympathy for the observation of Hill J in *R v. Barbosa* (1994), 92 CCC (3d) 131 (Ont. Ct. (Gen. Div.)), to this effect (at p. 141):

> In addressing the disclosure of records, relating to past treatment, analysis, assessment or care of a complainant, it is necessary to remember that the pursuit of full answer and defence on behalf of an accused person should be achieved without indiscriminately or arbitrarily eradicating the privacy of the complainant. *Systemic revictimization of a complainant fosters disrepute for the criminal justice system.* [Emphasis added.]

(iii) Balancing Competing Values

[129] As Lamer CJ recently noted for the majority in *Dagenais, supra*, at p. 877, competing constitutional considerations must be balanced with particular care:

> A hierarchical approach to rights, which places some over others, must be avoided, both when interpreting the *Charter* and when developing the common law. When the protected

rights of two individuals come into conflict ... *Charter* principles require a balance to be achieved that fully respects the importance of both sets of rights.

Notwithstanding my agreement with this proposition, I would emphasize that the imagery of conflicting rights which it conjures up may not always be appropriate. One such example is the interrelation between the equality rights of complainants in sexual assault trials and the rights of the accused to a fair trial. The eradication of discriminatory beliefs and practices in the conduct of such trials will enhance rather than detract from the fairness of such trials. Conversely, sexual assault trials that are fair will promote the equality of women and children, who are most often the victims.

[130] From my earlier remarks, moreover, it should be clear that I am satisfied that witnesses have a right to privacy in relation to private documents and records (i.e. documents and records in which they hold a reasonable expectation of privacy) which are not a part of the Crown's "case to meet" against the accused. They are entitled not to be deprived of their reasonable expectation of privacy except in accordance with the principles of fundamental justice. In cases such as the present one, any interference with the individual's right to privacy comes about as a result of another person's assertion that this interference is necessary in order to make full answer and defence. As important as the right to full answer and defence may be, it must co-exist with other constitutional rights, rather than trample them: *Dagenais, supra*, at p. 877. Privacy and equality must not be sacrificed willy-nilly on the altar of trial fairness.

[131] The proper approach to be taken in contexts involving competing constitutional rights may be analogized from *Dagenais*, at p. 891. In particular, since an applicant seeking production of private records from third parties is seeking to invoke the power of the state to violate the privacy rights of other individuals, the applicant must show that the use of the state power to compel production is justified in a free and democratic society. If it is not, then the other person's privacy rights will have been infringed in a manner that is contrary to the principles of fundamental justice.

[132] The use of state power to compel production of private records will be justified in a free and democratic society when the following criteria are applied. First, production should only be granted when it is shown that the accused cannot obtain the information sought by any other reasonably available and effective alternative means. Second, production which infringes upon a right to privacy must be as limited as reasonably possible to fulfil the right to make full answer and defence. Third, arguments urging production must rest upon permissible chains of reasoning, rather than upon discriminatory assumptions and stereotypes. Finally, there must be a proportionality between the salutary effects of production on the accused's right to make full answer and defence as compared with the deleterious effects on the party whose private records are being produced. The measure of proportionality must reflect the extent to which a reasonable expectation of privacy vests in the particular records, on the one hand, and the importance of the issue to which the evidence relates, on the other. Moreover, courts must remain alive to the fact that, in certain cases, the deleterious effects of production may demonstrably include negative effects on the complainant's course of therapy, threatening psychological harm to the individual concerned and thereby resulting in a concomitant deprivation of the individual's security of the person.

[133] All of the above considerations must be borne in mind when formulating an appropriate approach to the difficult issue raised in this appeal. Using these ground rules

to structure our analysis, it is now possible to elaborate upon an approach to production of third parties' private records that, it is hoped, will maintain the greatest possible degree of proportionality in reconciling the equally important constitutional concerns of full answer and defence, privacy, and equality without discrimination.

. . .

(b) Application for Production

[In light of these constitutional values, L'Heureux-Dubé J proposed a two-stage test for production of third parties' private records. At the first stage, the accused would have to demonstrate that the records were "*likely to be relevant*" either to an issue in the proceeding or to the competence of the subject to testify." She described this burden as "a significant one" and held that it could not be satisfied by "a bare, unsupported assertion that the records might impact on 'recent complaint' or 'the kind of person' the witness is," or by "the mere fact that a witness has a medical or psychiatric record" or "the mere fact that a witness received treatment or counselling after a sexual assault." If the trial found that the records were likely to be relevant, then at the second stage the judge had to decide whether to order "production of the records to the court for inspection" *and* had to decide "whether, and to what extent, they should be produced to the accused." In making both of these decisions, the judge had to "balance the salutary and deleterious effects ... having regard to the accused's right to make full answer and defence, and the effect of such production on the privacy and equality rights of the subject of the records."]

[155] In *Dagenais*, the Court assessed proportionality by examining and weighing the salutary and deleterious effects of the rights infringements in question. I believe that such a process was already implicit in *Seaboyer*, in which this Court sought to achieve a measure of proportionality between the right to privacy and the right to a fair trial. In my view, an analogous approach is appropriate in the disclosure context. Once a court has reviewed the records, production should only be ordered in respect of those records, or parts of records, that have significant probative value that is not substantially outweighed by the danger of prejudice to the proper administration of justice or by the harm to the privacy rights of the witness or to the privileged relation. See also Stuesser, "Reconciling Disclosure and Privilege" (1994), 30 CR (4th) 67, at pp. 71-72.

[156] Although this list is not exhaustive, the following factors should be considered in this determination: (1) the extent to which the record is necessary for the accused to make full answer and defence; (2) the probative value of the record in question; (3) the nature and extent of the reasonable expectation of privacy vested in that record; (4) whether production of the record would be premised upon any discriminatory belief or bias; (5) the potential prejudice to the complainant's dignity, privacy or security of the person that would be occasioned by production of the record in question; (6) the extent to which production of records of this nature would frustrate society's interest in encouraging the reporting of sexual offences and the acquisition of treatment by victims; and (7) the effect on the integrity of the trial process of producing, or failing to produce, the record, having in mind the need to maintain consideration in the outcome.

[157] According to the Chief Justice and Sopinka J, society's interest in encouraging victims of sexual assault to report the offences and to obtain treatment "is not a paramount

consideration" (para. 33), and the effect of production on the integrity of the trial process should not be considered at all, in assessing whether the guardians of therapeutic records should be compelled to produce them to the defence. I can see no reason to reduce the relative importance of these factors, let alone exclude them, when balancing the salutary and deleterious effects of a production order.

[158] This Court has already recognized that society has a legitimate interest in encouraging the reporting of sexual assault and that this social interest is furthered by protecting the privacy of complainants: *Seaboyer, supra*, at pp. 605-6. Parliament, too, has recognized this important interest in s. 276(3)(b) of the *Criminal Code*. While *Seaboyer* and s. 276(3)(b) relate to the admissibility of evidence regarding the past sexual conduct of the complainant, the same reasoning applies here. The compelled production of therapeutic records is a serious invasion of complainants' privacy which has the potential to deter sexual assault victims from reporting offences or, if they do report them, from seeking treatment.

[Lamer CJC and Sopinka J, dissenting in the result but speaking for the majority (Lamer CJC and Sopinka, Cory, Iacobucci, and Major JJ) on this point, said:]

LAMER CJC and SOPINKA J:

[17] In our opinion, the balancing approach we established in *Stinchcombe* can apply with equal force in the context of *production*, where the information sought is in the hands of a third party. Of course, the balancing process must be modified to fit the context in which it is applied. In cases involving production, for example, we are concerned with the competing claims of a constitutional right to privacy in the information on the one hand, and the right to full answer and defence on the other. We agree with L'Heureux-Dubé J that a constitutional right to privacy extends to information contained in many forms of third party records.

[18] In recognizing that all individuals have a right to privacy which should be protected as much as is reasonably possible, we should not lose sight of the possibility of occasioning a miscarriage of justice by establishing a procedure which unduly restricts an accused's ability to access information which may be necessary for meaningful full answer and defence. In *R v. Seaboyer*, [1991] 2 SCR 577, at p. 611, we recognized that:

> Canadian courts ... have been extremely cautious in restricting the power of the accused to call evidence in his or her defence, a reluctance founded in the fundamental tenet of our judicial system that an innocent person must not be convicted.

Indeed, so important is the societal interest in preventing a miscarriage of justice that our law requires the state to disclose the identity of an informer in certain circumstances, despite the fact that the revelation may jeopardize the informer's safety.

(b) The First Stage: Establishing "Likely Relevance"

[19] When the defence seeks information in the hands of a third party (as compared to the state), the following considerations operate so as to require a shifting of the onus and a higher threshold of relevance:

(1) the information is not part of the state's "case to meet" nor has the state been granted access to the information in preparing its case; and

(2) third parties have no obligation to assist the defence.

In light of these considerations, we agree with L'Heureux-Dubé J that, at the first stage in the production procedure, the onus should be on the accused to satisfy a judge that the information is *likely to be relevant*. The onus we place on the accused should not be interpreted as an evidential burden requiring evidence and a *voir dire* in every case. It is simply an initial threshold to provide a basis for production which can be satisfied by oral submissions of counsel. It is important to recognize that the accused will be in a very poor position to call evidence given that he has never had access to the records.

. . .

[21] According to L'Heureux-Dubé J, once the accused meets the "likely relevance" threshold, he or she must then satisfy the judge that the salutary effects of ordering the documents produced to the court for inspection outweigh the deleterious effects of such production. We are of the view that this balancing should be undertaken at the second stage of the procedure. The "likely relevance" stage should be confined to a question of whether the right to make full answer and defence is implicated by information contained in the records. Moreover, a judge will only be in an informed position to engage in the required balancing analysis once he or she has had an opportunity to review the records in question.

. . .

[25] ...

> What troubles me about this [the majority's] approach is that it puts on a plaintiff [the] burden of proving how the documents, which are admittedly relevant, can be of assistance. How can he do that? He has never seen them; they are confidential and so unavailable. To some extent, then, what the documents contain must be a matter of speculation.

We are of the view that the concern expressed in these cases applies with equal force in the case at bar, where the ultimate goal is the search for truth rather than the suppression of potentially relevant evidence.

[26] [I]t should be remembered that in most cases, an accused will not be privy to the existence of third party records which are maintained under strict rules of confidentiality. Generally speaking, an accused will only become aware of the existence of records because of something which arises in the course of the criminal case. For example, the complainant's psychiatrist, therapist or social worker may come forward and reveal his or her concerns about the complainant (as occurred in *R v. Ross* (1993), 79 CCC (3d) 253 (NSCA), and *R v. Ross* (1993), 81 CCC (3d) 234 (NSCA)). In other cases, the complainant may reveal at the preliminary inquiry or in his or her statement to the police that he or she decided to lay a criminal charge against the accused following a visit with a particular therapist. There is a possibility of materiality where there is a "reasonably close temporal connection between" the creation of the records and the date of the alleged commission of the offence (*R v. Osolin*, [1993] 4 SCR 595, at p. 673) or in cases of historical events, as in this case, a close temporal connection between the creation of the records and the decision to bring charges against the accused.

. . .

[29] By way of illustration only, we are of the view that there are a number of ways in which information contained in third party records may be relevant, for example, in sexual assault cases:

(1) [T]hey may contain information concerning the unfolding of events underlying the criminal complaint. See *Osolin*, *supra*, and *R v. R.S.* (1985), 19 CCC (3d) 115 (Ont. CA).

(2) [T]hey may reveal the use of a therapy which influenced the complainant's memory of the alleged events. For example, in *R v. L.(D.O.)*, [1993] 4 SCR 419, at p. 447, L'Heureux-Dubé J recognized the problem of contamination when she stated, in the context of the sexual abuse of children, that "the fear of contaminating required testimony has forced the delay of needed therapy and counselling." See too *R v. Norman* (1993), 87 CCC (3d) 153 (Ont. CA).

(3) [T]hey may contain information that bears on the complainant's "credibility, including testimonial factors such as the quality of their perception of events at the time of the offence, and their memory since." See *R v. R.(L.)*, *supra*, at p. 398; *R v. Hedstrom* (1991), 63 CCC (3d) 261 (BCCA); *R v. Ross* (1993), 81 CCC (3d) 234 (NSCA); *Toohey v. Metropolitan Police Commissioner*, [1965] 1 All ER 506 (HL).

As a result, we disagree with L'Heureux-Dubé J's assertion that therapeutic records will only be relevant to the defence in rare cases.

NOTES AND QUESTIONS

In response to *O'Connor*, Parliament enacted ss 278.1 through 278.9 of the *Criminal Code*. The procedure created by these provisions differs in several important ways from the procedure outlined by the majority in *O'Connor*. First, at the first stage of establishing "likely relevance," s 278.3(4) states:

(4) Any one or more of the following assertions by the accused are not sufficient on their own to establish that the record is likely relevant to an issue at trial or to the competence of a witness to testify:

(a) that the record exists;

(b) that the record relates to medical or psychiatric treatment, therapy or counselling that the complainant or witness has received or is receiving;

(c) that the record relates to the incident that is the subject-matter of the proceedings;

(d) that the record may disclose a prior inconsistent statement of the complainant or witness;

(e) that the record may relate to the credibility of the complainant or witness;

(f) that the record may relate to the reliability of the testimony of the complainant or witness merely because the complainant or witness has received or is receiving psychiatric treatment, therapy or counselling;

(g) that the record may reveal allegations of sexual abuse of the complainant by a person other than the accused;

(h) that the record relates to the sexual activity of the complainant with any person, including the accused;

(i) that the record relates to the presence or absence of a recent complaint;

(j) that the record relates to the complainant's sexual reputation; or

(k) that the record was made close in time to a complaint or to the activity that forms the subject-matter of the charge against the accused.

Does this mean that even if the accused can establish *all* of these grounds, the records may not be produced to the judge?

Second, at the first stage, s 278.5(1) requires not only that the record be "likely relevant" but that its production to the trial judge be "necessary in the interests of justice."

Third, s 278.5(2) lists eight factors relevant to production at the first stage:

(2) In determining whether to order the production of the record or part of the record for review pursuant to subsection (1), the judge shall consider the salutary and deleterious effects of the determination on the accused's right to make a full answer and defence and on the right to privacy, personal security and equality of the complainant or witness, as the case may be, and any other person to whom the record relates. In particular, the judge shall take the following factors into account:

(a) the extent to which the record is necessary for the accused to make a full answer and defence;

(b) the probative value of the record;

(c) the nature and extent of the reasonable expectation of privacy with respect to the record;

(d) whether production of the record is based on a discriminatory belief or bias;

(e) the potential prejudice to the personal dignity and right to privacy of any person to whom the record relates;

(f) society's interest in encouraging the reporting of sexual offences;

(g) society's interest in encouraging the obtaining of treatment by complainants of sexual offences; and

(h) the effect of the determination on the integrity of the trial process.

Fourth, at the second stage of deciding whether to order production of the record to the accused, s 278.7(2) states (contrast the five factors listed by Lamer CJC and Sopinka J at para 31 of *O'Connor* at the second stage):

(d) The Role of the Judge at the Second Stage: Balancing Full Answer and Defence and Privacy

[30] We agree with L'Heureux-Dubé J. that "upon their production to the court, the judge should examine the records to determine whether, and to what extent, they should be produced to the accused" (para. 153). We also agree that in making that determination, the judge must examine and weigh the salutary and deleterious effects of a production order and determine whether a non-production order would constitute a reasonable limit on the ability of the accused to make full answer and defence. In some cases, it may be possible for the presiding judge to provide a judicial summary of the records to counsel to enable them to assist in determining whether the material should be produced. This, of course, would depend on the specific facts of each particular case.

[31] We also agree that, in balancing the competing rights in question, the following factors should be considered: "(1) the extent to which the record is necessary for the accused to make

full answer and defence; (2) the probative value of the record in question; (3) the nature and extent of the reasonable expectation of privacy vested in that record; (4) whether production of the record would be premised upon any discriminatory belief or bias" and "(5) the potential prejudice to the complainant's dignity, privacy or security of the person that would be occasioned by production of the record in question" (para. 156).

[32] However, L'Heureux-Dubé J. also refers to two other factors that she believes must be considered. She suggests that the judge should take account of "the extent to which production of records of this nature would frustrate society's interest in encouraging the reporting of sexual offences and the acquisition of treatment by victims" as well as "the effect on the integrity of the trial process of producing, or failing to produce, the record, having in mind the need to maintain consideration in the outcome" (para. 156). This last factor is more appropriately dealt with at the admissibility stage and not in deciding whether the information should be produced. As for society's interest in the reporting of sexual crimes, we are of the opinion that there are other avenues available to the judge to ensure that production does not frustrate the societal interests that may be implicated by the production of the records to the defence. ...

[33] Consequently, the societal interest is not a paramount consideration in deciding whether the information should be provided. It is, however, a relevant factor which should be taken into account in weighing the competing interests. ...

Given that the procedure outlined in *O'Connor* was supposed to reflect a constitutional balancing of the accused's and the complainant's rights, there was a strong argument to be made that the revisions to the Code were unconstitutional. But in *R v Mills*, [1999] 3 SCR 668, the Supreme Court upheld the provisions. In *Mills*, the court noted (at para 20) that "[t]he law develops through dialogue between courts and legislatures" and "[a]gainst the backdrop of *O'Connor*, Parliament was free to craft its own solution to the problem consistent with the Charter."

In *R v McNeil*, 2009 SCC 3, [2009] 1 SCR 66, the Supreme Court explained the differences between the two regimes and why it decided that both are constitutionally valid:

[30] It is important to note that the common law likely relevance threshold in *O'Connor* differs significantly from the statutory likely relevance threshold set by Parliament for the production of records containing personal information in sexual assault proceedings under the *Mills* regime (see s. 278.3(4) of the *Criminal Code*). As this Court explained at some length in *Mills*, a range of permissible regimes can meet constitutional standards. It was therefore open to Parliament to craft its own solution to address the particular concerns arising from disclosure of third party records in sexual proceedings. In doing so, Parliament "sought to recognize the prevalence of sexual violence against women and children and its disadvantageous impact on their rights, ... and to reconcile fairness to complainants with the rights of the accused" (*Mills*, at para. 59). The following differences between the two regimes are particularly noteworthy.

[31] First, the likely relevance standard adopted by Parliament under the *Mills* regime is tailored to counter speculative myths, stereotypes and generalized assumptions about sexual assault victims and about the usefulness of private records in sexual assault proceedings. Such generalized views need not be countered at large in respect of all third party records that fall outside the *Mills* regime. The general common law threshold of likely relevance under *O'Connor* is intended rather to screen applications to ensure the proper use of state authority in compelling production of third party records and to establish the appropriateness of the application so as to avoid squandering scarce judicial resources.

[32] Second, while the *Mills* regime retains the two-stage framework set out in *O'Connor*, it differs significantly in that much of the balancing of the competing interests is effected at the first stage in determining whether production should be made to the court for inspection. This reflects Parliament's assumption that a reasonable expectation of privacy exists in the types of records targeted by the statutory regime: see *R v. Clifford* (2002), 163 CCC (3d) 3 (Ont. CA), at paras. 48-49. An equivalent presumption of privacy does not attach in respect of all third party records that fall outside the *Mills* regime. Hence, any balancing of competing interests is reserved for the second stage of the *O'Connor* regime, when the documents can be inspected by the court to better ascertain the nature of the privacy interest, if any. Because of these significant differences, it is important not to transpose the *Mills* regime into the *O'Connor* production hearing in respect of documents to which the statutory dispositions do not apply.

The provisions at issue in *Mills* apply to the sexual offences: see s 278.2(1). *O'Connor* applies to all other criminal contexts and has helpfully summarized *McNeil* at para 27:

(1) The accused first obtains a *subpoena duces tecum* under ss. 698(1) and 700(1) of the *Criminal Code* and serves it on the third party record holder. The subpoena compels the person to whom it is directed to attend court with the targeted records or materials.

(2) The accused also brings an application, supported by appropriate affidavit evidence, showing that the records sought are likely to be relevant in his or her trial. Notice of the application is given to the prosecuting Crown, the person who is the subject of the records and any other person who may have a privacy interest in the records targeted for production.

(3) The *O'Connor* application is brought before the judge seized with the trial, although it may be heard before the trial commences. If production is unopposed, of course, the application for production becomes moot and there is no need for a hearing.

(4) If the record holder or some other interested person advances a well-founded claim that the targeted documents are privileged, in all but the rarest cases where the accused's innocence is at stake, the existence of privilege will effectively bar the accused's application for production of the targeted documents, regardless of their relevance. Issues of privilege are therefore best resolved at the outset of the *O'Connor* process.

(5) Where privilege is not in question, the judge determines whether production should be compelled in accordance with the two-stage test established in *O'Connor*. At the first stage, if satisfied that the record is likely relevant to the proceeding against the accused, the judge may order production of the record for the court's inspection. At the next stage, with the records in hand, the judge determines whether, and to what extent, production should be ordered to the accused.

NOTE

McNeil addressed a claim by an accused to "serious misconduct information" about an investigating officer. The court held that the Crown must disclose misconduct information—for example, convictions under the *Criminal Code*—where that information could reasonably have an effect on a prosecution. The Crown has a duty to inquire and the police have a duty to disclose when put on notice of relevant information. If the Crown does not, and ought not, have relevant information, and thus is not required to produce it under its constitutionally mandated disclosure obligation, the accused can seek access to third-party information through the *O'Connor* regime.

IX. IMPLIED/DEEMED UNDERTAKING OF CONFIDENTIALITY IN DISCOVERY

Evidence compelled (by the discovery rules) by pre-trial or hearing discovery from a party to civil litigation can be used by parties to the litigation solely for the purpose of the litigation in which it was obtained. Parties (and of course their counsel) are "deemed" to have given this "undertaking" at both common law and civil law. In addition, the rule is contained in statutory provision, rules of court or tribunals, or professional ethics. The Supreme Court of Canada provided a comprehensive treatment of the implied undertaking rule, its rationale, exceptions, and means of enforcement in *Juman v Doucette*.

Juman v Doucette

2008 SCC 8, [2008] 1 SCR 157

McLachlin CJ and Bastarache, Binnie, LeBel, Deschamps, Fish,

Abella, Charron, and Rothstein JJ (6 March 2008)

BINNIE J:

[1] The principal issue raised on this appeal is the scope of the "implied undertaking rule" under which evidence compelled during pre-trial discovery from a party to civil litigation can be used by the parties only for the purpose of the litigation in which it was obtained. The issue arises in the context of alleged child abuse, a matter of great importance and concern in our society. The Attorney General of British Columbia rejects the existence of an implied undertaking rule in British Columbia (factum, at para. 4). Alternatively, if there is such a rule, he says it does not extend to *bona fide* disclosures of criminal activity. In his view the parties may, without court order, share with the police any discovery documents or oral testimony that tend to show criminal misconduct.

[2] In the further alternative, the Attorney General argues that the existence of an implied undertaking would not in any way inhibit the ability of the authorities, who are not parties to it, to obtain a subpoena *duces tecum* or to seize documents or a discovery transcript pursuant to a search warrant issued under s. 487 of the *Criminal Code*, RSC 1985, c. C-46.

[3] The British Columbia Court of Appeal held that the implied undertaking rule "does not extend to *bona fide* disclosure of criminal conduct" ((2006), 55 BCLR (4th) 66, 2006 BCCA 262, at para. 56). This ruling is stated too broadly, in my opinion. The rationale of the implied undertaking rule rests on the statutory compulsion that requires a party to make documentary and oral discovery regardless of privacy concerns and whether or not it tends to self-incriminate. The more serious the criminality, the greater would be the reluctance of a party to make disclosure fully and candidly, and the greater is the need for broad protection to facilitate his or her cooperation in civil litigation. It is true, as the chambers judge acknowledged, that there is an "immediate and serious danger" exception

to the usual requirement for a court order prior to disclosure ((2005), 45 BCLR (4th) 108, 2005 BCSC 400, at paras. 28-29), but the exception is much narrower than is suggested by the *dictum* of the Court of Appeal, and it does not cover the facts of this case. In my view a party is not in general free to go without a court order to the police or any non-party with what it may view as "criminal conduct," which is a label that covers many shades of suspicion or rumour or belief about many different offences from the mundane to the most serious. The qualification added by the Court of Appeal, namely that the whistle blower must act *bona fides*, does not alleviate the difficulty. Many a tip to the police is tinged with self-interest. At what point does the hope of private advantage rob the communication of its *bona fides*? The lines need to be clear because, as the Court of Appeal itself noted, "non-*bona fide* disclosure of alleged criminal conduct would attract serious civil sanctions for contempt" (para. 56 (emphasis added)).

[4] Thus the rule is that both documentary and oral information obtained on discovery, including information thought by one of the parties to disclose some sort of criminal conduct, *is* subject to the implied undertaking. It is not to be used *by the other parties* except for the purpose of that litigation, unless and until the scope of the undertaking is varied by a court order or other judicial order or a situation of immediate and serious danger emerges.

[5] Here, because of the facts, much of the appellant's argument focussed on her right to protection against self-incrimination, but the implied undertaking rule is broader than that. It includes the wrongdoing of persons other than the examinee and covers innocuous information that is neither confidential nor discloses any wrongdoing at all. Here, if the parents of the victim or other party wished to disclose the appellant's transcript to the police, he or she or they could have made an application to the BC Supreme Court for permission to make disclosure, but none of them did so, and none of them is party to the current proceeding. The applicants are the Vancouver Police Department and the Attorney General of British Columbia supported by the Attorney General of Canada. None of these authorities is party to the undertaking. They have available to them the usual remedies of subpoena *duces tecum* or a search warrant under the *Criminal Code*. If at this stage they do not have the grounds to obtain a search warrant, it is not open to them to build their case on the compelled testimony of the appellant. Further, even if the authorities were thereby to obtain access to this compelled material, it would still be up to the court at the proceedings (if any) where it is sought to be introduced to determine its admissibility.

[6] I agree with the chambers judge that the balance of interests relevant to whether disclosure should be made by a party of alleged criminality is better evaluated by a court than by one of the litigants who will generally be self-interested. Discoveries (both oral and documentary) are likely to run more smoothly if none of the disputants are in a position to go without a court order to the police, or regulators or other authorities with their suspicions of wrongdoing, or to use the material obtained for any other purpose collateral or ulterior to the action in which the discovery is obtained. Of course the implied undertaking does not bind the Attorney General and the police (who are not parties to it) from seeking a search warrant in the ordinary way to obtain the discovery transcripts if they have the grounds to do so. Apparently, no such application has been made. At this stage the matter has proceeded only to the point of determining whether or not the implied undertaking permits "the *bona fide* disclosure of criminal conduct" without court order (BCCA, at para. 56). In my view it does not do so in the circumstances disclosed here. I would allow the appeal.

I. Facts

[7] The appellant, a childcare worker, provided day services in her home. A 16-month-old child, Jade Doucette, suffered a seizure while in the appellant's care. The child was later determined to have suffered a brain injury. She and her parents sued the owners and operators of the day-care centre for damages, alleging that Jade's injury resulted from its negligence and that of the appellant.

[8] The appellant's defence alleges, in part, that Jade suffered a number of serious mishaps, including a bicycle accident while riding as a passenger with her father, none of which involved the appellant, and none of which were disclosed to the appellant when the child was delivered into her care (Statement of Defence, at para. 3).

[9] The Vancouver Police have for several years been conducting an investigation, which is still ongoing. In May 2004, the Vancouver police arrested the appellant. She was questioned in the absence of her counsel (AR, at p. 179). She was later released. In August 2004, the appellant and her husband received notices that their private communications had been intercepted by the police pursuant to s. 196 of the *Criminal Code*. To date, no criminal charges have been laid. In furtherance of that investigation, the authorities seek access to the appellant's discovery transcript.

[10] In November 2004, the appellant brought an interlocutory motion to prohibit the parties to the civil proceeding from providing the transcripts of discovery (which had not yet been held) to the police. She also sought to prevent the release of information from the transcripts to the police or the Attorney General of British Columbia and a third motion to prohibit the Attorney General of British Columbia, the police and the RCMP from obtaining and using copies of the transcripts and solicitor's notes without further court order. She relied upon the implied undertaking rule.

[11] The Attorney General of British Columbia opposed the appellant's motions and brought his own cross-motion for an order (if necessary) varying the legal undertaking to permit release of the transcripts to police. He also brought a second motion for an order permitting the police to apply for the transcripts by way of search warrant, subpoena or other investigative means in the usual way.

[12] The appellant was examined for discovery for four days between June 2005 and September 2006. She claimed the protection of the *Canada Evidence Act*, RSC 1985, c. C-5, the British Columbia *Evidence Act*, RSBC 1996, c. 124, and (though an explicit claim was not necessary) of the *Canadian Charter of Rights and Freedoms*, and says that she answered all the appropriate questions put to her. The transcripts are now in the possession of the parties and/or their counsel.

[13] In 2006, the underlying claim was settled. The appellant's discovery was never entered into evidence at a trial nor its contents disclosed in open court.

II. Judicial History

A. Supreme Court of British Columbia (Shaw J) (2005), 45 BCLR (4th) 108, 2005 BCSC 400

[14] The chambers judge observed that an examination for discovery is statutorily compelled testimony by rule 27 of the BC *Rules of Court*, BC Reg. 221/90. As a general rule, there exists in British Columbia an implied undertaking in civil actions that the

parties and their lawyers will use discovery evidence strictly for the purposes of the court case. Discovery exists because getting at the truth in the pursuit of justice is an important social goal, but so (he held) is limiting the invasion of the examinee's privacy. Evidence taken on oral discovery comes within the scope of the undertaking. He noted that the court has the discretionary power to grant exemptions from or variations to the undertaking, and that in the exercise of that discretion courts must balance the need for disclosure against the right to privacy.

[15] The chambers judge rejected the contention that the implied undertaking does not apply to evidence of crimes. Considerations of practicality supported keeping evidence of crimes within the scope of the undertaking because such evidence could vary from mere suspicion to blatant admissions and from minor to the most serious offences. It was better to leave the discretionary power of relief to the courts.

[16] As to the various arguments asserted by the appellant under ss. 7, 11(c) and 13 of the *Charter*, the chambers judge concluded that "[t]he state is forbidden to use its investigatory powers to violate the confidentiality requirement of solicitor–client privilege; so too, in my view, should the state be forbidden to violate the confidentiality protected by discovery privilege" (para. 62). In his view, it was not open to the police to seize the transcript under a search warrant.

B. Court of Appeal for British Columbia (Newbury, Low and Kirkpatrick JJA) (2006), 55 BCLR (4th) 66, 2006 BCCA 262

[17] The Court of Appeal allowed the appeal. In its view, the parties were at liberty to disclose the appellant's discovery evidence to the police to assist in the criminal investigation. Further, the authorities could obtain the discovery evidence by lawful investigative means such as subpoenas and search warrants.

[18] Kirkpatrick JA, speaking for a unanimous court, noted the English law on the implied undertaking of confidentiality had been applied in British Columbia only in recent years. See *Hunt v. T & N plc* (1995), 4 BCLR (3d) 110. In that case, however, the British Columbia Court of Appeal had held that "[t]he obligation the law imposes is one of confidentiality from improper publication. It does not supersede all other legal, social or moral duties" (para. 65; quoted at para. 32). Thus, in Kirkpatrick JA's opinion, "the undertaking in the action cannot form a shield from the detection and prosecution of crimes in which the public has an overriding interest" (para. 48).

[19] Kirkpatrick JA then turned to the *Charter* issues in the case. She noted that no charges had been laid against the appellant and therefore that ss. 11(c) (which applies to persons "charged with an offence") and 13 (which provides use immunity) were not engaged. The appellant was not in any imminent danger of deprivation of her right to liberty or security, and therefore any s. 7 claim was premature. Kirkpatrick JA declared that an implied undertaking, being just a rule of civil procedure, should not be given "constitutional status." Discovery material is not immune to search or seizure. The appeal was therefore allowed.

III. Analysis

[20] The root of the implied undertaking is the statutory compulsion to participate fully in pre-trial oral and documentary discovery. If the opposing party seeks information

that is relevant and is not protected by privilege, it must be disclosed even if it tends to self-incrimination. See BC *Rules of Court*, rules 27(2), 44, 60(41), 60(42) and 64(1); *Ross v. Henriques*, [2007] BCJ no. 2023 (QL), 2007 BCSC 1381, at paras. 180-81. In Quebec, see *Lac d'Amiante du Québec Ltée v. 2858-0702 Québec Inc.*, [2001] 2 SCR 743, 2001 SCC 51, at para. 42. In Ontario, see *Stickney v. Trusz* (1973), 2 OR (2d) 469 (HCJ), aff'd (1974), 3 OR (2d) 538 (Div. Ct.), at p. 539, aff'd (1974), 3 OR (2d) 538 (p. 539) (CA), leave to appeal ref'd, [1974] SCR xii. The rule in common law jurisdictions was affirmed post-*Charter* in *Tricontinental Investments Co. v. Guarantee Co. of North America* (1982), 39 OR (2d) 614 (HCJ), and has been applied to public inquiries, *Phillips v. Nova Scotia (Commission of Inquiry into the Westray Mine Tragedy)*, [1995] 2 SCR 97.

[21] The Attorney General of British Columbia submits that *Lac d'Amiante*, which was based on the Quebec *Code of Civil Procedure*, RSQ, c. C-25, "was wrongly decided" (factum, at para. 16). An implied undertaking not to disclose pre-trial documentary and oral discovery for purposes other than the litigation in which it was obtained is, he argues, contrary to the "open court" principle stated in *Attorney General of Nova Scotia v. MacIntyre*, [1982] 1 SCR 175, and *Edmonton Journal v. Alberta (Attorney General)*, [1989] 2 SCR 1326 (factum, at para. 6). The Vancouver Police support this position (factum, at para. 48). The argument is based on a misconception. Pre-trial discovery does not take place in open court. The vast majority of civil cases never go to trial. Documents are inspected or exchanged by counsel at a place of their own choosing. In general, oral discovery is not conducted in front of a judge. The only point at which the "open court" principle is engaged is when, if at all, the case goes to trial and the discovered party's documents or answers from the discovery transcripts are introduced as part of the case at trial.

[22] In *Attorney General of Nova Scotia v. MacIntyre*, relied on by the Vancouver Police as well as by the Attorney General of British Columbia, the contents of the affidavit in support of the search warrant application were made public, but not until after the search warrant had been executed, and "the purposes of the policy of secrecy are largely, if not entirely, accomplished" (p. 188). At that point the need for public access and public scrutiny prevail. Here the action has been settled but the policies reflected in the implied undertaking (privacy and the efficient conduct of civil litigation generally) remain undiminished. Nor is *Edmonton Journal* helpful to the respondents. In that case the court struck down a "sweeping" Alberta prohibition against publication of matrimonial proceedings, including publication of the "comments of counsel and the presiding judge." In the face of such prohibition, the court asked, "how then is the community to know if judges conduct themselves properly" (p. 1341). No such questions of state accountability arise in pre-trial discoveries. The situations are simply not analogous.

A. The Rationale for the Implied Undertaking

[23] Quite apart from the cases of exceptional prejudice, as in disputes about trade secrets or intellectual property, which have traditionally given rise to express confidentiality orders, there are good reasons to support the existence of an implied (or, in reality, a court-imposed) undertaking.

[24] In the first place, pre-trial discovery is an invasion of a private right to be left alone with your thoughts and papers, however embarrassing, defamatory or scandalous. At least one side in every lawsuit is a reluctant participant. Yet a proper pre-trial discovery is

essential to prevent surprise or "litigation by ambush," to encourage settlement once the facts are known, and to narrow issues even where settlement proves unachievable. Thus, rule 27(22) of the BC *Rules of Court* compels a litigant to answer all relevant questions posed on an examination for discovery. Failure to do so can result in punishment by way of imprisonment or fine pursuant to rules 56(1), 56(4) and 2(5). In some provinces, the rules of practice provide that individuals who are not even parties can be ordered to submit to examination for discovery on issues relevant to a dispute in which they may have no direct interest. It is not uncommon for plaintiff's counsel aggressively to "sue everyone in sight" not with any realistic hope of recovery but to "get discovery." Thus, for the out-of-pocket cost of issuing a statement of claim or other process, the gate is swung open to investigate the private information and perhaps highly confidential documents of the examinee in pursuit of allegations that might in the end be found to be without any merit at all.

[25] The public interest in getting at the truth in a civil action outweighs the examinee's privacy interest, but the latter is nevertheless entitled to a measure of protection. The answers and documents are compelled by statute solely for the purpose of the civil action and the law thus requires that the invasion of privacy should generally be limited to the level of disclosure necessary to satisfy that purpose and that purpose alone. Although the present case involves the issue of self-incrimination of the appellant, that element is not a necessary requirement for protection. Indeed, the disclosed information need not even satisfy the legal requirements of confidentiality set out in *Slavutych v. Baker*, [1976] 1 SCR 254. The general idea, metaphorically speaking, is that whatever is disclosed in the discovery room stays in the discovery room unless eventually revealed in the courtroom or disclosed by judicial order.

[26] There is a second rationale supporting the existence of an implied undertaking. A litigant who has some assurance that the documents and answers will not be used for a purpose collateral or ulterior to the proceedings in which they are demanded will be encouraged to provide a more complete and candid discovery. This is of particular interest in an era where documentary production is of a magnitude ("litigation by avalanche") as often to preclude careful pre-screening by the individuals or corporations making production. See *Kyuquot Logging Ltd. v. British Columbia Forest Products Ltd.* (1986), 5 BCLR (2d) 1 (CA), *per* Esson JA dissenting, at pp. 10-11.

[27] For good reason, therefore, the law imposes on the parties to civil litigation an undertaking *to the court* not to use the documents or answers for any purpose other than securing justice in the civil proceedings in which the answers were compelled (whether or not such documents or answers were in their origin confidential or incriminatory in nature). See *Home Office v. Harman*, [1983] 1 AC 280 (HL); *Lac d'Amiante*; *Hunt v. T & N plc*; *Shaw Estate v. Oldroyd*, [2007] BCJ no. 1310 (QL), 2007 BCSC 866, at para. 21; *Rayman Investments and Management Inc. v. Canada Mortgage and Housing Corp.*, [2007] BCJ no. 628 (QL), 2007 BCSC 384; *Wilson v. McCoy* (2006), 59 BCLR (4th) 1, 2006 BCSC 1011; *Laxton Holdings Ltd. v. Madill*, [1987] 3 WWR 570 (Sask. CA); *Blake v. Hudson's Bay Co.*, [1988] 1 WWR 176 (Man. QB); *755568 Ontario Ltd. v. Linchris Homes Ltd.* (1990), 1 OR (3d) 649 (Gen. Div.); *Rocca Enterprises Ltd. v. University Press of New Brunswick Ltd.* (1989), 103 NBR (2d) 224 (QB); *Eli Lilly and Co. v. Interpharm Inc.* (1993), 161 NR 137 (FCA). A number of other decisions are helpfully referenced in W.A. Stevenson and J.E. Côté, *Civil Procedure Encyclopedia* (2003), Vol. 2, at pp. 42-36 *et seq.*; and C. Papile, "The Implied Undertaking Revisited" (2006), 32 *Adv. Q* 190, at pp. 194-96.

[28] The need to protect the privacy of the pre-trial discovery is recognized even in common law jurisdictions where there is no implied undertaking. See J. B. Laskin, "The Implied Undertaking" (a paper presented to the CBA-Ontario, CLE Conference on *Privilege and Confidential Information in Litigation—Current Developments and Future Trends*, October 19, 1991), at pp. 36-40. Rule 26(c) of the United States *Federal Rules of Civil Procedure* provides that a court may, upon a showing of "good cause," grant a protective order to maintain the confidentiality of information disclosed during discovery. The practical effect is that the courts routinely make confidentiality orders limited to pre-trial disclosure to protect a party or person being discovered "from annoyance, embarrassment, oppression, or undue burden or expense." See, e.g., *Cipollone v. Liggett Group, Inc.*, 785 F.2d 1108 (3d Cir. 1986).

B. Remedies for Breach of the Implied Undertaking

[29] Breach of the undertaking may be remedied by a variety of means including a stay or dismissal of the proceeding, or striking a defence, or, in the absence of a less drastic remedy, contempt proceedings for breach of the undertaking owed to the court. See *Lac d'Amiante*, at para. 64, and *Goodman v. Rossi* (1995), 125 DLR (4th) 613 (Ont. CA), at p. 624.

C. Exceptional Circumstances May Trump the Implied Undertaking

[30] The undertaking is imposed in recognition of the examinee's privacy interest, and the public interest in the efficient conduct of civil litigation, but those values are not, of course, absolute. They may, in turn, be trumped by a more compelling public interest. Thus, where the party being discovered does not consent, a party bound by the undertaking may apply to the court for leave to use the information or documents otherwise than in the action, as described in *Lac d'Amiante*, at para. 77:

> Before using information, however, the party in question will have to apply for leave, specifying the purposes of using the information and the reasons why it is justified, and both sides will have to be heard on the application.

In such an application the judge would have access to the documents or transcripts at issue.

D. Applications Should Be Dealt with Expeditiously

[31] The injury to Jade Doucette occurred on November 19, 2001. The police investigation was launched shortly thereafter. Almost four years ago the appellant was (briefly) arrested. Three and a half years ago the present court applications were launched. Over two years ago the appellant was examined for discovery. It is apparent that in many of these cases delay will defeat the purpose of the application. It is important that they proceed expeditiously.

E. Criteria on the Application for a Modification or Variance of the Implied Undertaking

[32] An application to modify or relieve against an implied undertaking requires an applicant to demonstrate to the court on a balance of probabilities the existence of a public

interest of greater weight than the values the implied undertaking is designed to protect, namely privacy and the efficient conduct of civil litigation. In a case like the present, of course, there weighs heavily in the balance the right of a suspect to remain silent in the face of a police investigation, and the right not to be compelled to incriminate herself. The chambers judge took the view (I think correctly) that in this case that factor was decisive. In other cases the mix of competing values may be different. What is important in each case is to recognize that unless an examinee is satisfied that the undertaking will only be modified or varied by the court in exceptional circumstances, the undertaking will not achieve its intended purpose.

[33] Reference was made to *Crest Homes plc v. Marks*, [1987] 2 All ER 1074, where Lord Oliver said, on behalf of the House of Lords, that the authorities "illustrate no general principle beyond this, that the court will not release or modify the implied undertaking given on discovery save in special circumstances and where the release or modification will not occasion injustice to the person giving discovery" (p. 1083). I would prefer to rest the discretion on a careful weighing of the public interest asserted by the applicant (here the prosecution of a serious crime) against the public interest in protecting the right against self-incrimination as well as upholding a litigant's privacy and promoting an efficient civil justice process. What is important is the identification of the competing values, and the weighing of one in the light of the others, rather than setting up an absolute barrier to occasioning any "injustice to the person giving discovery." Prejudice, possibly amounting to injustice, to a particular litigant may exceptionally be held justified by a higher public interest, as in the case of the accused whose solicitor–client confidences were handed over to the police in *Smith v. Jones*, [1999] 1 SCR 455, a case referred to in the courts below, and discussed hereafter. Of course any perceived prejudice to the examinee is a factor that will always weigh heavily in the balance. It may be argued that disclosure to the police of the evil secrets of the psychopath at issue in *Smith v. Jones* may have been prejudicial to him but was not an "injustice" in the overall scheme of things, but such a gloss would have given cold comfort to an accused who made his disclosures in the expectation of confidentiality. If public safety trumps solicitor–client privilege despite a measure of injustice to the (unsympathetic) accused in *Smith v. Jones*, it can hardly be disputed in this jurisdiction that the implied undertaking rule would yield to such a higher public interest as well.

[34] Three Canadian provinces have enacted rules governing when relief should be given against such implied or "deemed" undertakings, (see *Queen's Bench Rules*, MR 553/88, r. 30.1 (Manitoba), *Rules of Civil Procedure*, RRO 1990, Reg. 194, r. 30.1 (Ontario), and *Rules of Civil Procedure*, r. 30.1 (Prince Edward Island)). I believe the test formulated therein (in identical terms) is apt as a reflection of the common law more generally, namely:

> If satisfied that the interest of justice outweighs any prejudice that would result to a party who disclosed evidence, the court may order that [the implied or "deemed" undertaking] does not apply to the evidence or to information obtained from it, and may impose such terms and give such direction as are just.

[35] The case law provides some guidance to the exercise of the court's discretion. For example, where discovery material in one action is sought to be used in another action with the same or similar parties and the same or similar issues, the prejudice to the examinee is virtually non-existent and leave will generally be granted. See *Lac Minerals Ltd. v.*

New Cinch Uranium Ltd. (1985), 50 OR (2d) 260 (HCJ), at pp. 265-66; *Crest Homes*, at p. 1083; *Miller (Ed) Sales & Rentals Ltd. v. Caterpillar Tractor Co.* (1988), 90 AR 323 (CA); *Harris v. Sweet*, [2005] BCJ no. 1520 (QL), 2005 BCSC 998; *Scuzzy Creek Hydro & Power Inc. v. Tercon Contractors Ltd.* (1998), 27 CPC (4th) 252 (BCSC).

[36] On the other hand, courts have generally not favoured attempts to use the discovered material for an extraneous purpose, or for an action wholly unrelated to the purposes of the proceeding in which discovery was obtained in the absence of some compelling public interest. See, e.g., *Lubrizol Corp. v. Imperial Oil Ltd.* (1990), 33 CPR (3d) 49 (FCTD), at p. 51. In *Livent Inc. v. Drabinsky* (2001), 53 OR (3d) 126 (SCJ), the court held that a non-party to the implied undertaking could in unusual circumstances apply to have the undertaking varied, but that relief in such cases would virtually never be given (p. 130).

[37] Some applications have been refused on the basis that they demonstrate precisely the sort of mischief the implied undertaking rule was designed to avoid. In *755568 Ontario Ltd.*, for example, the plaintiff sought leave to send the defendant's discovery transcripts to the police. The court concluded that the plaintiff's strategy was to enlist the aid of the police to discover further evidence in support of the plaintiff's claim and/or to pressure the defendant to settle (p. 655).

(i) The Balancing of Interests

[38] As stated, the onus in each case will be on the applicant to demonstrate a superior public interest in disclosure, and the court will be mindful that an undertaking should only be set aside in exceptional circumstances. In what follows I do not mean to suggest that the categories of superior public interest are fixed. My purpose is illustrative rather than exhaustive. However, to repeat, an undertaking designed in part to encourage open and generous discovery by assuring parties being discovered of confidentiality will not achieve its objective if the confidentiality is seen by reluctant litigants to be too readily set aside.

(ii) Statutory Exceptions

[39] The implied undertaking rule at common law, and in those jurisdictions which have enacted rules, more or less codifying the common law, is subject to legislative override. In the present case for example, the Attorney General of British Columbia and the Vancouver Police rely on s. 14 of the *Child, Family and Community Service Act*, RSBC 1996, c. 46, which provides that:

(1) A person who has reason to believe that a child needs protection under section 13 must promptly report the matter to a director or a person designated by a director.

(2) Subsection (1) applies even if the information on which the belief is based

(a) is privileged, except as a result of a solicitor–client relationship, or

(b) is confidential and its disclosure is prohibited under another Act.

It is apparent from the extensive police investigation to date and the appearance of the Attorneys General and the Vancouver Police in these proceedings that a report was made to the authorities. We do not know the details. Undoubtedly, a report could have been made without reference to anything said or produced at discovery. At this point the matter has proceeded beyond a mere "report" and involves the collection of evidence. This will require, in the ordinary way laid down by Parliament in s. 487 of the *Criminal Code*, the application for a search warrant or a subpoena *duces tecum* at trial, if there is a trial.

(iii) Public Safety Concerns

[40] One important public interest flagged by the chambers judge was the "public safety" issue raised by way of analogy to *Smith v. Jones*, a case dealing with solicitor–client privilege. While solicitor–client privilege constitutes an interest higher than the privacy interest at issue here, the chambers judge used the case to illustrate the relevant balancing of interests. There, a psychiatrist was retained by defence counsel to prepare an assessment of the accused for purposes of the defence generally, including potential submissions on sentencing in the event of a conviction. During his interview with the psychiatrist, the accused described in considerable detail his plan to kidnap, rape and kill prostitutes. The psychiatrist concluded the accused was a dangerous individual who would, more likely than not, commit future offences unless he received immediate psychiatric treatment. The psychiatrist wished to take his concerns to the police and applied to the court for leave to do so notwithstanding that the psychiatrist's only access to the accused was under the umbrella of solicitor–client privilege. In such a case the accused/client would undoubtedly consider himself to be the victim of an injustice, but our Court held that the privilege yielded to "clear and imminent threat of serious bodily harm to an identifiable group … if this threat is made in such a manner that a sense of urgency is created" (para. 84). Further, in circumstances of "immediate and serious danger," the police may be contacted without leave of the court (paras. 96-97). If a comparable situation arose in the context of an implied undertaking, the proper procedure would be for the concerned party to make application to a chambers judge but if, as discussed in *Smith v. Jones* there existed a situation of "immediate and serious danger," the applicant would be justified in going directly to the police, in my opinion, without a court order.

(iv) Impeaching Inconsistent Testimony

[41] Another situation where the deponent's privacy interest will yield to a higher public interest is where the deponent has given contradictory testimony about the same matters in successive or different proceedings. If the contradiction is discovered, the implied undertaking rule would afford no shield to its use for purposes of impeachment. In provinces where the implied undertaking rule has been codified, there is a specific provision that the undertaking "does not prohibit the use of evidence obtained in one proceeding, or information obtained from such evidence, to impeach the testimony of a witness in another proceeding": see Manitoba r. 30.1(6), Ontario r. 30.1.01(6), Prince Edward Island r. 30.1.01(6). While statutory, this provision, in my view, also reflects the general common law in Canada. An undertaking implied by the court (or imposed by the legislature) to make civil litigation more effective should not permit a witness to play games with the administration of justice: *R v. Henry*, [2005] 3 SCR 609, 2005 SCC 76. Any other outcome would allow a person accused of an offence "[w]ith impunity [to] tailor

his evidence to suit his needs in each particular proceeding" (*R v. Nedelcu* (2007), 41 CPC (6th) 357 (Ont. SCJ), at paras. 49-51).

(v) The Suggested "Crimes" Exception

[42] As stated, Kirkpatrick JA concluded that "the undertaking in the action cannot form a shield from the detection and prosecution of crimes in which the public has an overriding interest" (para. 48). In her view,

> a party obtaining production of documents or transcriptions of oral examination of discovery is under a general obligation, in most cases, to keep such document confidential. A party seeking to use the discovery evidence other than in the proceedings in which it is produced must obtain the permission of the disclosing party or leave of the court. However, the obligation of confidentiality does not extend to *bona fide* disclosure of criminal conduct. On the other hand, non-*bona fide* disclosure of alleged criminal conduct would attract serious civil sanctions for contempt. [para. 56]

[43] The chambers judge put his finger on one of the serious difficulties with such an exception. He wrote:

> [C]onsiderations of practicality support keeping evidence of crimes within the scope of the undertaking. In this regard, it should be understood that evidence relating to a crime may vary from mere suspicion to blatant admissions, from peripheral clues to direct evidence, from minor offences to the most heinous. There are also many shades and variations in between these extremes. [para. 27]

This difficulty is compounded by the fact that parties to civil litigation are often quick to see the supposed criminality in what their opponents are up to, or at least to appreciate the tactical advantage that threats to go to the police might achieve, and to pose questions to the examinee to lay the basis for such an approach: see *755568 Ontario Ltd.*, at p. 656. The rules of discovery were not intended to constitute litigants as private attorneys general.

[44] The chambers judge took the view that "leaving the discretionary power of exemption or variation with the courts is preferable to giving litigants the power to report to the police, without a court order, anything that might relate to a criminal offence" (para. 27). I agree. On such an application the court will be able to weigh against the examinee's privacy interest the seriousness of the offence alleged, the "evidence" or admissions said to be revealed in the discovery process, the use to which the applicant or police may put this material, whether there is evidence of malice or spite on the part of the applicant, and such other factors as appear to the court to be relevant to the exercise of its discretion. This will include recognition of the potential adverse effects if the protection of the implied undertaking is seen to be diluted or diminished.

[45] Kirkpatrick JA noted that in some circumstances

> neither party has an interest in or is willing to seek court ordered relief from the disclosure of information under the undertaking or otherwise. Nor does it [the chambers judge's approach] contemplate non-exigent circumstances of disclosed criminal conduct. It is easy to imagine a situation in which criminal conduct is disclosed in the discovery process, but no one apprehends that immediate harm is likely to result. [para. 55]

This is true, but it presupposes that the police are entitled to be handed a transcript of statutorily compelled answers which they themselves have no authority to compel, thereby using the civil discovery process to obtain indirectly what the police have no right to obtain directly. Such a rule, if accepted, would undermine the freedom of a suspect to cooperate or refuse to cooperate with the police, which is an important element of our criminal law.

[46] In reaching her decision, Kirkpatrick JA relied on *dicta* of the House of Lords in *Rank Film Distributors Ltd. v. Video Information Centre*, [1982] AC 380 (p. 425). Lord Fraser said:

> If a defendant's answers to interrogatories tend to show that he has been guilty of a serious offence I cannot think that there would be anything improper in his opponent reporting the matter to the criminal authorities with a view to prosecution, certainly if he had first obtained leave from the court which ordered the interrogatories, and probably without such leave.
> [p. 447]

These observations, however, must be read in light of the fact that in England, unlike British Columbia, there existed at the time (since amended) "a privilege against compulsory self-incrimination by discovery or by answering interrogatories" (p. 446). There was thus absent from the English procedure the very foundation of the appellant's case, namely that she had *no* right to refuse to answer questions on discovery that might incriminate her, because she was obliged by statute to give the truth, the whole truth and nothing but the truth.

[47] It is true that solicitor–client privilege includes a "crime" exception, but here again there is no proper analogy to an implied undertaking. In *Solosky v. The Queen*, [1980] 1 SCR 821, Dickson J observed at p. 835:

> [I]f a client seeks guidance from a lawyer in order to facilitate the commission of a crime or a fraud, the communication will not be privileged and it is immaterial whether the lawyer is an unwitting dupe or knowing participant.

See also *R v. Campbell*, [1999] 1 SCR 565. Abuse of solicitor–client privilege to facilitate criminality is contrary to its purpose. Adoption of the implied undertaking to facilitate full disclosure on discovery *even by crooks* is of the very essence of its purpose. In England, the weight of authority now seems to favour requiring leave of the court where the protected material relates to alleged criminality. See *Attorney-General for Gibraltar v. May*, [1999] 1 WLR 998 (CA), at pp. 1007-8; *Bank of Crete S.A. v. Koskotas (No. 2)*, [1992] 1 WLR 919 (Ch. D), at p. 922; *Sybron Corp. v. Barclays Bank Plc.*, [1985] 1 Ch. 299, at p. 326. The same practice prevails in Australia: *Bailey v. Australian Broadcasting Corp.*, [1995] 1 Qd. R 476 (SC); *Commonwealth v. Temwood Holdings Pty Ltd.* (2001), 25 WAR 31, [2001] WASC 282.

[48] In reaching her conclusion, Kirkpatrick JA rejected the view expressed in *755568 Ontario Ltd.* and *Perrin v. Beninger*, [2004] OJ no. 2353 (QL) (SCJ), that the public interest in investigating possible crimes is *not* in all cases sufficient to relieve against the undertaking. It is inherent in any balancing exercise that one interest will not always and in every circumstance prevail over other interests. It will depend on the facts. In *Tyler v. MNR*, [1991] 2 FC 68 (CA), in a somewhat analogous situation of statutory compulsion, the appellant was charged with narcotics offences. Revenue Canada, on reading about the

charges in a newspaper, began to investigate the possibility that the appellant had not reported all of his income in earlier years. The Minister invoked his statutory powers to compel information from the appellant, who sought to prevent the Minister from communicating any information thereby obtained to the RCMP. Stone JA, speaking for a unanimous Federal Court of Appeal, agreed that the Minister should be permitted to continue using his compulsory audit for *Income Tax Act* purposes but prohibited the Minister from sharing the information compulsorily obtained from the appellant with the RCMP. Stone JA was of the view that the prosecution of crime did not necessarily trump a citizen's privacy interest in the disclosure of statutorily compelled information and I agree with him.

[49] The BC Court of Appeal qualified its "crimes" exception by the requirement that the communication to the police be made in good faith. Aside from the difficulties in applying such a requirement, as previously mentioned, I do not see how a "good faith" requirement is consistent with the court's rationale for granting relief against the undertaking. If, as the hypothesis requires, it is determined in a particular case that the public interest in investigating a crime and bringing the perpetrators to justice is paramount to the examinee's privacy interest, the good faith of the communication should no more be an issue here than in the case of any other informant. Informants are valued for what they can tell not for their worthy motives.

[50] Finally, Kirkpatrick JA feared that

> if an application to court is required before a party may disclose the alleged conduct, the perpetrator of the crime may be notified of the disclosure and afforded the opportunity to destroy or hide evidence or otherwise conceal his or her involvement in the alleged crime. [para. 55]

This concern is largely remedied by permitting the party wishing to be relieved of the obligation of confidentiality to apply to the court *ex parte*. It would be up to the chambers judge to determine whether the circumstances justify proceeding *ex parte*, or whether the deponent and other parties to the proceeding should be notified of the application.

F. Continuing Nature of the Implied Undertaking

[51] As mentioned earlier, the lawsuit against the appellant and others was settled in 2006. As a result the appellant was not required to give evidence at a civil trial; nor were her examination for discovery transcripts ever read into evidence. The transcripts remain in the hands of the parties and their lawyer. Nevertheless, the implied undertaking continues. The fact that the settlement has rendered the discovery moot does not mean the appellant's privacy interest is also moot. The undertaking continues to bind. When an adverse party incorporates the answers or documents obtained on discovery as part of the court record at trial the undertaking is spent, but not otherwise, except by consent or court order. See *Lac d'Amiante*, at paras. 70 and 76; *Shaw Estate v. Oldroyd*, at paras. 20-22. It follows that decisions to the contrary, such as the decision of the House of Lords in *Home Office v. Harman* (where a narrow majority held that the implied undertaking not to disclose documents obtained on discovery continued even after the documents in question had been read aloud in open court), should not be followed in this country. The effect of the *Harman* decision has been reversed by a rule change in its country of origin.

G. Who Is Entitled to Notice of an Application to Modify or Vary the Implied Undertaking?

[52] While the issue of notice will be for the chambers judge to decide on the facts of any particular case, I do not think that in general the police are entitled to notice of such an application. Nor are the media. The only parties with a direct interest, other than the applicant, are the deponent and the other parties to the litigation.

H. Application to Modify or Vary an Implied Undertaking by Strangers to It

[53] I would not preclude an application to vary an undertaking by a non-party on the basis of standing, although I agree with *Livent Inc. v. Drabinsky* that success on such an application would be unusual. What has already been said provides some illustrations of potential third party applicants. In this case the Attorney General of British Columbia, supported by the Vancouver Police, demonstrated a sufficient interest in the appellant's transcripts to be given standing to apply. Their objective was to obtain evidence that would help explain the events under investigation, and possibly to incriminate the appellant. I think it would be quite wrong for the police to be able to take advantage of statutorily compelled testimony in civil litigation to undermine the appellant's right to silence and the protection against self-incrimination afforded him by the criminal law. Accordingly, in my view, the present application was rightly dismissed by the chambers judge. On the other hand, a non-party engaged in *other* litigation with an examinee, who learns of potentially contradicting testimony by the examinee in a discovery to which that other person is not a party, would have standing to seek to obtain a modification of the implied undertaking and for the reasons given above may well succeed. Of course if the undertaking is respected by the parties to it, then non-parties will be unlikely to possess enough information to make an application for a variance in the first place that is other than a fishing expedition. But the possibility of third party applications exists, and where duly made the competing interests will have to be weighed, keeping in mind that an undertaking too readily set aside sends the message that such undertakings are unsafe to be relied upon, and will therefore not achieve their broader purpose.

I. Use Immunity

[54] Reference was earlier made to the fact that at her discovery the appellant claimed the benefit of s. 5 of the *Canada Evidence Act* which eliminates the right formerly enjoyed by a witness to refuse to answer "any question on the ground that the answer to the question may tend to criminate him, or may tend to establish his liability to a civil proceeding at the instance of the Crown or of any person" (s. 5(1)). Answers given under objection, however, "shall not be used or admissible in evidence against him in any criminal trial or other criminal proceeding against him thereafter taking place, other than a prosecution for perjury" (s. 5(2)). Similar protection is provided under s. 4 of the British Columbia *Evidence Act*. Section 13 of the *Charter* applies without need of objection. Derivative use immunity is a question for the criminal court at any trial that may be held: *R v. S. (R.J.)*, [1995] 1 SCR 451, at paras. 191-92 and 204. The appellant's statutory or *Charter* rights are not in peril in the present appeal and her claims to *Charter* relief at this stage were properly dismissed.

J. Implied Undertaking Is No Bar to Persons Not a Party to It

[55] None of the parties to the original civil litigation applied to vary the undertaking. Neither the Attorneys General nor the police are parties to the implied undertaking and they are not bound by its terms. If the police, as strangers to the undertaking, have grounds, they can apply for a search warrant under s. 487 of the *Criminal Code* in the ordinary way.

[56] The appellant's discovery transcript and documents, while protected by an implied undertaking of the parties to the court, are not themselves privileged, and are not exempt from seizure: *R v. Serendip Physiotherapy Clinic* (2004), 189 CCC (3d) 417 (Ont. CA), at para. 35. A search warrant, where available, only gives the police access to the material. It does not authorize its use of the material in any proceedings that may be initiated.

[57] If criminal charges are brought, the prosecution may also compel a witness to produce a copy of the documents or transcripts in question from his or her possession by a subpoena *duces tecum*. The trial judge would then determine what, if any use could be made of the material, having regard to the appellant's *Charter* rights and any other relevant considerations. None of these issues arise for decision on the present appeal.

K. Disposition of the Present Appeal

[58] As stated, none of the parties bound by the implied undertaking made application to the court to be relieved from its obligations. The application is made solely by the Attorney General of British Columbia to permit

> any person in lawful possession of the transcript to provide a copy to the police or to the Attorney-General to assist in the investigation and/or prosecution of any criminal offence which may have occurred. [BCSC, at para. 6]

While I would not deny the Attorney General standing to seek to vary an implied undertaking to which he is not a party, I agree with the chambers judge that his application should be rejected on the facts of this case. The purpose of the application was to sidestep the appellant's silence in the face of police investigation of her conduct. The authorities should not be able to obtain indirectly a transcript which they are unable to obtain directly through a search warrant in the ordinary way because they lack the grounds to justify it.

IV. Disposition

[59] I would allow the appeal with costs to the appellant both here and in the courts below.

PROBLEM (R v GALLOWAY)

It will be remembered from the segment of the case study introduced at the end of Chapter 7, Character that at one point during their lengthy investigation, the police had focused their attention on an individual named Kevin Grey.

You will recall that Grey is 28 years old and lives with his parents on a rural property about 3 kilometres from the Galloways. Grey has an extensive criminal record dating back to his teenage years, mostly relating to drug offences. That record includes three prior convictions for breaking and entering, as well as two prior convictions for simple assault and one conviction for assault causing bodily harm.

With respect to the prior break-ins, they all related to rural properties within a 10-kilometre radius of the Galloways' home. In each case, Grey burglarized barns and garages, never homes, stealing tools, gardening equipment, ATVs, and snowmobiles.

During their investigation, police interviewed Grey. He readily acknowledged his earlier crimes, but reports that he has been clean and sober since the fall of 2015 and has not been involved in crime since then. He denied involvement in the Galloway homicide and insisted that he was at home, with his parents, on the evening of Sunday, March 27, 2016. His parents corroborated his alibi.

The latent partial palm print on the snow blower was compared to Grey's known prints and eliminated. Grey was asked to produce the shoes he was wearing in April 2016, but was unable to do so. He claimed that he spilt paint on the shoes and had thrown them out.

The attention of police was drawn to Grey as a result of a tip police received from a confidential informant. As part of disclosure, the Crown revealed to the defence that police had received a confidential tip from an informant who reported that he overheard a drunken Grey speaking to some companions about "a break-in we did that went sideways" and reportedly commenting that "that lady put up a hell of a fight, but when she punched me I just lost it."

When police interviewed Grey they accused him of telling people that he had been involved in a break-in that had gone badly and ended in a woman's death; Grey categorically denied this.

The interview of Grey was not a standard police interview. Grey initially refused to speak with police. He ultimately sat down with investigators after lengthy negotiations with his criminal lawyer. The statement he gave was "induced," meaning that it was given on the understanding that it would not be admissible in evidence against him if he was ever charged with a crime. (Essentially, through this arrangement, the parties are agreeing that the statement is not "voluntary"; it's a procedure that allows police to gain access to information that they would not otherwise obtain, with no downside risk for the individual involved.)

The police ultimately decided that the confidential informant had not actually overheard Grey confessing. Rather, they surmised that the informant had pieced together information from snippets of conversations he overheard and combined that with rumours that were circulating among Grey's circle of friends. As a result, the police "cleared" Grey and focused their attention exclusively on Martin Galloway. This is all that the Crown is prepared to reveal by way of disclosure.

At trial, the defence brings an application seeking the following:

1. *Disclosure of the identity of the confidential informant who reportedly overheard Grey's confession.* If you were defence counsel, what arguments would you make in seeking access to this information? How would the Crown likely respond? Is the defence entitled to this information?

2. *Disclosure of Grey's defence lawyer's notes relating to the interviews he conducted with his client in the lead-up to his induced statement to police.* If you were defence counsel for Martin Galloway, what arguments would you make in seeking access to this information? How would the Crown likely respond? What, if any, obligations would Kevin Grey's criminal lawyer have in response to such an application? Is Martin Galloway entitled to this information?

PART IV

Further Aspects of Proof

Proof Without Evidence

Evidence is required only where facts are disputed. The law provides a number of devices that enable facts to be established without evidence being led in the traditional manner. In this chapter we consider two of these devices: formal admissions by parties and judicial notice.

I. FORMAL ADMISSIONS

In any proceeding a party may admit facts, dispensing with the need for the other party to prove them. Formal admissions should not be confused with the party admissions exception to the rule against hearsay (on which, see Chapter 4, Section II.F).

A. Criminal Cases

1. Guilty Pleas

A person accused of a criminal offence may plead guilty. Indeed, most do. A plea of guilty is a formal admission of the facts necessary to establish the elements of the offence, as particularized in the indictment or information; it is not an admission of any further facts that may be alleged by the Crown. For example, an accused charged with assault who pleads guilty is admitting that he intentionally applied force to the complainant, knowing or being reckless as to the complainant's non-consent, but he is not thereby admitting that any particular degree of force was used or that any particular number of blows was struck. If proof of further facts is required for other purposes, those facts must be agreed to or proved. If the

Crown wishes to rely on further facts for the purpose of sentencing, for example, absent agreement the Crown will need to prove those further facts it alleges beyond a reasonable doubt in the sentencing hearing (see *R v Gardiner*, [1982] 2 SCR 368, and *Criminal Code*, s 724(3)). An accused who pleads guilty also waives several procedural rights that would attend a trial: non-compellability as a witness, the right to remain silent, and the right to offer full answer and defence to the charge. For this reason the plea inquiry is important, and also independent, in that the trial judge is not bound by any agreement that may have been made between the accused or counsel and the prosecutor: *R v DMG*, 2011 ONCA 343. The trial judge must find that the relevant facts support the particular charges to which the accused is pleading guilty: *R v Fones*, 2012 MBCA 110. The trial judge usually does this by reviewing an Agreed Statement of Facts that will be filed by the Crown in support of the guilty plea: *R v DMG*, above. (Agreed Statements of Fact are discussed below.)

The trial judge's duty to inquire into the genuineness of a guilty plea was addressed in *Adgey v R*, [1975] 2 SCR 426, (1973), 13 CCC (2d) 177, which holds that an accused may change his plea if he can persuade a court that there are "valid grounds" to do so, adding that it "would be unwise to attempt to define all that which might be embraced within the phrase 'valid grounds'" (at 431 SCR).The plea inquiry is mandatory under s 606 of the *Criminal Code*, whether or not the accused is represented by counsel, but failure to make a "full" inquiry is not necessarily fatal: *R v Leiviska*, 2011 BCCA 145. Subsections 606(1.1) and (1.2) state:

> 606.(1.1) A court may accept a plea of guilty only if it is satisfied that the accused
>
> > (a) is making the plea voluntarily; and
> >
> > (b) understands
> >
> > > (i) that the plea is an admission of the essential elements of the offence,
> > >
> > > (ii) the nature and consequences of the plea, and
> > >
> > > (iii) that the court is not bound by any agreement made between the accused and the prosecutor.
>
> (1.2) The failure of the court to fully inquire whether the conditions set out in subsection (1.1) are met does not affect the validity of the plea.

The burden lies on the accused to establish on a balance of probabilities that the guilty plea should be withdrawn by the trial judge (if sentencing is scheduled for a later date), or set aside by the appeal court: *R v Le*, 2013 BCCA 455; *R v Sutton*, 2012 NLCA 35. Trial judges are granted considerable discretion in managing the plea inquiry: *R v Lewis*, 2012 SKCA 81.

As explained by the Ontario Court of Appeal in *R v Eizenga*, 2011 ONCA 113 at para 44, "[a] trial judge has the discretion to accept or not to accept a guilty plea. Up until the time of sentencing, a trial judge also has the discretion to permit an accused person to withdraw a guilty plea and to enter a new one. Provided the trial judge has exercised his or her discretion judicially, an appellate court will not lightly interfere: *R. v. Adgey* [above]."

In deciding the validity of a guilty plea, judges consider a range of factors, including whether the plea was voluntary, unequivocal, and properly informed (that is, the accused was aware of the nature of the allegation, the effect of a plea, and the consequences of it), and whether justice has been done overall. These were considered in detail by Doherty JA in the leading decision of *R v T (R)* (1992), 10 OR (3d) 514, 17 CR (4th) 247 (CA) and approved by the Supreme Court of Canada In *R v Taillefer; R v Duguay*, 2003 SCC 70, [2003] 3 SCR 307. *Taillefer* held that an otherwise valid plea may nonetheless be withdrawn if the constitutional rights of the accused have been infringed (at para 112): "the Crown's breach of its duty to disclose all of the relevant evidence led to a serious infringement of the appellant's right to make full answer and defence. That breach cast doubt on the validity of the appellant's admission of guilt and the waiver of the presumption of innocence that pleading guilty involved." See also the discussion in *R v Henry*, 2011 ONCA 289.

Convictions arising from guilty pleas tendered as a result of the now discredited evidence of pathologist Dr. Charles Taylor in Ontario, discussed in Chapter 5, Opinion Evidence, have been set aside in a series of cases: *R v Shepherd*, 2016 ONCA 188, *R v Kumar*, 2011 ONCA 120, and *R v Brant*, 2011 ONCA 362. In 2007 the commissioned *Inquiry into Paediatric Forensic Pathology* conducted by Justice Goudge concluded that Dr. Smith had made profound mistakes in 20 paediatric autopsy reports. The court in *Kumar* explained its jurisdiction to set aside a guilty plea and why it was vital to do so on the facts (at para 34):

> As this court explained in *R. v. Hanemaayer* (2008), 234 C.C.C. (3d) 3 and *R. v. T.(R.)* (1992), 10 O.R. (3d) 514, even though an appellant's plea of guilty appears to meet all the traditional tests for a valid guilty plea, the court retains a discretion, to be exercised in the interests of justice, to receive fresh evidence to explain the circumstances that led to the guilty plea and that demonstrate a miscarriage of justice occurred. In our view, this is one of those cases. The circumstances are compelling. At the time he pleaded guilty, the appellant was facing a charge of second degree murder. He was relatively new to Canada and was unfamiliar with the language and the legal system. At the time of the infant's death, his wife had just returned from hospital after major surgery for a brain tumour. He was facing loss of his liberty for at least ten years, loss of custody of his remaining child and deportation. Competent counsel had been unable to obtain opinion evidence to refute the opinion of the then leading expert in the province that the appellant had intentionally caused the death of his child. Like in *Hanemaayer*, the appellant faced a terrible dilemma. The justice system now held out a powerful inducement: a reduced charge, a much-reduced sentence (90 days instead of a minimum of ten years), all but the elimination of the possibility of deportation, and access to his surviving child. Given the persuasive value of the fresh expert evidence that shows that the conviction was unreasonable, this is a proper case to set aside the guilty plea to avoid a miscarriage of justice.

And in *Shepherd* (at para 20):

> Maria Shepherd pleaded guilty on the basis of the cause and mechanism of death advanced by Dr. Charles Smith—a significant blow, indeed a fatal blow to the back of the head while wearing a watch. The fresh evidence has thoroughly discredited that mechanism and cause of death. As a result, the plea of guilty, in our view, can no longer be said to be informed. Nor can the conviction recorded on that basis be considered reasonable or supported by the evidence. There is no demonstrated nexus between Maria Shepherd's conduct and her stepdaughter's death. It follows that the plea of guilty entered and the conviction the trial judge recorded must be set aside.

Case law on whether the plea can be set aside on appeal on the basis that the specific sentence (for example, a mandatory firearms prohibition) or its collateral consequences (for example, an immigration, tax, employment, civil, or regulatory impact) was unexpected varies considerably. The Newfoundland Court of Appeal has held that where a "plea was made voluntarily and upon a full understanding of the charge and its consequences, the consequences being the possible sentence to be imposed by the court" it could not be withdrawn. See *R v Mahoney*, 2000 NFCA 62, 197 Nfld & PEIR 1 at 4. The Supreme Court of Canada has expressed itself in a similar manner in *R v Lyons*, [1987] 2 SCR 309 at 372: "Subsequent dissatisfaction with the 'way things turned out' or with the sentence received is not, in my view, a sufficient reason to move this Court to inquire into the reasons behind the election or plea of an offender, particularly where there is nothing to suggest that these were anything other than informed and voluntary acts."

The variation in the case law appears to turn on the meaning of the term "informed" and, if the accused had counsel, whether counsel advised the accused of particular consequences of the guilty plea. For examples of the different approaches across the country, see the following cases: *R v Quick*, 2016 ONCA 95 (guilty plea invalid: realistic likelihood that accused truck driver who was not informed of an automatic and indefinite licence suspension under provincial legislation would not have pleaded guilty); *R v Aujla*, 2015 ONCA 325 (guilty plea invalid: failure to understand the immigration consequences of a guilty plea under the *Criminal Code* may render the plea uninformed); *R v Miller*, 2010 BCCA 39 (guilty plea valid: additional penalty points on accused's driver's licence is an administrative function unrelated to court proceedings); *R v Lennon*, 2012 ABCA 53 (guilty plea valid: disappointed expectations regarding consequences for driving are insufficient grounds to set aside the plea); *R v Riley*, 2011 NSCA 52 (guilty plea valid: no evidence that accused would have pleaded differently had he been informed of a mandatory firearms ban).

2. *Agreed Statements of Fact*

The *Criminal Code* authorizes an accused person to admit facts short of pleading guilty to the offence:

> 655. Where an accused is on trial for an indictable offence, he or his counsel may admit any fact alleged against him for the purpose of dispensing with proof thereof.

Thus, for example, a person charged with murder might admit having killed the victim but claim that he acted in self-defence. Crown counsel and defence counsel will usually negotiate an Agreed Statement of Facts, which becomes a formal admission pursuant to s 655 of the *Criminal Code*. These facts may dispense with issues such as identity or jurisdiction and can greatly streamline trials. An Agreed Statement of Facts may also be used in support of other evidence applications, such as an application by the Crown to introduce similar fact evidence: see *R v TLM*, 2012 SCC 6. An Agreed Statement of Facts contains facts alleged by the Crown, and accepted as true by the accused: *R v Castellani*, [1970] SCR 310. It accompanies guilty pleas, discussed above. A formal admission under s 655 is conclusive proof of the facts contained in the agreed statement; these facts cannot be contradicted. By way of contrast, party (informal) admissions can be rebutted: *R v Falconer*, 2016 NSCA 22.

Agreed Statements of Facts can be used in a number of other ways that raise interesting and important issues. For example, often one of two co-accused may plead guilty to an offence, and an Agreed Statement of Facts will be put forward to support that plea, while the other accused chooses to go to trial. The first accused—now convicted—could later be called as a Crown witness at the co-accused's trial, and offer evidence inconsistent with the Agreed Statement of Facts. If the relevant conditions regarding impeachment are met, the Agreed Statement of Facts can be used as a prior inconsistent statement, as discussed in Chapter 6, Credibility. Further, if the inconsistent evidence is such that the witness is essentially recanting the statements contained in the Agreed Statement of Facts, then, as explained in the discussion on the principled approach to hearsay exceptions in Chapter 4, Hearsay, the Agreed Statement of Facts may be admissible for the truth of its contents.

An excellent illustration is provided by *R v Youvarajah*, 2013 SCC 41. Here, a witness recanted the portions of the Agreed Statement of Facts which was filed in support of his guilty plea and which implicated the accused, replacing them with assertions that exonerated the accused. The trial judge's decision to deny the Crown's application to use the Agreed Statement of Facts for the truth of its contents against the accused was upheld by a majority of the Supreme Court of Canada on the basis that the Agreed Statement of Facts lacked sufficient threshold reliability. An opposite result was reached in *R v Kanagalingam*, 2014 ONCA 727, which serves as a reminder that the hearsay analysis is contextual: Agreed Statements of Fact may or may not be admissible for their truth in subsequent proceedings where the former accused is now a witness.

In another scenario, the trial judge declares a mistrial, or there is a successful appeal from conviction and a new trial is ordered, in a matter where there was an Agreed Statement of Facts between the Crown and the accused on particular issues. At the new trial, the accused may seek to resile from the Agreed Statement of Facts. This attempt by an accused was denied in *R v Baksh* (2005), 199 CCC (3d) 201 (Ont Sup Ct J), aff'd 2008 ONCA 116, leave to appeal refused [2008] SCCA No 155 (QL). The court held that at the new trial, the Agreed Statement of Facts could be admitted as part of the Crown's case as an ordinary party admission, at which point the accused is entitled to explain or rebut it, as is the case with all party (informal) admissions.

B. Civil Cases

One of the purposes of pleadings in modern civil procedure is to narrow the range of factual disagreement between the parties. So a statement of defence is typically required to contain, among other things, a list of the allegations in the plaintiff's statement of claim that the defendant does not contest: see, for example, Ontario *Rules of Civil Procedure*, r 25.07; British Columbia *Supreme Court Civil Rules*, r 3-3(2)(a) and form 2. Similarly, a party may formally request that another party admit facts: see, for example, British Columbia *Supreme Court Civil Rules*, r 7-7. Facts may also be expressly admitted by counsel in the course of the trial.

Once a party has formally admitted a fact, should the party be allowed to resile from the admission? Does it matter whether, or to what extent, the other party has relied on the admission? Does it matter whether the evidence led concerning other matters cast serious doubt on the fact admitted? In *Tunner v Novak* (1993), 76 BCLR (2d) 255 (CA), the British Columbia Court of Appeal dealt with the issue of the consequences of an oral admission of facts by counsel. In this case a real estate transaction was repudiated by the purchaser on the basis of misrepresentations by the vendors' agents. The vendors sued and proceeded by way of a summary trial under r 18A of the British Columbia *Rules of Court* (1990). At the outset of the proceeding, counsel for the vendors accepted the allegations of fact set out in the purchaser's affidavits. The position of the vendors was that the statements did not amount to a misrepresentation at law. The real estate agents of both the purchaser and vendors were named as third parties by the purchaser. The chambers judge noted that all counsel agreed to the concession by vendors' counsel and the summary trial proceeded, with counsel for the third parties participating. The judge found that there was a misrepresentation entitling the purchaser to repudiate. On appeal, new counsel for the vendors' real estate agents argued that the concession by vendors' counsel could not be used to make a finding of fact in a summary trial. The Court of Appeal rejected this claim (at 261-62):

> He says an admission or, to use his phrase, a provisional acceptance, of a fact cannot constitute a finding of fact. If he is right, the judgment is a nullity and there must be a new trial.
>
> But this and similar objections fail in light of the purpose and effect of admissions. The relevant propositions are compendiously stated in *The Law of Evidence in Canada*, 2nd ed. (Toronto: Butterworths, 1999), by Sopinka, Lederman and Bryant, at [pp 971-72]:
>
>> A formal admission in civil proceedings is a concession made by a party to the proceeding that a certain fact or issue is not in dispute. Formal admissions made for the purpose of dispensing with proof at trial are conclusive as to the matters admitted. As to these matters other evidence is precluded as being irrelevant, but, if such evidence is adduced the court is bound to act on the admission even if the evidence contradicts it. ...
>>
>> A formal admission may be made: (1) by a statement in the pleadings or by failure to deliver pleadings, (2) by an agreed statement of facts filed at the trial, (3) by an oral statement made by counsel at trial, or even counsel's silence in the face of statements made to the trial judge by the opposing counsel with the intention that the statements be relied on by the judge, (4) by a letter written by a party's solicitor prior to trial; or (5) by a reply or failure to reply to a request to admit facts.
>
> In my view the concession made by counsel was a formal admission concurred in by the purchaser and the third parties. Accordingly, it was not open to the parties or the judge to controvert what was admitted for the purpose of dispensing with proof of the facts relied upon to establish the representation found by the chambers judge to be an innocent misrepresentation. In the circumstances of this case I think this extends to the third parties. Royal LePage and Ms. Bardell [the vendors' real estate agents] did not stand aloof at the summary trial. They contested the purchaser's allegations of misrepresentation vigorously, as they did in this Court. By so doing, they must be taken to have accepted the risk of an adverse finding. I think this is also so with respect to the purchaser's agents.
>
> For the purposes of the summary trial and of this appeal, findings of fact founded on the concession made by counsel are as though proof of the relevant facts had been tendered at trial.

The court declined to resolve the controversy over whether the admission can "survive" the particular proceeding and apply if a new trial were ordered, but seemed inclined to agree with Sopinka, Lederman & Bryant, *The Law of Evidence in Canada*, 2nd ed (Toronto: Butterworths, 1999) at 1052-53 that it would no longer be binding in a subsequent trial but could be introduced as an informal admission with the admitting party having the usual right to try to explain or contradict it. This is consistent with the approach taken in criminal cases, described in *Baksh*, above.

II. JUDICIAL NOTICE

Generally speaking, the court is not supposed to know anything about the facts of a case until the parties lead evidence relevant to those facts. The doctrine of judicial notice is an exception to this general rule. Under the doctrine, a judge may under certain circumstances take notice of a fact despite a lack of relevant and admissible evidence. That it is an exception to the rule does not necessarily mean judicial notice is an exceptional process. Justice Binnie of the Supreme Court of Canada contested that assumption in "Judicial Notice: How Much Is Too Much?" in Law Society of Upper Canada, *Special Lectures 2003: The Law of Evidence* (Toronto: Irwin Law, 2004) 543:

> I once thought judicial notice was a rather exceptional procedure. It allows a court to accept as facts matters that have not been established in the evidence either by *viva voce* testimony or in authenticated documents. By "facts" I do not merely mean the facts of who did what and to whom in the particular dispute but also the facts or perceptions that go into the evaluation of that evidence by the judge or the juror, as well as the facts that provide the rationale for the legal rules that govern the outcome of the case.
>
> I am going to suggest here that, rather than being an exceptional procedure, judicial notice is the rule. In other words, what is actually established in court using the complex rules of evidence … is merely the tip of the iceberg. Facts judicially noticed rest on a vast submerged universe of un-proven fact, intuition, conjecture, out-of-court perception, and other mental baggage brought into court by the judge and jurors, representing the product of their collective life experiences, most of which is not accessible for contradiction to contending counsel in any precise detail.

The test for taking judicial notice is simple (see Section II.A, below), and its application is influenced by the categorization of judicially noticed facts into one of two types: adjudicative facts or non-adjudicative facts. The latter category includes "legislative" and "social" facts. Adjudicative facts are the "who, what, where, when, and why" facts resolved to decide the facts in dispute between the parties, and the test for these being judicially noticed is strict. Facts that do not relate directly to the facts in dispute, but rather to the context in which the adjudi-cation occurs, are "legislative" in relation to legislation or judicial policy, and "social" when they relate to the fact-finding process. Depending on the significance of non-adjudicative facts, it may be somewhat easier to have these judicially noticed. These labels are newly embraced in the cases but judicial notice doctrine is old, and has occupied the attention of some of the greatest treatise writers in evidence law. Old and new commentators struggle because judi-cial notice and the act of judicial reasoning are actually complexly intertwined.

Professor Thayer, from the United States, famously observed in 1890: "[i]n conducting a process of judicial reasoning, as of other reasoning, not a step can be taken without assuming something which has not been proved; and the capacity to do this, with competent judg-ment and efficiency, is imputed to judges and juries as part of their necessary mental outfit." (James Thayer, *A Preliminary Treatise on the Laws of Evidence at the Common Law* (1898) 279-80, internal citations omitted.) Given that legal reasoning depended upon unproven but reliable assumptions, Thayer argued that judicial notice should be more widely used. He believed that a judge was entitled to make *prima facie* assumptions about notoriety and if counsel disagreed, they could introduce rebutting evidence (at 300). Further, Thayer believed that "[c]ourts may judicially notice much which they cannot be required to notice," implying a wide discretion in judges to decide one way or another (at 309).

Professor Morgan, also of the United States, expressed concern about the device and the enormous potential for its abuse by judges. He argued: "[t]o warrant such judicial notice the probability must be so great as to make the truth of the proposition notoriously indisput-able among reasonable men." (Morgan, "Judicial Notice" (1944) 57 Harv L Rev 269 at 274.) Once something met that requirement (after submissions and, if necessary, evidence led by the parties) it would be illogical to then permit counsel to rebut the fact since, by definition, it is irrebuttable (at 279). The rationale for judicial notice is, for Professor Morgan, simply rationality itself.

A third academic writer whose arguments have had an enormous impact in Canadian courts is Kenneth Culp Davis. He authored the distinction between adjudicative facts (those that relate to the parties) and legislative facts (those that relate to the law and its policy and not to specific individuals). (Kenneth Culp Davis, "Judicial Notice" (1955) 55 Colum L Rev 945 at 952.) According to Professor Davis, a court must come to its decision about judicial notice by considering three factors: whether the fact in issue is close to the centre of the controversy between the parties, or merely background or near the periphery of the dispute; whether the facts are adjudicative or legislative; and the degree of certainty or doubt with respect to the particular fact (at 977).

At its core, the doctrine requires attention to concepts of certainty and adversarial fairness; as a result, the doctrine of judicial notice inevitably triggers an ongoing and healthy debate about legitimacy in the legal system. Justice Binnie summarizes the debate as "something of a doctrinal dog's breakfast" (*supra* at 547). As you read the cases that follow, consider how, at different times, Canadian courts have followed Thayer or Morgan or Davis, or an eclectic mix of all three. Also consider these issues: (1) what is the proper role of efficiency in the legal system? (2) is there a distinction between a rational decision and a legitimate one in law? (3) is there any difference between a trial and an appeal judge with regard to the test? (4) if a judge is convinced that judicial notice of a fact should be taken, is that the end of the dispute? (5) is the recently introduced distinction between facts and inferences in the cases a stable one? and (6) what is the correct interplay between judicial notice and social framework facts and expert evidence rules? The most recent decision of the Supreme Court of Canada, in *R v Spence*, 2005 SCC 71, authored by Justice Binnie, reviews much of the intellectual history and acknowledges many of these issues. Finally, while the Supreme Court of Canada has held that the standard of review for findings of fact—whether adjudicative, legislative, or social—is palpable and overriding error (*Canada (Attorney General) v Bedford*, 2013 SCC 72 at para 56), an error in the application of the test for judicial notice constitutes an error of law.

A. The Test for Judicial Notice

The Supreme Court of Canada has consistently defined the test for judicial notice as follows (*Newfoundland (Treasury Board) v NAPE*, 2004 SCC 66 at para 56, [2004] 3 SCR 381, adopting *R v Find*, 2001 SCC 32 at para 48, [2001] 1 SCR 863):

> Judicial notice dispenses with the need for proof of facts that are clearly uncontroversial or beyond reasonable dispute. Facts judicially noticed are not proved by evidence under oath. Nor are they tested by cross-examination. Therefore, the threshold for judicial notice is strict: a court may properly take judicial notice of facts that are either: (1) so notorious or generally accepted as not to be the subject of debate among reasonable persons; *or (2) capable of immediate and accurate demonstration by resort to readily accessible sources of indisputable accuracy* …. [Emphasis added.]

This test, which comes from Professor Morgan, is referred to in *Spence* (excerpted below) as the "gold standard," and is in contrast to the more general and generous approach of Professor Thayer, noted previously.

B. Judicial Acceptance of the Difference Between Adjudicative and Non-Adjudicative (Legislative and Social) Facts

In *Danson v Ontario (Attorney General)*, [1990] 2 SCR 1086, the Supreme Court of Canada initially drew the distinction between adjudicative and legislative facts. Only later, with *Spence*, does the court adopt the category of "non-adjudicative" as encompassing both legislative and social facts and as potentially attracting a less stringent test:

> It is necessary to draw a distinction at the outset between two categories of facts in constitutional litigation: "adjudicative facts" and "legislative facts." These terms derive from Davis, *Administrative Law Treatise* (1958), vol. 2, para. 15.03, p. 353. (See also Morgan, "Proof of Facts in Charter Litigation," in Sharpe, ed., *Charter Litigation* (1987).) Adjudicative facts are those that concern the immediate parties: in Davis's words, "who did what, where, when, how and with what motive or intent … ." Such facts are specific, and must be proved by admissible evidence. Legislative facts are those that establish the purpose and background of legislation, including its social, economic and cultural context. Such facts are of a more general nature, and are subject to less stringent admissibility requirements.

While the distinction is well established, it must also be noted that even the Supreme Court of Canada has admitted that "the distinction between legislative and adjudicative facts may be harder to maintain in practice than in theory" (per McLachlin J (as she then was) in *RJR-MacDonald Inc v Canada (Attorney General)*, [1995] 3 SCR 199 at para 141). In *Danson*, a lawyer brought an application for a declaration that r 57.07 of the Ontario *Rules of Civil Procedure* was constitutionally invalid. The rule provides for the assessment of costs against solicitors personally in some circumstances. No affidavits were filed in support of the application. The Attorney General brought a motion to quash the application on the ground that the only rule authorizing it was r 14.05(3), which requires, among other things, that "it is unlikely that there will be any material facts in dispute" and that the facts were likely to be disputed. The motion was dismissed and the Attorney General's appeal to the Divisional Court was dismissed, but a further appeal to the Court of Appeal was allowed and the application was quashed. The Supreme Court unanimously affirmed the Court of Appeal's decision:

> In the present case, the appellant contends that he ought to be entitled to proceed with his application under Rule 14.05(3)(h) in the complete absence of adjudicative facts, and, moreover, that it is sufficient that he present in argument (but not prove by affidavit or otherwise) legislative "facts," in the form of textbooks and academic material about the prevailing understanding of the concept of the independence of the bar, and material concerning the legislative history of the impugned rules. In the view I take of this matter, the appellant is not entitled to proceed with the application as presently constituted.
>
> In the time between the granting of leave to appeal in this matter and the hearing of the appeal, this Court heard and decided *MacKay v. Manitoba*, [1989] 2 SCR 357 … . Cory J, speaking for a unanimous Court, stated, at pp. 361-62:
>
>> *Charter* decisions should not and must not be made in a factual vacuum. To attempt to do so would trivialize the *Charter* and inevitably result in ill-considered opinions. The presentation of facts is not, as stated by the respondent, a mere technicality; rather, it is essential to a proper consideration of *Charter* issues. … *Charter* decisions cannot be based upon the unsupported hypotheses of enthusiastic counsel.

Later, Cory J stated, at p. 366:

> A factual foundation is of fundamental importance on this appeal. It is not the purpose of the legislation which is said to infringe the *Charter* but its effects. If the deleterious effects are not established there can be no *Charter* violation and no case has been made out. Thus the absence of a factual base is not just a technicality that could be overlooked, but rather it is a flaw that is fatal to the appellants' position.

This is not to say that such facts must be established in all *Charter* challenges. Each case must be considered on its own facts (or lack thereof). As Beetz J pointed out in *Manitoba (Attorney General) v. Metropolitan Stores Ltd.*, [1987] 1 SCR 110, at p. 133:

> There may be rare cases where the question of constitutionality will present itself as a simple question of law alone which can be finally settled by a motion judge. A theoretical example which comes to mind is one where Parliament or a legislature would purport to pass a law imposing the beliefs of a state religion. Such a law would violate s. 2(a) of the *Canadian Charter of Rights and Freedoms*, could not possibly be saved under s. 1 of the *Charter*, and might perhaps be struck down right away; see *Attorney General of Quebec v. Quebec Association of Protestant School Boards*, [1984] 2 SCR 66, at p. 88. *It is trite to say that these cases are exceptional.* [Emphasis added.]

The unconstitutional purpose of Beetz J's hypothetical law is found on the face of the legislation, and requires no extraneous evidence to flesh it out. It is obvious that this is not one of those exceptional cases. In general, any *Charter* challenge based upon allegations of the unconstitutional effects of impugned legislation must be accompanied by admissible evidence of the alleged effects. In the absence of such evidence, the courts are left to proceed in a vacuum, which, in constitutional cases as in nature, has always been abhorred. As Morgan put it, op. cit., at p. 162: "... the process of constitutional litigation remains firmly grounded in the discipline of the common law methodology."

The present case is, for these purposes, indistinguishable from *MacKay*, and I would respectfully adopt and apply Cory J's comments to these circumstances. The appellant here seeks to attack the impugned rules on the basis of their alleged effects upon the legal profession in Ontario. It would be, in my view, difficult if not impossible for a motions judge to assess the merits of the appellant's application under Rule 14.05(3)(h) without evidence of those effects, by way of adjudicative facts (i.e., actual instances of the use or threatened use of the impugned rules) and legislative facts (i.e., the purpose, history and perceptions among the profession of the impugned rules).

We have discovered by a roundabout route that the appellant is in possession of the facts he needs to bring his challenge, by way of application, to a conclusion on the merits if he so chooses. As the application is presently framed, however, it cannot proceed without a factual foundation. It is not necessary that the appellant prove that the impugned rules were applied against him personally (standing not being an issue); but he must present admissible evidence that the effects of the impugned rules violate provisions of the *Charter*.

The Supreme Court of Canada made a similar critique in another constitutional case, reminding counsel that "[t]he concept of 'legislative fact' does not, however, provide an excuse to put before the court controversial evidence to the prejudice of the opposing party without providing a proper opportunity for its truth to be tested. In this application, PSBAA is endeavouring to adduce apparently controversial material without the intermediary of a knowledgeable witness." (See *Public School Boards' Assn of Alberta v Alberta (Attorney General)*, 2000 SCC 2 at para 5, [2000] 1 SCR 44.) In *R v Malmo-Levine; R v Caine*, 2003 SCC 74 at para 28, [2003] 3 SCR 571, the court noted that while, following *Danson* (discussed above), the requirements for judicial notice are less strict for legislative facts, "courts should nevertheless proceed cautiously to take judicial notice even as 'legislative facts' of matters that are reasonably open to dispute, particularly where they relate to an issue that could be dispositive."

On the other hand, there are several cases that suggest that the court does not insist on the rule that evidence be led to support Charter claims, even those that are central to the dispute between the parties. In its first major equality case under s 15 of the Charter, *Andrews v Law Society of British Columbia*, [1989] 1 SCR 143, the court employed judicial notice in concluding that non-citizenship was analogous to grounds listed in s 15(1) and a basis for disadvantageous treatment. In *Vriend v Alberta*, [1998] 1 SCR 493 at para 13, the court noted without disapproval that the trial judge was satisfied that the discrimination homosexuals suffer "is so notorious that [she could] take judicial notice of it without evidence." In *Newfoundland (Treasury Board) v NAPE*, 2004 SCC 66, [2004] 3 SCR 381, the court used the device of judicial notice under s 1 of the Charter to conclude that the Newfoundland government was facing a severe economic crisis and was thereby justified in erasing an obligation to pay $24 million under a pay equity agreement with public sector unions. The unions argued that the record on the s 1 issue was fatally deficient. The court reasoned:

[55] As with any matter that must be approached with close attention to context, the evidence led in support of a s. 1 justification is very important to the outcome. The only evidence before the Board consisted of an extract from *Hansard* and some budget documents. The government witnesses were not employed in the relevant policy group at the time.

[56] Ordinarily such a casually introduced s. 1 record would be a matter of serious concern. However the essential subject matter of the s. 1 justification in this case consists of the public accounts of the Province that are filed with the House of Assembly, and comments by the Minister of Finance and the President of the Treasury Board as to what they thought the accounts disclosed and what they proposed to do about it, which are reported in *Hansard*. This is all material of which courts may take judicial notice, as noted in *R v. Find* [excerpted below], at para. 48:

. . .

[57] The purpose of judicial notice is not only to dispense with unnecessary proof but to avoid a situation where a court, on the evidence, reaches a factual conclusion which contradicts "readily accessible sources of indisputable accuracy," and which would therefore bring into question the accuracy of the court's own fact-finding processes. A finding on the evidence led by the parties, for example, that the Newfoundland deficit in 1988 was $5 million whereas anyone could ascertain from the public accounts that it was $120 million would create a serious anomaly. As Professor Morgan famously wrote:

... [the court] cannot adjust legal relations among members of society and thus fulfill the sole purpose of its creation if it permits the parties to take issue on, and thus secure results contrary to, what is so notoriously true as not to be the subject of reasonable dispute ... .

(E.M. Morgan, "Judicial Notice" (1944), 57 *Harv. L Rev.* 269, at p. 273)

[58] The Board was critical of the government in failing to call witnesses who could describe at first hand what alternatives were examined to secure cost reductions that might, if adopted, have avoided a deferral of pay equity. I agree with the Board that the government ought to have called witnesses who were better placed to explain the government accounts and ministerial

observations. However, in the context of this particular subject matter, I do not agree that failure to do so was fatal to the government's s. 1 case. There are serious limits to how far the courts can penetrate Cabinet privilege in order to require information about the deliberations of the Executive Council: *Canada (Auditor General) v. Canada (Minister of Energy, Mines and Resources)*, [1989] 2 SCR 49, at p. 89. What transpires in the budgetary process, of course, lies at the high end of Cabinet confidences, and here there was no need to precipitate a confrontation between the courts and the government. In my view, the material brought to the Board's attention, and of which we may take judicial notice, is sufficient for the purposes of disposing of this appeal.

(2) Was There a Pressing and Substantial Legislative Objective?

[59] It cannot reasonably be disputed that the provincial government faced a severe fiscal crisis in the spring of 1991. ...

In light of this more recent authority, and after reading the material in the rest of this chapter, you may wish to ask whether the Supreme Court was right to dismiss Danson's appeal.

C. Adjudicative Facts

R v Potts

(1982), 36 OR (2d) 195 (CA), leave to appeal refused, [1982] 1 SCR xi
Lacourcière, Houlden, and Thorson JJA (24 February 1982)

[The accused was charged with speeding contrary to s 5(1) of the *National Capital Commission Traffic and Property Regulations*, CRC 1978, c 1044, on Colonel By Drive. The regulations applied to "driveways," that is, roads that were "under the control and management of, or vested in the name of" the National Capital Commission (NCC). The Crown led no evidence as to whether Colonel By Drive was such a road. A justice of the peace convicted the accused. An appeal by way of stated case was allowed, and the Crown appealed further.]

THORSON JA: ...

. . .

[Mr. Rutherford, on behalf of the appellant, submitted] that it was open to the justice of the peace at trial to conclude that Colonel By Drive in the City of Ottawa was a "driveway" within the meaning of the regulations in question by considering that the acts of control and management by the NCC over Colonel By Drive were sufficiently notorious in the City of Ottawa that judicial notice could properly be taken of them. This, therefore, was unlike a case where the court has purported to take judicial notice of such things as the location of a municipal boundary, the limits of federal and provincial jurisdiction as a matter of law, or the existence of title to land.

Mr. Rutherford then invited the Court to consider a "typical" driveway location "somewhere" in the National Capital area in terms of what any ordinary person, travelling along the driveway and observing the passing scene, could expect to encounter if in fact that driveway happened to be under the control and management of the NCC. The picture he painted of such a "typical" driveway (which might or might not be Colonel By Drive) was of a broad, generally well-tended and beautifully landscaped thoroughfare following along the contours of perhaps the Ottawa River or perhaps the Rideau Canal, kept salted and sanded in the winter months by work crews in vehicles bearing the insignia of the NCC, and kept groomed and in repair in other more salubrious seasons by crews working out of similar NCC vehicles. In the springtime the traveller along such a driveway could expect to encounter nearby vast beds of tulips, the famed (and no doubt judicially noticeable) royal Dutch gift of thanks to the Canadian people. On Sunday mornings in the summertime, the same traveller could expect to meet NCC personnel placing barriers across the roadway reserving it for a time for use only by people on bicycles, and in the wintertime he might see similar barriers being erected by NCC personnel to protect skaters seeking to gain access to what could be the Rideau Canal, at locations where skaters' huts maintained by the NCC are to be found.

In all seasons, a further significant indication of the Commission's "presence" would be the distinctive "white-on-black" NCC traffic signs to be seen at intervals along the whole length of the driveway, displaying in both official languages and over the Commission's name such information as the name of the driveway and its posted maximum speed. Finally the motorist on the driveway would soon enough observe that the entire driveway was being patrolled by police vehicles bearing the markings of the Royal Canadian Mounted Police and manned, one might guess, by personnel of the same organizational persuasion. From this it could further be guessed that the driveway in question was under an administration different from that governing streets and highways elsewhere in the City of Ottawa which are municipally or provincially policed.

The point, of course, of counsel's most vivid and evocative imagery, which I have sought to reproduce faithfully here, is that all of these things would be readily observable factual manifestations of the NCC's control and management of a "typical" driveway if that driveway happened to come under the control and management of the NCC. The further point to which this in turn leads is that in the instant case of Colonel By Drive, these very same manifestations of the Commission's control and management are so familiarly present, and they are so compelling of the obvious inference which is to be drawn from the fact of their presence, as to make it "notorious" in the City of Ottawa that Colonel By Drive is indeed under the control and management of the Commission and is thus "property of the Commission" within the meaning of its Traffic and Property Regulations.

Counsel for the respondent did not at any earlier stage in this case contest the fact that his client was breaking *some* speed limit in Ontario when the vehicle his client was driving was clocked by the radar unit at 123 km. More significantly, however, counsel for the respondent did not at any earlier stage seek to argue that Colonel By Drive was not property of the Commission, or that the finding made at trial based on the matter judicially noticed would not have been warranted if some evidence had been led to establish the status of the driveway as "property of the Commission," to which the regulations rather than the ordinarily applicable provincial *Highway Traffic Act*, RSO 1980, c. 198, was an essential element of the Crown's case, and in the absence of any evidence as to that matter it was not proved, nor could it be, by the taking of judicial notice of it.

• • •

I think the justice of the peace acted entirely properly in taking judicial notice of the status of this driveway in the case before him.

Judicial notice, it has been said, is the acceptance by a court or judicial tribunal, without the requirement of proof, of the truth of a particular fact or state of affairs that is of such general or common knowledge in the community that proof of it can be dispensed with. The doctrine is thus said to be an exception to the general rule that a judge or jury may consider only evidence which has been tendered in court and may not act on personal knowledge (see McWilliams, *Canadian Criminal Evidence* (1974), at p. 379). As Lord Sumner put it in *Commonwealth Shipping Representative v. Peninsular & Oriental Branch Service*, [1923] AC 191 at 211:

> [T]o require that a judge should affect a cloistered aloofness from facts that every other man in Court is fully aware of, and should insist on having proof on oath of what, as a man of the world, he knows already better than any witness can tell him, is a rule that may easily become pedantic and futile.

Thus it has been held that, generally speaking, a court may properly take judicial notice of any fact or matter which is so generally known and accepted that it cannot reasonably be questioned, or any fact or matter which can readily be determined or verified by resort to sources whose accuracy cannot reasonably be questioned.

As to what constitutes general or "common" knowledge, the following passage in McWilliams at p. 380, citing G.D. Nokes in "The Limits of Judicial Notice," 74 LQR 59 (1958) at p. 67, is, I think, instructive:

> Judicial notice of matters of fact is founded upon that fund of knowledge and experience which is common to both judges and jurors and is not confined to the Bench. In many cases no reference is made during the trial to this aspect of judicial notice; if the fact is relevant, everyone in court will assume that rain falls, for example; and there is no ascertainable limit to the matters which are thus silently noticed by both judge and jury. But when a fact less obviously forms part of mankind's fund of common knowledge, it may be necessary for counsel to request the judge to take judicial notice; *and in such cases the judge must exercise a discretion whether to do so, which is merely another way of saying that he must decide whether the fact falls within the rule as being notorious.* ... [C]ommon knowledge differs with time and place, so a fact which was notorious a century ago may no longer be the appropriate subject of notice, and a fact may be common knowledge only among a class of the community, such as those interested in a particular sport ... Thirdly, though a judge may consider a fact to be the appropriate subject of notice, he may not himself remember or profess to know it, and therefore he may take steps to acquire the necessary knowledge.
>
>   • • •
>
>   Little assistance can be had by a search of the authorities for exactly similar cases. ... What may be a proper subject of judicial notice at one time or place may not be at another.
>
>   • • •

There are, it seems to me, at least two distinct threads running through these cases. The first has to do with the standard to be applied in determining what is common knowledge, and the point which the cases make is that what constitutes common knowledge is to be judged by reference to that which is common knowledge in the community where and when the issue is being tried. The second has to do with the proper function of an appellate court, sitting on an appeal from a decision applying a community standard of common knowledge. Each of these merits a brief comment.

Where judicial notice of some matter is taken by a trial court, the trier of the facts (whether judge alone or jury) may or may not share the knowledge that is said to be common knowledge in the community or in a particular class of the community. If it happens that the court does share a personal knowledge of that which is commonly known in the community, well and good. If not, however, the matter may still be judicially noticed, but the court is put on its inquiry as to whether the matter is or is not one which may properly be made part of the case before it without formal proof thereof. Conversely there is the situation where the knowledge that the court has about a particular matter is knowledge of a kind which the court is required to apply repeatedly in the cases that come before it day by day. In *R v. Miller* (1971), 4 CCC (2d) 70, 15 CRNS 164, the learned County Court judge, speaking of the procedures that are involved in taking samples of a person's breath for breathalyzer testing, concluded that, on the authorities he had reviewed, "it is possible for a Court to take judicial notice of matters that are repeatedly before it" (p. 80 CCC). While in principle this appears to make a good deal of sense, at least where the matters being noticed are not really disputed, it is nevertheless clear that a trial court is not justified in acting on its own personal knowledge of or familiarity with a particular matter, alone and without more.

As for an appellant court, the cases also make it clear that it is not its function to adjudicate upon the correctness of a trial court's decision to take judicial notice of some fact or matter known locally, relying solely upon the appellate court's knowledge of (or, for that matter, its lack of knowledge of) that which was noticed in the court below, unless of course that same knowledge is in the larger public domain. While no member of an appellate court is obliged to "check at the doorway to the court-house" his own personal knowledge and experience of the world around him, in the very nature of an appellate court, particularly in a jurisdiction as geographically vast as Ontario, it is highly improbable that each of its members will share personally in the knowledge that is "common knowledge" in the diverse communities from which it draws its cases. It is, for example, no more than pure chance that the writer of these reasons, as a result of long residence in the City of Ottawa, happens to be very familiar with the driveway known as Colonel By Drive, that he has many times seen and admired Mr. Rutherford's pictured tulips, skated along his canal, cycled along the driveway, and of course, made dutiful mental note of the speed limit posted on its traffic signs. Yet all this is indeed "immaterial," as Morden JA correctly stated in *R v. Bednarz* [(1961), 130 CCC 398 (Ont CA)]. What in my opinion is material is that the justice of the peace in Ottawa who heard this case was warranted in making the decision he did regarding the status of this driveway as "property of the Commission," on the basis of the public notoriety of that matter in the National Capital area.

. . .

In this case, it was not until after the taking of evidence had been concluded without any evidence having been given by the respondent that the latter's counsel first raised the point that no evidence had been adduced by the Crown as to the status of this driveway. Counsel of course was within his rights in waiting until then to raise this point, but even then the driveway's status as property of the Commission was not disputed by him. In my opinion its status was not disputed, as clearly as it could have been, precisely because it could only have been obvious to all those who took part in the trial what the outcome of the dispute would have been. In these circumstances, I cannot accept that it was incumbent upon the Crown to prove a matter which did not need to be proved, or that the justice of the peace erred in proceeding to convict the respondent in the absence of its proof.

For the reasons given, I would allow the appeal, set aside the acquittal and restore the conviction of the respondent for the offence charged in the information.

QUESTION

Would it be proper for a sentencing judge to take judicial notice of the evil represented by a large number of offences related to drinking and driving committed in the particular district in which the offence occurred? See *R v Lacasse*, 2015 SCC 64.

R v Zundel (No 1)
(1987), 58 OR (2d) 129, 31 CCC (3d) 97 (CA)
Howland CJO and Brooke, Martin, Lacourcière, and Houlden JJA
(23 January 1987)

[The accused published a pamphlet titled "Did Six Million Really Die?" in which he argued, in his words, that "the allegation that 6 million Jews died during the Second World War, as a direct result of official German policy of extermination, is utterly unfounded." He was charged with spreading false news that he knew to be false contrary to s 177 of the *Criminal Code*, RSC 1970, c C-34. His defences were that the pamphlet was not false or, in the alternative, that he did not know it was false. The Crown led the expert evidence of a historian, Dr. Raul Hilberg, who gave an opinion to the effect that "over five million Jews were systematically annihilated by the Nazi government of Germany." The defence led the expert evidence of Dr. Robert Faurisson, whose opinion was that the Nazi government had no policy of extermination and that the number of persons killed in concentration camps was much lower than generally stated.]

BY THE COURT: …

. . .

Counsel for the Crown contended that the trial judge erred in rejecting the Crown's application that he take judicial notice of the Holocaust and, accordingly, the appellant suffered no prejudice even if the evidence of Dr. Hilberg was inadmissible.

At the end of the Crown's case, Crown counsel requested that the judge take judicial notice of the Holocaust. The judge in his ruling rejecting the Crown's application stated that the Crown had requested the court to take judicial notice of two things. Firstly, that millions of Jews were annihilated in Europe during the years 1933 to 1945 because of a "premeditated policy of the hierarchy of Nazi Germany." Secondly, the means of annihilation included mass shootings of Jews, their deliberate starvation, privation and death by gassing. The judge, after careful consideration of lengthy submissions by both Crown counsel and defence counsel, said that, however tempted he might be to grant the Crown's application, it would have the effect, in the eyes of the public, as well as perhaps in the eyes of the jury and the accused, of not providing the accused with an opportunity to make full answer and defence. To grant the motion would have the effect of "substantially eliminating a portion of the duty incumbent on the Crown in so far as the guilt of the accused is concerned."

The application to the court to take judicial notice of the Holocaust was renewed after the conclusion of the defence evidence on the basis that the bulk of the defence evidence had related to the appellant's belief in the truth of the pamphlet and that there was no evidence called "to cast a doubt" on the two matters that the court had earlier been requested to notice. The court in rejecting the second application stated that the Crown alleged that the accused had published something that was inherently false and the Crown had the burden of proving that allegation.

[The court referred to *Potts*, above, and continued:]

It was the view of both Thayer and Wigmore that taking judicial notice of a fact or matter does not import that the matter is indisputable; it is not necessarily anything more than a *prima facie* recognition of the matter as true without the offering of evidence by the party who should ordinarily have done so, but the opponent is not prevented from disputing the matter by evidence, if he believes it disputable: see Thayer, *A Preliminary Treatise on Evidence at the Common Law* (1898), pp. 308-9; *Wigmore on Evidence*, 3d. ed., vol. 9, p. 535.

The generally accepted modern view, however, is that where the court takes judicial notice of a matter, the judicial notice is final: see Morgan, "Judicial Notice" (1944), 57 *Harv. L Rev.* 269; Nokes, "The Limits of Judicial Notice" (1958), 74 *LQ Rev.* pp. 59-63; McNaughton, "Judicial Notice—Excerpts Relating to the Morgan-Wigmore Controversy" (1961), 14 *Vand. L Rev.* 779. When a court takes judicial notice of a fact, it declares that it will find the fact exists *or direct the jury to do so*: see *Cross on Evidence*, 6th ed., pp. 62-3.

It is well established that the court may take judicial notice of an historical fact. The court may, on its own initiative, consult historical works or documents, or the court may be referred to them: see *Read et al. v. Bishop of Lincoln*, [1892] AC 644; *R v. Bartleman* (1984), 13 CCC (3d) 488 at pp. 491-2, 12 DLR (4th) 73 at p. 77 (BCCA). The court may even hear sworn testimony before judicial notice is taken: see *McQuaker v. Goddard*, [1940] 1 KB 687.

As Professor Cross points out, the distinction between the process of taking judicial notice and the reception of evidence begins to fade when the judge makes inquiries before deciding to take judicial notice of a matter. He points out that if learned treatises are consulted, it is not easy to say whether evidence is being received under an exception to the hearsay rule or whether the judge is equipping himself to take judicial notice. The resemblance of taking judicial notice to the reception of evidence is even more marked when sworn testimony is heard before judicial notice is taken. He concludes, however, that even where the processes of taking judicial notice and receiving evidence approximate most closely, they are essentially different: see *Cross on Evidence*, 6th ed., pp. 67-8. The essential difference is that when the judge is equipping himself to take judicial notice, the hearsay rule does not apply.

Professor Morgan in his famous article, previously mentioned, states at pp. 286-7:

> The party seeking judicial notice has the burden of convincing the judge that (a) the matter is so notorious as not to be the subject of dispute among reasonable men or (b) the matter is capable of immediate accurate demonstration by resort to readily accessible sources of indisputable accuracy. There is no artificial limit upon the sources of information which he may furnish the judge, and none upon those which the judge may consult of his own motion. The opponent likewise is not restricted by rules of evidence in offering, or inducing the judge to consult, reliable repositories of relevant data. If the judge believes it doubtful whether the matter falls within the domain of judicial notice, or if the sources available are inadequate,

he leaves the subject within the domain of evidence, and all the ordinary rules applicable to the process of resolving an ordinary issue of fact are enforced.

Professor Pattenden also states that a judge can take judicial notice of an opinion which rests on hearsay: [1982] *Crim. L Rev.* at pp. 91-2 and 96.

Judicial notice may be taken of an evidential fact or a fact in issue: see Thayer, *A Preliminary Treatise on Evidence at the Common Law*, at p. 306; *Phipson on Evidence*, 13th ed., p. 26. The judge here was requested to take judicial notice of a fact in issue which was an essential element of the Crown's case. The judges, however, have a wide discretion as to matters of which they will take judicial notice and may notice matters which they cannot be required to notice: see *Thayer, A Preliminary Treatise on Evidence at the Common Law*, p. 309; *Phipson on Evidence*, 13th ed., p. 26.

In the present case, the prosecution was required to prove, *inter alia*, (a) that the pamphlet was false, and (b) that the appellant subjectively knew that it was false. There was no direct evidence of the appellant's knowledge of the falsity of the pamphlet, such as an admission, and, indeed, the defence position was (a) that it was true and (b) even if it was not true the appellant honestly believed it to be true. The Crown, in order to succeed, was required to prove by circumstantial evidence of inference that the appellant knew the pamphlet was false. If the jury on the evidence concluded that the existence of the Holocaust was so notorious as to be indisputable by reasonable men and women, that would be a circumstance, but only a circumstance, from which the jury might infer that the appellant knew that the pamphlet was false, but the jury would not be required to draw that inference. However, if the trial judge had taken judicial notice of the existence of the Holocaust, he would have been required to so declare to the jury and to direct them to find that the Holocaust existed, which would have been gravely prejudicial to the defence in so far as it would influence the drawing of the inference concerning the appellant's knowledge of the falsity of the pamphlet. In our view, the judge exercised his discretion judicially in refusing to take judicial notice of the Holocaust.

Since we have held that the evidence of Dr. Hilberg was admissible, it is unnecessary to consider whether we might properly take judicial notice of those matters of which the trial judge declined to take judicial notice, and invoke s. 613(1)(b)(iii) of the Code with respect to the alleged error in admitting Dr. Hilberg's evidence.

NOTE

Zundel's appeal was allowed on other grounds and a new trial was ordered. He was again convicted, and he again appealed.

R v Zundel (No 2)
(1990), 53 CCC (3d) 161 (Ont CA)
Brooke, Morden, and Galligan JJA (5 February 1990)

BY THE COURT: ... At the opening of the trial now in question, Crown counsel requested that the judge take judicial notice of the Holocaust, being the historical fact that during the Second World War, the National Socialist Regime of Adolf Hitler pursued a policy which had as its goal the extermination of the Jews of Europe.

During the lengthy submissions of both counsel, guided by the considerations set out in *Zundel (No. 1)*, the trial judge attempted to discern the issues of fact, contentious and otherwise.

Crown counsel contended that he would prove the falsity of some 25 assertions of fact contained in the pamphlet. He submitted that to take judicial notice as requested would not prove the falsity of any of those facts nor assist the Crown in discharging the burden of proving that Mr. Zundel knew that the pamphlet was false. He also submitted that to take judicial notice as requested would in no way be prejudicial to the defence raising a reasonable doubt with respect to any issue in the case. In other words, it was the Crown's submission that to take judicial notice as requested would not assist the Crown in discharging the burden of proof on any of the elements of the offence or on any of the evidentiary issues in relation to them. The facts were simply a necessary piece of background.

For the defence, it was submitted that to take judicial notice as requested was tantamount to taking judicial notice of an official policy of genocide, which would have been highly prejudicial to the defence with respect to the controverted issues of fact referred to by the Crown. Defence counsel submitted that it would be a misstatement to express the thesis of the pamphlet as "the Holocaust did not happen." The pamphlet, he said, asserts that the allegation that six million Jews died during the Second World War as a direct result of official German policy of extermination is utterly unfounded. Defence counsel distinguished several elements, including the numbers, whether or not there was an official policy of extermination, and finally, the existence of the gas chambers.

During defence counsel's submissions, the court asked him whether it would be different were the court to instruct the jury that they must take judicial notice that there was, in Europe, during the crucial years, the murder of many Jews by the Nazis as opposed to telling the jury that there was a systematic policy of government to that effect. Defence counsel replied:

> I think I can tell Your Honour that if the first statement was made, the problem isn't even disputed ... by this booklet ... So then, if that's the case, if that's not in dispute, why take judicial notice of it?

In his ruling, the trial judge noted the difference between the subject-matter of the request for judicial notice in *Zundel (No. 1)* and the timing of that request and the request made to him. He concluded that the decision of the Court of Appeal in *Zundel (No. 1)* made it clear that while a judge could take judicial notice of the matters requested, in the circumstances the judge at the first trial had not erred in declining to take judicial notice. However, the trial judge was of the view that, in this second case, the court should take judicial notice of the Holocaust in a narrow way. He said: "The mass murder and extermination of Jews of Europe by the Nazi regime during the Second World War is so notorious as not to be the subject of dispute among reasonable persons."

But he declined to take judicial notice of whether or not what had occurred was by reason of a policy. In this regard he said:

> In this case, the jury will be instructed by me that the Crown need not establish there was mass murder and extermination of Jews in Europe by the Nazi regime during the Second World War. I have deliberately refrained from discussing whether there was a policy, because the question of whether there was a policy or not, while not irrelevant to the defence, is not an essential fact on the question of the Holocaust.

He noted the Crown's intention to prove the falsity of some 25 assertions of fact contained in the pamphlet and noted that Mr. Zundel would have the opportunity to demonstrate the truth of these individual assertions. He emphasized in his ruling that the Crown bears the burden of proving that the accused knew the contents of the pamphlet were false.

Following the opening remarks of Crown and defence counsel, the trial judge gave instructions to the jury as to the historical fact of which he had taken judicial notice. He correctly reviewed the essential elements of the offence with which the accused was charged and directed them that the Holocaust

> … which is defined, in essence, as the mass murder and extermination of Jews in Europe by the Nazi regime during the Second World War, is a historical fact which is so notorious as not to be the subject of dispute among reasonable persons and I direct you now as I would later, to accept it as a fact … but you will keep in mind that this offence alleged against the accused is directed to the publication of the pamphlet, and it must be of statements or tales which are false, and the Crown must establish that the publication is false and it must be false to the knowledge of the person who publishes it.

We think the trial judge took judicial notice of non-contentious historical facts which were background and declined to take judicial notice of historical facts which the Crown had to demonstrate in proving that specific statements or allegations in the pamphlet were false, and that the accused knew them to be false when he published them. These latter were issues of fact for the jury, and the trial judge had no intention of resolving their proof by judicial notice or of diminishing the accused's right to make full answer and defence with respect to these facts. He did not take judicial notice of any policy of the National Socialist government and/or Adolf Hitler, he did not take judicial notice of the specific numbers of persons who died and he did not take judicial notice of the use of gas chambers.

Defence counsel recognized this and its significance in relation to the specific statements in the pamphlet which the Crown alleged to be false. In opening his address to the jury with respect to judicial notice, defence counsel said to them:

> His Honour will tell you what he says is reasonable for reasonable men to contest. But it won't include the six million, it won't include the gas chambers and it won't include the official plan. That's basically what this book is all about. These three items are opinion and can be debated by reasonable people.
>
> That is not to dispute the Jewish tragedy of mass murder of some Jews by some Nazis during World War II, which His Honour will tell you is a fact. The judicial ruling goes no further than that.

Should Judicial Notice Have Been Taken?

There can be no doubt that the information and authorities to which the trial judge was referred and upon which he relied were quite sufficient to justify his taking judicial notice of the Holocaust as he did, and that such historical facts are so notorious as not to be the subject of dispute amongst reasonable persons. He heard extensive submissions in this regard. The information and authorities referred to were in part reviewed before us, but we have heard nothing that would cause us to doubt his judgment on this issue. We are not persuaded that he erred in the exercise of his discretion. This case, on the facts relevant to this issue, is quite different from *Zundel (No. 1)* and as stated, judicial notice was taken of historical facts which were not in contention and which were no more than background.

The Crown proceeded to adduce evidence going to the proof of the falsehood of many of the specific statements in the pamphlet, from which the jury could infer that those statements were false. The defence led evidence to the contrary. However, the judicial notice taken by the trial judge was of such a limited scope that it could not have prejudiced the defence.

NOTE

Zundel's appeal was dismissed. He appealed to the Supreme Court of Canada and was acquitted when the court declared the offence of spreading false news to be unconstitutional: see *R v Zundel*, [1992] 2 SCR 731, 75 CCC (3d) 449.

R v Krymowski
2005 SCC 7, [2005] 1 SCR 101
McLachlin CJ and Major, Bastarache, Binnie, LeBel, Deschamps,
Fish, Abella, and Charron JJ (24 February 2005)

CHARRON J:

I. Introduction

[1] The respondents were charged with the wilful promotion of hatred arising from their participation in a demonstration to protest against the entry of Roma refugee claimants into Canada. At the conclusion of the Crown's case, the defence called no evidence and argued that the Crown had failed to prove that the wilful promotion of hatred was against "Roma," as particularized in the information. Counsel argued that the evidence showed only that the actions of the demonstrators were directed toward "gypsies" and that there was "no evidence that Roma is the same as Gypsies, similar to Gypsies, related to Gypsies." The trial judge refused to accede to the Crown's requests that he take judicial notice of the shared meaning of the terms, or that he permit the amendment of the information or a reopening of the Crown's case to address this point. He accepted the defence argument that the Crown had failed to establish an essential element of the offence and acquitted the respondents (2000 CarswellOnt 5870 (Ont. CJ)). The Crown's appeal to the summary conviction appeal court was dismissed (2002 CarswellOnt 5516 (Ont. SCJ)) as was its further appeal to the Court of Appeal for Ontario ((2003), 65 OR (3d) 75 (Ont. CA)). Leave to appeal to this Court was granted pursuant to s. 40 of the *Supreme Court Act*, RSC 1985, c. S-26.

[2] In my view, the trial judge erred in law in finding, in effect, that it was necessary for the Crown to prove that the terms "gypsies" and "Roma" were interchangeable. In focussing on this narrow issue, he failed to consider whether, on the totality of the evidence, the Crown had established that "Roma" were targeted by the accused. Because I have concluded that there must be a new trial, I will only review the facts to the extent necessary to dispose of the appeal.

II. Background

[3]   Some weeks prior to this incident, there was a large influx of Roma refugee claimants into Canada which attracted considerable media attention and gave rise to some public controversy. On August 26, 1997, about 25 persons participated in a demonstration in front of the Lido Motel in Scarborough, Ontario, which at that time was temporarily housing the refugees while they awaited the outcome of their claims. The demonstration included chants and placards. The placards stated, among other things, "Honk if you hate Gypsies," "Canada is not a trash can," "You're a Cancer to Canada" and "G.S.T.—Gypsies Suck Tax." The chants included statements such as "Gypsies Out," "How do you like Canada now?" and "White power." Some participants were seen giving the "Sieg Heil" Nazi salute. Nazi and American Confederate flags were used in the demonstration. Some of the clothing, accessories and footwear worn by the demonstrators was described as typical "Skin head" accoutrements.

[4]   The Crown alleged that the respondents were amongst the demonstrators. Separate informations establishing the charges under s. 319(2) of the *Criminal Code*, RSC 1985, c. C-46, against both the adults and young persons accused in this matter read as follows:

> [The respondents] did wilfully promote hatred against an identifiable group, to wit Roma, by communicating statements, including the written statements: "Honk if you hate Gypsies," "Canada is not a Trash Can," and "You're a cancer to Canada," contrary to the *Criminal Code* of Canada.

The trial was held for the adult respondents, at the end of which the evidence was admitted in the young person proceeding. For convenience, I will refer to the two separate proceedings as one.

[5]   During the course of the trial, the respondents admitted that the Roma were an identifiable group within the meaning of s. 319(2). The admission was confirmed by letter from counsel stating that "the Roma people are an identifiable group which were historically persecuted by the Nazis." Two pages from an article about Nazi persecution of Roma authored by Ian Hancock were attached to the letter. The article referred to Roma and gypsies interchangeably. However, counsel's letter expressly stated that the article excerpt was admitted solely as background and not as any further admission. The record is replete with examples showing that the witnesses, Crown counsel, both defence counsel and the trial judge referred to the refugee claimants indiscriminately as "Roma," "Gypsy Roma" or "Romani Gypsies" throughout the proceedings.

[6]   At the conclusion of the Crown's case, the defence called no evidence and closed its case. Following the Crown's closing arguments, the defence made its closing submissions, the main argument being that the Crown had failed to prove an essential element of the offence as charged, namely that the accused wilfully promoted hatred *against Roma*, as all evidence pointed to "gypsies," and no evidence linked "gypsies" to Roma.

[7]   In reply, the Crown submitted that the court could infer, from the wording of the informations, that "Roma" was referable to "gypsy." The trial judge rejected that suggestion. Alternatively, the Crown argued that the court could take judicial notice of that fact, relying on the Hancock article and the author's interchangeable use of the terms "Roma" and "gypsy." The trial judge was unwilling to accept that position. The Crown therefore asked that the informations be amended by inserting the words "a.k.a. gypsies" after the

word "Roma." Following a two-day adjournment, the matter was argued more fully. The Crown again invited the court to take judicial notice of the synonymy of "Roma" and "gypsies" based on five dictionary definitions containing definitions of "Roma" and its varying forms ("Rom"; "Romany") and "gypsy."

[8] According to the trial judge, the dictionaries did not evince a sufficient degree of uniformity in definitions because several definitions of "Rom" and "Roma" referred only to male gypsies and some dictionary and internet definitions of "gypsy" presented by the defence contained no reference to "Roma." For this reason, and since the issue was "vital and highly contentious," he concluded that the court should not exercise its discretion and take judicial notice on this matter.

. . .

[10] The trial judge then dismissed the charge against all respondents finding that there was "no evidence whatsoever, or in any form, establishing beyond a reasonable doubt the willful promotion of hatred against Roma or that Roma are one and the same as or also known as Gypsies" nor was there any evidence that "Gypsies is a pejorative term for Roma as contended by the Crown" (paras. 35-36).

. . .

[13] The gist of the offence under s. 319(2) of the *Criminal Code* is the wilful promotion of hatred against any identifiable group. ...

. . .

[17] In short, it was necessary for the Crown in this case to prove that the respondents, by communicating statements other than in private conversation, wilfully promoted hatred against a section of the public distinguished by colour, race, religion or ethnic origin. The arguments presented at trial and on this appeal all only relate to the requirement that the hatred be against an identifiable group as so defined. The Crown in this case particularized this group as being "Roma." The defence conceded that Roma are an identifiable group within the meaning of s. 319(2). The sole remaining question in respect of this essential element of the offence became whether Roma were the target of the respondents' conduct.

[18] As noted earlier, the informations also particularized the manner in which the offence was committed: "by communicating statements, including the written statements: 'Honk if you hate Gypsies,' 'Canada is not a Trash Can,' and 'You're a cancer to Canada.'" Particulars define the factual transaction that the prosecution must prove to support a conviction: *R v. McCune* (1998), 131 CCC (3d) 152 (BCCA); *R v. Groot*, [1999] 3 SCR 664 (SCC). To make out the offence, however, there was no need to prove any "interchangeability" between the specific hateful terms employed and the name by which the target group was identified in the information. The relevant questions to be asked with respect to this element of the offence were whether the Crown had proved beyond a reasonable doubt that the respondents made some or all of the statements alleged in the information and whether the statements made, as a matter of fact, promoted hatred of the Roma.

[19] It was incumbent upon the trial judge to look at the totality of the evidence and draw appropriate inferences to determine whether the respondents intended to target "any section of the public distinguished by colour, race, religion or ethnic origin," in this case, the Roma people. Several items of evidence potentially related to this issue. The reference to "gypsies" was but one item of evidence to consider. To illustrate the point, it may be useful to consider whether the offence could be made out even if the demonstrators

had made the same statements but without using the word "gypsies." Among other things, the trial judge in his reasons for judgment referred to the following evidence as fact: (1) the motel outside of which the respondents demonstrated was temporarily housing the refugee claimants who were awaiting the outcome of their claims; (2) some of the participants were seen giving the "Sieg Heil" Nazi salute; (3) Nazi and American Confederate flags were used in the demonstration; and (4) the chant "White Power" was heard during the demonstration. Furthermore, the defence concession expressly linked Nazi persecution to the "Roma people."

[20] Hence, the ethnic flavour to the demonstration, the fact that it was situated outside a motel housing refugee claimants who were at times described by the witnesses as Roma, and the fact that Roma people are a group historically persecuted by the Nazis while the Nazi theme was apparent at the demonstration were all factors to consider, in addition to the actual words used, in determining whether Roma were the target of the hate speech. In focussing entirely on one of the specific statements particularized in the information, the trial judge misdirected himself as to the essential elements of the offence. In doing so, he erred in law.

[21] In addition, I will deal briefly with judicial notice in the context in which it arose in this case.

[22] A court may accept without the requirement of proof facts that are either "(1) so notorious or generally accepted as not to be the subject of debate among reasonable persons; or (2) capable of immediate and accurate demonstration by resort to readily accessible sources of indisputable accuracy": *R v. Find*, [2001] 1 SCR 863 (SCC), at para. 48. The dictionary meaning of words may fall within the latter category: see J. Sopinka, S.N. Lederman and A.W. Bryant, *The Law of Evidence in Canada* (2nd ed. 1999), at § 19.13 and § 19.22.

[23] The Crown presented the trial judge with five dictionaries demonstrating a relationship between "Roma" and "gypsy." For example, the *New Oxford Dictionary of English* (1998) contained the following definitions:

> **gypsy** (also **gipsy**): **noun** (pl. **-ies**) a member of a travelling people with dark skin and hair, speaking a language, (Romany) related to Hindi, and traditionally living by seasonal work, itinerant trade, and fortune-telling. Gypsies are now found mostly in Europe, parts of North Africa, and North America, but are believed to have originated in the Indian subcontinent.
>
> **Rom: noun** (pl. **Roma**/…) a gypsy, especially a man.
> —origin mid 19th cent.: abbreviation of **ROMANY**.
>
> **Romany: noun** (pl. **-ies**) **1** (mass noun) the language of the gypsies, which is an Indo-European language related to Hindi. It is spoken by a dispersed group of about 1 million people, and has many dialects.
> **2** A gypsy.

[24] The dictionary definitions presented to the trial judge hence showed that "gypsy" can refer to an ethnic group properly known as "Roma," "Rom," or "Romany." I see no reason why the trial judge should not have taken judicial notice of that fact and then considered it, together with the rest of the evidence, to determine whether there was proof beyond a reasonable doubt that the respondents did in fact intend to target Roma.

V. Disposition

[25] For these reasons, I would allow the appeal, set aside the acquittals and order new trials.

NOTES AND QUESTIONS

1. Is the approach to judicial notice of historical facts in *Zundel (No 1)* consistent with *Zundel (No 2)*?

2. In these cases courts struggle when asked to take judicial notice of a central or dispositive fact. Why was it appropriate to take judicial notice in *Krymowski* but not in *Zundel (No 1)*? Would you be prepared to take judicial notice that "ecstasy" is indeed N-methyl-3,4-methylenedioxyamphetamine (N,alpha-dimethyl-1,3-benzodioxole-5-ethanamine)? See *Saad v United States of America* (2004), 183 CCC (3d) 97 (Ont CA). Would you take judicial notice that condom use during sex always negates a significant risk of serious bodily harm? See *R v Mabior*, 2012 SCC 47.

3. There are several cases in which courts of appeal have admonished trial judges who took judicial notice of facts without advising the parties. Compare *Dean v Brown*, 2002 NSCA 124, 209 NSR (2d) 70 with *Cronk v Canadian General Insurance Co* (1995), 25 OR (3d) 505 (CA). On the other hand, Justice Binnie has argued that "[t]he Court will, if necessary, unleash its own research machinery on matters of legislative fact or social fact that turn out to be important but that the parties failed to address in their evidence." (*Supra* at 560.) After noting some authority for this point, he explained why the Supreme Court of Canada may proceed in this manner: "The correct resolution of these [Charter] cases has an importance well beyond the interest of the immediate parties. Those affected by the result who are not before the Court should not be burdened by a result that is produced by inadequate counsel-work. This may on occasion require a more aggressive resort to judicial notice, but this is preferable, if appropriate care is taken, to a potential miscarriage of justice." (*Ibid* at 561.)

D. Legislative Facts

As explained in *Danson* above, legislative facts are those "that establish the purpose and background of legislation, including its social, economic and cultural context." Should legislative facts also be taken to include facts about the empirical effects of legislation, for example, for the purposes of determining whether a limit on a Charter right should be upheld under s 1?

In many cases the dispute is not about a particular law, legislative policy, or legislative effects—classic "legislative facts"—but rather about society or human behaviour. These are called "social" framework or context facts and are often the subject of judicial notice. For example, rather than require proof in every family law case that women tend to suffer in financial terms upon marital breakdown as contrasted to men, or that it costs more to raise a child as the child gets older, the Supreme Court of Canada has taken judicial notice of these social facts (see *Moge v Moge*, [1992] 3 SCR 813 and *Willick v Willick*, [1994] 3 SCR 670). None of this is completely uncontroversial, but it is justified on the basis that it would be inefficient to make parties repeat the expensive exercise of proving points that arise in countless marital breakdown cases. More complicated are cases where counsel assert that the general social facts lead to particular inferences that are then relied on to support a Charter claim in a specific case. This move from the general to the particular can be fraught with dangers, as explained by the Supreme Court of Canada in the two major cases below: *R v Find* and *R v Spence*.

Accused persons have the right to challenge a potential juror "for cause" if it can be established that a juror may not be impartial. In both cases the accused chose a trial by jury. In *Find*, a male accused was charged with sexual offences against children; in *Spence*, a black accused was charged with robbing an East Asian man. In the earlier decision in *R v Williams*, [1998] 1 SCR 1128, the court held that widespread prejudice against the accused's racial group may permit an accused to challenge for cause. In *Find*, the accused argued that a court could take judicial notice that the nature of the crimes gave rise to a realistic possibility that some prospective jurors might harbour such prejudice that they would be unable to act impartially and try the case solely on the evidence before them. In *Spence*, the accused sought to challenge potential jurors for cause, arguing that jurors who are East Indian may feel a natural sympathy for a victim of the same race and that race-based sympathy for the victim aggravates or compounds the potential racial prejudice against a black accused.

R v Find
2001 SCC 32, [2001] 1 SCR 863
McLachlin CJ and L'Heureux-Dubé, Gonthier, Iacobucci, Major,
Bastarache, Binnie, Arbour, and LeBel JJ (24 May 2001)

McLACHLIN CJ:

. . .

[6] The appellant was tried on 21 counts of sexual assault involving three complainants, who ranged between the ages of 6 and 12 at the time of the alleged offences. Prior to jury selection, defence counsel applied to challenge potential jurors for cause. No evidence was led in support of this application; rather, defence counsel contended a realistic potential for juror partiality arose from the ages of the alleged victims, the high number of alleged assaults, and the alleged use of violence. Defence counsel proposed that the following questions be put to potential jurors:

> Do you have strong feelings about the issue of rape and violence on young children?
>
> If so, what are those feelings based on?
>
> Would those strong feelings concerning the rape and violence on young children prevent you from giving Mr. Find a fair trial based solely on the evidence given during the trial of this case?

The trial judge, in a brief oral ruling, dismissed the application on the basis that it simply "doesn't fall anywhere near the dicta of the Court of Appeal in *Regina v. Parks*" (in *R v. Parks* (1993), 84 CCC (3d) 353 (Ont. CA), the Ontario Court of Appeal held that the accused was entitled to challenge potential jurors for cause on the basis of racial prejudice).

[7] Later, during the process of empanelling the jury, a potential juror spontaneously offered that he had two children, stating "I just don't think I could separate myself from my feelings towards them and separate the case." This prospective juror was peremptorily challenged, and defence counsel renewed the request to challenge for cause, to no avail. The appellant was tried and convicted on 17 of the 21 counts.

[8] The appellant appealed on the ground, *inter alia*, that the trial judge erred in not allowing challenges for cause. The spontaneous admission of the potential juror during the selection process was the only evidence relied upon before the Ontario Court of Appeal. The majority, *per* McMurtry CJO, held that this admission did not demonstrate a realistic potential for partiality and offered no evidentiary basis for allowing challenges for cause: (1999), 126 OAC 261 (Ont. CA), at para. 8. Since no other evidence was led, the appellant could succeed only if the court could take judicial notice of a widespread bias in the community in relation to sexual offences of this kind. The majority held that judicial notice could not be taken of that fact, for the reasons articulated in *R v. K. (A.)* (1999), 45 OR (3d) 641 (Ont. CA), a judgment released concurrently. Moldaver JA dissented on the challenge for cause issue, also relying on his reasons from *K. (A.)*. Since both opinions import the substance of their reasons from the companion case of *K. (A.)*, it is necessary to consider this case in some detail.

[9] *K. (A.)* involved two brothers charged with the sexual assault of children aged 4 to 12 years at the time of the alleged assaults. The majority of the Court of Appeal, *per* Charron JA, upheld the trial judge's decision to deny challenges for cause, while allowing the appeal on other grounds. Charron JA emphasized the distinction between racial prejudice and prejudice against persons charged with sexual assault, arguing that the first goes to a want of indifference towards the accused while the second relates to a want of indifference towards the nature of the crime. The connection between racial prejudice and a particular accused is direct and logical, whereas "strong attitudes about a particular crime, even when accompanied by intense feelings of hostility and resentment towards those who commit the crime, will rarely, if ever, translate into partiality in respect of the accused" (para. 41). She rejected the argument that this Court's decision in *Williams*, … [*R v Williams*, [1998] 1 SCR 1128], expanded the right to challenge for cause. While *Williams* recognized the possibility of bias arising from the nature of an offence, it did not eliminate the need to show a realistic potential for partiality, which remains the governing test for challenges for cause. This test was not met in the case before the court.

[10] Charron JA found little support for the accused's application in statistics indicating widespread sexual abuse in Canadian society. These statistics, she observed, only demonstrate the prevalence of abuse; they do not indicate a resultant bias, let alone the nature of that bias or its impact on jury deliberation. To her mind, they did not support the inference that there exists a realistic risk of juror partiality. As to the appellant's contention that widespread attitudes about sexual offences may cause jurors to act contrary to their oath, Charron JA concluded that the material before the court did not describe the alleged attitudes, or indicate how they would affect juror behaviour. She noted that the work of Professor Neil Vidmar, often advanced in support of the concept of generic prejudice, is the subject of heated debate and suffers from a number of flaws, most notably a lack of attention to the impact of juror attitudes on deliberation behaviour.

[11] Charron JA also found that the presence of "strong feelings, opinions and beliefs" is not so notorious as to be the subject of judicial notice—in fact, it was unclear exactly what beliefs and opinions were being targeted for judicial notice. Beliefs and opinions regarding allegations of sexual abuse are all over the map: some believe children never lie about abuse, others believe that children are especially susceptible to the influence of adults, and that their testimony should not be relied upon; some believe the trial system to be stacked in favour of the accused, others the complainant. Even if these opinions and

beliefs are accepted as widespread, they are likely to be diffused in deliberation. The exist-ence of feelings, opinions and beliefs about the crime of sexual assault does not translate into partiality—jurors are neither presumed, nor desired, to function as blank slates.

[12] Finally, Charron JA remained unconvinced by evidence that a high proportion of prospective jurors were successfully challenged for cause in cases where challenges were allowed. She found it "impossible to draw any meaningful inference from the answers provided by the jurors when confronted with general questions such as those found ... in this case and in other cases relied upon" (*K. (A.)*, *supra*, at para. 51). Many of the re-sponses demonstrated nothing more than that the candidate would have difficulty hearing the case. No meaningful direction had been provided by the trial judge on the nature of jury duty or the meaning of impartiality, and no distinction drawn between partiality and the beliefs, emotions and opinions that influence all decision making.

[13] Moldaver JA, dissenting on this issue, was satisfied that a "realistic potential" of juror partiality arises from the nature of sexual assault charges, grounding a right in the accused to challenge prospective jurors for cause. Considering the evidence in its entirety, and taking judicial notice of what he found to be notorious facts, he made a number of preliminary findings: (1) sexual abuse impacts a large percentage of the population, supporting a reasonable inference that any jury panel may contain victims, perpetrators and people closely associated with them; (2) the effects of sexual abuse, or wrongful al-legations, are potentially devastating and lifelong; (3) sexual assault tends to be committed along gender lines; (4) women and children have been subjected to systemic discrimin-ation, including in the justice system—recent changes have gone too far for some, but not far enough for others; (5) where challenges for cause have been permitted, literally hun-dreds of potential jurors have been found partial; and (6) unlike many crimes, a wide variety of stereotypes and beliefs surround the crime of sexual abuse.

[14] Moldaver JA concluded that these factors, in combination, raised a realistic concern about juror partiality. At the very least, they left him in doubt, which should be resolved in favour of the accused: *Williams*, *supra*, at para. 22. While asserting that chal-lenges for cause based on the nature of the offence are exceptional, he concluded that "unlike other crimes, by its nature, the crime of sexual abuse can give rise to intense and deep-seated biases that may be immune to judicial cleansing and highly prejudicial to an accused" (*K. (A.)*, *supra*, at para. 189).

[15] Two arguments held particular sway with Moldaver JA. First, he accepted that the high incidence of juror disqualification where challenges for cause were allowed disclosed the existence of a widespread bias against persons charged with sexual assault. Second, he adopted Professor David Paciocco's theory that the prevalence of sexual as-sault and the politicization of this offence have created two groups of people, "dogmatists" and "victims," both of which contain people who may be unable to set aside their political convictions or experiences with abuse to render an impartial decision.

· · ·

[25] One ground for challenge for cause is that a prospective juror is "not indifferent between the Queen and the accused": *Criminal Code*, s. 638(1)(*b*). If the judge is satisfied that a realistic potential for juror partiality exists, he or she may permit the requested challenges for cause. If challenged for cause, the impartiality of the candidate is tried by two triers of fact, usually two previously sworn jurors: *Criminal Code*, s. 640(2). Absent elimination, the juror is sworn and takes his or her place in the jury box. After the full

complement of 12 jurors is empanelled, the accused is placed in their charge, and the trial commences.

[26] The Canadian system of selecting jurors may be contrasted with procedures prevalent in the United States. In both countries the aim is to select a jury that will decide the case impartially. The Canadian system, however, starts from the presumption that jurors are capable of setting aside their views and prejudices and acting impartially between the prosecution and the accused upon proper instruction by the trial judge on their duties. This presumption is displaced only where potential bias is either clear and obvious (addressed by judicial pre-screening), or where the accused or prosecution shows reason to suspect that members of the jury array may possess biases that cannot be set aside (addressed by the challenge for cause process). The American system, by contrast, treats all members of the jury pool as presumptively suspect, and hence includes a preliminary *voir dire* process, whereby prospective jurors are frequently subjected to extensive questioning, often of a highly personal nature, to guide the respective parties in exercising their peremptory challenges and challenges for cause.

· · ·

B. The Test: When Should Challenges for Cause Be Granted Under Section 638(1)(b)?

1. The Test for Partiality

· · ·

[32] As a practical matter, establishing a realistic potential for juror partiality generally requires satisfying the court on two matters: (1) that a widespread bias exists in the community; and (2) that some jurors may be incapable of setting aside this bias, despite trial safeguards, to render an impartial decision. These two components of the challenge for cause test reflect, respectively, the *attitudinal* and *behavioural* components of partiality: *Parks, supra*, at pp. 364-65; *R v. B. (A.)* (1997), 115 CCC (3d) 421 (Ont. CA), at pp. 435-36.

[33] These two components of the test involve distinct inquiries. The first is concerned with the existence of a material bias, and the second with the potential effect of the bias on the trial process. However, the overarching consideration, in all cases, is whether there exists a realistic potential for partial juror behaviour. The two components of this test serve to ensure that all aspects of the issue are examined. They are not water-tight compartments, but rather guidelines for determining whether, on the record before the court, a realistic possibility exists that some jurors may decide the case on the basis of preconceived attitudes or beliefs, rather than the evidence placed before them.

[34] The test for partiality involves two key concepts: "bias" and "widespread." It is important to understand how each term is used.

[35] The *New Oxford Dictionary of English* (1998), at p. 169, defines "bias" as "prejudice in favour of or against one thing, person, or group compared with another, especially in a way considered to be unfair." "Bias," in the context of challenges for cause, refers to an attitude that could lead jurors to discharge their function in the case at hand in a prejudicial and unfair manner.

[36] It is evident from the definition of bias that not every emotional or stereotypical attitude constitutes bias. Prejudice capable of unfairly affecting the outcome of the case is required. Bias is not determined at large, but in the context of the specific case. What

must be shown is a bias that could, as a matter of logic and experience, incline a juror to a certain party or conclusion in a manner that is unfair. This is determined without regard to the cleansing effect of trial safeguards and the direction of the trial judge, which become relevant only at the second stage consideration of the behavioural effect of the bias.

[37] Courts have recognized that "bias" may flow from a number of different attitudes, including: a personal interest in the matter to be tried ... ; prejudice arising from prior exposure to the case, as in the case of pre-trial publicity ... ; and prejudice against members of the accused's social or racial group (*Williams*, *supra*, at para. 14).

[38] In addition, some have suggested that bias may result from the nature and circumstances of the offence with which the accused is charged: *R v. L. (R.)* (1996), 3 CR (5th) 70 (Ont. Ct. (Gen. Div.)); *R v. Mattingly* (1994), 28 CR (4th) 262 (Ont. Ct. (Gen. Div.)); N. Vidmar, "Generic Prejudice and the Presumption of Guilt in Sex Abuse Trials" (1997), 21 *Law & Hum. Behav.* 5. In *Williams*, *supra*, at para. 10, this Court referred to Vidmar's suggestion that bias might, in some cases, flow from the nature of the offence. However, the Court has not, prior to this case, directly considered this kind of bias.

[39] The second concept, "widespread," relates to the prevalence or incidence of the bias in question. Generally speaking, the alleged bias must be established as sufficiently pervasive in the community to raise the possibility that it may be harboured by one or more members of a representative jury pool (although, in exceptional circumstances, a less prevalent bias may suffice, provided it raises a realistic potential of juror partiality: *Williams*, *supra*, at para. 43). If only a few individuals in the community hold the alleged bias, the chances of this bias tainting the jury process are negligible. For this reason, a court must generally be satisfied that the alleged bias is widespread in the community before a right to challenge for cause may flow.

[40] If widespread bias is shown, a second question arises: may some jurors be unable to set aside their bias despite the cleansing effect of the judge's instructions and the trial process? This is the behavioural component of the test. The law accepts that jurors may enter the trial with biases. But the law presumes that jurors' views and biases will be cleansed by the trial process. It therefore does not permit a party to challenge their right to sit on the jury because of the existence of widespread bias alone.

[The court then discussed the evolution of trial procedure to counter biases, and explained that diversity of views and outlooks, rather than the jettisoning of them, is critical to the jury system.]

2. *Proof: How a Realistic Potential for Partiality May Be Established*

[46] A party may displace the presumption of juror impartiality by calling evidence, by asking the judge to take judicial notice of facts, or both. In addition, the judge may draw inferences from events that occur in the proceedings and may make common sense inferences about how certain biases, if proved, may affect the decision-making process.

[47] The first branch of the inquiry—establishing relevant widespread bias requires evidence, judicial notice or trial events demonstrating a pervasive bias in the community. The second stage of the inquiry—establishing a behavioural link between widespread attitudes and juror conduct—may be a matter of proof, judicial notice, or simply reasonable inference as to how bias might influence the decision-making process: *Williams*, *supra*, at para. 23.

[48] In this case, the appellant relies heavily on proof by judicial notice. Judicial notice dispenses with the need for proof of facts that are clearly uncontroversial or beyond reasonable dispute. Facts judicially noticed are not proved by evidence under oath. Nor are they tested by cross-examination. Therefore, the threshold for judicial notice is strict: a court may properly take judicial notice of facts that are either: (1) so notorious or generally accepted as not to be the subject of debate among reasonable persons; or (2) capable of immediate and accurate demonstration by resort to readily accessible sources of indisputable accuracy: *R v. Potts* (1982), 66 CCC (2d) 219 (Ont. CA); J. Sopinka, S.N. Lederman and A.W. Bryant, *The Law of Evidence in Canada* (2nd ed. 1999), at p. 1055.

[49] The scientific and statistical nature of much of the information relied upon by the appellant further complicates this case. Expert evidence is by definition neither notorious nor capable of immediate and accurate demonstration. This is why it must be proved through an expert whose qualifications are accepted by the court and who is available for cross-examination. As Doherty JA stated in *R v. Alli* (1996), 110 CCC (3d) 283 (Ont. CA), at p. 285: "[a]ppellate analysis of untested social science data should not be regarded as the accepted means by which the scope of challenges for cause based on generic prejudice will be settled."

C. Were the Grounds for Challenge for Cause Present in This Case?

[50] To challenge prospective jurors for cause, the appellant must displace the presumption of juror impartiality by showing a realistic potential for partiality. To do this, the appellant must demonstrate the existence of a widespread bias arising from the nature of the charges against him (the "attitudinal" component), that raises a realistic potential for partial juror behaviour despite the safeguards of the trial process (the "behavioural" component). I will discuss each of these requirements in turn as they apply to this case.

1. Widespread Bias

[51] In this case, the appellant alleges that the nature and the circumstances of the offence with which he is charged give rise to a bias that could unfairly incline jurors against him or toward his conviction. He further alleges that this bias is widespread in the community. In support of this submission, the appellant relies on the following propositions from Moldaver JA's dissent in *K. (A.)*, *supra*, at para. 166. The parties generally agree on these facts, but dispute the conclusions to be drawn from them:

- Studies and surveys conducted in Canada over the past two decades reveal that a large percentage of the population, both male and female, have been the victims of sexual abuse. From this, it is reasonable to infer that any given jury panel may contain victims of sexual abuse, perpetrators and people closely associated with them.
- The harmful effects of sexual abuse can prove devastating not only to those who have been victimized, but those closely related to them. Tragically, many victims remain traumatized and psychologically scarred for life. By the same token, for those few individuals who have been wrongfully accused of sexual abuse, the effects can also be devastating.
- Sexual assault tends to be committed along gender lines. As a rule, it is women and children who are victimized by men.

- Women and children have been subjected to systemic discrimination reflected in both individual and institutional conduct, including the criminal justice system. As a result of widespread media coverage and the earnest and effective efforts of lobby groups in the past decade, significant and long overdue changes have come about in the criminal justice system. For some, the changes have not gone far enough; for others, too far.
- Where challenges for cause have been permitted in cases involving allegations of sexual abuse, literally hundreds of prospective jurors have been found to be partial by the triers of fact. In those cases where trial judges have refused to permit the challenge, choosing instead to vet the panel at large for bias, the numbers are equally substantial.
- Unlike many crimes, there are a wide variety of stereotypical attitudes and beliefs surrounding the crime of sexual abuse.

[52] While the parties agree on these basic facts, they disagree on whether they demonstrate widespread bias. The appellant called no evidence, expert or otherwise, on the incidence or likely effect of prejudice stemming from the nature of the offences with which he is charged. Instead, he asks the Court to take judicial notice of a widespread bias arising from allegations of the sexual assault of children. The Crown, by contrast, argues that the facts on which it agrees do not translate into bias, much less widespread bias.

[53] The appellant relies on the following: (a) the incidence of victimization and its effect on members of the jury pool; (b) the strong views held by many about sexual assault and the treatment of this crime by the criminal justice system; (c) myths and stereotypes arising from widespread and deeply entrenched attitudes about sexual assault; (d) the incidence of intense emotional reactions to sexual assault, such as a strong aversion to the crime or undue empathy for its victims; (e) the experience of Ontario trial courts, where hundreds of potential jurors in such cases have been successfully challenged as partial; and (f) social science research indicating a "generic prejudice" against the accused in sexual assault cases. He argues that these factors permit the Court to take judicial notice of widespread bias arising from charges of sexual assault of children.

[54] It is worth reminding ourselves that at this stage we are concerned solely with the nature and prevalence of the alleged biases (i.e., the "attitudinal" component), and not their amenability to cleansing by the trial process, which is the focus of the "behavioural" component.

(a) Incidence of Victimization

[55] The appellant argues that the prevalence and potentially devastating impact of sexual assault permit the Court to conclude that any given jury pool is likely to contain victims or those close to them who may harbour a prejudicial bias as a consequence of their experiences.

[56] The Crown acknowledges both the widespread nature of abuse and its potentially traumatic impact. Neither of these facts is in issue. Nor is it unreasonable to conclude from these facts that victims of sexual assault, or those close to them, may turn up in a jury panel. What is disputed is whether this widespread victimization permits the Court to conclude, without proof, that the victims and those who share their experience are biased, in the sense that they may harbour prejudice against the accused or in favour of the Crown when trying sexual assault charges.

[57] The only social science research before us on the issue of victim empathy is a study by R.L. Wiener, A.T. Feldman Wiener and T. Grisso, "Empathy and Biased Assimilation of Testimonies in Cases of Alleged Rape" (1989) 13 *Law & Hum. Behav.* 343. The appellant cites this study for the proposition that those participants acquainted in some way with a rape victim demonstrated a greater tendency, under the circumstances of the study, to find a defendant guilty. However, as the Crown notes, this study offers no evidence that victim status *in itself* impacts jury verdicts. In fact, the study found no correlation between degree of empathy for rape victims and tendency to convict, nor did it find higher degrees of victim empathy amongst those persons acquainted with rape victims. Further, the study was limited to a small sample of participants. It made no attempt to simulate an actual jury trial, and did not involve a deliberation process or an actual verdict. In the absence of expert testimony, tested under cross-examination, as to the conclusions properly supported by this study, I can only conclude that it provides little assistance in establishing the existence of widespread bias arising from the incidence of sexual assault in Canadian society.

[58] Moldaver JA concluded that the prevalence of sexual assault in Canadian society and its traumatic and potentially lifelong effects, [*sic*] provided a realistic basis to believe that victims of this crime may harbor intense and deep-seated biases. In arriving at this conclusion, he expressly relied on an unpublished article by Professor David Paciocco, "Challenges for Cause in Jury Selection after *Regina v. Parks*: Practicalities and Limitations," Canadian Bar Association—Ontario, February 11, 1995, which he quoted at para. 176 for the proposition that "[o]ne cannot help but believe that these deep scars would, for some, prevent them from adjudicating sexual offence violations impartially."

[59] This is, however, merely the statement of an assumption, offered without a supporting foundation of evidence or research. Courts must approach sweeping and untested "common sense" assumptions about the behaviour of abuse victims with caution: see *R v. Seaboyer*, [1991] 2 SCR 577 (*per* L'Heureux-Dubé J, dissenting in part); *R v. Lavallee*, [1990] 1 SCR 852, at pp. 870-72 (*per* Wilson J). Certainly these assumptions are not established beyond reasonable dispute, or documented with indisputable accuracy, so as to permit the Court to take judicial notice of them.

[60] I conclude that while widespread victimization may be a factor to be considered, standing alone it fails to establish widespread bias that might lead jurors to discharge their task in a prejudicial and unfair manner.

(b) Strongly Held Views Relating to Sexual Offences

[61] The appellant submits that the politicized and gender-based nature of sexual offences gives rise to firmly held beliefs, opinions and attitudes that establish widespread bias in cases of sexual assault.

[62] This argument found favour with Moldaver JA in *K. (A.)*. Moldaver JA judicially noticed the tendency of sexual assault to be committed along gender lines. He also took judicial notice of the systemic discrimination women and children have faced in the criminal justice system, and the fact that recent reforms have gone too far for some and not far enough for others. From this foundation of facts, he inferred that the gender-based and politicized nature of sexual offences leads to a realistic possibility that some members of the jury pool, as a result of their political beliefs, will harbour deep-seated and virulent

biases that might prove resistant to judicial cleansing. Quoting from the work of Professor Paciocco, Moldaver JA emphasized that strong political convictions and impartiality are not necessarily incongruous, but that for some "feminists" "commitment gives way to zealotry and dogma." The conviction that the justice system and its rules are incapable of protecting women and children, it is argued, may lead some potential jurors to disregard trial directions and rules safeguarding the presumption of innocence. Little regard for judicial direction can be expected from "those who see the prosecution of sexual offenders as a battlefront in a gender based war" (para. 177).

[63] The appellant supports this reasoning, adding that the polarized, politically charged nature of sexual offences results in two prevalent social attitudes: first, that the criminal justice system is incapable of dealing with an "epidemic" of abuse because of its male bias or the excessive protections it affords the accused; and second, that conviction rates in sexual offence cases are unacceptably low. These beliefs, he alleges, may jeopardize the accused's right to a fair trial. For example, jurors harbouring excessive political zeal may ignore trial directions and legal rules perceived as obstructing the "truth" of what occurred, or may simply "cast their lot" with the victim. All this, the appellant submits, amounts to widespread bias in the community incompatible with juror impartiality.

[64] The appellant does not deny that jurors trying any serious offence may hold strong views about the relevant law. Nor does he suggest such views raise concerns about bias in the trial of most offences. Few rules of criminal law attract universal support, and many engender heated debate. The treatment of virtually all serious crimes attracts sharply divided opinion, fervent criticism, and advocacy for reform. General disagreement or criticism of the relevant law, however, does not mean a prospective juror is inclined to take the law into his or her own hands at the expense of an individual accused.

[65] The appellant's submission reduces to this: while strong views on the law do not ordinarily indicate bias, an exception arises in the case of sexual assaults on children. The difficulty, however, is that there is nothing in the material that supports this contention, nor is it self-evident. There is no indication that jurors are more willing to cross the line from opinion to prejudice in relation to sexual assault than for any other serious crime. It is therefore far from clear that strongly held views about sexual assault translate into bias, in the required sense of a tendency to act in an unfair and prejudicial manner.

[66] Moreover, assuming that the strong views people may hold about sexual assault raise the possibility of bias, how widespread such views are in Canadian society remains a matter of conjecture. The material before the Court offers no measure of the prevalence in Canadian society of the specific attitudes identified by the appellant as corrosive of juror impartiality. Some people may indeed believe that the justice system is faltering in the face of an epidemic of abuse and that perpetrators of this crime too often escape conviction; yet, it is far from clear that these beliefs are prevalent in our society, let alone that they translate into bias on a widespread scale.

(c) Myths and Stereotypes About Sexual Offences

[67] The appellant suggests that the strong views that surround the crime of sexual assault may contribute to widespread myths and stereotypes that undermine juror impartiality. In any given jury pool, he argues, some people may reason from the prevalence of abuse to the conclusion that the accused is likely guilty; some may assume children

never lie about abuse; and some may reason that the accused is more likely to be guilty because he is a man.

[68] Again, however, the proof falls short. Although these stereotypical beliefs clearly amount to bias that might incline some people against the accused or toward conviction, it is neither notorious nor indisputable that they enjoy widespread acceptance in Canadian society. Myths and stereotypes do indeed pervade public perceptions of sexual assault. Some favour the accused, others the Crown. In the absence of evidence, however, it is difficult to conclude that these stereotypes translate into widespread bias.

(d) Emotional Nature of Sexual Assault Trials

[69] The appellant asks the Court to take judicial notice of the emotional nature of sexual assault trials and to conclude that fear, empathy for the victim, and abhorrence of the crime establish widespread bias in the community. His concern is that jurors, faced with allegations of sexual assaults of children, may act on emotion rather than reason. This is particularly the case, he suggests, for past victims of abuse, for whom the moral repugnancy of the crime may be amplified. He emphasizes that the presumption of innocence in criminal trials demands the acquittal of the "probably" guilty. An intense aversion to sexual crimes, he argues, may incline some jurors to err on the side of conviction in such circumstances. Undue empathy for the victim, he adds, may also prompt a juror to "validate" the complaint with a guilty verdict, rather than determine guilt or innocence according to the law.

[70] Crimes commonly arouse deep and strong emotions. They represent a fundamental breach of the perpetrator's compact with society. Crimes make victims, and jurors cannot help but sympathize with them. Yet these indisputable facts do not necessarily establish bias, in the sense of an attitude that could unfairly prejudice jurors against the accused or toward conviction. Many crimes routinely tried by jurors are abhorrent. Brutal murders, ruthless frauds and violent attacks are standard fare for jurors. Abhorred as they are, these crimes seldom provoke suggestions of bias incompatible with a fair verdict.

[71] One cannot automatically equate strong emotions with an unfair and prejudicial bias against the accused. Jurors are not expected to be indifferent toward crimes. Nor are they expected to remain neutral toward those shown to have committed such offences. If this were the case, prospective jurors would be routinely and successfully challenged for cause as a preliminary stage in the trial of all serious criminal offences. Instead, we accept that jurors often abhor the crime alleged to have been committed—indeed there would be cause for alarm if representatives of a community did *not* deplore heinous criminal acts. It would be equally alarming if jurors did not feel empathy or compassion for persons shown to be victims of such acts. These facts alone do not establish bias. There is simply no indication that these attitudes, commendable in themselves, unfairly prejudice jurors against the accused or toward conviction. They are common to the trial of many serious offences and have never grounded a right to challenge for cause.

[72] Recognizing this fact, the appellant and the intervener Criminal Lawyers' Association ("CLA") contend that allegations of sexual offences against children incite emotional reactions of an intensity *above and beyond* those invoked by other criminal acts. Such offences, they contend, stand alone in their capacity to inflame jurors and cloud reason. Moldaver JA, dissenting in *K. (A.)*, distinguished sexual offences from most other despicable

criminal acts, on the basis that "sexual assault trials tend to be emotionally charged, particularly in cases of child abuse, where the mere allegation can trigger feelings of hostility, resentment and disgust in the minds of jurors" (para. 188).

[73] The proposition that sexual offences are generically different from other crimes in their ability to arouse strong passion is not beyond reasonable debate or capable of immediate and accurate demonstration. As such, it does not lend itself to judicial notice. Nor was evidence led on this issue. Some may well react to allegations of a sexual crime with emotions of the intensity described by the appellant. Yet how prevalent such emotions are in Canadian society remains a matter of conjecture. The Court simply cannot reach conclusions on these controversial matters in an evidentiary vacuum. As a result, the appellant has not established the existence of an identifiable bias arising from the emotionally charged nature of sexual crimes, or the prevalence of this bias should it in fact exist.

(e)   The History of Challenges for Cause in Ontario

[74] The appellant refers this Court to the experience of Ontario trial courts where judges have allowed defence counsel to challenge prospective jurors for cause in cases involving allegations of sexual assault: see Vidmar, *supra*, at p. 5; D.M. Tanovich, D.M. Paciocco, S. Skurka, *Jury Selection in Criminal Trials: Skills, Science, and the Law* (1997), at pp. 239-42. These sources, cataloguing 34 cases, indicate that hundreds of potential jurors have been successfully challenged for cause as not indifferent between the Crown and the accused. It is estimated that 36 percent of the prospective jurors challenged were disqualified.

[75] The appellant argues that the fact that hundreds of prospective jurors have been found to be partial is in itself sufficient evidence of widespread bias arising from sexual assault trials. This is proof, he asserts, that the social realities surrounding sexual assault trials give rise to prejudicial beliefs, attitudes and emotions on a widespread scale in Canadian communities.

[76] The Crown disagrees. It argues first, that the survey lacks validity because of methodological defects, and second, that even if the results are accepted, the successful challenges do not demonstrate a widespread bias, but instead may be attributed to other causes.

[77] The first argument against the survey is that its methodology is unsound. The Crown raises a number of concerns: the survey is entirely anecdotal, not comprehensive or random; not all of the questions asked of prospective jurors are indicated; there is no way in which to assess the directions, if any, provided by the trial judge, especially in relation to the distinction between strong opinions or emotions and partiality; and no comparative statistics are provided contrasting these results with the experience in other criminal law contexts. The intervener CLA concedes that the survey falls short of scientific validity, but contends that it nevertheless documents a phenomena of considerable significance. Hundreds of prospective jurors disqualified on the grounds of bias by impartial triers of fact must, it is argued, displace the presumption of juror impartiality. Nonetheless, the lack of methodological rigour and the absence of expert evidence undermine the suggestion that the Ontario experience establishes widespread bias.

[78] The second argument against the survey is that the questions asked were so general, and the information elicited so scarce, that no meaningful inference can be drawn from the responses given by challenged jurors or from the number of potential jurors

disqualified. Charron JA, for the majority in *K. (A.)*, observed that prospective jurors in that case received no meaningful instruction on the nature of jury duty or the meaning and importance of impartiality. Further, they often indicated confusion at the questions posed to them or asked that the questions be repeated. In the end, numerous prospective jurors were disqualified for offering little more than that they would find it difficult to hear a case of this nature, or that they held strong emotions about the sexual abuse of children.

[79] The challenge for cause process rests to a considerable extent on self-assessment of impartiality by the challenged juror, and the response to questions on challenge often will be little more than an affirmation or denial of one's own ability to act impartially in the circumstances of the case. In the absence of guidance, prospective jurors may conflate disqualifying bias with a legitimate apprehension about sitting through a case involving allegations of sexual abuse of children, or the strong views or emotions they may hold on this subject.

[80] Where potential jurors are challenged for racial bias, the risk of social disapprobation and stigma supports the veracity of admissions of potential partiality. No similar indicia of reliability attach to the frank and open admission of concern about one's ability to approach and decide a case of alleged child sexual abuse judiciously. While a prospective juror's admission of racial prejudice may suggest partiality, the same cannot be said of an admission of abhorrence or other emotional attitude toward the sexual abuse of children. We do not know whether the potential jurors who professed concerns about serving on juries for sexual assault charges were doing so because they were biased, or for other reasons. We do not know whether they were told that strong emotions and beliefs would not in themselves impair their duty of impartiality, or whether they were informed of the protections built into the trial process.

[81] In fact, the number of prospective jurors disqualified, although relied on as support for judicial notice of widespread bias, is equally consistent with the conclusion that the challenge processes, despite the best intentions of the participants, disqualified prospective jurors for acknowledging the intense emotions, beliefs, experiences and misgivings anyone might experience when confronted with the prospect of sitting as a juror on a case involving charges of sexual assault of children. As discussed, the mere presence of strong emotions and opinions cannot be equated automatically with bias against the accused or toward conviction.

[82] It follows that the survey of past challenge for cause cases involving charges of sexual assault does not without more establish widespread bias arising from these charges.

(f) Social Science Evidence of "Generic Prejudice"

[83] The appellant argues that social science research, particularly that of Vidmar, supports the contention that social realities, such as the prevalence of sexual abuse and its politically charged nature, translate into a widespread bias in Canadian society.

[84] In *Williams, supra*, the Court referred to Vidmar's research in concluding that the partiality targeted by s. 638(1)(*b*) was not limited to biases arising from a direct interest in the proceeding or pre-trial exposure to the case, but could arise from *any* of a variety of sources, including the "nature of the crime itself" (para. 10). However, recognition that the nature of an offence may give rise to "generic prejudice" does not obviate the need for proof. Labels do not govern the availability of challenges for cause. Regardless of how a

case is classified, the ultimate issue is whether a realistic possibility exists that some potential jurors may try the case on the basis of prejudicial attitudes and beliefs, rather than the evidence offered at trial. The appellant relies on the work of Vidmar for the proposition that such a possibility does in fact arise from allegations of sexual assault.

[85] Vidmar is known for the theory of a "generic prejudice" against accused persons in sexual assault trials and for the conclusion that the attitudes and beliefs of jurors are frequently reflected in the verdicts of juries on such trials. However, the conclusions of Vidmar do not assist in finding widespread bias. His theory that a "generic prejudice" exists against those charged with sexual assault, although in the nature of expert evidence, has not been proved. Nor can the Court take judicial notice of this contested proposition. With regard to the behaviour of potential jurors, the Court has no foundation in this case to draw an inference of partial juror conduct, as discussed in more detail below, under the behavioural stage of the partiality test.

[86] Vidmar himself acknowledges the limitations of his research. He concedes that the notion of "generic prejudice" lacks scientific validity, and that none of the studies he relies on actually asked the questions typically asked of Canadian jurors, including whether they can impartially adjudicate guilt or innocence in a sexual assault trial: Vidmar, *supra*. Moreover, the authorities Vidmar relies on are almost exclusively "confined to examination of public attitudes towards certain criminal acts, especially child sexual abuse. Not surprisingly, it appears the public is quite disapproving of persons who have sexually abused children, and of such conduct itself": *R v. Hillis*, [1996] OJ No. 2739 (Gen. Div.) (QL), at para. 7. While judicial notice may be taken of the uncontested fact that sexual crimes are almost universally abhorred, this does not establish widespread bias arising from sexual assault trials.

[87] The attempt of Vidmar and others to conduct scientific research on jury behaviour is commendable. Unfortunately, research into the effect of juror attitudes on deliberations and verdicts is constrained by the almost absolute prohibition in s. 649 of the *Criminal Code* against the disclosure by jury members of information relating to the jury's proceedings. More comprehensive and scientific assessment of this and other aspects of the criminal law and criminal process would be welcome. Should Parliament reconsider this prohibition, it may be that more helpful research into the Canadian experience would emerge. But for now, social science evidence appears to cast little light on the extent of any "generic prejudice" relating to charges of sexual assault, or its relationship to jury verdicts.

(g) Conclusions on the Existence of a Relevant, Widespread Bias

[88] Do the factors cited by the appellant, taken together, establish widespread bias arising from charges relating to sexual abuse of children? In my view, they do not. The material presented by the appellant, considered in its totality, falls short of grounding judicial notice of widespread bias in Canadian society against the accused in such trials. At best, it establishes that the crime of sexual assault, like many serious crimes, frequently elicits strong attitudes and emotions.

[89] However, the two branches of the test for partiality are not water-tight compartments. Given the challenge of proving facts as elusive as the nature and scope of prejudicial attitudes, and the need to err on the side of caution, I prefer not to resolve this case entirely at the first, attitudinal stage. Out of an abundance of caution, I will proceed to consider the potential impact, if any, of the alleged biases on juror behaviour.

2. Is It Reasonable to Infer That Some Jurors May Be Incapable of Setting Aside Their Biases Despite Trial Safeguards?

[90] The fact that members of the jury pool may harbour prejudicial attitudes, opinions or feelings is not, in itself, sufficient to support an entitlement to challenge for cause. There must also exist a realistic possibility that some jurors may be unable or unwilling to set aside these prejudices to render a decision in strict accordance with the law. This is referred to as the behavioural aspect of the test for partiality.

[91] The applicant need not always adduce direct evidence establishing this link between the bias in issue and detrimental effects on the trial process. Even in the absence of such evidence, a trial judge may reasonably infer that some strains of bias by their very nature may prove difficult for jurors to identify and eliminate from their reasoning.

[92] This inference, however, is not automatic. Its strength varies with the nature of the bias in issue, and its amenability to judicial cleansing. In *Williams*, the Court inferred a behavioural link between the pervasive racial prejudice established on the evidence and the possibility that some jurors, consciously or not, would decide the case based on prejudice and stereotype. Such a result, however, is not inevitable for every form of bias, prejudice or preconception. In some circumstances, the appropriate inference is that the "predispositions can be safely regarded as curable by judicial direction": *Williams, supra*, at para. 24.

[93] Fundamental distinctions exist between the racial prejudice at issue in *Williams* and a more general bias relating to the nature of the offence itself. These differences relate both to the nature of these respective biases, and to their susceptibility (or resistance) to cleansing by the trial process. It may be useful to examine these differences before embarking on a more extensive consideration of the potential effects on the trial process, if any, of the biases alleged in the present case.

[94] The first difference is that race may impact more directly on the jury's decision than bias stemming from the nature of the offence. As Moldaver JA stated in *Betker* [*R v Betker* (1997), 33 OR (3d) 321 (CA)] at p. 441, "[r]acial prejudice is a form of bias directed against a particular class of accused by virtue of an identifiable immutable characteristic. There is a direct and logical connection between the prejudice asserted and the particular accused." By contrast, the aversion, fear, abhorrence, and beliefs alleged to surround sexual assault offences may lack this cogent and irresistible connection to the accused. Unlike racial prejudice, they do not point a finger at a particular accused.

[95] Second, trial safeguards may be less successful in cleansing racial prejudice than other types of bias, as recognized in *Williams*. As Doherty JA observed in *Parks, supra*, at p. 371: "[i]n deciding whether the post-jury selection safeguards against partiality provide a reliable antidote to racial bias, the nature of that bias must be emphasized." The nature of racial prejudice—in particular its subtle, systemic and often unconscious operation—compelled the inference in *Williams* that some people might be incapable of effacing, or even identifying, its influence on their reasoning. In reaching this conclusion, the Court emphasized the "invasive and elusive" operation of racial prejudice and its foundation "on preconceptions and unchallenged assumptions that unconsciously shape the daily behaviour of individuals" (paras. 21-22).

[96] The biases alleged in this case, by contrast, may be more susceptible to cleansing by the rigours of the trial process. They are more likely to be overt and acknowledged than is racial prejudice, and hence more easily removed. Jurors are more likely to recognize and counteract them. The trial judge is more likely to address these concerns in the course

of directions to the jury, as are counsel in their addresses. Offence-based bias has concerned the trial process throughout its long evolution, and many of the safeguards the law has developed may be seen as a response to it.

[97] Against this background, I turn to the question of whether the biases alleged to arise from the nature of sexual assault, if established, might lead jurors to decide the case in an unfair and prejudicial way, despite the cleansing effect of the trial process.

[98] First, the appellant contends that some jurors, whether victims, friends of victims, or simply people holding strong views about sexual assault, may not be able to set aside strong beliefs about this crime—for example, that the justice system is biased against complainants, that there exists an epidemic of abuse that must be halted, or that conviction rates are too low—and decide the case solely on its merits. Some jurors, he says, may disregard rules of law that are perceived as obstructing the "truth" of what occurred. Others may simply "cast their lot" with groups that have been victimized. These possibilities, he contends, support a reasonable inference that strong opinions may translate into a realistic potential for partial juror conduct.

[99] This argument cannot succeed. As discussed, strongly held political views do not necessarily suggest that jurors will act unfairly in an actual trial. Indeed, passionate advocacy for law reform may be an expression of the highest respect for the rule of law, not a sign that one is willing to subvert its operation at the expense of the accused. As Moldaver JA eloquently observed in *Betker*, *supra*, at p. 447, "the test for partiality is not whether one seeks to change the law but whether one is capable of upholding the law ... ."

[100] In the absence of evidence that such beliefs and attitudes may affect jury behaviour in an unfair manner, it is difficult to conclude that they will not be cleansed by the trial process. Only speculation supports the proposition that jurors will act on general opinions and beliefs to the detriment of an individual accused, in disregard of their oath or affirmation, the presumption of innocence, and the directions of the trial judge.

[101] The appellant also contends that myths and stereotypes attached to the crime of sexual assault may unfairly inform the deliberation of some jurors. However, strong, sometimes biased, assumptions about sexual behaviour are not new to sexual assault trials. Traditional myths and stereotypes have long tainted the assessment of the conduct and veracity of complainants in sexual assault cases—the belief that women of "unchaste" character are more likely to have consented or are less worthy of belief; that passivity or even resistance may in fact constitute consent; and that some women invite sexual assault by reason of their dress or behaviour, to name only a few. Based on overwhelming evidence from relevant social science literature, this Court has been willing to accept the prevailing existence of such myths and stereotypes: see, for example, *Seaboyer*, *supra*; *R v. Osolin*, [1993] 4 SCR 595, at pp. 669-71; *R v. Ewanchuk*, [1999] 1 SCR 330, at paras. 94-97.

[102] Child complainants may similarly be subject to stereotypical assumptions, such as the belief that stories of abuse are probably fabricated if not reported immediately, or that the testimony of children is inherently unreliable: *R v. W. (R.)*, [1992] 2 SCR 122; *R v. D. (D.)*, [2000] 2 SCR 275, 2000 SCC 43; N. Bala, "Double Victims: Child Sexual Abuse and the Canadian Criminal Justice System" in W.S. Tarnopolsky, J. Whitman and M. Ouellette, eds., *Discrimination in the Law and the Administration of Justice* (1993), 231.

[103] These myths and stereotypes about child and adult complainants are particularly invidious because they comprise part of the fabric of social "common sense" in which we

are daily immersed. Their pervasiveness, and the subtlety of their operation, create the risk that victims of abuse will be blamed or unjustly discredited in the minds of both judges and jurors.

[104] Yet the prevalence of such attitudes has never been held to justify challenges for cause as of right by Crown prosecutors. Instead, we have traditionally trusted the trial process to ensure that such attitudes will not prevent jurors from acting impartially. We have relied on the rules of evidence, statutory protections, and guidance from the judge and counsel to clarify potential misconceptions and promote a reasoned verdict based solely on the merits of the case.

[105] Absent evidence to the contrary, there is no reason to believe that stereotypical attitudes about accused persons are more elusive of these cleansing measures than stereotypical attitudes about complainants. It follows that the myths and stereotypes alleged by the appellant, even if widespread, provide little support for any inference of a behavioural link between these beliefs and the potential for juror partiality.

[106] Finally, the appellant argues that the strong emotions evoked by allegations of sexual assault, especially in cases involving child complainants, may distort the reasoning of some jurors. He emphasizes that a strongly held aversion to the offence may incline some jurors to err on the side of conviction. Others may be swayed by "undue empathy" for the alleged victim, perceiving the case as a rejection or validation of the complainant's claim, rather than a determination of the accused's guilt or innocence according to law.

[107] Again, absent evidence, it is highly speculative to suggest that the emotions surrounding sexual crimes will lead to prejudicial and unfair juror behaviour. As discussed, the safeguards of the trial process and the instructions of the trial judge are designed to replace emotional reactions with rational, dispassionate assessment. Our long experience in the context of the trial of other serious offences suggests that our faith in this cleansing process is not misplaced. The presumption of innocence, the oath or affirmation, the diffusive effects of collective deliberation, the requirement of jury unanimity, specific directions from the trial judge and counsel, a regime of evidentiary and statutory protections, the adversarial nature of the proceedings and their general solemnity, and numerous other precautions both subtle and manifest—all collaborate to keep the jury on the path to an impartial verdict despite offence-based prejudice. The appellant has not established that the offences with which he is charged give rise to a strain of bias that is uniquely capable of eluding the cleansing effect of these trial safeguards.

[108] It follows that even if widespread bias were established, we cannot safely infer, on the record before the Court, that it would lead to unfair, prejudicial and partial juror behaviour. This is not to suggest that an accused can never be prejudiced by the mere fact of the nature and circumstances of the charges he or she faces; rather, the inference between social attitudes and jury behaviour is simply far less obvious and compelling in this context, and more may be required to satisfy a court that this inference may be reasonably drawn. The nature of offence-based bias, as discussed, suggests that the circumstances in which it is found to be both widespread in the community and resistant to the safeguards of trial may prove exceptional. Nonetheless, I would not foreclose the possibility that such circumstances may arise. If widespread bias arising from sexual assault were established in a future case, it would be for the court in that case to determine whether this bias gives rise to a realistic potential for partial juror conduct in the community from which the

jury pool is drawn. I would only caution that in deciding whether to draw an inference of adverse effect on jury behaviour the court should take into account the nature of the bias and its susceptibility to cleansing by the trial process.

VI. Conclusion

[109] The case for widespread bias arising from the nature of charges of sexual assault on children is tenuous. Moreover, even if the appellant had demonstrated widespread bias, its link to actual juror behaviour is speculative, leaving the presumption that it would be cleansed by the trial process firmly in place. Many criminal trials engage strongly held views and stir up powerful emotions—indeed, even revulsion and abhorrence. Such is the nature of the trial process. Absent proof, we cannot simply assume that strong beliefs and emotions translate into a realistic potential for partiality, grounding a right to challenge for cause. I agree with the majority of the Court of Appeal that the appellant has not established that the trial judge erred in refusing to permit him to challenge prospective jurors for cause.

[110] I would dismiss the appeal and affirm the conviction.

R v Spence
2005 SCC 71
Major, Binnie, LeBel, Deschamps, Fish, Abella, and Charron JJ
(2 December 2005)

BINNIE J:

[48] It is not to be doubted that evidence of *how* and *to what extent* racial discrimination affects the behaviour of jurors is difficult to come by, as noted by Finlayson JA in *Koh* [*R v Koh* (1998), 131 CCC (3d) 257 (Ont CA)] (paras. 28 and 41). The intervener, African Canadian Legal Clinic, in a useful submission that went beyond the more case law oriented argument of the respondent, urged the Court to fill the evidentiary gap with the taking of judicial notice that where the complainant is also a member of a visible minority

> [r]acial bias can affect the fairness of the trial process … for example affecting juror assessment of credibility and weight of the evidence, shaping information received during the trial, consideration of the accused's propensity for criminality, and favouring of the Crown or witnesses. During the trial process stereotypes relating to both the complainant and the accused may interact and affect a potential juror. The operation of biases in this context is potentially harmful, unpredictable, and can skew the outcome in innumerable ways.
>
> Juror impartiality may arise from a favouring of the victim over the accused because the victim is from the same racialized group as the juror. [paras. 34-35]

[49] In taking this broad approach to judicial notice, the intervener was perhaps invoking the work of the great American expert on the law of evidence, Professor James Thayer, who wrote in 1890 that "courts may and should notice without proof, and assume

as known by others, whatever, as the phrase is, *everybody* knows" (emphasis added) (J.B. Thayer, "Judicial Notice and the Law of Evidence" (1889-90), 3 *Harv. L Rev.* 285, at p. 305). In taking this view, he is largely supported by Dean Wigmore. (See J.H. Wigmore, *Evidence in Trials at Common Law* (Chadbourn rev. 1981), vol. 9, at p. 732.) From time to time, similarly broad statements have issued from this Court. ...

[50] Professor Thayer's view was that "[i]n conducting a process of judicial reasoning, as of other reasoning, not a step can be taken without assuming something which has not been proved" (pp. 287-88). I would add the comment of Scrutton LJ:

> It is difficult to know what judges are allowed to know, though they are ridiculed if they pretend not to know.
>
> (*Tolley v. Fry*, [1930] 1 KB 467 (CA), at p. 475)

This is true, so far as it goes. ...

[51] Thayer's approach to judicial notice has its role but I do not think it helps us to solve the issue posed by the African Canadian Legal Clinic. There are at least three difficulties standing in its way. Firstly what "everybody knows" may be wrong. Until *Parks* [*R v Parks* (1993), 84 CCC (3d) 353 (Ont CA)], "everybody" knew the solemnity of a criminal trial and careful jury instructions from the judge meant there was little possibility that potential jurors in Toronto would be influenced by racial prejudice ... . Secondly, there is the problem of trial fairness. Where do these facts come from and how are the parties going to address them? How can parties who are prejudiced by the taking of judicial notice rebut what "everybody" knows unless a plausible source is put to them for their comment and potential disagreement? (See *R v. Parnell* (1995), 98 CCC (3d) 83 (Ont. CA), at p. 94.) A third problem is that judges occasionally contradict each other about some "fact" that "everybody" knows, even on the same court in the same case. ...

[52] While courts have accepted the widespread existence of racism, and the likelihood that anti-black racism is aggravated when the alleged victim is white, there is no similar consensus that "everybody knows" a juror of a particular race is likely to favour a complainant or witness of the same race, despite the trial safeguards and the trial judge's instruction to the contrary.

[53] Still less can it be said that such favouritism satisfies the more stringent test of judicial notice adopted by this Court in *Find*, at para. 48 ... .

[54] This stricter formulation adopted in *Find* was originally put forward by Professor E.M. Morgan in "Judicial Notice" (1943-1944), 57 *Harv. L Rev.* 269. ... I do not think the African Canadian Legal Clinic's view of race-based sympathy for victims (or partiality in favour of certain witnesses) is so notoriously correct as "not to be the subject of debate among reasonable persons." Nor is it capable of immediate demonstration by resort to "readily accessible sources of indisputable accuracy" (*Find*, at para. 48).

[55] Unlike Professor Thayer, for whom judicial notice created a rebuttable presumption of accuracy, Professor Morgan (p. 273) necessarily concluded that if certain facts were properly made subject to judicial notice, they were, by definition, not open to rebuttal. In this, he was supported by Professor C.T. McCormick, who wrote that "a ruling that a fact will be judicially noticed precludes contradictory evidence"; see "Judicial Notice" (1951-1952), 5 *Vand. L Rev.* 296, at p. 322. In *R v. Zundel* (1987), 31 CCC (3d) 97 (Ont. CA) the court said that "[t]he generally accepted modern view ... is that where the court

takes judicial notice of a matter, the judicial notice is final" (p. 150). On this view, acceptance through judicial notice of the broad race-based thesis of the intervener African Canadian Legal Clinic would not only stretch the elasticity of judicial notice, it would create a set of irrebuttable presumptions about how individuals called to jury duty can be expected to think. If there is one thing most of the social science studies agree upon, it is that much work remains to be done in Canada within the limits imposed by s. 649 of the *Criminal Code* to clarify our working assumptions about jury behaviour.

[56] It could be argued that the requirements of judicial notice accepted in *Find* should be relaxed in relation to such matters as laying a factual basis for the exercise of a discretion to permit challenges for cause. These are matters difficult to prove, and they do not strictly relate to the adjudication of guilt or innocence, but rather to the framework within which that adjudication is to take place. Such non-adjudicative facts are now generally called "social facts" when they relate to the fact-finding process and "legislative facts" in relation to legislation or judicial policy. Juror partiality is a question of fact, and what the African Canadian Legal Clinic invites us to do is to take judicial notice of the "social facts" of different aspects of racism.

[57] "Social fact" evidence has been defined as social science research that is used to construct a frame of reference or background context for deciding factual issues crucial to the resolution of a particular case: see, e.g., C. L'Heureux-Dubé, "Re-examining the Doctrine of Judicial Notice in the Family Law Context" (1994), 26 *Ottawa L Rev.* 551, at p. 556. As with their better known "legislative fact" cousins, "social facts" are general. They are not specific to the circumstances of a particular case, but if properly linked to the adjudicative facts, they help to explain aspects of the evidence. Examples are the Court's acceptance of the "battered wife syndrome" to explain the wife's conduct in *R v. Lavallee*, [1990] 1 SCR 852, or the effect of the "feminization of poverty" judicially noticed in *Moge v. Moge*, [1992] 3 SCR 813, at p. 853, and of the systemic or background factors that have contributed to the difficulties faced by aboriginal people in both the criminal justice system and throughout society at large in *R v. Wells*, [2000] 1 SCR 207, 2000 SCC 10, at para. 53, and in *R v. Gladue*, [1999] 1 SCR 688, at para. 83.

[58] No doubt there is a useful distinction between adjudicative facts (the where, when and why of what the accused is alleged to have done) and "social facts" and "legislative facts" which have relevance to the reasoning process and may involve broad considerations of policy: Paciocco and Stuesser [*The Law of Evidence*, 2nd ed (Toronto: Irwin Law, 1999)], at p. 286. However, simply categorizing an issue as "social fact" or "legislative fact" does not license the court to put aside the need to examine the trustworthiness of the "facts" sought to be judicially noticed. Nor are counsel encouraged to bootleg "evidence in the guise of authorities": *Public School Boards' Assn. of Alberta v. Alberta (Attorney General)*, [1999] 3 SCR 845, at para. 3.

[59] The distinction between legislative and adjudicative facts was formulated by the astute administrative law expert, Kenneth Culp Davis, who thought it important to distinguish for purposes of judicial notice between "adjudicative" fact (where he thought the Morgan criteria should apply) and "legislative" fact (where he tended to side with Thayer): K.C. Davis, *Administrative Law Treatise* (2nd ed. 1980), vol. 3, at p. 139. The proof of facts about widespread racism in the community, and whether or not it is so strong as to create a "realistic possibility" of overcoming a juror's presumed impartiality, has to do with juries in general and judicial policy towards their composition. Such matters, according to

Sopinka J, "are subject to less stringent admissibility requirements": *Danson v. Ontario (Attorney General)*, [1990] 2 SCR 1086, at p. 1099. The "less stringent" standard was not defined.

[60] Professor Davis' useful distinction between adjudicative facts and legislative facts is part of his larger insight, highly relevant for present purposes, that the permissible scope of judicial notice should vary according to the nature of the issue under consideration. For example, more stringent proof may be called for of facts that are close to the center of the controversy between the parties (whether social, legislative or adjudicative) as distinguished from background facts at or near the periphery.

[61] To put it another way, the closer the fact approaches the dispositive issue, the more the court ought to insist on compliance with the stricter Morgan criteria. Thus in *Find*, the Court's consideration of alleged juror bias arising out of the repellant nature of the offences against the accused did not relate to the issue of guilt or innocence, and was not "adjudicative" fact in that sense, but nevertheless the Court insisted on compliance with the Morgan criteria because of the centrality of the issue, which was hotly disputed, to the disposition of the appeal. While some learned commentators seek to limit the Morgan criteria to adjudicative fact (see, e.g., Paciocco and Stuesser, at p. 286; McCormick, at p. 316), I believe the Court's decision in *Find* takes a firmer line. I believe a review of our jurisprudence suggests that the Court will start with the Morgan criteria, whatever may be the type of "fact" that is sought to be judicially noticed. The Morgan criteria represent the gold standard and, if satisfied, the "fact" will be judicially noticed, and that is the end of the matter.

[62] If the Morgan criteria are not satisfied, and the fact is "adjudicative" in nature, the fact will not be judicially recognized, and that too is the end of the matter.

[63] It is when dealing with social facts and legislative facts that the Morgan criteria, while relevant, are not necessarily conclusive. There are levels of notoriety and indisputability. Some legislative "facts" are necessarily laced with supposition, prediction, presumption, perception and wishful thinking. Outside the realm of adjudicative fact, the limits of judicial notice are inevitably somewhat elastic. Still, the Morgan criteria will have great weight when the legislative fact or social fact approaches the dispositive issue. For example, in *R v. Advance Cutting & Coring Ltd.*, [2001] 3 SCR 209, 2001 SCC 70, LeBel J observed:

> The fact that unions intervene in political social debate is well known and well documented and might be the object of judicial notice. ...
>
> Taking judicial notice of the fact that Quebec unions have a constant ideology, act in constant support of a particular cause or policy, and seek to impose that ideology on their members seems far more controversial. It would require a leap of faith and logic, absent a proper factual record on the question. [paras. 226-27]

See also *Gladue*, at para. 83.

[64] The reality is that in many Charter cases (for example), the adjudicative facts are admitted. It is the legislative facts or social facts that are likely to prove dispositive (e.g., *R v. Sharpe*, [2001] 1 SCR 45, 2001 SCC 2; *R v. Butler*, [1992] 1 SCR 452; *Little Sisters Book and Art Emporium v. Canada (Minister of Justice)*, [2000] 2 SCR 1120, 2000 SCC 69). The Court in those cases was rightly careful to keep judicial notice on a relatively short leash, while at the same time acknowledging that facts cannot be demonstrated with greater precision than the subject matter permits.

[65] When asked to take judicial notice of matters falling between the high end already discussed where the Morgan criteria will be insisted upon, and the low end of background facts where the court will likely proceed (consciously or unconsciously) on the basis that the matter is beyond serious controversy, I believe a court ought to ask itself whether such "fact" would be accepted by reasonable people who have taken the trouble to inform themselves on the topic as not being the subject of reasonable dispute *for the particular purpose for which it is to be used*, keeping in mind that the need for reliability and trustworthiness increases directly with the centrality of the "fact" to the disposition of the controversy.

. . .

[67] Here, the respondent and the African Canadian Legal Clinic are asking the Court to make some fundamental shifts in the law's understanding of how juries function and how the selection of their members should be approached. Their submissions carry us well beyond the specific context in which *Williams* [*R v Williams*, [1998] 1 SCR 1128] and *Parks* were decided. The facts of which they ask us to take judicial notice would be dispositive of the appeal; yet they are neither notorious nor easily verified by reference to works of "indisputable accuracy." We are urged to pile inference onto inference. To take judicial notice of such matters for this purpose would, in my opinion, be to take even a generous view of judicial notice a leap too far. We do not know whether a favourable predisposition based on race—to the extent it exists—is any more prevalent than it is for people who share the same religion, or language, or national origin, or old school. On the present state of our knowledge, I think we should decline, at least for now, to proceed by way of judicial notice down the road the African Canadian Legal Clinic has laid out for us.

[68] I would add this comment: in *R v. Malmo-Levine*, [2003] 3 SCR 571, 2003 SCC 74, a majority of our Court expressed a preference for social science evidence to be presented through an expert witness who could be cross-examined as to the value and weight to be given to such studies and reports. This is the approach that had been taken by the litigants in *Sharpe, Little Sisters, Malmo-Levine* itself and subsequently in *Canadian Foundation for Children, Youth and the Law v. Canada (Attorney General)*, [2004] 1 SCR 76, 2004 SCC 4. We said in *Malmo-Levine* that

> ... courts should nevertheless proceed cautiously to take judicial notice even as "legislative facts" of matters ... are reasonably open to dispute, particularly where they relate to an issue that could be dispositive. [para. 28]

The suggestion that even legislative fact and social "facts" should be established by expert testimony rather than reliance on judicial notice was also made in cases as different from one another as *Find, Moysa* [*Moysa v Alberta (Labour Relations Board)*, [1989] 1 SCR 1572], *Danson*, at p. 1101, *Symes v. Canada*, [1993] 4 SCR 695, *Waldick v. Malcolm*, [1991] 2 SCR 456, at pp. 472-73, *Stoffman v. Vancouver General Hospital*, [1990] 3 SCR 483, at pp. 549-50, *R v. Penno*, [1990] 2 SCR 865, at pp. 881-82, and *MacKay v. Manitoba*, [1989] 2 SCR 357. Litigants who disregard the suggestion proceed at some risk.

[69] I accept that, as Finlayson JA pointed out in *Koh*, sometimes expert testimony is hard to come by and may in any event be beyond the resources of the particular litigants. As will be seen, I think such considerations in the context of challenges for cause are better addressed as part of the court's concern for trial fairness and the necessary perception of fairness, rather than being allowed to dilute the principled exercise of judicial notice.

NOTES AND QUESTIONS

1. In *R v Butler*, [1992] 1 SCR 452, the Supreme Court rejected a constitutional challenge to the obscenity provisions of the *Criminal Code*. The court held that the obscenity provisions violated s 2(b), but were justified under s 1. An important element of the court's s 1 analysis was the empirical proposition that pornography is harmful to women. On the "rational connection" branch of the *Oakes* test, the court referred to several government reports concerning the effect of pornography on behaviour and attitudes toward women. Those reports, in turn, relied on numerous empirical studies. Sopinka J, speaking for the majority, recognized that the social science evidence was "inconclusive," but held that it nonetheless provided Parliament with a "reasoned apprehension of harm" flowing from pornographic materials. This reasoned apprehension was sufficient to satisfy the requirement of rational connection. It appears that none of these empirical studies was put before the trial judge (see *R v Butler* (1989), 60 Man R (2d) 82, 50 CCC (3d) 97 (QB)). Was the court taking judicial notice of these studies? If so, was that a proper thing for an appellate court to do? If not, what exactly was the court doing? See also *R v Hawkins* (1993), 15 OR (3d) 549, 86 CCC (3d) 246 (CA).

2. In *R v Khawaja*, 2010 ONCA 862, the court overturned the trial judge's finding that the motive clause in anti-terrorism legislation would inhibit persons who wished to engage in conduct that is outside the definition of "terrorist activity" from expressing certain beliefs and opinions that might be shared by those who were engaged in terrorist activity. The appeal court held:

> [123] The trial judge did not suggest that he was taking judicial notice of the "chilling effect" of the motive clause, although that is what he did. Accepting that the scope of judicial notice is broader in respect of non-adjudicative social facts, such as the potential "chilling effect" of legislation, judicial notice still requires that the fact of which judicial notice is taken be one that is not open to reasonable dispute after due inquiry. ...
>
> [124] The contention that a segment of the community is reluctant to exercise its rights under s. 2 because of the motive clause in the anti-terrorism legislation comes nowhere near to meeting the standard required before judicial notice can be taken.

By contrast, the court upheld the trial judge's explicit taking of judicial notice of the following facts with respect to the war in Afghanistan: (1) the internationally recognized government of Afghanistan is backed by a coalition of western nations, including Canada, pursuant to various United Nations Security Council Resolutions; (2) insurgents in Afghanistan are conducting armed warfare against the coalition forces, the local government, and that part of the local population that supports them; (3) Canadian forces have sustained fatal casualties as a result of insurgent fighting in Afghanistan; and (4) the purpose of the armed insurgent attacks is to intimidate those assisting in or supporting the peaceful reconstruction of Afghanistan and to compel those persons to desist from those efforts (at paras 172-173).

The further appeal to the Supreme Court of Canada was dismissed: 2012 SCC 69. With respect to judicial notice of a "chilling effect," the court affirmed the reasons of the Court of Appeal, above, and added:

> [79] In some situations, a chilling effect can be inferred from known facts and experience. For example, no reasonable person would dispute that a law that makes the press liable in damages for responsible reporting on political figures will probably have a chilling effect on what the press says. In such a case, it may be unnecessary to call evidence of a chilling effect. Therefore, if the

Court of Appeal is understood as suggesting that a claimant under s. 2 of the *Charter* must always call evidence of a chilling effect, I could not agree.

[80] However, in this case, it is impossible to infer, without evidence, that the motive clause will have a chilling effect on the exercise of s. 2 freedoms by people holding religious or ideological views similar to those held by some terrorists. The reasons of the Court of Appeal detail why such an inference cannot be made.

The Supreme Court also agreed with the judges below on the propriety of taking judicial notice of the facts relating to the war in Afghanistan, as these facts were "beyond contestation" (at para 99).

3. In *R v Ipeelee*, 2012 SCC 13, the court identified as a problem the fact that some courts were hesitant to take judicial notice of the systemic and background factors affecting Aboriginal peoples in Canada. It held that judges *must* do so in order to achieve proper sentencing outcomes for Aboriginal offenders (at para 60):

> To be clear, courts must take judicial notice of such matters as the history of colonialism, displacement, and residential schools and how that history continues to translate into lower educational attainment, lower incomes, higher unemployment, higher rates of substance abuse and suicide, and of course higher levels of incarceration for Aboriginal peoples. These matters, on their own, do not necessarily justify a different sentence for Aboriginal offenders. Rather, they provide the necessary *context* for understanding and evaluating the case-specific information presented by counsel.

4. In *Find*, above, at para 102, the court referred to its prior decision in *R v DD*, 2000 SCC 43, [2000] 2 SCR 275 for the proposition that children alleging sexual assault are subject to the invidious myth that their allegation is fabricated unless it is made immediately. In response to this, the court held in that case:

> [65] A trial judge should recognize and so instruct a jury that there is no inviolable rule on how people who are the victims of trauma like a sexual assault will behave. Some will make an immediate complaint, some will delay in disclosing the abuse, while some will never disclose the abuse. Reasons for delay are many and at least include embarrassment, fear, guilt, or a lack of understanding and knowledge. In assessing the credibility of a complainant, the timing of the complaint is simply one circumstance to consider in the factual mosaic of a particular case. A delay in disclosure, standing alone, will never give rise to an adverse inference against the credibility of the complainant.
>
> [66] It was submitted that it is preferable to introduce the concept contained in Dr. Marshall's evidence to the jury by way of expert testimony rather than by judicial instruction. In my view, this argument is flawed. There is nothing to be gained from a cross-examination of the simple and irrefutable proposition advanced in this case by the expert. As well, there is no benefit to be derived from the added flexibility of expert evidence since the undeniable nature of the proposition does not lend itself to future advancements in knowledge and understanding.

Is this an example of judicial notice? For a recent and failed effort to obtain judicial notice that statements given after domestic disputes are unreliable (for the purposes of a hearsay exception), see *R v Johnson*, 2004 NSCA 91, 188 CCC (3d) 214.

E. Judicial Notice of Law

At common law and under statute in Canada (see, for example, *Canada Evidence Act*, ss 17-18), judges *must* take judicial notice of the domestic law. On occasion this is forgotten.

R v St Lawrence Cement Inc
(2002), 60 OR (3d) 712 (CA)
Charron, Borins, and Feldman JJA (2 August 2002)

[The accused was acquitted of operating a vehicle with emissions above those permitted under the *Drive Clean Guide* published by the Ministry of the Environment of Ontario, on the basis that the Crown had not proved the Guide. The acquittal was initially upheld on appeal but then overturned by the Ontario Court of Appeal for reasons excerpted below.]

BORINS JA:
    [15] The doctrine of judicial notice is the vehicle by which statutes and subordinate legislation are proved. At common law, judicial notice has always been taken of a public Act of Parliament or a provincial legislature. No evidence has ever been required concerning its passage through Parliament or a legislature, nor of its contents. The common law rule has been codified and is found in s. 7(1) of the *Interpretation Act* [RSO 1990, c I.11]. A similar provision in respect to regulations published in *The Ontario Gazette* is in s. 5(4)(b) of the *Regulations Act*. There is no need to prove that a regulation has been published to rely on s. 5(4) [RSO 1990, c R.21]. Publication is presumed, subject to proof to the contrary. Indeed, it can be said that statutes and regulations are the everyday companions of judges and counsel and so it should come as no surprise that a judge is not merely permitted to take judicial notice of these sources of domestic law, but a judge is required to do so. In addition, various statutory provisions provide that judicial notice shall be taken of the seals and signatures of various persons in official documents, and of certified copies of certain documents: *Evidence Act*, RSO 1990, c. E.23, ss. 27, 29, 32, 36.
    [16] The doctrine of judicial notice is one of common sense. ... At common law, judges are required to take judicial notice of domestic law, which includes legislation enacted by Parliament and provincial legislatures. See S. Schiff, *Evidence in the Litigation Process*, 4th ed. (Scarborough, Ont.: Carswell, 1993) Vol. 2, at 1051-1052. The common law rule that the court is required to take judicial notice of statute law has been codified throughout Canada. As Sopinka, Lederman and Bryant [*The Law of Evidence in Canada*, 2nd ed (Toronto: Butterworths, 1999)] state at pp. 1060-1061:

> There are innumerable instances in which the court is required by statute to take judicial notice. Thus, courts throughout Canada are bound to take judicial notice of Acts, public or private, of the federal Parliament and of the legislature of the province by which they are passed. The statutory provisions generally extend to ordinances, orders-in-council, proclamations and regulations. [Footnotes omitted.]

The requirement that the court must take judicial notice of statutes and regulations avoids the cumbersome and slow process of common law proof by witnesses to authenticate legislation.

[17] As the justice of the peace was required to take judicial notice of the regulation, it is necessary to determine whether the Guide was part of the regulation and, as such, should have been judicially noticed. As I have indicated, although the respondent agrees that the Guide was properly adopted, and thereby incorporated by reference, in s. 12(2) of the regulation, it maintains that because its text was not published in *The Ontario Gazette* at the time of the regulation's publication, it had to be independently proved. I do not agree.

. . .

[19] In a case not unlike this appeal, the British Columbia Court of Appeal held that incorporation by reference was complete without publication of the text of the incorporated documents in the *Canada Gazette*: *R v. Sims* (2000), 148 CCC (3d) 308 (BCCA). The court held that it was unnecessary to publish a regulatory standard incorporated by reference together with the regulation before a prosecution based on contravention of the standard could be pursued. It further held at p. 318 that incorporation by reference does not require that the text of the incorporated document be reproduced in the incorporating statute or regulation. See, also, *Denison Mines Ltd. v. Ontario (Securities Commission)* (1981), 32 OR (2d) 469, 122 DLR (3d) 98 (Div. Ct.).

[20] I would adopt and apply the following statement of the law of Rowles JA in *Sims* at p. 315 CCC:

> When material is incorporated by reference into a statute or regulation it becomes an integral part of the incorporating instrument as if reproduced therein. ...

[21] It follows, therefore, that because the text of the Guide was effectively written into s. 12(2) of the regulation by the doctrine of incorporation by reference, and because the regulation had been published in *The Ontario Gazette*, the Crown was not required to prove the Guide. The justice of the peace was required to take judicial notice of it [footnote omitted].

NOTE

While it is clear that courts must take judicial notice of the prior decisions of their own court, it is important to distinguish taking notice of the fact of a decision and the holding of law in it (proper) and taking judicial notice of the facts in a decision (generally improper unless the doctrines of *res judicata*, estoppel, abuse of process, or related principles apply). See, for example, *R v Levkovic*, 2010 ONCA 830 at paras 44-50, 103 OR (3d) 1 (affirmed without reference to this point: 2013 SCC 25), and the treatment of prior decisions in subsequent proceedings in *British Columbia (Attorney General) v Malik*, 2011 SCC 18 at para 38 and *R v Jesse*, 2012 SCC 21 at para 47.

PROBLEM (R v GALLOWAY)

Consider the following questions:

1. At trial, would it be possible for the defence to admit that the killing of Angela Galloway was a murder while contesting that Martin Galloway perpetrated that murder? Is the Crown's consent required before such an "admission" can be made? Are there tactical reasons why either the defence or the Crown would or would not want to make or accept such an admission?

2. You will remember that in advancing its case, the Crown contends that Martin Galloway lied about performing CPR on Angela. In making this claim, the Crown points to the fact that Martin had virtually no blood on him when emergency personnel arrived (there were only a few spots of blood on his T-shirt), arguing that he should have been covered in blood if he had performed CPR on the blood-soaked victim. The Crown doesn't call any expert evidence to support this theory. Rather, it asserts that this is simply something that can be inferred from the proven facts. During the pre-charge conference, the Crown asks the judge to give the jury an instruction to this effect. The defence objects, taking the position that without expert evidence, the Crown's argument goes beyond the pale of the sort of matters over which judicial notice should be taken. Who has the better argument?

Burden and Quantum of Proof

When all the evidence is in, the trier of fact has to decide what the facts are. In doing so, the trier of fact must take account of which party has the burden of proof, the degree of proof, the proper approach to inferring facts from evidence, and any presumptions that may or must be applied. This chapter provides an introduction to these topics.

I. EVIDENTIARY AND PERSUASIVE BURDENS

Before turning to the degree or quantum of proof that must be satisfied, we consider two different types of burden of proof: the *persuasive* burden and the *evidentiary* burden.

The *persuasive burden* of proof is on the party who, in law, is required to establish the relevant facts to succeed. As Cross put it, "It is the burden borne by the party who will lose the issue unless he satisfies the tribunal of fact to the appropriate degree of conviction." (Rupert Cross, *Evidence* (London: Butterworths, 1958) at 63.) In a civil action, the plaintiff normally bears the persuasive burden, while in a criminal trial, the prosecution normally bears the persuasive burden, although the location of the persuasive burden may vary, depending on the issue at hand. The trier of fact applies the persuasive burden to the evidence to decide which party has established its case to the required degree of proof (see Sections II and III).

The *evidentiary burden* of proof is on the party whose duty it is to raise an issue. A party under an evidentiary burden must adduce or point to some relevant evidence capable of supporting a decision in the party's favour on an issue before that issue can go to the trier of fact. To use Cross's words again, "It is the burden of producing sufficient evidence to justify a finding in favour of the party who bears it." (Cross, *supra* at 64.) But the evidentiary burden does not have to be in the same place as the persuasive burden. There may be cases where one party has a duty to satisfy an evidentiary burden on a particular issue, and, once that burden is satisfied, the other party bears the persuasive burden. For example, in a criminal case, the Crown ordinarily bears both the evidentiary burden and the persuasive burden with respect to the elements of the offence charged, but the accused typically bears an evidentiary burden with respect to most of the standard justifications and excuses; once the accused has satisfied the evidentiary burden, the Crown must disprove the excuse or justification beyond a reasonable doubt.

II. BURDEN AND DEGREE OF PROOF IN CIVIL PROCEEDINGS

In civil proceedings, the plaintiff typically bears both the evidentiary and the persuasive burden on all the elements of the action. The plaintiff has to lead evidence capable of supporting the facts that the plaintiff alleges, and the plaintiff must then satisfy the trier of fact on a balance of probabilities that the facts alleged are true. (This general rule has some significant exceptions; for example, in an action for defamation, a defendant who raises a defence of justification must establish that defence on a balance of probabilities.) In this section, we provide a brief introduction to these burdens of proof, as well as to the motion for a non-suit and the motion for summary judgment.

A. Motion for a Non-Suit

At the close of the plaintiff's case, the defendant may argue that the plaintiff has not met his or her evidentiary burden. This argument takes the form of a motion for a non-suit: the defendant argues that the plaintiff has not led evidence capable of supporting one or more of the elements of the cause of action. When the defendant makes the motion, he or she must decide whether to call any evidence. In some Canadian jurisdictions, the decision to call evidence means that the motion for a non-suit is abandoned; in other jurisdictions, the decision to call evidence means only that the trial judge will reserve judgment on the motion until all the evidence has been heard.

The motion for a non-suit is determined by the trial judge. In *Hall v Pemberton* (1974), 5 OR (2d) 438, 50 DLR (3d) 518 (CA), Jessup JA described the test to be applied on a motion for a non-suit as follows:

> In this action defendant's counsel moved for a nonsuit at the conclusion of the plaintiffs' case and elected to call no evidence. The learned trial Judge granted the nonsuit. In view of the disposition which we think should be made of this case, I do not propose to discuss the evidence.
>
> The principle which this Court must apply is stated by Lord Penzance in *Parfitt v. Lawless* (1872), 41 LJP & M 68 at pp. 71-2 where he said:
>
>> I conceive, therefore, that in judging whether there is any case evidence for a jury the Judge must weigh the evidence given, must assign what he conceives to be the most

favourable meaning which can reasonably be attributed to any ambiguous statements, and determine on the whole what tendency the evidence has to establish the issue.

and:

From every fact that is proved, legitimate and reasonable inferences may of course be drawn, and all that is fairly deducible from the evidence is as much proved, for the purpose of a prima facie case, as if it had been proved directly. I conceive, therefore, that in discussing whether there is in any case evidence to go to the jury, what the Court has to consider is this, whether, assuming the evidence to be true, and adding to the direct proof all such inferences of fact as in the exercise of a reasonable intelligence the jury would be warranted in drawing from it, there is sufficient to support the issue.

We are all of the opinion that there was evidence in this case which if accepted by the jury (and from our point of view we must assume that would be done) would support an inference that the defendant was responsible for the telephone calls which are the subject of the complaint in the action.

It must be stressed that avoidance of a non-suit means only that the plaintiff has established a case fit to go to the trier of fact; it does not mean that the plaintiff will ultimately be successful in the action. But where the trier of fact is the jury rather than the judge, the case may go to the jury while the trial judge's decision on the motion for a non-suit is under reserve. In *McKenzie v Bergin*, [1937] OWN 200 (CA), Middleton JA explained this procedure as follows:

(1) The trial Judge should not, of his own motion, undertake to non-suit, but in all cases it should be left for counsel for the defendant to move for a non-suit if he desires to do so.

(2) Even if counsel for the defendant moves for a non-suit, it would be wise and convenient if the trial Judge would reserve his decision on the motion for a non-suit and ask the defendant if he desires to put in evidence. If the defendant desires to put in evidence, the case should proceed and the jury's finding obtained. If the learned trial Judge then decides that the non-suit should be granted he could dismiss the action and, if appeal were taken, this Court would have all the facts before it, including the assessment of damages, and if it should be of the opinion that the non-suit should not have been granted the action could finally be disposed of.

(3) If on the other hand the defendant said he did not desire to put in any evidence but rested his case on the weakness of the plaintiff's case, then the learned trial Judge could properly dispose of the motion for non-suit.

For an example, see *Babineau v Babineau* (1981), 32 OR (2d) 545 (HCJ), aff'd (1982), 37 OR (2d) 527 (CA). Is this rule preferable to the rule that the defendant who calls evidence must abandon the motion?

B. Proof on a Balance of Probabilities

As noted above, in most types of civil proceedings, the plaintiff must prove his or her allegations on a balance of probabilities. It is clear from *Lifchus*, excerpted below in Section III.C, and from all the case law concerning proof in criminal matters, that proof on a balance of probabilities is less demanding than proof beyond a reasonable doubt. Various expressions have been used to describe the requirement of proof on a balance of probabilities: proof to this standard has been described as requiring that the trier of fact (1) find the fact alleged "more probable than not" (*Miller v Minister of Pensions*, [1947] 2 All ER 372 at 374, per Denning J);

and (2) "on the basis of a preponderance of probability ... be reasonably satisfied" of the fact alleged (*Smith v Smith*, [1952] 2 SCR 312 at 331-32, per Cartwright J).

At times, it has been suggested that the standard should be applied in a more exacting manner where the allegations are especially grave. For example, where a plaintiff alleges fraud, professional misconduct, or criminal conduct, particularly sexual assault against minors, the stigma that could result from an adverse finding has led some to suggest the need for proof to "a degree of probability which is commensurate with the occasion." (See *Bater v Bater*, [1950] 2 All ER 458 at 459 (CA), per Lord Denning.)

The Supreme Court of Canada has categorically rejected this view. In *FH v McDougall*, 2008 SCC 53 at para 40, [2008] 3 SCR 41, the court emphasized the impracticality of applying vary-ing standards to different types of claims, making clear that

> there is only one civil standard of proof at common law and that is proof on a balance of probabil-ities. Of course, context is all important and a judge should not be unmindful, where appropriate, of inherent probabilities or improbabilities or the seriousness of the allegations or consequences. However, these considerations do not change the standard of proof.

C. Summary Judgment

All of the Canadian common law provinces have, as part of their rules of court, a rule permit-ting some form of summary judgment—that is, judgment without trial—in civil matters. The relevant Ontario rule (*Rules of Civil Procedure*, RRO 1990, Reg 194, r 20.01) reads as follows:

> 20.01(1) A plaintiff may, after the defendant has delivered a statement of defence or served a notice of motion, move with supporting affidavit material or other evidence for summary judg-ment on all or part of the claim in the statement of claim.
>
> (2) The plaintiff may move, without notice, for leave to serve a notice of motion for summary judgment together with the statement of claim, and leave may be given where special urgency is shown, subject to such directions as are just.
>
> (3) A defendant may, after delivering a statement of defence, move with supporting affidavit material or other evidence for summary judgment dismissing all or part of the claim in the state-ment of claim.

The relevant Newfoundland and Labrador rule (*Rules of the Supreme Court, The Judicature Act*, SNL 1986, c 42, Schedule D, r 17.01) reads as follows:

> 17.01(1) Where the defendant has filed a defence or appeared on a hearing under an ori-ginating document, the plaintiff may, on the ground that the defendant has no defence to a claim in the originating document or a part thereof or has no defence to such a claim or part except to the amount of any damages claimed, apply to the Court to enter judgment against the defendant.
>
> (2) This rule applies to every proceeding begun by statement of claim other than one which includes
>
> (a) a claim by the plaintiff for libel, slander, malicious prosecution, false imprisonment, seduction, breach of promise of marriage or for specific performance; or
>
> (b) a claim by the plaintiff if based upon an allegation of fraud.

What are the differences between the Ontario rule and the Newfoundland and Labrador rule? The other common law provinces have rules broadly similar to the Ontario rule: see *Court of Queen's Bench Rules*, Man Reg 553/88, r 20.01; *Rules of Court*, NB Reg 82-73, r 22.01; Prince Edward Island, *Rules of Civil Procedure*, r 20.01; *Alberta Rules of Court*, Alta Reg 124/2010, Division 2; *Supreme Court Civil Rules*, BC Reg 168/2009, r 9-6; *The Queen's Bench Rules*, SaskGaz December 27, 2013, 2684, Part 7, Division 2; and *Nova Scotia Civil Procedure Rules*, Royal Gaz Nov 19, 2008, r 13.

A motion for summary judgment differs from a motion for a non-suit not just in its timing but also in the issue to be addressed: in a motion for summary judgment, the moving party is *not* claiming that the responding party has led no evidence capable of establishing the elements of a cause of action; rather, the moving party asserts that the responding party's case is so weak that it is not worth bringing to trial. A motion for summary judgment differs from an application to determine a question of law in that the latter application requires an *agreement* as to the facts, whereas the former motion involves a *disagreement* about the facts.

Given that a successful motion for summary judgment precludes a trial, even though both parties have pleaded a proper cause of action and the facts remain disputed, what standard should the judge hearing the motion apply? In *Pizza Pizza Ltd v Gillespie* (1990), 75 OR (2d) 225 (Gen Div), Henry J described the judge's decision on a motion for summary judgment as follows:

> Rule 20 contemplates a radically new attitude to motions for judgment; the objective is to screen out claims that in the opinion of the court, based on evidence furnished as directed by the rule, ought not to proceed to trial because they cannot survive the "good hard look."
>
> There is no arbitrary or fixed criterion that the motions judge must apply. It is a case by case decision to be made on the law and on the facts that he is able to find on the evidence submitted to him in support of the claim or defence, whether the plaintiff has laid a proper foundation in its affidavit and other evidence to sustain the claims made.
>
> It is not sufficient for the responding party to say that more and better evidence will (or may) be available at trial. The occasion is now. The respondent must set out specific facts and coherent evidence organized to show that there is a genuine issue for trial.
>
> Apparent factual conflict in evidence does not end the inquiry.
>
> The court may, on a common sense basis, draw inferences from the evidence.
>
> The court may look at the overall credibility of the plaintiff's action, i.e., does the plaintiff's case have the ring of truth about it such that it would justify consideration by the trier of fact?
>
> Matters of credibility requiring resolution in a case of conflicting evidence ought to go to trial; however, that depends upon the circumstances of the case; the court in taking the "hard look" at the merits must decide if any conflict is more apparent than real, i.e., whether there is really an issue of credibility that must be resolved in order to adjudicate on the merits.
>
> Motions under Rule 20 must be made sparingly and judiciously; the court will control abuse of this process if necessary by its order for costs.

The evidence filed by the parties in *Pizza Pizza* disclosed few, if any, issues of credibility that would have to be resolved in a trial, and Henry J granted summary judgment to the defendant. For a case in which credibility issues were central, see *Irving Ungerman Ltd v Galanis* (1991), 4 OR (3d) 545 (CA).

III. BURDEN AND DEGREE OF PROOF IN PENAL PROCEEDINGS

A. Directed Verdict, Committal to Stand Trial, and Extradition

The directed verdict of acquittal is the criminal analogue of the non-suit. At the end of the prosecution's case, the accused may ask the trial judge to rule that the Crown has not discharged its evidentiary burden—that is, that the Crown has not led evidence capable of establishing the elements of the offence. But the accused is not required to elect whether to call evidence before the judge decides the motion. In *R v Monteleone*, [1987] 2 SCR 154, McIntyre J, speaking for a unanimous court, described the test for a directed verdict of acquittal as follows:

> Where there is before the court any admissible evidence, whether direct or circumstantial, which, if believed by a properly charged jury acting reasonably, would justify a conviction, the trial judge is not justified in directing a verdict of acquittal. It is not the function of the trial judge to weigh the evidence, to test its quality or reliability once a determination of its admissibility has been made. It is not for the trial judge to draw inferences of fact from the evidence before him. These functions are for the trier of fact, the jury.

The Supreme Court has repeatedly held that the Crown's burden to avoid a directed verdict of acquittal is the same as the standard to be applied in committing the accused for trial at a preliminary inquiry and committing a fugitive for extradition. In *Monteleone*, the court stated that the prohibition on assessing the reliability of evidence applied equally to direct and circumstantial evidence. That stance was modified in the following decision.

R v Arcuri

2001 SCC 54, [2001] 2 SCR 828

McLachlin CJ and L'Heureux-Dubé, Gonthier, Iacobucci, Major, Bastarache, Binnie, Arbour, and LeBel JJ (14 September 2001)

McLACHLIN CJ:

[2] The accused was charged with the first degree murder of Enio Mora, who was to all appearances his close friend. At the preliminary hearing, the Crown's case against the accused was entirely circumstantial. The accused called two witnesses whose testimony was arguably exculpatory. The issue was whether the evidence was sufficient to warrant committing the accused to trial.

[3] The Crown's evidence was to the following effect. Mora was found dead in the trunk of his Cadillac at about 4:00 p.m. on September 11th, 1996. The Cadillac was parked on the north side of Teston Road, between Pine Valley Drive and Weston Road in the City of Vaughan, which is located north of Toronto. Mora had been shot four times in the left temple at close range.

[4] The Crown presented no evidence purporting to establish when Mora's Cadillac was first parked at the place it was discovered. However, one witness testified that the car was not parked there when he passed the area at 10:45 a.m. Several witnesses testified that they saw the car at around 2:00 p.m., or soon after.

[5] The principal evidence linking the accused to the crime consisted of a bundle of clothes discovered by the side of Pine Valley Drive by Onido Salerno, a local farmer. On September 11th, Salerno was working outside on his farm, which is on Pine Valley Drive just south of Teston Road. At about 2:00 p.m., Salerno saw a black or blue car, a Buick or Oldsmobile with a chrome stripe along the side, stop on the road in front of him. The driver and a passenger got out and left something in the ditch by the side of the road. The two then got back in the car and drove off. After the car had driven off, Salerno went to see what the men had left in the ditch. He found a pair of beige pants, a shirt spotted with blood, a pair of shoes, and a full package of Freedent gum. Salerno later viewed photographs at the police station and identified the driver of the car he had seen to be someone other than the accused. The Crown maintained that the man Salerno had seen was the accused.

[6] The Crown presented evidence as to the whereabouts of the deceased and the accused on the morning of September 11th. Nick Nesci, a real estate broker and long-time acquaintance of the accused, stated that the accused had arrived at his office some time soon after 10:00 a.m. One of Nesci's clients, Nicola Galiffe, had a 10:00 a.m. appointment with Nesci and was already in the office. Mora arrived at about 10:20 or 10:30 a.m., to follow up on an offer Nesci had made to get him a good price on an exercise treadmill. Nesci left his office at about 11:00 a.m. for an appointment. He left Galiffe, Mora, and the accused standing outside his office, "talking like old friends". That was the last he saw of them that day, and the last he saw of Mora.

[7] Galiffe was not called as a witness but he submitted a signed statement to the police stating that he, Mora, and the accused went for coffee after leaving Nesci's office.

[8] Some time on the morning of September 11th, Mora paged Giancarlo Serpe, an acquaintance, to ask him to meet for coffee at 11:30 a.m. The two apparently met for coffee on a daily basis. They met for about 20 minutes or half an hour. In examination-in-chief, Serpe stated that Mora left the donut shop at about 11:30. On cross-examination, he stated that it was about 12:00 noon. In any event it seems he is the last witness to have seen Mora alive.

[9] The accused cooperated with the police investigation. In the course of one interview, he stated that he had been in Mora's car on September 10th. The police therefore asked him to provide "elimination prints"; he agreed. He also agreed to provide a buccal swab for D.N.A. testing.

[10] Forensic tests revealed that the D.N.A. profile taken from the collar of the shirt found by Onido Salerno matched that of the accused and that the blood on the shirt was Mora's. The accused was arrested on December 3rd and charged with first degree murder. A packet of Freedent gum was found on his person. The shirt the accused was wearing at the time of his arrest was about the same size as the shirt that Onido Salerno had found. The pants were the same size. From the accused's residence, the police seized, among other things, several packages of Freedent gum, many pairs of shoes, many pairs of pants, several rounds of .22 calibre bullets, a .22 calibre rifle, and a double-barreled shotgun. Many of the shoes and most of the pants were the same size as those that Onido Salerno had found on Pine Valley Drive. The laces on some pairs of shoes were tied in double knots, as had been the laces on the pair of shoes that Onido Salerno had found. According to an R.C.M.P. expert who examined several of the shoes, it was "highly probable" that the person who had worn the shoes that Onido Salerno had found was the same person who had worn the shoes found in the accused's residence. The accused's car was seized

on December 4th. It was a blue, 1989, 4-door Buick Park Avenue, with a wide chrome strip along the bottom of the fenders and doors. Inside the car, the police found, among other things, Freedent gum and a pair of boots.

[11] The police theorized that Mora had been murdered at a farm located at 10367 Weston Road. The distance between the farm and the place Mora's car was found could be traveled in slightly over a minute, driving at 65 kilometres per hour. The farm is owned by Nicola DiLorenzo, for whom the accused had worked "a long time ago." DiLorenzo stated that he had never seen the accused at the farm. However, the accused's son has done work for DiLorenzo. Soil samples taken from one of the barns matched soil found on Mora's clothing and shoes as well as on the shoes found by Onido Salerno on Pine Valley Drive. The police also found feathers and feather fragments similar to those found with Mora's body, on the boots found in the accused's car, and on the shirt and pants found by Salerno. In a subsequent search, the police found four .22 calibre live rounds of ammunition, a .22 calibre shell case, and a .22 calibre ammunition container.

[12] The accused called witnesses whose testimony was arguably exculpatory. Michael Fiorillo, the owner of the real estate company with which Nesci is employed, testified that he saw Galiffe, Mora, and the accused leave his premises at about 11:00 a.m. He also stated that he saw Galiffe and the accused in the same parking lot between 1:30 and 2:00 p.m., but closer to 2:00 p.m. At that time, the accused was getting into his car. Galiffe was getting into his own car. Carmelo Suppo, a travel agent and long-time friend of the accused, testified that the accused had visited her on September 11th between about 2:00 p.m. and 2:30 p.m. No evidence was offered by the Crown or by the accused as to how long it would take to drive from the place the clothing was found on Pine Valley Drive to Mr. Fiorillo's office or Ms. Suppo's office. The accused suggested, however, that the testimony of Fiorillo and Suppo was exculpatory as it suggested lack of opportunity.

• • •

[21] The question to be asked by a preliminary inquiry judge under s. 548(1) of the *Criminal Code* is the same as that asked by a trial judge considering a defence motion for a directed verdict, namely, "whether or not there is any evidence upon which a reasonable jury properly instructed could return a verdict of guilty": *Shephard*, … [*United States of America v Shephard*, [1977] 2 SCR 1067], at p. 1080; see also *R. v. Monteleone*, [1987] 2 S.C.R. 154 at p. 160. Under this test, a preliminary inquiry judge must commit the accused to trial "in any case in which there is admissible evidence which could, if it were believed, result in a conviction": *Shephard*, at p. 1080.

[22] The test is the same whether the evidence is direct or circumstantial: see *Mezzo v. Queen*, [1986] 1 S.C.R. 802, at pp. 842-43; *Monteleone, supra*, at p. 161. The nature of the judge's task, however, varies according to the type of evidence that the Crown has advanced. Where the Crown's case is based entirely on direct evidence, the judge's task is straightforward. By definition, the only conclusion that needs to be reached in such a case is whether the evidence is true … . It is for the jury to say whether and how far the evidence is to be believed: see *Shephard, supra*, at pp. 1086-87. Thus if the judge determines that the Crown has presented direct evidence as to every element of the offence charged, the judge's task is complete. If there is direct evidence as to every element of the offence, the accused must be committed to trial.

[23] The judge's task is somewhat more complicated where the Crown has not presented direct evidence as to every element of the offence. The question then becomes whether the remaining elements of the offence—that is, those elements as to which the Crown has not

advanced direct evidence—may reasonably be inferred from the circumstantial evidence. Answering this question inevitably requires the judge to engage in a limited weighing of the evidence because, with circumstantial evidence, there is, by definition, an inferential gap between the evidence and the matter to be established—that is, an inferential gap *beyond* the question of whether the evidence should be believed ... The judge must therefore weigh the evidence, in the sense of assessing whether it is reasonably capable of supporting the inferences that the Crown asks the jury to draw. This weighing, however, is limited. The judge does not ask whether she herself would conclude that the accused is guilty. Nor does the judge draw factual inferences or assess credibility. The judge asks only whether the evidence, *if believed*, could reasonably support an inference of guilt.

· · ·

[25] Notwithstanding certain confusing language in *Mezzo, supra,* and *Monteleone, supra,* nothing in this Court's jurisprudence calls into question the continuing validity of the common law rule ... .

· · ·

[26] In *Monteleone, supra,* the accused was charged with setting fire to his own clothing store. The evidence was entirely circumstantial. The question was whether the trial judge had erred in directing an acquittal on the grounds that the "cumulative effect [of the evidence] gives rise to suspicion only, and cannot justify the drawing of an inference of guilt": *Monteleone,* at p. 159. In ordering a new trial, McIntyre J. wrote that "[i]t is not the function of the trial judge to weigh the evidence, [or] ... to draw inferences of fact from the evidence before him": *Monteleone,* at p. 161. Again, however, the remainder of the reasons make clear that by "weighing" McIntyre J. was referring to the final drawing of inferences from the facts (which task, again, is within the exclusive province of the jury), not to the task of assessing whether guilt could reasonably be inferred. Indeed, the reasons explicitly reaffirm the common law rule that the judge must determine whether "there is before the court any admissible evidence, whether direct or circumstantial, which, if believed by a properly charged jury acting reasonably, would justify a conviction": *Monteleone,* p. 161.

· · ·

[29] The question that arises in the case at bar is whether the preliminary inquiry judge's task differs where the defence tenders exculpatory evidence, as is its prerogative under s. 541. In my view, the task is essentially the same, in situations where the defence calls exculpatory evidence, whether it be direct or circumstantial. Where the Crown adduces direct evidence on all the elements of the offence, the case must proceed to trial, regardless of the existence of defence evidence, as by definition the only conclusion that needs to be reached is whether the evidence is true. However, where the Crown's evidence consists of, or includes, circumstantial evidence, the judge must engage in a limited weighing of the whole of the evidence (i.e., including any defence evidence) to determine whether a reasonable jury properly instructed could return a verdict of guilty.

[30] In performing the task of limited weighing, the preliminary inquiry judge does not draw inferences from facts. Nor does she assess credibility. Rather, the judge's task is to determine whether, *if the Crown's evidence is believed*, it would be reasonable for a properly instructed jury to infer guilt. Thus, this task of "limited weighing" never requires consideration of the inherent reliability of the evidence itself. It should be regarded, instead, as an assessment of the reasonableness of the inferences to be drawn from the circumstantial evidence.

· · ·

[33] With those principles in mind, I turn, then, to the question of whether Lampkin Prov. J. properly interpreted and applied the law in this case. ...

· · ·

[35] ... I am not persuaded that Lampkin Prov. J. reached the wrong result. Before committing the appellant to trial, the preliminary inquiry justice thoroughly surveyed the circumstantial evidence that had been presented by the Crown—principally the sighting of a car similar to the appellant's on Pine Valley Drive just after 2:00 p.m., the sighting of a man similar in appearance to the accused exiting the car and leaving clothes in the ditch, the DNA evidence linking the accused to the shirt left in the ditch, the foot-imprint evidence linking the accused to the shoes left in the ditch, the evidence that blood on the shirt was Mora's, and the evidence that soil on the shoes matched soil found on Mora's body and at the presumed murder site. Lampkin Prov. J. also surveyed the evidence proffered by the defence. Indeed, he identified at para. 89 eleven arguments that favoured the accused, including the "absolute and complete absence of any evidence of motive or possibility of gain", and the absence of evidence of animus. Only after considering "the evidence as a whole" did Lampkin Prov. J. commit the appellant to trial.

[36] As to the appellant's argument that Lampkin Prov. J. did not place sufficient weight on the absence of evidence of opportunity, I note that there was no independent evidence as to the accused's whereabouts between the hours of about 11:30 a.m. and 2:00 p.m. The evidence of the accused's whereabouts before and after those times came from Michael Fiorillo and Carmelo Suppo. This evidence was of course testimonial, and its credibility was therefore a matter for the jury.

· · ·

[37] For the foregoing reasons, I conclude that the appeal should be dismissed.

Appeal dismissed.

NOTES AND QUESTIONS

The court in *Arcuri* stated that an issue must go to the trier of fact if there is direct evidence on that issue, no matter how weak. That proposition must now be read in light of *R v Hay*, 2013 SCC 61 at para 41, [2013] 3 SCR 694 (directed verdict must be awarded where identification evidence "would necessarily leave reasonable doubt in the mind of a reasonable juror") and *United States of America v Ferras; United States of America v Latty*, 2006 SCC 33 at paras 39-50, [2006] 2 SCR 77 (judge may decline to extradite if evidence is "manifestly unreliable"). Can you think of any other circumstances in which a more robust evaluation of the evidence should be required?

B. Putting a Defence in Issue

It is well established that a trial judge is required to charge the jury regarding all defences that arise on the evidence in the case; but a mere assertion by the accused that a defence should be left to the jury does not, by itself, put a defence in play. The trial judge is required to exercise some judgment as to whether the evidence supports a defence to the extent that the jury should consider it. The test for leaving a defence with the jury is sometimes called the "air of reality" test. In *Pappajohn v R*, [1980] 2 SCR 120, 52 CCC (2d) 481, McIntyre J described this test as follows:

It is well established that it is the duty of a trial judge, in giving directions to a jury, to draw to their attention and to put before them fairly and completely the theory of the defence. In performing this task, it is also clear that the trial judge must put before the jury any defences which may be open to the accused upon the evidence, whether raised by the accused's counsel or not. He must give all necessary instructions on the law relating to such defences, review the relevant evidence and relate it to the law applicable. This, however, does not mean that the trial judge becomes bound to put every defence suggested to him by counsel. Before any obligation arises to put defences, there must be in the evidence some basis upon which the defence can rest, and it is only where such an evidentiary basis is present that a trial judge must put a defence. Indeed, where it is not present he should not put a defence, for to do so would only be to confuse.

What is the standard which the judge must apply in considering this question? Ordinarily, when there is any evidence of a matter of fact the proof of which may be relevant to the guilt or innocence of an accused, the trial judge must leave that evidence to the jury so that they may reach their own conclusion upon it. Where, however, the trial judge is asked to put a specific defence to the jury, he is not concerned only with the existence or non-existence of evidence of fact. He must consider, assuming that the evidence relied upon by the accused to support a defence is true, whether that evidence is sufficient to justify the putting of the defence.

In *R v Cinous*, 2002 SCC 29, [2002] 2 SCR 3, 162 CCC (3d) 129, McLachlin CJ for the majority described the "air of reality" test as follows:

[50] The principle that a defence should be put to a jury if and only if there is an evidential foundation for it has long been recognized by the common law. This venerable rule reflects the practical concern that allowing a defence to go to the jury in the absence of an evidential foundation would invite verdicts not supported by the evidence, serving only to confuse the jury and get in the way of a fair trial and true verdict. Following *Pappajohn*, *supra*, the inquiry into whether there is an evidential foundation for a defence is referred to as the air of reality test. See *R v. Park*, [1995] 2 SCR 836, at para. 11.

[51] The basic requirement of an evidential foundation for defences gives rise to two well-established principles. First, a trial judge must put to the jury all defences that arise on the facts, whether or not they have been specifically raised by an accused. Where there is an air of reality to a defence, it should go to the jury. Second, a trial judge has a positive duty to keep from the jury defences lacking an evidential foundation. A defence that lacks an air of reality should be kept from the jury. ... This is so even when the defence lacking an air of reality represents the accused's only chance for an acquittal, as illustrated by *R v. Latimer*, [2001] 1 SCR 3.

[52] It is trite law that the air of reality test imposes a burden on the accused that is merely evidential, rather than persuasive. ... The air of reality test is concerned only with whether or not a putative defence should be "put in play," that is, submitted to the jury for consideration. This idea was crucial to the finding in *R v. Osolin*, [1993] 4 SCR 595, that the air of reality test is consistent with the presumption of innocence guaranteed by s. 11(d) of the *Canadian Charter of Rights and Freedoms*.

[53] In applying the air of reality test, a trial judge considers the totality of the evidence, and assumes the evidence relied upon by the accused to be true. See *Osolin*, *supra*; *Park*, *supra*. The evidential foundation can be indicated by evidence emanating from the examination in chief or cross-examination of the accused, of defence witnesses, or of Crown witnesses. It can also rest upon the factual circumstances of the case or from any other evidential source on the record. There is no requirement that the evidence be adduced by the accused. See *Osolin*, *supra*; *Park*, *supra*; *R v. Davis*, [1999] 3 SCR 759.

[54] The threshold determination by the trial judge is not aimed at deciding the substantive merits of the defence. That question is reserved for the jury. See *R v. Finta*, [1994] 1 SCR 701; *R v. Ewanchuk*, [1999] 1 SCR 330. The trial judge does not make determinations about the credibility of witnesses, weigh the evidence, make findings of fact, or draw determinate factual inferences. See *R v. Bulmer*, [1987] 1 SCR 782; *Park, supra*. Nor is the air of reality test intended to assess whether the defence is likely, unlikely, somewhat likely, or very likely to succeed at the end of the day. The question for the trial judge is whether the evidence discloses a real issue to be decided by the jury, and not how the jury should ultimately decide the issue.

[55] Whether or not there is an air of reality to a defence is a question of law, subject to appellate review. It is an error of law to put to the jury a defence lacking an air of reality, just as it is an error of law to keep from the jury a defence that has an air of reality. See *Osolin, supra*; *Park, supra*; *Davis, supra*. The statements that "there is an air of reality" to a defence and that a defence "lacks an air of reality" express a legal conclusion about the presence or absence of an evidential foundation for a defence.

[56] The considerations discussed above have led this Court to reject unequivocally the argument that the air of reality test licenses an encroachment by trial judges on the jury's traditional function as arbiter of fact. ...

[57] This Court has held on many occasions that a single air of reality test applies to all defences. *Osolin, supra*; *Park, supra*, at para. 12. The test has been applied uniformly to a wide range of defences over the years. These include the defence of honest but mistaken belief in consent in sexual assault cases (*Pappajohn, supra*; *Bulmer, supra*; *Osolin, supra*; *Park, supra*; *R v. Esau*, [1997] 2 SCR 777; *Ewanchuk, supra*; *Davis, supra*), and other defences such as intoxication (*R v. Robinson*, [1996] 1 SCR 683; *R v. Lemky*, [1996] 1 SCR 757), necessity (*Latimer, supra*), duress (*R v. Ruzic*, [2001] 1 SCR 687), provocation (*R v. Thibert*, [1996] 1 SCR 37), and self-defence (*Brisson v. The Queen*, [1982] 2 SCR 227; *R v. Hebert*, [1996] 2 SCR 272). Adopting different evidential standards for different classes of cases would constitute a sharp break with the authorities.

Once a defence survives the air of reality test and is put to the jury, the Crown is normally obliged to disprove it beyond a reasonable doubt in order to obtain a conviction. In light of *Cinous*, how does the "air of reality" standard compare with the test for avoiding a directed verdict of acquittal? Is there, or should there be, any difference between the two standards?

The defence of mental disorder (see s 16 of the *Criminal Code*) has to be established on a balance of probabilities by the party who raises the defence. Should this difference in the persuasive burden make any difference to the evidentiary burden that applies to the party who wants to raise the defence?

Until recently, the defence of non-insane automatism was like any other defence in that the accused had only to raise a reasonable doubt to be acquitted. This rule seemed anomalous to some commentators, in that the central issue in most cases of automatism is whether the automatism was of the non-insane or insane variety: if the former, it would be sufficient for the accused to raise a reasonable doubt; if the latter, the accused (or the Crown) had to prove it on a balance of probabilities. In *R v Stone*, [1999] 2 SCR 290, 134 CCC (3d) 353, Bastarache J for the majority held that the defence of automatism, whether insane or non-insane, had to be established by the accused on a balance of probabilities. He said at para 173 that this change in the law concerning the persuasive burden of proof had implications for the evidentiary burden on the accused: "The relationship between the burdens associated with automatism dictates that any change in the legal burden of automatism will necessarily result in a change to the evidentiary or proper foundation burden associated with this defence." He summarized the required change in the evidentiary burden as follows:

[192] To sum up, in order to satisfy the evidentiary or proper foundation burden in cases involving claims of automatism, the defence must make an assertion of involuntariness and call expert psychiatric or psychological evidence confirming that assertion. However, it is an error of law to conclude that this defence burden has been satisfied simply because the defence has met these two requirements. The burden will only be met where the trial judge concludes that there is evidence upon which a properly instructed jury could find that the accused acted involuntarily on a balance of probabilities. In reaching this conclusion, the trial judge will first examine the psychiatric or psychological evidence and inquire into the foundation and nature of the expert opinion. The trial judge will also examine all other available evidence, if any. Relevant factors are not a closed category and may, by way of example, include: the severity of the triggering stimulus, corroborating evidence of bystanders, corroborating medical history of automatistic-like dissociative states, whether there is evidence of a motive for the crime, and whether the alleged trigger of the automatism is also the victim of the automatistic violence. I point out that no single factor is meant to be determinative. Indeed, there may be cases in which the psychiatric or psychological evidence goes beyond simply corroborating the accused's version of events, for example, where it establishes a documented history of automatistic-like dissociative states. Furthermore, the ever advancing state of medical knowledge may lead to a finding that other types of evidence are also indicative of involuntariness. I leave it to the discretion and experience of trial judges to weigh all of the evidence available on a case-by-case basis and to determine whether a properly instructed jury could find that the accused acted involuntarily on a balance of probabilities.

Do you agree with this approach? If the evidentiary burden on the accused with respect to non-insane automatism is elevated because of the requirement of proof on a balance of probabilities, should the evidentiary burden on the Crown to avoid a directed verdict of acquittal be elevated beyond the *Monteleone/Arcuri* standard because of the requirement of proof beyond a reasonable doubt? Or are there policy concerns at play in the one case that do not apply in the other?

In *R v Fontaine*, 2004 SCC 27, [2004] 1 SCR 702, a unanimous Supreme Court, per Fish J, held that in a case of mental disorder (insane) automatism, "the evidential burden is discharged *if there is some evidence upon which a properly instructed jury could reasonably decide the issue*" (para 14). He added that the factors mentioned by Bastarache J in para 192 of *Stone* "can no longer, in the light of *Cinous*, be seen to inform the judge's legal determination whether the required evidential burden has been met," though "they may be expected to afford both structure and guidance" to the trier of fact in deciding whether the persuasive burden is satisfied (para 88). Should *Stone* still be considered authoritative in cases of non-mental-disorder (non-insane) automatism?

C. Proof Beyond a Reasonable Doubt

1. Defining the Standard

The requirement that the Crown prove the accused's guilt beyond a reasonable doubt is a cornerstone of criminal procedure in the common law world. The requirement of proof beyond a reasonable doubt is a common law doctrine: s 6 of the *Criminal Code* codifies the presumption of innocence, but says nothing about the quantum of proof required to displace that presumption. In *R v Oakes*, [1986] 1 SCR 103, 24 CCC (3d) 321, Dickson J held that the requirement of proof beyond a reasonable doubt was enshrined as part of the presumption of innocence guaranteed by s 11(d) of the Charter: see the excerpt in Section V.B, below.

The precise content of concept of proof beyond a reasonable doubt has been difficult to specify. It is clear that to convict on a standard of proof beyond a reasonable doubt, the jury must be satisfied of something more than probable guilt, but need not be *absolutely* sure of guilt. In the following case, the Supreme Court attempted to provide some guidance for trial judges in explaining the concept.

R v Lifchus
[1997] 3 SCR 320, 118 CCC (3d) 1
Lamer CJ and La Forest, L'Heureux-Dubé, Sopinka, Gonthier, Cory, McLachlin,
Iacobucci, and Major JJ (18 September 1997)

[The accused, a stockbroker, was convicted of fraud. He appealed his conviction on the ground that the trial judge had not properly explained the concept of reasonable doubt to the jury. The Manitoba Court of Appeal agreed, and ordered a new trial. The Crown appealed to the Supreme Court of Canada.]

CORY J (Lamer CJ and Sopinka, McLachlin, Iacobucci, and Major JJ concurring):
. . .

A. *The Fundamental Importance of Understanding the Onus Resting upon the Crown*

[13] The onus resting upon the Crown to prove the guilt of the accused beyond a reasonable doubt is inextricably linked to the presumption of innocence. That jurors clearly understand the meaning of the term is of fundamental importance to our criminal justice system. It is one of the principal safeguards which seeks to ensure that no innocent person is convicted. The *Marshall, Morin* and *Milgaard* cases serve as a constant reminder that our system, with all its protections for the accused, can still make tragic errors. A fair trial must be the goal of criminal justice. There cannot be a fair trial if jurors do not clearly understand the basic and fundamentally important concept of the standard of proof that the Crown must meet in order to obtain a conviction.

[14] No matter how exemplary the directions to the jury may be in every other respect if they are wanting in this aspect the trial must be lacking in fairness. It is true the term has come echoing down the centuries in words of deceptive simplicity. Yet jurors must appreciate their meaning and significance. They must be aware that the standard of proof is higher than the standard applied in civil actions of proof based upon a balance of probabilities yet less than proof to an absolute certainty.

(1) *Should a Trial Judge Explain "Reasonable Doubt" to the Jury?*

[15] In both its written submissions and during the oral hearing of this appeal, the Crown very fairly and properly conceded that there is good authority for the proposition that Canadian juries should be given a definition of "reasonable doubt."

[16] In some jurisdictions, most notably the United Kingdom, the position appears to be that there is no need to define "reasonable doubt" beyond telling jurors that they cannot convict unless they are "sure" that the accused is guilty. Indeed, some very eminent jurists have espoused the view that, because the words "reasonable doubt" are readily understood by jurors, it may even be unwise to attempt a definition (Glanville Williams, *Criminal Law: The General Part* (2nd ed. 1961), at p. 873; and *Textbook of Criminal Law* (2nd ed. 1983), at p. 43; *Wigmore on Evidence*, vol. 9 (Chadbourn rev. 1981), [para] 2497, at pp. 412-15).

[Cory J referred to *Victor v Nebraska*, 127 L Ed (2d) 583 (1994); *R v Tyhurst* (1992), 79 CCC (3d) 238 (BCCA); *R v Jenkins* (1996), 29 OR (3d) 30, 107 CCC (3d) 440 (CA); and *R v Brydon*, [1995] 4 SCR 253. In all of these cases, it was held that the trial judge ought to explain the concept of reasonable doubt to the jury.]

[22] The phrase "beyond a reasonable doubt," [*sic*] is composed of words which are commonly used in everyday speech. Yet, these words have a specific meaning in the legal context. This special meaning of the words "reasonable doubt" may not correspond precisely to the meaning ordinarily attributed to them. In criminal proceedings, where the liberty of the subject is at stake, it is of fundamental importance that jurors fully understand the nature of the burden of proof that the law requires them to apply. An explanation of the meaning of proof beyond a reasonable doubt is an essential element of the instructions that must be given to a jury. That a definition is necessary can be readily deduced from the frequency with which juries ask for guidance with regard to its meaning. It is therefore essential that the trial judge provide the jury with an explanation of the expression.

(2) How Should the Expression "Reasonable Doubt" Be Explained to the Jury?

(a) What Should Be Avoided?

[23] Perhaps a consideration of how to define the expression can begin by setting out common definitions which should be avoided. For example, a reasonable doubt should not be described as an "ordinary" concept. Jurors should not be invited to apply to the determination of guilt in a criminal trial the same standard of proof that they would apply to the decisions they are required to make in their everyday lives, or even to the most important of these decisions. In this aspect, I agree with the comments of Scott CJM set out in the judgment below (at pp. 234-35):

> Reasonable doubt, no matter how elusive the concept, cannot be equated to an ordinary everyday phrase. It is not, as we have seen, a "perfectly ordinary concept"—far from it. The reason for this is that the word "reasonable" can, depending on the circumstances, have two very different meanings. The first is the meaning thoroughly canvassed by Wood JA in *Brydon*. The other more common use is that in ordinary parlance: we hold "reasonable" views, we have "reasonable" opinions, and we make "reasonable" prognostications. *This is the standard by which we make our everyday decisions and by which we habitually govern ourselves. It is a standard of probability and, often within that, at the low end of the scale. It is very different from the criminal standard of proof which requires a much higher degree of certitude to arrive at a conclusion of guilt.*

To instruct the jury that reasonable doubt means nothing more than the "everyday sense" of the words is misleading and constitutes reversible error. [Emphasis added.]

[24] Ordinarily even the most important decisions of a lifetime are based upon carefully calculated risks. They are made on the assumption that certain events will in all likelihood take place or that certain facts are in all probability true. Yet to invite jurors to apply to a criminal trial the standard of proof used for even the important decisions in life runs the risk of significantly reducing the standard to which the prosecution must be held.

[25] Nor is it helpful to describe proof beyond a reasonable doubt simply as proof to a "moral certainty." I agree with Wood JA in *Brydon*, *supra*, and with Proulx JA in *R v. Girard* (1996), 109 CCC (3d) 545 (Que. CA), at p. 554, that this expression, although at one time perhaps clear to jurors, is today neither descriptive nor helpful. Moreover, as the United States Supreme Court recognized in *Victor*, *supra*, at pp. 596-97, there is great strength and persuasion in the position put forward that "moral certainty" may not be equated by jurors with "evidentiary certainty." Thus, if the standard of proof is explained as equivalent to "moral certainty," without more, jurors may think that they are entitled to convict if they feel "certain," even though the Crown has failed to prove its case beyond a reasonable doubt. In other words, different jurors may have different ideas about the level of proof required before they are "morally certain" of the accused's guilt. Like the United States Supreme Court, I think that this expression, although not necessarily fatal to a charge on reasonable doubt, should be avoided.

[26] Finally, qualifications of the word "doubt," other than by way of the adjective "reasonable," should be avoided. For instance, instructing the jury that a "reasonable doubt" is a "haunting" doubt, a "substantial" doubt or a "serious" doubt, may have the effect of misleading the jury (*Boucher v. The Queen*, [1955] SCR 16). What may be considered to be "haunting," "substantial" or "serious" is bound to vary with the background and perceptions of each individual juror. As a result of the use of these words jurors will be likely to understand that they should apply a standard of proof that could be higher or lower than that required. Similarly, to advise jurors that a "reasonable doubt" is a doubt which is so serious as to prevent them from eating or sleeping is manifestly misleading (*Girard, supra; R v. Bergeron* (1996), 109 CCC (3d) 571 (Que. CA), at p. 576). These words would lead a juror to set an unacceptably high standard of certainty.

(b) What Should Be Included in the Definition?

[27] First, it must be made clear to the jury that the standard of proof beyond a reasonable doubt is vitally important since it is inextricably linked to that basic premise which is fundamental to all criminal trials: the presumption of innocence. The two concepts are forever as closely linked as Romeo with Juliet or Oberon with Titania and they must be presented together as a unit. If the presumption of innocence is the golden thread of criminal justice then proof beyond a reasonable doubt is the silver and these two threads are forever intertwined in the fabric of criminal law. Jurors must be reminded that the burden of proving beyond a reasonable doubt that the accused committed the crime rests with the prosecution throughout the trial and never shifts to the accused.

[28] It will be recalled that, in *Brydon*, Wood JA defined a "reasonable doubt" as "a doubt for which one can give a reason, so long as the reason given is logically connected

to the evidence" (p. 525). This was the definition adopted in the Court below. However the idea that jurors should be instructed that a reasonable doubt is a doubt "for which one can give a reason" is not without its forceful detractors. Indeed it was expressly rejected by the Ontario Court of Appeal in *R v. Ford* (1991), 12 WCB (2d) 576. The view has been expressed that this instruction works to the detriment of the "inarticulate" juror. In short, the fear is that a juror who has a reasonable doubt which he or she is unable to concisely articulate to fellow jurors or even to herself, [*sic*] may erroneously conclude that the doubt is not reasonable. Wood JA dismissed this objection stating (at p. 525):

> ... I am not impressed by the notion that modern-day jurors are likely to be lacking in intelligence or "inarticulate" in the sense, or to the degree, that they would be unable either to engage in the limited reasoning process which such an instruction demands or be afraid to speak out and express their views in that respect to their fellow jurors. ...
>
> However, assuming that there may be some jurors who will find it difficult to communicate their closely held personal views to their fellow jurors, either because they are generally shy or because they have difficulty expressing themselves in conversation with others, that difficulty can be overcome by an instruction cast in terms which does no more than require that they be able to give themselves a reason for the doubt they hold. ...

[29] Nonetheless there is still another problem with this definition. It is that certain doubts, although reasonable, are simply incapable of articulation. For instance, there may be something about a person's demeanor in the witness box which will lead a juror to conclude that the witness is not credible. It may be that the juror is unable to point to the precise aspect of the witness's demeanor which was found to be suspicious, and as a result cannot articulate either to himself or others exactly why the witness should not be believed. A juror should not be made to feel that the overall, perhaps intangible, effect of a witness's demeanor cannot be taken into consideration in the assessment of credibility.

[30] It follows that it is certainly not essential to instruct jurors that a reasonable doubt is a doubt for which a reason can be supplied. To do so may unnecessarily complicate the task of the jury. It will suffice to instruct the jury that a reasonable doubt is a doubt based on reason and common sense which must be logically based upon the evidence or lack of evidence.

[31] It will be helpful in defining the term to explain to jurors those elements that should not be taken into consideration. They should be instructed that a reasonable doubt cannot be based on sympathy or prejudice. Further they should be told that a reasonable doubt must not be imaginary or frivolous. As well they must be advised that the Crown is not required to prove its case to an absolute certainty since such an unrealistically high standard could seldom be achieved.

[32] Members of the jury panel may have heard of the "balance of probabilities" or sat on a civil case and been instructed as to the standard used in those cases. It is important that jurors be told that they are not to apply that standard in the context of the criminal trial. They should be told that proof establishing a probability of guilt is not sufficient to establish guilt beyond a reasonable doubt. The instructions explaining what the standard is not will help jurors to understand what it is.

[33] In the United Kingdom juries are instructed that they may convict if they are "sure" or "certain" of the accused's guilt. Yet, in my view that instruction standing alone

is both insufficient and potentially misleading. Being "certain" is a conclusion which a juror may reach, but it does not indicate the route the juror should take in order to arrive at the conclusion.

[34] It is only *after* proper instructions have been given as to the meaning of the expression "beyond a reasonable doubt" that a jury may be advised that they can convict if they are "certain" or "sure" that the accused is guilty.

[35] In some jurisdictions, after the jury has been selected, the trial judge will provide some brief basic instructions as to the nature of a criminal trial and the fundamental principles that will be applied. This is such a sound, sensible and salutary practice that it should be undertaken in all jurisdictions. Obviously it will be of great assistance to jurors if, at the beginning of the trial, they are advised of the applicable basic principles. If that procedure is followed, it would be helpful to advise the jury at this time, as well as at the conclusion of the trial, of the presumption of innocence and the burden of proof beyond a reasonable doubt which the Crown must meet.

(c) Summary

[36] Perhaps a brief summary of what the definition should and should not contain may be helpful. It should be explained that:

- the standard of proof beyond a reasonable doubt is inextricably intertwined with that principle fundamental to all criminal trials, the presumption of innocence;
- the burden of proof rests on the prosecution throughout the trial and never shifts to the accused;
- a reasonable doubt is not a doubt based upon sympathy or prejudice;
- rather, it is based upon reason and common sense;
- it is logically connected to the evidence or absence of evidence;
- it does not involve proof to an absolute certainty; it is not proof beyond *any* doubt nor is it an imaginary or frivolous doubt; and
- more is required than proof that the accused is probably guilty—a jury which concludes only that the accused is probably guilty must acquit.

[37] On the other hand, certain references to the required standard of proof should be avoided. For example:

- describing the term "reasonable doubt" as an ordinary expression which has no special meaning in the criminal law context;
- inviting jurors to apply to the task before them the same standard of proof that they apply to important, or even the most important, decisions in their own lives;
- equating proof "beyond a reasonable doubt" to proof "to a moral certainty";
- qualifying the word "doubt" with adjectives other than "reasonable," such as "serious," "substantial" or "haunting," which may mislead the jury; and
- instructing jurors that they may convict if they are "sure" that the accused is guilty, before providing them with a proper definition as to the meaning of the words "beyond a reasonable doubt."

[38] A charge which is consistent with the principles set out in these reasons will suffice regardless of the particular words used by the trial judge. Nevertheless, it may, as suggested

in *Girard*, *supra*, at p. 556, be useful to set out a "model charge" which could provide the necessary instructions as to the meaning of the phrase beyond a reasonable doubt.

(3) Suggested Charge

[39] Instructions pertaining to the requisite standard of proof in a criminal trial of proof beyond a reasonable doubt might be given along these lines:

> The accused enters these proceedings presumed to be innocent. That presumption of innocence remains throughout the case until such time as the Crown has on the evidence put before you satisfied you beyond a reasonable doubt that the accused is guilty.
>
> What does the expression "beyond a reasonable doubt" mean?
>
> The term "beyond a reasonable doubt" has been used for a very long time and is a part of our history and traditions of justice. It is so engrained in our criminal law that some think it needs no explanation, yet something must be said regarding its meaning.
>
> A reasonable doubt is not an imaginary or frivolous doubt. It must not be based upon sympathy or prejudice. Rather, it is based on reason and common sense. It is logically derived from the evidence or absence of evidence.
>
> Even if you believe the accused is probably guilty or likely guilty, that is not sufficient. In those circumstances you must give the benefit of the doubt to the accused and acquit because the Crown has failed to satisfy you of the guilt of the accused beyond a reasonable doubt.
>
> On the other hand you must remember that it is virtually impossible to prove anything to an absolute certainty and the Crown is not required to do so. Such a standard of proof is impossibly high.
>
> In short if, based upon the evidence before the Court, you are sure that the accused committed the offence you should convict since this demonstrates that you are satisfied of his guilt beyond a reasonable doubt.

[40] This is not a magic incantation that needs to be repeated word for word. It is nothing more than a suggested form that would not be faulted if it were used. For example, in cases where a reverse onus provision must be considered, it would be helpful to bring to the attention of the jury either the evidence which might satisfy that onus or the absence of evidence applicable to it. Any form of instruction that complied with the applicable principles and avoided the pitfalls referred to would be satisfactory.

[41] Further, it is possible that an error in the instructions as to the standard of proof may not constitute a reversible error. It was observed in *R v. W.(D.)*, [1991] 1 SCR 742, at p. 758, that the verdict ought not be disturbed "if the charge, when read as a whole, makes it clear that the jury could not have been under any misapprehension as to the correct burden and standard of proof to apply." On the other hand, if the charge as a whole gives rise to the reasonable likelihood that the jury misapprehended the standard of proof, then as a general rule the verdict will have to be set aside and a new trial directed.

(4) The Charge in This Case

[42] The relevant part of the trial judge's charge was in these words:

When I use the words "proof beyond a reasonable doubt," I use those words in their ordinary, natural every day sense. There isn't one of you who hasn't said, gosh I've got a doubt about such and so. Perfectly every day word. There isn't one of you who doesn't have a notion of reasonable. That, too, is a perfectly ordinary concept.

... On your review of the evidence if you are left with a doubt as to whether the Crown has proved one of those essential elements and if that doubt is a reasonable one then the accused must be acquitted of the evidence.

On the other hand, if having reviewed all of the evidence, you are not left with a reasonable doubt as to whether any of those essential elements have been proved, in other words if you are satisfied beyond that point of reasonable doubt, the accused must be convicted. The words "doubt" the words "reasonable" [sic] are ordinary, every day words that I am sure you understand.

[43] Like Scott CJM, I am of the view that this charge was insufficient. To begin with, the trial judge did not provide a definition of "reasonable doubt." This expression must be explained to the jury. Further, the trial judge told the jurors to evaluate the concept of reasonable doubt as if these were "ordinary, every day words." For the reasons set out earlier, this is an unacceptable direction. The expression "beyond a reasonable doubt" cannot be equated to the everyday use made in today's society of the words "reasonable" and "doubt." Rather, in the context of a criminal trial they have a specific meaning. Unfortunately, the trial judge failed to explain the standard of proof fully and properly to the jury. This failure constituted an error of law in a fundamentally important aspect of this criminal trial.

[44] It is true that the charge as a whole must be considered. Yet, the trial judge did not provide any further guidance to the jury concerning the meaning of proof beyond a reasonable doubt. It follows that this serious error was not saved by further instructions. This is unfortunate, since the trial judge's charge, in all other respects, was, as Scott CJM observed, "a model of clarity and conciseness" (p. 235). Nevertheless, the error was serious and gave rise to the reasonable likelihood that the jury misapprehended the burden of proof which they were required to apply.

[Cory J held that the trial judge's error could not be cured by application of the proviso in s 686(1)(b)(iii) of the *Criminal Code*. L'Heureux-Dubé J, La Forest and Gonthier JJ concurring, concurred in the result. The Crown's appeal was dismissed.]

NOTES AND QUESTIONS

In subsequent cases, many of them involving jury instructions that were delivered before *Lifchus* was decided, the Supreme Court has held that a jury charge is acceptable as long as it is in "substantial compliance" with the principles expressed in *Lifchus*. See particularly *R v Starr*, 2000 SCC 40, [2000] 2 SCR 144, *R v Beauchamp*, 2000 SCC 54, [2000] 2 SCR 720, and *R v Cinous*, 2002 SCC 29, [2002] 2 SCR 3.

1. How would you determine "substantial compliance" with *Lifchus*?

2. Would a brief instruction that contained no errors but did not provide much explanation of the concept be better or worse than a longer instruction that contained several errors

but clearly distinguished between proof on a balance of probabilities and proof beyond a reasonable doubt?

3. Would it make any difference whether the instruction was delivered before or after the decision in *Lifchus* was released?

2. Applying the Standard

R v Morin
[1988] 2 SCR 345, 44 CCC (3d) 193
Dickson CJ and McIntyre, La Forest, Wilson, Lamer, and Sopinka JJ
(17 November 1988)

[The accused was charged with the first-degree murder of a young girl. The Crown's case rested largely on circumstantial evidence and on statements that the accused had allegedly made to a cellmate and to an undercover officer. The accused's defence was that he had not committed the crime or that, if he had, he was insane. He was acquitted. The Crown's appeal to the Ontario Court of Appeal was allowed and a new trial was ordered. Morin appealed to the Supreme Court of Canada.]

SOPINKA J (Dickson CJ and McIntyre and La Forest JJ concurring):

[22] The following are the relevant excerpts from the charge to the jury set out in the order in which they occurred:

1. Concerning Evidence
You are not obliged to accept any part of the evidence of a witness just because there is no denial of it. If you have a reasonable doubt about any of the evidence, you will give the benefit of that doubt to the accused with respect to such evidence. *Having decided what evidence you consider worthy of belief, you will consider it as a whole, of course, in arriving at your verdict.* [Emphasis added.]

2. Concerning Burden of Proof
The accused is entitled to the benefit of reasonable doubt on the whole of the case and on each and every issue in the case.

Proof beyond a reasonable doubt does not apply to the individual items of evidence or the separate pieces of evidence in the case, but to the total body of evidence upon which the Crown relies to prove guilt. Before you can convict you must be satisfied beyond a reasonable doubt of his guilt.

3. Concerning Hairs and Fibres
It seems to me that this evidence does not go beyond proving that Christine could have been in the Honda motor vehicle and that the accused could have been at the scene of the killing, and of course that is not proof beyond a reasonable doubt

4. Concerning Appellant's Statements to Hobbs
I was going to go on to say that if you find that the evidence of the accused at trial here represents the correct interpretation of those tapes and transcripts, or parts of the tapes and transcripts, or if you have a reasonable doubt that that might be so, you will give him the benefit of the doubt as to those parts of the tapes or transcripts and adopt his interpretation.

5. Concerning Appellant's Statement to Inmate May

Now, as to that evidence, in relation to that part of the tape that I have just read, if you find the evidence of the accused at trial represents the correct interpretation of that exchange, or if you have a reasonable doubt that that may be so, you will give the benefit of the doubt to the accused and adopt his interpretation.

[23] In my opinion, based on my reading of the charge as a whole, a jury would likely have concluded that in examining the evidence they were to give the accused the benefit of the doubt in respect of *any* evidence. This process of examination and elimination would occur during the so-called "fact-finding" stage, to use the appellant's phrase. The evidence as a whole to which the jury was to apply itself in order to determine guilt or innocence was the residuum after the "fact-finding" stage. There is no other way of reading the first excerpt from the charge.

[24] The appellant contends, however, that the second excerpt corrected this error. Cory JA agreed that it and the instruction as to alibi "do much to rectify the errors made on this subject" (p. 62). The second excerpt refers to the "whole of the case" and the "total body of evidence." Having been told earlier that the "whole" upon which the verdict was to be based consisted of the evidence that had been accepted, I am not satisfied that the jury would have interpreted this passage as a correction. Rather, they might very well have assumed that the earlier definition of the "whole" still applied. At best, from the appellant's standpoint the jury would be confused. Subsequent passages in the charge illustrate what is meant by the first excerpt, and would confirm that individual pieces of evidence were to be examined by reference to the criminal standard.

· · ·

[28] The appellant submits, citing *R v. Challice* (1979), 45 CCC (2d) 546 (Ont. CA), that different considerations apply where the credibility of defence evidence is at issue. In such cases the argument is that the defence evidence does not have to be believed, but "only has to raise a reasonable doubt." That does not mean, however, that the defence evidence or the evidence which it contradicts or explains is to be examined piecemeal. The judgment of Morden JA in *Challice*, which the appellant agrees expresses the traditional view and is consistent with the judgment of this court in *Nadeau v. The Queen*, [1984] 2 SCR 570, 15 CCC (3d) 499, and *R v. Thatcher*, [1987] 1 SCR 652, 32 CCC (3d) 481, affirming 24 CCC (3d) 449, correctly states the law in the following passage:

Understandably, a jury have to give careful consideration to issues of credibility when deliberating upon their verdict, and with respect to various pieces of evidence they may have differing views: total acceptance, total rejection, or something in between. *An effective and desirable way of recognizing this necessary part of the process, and putting it to the jury in a way that accurately comports with their duty respecting the burden and standard of proof, is to instruct the jury that it is not necessary for them to believe the defence evidence on a vital issue—but that it is sufficient if it, viewed in the context of all the evidence,* leaves them in a state of reasonable doubt as to the accused's guilt. See *R v. Lobell*, [1957] 1 QB 547 at p. 551, *per* Lord Goddard, CJ. [Emphasis added.]

[29] Nothing in *Nadeau* supports the appellant's submission. In that case the trial judge charged the jury in effect that they should accept either the Crown's version of the facts or that of the accused. He added that the accused was entitled to the benefit of the

doubt only if the versions were equally consistent with the evidence. The judgment of Lamer J makes it plain that the accused's version is entitled to the benefit of the doubt unless, when it is considered in light of all the evidence, the jury is satisfied beyond a reasonable doubt that the Crown's version is correct. He said (at p. 573):

> The jurors cannot accept his [a Crown witness's] version, or any part of it, unless they are satisfied beyond all reasonable doubt, *having regard to all the evidence*, that the events took place in this manner, otherwise, the accused is entitled, unless a fact has been established beyond a reasonable doubt, to the finding of fact the most favourable to him, provided of course that it is based on evidence in the record and not mere speculation. [Emphasis added.]

[30] There is nothing in the judgment in the *Thatcher* case, *supra*, which is inconsistent with this view.

[31] The effect of the misdirections referred to above may very well have been that the jury examined evidence that was crucial to the Crown's case in bits and pieces. Standing alone or pitted against the evidence of the accused without the support of other evidence, much of this evidence might have been discarded as not measuring up to the test. When the jury came to consider the Crown's case as a whole, there may not have been very much left of it. We cannot know for certain, but this scenario is a very likely one and the charge therefore constituted a serious misdirection.

[32] This conclusion is sufficient to dispose of this ground of appeal without addressing the second point in the appellant's argument: the submission that it is a correct instruction to a jury that they are to apply the criminal standard in two stages—the fact-finding stage and the verdict, or guilt, stage. Since, however, it was an attempt to do so by the trial judge that led to the difficulties in the charge, I propose to consider this point.

[33] The authorities reviewed above are clear that the jury is not to examine the evidence piecemeal by reference to the criminal standard. Otherwise, there is virtually no guidance in previous cases as to what legal rules, if any, apply to the process of weighing the evidence. Attempts to formulate such rules have been frowned upon.

[Sopinka J next considered a number of authorities that disapprove of piecemeal consideration of individual pieces of evidence.]

[38] In practice it is not practical, because the jury would have to agree on not only the same facts but what individual facts prove. Individual facts do not necessarily establish guilt, but are a link in the chain of ultimate proof. It is not possible, therefore, to require the jury to find facts proved beyond a reasonable doubt without identifying *what it is* that they prove beyond a reasonable doubt. Since the same fact may give rise to different inferences tending to establish guilt or innocence, the jury might discard such facts on the basis that there is doubt as to what they prove.

[39] The concern which proponents of the two-stage process express is that facts which are doubtful will be used to establish guilt. The answer to this concern is that a chain is only as strong as its weakest link. If facts which are essential to a finding of guilt are still doubtful notwithstanding the support of other facts, this will produce a doubt in the mind of the jury that guilt has been proved beyond a reasonable doubt.

[40] I conclude from the foregoing that the facts are for the jury to determine, subject to an instruction by the trial judge as to the law. While the charge may and often does

include many helpful tips on the weighing of evidence, such as observing demeanour, taking into the account the interest of the witness and so forth, the law lays down only one basic requirement: during the process of deliberation the jury or other trier of fact must consider the evidence as a whole and determine whether guilt is established by the prosecution beyond a reasonable doubt. This of necessity requires that each element of the offence or issue be proved beyond a reasonable doubt. Beyond this injunction it is for the trier of fact to determine how to proceed. To intrude in this area is, as pointed out by North P, an intrusion into the province of the jury.

[41] The reason we have juries is so that lay persons and not lawyers decide the facts. To inject into the process artificial legal rules with respect to the natural human activity of deliberation and decision would tend to detract from the value of the jury system. Accordingly, it is wrong for a trial judge to lay down additional rules for the weighing of the evidence. Indeed, it is unwise to attempt to elaborate on the basic requirement referred to above. I would make two exceptions. The jury should be told that the facts are not to be examined separately and in isolation with reference to the criminal standard. This instruction is a necessary corollary to the basic rule referred to above. Without it there is some danger that a jury might conclude that the requirement that each issue or element of the offence be proved beyond a reasonable doubt demands that individual items of evidence be so proved.

[Wilson J, Lamer J concurring, agreed that the trial judge's charge to the jury was erroneous, but for slightly different reasons.]

WILSON J (Lamer J concurring):

. . .

[95] … How could one come to a conclusion with any degree of certainty if one has reasonable doubts about the facts upon which the conclusion is based?

[96] Was the trial judge in error, then, in the passages from the charge cited above? In my view, he was. While the trial judge was correct to direct the jury not to use facts that were not proved beyond a reasonable doubt in order to found a conviction, he erred in suggesting (or seeming to suggest) that each fact should be assessed in isolation from the others. What he should have told the jury, in my opinion, is: that in their ultimate determination of guilt they could rely only on facts which, when assessed in the context of all the facts, they found to have been proved beyond a reasonable doubt; that they must not make a finding of guilt on doubtful facts; but that facts which might seem doubtful when viewed in isolation might become completely credible against the backdrop of all the other facts.

NOTES AND QUESTIONS

At his second trial, Morin was found guilty of first-degree murder. His second appeal to the Ontario Court of Appeal was allowed when DNA testing excluded him as the killer.

What is the difference between the approach of Sopinka J and that of Wilson J? Is it possible to imagine a case in which a jury, reasoning logically, would reach a different conclusion if they followed the approach of Wilson J rather than that of Sopinka J?

In *R v W (D)*, [1991] 1 SCR 742, Cory J for a unanimous court held that where the accused testifies, the following instruction should be included in the charge to the jury:

First, if you believe the evidence of the accused, obviously you must acquit.

Second, if you do not believe the testimony of the accused but you are left in reasonable doubt by it, you must acquit.

Third, even if you are not left in doubt by the evidence of the accused, you must ask yourself whether, on the basis of the evidence which you do accept, you are convinced beyond a reasonable doubt by that evidence of the guilt of the accused.

Is this instruction consistent with the holding in *Morin*?

Even if the accused does not testify, courts have held that the *W (D)* instruction should be given when the defence presents or points to other evidence that could result in acquittal. See *R v D (B)*, 2011 ONCA 51 at paras 105-114. Whether or not the accused testifies, however, the instruction is mandatory only when "credibility is a central or significant issue." (*R v Daley*, 2007 SCC 53 at para 106.) For applications of *W (D)* in cases where the accused testifies that an incriminating statement made by him or her before trial is untrue, see *R v MacKenzie*, [1993] 1 SCR 212 at 239; *R v Mayuran*, 2012 SCC 31 at paras 39-43.

W (D) has been criticized for being almost too simplistic in the direction that it provides. In practice, greater nuance may sometimes be necessary. The Supreme Court acknowledged as much in *R v JHS*, 2008 SCC 30, [2008] 2 SCR 152:

[10] The precise formulation of the *W. (D.)* questions has been criticized. As to the first question, the jury may believe inculpatory elements of the statements of an accused but reject the exculpatory explanation. In *R v. Latimer*, [2001] 1 SCR 3, 2001 SCC 1, the accused did not testify, but his description of the killing of his daughter was put into evidence by way of statements to the police. His description of the event itself was obviously believed. The exculpatory explanation did not amount to a defence at law. He was convicted. The principle that a jury may believe some, none, or all of the testimony of any witness, including that of an accused, suggests to some critics that the first *W. (D.)* question is something of an oversimplification.

[11] As to the second question, some jurors may wonder how, if they believe *none* of the evidence of the accused, such rejected evidence may nevertheless *of itself* raise a reasonable doubt. Of course, some elements of the evidence of an accused may raise a reasonable doubt, even though the bulk of it is rejected. Equally, the jury may simply conclude that they do not know whether to believe the accused's testimony or not. In either circumstance the accused is entitled to an acquittal.

[12] The third question, again, is taken by some critics as failing to contemplate a jury's acceptance of inculpatory bits of the evidence of an accused but not the exculpatory elements. In light of these possible sources of difficulty, Wood JA in *H. (C.W.)* suggested an additional instruction:

I would add one more instruction in such cases, which logically ought to be second in the order, namely: "If, after a careful consideration of all the evidence, you are unable to decide whom to believe, you must acquit." [p. 155]

[13] In short the *W. (D.)* questions should not have attributed to them a level of sanctity or immutable perfection that their author never claimed for them. *W. (D.)*'s message that it must be made crystal clear to the jury that the burden *never* shifts from the Crown to prove *every* element of the offence beyond a reasonable doubt is of fundamental importance but its application

should not result in a triumph of form over substance. In *R v. S. (W.D.)*, [1994] 3 SCR 521, Cory J reiterated that the *W. (D.)* instructions need not be given "word for word as some magic incantation" (p. 533). In *R v. Avetysan*, [2000] 2 SCR 745, 2000 SCC 56, Major J for the majority pointed out that in any case where credibility is important "[t]he question is really whether, in substance, the trial judge's instructions left the jury with the impression that it had to choose between the two versions of events" (para. 19). The main point is that lack of credibility on the part of the accused does not equate to proof of his or her guilt beyond a reasonable doubt.

D. Strict Liability Offences

In *R v Sault Ste Marie*, [1978] 2 SCR 1299, 40 CCC (2d) 353, Dickson J, speaking for a unanimous court, considered the fault element and the burden of proof for criminal and quasi-criminal offences:

> Public welfare offences involve a shift of emphasis from the protection of individual interests to the protection of public and social interests: see F.B. Sayre, "Public Welfare Offenses" (1933), 33 *Columbia Law Rev.* 55; Hall, *General Principles of Criminal Law*, c. 13 (1947), at 427; R.M. Perkins, "Civil Offense" (1952), 100 *U of Pa. L Rev.* 832; Jobson, "Far From Clear" (1975-76), 18 *Crim. LQ* 294. The unfortunate tendency in many past cases has been to see the choice as between two stark alternatives: (i) full *mens rea*; or (ii) absolute liability. In respect of public welfare offences (within which category pollution offences fall) where full *mens rea* is not required, absolute liability has often been imposed. English jurisprudence has consistently maintained this dichotomy: see *Criminal Law, Evidence and Procedure*, 11 Hals., 4th ed., at 202, para. 18. There has, however, been an attempt in Australia, in many Canadian courts, and indeed in England, to seek a middle position, fulfilling the goals of public welfare offences while still not punishing the entirely blameless. There is an increasing and impressive stream of authority which holds that where an offence does not require full *mens rea*, it is nevertheless a good defence for the defendant to prove that he was not negligent.
>
> Dr. Glanville Williams has written: "There is a half-way house between *mens rea* and strict responsibility which has not yet been properly utilized, and that is responsibility for negligence" (*Criminal Law: General Part*, 2nd ed. (1961), at 262). Morris and Howard, in *Studies in Criminal Law* (1964), at 200, suggest that strict responsibility might with advantage be replaced by a doctrine of responsibility for negligence strengthened by a shift in the burden of proof. The defendant would be allowed to exculpate himself by proving affirmatively that he was not negligent. Professor Howard ("Strict Responsibility in the High Court of Australia" (1960), 76 *LQR* 547) offers the comment that English law of strict responsibility in minor statutory offences is distinguished only by its irrationality, and then has this to say in support of the position taken by the Australian High Court, at p. 548:
>
> > Over a period of nearly sixty years since its inception the High Court has adhered with consistency to the principle that there should be no criminal responsibility without fault, however minor the offence. It has done so by utilizing the very half-way house to which Dr. Williams refers, responsibility for negligence.
>
> In his work, "Public Welfare Offenses," at p. 78, Professor Sayre suggests that if the penalty is really slight, involving, for instance, a maximum fine of $25, particularly if adequate enforcement depends upon wholesale prosecution, or if the social danger arising from violation is serious, the

doctrine of basing liability upon mere activity rather than fault, [*sic*] is sound. He continues, however, at p. 79:

> On the other hand, some public welfare offenses involve a possible penalty of imprisonment or heavy fine. In such cases it would seem sounder policy to maintain the orthodox requirement of a guilty mind but to shift the burden of proof to the shoulders of the defendant to establish his lack of a guilty intent if he can. For public welfare offenses defendants may be convicted by proof of the mere act of violation; but, if the offense involves a possible prison penalty, the defendant should not be denied the right of bringing forward affirmative evidence to prove that the violation was the result of no fault on his part.

and at p. 82:

> It is fundamentally unsound to convict a defendant for a crime involving a substantial term of imprisonment without giving him the opportunity to prove that his action was due to an honest and reasonable mistake of fact or that he acted without guilty intent. If the public danger is widespread and serious, the practical situation can be met by shifting to the shoulders of the defendant the burden of proving a lack of guilty intent.

The doctrine proceeds on the assumption that the defendant could have avoided the *prima facie* offence through the exercise of reasonable care and he is given the opportunity of establishing, if he can, that he did in fact exercise such care.

. . .

The correct approach, in my opinion, is to relieve the Crown of the burden of proving *mens rea*, having regard to *Pierce Fisheries* and to the virtual impossibility in most regulatory cases of proving wrongful intention. In a normal case, the accused alone will have knowledge of what he has done to avoid the breach and it is not improper to expect him to come forward with the evidence of due diligence. This is particularly so when it is alleged, for example, that pollution was caused by the activities of a large and complex corporation. Equally, there is nothing wrong with rejecting absolute liability and admitting the defence of reasonable care.

In this doctrine it is not up to the prosecution to prove negligence. Instead, it is open to the defendant to prove that all due care has been taken. This burden falls upon the defendant as he is the only one who will generally have the means of proof. This would not seem unfair as the alternative is absolute liability which denies an accused any defence whatsoever. While the prosecution must prove beyond a reasonable doubt that the defendant committed the prohibited act, the defendant must only establish on the balance of probabilities that he has a defence of reasonable care.

I conclude, for the reasons which I have sought to express, that there are compelling grounds for the recognition of three categories of offences rather than the traditional two:

1. Offences in which *mens rea*, consisting of some positive state of mind such as intent, knowledge, or recklessness, must be proved by the prosecution either as an inference from the nature of the act committed, or by additional evidence.

2. Offences in which there is no necessity for the prosecution to prove the existence of *mens rea*; the doing of the prohibited act *prima facie* imports the offence, leaving it open to the accused to avoid liability by proving that he took all reasonable care. This involves consideration of what a reasonable man would have done in the circumstances. The defence will be available if the accused reasonably believed in a mistaken set of facts

which, if true, would render the act or omission innocent, or if he took all reasonable steps to avoid the particular event. These offences may properly be called offences of strict liability. Mr. Justice Estey so referred to them in *Hickey*'s case.

3. Offences of absolute liability where it is not open to the accused to exculpate himself by showing that he was free of fault.

Offences which are criminal in the true sense fall in the first category. Public welfare offences would, *prima facie*, be in the second category. They are not subject to the presumption of full *mens rea*. An offence of this type would fall in the first category only if such words as "wilfully," "with intent," "knowingly," or "intentionally" are contained in the statutory provision creating the offence. On the other hand, the principle that punishment should in general not be inflicted on those without fault applies. Offences of absolute liability would be those in respect of which the Legislature had made it clear that guilt would follow proof merely of the proscribed act. The over-all regulatory pattern adopted by the Legislature, the subject-matter of the legislation, the importance of the penalty, and the precision of the language used will be primary considerations in determining whether the offence falls into the third category.

Sault Ste Marie was decided before the Charter, but is still the leading case on the meaning of fault and on the burden of proof in regulatory offences. Do you accept Dickson J's rationale for creating a "half-way house" of due diligence between full *mens rea* and absolute liability? Does that rationale extend to placing a persuasive burden on the accused on the issue of due diligence?

IV. CONSTITUTIONAL LITIGATION

If it is necessary to establish facts in constitutional litigation, who should have the burden of proof, and what quantum of proof should be required? It is well established in Charter litigation that the applicant bears the burden of establishing, on a balance of probabilities, the facts relevant to a claim that a Charter right has been infringed. In *R v Oakes*, [1986] 1 SCR 103, 24 CCC (3d) 321, Dickson CJ made the following comments about the burden and quantum of proof where s 1 of the Charter is invoked:

The standard of proof under s. 1 is the civil standard, namely, proof by a preponderance of probability. The alternative criminal standard, proof beyond a reasonable doubt, would, in my view, be unduly onerous on the party seeking to limit. Concepts such as "reasonableness," "justifiability" and "free and democratic society" are simply not amenable to such a standard. Nevertheless, the preponderance of probability test must be applied rigorously. Indeed, the phrase "demonstrably justified" in s. 1 of the *Charter* supports this conclusion. ...

. . .

Having regard to the fact that s. 1 is being invoked for the purpose of justifying a violation of the constitutional rights and freedoms the *Charter* was designed to protect, a very high degree of probability will be, in the words of Lord Denning, "commensurate with the occasion." Where evidence is required in order to prove the constituent elements of a s. 1 inquiry, and this will generally be the case, it should be cogent and persuasive and make clear to the court the consequences of imposing or not imposing the limit: see *Law Society of Upper Canada v. Skapinker*, [1984] 1 SCR 357 at p. 384; *Re Singh and Minister of Employment & Immigration*, [1985] 1 SCR 177 at p. 217. A court will also need to know what alternative measures for implementing the objective were available to the legislators when they made their decisions. I should add, however, that there may be cases where certain elements of the s. 1 analysis are obvious or self-evident.

Dickson CJ might have added that in some cases courts will take judicial notice of facts relevant to a s 1 justification. What is the practical effect of the holding that the elements of a s 1 justification be proved by "cogent and persuasive" evidence? Can this statement be reconciled with the court's pronouncement in *McDougall*, *supra*, that the quantum of proof associated with the balance of probabilities standard never shifts? Are you aware of any constitutional cases where the quantum of proof has made a difference to the outcome?

In *R v Collins*, [1987] 1 SCR 265, the court held that in an application to exclude evidence under s 24 of the Charter, the applicant bears the burden of establishing, on a balance of probabilities, both the Charter violation and the standard for exclusion under s 24(2). In light of the reasoning in *Oakes* about the burden of proof for a s 1 justification, why should a person whose rights have been violated have to show that admission of the evidence thereby obtained will bring the administration of justice into disrepute? If the state has obtained evidence unconstitutionally, should it have to overcome a presumption that its admission would bring the administration of justice into disrepute? In light of the *Grant* test for exclusion (see Chapter 8, Section II.C), does the location of the burden of proof on s 24(2) issues make any difference?

V. PRESUMPTIONS AND REVERSE ONUSES

A. Presumptions

A presumption is a legal device enabling, or requiring, a trier of fact to reach a conclusion about a particular fact either where there is no evidence about that fact, or where a legal rule states that the fact may, or must, be inferred from other facts. Cross reminds us that there are two different kinds of presumptions and that it is important to keep the distinction between them in mind:

> In the first place, a presumption sometimes means nothing more than a conclusion which must be drawn until the contrary is proved; secondly, and more frequently, it denotes a conclusion that a fact (conveniently called the "presumed fact") exists which may, or must, be drawn if some other fact (conveniently called the "basic fact") is proved or admitted.

(Rupert Cross, *Evidence* (London: Butterworths, 1958) at 84.)

In *R v Oakes*, [1986] 1 SCR 103, 24 CCC (3d) 321, Dickson CJ elaborated on this distinction as follows:

> Presumptions can be classified into two general categories: presumptions *without* basic facts and presumptions *with* basic facts. A presumption without a basic fact is simply a conclusion which is to be drawn until the contrary is proved. A presumption with a basic fact entails a conclusion to be drawn upon proof of the basic fact (see *Cross on Evidence*, 5th ed. (1979), pp. 122-23).
>
> Basic fact presumptions can be further categorized into permissive and mandatory presumptions. A permissive presumption leaves it optional as to whether the inference of the presumed fact is drawn following proof of the basic fact. A mandatory presumption requires that the inference be made.

Presumptions may also be either rebuttable or irrebuttable. If a presumption is rebuttable, there are three potential ways the presumed fact can be rebutted. First, the accused may be required merely to raise a reasonable doubt as to its existence. Secondly, the accused may have an evidentiary burden to adduce sufficient evidence to bring into question the truth of the presumed fact. Thirdly, the accused may have a legal or persuasive burden to prove on a balance of probabilities the non-existence of the presumed fact.

Finally, presumptions are often referred to as either presumptions of law or presumptions of fact. The latter entail "frequently recurring examples of circumstantial evidence" (*Cross on Evidence*, at p. 124) while the former involve actual legal rules.

Dickson CJ's typology of presumptions might be illustrated with the following examples (among others).

The presumption of innocence is, of course, a basic concept in our system of criminal justice. It originated at common law, is specifically mentioned in s 6 of the *Criminal Code*, and is enshrined in s 11(d) of the Charter. It holds that the trier of fact cannot find the accused guilty unless his or her guilt is proved to the required standard. The presumption of innocence therefore falls into Cross's first category; to use Dickson CJ's terms, it is a mandatory (but rebuttable) presumption that does not depend on basic facts.

The presumption that a person intends the natural consequences of his or her actions has a long common law history (for some of this history, see KJM Smith, *Lawyers, Legislators and Theorists: Developments in English Criminal Jurisprudence, 1800-1957* (Oxford: Clarendon Press, 1998) at 143-66). This presumption would enable the trier of fact to find the presumed fact— the accused's intent—upon proof of the basic fact—the accused's conduct. There have been times in the history of English criminal law when this presumption has been considered both mandatory and irrebuttable; but, at least since the decision in *R v Giannotti*, [1956] OR 349, 115 CCC 203 (CA), it has been clear in Canada that the presumption does not have the legal status of the presumption of innocence or of the many statutory presumptions found in the *Criminal Code*. Indeed, in *R v Beyo* (2000), 47 OR (3d) 712, 144 CCC (3d) 15 at para 37 (CA), Rosenberg JA said: "there is no presumption that a person intends the natural consequences of his acts." What Rosenberg JA meant, it is submitted, is that the trier of fact may use the presumption, but only as a common sense tool for reasoning; in other words, this presumption is both permissive and rebuttable. In the absence of any other evidence about the accused's intent, the trier of fact may (but need not) infer that the accused intended the natural consequences of his or her acts; the presumption is therefore permissive, not mandatory. And, even where the trier of fact might be tempted to infer intent from the natural consequences of action, the accused can lead or point to evidence of mistake, incapacity, intoxication, or any other factor that might have negated his or her intent; the presumption is therefore rebuttable. See *R v Seymour*, [1996] 2 SCR 252 at paras 19-24; *R v Walle*, 2012 SCC 41 at paras 55-68; *R v Luciano*, 2011 ONCA 89 at para 79.

Where a presumption is rebuttable, what is required to rebut it? Typically, presumptions that fall into Cross's first category can be rebutted only by proof of a party's case to the required standard. So the presumption of innocence, as we have seen, can be rebutted only by proof of guilt beyond a reasonable doubt. Presumptions that fall into Cross's second category can often be rebutted merely by raising evidence that has the effect of putting a basic fact into question; the presumption is then spent, so to speak, and the parties must prove or disprove the relevant fact without the assistance of the presumption. Consider, for example, s 286.2(3) of the *Criminal Code*, which provides:

> 286.2(3) … evidence that a person lives with or is habitually in the company of a person who offers or provides sexual services for consideration is, in the absence of evidence to the contrary, proof that the person received a financial or other material benefit from those services.

This is a classic presumption of the second sort described by Cross: once the Crown proves the basic fact (that the accused "lives with or is habitually in the company of a person who offers or provides sexual services for consideration"), the trier of fact must infer the presumed fact (that the accused lives on the avails of prostitution). But what is the effect of the phrase "received a financial or other material benefit from those services" on this presumption? Does it mean that, once the basic fact is proved, the accused must prove, to some standard, that he or she does *not* live on the avails of prostitution? Or does it mean only that if the accused is able to lead (or to point to) "evidence to the contrary," the presumption has no further effect, so that the trier of fact must determine guilt or innocence without the aid of s 286.2(3)? In *R v Downey*, [1992] 2 SCR 10, 72 CCC (3d) 1, Cory J speaking for the majority said that the predecessor to s 286.2(3) imposed only an evidentiary burden on the accused, so that the presumption means that the accused "need only point to evidence capable of raising a reasonable doubt on this issue."

QUESTIONS AND PROBLEMS

1. Section 258(1)(a) of the *Criminal Code* provides that for proceedings in respect of certain impaired driving offences, "where it is proved that the accused occupied the seat or position ordinarily occupied by a person who operates a motor vehicle … , the accused shall be deemed to have had the care or control of the vehicle … , unless the accused establishes that the accused did not occupy that seat or position for the purpose of setting the vehicle … in motion." What kind of presumption does this section create? What is required to rebut the presumption? Once the presumption is rebutted, what is the effect on proof of the elements of the underlying offence of having care or control while impaired (bearing in mind that an intention or a purpose to set a vehicle in motion is *not* an element of that offence)? See *R v Whyte*, [1988] 2 SCR 3, 42 CCC (3d) 97.

2. In *Re Beckon* (1992), 9 OR (3d) 256 (CA), Morden ACJO described the presumption against suicide in the following terms:

> I turn now to the presumption against suicide. It is referred to in many cases but it is sufficient to refer to its treatment in one of the more recent decisions, that of the Newfoundland Court of Appeal in *Greening v. Commercial Union Assurance Co.* (1987), [1988] ILR 1-2300, 68 Nfld. & PEIR 41. Suicide was raised as a defence to a claim on a life insurance policy. I agree with the court's conclusion (at pp. 8896-97 ILR, pp. 45-46 Nfld. & PEIR) that the presumption against suicide allocates the burden of proof to the party alleging suicide and, also, requires, within the civil standard of balance of probabilities, a high standard of proof. The court referred, among other decisions, to *London Life Insurance Co. v. Lang Shirt Co.*, [1929] SCR 117; *London Life Insurance Co. v. Chase*, [1963] SCR 207, and *Bater v. Bater*, [1951] P 35, [1950] 2 All ER 458 (CA).
>
> I think that the presumption against suicide should be referred to in a charge to a jury in connection with the burden and standard of proof relating to the issue of suicide. However, I would not regard the absence of such a reference as being necessarily fatal, provided that the charge clearly places the burden of proving suicide on the person alleging it and, also, makes clear, in a reasoned manner, the high standard of probability that must be met before suicide can be found.

… I appreciate the practical impact that a coroner's jury's verdict can have, but it seems to me that coroners' proceedings are more like civil proceedings than criminal proceedings. In the latter, the liberty of the accused is at stake, a fact that is frequently referred to as justifying the criminal standard. This is not the case with respect to a coroner's proceedings. On the other hand, in a civil proceeding of the kind to which I have referred, not only may the actual finding of suicide affect the family of the deceased in the same way as a finding in coroner's proceedings, there is also the direct legal effect of a finding of suicide on the rights of the parties which is not present in coroners' proceedings.

Without intending to suggest precise wording, I think that, if one of the possibilities on the evidence is suicide, a proper instruction would be along the following lines. Suicide is not to be presumed. In fact, there is a presumption against it. The finding must be against suicide unless the jury is satisfied, on a balance of probability, that the means of death was suicide. The degree of probability is a high one and, before being satisfied that it has been met, the jury should take into account that suicide is not a natural act and that the allegation of suicide is a serious one with grave consequences. The evidence establishing the probability of suicide should be clear and cogent.

What kind of presumption is the presumption against suicide? What is required to rebut it, and why? Does the fact that there is a presumption against suicide have anything to do with the quantum of proof imposed on a party seeking to establish suicide? If not, what is the rationale for elevating the quantum beyond the usual civil standard of proof on a balance of probabilities? And if the quantum for establishing suicide is elevated, does this conflict with *McDougall, supra*?

B. Reverse Onuses

A "reverse onus" puts the burden of proof on the party who does not normally have it. One might say that a reverse onus changes a presumption that would otherwise apply in the proceedings. In *Oakes*, the Supreme Court considered the constitutionality of a reverse onus of this sort.

R v Oakes

[1986] 1 SCR 103, 24 CCC (3d) 321

Dickson CJ and Estey, McIntyre, Chouinard, Lamer, Wilson, and Le Dain JJ

(28 February 1986)

[The accused was found in possession of eight vials of hashish and $619.45 in cash. He told the police that he had bought ten vials of hashish for his own use and that the cash was from a workers' compensation cheque. He was charged with possession of a narcotic for the purpose of trafficking, contrary to s 4(2) of the *Narcotic Control Act*, RSC 1970, c N-1. The Crown relied on s 8 of the Act, which read as follows:

> 8. In any prosecution for a violation of subsection 4(2), if the accused does not plead guilty, the trial shall proceed as if it were a prosecution for an offence under section 3, and after the close of the case for the prosecution and after the accused has had an opportunity to

make full answer and defence, the court shall make a finding as to whether or not the accused was in possession of the narcotic contrary to section 3; if the court finds that the accused was not in possession of the narcotic contrary to section 3, he shall be acquitted but if the court finds that the accused was in possession of the narcotic contrary to section 3, he shall be given an opportunity of establishing that he was not in possession of the narcotic for the purpose of trafficking, and thereafter the prosecutor shall be given an opportunity of adducing evidence to establish that the accused was in possession of the narcotic for the purpose of trafficking; if the accused establishes that he was not in possession of the narcotic for the purpose of trafficking he shall be acquitted of the offence as charged but he shall be convicted of an offence under section 3 and sentenced accordingly; and if the accused fails to establish that he was not in possession of the narcotic for the purpose of trafficking, he shall be convicted of the offence as charged and sentenced accordingly.

The accused pleaded guilty to simple possession. The accused's argument that s 8 was unconstitutional succeeded at trial and on appeal to the Ontario Court of Appeal, so he was acquitted of the charge under s 4(2). The Crown appealed to the Supreme Court of Canada.]

DICKSON CJ (Chouinard, Lamer, Wilson, and Le Dain JJ concurring):

Does Section 8 of the Narcotic Control Act Violate Section 11(d) of the Charter?

(a) The Meaning of Section 8

. . .

[21] To return to s. 8 of the *Narcotic Control Act*, it is my view that, upon a finding beyond a reasonable doubt of possession of a narcotic, the accused has the legal burden of proving on a balance of probabilities that he or she was not in possession of the narcotic for the purpose of trafficking. Once the basic fact of possession is proven, a mandatory presumption of law arises against the accused that he or she had the intention to traffic. Moreover, the accused will be found guilty of the offence of trafficking unless he or she can rebut this presumption on a balance of probabilities. This interpretation of s. 8 is supported by the courts in a number of jurisdictions ... .

[Dickson CJ then reviewed some of the conflicting interpretations of s 8 in the lower courts.]

[26] I conclude that s. 8 of the *Narcotic Control Act* contains a reverse onus provision imposing a legal burden on an accused to prove on a balance of probabilities that he or she was not in possession of a narcotic for the purpose of trafficking. It is therefore necessary to determine whether s. 8 of the *Narcotic Control Act* offends the right to be "presumed innocent until proven guilty" as guaranteed by s. 11(d) of the *Charter*.

(b) The Presumption of Innocence and Section 11(d) of the Charter

[27] Section 11(d) of the *Charter* constitutionally entrenches the presumption of innocence as part of the supreme law of Canada. ...

[28] To interpret the meaning of s. 11(d), it is important to adopt a purposive approach. As this Court stated in *R v. Big M Drug Mart Ltd.* (1985), 18 CCC (3d) 385 at pp. 423-24, [1985] 1 SCR 295 at p. 344:

> The meaning of a right or freedom guaranteed by the *Charter* was to be ascertained by an analysis of the *purpose* of such a guarantee; it was to be understood, in other words, in the light of the interests it was meant to protect.
>
> In my view, this analysis is to be undertaken, and the purpose of the right or freedom in question is to be sought by reference to the character and the larger objects of the *Charter* itself, to the language chosen to articulate the specific right or freedom, to the historical origins of the concepts enshrined, and where applicable, to the meaning and purpose of the other specific rights and freedoms ... .

To identify the underlying purpose of the *Charter* right in question, therefore, it is important to begin by understanding the cardinal values it embodies.

[29] The presumption of innocence is a hallowed principle lying at the very heart of criminal law. Although protected expressly in s. 11(d) of the *Charter*, the presumption of innocence is referable and integral to the general protection of life, liberty and security of the person contained in s. 7 of the *Charter*: see *Reference re s. 94(2) of Motor Vehicle Act* (1985), 23 CCC (3d) 289. The presumption of innocence protects the fundamental liberty and human dignity of any and every person accused by the State of criminal conduct. An individual charged with a criminal offence faces grave social and personal consequences, including potential loss of physical liberty, subjection to social stigma and ostracism from the community, as well as other social, psychological and economic harms. In light of the gravity of these consequences, the presumption of innocence is crucial. It ensures that until the State proves an accused's guilt beyond all reasonable doubt, he or she is innocent. This is essential in a society committed to fairness and social justice. The presumption of innocence confirms our faith in humankind; it reflects our belief that individuals are decent and law-abiding members of the community until proven otherwise.

[30] The presumption of innocence has enjoyed long-standing recognition at common law. In the leading case, *Woolmington v. Director of Public Prosecutions*, [1935] AC 462 (HL), Viscount Sankey LC wrote at pp. 481-2:

> Throughout the web of the English Criminal Law one golden thread is always to be seen, that it is the duty of the prosecution to prove the prisoner's guilt subject to what I have already said as to the defence of insanity and subject also to any statutory exception. If, at the end of and on the whole of the case, there is a reasonable doubt, created by the evidence given by either the prosecution or the prisoner, as to whether the prisoner killed the deceased with a malicious intention, the prosecution has not made out the case and the prisoner is entitled to an acquittal. No matter what the charge or where the trial, the principle that the prosecution must prove the guilt of the prisoner is part of the common law of England and no attempt to whittle it down can be entertained.

Subsequent Canadian cases have cited the *Woolmington* principle with approval: see, for example, *Manchak v. The King* (1938), 70 CCC 161 at 167, [1938] SCR 341 at 349; *R v. City of Sault Ste. Marie* (1978), 40 CCC (2d) 353 at 366-7, [1978] 2 SCR 1299 at 1316.

[31] Further evidence of the widespread acceptance of the principle of the presumption of innocence is its inclusion in the major international human rights documents.

Article 11(1) of the *Universal Declaration of Human Rights*, adopted December 10, 1948, by the General Assembly of the United Nations, provides:

> Article 11
>   1. Everyone charged with a penal offence has the right to be presumed innocent until proved guilty according to law in a public trial at which he has had all the guarantees necessary for his defence.

In the *International Covenant on Civil and Political Rights*, 1966, art. 14(2) states:

> Article 14
>   2. Everyone charged with a criminal offence shall have the right to be presumed innocent until proved guilty according to law.

Canada acceded to this covenant, and the optional protocol which sets up machinery for implementing the covenant, on May 19, 1976. Both came into effect on August 19, 1976.

[32] In light of the above, the right to be presumed innocent until proven guilty requires that s. 11(d) have, at a minimum, the following content. First, an individual must be proven guilty beyond a reasonable doubt. Secondly, it is the State which must bear the burden of proof. As Mr. Justice Lamer stated in *Dubois v. The Queen* (1985), 22 CCC (3d) 513 at 531, [1985] 2 SCR 350:

> Section 11(d) imposes upon the Crown the burden of proving the accused's guilt beyond a reasonable doubt as well as that of making out the case against the accused before he or she need respond, either by testifying or by calling other evidence.

Third, criminal prosecutions must be carried out in accordance with lawful procedures and fairness. The latter part of s. 11(d), which requires the proof of guilt "according to law in a fair and public hearing by an independent and impartial tribunal," underlines the importance of this procedural requirement.

(c) Authorities on Reverse Onus Provisions and the Presumption of Innocence

[Dickson CJ reviewed a number of Canadian and American authorities, as well as jurisprudence under the European Convention on Human Rights.]

(d) Conclusion Regarding Section 11(d) of the Charter and Section 8 of the Narcotic Control Act

[56] This review of the authorities lays the groundwork for formulating some general conclusions regarding reverse onus provisions and the presumption of innocence in s. 11(d). We can then proceed to apply these principles to the particulars of s. 8 of the *Narcotic Control Act*.

[57] In general one must, I think, conclude that a provision which requires an accused to disprove on a balance of probabilities the existence of a presumed fact, which is an important element of the offence in question, violates the presumption of innocence in s. 11(d). If an accused bears the burden of disproving on a balance of probabilities an essential element of an offence, it would be possible for a conviction to occur despite the existence of a reasonable doubt. This would arise if the accused adduced sufficient evidence

to raise a reasonable doubt as to his or her innocence but did not convince the jury on a balance of probabilities that the presumed fact was untrue.

[58] The fact that the standard is only the civil one does not render a reverse onus clause constitutional. As Sir Rupert Cross commented in the *Rede Lectures*, "The Golden Thread of the English Criminal Law: The Burden of Proof," delivered in 1976 at the University of Toronto, at pp. 114:

> It is sometimes said that exceptions to the Woolmington rule are acceptable because, whenever the burden of proof on any issue in a criminal case is borne by the accused, he only has to satisfy the jury on the balance of probabilities, whereas on issues on which the Crown bears the burden of proof the jury must be satisfied beyond a reasonable doubt. ... The fact that the standard is lower when the accused bears the burden of proof than it is when the burden of proof is borne by the prosecution is no answer to my objection to the existence of exceptions to the Woolmington rule as it does not alter the fact that a jury or bench of magistrates may have to convict the accused although they are far from sure of his guilt.

[59] As we have seen, the potential for a rational connection between the basic fact and the presumed fact to justify a reverse onus provision has been elaborated in some of the cases discussed above and is now known as the "rational connection test." In the context of s. 11(d), however, the following question arises: if we apply the rational connection test to the consideration of whether s. 11(d) has been violated, are we adequately protecting the constitutional principle of the presumption of innocence? As Professors MacKay and Cromwell point out in their article "Oakes: A Bold Initiative Impeded by Old Ghosts" (1983), 32 CR (3d) 221, at p. 233:

> The rational connection test approves a provision that forces the trier to infer a fact that may be simply rationally connected to the proved fact. Why does it follow that such a provision does not offend the constitutional right to be proved guilty beyond a reasonable doubt?

A basic fact may rationally tend to prove a presumed fact, but not prove its existence beyond a reasonable doubt. An accused person could thereby be convicted despite the presence of a reasonable doubt. This would violate the presumption of innocence.

[60] I should add that this questioning of the constitutionality of the "rational connection test" as a guide to interpreting s. 11(d) does not minimize its importance. The appropriate stage for invoking the rational connection test, however, is under s. 1 of the *Charter*. This consideration did not arise under the *Canadian Bill of Rights* because of the absence of an equivalent to s. 1. At the Court of Appeal level in the present case, Martin JA sought to combine the analysis of ss. 11(d) and 1 to overcome the limitations of the *Canadian Bill of Rights* jurisprudence. To my mind, it is highly desirable to keep ss. 1 and 11(d) analytically distinct. Separating the analysis into two components is consistent with the approach this Court has taken to the *Charter* to date (see *R v. Big M Drug Mart Ltd.* (1985), 18 CCC (3d) 385, [1985] 1 SCR 295; *Hunter et al. v. Southam Inc.* (1984), 14 CCC (3d) 97, [1984] 2 SCR 145; *Law Society of Upper Canada v. Skapinker* (1984), 11 CCC (3d) 481, [1984] 1 SCR 357).

[61] To return to s. 8 of the *Narcotic Control Act*, I am in no doubt whatsoever that it violates s. 11(d) of the *Charter* by requiring the accused to prove on a balance of probabilities that he was not in possession of the narcotic for the purpose of trafficking. Mr. Oakes is compelled by s. 8 to prove he is *not* guilty of the offence of trafficking. He is thus

denied his right to be presumed innocent and subjected to the potential penalty of life imprisonment unless he can rebut the presumption. This is radically and fundamentally inconsistent with the societal values of human dignity and liberty which we espouse, and is directly contrary to the presumption of innocence enshrined in s. 11(d). Let us turn now to s. 1 of the *Charter*.

Is Section 8 of the Narcotic Control Act a Reasonable and Demonstrably Justified Limit Pursuant to Section 1 of the Charter?

[Dickson CJ, after outlining the now-famous "*Oakes* test," held that the violation of s 11(d) was not justified under s 1.]

[73] The starting point for formulating a response to this question is, as stated above, the nature of Parliament's interest or objective which accounts for the passage of s. 8 of the *Narcotic Control Act*. According to the Crown, s. 8 of the *Narcotic Control Act* is aimed at curbing drug trafficking by facilitating the conviction of drug traffickers. In my opinion, Parliament's concern that drug trafficking be decreased can be characterized as substantial and pressing. The problem of drug trafficking has been increasing since the 1950's at which time there was already considerable concern: see *Report of the Special Committee on Traffic in Narcotic Drugs, Appendix to Debates of the Senate, Canada, Session 1955*, pp. 690-700; see also *Final Report, Commission of Inquiry into the Non-Medical Use of Drugs* (Ottawa, 1973). Throughout this period, numerous measures were adopted by free and democratic societies, at both the international and national levels.

[74] At the international level, on June 23, 1953, the *Protocol for Limiting and Regulating the Cultivation of the Poppy Plant, the Production of, International and Wholesale Trade in, and Use of Opium*, to which Canada is a signatory, was adopted by the United Nations Opium Conference held in New York. *The Single Convention on Narcotic Drugs*, 1961, was acceded to in New York on March 30, 1961. This treaty was signed by Canada on March 30, 1961. It entered into force on December 13, 1964. As stated in the preamble, "addiction to narcotic drugs constitutes a serious evil for the individual and is fraught with social and economic danger to mankind. ..."

[75] At the national level, statutory provisions have been enacted by numerous countries which, *inter alia*, attempt to deter drug trafficking by imposing criminal sanctions: see, for example, *Misuse of Drugs Act*, 1975 (NZ), No. 116; *Misuse of Drugs Act*, 1971 (UK), c. 38.

[76] The objective of protecting our society from the grave ills associated with drug trafficking, is, in my view, one of sufficient importance to warrant overriding a constitutionally protected right or freedom in certain cases. Moreover, the degree of seriousness of drug trafficking makes its acknowledgement as a sufficiently important objective for the purposes of s. 1, to a large extent, self-evident. The first criterion of a s. 1 inquiry, therefore, has been satisfied by the Crown.

[77] The next stage of inquiry is a consideration of the means chosen by Parliament to achieve its objective. The means must be reasonable and demonstrably justified in a free and democratic society. As outlined above, this proportionality test should begin with a consideration of the rationality of the provision: is the reverse onus clause in s. 8 rationally related to the objective of curbing drug trafficking? At a minimum, this requires

that s. 8 be internally rational; there must be a rational connection between the basic fact of possession and the presumed fact of possession for the purpose of trafficking. Otherwise, the reverse onus clause could give rise to unjustified and erroneous convictions for drug trafficking of persons guilty only of possession of narcotics.

[78]   In my view, s. 8 does not survive this rational connection test. As Martin JA of the Ontario Court of Appeal concluded, possession of a small or negligible quantity of narcotics does not support the inference of trafficking. In other words, it would be irrational to infer that a person had an intent to traffic on the basis of his or her possession of a very small quantity of narcotics. The presumption required under s. 8 of the *Narcotic Control Act* is overinclusive and could lead to results in certain cases which would defy both rationality and fairness. In light of the seriousness of the offence in question, which carries with it the possibility of imprisonment for life, I am further convinced that the first component of the proportionality test has not been satisfied by the Crown.

[79]   Having concluded that s. 8 does not satisfy this first component of proportionality, it is unnecessary to consider the other two components.

[The Crown's appeal was dismissed. Estey J, McIntyre J concurring, concurred in the result.]

QUESTIONS

In light of *Oakes* and of subsequent cases interpreting and applying s 1 of the Charter, consider the following questions:

1.   Do you agree with Dickson CJ's holding that the limitation on the right was not rationally connected with its objective? How do you think the Supreme Court would approach that question today? How would you apply the other elements of the *Oakes* test to the s 11(d) violation?

2.   As we saw in Section III.D, above, most regulatory offences are deemed to be offences of strict liability: the Crown is required to prove the *actus reus* beyond a reasonable doubt, and the accused is then afforded an opportunity to establish the defence of due diligence on a balance of probabilities. Do offences of strict liability offend s 11(d) of the Charter? If so, could they be justified under s 1? Does the regulatory setting of most offences of strict liability matter? Does it depend on which particular regulatory offence is at issue? See *R v Wholesale Travel Group Inc*, [1991] 3 SCR 154, 67 CCC (3d) 193.

3.   In criminal proceedings, the accused may face an evidentiary burden, either by virtue of statute or at common law, to adduce or point to evidence that is capable of raising a reasonable doubt on an issue. Does a statute or common law rule that places an evidentiary burden on an accused infringe s 11(d) of the Charter? If so, could that infringement be justified under s 1? See *R v Downey*, [1992] 2 SCR 10, 72 CCC (3d) 1 and *R v Osolin*, [1993] 4 SCR 595, 86 CCC (3d) 481.

4.   Section 394 of the *Criminal Code* concerns fraudulent transactions relating to mines and minerals. Section 394(1)(b) formerly read as follows:

394(1)   Every one is guilty of an indictable offence and liable to imprisonment for a term not exceeding five years who ...

(b)   sells or purchases any rock, mineral, or other substance that contains precious metals or unsmelted, untreated, unmanufactured, or partly smelted, partly treated or partly manufactured precious metals, unless he establishes that he is the owner or agent of the owner or is acting under lawful authority.

Did this section offend s 11(d) of the Charter? Could it be justified under s 1? See *R v Laba*, [1994] 3 SCR 965, 94 CCC (3d) 385.

In 1999, s 394 was substantially amended, and the reverse onus clause in the former s 394(1)(b) was replaced with the following presumption, which applies to sales and purchases of unrefined minerals:

> 394(4) In any proceeding in relation to subsection (2) or (3), in the absence of evidence raising a reasonable doubt to the contrary, it is presumed that
>   (a) in the case of a sale, the seller is not the owner of the valuable mineral or the owner's agent or someone otherwise acting under lawful authority; and
>   (b) in the case of a purchase, the purchaser, when buying the valuable mineral, had reason to believe that the seller was not the owner of the mineral or the owner's agent or someone otherwise acting under lawful authority.

What kind of a presumption is this? Does it offend s 11(d) of the Charter? If so, can it be justified under s 1?

5. Consider s 258(1)(a) of the Code, reproduced in Section V.A, above. Does this section offend s 11(d) of the Charter? Can it be justified under s 1? See *R v Whyte*, [1988] 2 SCR 3, 42 CCC (3d) 97.

VI. APPELLATE REVIEW OF FACTUAL FINDINGS

A. Civil Proceedings

Stein v The "Kathy K"
[1976] 2 SCR 802, 62 DLR (3d) 1
Martland, Judson, Ritchie, Spence, and Dickson JJ (7 October 1975)

RITCHIE J:

This is an appeal from a judgment of the Federal Court of Appeal (Thurlow J dissenting) setting aside the judgment rendered at trial by Mr. Justice Heald and dismissing the action brought by the widow and executors of the late Charles Simmon Stein who lost his life in the waters of English Bay, Vancouver, when the small sailboat in which he was acting as crew for his son, Ross Stein, collided with the unmanned barge S.N. No. 1 which was then in tow of a tug known as Storm Point. The reasons for judgment of the learned trial judge are reported in [1972] FC 585 and those of the Court of Appeal in [1974] 1 FC 657.

• • •

In the course of his reasons for judgment, in which he made a careful review of the evidence, Mr. Justice Heald concluded that the "crew" of the sailboat 505 were negligent in that they failed to keep a proper look-out and that the tug was also guilty of negligent conduct causative of the collision and he apportioned that fault "on the basis of 75 per cent to the tugboat 'Storm Point' and 25 per cent to the 505 sailboat skippered by Ross Stein." (See [1972] FC pp. 599 to 600.)

In reaching the conclusion that the sailboat was entirely to blame, Chief Justice Jackett, who delivered the judgment on behalf of the majority of the Court of Appeal, appears to have ignored the various findings of fact made by the trial judge, in favour of his own appreciation of "the balance of probability." In this regard he states in [1974] 1 FC at p. 661:

> Any attempt to trace with precision the respective courses of speed of the tug (with its barge) and the sailing boat in relation to each other and to determine with precision what steps were taken at particular points of time on the respective vessels is doomed to failure having regard to the state of the evidence. I accordingly limit myself to a statement in general terms of what, as I appreciate it on the balance of probability, did happen.

With the greatest respect for the learned Chief Justice, I do not consider that this approach to the determination of the facts is justified under the circumstances, particularly having regard to the fact that evidence was taken from the individuals in charge of the respective vessels and that findings of credibility were involved in the trial judge's conclusions. I think that under such circumstances the accepted approach of a court of appeal is to test the findings made at trial on the basis of whether or not they were clearly wrong rather than whether they accorded with that court's view of the balance of probability.

In this regard reference may be had to the case of *S.S. Honestroom (Owners) v. S.S. Sagaporack (Owners)*, [1927] AC 37, where Lord Sumner said, at pp. 47-8:

> [N]ot to have seen the witnesses puts appellate judges in a permanent position of disadvantage as against the trial judge, and unless it can be shown that he has failed to use or has palpably misused his advantage, the higher Court ought not to take the responsibility of reversing conclusions so arrived at, merely on the result of their own comparisons and criticisms of the witnesses *and of their own view of the probabilities of the case*. The course of the trial and the whole substance of the judgment must be looked at, and the matter does not depend on the question whether a witness has been cross-examined to credit or has been pronounced by the judge in terms to be unworthy of it. If his estimate of the man forms any substantial part of his reasons for his judgment the trial judge's conclusion of fact should, as I understand the decisions, be let alone. In *The Julia*, (1860) 14 Moo. PC 210, 235, Lord Kingsdown says: "They, who require this Board, under such circumstances, to reverse a decision of the Court below, upon a point of this description, undertake a task of great and almost insuperable difficulty. ... We must, in order to reverse, not merely entertain doubts whether the decision below is right, but be convinced that it is wrong."

(The italics are my own.)

In the same case, Lord Sumner adopts the practice laid down by James LJ in *The Sir Robert Peel* (1880), 4 Asp. MLC 321, at p. 322, where he said:

> The Court will not depart from the rule it has laid down that it will not overrule the decision of the Court below on a question of fact in which the judge has had the advantage of seeing the witnesses and observing their demeanour, unless they find some governing fact which in relation to others has created a wrong impression.

These passages were expressly adopted by Martland J, when delivering the judgment of this Court in *Prudential Trust Co. Ltd. v. Forseth*, [1960] SCR 210, at pp. 216-7, where he also adopted the following passage from the judgment of Lord Shaw in *Clarke v. Edinburgh*

Tramways Co., [1919] SC (HL) 35, at p. 36, which is quoted by Lord Sankey in *Powell v. Streatham Manor Nursing Home*, [1935] AC 243, at p. 250:

> "Am I—who sits here without those advantages, sometimes broad and sometimes subtle, which are the privilege of the Judge who heard and tried the case—in a position, not having those privileges, to come to a clear conclusion that the Judge who had them was plainly wrong? If I cannot be satisfied in my own mind that the Judge with those privileges was plainly wrong, then it appears to me to be my duty to defer to his judgment."

These authorities are not to be taken as meaning that the findings of fact made at trial are immutable, but rather that they are not to be reversed unless it can be established that the learned trial judge made some palpable and overriding error which affected his assessment of the facts. While the Court of Appeal is seized with the duty of re-examining the evidence in order to be satisfied that no such error occurred, it is not, in my view, part of its function to substitute its assessment of the balance of probability for the findings of the judge who presided at the trial.

Applying the test recognized in these authorities, I am unable to conclude that the learned trial judge in the present case was plainly wrong in any of the relevant findings of fact made in the course of his reasons for judgment, but I note and will consider hereafter the fact that the Court of Appeal were advised by assessors whose advice differed in one material aspect from that of the assessors sitting with the learned trial judge so that at least to this extent different considerations applied at trial and on appeal.

[After an extensive review of the evidence, Ritchie J held that the Court of Appeal should not have changed the trial judge's factual findings, and that the trial judge's judgment should be restored.]

QUESTIONS

1. What features of the trial process justify this restrictive approach to revisiting factual findings on appeal?

2. How would you determine whether a trial judge's findings were affected by "palpable and overriding error?" See *Housen v Nikolaisen*, 2002 SCC 33 at paras 10-18, [2002] 2 SCR 235; *HL v Canada (Attorney General)*, 2005 SCC 25 at paras 52-76, [2005] 1 SCR 401.

B. Criminal Proceedings

Generally speaking, courts of appeal will apply the same deference to factual findings in criminal matters as in civil matters. Rights of appeal to provincial courts of appeal in criminal proceedings by way of indictment are governed by s 675 of the *Criminal Code*. Section 675(1)(a)(ii) provides that an accused may appeal from conviction "on any ground of appeal that involves a question of fact or a question of mixed law and fact, with leave of the court of appeal or a judge thereof." This procedure is rarely invoked, and the holding in *Biniaris*, below, that the reasonableness of a conviction is a question of law will certainly not increase its utility. The Crown's right of appeal in s 676(1) is limited to "a question of law alone." The Crown therefore cannot appeal an acquittal on the ground that the trier of fact ought to have found a fact that would have led to a conviction; the Crown can appeal a factual finding only in-directly, by pointing to some error of law that tainted the fact-finding process.

Appeals from the provincial courts of appeal to the Supreme Court of Canada are created by ss 691 to 693 of the Code. In general, an appeal to the Supreme Court has to be on a ques-tion of law: the Supreme Court has no jurisdiction to review factual findings as such.

Accused persons who appeal from conviction frequently argue that the conviction was unreasonable. The jurisdiction of a Court of Appeal to allow an appeal on this ground is es-tablished by s 686(1)(a)(i) of the *Criminal Code*. In *Biniaris*, the Supreme Court reconsidered the nature of this jurisdiction.

R v Biniaris
2000 SCC 15, [2000] 1 SCR 381
Lamer CJ and L'Heureux-Dubé, Gonthier, McLachlin, Iacobucci, Major,
Bastarache, Binnie, and Arbour JJ (13 April 2000)

[The accused and another were, in separate proceedings, convicted of second-degree murder. A majority of the British Columbia Court of Appeal held that the conviction was unreasonable and substituted a conviction for manslaughter, on the ground that his par-ticipation in the assault was very brief and the evidence of his intention was "unclear." The majority said that murder "was perhaps an open verdict ... but very thinly supported by the evidence." The dissenting judge held that the verdict was reasonable because it was open to the jury to find that the accused was part of a joint endeavour and had the required intent. The Crown's appeal to the Supreme Court of Canada was allowed and the conviction was restored. The court held that the question of the reasonableness of a conviction was a question of law, thus giving either the accused or the Crown a right to appeal to the Supreme Court if a judge of the Court of Appeal dissents on this point. The court went on to describe the process of determining whether a verdict of conviction is unreasonable.]

ARBOUR J:

[36] The test for an appellate court determining whether the verdict of a jury or the judgment of a trial judge is unreasonable or cannot be supported by the evidence has been unequivocally expressed in *R v. Yebes*, [1987] 2 SCR 168, as follows:

> [C]urial review is invited whenever a jury goes beyond a reasonable standard. ... [T]he test is "whether the verdict is one that a properly instructed jury acting judicially, [*sic*] could reasonably have rendered."
>
> (*Yebes*, *supra*, at p. 185 (quoting *Corbett v. The Queen*, [1975] 2 SCR 275, at p. 282, *per* Pigeon J).)

That formulation of the test imports both an objective assessment and, to some extent, a subjective one. It requires the appeal court to determine what verdict a reasonable jury, properly instructed, could judicially have arrived at, and, in doing so, to review, analyse and, within the limits of appellate disadvantage, weigh the evidence. This latter process is usually understood as referring to a subjective exercise, requiring the appeal court to examine the weight of the evidence, rather than its bare sufficiency. The test is therefore mixed, and it is more helpful to articulate what the application of that test entails, than to characterize it as either an objective or a subjective test.

[37] The *Yebes* test is expressed in terms of a verdict reached by a jury. It is, however, equally applicable to the judgment of a judge sitting at trial without a jury. The review for unreasonableness on appeal is different, however, and somewhat easier when the judgment under attack is that of a single judge, at least when reasons for judgment of some substance are provided. In those cases, the reviewing appellate court may be able to identify a flaw in the evaluation of the evidence, or in the analysis, that will serve to explain the unreasonable conclusion reached, and justify the reversal. For example, in *R v. Burke*, [1996] 1 SCR 474, this Court was in a position to identify the deficiencies in the trial judge's analysis of the evidence which led to her unreasonable conclusions in respect of the three counts of indecent assault facing the accused. In that case, Sopinka J found that the trial judge had ignored the possibility of collusion or corroboration between witnesses before accepting their "strikingly similar" evidence, had not been alive to circumstances (i.e., the absence of physical traces of an alleged indecent assault which, if true, should have left observable marks) which caused great concern about the reliability of evidence adduced in support of allegations of a bizarre nature, and had relied uncritically on unorthodox identification evidence. Similarly, in *R v. Reitsma*, [1998] 1 SCR 769, rev'g. (1997), 97 BCAC 303, this Court agreed with Rowles JA, dissenting, that the trial judge had failed to advert to deficiencies in the pre-trial identification procedure and the short-coming of "in-dock" identification. Finally, in *R v. O'Connor* (1998), 123 CCC (3d) 487 (BC CA), at pp. 492-93 and 518-20, the trial judge accepted the accused's evidence that he was not present at the place where the offence was alleged to have been committed, and yet convicted the accused. This logical inconsistency was relied upon by the Court of Appeal to explain the unreasonableness of the verdict. These examples demonstrate that in trials by judge alone, the court of appeal often can and should identify the defects in the analysis that led the trier of fact to an unreasonable conclusion. The court of appeal will therefore be justified to intervene and set aside a verdict as unreasonable when the reasons of the trial judge reveal that he or she was not alive to an applicable legal principle, or entered a verdict inconsistent with the factual conclusions reached. These discernible defects are themselves sometimes akin to a separate error of law, and therefore easily sustain the conclusion that the unreasonable verdict which rests upon them also raises a question of law.

[38] The exercise of appellate review is considerably more difficult when the court of appeal is required to determine the alleged unreasonableness of a verdict reached by a jury. If there are no errors in the charge, as must be assumed, there is no way of determining the basis upon which the jury reached its conclusion. But this does not dispense the reviewing court from the need to articulate the basis upon which it finds that the conclusion reached by the jury was unreasonable. It is insufficient for the court of appeal to refer to a vague unease, or a lingering or lurking doubt based on its own review of the evidence. This "lurking doubt" may be a powerful trigger for thorough appellate scrutiny of the evidence, but it is not, without further articulation of the basis for such doubt, a proper basis upon which to interfere with the findings of a jury. In other words, if, after reviewing the evidence at the end of an error-free trial which led to a conviction, the appeal court judge is left with a lurking doubt or feeling of unease, that doubt, which is not in itself sufficient to justify interfering with the conviction, may be a useful signal that the verdict

was indeed reached in a non-judicial manner. In that case, the court of appeal must proceed further with its analysis.

[39] When a jury which was admittedly properly instructed returns what the appeal court perceives to be an unreasonable conviction, the only rational inference, if the test in *Yebes* is followed, is that the jury, in arriving at that guilty verdict, was not acting judicially. This conclusion does not imply an impeachment of the integrity of the jury. It may be that the jury reached its verdict pursuant to an analytical flaw similar to the errors occasionally incurred in the analysis of trial judges and revealed in their reasons for judgment. Such error would of course not be apparent on the face of the verdict by a jury. But the unreasonableness itself of the verdict would be apparent to the legally trained reviewer when, in all the circumstances of a given case, judicial fact-finding precludes the conclusion reached by the jury. Judicial appreciation of the evidence is governed by rules that dictate the required content of the charge to the jury. These rules are sometimes expressed in terms of warnings, mandatory or discretionary sets of instructions by which a trial judge will convey the product of accumulated judicial experience to the jury, who, by definition, is new to the exercise. For instance, a judge may need to warn the jury about the frailties of eye-witness identification evidence. Similarly, years of judicial experience has revealed the possible need for special caution in evaluating the evidence of certain witnesses, such as accomplices, who may, to the uninitiated, seem particularly knowledgeable and therefore credible. Finally, judicial warnings may be required when the jury has heard about the criminal record of the accused, or about similar fact evidence. But these rules of caution cannot be exhaustive, they cannot capture every situation, and cannot be formulated in every case as a requirement of the charge. Rather, after the jury has been adequately charged as to the applicable law, and warned, if necessary, about drawing possibly unwarranted conclusions, it remains that in some cases, the totality of the evidence and the peculiar factual circumstances of a given case will lead an experienced jurist to conclude that the fact-finding exercise applied at trial was flawed in light of the unreasonable result that it produced.

[40] When an appellate court arrives at that conclusion, it does not act as a "thirteenth juror," nor is it "usurping the function of the jury." In concluding that no properly instructed jury acting judicially could have convicted, the reviewing court inevitably is concluding that these particular jurors who convicted must not have been acting judicially. In that context, acting judicially means not only acting dispassionately, applying the law and adjudicating on the basis of the record and nothing else. It means, in addition, arriving at a conclusion that does not conflict with the bulk of judicial experience. This, in my view, is the assessment that must be made by the reviewing court. It requires not merely asking whether twelve properly instructed jurors, acting judicially, could reasonably have come to the same result, but doing so through the lens of judicial experience which serves as an additional protection against an unwarranted conviction.

[41] It is not particularly significant to describe this judicial oversight as either objective or subjective. It is exercised by an appeal court and therefore it will invariably draw on a collection of judicial experiences. Because of its judicial character, and because it purports to identify features of a case that will give experienced jurists cause for concern, it is imperative that the reviewing court articulate as precisely as possible what features of the case suggest that the verdict reached by the jury was unreasonable, despite the fact that it was not tainted by any erroneous instructions as to the applicable law. In some cases, the

articulation of the grounds upon which an appellate court concludes that a conviction was unreasonable may elucidate previously unidentified dangers in evidence and give rise to additional warnings to the jury in subsequent cases. Most of the time, it will simply point to a case that presented itself with several causes for concern, none of which, in isolation, might have required that the jury be warned in any particular way. There are many illustrations from the case law of verdicts having been found unreasonable essentially on the strength of accumulated judicial experience. Concerns about various aspects of the frailty of identification evidence have been a recurrent basis, by itself or together with other considerations, for overturning verdicts as unreasonable. See, e.g., *Burke, supra*; *Reitsma, supra*; *R v. Keeper* (1993), 88 Man. R (2d) 156 (CA); *R v. Malcolm* (1993), 81 CCC (3d) 196 (Ont. CA); *R v. Tat* (1997), 117 CCC (3d) 481 (Ont. CA); *R v. N.D.*, [1993] OJ No. 2139 (QL) (CA). Judicial experience has also been relied upon to question the reasonableness of verdicts in cases of sexual misconduct presenting troubling features such as allegations of sexual touching of a bizarre nature (see, e.g., *Burke, supra*; *R v. C.V.*, [1993] OJ No. 1512 (QL) (CA); *R v. L.(J.H.H.P.)* (1992), 75 CCC (3d) 165 (Man. CA)), or the possibility of collusion between witnesses (see, e.g., *Burke, supra*). Finally, the experience of the courts has occasionally been brought to bear, although not always explicitly, on the assessment of verdicts rejecting a defence with respect to which there may be unjustified skepticism or even prejudice because those relying on such justifications or excuses may be viewed as simply trying to avoid responsibility for their actions. See, e.g., *R v. Vaillancourt* (1999), 136 CCC (3d) 530 (Que. CA); *R v. Molodowic* (2000), 143 CCC (3d) 31.

[42] It follows from the above that the test in *Yebes* continues to be the binding test that appellate courts must apply in determining whether the verdict of the jury is unreasonable or cannot be supported by the evidence. To the extent that it has a subjective component, it is the subjective assessment of an assessor with judicial training and experience that must be brought to bear on the exercise of reviewing the evidence upon which an allegedly unreasonable conviction rests. That, in turn, requires the reviewing judge to import his or her knowledge of the law and the expertise of the courts, gained through the judicial process over the years, not simply his or her own personal experience and insight. It also requires that the reviewing court articulate as explicitly and as precisely as possible the grounds for its intervention. I wish to stress the importance of explicitness in the articulation of the reasons that support a finding that a verdict is unreasonable or cannot be supported by the evidence. Particularly since this amounts to a question of law that may give rise to an appeal, either as of right or by leave, the judicial process requires clarity and transparency as well as accessibility to the legal reasoning of the court of appeal. When there is a dissent in the court of appeal on the issue of the reasonableness of the verdict, both the spirit and the letter of s 677 of the *Criminal Code* should be complied with. This Court should be supplied with the grounds upon which the verdict was found to be, or not to be, unreasonable.

NOTES AND QUESTIONS

In light of *Biniaris,* it is apparent that the reasonableness of a finding of guilt is a question of law for the purpose of defining rights of appeal. But is the exercise that the appellate judge undertakes one of law or of fact? To what extent should the deferential approach to factual findings articulated in the civil context apply here?

In his dissenting reasons in *R v Beaudry*, 2007 SCC 5 at para 97, [2007] 1 SCR 190, Fish J concluded (and a majority of the court agreed) that in judge-alone trials, a conviction must be overturned and a new trial ordered even if the verdict is supported by the evidence, if the reasons for the decision are "illogical on their face." See also *R v Sinclair*, 2011 SCC 40, [2011] 3 SCR 3; *R v WH*, 2013 SCC 22 at para 26, [2013] 2 SCR 180.

PROBLEM (R v GALLOWAY)

During the charge to the jury, at one point, the trial judge said the following:

> Members of the jury, you will remember the evidence of the pathologist that Angela Galloway died as a result of extreme blunt force trauma to the head. You will also remember the evidence regarding the axe that was found between her body and that pile of firewood located in the drive shed. You will recall the evidence that the axe was tested and determined through DNA analysis to have Angela's blood on it. Finally, you will recall that when shown the axe the pathologist testified that it was consistent with the sort of implement that caused the severe head injuries that led to Angela's death. Returning to the law, for a moment. In deciding whether or not the prosecution has established that the killing of Angela Galloway was murder, as opposed to manslaughter, the key difference is a question of intention. To be murder, the perpetrator must either have intended to cause Angela's death or have intended to cause her bodily harm that the perpetrator knew was likely to cause death and was reckless whether death ensued. Members of the jury, because we can never see into another person's mind, the law entitles you to draw an inference that a sane and sober person intends the natural consequences of his or her actions. Therefore, in deciding as between manslaughter and murder, you may infer that whoever forcefully struck Angela Galloway to the head with that axe may have intended the natural consequences of that act.

Is the above instruction correct, or do you think it is something that either defence counsel or Crown counsel should take exception to?

In the course of instructing the jury, the trial judge also said the following:

> Members of the jury, in the end, this case boils down to one very basic question: was Angela Galloway killed during a botched burglary or was she killed by her husband, the accused, Martin Galloway? You will remember that Mr. Galloway is presumed to be innocent. He is not required to prove anything. It is the Crown that must establish his guilt beyond a reasonable doubt. In deciding whether or not the Crown has discharged its burden, you must be sure that the guilt of the accused is the only reasonable inference to be drawn from the proven facts. If, on the evidence, you think it equally likely that Angela Galloway was killed in a botched burglary, then you have a reasonable doubt and you must find the accused not guilty.

Is the above instruction correct, or do you think it is something that either defence or Crown counsel should take exception to?